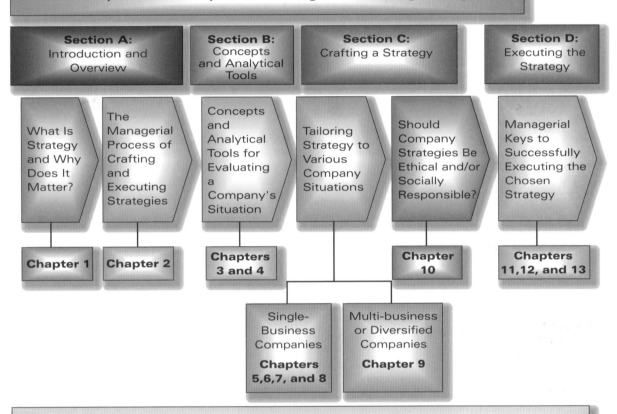

Part I: Concepts and Techniques for Crafting and Executing Strategy

Section A: Introduction and Overview

Section B: Concepts and Analytical Tools

Section C: Crafting a Strategy

Section D: Executing the Strategy

What Is Strategy and Why Does It Matter?

The Managerial Process of Crafting and Executing Strategies

Concepts and Analytical Tools for Evaluating a Company's Situation

Tailoring Strategy to Various Company Situations

Should Company Strategies Be Ethical and/or Socially Responsible?

Managerial Keys to Successfully Executing the Chosen Strategy

Chapter 1

Chapter 2

Chapters 3 and 4

Chapter 10

Chapters 11,12, and 13

Single-Business Companies
Chapters 5,6,7, and 8

Multi-business or Diversified Companies
Chapter 9

Part II: Cases in Crafting and Executing Strategy

Section A: Crafting Strategy in Single-Business Companies (20 cases)
Section B: Crafting Strategy in Diversified Companies (2 cases)
Section C: Implementing and Executing Strategy (8 cases)
Section D: Strategy, Ethics, and Social Responsibility (3 cases)

IMPORTANT

HERE IS YOUR REGISTRATION CODE TO ACCESS MCGRAW-HILL
PREMIUM CONTENT AND MCGRAW-HILL ONLINE RESOURCES

For key premium online resources you need THIS CODE to
gain access. Once the code is entered, you will be able to
use the web resources for the length of your course.

Access is provided only if you have purchased a new book.

If the registration code is missing from this book, the registration screen on our
website, and within your WebCT or Blackboard course will tell you how to obtain
your new code. Your registration code can be used only once to establish
access. It is not transferable

To gain access to these online resources

1. USE your web browser to go to: **http://www.mhhe.com/thompson**

2. CLICK on "First Time User"

3. ENTER the Registration Code printed on the tear-off bookmark on the right

4. After you have entered your registration code, click on "Register"

5. FOLLOW the instructions to setup your personal UserID and Password

6. WRITE your UserID and Password down for future reference. Keep it in a safe place.

If your course is using WebCT or Blackboard, you'll be able to use this code to
access the McGraw-Hill content within your instructor's online course.

To gain access to the McGraw-Hill content in your instructor's WebCT or
Blackboard course simply log into the course with the user ID and Password
provided by your instructor. Enter the registration code exactly as it appears to
the right when prompted by the system. You will only need to use this code the
first time you click on McGraw-Hill content.

These instructions are specifically for student access. Instructors are not required
to register via the above instructions.

The McGraw-Hill Companies

**McGraw-Hill
Irwin**

Thank you, and welcome to your
McGraw-Hill/Irwin Online Resources.

Thompson/Strickland/Gamble

Crafting & Executing Strategy: The Quest for Competitive Advantage: Concepts & Cases. 15/e
Crafting & Executing Strategy: Text and Readings. 15/e
ISBN 13: 978-0-07-326939-9; ISBN 10: 0-07-326939-5

THE PREMIMUM CONTENT INCLUDES:

- **Case-TUTOR**—Downloadable software w/assignment questions for all 35 cases in the text, plus analytically-structured exercises for 11 of the cases

- **PowerWeb**—Articles, Weekly Update Archive, and News Feeds

- **Build Your Management Skills**—Interactive self-assessment and concept review exercises

Crafting and Executing Strategy

The Quest for Competitive Advantage

Concepts and Cases

Crafting and Executing Strategy

The Quest for Competitive Advantage

Concepts and Cases

15th Edition

Arthur A. Thompson, Jr.
University of Alabama

A. J. Strickland III
University of Alabama

John E. Gamble
University of South Alabama

McGraw-Hill Irwin

Boston   Burr Ridge, IL   Dubuque, IA   Madison, WI   New York
San Francisco   St. Louis   Bangkok   Bogotá   Caracas   Kuala Lumpur
Lisbon   London   Madrid   Mexico City   Milan   Montreal   New Delhi
Santiago   Seoul   Singapore   Sydney   Taipei   Toronto

McGraw-Hill
Irwin

CRAFTING AND EXECUTING STRATEGY: THE QUEST FOR COMPETITIVE ADVANTAGE:
CONCEPTS AND CASES

Published by McGraw-Hill/Irwin, a business unit of The McGraw-Hill Companies, Inc., 1221 Avenue
of the Americas, New York, NY, 10020. Copyright © 2007 by The McGraw-Hill Companies, Inc. All
rights reserved. No part of this publication may be reproduced or distributed in any form or by any
means, or stored in a database or retrieval system, without the prior written consent of The McGraw-Hill
Companies, Inc., including, but not limited to, in any network or other electronic storage or transmission,
or broadcast for distance learning.

Some ancillaries, including electronic and print components, may not be available to customers outside
the United States.

This book is printed on acid-free paper.

3 4 5 6 7 8 9 0 DOW/DOW 0 9 8 7

ISBN-13: 978-0-07-296943-6
ISBN-10: 0-07-296943-1

Editorial director: *John E. Biernat*
Executive editor: *John Weimeister*
Managing developmental editor: *Laura Hurst Spell*
Marketing director: *Ellen Cleary*
Media producer: *Benjamin Curless*
Project manager: *Harvey Yep*
Lead production supervisor: *Rose Hepburn*
Designer: *Cara David*
Photo research coordinator: *Lori Kramer*
Media project manager: *Joyce J. Chappetto*
Cover design: *Cara David*
Interior design: *Cara David*
Typeface: *10.5/12 Times New Roman*
Compositor: *Laserwords Private Limited*
Printer: *R. R. Donnelley*
Cover Image: *(c) Stockbyte*

Library of Congress Cataloging-in-Publication Data
Thompson, Arthur A., 1940-
    Crafting and executing strategy : the quest for competitive advantage : concepts and
cases / Arthur A. Thompson, A. J. Strickland, John E. Gamble. -- 15th ed.
        p. cm.
    Includes bibliographical references and index.
    ISBN-13: 978-0-07-296943-6 (alk. paper)
    ISBN-10: 0-07-296943-1 (alk. paper)
    1. Strategic planning. 2. Strategic planning--Case studies. I. Strickland, A. J.
(Alonzo J.) II. Gamble, John (John E.) III. Title.
    HD30.28.T53 2007
    658.4' 012--dc22

                                                                                    2006011853

www.mhhe.com

To our families and especially our wives:
Hasseline, Kitty, and Debra

About the Authors

Arthur A. Thompson, Jr., earned his B.S. and Ph.D. degrees in economics from The University of Tennessee, spent three years on the economics faculty at Virginia Tech, and served on the faculty of The University of Alabama's College of Commerce and Business Administration for 24 years. In 1974 and again in 1982, Dr. Thompson spent semester-long sabbaticals as a visiting scholar at the Harvard Business School.

His areas of specialization are business strategy, competition and market analysis, and the economics of business enterprises. In addition to publishing over 30 articles in some 25 different professional and trade publications, he has authored or co-authored five textbooks and six computer-based simulation exercises that are used in colleges and universities worldwide.

Dr. Thompson spends much of his off-campus time giving presentations, putting on management development programs, working with companies, and helping operate a business simulation enterprise in which he is a major partner.

Dr. Thompson and his wife of 45 years have two daughters, two grandchildren, and two Yorkshire terriers.

Dr. A. J. (Lonnie) Strickland, a native of North Georgia, attended the University of Georgia, where he received a bachelor of science degree in math and physics in 1965. Afterward he entered the Georgia Institute of Technology, where he received a master of science in industrial management. He earned a PhD in business administration from Georgia State University in 1969. He currently holds the title of Professor of Strategic Management in the Graduate School of Business at The University of Alabama.

Dr. Strickland's experience in consulting and executive development is in the strategic management area, with a concentration in industry and competitive analysis. He has developed strategic planning systems for such firms as the Southern Company, BellSouth, South Central Bell, American Telephone and Telegraph, Gulf States Paper, Carraway Methodist Medical Center, Delco Remy, Mark IV Industries, Amoco Oil Company, USA Group, General Motors, and Kimberly Clark Corporation (Medical Products). He is a very popular speaker on the subject of implementing strategic change and serves on several corporate boards.

John E. Gamble is currently Associate Dean and Professor of Management in the Mitchell College of Business at the University of South Alabama. His teaching specialty at USA is strategic management and he also conducts a course in strategic management in Germany, which is sponsored by the University of Applied Sciences in Worms.

Dr. Gamble's research interests center on strategic issues in entrepreneurial, health care, and manufacturing settings. His work has been published in various scholarly journals and he is the author or co-author of more than 30 case studies published in an assortment of strategic management and strategic marketing texts. He has done consulting on industry and market analysis for clients in a diverse mix of industries.

Professor Gamble received his Ph.D. in management from The University of Alabama in 1995. Dr. Gamble also has a Bachelor of Science degree and a Master of Arts degree from The University of Alabama.

The Preface

The hallmark of this 15th edition is a fresh, refined presentation in every chapter and a powerhouse collection of cases. A bigger portion of each chapter has been revised and rewritten than in any previous edition. Coverage was trimmed in some areas, expanded in others. Every paragraph on every page of the 14th edition was revisited, producing a host of both major and minor changes in exposition. Pains were taken to improve and enliven the explanations of core concepts and analytical tools. The latest research findings from the literature and cutting-edge strategic practices of companies have been incorporated to keep step with both theory and practice. Scores of new examples have been added to complement the new and updated Illustration Capsules. More chapter-end exercises have been included. The result is a text treatment with more punch, greater clarity, and improved classroom effectiveness. But none of the changes have altered the fundamental character that has driven the text's success over the years. The chapter content continues to be solidly mainstream and balanced, mirroring *both* the best academic thinking and the pragmatism of real-world strategic management.

Complementing the text presentation is a truly appealing lineup of 33 diverse, timely, and thoughtfully crafted cases. Many involve high-profile companies, and all are framed around issues and circumstances tightly linked to the content of the 13 chapters, thus pushing students to apply the concepts and analytical tools they have read about. We are confident you will be impressed with how well these cases will teach and the amount of student interest they will spark. And there's a comprehensive package of support materials that are a breeze to use, highly effective, and flexible enough to fit most any course design.

A TEXT WITH ON-TARGET CONTENT

In our view, for a senior/MBA-level strategy text to qualify as having on-target content, it must:

- Explain core concepts in language that students can grasp and provide examples of their relevance and use by actual companies.
- Take care to thoroughly describe the tools of strategic analysis, how they are used, and where they fit into the managerial process of crafting and executing strategy.
- Be up-to-date and comprehensive, with solid coverage of the landmark changes in competitive markets and company strategies being driven by globalization and Internet technology.
- Focus squarely on what every student needs to know about crafting, implementing, and executing business strategies in today's market environments.
- Contain freshly researched, value-adding cases that feature interesting products and companies, illustrate the important kinds of strategic challenges managers face, link closely to the chapter content, contain valuable teaching points, and ignite lively class discussions.

We believe this 15th edition measures up on all five of these criteria. Chapter discussions cut straight to the chase about what students really need to know. Our explanations of core concepts and analytical tools are covered in enough depth to make them understandable and usable, the rationale being that a shallow explanation carries little punch and has almost no instructional value. All the chapters are flush with convincing examples that students can easily relate to. There's a straightforward, integrated flow from one chapter to the next. All the latest research findings pertinent to a first course in strategy have been woven into the chapters. We have deliberately adopted a pragmatic, down-to-earth writing style, not only to better communicate to an audience of students (who, for the most part, will soon be practicing managers) but also to convince readers that the subject matter deals directly with what managers and companies do in the real world.

And, thanks to the excellent case research and case writing being done by colleagues in strategic management, this edition contains a set of high-interest cases with an unusual ability to work magic in the classroom. Great cases make it far easier for you to drive home valuable lessons in the whys and hows of successfully crafting and executing strategy.

ORGANIZATION, CONTENT, AND FEATURES OF THE TEXT CHAPTERS

The 13 chapters in this edition are arranged in the same order as the 14th edition and cover essentially the same topics. But every chapter has been given a refreshing facelift that includes the latest thinking and evidence from the literature, more refined presentations, and a greater number of current examples. The latest developments in the theory and practice of strategic management have been ingrained in every chapter to keep the content solidly in the mainstream of contemporary strategic thinking. You'll find up-to-date coverage of the continuing march of industries and companies to wider globalization, the growing scope and strategic importance of collaborative alliances, the spread of high-velocity change to more industries and company environments, and how online technology is driving fundamental changes in both strategy and internal operations in companies across the world.

No other leading strategy text comes close to matching our coverage of the resource-based theory of the firm. The resource-based view of the firm is prominently and comprehensively integrated into our coverage of crafting both single-business and multibusiness strategies. Chapters 3 through 9 emphasize that a company's strategy must be matched *both* to its external market circumstances and to its internal resources and competitive capabilities. Moreover, Chapters 11, 12, and 13, on various aspects of executing strategy, have a strong resource-based perspective that makes it unequivocally clear how and why the tasks of assembling intellectual capital and building core competencies and competitive capabilities are absolutely critical to successful strategy execution and operating excellence.

No other leading strategy text comes close to matching our coverage of business ethics, values, and social responsibility. We have embellished the highly important Chapter 10, "Strategy, Ethics, and Social Responsibility," with new discussions and material so that it can better fulfill the important functions of (1) alerting students to the role and importance of incorporating business ethics and social responsibility into decision making and (2) addressing the accreditation requirements of the AACSB that business ethics be visibly and thoroughly embedded in the core curriculum. Moreover, there are discussions of the roles of values and ethics in Chapters 1, 2, 11, and 13, thus providing you with a meaty, comprehensive treatment of business ethics and socially responsible behavior as they apply to crafting and executing company strategies.

The following rundown summarizes the noteworthy chapter features and topical emphasis in this edition:

- Chapter 1 continues to focus on the central questions of "What is strategy?" and "Why is it important?" It defines what is meant by the term *strategy*, identifies the different elements of a company's strategy, and explains why management efforts to craft a company's strategy entail a quest for competitive advantage. Following Henry Mintzberg's pioneering research, we stress how and why a company's strategy is partly planned and partly reactive, and why a company's strategy tends to evolve over time. There's an enhanced discussion of what is meant by the term *business model* and how it relates to the concept of strategy. The thrust of this first chapter is to convince students that good strategy + good strategy execution = good management. The chapter is a perfect accompaniment for your opening-day lecture on what the course is all about and why it matters.

- Chapter 2 delves into the managerial process of actually crafting and executing a strategy—it makes a great assignment for the second day of class and is a perfect follow-on to your first day's lecture. The focal point of the chapter is the five-step managerial process of crafting and executing strategy: (1) forming a strategic vision of where the company is headed and why, (2) setting objectives and performance targets that measure the company's progress, (3) crafting a strategy to achieve these targets and move the company toward its market destination, (4) implementing and executing the strategy, and (5) monitoring progress and making corrective adjustments as needed. Students are introduced to such core concepts as strategic visions, mission statements, strategic versus financial objectives, and strategic intent. There's a section underscoring that *all managers are on a company's strategy-making, strategy-executing team* and that a company's strategic plan is a collection of strategies devised by different managers at different levels in the organizational hierarchy. The chapter winds up with a substantially expanded section on corporate governance.

- Chapter 3 sets forth the now-familiar analytical tools and concepts of industry and competitive analysis and demonstrates the importance of tailoring strategy to fit the circumstances of a company's industry and competitive environment. The standout feature of this chapter is a presentation of Michael E. Porter's "five-forces model of competition" that we think is the clearest, most straightforward discussion of any text in the field. Globalization and Internet technology are treated as potent driving forces capable of reshaping industry competition—their roles as change agents have become factors that most companies in most industries must reckon with in forging winning strategies.

- Chapter 4 establishes the equal importance of doing solid company situation analysis as a basis for matching strategy to organizational resources, competencies, and competitive capabilities. The roles of core competencies and organizational resources and capabilities in creating customer value and helping build competitive advantage are *center stage* in the discussions of company resource strengths and weaknesses. SWOT analysis is cast as a simple, easy-to-use way to assess a company's resources and overall situation. There is much-clearer coverage of value chain analysis, benchmarking, and competitive strength assessments—standard tools for appraising a company's relative cost position and market standing vis-à-vis rivals. *An important addition to this chapter is a table showing how key financial and operating ratios are calculated and how to interpret them;* students will find this table handy in doing the number-crunching needed to evaluate whether a company's strategy is delivering good financial performance.

- Chapter 5 deals with a company's quest for competitive advantage and is framed around the five generic competitive strategies—low-cost leadership, differentiation, best-cost provider, focused differentiation, and focused low-cost provider.

- Chapter 6 extends the coverage of the previous chapter and deals with what *other strategic actions* a company can take to complement its choice of a basic competitive strategy. The chapter features sections on what use to make of strategic alliances and collaborative partnerships; merger and acquisition strategies; vertical integration strategies; outsourcing strategies; offensive and defensive strategies; and the different types of Web site strategies that companies can employ to position themselves in the marketplace. The discussion of offensive strategies has been totally overhauled and features a new section on blue ocean strategy. The concluding section of this chapter provides a much enhanced treatment of first-mover advantages and disadvantages.

- Chapter 7 explores the full range of strategy options for competing in foreign markets: export strategies; licensing; franchising; multicountry strategies; global strategies; and collaborative strategies involving heavy reliance on strategic alliances and joint ventures. The spotlight is trained on two strategic issues unique to competing multinationally: (1) whether to customize the company's offerings in each different country market to match the tastes and preferences of local buyers or whether to offer a mostly standardized product worldwide, and (2) whether to employ essentially the same basic competitive strategy in the markets of all countries where it operates or whether to modify the company's competitive approach country by country as needed to fit the specific market conditions and competitive circumstances it encounters. There's also coverage of the concepts of profit sanctuaries and cross-market subsidization, the ways to achieve competitive advantage by operating multinationally, the special issues of competing in the markets of emerging countries; and the strategies that local companies in emerging countries can use to defend against global giants.

- The role of Chapter 8 is to hammer home the points made in Chapters 3 and 4 that winning strategies have to be matched both to industry and competitive conditions and to company resources and capabilities. The first portion of the chapter covers the broad strategy options for companies competing in six representative industry and competitive situations: (1) emerging industries; (2) rapid-growth industries; (3) mature, slow-growth industries; (4) stagnant or declining industries; (5) turbulent, high-velocity industries; and (6) fragmented industries. The second portion of the chapter looks at matching strategy to the resources and capabilities of four representative types of companies: (1) companies pursuing rapid growth, (2) companies in industry-leading positions, (3) companies in runner-up positions, and (4) companies in competitively weak positions or plagued by crisis conditions. The detail with which these 10 concrete examples are covered in Chapter 8 should enable you to convince students why it is management's job to craft a strategy that is tightly matched to a company's internal and external circumstances.

- Our rather meaty treatment of diversification strategies for multibusiness enterprises in Chapter 9 begins by laying out the various paths for becoming diversified, explains how a company can use diversification to create or compound competitive advantage for its business units, and examines the strategic options an already-diversified company has to improve its overall performance. In the middle part of the chapter, the analytical spotlight is on the techniques and procedures for assessing the strategic attractiveness of a diversified company's business portfolio—the relative attractiveness of the various businesses the company has diversified into, a multi-industry company's competitive strength in each of its lines of business, and the *strategic fits* and *resource fits* among a diversified company's different businesses. The chapter concludes with a brief survey of a company's four main postdiversification strategy alternatives: (1) broadening the diversification base, (2) divesting some businesses and retrenching to a narrower diversification base, (3) restructuring the makeup of the company's business lineup, and (4) multinational diversification.

- Chapter 10 reflects the very latest in the literature on (1) whether and why a company has a *duty* to operate according to ethical standards and (2) whether and why a company has a *duty* or *obligation* to contribute to the betterment of society independent of the needs and preferences of the customers it serves. Is there a credible business case for operating ethically and/or operating in a socially responsible manner? The opening section of the chapter addresses whether ethical standards are universal (as maintained by the school of ethical universalism) or dependent on local norms and situational circumstances (as maintained by the school of ethical relativism) or a combination of both (as maintained by integrative social contracts theory). Following this is a section on the three categories of managerial morality (moral, immoral, and amoral), a section on the drivers of unethical strategies and shady business behavior, a section on the approaches to managing a company's ethical conduct, a section on linking a company's strategy to its ethical principles and core values, a section on the concept of a "social responsibility strategy," and sections that explore the business case for ethical and socially responsible behavior. The chapter will give students some serious ideas to chew on and, hopefully, will make them far more ethically conscious. It has been written as a stand-alone chapter that can be assigned in the early, middle, or late part of the course.

- The three-chapter module on executing strategy (Chapters 11–13) is anchored around a pragmatic, compelling conceptual framework: (1) building the resource strengths and organizational capabilities needed to execute the strategy in competent fashion; (2) allocating ample resources to strategy-critical activities; (3) ensuring that policies and procedures facilitate rather than impede strategy execution; (4) instituting best practices and pushing for continuous improvement in how value chain activities are performed; (5) installing information and operating systems that enable company personnel to better carry out their strategic roles proficiently; (6) tying rewards and incentives directly to the achievement of performance targets and good strategy execution; (7) shaping the work environment and corporate culture to fit the strategy; and (8) exerting the internal leadership needed to drive execution forward.

  We have reworked and refreshed the content all three chapters. You will see thoroughly overhauled discussions of staffing the organization, building capabilities, instilling a corporate culture, leading the strategy-execution process, and adopting best practices and Six Sigma in facilitating the drive for operating excellence.

As with the 14th edition, the recurring theme of these Chapters 11–13 is that implementing and executing strategy entails figuring out the specific actions, behaviors, and conditions that are needed for a smooth strategy-supportive operation and then following through to get things done and deliver results—the goal here is to ensure that students understand the strategy-implementing/strategy-executing phase is a make-things-happen and make-them-happen-right kind of managerial exercise.

We have done our best to ensure that the 13 chapters hit the bull's-eye in covering the essentials of a senior/MBA course in strategy and convey the best thinking of academics and practitioners. The number of examples in each chapter has been dramatically expanded. There are new and updated "strategy in action" capsules in each chapter that tie core concepts to real-world management practice. We've provided a host of interesting chapter-end exercises that you can use as a basis for class discussion or written assignments or team presentations. We are confident you'll find this 13-chapter presentation superior to our prior editions as concerns coverage, readability, and convincing examples. The ultimate test of the text, of course, is the positive pedagogical impact it has in the classroom. If this edition sets a more effective stage for your lectures and does a better job of helping you persuade students that the discipline of strategy merits their rapt attention, then it will have fulfilled its purpose.

THE CASE COLLECTION

The 33 cases included in this edition are the very latest and best that we could find. The lineup is flush with interesting companies and valuable lessons for students in the art and science of crafting and executing strategy. And there's a good blend of cases from a length perspective—close to one-third are under 15 pages yet offer plenty for students to chew on; about one-third are medium-length cases; and one-third are longer, detail-rich cases, the 33 cases average just under 17 pages in length.

At least 26 of the 33 cases involve companies, products, or people that students will have heard of, know about from personal experience, or can easily identify with. There are four dot-com company cases, plus several others that will provide students with insight into the special demands of competing in industry environments where technological developments are an everyday event, product life cycles are short, and competitive maneuvering among rivals comes fast and furious. Over 20 of the cases involve situations where company resources and competitive capabilities play as large a role in the strategy-making, strategy-executing scheme of things as industry and competitive conditions do. Scattered throughout the lineup are 10 cases concerning non-U.S. companies, globally competitive industries, and/or cross-cultural situations; these cases, in conjunction with the globalized content of the text chapters, provide ample material for linking the study of strategic management tightly to the ongoing globalization of the world economy. You'll also find 7 cases dealing with the strategic problems of family-owned or relatively small entrepreneurial businesses and 23 cases involving public companies about which students can do further research on the Internet. Eleven of the cases (Starbucks, JetBlue Airways, Competition in the MP3 Player Industry, Netflix, Krispy Kreme Doughnuts, eBay, Google, Harley-Davidson, Wal-Mart, Monsanto, and Merck-Vioxx) have accompanying videotape segments.

We believe you will find the collection of 33 cases quite appealing, eminently teachable, and very suitable for drilling students in the use of the concepts and analytical treatments in Chapters 1 through 13. With this case lineup, you should have no difficulty whatsoever choosing a set of cases to assign that will capture the interest of students from start to finish.

TWO ACCOMPANYING ONLINE, FULLY-AUTOMATED SIMULATION EXERCISES—*THE BUSINESS STRATEGY GAME* AND *GLO-BUS*

The Business Strategy Game and *GLO-BUS: Developing Winning Competitive Strategies*—two competition-based strategy simulations that are delivered online and that feature automated processing of decisions and grading of performance—are being marketed by the publisher as companion supplements for use with this and other texts in the field. *The Business Strategy Game* is the world's leading strategy simulation, having been played by well over 400,000 students at universities across the world. *GLO-BUS,* a somewhat simpler online simulation introduced in 2004, has been played by over 15,000 students at more than 125 universities across the world.

We think there are compelling reasons for using a simulation as a cornerstone, if not a centerpiece, of strategy courses for seniors and MBA students:

- Assigning students to run a company that competes head-to-head against companies run by other class members *gives students immediate opportunity to experiment with various strategy options and to gain proficiency in applying the core concepts and analytical tools that they have been reading about in the chapters.* The whole teaching/learning enterprise is facilitated when what the chapters have to say about the managerial tasks of crafting and executing strategy matches up with the strategy-making challenges that students confront in the simulation.

- Most *students desperately need the experience of actively managing a close-to-real-life company where they can practice and hone their skills* in thinking strategically, evaluating changing industry and competitive conditions, assessing a company's financial and competitive condition, and crafting and executing a strategy that delivers good results and produces sustainable competitive advantage. Strategy simulations put students through a drill where they can improve (1) their business acumen, (2) their ability to make good bottom-line decisions in the face of uncertain market and competitive conditions, and (3) their proficiency in weaving functional area decisions into a cohesive strategy. *Such skills building is the essence of senior and MBA courses in business strategy.*

- Students are *more motivated* to buckle down and figure out what strategic moves will make their simulation company perform better than they are to wrestle with the strategic issues posed in an assigned case (which entails reading the case thoroughly, diagnosing the company's situation, and proposing well-reasoned action recommendations). In a strategy simulation, students have to take the analysis of market conditions, the strategies and actions of competitors, and the condition of their company *seriously*—they are held fully accountable for their decisions and their company's performance. It is to students' advantage to avoid faulty analysis and flawed strategies—*nothing gets students' attention quicker than the adverse grade consequences of a decline in their company's performance or the loss of an industry position.* And no other type of assignment does a better job of spurring students to fully exercise their strategic wits and analytical prowess—*company co-managers have a strong grade incentive to spend quality time debating and deciding how best to boost the performance of their company.*

In class discussions of cases, however, students take on the more passive and detached role of outside observers providing their thoughts about a company's situation. It is sometimes hard to get students to think long and hard about the company in the assigned case or what needs to be done to improve its future performance. They may well not see an immediate or alarming impact on their grade if their case preparation is skimpy or their analysis of the company's situation is deficient or their recommendations about what the company should do are suboptimal or even off-the-wall. Thus, while case analysis absolutely needs to be an essential part of senior/MBA courses in strategy, case assignments fall short of strategy simulations in their capacity to motivate students to do first-rate strategic analysis and come up with insightful action recommendations.

- *A competition-based strategy simulation adds an enormous amount of student interest and excitement*—a head to-head competitive battle for market share and industry leadership *stirs students' competitive juices and emotionally engages them in the subject matter.* Being an active manager in running a company in which they have a stake makes their task of learning about crafting and executing winning strategies more enjoyable. Their company becomes "real" and takes on a life of its own as the simulation unfolds—and it doesn't take long for students to establish a healthy rivalry with other class members who are running rival companies. Because the competition in the simulation typically gets very personal, most students become immersed in what's going on in their industry—as compared to the more impersonal engagement that occurs when they are assigned a case to analyze.

- A first-rate simulation produces a "Wow! Not only is this fun, but I am learning a lot" reaction from students. *The element of competition ingrained in strategy simulations stirs students' competitive juices and emotionally engages them in the subject matter.* Most students will thoroughly enjoy the *learn-by-doing* character of a simulation, recognize the practical value of having to make all kinds of decisions and run a whole company, and gain confidence from working with all the financial and operating statistics—all of which tends to (1) make the strategy course *a livelier, richer learning experience,* and (2) result in higher instructor evaluations at the end of the course.

- Strategy simulations like *The Business Strategy Game* or *GLO-BUS* that have exceptionally close ties between the industry and company circumstances in the simulation and the topics covered in the text chapters *provide instructors with a host of first-rate examples of how the material in the text applies both to the experience that students are having in running their companies and to real-world management.* Since *students can easily relate to these examples,* they are much more apt to say "Aha! Now I see how this applies and why I need to know about it and use it." The host of examples the simulation experience provides to create this "Aha!" effect thus adds real value. (There is information posted in the Instructor Centers for both *The Business Strategy Game* and *GLO-BUS* showing specific links between the pages of this text and the simulation.)

- Because a simulation involves making decisions relating to production operations, worker compensation and training, sales and marketing, distribution, customer service, and finance and requires analysis of company financial statements and market data, *the simulation helps students synthesize the knowledge gained in a variety of different business courses. The cross-functional, integrative nature of a strategy simulation helps make courses in strategy much more of a true capstone experience.*

In sum, *a three-pronged text–case–simulation course model has significantly more teaching/learning power than the traditional text–case combination.* Indeed, a very convincing argument can be made that a competition-based strategy simulation is *the single most powerful vehicle that instructors can use to effectively teach the discipline of business and competitive strategy and to build student proficiencies in crafting and executing a winning strategy.* Mounting instructor recognition of the teaching/learning effectiveness of a good strategy simulation accounts for why strategy simulations have earned a prominent place in so many of today's strategy courses.

And, happily, there's another positive side benefit to using a simulation—*it lightens the grading burden for instructors.* Since a simulation can entail 20 or more hours of student time over the course of a term (depending on the number of decisions and the extent of accompanying assignments), most adopters compensate by trimming the total number of assigned cases or substituting the simulation for one (or two) written cases and/or an hour exam. This results in less time spent grading, because both *The Business Strategy Game* and *GLO-BUS* have built-in grading features that require no instructor effort (beyond setting the grading weights).

A Bird's-Eye View of The Business Strategy Game

The setting for *The Business Strategy Game* (*BSG*) is the global athletic footwear industry (there can be little doubt in today's world that a globally competitive strategy simulation is *vastly superior* to a simulation with a domestic-only setting). Global market demand for footwear grows at the rate of 7–9 percent annually for the first five years and 5–7 percent annually for the second five years. However, market growth rates vary by geographic region—North America, Latin America, Europe-Africa, and Asia-Pacific.

Companies begin the simulation producing branded and private-label footwear in two plants, one in North America and one in Asia. They have the option to establish production facilities in Latin America and Europe-Africa, either by constructing new plants or buying previously constructed plants that have been sold by competing companies. Company co-managers exercise control over production costs based on the styling and quality they opt to manufacture, plant location (wages and incentive compensation vary from region to region), the use of best practices and Six Sigma programs to reduce the production of defective footwear and to boost worker productivity, and compensation practices.

All newly produced footwear is shipped in bulk containers to one of four geographic distribution centers. All sales in a geographic region are made from footwear inventories in that region's distribution center. Costs at the four regional distribution centers are a function of inventory storage costs, packing and shipping fees, import tariffs paid on incoming pairs shipped from foreign plants, and exchange rate impacts. At the start of the simulation, import tariffs average $4 per pair in Europe-Africa, $6 per pair in Latin America, and $8 in the Asia-Pacific region. However, the Free Trade Treaty of the Americas allows tariff-free movement of footwear between North America and Latin America. Instructors have the option to alter tariffs as the game progresses.

Companies market their brand of athletic footwear to footwear retailers worldwide and to individuals buying online at the company's Web site. Each company's sales and market share in the branded footwear segments hinge on its competitiveness on 11 factors: attractive pricing, footwear styling and quality, product-line breadth, advertising, the use of mail-in rebates, the appeal of celebrities endorsing a company's brand, success in convincing footwear retailers dealers to carry its brand, the number of weeks it takes to fill retailer orders, the effectiveness of a company's online sales effort at its Web site, and customer loyalty. Sales of private-label footwear hinge solely on being the low-price bidder.

All told, company co-managers make 47 types of decisions each period that cut across production operations (up to 10 decisions each plant, with a maximum of 4 plants), plant capacity additions/sales/upgrades (up to 6 decisions per plant), worker compensation and training (3 decisions per plant), shipping (up to 8 decisions each plant), pricing and marketing (up to 10 decisions in 4 geographic regions), bids to sign celebrities (2 decision entries per bid), and financing of company operations (up to 8 decisions).

Each time company co-managers make a decision entry, an assortment of on-screen calculations instantly shows the projected effects on unit sales, revenues, market shares, unit costs, profit, earnings per share, ROE, and other operating statistics. The on-screen calculations help team members evaluate the relative merits of one decision entry versus another and put together a promising strategy.

Companies can employ any of the five generic competitive strategy options in selling branded footwear—low-cost leadership, differentiation, best-cost provider, focused low-cost, and focused differentiation. They can pursue essentially the same strategy worldwide or craft slightly or very different strategies for the Europe-Africa, Asia-Pacific, Latin America, and North America markets. They can strive for competitive advantage based on more advertising or a wider selection of models or more appealing styling/quality, or bigger rebates, and so on.

Any well-conceived, well-executed competitive approach is capable of succeeding, provided it is not overpowered by the strategies of competitors or defeated by the presence of too many copycat strategies that dilute its effectiveness. The challenge for each company's management team is to craft and execute a competitive strategy that produces good performance on five measures: earnings per share, return on equity investment, stock price appreciation, credit rating, and brand image.

All activity for *The Business Strategy Game* takes place at www.bsg-online.com.

A Bird's-Eye View of GLO-BUS

The industry setting for *GLO-BUS* is the digital camera industry. Global market demand grows at the rate of 8–10 percent annually for the first five years and 4–6 percent annually for the second five years. Retail sales of digital cameras are seasonal, with about 20 percent of consumer demand coming in each of the first three quarters of each calendar year and 40 percent coming during the big fourth-quarter retailing season.

Companies produce entry-level and upscale, multifeatured cameras of varying de-signs and quality in a Taiwan assembly facility and ship assembled cameras directly to retailers in North America, Asia-Pacific, Europe-Africa, and Latin America. All cameras are assembled as retail orders come in and shipped immediately upon completion of the assembly process—companies maintain no finished-goods inventories, and all parts and components are delivered on a just-in-time basis (which eliminates the need to track inventories and simplifies the accounting for plant operations and costs). Company co-managers exercise control over production costs based on the designs and components they specify for their cameras, workforce compensation and training, the length of warranties offered (which affects warranty costs), the amount spent for technical support provided to buyers of the company's cameras, and their management of the assembly process.

Competition in each of the two product market segments (entry-level and multifeatured digital cameras) is based on 10 factors: price, camera performance and quality, number of quarterly sales promotions, length of promotions in weeks, the size of the promotional discounts offered, advertising, the number of camera models, size of retail dealer network, warranty period, and the amount/caliber of technical support provided to camera buyers. Low-cost leadership, differentiation strategies, best-cost provider strategies, and focus strategies are all viable competitive options. Rival companies can strive to be the clear market leader in either entry-level cameras, upscale multifeatured cameras, or both. They can focus on one or two geographic regions or strive for geographic balance. They can pursue essentially the same strategy worldwide or craft slightly or very different strategies for the Europe-Africa, Asia-Pacific, Latin America, and North America markets. Just as with *The Business Strategy Game,* most any well-conceived, well-executed competitive approach is capable of succeeding, *provided it is not overpowered by the strategies of competitors or defeated by the presence of too many copycat strategies that dilute its effectiveness.*

Company co-managers make 44 types of decisions each period, ranging from R&D, camera components, and camera performance (10 decisions) to production operations and worker compensation (15 decisions) to pricing and marketing (15 decisions) to the financing of company operations (4 decisions). Each time participants make a decision entry, an assortment of on-screen calculations instantly shows the projected effects on unit sales, revenues, market shares, unit costs, profit, earnings per share, ROE, and other operating statistics. These on-screen calculations help team members evaluate the relative merits of one decision entry versus another and stitch the separate decisions into a cohesive and promising strategy. Company performance is judged on five criteria: earnings per share, return on equity investment, stock price, credit rating and brand image.

All activity for *GLO-BUS* occurs at www.glo-bus.com.

Administration and Operating Features of the Two Simulations

The online delivery and user-friendly designs of both *BSG* and *GLO-BUS* make them incredibly easy to administer, even for first-time users. And the menus and controls are so similar that you can readily switch between the two simulations or use one in your undergraduate class and the other in a graduate class. If you have not yet used either of the two simulations, you may find the following of particular interest:

- Time requirements for instructors are minimal. Setting up the simulation for your course is done online and takes about 10–15 minutes. Once setup is completed, no other administrative actions are required beyond that of moving participants to a different team (should the need arise) and monitoring the progress of the simulation (to whatever extent desired).

- There's no software for students or administrators to download and no disks to fool with. All work must be done online and the speed for participants using dial-up modems is quite satisfactory. The servers dedicated to hosting the two simulations have appropriate back-up capability and are maintained by a prominent Web-hosting service that guarantees 99.99 percent reliability on a 24/7/365 basis—as long as students or instructors are connected to the Internet, the servers are virtually guaranteed to be operational.

- Participant's Guides are delivered at the Web site—students can read the Guide on their monitors or print out a copy, as they prefer.

- There are extensive built-in "Help" screens explaining (1) each decision entry, (2) the information on each page of the Industry Reports, and (3) the numbers presented in the Company Reports. *The Help screens allow company co-managers to figure things out for themselves, thereby curbing the need for students to always run to the instructor with questions about "how things work."*

- The results of each decision are processed automatically and are typically available to all participants *15 minutes* after the decision deadline specified by the instructor/game administrator.

- Participants and instructors are notified via e-mail when the results are ready.

- Decision schedules are instructor-determined. Decisions can be made once per week, twice per week, or even twice daily, depending on how instructors want to conduct the exercise. One popular decision schedule involves 1 or 2 practice decisions, 6–10 regular decisions, and weekly decisions across the whole term. A second popular schedule is 1 or 2 practice decisions, 6–8 regular decisions, and biweekly decisions, all made during the last 4 to 6 weeks of the course (when it can be assumed that students have pretty much digested the contents of Chapters 1–6, gotten somewhat comfortable with what is involved in crafting strategy for a single-business company situation, and have prepared several assigned cases). A third popular schedule is to use the simulation as a "final exam" for the course, with daily decisions (Monday through Friday) for the last two weeks of the term.

- Instructors have the flexibility to prescribe 0, 1, or 2 practice decisions and from 3 to 10 regular decisions.

- Company teams can be composed of 1 to 5 players each and the number of companies in a single industry can range from 4 to 12. If your class size is too large for a single industry, then it is a simple matter to create two or more industries for a single class section.

- Following each decision, participants are provided with a complete set of reports—a six-page Industry Report, a one-page Competitive Intelligence report for each geographic region that includes strategic group maps and bulleted lists of competitive strengths and weaknesses, and a set of Company Reports (income statement, balance sheet, cash flow statement, and assorted production, marketing, and cost statistics).

- Two "open-book" multiple-choice tests of 20 questions (optional, but strongly recommended) are included as part of each of the two simulations. The quizzes are taken online and automatically graded, with scores reported instantaneously to participants and automatically recorded in the instructor's electronic gradebook. Students are automatically provided with three sample questions for each test.

- Both simulations contain a three-year strategic plan option that you can assign. Scores on the plan are automatically recorded in the instructor's online gradebook.
- At the end of the simulation, you can have students complete online peer evaluations. (Again, the scores are automatically recorded in your online gradebook.)
- Both simulations have a Company Presentation feature that enables students to easily prepare PowerPoint slides for use in describing their strategy and summarizing their company's performance in a presentation either to the class, the instructor, or an "outside" board of directors.

For more details on either simulation, please consult the Instructor's Manual or visit the simulation Web sites (www.bsg-online.com and www.glo-bus.com). The Web sites provide a wealth of information, including a "Guided Tour" link that takes about five minutes. Once you register (there's no obligation), you'll be able to access the Instructor's Guide and a set of PowerPoint Presentation slides that you can skim to preview the two simulations in some depth. The simulation authors will be glad to provide you with a personal tour of either or both Web sites (while you are on your PC) and walk you through the many features that are built into the simulations. We think you'll be quite impressed with the capabilities that have been programmed into *The Business Strategy Game and GLO-BUS,* the simplicity with which both simulations can be administered, and their exceptionally tight connection to the text chapters, core concepts, and standard analytical tools.

Adopters of the text who also want to incorporate use of either of the two simulation supplements should instruct their bookstores to order the "book-simulation package"—the publisher has a special ISBN for new texts that contain a special card shrink-wrapped with each text; printed on the enclosed card is a prepaid access code that student can use to register for either simulation and gain full access to the student portion of the Web site.

STUDENT SUPPORT MATERIALS FOR THE 15TH EDITION

Key Points Summaries

At the end of each chapter is a synopsis of the core concepts, analytical tools, and other key points discussed in the chapter. These chapter-end synopses, along with the margin notes scattered throughout each chapter, help students focus on basic strategy principles, digest the messages of each chapter, and prepare for tests.

Chapter-End Exercises

Each chapter contains a much-embellished set of exercises that you can use as the basis for class discussion, oral presentation assignments, and/or short written reports. A few of the exercises (and many of the Illustration Capsules) qualify as "mini-cases"; these can be used to round out the rest of a 75-minute class period should your lecture on a chapter only last for 50 minutes.

A Value-Added Web Site

Students use the code that comes on the inside page of each new copy of the text to gain access to the publisher's Web site for the 15th edition; students having a used text can purchase access to the site for a very modest fee. The student section of www.mhhe.com/thompson contains a number of helpful aids:

- Self-scoring 20-question chapter tests that students can take to measure their grasp of the material presented in each of the 13 chapters.
- A "Guide to Case Analysis" containing sections on what a case is, why cases are a standard part of courses in strategy, preparing a case for class discussion, doing a written case analysis, doing an oral presentation, and using financial ratio analysis to assess a company's financial condition. We suggest having students read this Guide prior to the first class discussion of a case.
- A select number of PowerPoint slides for each chapter.

PowerWeb

With each new book, students gain access to the publisher's PowerWeb site offering current news, articles from 6,300 premium sources, a Web research guide, current readings from annual editions, and links to related sites.

Case-Tutor Software

One of the most important and useful student aids at the 15th edition's Web site is a set of downloadable files called Case-Tutor that consists of (1) files containing assignment questions for all 35 cases in the text and (2) files containing analytically structured exercises for 11 of the cases—these 11 "case preparation exercises" coach students in doing the strategic thinking needed to arrive at solid answers to the assignment questions for that case. Conscientious completion of the case preparation exercises helps students gain quicker command of the concepts and analytical techniques and points them toward doing good strategic analysis. The 11 cases with an accompanying case preparation exercise are indicated by the Case-Tutor logo in the case listing section of the Table of Contents. (The Case-Tutor logo also appears on the first page of cases for which there is an exercise.)

INSTRUCTOR SUPPORT MATERIALS FOR THE 15TH EDITION

Instructor's Manual

The accompanying Instructor's Manual contains a section on suggestions for organizing and structuring your course, sample syllabi and course outlines, a set of lecture notes on each chapter, a copy of the test bank, and comprehensive teaching notes for each of cases.

Test Bank

There is a test bank prepared by the co-authors containing over 1,200 multiple-choice questions and short-answer/essay questions.

EZ-Test

A computerized version of the test bank, EZ-Test allows you to generate tests quite conveniently and to add in your own questions.

PowerPoint Slides

To facilitate delivery preparation of your lectures and to serve as chapter outlines, you'll have access to approximately 500 colorful and professional-looking slides displaying core concepts, analytical procedures, key points, and all the figures in the text chapters. The slides, prepared in close collaboration with the text authors, are the creation of Professor Jana Kuzmicki of Troy State University.

Accompanying Case Videos

Eleven of the cases (Starbucks, JetBlue Airways, Netflix, Krispy Kreme Doughnuts, Competition in the MP3 Player Industry, eBay, Google, Harley-Davidson, Wal-Mart, Monsanto, and Merck-Vioxx) have accompanying videotape segments that can be shown in conjunction with the case discussions. Suggestions for using each video are contained in the teaching note for that case.

The Business Strategy Game *and* GLO-BUS
Online Simulations

Using one of the two companion simulations is a powerful and constructive way of emotionally connecting students to the subject matter of the course. We know of no more effective and interesting way to stimulate the competitive energy of students and prepare them for the rigors of real-world business decision making than to have them match strategic wits with classmates in running a company in head-to-head competition for global market leadership.

Instructor's Resource CD-ROM

The complete Instructor's Manual and the accompanying PowerPoint slides have been installed on an Instructor's Resource CD that the publisher provides to adopters.

We've done our level best in this 15th edition to provide you with a full-featured teaching/learning package that squarely targets what every business student needs to know about crafting and executing business strategies, that is diverse enough to keep the nature of student assignments varied and interesting, and that wins the applause of students. The intent has been to raise the bar for what a text package in the discipline of strategy ought to deliver and to equip you with all the resources and materials you'll need to design and deliver a course that is on the cutting-edge and pedagogically effective.

ACKNOWLEDGMENTS

We heartily acknowledge the contributions of the case researchers whose case-writing efforts appear herein and the companies whose cooperation made the cases possible. To each one goes a very special thank-you. We cannot overstate the importance of timely, carefully researched cases in contributing to a substantive study of strategic management issues and practices. From a research standpoint, strategy-related cases are invaluable in exposing the generic kinds of strategic issues that companies face, in forming hypotheses about strategic behavior, and in drawing experienced-based generalizations about the practice of strategic management. From an instructional standpoint, strategy cases give students essential practice in diagnosing and evaluating the strategic situations of companies and organizations, in applying the concepts and tools of strategic analysis, in weighing strategic options and crafting strategies, and in tackling the challenges of successful strategy execution. Without a continuing stream of fresh, well-researched, and well-conceived cases, the discipline of strategic management would lose its close ties to the very institutions whose strategic actions and behavior it is aimed at explaining. There's no question, therefore, that first-class case research constitutes a valuable scholarly contribution to the theory and practice of strategic management.

In addition, a great number of colleagues and students at various universities, business acquaintances, and people at McGraw-Hill provided inspiration, encouragement, and counsel during the course of this project. Like all text authors in the strategy field, we are intellectually indebted to the many academics whose research and writing have blazed new trails and advanced the discipline of strategic management. The following reviewers provided seasoned advice and splendid suggestions for improving the chapters in this 15th edition:

Lynne Patten, *Clark Atlanta University*

Nancy E. Landrum, *Morehead State University*

Jim Goes, *Walden University*

Jon Kalinowski, *Minnesota State University–Mankato*

Rodney M. Walter Jr., *Western Illinois University*

Judith D. Powell, *Virginia Union University*

We also express our thanks to Seyda Deligonul, David Flanagan, Esmerelda Garbi, Mohsin Habib, Kim Hester, Jeffrey E. McGee, Diana J. Wong, F. William Brown, Anthony F. Chelte, Gregory G. Dess, Alan B. Eisner, John George, Carle M. Hunt, Theresa Marron-Grodsky, Sarah Marsh, Joshua D. Martin, William L. Moore, Donald Neubaum, George M. Puia, Amit Shah, Lois M. Shelton, Mark Weber, Steve Barndt, J. Michael Geringer, Ming-Fang Li, Richard Stackman, Stephen Tallman, Gerardo R. Ungson, James Boulgarides, Betty Diener, Daniel F. Jennings, David Kuhn, Kathryn Martell, Wilbur Mouton, Bobby Vaught, Tuck Bounds, Lee Burk, Ralph Catalanello, William Crittenden, Vince Luchsinger, Stan Mendenhall, John Moore, Will Mulvaney, Sandra Richard, Ralph Roberts, Thomas Turk, Gordon VonStroh, Fred Zimmerman, S. A. Billion, Charles Byles, Gerald L. Geisler, Rose Knotts, Joseph Rosenstein, James B. Thurman, Ivan Able, W. Harvey Hegarty, Roger Evered, Charles B. Saunders, Rhae

M. Swisher, Claude I. Shell, R. Thomas Lenz, Michael C. White, Dennis Callahan, R. Duane Ireland, William E. Burr II, C. W. Millard, Richard Mann, Kurt Christensen, Neil W. Jacobs, Louis W. Fry, D. Robley Wood, George J. Gore, and William R. Soukup. These reviewers provided valuable guidance in steering our efforts to improve earlier editions.

As always, we value your recommendations and thoughts about the book. Your comments regarding coverage and contents will be taken to heart, and we always are grateful for the time you take to call our attention to printing errors, deficiencies, and other shortcomings. Please e-mail us at athompso@cba.ua.edu, astrickl@cba.ua.edu, or jgamble@usouthal.edu; fax us at (205) 348-6695; or write us at P.O. Box 870225, Department of Management and Marketing, The University of Alabama, Tuscaloosa, Alabama 35487-0225.

Arthur A.Thompson

A. J. Strickland

John E. Gamble

Guided Tour

Chapter Structure and Organization

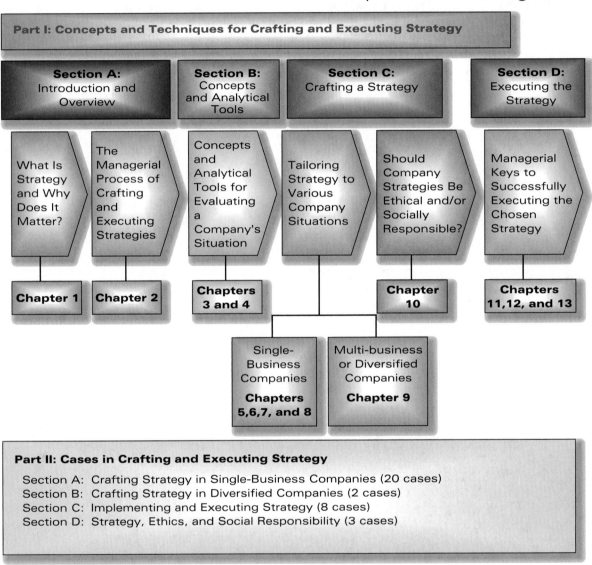

Part I: Concepts and Techniques for Crafting and Executing Strategy

Section A: Introduction and Overview

Section B: Concepts and Analytical Tools

Section C: Crafting a Strategy

Section D: Executing the Strategy

What Is Strategy and Why Does It Matter?

The Managerial Process of Crafting and Executing Strategies

Concepts and Analytical Tools for Evaluating a Company's Situation

Tailoring Strategy to Various Company Situations

Should Company Strategies Be Ethical and/or Socially Responsible?

Managerial Keys to Successfully Executing the Chosen Strategy

Chapter 1

Chapter 2

Chapters 3 and 4

Chapter 10

Chapters 11,12, and 13

Single-Business Companies
Chapters 5,6,7, and 8

Multi-business or Diversified Companies
Chapter 9

Part II: Cases in Crafting and Executing Strategy

Section A: Crafting Strategy in Single-Business Companies (20 cases)
Section B: Crafting Strategy in Diversified Companies (2 cases)
Section C: Implementing and Executing Strategy (8 cases)
Section D: Strategy, Ethics, and Social Responsibility (3 cases)

chapter one

What Is Strategy and Why Is It Important?

Strategy means making clear-cut choices about how to compete.
—**Jack Welch**
Former CEO, General Electric

A strategy is a commitment to undertake one set of actions rather than another.
—**Sharon Oster**
Professor, Yale University

The process of developing superior strategies is part planning, part trial and error, until you hit upon something that works.
—**Costas Markides**
Professor, London Business School

Without a strategy the organization is like a ship without a rudder.
—**Joel Ross and Michael Kami**
Authors and Consultants

Managers face three central questions in evaluating their company's business prospects: What's the company's present situation? Where does the company need to go from here? How should it get there? Arriving at a probing answer to the question "What's the company's present situation?" prompts managers to evaluate industry conditions and competitive pressures, the company's current performance and market standing, its resource strengths and capabilities, and its competitive weaknesses. The question "Where does the company need to go from here?" pushes managers to make choices about the direction the company should be headed—what new or different customer groups and customer needs it should endeavor to satisfy, what market positions it should be staking out, what changes in its business makeup are needed. The question "How should it get there?" challenges managers to craft and execute a strategy capable of moving the company in the intended direction, growing its business, and improving its financial and market performance.

In this opening chapter, we define the concept of strategy and describe its many facets. We shall indicate the kinds of actions that determine what a company's strategy is, why strategies are partly proactive and partly reactive, and why company strategies tend to evolve over time. We will look at what sets a winning strategy apart from ho-hum or flawed strategies and why the caliber of a company's strategy determines whether it will enjoy a competitive advantage or be burdened by competitive disadvantage. By the end of this chapter, you will have a pretty clear idea of why the tasks of crafting and executing strategy are core management functions and why excellent execution of an excellent strategy is the most reliable recipe for turning a company into a standout performer.

WHAT DO WE MEAN BY *STRATEGY*?

A company's **strategy** is management's action plan for running the business and conducting operations. The crafting of a strategy represents a managerial *commitment to pursue a particular set of actions* in growing the business, attracting and pleasing customers, competing successfully, conducting operations, and improving the company's financial and market performance. Thus a company's strategy is all about *how—how* management intends to grow the business, *how* it will build a loyal clientele and outcompete rivals, *how* each functional piece of the business (research and development,

Each chapter begins with a series of pertinent **quotes** and an introductory preview of its contents.

Illustration Capsule 1.2

Microsoft and Red Hat: Two Contrasting Business Models

The strategies of rival companies are often predicated on strikingly different business models. Consider, for example, the business models for Microsoft and Red Hat in operating system software for personal computers (PCs).

Microsoft's business model for making money from its Windows operating system products is based on the following revenue-cost-profit economics:

- Employ a cadre of highly skilled programmers to develop proprietary code; keep the source code hidden so as to keep the inner workings of the software proprietary.
- Sell the resulting operating system and software package to PC makers and to PC users at relatively attractive prices (around $75 to PC makers and about $100 at retail to PC users); strive to maintain a 90 percent or more market share of the 150 million PCs sold annually worldwide.
- Strive for big-volume sales. Most of Microsoft's costs arise on the front end in developing the software and are thus fixed; the variable costs of producing and packaging the CDs provided to users are only a couple of dollars per copy—once the break-even volume is reached, Microsoft's revenues from additional sales are almost pure profit.
- Provide a modest level of technical support to users at no cost.
- Keep rejuvenating revenues by periodically introducing next-generation software versions with features that will induce PC users to upgrade the operating system on previously purchased PCs to the new version.

Red Hat, a company formed to market its own version of the Linux open-source operating system, employs a business model based on sharply different revenue-cost-profit economics:

- Rely on the collaborative efforts of volunteer programmers from all over the world who contribute bits and pieces of code to improve and polish the Linux system. The global community of thousands of programmers who work on Linux in their spare time do what they do because they love it, because they are fervent believers that all software should be free (as in free speech), and in some cases because they are anti-Microsoft and want to have a part in undoing what they see as a Microsoft monopoly.

- Collect and test enhancements and new applications submitted by the open-source community of volunteer programmers. Linux's originator, Linus Torvalds, and a team of 300-plus Red Hat engineers and software developers evaluate which incoming submissions merit inclusion in new releases of Linux—the evaluation and integration of new submissions are Red Hat's only upfront product development costs.
- Market the upgraded and tested family of Red Hat products to large enterprises and charge them a subscription fee that includes 24/7 support within one hour in seven languages. Provide subscribers with updated versions of Linux every 12–18 months to maintain the subscriber base.
- Make the source code open and available to all users, allowing them to create a customized version of Linux.
- Capitalize on the specialized expertise required to use Linux in multiserver, multiprocessor applications by providing fees-based training, consulting, software customization, and client-directed engineering to Linux users. Red Hat offers Linux certification training programs at all skill levels at more than 60 global locations—Red Hat certification in the use of Linux is considered the best in the world.

Microsoft's business model—sell proprietary code software and give service away free—is a proven moneymaker that generates billions in profits annually. In contrast, the jury is still out on Red Hat's business model of selling subscriptions to open-source software to large corporations and deriving substantial revenues from the sales of technical support (included in the subscription cost), training, consulting, software customization, and engineering to generate revenues sufficient to cover costs and yield a profit. Red Hat posted losses of $140 million on revenues of $79 million in fiscal year 2002 and losses of $6.6 million on revenues of $91 million in fiscal year 2003, but it earned $14 million on revenues of $126 million in fiscal 2004. The profits came from a shift in Red Hat's business model that involved putting considerably more emphasis on getting large corporations to purchase subscriptions to the latest Linux updates. In 2005, about 75 percent of Red Hat's revenues came from large enterprise subscriptions, compared to about 53 percent in 2003.

Source: Company documents and information posted on www.microsoft.com and www.redhat.com. (accessed August 10, 2005).

In-depth examples–
Illustration Capsules–
appear in boxes throughout each chapter to illustrate important chapter topics, connect the text presentation to real world companies, and convincingly demonstrate "strategy in action." Some can be used as "mini-cases" for purposes of class discussion.

Margin notes define core concepts and call attention to important ideas and principles.

Strategy and the Quest for Competitive Advantage

The heart and soul of any strategy are the actions and moves in the marketplace that managers are taking to improve the company's financial performance, strengthen its long-term competitive position, and gain a competitive edge over rivals. A creative, distinctive strategy that sets a company apart from rivals and yields a competitive advantage is a company's most reliable ticket for earning above-average profits. Competing in the marketplace with a competitive advantage tends to be more profitable than competing with no advantage. And a company is almost certain to earn significantly higher profits when it enjoys a competitive advantage as opposed to when it is hamstrung by competitive disadvantage. Furthermore, if a company's competitive edge holds promise for being durable and sustainable (as opposed to just temporary), then so much the better for both the strategy and the company's future profitability. It's nice when a company's strategy produces at least a temporary competitive edge, but a **sustainable competitive advantage** is plainly much better. What makes a competitive advantage sustainable as opposed to temporary are actions and elements in the strategy that cause an attractive number of buyers to have a *lasting preference* for a company's products or services as compared to the offerings of competitors. Competitive advantage is the key to above-average profitability and financial performance because strong buyer preferences for the company's product offering translate into higher sales volumes (Wal-Mart) and/or the ability to command a higher price (Häagen-Dazs), thus driving up earnings, return on investment, and other measures of financial performance.

Four of the most frequently used and dependable strategic approaches to setting a company apart from rivals, building strong customer loyalty, and winning a sustainable competitive advantage are:

Core Concept
A company achieves *sustainable competitive advantage* when an attractive number of buyers prefer its products or services over the offerings of competitors and when the basis for this preference is durable.

Figures scattered throughout the chapters provide conceptual and analytical frameworks.

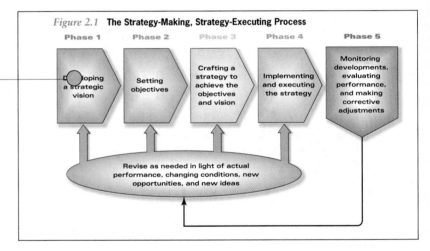

Figure 2.1 **The Strategy-Making, Strategy-Executing Process**

Phase 1 — Developing a strategic vision

Phase 2 — Setting objectives

Phase 3 — Crafting a strategy to achieve the objectives and vision

Phase 4 — Implementing and executing the strategy

Phase 5 — Monitoring developments, evaluating performance, and making corrective adjustments

Revise as needed in light of actual performance, changing conditions, new opportunities, and new ideas

ist and poet Ralph Waldo Emerson: "Commerce is a game of skill which many people play, but which few play well." If the content of this book helps you become a more savvy player and equips you to succeed in business, then your journey through these pages will indeed be time well spent.

Key Points

The tasks of crafting and executing company strategies are the heart and soul of managing a business enterprise and winning in the marketplace. A company's strategy is the game plan management is using to stake out a market position, conduct its operations, attract and please customers, compete successfully, and achieve organizational objectives. The central thrust of a company's strategy is undertaking moves to build and strengthen the company's long-term competitive position and financial performance and, ideally, gain a competitive advantage over rivals that then becomes a company's ticket to above-average profitability. A company's strategy typically evolves and reforms over time, emerging from a blend of (1) proactive and purposeful actions on the part of company managers and (2) as-needed reactions to unanticipated developments and fresh market conditions.

Key Points sections at the end of each chapter provide a handy summary of essential ideas and things to remember.

the company's product offerings and competitive approaches will generate a revenue stream and have an associated cost structure that produces attractive earnings and return on investment—in effect, a company's business model sets forth the economic logic for making money in a particular business, given the company's current strategy.

A winning strategy fits the circumstances of a company's external situation and its internal resource strengths and competitive capabilities, builds competitive advantage, and boosts company performance.

Crafting and executing strategy are core management functions. Whether a company wins or loses in the marketplace is directly attributable to the caliber of a company's strategy and the proficiency with which the strategy is executed.

Exercises

1. Go to Red Hat's Web site (www.redhat.com) and check whether the company's recent financial reports indicate that its business model is working. Is the company sufficiently profitable to validate its business model and strategy? Is its revenue stream from selling training, consulting, and engineering services growing or declining as a percentage of total revenues? Does your review of the company's recent financial performance suggest that its business model and strategy are changing? Read the company's latest statement about its business model and about why it is pursuing the subscription approach (as compared to Microsoft's approach of selling copies of its operating software directly to PC manufacturers

Value-added **exercises** at the end of each chapter provide a basis for class discussion, oral presentations, and written assignments. Several chapters have exercises that qualify as "mini-cases."

33 cases detailing the strategic circumstances of actual companies and providing practice in applying the concepts and tools of strategic analysis.

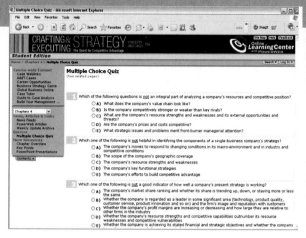

Web site: www.mhhe.com/thompson

The student portion of the Web site features a "Guide to Case Analysis," with special sections on what a case is, why cases are a standard part of courses in strategy, preparing a case for class discussion, doing a written case analysis, doing an oral presentation, and using financial ratio analysis to assess a company's financial condition. In addition, there are 20-question self-scoring chapter tests and a select number of PowerPoint slides for each chapter.

Case-TUTOR: A set of downloadable files containing assignment questions for each of the 33 cases in the text, plus analytically-structured exercises for 11 of the cases that coach students in doing the strategic thinking needed to arrive at solid answers to the assignment questions for that case. Conscientious completion of the 11 case exercises aids quicker command of the concepts and analytical techniques and facilitates good strategic analysis and thorough preparation of assigned cases.

The Business Strategy Game or GLO-BUS Simulation Exercises Either one of these text supplements involves teams of students managing companies in a head-to-head contest for global market leadership. Company co-managers have to make decisions relating to product quality, production, work force compensation and training, pricing and marketing, and financing of company operations. The challenge is to craft and execute a strategy that is powerful enough to deliver good financial performance despite the competitive efforts of rival companies. Each company competes in North America, Latin America, Europe-Africa, and Asia-Pacific.

PowerWeb With each new book, students gain access to publisher's PowerWeb site offering current news, articles from 6,300 premium sources, a Web research guide, current readings from annual editions, and links to related sites.

Brief Contents

Table of Contents

6. Supplementing the Chosen Competitive Strategy:
Other Important Strategy Choices   160

Illustration Capsules

9.1. Related Diversification at L'Oréal, Johnson & Johnson, PepsiCo, and Darden Restaurants   277

9.2. Unrelated Diversification at General Electric, United Technologies, American Standard, and Lancaster Colony   281

9.3. Managing Diversification at Johnson & Johnson: The Benefits of Cross-Business Strategic Fits   302

9.4. Lucent Technology's Retrenchment Strategy   304

9.5. The Global Scope of Four Prominent Diversified Multinational Corporations   309

10. Strategy, Ethics, and Social Responsibility   316

What Do We Mean by *Business Ethics?*   317

Where Do Ethical Standards Come From—Are They Universal or Dependent on Local Norms and Situational Circumstances?   318
    The School of Ethical Universalism   318
    The School of Ethical Relativism   319
    Ethics and Integrative Social Contracts Theory   322

The Three Categories of Management Morality   323
    Evidence of Managerial Immorality in the Global Business Community   325

Do Company Strategies Need to Be Ethical?   327
    What Are the Drivers of Unethical Strategies and Business Behavior?   328
    Approaches to Managing a Company's Ethical Conduct   333

Why Should Company Strategies Be Ethical?   338
    The Moral Case for an Ethical Strategy   338
    The Business Case for an Ethical Strategy   338

Linking a Company's Strategy to Its Ethical Principles and Core Values   341

Strategy and Social Responsibility   342
    What Do We Mean by Social Responsibility?   342
    Crafting a Social Responsibility Strategy: The Starting Point for Demonstrating a Social Conscience   345
    The Moral Case for Corporate Social Responsibility   346
    The Business Case for Socially Responsible Behavior   347
    The Well-Intentioned Efforts of Do-Good Executives Can Be Controversial   349
    How Much Attention to Social Responsibility Is Enough?   351
    Linking Social Performance Targets to Executive Compensation   352

Illustration Capsules

10.1. Marsh & McLennan's Ethically Flawed Strategy   329

10.2. Philip Morris USA's Strategy for Marlboro Cigarettes: Ethical or Unethical?   334

10.3. A Test of Your Business Ethics   340

13. Corporate Culture and Leadership: Keys to Good Strategy Execution   414

part one

1

Concepts and Techniques for Crafting and Executing Strategy

What Is Strategy and Why Is It Important?

Strategy means making clear-cut choices about how to compete.

—Jack Welch
Former CEO, General Electric

A strategy is a commitment to undertake one set of actions rather than another.

—Sharon Oster
Professor, Yale University

The process of developing superior strategies is part planning, part trial and error, until you hit upon something that works.

—Costas Markides
Professor, London Business School

Without a strategy the organization is like a ship without a rudder.

—Joel Ross and Michael Kami
Authors and Consultants

M anagers face three central questions in evaluating their company's business prospects: What's the company's present situation? Where does the company need to go from here? How should it get there? Arriving at a probing answer to the question "What's the company's present situation?" prompts managers to evaluate industry conditions and competitive pressures, the company's current performance and market standing, its resource strengths and capabilities, and its competitive weaknesses. The question "Where does the company need to go from here?" pushes managers to make choices about the direction the company should be headed—what new or different customer groups and customer needs it should endeavor to satisfy, what market positions it should be staking out, what changes in its business makeup are needed. The question "How should it get there?" challenges managers to craft and execute a strategy capable of moving the company in the intended direction, growing its business, and improving its financial and market performance.

In this opening chapter, we define the concept of strategy and describe its many facets. We shall indicate the kinds of actions that determine what a company's strategy is, why strategies are partly proactive and partly reactive, and why company strategies tend to evolve over time. We will look at what sets a winning strategy apart from ho-hum or flawed strategies and why the caliber of a company's strategy determines whether it will enjoy a competitive advantage or be burdened by competitive disadvantage. By the end of this chapter, you will have a pretty clear idea of why the tasks of crafting and executing strategy are core management functions and why excellent execution of an excellent strategy is the most reliable recipe for turning a company into a standout performer.

WHAT DO WE MEAN BY *STRATEGY?*

A company's **strategy** is management's action plan for running the business and conducting operations. The crafting of a strategy represents a managerial *commitment to pursue a particular set of actions* in growing the business, attracting and pleasing customers, competing successfully, conducting operations, and improving the company's financial and market performance. Thus a company's strategy is all about *how—how* management intends to grow the business, *how* it will build a loyal clientele and outcompete rivals, *how* each functional piece of the business (research and development,

Core Concept

A company's *strategy* consists of the competitive moves and business approaches that managers are employing to grow the business, attract and please customers, compete successfully, conduct operations, and achieve the targeted levels of organizational performance.

supply chain activities, production, sales and marketing, distribution, finance, and human resources) will be operated, *how* performance will be boosted. In choosing a strategy, management is in effect saying, "Among all the many different business approaches and ways of competing we could have chosen, we have decided to employ this particular combination of competitive and operating approaches in moving the company in the intended direction, strengthening its market position and competitiveness, and boosting performance." The strategic choices a company makes are seldom easy decisions, and some of them may turn out to be wrong—but that is not an excuse for not deciding on a concrete course of action.[1]

In most industries companies have considerable freedom in choosing the hows of strategy.[2] Thus, some rivals strive to improve their performance and market standing by achieving lower costs than rivals, while others pursue product superiority or personalized customer service or the development of competencies and capabilities that rivals cannot match. Some target the high end of the market, while others go after the middle or low end; some opt for wide product lines, while others concentrate their energies on a narrow product lineup. Some competitors position themselves in only one part of the industry's chain of production/distribution activities (preferring to be just in manufacturing or wholesale distribution or retailing), while others are partially or fully integrated, with operations ranging from components production to manufacturing and assembly to wholesale distribution or retailing. Some competitors deliberately confine their operations to local or regional markets; others opt to compete nationally, internationally (several countries), or globally (all or most of the major country markets worldwide). Some companies decide to operate in only one industry, while others diversify broadly or narrowly, into related or unrelated industries, via acquisitions, joint ventures, strategic alliances, or internal start-ups.

At companies intent on gaining sales and market share at the expense of competitors, managers typically opt for offensive strategies, frequently launching fresh initiatives of one kind or another to make the company's product offering more distinctive and appealing to buyers. Companies already in a strong industry position are more prone to strategies that emphasize gradual gains in the marketplace, fortifying the company's market position, and defending against the latest maneuvering of rivals and other developments that threaten the company's well-being. Risk-averse companies often prefer conservative strategies, preferring to follow the successful moves of pioneering companies whose managers are more entrepreneurial and willing to take the risks of being first to make a bold and perhaps pivotal move that reshapes the contest among market rivals.

There is no shortage of opportunity to fashion a strategy that both tightly fits a company's own particular situation and is discernibly different from the strategies of rivals. In fact, a company's managers normally attempt to make strategic choices about the key building blocks of its strategy that differ from the choices made by competitors— not 100 percent different but at least different in several important respects. A strategy stands a better chance of succeeding when it is predicated on actions, business approaches, and competitive moves aimed at (1) appealing to buyers in ways that set a company apart from rivals and (2) carving out its own market position. Simply copying what successful companies in the industry are doing and trying to mimic their market position rarely works. Rather, there needs to be some distinctive "aha" element to the strategy that draws in customers and produces a competitive edge. Carbon-copy strategies among companies in the same industry are the exception rather than the rule.

For a concrete example of the actions and approaches that comprise strategy, see Illustration Capsule 1.1, which describes Comcast's strategy to revolutionize the cable TV business.

Comcast's Strategy to Revolutionize the Cable Industry

In 2004–2005 cable TV giant Comcast put the finishing touches on a bold strategy to change the way people watched television and to grow its business by introducing Internet phone service. With revenues of $18 billion and almost 22 million of the 74 million U.S. cable subscribers, Comcast became the industry leader in the U.S. market in 2002 when it acquired AT&T Broadband, along with its 13 million cable subscribers, for about $50 billion. Comcast's strategy had the following elements:

- *Continue to roll out high-speed Internet or broadband service to customers via cable modems.* With more than 8 million customers that generated revenues approaching $5 billion annually, Comcast was already America's number one provider of broadband service. It had recently upgraded its broadband service to allow download speeds of up to six megabits per second—considerably faster than the DSL-type broadband service available over telephone lines.

- *Continue to promote a relatively new video-on-demand service that allowed digital subscribers to watch TV programs whenever they wanted to watch them.* The service allowed customers to use their remotes to choose from a menu of thousands of programs, stored on Comcast's servers as they were first broadcast, and included network shows, news, sports, and movies. Viewers with a Comcast DVR set-top box had the ability to pause, stop, restart, and save programs, without having to remember to record them when they were broadcast. Comcast had signed up more than 10 million of its cable customers for digital service, and it was introducing enhanced digital and high-definition television (HDTV) service in additional geographic markets at a brisk pace.

- *Promote a video-on-demand service whereby digital customers with a set-top box could order and watch pay-per-view movies using a menu on their remote.* Comcast's technology enabled viewers to call up the programs they wanted with a few clicks of the remote. In 2005, Comcast had almost 4000 program choices and customers were viewing about 120 million videos per month.

- *Partner with Sony, MGM, and others to expand Comcast's library of movie offerings.* In 2004, Comcast agreed to develop new cable channels using MGM and Sony libraries, which had a combined 7,500 movies and 42,000 TV shows—it took about 300 movies to feed a 24-hour channel for a month.

- *Use Voice over Internet Protocol (VoIP) technology to offer subscribers Internet-based phone service at a fraction of the cost charged by other providers.* VoIP is an appealing low-cost technology widely seen as the most significant new communication technology since the invention of the telephone. Comcast was on track to make its Comcast Digital Voice (CDV) service available to 41 million homes by year-end 2006. CDV had many snazzy features, including call forwarding, caller ID, and conferencing, thus putting Comcast in position to go after the customers of traditional telephone companies.

- *Use its video-on-demand and CDV offerings to combat mounting competition from direct-to-home satellite TV providers.* Satellite TV providers such as EchoStar and DIRECTV had been using the attraction of lower monthly fees to steal customers away from cable TV providers. Comcast believed that the appeal of video-on-demand and low-cost CDV service would overcome its higher price. And satellite TV providers lacked the technological capability to provide either two-way communications connection to homes (necessary to offer video-on-demand) or reliable high-speed Internet access.

- *Employ a sales force (currently numbering about 3,200 people) to sell advertising to businesses that were shifting some of their advertising dollars from sponsoring network programs to sponsoring cable programs.* Ad sales generated revenues of about $1.6 billion, and Comcast had cable operations in 21 of the 25 largest markets in the United States.

- *Significantly improve Comcast's customer service.* Most cable subscribers were dissatisfied with the caliber of customer service offered by their local cable companies. Comcast management believed that service would be a big issue given the need to support video-on-demand, cable modems, HDTV, phone service, and the array of customer inquiries and problems such services entailed. In 2004, Comcast employed about 12,500 people to answer an expected volume of 200 million phone calls. Newly hired customer service personnel were given five weeks of classroom training, followed by three weeks of taking calls while a supervisor listened in—it cost Comcast about $7 to handle each call. The company's goal was to answer 90 percent of calls within 30 seconds.

Sources: Information posted at www.comcast.com (accessed August 6, 2005); Marc Gunter, "Comcast Wants to Change the World, But Can It Learn to Answer the Phone?" *Fortune,* October 16, 2004, pp. 140–56; and Stephanie N. Mehta, "The Future Is on the Line," *Fortune,* July 26, 2004, pp. 121–30.

Strategy and the Quest for Competitive Advantage

The heart and soul of any strategy are the actions and moves in the marketplace that managers are taking to improve the company's financial performance, strengthen its long-term competitive position, and gain a competitive edge over rivals. A creative, distinctive strategy that sets a company apart from rivals and yields a competitive advantage is a company's most reliable ticket for earning above-average profits. Competing in the marketplace with a competitive advantage tends to be more profitable than competing with no advantage. And a company is almost certain to earn significantly higher profits when it enjoys a competitive advantage as opposed to when it is hamstrung by competitive disadvantage. Furthermore, if a company's competitive edge holds promise for being durable and sustainable (as opposed to just temporary), then so much the better for both the strategy and the company's future profitability. It's nice when a company's strategy produces at least a temporary competitive edge, but a **sustainable competitive advantage** is plainly much better. What makes a competitive advantage sustainable as opposed to temporary are actions and elements in the strategy that cause an attractive number of buyers to have a *lasting preference* for a company's products or services as compared to the offerings of competitors. Competitive advantage is the key to above-average profitability and financial performance because strong buyer preferences for the company's product offering translate into higher sales volumes (Wal-Mart) and/or the ability to command a higher price (Häagen-Dazs), thus driving up earnings, return on investment, and other measures of financial performance.

> **Core Concept**
> A company achieves *sustainable competitive advantage* when an attractive number of buyers prefer its products or services over the offerings of competitors and when the basis for this preference is durable.

Four of the most frequently used and dependable strategic approaches to setting a company apart from rivals, building strong customer loyalty, and winning a sustainable competitive advantage are:

1. *Striving to be the industry's low-cost provider, thereby aiming for a cost-based competitive advantage over rivals.* Wal-Mart and Southwest Airlines have earned strong market positions because of the low-cost advantages they have achieved over their rivals and their consequent ability to underprice competitors. Achieving lower costs than rivals can produce a durable competitive edge when rivals find it hard to match the low-cost leader's approach to driving costs out of the business. Despite years of trying, discounters like Kmart and Target have struck out trying to match Wal-Mart's frugal operating practices, super-efficient distribution systems, and its finely honed supply chain approaches that allow it to obtain merchandise from manufacturers at super-low prices.

2. *Outcompeting rivals based on such differentiating features as higher quality, wider product selection, added performance, value-added services, more attractive styling, technological superiority, or unusually good value for the money.* Successful adopters of differentiation strategies include Johnson & Johnson in baby products (product reliability), Harley-Davidson (bad-boy image and king-of-the-road styling), Chanel and Rolex (top-of-the-line prestige), Mercedes-Benz and BMW (engineering design and performance), L. L. Bean (good value), and Amazon. com (wide selection and convenience). Differentiation strategies can be powerful so long as a company is sufficiently innovative to thwart clever rivals in finding ways to copy or closely imitate the features of a successful differentiator's product offering.

3. *Focusing on a narrow market niche and winning a competitive edge by doing a better job than rivals of serving the special needs and tastes of buyers comprising*

the niche. Prominent companies that enjoy competitive success in a specialized market niche include eBay in online auctions, Jiffy Lube International in quick oil changes, McAfee in virus protection software, Starbucks in premium coffees and coffee drinks, Whole Foods Market in natural and organic foods, CNBC and The Weather Channel in cable TV.

4. *Developing expertise and resource strengths that give the company competitive capabilities that rivals can't easily imitate or trump with capabilities of their own.* FedEx has superior capabilities in next-day delivery of small packages. Walt Disney has hard-to-beat capabilities in theme park management and family entertainment. Over the years, Toyota has developed a sophisticated production system that allows it to produce reliable, largely defect-free vehicles at low cost. IBM has wide-ranging expertise in helping corporate customers develop and install cutting-edge information systems. Ritz-Carlton and Four Seasons have uniquely strong capabilities in providing their hotel guests with an array of personalized services. Very often, winning a durable competitive edge over rivals hinges more on building competitively valuable expertise and capabilities than it does on having a distinctive product. Clever rivals can nearly always copy the attributes of a popular or innovative product, but for rivals to match experience, know-how, and specialized competitive capabilities that a company has developed and perfected over a long period of time is substantially harder to duplicate and takes much longer.

The tight connection between competitive advantage and profitability means that the quest for sustainable competitive advantage always ranks center stage in crafting a strategy. The key to successful strategy making is to come up with one or more differentiating strategy elements that act as a magnet to draw customers and yield a lasting competitive edge. Indeed, what separates a powerful strategy from a run-of-the-mill or ineffective one is management's ability to forge a series of moves, both in the marketplace and internally, that sets the company apart from its rivals, tilts the playing field in the company's favor by giving buyers reason to prefer its products or services, and produces a sustainable competitive advantage over rivals. The bigger and more sustainable the competitive advantage, the better the company's prospects for winning in the marketplace and earning superior long-term profits relative to its rivals. Without a strategy that leads to competitive advantage, a company risks being outcompeted by stronger rivals and/or locked in to mediocre financial performance. Hence, company managers deserve no gold stars for coming up with a ho-hum strategy that results in ho-hum financial performance and a ho-hum industry standing.

Identifying a Company's Strategy

The best indicators of a company's strategy are its actions in the marketplace and the statements of senior managers about the company's current business approaches, future plans, and efforts to strengthen its competitiveness and performance. Figure 1.1 shows what to look for in identifying the key elements of a company's strategy.

Once it is clear what to look for, the task of identifying a company's strategy is mainly one of researching information about the company's actions in the marketplace and business approaches. In the case of publicly owned enterprises, the strategy is often openly discussed by senior executives in the company's annual report and 10-K report, in press releases and company news (posted on the company's Web site), and in the information provided to investors at the company's Web site. To maintain the confidence of investors and Wall Street, most public companies have to be fairly open about their strategies. Company executives typically lay out key elements of their strategies in

Figure 1.1   **Identifying a Company's Strategy—What to Look for**

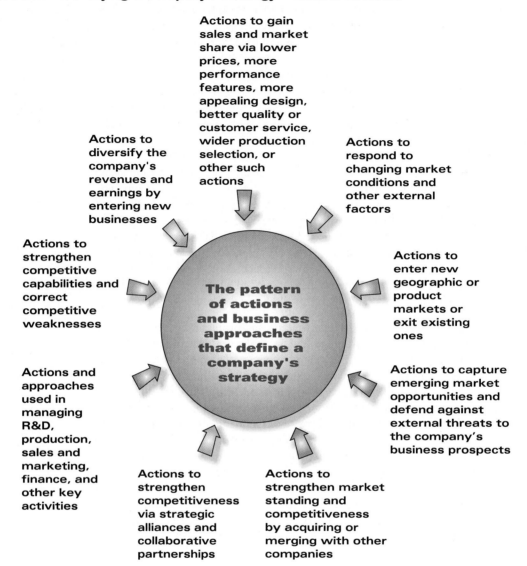

presentations to securities analysts (the accompanying PowerPoint slides are sometimes posted in the investor relations section of the company's Web site), and stories in the business media about the company often include aspects of the company's strategy. Hence, except for some about-to-be-launched moves and changes that remain under wraps and in the planning stage, there's usually nothing secret or undiscoverable about a company's present strategy.

Why a Company's Strategy Evolves over Time

Irrespective of where the strategy comes from—be it the product of top executives or the collaborative product of numerous company personnel—it is unlikely that the strategy, as originally conceived, will prove entirely suitable over time. Every company must be willing and ready to modify its strategy in response to changing market conditions, advancing technology, the fresh moves of competitors, shifting buyer needs and preferences, emerging market opportunities, new ideas for improving the strategy, and mounting evidence that the strategy is not working well. Thus, *a company's strategy is always a work in progress.*

Most of the time a company's strategy evolves incrementally from management's ongoing efforts to fine-tune this or that piece of the strategy and to adjust certain strategy elements in response to unfolding events. But, on occasion, major strategy shifts are called for, such as when a strategy is clearly failing and the company faces a financial crisis, when market conditions or buyer preferences change significantly, or when important technological breakthroughs occur. In some industries, conditions change at a fairly slow pace, making it feasible for the major components of a good strategy to remain in place for long periods. But in industries where industry and competitive conditions change frequently and in sometimes dramatic ways, the life cycle of a given strategy is short. Industry environments characterized by *high-velocity change* require companies to rapidly adapt their strategies.[3] For example, companies in industries with rapid-fire advances in technology—like medical equipment, electronics, and wireless devices—often find it essential to adjust one or more key elements of their strategies several times a year, sometimes even finding necessary to reinvent their approach to providing value to their customers. Companies in online retailing and the travel and resort industries find it necessary to adapt their strategies to accommodate sudden bursts of new spending or sharp drop-offs in demand, often updating their market prospects and financial projections every few months.

But regardless of whether a company's strategy changes gradually or swiftly, the important point is that a company's present strategy is always temporary and on trial, pending new ideas for improvement from management, changing industry and competitive conditions, and any other new developments that management believes warrant strategy adjustments. Thus, a company's strategy at any given point is fluid, representing the temporary outcome of an ongoing process that, on the one hand, involves reasoned and creative management efforts to craft an effective strategy and, on the other hand, involves ongoing responses to market change and constant experimentation and tinkering. Adapting to new conditions and constantly learning what is working well enough to continue and what needs to be improved is consequently a normal part of the strategy-making process and results in an evolving strategy.

> **Core Concept**
> Changing circumstances and ongoing management efforts to improve the strategy cause a company's strategy to evolve over time—a condition that makes the task of crafting a strategy a work in progress, not a one-time event.

> A company's strategy is shaped partly by management analysis and choice and partly by the necessity of adapting and learning by doing.

A Company's Strategy Is Partly Proactive and Partly Reactive

The evolving nature of a company's strategy means that the typical company strategy is a blend of (1) proactive actions to improve the company's financial performance and secure a competitive edge and (2) as-needed reactions to unanticipated developments and fresh market conditions (see Figure 1.2).[4] The biggest portion of a company's current strategy flows from previously initiated actions and business approaches that are working well enough to merit continuation and newly launched initiatives aimed at boosting financial performance and edging out rivals. Typically, managers proactively modify this or that aspect of their strategy as new learning emerges about which pieces of the strategy are working well and which aren't, and as they hit upon new ideas for strategy improvement. This part of management's action plan for running the company is deliberate and proactive, standing as the current product of management's latest and best strategy ideas.

Figure 1.2   **A Company's Strategy Is a Blend of Proactive Initiatives and Reactive Adjustments**

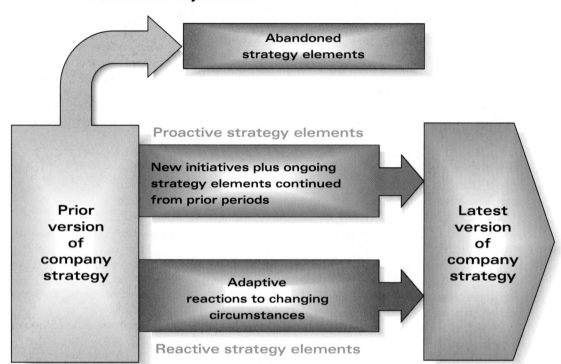

But managers must always be willing to supplement or modify all the proactive strategy elements with as-needed reactions to unanticipated developments. Inevitably, there will be occasions when market and competitive conditions take an unexpected turn that calls for some kind of strategic reaction or adjustment. Hence, a portion of a company's strategy is always developed on the fly, coming as a response to fresh strategic maneuvers on the part of rival firms, unexpected shifts in customer requirements and expectations, fast-changing technological developments, newly appearing market opportunities, a changing political or economic climate, or other unanticipated happenings in the surrounding environment. These adaptive strategy adjustments form the reactive strategy elements.

As shown in Figure 1.2, a company's strategy evolves from one version to the next as managers abandon obsolete or ineffective strategy elements, settle upon a set of *proactive/intended strategy elements*, and then adapt the strategy as new circumstances unfold, thus giving rise to *reactive/adaptive strategy elements*. A company's strategy thus tends to be a *combination* of proactive and reactive elements. In the process, some strategy elements end up being abandoned because they have become obsolete or ineffective.

STRATEGY AND ETHICS: PASSING THE TEST OF MORAL SCRUTINY

In choosing from among strategic alternatives, company managers are well advised to embrace actions that are aboveboard and can pass the test of moral scrutiny. Just keeping a company's strategic actions within the bounds of what is legal does not mean the strategy is ethical. Ethical and moral standards are not governed by what is legal. Rather, they involve issues of both right versus wrong and *duty*—what one *should* do. A strategy is ethical only if (1) it does not entail actions and behaviors that cross the line from "should do" to "should not do" (because such actions are unsavory, unconscionable, or injurious to other people or unnecessarily harmful to the environment) and (2) it allows management to fulfill its ethical duties to all stakeholders— owners/shareholders, employees, customers, suppliers, the communities in which it operates, and society at large.

> **Core Concept**
> A strategy cannot be considered ethical just because it involves actions that are legal. To meet the standard of being ethical, a strategy must entail actions that can pass moral scrutiny and that are aboveboard in the sense of not being shady, unconscionable, injurious to others, or unnecessarily harmful to the environment.

Admittedly, it is not always easy to categorize a given strategic behavior as definitely ethical or definitely unethical. Many strategic actions fall in a gray zone in between, and whether they are deemed ethical or unethical hinges on how clearly the boundaries are defined. For example, is it ethical for advertisers of alcoholic products to place ads in media having an audience of as much as 50 percent underage viewers? (In 2003, growing concerns about underage drinking prompted some beer and distilled spirits companies to agree to place ads in media with an audience at least 70 percent adult, up from a standard of 50 percent adult.) Is it ethical for an apparel retailer attempting to keep prices attractively low to source clothing from foreign man- ufacturers who pay substandard wages, use child labor, or subject workers to unsafe working conditions? Many people would say no, but some might argue that a company is not unethical simply because it does not police the business practices of its suppliers. Is it ethical for the makers of athletic uniforms, shoes, and other sports equipment to pay coaches large sums of money to induce them to use the manufacturer's products in their sport? (The compensation contracts of many college coaches include substantial payments from sportswear and sports equipment manufacturers, and the teams subse- quently end up wearing the uniforms and using the products of those manufacturers.) Is it ethical for manufacturers of life-saving drugs to charge higher prices in some countries than they charge in others? (This is a fairly common practice that has recently come under scrutiny because it raises the costs of health care for consumers who are charged higher prices.) Is it ethical for a company to turn a blind eye to the damage its operations do to the environment even though its operations are in compliance with current environmental regulations—especially if it has the know-how and the means to alleviate some of the environmental impacts by making relatively inexpensive changes in its operating practices?

Senior executives with strong ethical convictions are generally proactive in linking strategic action and ethics: They forbid the pursuit of ethically questionable business opportunities and insist that all aspects of company strategy reflect high ethi- cal standards.[5] They make it clear that all company personnel are expected to act with integrity, and they put organizational checks and balances into place to monitor behav- ior, enforce ethical codes of conduct, and provide guidance to employees regarding any gray areas. Their commitment to conducting the company's business in an ethical manner is genuine, not hypocritical.

Instances of corporate malfeasance, ethical lapses, and fraudulent accounting prac- tices at Enron, WorldCom, Tyco, Adelphia, HealthSouth, and other companies leave no room to doubt the damage to a company's reputation and business that can result from ethical misconduct, corporate misdeeds, and even criminal behavior on the part of company personnel. Aside from just the embarrassment and black marks that ac- company headline exposure of a company's unethical practices, the hard fact is that many customers and many suppliers are wary of doing business with a company that engages in sleazy practices or that turns a blind eye to illegal or unethical behavior on the part of employees. They are turned off by unethical strategies or behavior and, rather than become victims or get burned themselves, wary customers will quickly take their business elsewhere and wary suppliers will tread carefully. Moreover, employees with character and integrity do not want to work for a company whose strategies are shady or whose executives lack character and integrity. There's little lasting benefit to unethical strategies and behavior, and the downside risks can be substantial. Besides, such actions are plain wrong.

THE RELATIONSHIP BETWEEN A COMPANY'S STRATEGY AND ITS BUSINESS MODEL

Core Concept

A company's ***business model*** explains the rationale for why its business approach and strategy will be a moneymaker. Absent the ability to deliver good profitability, the strategy is not viable and the survival of the business is in doubt.

Closely related to the concept of strategy is the concept of a company's **business model.** While the word *model* conjures up images of ivory-tower ideas that may be loosely connected to the real world, such images do not apply here. A company's business model is management's story line for how the strategy will be a moneymaker. The story line sets forth the key components of the enterprise's business approach, indicates how revenues will be generated, and makes a case for why the strategy can deliver value to customers in a profitable manner.[6] A company's business model thus explains why its business approach and strategy will generate ample revenues to cover costs and capture a profit.

The nitty-gritty issue surrounding a company's business model is whether the chosen strategy makes good business sense. Why is there convincing reason to believe that the strategy is capable of producing a profit? How will the business generate its revenues? Will those revenues be sufficient to cover operating costs? Will customers see enough value in what the business does for them to pay a profitable price? The concept of a company's business model is, consequently, more narrowly focused than the concept of a company's business strategy. A company's strategy *relates broadly to its competitive initiatives and action plan for running the business* (but it may or may not lead to profitability). However, a company's business model zeros in on *how and why the business will generate revenues sufficient to cover costs and produce attractive profits and return on investment.* Absent the ability to deliver good profits, the strategy is not viable, the business model is flawed, and the business itself is in jeopardy of failing.

Companies that have been in business for a while and are making acceptable profits have a proven business model—because there is hard evidence that their strategies are capable of profitability. Companies that are in a start-up mode or that are losing money have questionable business models; their strategies have yet to produce good bottom-line results, putting their story line about how they intend to make money and their viability as business enterprises in doubt.

Magazines and newspapers employ a business model based on generating sufficient subscriptions and advertising to cover the costs of delivering their products to readers. Cable TV companies, cell-phone providers, record clubs, satellite radio companies, and Internet service providers also employ a subscription-based business model. The business model of network TV and radio broadcasters entails providing free programming to audiences but charging advertising fees based on audience size. McDonald's invented the business model for fast food—economical quick-service meals at clean, convenient locations. Wal-Mart has perfected the business model for big-box discount retailing—a model also used by Home Depot, Costco, and Target. Gillette's business model in razor blades involves selling a "master product"—the razor—at an attractively low price and then making money on repeat purchases—the razor blades. Printer manufacturers like Hewlett-Packard, Lexmark, and Epson pursue much the same business model as Gillette—selling printers at a low (virtually break-even) price and making large profit margins on the repeat purchases of printer supplies, especially ink cartridges. Companies like Dell and Avon employ a direct sales business model that helps keep prices low by cutting out the costs of reaching consumers through distributors and retail dealers. Illustration Capsule 1.2 discusses the contrasting business models of Microsoft and Red Hat.

WHAT MAKES A STRATEGY A WINNER?

Three questions can be used to test the merits of one strategy versus another and distinguish a winning strategy from a so-so or flawed strategy:

1. *How well does the strategy fit the company's situation?* To qualify as a winner, a strategy has to be well matched to industry and competitive conditions, a company's best market opportunities, and other aspects of the enterprise's external environment. At the same time, it has to be tailored to the company's resource strengths and weaknesses, competencies, and competitive capabilities. Unless a strategy exhibits tight fit with both the external and internal aspects of a company's overall situation, it is likely to produce less than the best possible business results.

> **Core Concept**
> A winning strategy must fit the enterprise's external and internal situation, build sustainable competitive advantage, and improve company performance.

2. *Is the strategy helping the company achieve a sustainable competitive advantage?* Winning strategies enable a company to achieve a competitive advantage that is durable. The bigger and more durable the competitive edge that a strategy helps build, the more powerful and appealing it is.

3. *Is the strategy resulting in better company performance?* A good strategy boosts company performance. Two kinds of performance improvements tell the most about the caliber of a company's strategy: (*a*) gains in profitability and financial strength, and (*b*) gains in the company's competitive strength and market standing.

Once a company commits to a particular strategy and enough time elapses to assess how well it fits the situation and whether it is actually delivering competitive advantage and better performance, then one can determine what grade to assign that strategy. Strategies that come up short on one or more of the above questions are plainly less appealing than strategies that pass all three test questions with flying colors.

Managers can also use the same questions to pick and choose among alternative strategic actions. A company evaluating which of several strategic options to employ can evaluate how well each option measures up against each of the three questions. The strategic option with the highest prospective passing scores on all three questions can be regarded as the best or most attractive strategic alternative.

Other criteria for judging the merits of a particular strategy include internal consistency and unity among all the pieces of strategy, the degree of risk the strategy poses as compared to alternative strategies, and the degree to which it is flexible and adaptable to changing circumstances. These criteria are relevant and merit consideration, but they seldom override the importance of the three test questions posed above.

Illustration Capsule 1.2

Microsoft and Red Hat: Two Contrasting Business Models

The strategies of rival companies are often predicated on strikingly different business models. Consider, for example, the business models for Microsoft and Red Hat in operating system software for personal computers (PCs).

Microsoft's business model for making money from its Windows operating system products is based on the following revenue-cost-profit economics:

- Employ a cadre of highly skilled programmers to develop proprietary code; keep the source code hidden so as to keep the inner workings of the software proprietary.

- Sell the resulting operating system and software package to PC makers and to PC users at relatively attractive prices (around $75 to PC makers and about $100 at retail to PC users); strive to maintain a 90 percent or more market share of the 150 million PCs sold annually worldwide.

- Strive for big-volume sales. Most of Microsoft's costs arise on the front end in developing the software and are thus fixed; the variable costs of producing and packaging the CDs provided to users are only a couple of dollars per copy—once the break-even volume is reached, Microsoft's revenues from additional sales are almost pure profit.

- Provide a modest level of technical support to users at no cost.

- Keep rejuvenating revenues by periodically introducing next-generation software versions with features that will induce PC users to upgrade the operating system on previously purchased PCs to the new version.

Red Hat, a company formed to market its own version of the Linux open-source operating system, employs a business model based on sharply different revenue-cost-profit economics:

- Rely on the collaborative efforts of volunteer programmers from all over the world who contribute bits and pieces of code to improve and polish the Linux system. The global community of thousands of programmers who work on Linux in their spare time do what they do because they love it, because they are fervent believers that all software should be free (as in free speech), and in some cases because they are anti-Microsoft and want to have a part in undoing what they see as a Microsoft monopoly.

- Collect and test enhancements and new applications submitted by the open-source community of volunteer programmers. Linux's originator, Linus Torvalds, and a team of 300-plus Red Hat engineers and software developers evaluate which incoming submissions merit inclusion in new releases of Linux—the evaluation and integration of new submissions are Red Hat's only up-front product development costs.

- Market the upgraded and tested family of Red Hat products to large enterprises and charge them a subscription fee that includes 24/7 support within one hour in seven languages. Provide subscribers with updated versions of Linux every 12–18 months to maintain the subscriber base.

- Make the source code open and available to all users, allowing them to create a customized version of Linux.

- Capitalize on the specialized expertise required to use Linux in multiserver, multiprocessor applications by providing fees-based training, consulting, software customization, and client-directed engineering to Linux users. Red Hat offers Linux certification training programs at all skill levels at more than 60 global locations—Red Hat certification in the use of Linux is considered the best in the world.

Microsoft's business model—sell proprietary code software and give service away free—is a proven money-maker that generates billions in profits annually. In contrast, the jury is still out on Red Hat's business model of selling subscriptions to open-source software to large corporations and deriving substantial revenues from the sales of technical support (included in the subscription cost), training, consulting, software customization, and engineering to generate revenues sufficient to cover costs and yield a profit. Red Hat posted losses of $140 million on revenues of $79 million in fiscal year 2002 and losses of $6.6 million on revenues of $91 million in fiscal year 2003, but it earned $14 million on revenues of $126 million in fiscal 2004. The profits came from a shift in Red Hat's business model that involved putting considerably more emphasis on getting large corporations to purchase subscriptions to the latest Linux updates. In 2005, about 75 percent of Red Hat's revenues came from large enterprise subscriptions, compared to about 53 percent in 2003.

Source: Company documents and information posted on www.microsoft.com and www.redhat.com. (accessed August 10, 2005).

WHY ARE CRAFTING AND EXECUTING STRATEGY IMPORTANT?

Crafting and executing strategy are top-priority managerial tasks for two very big reasons. First, there is a compelling need for managers to *proactively shape*, or *craft*, how the company's business will be conducted. A clear and reasoned strategy is management's prescription for doing business, its road map to competitive advantage, its game plan for pleasing customers and improving financial performance. Winning in the marketplace requires a well-conceived, opportunistic strategy, usually one characterized by strategic offensives to outinnovate and outmaneuver rivals and secure sustainable competitive advantage, then using this market edge to achieve superior financial performance. A powerful strategy that delivers a home run in the marketplace can propel a firm from a trailing position into a leading one, clearing the way for its products/services to become the industry standard. High-achieving enterprises are nearly always the product of astute, creative, proactive strategy making that sets a company apart from its rivals. Companies don't get to the top of the industry rankings or stay there with imitative strategies or with strategies built around timid actions to try to do better. And only a handful of companies can boast of strategies that hit home runs in the marketplace due to lucky breaks or the good fortune of having stumbled into the right market at the right time with the right product. There can be little argument that a company's strategy matters—and matters a lot.

Second, a *strategy-focused enterprise* is more likely to be a strong bottom-line performer than a company whose management views strategy as secondary and puts its priorities elsewhere. There's no escaping the fact that the quality of managerial strategy making and strategy execution has a highly positive impact on revenue growth, earnings, and return on investment. A company that lacks clear-cut direction, has vague or undemanding performance targets, has a muddled or flawed strategy, or can't seem to execute its strategy competently is a company whose financial performance is probably suffering, whose business is at long-term risk, and whose management is sorely lacking. In contrast, when crafting and executing a winning strategy drive management's whole approach to operating the enterprise, the odds are much greater that the initiatives and activities of different divisions, departments, managers, and work groups will be unified into a *coordinated, cohesive effort*. Mobilizing the full complement of company resources in a total team effort behind good execution of the chosen strategy and achievement of the targeted performance allows a company to operate at full power. The chief executive officer of one successful company put it well when he said:

> In the main, our competitors are acquainted with the same fundamental concepts and techniques and approaches that we follow, and they are as free to pursue them as we are. More often than not, the difference between their level of success and ours lies in the relative thoroughness and self-discipline with which we and they develop and execute our strategies for the future.

Good Strategy + Good Strategy Execution = Good Management

Crafting and executing strategy are core management functions. Among all the things managers do, nothing affects a company's ultimate success or failure more fundamentally than how well its management team charts the company's direction, develops

Core Concept
Excellent execution of an excellent strategy is the best test of managerial excellence—and the most reliable recipe for turning companies into standout performers.

competitively effective strategic moves and business approaches, and pursues what needs to be done internally to produce good day-in, day-out strategy execution and operating excellence. Indeed, *good strategy and good strategy execution are the most trustworthy signs of good management.* Managers don't deserve a gold star for designing a potentially brilliant strategy but failing to put the organizational means in place to carry it out in high-caliber fashion—weak implementation and execution undermine the strategy's potential and pave the way for shortfalls in customer satisfaction and company performance. Competent execution of a mediocre strategy scarcely merits enthusiastic applause for management's efforts either. The rationale for using the twin standards of good strategy making and good strategy execution to determine whether a company is well managed is therefore compelling: *The better conceived a company's strategy and the more competently it is executed, the more likely that the company will be a standout performer in the marketplace.*

Throughout the text chapters to come and the accompanying case collection, the spotlight is trained on the foremost question in running a business enterprise: What must managers do, and do well, to make a company a winner in the marketplace? The answer that emerges, and that becomes the message of this book, is that doing a good job of managing inherently requires good strategic thinking and good management of the strategy-making, strategy-executing process.

The mission of this book is to provide a solid overview of what every business student and aspiring manager needs to know about crafting and executing strategy. This requires exploring what good strategic thinking entails; presenting the core concepts and tools of strategic analysis; describing the ins and outs of crafting and executing strategy; and, through the cases, helping you build your skills both in diagnosing how well the strategy-making, strategy-executing task is being performed in actual companies and in prescribing actions for how the companies in question can improve their approaches to crafting and executing their strategies. At the very least, we hope to convince you that capabilities in crafting and executing strategy are basic to managing successfully and merit a place in a manager's tool kit.

As you tackle the following pages, ponder the following observation by the essayist and poet Ralph Waldo Emerson: "Commerce is a game of skill which many people play, but which few play well." If the content of this book helps you become a more savvy player and equips you to succeed in business, then your journey through these pages will indeed be time well spent.

Key Points

The tasks of crafting and executing company strategies are the heart and soul of managing a business enterprise and winning in the marketplace. A company's strategy is the game plan management is using to stake out a market position, conduct its operations, attract and please customers, compete successfully, and achieve organizational objectives. The central thrust of a company's strategy is undertaking moves to build and strengthen the company's long-term competitive position and financial performance and, ideally, gain a competitive advantage over rivals that then becomes a company's ticket to above-average profitability. A company's strategy typically evolves and reforms over time, emerging from a blend of (1) proactive and purposeful actions on the part of company managers and (2) as-needed reactions to unanticipated developments and fresh market conditions.

Closely related to the concept of strategy is the concept of a company's business model. A company's business model is management's story line for how and why the company's product offerings and competitive approaches will generate a revenue stream and have an associated cost structure that produces attractive earnings and return on investment—in effect, a company's business model sets forth the economic logic for making money in a particular business, given the company's current strategy.

A winning strategy fits the circumstances of a company's external situation and its internal resource strengths and competitive capabilities, builds competitive advantage, and boosts company performance.

Crafting and executing strategy are core management functions. Whether a company wins or loses in the marketplace is directly attributable to the caliber of a company's strategy and the proficiency with which the strategy is executed.

Exercises

1. Go to Red Hat's Web site (www.redhat.com) and check whether the company's recent financial reports indicate that its business model is working. Is the company sufficiently profitable to validate its business model and strategy? Is its revenue stream from selling training, consulting, and engineering services growing or declining as a percentage of total revenues? Does your review of the company's recent financial performance suggest that its business model and strategy are changing? Read the company's latest statement about its business model and about why it is pursuing the subscription approach (as compared to Microsoft's approach of selling copies of its operating software directly to PC manufacturers and individuals).

2. From your perspective as a cable or satellite service consumer, does Comcast's strategy as described in Illustration Capsule 1.1 seem to be well matched to industry and competitive conditions? Does the strategy seem to be keyed to maintaining a cost advantage, offering differentiating features, serving the unique needs of a niche, or developing resource strengths and competitive capabilities rivals can't imitate or trump (or a mixture of these)? Do you think Comcast's strategy has evolved in recent years? Why or why not? What is there about Comcast's strategy that can lead to sustainable competitive advantage?

3. In 2003, Levi Strauss & Company announced it would close its two remaining U.S. apparel plants to finalize its transition from a clothing manufacturer to a marketing, sales, and design company. Beginning in 2004, all Levi's apparel would be produced by contract manufacturers located in low-wage countries. As recently as 1990, Levi Strauss had produced 90 percent of its apparel in company-owned plants in the United States employing over 20,000 production workers. With every plant closing, Levi Strauss & Company provided severance and job retraining packages to affected workers and cash payments to small communities where its plants were located. However, the economies of many small communities had yet to recover and some employees had found it difficult to match their previous levels of compensation and benefits.

   Review Levi Strauss & Company's discussion of its Global Sourcing and Operating Guidelines at www.levistrauss.com/responsibility/conduct. Does the company's strategy fulfill the company's ethical duties to all stakeholders—owners/shareholders, employees, customers, suppliers, the communities in which it operates, and society at large? Does Levi Strauss's strategy to outsource all of its manufacturing operations to low-wage countries pass the moral scrutiny test given that 20,000 workers lost their jobs?

The Managerial Process of Crafting and Executing Strategy

Unless we change our direction we are likely to end up where we are headed.

—Ancient Chinese proverb

If we can know where we are and something about how we got there, we might see where we are trending—and if the outcomes which lie naturally in our course are unacceptable, to make timely change.

—Abraham Lincoln

If you don't know where you are going, any road will take you there.
—The Koran

Management's job is not to see the company as it is . . . but as it can become.
—John W. Teets
Former CEO

rafting and executing strategy are the heart and soul of managing a business enterprise. But exactly what is involved in developing a strategy and executing it proficiently? What are the various components of the strategy-making, strategy-executing process? And to what extent are company personnel—aside from top executives—involved in the process? In this chapter we present an overview of the managerial ins and outs of crafting and executing company strategies. Special attention will be given to management's direction-setting responsibilities—charting a strategic course, setting performance targets, and choosing a strategy capable of producing the desired outcomes. We will also examine which kinds of strategic decisions are made at which levels of management and the roles and responsibilities of the company's board of directors in the strategy-making, strategy-executing process.

WHAT DOES THE STRATEGY-MAKING, STRATEGY-EXECUTING PROCESS ENTAIL?

The managerial process of crafting and executing a company's strategy consists of five interrelated and integrated phases:

1. *Developing a strategic vision* of where the company needs to head and what its future product/market/customer technology focus should be.
2. *Setting objectives* and using them as yardsticks for measuring the company's performance and progress.
3. *Crafting a strategy to achieve the objectives* and move the company along the strategic course that management has charted.
4. *Implementing and executing the chosen strategy efficiently and effectively.*
5. *Evaluating performance and initiating corrective adjustments* in the company's long-term direction, objectives, strategy, or execution in light of actual experience, changing conditions, new ideas, and new opportunities.

Figure 2.1 displays this five-phase process. Let's examine each phase in enough detail to set the stage for the forthcoming chapters and give you a bird's-eye view of what this book is about.

Figure 2.1 **The Strategy-Making, Strategy-Executing Process**

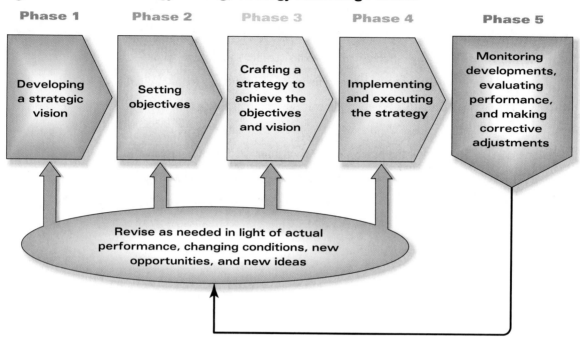

DEVELOPING A STRATEGIC VISION: PHASE 1 OF THE STRATEGY-MAKING, STRATEGY-EXECUTING PROCESS

Very early in the strategy-making process, a company's senior managers must wrestle with the issue of what path the company should take and what changes in the company's product/market/customer/technology focus would improve its market position and future prospects. Deciding to commit the company to one path versus another pushes managers to draw some carefully reasoned conclusions about how to modify the company's business makeup and what market position it should stake out. A number of direction-shaping factors need to be considered in deciding where to head and why such a direction makes good business sense—see Table 2.1.

Top management's views and conclusions about the company's direction and future product/market/customer/technology focus constitute a **strategic vision** for the company. A strategic vision delineates management's aspirations for the business, providing a panoramic view of "where we are going" and a convincing rationale for why this makes good business sense for the company. A strategic vision thus points an organization in a particular direction, charts a strategic path, and molds organizational identity.A clearly articulated strategic vision communicates management's aspirations to stakeholders and helps steer the energies of company personnel in a common direction. For instance, Henry Ford's vision of a car in every garage had power because it captured the imagination of others, aided internalefforts to mobilize the Ford Motor Company's resources, and served as a reference point for gauging the merits of the company's strategic actions.

Core Concept
A *strategic vision* describes the route a company intends to take in developing and strengthening its business. It lays out the company's strategic course in preparing for the future.

Table 2.1   **Factors to Consider in Deciding to Commit the Company to One Path versus Another**

External Considerations	Internal Considerations
• Is the outlook for the company promising if it simply maintains its product/market/customer/technology focus? Does sticking with the company's current strategic course present attractive growth opportunities? • Are changes under way in the market and competitive landscape acting to enhance or weaken the company's prospects? • What, if any, new customer groups and/or geographic markets should the company get in position to serve? • Which emerging market opportunities should the company pursue? Which ones should not be pursued? • Should the company plan to abandon any of the markets, market segments, or customer groups it is currently serving?	• What are the company's ambitions? What industry standing should the company have? • Will the company's present business generate sufficient growth and profitability in the years ahead to please shareholders? • What organizational strengths ought to be leveraged in terms of adding new products or services and getting into new businesses? • Is the company stretching its resources too thin by trying to compete in too many markets or segments, some of which are unprofitable? • Is the company's technological focus too broad or too narrow? Are any changes needed?

Well-conceived visions are *distinctive* and *specific* to a particular organization; they avoid generic feel-good statements like "We will become a global leader and the first choice of customers in every market we choose to serve"—which could apply to any of hundreds of organizations.[1] And they are not the product of a committee charged with coming up with an innocuous but well-meaning one-sentence vision that wins consensus approval from various stakeholders. Nicely worded vision statements with no specifics about the company's product/market/customer/technology focus fall well short of what it takes for a vision to measure up. A strategic vision proclaiming management's quest "to be the market leader" or "to be the first choice of customers" or "to be the most innovative" or "to be recognized as the best company in the industry" offers scant guidance about a company's direction and what changes and challenges lie on the road ahead.

For a strategic vision to function as a valuable managerial tool, it must (1) provide understanding of what management wants its business to look like and (2) provide managers with a reference point in making strategic decisions and preparing the company for the future. It must say something definitive about how the company's leaders intend to position the company beyond where it is today. A good vision always needs to be a bit beyond a company's reach, but progress toward the vision is what unifies the efforts of company personnel. Table 2.2 lists some characteristics of an effectively worded strategic vision.

A sampling of strategic visions currently in use shows a range from strong and clear to overly general and generic. A surprising number of the visions found on company Web sites and in annual reports are vague and unrevealing, saying very little about the company's future product/market/customer/technology focus. Some are nice-sounding but say little. Others read like something written by a committee to win the support of different stakeholders. And some are so short on specifics as to apply to most any company in any industry. Many read like a public relations statement—high-sounding words that someone came up with because it is fashionable for companies to have an official vision statement.[2] Table 2.3 provides a list of the most

Table 2.2   **Characteristics of an Effectively Worded Strategic Vision**

Graphic	Paints a picture of the kind of company that management is trying to create and the market position(s) the company is striving to stake out.
Directional	Is forward-looking; describes the strategic course that management has charted and the kinds of product/market/customer/technology changes that will help the company prepare for the future.
Focused	Is specific enough to provide managers with guidance in making decisions and allocating resources.
Flexible	Is not a once-and-for-all-time statement—the directional course that management has charted may have to be adjusted as product/market/customer/technology circumstances change.
Feasible	Is within the realm of what the company can reasonably expect to achieve in due time.
Desirable	Indicates why the chosen path makes good business sense and is in the long-term interests of stakeholders (especially shareowners, employees, and customers).
Easy to communicate	Is explainable in 5–10 minutes and, ideally, can be reduced to a simple, memorable slogan (like Henry Ford's famous vision of "a car in every garage").

Source: Based partly on John P. Kotter, *Leading Change* (Boston: Harvard Business School Press, 1996), p. 72.

common shortcomings in strategic vision statements. The one- or two-sentence vision statements most companies make available to the public, of course, provide only a glimpse of what company executives are really thinking and the strategic course they have charted—company personnel nearly always have a much better understanding of where the company is headed and why that is revealed in the official vision. But the real purpose of a strategic vision is to serve as a management tool for giving the organization a sense of direction. Like any tool, it can be used properly or improperly, either clearly conveying a company's strategic course or not.

Table 2.3   **Common Shortcomings in Company Vision Statements**

Vague or incomplete	Is short on specifics about where the company is headed or what the company is doing to prepare for the future.
Not forward-looking	Does not indicate whether or how management intends to alter the company's current product/market/customer/technology focus.
Too broad	Is so umbrella-like and all-inclusive that the company could head in most any direction, pursue most any opportunity, or enter most any business.
Bland or uninspiring	Lacks the power to motivate company personnel or inspire shareholder confidence about the company's direction or future prospects.
Not distinctive	Provides no unique company identity; could apply to companies in any of several industries (or at least several rivals operating in the same industry or market arena).
Too reliant on superlatives	Does not say anything specific about the company's strategic course beyond the pursuit of such lofty accolades as *best, most successful, recognized leader, global or worldwide leader,* or *first choice of customers.*

Sources: Based on information in Hugh Davidson, *The Committed Enterprise: How to Make Vision and Values Work* (Oxford: Butterworth Heinemann, 2002), Chapter 2, and Michel Robert, *Strategy Pure and Simple II* (New York: McGraw-Hill, 1992), Chapters 2, 3, and 6.

Illustration Capsule 2.1

Examples of Strategic Visions—How Well Do They Measure Up?

Using the information in Tables 2.2 and 2.3, critique the following strategic visions and rank them from 1 (best) to 7 (in need of substantial improvement).

RED HAT

To extend our position as the most trusted Linux and open source provider to the enterprise. We intend to grow the market for Linux through a complete range of enterprise Red Hat Linux software, a powerful Internet management platform, and associated support and services.

WELLS FARGO

We want to satisfy all of our customers' financial needs, help them succeed financially, be the premier provider of financial services in every one of our markets, and be known as one of America's great companies.

HILTON HOTELS CORPORATION

Our vision is to be the first choice of the world's travelers. Hilton intends to build on the rich heritage and strength of our brands by:

- Consistently delighting our customers
- Investing in our team members
- Delivering innovative products and services
- Continuously improving performance
- Increasing shareholder value

- Creating a culture of pride
- Strengthening the loyalty of our constituents

THE DENTAL PRODUCTS DIVISION OF 3M CORPORATION

Become THE supplier of choice to the global dental professional markets, providing world-class quality and innovative products.

[*Note:* All employees of the division wear badges bearing these words, and whenever a new product or business procedure is being considered, management asks "Is this representative of THE leading dental company?"]

CATERPILLAR

Be the global leader in customer value.

eBAY

Provide a global trading platform where practically anyone can trade practically anything.

H. J. HEINZ COMPANY

Be the world's premier food company, offering nutritious, superior tasting foods to people everywhere. Being the premier food company does not mean being the biggest but it does mean being the best in terms of consumer value, customer service, employee talent, and consistent and predictable growth.

Sources: Company documents and Web sites.

Illustration Capsule 2.1 provides examples of strategic visions of several prominent companies. See if you can tell which ones are mostly meaningless or nice-sounding and which ones are managerially useful in communicating "where we are headed and the kind of company we are trying to become".

A Strategic Vision Covers Different Ground than the Typical Mission Statement

The defining characteristic of a well-conceived *strategic vision* is what it says about the company's *future strategic course*—"the direction we are headed and what our future product/market/customer/technology focus will be."

In contrast, the *mission statements* that one finds in company annual reports or posted on company Web sites typically provide a brief overview of the company's *present* business purpose and raison d'être, and sometimes its geographic coverage or standing as a market leader. They may or may not single out the company's present products/services, the buyer needs it is seeking to satisfy, the customer groups it serves, or its technological and business capabilities. But rarely do company mission statements say anything about where the company is headed, the anticipated changes in its business, or its aspirations; hence, they lack the essential forward-looking quality of a strategic vision in specifying a company's direction and *future* product/market/customer/technology focus.

Consider, for example, the mission statement of Trader Joe's (a specialty grocery chain):

> The mission of Trader Joe's is to give our customers the best food and beverage values that they can find anywhere and to provide them with the information required for informed buying decisions. We provide these with a dedication to the highest quality of customer satisfaction delivered with a sense of warmth, friendliness, fun, individual pride, and company spirit.

Note that Trader Joe's mission statement does a good job of conveying "who we are, what we do, and why we are here," but provides no sense of "where we are headed." (Some companies use the term *business purpose* instead of *mission statement* in describing themselves; in practice, there seems to be no meaningful difference between the terms *mission statement* and *business purpose*—which one is used is a matter of preference.)

> The distinction between a strategic vision and a mission statement is fairly clear-cut: A strategic vision portrays a company's *future* business scope ("where we are going"), whereas a company's mission typically describes its *present* business and purpose ("who we are, what we do, and why we are here").

There is value in distinguishing between the forward-looking concept of a strategic vision and the here-and-now theme of the typical mission statement. Thus, to mirror actual practice, we will use the term *mission statement* to refer to an enterprise's description of its *present* business and its purpose for existence. Ideally, a company mission statement is sufficiently descriptive to *identify the company's products/services and specify the buyer needs it seeks to satisfy, the customer groups or markets it is endeavoring to serve, and its approach to pleasing customers.* Not many company mission statements fully reveal *all* of these facets (and a few companies have worded their mission statements so obscurely as to mask what they are about), but most company mission statements do a decent job of indicating "who we are, what we do, and why we are here."

An example of a well-formed mission statement with ample specifics is that of the U.S. government's Occupational Safety and Health Administration (OSHA): "to assure the safety and health of America's workers by setting and enforcing standards; providing training, outreach, and education; establishing partnerships; and encouraging continual improvement in workplace safety and health." Google's mission statement, while short, still captures the essence of the company: "to organize the world's information and make it universally accessible and useful." Likewise, Blockbuster has a brief mission statement that cuts right to the chase: "To help people transform ordinary nights into BLOCKBUSTER nights by being their complete source for movies and games."

An example of a not-so-revealing mission statement is that of the present-day Ford Motor Company: "We are a global family with a proud heritage passionately committed to providing personal mobility for people around the world. We anticipate consumer need and deliver outstanding products and services that improve people's lives." A person who has never heard of Ford would not know from reading the company's mission statement that it is a global producer of motor vehicles. Similarly, Microsoft's mission statement—"to help people and businesses throughout the world realize their full potential"—says nothing about its products or business makeup and could apply to many companies in many different industries. Coca-Cola, which markets nearly 400 beverage brands in over 200 countries, also has an overly general mission statement: "to benefit and refresh everyone it touches." A mission statement that provides scant indication of "who we are and what we do" has no substantive value.

Occasionally, companies couch their mission statements in terms of making a profit. This is misguided. Profit is more correctly an *objective* and a *result* of what a company does. Moreover, earning a profit is the obvious intent of every commercial enterprise. Such companies as BMW, McDonald's, Shell Oil, Procter & Gamble, Nintendo, and Nokia are each striving to earn a profit for shareholders; but plainly the fundamentals of their businesses are substantially different when it comes to "who we are and what we do." It is management's answer to "Make a profit doing what and for whom?" that reveals a company's true substance and business purpose. *A well-conceived mission statement distinguishes a company's business makeup from that of other profit-seeking enterprises in language specific enough to give the company its own identity.*

Communicating the Strategic Vision

Effectively communicating the strategic vision down the line to lower-level managers and employees is as important as choosing a strategically sound long-term direction. Not only do people have a need to believe that senior management knows where it's trying to take the company and understand what changes lie ahead both externally and internally, but unless and until frontline employees understand why the strategic course that management has charted is reasonable and beneficial, they are unlikely to rally behind managerial efforts to get the organization moving in the intended direction.

Winning the support of organization members for the vision nearly always means putting "where we are going and why" in writing, distributing the written vision organizationwide, and having executives personally explain the vision and its rationale to as many people as feasible. Ideally, executives should present their vision for the company in a manner that reaches out and grabs people. An engaging and convincing strategic vision has enormous motivational value—for the same reason that a stonemason is more inspired by "building a great cathedral for the ages" than by "laying stones to create floors and walls." When managers articulate a vivid and compelling case for where the company is headed, organization members begin to say, "This is interesting and has a lot of merit. I want to be involved and do my part to helping make it happen." The more that a vision evokes positive support and excitement, the greater its impact in terms of arousing a committed organizational effort and getting company personnel to move in a common direction.[3] Thus executive ability to paint a convincing and inspiring picture of a company's journey and destination is an important element of effective strategic leadership.

> **Core Concept**
> An effectively communicated vision is a valuable management tool for enlisting the commitment of company personnel to actions that get the company moving in the intended direction.

Expressing the Essence of the Vision in a Slogan   The task of effectively conveying the vision to company personnel is assisted when management can capture the vision of where to head in a catchy or easily remembered slogan. A number of organizations have summed up their vision in a brief phrase:

- Levi Strauss & Company: "We will clothe the world by marketing the most appealing and widely worn casual clothing in the world."
- Nike: "To bring innovation and inspiration to every athlete in the world."

- Mayo Clinic: "The best care to every patient every day."
- Scotland Yard: "To make London the safest major city in the world."
- Greenpeace: "To halt environmental abuse and promote environmental solutions."
- Charles Schwab: "To provide customers with the most useful and ethical financial services in the world."

> Strategic visions become real only when the vision statement is imprinted in the minds of organization members and then translated into hard objectives and strategies.

Creating a short slogan to illuminate an organization's direction and purpose and then using it repeatedly as a reminder of "where we are headed and why" helps rally organization members to hurdle whatever obstacles lie in the company's path and maintain their focus.

Breaking Down Resistance to a New Strategic Vision   It is particularly important for executives to provide a compelling rationale for a dramatically *new* strategic vision and company direction. When company personnel don't understand or accept the need for redirecting organizational efforts, they are prone to resist change. Hence, reiterating the basis for the new direction, addressing employee concerns head-on, calming fears, lifting spirits, and providing updates and progress reports as events unfold all become part of the task of mobilizing support for the vision and winning commitment to needed actions.

Just stating the case for a new direction once is not enough. Executives must repeat the reasons for the new direction often and convincingly at company gatherings and in company publications, and they must reinforce their pronouncements with updates about how the latest information confirms the choice of direction and the validity of the vision. Unless and until more and more people are persuaded of the merits of management's new vision and the vision gains wide acceptance, it will be a struggle to move the organization down the newly chosen path.

Recognizing Strategic Inflection Points   Sometimes there's an order-of-magnitude change in a company's environment that dramatically alters its prospects and mandates radical revision of its strategic course. Intel's former chairman Andrew Grove has called such occasions *strategic inflection points*—Illustration Capsule 2.2 relates Intel's two encounters with strategic inflection points and the resulting alterations in its strategic vision. As the Intel example forcefully demonstrates, when a company reaches a strategic inflection point, management has some tough decisions to make about the company's course. Often it is a question of what to do to sustain company success, not just how to avoid possible disaster. Responding quickly to unfolding changes in the marketplace lessens a company's chances of becoming trapped in a stagnant or declining business or letting attractive new growth opportunities slip away.

Understanding the Payoffs of a Clear Vision Statement   In sum, a well-conceived, forcefully communicated strategic vision pays off in several respects: (1) it crystallizes senior executives' own views about the firm's long-term direction; (2) it reduces the risk of rudderless decision making; (3) it is a tool for winning the support of organizational members for internal changes that will help make the vision a reality; (4) it provides a beacon for lower-level managers in forming departmental missions, setting departmental objectives, and crafting functional and departmental strategies that are in sync with the company's overall strategy; and (5) it helps an organization prepare for the future. When management is able to demonstrate significant progress in achieving these five benefits, the first step in organizational direction setting has been successfully completed.

Illustration Capsule 2.2
Intel's Two Strategic Inflection Points

Intel Corporation has encountered two strategic inflection points within the past 20 years. The first came in the mid-1980s, when memory chips were Intel's principal business and Japanese manufacturers, intent on dominating the memory chip business, began cutting their prices 10 percent below the prices charged by Intel and other U.S. memory chip manufacturers. Each time U.S. companies matched the Japanese price cuts, the Japanese manufacturers responded with another 10 percent price cut. Intel's management explored a number of strategic options to cope with the aggressive pricing of its Japanese rivals—building a giant memory chip factory to overcome the cost advantage of Japanese producers, investing in research and development (R&D) to come up with a more advanced memory chip, and retreating to niche markets for memory chips that were not of interest to the Japanese.

At the time, Gordon Moore, Intel's chairman and cofounder, and Andrew Grove, Intel's chief executive officer (CEO), jointly concluded that none of these options offered much promise and that the best long-term solution was to abandon the memory chip business even though it accounted for 70 percent of Intel's revenue. Grove, with the concurrence of both Moore and the board of directors, then proceeded to commit Intel's full energies to the business of developing ever more powerful microprocessors for personal computers. Intel had invented microprocessors in the early 1970s but had recently been concentrating on memory chips because of strong competition and excess capacity in the market for microprocessors.

Grove's bold decision to withdraw from memory chips, absorb a $173 million write-off in 1986, and go all out in microprocessors produced a new strategic vision for Intel—becoming the preeminent supplier of microprocessors to the personal computing industry, making the personal computer (PC) the central appliance in the workplace and the home, and being the undisputed leader in driving PC technology forward. Grove's new vision for Intel and the strategic course he charted in 1985 produced spectacular results. Since 1996, over 80 percent of the world's PCs have been made with Intel microprocessors and Intel has become the world's most profitable chip maker.

Intel encountered a second inflection point in 1998, opting to refocus on becoming the preeminent building-block supplier to the Internet economy and spurring efforts to make the Internet more useful. Starting in early 1998 and responding to the mushrooming importance of the Internet, Intel's senior management launched major new initiatives to direct attention and resources to expanding the capabilities of both the PC platform and the Internet. It was this strategic inflection point that led to Intel's latest strategic vision of playing a major role in getting a billion computers connected to the Internet worldwide, installing millions of servers, and building an Internet infrastructure that would support trillions of dollars of e-commerce and serve as a worldwide communication medium.

Source: Andrew S. Grove, *Only the Paranoid Survive* (New York: Doubleday-Currency, 1996), company documents and press releases, and information posted at www.intel.com.

Linking the Vision/Mission with Company Values

Many companies have developed a statement of values to guide the company's pursuit of its vision/mission, strategy, and ways of operating. By **values** (or *core values,* as they are often called)*,* we mean the beliefs, traits, and ways of doing things that management has determined should guide the pursuit of its vision and strategy, the conduct of company's operations, and the behavior of company personnel.

Values, good and bad, exist in every organization. They relate to such things as fair treatment, integrity, ethical behavior, innovation, teamwork, top-notch quality, superior customer service, social responsibility, and community citizenship. Most companies have built their statements of values around four to eight traits that company personnel are expected to display and that are supposed to be mirrored in how the company conducts its business.

> **Core Concept**
> A company's **values** are the beliefs, traits, and behavioral norms that company personnel are expected to display in conducting the company's business and pursuing its strategic vision and strategy.

At Kodak, the core values are respect for the dignity of the individual, uncompromising integrity, unquestioned trust, constant credibility, continual improvement and personal renewal, and open celebration of individual and team achievements. Home Depot embraces eight values (entrepreneurial spirit, excellent customer service, giving back to the community, respect for all people, doing the right thing, taking care of people, building strong relationships, and creating shareholder value) in its quest to be the world's leading home improvement retailer by operating warehouse stores filled with a wide assortment of products at the lowest prices with trained associates giving absolutely the best customer service in the industry. Toyota preaches respect for and development of its employees, teamwork, getting quality right the first time, learning, continuous improvement, and embracing change in its pursuit of low-cost, top-notch manufacturing excellence in motor vehicles.[4] DuPont stresses four values—safety, ethics, respect for people, and environmental stewardship; the first three have been in place since the company was founded 200 years ago by the DuPont family. Heinz uses the acronym PREMIER to identify seven values that "define to the world and to ourselves who we are and what we stand for":

- *P*assion . . . to be passionate about winning and about our brands, products and people, thereby delivering superior value to our shareholders.
- *R*isk Tolerance . . . to create a culture where entrepreneurship and prudent risk taking are encouraged and rewarded.
- *E*xcellence . . . to be the best in quality and in everything we do.
- *M*otivation . . . to celebrate success, recognizing and rewarding the achievements of individuals and teams.
- *I*nnovation . . . to innovate in everything, from products to processes.
- *E*mpowerment . . . to empower our talented people to take the initiative and to do what's right.
- *R*espect . . . to act with integrity and respect towards all.

Do companies practice what they preach when it comes to their professed values? Sometimes no, sometimes yes—at runs the gamut. At one extreme are companies with window-dressing values; the values statement is merely a collection of nice words and phrases that may be given lip service by top executives but have little discernible impact on either how company personnel behave or how the company operates. Such companies have values statements because such statements are in vogue and are seen as making the company look good. At the other extreme are companies whose executives take the stated values very seriously—the values are widely adopted by company personnel, are ingrained in the corporate culture, and are mirrored in how company personnel conduct themselves and the company's business on a daily basis. Top executives at companies on this end of the values-statement gamut genuinely believe in the importance of grounding company operations on sound values and ways of doing business. In their view, holding company personnel accountable for displaying the stated values is a way of infusing the company with the desired character, identity, and behavioral norms—the values become the company's equivalent of DNA.

At companies where the stated values are real rather than cosmetic, managers connect values to the pursuit of the strategic vision and mission in one of two ways. In companies with long-standing values that are deeply entrenched in the corporate culture, senior managers are careful to craft a vision, mission, and strategy that match established values, and they reiterate how the values-based behavioral norms contribute to the company's business success. If the company changes to a different vision or strategy, executives take care to explain how and why the core values continue to be relevant. Few companies with sincere commitment to established core values ever undertake strategic moves that conflict with ingrained values.

In new companies or companies with weak or incomplete sets of values, top management considers what values, behaviors, and business conduct should characterize the company and that will help drive the vision and strategy forward. Then values and behaviors that complement and support vision are drafted and circulated among managers and employees for discussion and possible modification. A final values statement that incorporates the desired behaviors and traits and that connects to the vision/mission is then officially adopted. Some companies combine their vision and values into a single statement or document, circulate it to all organization members, and in many instances post the vision/mission and values statement on the company's Web site. Illustration Capsule 2.3 describes the connection between Yahoo's mission and its core values.

Of course, a wide gap sometimes opens between a company's stated values and its actual business practices. Enron, for example, touted four corporate values— respect, integrity, communication, and excellence—but some top officials engaged in dishonest and fraudulent maneuvers that were concealed by "creative" accounting; the lack of integrity on the part of Enron executives and their deliberate failure to accurately communicate with shareholders and regulators in the company's financial filings led directly to the company's dramatic bankruptcy and implosion over a six-week period, along with criminal indictments, fines, or jail terms for over a dozen Enron executives. Once one of the world's most distinguished public accounting firms, Arthur Andersen was renowned for its commitment to the highest standards of audit integrity, but its high-profile audit failures and ethical lapses at Enron, WorldCom, and other companies led to Andersen's demise—in 2002, it was indicted for destroying Enron-related documents to thwart investigators.

SETTING OBJECTIVES: PHASE 2 OF THE STRATEGY-MAKING, STRATEGY-EXECUTING PROCESS

The managerial purpose of setting **objectives** is to convert the strategic vision into specific performance targets—results and outcomes the company's management wants to achieve. Objectives represent a managerial commitment to achieving particular results and outcomes. Well-stated objectives are *quantifiable,* or *measurable,* and contain a *deadline for achievement.* As Bill Hewlett, cofounder of Hewlett-Packard, shrewdly observed, "You cannot manage what you cannot measure. . . . And what gets measured gets done."[5] Concrete, measurable objectives are managerially valuable because they serve as yardsticks for tracking a company's performance and progress—a company that consistently meets or beats its performance targets is generally a better overall performer than a company that frequently falls short of achieving its objectives. Indeed, the experiences of countless companies and managers teach that precisely spelling out *how much* of *what kind* of performance *by when* and then pressing forward with actions and incentives calculated to help achieve the targeted outcomes greatly improve a company's actual performance. Such an approach definitely beats setting vague targets like "maximize profits," "reduce costs," "become more efficient," or "increase sales," which specify neither how much nor when. Similarly, exhorting

Core Concept
Objectives are an organization's performance targets—the results and outcomes management wants to achieve. They function as yardsticks for measuring how well the organization is doing.

Illustration Capsule 2.3

The Connection between Yahoo's Mission and Core Values

Our mission is to be the most essential global Internet service for consumers and businesses. How we pursue that mission is influenced by a set of core values—the standards that guide interactions with fellow Yahoos, the principles that direct how we service our customers, the ideals that drive what we do and how we do it. Many of our values were put into practice by two guys in a trailer some time ago; others reflect ambitions as our company grows. All of them are what we strive to achieve every day.

EXCELLENCE

We are committed to winning with integrity. We know leadership is hard won and should never be taken for granted. We aspire to flawless execution and don't take shortcuts on quality. We seek the best talent and promote its development. We are flexible and learn from our mistakes.

INNOVATION

We thrive on creativity and ingenuity. We seek the innovations and ideas that can change the world. We anticipate market trends and move quickly to embrace them. We are not afraid to take informed, responsible risk.

CUSTOMER FIXATION

We respect our customers above all else and never forget that they come to us by choice. We share a personal responsibility to maintain our customers' loyalty and trust. We listen and respond to our customers and seek to exceed their expectations.

TEAMWORK

We treat one another with respect and communicate openly. We foster collaboration while maintaining individual accountability. We encourage the best ideas to surface from anywhere within the organization. We appreciate the value of multiple perspectives and diverse expertise.

COMMUNITY

We share an infectious sense of mission to make an impact on society and empower consumers in ways never before possible. We are committed to serving both the Internet community and our own communities.

FUN

We believe humor is essential to success. We applaud irreverence and don't take ourselves too seriously. We celebrate achievement. We yodel.

WHAT YAHOO DOESN'T VALUE

At the end of its values statement, Yahoo made a point of singling out 54 things that it did not value, including bureaucracy, losing, good enough, arrogance, the status quo, following, formality, quick fixes, passing the buck, micromanaging, Monday morning quarterbacks, 20/20 hindsight, missing the boat, playing catch-up, punching the clock, and "shoulda coulda woulda."

Source: http://docs.yahoo.com/info/values (accessed August 20, 2005).

company personnel to try hard or do the best they can, and then living with whatever results they deliver, is clearly inadequate.

The Imperative of Setting Stretch Objectives Ideally, managers ought to use the objective-setting exercise as a tool for *stretching an organization to perform at its full potential and deliver the best possible results.* Challenging company personnel to go all out and deliver "stretch" gains in performance pushes an enterprise to be more inventive, to exhibit more urgency in improving both its financial performance and its business position, and to be more intentional and focused in its actions. Stretch objectives spur exceptional performance and help companies guard against contentment with modest gains in organizational performance. As Mitchell Leibovitz, former CEO of the auto parts and service retailer Pep Boys, once said, "If you want to have ho-hum results, have ho-hum objectives." *There's no better way to avoid ho-hum results than by setting stretch objectives and*

> Setting stretch objectives is an effective tool for avoiding ho-hum results.

using compensation incentives to motivate organization members to achieve the stretch performance targets.

What Kinds of Objectives to Set: The Need for a Balanced Scorecard

Two very distinct types of performance yardsticks are required: those relating to *financial performance* and those relating to *strategic performance*—outcomes that indicate a company is strengthening its marketing standing, competitive vitality, and future business prospects. Examples of commonly used **financial objectives** and **strategic objectives** include the following:

Core Concept
Financial objectives relate to the financial performance targets management has established for the organization to achieve. ***Strategic objectives*** relate to target outcomes that indicate a company is strengthening its market standing, competitive vitality, and future business prospects.

Financial Objectives	Strategic Objectives
• An *x* percent increase in annual revenues • Annual increases in after-tax profits of *x* percent • Annual increases in earnings per share of *x* percent • Annual dividend increases • Larger profit margins • An *x* percent return on capital employed (ROCE) or return on equity (ROE) • Increased shareholder value—in the form of an upward trending stock price and annual dividend increases • Strong bond and credit ratings • Sufficient internal cash flows to fund new capital investment • Stable earnings during periods of recession	• Winning an *x* percent market share • Achieving lower overall costs than rivals • Overtaking key competitors on product performance or quality or customer service • Deriving *x* percent of revenues from the sale of new products introduced within the past five years • Achieving technological leadership • Having better product selection than rivals • Strengthening the company's brand-name appeal • Having stronger national or global sales and distribution capabilities than rivals • Consistently getting new or improved products to market ahead of rivals

Achieving acceptable financial results is a must. Without adequate profitability and financial strength, a company's pursuit of its strategic vision, as well as its long-term health and ultimate survival, is jeopardized. Furthermore, subpar earnings and a weak balance sheet not only alarm shareholders and creditors but also put the jobs of senior executives at risk. However, good financial performance, by itself, is not enough. Of equal or greater importance is a company's strategic performance—outcomes that indicate whether a company's market position and competitiveness are deteriorating, holding steady, or improving.

The Case for a Balanced Scorecard: Improved Strategic Performance Fosters Better Financial Performance   A company's financial performance measures are really *lagging indicators* that reflect the results of past decisions and organizational activities.[6] But a company's past or current financial performance is not a reliable indicator of its future prospects—poor financial performers often turn things around and do better, while good financial performers can fall on hard times. The best and most reliable *leading indicators* of a company's future financial performance and business prospects are strategic outcomes that indicate whether the

Core Concept
A company that pursues and achieves strategic outcomes that boost its competitiveness and strength in the marketplace is in much better position to improve its future financial performance.

company's competitiveness and market position are stronger or weaker. For instance, if a company has set aggressive strategic objectives and is achieving them—such that its competitive strength and market position are on the rise, then there's reason to expect that its *future* financial performance will be better than its current or past performance. If a company is losing ground to competitors and its market position is slipping—outcomes that reflect weak strategic performance (and, very likely, failure to achieve its strategic objectives), then its ability to maintain its present profitability is highly suspect. Hence, the degree to which a company's managers set, pursue, and achieve stretch strategic objectives tends to be a reliable leading indicator of whether its future financial performance will improve or stall.

Consequently, a *balanced scorecard* for measuring company performance—one that tracks the achievement of both financial objectives and strategic objectives—is optimal.[7] Just tracking a company's financial performance overlooks the fact that what ultimately enables a company to deliver better financial results from its operations is the achievement of strategic objectives that improve its competitiveness and market strength. Indeed, *the surest path to boosting company profitability quarter after quarter and year after year is to relentlessly pursue strategic outcomes that strengthen the company's market position and produce a growing competitive advantage over rivals.*

Roughly 36 percent of global companies and over 100 nonprofit and governmental organizations used the balanced scorecard approach in 2001.[8] A more recent survey of 708 companies on five continents found that 62 percent were using a balanced scorecard to track performance.[9] Organizations that have adopted the balanced scorecard approach to setting objectives and measuring performance include Exxon Mobil, CIGNA, United Parcel Service, Sears, Nova Scotia Power, BMW, AT&T Canada, Chemical Bank, DaimlerChrysler, DuPont, Motorola, Siemens, Wells Fargo, Wendy's, Saatchi & Saatchi, Duke Children's Hospital, U.S. Department of the Army, Tennessee Valley Authority, the United Kingdom's Ministry of Defense, the University of California at San Diego, and the City of Charlotte, North Carolina.[10]

Illustration Capsule 2.4 shows selected objectives of five prominent companies—all employ a combination of strategic and financial objectives.

Both Short-Term and Long-Term Objectives Are Needed   As a rule, a company's set of financial and strategic objectives ought to include both near-term and longer-term performance targets. Having quarterly and annual objectives focuses attention on delivering immediate performance improvements. Targets to be achieved within three to five years prompt considerations of what to do *now* to put the company in position to perform better later. A company that has an objective of doubling its sales within five years can't wait until the third or fourth year to begin growing its sales and customer base. By spelling out annual (or perhaps quarterly) performance targets, management indicates the *speed* at which longer range targets are to be approached. Long-term objectives take on particular importance because it is generally in the best interest of shareholders for companies to be managed for optimal long-term performance. When trade-offs have to be made between achieving long-run objectives and achieving short-run objectives, long-run objectives should take precedence (unless the achievement of one or more short-run performance targets have unique importance). Shareholders are seldom well-served by repeated management actions that sacrifice better long-term performance in order to make quarterly or annual targets.

Strategic Intent: Relentless Pursuit of an Ambitious Strategic Objective
Very ambitious companies often establish a long-term strategic objective that clearly

Illustration Capsule 2.4
Examples of Company Objectives

NISSAN

Increase sales to 4.2 million cars and trucks by 2008 (up from 3 million in 2003); cut purchasing costs 20% and halve the number of suppliers; have zero net debt; maintain a return on invested capital of 20%; maintain a 10% or better operating margin.

McDONALD'S

Place more emphasis on delivering an exceptional customer experience; add approximately 350 net new McDonald's restaurants; reduce general and administrative spending as a percent of total revenues; achieve systemwide sales and revenue growth of 3% to 5%, annual operating income growth of 6% to 7%, and annual returns on incremental invested capital in the high teens.

H. J. HEINZ COMPANY

Achieve 4–6% sales growth, 7–10% growth in operating income, EPS in the range of $2.35 to $2.45, and operating free cash flow of $900 million to $1 billion in fiscal 2006; pay dividends equal to 45–50 percent of earnings; increase the focus on the company's 15 power brands and give top resource priority to those brands with number one and two market positions; continue to introduce new and improved food products; add to the Heinz portfolio of brands by acquiring companies with brands that complement existing brands; increase sales in Russia, Indonesia, China and India by 50 percent in fiscal year 2006 to roughly 6 percent of total sales; and by the end of fiscal 2008, derive approximately 50 percent of sales and profits from North America, 30 percent from Europe, and 20 percent from all other markets.

SEAGATE TECHNOLOGY

Solidify the company's No. 1 position in the overall market for hard-disk drives; get more Seagate drives into popular consumer electronics products; take share away from Western Digital in providing disk drives for Microsoft's Xbox; maintain leadership in core markets and achieve leadership in emerging markets; grow revenues by 10 percent per year; maintain gross margins of 24–26 percent; hold internal operating expenses to 13–13.5 percent of revenue.

3M CORPORATION

To achieve long term sales growth of 5–8% organic plus 2–4% from acquisitions; annual growth in earnings per share of 10% or better, on average; a return on stockholders' equity of 20%–25%; a return on capital employed of 27% or better; double the number of qualified new 3M product ideas and triple the value of products that win in the marketplace; and build the best sales and marketing organization in the world.

Sources: Information posted on company Web sites (accessed August 21, 2005); and "Nissan's Smryna Plant Produces 7 Millionth Vehicle," *Automotive Intelligence News,* August 2, 2005, p. 5.

signals **strategic intent** to be a winner in the marketplace, often against long odds.[11] A company's strategic intent can entail unseating the existing industry leader, becoming the dominant market share leader, delivering the best customer service of any company in the industry (or the world), or turning a new technology into products capable of changing the way people work and live. Nike's strategic intent during the 1960s was to overtake Adidas; this intent connected nicely with Nike's core purpose "to experience the emotion of competition, winning, and crushing competitors." Canon's strategic intent in copying equipment was to "beat Xerox." For some years, Toyota has been driving to overtake General Motors as the world's largest motor vehicle producer—and it surpassed Ford Motor Company in total vehicles sold in 2003, to move into second place. Toyota has expressed its strategic intent in the form of a global market share objective of 15 percent by 2010, up from 5 percent in 1980 and 10 percent in 2003. Starbucks' strategic intent is to make the Starbucks brand the world's most recognized and respected brand.

> **Core Concept**
> A company exhibits *strategic intent* when it relentlessly pursues an ambitious strategic objective, concentrating the full force of its resources and competitive actions on achieving that objective.

Ambitious companies that establish exceptionally bold strategic objectives and have an unshakable commitment to achieving them almost invariably begin with strategic intents that are out of proportion to their immediate capabilities and market grasp. But they pursue their strategic target relentlessly, sometimes even obsessively. They rally the organization around efforts to make the strategic intent a reality. They go all out to marshal the resources and capabilities to close in on their strategic target (which is often global market leadership) as rapidly as they can. They craft potent offensive strategies calculated to throw rivals off-balance, put them on the defensive, and force them into an ongoing game of catch-up. They deliberately try to alter the market contest and tilt the rules for competing in their favor. As a consequence, capably managed up-and-coming enterprises with strategic intents exceeding their present reach and resources are a force to be reckoned with, often proving to be more formidable competitors over time than larger, cash-rich rivals that have modest strategic objectives and market ambitions.

The Need for Objectives at All Organizational Levels   Objective setting should not stop with top management's establishing of companywide performance targets. Company objectives need to be broken down into performance targets for each of the organization's separate businesses, product lines, functional departments, and individual work units. Company performance can't reach full potential unless each organizational unit sets and pursues performance targets that contribute directly to the desired companywide outcomes and results. Objective setting is thus a top-down process that must extend to the lowest organizational levels. And it means that each organizational unit must take care to set performance targets that support—rather than conflict with or negate—the achievement of companywide strategic and financial objectives.

The ideal situation is a team effort in which each organizational unit strives to produce results in its area of responsibility that contribute to the achievement of the company's performance targets and strategic vision. Such consistency signals that organizational units know their strategic role and are on board in helping the company move down the chosen strategic path and produce the desired results.

Objective Setting Needs to Be Top-Down Rather than Bottom-Up   To appreciate why a company's objective-setting process needs to be more top-down than bottom-up, consider the following example. Suppose the senior executives of a diversified corporation establish a corporate profit objective of $500 million for next year. Suppose further that, after discussion between corporate management and the general managers of the firm's five different businesses, each business is given a stretch profit objective of $100 million by year-end (i.e., if the five business divisions contribute $100 million each in profit, the corporation can reach its $500 million profit objective). A concrete result has thus been agreed on and translated into measurable action commitments at two levels in the managerial hierarchy. Next, suppose the general manager of business unit A, after some analysis and discussion with functional area managers, concludes that reaching the $100 million profit objective will require selling 1 million units at an average price of $500 and producing them at an average cost of $400 (a $100 profit margin times 1 million units equals $100 million profit). Consequently, the general manager and the manufacturing manager settle on a production objective of 1 million units at a unit cost of $400; and the general manager and the marketing manager agree on a sales objective of 1 million units and a target selling price of $500. In turn, the marketing manager, after consultation with regional sales personnel, breaks the sales objective of 1 million units into unit sales targets for each sales territory, each item in the product line, and each salesperson. It is logical for organizationwide objectives and strategy to be established first so they can guide objective setting and strategy making at lower levels.

A top-down process of setting companywide performance targets first and then insisting that the financial and strategic performance targets established for business units, divisions, functional departments, and operating units be directly connected to the achievement of company objectives has two powerful advantages: One, it helps produce *cohesion* among the objectives and strategies of different parts of the organization. Two, it helps *unify internal efforts* to move the company along the chosen strategic path. If top management, desirous of involving many organization members, allows objective setting to start at the bottom levels of an organization without the benefit of companywide performance targets as a guide, then lower-level organizational units have no basis for connecting their performance targets to the company's. Bottom-up objective setting, with little or no guidance from above, nearly always signals an absence of strategic leadership on the part of senior executives.

CRAFTING A STRATEGY: PHASE 3 OF THE STRATEGY-MAKING, STRATEGY-EXECUTING PROCESS

The task of crafting a strategy entails answering a series of hows: *how* to grow the business, *how* to please customers, *how* to outcompete rivals, *how* to respond to changing market conditions, *how* to manage each functional piece of the business and develop needed competencies and capabilities, *how* to achieve strategic and financial objectives. It also means exercising astute entrepreneurship in choosing among the various strategic alternatives—proactively searching for opportunities to do new things or to do existing things in new or better ways.[12] The faster a company's business environment is changing, the more critical the need for its managers to be good entrepreneurs in diagnosing the direction and force of the changes under way and in responding with timely adjustments in strategy. Strategy makers have to pay attention to early warnings of future change and be willing to experiment with dare-to-be-different ways to alter their market position in preparing for new market conditions. When obstacles unexpectedly appear in a company's path, it is up to management to adapt rapidly and innovatively. *Masterful strategies come partly (maybe mostly) by doing things differently from competitors where it counts—outinnovating them, being more efficient, being more imaginative, adapting faster—rather than running with the herd.* Good strategy making is therefore inseparable from good business entrepreneurship. One cannot exist without the other.

Who Participates in Crafting a Company's Strategy?

A company's senior executives obviously have important strategy-making roles. The chief executive officer (CEO) wears the mantles of chief direction setter, chief objective setter, chief strategy maker, and chief strategy implementer for the total enterprise. Ultimate responsibility for *leading* the strategy-making, strategy-executing process rests with the CEO. In some enterprises the CEO functions as strategic visionary and chief architect of strategy, personally deciding what the key elements of the company's strategy will be, although others may well assist with data gathering and analysis, and the CEO may seek the advice of other senior managers and key employees in fashioning an overall strategy and deciding on important strategic moves. A CEO-centered approach to strategy development is characteristic of small owner-managed companies and sometimes large corporations that have been founded by the present CEO or that have CEOs with strong strategic leadership skills. Meg Whitman at eBay, Andrea Jung at Avon, Jeffrey Immelt at General Electric, and Howard Schultz at Starbucks are prominent examples of corporate CEOs who have wielded a heavy hand in shaping their company's strategy.

In most companies, however, strategy is the product of more than just the CEO's handiwork. Typically, other senior executives—business unit heads, the chief financial officer, and vice presidents for production, marketing, human resources, and other functional departments—have influential strategy-making roles and help fashion the chief strategy components. Normally, a company's chief financial officer (CFO) is in charge of devising and implementing an appropriate financial strategy; the production vice president takes the lead in developing the company's production strategy; the marketing vice president orchestrates sales and marketing strategy; a brand manager is in charge of the strategy for a particular brand in the company's product lineup; and so on.

But even here it is a mistake to view strategy making as a *top* management function, the exclusive province of owner-entrepreneurs, CEOs, and other senior executives. The more that a company's operations cut across different products, industries, and geographical areas, the more that headquarters executives have little option but to delegate considerable strategy-making authority to down-the-line managers in charge of particular subsidiaries, divisions, product lines, geographic sales offices, distribution centers, and plants. On-the-scene managers with authority over specific operating units are in the best position to evaluate the local situation in which the strategic choices must be made and can be expected to have detailed familiarity with local market and competitive conditions, customer requirements and expectations, and all the other aspects surrounding the strategic issues and choices in their arena of authority. This gives them an edge over headquarters executives in keeping the local aspects of the company's strategy responsive to local market and competitive conditions.

Take a company like Toshiba, a $43 billion corporation with 300 subsidiaries, thousands of products, and operations extending across the world. While top-level Toshiba executives may well be personally involved in shaping Toshiba's *overall* strategy and fashioning *important* strategic moves, it doesn't follow that a few senior executives at Toshiba headquarters have either the expertise or a sufficiently detailed understanding of all the relevant factors to wisely craft all the strategic initiatives taken for 300 subsidiaries and thousands of products. They simply cannot know enough about the situation in every Toshiba organizational unit to decide upon every strategy detail and direct every strategic move made in Toshiba's worldwide organization. Rather, it takes involvement on the part of Toshiba's whole management team—top executives, subsidiary heads, division heads, and key managers in such geographic units as sales offices, distribution centers, and plants—to craft the thousands of strategic initiatives that end up comprising the whole of Toshiba's strategy. The same can be said for a company like General Electric, which employs 300,000 people in businesses ranging from jet engines to plastics, power generation equipment to appliances, medical equipment to TV broadcasting, and locomotives to financial services (among many others) and that sells to customers in over 100 countries.

While managers farther down in the managerial hierarchy obviously have a narrower, more specific strategy-making role than managers closer to the top, the important understanding here is that in most of today's companies *every company manager typically has a strategy-making role—ranging from minor to major—for the area he or she heads.* Hence, any notion that an organization's strategists are at the top of the management hierarchy and that midlevel and frontline personnel merely carry out the strategic directives of senior managers needs to be cast aside. In companies with wide-ranging operations, it is far more accurate to view strategy making as a *collaborative or team effort* involving managers (and sometimes key employees) down through the whole organizational hierarchy.

> **Core Concept**
> In most companies, crafting and executing strategy is a team effort in which every manager has a role for the area he or she heads. It is flawed thinking to view crafting and executing strategy as something only high-level managers do.

In fact, the necessity of delegating some strategy-making authority to down-the-line managers has resulted in it being fairly common for key pieces of a company's strategy to originate in a company's middle and lower ranks.[13] Electronic Data Systems conducted a yearlong strategy review involving 2,500 of its 55,000 employees and coordinated by a core of 150 managers and staffers from all over the world.[14] J. M. Smucker, best-known for its jams and jellies, formed a team of 140 employees (7 percent of its 2,000-person workforce) who spent 25 percent of their time over a six-month period looking for ways to rejuvenate the company's growth. Involving teams of people to dissect complex situations and come up with strategic solutions is an often-used component of the strategy-making process because many strategic issues are complex or cut across multiple areas of expertise and operating units, thus calling for the contributions of many disciplinary experts and the collaboration of managers from different parts of the organization. A valuable strength of collaborative strategy-making is that the team of people charged with crafting the strategy can easily include the very people who will also be charged with implementing and executing it. Giving people an influential stake in crafting the strategy they must later help implement and execute not only builds motivation and commitment but also means those people can be held accountable for putting the strategy into place and making it work—the excuse of "It wasn't my idea to do this" won't fly.

The Strategy-Making Role of Corporate Intrapreneurs   In some companies, top management makes a regular practice of encouraging individuals and teams to develop and champion proposals for new product lines and new business ventures. The idea is to unleash the talents and energies of promising "corporate intrapreneurs," letting them try out untested business ideas and giving them the room to pursue new strategic initiatives. Executives judge which proposals merit support, give the chosen intrapreneurs the organizational and budgetary support they need, and let them proceed freely. Thus, important pieces of company strategy can originate with those intrapreneurial individuals and teams who succeed in championing a proposal through the approval stage and then end up being charged with the lead role in launching new products, overseeing the company's entry into new geographic markets, or heading up new business ventures. W. L. Gore and Associates, a privately owned company famous for its Gore-Tex waterproofing film, is an avid and highly successful practitioner of the corporate intrapreneur approach to strategy making. Gore expects all employees to initiate improvements and to display innovativeness. Each employee's intrapreneurial contributions are prime considerations in determining raises, stock option bonuses, and promotions. Gore's commitment to intrapreneurship has produced a stream of product innovations and new strategic initiatives that have kept the company vibrant and growing for nearly two decades.

A Company's Strategy-Making Hierarchy

It thus follows that *a company's overall strategy is a collection of strategic initiatives and actions* devised by managers and key employees up and down the whole organizational hierarchy. The larger and more diverse the operations of an enterprise, the more points of strategic initiative it has and the more managers and employees at more levels of management that have a relevant strategy-making role. Figure 2.2 shows who is generally responsible for devising what pieces of a company's overall strategy.

In diversified, multibusiness companies where the strategies of several different businesses have to be managed, the strategy-making task involves four distinct types or levels of strategy, each of which involves different facets of the company's overall strategy:

1. *Corporate strategy* consists of the kinds of initiatives the company uses to establish business positions in different industries, the approaches corporate executives pursue to boost the combined performance of the set of businesses the company has diversified into, and the means of capturing cross-business synergies and turning them into competitive advantage. Senior corporate executives normally have lead responsibility for devising corporate strategy and for choosing from among whatever recommended actions bubble up from the organization below. Key business-unit heads may also be influential, especially in strategic decisions affecting the businesses they head. Major strategic decisions are usually reviewed and approved by the company's board of directors. We will look deeper into the strategy-making process at diversified companies when we get to Chapter 9.

2. *Business strategy* concerns the actions and the approaches crafted to produce successful performance in one specific line of business. The key focus is crafting responses to changing market circumstances and initiating actions to strengthen market position, build competitive advantage, and develop strong competitive capabilities. Orchestrating the development of business-level strategy is the responsibility of the manager in charge of the business. The business head has at least two other strategy-related roles: (*a*) seeing that lower-level strategies are well conceived, consistent, and adequately matched to the overall business strategy, and (*b*) getting major business-level strategic moves approved by corporate-level officers (and sometimes the board of directors) and keeping them informed of emerging strategic issues. In diversified companies, business-unit heads may have the additional obligation of making sure business-level objectives and strategy conform to corporate-level objectives and strategy themes.

3. *Functional-area strategies* concern the actions, approaches, and practices to be employed in managing particular functions or business processes or key activities within a business. A company's marketing strategy, for example, represents the managerial game plan for running the sales and marketing part of the business. A company's product development strategy represents the managerial game plan for keeping the company's product lineup fresh and in tune with what buyers are looking for. Functional strategies add specifics to the hows of business-level strategy. Plus, they aim at establishing or strengthening a business unit's competencies and capabilities in performing strategy-critical activities so as to enhance the business's market position and standing with customers. The primary role of a functional strategy is to *support* the company's overall business strategy and competitive approach.

   Lead responsibility for functional strategies within a business is normally delegated to the heads of the respective functions, with the general manager of

Figure 2.2   **A Company's Strategy-Making Hierarchy**

Orchestrated by the CEO and other senior executives.

Corporate Strategy

The companywide game plan for managing a set of businesses

In the case of a single-business company, these two levels of the strategy-making hierarchy merge into one level—*business strategy*—that is orchestrated by the company's CEO and other top executives.

Two-Way Influence

Orchestrated by the general managers of each of the company's different lines of business, often with advice and input from the heads of functional area activities within each business and other key people.

Business Strategy (one for each business the company has diversified into)

• How to strengthen market position and build competitive advantage
• Actions to build competitive capabilities

Two-Way Influence

Crafted by the heads of major functional activities within a particular business—often in collaboration with other key people.

Functional-area strategies within each business

• Add relevant detail to the hows of overall business strategy
• Provide a game plan for managing a particular activity in ways that support the overall business strategy

Two-Way Influence

Crafted by brand managers; the operating managers of plants, distribution centers, and geographic units; and the managers of strategically important activities like advertising and Web site operations—often key employees are involved.

Operating strategies within each business

• Add detail and completeness to business and functional strategy
• Provide a game plan for managing specific lower-echelon activities with strategic significance

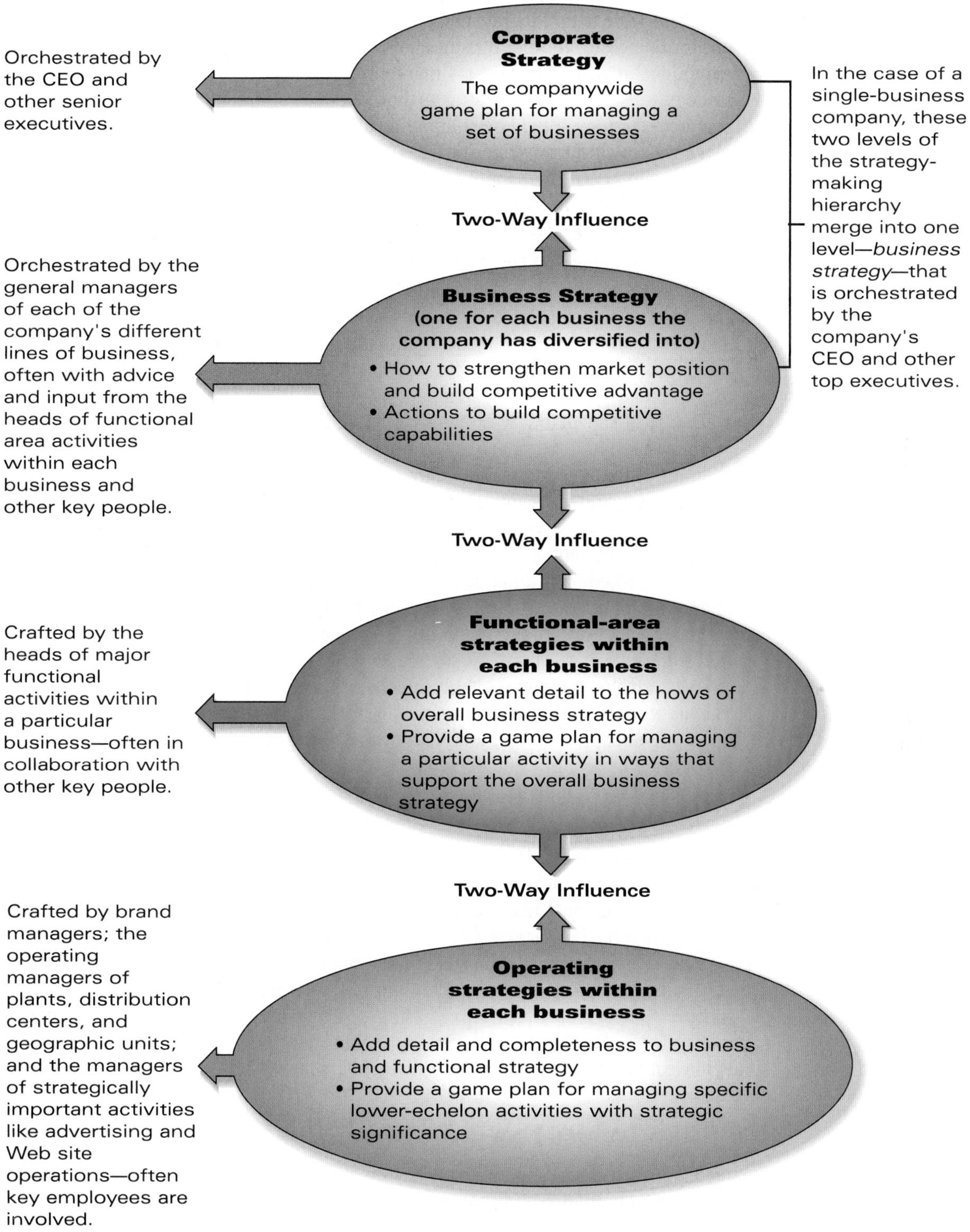

the business having final approval and perhaps even exerting a strong influence over the content of particular pieces of the strategies. To some extent, functional managers have to collaborate and coordinate their strategy-making efforts to avoid uncoordinated or conflicting strategies. For the overall business strategy to have maximum impact, a business's marketing strategy, production strategy, finance strategy, customer service strategy, product development strategy, and human resources strategy should be compatible and mutually reinforcing rather than each serving its own narrower purposes. If inconsistent functional-area strategies are sent up the line for final approval, the business head is responsible for spotting the conflicts and getting them resolved.

4. *Operating strategies* concern the relatively narrow strategic initiatives and approaches for managing key operating units (plants, distribution centers, geographic units) and specific operating activities with strategic significance (advertising campaigns, the management of specific brands, supply chain–related activities, and Web site sales and operations). A plant manager needs a strategy for accomplishing the plant's objectives, carrying out the plant's part of the company's overall manufacturing game plan, and dealing with any strategy-related problems that exist at the plant. A company's advertising manager needs a strategy for getting maximum audience exposure and sales impact from the ad budget. Operating strategies, while of limited scope, add further detail and completeness to functional strategies and to the overall business strategy. Lead responsibility for operating strategies is usually delegated to frontline managers, subject to review and approval by higher-ranking managers.

   Even though operating strategy is at the bottom of the strategy-making hierarchy, its importance should not be downplayed. A major plant that fails in its strategy to achieve production volume, unit cost, and quality targets can undercut the achievement of company sales and profit objectives and wreak havoc with strategic efforts to build a quality image with customers. Frontline managers are thus an important part of an organization's strategy-making team because many operating units have strategy-critical performance targets and need to have strategic action plans in place to achieve them. One cannot reliably judge the strategic importance of a given action simply by the strategy level or location within the managerial hierarchy where it is initiated.

In single-business enterprises, the corporate and business levels of strategy making merge into one level—business strategy—because the strategy for the whole company involves only one distinct line of business. Thus, a single-business enterprise has three levels of strategy: business strategy for the company as a whole, functional-area strategies for each main area within the business, and operating strategies undertaken by lower-echelon managers to flesh out strategically significant aspects for the company's business and functional-area strategies. Proprietorships, partnerships, and owner-managed enterprises may have only one or two strategy-making levels since their strategy-making, strategy-executing process can be handled by just a few key people.

Uniting the Strategy-Making Effort

Ideally, the pieces of a company's strategy up and down the strategy hierarchy should be cohesive and mutually reinforcing, fitting together like a jigsaw puzzle. To achieve such unity, the strategizing process requires leadership from the top. It is the responsibility of top executives to provide strategy-making direction and clearly articulate key strategic themes that paint the white lines for lower-level strategy-making efforts. *Mid-level and frontline managers cannot craft unified strategic moves without first understanding the company's long-term direction and knowing the major components of the overall and business strategies that their strategy-making efforts are supposed to support and enhance.* Thus, as a general rule, strategy making must start at the top of the organization and then proceed downward through the hierarchy from the corporate level to the business level and then from the business level to the associated functional and operating levels. Strategy cohesion requires that business-level strategies complement and be compatible with the overall corporate strategy. Likewise, functional and operating strategies have to complement and support the overall business-level strategy of which they are a part. When the strategizing process is mostly top-down, with lower-level strategy-making efforts taking their cues from the higher-level strategy elements they are supposed to complement and support, there's less potential for strategy conflict between different levels. An absence of strong strategic leadership from the top sets the stage for some degree of strategic disunity. The strategic disarray that occurs in an organization when there is weak leadership and too few strategy guidelines coming from top executives is akin to what would happen to a football team's offensive performance if the quarterback decided not to call a play for the team but instead let each player do whatever he/thought would work best at his respective position. In business, as in sports, all the strategy makers in a company are on the same team and the many different pieces of the overall strategy crafted at various organizational levels need to be in sync. *Anything less than a unified collection of strategies weakens the overall strategy and is likely to impair company performance.*

> **Core Concept**
> A company's strategy is at full power only when its many pieces are united.

There are two things that top-level executives can do to drive consistent strategic action down through the organizational hierarchy. One is to effectively communicate the company's vision, objectives, and major strategy components to down-the-line managers and key personnel. The greater the numbers of company personnel who know, understand, and buy into the company's long-term direction and overall strategy, the smaller the risk that organization units will go off in conflicting strategic directions when strategy making is pushed down to frontline levels and many people are given a strategy-making role. The second is to exercise due diligence in reviewing lower-level strategies for consistency and support of higher level strategies. Any strategy conflicts must be addressed and resolved, either by modifying the lower-level strategies with conflicting elements or by adapting the higher-level strategy to accommodate what may be more appealing strategy ideas and initiatives bubbling from below. Thus, the process of synchronizing the strategy initiatives up and down the organizational hierarchy does not necessarily mean that lower-level strategies must be changed whenever conflicts and inconsistencies are spotted. When more attractive strategies ideas originate at lower organizational levels, it makes sense to adapt higher-level strategies to accommodate them.

A Strategic Vision + Objectives + Strategy = A Strategic Plan

Developing a strategic vision and mission, setting objectives, and crafting a strategy are basic direction-setting tasks. They map out where a company is headed, the targeted strategic and financial outcomes, and the competitive moves and internal action approaches to be used in achieving the desired business results. Together, they constitute a **strategic plan** for coping with industry and competitive conditions, the expected actions of the industry's key players, and the challenges and issues that stand as obstacles to the company's success.[15]

> **Core Concept**
> A *strategic plan* lays out the company's future direction, performance targets, and strategy.

In companies that do regular strategy reviews and develop explicit strategic plans, the strategic plan usually ends up as a written document that is circulated to most managers and perhaps selected employees. Near-term performance targets are the part of the strategic plan most often spelled out explicitly and communicated to managers and employees. A number of companies summarize key elements of their strategic plans in the company's annual report to shareholders, in postings on their Web site, or in statements provided to the business media. Other companies, perhaps for reasons of competitive sensitivity, make only vague, general statements about their strategic plans. In small, privately owned companies, it is rare for strategic plans to exist in written form. Small companies' strategic plans tend to reside in the thinking and directives of owners/ executives, with aspects of the plan being revealed in meetings and conversations with company personnel, and the understandings and commitments among managers and key employees about where to head, what to accomplish, and how to proceed.

IMPLEMENTING AND EXECUTING THE STRATEGY: PHASE 4 OF THE STRATEGY-MAKING, STRATEGY-EXECUTING PROCESS

Managing the implementation and execution of strategy is an operations-oriented, make-things-happen activity aimed at performing core business activities in a strategy-supportive manner. It is easily the most demanding and time-consuming part of the strategy management process. Converting strategic plans into actions and results tests a manager's ability to direct organizational change, motivate people, build and strengthen company competencies and competitive capabilities, create and nurture a strategy-supportive work climate, and meet or beat performance targets. Initiatives to put the strategy in place and execute it proficiently have to be launched and managed on many organizational fronts.

Management's action agenda for implementing and executing the chosen strategy emerges from assessing what the company will have to do differently or better, given its particular operating practices and organizational circumstances, to execute the strategy competently and achieve the targeted financial and strategic performance. Each company manager has to think through the answer to "What has to be done in my area to execute my piece of the strategic plan, and what actions should I take to get the process under way?" How much internal change is needed depends on how much of the strategy is new, how far internal practices and competencies deviate from what the strategy requires, and how well the present work climate/culture supports good strategy execution. Depending on the amount of internal change involved, full implementation and proficient execution of company strategy (or important new pieces thereof) can take several months to several years.

In most situations, managing the strategy execution process includes the following principal aspects:

- Staffing the organization with the needed skills and expertise, consciously building and strengthening strategy-supportive competencies and competitive capabilities, and organizing the work effort.
- Allocating ample resources to those activities critical to strategic success.
- Ensuring that policies and procedures facilitate rather than impede effective execution.

- Using best practices to perform core business activities and pushing for continuous improvement. Organizational units have to periodically reassess how things are being done and diligently pursue useful changes and improvements.
- Installing information and operating systems that enable company personnel to better carry out their strategic roles day in and day out.
- Motivating people to pursue the target objectives energetically and, if need be, modifying their duties and job behavior to better fit the requirements of successful strategy execution.
- Tying rewards and incentives directly to the achievement of performance objectives and good strategy execution.
- Creating a company culture and work climate conducive to successful strategy execution.
- Exerting the internal leadership needed to drive implementation forward and keep improving on how the strategy is being executed. When stumbling blocks or weaknesses are encountered, management has to see that they are addressed and rectified in timely and effective fashion.

Good strategy execution requires diligent pursuit of operating excellence. It is a job for a company's whole management team. And success hinges on the skills and cooperation of operating managers who can push needed changes in their organization units and consistently deliver good results. Strategy implementation can be considered successful if things go smoothly enough that the company meets or beats its strategic and financial performance targets and shows good progress in achieving management's strategic vision.

EVALUATING PERFORMANCE AND INITIATING CORRECTIVE ADJUSTMENTS: PHASE 5 OF THE STRATEGY-MAKING, STRATEGY-EXECUTING PROCESS

The fifth phase of the strategy management process—monitoring new external developments, evaluating the company's progress, and making corrective adjustments—is the trigger point for deciding whether to continue or change the company's vision, objectives, strategy, or strategy execution methods. So long as the company's direction and strategy seem well matched to industry and competitive conditions, and performance targets are being met, company executives may well decide to stay the course. Simply fine-tuning the strategic plan and continuing with efforts to improve strategy execution are sufficient.

> **Core Concept**
> A company's vision, objectives, strategy, and approach to strategy execution are never final; managing strategy is an ongoing process, not an every-now-and-then task.

But whenever a company encounters disruptive changes in its environment, questions need to be raised about the appropriateness of its direction and strategy. If a company experiences a downturn in its market position or persistent shortfalls in performance, then company managers are obligated to ferret out the causes—do they relate to poor strategy, poor strategy execution, or both?—and take timely corrective action. A company's direction, objectives, and strategy have to be revisited anytime external or internal conditions warrant. It is to be expected that a company will modify its strategic vision, direction, objectives, and strategy over time.

Likewise, it is not unusual for a company to find that one or more aspects of its strategy implementation and execution are not going as well as intended. Proficient strategy execution is always the product of much organizational learning. It is achieved unevenly—coming quickly in some areas and proving nettlesome in others. It is both normal and desirable to periodically assess strategy execution to determine which aspects are working well and which need improving. Successful strategy execution entails vigilantly searching for ways to improve and then making corrective adjustments whenever and wherever it is useful to do so.

CORPORATE GOVERNANCE: THE ROLE OF THE BOARD OF DIRECTORS IN THE STRATEGY-MAKING, STRATEGY-EXECUTING PROCESS

Although senior managers have *lead responsibility* for crafting and executing a company's strategy, it is the duty of the board of directors to exercise *strong oversight* and see that the five tasks of strategic management are done in a manner that benefits shareholders (in the case of investor-owned enterprises) or stakeholders (in the case of not-for-profit organizations). In watching over management's strategy-making, strategy-executing actions and making sure that executive actions are not only proper but also aligned with the interests of stakeholders, a company's board of directors has four important obligations to fulfill:

1. *Be inquiring critics and oversee the company's direction, strategy, and business approaches.* Board members must ask probing questions and draw on their business acumen to make independent judgments about whether strategy proposals have been adequately analyzed and whether proposed strategic actions appear to have greater promise than alternatives. If executive management is bringing well-supported and reasoned strategy proposals to the board, there's little reason for board members to aggressively challenge or pick apart everything put before them. Asking incisive questions is usually sufficient to test whether the case for management's proposals is compelling. However, when the company's strategy is failing or is plagued with faulty execution, and certainly when there is a precipitous collapse in profitability, board members have a duty to express their concerns about the validity of the strategy and/or operating methods, initiate debate about the company's strategic path, hold one-on-one discussions with key executives and other board members, and perhaps directly intervene as a group to alter the company's executive leadership and, ultimately, its strategy and business approaches.

2. *Evaluate the caliber of senior executives' strategy-making and strategy-executing skills.* The board is always responsible for determining whether the current CEO is doing a good job of strategic leadership (as a basis for awarding salary increases and bonuses and deciding on retention or removal). Boards must also exercise due diligence in evaluating the strategic leadership skills of other senior executives in line to succeed the CEO. When the incumbent CEO steps down or leaves for a position elsewhere, the board must elect a successor, either going with an insider or deciding that a better-qualified outsider is needed to perhaps radically change the company's strategic course.

3. *Institute a compensation plan for top executives that rewards them for actions and results that serve stakeholder interests, and most especially those of shareholders.* A basic principle of corporate governance is that the owners of a corporation delegate operating authority and managerial control to top management in return for compensation. In their role as an *agent* of shareholders, top executives have a

clear and unequivocal duty to make decisions and operate the company in accord with shareholder interests (but this does not mean disregarding the interests of other stakeholders, particularly those of employees, with whom they also have an agency relationship). Most boards of directors have a compensation committee, composed entirely of outside directors, to develop a salary and incentive compensation plan that makes it in the self-interest of executives to operate the business in a manner that benefits the owners; the compensation committee's recommendations are presented to the full board for approval. But in addition to creating compensation plans intended to align executive actions with owner interests, the board of directors must put a halt to self-serving executive perks and privileges that simply line the financial pockets of executives. Numerous media reports have recounted instances in which boards of directors have gone along with opportunistic executive efforts to secure excessive, if not downright obscene, compensation of one kind or another (multimillion-dollar interest-free loans, personal use of corporate aircraft, lucrative severance and retirement packages, outsized stock incentive awards, and so on).

4. *Oversee the company's financial accounting and financial reporting practices.* While top managers, particularly the company's CEO and CFO, are primarily responsible for seeing that the company's financial statements fairly and accurately report the results of the company's operations, it is well established that board members have a fiduciary duty to protect shareholders by exercising oversight of the company's financial practices, ensuring that generally accepted accounting principles (GAAP) are properly used in preparing the company's financial statements, and determining whether proper financial controls are in place to prevent fraud and misuse of funds. Virtually all boards of directors monitor the financial reporting activities by appointing an audit committee, always composed entirely of outside directors. The members of the audit committee have lead responsibility for overseeing the company's financial officers and consulting with both internal and external auditors to ensure accurate financial reporting and adequate financial controls.

   The number of prominent companies penalized because of the actions of scurrilous or out-of-control CEOs and CFOs, the growing propensity of disgruntled stockholders to file lawsuits alleging director negligence, and the escalating costs of liability insurance for directors all underscore the responsibility that a board of directors has for overseeing a company's strategy-making, strategy-executing process and ensuring that management actions are proper and responsible. Moreover, holders of large blocks of shares (mutual funds and pension funds), regulatory authorities, and the financial press consistently urge that board members, especially outside directors, be active and diligent in their oversight of company strategy and maintain a tight rein on executive actions.

Every corporation should have a strong, independent board of directors that (1) is well informed about the company's performance, (2) guides and judges the CEO and other top executives, (3) has the courage to curb inappropriate or unduly risky management actions, (4) certifies to shareholders that the CEO is doing what the board expects, (5) provides insight and advice to management, and (6) is intensely involved in debating the pros and cons of key decisions and actions.[14] Boards of directors that lack the backbone to challenge a strong-willed or imperial CEO or that rubber-stamp most anything the CEO recommends without probing inquiry and debate (perhaps because the board is stacked with the CEO's cronies) abdicate their duty to represent and protect shareholder interests. The whole fabric of effective corporate governance is undermined when boards of directors shirk their responsibility to maintain ultimate control over the company's strategic direction, the major elements of its strategy, the business approaches management is using to implement and execute the strategy, executive compensation, and the financial reporting process. Thus, even though lead responsibility for crafting and executing strategy falls to top executives, boards of directors have a very important oversight role in the strategy-making, strategy-executing process.

Key Points

The managerial process of crafting and executing a company's strategy consists of five interrelated and integrated phases:

1. *Developing a strategic vision* of where the company needs to head and what its future product/market/customer/technology focus should be. This managerial step provides long-term direction, infuses the organization with a sense of purposeful action, and communicates management's aspirations to stakeholders.

2. *Setting objectives* to spell out for the company *how much* of *what kind* of performance is expected, and *by when.* The objectives need to require a significant amount of organizational stretch. A balanced scorecard approach for measuring company performance entails setting both *financial objectives* and *strategic objectives.*

3. *Crafting a strategy to achieve the objectives* and move the company along the strategic course that management has charted. Crafting strategy is concerned principally with forming responses to changes under way in the external environment, devising competitive moves and market approaches aimed at producing sustainable competitive advantage, building competitively valuable competencies and capabilities, and uniting the strategic actions initiated in various parts of the company. The more that a company's operations cut across different products, industries, and geographical areas, the more that strategy making becomes a *team effort* involving managers and company personnel at many organizational levels. The total strategy that emerges in such companies is really a collection of strategic actions and business approaches initiated partly by senior company executives, partly by the heads of major business divisions, partly by functional-area managers, and partly by frontline operating managers. The larger and more diverse the operations of an enterprise, the more points of strategic initiative it has and the more managers and employees at more levels of management that have a relevant strategy-making role. A single business enterprise has three levels of strategy—business strategy for the company as a whole, functional-area strategies for each main area within the business, and operating strategies undertaken by lower-echelon managers to flesh out strategically significant aspects for the company's business and functional-area strategies. In diversified, multibusiness companies, the strategy-making task involves four distinct types or levels of strategy: corporate strategy for the company as a whole, business strategy (one for each business the company has diversified into), functional-area strategies within each business, and operating strategies. Typically, the strategy-making task is more top-down than bottom-up, with higher-level strategies serving as the guide for developing lower-level strategies.

4. *Implementing and executing the chosen strategy efficiently and effectively.* Managing the implementation and execution of strategy is an operations-oriented, make-things-happen activity aimed at shaping the performance of core business activities in a strategy-supportive manner. Management's handling of the strategy implementation process can be considered successful if things go smoothly

enough that the company meets or beats its strategic and financial performance targets and shows good progress in achieving management's strategic vision.

5. *Evaluating performance and initiating corrective adjustments* in vision, long-term direction, objectives, strategy, or execution in light of actual experience, changing conditions, new ideas, and new opportunities. This phase of the strategy management process is the trigger point for deciding whether to continue or change the company's vision, objectives, strategy, and/or strategy execution methods.

A company's strategic vision, objectives, and strategy constitute a *strategic plan* for coping with industry and competitive conditions, outcompeting rivals, and addressing the challenges and issues that stand as obstacles to the company's success.

Boards of directors have a duty to shareholders to play a vigilant role in overseeing management's handling of a company's strategy-making, strategy-executing process. A company's board is obligated to (1) critically appraise and ultimately approve strategic action plans; (2) evaluate the strategic leadership skills of the CEO and others in line to succeed the incumbent CEO; (3) institute a compensation plan for top executives that rewards them for actions and results that serve stakeholder interests, most especially those of shareholders; and (4) ensure that the company issues accurate financial reports and has adequate financial controls.

Exercises

1. Go to the Investors section of Heinz's Web site (www.heinz.com) and read the letter to the shareholders in the company's fiscal 2003 annual report. Is the vision for Heinz articulated by Chairman and CEO William R. Johnson sufficiently clear and well defined? Why or why not? Are the company's objectives well stated and appropriate? What about the strategy that Johnson outlines for the company? If you were a shareholder, would you be satisfied with what Johnson has told you about the company's direction, performance targets, and strategy?

2. Consider the following mission statement of the American Association of Retired People (AARP):

AARP Mission Statement

- AARP is a nonprofit, nonpartisan membership organization for people age 50 and over.
- AARP is dedicated to enhancing quality of life for all as we age. We lead positive social change and deliver value to members through information, advocacy and service.
- AARP also provides a wide range of unique benefits, special products, and services for our members. These benefits include AARP Web site at www.aarp.org, "AARP The Magazine," the monthly "AARP Bulletin," and a Spanish-language newspaper, "Segunda Juventud."
- Active in every state, the District of Columbia, Puerto Rico, and the U.S. Virgin Islands, AARP celebrates the attitude that age is just a number and life is what you make it.

Is AARP's mission statement well-crafted? Does it do an adequate job of indicating "who we are, what we do, and why we are here"? Why or why not?

3. How would you rewrite/restate the strategic vision for Caterpillar in Illustration Capsule 2.1 so as to better exemplify the characteristics of effective vision statements presented in Tables 2.2 and 2.3? Visit www.caterpillar.com to get more information about Caterpillar and figure out how a more appropriate strategic vision might be worded.

chapter three

Evaluating a Company's External Environment

Analysis is the critical starting point of strategic thinking.

—Kenichi Ohmae
Consultant and Author

Things are always different—the art is figuring out which differences matter.

—Laszlo Birinyi
Investments Manager

Competitive battles should be seen not as one-shot skirmishes but as a dynamic multiround game of moves and countermoves.

—Anil K. Gupta
Professor

M anagers are not prepared to act wisely in steering a company in a different direction or altering its strategy until they have a deep understanding of the pertinent factors surrounding the company's situation. As indicated in the opening paragraph of Chapter 1, one of the three central questions that managers must address in evaluating their company's business prospects is "What's the company's present situation?" Two facets of a company's situation are especially pertinent: (1) the industry and competitive environment in which the company operates and the forces acting to reshape this environment, and (2) the company's own market position and competitiveness—its resources and capabilities, its strengths and weaknesses vis-à-vis rivals, and its windows of opportunity.

Insightful diagnosis of a company's external and internal environment is a prerequisite for managers to succeed in crafting a strategy that is an excellent fit with the company's situation, is capable of building competitive advantage, and holds good prospect for boosting company performance—the three criteria of a winning strategy. As depicted in Figure 3.1, the task of crafting a strategy thus should always begin with an appraisal of the company's external and internal situation (as a basis for developing strategic vision of where the company needs to head), then move toward an evaluation of the most promising alternative strategies and business models, and culminate in choosing a specific strategy.

This chapter presents the concepts and analytical tools for zeroing in on those aspects of a single-business company's external environment that should be considered in making strategic choices. Attention centers on the competitive arena in which a company operates, the drivers of market change, and what rival companies are doing. In Chapter 4 we explore the methods of evaluating a company's internal circumstances and competitiveness.

THE STRATEGICALLY RELEVANT COMPONENTS OF A COMPANY'S EXTERNAL ENVIRONMENT

All companies operate in a "macroenvironment" shaped by influences emanating from the economy at large; population demographics; societal values and lifestyles; governmental legislation and regulation; technological factors; and, closer to home, the

Figure 3.1   **From Thinking Strategically about the Company's Situation to Choosing a Strategy**

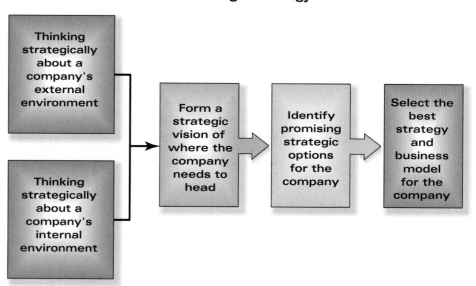

industry and competitive arena in which the company operates (see Figure 3.2). Strictly speaking, a company's macroenvironment includes *all relevant factors and influences* outside the company's boundaries; by relevant, we mean important enough to have a bearing on the decisions the company ultimately makes about its direction, objectives, strategy, and business model. Strategically relevant influences coming from the outer ring of the macroenvironment can sometimes have a high impact on a company's business situation and have a very significant impact on the company's direction and strategy. The strategic opportunities of cigarette producers to grow their business are greatly reduced by antismoking ordinances and the growing cultural stigma attached to smoking. Motor vehicle companies must adapt their strategies (especially as concerns the fuel mileage of their vehicles) to customer concerns about gasoline prices. The demographics of an aging population and longer life expectancies are having a dramatic impact on the business prospects and strategies of health care and prescription drug companies. Companies in most all industries have to craft strategies that are responsive to environmental regulations, growing use of the Internet and broadband technology, and energy prices. Companies in the food-processing, restaurant, sports, and fitness industries have to pay special attention to changes in lifestyles, eating habits, leisure-time preferences, and attitudes toward nutrition and exercise in fashioning their strategies.

Happenings in the outer ring of the macroenvironment may occur rapidly or slowly, with or without advance warning. The impact of outer-ring factors on a company's choice of strategy can range from big to small. But even if the factors in the outer ring of the macroenvironment change slowly or have such a comparatively low impact on a company's situation that only the edges of a company's direction and strategy are affected, there are enough strategically relevant outer-ring trends and events to justify a watchful eye. As company managers scan the external environment, they must be alert for potentially important outer-ring developments, assess their impact and influence, and adapt the company's direction and strategy as needed.

Figure 3.2   **The Components of a Company's Macroenvironment**

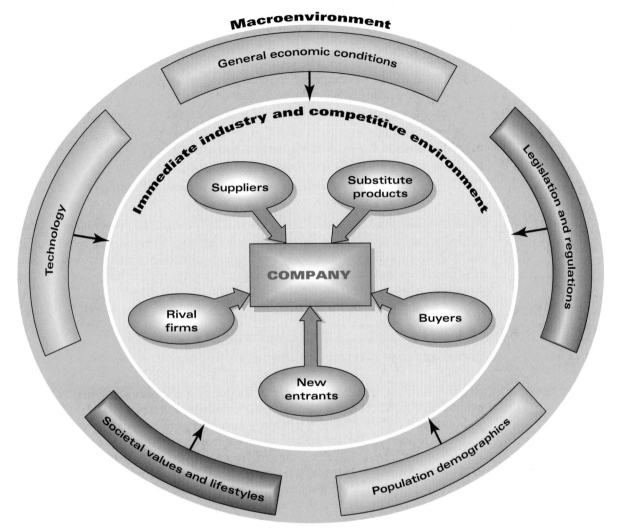

However, the factors and forces in a company's macroenvironment having the *biggest* strategy-shaping impact typically pertain to the company's immediate industry and competitive environment—competitive pressures, the actions of rivals firms, buyer behavior, supplier-related considerations, and so on. Consequently, it is on a company's industry and competitive environment that we concentrate our attention in this chapter.

THINKING STRATEGICALLY ABOUT A COMPANY'S INDUSTRY AND COMPETITIVE ENVIRONMENT

To gain a deep understanding of a company's industry and competitive environment, managers do not need to gather all the information they can find and spend lots of time digesting it. Rather, the task is much more focused. Thinking strategically about a company's industry and competitive environment entails using some well-defined concepts and analytical tools to get clear answers to seven questions:

1.   What are the industry's dominant economic features?
2.   What kinds of competitive forces are industry members facing and how strong is each force?
3.   What forces are driving industry change and what impacts will they have on competitive intensity and industry profitability?
4.   What market positions do industry rivals occupy—who is strongly positioned and who is not?
5.   What strategic moves are rivals likely to make next?
6.   What are the key factors for future competitive success?
7.   Does the outlook for the industry present the company with sufficiently attractive prospects for profitability?

Analysis-based answers to these questions provide managers with the understanding needed to craft a strategy that fits the company's external situation. The remainder of this chapter is devoted to describing the methods of obtaining solid answers to the seven questions and explaining how the nature of a company's industry and competitive environment weighs upon the strategic choices of company managers.

QUESTION 1: WHAT ARE THE INDUSTRY'S DOMINANT ECONOMIC FEATURES?

Because industries differ so significantly, analyzing a company's industry and competitive environment begins with identifying an industry's dominant economic features and forming a picture of what the industry landscape is like. An industry's dominant economic features are defined by such factors as market size and growth rate, the number and sizes of buyers and sellers, the geographic boundaries of the market (which can extend from local to worldwide), the degree to which sellers' products are differentiated, the pace of product innovation, market supply/demand conditions, the pace of technological change, the extent of vertical integration, and the extent to which costs are affected by scale economies (i.e., situations in which large-volume operations result in lower unit costs) and learning/experience curve effects (i.e., situations in which costs decline as a company gains knowledge and experience). Table 3.1 provides a convenient summary of what economic features to look at and the corresponding questions to consider in profiling an industry's landscape.

Getting a handle on an industry's distinguishing economic features not only sets the stage for the analysis to come but also promotes understanding of the kinds of strategic moves that industry members are likely to employ. For example, in industries characterized by one product advance after another, companies must invest in research and development (R&D) and develop strong product innovation capabilities—a strategy of continuous product innovation becomes a condition of survival in such industries as video games, mobile phones, and pharmaceuticals. An industry that has recently passed through the rapid-growth stage and is looking at single-digit percentage increases in buyer demand is likely to be experiencing a competitive shake-out and much stronger strategic emphasis on cost reduction and improved customer service.

In industries like semiconductors, strong *learning/experience curve effects* in manufacturing cause unit costs to decline about 20 percent each time *cumulative* production

Table 3.1   **What to Consider in Identifying an Industry's Dominant Economic Features**

Economic Feature	Questions to Answer
Market size and growth rate	• How big is the industry and how fast is it growing? • What does the industry's position in the life cycle (early development, rapid growth and takeoff, early maturity and slowing growth, saturation and stagnation, decline) reveal about the industry's growth prospects?
Number of rivals	• Is the industry fragmented into many small companies or concentrated and dominated by a few large companies? • Is the industry going through a period of consolidation to a smaller number of competitors?
Scope of competitive rivalry	• Is the geographic area over which most companies compete local, regional, national, multinational, or global? • Is having a presence in the foreign country markets becoming more important to a company's long-term competitive success?
Number of buyers	• Is market demand fragmented among many buyers? • Do some buyers have bargaining power because they purchase in large volume?
Degree of product differentiation	• Are the products of rivals becoming more differentiated or less differentiated? • Are increasingly look-alike products of rivals causing heightened price competition?
Product innovation	• Is the industry characterized by rapid product innovation and short product life cycles? • How important is R&D and product innovation? • Are there opportunities to overtake key rivals by being first-to-market with next-generation products?
Supply/demand conditions	• Is a surplus of capacity pushing prices and profit margins down? • Is the industry overcrowded with too many competitors? • Are short supplies creating a sellers' market?
Pace of technological change	• What role does advancing technology play in this industry? • Are ongoing upgrades of facilities/equipment essential because of rapidly advancing production process technologies? • Do most industry members have or need strong technological capabilities?
Vertical integration	• Do most competitors operate in only one stage of the industry (parts and components production, manufacturing and assembly, distribution, retailing) or do some competitors operate in multiple stages? • Is there any cost or competitive advantage or disadvantage associated with being fully or partially integrated?
Economies of scale	• Is the industry characterized by economies of scale in purchasing, manufacturing, advertising, shipping, or other activities? • Do companies with large-scale operations have an important cost advantage over small-scale firms?
Learning/experience curve effects	• Are certain industry activities characterized by strong learning/experience curve effects ("learning by doing") such that unit costs decline as a company's experience in performing the activity builds? • Do any companies have significant cost advantages because of their learning/experience in performing particular activities?

volume doubles. With a 20 percent experience curve effect, if the first 1 million chips cost $100 each, the unit cost would be $80 (80 percent of $100) by a production volume of 2 million, the unit cost would be $64 (80 percent of $80) by a production volume of 4 million, and so on.[1] The bigger the learning/experience curve effect, the bigger the cost advantage of the company with the largest *cumulative* production volume.

Thus, when an industry is characterized by important learning/experience curve effects (or by economies of scale), industry members are strongly motivated to adopt volume-increasing strategies to capture the resulting cost-saving economies and maintain their competitiveness. Unless small-scale firms succeed in pursuing strategic options that allow them to grow sales sufficiently to remain cost-competitive with larger-volume rivals, they are unlikely to survive. The bigger the learning/experience curve effects and/or scale economies in an industry, the more imperative it becomes for competing sellers to pursue strategies to win additional sales and market share—the company with the biggest sales volume gains sustainable competitive advantage as the low-cost producer.

QUESTION 2: WHAT KINDS OF COMPETITIVE FORCES ARE INDUSTRY MEMBERS FACING?

The character, mix, and subtleties of the competitive forces operating in a company's industry are never the same from one industry to another. Far and away the most powerful and widely used tool for systematically diagnosing the principal competitive pressures in a market and assessing the strength and importance of each is the *five-forces model of competition.*[2] This model, depicted in Figure 3.3, holds that the state of competition in an industry is a composite of competitive pressures operating in five areas of the overall market:

1. Competitive pressures associated with the market maneuvering and jockeying for buyer patronage that goes on among *rival sellers* in the industry.
2. Competitive pressures associated with the threat of *new entrants* into the market.
3. Competitive pressures coming from the attempts of companies in other industries to win buyers over to their own *substitute products.*
4. Competitive pressures stemming from *supplier* bargaining power and supplier–seller collaboration.
5. Competitive pressures stemming from *buyer* bargaining power and seller–buyer collaboration.

The way one uses the five-forces model to determine the nature and strength of competitive pressures in a given industry is to build the picture of competition in three steps:

- *Step 1:* Identify the specific competitive pressures associated with each of the five forces.
- *Step 2:* Evaluate how strong the pressures comprising each of the five forces are (fierce, strong, moderate to normal, or weak).
- *Step 3:* Determine whether the collective strength of the five competitive forces is conducive to earning attractive profits.

Figure 3.3   **The Five-Forces Model of Competition: A Key Analytical Tool**

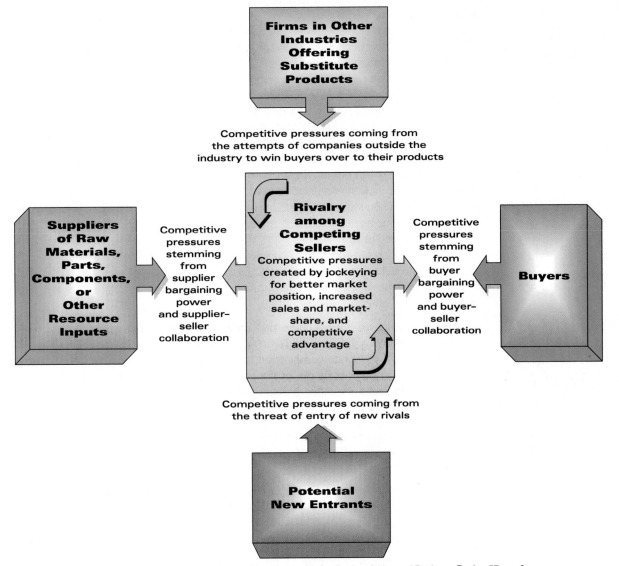

Source: Adapted from Michael E. Porter, "How Competitive Forces Shape Strategy," *Harvard Business Review* 57, no. 2 (March–April 1979), pp. 137–45.

Competitive Pressures Associated with the Jockeying among Rival Sellers

The strongest of the five competitive forces is nearly always the market maneuvering and jockeying for buyer patronage that goes on among rival sellers of a product or service. In effect, *a market is a competitive battlefield* where there's no end to the jockeying for buyer patronage. Rival sellers are prone to employ whatever weapons they have in their business arsenal to improve their market positions, strengthen their market position with buyers, and earn good profits. The challenge is to craft a competitive strategy that, at the very least, allows a company to hold its own against rivals and that, ideally, *produces a competitive edge over rivals.* But competitive contests are ongoing and dynamic. When one firm makes a strategic move that produces good results, its rivals typically respond with offensive or defensive countermoves, shifting their strategic emphasis from one combination of product attributes, marketing tactics, and capabilities to another. This pattern of action and reaction, move and countermove, adjust and readjust produces a continually evolving competitive landscape in which the market battle ebbs and flows, sometimes takes unpredictable twists and turns, and produces winners and losers. But the winners—the current market leaders— have no guarantees of continued leadership; their market success is no more durable than the power of their strategies to fend off the strategies of ambitious challengers. In every industry, the ongoing jockeying of rivals leads to one or another companies gaining or losing momentum in the marketplace according to whether their latest strategic maneuvers succeed or fail.

Figure 3.4 shows a sampling of competitive weapons that firms can deploy in battling rivals and indicates the factors that influence the intensity of their rivalry. A brief discussion of some of the factors that influence the tempo of rivalry among industry competitors is in order:[3]

- *Rivalry intensifies when competing sellers are active in launching fresh actions to boost their market standing and business performance.* One indicator of active rivalry is lively price competition, a condition that puts pressure on industry members to drive costs out of the business and threatens the survival of high-cost companies. Another indicator of active rivalry is rapid introduction of next-generation products—when one or more rivals frequently introduce new or improved products, competitors that lack good product innovation capabilities feel considerable competitive heat to get their own new and improved products into the marketplace quickly. Other indicators of active rivalry among industry members include:
  - Whether industry members are racing to differentiate their products from rivals by offering better performance features or higher quality or improved customer service or a wider product selection.
  - How frequently rivals resort to such marketing tactics as special sales promotions, heavy advertising, rebates, or low-interest-rate financing to drum up additional sales.
  - How actively industry members are pursuing efforts to build stronger dealer networks or establish positions in foreign markets or otherwise expand their distribution capabilities and market presence.
  - How hard companies are striving to gain a market edge over rivals by developing valuable expertise and capabilities that rivals are hard pressed to match.

  Normally, competitive jockeying among rival sellers is active and fairly intense because competing companies are highly motivated to launch whatever fresh actions and creative market maneuvers they can think of to try to strengthen their market positions and business performance.
- *Rivalry intensifies as the number of competitors increases and as competitors become more equal in size and capability.* Rivalry is not as vigorous in microprocessors for PCs, where Advanced Micro Devices (AMD) is one of the few

Figure 3.4   **Weapons for Competing and Factors Affecting the Strength of Rivalry**

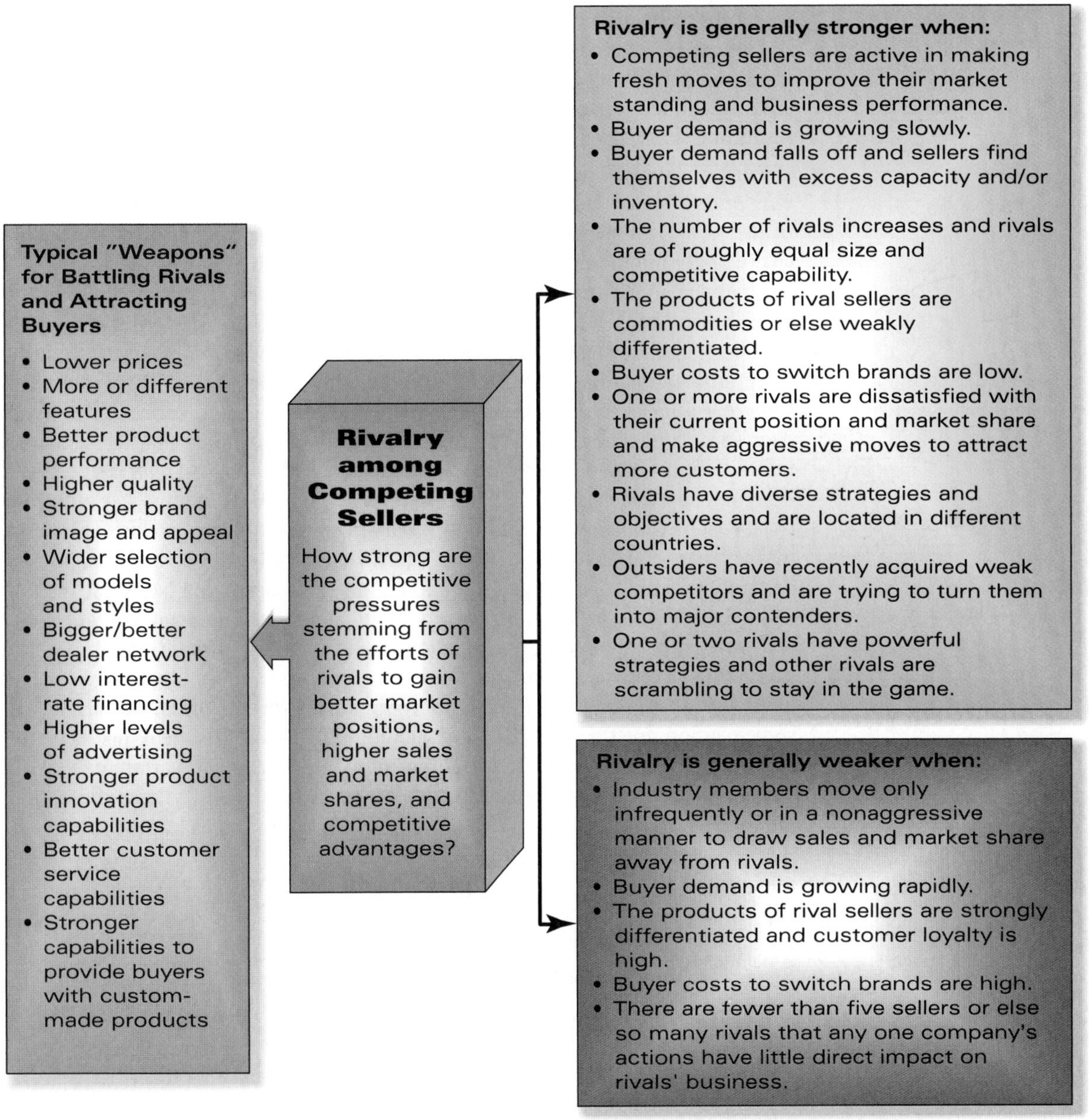

Typical "Weapons" for Battling Rivals and Attracting Buyers

- Lower prices
- More or different features
- Better product performance
- Higher quality
- Stronger brand image and appeal
- Wider selection of models and styles
- Bigger/better dealer network
- Low interest-rate financing
- Higher levels of advertising
- Stronger product innovation capabilities
- Better customer service capabilities
- Stronger capabilities to provide buyers with custom-made products

Rivalry among Competing Sellers

How strong are the competitive pressures stemming from the efforts of rivals to gain better market positions, higher sales and market shares, and competitive advantages?

Rivalry is generally stronger when:
- Competing sellers are active in making fresh moves to improve their market standing and business performance.
- Buyer demand is growing slowly.
- Buyer demand falls off and sellers find themselves with excess capacity and/or inventory.
- The number of rivals increases and rivals are of roughly equal size and competitive capability.
- The products of rival sellers are commodities or else weakly differentiated.
- Buyer costs to switch brands are low.
- One or more rivals are dissatisfied with their current position and market share and make aggressive moves to attract more customers.
- Rivals have diverse strategies and objectives and are located in different countries.
- Outsiders have recently acquired weak competitors and are trying to turn them into major contenders.
- One or two rivals have powerful strategies and other rivals are scrambling to stay in the game.

Rivalry is generally weaker when:
- Industry members move only infrequently or in a nonaggressive manner to draw sales and market share away from rivals.
- Buyer demand is growing rapidly.
- The products of rival sellers are strongly differentiated and customer loyalty is high.
- Buyer costs to switch brands are high.
- There are fewer than five sellers or else so many rivals that any one company's actions have little direct impact on rivals' business.

challengers to Intel, as it is in fast-food restaurants, where numerous sellers are actively jockeying for buyer patronage. Up to a point, the greater the number of competitors, the greater the probability of fresh, creative strategic initiatives. In addition, when rivals are nearly equal in size and capability, they can usually compete on a fairly even footing, making it harder for one or two firms to win commanding market shares and confront weaker market challenges from rivals.

- *Rivalry is usually stronger in slow-growing markets and weaker in fast-growing markets.* Rapidly expanding buyer demand produces enough new business for all industry members to grow. Indeed, in a fast-growing market, a company may find itself stretched just to keep abreast of incoming orders, let alone devote resources to stealing customers away from rivals. But in markets where growth is sluggish or where buyer demand drops off unexpectedly, expansion-minded firms and firms with excess capacity often are quick to cut prices and initiate other sales-increasing tactics, thereby igniting a battle for market share that can result in a shake-out of weak, inefficient firms.

- *Rivalry is usually weaker in industries comprised of so many rivals that the impact of any one company's actions is spread thin across all industry members; likewise, it is often weak when there are fewer than five competitors.* A progressively larger number of competitors can actually begin to weaken head-to-head rivalry once an industry becomes populated with so many rivals that the impact of successful moves by any one company is spread thin across many industry members. To the extent that a company's strategic moves ripple out to have little discernible impact on the businesses of its many rivals, then industry members soon learn that it is not imperative to respond every time one or another rival does something to enhance its market position—an outcome that weakens the intensity of head-to-head battles for market share. Rivalry also *tends* to be weak if an industry consists of just two or three or four sellers. In a market with few rivals, each competitor soon learns that aggressive moves to grow its sales and market share can have immediate adverse impact on rivals' businesses, almost certainly provoking vigorous retaliation and risking an all-out battle for market share that is likely to lower the profits of all concerned. Companies that have a few strong rivals thus come to understand the merits of *restrained* efforts to wrest sales and market share from competitors as opposed to undertaking hard-hitting offensives that escalate into a profit-eroding arms-race or price war. However, some caution must be exercised in concluding that rivalry is weak just because there are only a few competitors. Thus, although occasional warfare can break out (the fierceness of the current battle between Red Hat and Microsoft and the decades-long war between Coca-Cola and Pepsi are prime examples), competition among the few normally produces a live-and-let-live approach to competing because rivals see the merits of restrained efforts to wrest sales and market share from competitors as opposed to undertaking hard-hitting offensives that escalate into a profit-eroding arms race or price war.

- *Rivalry increases when buyer demand falls off and sellers find themselves with excess capacity and/or inventory.* Excess supply conditions create a "buyers' market," putting added competitive pressure on industry rivals to scramble for profitable sales levels (often by price discounting).

- *Rivalry increases as it becomes less costly for buyers to switch brands.* The less expensive it is for buyers to switch their purchases from the seller of one brand to the s eller of another brand, the easier it is for sellers to steal customers away from rivals. But the higher the costs buyers incur to switch brands, the less prone they are to brand switching. Even if consumers view one or more rival brands as more attractive, they may not be inclined to switch because of the added time and inconvenience or the psychological costs of abandoning a familiar brand. Distributors and retailers may not switch to the brands of rival manufacturers because they are hesitant to sever long-standing supplier relationships, incur any technical support costs or retraining expenses in making the switchover, go to the trouble of testing the quality and reliability of the rival brand, or devote resources to marketing the new brand (especially if the brand is lesser known).

Apple Computer, for example, has been unable to convince PC users to switch from Windows-based PCs because of the time burdens and inconvenience associated with learning Apple's operating system and because so many Windows-based applications will not run on a MacIntosh due to operating system incompatibility. Consequently, unless buyers are dissatisfied with the brand they are presently purchasing, high switching costs can significantly weaken the rivalry among competing sellers.

- *Rivalry increases as the products of rival sellers become more standardized and diminishes as the products of industry rivals become more strongly differentiated.* When the offerings of rivals are identical or weakly differentiated, buyers have less reason to be brand-loyal—a condition that makes it easier for rivals to convince buyers to switch to their offering. And since the brands of different sellers have comparable attributes, buyers can shop the market for the best deal and switch brands at will. In contrast, strongly differentiated product offerings among rivals breed high brand loyalty on the part of buyers—because many buyers view the attributes of certain brands as better suited to their needs. Strong brand attachments make it tougher for sellers to draw customers away from rivals. Unless meaningful numbers of buyers are open to considering new or different product attributes being offered by rivals, the high degrees of brand loyalty that accompany strong product differentiation work against fierce rivalry among competing sellers. *The degree of product differentiation also affects switching costs.* When the offerings of rivals are identical or weakly differentiated, it is usually easy and inexpensive for buyers to switch their purchases from one seller to another. Strongly differentiated products raise the probability that buyers will find it costly to switch brands.

- *Rivalry is more intense when industry conditions tempt competitors to use price cuts or other competitive weapons to boost unit volume.* When a product is perishable, seasonal, or costly to hold in inventory, competitive pressures build quickly anytime one or more firms decide to cut prices and dump supplies on the market. Likewise, whenever fixed costs account for a large fraction of total cost, such that unit costs tend to be lowest at or near full capacity, then firms come under significant pressure to cut prices or otherwise try to boost sales whenever they are operating below full capacity. Unused capacity imposes a significant cost-increasing penalty because there are fewer units over which to spread fixed costs. The pressure of high fixed costs can push rival firms into price concessions, special discounts, rebates, low-interest-rate financing, and other volume-boosting tactics.

- *Rivalry increases when one or more competitors become dissatisfied with their market position and launch moves to bolster their standing at the expense of rivals.* Firms that are losing ground or in financial trouble often pursue aggressive (or perhaps desperate) turnaround strategies that can involve price discounts, more advertising, acquisition of or merger with other rivals, or new product introductions—such strategies can turn competitive pressures up a notch.

- *Rivalry becomes more volatile and unpredictable as the diversity of competitors increases in terms of visions, strategic intents, objectives, strategies, resources, and countries of origin.* A diverse group of sellers often contains one or more mavericks willing to try novel or high-risk or rule-breaking market approaches, thus generating a livelier and less predictable competitive environment. Globally competitive markets often contain rivals with different views about where the industry is headed and a willingness to employ perhaps radically different competitive approaches. Attempts by cross-border rivals to gain stronger footholds in each other's domestic markets usually boost the intensity of rivalry, especially when the aggressors have lower costs or products with more attractive features.

- *Rivalry increases when strong companies outside the industry acquire weak firms in the industry and launch aggressive, well-funded moves to transform their newly acquired competitors into major market contenders.* A concerted effort to turn a weak rival into a market leader nearly always entails launching well-financed strategic initiatives to dramatically improve the competitor's product offering, excite buyer interest, and win a much bigger market share—actions that, if successful, put added pressure on rivals to counter with fresh strategic moves of their own.

- *A powerful, successful competitive strategy employed by one company greatly intensifies the competitive pressures on its rivals to develop effective strategic responses or be relegated to also-ran status.*

Rivalry can be characterized as *cutthroat* or *brutal* when competitors engage in protracted price wars or habitually employ other aggressive tactics that are mutually destructive to profitability. Rivalry can be considered *fierce* to *strong* when the battle for market share is so vigorous that the profit margins of most industry members are squeezed to bare-bones levels. Rivalry can be characterized as *moderate* or *normal* when the maneuvering among industry members, while lively and healthy, still allows most industry members to earn acceptable profits. Rivalry is *weak* when most companies in the industry are relatively well satisfied with their sales growth and market shares, rarely undertake offensives to steal customers away from one another, and have comparatively attractive earnings and returns on investment.

Competitive Pressures Associated with the Threat of New Entrants

Several factors determine whether the threat of new companies entering the marketplace poses significant competitive pressure (see Figure 3.5). One factor relates to the size of the pool of likely entry candidates and the resources at their command. As a rule, the bigger the pool of entry candidates, the stronger the threat of potential entry. This is especially true when some of the likely entry candidates have ample resources and the potential to become formidable contenders for market leadership. Frequently, the strongest competitive pressures associated with potential entry come not from outsiders, but from current industry participants looking for growth opportunities. *Existing industry members are often strong candidates for entering market segments or geographic areas where they currently do not have a market presence.* Companies already well established in certain product categories or geographic areas often possess the resources, competencies, and competitive capabilities to hurdle the barriers of entering a different market segment or new geographic area.

A second factor concerns whether the likely entry candidates face high or low entry barriers. High barriers reduce the competitive threat of potential entry, while low barriers make entry more likely, especially if the industry is growing and offers attractive profit opportunities. The most widely encountered barriers that entry candidates must hurdle include:[4]

- *The presence of sizable economies of scale in production or other areas of operation*—When incumbent companies enjoy cost advantages associated with

Figure 3.5   **Factors Affecting the Threat of Entry**

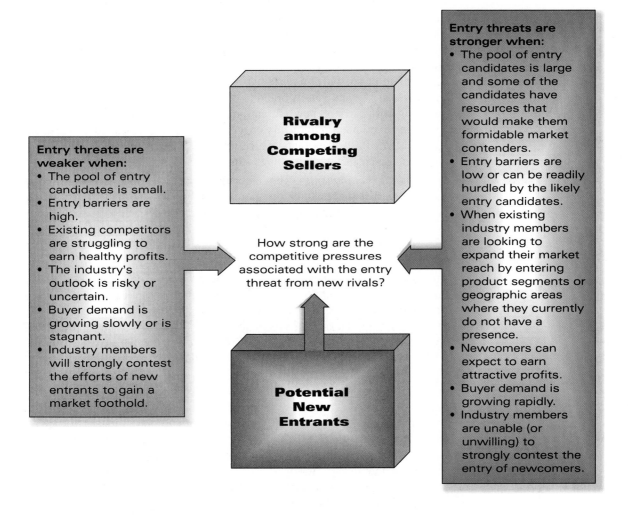

Entry threats are weaker when:
- The pool of entry candidates is small.
- Entry barriers are high.
- Existing competitors are struggling to earn healthy profits.
- The industry's outlook is risky or uncertain.
- Buyer demand is growing slowly or is stagnant.
- Industry members will strongly contest the efforts of new entrants to gain a market foothold.

Rivalry among Competing Sellers

How strong are the competitive pressures associated with the entry threat from new rivals?

Potential New Entrants

Entry threats are stronger when:
- The pool of entry candidates is large and some of the candidates have resources that would make them formidable market contenders.
- Entry barriers are low or can be readily hurdled by the likely entry candidates.
- When existing industry members are looking to expand their market reach by entering product segments or geographic areas where they currently do not have a presence.
- Newcomers can expect to earn attractive profits.
- Buyer demand is growing rapidly.
- Industry members are unable (or unwilling) to strongly contest the entry of newcomers.

large-scale operation, outsiders must either enter on a large scale (a costly and perhaps risky move) or accept a cost disadvantage and consequently lower profitability. Trying to overcome the disadvantages of small size by entering on a large scale at the outset can result in long-term overcapacity problems for the new entrant (until sales volume builds up), and it can so threaten the market shares of existing firms that they launch strong defensive maneuvers (price cuts, increased advertising and sales promotion, and similar blocking actions) to maintain their positions and make things hard on a newcomer.

- *Cost and resource disadvantages not related to scale of operation*—Aside from enjoying economies of scale, there are other reasons why existing firms may have low unit costs that are hard to replicate by newcomers. Industry incumbents can have cost advantages that stem from learning/experience curve effects, the possession of key patents or proprietary technology, partnerships with the best and cheapest suppliers of raw materials and components, favorable locations, and low fixed costs (because they have older facilities that have been mostly depreciated).

- *Strong brand preferences and high degrees of customer loyalty*—The stronger the attachment of buyers to established brands, the harder it is for a newcomer to break into the marketplace. In such cases, a new entrant must have the financial resources to spend enough on advertising and sales promotion to overcome customer loyalties and build its own clientele. Establishing brand recognition and building customer loyalty can be a slow and costly process. In addition, if it is difficult or costly for a customer to switch to a new brand, a new entrant must persuade buyers that its brand is worth the switching costs. To overcome switching-cost barriers, new entrants may have to offer buyers a discounted price or an extra margin of quality or service. All this can mean lower expected profit margins for new entrants, which increases the risk to start-up companies dependent on sizable early profits to support their new investments.

- *High capital requirements*—The larger the total dollar investment needed to enter the market successfully, the more limited the pool of potential entrants. The most obvious capital requirements for new entrants relate to manufacturing facilities and equipment, introductory advertising and sales promotion campaigns, working capital to finance inventories and customer credit, and sufficient cash to cover start-up costs.

- *The difficulties of building a network of distributors or retailers and securing adequate space on retailers' shelves*—A potential entrant can face numerous distribution channel challenges. Wholesale distributors may be reluctant to take on a product that lacks buyer recognition. Retailers have to be recruited and convinced to give a new brand ample display space and an adequate trial period. When existing sellers have strong, well-functioning distributor or retailer networks, a newcomer has an uphill struggle in squeezing its way in. Potential entrants sometimes have to "buy" their way into wholesale or retail channels by cutting their prices to provide dealers and distributors with higher markups and profit margins or by giving them big advertising and promotional allowances. As a consequence, a potential entrant's own profits may be squeezed unless and until its product gains enough consumer acceptance that distributors and retailers are anxious to carry it.

- *Restrictive regulatory policies*—Government agencies can limit or even bar entry by requiring licenses and permits. Regulated industries like cable TV, telecommunications, electric and gas utilities, radio and television broadcasting, liquor retailing, and railroads entail government-controlled entry. In international markets, host governments commonly limit foreign entry and must approve all foreign investment applications. Stringent government-mandated safety regulations and environmental pollution standards are entry barriers because they raise entry costs.

- *Tariffs and international trade restrictions*—National governments commonly use tariffs and trade restrictions (antidumping rules, local content requirements, quotas, etc.) to raise entry barriers for foreign firms and protect domestic producers from outside competition.

- *The ability and inclination of industry incumbents to launch vigorous initiatives to block a newcomer's successful entry*—Even if a potential entrant has or can acquire the needed competencies and resources to attempt entry, it must still worry about the reaction of existing firms.[5] Sometimes, there's little that incumbents can do to throw obstacles in an entrant's path—for instance, existing restaurants have little in their arsenal to discourage a new restaurant from opening or to dissuade people from trying the new restaurant. But there are times when incumbents do all they can to make it difficult for a new entrant, using price cuts, increased advertising, product improvements, and whatever else they can think of to prevent the entrant from building a clientele. Cable TV companies vigorously fight the entry of satellite TV companies; Sony and Nintendo have mounted strong defenses to thwart Microsoft's entry in videogames with its Xbox; existing hotels try to combat the opening of new hotels with loyalty programs, renovations of their own, the addition of new services, and so on. A potential entrant can have second thoughts when financially strong incumbent firms send clear signals that they will give newcomers a hard time.

Whether an industry's entry barriers ought to be considered high or low depends on the resources and competencies possessed by the pool of potential entrants. Companies with sizable financial resources, proven competitive capabilities, and a respected brand name may be able to hurdle an industry's entry barriers rather easily. Small start-up enterprises may find the same entry barriers insurmountable. Thus, how hard it will be for potential entrants to compete on a level playing field is always relative to the financial resources and competitive capabilities of likely entrants. For example, when Honda opted to enter the U.S. lawn-mower market in competition against Toro, Snapper, Craftsman, John Deere, and others, it was easily able to hurdle entry barriers that would have been formidable to other newcomers because it had long-standing expertise in gasoline engines and because its well-known reputation for quality and durability gave it instant credibility with shoppers looking to buy a new lawn mower. Honda had to spend relatively little on advertising to attract buyers and gain a market foothold, distributors and dealers were quite willing to handle the Honda lawn-mower line, and Honda had ample capital to build a U.S. assembly plant.

In evaluating whether the threat of additional entry is strong or weak, company managers must look at (1) how formidable the entry barriers are for each type of potential entrant—start-up enterprises, specific candidate companies in other industries, and current industry participants looking to expand their market reach—and (2) how attractive the growth and profit prospects are for new entrants. Rapidly growing market demand and high potential profits act as magnets, motivating potential entrants to commit the resources needed to hurdle entry barriers.[6] When profits are sufficiently attractive, entry barriers are unlikely to be an effective entry deterrent. At most, they limit the pool of candidate entrants to enterprises with the requisite competencies and resources and with the creativity to fashion a strategy for competing with incumbent firms.

Hence, *the best test of whether potential entry is a strong or weak competitive force in the marketplace is to ask if the industry's growth and profit prospects are strongly attractive to potential entry candidates.* When the answer is no, potential entry is a weak competitive force. When the answer is yes and there are entry candidates with sufficient expertise and resources, then potential entry adds significantly to competitive pressures in the marketplace. The stronger the threat of entry, the more that incumbent firms are driven to seek ways to fortify their positions against newcomers, pursuing strategic moves not only to protect their market shares but also to make entry more costly or difficult.

One additional point: *The threat of entry changes as the industry's prospects grow brighter or dimmer and as entry barriers rise or fall.* For example, in the pharmaceutical industry the expiration of a key patent on a widely prescribed drug virtually guarantees that one or more drug makers will enter with generic offerings of their own. Growing use of the Internet for shopping is making it much easier for Web-based retailers to enter into competition

High entry barriers and weak entry threats today do not always translate into high entry barriers and weak entry threats tomorrow.

against such well-known retail chains as Sears, Circuit City, and Barnes and Noble. In international markets, entry barriers for foreign-based firms fall as tariffs are lowered, as host governments open up their domestic markets to outsiders, as domestic wholesalers and dealers seek out lower-cost foreign-made goods, and as domestic buyers become more willing to purchase foreign brands.

Competitive Pressures from the Sellers of Substitute Products

Companies in one industry come under competitive pressure from the actions of companies in a closely adjoining industry whenever buyers view the products of the two industries as good substitutes. For instance, the producers of sugar experience competitive pressures from the sales and marketing efforts of the makers of artificial sweeteners. Similarly, the producers of eyeglasses and contact lenses are currently facing mounting competitive pressures from growing consumer interest in corrective laser surgery. Newspapers are feeling the competitive force of the general public turning to cable news channels for late-breaking news and using Internet sources to get information about sports results, stock quotes, and job opportunities. The makers of videotapes and VCRs have watched demand evaporate as more and more consumers have been attracted to substitute use of DVDs and DVD recorders/players. Traditional providers of telephone service like BellSouth, AT&T, Verizon, and Qwest are feeling enormous competitive pressure from cell phone providers, as more and more consumers find cell phones preferable to landline phones.

Just how strong the competitive pressures are from the sellers of substitute products depends on three factors:

1. *Whether substitutes are readily available and attractively priced.* The presence of readily available and attractively priced substitutes creates competitive pressure by placing a ceiling on the prices industry members can charge without giving customers an incentive to switch to substitutes and risking sales erosion.[7] This price ceiling, at the same time, puts a lid on the profits that industry members can earn unless they find ways to cut costs. When substitutes are cheaper than an industry's product, industry members come under heavy competitive pressure to reduce their prices and find ways to absorb the price cuts with cost reductions.

2. *Whether buyers view the substitutes as being comparable or better in terms of quality, performance, and other relevant attributes.* The availability of substitutes inevitably invites customers to compare performance, features, ease of use, and other attributes as well as price. For example, ski boat manufacturers are experiencing strong competition from personal water-ski craft because water sports enthusiasts see personal water skis as fun to ride and less expensive. The users of paper cartons constantly weigh the performance trade-offs with plastic containers and metal cans. Camera users consider the convenience and performance trade-offs when deciding whether to substitute a digital camera for a film-based camera. Competition from good-performing substitutes unleashes competitive pressures on industry participants to incorporate new performance features and attributes that makes their product offerings more competitive.

3. *Whether the costs that buyers incur in switching to the substitutes are high or low.* High switching costs deter switching to substitutes, while low switching costs make it easier for the sellers of attractive substitutes to lure buyers to their offering.[8] Typical switching costs include the time and inconvenience that may be involved, the costs of additional equipment, the time and cost in testing the quality

Figure 3.6   **Factors Affecting Competition from Substitute Products**

Firms in Other Industries Offering Substitute Products

Competitive pressures from substitutes are weaker when:
- Good substitutes are not readily available or don't exist.
- Substitutes are higher priced relative to the performance they deliver.
- End users have high costs in switching to substitutes.

How strong are competitive pressures coming from the attempts of companies outside the industry to win buyers over to their products?

Competitive pressures from substitutes are stronger when:
- Good substitutes are readily available or new ones are emerging.
- Substitutes are attractively priced.
- Substitutes have comparable or better performance features.
- End users have low costs in switching to substitutes.
- End users grow more comfortable with using substitutes

Rivalry among Competing Sellers

Signs That Competition from Substitutes Is Strong
- Sales of substitutes are growing faster than sales of the industry being analyzed (an indication that the sellers of substitutes are drawing customers away from the industry in question).
- Producers of substitutes are moving to add new capacity.
- Profits of the producers of substitutes are on the rise.

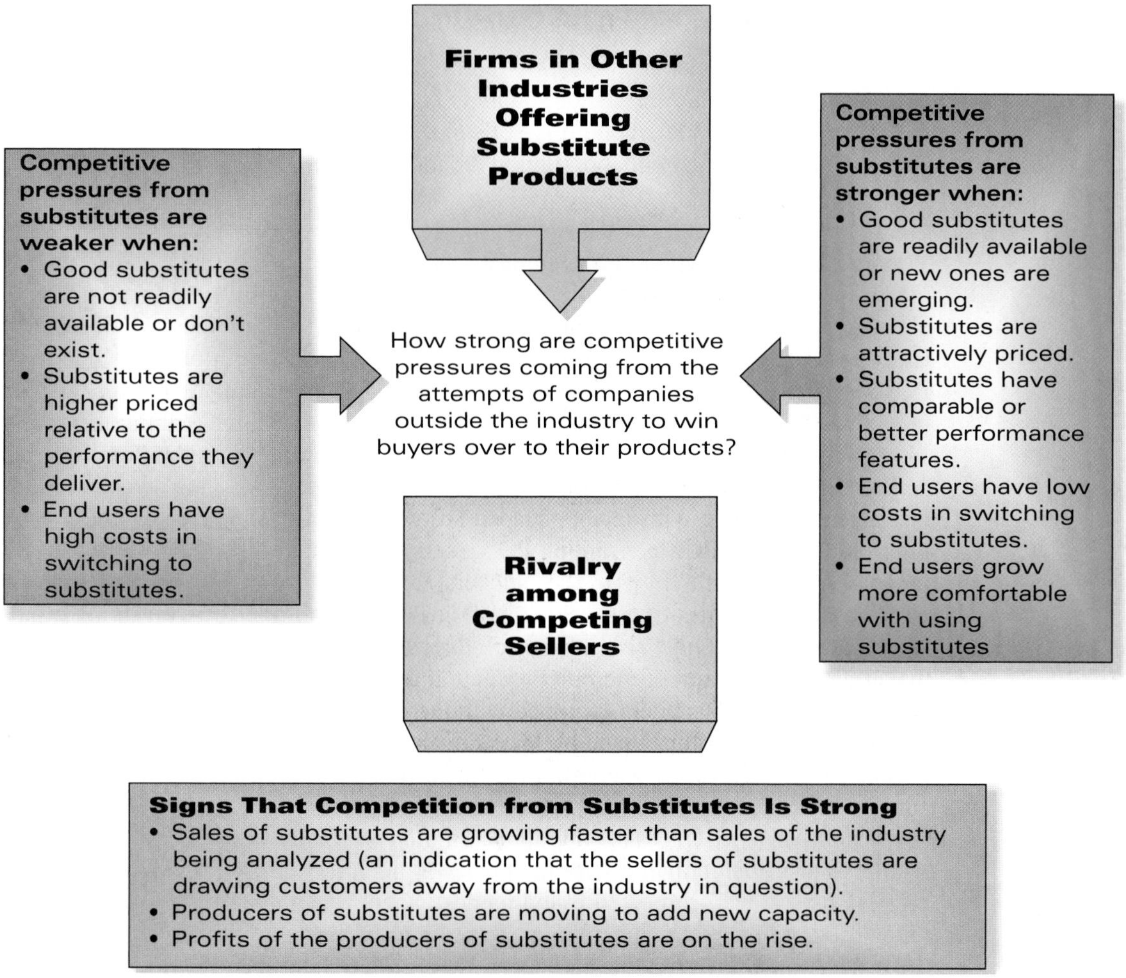

and reliability of the substitute, the psychological costs of severing old supplier relationships and establishing new ones, payments for technical help in making the changeover, and employee retraining costs. High switching costs can materially weaken the competitive pressures that industry members experience from substitutes unless the sellers of substitutes are successful in offsetting the high switching costs with enticing price discounts or additional performance enhancements.

Figure 3.6 summarizes the conditions that determine whether the competitive pressures from substitute products are strong, moderate, or weak.

As a rule, the lower the price of substitutes, the higher their quality and performance, and the lower the user's switching costs, the more intense the competitive pressures posed by substitute products. Other market indicators of the competitive strength of substitute products include (1) whether the sales of substitutes are growing faster than the sales of the industry being analyzed (a sign that the sellers of substitutes may be drawing customers away from the industry in question), (2) whether the producers of substitutes are moving to add new capacity, and (3) whether the profits of the producers of substitutes are on the rise.

Competitive Pressures Stemming from Supplier Bargaining Power and Supplier–Seller Collaboration

Whether supplier–seller relationships represent a weak or strong competitive force depends on (1) whether the major suppliers can exercise sufficient bargaining power to influence the terms and conditions of supply in their favor, and (2) the nature and extent of supplier–seller collaboration in the industry.

How Supplier Bargaining Power Can Create Competitive Pressures

Whenever the major suppliers to an industry have considerable leverage in determining the terms and conditions of the item they are supplying, then they are in a position to exert competitive pressure on one or more rival sellers. For instance, Microsoft and Intel, both of which supply personal computer (PC) makers with products that most PC users consider essential, are known for using their dominant market status not only to charge PC makers premium prices but also to leverage PC makers in other ways. Microsoft pressures PC makers to load only Microsoft products on the PCs they ship and to position the icons for Microsoft software prominently on the screens of new computers that come with factory-loaded software. Intel pushes greater use of Intel microprocessors in PCs by granting PC makers sizable advertising allowances on PC models equipped with "Intel Inside" stickers; it also tends to give PC makers that use the biggest percentages of Intel chips in their PC models top priority in filling orders for newly introduced Intel chips. Being on Intel's list of preferred customers helps a PC maker get an allocation of the first production runs of Intel's latest and greatest chips and thus get new PC models equipped with these chips to market ahead of rivals who are heavier users of chips made by Intel's rivals. The ability of Microsoft and Intel to pressure PC makers for preferential treatment of one kind or another in turn affects competition among rival PC makers.

Several other instances of supplier bargaining power are worth citing. Small-scale retailers must often contend with the power of manufacturers whose products enjoy prestigious and well-respected brand names; when a manufacturer knows that a retailer needs to stock the manufacturer's product because consumers expect to find the product on the shelves of retail stores where they shop, the manufacturer usually has some degree of pricing power and can also push hard for favorable shelf displays. Motor vehicle manufacturers typically exert considerable power over the terms and conditions with which they supply new vehicles to their independent automobile dealerships. The operators of franchised units of such chains as McDonald's, Dunkin' Donuts, Pizza Hut, Sylvan Learning Centers, and Hampton Inns must frequently agree not only to source some of their supplies from the franchisor at prices and terms favorable to that franchisor but also to operate their facilities in a manner largely dictated by the franchisor.

Strong supplier bargaining power is a competitive factor in industries where unions have been able to organize the workforces of some industry members but not others; those industry members that must negotiate wages, fringe benefits, and working conditions with powerful unions (which control the supply of labor) often find themselves with higher labor costs than their competitors with nonunion labor forces. The bigger the gap between union and nonunion labor costs in an industry, the more that unionized industry members must scramble to find ways to relieve the competitive pressure associated with their disadvantage on labor costs. High labor costs are proving a huge competitive liability to unionized supermarket chains like Kroger and Safeway in trying to combat the market share gains being made by Wal-Mart in supermarket retailing—Wal-Mart has a nonunion workforce, and the prices for supermarket items at its Supercenters tend to run 5 to 20 percent lower than those at unionized supermarket chains.

The factors that determine whether any of the suppliers to an industry are in a position to exert substantial bargaining power or leverage are fairly clear-cut:[9]

- *Whether the item being supplied is a commodity that is readily available from many suppliers at the going market price.* Suppliers have little or no bargaining power or leverage whenever industry members have the ability to source their requirements at competitive prices from any of several alternative and eager suppliers, perhaps dividing their purchases among two or more suppliers to promote lively competition for orders. The suppliers of commodity items have market power only when supplies become quite tight and industry members are so eager to secure what they need that they agree to terms more favorable to suppliers.

- *Whether a few large suppliers are the primary sources of a particular item.* The leading suppliers may well have pricing leverage unless they are plagued with excess capacity and are scrambling to secure additional orders for their products. Major suppliers with good reputations and strong demand for the items they supply are harder to wring concessions from than struggling suppliers striving to broaden their customer base or more fully utilize their production capacity.

- *Whether it is difficult or costly for industry members to switch their purchases from one supplier to another or to switch to attractive substitute inputs.* High switching costs signal strong bargaining power on the part of suppliers, whereas low switching costs and ready availability of good substitute inputs signal weak bargaining power. Soft-drink bottlers, for example, can counter the bargaining power of aluminum can suppliers by shifting or threatening to shift to greater use of plastic containers and introducing more attractive plastic container designs.

- *Whether certain needed inputs are in short supply.* Suppliers of items in short supply have some degree of pricing power, whereas a surge in the availability of particular items greatly weakens supplier pricing power and bargaining leverage.

- *Whether certain suppliers provide a differentiated input that enhances the performance or quality of the industry's product.* The more valuable that a particular input is in terms of enhancing the performance or quality of the products of industry members or of improving the efficiency of their production processes, the more bargaining leverage its suppliers are likely to possess.

- *Whether certain suppliers provide equipment or services that deliver valuable cost-saving efficiencies to industry members in operating their production processes.* Suppliers who provide cost-saving equipment or other valuable or necessary production-related services are likely to possess bargaining leverage. Industry members that do not source from such suppliers may find themselves at a cost disadvantage and thus under competitive pressure to do so (on terms that are favorable to the suppliers).

- *Whether suppliers provide an item that accounts for a sizable fraction of the costs of the industry's product.* The bigger the cost of a particular part or component, the more opportunity for the pattern of competition in the marketplace to be affected by the actions of suppliers to raise or lower their prices.

- *Whether industry members are major customers of suppliers.* As a rule, suppliers have less bargaining leverage when their sales to members of this one industry constitute a big percentage of their total sales. In such cases, the well-being of suppliers is closely tied to the well-being of their major customers.

Suppliers then have a big incentive to protect and enhance their customers' competitiveness via reasonable prices, exceptional quality, and ongoing advances in the technology of the items supplied.

- *Whether it makes good economic sense for industry members to integrate backward and self-manufacture items they have been buying from suppliers.* The make-or-buy issue generally boils down to whether suppliers who specialize in the production of a particular part or component and make them in volume for many different customers have the expertise and scale economies to supply as good or better component at a lower cost than industry members could achieve via self-manufacture. Frequently, it is difficult for industry members to self-manufacture parts and components more economically than they can obtain them from suppliers who specialize in making such items. For instance, most producers of outdoor power equipment (lawn mowers, rotary tillers, leaf blowers, etc.) find it cheaper to source the small engines they need from outside manufacturers who specialize in small-engine manufacture rather than make their own engines because the quantity of engines they need is too small to justify the investment in manufacturing facilities, master the production process, and capture scale economies. Specialists in small-engine manufacture, by supplying many kinds of engines to the whole power equipment industry, can obtain a big enough sales volume to fully realize scale economies, become proficient in all the manufacturing techniques, and keep costs low. As a rule, suppliers are safe from the threat of self-manufacture by their customers *until* the volume of parts a customer needs becomes large enough for the customer to justify backward integration into self-manufacture of the component. Suppliers also gain bargaining power when they have the resources and profit incentive to integrate forward into the business of the customers they are supplying and thus become a strong rival.

Figure 3.7 summarizes the conditions that tend to make supplier bargaining power strong or weak.

How Seller–Supplier Partnerships Can Create Competitive Pressures   In more and more industries, sellers are forging strategic partnerships with select suppliers in efforts to (1) reduce inventory and logistics costs (e.g., through just-in-time deliveries), (2) speed the availability of next-generation components, (3) enhance the quality of the parts and components being supplied and reduce defect rates, and (4) squeeze out important cost savings for both themselves and their suppliers. Numerous Internet technology applications are now available that permit real-time data sharing, eliminate paperwork, and produce cost savings all along the supply chain. The many benefits of effective seller–supplier collaboration can translate into competitive advantage for industry members that do the best job of managing supply chain relationships.

Dell Computer has used strategic partnering with key suppliers as a major element in its strategy to be the world's lowest-cost supplier of branded PCs, servers, and workstations. Because Dell has managed its supply chain relationships in ways that contribute to a low-cost, high-quality competitive edge in components supply, it has put enormous pressure on its PC rivals to try to imitate its supply chain management practices. Effective partnerships with suppliers on the part of one or more industry members can thus become a major source of competitive pressure for rival firms.

The more opportunities that exist for win–win efforts between a company and its suppliers, the less their relationship is characterized by who has the upper hand in

Figure 3.7   **Factors Affecting the Bargaining Power of Suppliers**

Supplier bargaining power is stronger when:
- Industry members incurs high costs in switching their purchases to alternative suppliers.
- Needed inputs are in short supply (which gives suppliers more leverage in setting prices).
- A supplier has a differentiated input that enhances the quality or performance of sellers' products or is a valuable or critical part of sellers' production process.
- There are only a few suppliers of a particular input.
- Some suppliers threaten to integrate forward into the business of industry members and perhaps become a powerful rival.

Supplier bargaining power is weaker when:
- The item being supplied is a commodity that is readily available from many suppliers at the going market price.
- Seller switching costs to alternative suppliers are low.
- Good substitute inputs exist or new ones emerge.
- There is a surge in the availability of supplies (thus greatly weakening supplier pricing power).
- Industry members account for a big fraction of suppliers' total sales and continued high volume purchases are important to the well-being of suppliers.
- Industry members are a threat to integrate backward into the business of suppliers and to self-manufacture their own requirements.
- Seller collaboration or partnering with selected suppliers provides attractive win–win opportunities.

bargaining with the other. Collaborative partnerships between a company and a supplier tend to last so long as the relationship is producing valuable benefits for both parties. Only if a supply partner is falling behind alternative suppliers is a company likely to switch suppliers and incur the costs and trouble of building close working ties with a different supplier.

Competitive Pressures Stemming from Buyer Bargaining Power and Seller–Buyer Collaboration

Whether seller–buyer relationships represent a weak or strong competitive force depends on (1) whether some or many buyers have sufficient bargaining leverage to obtain price concessions and other favorable terms and conditions of sale, and (2) the extent and competitive importance of seller–buyer strategic partnerships in the industry.

How Buyer Bargaining Power Can Create Competitive Pressures   As with suppliers, the leverage that certain types of buyers have in negotiating favorable terms can range from weak to strong. Individual consumers, for example, rarely have much bargaining power in negotiating price concessions or other favorable terms with sellers; the primary exceptions involve situations in which price haggling is customary, such as the purchase of new and used motor vehicles, homes, and certain big-ticket items like luxury watches, jewelry, and pleasure boats. For most consumer goods and services, individual buyers have no bargaining leverage—their option is to pay the seller's posted price or take their business elsewhere.

In contrast, large retail chains like Wal-Mart, Best Buy, Staples, and Home Depot typically have considerable negotiating leverage in purchasing products from manufacturers because of manufacturers' need for broad retail exposure and the most appealing shelf locations. Retailers may stock two or three competing brands of a product but rarely all competing brands, so competition among rival manufacturers for visibility on the shelves of popular multistore retailers gives such retailers significant bargaining strength. Major supermarket chains like Kroger, Safeway, and Royal Ahold, which provide access to millions of grocery shoppers, have sufficient bargaining power to demand promotional allowances and lump-sum payments (called slotting fees) from food products manufacturers in return for stocking certain brands or putting them in the best shelf locations. Motor vehicle manufacturers have strong bargaining power in negotiating to buy original equipment tires from Goodyear, Michelin, Bridgestone/Firestone, Continental, and Pirelli not only because they buy in large quantities but also because tire makers believe they gain an advantage in supplying replacement tires to vehicle owners if their tire brand is original equipment on the vehicle. "Prestige" buyers have a degree of clout in negotiating with sellers because a seller's reputation is enhanced by having prestige buyers on its customer list.

Even if buyers do not purchase in large quantities or offer a seller important market exposure or prestige, they gain a degree of bargaining leverage in the following circumstances:[10]

- *If buyers' costs of switching to competing brands or substitutes are relatively low*—Buyers who can readily switch brands or source from several sellers have more negotiating leverage than buyers who have high switching costs. When the products of rival sellers are virtually identical, it is relatively easy for buyers to switch from seller to seller at little or no cost and anxious sellers may be willing to make concessions to win or retain a buyer's business.

- *If the number of buyers is small or if a customer is particularly important to a seller*—The smaller the number of buyers, the less easy it is for sellers to find alternative buyers when a customer is lost to a competitor. The prospect of losing a customer not easily replaced often makes a seller more willing to grant concessions of one kind or another.

- *If buyer demand is weak and sellers are scrambling to secure additional sales of their products*—Weak or declining demand creates a "buyers' market"; conversely, strong or rapidly growing demand creates a "sellers' market" and shifts bargaining power to sellers.

- *If buyers are well informed about sellers' products, prices, and costs*—The more information buyers have, the better bargaining position they are in. The mushrooming availability of product information on the Internet is giving added bargaining power to individuals. Buyers can easily use the Internet to compare prices and features of vacation packages, shop for the best interest rates on mortgages and loans, and find the best prices on big-ticket items such as digital cameras. Bargain-hunting individuals can shop around for the best deal on the Internet and use that information to negotiate a better deal from local retailers; this method is becoming commonplace in buying new and used motor vehicles. Further, the Internet has created opportunities for manufacturers, wholesalers, retailers, and sometimes individuals to join online buying groups to pool their purchasing power and approach vendors for better terms than could be gotten individually. A multinational manufacturer's geographically scattered purchasing groups can use Internet technology to pool their orders with parts and components suppliers and bargain for volume discounts. Purchasing agents at some companies are banding together at third-party Web sites to pool corporate purchases to get better deals or special treatment.

- *If buyers pose a credible threat of integrating backward into the business of sellers*—Companies like Anheuser-Busch, Coors, and Heinz have integrated backward into metal can manufacturing to gain bargaining power in obtaining the balance of their can requirements from otherwise powerful metal can manufacturers. Retailers gain bargaining power by stocking and promoting their own private-label brands alongside manufacturers' name brands. Wal-Mart, for example, has elected to compete against Procter & Gamble (P&G), its biggest supplier, with its own brand of laundry detergent, called Sam's American Choice, which is priced 25 to 30 percent lower than P&G's Tide.

- *If buyers have discretion in whether and when they purchase the product*—Many consumers, if they are unhappy with the present deals offered on major appliances or hot tubs or home entertainment centers, may be in a position to delay purchase until prices and financing terms improve. If business customers are not happy with the prices or security features of bill-payment software systems, they can either delay purchase until next-generation products become available or attempt to develop their own software in-house. If college students believe that the prices of new textbooks are too high, they can purchase used copies.

Figure 3.8 highlights the factors causing buyer bargaining power to be strong or weak.

A final point to keep in mind is that *not all buyers of an industry's product have equal degrees of bargaining power with sellers*, and some may be less sensitive than others to price, quality, or service differences. For example, independent tire retailers have less bargaining power in purchasing tires than do Honda, Ford, and DaimlerChrysler (which buy in much larger quantities), and they are also less sensitive to quality. Motor vehicle manufacturers are very particular about tire quality and tire performance because of the effects on vehicle performance, and they drive a hard bargain with tire manufacturers on both price and quality. Apparel manufacturers confront significant bargaining power when selling to big retailers like JCPenney, Macy's, or L. L. Bean but they can command much better prices selling to small owner-managed apparel boutiques.

How Seller–Buyer Partnerships Can Create Competitive Pressures   Partnerships between sellers and buyers are an increasingly important element of the competitive picture in *business-to-business relationships* (as opposed to business-to-consumer relationships). Many sellers that provide items to business customers have found it in their mutual interest to collaborate closely on such matters as just-in-time deliveries, order processing, electronic invoice payments, and data sharing. Wal-Mart, for example, provides the manufacturers with which it does business (like Procter & Gamble) with daily sales at each of its stores so that the manufacturers can maintain sufficient inventories at Wal-Mart's distribution centers to keep the shelves at each Wal-Mart store amply stocked. Dell has partnered with its largest PC customers to create

Figure 3.8 **Factors Affecting the Bargaining Power of Buyers**

Buyer bargaining power is stronger when:
- Buyer switching costs to competing brands or substitute products are low.
- Buyers are large and can demand concessions when purchasing large quantities.
- Large-volume purchases by buyers are important to sellers.
- Buyer demand is weak or declining.
- There are only a few buyers—so that each one's business is important to sellers.
- Identity of buyer adds prestige to the seller's list of customers.
- Quantity and quality of information available to buyers improves.
- Buyers have the ability to postpone purchases until later if they do not like the present deals being offered by sellers.
- Some buyers are a threat to integrate backward into the business of sellers and become an important competitor.

Buyer bargaining power is weaker when:
- Buyers purchase the item infrequently or in small quantities.
- Buyer switching costs to competing brands are high.
- There is a surge in buyer demand that creates a "sellers' market."
- A seller's brand reputation is important to a buyer.
- A particular seller's product delivers quality or performance that is very important to buyer and that is not matched in other brands.
- Buyer collaboration or partnering with selected sellers provides attractive win–win opportunities.

online systems for over 50,000 corporate customers, providing their employees with information on approved product configurations, global pricing, paperless purchase orders, real-time order tracking, invoicing, purchasing history, and other efficiency tools. Dell loads a customer's software at the factory and installs asset tags so that customer setup time is minimal; it also helps customers upgrade their PC systems to next-generation hardware and software. Dell's partnerships with its corporate customers have put significant competitive pressure on other PC makers.

Is the Collective Strength of the Five Competitive Forces Conducive to Good Profitability?

Scrutinizing each of the five competitive forces one by one provides a powerful diagnosis of what competition is like in a given market. Once the strategist has gained an understanding of the specific competitive pressures comprising each force and determined whether these pressures constitute a strong, moderate, or weak competitive force, the next step is to evaluate the collective strength of the five forces and determine whether the state of competition is conducive to good profitability. Is the collective impact of the five competitive forces stronger than "normal"? Are some of the competitive forces sufficiently strong to undermine industry profitability? Can companies in this industry reasonably expect to earn decent profits in light of the prevailing competitive forces?

Is the Industry Competitively Attractive or Unattractive?   *As a rule, the stronger the collective impact of the five competitive forces, the lower the combined profitability of industry participants.* The most extreme case of a competitively unattractive industry is when all five forces are producing strong competitive pressures: Rivalry among sellers is vigorous, low entry barriers allow new rivals to gain a market foothold, competition from substitutes is intense, and both suppliers and customers are able to exercise considerable bargaining leverage. Fierce to strong competitive pressures coming from all five directions nearly always drive industry profitability to unacceptably low levels, frequently producing losses for many industry members and forcing some out of business. But an industry can be competitively unattractive even when not all five competitive forces are strong. Intense competitive pressures from just two or three of the five forces may suffice to destroy the conditions for good profitability and prompt some companies to exit the business. The manufacture of disk drives, for example, is brutally competitive; IBM recently announced the sale of its disk drive business to Hitachi, taking a loss of over $2 billion on its exit from the business. Especially intense competitive conditions seem to be the norm in tire manufacturing and apparel, two industries where profit margins have historically been thin.

> The stronger the forces of competition, the harder it becomes for industry members to earn attractive profits.

In contrast, when the collective impact of the five competitive forces is moderate to weak, an industry is competitively attractive in the sense that industry members can reasonably expect to earn good profits and a nice return on investment. The ideal competitive environment for earning superior profits is one in which both suppliers and customers are in weak bargaining positions, there are no good substitutes, high barriers block further entry, and rivalry among present sellers generates only moderate competitive pressures. Weak competition is the best of all possible worlds for also-ran companies because even they can usually eke out a decent profit—if a company can't make a decent profit when competition is weak, then its business outlook is indeed grim.

In most industries, the collective strength of the five competitive forces is somewhere near the middle of the two extremes of very intense and very weak, typically ranging from slightly stronger than normal to slightly weaker than normal and typically allowing well-managed companies with sound strategies to earn attractive profits.

Matching Company Strategy to Competitive Conditions   Working through the five-forces model step by step not only aids strategy makers in assessing whether the intensity of competition allows good profitability but also promotes sound strategic thinking about how to better match company strategy to the specific competitive character of the marketplace. Effectively matching a company's strategy to prevailing competitive conditions has two aspects:

> A company's strategy is increasingly effective the more it provides some insulation from competitive pressures and shifts the competitive battle in the company's favor.

1. Pursuing avenues that shield the firm from as many of the different competitive pressures as possible.
2. Initiating actions calculated to produce sustainable competitive advantage, thereby shifting competition in the company's favor, putting added competitive pressure on rivals, and perhaps even defining the business model for the industry.

But making headway on these two fronts first requires identifying competitive pressures, gauging the relative strength of each of the five competitive forces, and gaining a deep enough understanding of the state of competition in the industry to know which strategy buttons to push.

QUESTION 3: WHAT FACTORS ARE DRIVING INDUSTRY CHANGE AND WHAT IMPACTS WILL THEY HAVE?

An industry's present conditions don't necessarily reveal much about the strategically relevant ways in which the industry environment is changing. All industries are characterized by trends and new developments that gradually or speedily produce changes important enough to require a strategic response from participating firms. A popular hypothesis states that industries go through a life cycle of takeoff, rapid growth, early maturity and slowing growth, market saturation, and stagnation or decline. This hypothesis helps explain industry change—but it is far from complete.[11] There are more causes of industry change than an industry's normal progression through the life cycle—these need to be identified and their impacts understood.

The Concept of Driving Forces

Core Concept
Industry conditions change because important forces are *driving* industry participants (competitors, customers, or suppliers) to alter their actions; the **driving forces** in an industry are the *major underlying causes* of changing industry and competitive conditions—they have the biggest influence on how the industry landscape will be altered. Some driving forces originate in the outer ring of macroenvironment and some originate from the inner ring.

While it is important to track where an industry is in the life cycle, there's more analytical value in identifying the other factors that may be even stronger drivers of industry and competitive change. The point to be made here is that industry and competitive conditions change because forces are enticing or pressuring certain industry participants (competitors, customers, suppliers) to alter their actions in important ways.[12] The most powerful of the change agents are called **driving forces** because they have the biggest influences in reshaping the industry landscape and altering competitive conditions. Some driving forces originate in the outer ring of the company's macroenvironment (see Figure 3.2), but most originate in the company's more immediate industry and competitive environment.

Driving-forces analysis has three steps: (1) identifying what the driving forces are; (2) assessing whether the drivers of change are, on the whole, acting to make the industry more or less attractive; and (3) determining what strategy changes are needed to prepare for the impacts of the driving forces. All three steps merit further discussion.

Identifying an Industry's Driving Forces

Many developments can affect an industry powerfully enough to qualify as driving forces. Some drivers of change are unique and specific to a particular industry situation, but most drivers of industry and competitive change fall into one of the following categories:[13]

- *Emerging new Internet capabilities and applications*—Since the late 1990s, the Internet has woven its way into everyday business operations and the social fabric of life all across the world. Mushrooming Internet use, growing acceptance of Internet shopping, the emergence of high-speed Internet service and Voice over Internet Protocol (VoIP) technology, and an ever-growing series of Internet applications and capabilities have been major drivers of change in industry after industry. Companies are increasingly using online technology (1) to collaborate closely with suppliers and streamline their supply chains and (2) to revamp internal operations and squeeze out cost savings. Manufacturers can use their Web sites to access customers directly rather than distribute exclusively through traditional wholesale and retail channels. Businesses of all types can use Web stores to extend their geographic reach and vie for sales in areas where they formerly did not have a presence. The ability of companies to reach consumers via the Internet increases the number of rivals a company faces and often escalates rivalry by pitting pure online sellers against combination brick-and-click sellers against pure brick-and-mortar sellers. The Internet gives buyers unprecedented ability to research the product offerings of competitors and shop the market for the best value. Mounting ability of consumers to download music from the Internet via either file sharing or online music retailers has profoundly and re-shaped the music industry and the business of traditional brick-and-mortar music retailers. Widespread use of e-mail has forever eroded the business of providing fax services and the first-class mail delivery revenues of government postal services worldwide. Videoconferencing via the Internet can erode the demand for business travel. Online course offerings at universities have the potential to revolutionize higher education. The Internet of the future will feature faster speeds, dazzling applications, and over a billion connected gadgets performing an array of functions, thus driving further industry and competitive changes. But Internet-related impacts vary from industry to industry. The challenges here are to assess precisely how emerging Internet developments are altering a particular industry's landscape and to factor these impacts into the strategy-making equation.

- *Increasing globalization*—Competition begins to shift from primarily a regional or national focus to an international or global focus when industry members begin seeking out customers in foreign markets or when production activities begin to migrate to countries where costs are lowest. Globalization of competition really starts to take hold when one or more ambitious companies precipitate a race for worldwide market leadership by launching initiatives to expand into more and more country markets. Globalization can also be precipitated by the blossoming of consumer demand in more and more countries and by the actions of government officials in many countries to reduce trade barriers or open up once-closed markets to foreign competitors, as is occurring in many parts of Europe, Latin America, and Asia. Significant differences in labor costs among countries give manufacturers a strong incentive to locate plants for labor-intensive products in low-wage countries and use these plants to supply market demand across the world. Wages in China, India, Singapore, Mexico, and Brazil, for example, are about one-fourth those in the United States, Germany, and Japan. The forces of globalization are sometimes such a strong driver that companies find it highly advantageous, if not necessary, to spread their operating reach into more and more country markets. Globalization is very much a driver of industry change in such industries as credit cards, cell phones, digital cameras, golf and ski equipment, motor vehicles, steel, petroleum, personal computers, video games, public accounting, and textbook publishing.

- *Changes in an industry's long-term growth rate*—Shifts in industry growth up or down are a driving force for industry change, affecting the balance between industry supply and buyer demand, entry and exit, and the character and strength of competition. An upsurge in buyer demand triggers a race among established firms and newcomers to capture the new sales opportunities; ambitious companies with trailing market shares may see the upturn in demand as a golden opportunity to launch offensive strategies to broaden their customer base and move up several notches in the industry standings. A slowdown in the rate at which demand is growing nearly always portends mounting rivalry and increased efforts by some firms to maintain their high rates of growth by taking sales and market share away from rivals. If industry sales suddenly turn flat or begin to shrink after years of rising at double-digit levels, competition is certain to intensify as industry members scramble for the available business and as mergers and acquisitions result in industry consolidation to a smaller number of competitively stronger participants. Stagnating sales usually prompt both competitively weak and growth-oriented companies to sell their business operations to those industry members who elect to stick it out; as demand for the industry's product continues to shrink, the remaining industry members may be forced to close inefficient plants and retrench to a smaller production base—all of which results in a much-changed competitive landscape.

- *Changes in who buys the product and how they use it*—Shifts in buyer demographics and new ways of using the product can alter the state of competition by opening the way to market an industry's product through a different mix of dealers and retail outlets; prompting producers to broaden or narrow their product lines; bringing different sales and promotion approaches into play; and forcing adjustments in customer service offerings (credit, technical assistance, maintenance, and repair). The mushrooming popularity of downloading music from the Internet, storing music files on PC hard drives, and burning custom discs has forced recording companies to reexamine their distribution strategies and raised questions about the future of traditional retail music stores; at the same time, it has stimulated sales of disc burners and blank discs. Longer life expectancies and growing percentages of relatively well-to-do retirees are driving changes in such industries as health care, prescription drugs, recreational living, and vacation travel. The growing percentage of households with PCs and Internet access is opening opportunities for banks to expand their electronic bill-payment services and for retailers to move more of their customer services online.

- *Product innovation*—Competition in an industry is always affected by rivals racing to be first to introduce one new product or product enhancement after another. An ongoing stream of product innovations tends to alter the pattern of competition in an industry by attracting more first-time buyers, rejuvenating industry growth, and/or creating wider or narrower product differentiation among rival sellers. Successful new product introductions strengthen the market positions of the innovating companies, usually at the expense of companies that stick with their old products or are slow to follow with their own versions of the new product. Product innovation has been a key driving force in such industries as digital cameras, golf clubs, video games, toys, and prescription drugs.

- *Technological change and manufacturing process innovation*—Advances in technology can dramatically alter an industry's landscape, making it possible to produce new and better products at lower cost and opening up whole new industry frontiers. For instance, Voice over Internet Protocol (VoIP) technology has spawned low-cost, Internet-based phone networks that are stealing large numbers of customers away from traditional telephone companies worldwide (whose higher cost technology depends on hardwired connections via overhead and underground telephone lines). Flat-screen technology for PC monitors is killing the demand for conventional cathode ray tube (CRT) monitors. Liquid crystal display (LCD), plasma screen technology, and high-definition technology are precipitating a revolution in the television industry and driving use of cathode ray technology (CRT) into the background. MP3 technology is transforming how people listen to music. Digital technology is driving huge changes in the camera and film industries. Satellite radio technology is allowing satellite radio companies with their largely commercial-free programming to draw millions of listeners away from traditional radio stations whose revenue streams from commercials are dependent on audience size. Technological developments can also produce competitively significant changes in capital requirements, minimum efficient plant sizes, distribution channels and logistics, and learning/experience curve effects. In the steel industry, ongoing advances in electric arc minimill technology (which involve recycling scrap steel to make new products) have allowed steelmakers with state-of-the-art minimills to gradually expand into the production of more and more steel products, steadily taking sales and market share from higher-cost integrated producers (which make steel from scratch using iron ore, coke, and traditional blast furnace technology). Nucor Corporation, the leader of the minimill technology revolution in the United States, began operations in 1970 and has ridden the wave of technological advances in minimill technology to become the biggest U.S. steel producer (as of 2004) and rank among the lowest-cost producers in the world. In a space of 30 years, advances in minimill technology have changed the face of the steel industry worldwide.

- *Marketing innovation*—When firms are successful in introducing new ways to *market* their products, they can spark a burst of buyer interest, widen industry demand, increase product differentiation, and lower unit costs—any or all of which can alter the competitive positions of rival firms and force strategy revisions. Online marketing is shaking up competition in electronics (where there are dozens of online electronics retailers, often with deep-discount prices) and office supplies (where Office Depot, Staples, and Office Max are using their Web sites to market office supplies to corporations, small businesses, schools and universities, and government agencies). Increasing numbers of music artists are marketing their recordings at their own Web sites rather than entering into contracts with recording studios that distribute through online and brick-and-mortar music retailers.

- *Entry or exit of major firms*—The entry of one or more foreign companies into a geographic market once dominated by domestic firms nearly always shakes up competitive conditions. Likewise, when an established domestic firm from another industry attempts entry either by acquisition or by launching its own start-up venture, it usually applies its skills and resources in some innovative fashion that pushes competition in new directions. Entry by a major firm thus often produces a new ball game, not only with new key players but also with new rules for competing. Similarly, exit of a major firm changes the competitive structure by reducing the number of market leaders (perhaps increasing the dominance of the leaders who remain) and causing a rush to capture the exiting firm's customers.

- *Diffusion of technical know-how across more companies and more countries*— As knowledge about how to perform a particular activity or execute a particular manufacturing technology spreads, the competitive advantage held by firms originally possessing this know-how erodes. Knowledge diffusion can occur through scientific journals, trade publications, on-site plant tours, word of mouth among suppliers and customers, employee migration, and Internet sources. It can also occur when those possessing technological knowledge license others to use that knowledge for a royalty fee or team up with a company interested in turning the technology into a new business venture. Quite often, technological know-how can be acquired by simply buying a company that has the wanted skills, patents, or manufacturing capabilities. In recent years, *rapid technology transfer across national boundaries has been a prime factor in causing industries to become more globally competitive.* As companies worldwide gain access to valuable technical know-how, they upgrade their manufacturing capabilities in a long-term effort to compete head-on with established companies. Cross-border technology transfer has made the once domestic industries of automobiles, tires, consumer electronics, telecommunications, computers, and others increasingly global.

- *Changes in cost and efficiency*—Widening or shrinking differences in the costs among key competitors tend to dramatically alter the state of competition. The low cost of fax and e-mail transmission has put mounting competitive pressure on the relatively inefficient and high-cost operations of the U.S. Postal Service—sending a one-page fax is cheaper and far quicker than sending a first-class letter; sending e-mail is faster and cheaper still. In the steel industry, the lower costs of companies using electric-arc furnaces to recycle scrap steel into new steel products has forced traditional manufacturers that produce steel from iron ore using blast furnace technology to overhaul their plants and to withdraw totally from making those steel products where they could no longer be cost competitive. Shrinking cost differences in producing multifeatured mobile phones is turning the mobile phone market into a commodity business and causing more buyers to base their purchase decisions on price.

- *Growing buyer preferences for differentiated products instead of a commodity product (or for a more standardized product instead of strongly differentiated products)*—When buyer tastes and preferences start to diverge, sellers can win a loyal following with product offerings that stand apart from those of rival sellers. In recent years, beer drinkers have grown less loyal to a single brand and have begun to drink a variety of domestic and foreign beers; as a consequence, beer manufacturers have introduced a host of new brands and malt beverages with different tastes and flavors. Buyer preferences for motor vehicles are becoming increasingly diverse, with few models generating sales of more than 250,000 units annually. When a shift from standardized to differentiated products occurs, the driver of change is the contest among rivals to cleverly outdifferentiate one another.

  However, buyers sometimes decide that a standardized, budget-priced product suits their requirements as well as or better than a premium-priced product with lots of snappy features and personalized services. Online brokers, for example, have used the lure of cheap commissions to attract many investors willing to place their own buy–sell orders via the Internet; growing acceptance of online trading has put significant competitive pressures on full-service brokers whose business model has always revolved around convincing clients of the value of asking for personalized advice from professional brokers and paying their high commission fees to make trades. Pronounced shifts toward greater product standardization usually spawn lively price competition and force rival sellers to drive down their costs to maintain profitability. The lesson here is that competition is driven partly by whether the market forces in motion are acting to increase or decrease product differentiation.

- *Reductions in uncertainty and business risk*—An emerging industry is typically characterized by much uncertainty over potential market size, how much time and money will be needed to surmount technological problems, and what distribution channels and buyer segments to emphasize. Emerging industries tend to attract only risk-taking entrepreneurial companies. Over time, however, if the business model of industry pioneers proves profitable and market demand for the product appears durable, more conservative firms are usually enticed to enter the market. Often, these later entrants are large, financially strong firms looking to invest in attractive growth industries.

  Lower business risks and less industry uncertainty also affect competition in international markets. In the early stages of a company's entry into foreign markets, conservatism prevails and firms limit their downside exposure by using less risky strategies like exporting, licensing, joint marketing agreements, or joint ventures with local companies to accomplish entry. Then, as experience accumulates and perceived risk levels decline, companies move more boldly and more independently, making acquisitions, constructing their own plants, putting in their own sales and marketing capabilities to build strong competitive positions in each country market, and beginning to link the strategies in each country to create a more globalized strategy.

- *Regulatory influences and government policy changes*—Government regulatory actions can often force significant changes in industry practices and strategic approaches. Deregulation has proved to be a potent pro-competitive force in the airline, banking, natural gas, telecommunications, and electric utility industries. Government efforts to reform Medicare and health insurance have become potent driving forces in the health care industry. In international markets, host governments can drive competitive changes by opening their domestic markets to foreign participation or closing them to protect domestic companies. Note that this driving force is spawned by forces in a company's macroenvironment.

- *Changing societal concerns, attitudes, and lifestyles*—Emerging social issues and changing attitudes and lifestyles can be powerful instigators of industry change. Growing antismoking sentiment has emerged as a major driver of change in the tobacco industry; concerns about terrorism are having a big impact on the travel industry. Consumer concerns about salt, sugar, chemical additives, saturated fat, cholesterol, carbohydrates, and nutritional value have forced food producers to revamp food-processing techniques, redirect R&D efforts into the use of healthier ingredients, and compete in developing nutritious, good-tasting products. Safety concerns have driven product design changes in the automobile, toy, and outdoor power equipment industries, to mention a few. Increased interest in physical fitness has spawned new industries in exercise equipment, biking, outdoor apparel, sports gyms and recreation centers, vitamin and nutrition supplements, and medically supervised diet programs. Social concerns about air and water pollution have forced industries to incorporate expenditures for controlling pollution into their cost structures. Shifting societal concerns, attitudes, and lifestyles alter the pattern of competition, usually favoring those

Table 3.2 **The Most Common Driving Forces**

1. Emerging new Internet capabilities and applications
2. Increasing globalization
3. Changes in an industry's long-term growth rate
4. Changes in who buys the product and how they use it
5. Product innovation
6. Technological change and manufacturing process innovation
7. Marketing innovation
8. Entry or exit of major firms
9. Diffusion of technical know-how across more companies and more countries
10. Changes in cost and efficiency
11. Growing buyer preferences for differentiated products instead of a commodity product (or for a more standardized product instead of strongly differentiated products)
12. Reductions in uncertainty and business risk
13. Regulatory influences and government policy changes
14. Changing societal concerns, attitudes, and lifestyles

players that respond quickly and creatively with products targeted to the new trends and conditions. As with the preceding driving force, this driving force springs from factors at work in a company's macroenvironment.

Table 3.2 lists these 14 most common driving forces.

That there are so many different potential driving forces explains why it is too simplistic to view industry change only in terms of moving through the different stages in an industry's life cycle and why a full understanding of all types of change drivers is a fundamental part of industry analysis. However, while many forces of change may be at work in a given industry, no more than three or four are likely to be true driving forces powerful enough to qualify as the *major determinants* of why and how the industry is changing. Thus company strategists must resist the temptation to label every change they see as a driving force; the analytical task is to evaluate the forces of industry and competitive change carefully enough to separate major factors from minor ones.

Assessing the Impact of the Driving Forces

An important part of driving-forces analysis is to determine whether the collective impact of the driving forces will be to increase or decrease market demand, make competition more or less intense, and lead to higher or lower industry profitability.

Just identifying the driving forces is not sufficient, however. The second, and more important, step in driving-forces analysis is to determine whether the prevailing driving forces are, on the whole, acting to make the industry environment more or less attractive. Answers to three questions are needed here:

1. Are the driving forces collectively acting to cause demand for the industry's product to increase or decrease?
2. Are the driving forces acting to make competition more or less intense?
3. Will the combined impacts of the driving forces lead to higher or lower industry profitability?

Getting a handle on the collective impact of the driving forces usually requires looking at the likely effects of each force separately, since the driving forces may not all be pushing change in the same direction. For example, two driving forces may be acting to spur demand for the industry's product while one driving force may be working to curtail demand. Whether the net effect on industry demand is up or down hinges on which driving forces are the more powerful. The analyst's objective here is to get a good grip on what external factors are shaping industry change and what difference these factors will make.

Developing a Strategy That Takes the Impacts of the Driving Forces into Account

The third step of driving-forces analysis—where the real payoff for strategy making comes—is for managers to draw some conclusions about what strategy adjustments will be needed to deal with the impacts of the driving forces. The real value of doing driving-forces analysis is to gain better understanding of what strategy adjustments will be needed to cope with the drivers of industry change and the impacts they are likely to have on market demand, competitive intensity, and industry profitability. In short, the strategy-making challenge that flows from driving-forces analysis is what to do to prepare for the industry and competitive changes being wrought by the driving forces. Indeed, without understanding the forces driving industry change and the impacts these forces will have on the character of the industry environment and on the company's business over the next one to three years, managers are ill-prepared to craft a strategy tightly matched to emerging conditions. Similarly, if managers are uncertain about the implications of one or more driving forces, or if their views are incomplete or off base, it's difficult for them to craft a strategy that is responsive to the driving forces and their consequences for the industry. So driving-forces analysis is not something to take lightly; it has practical value and is basic to the task of thinking strategically about where the industry is headed and how to prepare for the changes ahead.

> Driving-forces analysis, when done properly, pushes company managers to think about what's around the corner and what the company needs to be doing to get ready for it.

> The real payoff of driving-forces analysis is to help managers understand what strategy changes are needed to prepare for the impacts of the driving forces.

QUESTION 4: WHAT MARKET POSITIONS DO RIVALS OCCUPY—WHO IS STRONGLY POSITIONED AND WHO IS NOT?

Since competing companies commonly sell in different price/quality ranges, emphasize different distribution channels, incorporate product features that appeal to different types of buyers, have different geographic coverage, and so on, it stands to reason that some companies enjoy stronger or more attractive market positions than other companies. Understanding which companies are strongly positioned and which are weakly positioned is an integral part of analyzing an industry's competitive structure. The best technique for revealing the market positions of industry competitors is **strategic group mapping.**[14] This analytical tool is useful for comparing the market positions of each firm separately or for grouping them into like positions when an industry has so many competitors that it is not practical to examine each one in depth.

> **Core Concept**
> *Strategic group mapping* is a technique for displaying the different market or competitive positions that rival firms occupy in the industry.

Using Strategic Group Maps to Assess the Market Positions of Key Competitors

A **strategic group** consists of those industry members with similar competitive approaches and positions in the market.[15] Companies in the same strategic group can resemble one another in any of several ways: They may have comparable product-line breadth, sell in the same price/quality range, emphasize the same distribution channels, use essentially

> **Core Concept**
> A **strategic group** is a cluster of industry rivals that have similar competitive approaches and market positions.

the same product attributes to appeal to similar types of buyers, depend on identical technological approaches, or offer buyers similar services and technical assistance.[16] An industry contains only one strategic group when all sellers pursue essentially identical strategies and have comparable market positions. At the other extreme, an industry may contain as many strategic groups as there are competitors when each rival pursues a distinctively different competitive approach and occupies a substantially different market position.

The procedure for constructing a *strategic group map* is straightforward:

- Identify the competitive characteristics that differentiate firms in the industry. Typical variables are price/quality range (high, medium, low); geographic coverage (local, regional, national, global); degree of vertical integration (none, partial, full); product-line breadth (wide, narrow); use of distribution channels (one, some, all); and degree of service offered (no-frills, limited, full).
- Plot the firms on a two-variable map using pairs of these differentiating characteristics.
- Assign firms that fall in about the same strategy space to the same strategic group.
- Draw circles around each strategic group, making the circles proportional to the size of the group's share of total industry sales revenues.

This produces a two-dimensional diagram like the one for the retailing industry in Illustration Capsule 3.1.

Several guidelines need to be observed in mapping the positions of strategic groups in the industry's overall strategy space.[17] First, the two variables selected as axes for the map should *not* be highly correlated; if they are, the circles on the map will fall along a diagonal and strategy makers will learn nothing more about the relative positions of competitors than they would by considering just one of the variables. For instance, if companies with broad product lines use multiple distribution channels while companies with narrow lines use a single distribution channel, then looking at broad versus narrow product lines reveals just as much about who is positioned where as looking at single versus multiple distribution channels; that is, one of the variables is redundant. Second, the variables chosen as axes for the map should expose big differences in how rivals position themselves to compete in the marketplace. This, of course, means analysts must identify the characteristics that differentiate rival firms and use these differences as variables for the axes and as the basis for deciding which firm belongs in which strategic group. Third, the variables used as axes don't have to be either quantitative or continuous; rather, they can be discrete variables or defined in terms of distinct classes and combinations. Fourth, drawing the sizes of the circles on the map proportional to the combined sales of the firms in each strategic group allows the map to reflect the relative sizes of each strategic group. Fifth, if more than two good competitive variables can be used as axes for the map, several maps can be drawn to give different exposures to the competitive positioning relationships present

Illustration Capsule 3.1

Comparative Market Positions of Selected Retail Chains: A Strategic Group Map Application

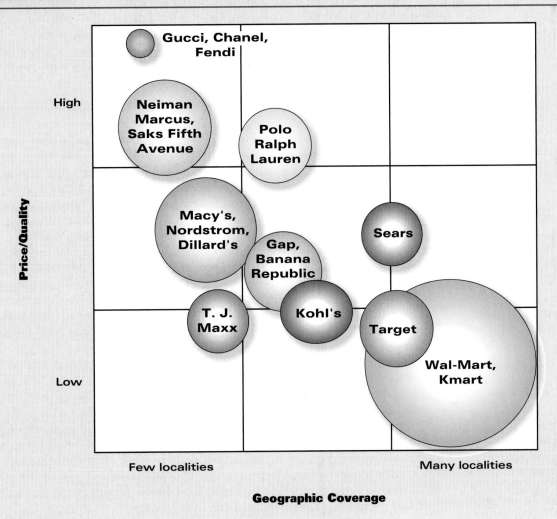

Note: Circles are drawn roughly proportional to the sizes of the chains, based on revenues.

in the industry's structure. Because there is not necessarily one best map for portraying how competing firms are positioned in the market, it is advisable to experiment with different pairs of competitive variables.

What Can Be Learned from Strategic Group Maps?

Strategic group maps are revealing in several respects. The most important has to do with which rivals are similarly positioned and are thus close rivals and which are distant rivals. Generally speaking, *the closer strategic groups are to each other on the*

Strategic group maps reveal which companies are close competitors and which are distant competitors.

map, the stronger the cross-group competitive rivalry tends to be. Although firms in the same strategic group are the closest rivals, the next closest rivals are in the immediately adjacent groups.[18] Often, firms in strategic groups that are far apart on the map hardly compete at all. For instance, Wal-Mart's clientele, merchandise selection, and pricing points are much too different to justify calling them close competitors of Neiman Marcus or Saks Fifth Avenue in retailing. For the same reason, Timex is not a meaningful competitive rival of Rolex, and Subaru is not a close competitor of Lincoln or Mercedes-Benz.

The second thing to be gleaned from strategic group mapping is that *not all positions on the map are equally attractive.* Two reasons account for why some positions can be more attractive than others:

1. *Prevailing competitive pressures and industry driving forces favor some strategic groups and hurt others.*[19] Discerning which strategic groups are advantaged and disadvantaged requires scrutinizing the map in light of what has also been learned from the prior analysis of competitive forces and driving forces. Quite often the strength of competition varies from group to group—there's little reason to believe that all firms in an industry feel the same degrees of competitive pressure, since their strategies and market positions may well differ in important respects. For instance, the competitive battle among Wal-Mart, Target, and Sears/Kmart (Kmart acquired Sears in 2005) is more intense (with consequently smaller profit margins) than the rivalry among Gucci, Chanel, Fendi, and other high-end fashion retailers. Likewise, industry driving forces may be acting to grow the demand for the products of firms in some strategic groups and shrink the demand for the products of firms in other strategic groups—as is the case in the radio broadcasting industry where satellite radio firms like XM and Sirius stand to gain market ground at the expense of commercial-based radio broadcasters due to the impacts of such driving forces as technological advances in satellite broadcasting, growing buyer preferences for more diverse radio programming, and product innovation in satellite radio devices. Firms in strategic groups that are being adversely impacted by intense competitive pressures or driving forces may try to shift to a more favorably situated group. But shifting to a different position on the map can prove difficult when entry barriers for the target strategic group are high. Moreover, attempts to enter a new strategic group nearly always increase competitive pressures in the target strategic group. If certain firms are known to be trying to change their competitive positions on the map, then attaching arrows to the circles showing the targeted direction helps clarify the picture of competitive maneuvering among rivals.

Core Concept
Not all positions on a strategic group map are equally attractive.

2. *The profit potential of different strategic groups varies due to the strengths and weaknesses in each group's market position.* The profit prospects of firms in different strategic groups can vary from good to ho-hum to poor because of differing growth rates for the principal buyer segments served by each group, differing degrees of competitive rivalry within strategic groups, differing degrees of exposure to competition from substitute products outside the industry, and differing degrees of supplier or customer bargaining power from group to group.

Thus, part of strategic group map analysis always entails drawing conclusions about where on the map is the "best" place to be and why. Which companies/strategic groups are destined to prosper because of their positions? Which companies/strategic groups seem destined to struggle because of their positions? What accounts for why some parts of the map are better than others?

QUESTION 5: WHAT STRATEGIC MOVES ARE RIVALS LIKELY TO MAKE NEXT?

Unless a company pays attention to what competitors are doing and knows their strengths and weaknesses, it ends up flying blind into competitive battle. As in sports, scouting the opposition is essential. *Competitive intelligence* about rivals' strategies, their latest actions and announcements, their resource strengths and weaknesses, the efforts being made to improve their situation, and the thinking and leadership styles of their executives is valuable for predicting or anticipating the strategic moves competitors are likely to make next in the marketplace. Having good information to predict the strategic direction and likely moves of key competitors allows a company to prepare defensive countermoves, to craft its own strategic moves with some confidence about what market maneuvers to expect from rivals, and to exploit any openings that arise from competitors' missteps or strategy flaws.

> Good scouting reports on rivals provide a valuable assist in anticipating what moves rivals are likely to make next and outmaneuvering them in the marketplace.

Identifying Competitors' Strategies and Resource Strengths and Weaknesses

Keeping close tabs on a com.petitor's strategy entails monitoring what the rival is doing in the marketplace, what its management is saying in company press releases, information posted on the company's Web site (especially press releases and the presentations management has recently made to securities analysts), and such public documents as annual reports and 10-K filings, articles in the business media, and the reports of securities analysts. (Figure 1.1 in Chapter 1 indicates what to look for in identifying a company's strategy.) Company personnel may be able to pick up useful information from a rival's exhibits at trade shows and from conversations with a rival's customers, suppliers, and former employees.[20] Many companies have a competitive intelligence unit that sifts through the available information to construct up-to-date strategic profiles of rivals—their current strategies, resource strengths and competitive capabilities, competitive shortcomings, press releases, and recent executive pronouncements. Such profiles are typically updated regularly and made available to managers and other key personnel.

Those who gather competitive intelligence on rivals, however, can sometimes cross the fine line between honest inquiry and unethical or even illegal behavior. For example, calling rivals to get information about prices, the dates of new product introductions, or wage and salary levels is legal, but misrepresenting one's company affiliation during such calls is unethical. Pumping rivals' representatives at trade shows is ethical only if one wears a name tag with accurate company affiliation indicated. Avon Products at one point secured information about its biggest rival, Mary Kay Cosmetics (MKC), by having its personnel search through the garbage bins outside MKC's headquarters.[21] When MKC officials learned of the action and sued, Avon claimed it did nothing illegal, since a 1988 Supreme Court case had ruled that trash left on public property (in this case, a sidewalk) was anyone's for the taking. Avon even produced a videotape of its removal of the trash at the MKC site. Avon won the lawsuit—but Avon's action, while legal, scarcely qualifies as ethical.

In sizing up competitors, it makes sense for company strategists to make three assessments:

1. Which competitor has the best strategy? Which competitors appear to have flawed or weak strategies?

2. Which competitors are poised to gain market share, and which ones seem destined to lose ground?

3. Which competitors are likely to rank among the industry leaders five years from now? Do one or more up-and-coming competitors have powerful strategies and sufficient resource capabilities to overtake the current industry leader?

The industry's *current* major players are generally easy to identify, but some of the leaders may be plagued with weaknesses that are causing them to lose ground; other notable rivals may lack the resources and capabilities to remain strong contenders given the superior strategies and capabilities of up-and-coming companies. In evaluating which competitors are favorably or unfavorably positioned to gain market ground, company strategists need to focus on why there is potential for some rivals to do better or worse than other rivals. Usually, a competitor's prospects are a function of whether it is in a strategic group that is being favored or hurt by competitive pressures and driving forces, whether its strategy has resulted in competitive advantage or disadvantage, and whether its resources and capabilities are well suited for competing on the road ahead.

> Today's market leaders don't automatically become tomorrow's.

Predicting Competitors' Next Moves

Predicting the next strategic moves of competitors is the hardest yet most useful part of competitor analysis. Good clues about what actions a specific company is likely to undertake can often be gleaned from how well it is faring in the marketplace, the problems or weaknesses it needs to address, and how much pressure it is under to improve its financial performance. Content rivals are likely to continue their present strategy with only minor fine-tuning. Ailing rivals can be performing so poorly that fresh strategic moves are virtually certain. Ambitious rivals looking to move up in the industry ranks are strong candidates for launching new strategic offensives to pursue emerging market opportunities and exploit the vulnerabilities of weaker rivals.

Since the moves a competitor is likely to make are generally predicated on the views their executives have about the industry's future and their beliefs about their firm's situation, it makes sense to closely scrutinize the public pronouncements of rival company executives about where the industry is headed and what it will take to be successful, what they are saying about their firm's situation, information from the grapevine about what they are doing, and their past actions and leadership styles. Other considerations in trying to predict what strategic moves rivals are likely to make next include the following:

- Which rivals badly need to increase their unit sales and market share? What strategic options are they most likely to pursue: lowering prices, adding new models and styles, expanding their dealer networks, entering additional geographic markets, boosting advertising to build better brand-name awareness, acquiring a weaker competitor, or placing more emphasis on direct sales via their Web site?

- Which rivals have a strong incentive, along with the resources, to make major strategic changes, perhaps moving to a different position on the strategic group map? Which rivals are probably locked in to pursuing the same basic strategy with only minor adjustments?

- Which rivals are good candidates to be acquired? Which rivals may be looking to make an acquisition and are financially able to do so?

- Which rivals are likely to enter new geographic markets?
- Which rivals are strong candidates to expand their product offerings and enter new product segments where they do not currently have a presence?

To succeed in predicting a competitor's next moves, company strategists need to have a good feel for each rival's situation, how its managers think, and what the rival's best strategic options are. Doing the necessary detective work can be tedious and time-consuming, but scouting competitors well enough to anticipate their next moves allows managers to prepare effective countermoves (perhaps even beat a rival to the punch) and to take rivals' probable actions into account in crafting their own best course of action.

> Managers who fail to study competitors closely risk being caught napping when rivals make fresh and perhaps bold strategic moves.

QUESTION 6: WHAT ARE THE KEY FACTORS FOR FUTURE COMPETITIVE SUCCESS?

An industry's **key success factors (KSFs)** are those competitive factors that most affect industry members' ability to prosper in the marketplace—the particular strategy elements, product attributes, resources, competencies, competitive capabilities, and market achievements that spell the difference between being a strong competitor and a weak competitor—and sometimes between profit and loss. KSFs by their very nature are so important to future competitive success that *all firms* in the industry must pay close attention to them or risk becoming an industry also-ran. To indicate the significance of KSFs another way, how well a company's product offering, resources, and capabilities measure up against an industry's KSFs determines just how financially and competitively successful that company will be. Identifying KSFs, in light of the prevailing and anticipated industry and competitive conditions, is therefore always a top-priority analytical and strategy-making consideration. Company strategists need to understand the industry landscape well enough to separate the factors most important to competitive success from those that are less important.

> **Core Concept**
> **Key success factors** are the product attributes, competencies, competitive capabilities, and market achievements with the greatest impact on future competitive success in the marketplace.

In the beer industry, the KSFs are full utilization of brewing capacity (to keep manufacturing costs low), a strong network of wholesale distributors (to get the company's brand stocked and favorably displayed in retail outlets where beer is sold), and clever advertising (to induce beer drinkers to buy the company's brand and thereby pull beer sales through the established wholesale/retail channels). In apparel manufacturing, the KSFs are appealing designs and color combinations (to create buyer interest) and low-cost manufacturing efficiency (to permit attractive retail pricing and ample profit margins). In tin and aluminum cans, because the cost of shipping empty cans is substantial, one of the keys is having can-manufacturing facilities located close to end-use customers. Key success factors thus vary from industry to industry, and even from time to time within the same industry, as driving forces and competitive conditions change. Table 3.3 lists the most common types of industry key success factors.

An industry's key success factors can usually be deduced from what was learned from the previously described analysis of the industry and competitive environment. Which factors are most important to future competitive success flow directly from the industry's dominant characteristics, what competition is like, the impacts of the driving forces, the comparative market positions of industry members, and the likely

Table 3.3   **Common Types of Industry Key Success Factors**

Technology-related KSFs	• Expertise in a particular technology or in scientific research (important in pharmaceuticals, Internet applications, mobile communications, and most high-tech industries) • Proven ability to improve production processes (important in industries where advancing technology opens the way for higher manufacturing efficiency and lower production costs)
Manufacturing-related KSFs	• Ability to achieve scale economies and/or capture learning/experience curve effects (important to achieving low production costs) • Quality control know-how (important in industries where customers insist on product reliability) • High utilization of fixed assets (important in capital-intensive, high-fixed-cost industries) • Access to attractive supplies of skilled labor • High labor productivity (important for items with high labor content) • Low-cost product design and engineering (reduces manufacturing costs) • Ability to manufacture or assemble products that are customized to buyer specifications
Distribution-related KSFs	• A strong network of wholesale distributors/dealers • Strong direct sales capabilities via the Internet and/or having company-owned retail outlets • Ability to secure favorable display space on retailer shelves
Marketing-related KSFs	• Breadth of product line and product selection • A well-known and well-respected brand name • Fast, accurate technical assistance • Courteous, personalized customer service • Accurate filling of buyer orders (few back orders or mistakes) • Customer guarantees and warranties (important in mail-order and online retailing, big-ticket purchases, new product introductions) • Clever advertising
Skills and capability-related KSFs	• A talented workforce (important in professional services like accounting and investment banking) • National or global distribution capabilities • Product innovation capabilities (important in industries where rivals are racing to be first-to-market with new product attributes or performance features) • Design expertise (important in fashion and apparel industries) • Short delivery time capability • Supply chain management capabilities • Strong e-commerce capabilities—a user-friendly Web site and/or skills in using Internet technology applications to streamline internal operations
Other types of KSFs	• Overall low costs (not just in manufacturing) so as to be able to meet customer expectations of low price • Convenient locations (important in many retailing businesses) • Ability to provide fast, convenient after-the-sale repairs and service • A strong balance sheet and access to financial capital (important in newly emerging industries with high degrees of business risk and in capital-intensive industries) • Patent protection

next moves of key rivals. In addition, the answers to three questions help identify an industry's key success factors:

1. On what basis do buyers of the industry's product choose between the competing brands of sellers? That is, what product attributes are crucial?
2. Given the nature of competitive rivalry and the competitive forces prevailing in the marketplace, what resources and competitive capabilities does a company need to have to be competitively successful?
3. What shortcomings are almost certain to put a company at a significant competitive disadvantage?

Only rarely are there more than five or six key factors for future competitive success. And even among these, two or three usually outrank the others in importance. Managers should therefore bear in mind the purpose of identifying key success factors—to determine which factors are most important to future competitive success—and resist the temptation to label a factor that has only minor importance a KSF. To compile a list of every factor that matters even a little bit defeats the purpose of concentrating management attention on the factors truly critical to long-term competitive success.

Correctly diagnosing an industry's KSFs raises a company's chances of crafting a sound strategy. The goal of company strategists should be to design a strategy aimed at stacking up well on all of the industry's future KSFs and trying to be *distinctively better* than rivals on one (or possibly two) of the KSFs. Indeed, companies that stand out or excel on a particular KSF are likely to enjoy a stronger market position—*being distinctively better than rivals on one or two key success factors tends to translate into competitive advantage.* Hence, using the industry's KSFs as *cornerstones* for the company's strategy and trying to gain sustainable competitive advantage by excelling at one particular KSF is a fruitful competitive strategy approach.[22]

> **Core Concept**
> A sound strategy incorporates the intent to stack up well on all of the industry's key success factors and to excel on one or two KSFs.

QUESTION 7: DOES THE OUTLOOK FOR THE INDUSTRY PRESENT THE COMPANY WITH AN ATTRACTIVE OPPORTUNITY?

The final step in evaluating the industry and competitive environment is to use the preceding analysis to decide whether the outlook for the industry presents the company with a sufficiently attractive business opportunity. The important factors on which to base such a conclusion include:

- The industry's growth potential.
- Whether powerful competitive forces are squeezing industry profitability to subpar levels and whether competition appears destined to grow stronger or weaker.
- Whether industry profitability will be favorably or unfavorably affected by the prevailing driving forces.
- The degrees of risk and uncertainty in the industry's future.
- Whether the industry as a whole confronts severe problems—regulatory or environmental issues, stagnating buyer demand, industry overcapacity, mounting competition, and so on.

- The company's competitive position in the industry vis-à-vis rivals. (Being a well-entrenched leader or strongly positioned contender in a lackluster industry may present adequate opportunity for good profitability; however, having to fight a steep uphill battle against much stronger rivals may hold little promise of eventual market success or good return on shareholder investment, even though the industry environment is attractive.)

- The company's potential to capitalize on the vulnerabilities of weaker rivals, perhaps converting a relatively unattractive *industry* situation into a potentially rewarding *company* opportunity.

- Whether the company has sufficient competitive strength to defend against or counteract the factors that make the industry unattractive.

- Whether continued participation in this industry adds importantly to the firm's ability to be successful in other industries in which it may have business interests.

Core Concept
The degree to which an industry is attractive or unattractive is not the same for all industry participants and all potential entrants; the attractiveness of the opportunities an industry presents depends heavily on whether a company has the resource strengths and competitive capabilities to capture them.

As a general proposition, *if an industry's overall profit prospects are above average, the industry environment is basically attractive; if industry profit prospects are below average, conditions are unattractive.* However, it is a mistake to think of a particular industry as being equally attractive or unattractive to all industry participants and all potential entrants. Attractiveness is relative, not absolute, and conclusions one way or the other have to be drawn from the perspective of a particular company. Industries attractive to insiders may be unattractive to outsiders. Companies on the outside may look at an industry's environment and conclude that it is an unattractive business for them to get into, given the prevailing entry barriers, the difficulty of challenging current market leaders with their particular resources and competencies, and the opportunities they have elsewhere. Industry environments unattractive to weak competitors may be attractive to strong competitors. A favorably positioned company may survey a business environment and see a host of opportunities that weak competitors cannot capture.

When a company decides an industry is fundamentally attractive and presents good opportunities, a strong case can be made that it should invest aggressively to capture the opportunities it sees and to improve its long-term competitive position in the business. When a strong competitor concludes an industry is relatively unattractive and lacking in opportunity, it may elect to simply protect its present position, investing cautiously if at all and looking for opportunities in other industries. A competitively weak company in an unattractive industry may see its best option as finding a buyer, perhaps a rival, to acquire its business.

Key Points

Thinking strategically about a company's external situation involves probing for answers to the following seven questions:

1. *What are the industry's dominant economic features?* Industries differ significantly on such factors as market size and growth rate, the number and relative sizes of both buyers and sellers, the geographic scope of competitive rivalry, the degree of product differentiation, the speed of product innovation, demand–supply conditions, the extent of vertical integration, and the extent of scale economies and learning-curve effects. In addition to setting the stage for the analysis to come,

identifying an industry's economic features also promotes understanding of the kinds of strategic moves that industry members are likely to employ.

2. *What kinds of competitive forces are industry members facing, and how strong is each force?* The strength of competition is a composite of five forces: (1) competitive pressures stemming from the competitive jockeying and market maneuvering among industry rivals, (2) competitive pressures associated with the market inroads being made by the sellers of substitutes, (3) competitive pressures associated with the threat of new entrants into the market, (4) competitive pressures stemming from supplier bargaining power and supplier–seller collaboration, and (5) competitive pressures stemming from buyer bargaining power and seller–buyer collaboration. The nature and strength of the competitive pressures associated with these five forces have to be examined force by force to identify the specific competitive pressures they each comprise and to decide whether these pressures constitute a strong or weak competitive force. The next step in competition analysis is to evaluate the collective strength of the five forces and determine whether the state of competition is conducive to good profitability. Working through the five-forces model step by step not only aids strategy makers in assessing whether the intensity of competition allows good profitability but also promotes sound strategic thinking about how to better match company strategy to the specific competitive character of the marketplace. Effectively matching a company's strategy to the particular competitive pressures and competitive conditions that exist has two aspects: (1) pursuing avenues that shield the firm from as many of the prevailing competitive pressures as possible, and (2) initiating actions calculated to produce sustainable competitive advantage, thereby shifting competition in the company's favor, putting added competitive pressure on rivals, and perhaps even defining the business model for the industry.

3. *What factors are driving industry change and what impact will they have on competitive intensity and industry profitability?* Industry and competitive conditions change because forces are in motion that create incentives or pressures for change. The first phase is to identify the forces that are driving change in the industry; the most common driving forces include the Internet and Internet technology applications, globalization of competition in the industry, changes in the long-term industry growth rate, changes in buyer composition, product innovation, entry or exit of major firms, changes in cost and efficiency, changing buyer preferences for standardized versus differentiated products or services, regulatory influences and government policy changes, changing societal and lifestyle factors, and reductions in uncertainty and business risk. The second phase of driving-forces analysis is to determine whether the driving forces, taken together, are acting to make the industry environment more or less attractive. Are the driving forces causing demand for the industry's product to increase or decrease? Are the driving forces acting to make competition more or less intense? Will the driving forces lead to higher or lower industry profitability?

4. *What market positions do industry rivals occupy—who is strongly positioned and who is not?* Strategic group mapping is a valuable tool for understanding the similarities, differences, strengths, and weaknesses inherent in the market positions of rival companies. Rivals in the same or nearby strategic groups are close competitors, whereas companies in distant strategic groups usually pose little or no immediate threat. The lesson of strategic group mapping is that some positions on the map are more favorable than others. The profit potential of different strategic groups varies due to strengths and weaknesses in each group's market

position. Often, industry driving forces and competitive pressures favor some strategic groups and hurt others.

5. *What strategic moves are rivals likely to make next?* This analytical step involves identifying competitors' strategies, deciding which rivals are likely to be strong contenders and which are likely to be weak, evaluating rivals' competitive options, and predicting their next moves. Scouting competitors well enough to anticipate their actions can help a company prepare effective countermoves (perhaps even beating a rival to the punch) and allows managers to take rivals' probable actions into account in designing their own company's best course of action. Managers who fail to study competitors risk being caught unprepared by the strategic moves of rivals.

6. *What are the key factors for future competitive success?* An industry's key success factors (KSFs) are the particular strategy elements, product attributes, competitive capabilities, and business outcomes that spell the difference between being a strong competitor and a weak competitor—and sometimes between profit and loss. KSFs by their very nature are so important to competitive success that *all firms* in the industry must pay close attention to them or risk becoming an industry also-ran. Correctly diagnosing an industry's KSFs raises a company's chances of crafting a sound strategy. The goal of company strategists should be to design a strategy aimed at stacking up well on all of the industry KSFs and trying to be *distinctively better* than rivals on one (or possibly two) of the KSFs. Indeed, using the industry's KSFs as *cornerstones* for the company's strategy and trying to gain sustainable competitive advantage by excelling at one particular KSF is a fruitful competitive strategy approach.

7. *Does the outlook for the industry present the company with sufficiently attractive prospects for profitability?* If an industry's overall profit prospects are above average, the industry environment is basically attractive; if industry profit prospects are below average, conditions are unattractive. Conclusions regarding industry attractive are a major driver of company strategy. When a company decides an industry is fundamentally attractive and presents good opportunities, a strong case can be made that it should invest aggressively to capture the opportunities it sees and to improve its long-term competitive position in the business. When a strong competitor concludes an industry is relatively unattractive and lacking in opportunity, it may elect to simply protect its present position, investing cautiously if at all and looking for opportunities in other industries. A competitively weak company in an unattractive industry may see its best option as finding a buyer, perhaps a rival, to acquire its business. On occasion, an industry that is unattractive overall is still very attractive to a favorably situated company with the skills and resources to take business away from weaker rivals.

A competently conducted industry and competitive analysis generally tells a clear, easily understood story about the company's external environment. Different analysts can have varying judgments about competitive intensity, the impacts of driving forces, how industry conditions will evolve, how good the outlook is for industry profitability, and the degree to which the industry environment offers the company an attractive business opportunity. However, while no method can guarantee that all analysts will come to identical conclusions about the state of industry and competitive conditions and an industry's future outlook, this doesn't justify shortcutting hardnosed strategic analysis and relying instead on opinion and casual observation. Managers become better strategists when they know what questions to pose and what tools to use. This is why this chapter has concentrated on suggesting the right questions to ask, explaining concepts and analytical approaches, and indicating the kinds of things to look for. There's no substitute for doing cutting edge strategic thinking about a company's external situation—anything less weakens managers' ability to craft strategies that are well matched to industry and competitive conditions.

Exercises

1. As the owner of a fast-food enterprise seeking a loan from a bank to finance the construction and operation of three new store locations, you have been asked to provide the loan officer with a brief analysis of the competitive environment in fast food. Draw a five-forces diagram for the fast-food industry, and briefly discuss the nature and strength of each of the five competitive forces in fast food. Do whatever Internet research is required to expand your understanding of competition in the fast-food industry and do a competent five-forces analysis.

2. Based on the strategic group map in Illustration Capsule 3.1: Who are Polo Ralph Lauren's closest competitors? Between which two strategic groups is competition the strongest? Why do you think no retailers are positioned in the upper right-hand corner of the map? Which company/strategic group faces the weakest competition from the members of other strategic groups?

3. With regard to the ice cream industry, which of the following factors might qualify as possible driving forces capable of causing fundamental change in the industry's structure and competitive environment?

   a. Increasing sales of frozen yogurt and frozen sorbets.

   b. The potential for additional makers of ice cream to enter the market.

   c. Growing consumer interest in low-calorie/low-fat/low-carb/sugar-free dessert alternatives.

   d. A slowdown in consumer purchases of ice cream products.

   e. Rising prices for milk, sugar, and other ice cream ingredients.

   f. A decision by Häagen-Dazs to increase its prices by 10 percent.

   g. A decision by Ben & Jerry's to add five new flavors to its product line.

Evaluating a Company's Resources and Competitive Position

Before executives can chart a new strategy, they must reach common understanding of the company's current position.

—W. Chan Kim and Rene Mauborgne

The real question isn't how well you're doing today against your own history, but how you're doing against your competitors.

—Donald Kress

Organizations succeed in a competitive marketplace over the long run because they can do certain things their customers value better than can their competitors.

—Robert Hayes, Gary Pisano, and David Upton

Only firms who are able to continually build new strategic assets faster and cheaper than their competitors will earn superior returns over the long term.

—C. C. Markides and P. J. Williamson

In Chapter 3 we described how to use the tools of industry and competitive analysis to assess a company's external environment and lay the groundwork for matching a company's strategy to its external situation. In this chapter we discuss the techniques of evaluating a company's resource capabilities, relative cost position, and competitive strength vis-á-vis its rivals. The analytical spotlight will be trained on five questions:

1. How well is the company's present strategy working?
2. What are the company's resource strengths and weaknesses, and its external opportunities and threats?
3. Are the company's prices and costs competitive?
4. Is the company competitively stronger or weaker than key rivals?
5. What strategic issues and problems merit front-burner managerial attention?

We will describe four analytical tools that should be used to probe for answers to these questions—SWOT analysis, value chain analysis, benchmarking, and competitive strength assessment. All four are valuable techniques for revealing a company's competitiveness and for helping company managers match their strategy to the company's own particular circumstances.

QUESTION 1: HOW WELL IS THE COMPANY'S PRESENT STRATEGY WORKING?

In evaluating how well a company's present strategy is working, a manager has to start with what the strategy is. Figure 4.1 shows the key components of a single-business company's strategy. The first thing to pin down is the company's competitive approach. Is the company striving to be a low-cost leader *or* stressing ways to differentiate its product offering from rivals? Is it concentrating its efforts on serving a broad spectrum of customers *or* a narrow market niche? Another strategy-defining consideration is the firm's competitive scope within the industry—what its geographic market coverage is and whether it operates in just a single stage of the industry's production/distribution chain or is vertically integrated across several stages. Another good indication of the company's strategy is whether the company has made moves recently to improve its competitive position and performance—for instance, by cutting prices, improving design, stepping up advertising, entering a new geographic market (domestic or foreign),

Figure 4.1   **Identifying the Components of a Single-Business Company's Strategy**

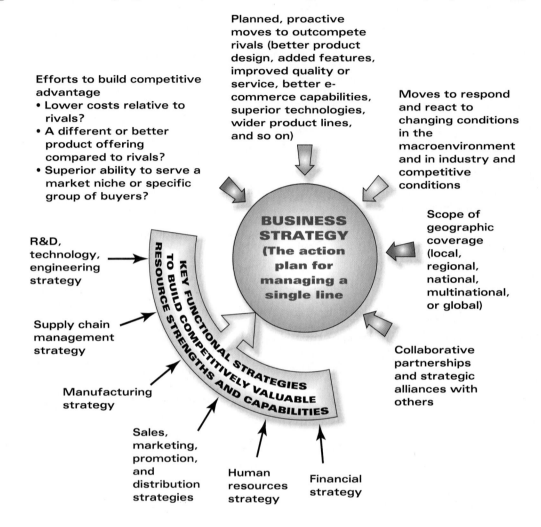

or merging with a competitor. The company's functional strategies in R&D, production, marketing, finance, human resources, information technology, and so on further characterize company strategy.

While there's merit in evaluating the strategy from a *qualitative* standpoint (its completeness, internal consistency, rationale, and relevance), the best *quantitative* evidence of how well a company's strategy is working comes from its results. The two best empirical indicators are (1) whether the company is achieving its stated financial and strategic objectives, and (2) whether the company is an above-average industry performer. Persistent shortfalls in meeting company performance targets and weak performance relative to rivals are reliable warning signs that the company suffers from poor strategy making, less-than-competent strategy execution, or both. Other indicators of how well a company's strategy is working include:

- Whether the firm's sales are growing faster, slower, or about the same pace as the market as a whole, thus resulting in a rising, eroding, or stable market share.

- Whether the company is acquiring new customers at an attractive rate as well as retaining existing customers.
- Whether the firm's profit margins are increasing or decreasing and how well its margins compare to rival firms' margins.
- Trends in the firm's net profits and return on investment and how these compare to the same trends for other companies in the industry.
- Whether the company's overall financial strength and credit rating are improving or on the decline.
- Whether the company can demonstrate continuous improvement in such internal performance measures as days of inventory, employee productivity, unit cost, defect rate, scrap rate, misfilled orders, delivery times, warranty costs, and so on.
- How shareholders view the company based on trends in the company's stock price and shareholder value (relative to the stock price trends at other companies in the industry).
- The firm's image and reputation with its customers.
- How well the company stacks up against rivals on technology, product innovation, customer service, product quality, delivery time, price, getting newly developed products to market quickly, and other relevant factors on which buyers base their choice of brands.

The stronger a company's current overall performance, the less likely the need for radical changes in strategy. The weaker a company's financial performance and market standing, the more its current strategy must be questioned. Weak performance is almost always a sign of weak strategy, weak execution, or both.

> The stronger a company's financial performance and market position, the more likely it has a well-conceived, well-executed strategy.

Table 4.1 provides a compilation of the financial ratios most commonly used to evaluate a company's financial performance and balance sheet strength.

QUESTION 2: WHAT ARE THE COMPANY'S RESOURCE STRENGTHS AND WEAKNESSES AND ITS EXTERNAL OPPORTUNITIES AND THREATS?

Appraising a company's resource strengths and weaknesses and its external opportunities and threats, commonly known as **SWOT analysis,** provides a good overview of whether the company's overall situation is fundamentally healthy or unhealthy. Just as important, a first-rate SWOT analysis provides the basis for crafting a strategy that capitalizes on the company's resources, aims squarely at capturing the company's best opportunities, and defends against the threats to its well-being.

> **Core Concept**
> **SWOT analysis** is a simple but powerful tool for sizing up a company's resource capabilities and deficiencies, its market opportunities, and the external threats to its future well-being.

Identifying Company Resource Strengths and Competitive Capabilities

A *resource strength* is something a company is good at doing or an attribute that enhances its competitiveness in the marketplace. Resource strengths can take any of several forms:

Table 4.1   **Key Financial Ratios: How to Calculate Them and What They Mean**

Ratio	How Calculated	What It Shows
Profitability ratios		
1. Gross profit margin	$\dfrac{\text{Sales} - \text{cost of goods sold}}{\text{Sales}}$	Shows the percentage of revenues available to cover operating expenses and yield a profit. Higher is better, and the trend should be upward.
2. Operating profit margin (or return on sales)	$\dfrac{\text{Sales} - \text{Operating expenses}}{\text{Sales}}$ or $\dfrac{\text{Operating income}}{\text{Sales}}$	Shows the profitability of current operations without regard to interest charges and income taxes. Higher is better, and the trend should be upward.
3. Net profit margin (or net return on sales)	$\dfrac{\text{Profits after taxes}}{\text{Sales}}$	Shows after-tax profits per dollar of sales. Higher is better, and the trend should be upward.
4. Return on total assets	$\dfrac{\text{Profits after taxes} + \text{Interest}}{\text{Total assets}}$	A measure of the return on total investment in the enterprise. Interest is added to after-tax profits to form the numerator since total assets are financed by creditors as well as by stockholders. Higher is better, and the trend should be upward.
5. Return on stockholders' equity	$\dfrac{\text{Profits after taxes}}{\text{Total stockholders' equity}}$	Shows the return stockholders are earning on their investment in the enterprise. A return in the 12–15 percent range is average, and the trend should be upward.
6. Earnings per share	$\dfrac{\text{Profits after taxes}}{\text{Number of shares of common stock outstanding}}$	Shows the earnings for each share of common stock outstanding. The trend should be upward, and the bigger the annual percentage gains, the better.
Liquidity ratios		
1. Current ratio	$\dfrac{\text{Current assets}}{\text{Current liabilities}}$	Shows a firm's ability to pay current liabilities using assets that can be converted to cash in the near term. Ratio should definitely be higher than 1.0; ratios of 2 or higher are better still.
2. Quick ratio (or acid-test ratio)	$\dfrac{\text{Current assets} - \text{Inventory}}{\text{Current liabilities}}$	Shows a firm's ability to pay current liabilities without relying on the sale of its inventories.
3. Working capital	Current assets – Current liabilities	Bigger amounts are better because the company has more internal funds available to (1) pay its current liabilities on a timely basis and (2) finance inventory expansion, additional accounts receivable, and a larger base of operations without resorting to borrowing or raising more equity capital.
Leverage ratios		
1. Debt-to-assets ratio	$\dfrac{\text{Total debt}}{\text{Total assets}}$	Measures the extent to which borrowed funds have been used to finance the firm's operations. Low fractions or ratios are better—high fractions indicate overuse of debt and greater risk of bankruptcy.

(Continued)

Table 4.1 **Continued**

Ratio	How Calculated	What It Shows
2. Debt-to-equity ratio	$$\frac{\text{Total debt}}{\text{Total stockholders' equity}}$$	Should usually be less than 1.0. High ratios (especially above 1.0) signal excessive debt, lower creditworthiness, and weaker balance sheet strength.
3. Long-term debt-to-equity ratio	$$\frac{\text{Long-term debt}}{\text{Total stockholders' equity}}$$	Shows the balance between debt and equity in the firm's *long-term* capital structure. Low ratios indicate greater capacity to borrow additional funds if needed.
4. Times-interest-earned (or coverage) ratio	$$\frac{\text{Operating income}}{\text{Interest expenses}}$$	Measures the ability to pay annual interest charges. Lenders usually insist on a minimum ratio of 2.0, but ratios above 3.0 signal better creditworthiness.
Activity ratios		
1. Days of inventory	$$\frac{\text{Inventory}}{\text{Cost of goods sold} \div 365}$$	Measures inventory management efficiency. Fewer days of inventory are usually better.
2. Inventory turnover	$$\frac{\text{Cost of goods sold}}{\text{Inventory}}$$	Measures the number of inventory turns per year. Higher is better.
3. Average collection period	$$\frac{\text{Accounts receivable}}{\text{Total sales} \div 365}$$ or $$\frac{\text{Accounts receivable}}{\text{Average daily sales}}$$	Indicates the average length of time the firm must wait after making a sale to receive cash payment. A shorter collection time is better.
Other important measures of financial performance		
1. Dividend yield on common stock	$$\frac{\text{Annual dividends per share}}{\text{Current market price per share}}$$	A measure of the return that shareholders receive in the form of dividends. A "typical" dividend yield in 2–3%. The dividend yield for fast-growth companies in often below 1% (may be even 0); the dividend yield for slow-growth companies can run 4–5%.
2. Price/earnings ratio	$$\frac{\text{Current market price per share}}{\text{Earnings per share}}$$	P/E ratios above 20 indicate strong investor confidence in a firm's outlook and earnings growth; firms whose future earnings are at risk or likely to grow slowly typically have ratios below 12.
3. Dividend payout ratio	$$\frac{\text{Annual dividends per share}}{\text{Earnings per share}}$$	Indicates the percentage of after-tax profits paid out as dividends.
4. Internal cash flow	After tax profits + Depreciation	A quick and rough estimate of the cash a company's business is generating after payment of operating expenses, interest, and taxes. Such amounts can be used for dividend payments or funding capital expenditures.

- *A skill, specialized expertise, or competitively important capability*—skills in low-cost operations, technological expertise, expertise in defect-free manufacture, proven capabilities in developing and introducing innovative products, cutting-edge supply chain management capabilities, expertise in getting new products to market quickly, strong e-commerce expertise, expertise in providing consistently good customer service, excellent mass merchandising skills, or unique advertising and promotional talents.

- *Valuable physical assets*—state-of-the-art plants and equipment, attractive real estate locations, worldwide distribution facilities, or ownership of valuable natural resource deposits.

- *Valuable human assets and intellectual capital*—an experienced and capable workforce, talented employees in key areas, cutting-edge knowledge in technology or other important areas of the business, collective learning embedded in the organization and built up over time, or proven managerial know-how.[1]

- *Valuable organizational assets*—proven quality control systems, proprietary technology, key patents, state-of-the-art systems for doing business via the Internet, ownership of important natural resources, a cadre of highly trained customer service representatives, a strong network of distributors or retail dealers, sizable amounts of cash and marketable securities, a strong balance sheet and credit rating (thus giving the company access to additional financial capital), or a comprehensive list of customers' e-mail addresses.

- *Valuable intangible assets*—a powerful or well-known brand name, a reputation for technological leadership, or strong buyer loyalty and goodwill.

- *An achievement or attribute that puts the company in a position of market advantage*—low overall costs relative to competitors, market share leadership, a superior product, a wider product line than rivals, wide geographic coverage, or award-winning customer service.

- *Competitively valuable alliances or cooperative ventures*—fruitful partnerships with suppliers that reduce costs and/or enhance product quality and performance; alliances or joint ventures that provide access to valuable technologies, specialized know-how, or geographic markets.

Core Concept
A company's resource strengths represent *competitive assets* and are big determinants of its competitiveness and ability to succeed in the marketplace.

A company's resource strengths represent its endowment of *competitive assets*. The caliber of a firm's resource strengths is a big determinant of its competitiveness—whether it has the wherewithal to be a strong competitor in the marketplace or whether its capabilities and competitive strengths are modest, thus relegating it to a trailing position in the industry.[2] Plainly, a company's resource strengths may or may not enable it to improve its competitive position and financial performance.

Assessing a Company's Competencies and Capabilities—What Activities Does It Perform Well?   One of the most important aspects of appraising a company's resource strengths has to do with its competence level in performing key pieces of its business—such as supply chain management, research and development (R&D), production, distribution, sales and marketing, and customer service. Which activities does it perform especially well? And are there any activities it performs better than rivals? A company's proficiency in conducting different facets of its operations can range from merely a competence in performing an activity to a core competence to a distinctive competence:

1. A **competence** is something an organization is good at doing. It is nearly always the product of experience, representing an accumulation of learning and the buildup

of proficiency in performing an internal activity. Usually a company competence originates with deliberate efforts to develop the organizational ability to do something, however imperfectly or inefficiently. Such efforts involve selecting people with the requisite knowledge and skills, upgrading or expanding individual abilities as needed, and then molding the efforts and work products of individuals into a cooperative group effort to create organizational ability. Then, as experience builds, such that the company gains proficiency in performing the activity consistently well and at an acceptable cost, the ability evolves into a true competence and company capability. Some competencies relate to fairly specific skills and expertise (like just-in-time inventory control or low-cost manufacturing efficiency or picking locations for new stores or designing an unusually appealing and user-friendly Web site); they spring from proficiency in a single discipline or function and may be performed in a single department or organizational unit. Other competencies, however, are inherently multidisciplinary and cross-functional—they are the result of effective collaboration among people with different expertise working in different organizational units. A competence in continuous product innovation, for example, comes from teaming the efforts of people and groups with expertise in market research, new product R&D, design and engineering, cost-effective manufacturing, and market testing.

> **Core Concept**
> A **competence** is an activity that a company has learned to perform well.

2. A **core competence** is a proficiently performed internal activity that is *central* to a company's strategy and competitiveness. A core competence is a more valuable resource strength than a competence because of the well-performed activity's core role in the company's strategy and the contribution it makes to the company's success in the marketplace. A core competence can relate to any of several aspects of a company's business: expertise in integrating multiple technologies to create families of new products, know-how in creating and operating systems for cost-efficient supply chain management, the capability to speed new or next-generation products to market, good after-sale service capabilities, skills in manufacturing a high-quality product at a low cost, or the capability to fill customer orders accurately and swiftly. A company may have more than one core competence in its resource portfolio, but rare is the company that can legitimately claim more than two or three core competencies. Most often, *a core competence is knowledge-based, residing in people and in a company's intellectual capital and not in its assets on the balance sheet.* Moreover, a core competence is more likely to be grounded in cross-department combinations of knowledge and expertise rather than being the product of a single department or work group. 3M Corporation has a core competence in product innovation—its record of introducing new products goes back several decades and new product introduction is central to 3M's strategy of growing its business. Ben & Jerry's Homemade, a subsidiary of Unilever, has a core competence in creating unusual flavors of ice cream and marketing them with catchy names like Chunky Monkey, Wavy Gravy, Chubby Hubby, The Gobfather, Dublin Mudslide, and Marsha Marsha Marshmallow.

> **Core Concept**
> A **core competence** is a *competitively important* activity that a company performs better than other internal activities.

3. A **distinctive competence** is a competitively valuable activity that a company *performs better than its rivals.* A distinctive competence thus signifies even greater proficiency than a core competence. But what is especially important about a distinctive competence is that the company enjoys *competitive superiority*

Core Concept
A *distinctive competence* is a competitively important activity that a company performs better than its rivals—it thus represents *a competitively superior resource strength.*

in performing that activity—a distinctive competence represents a level of proficiency that rivals do not have. Because a distinctive competence represents uniquely strong capability relative to rival companies, it qualifies as a *competitively superior resource strength* with competitive advantage potential. This is particularly true when the distinctive competence enables a company to deliver standout value to customers (in the form of lower costs and prices or better product performance or superior service). Toyota has worked diligently over several decades to establish a distinctive competence in low-cost, high-quality manufacturing of motor vehicles; its "lean production" system is far superior to that of any other automaker's, and the company is pushing the boundaries of its production advantage with a new type of assembly line—called the Global Body line—that costs 50 percent less to install and can be changed to accommodate a new model for 70 percent less than its previous production system.[3] Starbucks' distinctive competence in innovative coffee drinks and store ambience has propelled it to the forefront among coffee retailers.

The conceptual differences between a competence, a core competence, and a distinctive competence draw attention to the fact that a company's resource strengths and competitive capabilities are not all equal.[4] Some competencies and competitive capabilities merely enable market survival because most rivals have them—indeed, not having a competence or capability that rivals have can result in competitive disadvantage. If an apparel company does not have the competence to produce its apparel items cost-efficiently, it is unlikely to survive given the intensely price-competitive nature of the apparel industry. Every Web retailer requires a basic competence in designing an appealing and user-friendly Web site.

Core competencies are *competitively* more important resource strengths than competencies because they add power to the company's strategy and have a bigger positive impact on its market position and profitability. Distinctive competencies are even more competitively important. A distinctive competence is a competitively potent resource strength for three reasons: (1) it gives a company competitively valuable capability that is unmatched by rivals, (2) it has potential for being the cornerstone of the company's strategy, and (3) it can produce a competitive edge in the marketplace since it represents a level of proficiency that is superior to rivals. It is always easier for a company to build competitive advantage when it has a distinctive competence in performing an activity important to market success, when rival companies do not have offsetting competencies, and when it is costly and time-consuming for rivals to imitate the competence. A distinctive competence is thus potentially the mainspring of a company's success—unless it is trumped by more powerful resources possessed by rivals.

Core Concept
A distinctive competence is a competitively potent resource strength for three reasons: (1) it gives a company competitively valuable capability that is unmatched by rivals, (2) it can underpin and add real punch to a company's strategy, and (3) it is a basis for sustainable competitive advantage.

What Is the Competitive Power of a Resource Strength?

It is not enough to simply compile a list of a company's resource strengths and competitive capabilities. What is most telling about a company's resource strengths, individually and collectively, is how powerful they are in the marketplace. The competitive power of a resource strength is measured by how many of the following four tests it can pass:[5]

1. *Is the resource strength hard to copy?* The more difficult and more expensive it is to imitate a company's resource strength, the greater its potential competitive

value. Resources tend to be difficult to copy when they are unique (a fantastic real estate location, patent protection), when they must be built over time in ways that are difficult to imitate (a brand name, mastery of a technology), and when they carry big capital requirements (a cost-effective plant to manufacture cutting-edge microprocessors). Wal-Mart's competitors have failed miserably in their attempts over the past two decades to match Wal-Mart's super-efficient state-of-the-art distribution capabilities. Hard-to-copy strengths and capabilities are valuable competitive assets, adding to a company's market strength and contributing to sustained profitability.

2. *Is the resource strength durable—does it have staying power?* The longer the competitive value of a resource lasts, the greater its value. Some resources lose their clout in the marketplace quickly because of the rapid speeds at which technologies or industry conditions are moving. The value of Eastman Kodak's resources in film and film processing is rapidly being undercut by the growing popularity of digital cameras. The investments that commercial banks have made in branch offices is a rapidly depreciating asset because of growing use of direct deposits, debit cards, automated teller machines, and telephone and Internet banking options.

3. *Is the resource really competitively superior?* Companies have to guard against pridefully believing that their core competencies are distinctive competencies or that their brand name is more powerful than the brand names of rivals. Who can really say whether Coca-Cola's consumer marketing prowess is better than Pepsi-Cola's or whether the Mercedes-Benz brand name is more powerful than that of BMW or Lexus? Although many retailers claim to be quite proficient in product selection and in-store merchandising, a number run into trouble in the marketplace because they encounter rivals whose competencies in product selection and in-store merchandising are better than theirs. Apple's operating system for its MacIntosh PCs is by most accounts a world beater (compared to Windows XP), but Apple has failed miserably in converting its resource strength in operating system design into competitive success in the global PC market—it is an also-ran with a paltry 2–3 percent market share worldwide.

4. *Can the resource strength be trumped by the different resource strengths and competitive capabilities of rivals?* Many commercial airlines have invested heavily in developing the resources and capabilities to offer passengers safe, reliable flights at convenient times, along with an array of in-flight amenities. However, Southwest Airlines and JetBlue in the United States and Ryanair and easyJet in Europe have been quite successful deploying their resources in ways that enable them to provide commercial air services at radically lower fares. Amazon.com's strengths in online retailing of books have put a big dent in the business prospects of brick-and-mortar bookstores. Whole Foods Market has a resource lineup that enables it to merchandise a dazzling array of natural and organic food products in a supermarket setting, thus putting strong competitive pressure on Kroger, Safeway, Albertson's, and other prominent supermarket chains. The prestigious brand names of Cadillac and Lincoln have faded because Mercedes, BMW, Audi, and Lexus have used their resources to design, produce, and market more appealing luxury vehicles.

The vast majority of companies are not well endowed with standout resource strengths, much less with one or more competitively superior resources (or distinctive competencies) capable of passing all four tests with high marks. Most firms have a mixed bag of resources—one or two quite valuable, some good, many satisfactory to mediocre.

Companies in the top tier of their industry may have as many as two core competencies in their resource strength lineup. But only a few companies, usually the strongest industry leaders or up-and-coming challengers, have a resource strength that truly qualifies as a distinctive competence. Even so, a company can still marshal the resource strengths to be competitively successful without having a competitively superior resource or distinctive competence. A company can achieve considerable competitive vitality, maybe even competitive advantage, from a collection of good-to-adequate resource strengths that collectively give it competitive power in the marketplace. A number of fast-food chains—for example, Wendy's, Taco Bell, and Subway—have achieved a respectable market position competing against McDonald's with satisfactory sets of resource strengths and no apparent distinctive competence. The same can be said for Lowe's, which competes against industry leader Home Depot, and such regional banks as Compass, State Street, Keybank, PNC, BB&T, and AmSouth, which increasingly find themselves in competition with the top five U.S. banks—JPMorgan Chase, Bank of America, Citibank, Wachovia, and Wells Fargo.

> **Core Concept**
> A company's ability to succeed in the marketplace hinges to a considerable extent on the competitive power of its resources—the set of competencies, capabilities, and competitive assets at its command.

Identifying Company Resource Weaknesses and Competitive Deficiencies

A *resource weakness,* or *competitive deficiency,* is something a company lacks or does poorly (in comparison to others) or a condition that puts it at a disadvantage in the marketplace. A company's resource weaknesses can relate to (1) inferior or unproven skills, expertise, or intellectual capital in competitively important areas of the business; (2) deficiencies in competitively important physical, organizational, or intangible assets; or (3) missing or competitively inferior capabilities in key areas. *Internal weaknesses are thus shortcomings in a company's complement of resources and represent competitive liabilities.* Nearly all companies have competitive liabilities of one kind or another. Whether a company's resource weaknesses make it competitively vulnerable depends on how much they matter in the marketplace and whether they are offset by the company's resource strengths.

> **Core Concept**
> A company's resource strengths represent competitive assets; its resource weaknesses represent competitive liabilities.

Table 4.2 lists the kinds of factors to consider in compiling a company's resource strengths and weaknesses. Sizing up a company's complement of resource capabilities and deficiencies is akin to constructing a *strategic balance sheet,* where resource strengths represent *competitive assets* and resource weaknesses represent *competitive liabilities.* Obviously, the ideal condition is for the company's competitive assets to outweigh its competitive liabilities by an ample margin—a 50–50 balance is definitely not the desired condition!

Identifying a Company's Market Opportunities

Market opportunity is a big factor in shaping a company's strategy. Indeed, managers can't properly tailor strategy to the company's situation without first identifying its market opportunities and appraising the growth and profit potential each one holds. Depending on the prevailing circumstances, a company's opportunities can be plentiful or scarce, fleeting or lasting, and can range from wildly attractive (an absolute "must" to pursue) to marginally interesting (because the growth and profit potential are questionable) to unsuitable (because there's not a good match with the company's

Table 4.2   **What to Look for in Identifying a Company's Strengths, Weaknesses, Opportunities, and Threats**

Potential Resource Strengths and Competitive Capabilities	Potential Resource Weaknesses and Competitive Deficiencies
• A powerful strategy • Core competencies in _____ • A distinctive competence in _____ • A product that is strongly differentiated from those of rivals • Competencies and capabilities that are well matched to industry key success factors • A strong financial condition; ample financial resources to grow the business • Strong brand-name image/company reputation • An attractive customer base • Economy of scale and/or learning/experience curve advantages over rivals • Proprietary technology/superior technological skills/important patents • Superior intellectual capital relative to key rivals • Cost advantages over rivals • Strong advertising and promotion • Product innovation capabilities • Proven capabilities in improving production processes • Good supply chain management capabilities • Good customer service capabilities • Better product quality relative to rivals • Wide geographic coverage and/or strong global distribution capability • Alliances/joint ventures with other firms that provide access to valuable technology, competencies, and/or attractive geographic markets	• No clear strategic direction • Resources that are not well matched to industry key success factors • No well-developed or proven core competencies • A weak balance sheet; burdened with too much debt • Higher overall unit costs relative to key competitors • Weak or unproven product innovation capabilities • A product/service with ho-hum attributes or features inferior to those of rivals • Too narrow a product line relative to rivals • Weak brand image or reputation • Weaker dealer network than key rivals and/or lack of adequate global distribution capability • Behind on product quality, R&D, and/or technological know-how • In the wrong strategic group • Losing market share because . . . • Lack of management depth • Inferior intellectual capital relative to leading rivals • Subpar profitability because . . . • Plagued with internal operating problems or obsolete facilities • Behind rivals in e-commerce capabilities • Short on financial resources to grow the business and pursue promising initiatives • Too much underutilized plant capacity
Potential Market Opportunities	Potential External Threats to a Company's Future Prospects
• Openings to win market share from rivals • Sharply rising buyer demand for the industry's product • Serving additional customer groups or market segments • Expanding into new geographic markets • Expanding the company's product line to meet a broader range of customer needs • Using existing company skills or technological know-how to enter new product lines or new businesses • Online sales • Integrating forward or backward • Falling trade barriers in attractive foreign markets • Acquiring rival firms or companies with attractive technological expertise or capabilities • Entering into alliances or joint ventures to expand the firm's market coverage or boost its competitive capability • Openings to exploit emerging new technologies	• Increasing intensity of competition among industry rivals—may squeeze profit margins • Slowdowns in market growth • Likely entry of potent new competitors • Loss of sales to substitute products • Growing bargaining power of customers or suppliers • A shift in buyer needs and tastes away from the industry's product • Adverse demographic changes that threaten to curtail demand for the industry's product • Vulnerability to unfavorable industry driving forces • Restrictive trade policies on the part of foreign governments • Costly new regulatory requirements

resource strengths and capabilities). A checklist of potential market opportunities is included in Table 4.2.

While stunningly big or "golden" opportunities appear fairly frequently in volatile, fast-changing markets (typically due to important technological developments or rapidly shifting consumer preferences), they are nonetheless hard to see before most all companies in the industry identify them. The more volatile and thus unpredictable market conditions are, the more limited a company's ability to do market reconnaissance and spot important opportunities much ahead of rivals—there are simply too many variables in play for managers to peer into the fog of the future, identify one or more upcoming opportunities, and get a jump on rivals in pursuing it.[6] In mature markets, unusually attractive market opportunities emerge sporadically, often after long periods of relative calm—but future market conditions may be less foggy, thus facilitating good market reconnaissance and making emerging opportunities easier for industry members to detect. But in both volatile and stable markets, the rise of a golden opportunity is almost never under the control of a single company or manufactured by company executives—rather, it springs from the simultaneous alignment of several external factors. For instance, in China the recent upsurge in demand for motor vehicles was spawned by a convergence of many factors—increased disposable income, rising middle-class aspirations, a major road-building program by the government, the demise of employer-provided housing, and easy credit.[7] But golden opportunities are nearly always seized rapidly—and the companies that seize them are usually those that have been actively waiting, staying alert with diligent market reconnaissance, and preparing themselves to capitalize on shifting market conditions by patiently assembling an arsenal of competitively valuable resources—talented personnel, technical know-how, strategic partnerships, and a war chest of cash to finance aggressive action when the time comes.[8]

A company is well advised to pass on a particular market opportunity unless it has or can acquire the resources to capture it.

In evaluating a company's market opportunities and ranking their attractiveness, managers have to guard against viewing every *industry* opportunity as a *company* opportunity. Not every company is equipped with the resources to successfully pursue each opportunity that exists in its industry. Some companies are more capable of going after particular opportunities than others, and a few companies may be hopelessly outclassed. *The market opportunities most relevant to a company are those that match up well with the company's financial and organizational resource capabilities, offer the best growth and profitability, and present the most potential for competitive advantage.*

Identifying the External Threats to a Company's Future Profitability

Often, certain factors in a company's external environment pose *threats* to its profitability and competitive well-being. Threats can stem from the emergence of cheaper or better technologies, rivals' introduction of new or improved products, the entry of lower-cost foreign competitors into a company's market stronghold, new regulations that are more burdensome to a company than to its competitors, vulnerability to a rise in interest rates, the potential of a hostile takeover, unfavorable demographic shifts, adverse changes in foreign exchange rates, political upheaval in a foreign country where the company has facilities, and the like. A list of potential threats to a company's future profitability and market position is shown in Table 4.2.

External threats may pose no more than a moderate degree of adversity (all companies confront some threatening elements in the course of doing business), or they may be so imposing as to make a company's situation and outlook quite tenuous. On rare occasions, market shocks can give birth to a *sudden-death* threat that throws a company into an immediate crisis and battle to survive. Many of the world's major airlines have been plunged into unprecedented financial crisis by the perfect storm of the September 11, 2001, terrorist attacks, rising prices for jet fuel, mounting competition from low-fare carriers, shifting traveler preferences for low fares as opposed to lots of in-flight amenities, and out-of-control labor costs. It is management's job to identify the threats to the company's future prospects and to evaluate what strategic actions can be taken to neutralize or lessen their impact.

What Do the SWOT Listings Reveal?

SWOT analysis involves more than making four lists. The two most important parts of SWOT analysis are *drawing conclusions* from the SWOT listings about the company's overall situation, and *translating these conclusions into strategic actions* to better match the company's strategy to its resource strengths and market opportunities, to correct the important weaknesses, and to defend against external threats. Figure 4.2 shows the three steps of SWOT analysis.

> Simply making lists of a company's strengths, weaknesses, opportunities, and threats is not enough; the payoff from SWOT analysis comes from the conclusions about a company's situation and the implications for strategy improvement that flow from the four lists.

Just what story the SWOT listings tell about the company's overall situation is often revealed in the answers to the following sets of questions:

- Does the company have an attractive set of resource strengths? Does it have any strong core competencies or a distinctive competence? Are the company's strengths and capabilities well matched to the industry key success factors? Do they add adequate power to the company's strategy, or are more or different strengths needed? Will the company's current strengths and capabilities matter in the future?

- How serious are the company's weaknesses and competitive deficiencies? Are they mostly inconsequential and readily correctable, or could one or more prove fatal if not remedied soon? Are some of the company's weaknesses in areas that relate to the industry's key success factors? Are there any weaknesses that if uncorrected, would keep the company from pursuing an otherwise attractive opportunity? Does the company have important resource gaps that need to be filled for it to move up in the industry rankings and/or boost its profitability?

- Do the company's resource strengths and competitive capabilities (its competitive assets) outweigh its resource weaknesses and competitive deficiencies (its competitive liabilities) by an attractive margin?

- Does the company have attractive market opportunities that are well suited to its resource strengths and competitive capabilities? Does the company lack the resources and capabilities to pursue any of the most attractive opportunities?

- Are the threats alarming, or are they something the company appears able to deal with and defend against?

Figure 4.2 **The Three Steps of SWOT Analysis: Identify, Draw Conclusions, Translate into Strategic Action**

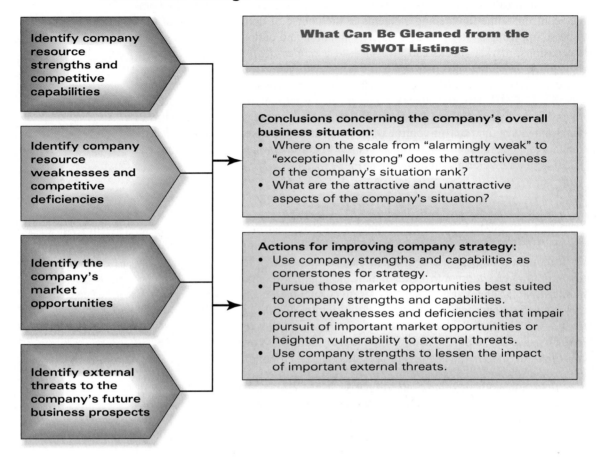

- All things considered, how strong is the company's overall situation? Where on a scale of 1 to 10 (1 being alarmingly weak and 10 exceptionally strong) should the firm's position and overall situation be ranked? What aspects of the company's situation are particularly attractive? What aspects are of the most concern?

The final piece of SWOT analysis is to translate the diagnosis of the company's situation into actions for improving the company's strategy and business prospects. The following questions point to implications the SWOT listings have for strategic action:

- Which competitive capabilities need to be strengthened immediately, so as to add greater power to the company's strategy and boost sales and profitability? Do new types of competitive capabilities need to be put in place to help the company better respond to emerging industry and competitive conditions? Which resources and capabilities need to be given greater emphasis, and which merit less emphasis? Should the company emphasize leveraging its existing resource strengths and capabilities, or does it need to create new resource strengths and capabilities?

- What actions should be taken to reduce the company's competitive liabilities? Which weaknesses or competitive deficiencies are in urgent need of correction?

- Which market opportunities should be top priority in future strategic initiatives (because they are good fits with the company's resource strengths and competitive capabilities, present attractive growth and profit prospects, and/or offer the best potential for securing competitive advantage)? Which opportunities should be ignored, at least for the time being (because they offer less growth potential or are not suited to the company's resources and capabilities)?
- What should the company be doing to guard against the threats to its well-being?

A company's resource strengths should generally form the cornerstones of strategy because they represent the company's best chance for market success.[9] As a rule, strategies that place heavy demands on areas where the company is weakest or has unproven ability are suspect and should be avoided. If a company doesn't have the resources and competitive capabilities around which to craft an attractive strategy, managers need to take decisive remedial action either to upgrade existing organizational resources and capabilities and add others as needed or to acquire them through partnerships or strategic alliances with firms possessing the needed expertise. Plainly, managers have to look toward correcting competitive weaknesses that make the company vulnerable, hold down profitability, or disqualify it from pursuing an attractive opportunity.

At the same time, sound strategy making requires sifting through the available market opportunities and aiming strategy at capturing those that are most attractive and suited to the company's circumstances. Rarely does a company have the resource depth to pursue all available market opportunities simultaneously without spreading itself too thin. How much attention to devote to defending against external threats to the company's market position and future performance hinges on how vulnerable the company is, whether there are attractive defensive moves that can be taken to lessen their impact, and whether the costs of undertaking such moves represent the best use of company resources.

QUESTION 3: ARE THE COMPANY'S PRICES AND COSTS COMPETITIVE?

Company managers are often stunned when a competitor cuts its price to "unbelievably low" levels or when a new market entrant comes on strong with a very low price. The competitor may not, however, be "dumping" (an economic term for selling at prices that are below cost), buying its way into the market with a super-low price, or waging a desperate move to gain sales—it may simply have substantially lower costs. One of the most telling signs of whether a company's business position is strong or precarious is whether its prices and costs are competitive with industry rivals. For a company to compete successfully, its costs must be *in line* with those of close rivals.

> The higher a company's costs are above those of close rivals, the more competitively vulnerable it becomes.

Price–cost comparisons are especially critical in a commodity-product industry where the value provided to buyers is the same from seller to seller, price competition is typically the ruling market force, and low-cost companies have the upper hand. But even in industries where products are differentiated and competition centers on the different attributes of competing brands as much as on price, rival companies have to keep their costs in line and make sure that any added costs they incur, and any price premiums they charge, create ample value that buyers are willing to pay extra for.

While some cost disparity is justified so long as the products or services of closely competing companies are sufficiently differentiated, a high-cost firm's market position becomes increasingly vulnerable the more its costs exceed those of close rivals.

Two analytical tools are particularly useful in determining whether a company's prices and costs are competitive: value chain analysis and benchmarking.

The Concept of a Company Value Chain

Core Concept
A company's *value chain* identifies the primary activities that create customer value and the related support activities.

Every company's business consists of a collection of activities undertaken in the course of designing, producing, marketing, delivering, and supporting its product or service. All of the various activities that a company performs internally combine to form a **value chain**—so called because the underlying intent of a company's activities is to do things that ultimately *create value for buyers*. A company's value chain also includes an allowance for profit because a markup over the cost of performing the firm's value-creating activities is customarily part of the price (or total cost) borne by buyers—unless an enterprise succeeds in creating and delivering sufficient value to buyers to produce an attractive profit, it can't survive for long.

As shown in Figure 4.3, a company's value chain consists of two broad categories of activities: the *primary activities* that are foremost in creating value for customers and the requisite *support activities* that facilitate and enhance the performance of the primary activities.[10] For example, the primary value-creating activities for a maker of bakery goods include supply chain management, recipe development and testing, mixing and baking, packaging, sales and marketing, and distribution; related support activities include quality control, human resource management, and administration. A wholesaler's primary activities and costs deal with merchandise selection and purchasing, inbound shipping and warehousing from suppliers, and outbound distribution to retail customers. The primary activities for a department store retailer include merchandise selection and buying, store layout and product display, advertising, and customer service; its support activities include site selection, hiring and training, and store maintenance, plus the usual assortment of administrative activities. A hotel chain's primary activities and costs are in site selection and construction, reservations, operation of its hotel properties (check-in and check-out, maintenance and housekeeping, dining and room service, and conventions and meetings), and managing its lineup of hotel locations; principal support activities include accounting, hiring and training hotel staff, advertising, building a brand and reputation, and general administration. Supply chain management is a crucial activity for Nissan and Amazon.com but is not a value chain component at Google or a TV and radio broadcasting company. Sales and marketing are dominant activities at Procter & Gamble and Sony but have minor roles at oil drilling companies and natural gas pipeline companies. Delivery to buyers is a crucial activity at Domino's Pizza but comparatively insignificant at Starbucks. Thus, what constitutes a primary or secondary activity varies according to the specific nature of a company's business, meaning that you should view the listing of the primary and support activities in Figure 4.3 as illustrative rather than definitive.

A Company's Primary and Support Activities Identify the Major Components of Its Cost Structure   Segregating a company's operations into different types of primary and support activities is the first step in understanding its cost structure. Each activity in the value chain gives rise to costs and ties up assets.

Figure 4.3 **A Representative Company Value Chain**

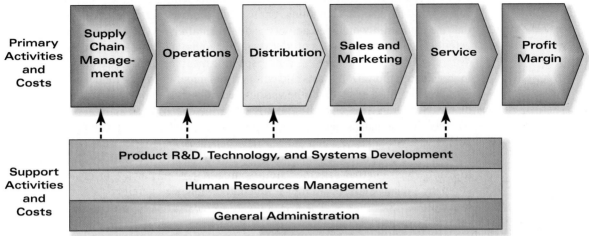

PRIMARY ACTIVITIES

- **Supply chain management**—activities, costs, and assets associated with purchasing fuel, energy, raw materials, parts and components, merchandise, and consumable items from vendors; receiving, storing, and disseminating inputs from suppliers; inspection; and inventory management.

- **Operations**—activities, costs, and assets associated with converting inputs into final product from (production, assembly, packaging, equipment maintenance, facilities, operations, quality assurance, environmental protection).

- **Distribution**—activities, costs, and assets dealing with physically distributing the product to buyers (finished goods warehousing, order processing, order picking and packing, shipping, delivery vehicle operations, establishing and maintaining a network of dealers and distributors).

- **Sales and marketing**—activities, costs, and assets related to sales force efforts, advertising and promotion, market research and planning, and dealer/distributor support.

- **Service**—activities, costs, and assets associated with providing assistance to buyers, such as installation, spare parts delivery, maintenance and repair, technical assistance, buyer inquiries, and complaints.

SUPPORT ACTIVITIES

- **Product R&D, technology, and systems development**—activities, costs, and assets relating to product R&D, process R&D, process design improvement, equipment design, computer software development, telecommunications systems, computer-assisted design and engineering, database capabilities, and development of computerized support systems.

- **Human resources management**—activities, costs, and assets associated with the recruitment, hiring, training, development, and compensation of all types of personnel; labor relations activities; and development of knowledge-based skills and core competencies.

- **General administration**—activities, costs, and assets relating to general management, accounting and finance, legal and regulatory affairs, safety and security, management information systems, forming strategic alliances and collaborating with strategic partners, and other overhead functions.

Source: Based on the discussion in Michael E. Porter, *Competitive Advantage* (New York: Free Press, 1985), pp. 37–43.

Assigning the company's operating costs and assets to each individual activity in the chain provides cost estimates and capital requirements—a process that accountants call activity-based cost accounting. Quite often, there are links between activities such that the manner in which one activity is done can affect the costs of performing other activities. For instance, how a product is designed has a huge impact on the number of different parts and components, their respective manufacturing costs, and the expense of assembling the various parts and components into a finished product.

The combined costs of all the various activities in a company's value chain define the company's internal cost structure. Further, the cost of each activity contributes to whether the company's overall cost position relative to rivals is favorable or unfavorable. The tasks of value chain analysis and benchmarking are to develop the data for comparing a company's costs activity-by-activity against the costs of key rivals and to learn which internal activities are a source of cost advantage or disadvantage. A company's relative cost position is a function of how the overall costs of the activities it performs in conducting business compare to the overall costs of the activities performed by rivals.

Why the Value Chains of Rival Companies Often Differ

A company's value chain and the manner in which it performs each activity reflect the evolution of its own particular business and internal operations, its strategy, the approaches it is using to execute its strategy, and the underlying economics of the activities themselves.[11] Because these factors differ from company to company, the value chains of rival companies sometimes differ substantially—a condition that complicates the task of assessing rivals' relative cost positions. For instance, music retailers like Blockbuster and Musicland, which purchase CDs from recording studios and wholesale distributors and sell them in their own retail store locations, have value chains and cost structures different from those of rival online music stores like Apple's iTunes and Musicmatch, which sell downloadable music files directly to music shoppers. Competing companies may differ in their degrees of vertical integration. The operations component of the value chain for a manufacturer that *makes* all of its own parts and assembles them into a finished product differs from the operations component of a rival producer that *buys* the needed parts from outside suppliers and performs assembly operations only. Likewise, there is legitimate reason to expect value chain and cost differences between a company that is pursuing a low-cost/low-price strategy and a rival that is positioned on the high end of the market. The costs of certain activities along the low-cost company's value chain should indeed be relatively low, whereas the high-end firm may understandably be spending relatively more to perform those activities that create the added quality and extra features of its products.

Moreover, cost and price differences among rival companies can have their origins in activities performed by suppliers or by distribution channel allies involved in getting the product to end users. Suppliers or wholesale/retail dealers may have excessively high cost structures or profit margins that jeopardize a company's cost-competitiveness even though its costs for internally performed activities are competitive. For example, when determining Michelin's cost-competitiveness vis-à-vis Goodyear and Bridgestone in supplying replacement tires to vehicle owners, we have to look at more than whether Michelin's tire manufacturing costs are above or below Goodyear's and Bridgestone's. Let's say that a motor vehicle owner looking for a new set of tires has to pay $400 for a set of Michelin tires and only $350 for a set of Goodyear or Bridgestone tires. Michelin's $50 price disadvantage can stem not only from higher manufacturing costs (reflecting, perhaps, the added costs of Michelin's strategic efforts to build a better-quality tire with more performance features) but also from (1) differences in what the three tire makers pay their suppliers for materials and tire-making components, and (2) differences in the operating efficiencies, costs, and markups of Michelin's wholesale–retail dealer outlets versus those of Goodyear and Bridgestone.

The Value Chain System for an Entire Industry

As the tire industry example makes clear, a company's value chain is embedded in a larger system of activities that includes the value chains of its suppliers and the value chains of whatever distribution channel allies it uses in getting its product or service to end users.[12] Suppliers' value chains are relevant because suppliers perform activities and incur costs in creating and delivering the purchased inputs used in a company's own value-creating activities. The costs, performance features, and quality of these inputs influence a company's own costs and product differentiation capabilities. Anything a company can do to help its suppliers' drive down the costs of their value chain activities or improve the quality and performance of the items being supplied can enhance its own competitiveness—a powerful reason for working collaboratively with suppliers in managing supply chain activities.[13]

The value chains of forward channel partners and/or the customers to whom a company sells are relevant because (1) the costs and margins of a company's distributors and retail dealers are part of the price the ultimate consumer pays, and (2) the activities that distribution allies perform affect customer satisfaction. For these reasons, companies normally work closely with their forward channel allies (who are their direct customers) to perform value chain activities in mutually beneficial ways. For instance, motor vehicle manufacturers work closely with their local automobile dealers to keep the retail prices of their vehicles competitive with rivals' models and to ensure that owners are satisfied with dealers' repair and maintenance services. Some aluminum can producers have constructed plants next to beer breweries and deliver cans on overhead conveyors directly to the breweries' can-filling lines; this has resulted in significant savings in production scheduling, shipping, and inventory costs for both container producers and breweries.[14] Many automotive parts suppliers have built plants near the auto assembly plants they supply to facilitate just-in-time deliveries, reduce warehousing and shipping costs, and promote close collaboration on parts design and production scheduling. Irrigation equipment companies, suppliers of grape-harvesting and winemaking equipment, and firms making barrels, wine bottles, caps, corks, and labels all have facilities in the California wine country to be close to the nearly 700 winemakers they supply.[15] The lesson here is that a company's value chain activities are often closely linked to the value chains of their suppliers and the forward allies or customers to whom they sell.

As a consequence, *accurately assessing a company's competitiveness from the perspective of the consumers who ultimately use its products or services thus requires that company managers understand an industry's entire value chain system for delivering a product or service to customers, not just the company's own value chain.* A typical industry value chain that incorporates the value chains of suppliers and forward channel allies (if any) is shown in Figure 4.4. However, industry value chains

> A company's cost-competitiveness depends not only on the costs of internally performed activities (its own value chain) but also on costs in the value chains of its suppliers and forward channel allies.

Figure 4.4 **Representative Value Chain for an Entire Industry**

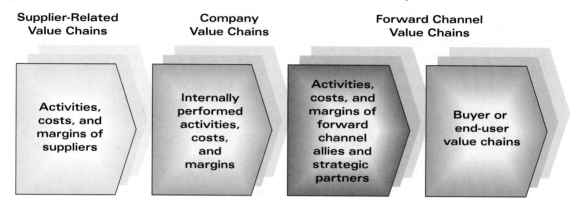

Source: Based in part on the single-industry value chain displayed in Michael E. Porter, *Competitive Advantage* (New York: Free Press, 1985), p. 35.

vary significantly by industry. The primary value chain activities in the pulp and paper industry (timber farming, logging, pulp mills, and papermaking) differ from the primary value chain activities in the home appliance industry (parts and components manufacture, assembly, wholesale distribution, retail sales). The value chain for the soft-drink industry (processing of basic ingredients and syrup manufacture, bottling and can filling, wholesale distribution, advertising, and retail merchandising) differs from that for the computer software industry (programming, disk loading, marketing, distribution). Producers of bathroom and kitchen faucets depend heavily on the activities of wholesale distributors and building supply retailers in winning sales to homebuilders and do-it-yourselfers, but producers of papermaking machines internalize their distribution activities by selling directly to the operators of paper plants. Illustration Capsule 4.1 shows representative costs for various activities performed by the producers and marketers of music CDs.

Activity-Based Costing: A Tool for Assessing a Company's Cost Competitiveness

Once the company has identified its major value chain activities, the next step in evaluating its cost competitiveness involves determining the costs of performing specific value chain activities, using what accountants call activity-based costing.[16] Traditional accounting identifies costs according to broad categories of expenses—wages and salaries, employee benefits, supplies, maintenance, utilities, travel, depreciation, R&D, interest, general administration, and so on. But activity-based cost accounting involves establishing expense categories for specific value chain activities and assigning costs to the activity responsible for creating the cost. An illustrative example is shown in Table 4.3. Perhaps 25 percent of the companies that have explored the feasibility of activity-based costing have adopted this accounting approach.

Illustration Capsule 4.1

Estimated Value Chain Costs for Recording and Distributing Music CDs through Traditional Music Retailers

The following table presents the representative costs and markups associated with producing and distributing a music CD retailing for $15 in music stores (as opposed to Internet sources).

Value Chain Activities and Costs in Producing and Distributing a CD		
1. Record company direct production costs:		$2.40
Artists and repertoire	$0.75	
Pressing of CD and packaging	1.65	
2. Royalties		0.99
3. Record company marketing expenses		1.50
4. Record company overhead		1.50
5. Total record company costs		6.39
6. Record company's operating profit		1.86
7. Record company's selling price to distributor/wholesaler		8.25
8. Average wholesale distributor markup to cover distribution activities and profit margins		1.50
9. Average wholesale price charged to retailer		9.75
10. Average retail markup over wholesale cost		5.25
11. Average price to consumer at retail		$15.00

Source: Developed from information in "Fight the Power," a case study prepared by Adrian Aleyne, Babson College, 1999.

The degree to which a company's costs should be disaggregated into specific activities depends on how valuable it is to develop cross-company cost comparisons for narrowly defined activities as opposed to broadly defined activities. Generally speaking, cost estimates are needed at least for each broad category of primary and secondary activities, but finer classifications may be needed if a company discovers that it has a cost disadvantage vis-à-vis rivals and wants to pin down the exact source or activity causing the cost disadvantage. It can also be necessary to develop cost estimates for activities performed in the competitively relevant portions of suppliers' and customers' value chains—which requires going to outside sources for reliable cost information.

Once a company has developed good cost estimates for each of the major activities in its value chain, and perhaps has cost estimates for subactivities within each primary/ secondary value chain activity, then it is ready to see how its costs for these activities compare with the costs of rival firms. This is where benchmarking comes in.

Table 4.3   **The Difference between Traditional Cost Accounting and Activity-Based Cost Accounting: A Supply Chain Activity Example**

Traditional Cost Accounting Categories for Supply Chain Activities		Cost of Performing Specific Supply Chain Activities Using Activity-Based Cost Accounting	
Wages and salaries	$450,000	Evaluate supplier capabilities	$150,000
Employee benefits	95,000	Process purchase orders	92,000
Supplies	21,500	Collaborate with suppliers on just-in-time deliveries	180,000
Travel	12,250		
Depreciation	19,000	Share data with suppliers	69,000
Other fixed charges (office space, utilities)	112,000	Check quality of items purchased	94,000
Miscellaneous operating expenses	40,250	Check incoming deliveries against purchase orders	50,000
	$750,000	Resolve disputes	15,000
		Conduct internal administration	100,000
			$750,000

Source: Developed from information in Terence P. Par, "A New Tool for Managing Costs," *Fortune,* June 14, 1993, pp. 124–29.

Benchmarking: A Tool for Assessing Whether a Company's Value Chain Costs Are in Line

Core Concept
Benchmarking is a potent tool for learning which companies are best at performing particular activities and then using their techniques (or "best practices") to improve the cost and effectiveness of a company's own internal activities.

Many companies today are **benchmarking** their costs of performing a given activity against competitors' costs (and/or against the costs of a noncompetitor that efficiently and effectively performs much the same activity in another industry). *Benchmarking is a tool that allows a company to determine whether its performance of a particular function or activity represents the "best practice" when both cost and effectiveness are taken into account.*

Benchmarking entails comparing how different companies perform various value chain activities—how materials are purchased, how suppliers are paid, how inventories are managed, how products are assembled, how fast the company can get new products to market, how the quality control function is performed, how customer orders are filled and shipped, how employees are trained, how payrolls are processed, and how maintenance is performed—and then making cross-company comparisons of the costs of these activities.[17] The objectives of benchmarking are to identify the best practices in performing an activity, to learn how other companies have actually achieved lower costs or better results in performing benchmarked activities, and to take action to improve a company's competitiveness whenever benchmarking reveals that its costs and results of performing an activity are not on a par with what other companies (either competitors or noncompetitors) have achieved.

Xerox became one of the first companies to use benchmarking when, in 1979, Japanese manufacturers began selling midsize copiers in the United States for $9,600 each—less than Xerox's production costs.[18] Xerox management suspected its Japanese competitors were dumping, but it sent a team of line managers to Japan, including the head of manufacturing, to study competitors' business processes and costs. With the aid of Xerox's joint venture partner in Japan, Fuji-Xerox, which knew the competitors well, the team found that Xerox's costs were excessive due to gross inefficiencies in the company's manufacturing processes and business practices. The findings triggered a major internal effort at Xerox to become cost-competitive and prompted Xerox to begin benchmarking 67 of its key work processes against companies identified as employing the best practices. Xerox quickly decided not to restrict its benchmarking efforts to its office equipment rivals but to extend them to any company regarded as world class in performing *any activity* relevant to Xerox's business. Other companies quickly picked up on Xerox's approach. Toyota managers got their idea for just-in-time inventory deliveries by studying how U.S. supermarkets replenished their shelves. Southwest Airlines reduced the turnaround time of its aircraft at each scheduled stop by studying pit crews on the auto racing circuit. Over 80 percent of Fortune 500 companies reportedly use benchmarking for comparing themselves against rivals on cost and other competitively important measures.

The tough part of benchmarking is not whether to do it, but rather how to gain access to information about other companies' practices and costs. Sometimes benchmarking can be accomplished by collecting information from published reports, trade groups, and industry research firms and by talking to knowledgeable industry analysts, customers, and suppliers. Sometimes field trips to the facilities of competing or noncompeting companies can be arranged to observe how things are done, ask questions, compare practices and processes, and perhaps exchange data on productivity, staffing levels, time requirements, and other cost components—but the problem here is that such companies, even if they agree to host facilities tours and answer questions, are unlikely to share competitively sensitive cost information. Furthermore, comparing one company's costs to another's costs may not involve comparing apples to apples if the two companies employ different cost accounting principles to calculate the costs of particular activities.

> Benchmarking the costs of company activities against rivals provides hard evidence of whether a company is cost-competitive.

However, a third and fairly reliable source of benchmarking information has emerged. The explosive interest of companies in benchmarking costs and identifying best practices has prompted consulting organizations (e.g., Accenture, A. T. Kearney, Benchnet—The Benchmarking Exchange, Towers Perrin, and Best Practices) and several councils and associations (e.g., the American Productivity and Quality Center, the Qualserve Benchmarking Clearinghouse, and the Strategic Planning Institute's Council on Benchmarking) to gather benchmarking data, distribute information about best practices, and provide comparative cost data without identifying the names of particular companies. Having an independent group gather the information and report it in a manner that disguises the names of individual companies avoid having the disclosure of competitively sensitive data and lessens the potential for unethical behavior on the part of company personnel in gathering their own data about competitors.Illustration Capsule 4.2 presents a widely recommended code of conduct for engaging in benchmarking that is intended to help companies avoid any improprieties in gathering and using benchmarking data.

Strategic Options for Remedying a Cost Disadvantage

Value chain analysis and benchmarking can reveal a great deal about a firm's cost competitiveness. Examining the costs of a company's own value chain activities and comparing them to rivals' indicates who has how much of a cost advantage or

Illustration Capsule 4.2

Benchmarking and Ethical Conduct

Because discussions between benchmarking partners can involve competitively sensitive data, conceivably raising questions about possible restraint of trade or improper business conduct, many benchmarking organizations urge all individuals and organizations involved in benchmarking to abide by a code of conduct grounded in ethical business behavior. Among the most widely used codes of conduct is the one developed by the American Productivity and Quality Center and advocated by the Qualserve Benchmarking Clearinghouse; it is based on the following principles and guidelines:

- Avoid discussions or actions that could lead to or imply an interest in restraint of trade, market and/or customer allocation schemes, price fixing, dealing arrangements, bid rigging, or bribery. Don't discuss costs with competitors if costs are an element of pricing.

- Refrain from the acquisition of trade secrets from another by any means that could be interpreted as improper including the breach or inducement of a breach of any duty to maintain secrecy. Do not disclose or use any trade secret that may have been obtained through improper means or that was disclosed by another in violation of duty to maintain its secrecy or limit its use.

- Be willing to provide the same type and level of information that you request from your benchmarking partner to your benchmarking partner.

- Communicate fully and early in the relationship to clarify expectations, avoid misunderstanding, and establish mutual interest in the benchmarking exchange.

- Be honest and complete.

- Treat benchmarking interchange as confidential to the individuals and companies involved. Information must not be communicated outside the partnering organizations without the prior consent of the benchmarking partner who shared the information.

- Use information obtained through benchmarking only for purposes stated to the benchmarking partner.

- The use or communication of a benchmarking partner's name with the data obtained or practices observed requires the prior permission of that partner.

- Respect the corporate culture of partner companies and work within mutually agreed-on procedures.

- Use benchmarking contacts designated by the partner company, if that is the company's preferred procedure.

- Obtain mutual agreement with the designated benchmarking contact on any hand-off of communication or responsibility to other parties.

- Make the most of your benchmarking partner's time by being fully prepared for each exchange.

- Help your benchmarking partners prepare by providing them with a questionnaire and agenda prior to benchmarking visits.

- Follow through with each commitment made to your benchmarking partner in a timely manner.

- Understand how your benchmarking partner would like to have the information he or she provides handled and used, and handle and use it in that manner.

Note: Identification of firms, organizations, and contacts visited is prohibited without advance approval from the organization.

Sources: The American Productivity and Quality Center, www.apqc.org, and the Qualserve Benchmarking Clearinghouse, www.awwa.org (accessed September 14, 2005).

disadvantage and which cost components are responsible. Such information is vital in strategic actions to eliminate a cost disadvantage or create a cost advantage. One of the fundamental insights of value chain analysis and benchmarking is that *a company's competitiveness on cost depends on how efficiently it manages its value chain activities relative to how well competitors manage theirs.*[19] There are three main areas in a company's overall value chain where important differences in the costs of competing firms can occur: a company's own activity segments, suppliers' part of the industry value chain, and the forward channel portion of the industry chain.

Remedying an Internal Cost Disadvantage   When a company's cost disadvantage stems from performing internal value chain activities at a higher cost than key rivals, then managers can pursue any of several strategic approaches to restore cost parity:[20]

1. Implement the use of best practices throughout the company, particularly for high-cost activities.

2. Try to eliminate some cost-producing activities altogether by revamping the value chain. Examples include cutting out low-value-added activities or bypassing the value chains and associated costs of distribution allies and marketing directly to end users. Dell has used this approach in PCs, and airlines have begun bypassing travel agents by getting passengers to purchase their tickets directly at airline Web sites.

3. Relocate high-cost activities (such as manufacturing) to geographic areas—such as China, Latin America, or Eastern Europe—where they can be performed more cheaply.

4. See if certain internally performed activities can be outsourced from vendors or performed by contractors more cheaply than they can be done in-house.

5. Invest in productivity-enhancing, cost-saving technological improvements (robotics, flexible manufacturing techniques, state-of-the-art electronic networking).

6. Find ways to detour around the activities or items where costs are high—computer chip makers regularly design around the patents held by others to avoid paying royalties; automakers have substituted lower-cost plastic and rubber for metal at many exterior body locations.

7. Redesign the product and/or some of its components to facilitate speedier and more economical manufacture or assembly.

8. Try to make up the internal cost disadvantage by reducing costs in the supplier or forward channel portions of the industry value chain—usually a last resort.

Remedying a Supplier-Related Cost Disadvantage   Supplier-related cost disadvantages can be attacked by pressuring suppliers for lower prices, switching to lower-priced substitute inputs, and collaborating closely with suppliers to identify mutual cost-saving opportunities.[21] For example, just-in-time deliveries from suppliers can lower a company's inventory and internal logistics costs and may also allow its suppliers to economize on their warehousing, shipping, and production scheduling costs—a win–win outcome for both. In a few instances, companies may find that it is cheaper to integrate backward into the business of high-cost suppliers and make the item in-house instead of buying it from outsiders. If a company strikes out in wringing savings out of its high-cost supply chain activities, then it must resort to finding cost savings either in-house or in the forward channel portion of the industry value chain to offset its supplier-related cost disadvantage.

Remedying a Cost Disadvantage Associated with Activities Performed by Forward Channel Allies   There are three main ways to combat a cost disadvantage in the forward portion of the industry value chain:

1. Pressure dealer-distributors and other forward channel allies to reduce their costs and markups so as to make the final price to buyers more competitive with the prices of rivals.

2. Work closely with forward channel allies to identify win–win opportunities to reduce costs. For example, a chocolate manufacturer learned that by shipping its bulk chocolate in liquid form in tank cars instead of 10-pound molded bars, it could not only save its candy bar manufacturing customers the costs associated with unpacking and melting but also eliminate its own costs of molding bars and packing them.

3. Change to a more economical distribution strategy, including switching to cheaper distribution channels (perhaps direct sales via the Internet) or perhaps integrating forward into company-owned retail outlets.

If these efforts fail, the company can either try to live with the cost disadvantage or pursue cost-cutting earlier in the value chain system.

Translating Proficient Performance of Value Chain Activities into Competitive Advantage

Performing value chain activities in ways that give a company the capabilities to either outmatch the competencies and capabilities of rivals or else beat them on costs are two good ways to secure competitive advantage.

A company that does a *first-rate job* of managing its value chain activities *relative to competitors* stands a good chance of achieving sustainable competitive advantage. As shown in Figure 4.5, outmanaging rivals in performing value chain activities can be accomplished in either or both of two ways: (1) by astutely developing core competencies and maybe a distinctive competence that rivals don't have or can't quite match and that are instrumental in helping it deliver attractive value to customers, and/or (2) by simply doing an overall better job than rivals of lowering its combined costs of performing all the various value chain activities, such that it ends up with a low-cost advantage over rivals.

The first of these two approaches begins with management efforts to build more organizational expertise in performing certain competitively important value chain activities, deliberately striving to develop competencies and capabilities that add power to its strategy and competitiveness. If management begins to make selected competencies and capabilities cornerstones of its strategy and continues to invest resources in building greater and greater proficiency in performing them, then over time one (or maybe several) of the targeted competencies/capabilities may rise to the level of a core competence. Later, following additional organizational learning and investments in gaining still greater proficiency, a core competence could evolve into a distinctive competence, giving the company superiority over rivals in performing an important value chain activity. Such superiority, if it gives the company significant competitive clout in the marketplace, can produce an attractive competitive edge over rivals and, more important, prove difficult for rivals to match or offset with competencies and capabilities of their own making. As a general rule, it is substantially harder for rivals to achieve best-in-industry proficiency in performing a key value chain activity than it is for them to clone the features and attributes of a hot-selling product or service.[22] This is especially true when a company with a distinctive competence avoids becoming complacent and works diligently to maintain its industry-leading expertise and capability. GlaxoSmithKline, one of the world's most competitively capable pharmaceutical companies, has built its business position around expert performance of a few competitively crucial activities: extensive R&D to achieve first discovery of new drugs, a carefully constructed approach to patenting, skill in gaining rapid and thorough clinical clearance through regulatory bodies, and unusually strong distribution and sales-force

Figure 4.5   **Translating Company Performance of Value Chain Activities into Competitive Advantage**

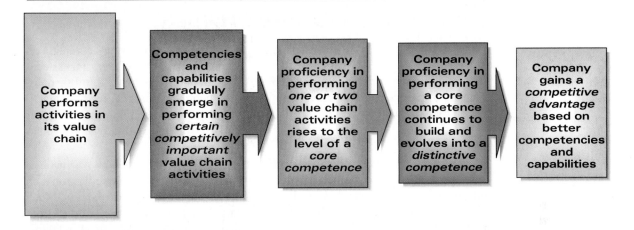

Option 1: Beat rivals in performing value chain activities more proficiently

Company performs activities in its value chain → Competencies and capabilities gradually emerge in performing *certain competitively important* value chain activities → Company proficiency in performing *one or two* value chain activities rises to the level of a *core competence* → Company proficiency in performing a core competence continues to build and evolves into a *distinctive competence* → Company gains a *competitive advantage* based on better competencies and capabilities

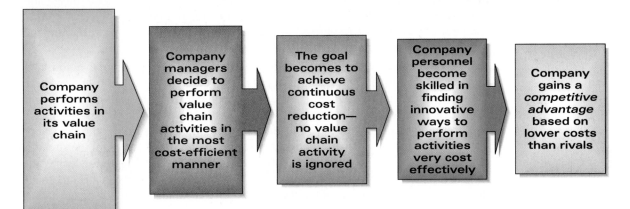

Option 2: Beat rivals in performing value chain activities more cheaply

Company performs activities in its value chain → Company managers decide to perform value chain activities in the most cost-efficient manner → The goal becomes to achieve continuous cost reduction— no value chain activity is ignored → Company personnel become skilled in finding innovative ways to perform activities very cost effectively → Company gains a *competitive advantage* based on lower costs than rivals

capabilities.[23] FedEx's astute management of its value chain has produced unmatched competencies and capabilities in overnight package delivery.

The second approach to building competitive advantage entails determined management efforts to be cost-efficient in performing value chain activities. Such efforts have to be ongoing and persistent, and they have to involve each and every value chain activity. The goal must be continuous cost reduction, not a one-time or on-again/off-again effort. Companies whose managers are truly committed to low-cost performance of value chain activities and succeed in engaging company personnel to discover innovative ways to drive costs out of the business have a real chance of gaining a durable low-cost edge over rivals. It is not as easy as it seems to imitate a company's low-cost practices. Companies like Wal-Mart, Dell, Nucor Steel, Southwest Airlines,

Toyota, and French discount retailer Carrefour have been highly successful in managing their values chains in a low-cost manner.

QUESTION 4: IS THE COMPANY COMPETITIVELY STRONGER OR WEAKER THAN KEY RIVALS?

Using value chain analysis and benchmarking to determine a company's competitiveness on price is necessary but not sufficient. A more comprehensive assessment needs to be made of the company's overall competitive strength. The answers to two questions are of particular interest: First, how does the company rank relative to competitors on each of the important factors that determine market success? Second, all things considered, does the company have a net competitive advantage or disadvantage versus major competitors?

An easy-to-use method for answering the two questions posed above involves developing quantitative strength ratings for the company and its key competitors on each industry key success factor and each competitively pivotal resource capability. Much of the information needed for doing a competitive strength assessment comes from previous analyses. Industry and competitive analysis reveals the key success factors and competitive capabilities that separate industry winners from losers. Benchmarking data and scouting key competitors provide a basis for judging the competitive strength of rivals on such factors as cost, key product attributes, customer service, image and reputation, financial strength, technological skills, distribution capability, and other competitively important resources and capabilities. SWOT analysis reveals how the company in question stacks up on these same strength measures.

Step 1 in doing a competitive strength assessment is to make a list of the industry's key success factors and most telling measures of competitive strength or weakness (6 to 10 measures usually suffice). Step 2 is to rate the firm and its rivals on each factor. Numerical rating scales (e.g., from 1 to 10) are best to use, although ratings of stronger ($+$), weaker ($-$), and about equal ($=$) may be appropriate when information is scanty and assigning numerical scores conveys false precision. Step 3 is to sum the strength ratings on each factor to get an overall measure of competitive strength for each company being rated. Step 4 is to use the overall strength ratings to draw conclusions about the size and extent of the company's net competitive advantage or disadvantage and to take specific note of areas of strength and weakness.

Table 4.5 provides two examples of competitive strength assessment, using the hypothetical ABC Company against four rivals. The first example employs an *unweighted rating system*. With unweighted ratings, each key success factor/competitive strength measure is assumed to be equally important (a rather dubious assumption). Whichever company has the highest strength rating on a given measure has an implied competitive edge on that factor; the size of its edge is mirrored in the margin of difference between its rating and the ratings assigned to rivals—a rating of 9 for one company versus ratings of 5, 4, and 3, respectively, for three other companies indicates a bigger advantage than a rating of 9 versus ratings of 8, 7, and 6. Summing a company's ratings on all the measures produces an overall strength rating. The higher a company's overall strength rating, the stronger its overall competitiveness versus rivals. The bigger the difference between a company's overall rating and the scores of *lower-rated* rivals, the greater its implied *net competitive advantage.* Conversely, the bigger the difference between a company's overall rating and the scores of *higher-rated* rivals, the greater its implied

Table 4.5 Illustrations of Unweighted and Weighted Competitive Strength Assessments

A. An Unweighted Competitive Strength Assessment

Key Success Factor/Strength Measure	ABC Co.	Strength Rating (Scale: 1 = Very weak; 10 = Very strong)			
		Rival 1	Rival 2	Rival 3	Rival 4
Quality/product performance	8	5	10	1	6
Reputation/image	8	7	10	1	6
Manufacturing capability	2	10	4	5	1
Technological skills	10	1	7	3	8
Dealer network/distribution capability	9	4	10	5	1
New product innovation capability	9	4	10	5	1
Financial resources	5	10	7	3	1
Relative cost position	5	10	3	1	4
Customer service capabilities	5	7	10	1	4
Unweighted overall strength rating	**61**	**58**	**71**	**25**	**32**

B. A Weighted Competitive Strength Assessment
(Rating Scale: 1 = Very weak; 10 = Very strong)

Key Success Factor/Strength Measure	Importance Weight	ABC Co.		Rival 1		Rival 2		Rival 3		Rival 4	
		Strength Rating	Score	Strength Rating	Score	Strength Rating	Score	Strength Rating	Score	Strength Rating	Score
Quality/product performance	0.10	8	0.80	5	0.50	10	1.00	1	0.10	6	0.60
Reputation/image	0.10	8	0.80	7	0.70	10	1.00	1	0.10	6	0.60
Manufacturing capability	0.10	2	0.20	10	1.00	4	0.40	5	0.50	1	0.10
Technological skills	0.05	10	0.50	1	0.05	7	0.35	3	0.15	8	0.40
Dealer network/distribution capability	0.05	9	0.45	4	0.20	10	0.50	5	0.25	1	0.05
New product innovation capability	0.05	9	0.45	4	0.20	10	0.50	5	0.25	1	0.05
Financial resources	0.10	5	0.50	10	1.00	7	0.70	3	0.30	1	0.10
Relative cost position	0.30	5	1.50	10	3.00	3	0.95	1	0.30	4	1.20
Customer service capabilities	0.15	5	0.75	7	1.05	10	1.50	1	0.15	4	0.60
Sum of importance weights	1.00										
Weighted overall strength rating		61	**5.95**	58	**7.70**	71	**6.85**	25	**2.10**	32	**3.70**

net competitive disadvantage. Thus, ABC's total score of 61 (see the top half of Table 4.5) signals a much greater net competitive advantage over Rival 4 (with a score of 32) than over Rival 1 (with a score of 58) but indicates a moderate net competitive disadvantage against Rival 2 (with an overall score of 71).

However, a better method is a *weighted rating system* (shown in the bottom half of Table 4.5) because the different measures of competitive strength are unlikely to be equally important. In an industry where the products/services of rivals are virtually identical, for instance, having low unit costs relative to rivals is nearly always the most important determinant of competitive strength. In an industry with strong product differentiation, the most significant measures of competitive strength

> A weighted competitive strength analysis is conceptually stronger than an unweighted analysis because of the inherent weakness in assuming that all the strength measures are equally important.

may be brand awareness, amount of advertising, product attractiveness, and distribution capability. In a weighted rating system each measure of competitive strength is assigned a weight based on its perceived importance in shaping competitive success. A weight could be as high as 0.75 (maybe even higher) in situations where one particular competitive variable is overwhelmingly decisive, or a weight could be as low as 0.20 when two or three strength measures are more important than the rest. Lesser competitive strength indicators can carry weights of 0.05 or 0.10. No matter whether the differences between the importance weights are big or little, *the sum of the weights must equal 1.0.*

Weighted strength ratings are calculated by rating each competitor on each strength measure (using the 1 to 10 rating scale) and multiplying the assigned rating by the assigned weight (a rating of 4 times a weight of 0.20 gives a weighted rating, or score, of 0.80). Again, the company with the highest rating on a given measure has an implied competitive edge on that measure, with the size of its edge reflected in the difference between its rating and rivals' ratings. The weight attached to the measure indicates how important the edge is. Summing a company's weighted strength ratings for all the measures yields an overall strength rating. Comparisons of the weighted overall strength scores indicate which competitors are in the strongest and weakest competitive positions and who has how big a net competitive advantage over whom.

Note in Table 4.5 that the unweighted and weighted rating schemes produce different orderings of the companies. In the weighted system, ABC Company drops from second to third in strength, and Rival 1 jumps from third to first because of its high strength ratings on the two most important factors. Weighting the importance of the strength measures can thus make a significant difference in the outcome of the assessment.

Interpreting the Competitive Strength Assessments

Competitive strength assessments provide useful conclusions about a company's competitive situation. The ratings show how a company compares against rivals, factor by factor or capability by capability, thus revealing where it is strongest and weakest, and against whom. Moreover, the overall competitive strength scores indicate how all the different factors add up—whether the company is at a net competitive advantage or disadvantage against each rival. The firm with the largest overall competitive strength rating enjoys the strongest competitive position, with the size of its net competitive advantage reflected by how much its score exceeds the scores of rivals.

> High competitive strength ratings signal a strong competitive position and possession of competitive advantage; low ratings signal a weak position and competitive disadvantage.

In addition, the strength ratings provide guidelines for designing wise offensive and defensive strategies. For example, consider the ratings and weighted scores in the bottom half of Table 4.5. If ABC Company wants to go on the offensive to win additional sales and market share, such an offensive probably needs to be aimed directly at winning customers away from Rivals 3 and 4 (which have lower overall strength scores) rather than Rivals 1 and 2 (which have higher overall strength scores). Moreover, while ABC has high ratings for quality/product performance (an 8 rating), reputation/image (an 8 rating), technological skills (a 10 rating), dealer network/distribution capability (a 9 rating), and new product innovation capability (a 9 rating), these strength measures have low importance weights—meaning that ABC has strengths in areas that don't translate into much competitive clout in the marketplace. Even so, it outclasses Rival 3 in all five areas, plus it enjoys lower costs than Rival 3: On relative cost position ABC has a 5 rating versus a 1 rating for Rival 3—and relative cost position carries the highest importance weight of all the strength measures. ABC also has greater competitive strength than Rival 3 as concerns customer service capabilities (which carries the second-highest importance weight). Hence, because ABC's strengths are in the very areas where Rival 3 is weak, ABC is in good position to attack Rival 3—it may well be able to persuade a number of Rival 3's customers to switch their purchases over to ABC's product.

But in mounting an offensive to win customers away from Rival 3, ABC should note that Rival 1 has an excellent relative cost position—its rating of 10, combined with the importance weight of 0.30 for relative cost, means that Rival 1 has meaningfully lower costs in an industry where low costs are competitively important. Rival 1 is thus strongly positioned to retaliate against ABC with lower prices if ABC's strategy offensive ends up drawing customers away from Rival 1. Moreover, Rival 1's very strong relative cost position vis-à-vis all the other companies arms it with the ability to use its lower-cost advantage to underprice all of its rivals and gain sales and market share at their expense. If ABC wants to defend against its vulnerability to potential price cutting by Rival 1, then it needs to aim a portion of its strategy at lowering its costs.

> A company's competitive strength scores pinpoint its strengths and weaknesses against rivals and point directly to the kinds of offensive/defensive actions it can use to exploit its competitive strengths and reduce its competitive vulnerabilities.

The point here is that a competitively astute company should use the strength assessment in deciding what strategic moves to make—which strengths to exploit in winning business away from rivals and which competitive weaknesses to try to correct. When a company has important competitive strengths in areas where one or more rivals are weak, it makes sense to consider offensive moves to exploit rivals' competitive weaknesses. When a company has important competitive weaknesses in areas where one or more rivals are strong, it makes sense to consider defensive moves to curtail its vulnerability.

QUESTION 5: WHAT STRATEGIC ISSUES AND PROBLEMS MERIT FRONT-BURNER MANAGERIAL ATTENTION?

The final and most important analytical step is to zero in on exactly what strategic issues that company managers need to address—and resolve—for the company to be more financially and competitively successful in the years ahead. This step involves drawing on the results of both industry and competitive analysis and the evaluations of the company's own competitiveness. The task here is to get a clear fix on exactly what strategic and competitive challenges confront the company, which of the company's competitive shortcomings need fixing, what obstacles stand in the way of improving the company's competitive position in the marketplace, and what specific problems

Zeroing in on the strategic issues a company faces and compiling a "worry list" of problems and roadblocks creates a strategic agenda of problems that merit prompt managerial attention.

merit front-burner attention by company managers. *Pinpointing the precise things that management needs to worry about sets the agenda for deciding what actions to take next to improve the company's performance and business outlook.*

The "worry list" of issues and problems that have to be wrestled with can include such things as *how* to stave off market challenges from new foreign competitors, *how* to combat the price discounting of rivals, *how* to reduce the company's high costs and pave the way for price reductions, *how* to sustain the company's present rate of growth in light of slowing buyer demand, *whether* to expand the company's product line, *whether* to correct the company's competitive deficiencies by acquiring a rival company with the missing strengths, *whether* to expand into foreign markets rapidly or cautiously, *whether* to reposition the company and move to a different strategic group, *what to do* about growing buyer interest in substitute products, and *what to do* to combat the aging demographics of the company's customer base. The worry list thus always centers on such concerns as "how to . . .," "what to do about . . .," and "whether to . . ."—the purpose of the worry list is to identify the specific issues/problems that management needs to address, not to figure out what specific actions to take. Deciding what to do—which strategic actions to take and which strategic moves to make—comes later (when it is time to craft the strategy and choose from among the various strategic alternatives).

Actually deciding upon a strategy and what specific actions to take is what comes *after* developing the list of strategic issues and problems that merit front-burner management attention.

If the items on the worry list are relatively minor—which suggests the company's strategy is mostly on track and reasonably well matched to the company's overall situation—then company managers seldom need to go much beyond fine-tuning of the present strategy. If, however, the issues and problems confronting the company are serious and indicate the present strategy is not well suited for the road ahead, the task of crafting a better strategy has got to go to the top of management's action agenda.

A good strategy must contain ways to deal with all the strategic issues and obstacles that stand in the way of the company's financial and competitive success in the years ahead.

Key Points

There are five key questions to consider in analyzing a company's own particular competitive circumstances and its competitive position vis-à-vis key rivals:

1. *How well is the present strategy working?* This involves evaluating the strategy from a qualitative standpoint (completeness, internal consistency, rationale, and suitability to the situation) and also from a quantitative standpoint (the strategic and financial results the strategy is producing). The stronger a company's current overall performance, the less likely the need for radical strategy changes. The weaker a company's performance and/or the faster the changes in its external situation (which can be gleaned from industry and competitive analysis), the more its current strategy must be questioned.

2. *What are the company's resource strengths and weaknesses, and its external opportunities and threats?* A SWOT analysis provides an overview of a firm's situation and is an essential component of crafting a strategy tightly matched to the company's situation. The two most important parts of SWOT analysis are (*a*) drawing conclusions about what story the compilation of strengths, weaknesses, opportunities, and threats tells about the company's overall situation, and

(*b*) acting on those conclusions to better match the company's strategy, to its resource strengths and market opportunities, to correct the important weaknesses, and to defend against external threats. A company's resource strengths, competencies, and competitive capabilities are strategically relevant because they are the most logical and appealing building blocks for strategy; resource weaknesses are important because they may represent vulnerabilities that need correction. External opportunities and threats come into play because a good strategy necessarily aims at capturing a company's most attractive opportunities and at defending against threats to its well-being.

3. *Are the company's prices and costs competitive?* One telling sign of whether a company's situation is strong or precarious is whether its prices and costs are competitive with those of industry rivals. Value chain analysis and benchmarking are essential tools in determining whether the company is performing particular functions and activities cost-effectively, learning whether its costs are in line with competitors, and deciding which internal activities and business processes need to be scrutinized for improvement. Value chain analysis teaches that how competently a company manages its value chain activities relative to rivals is a key to building a competitive advantage based on either better competencies and competitive capabilities or lower costs than rivals.

4. *Is the company competitively stronger or weaker than key rivals?* The key appraisals here involve how the company matches up against key rivals on industry key success factors and other chief determinants of competitive success and whether and why the company has a competitive advantage or disadvantage. Quantitative competitive strength assessments, using the method presented in Table 4.5, indicate where a company is competitively strong and weak, and provide insight into the company's ability to defend or enhance its market position. As a rule a company's competitive strategy should be built around its competitive strengths and should aim at shoring up areas where it is competitively vulnerable. When a company has important competitive strengths in areas where one or more rivals are weak, it makes sense to consider offensive moves to exploit rivals' competitive weaknesses. When a company has important competitive weaknesses in areas where one or more rivals are strong, it makes sense to consider defensive moves to curtail its vulnerability.

5. *What strategic issues and problems merit front-burner managerial attention?* This analytical step zeros in on the strategic issues and problems that stand in the way of the company's success. It involves using the results of both industry and competitive analysis and company situation analysis to identify a "worry list" of issues to be resolved for the company to be financially and competitively successful in the years ahead. The worry list always centers on such concerns as "how to . . .," "what to do about . . .," and "whether to . . ."—the purpose of the worry list is to identify the specific issues/problems that management needs to address. Actually deciding upon a strategy and what specific actions to take is what comes after the list of strategic issues and problems that merit front-burner management attention is developed.

Good company situation analysis, like good industry and competitive analysis, is a valuable precondition for good strategy making. A competently done evaluation of a company's resource capabilities and competitive strengths exposes strong and weak points in the present strategy and how attractive or unattractive the company's competitive position is and why. Managers need such understanding to craft a strategy that is well suited to the company's competitive circumstances.

Exercises

1. Review the information in Illustration Capsule 4.1 concerning the costs of the different value chain activities associated with recording and distributing music CDs through traditional brick-and-mortar retail outlets. Then answer the following questions:

    a. Does the growing popularity of downloading music from the Internet give rise to a new music industry value chain that differs considerably from the traditional value chain? Explain why or why not.

    b. What costs are cut out of the traditional value chain or bypassed when *online music retailers* (Apple, Sony, Microsoft, Musicmatch, Napster, Cdigix, and others) sell songs directly to online buyers? (Note: In 2005, online music stores were selling download-only titles for $0.79 to $0.99 per song and $9.99 for most albums.)

    c. What costs would be cut out of the traditional value chain or bypassed in the event that *recording studios* sell downloadable files of artists' recordings directly to online buyers?

    d. What happens to the traditional value chain if more and more music lovers use peer-to-peer file-sharing software to download music from the Internet to play music on their PCs or MP3 players or make their own CDs? (Note: It was estimated that, in 2004, about 1 billion songs were available for online trading and file sharing via such programs as Kazaa, Grokster, Shareaza, BitTorrent, and eDonkey, despite the fact that some 4,000 people had been sued by the Recording Industry Association of America for pirating copyrighted music via peer-to-peer file sharing.)

2. Using the information in Table 4.1 and the following financial statement information for Avon Products, calculate the following ratios for Avon for both 2003 and 2004:

    a. Gross profit margin.

    b. Operating profit margin.

    c. Net profit margin.

    d. Return on total assets.

    e. Return on stockholders' equity.

    f. Debt-to-equity ratio.

    g. Times-interest-earned.

    h. Days of inventory.

    i. Inventory turnover ratio.

    j. Average collection period.

    Based on these ratios, did Avon's financial performance improve, weaken, or remain about the same from 2003 to 2004?

Avon Products Inc., Consolidated Statements of Income
(in millions, except per share data)

	Years Ended December 31	
	2004	2003
Net sales	$7,656.2	$6,773.7
Other revenue	91.6	71.4
Total revenue	7,747.8	6,845.1
Costs, expenses and other:		
Cost of sales	2,911.7	2,611.8
Marketing, distribution and administrative expenses	3,610.3	3,194.4
Special charges, net	(3.2)	(3.9)
Operating profit	1,229.0	1,042.8
Interest expense	33.8	33.3
Interest income	(20.6)	(12.6)
Other expense (income), net	28.3	28.6
Total other expenses	41.5	49.3
Income before taxes and minority interest	1,187.5	993.5
Income taxes	330.6	318.9
Income before minority interest	856.9	674.6
Minority interest	(10.8)	(9.8)
Net income	$ 846.1	$ 664.8
Earnings per share:		
Basic	$ 1.79	$ 1.41
Diluted	$ 1.77	$ 1.39
Weighted-average shares outstanding (in millions):		
Basic	472.35	471.08
Diluted	477.96	483.13

Avon Products Inc. Consolidated Balance Sheets (in millions)

	December 31	
	2004	2003
Current assets		
Cash, including cash equivalents of $401.2 and $373.8	$ 769.6	$ 694.0
Accounts receivable (less allowances of $101.0 and $81.1)	599.1	553.2
Inventories	740.5	653.4
Prepaid expenses and other	397.2	325.5
Total current assets	$2,506.4	$2,226.1
Property, plant and equipment, at cost:		
Land	$ 61.7	$ 58.6
Buildings and improvements	886.8	765.9
Equipment	1,006.7	904.4
	1,955.2	1,728.9
Less accumulated depreciation	(940.4)	(873.3)
	1,014.8	855.6
Other assets	626.9	499.9
Total assets	$4,148.1	$3,581.6
Liabilities and shareholders' equity		
Current liabilities		
Debt maturing within one year	$ 51.7	$ 244.1
Accounts payable	490.1	400.1
Accrued compensation	164.5	149.5
Other accrued liabilities	360.1	332.6
Sales and taxes other than income	154.4	139.5
Income taxes	304.7	341.2
Total current liabilities	$1,525.5	$1,607.0
Long-term debt	$ 866.3	$ 877.7
Employee benefit plans	620.6	502.1
Deferred income taxes	12.1	50.6
Other liabilities (including minority interest of $42.5 and $46.0)	173.4	172.9
Total liabilities	$3,197.9	$3,210.3

(*Continued*)

	December 31	
	2004	**2003**
Shareholders' equity		
Common stock, par value $.25—authorized 1,500 shares; issued 728.61 and 722.25 shares	182.2	90.3
Additional paid-in capital	1,356.8	1,188.4
Retained earnings	2,693.5	2,202.4
Accumulated other comprehensive loss	(679.5)	(729.4)
Treasury stock, at cost—257.08 and 251.66 shares	(2,602.8)	(2,380.4)
Total shareholders' equity	950.2	371.3
Total liabilities and shareholders' equity	$4,148.1	$3,581.6

Source: Avon Products Inc., 2004 10-K

chapter five

The Five Generic Competitive Strategies

Which One to Employ?

Competitive strategy is about being different. It means deliberately choosing to perform activities differently or to perform different activities than rivals to deliver a unique mix of value.

—Michael E. Porter

Strategy . . . is about first analyzing and then experimenting, trying, learning, and experimenting some more.

—Ian C. McMillan and Rita Gunther McGrath

Winners in business play rough and don't apologize for it. The nicest part of playing hardball is watching your competitors squirm.

—George Stalk Jr. and Rob Lachenauer

The essence of strategy lies in creating tomorrow's competitive advantages faster than competitors mimic the ones you possess today.

—Gary Hamel and C. K. Prahalad

This chapter describes the *five basic competitive strategy options*—which of the five to employ is a company's first and foremost choice in crafting an overall strategy and beginning its quest for competitive advantage. A company's **competitive strategy** deals exclusively with the specifics of management's game plan for competing successfully—its specific efforts to please customers, its offensive and defensive moves to counter the maneuvers of rivals, its responses to whatever market conditions prevail at the moment, its initiatives to strengthen its market position, and its approach to securing a competitive advantage vis-à-vis rivals. Companies the world over are imaginative in conceiving competitive strategies to win customer favor. At most companies the aim, quite simply, is to do a significantly better job than rivals of providing what buyers are looking for and thereby secure an upper hand in the marketplace.

> **Core Concept**
> A *competitive strategy* concerns the specifics of management's game plan for competing successfully and securing a competitive advantage over rivals.

A company achieves competitive advantage whenever it has some type of edge over rivals in attracting buyers and coping with competitive forces. There are many routes to competitive advantage, but they all involve giving buyers what they perceive as superior value compared to the offerings of rival sellers. Superior value can mean a good product at a lower price; a superior product that is worth paying more for; or a best-value offering that represents an attractive combination of price, features, quality, service, and other appealing attributes. Delivering superior value—whatever form it takes—nearly always requires performing value chain activities differently than rivals and building competencies and resource capabilities that are not readily matched.

> **Core Concept**
> The objective of competitive strategy is to knock the socks off rival companies by doing a better job of satisfying buyer needs and preferences.

THE FIVE GENERIC COMPETITIVE STRATEGIES

There are countless variations in the competitive strategies that companies employ, mainly because each company's strategic approach entails custom-designed actions to fit its own circumstances and industry environment. The custom-tailored nature of each company's strategy makes the chances remote that any two companies—even companies in the same industry—will employ strategies that are exactly alike in every detail. Managers at different companies always have a slightly different spin on future market conditions and how to best align their company's strategy with these conditions; moreover, they have different notions of how they intend to outmaneuver rivals and what strategic options make the most sense for their particular company. However, when one strips away the details to get at the real substance, the biggest and most important differences among competitive strategies boil down to (1) whether a company's market target is broad or narrow, and (2) whether the company is pursuing a competitive advantage linked to low costs or product differentiation. Five distinct competitive strategy approaches stand out:[1]

1. A *low-cost provider strategy*—striving to achieve lower overall costs than rivals and appealing to a broad spectrum of customers, usually by underpricing rivals.

2. A *broad differentiation strategy*—seeking to differentiate the company's product offering from rivals' in ways that will appeal to a broad spectrum of buyers.

3. A *best-cost provider strategy*—giving customers more value for their money by incorporating good-to-excellent product attributes at a lower cost than rivals; the target is to have the lowest (best) costs and prices compared to rivals offering products with comparable attributes.

Figure 5.1   **The Five Generic Competitive Strategies: Each Stakes Out a Different Market Position**

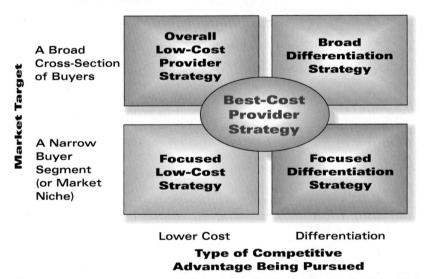

Source: This is an author-expanded version of a three-strategy classification discussed in Michael E. Porter, *Competitive Strategy: Techniques for Analyzing Industries and Competitors* (New York: Free Press, 1980), pp. 35–40.

4. *A focused (or market niche) strategy based on low costs*—concentrating on a narrow buyer segment and outcompeting rivals by having lower costs than rivals and thus being able to serve niche members at a lower price.

5. *A focused (or market niche) strategy based on differentiation*—concentrating on a narrow buyer segment and outcompeting rivals by offering niche members customized attributes that meet their tastes and requirements better than rivals' products.

Each of these five generic competitive approaches stakes out a different market position, as shown in Figure 5.1. Each involves distinctively different approaches to competing and operating the business. The remainder of this chapter explores the ins and outs of the five generic competitive strategies and how they differ.

LOW-COST PROVIDER STRATEGIES

Striving to be the industry's overall low-cost provider is a powerful competitive approach in markets with many price-sensitive buyers. A company achieves low-cost leadership when it becomes the industry's lowest-cost provider rather than just being one of perhaps several competitors with comparatively low costs. A low-cost provider's strategic target is meaningfully lower costs than rivals—but not necessarily the absolutely lowest possible cost. In striving for a cost advantage over rivals, managers must take care to include features and services that buyers consider essential—*a product offering that is too frills-free sabotages the attractiveness of the company's product and can turn buyers off even if it is priced lower than competing products.* For maximum effectiveness, companies employing a low-cost provider strategy need to achieve their cost advantage in ways difficult for rivals to copy or match. If rivals find it relatively easy or inexpensive to imitate the leader's low-cost methods, then the leader's advantage will be too short-lived to yield a valuable edge in the marketplace.

> **Core Concept**
> A low-cost leader's basis for competitive advantage is lower overall costs than competitors. Successful low-cost leaders are exceptionally good at finding ways to drive costs out of their businesses.

A company has two options for translating a low-cost advantage over rivals into attractive profit performance. Option 1 is to use the lower-cost edge to underprice competitors and attract price-sensitive buyers in great enough numbers to increase total profits. The trick to profitably underpricing rivals is either to keep the size of the price cut smaller than the size of the firm's cost advantage (thus reaping the benefits of both a bigger profit margin per unit sold and the added profits on incremental sales) or to generate enough added volume to increase total profits despite thinner profit margins (larger volume can make up for smaller margins provided the underpricing of rivals brings in enough extra sales). Option 2 is to maintain the present price, be content with the present market share, and use the lower-cost edge to earn a higher profit margin on each unit sold, thereby raising the firm's total profits and overall return on investment.

Illustration Capsule 5.1 describes Nucor Corporation's strategy for gaining low-cost leadership in manufacturing a variety of steel products.

The Two Major Avenues for Achieving a Cost Advantage

To achieve a low-cost edge over rivals, a firm's cumulative costs across its overall value chain must be lower than competitors' cumulative costs—and the means of achieving

Illustration Capsule 5.1

Nucor Corporation's Low-Cost Provider Strategy

Nucor Corporation is the world's leading minimill producer of such steel products as carbon and alloy steel bars, beams, sheet, and plate; steel joists and joist girders; steel deck; cold finished steel; steel fasteners; metal building systems; and light gauge steel framing. In 2004, it had close to $10 billion in sales, 9,000 employees, and annual production capacity of nearly 22 million tons, making it the largest steel producer in the United States and one of the 10 largest in the world. The company has pursued a strategy that has made it among the world's lowest-cost producers of steel and has allowed the company to consistently outperform its rivals in terms of financial and market performance.

Nucor's low-cost strategy aims to give it a cost and pricing advantage in the commodity-like steel industry and leaves no part of the company's value chain neglected. The key elements of the strategy include the following:

- Using electric arc furnaces where scrap steel and directly reduced iron ore are melted and then sent to a continuous caster and rolling mill to be shaped into steel products, thereby eliminating an assortment of production processes from the value chain used by traditional integrated steel mills. Nucor's minimill value chain makes the use of coal, coke, and iron ore unnecessary; cuts investment in facilities and equipment (eliminating coke ovens, blast furnaces, basic oxygen furnaces, and ingot casters); and requires fewer employees than integrated mills.

- Striving hard for continuous improvement in the efficiency of its plants and frequently investing in state-of-the-art equipment to reduce unit costs. Nucor is known for its technological leadership and its aggressive pursuit of production process innovation.

- Carefully selecting plant sites to minimize inbound and outbound shipping costs and to take advantage of low rates for electricity (electric arc furnaces are heavy users of electricity). Nucor tends to avoid locating new plants in geographic areas where labor unions are a strong influence.

- Hiring a nonunion workforce that uses team-based incentive compensation systems (often opposed by unions). Operating and maintenance employees and supervisors are paid weekly bonuses based on the productivity of their work group. The size of the bonus is based on the capabilities of the equipment employed and ranges from 80 percent to 150 percent of an employee's base pay; no bonus is paid if the equipment is not operating. Nucor's compensation program has boosted the company's labor productivity to levels nearly double the industry average while rewarding productive employees with annual compensation packages that exceed what their union counterparts earn by as much as 20 percent. Nucor has been able to attract and retain highly talented, productive, and dedicated employees. In addition, the company's healthy culture and results-oriented self-managed work teams allow the company to employ fewer supervisors than what would be needed with an hourly union workforce.

- Heavily emphasizing consistent product quality and has rigorous quality systems.

- Minimizing general and administrative expenses by maintaining a lean staff at corporate headquarters (fewer than 125 employees) and allowing only four levels of management between the CEO and production workers. Headquarters offices are modestly furnished and located in an inexpensive building. The company minimizes reports, paperwork, and meetings to keep managers focused on value-adding activities. Nucor is noted not only for its streamlined organizational structure but also for its frugality in travel and entertainment expenses—the company's top managers set the example by flying coach class, avoiding pricey hotels, and refraining from taking customers out for expensive dinners.

In 2001–2003, when many U.S. producers of steel products were in dire economic straits because of weak demand for steel and deep price discounting by foreign rivals, Nucor began acquiring state-of-the-art steelmaking facilities from bankrupt or nearly bankrupt rivals at bargain-basement prices, often at 20 to 25 percent of what it cost to construct the facilities. This has given Nucor much lower depreciation costs than rivals having comparable plants.

Nucor management's outstanding execution of its low-cost strategy and its commitment to drive down costs throughout its value chain has allowed it to compete aggressively on price, earn higher profit margins than rivals, and grow its business at a considerably faster rate than its integrated steel mill rivals.

Source: Company annual reports, news releases, and Web site.

the cost advantage must be durable. There are two ways to accomplish this:[2]

1. Do a better job than rivals of performing value chain activities more cost-effectively.
2. Revamp the firm's overall value chain to eliminate or bypass some cost-producing activities.

Let's look at each of the two approaches to securing a cost advantage.

Cost-Efficient Management of Value Chain Activities   For a company to do a more cost-efficient job of managing its value chain than rivals, managers must launch a concerted, ongoing effort to ferret out cost-saving opportunities in every part of the value chain. No activity can escape cost-saving scrutiny, and all company personnel must be expected to use their talents and ingenuity to come up with innovative and effective ways to keep costs down. All avenues for performing value chain activities at a lower cost than rivals have to be explored. Attempts to outmanage rivals on cost commonly involve such actions as:

1. *Striving to capture all available economies of scale.* Economies of scale stem from an ability to lower unit costs by increasing the scale of operation—there are many occasions when a large plant is more economical to operate than a small or medium-size plant or when a large distribution warehouse is more cost efficient than a small warehouse. Often, manufacturing economies can be achieved by using common parts and components in different models and/or by cutting back on the number of models offered (especially slow-selling ones) and then scheduling longer production runs for fewer models. In global industries, making separate products for each country market instead of selling a mostly standard product worldwide tends to boost unit costs because of lost time in model changeover, shorter production runs, and inability to reach the most economic scale of production for each country model.

2. *Taking full advantage of learning/experience curve effects.* The cost of performing an activity can decline over time as the learning and experience of company personnel builds. Learning/experience curve economies can stem from debugging and mastering newly introduced technologies, using the experiences and suggestions of workers to install more efficient plant layouts and assembly procedures, and the added speed and effectiveness that accrues from repeatedly picking sites for and building new plants, retail outlets, or distribution centers. Aggressively managed low-cost providers pay diligent attention to capturing the benefits of learning and experience and to keeping these benefits proprietary to whatever extent possible.

3. *Trying to operate facilities at full capacity.* Whether a company is able to operate at or near full capacity has a big impact on units costs when its value chain contains activities associated with substantial fixed costs. Higher rates of capacity utilization allow depreciation and other fixed costs to be spread over a larger unit volume, thereby lowering fixed costs per unit. The more capital-intensive the business, or the higher the percentage of fixed costs as a percentage of total costs, the more important that full-capacity operation becomes because there's such a stiff unit-cost penalty for underutilizing existing capacity. In such cases, finding ways to operate close to full capacity year-round can be an important source of cost advantage.

4. *Pursuing efforts to boost sales volumes and thus spread such costs as R&D, advertising, and selling and administrative costs out over more units.* The more units

a company sells, the more it lowers its unit costs for R&D, sales and marketing, and administrative overhead.

5. *Improving supply chain efficiency.* Many companies pursue cost reduction by partnering with suppliers to streamline the ordering and purchasing process via online systems, reduce inventory carrying costs via just-in-time inventory practices, economize on shipping and materials handling, and ferret out other cost-saving opportunities. A company with a core competence (or better still a distinctive competence) in cost-efficient supply chain management can sometimes achieve a sizable cost advantage over less adept rivals.

6. *Substituting the use of low-cost for high-cost raw materials or component parts.* If the costs of raw materials and parts are too high, a company can either substitute the use of lower-cost items or maybe even design the high-cost components out of the product altogether.

7. *Using online systems and sophisticated software to achieve operating efficiencies.* Data sharing, starting with customer orders and going all the way back to components production, coupled with the use of enterprise resource planning (ERP) and manufacturing execution system (MES) software, can make custom manufacturing just as cheap as mass production—and sometimes cheaper. Online systems and software can also greatly reduce production times and labor costs. Lexmark used ERP and MES software to cut its production time for inkjet printers from four hours to 24 minutes. Southwest Airlines uses proprietary software to schedule flights and assign flight crews cost-effectively.

8. *Adopting labor-saving operating methods.* Examples of ways for a company to economize on labor costs include the following: installing labor-saving technology, shifting production from geographic areas where labor costs are high to geographic areas where labor costs are low, avoiding the use of union labor where possible (because of work rules that can stifle productivity and because of union demands for above-market pay scales and costly fringe benefits), and using incentive compensation systems that promote high labor productivity.

9. *Using the company's bargaining power vis-à-vis suppliers to gain concessions.* Many large enterprises (e.g., Wal-Mart, Home Depot, the world's major motor vehicle producers) have used their bargaining clout in purchasing large volumes to wrangle good prices on their purchases from suppliers. Having greater buying power than rivals can be an important source of cost advantage.

10. *Being alert to the cost advantages of outsourcing and vertical integration.* Outsourcing the performance of certain value chain activities can be more economical than performing them in-house if outside specialists, by virtue of their expertise and volume, can perform the activities at lower cost. Indeed, outsourcing has in recent years become a widely used cost-reduction approach. However, there can be times when integrating the activities of either suppliers or distribution channel allies can allow an enterprise to detour suppliers or buyers who have an adverse impact on costs because of their considerable bargaining power.

In addition to the above means of achieving lower costs than rivals, managers can also achieve important cost savings by deliberately opting for an inherently economical strategy keyed to a frills-free product offering. For instance, a company can bolster its attempts to open up a durable cost advantage over rivals by:

- Having lower specifications for purchased materials, parts, and components than rivals do. Thus, a maker of personal computers (PCs) can use the cheapest hard drives, microprocessors, monitors, DVD drives, and other components it can find so as to end up with lower production costs than rival PC makers.

- Distributing the company's product only through low-cost distribution channels and avoiding high-cost distribution channels.
- Choosing to use the most economical method for delivering customer orders (even if it results in longer delivery times).

These strategy-related means of keeping costs low don't really involve "outmanaging" rivals, but they can nonetheless contribute materially to becoming the industry's low-cost leader.

Revamping the Value Chain to Curb or Eliminate Unnecessary Activities

Dramatic cost advantages can emerge from finding innovative ways to cut back on or entirely bypass certain cost-producing value chain activities. There are six primary ways companies can achieve a cost advantage by reconfiguring their value chains:

1. *Cutting out distributors and dealers by selling directly to customers.* Selling directly and bypassing the activities and costs of distributors or dealers can involve (1) having the company's own direct sales force (which adds the costs of maintaining and supporting a sales force but may well be cheaper than accessing customers through distributors or dealers) and/or (2) conducting sales operations at the company's Web site (Web site operations may be substantially cheaper than distributor or dealer channels). Costs in the wholesale/retail portions of the value chain frequently represent 35–50 percent of the price final consumers pay. There are several prominent examples in which companies have instituted a sell-direct approach to cutting costs out of the value chain. Software developers allow customers to download new programs directly from the Internet, eliminating the costs of producing and packaging CDs and cutting out the host of activities, costs, and markups associated with shipping and distributing software through wholesale and retail channels. By cutting all these costs and activities out of the value chain, software developers have the pricing room to boost their profit margins and still sell their products below levels that retailers would have to charge. The major airlines now sell most of their tickets directly to passengers via their Web sites, ticket counter agents, and telephone reservation systems, allowing them to save hundreds of millions of dollars in commissions once paid to travel agents.

2. *Replacing certain value chain activities with faster and cheaper online technology.* In recent years the Internet and Internet technology applications have become powerful and pervasive tools for conducting business and reengineering company and industry value chains. For instance, Internet technology has revolutionized supply chain management, turning many time-consuming and labor-intensive activities into paperless transactions performed instantaneously. Company procurement personnel can—with only a few mouse clicks—check materials inventories against incoming customer orders, check suppliers' stocks, check the latest prices for parts and components at auction and e-sourcing Web sites, and check FedEx delivery schedules. Various e-procurement software packages streamline the purchasing process by eliminating paper documents such as requests for quotations, purchase orders, order acceptances, and shipping notices. There's software that permits the relevant details of incoming customer orders to be instantly shared with the suppliers of needed parts and components. All this facilitates

just-in-time deliveries of parts and components and matching the production of parts and components to assembly plant requirements and production schedules, cutting out unnecessary activities and producing savings for both suppliers and manufacturers. Retailers can install online systems that relay data from cash register sales at the check-out counter back to manufacturers and their suppliers. Manufacturers can use online systems to collaborate closely with parts and components suppliers in designing new products and shortening the time it takes to get them into production. Online systems allow warranty claims and product performance problems involving supplier components to be instantly relayed to the relevant suppliers so that corrections can be expedited. Online systems have the further effect of breaking down corporate bureaucracies and reducing overhead costs. The whole back-office data management process (order processing, invoicing, customer accounting, and other kinds of transaction costs) can be handled fast, accurately, and with less paperwork and fewer personnel.

3. *Streamlining operations by eliminating low-value-added or unnecessary work steps and activities.* Examples include using computer-assisted design techniques, standardizing parts and components across models and styles, having suppliers collaborate to combine parts and components into modules so that products can be assembled in fewer steps, and shifting to an easy-to-manufacture product design. At Wal-Mart, some items supplied by manufacturers are delivered directly to retail stores rather than being routed through Wal-Mart's distribution centers and delivered by Wal-Mart trucks; in other instances, Wal-Mart unloads incoming shipments from manufacturers' trucks arriving at its distribution centers directly onto outgoing Wal-Mart trucks headed to particular stores without ever moving the goods into the distribution center. Many supermarket chains have greatly reduced in-store meat butchering and cutting activities by shifting to meats that are cut and packaged at the meat-packing plant and then delivered to their stores in ready-to-sell form.

4. *Relocating facilities so as to curb the need for shipping and handling activities.* Having suppliers locate facilities adjacent to the company's plant or locating the company's plants or warehouses near customers can help curb or eliminate shipping and handling costs.

5. *Offering a frills-free product.* Deliberately restricting a company's product offering to the essentials can help the company cut costs associated with snazzy attributes and a full lineup of options and extras. Activities and costs can also be eliminated by incorporating fewer performance and quality features into the product and by offering buyers fewer services. Stripping extras like first-class sections, meals, and reserved seating is a favorite technique of budget airlines like Southwest, Ryanair (Europe), easyJet (Europe), and Gol (Brazil).

6. *Offering a limited product line as opposed to a full product line.* Pruning slow-selling items from the product lineup and being content to meet the needs of most buyers rather than all buyers can eliminate activities and costs associated with numerous product versions and wide selection.

Illustration Capsule 5.2 describes how Wal-Mart has managed its value chain in the retail grocery portion of its business to achieve a dramatic cost advantage over rival supermarket chains and become the world's biggest grocery retailer.

Examples of Companies That Revamped Their Value Chains to Reduce Costs   Iowa Beef Packers (IBP), now a subsidiary of Tyson Foods, pioneered the

Ilustration Capsule 5.2

How Wal-Mart Managed Its Value Chain to Achieve a Huge Low-Cost Advantage over Rival Supermarket Chains

Wal-Mart has achieved a very substantial cost and pricing advantage over rival supermarket chains both by revamping portions of the grocery retailing value chain and by out-managing its rivals in efficiently performing various value chain activities. Its cost advantage stems from a series of initiatives and practices:

- Instituting extensive information sharing with vendors via online systems that relay sales at its check-out counters directly to suppliers of the items, thereby providing suppliers with real-time information on customer demand and preferences (creating an estimated 6 percent cost advantage). It is standard practice at Wal-Mart to collaborate extensively with vendors on all aspects of the purchasing and store delivery process to squeeze out mutually beneficial cost savings. Procter & Gamble, Wal-Mart's biggest supplier, went so far as to integrate its enterprise resource planning (ERP) system with Wal-Mart's.

- Pursuing global procurement of some items and centralizing most purchasing activities so as to leverage the company's buying power (creating an estimated 2.5 percent cost advantage).

- Investing in state-of-the-art automation at its distribution centers, efficiently operating a truck fleet that

makes daily deliveries to Wal-Mart's stores, and putting assorted other cost-saving practices into place at its headquarters, distribution centers, and stores (resulting in an estimated 4 percent cost advantage).

- Striving to optimize the product mix and achieve greater sales turnover (resulting in about a 2 percent cost advantage).

- Installing security systems and store operating procedures that lower shrinkage rates (producing a cost advantage of about 0.5 percent).

- Negotiating preferred real estate rental and leasing rates with real estate developers and owners of its store sites (yielding a cost advantage of 2 percent).

- Managing and compensating its workforce in a manner that produces lower labor costs (yielding an estimated 5 percent cost advantage)

Altogether, these value chain initiatives give Wal-Mart an approximately 22 percent cost advantage over Kroger, Safeway, and other leading supermarket chains. With such a sizable cost advantage, Wal-Mart has been able to under-price its rivals and become the world's leading supermarket retailer in little more than a decade.

Source: Developed by the authors from information at www.wal-mart.com (accessed September 15, 2004) and in Marco Iansiti and Roy Levien, "Strategy as Ecology," *Harvard Business Review* 82, no. 3 (March 2004), p. 70.

development of a cheaper value chain system in the beef-packing industry.[3] The traditional cost chain involved raising cattle on scattered farms and ranches; shipping them live to labor-intensive, unionized slaughtering plants; and then transporting whole sides of beef to grocery retailers whose butcher departments cut them into smaller pieces and packaged them for sale to grocery shoppers. IBP revamped the traditional chain with a radically different strategy: It built large automated plants employing nonunion workers near cattle supplies. Near the plants it arranged to set up large feed lots (or holding pens) where cattle were fed grain for a short time to fatten them up prior to slaughter. The meat was butchered at the processing plant into small, high-yield cuts. Some of the trimmed and boned cuts were vacuum-sealed in plastic casings for further butchering in supermarket meat departments, but others were trimmed and/or boned, put in plastic-sealed ready-to-sell trays, boxed, and shipped to retailers. IBP's strategy was to increase the volume of prepackaged, "case-ready" cuts that retail grocers could unpack from boxes and place directly into the meat case. In addition, IBP provided meat retailers with individually wrapped quick-frozen steaks, as well as precooked roasts, beef tip, and meatloaf selections that could be prepared in a matter of minutes. Iowa Beef's inbound cattle transportation expenses, traditionally a major cost item, were cut significantly by avoiding the weight losses that occurred when live animals were shipped long distances just prior to slaughter. Sizable major outbound shipping cost savings were achieved by not having to ship whole sides of beef, which had a high waste factor. Meat retailers had to do far less butchering to stock their meat cases. IBP value chain revamping was so successful that the company became the largest U.S. meatpacker.

Southwest Airlines has reconfigured the traditional value chain of commercial airlines to lower costs and thereby offer dramatically lower fares to passengers. Its mastery of fast turnarounds at the gates (about 25 minutes versus 45 minutes for rivals) allows its planes to fly more hours per day. This translates into being able to schedule more flights per day with fewer aircraft, allowing Southwest to generate more revenue per plane on average than rivals. Southwest does not offer in-flight meals, assigned seating, baggage transfer to connecting airlines, or first-class seating and service, thereby eliminating all the cost-producing activities associated with these features. The company's fast, user-friendly online reservation system facilitates e-ticketing and reduces staffing requirements at telephone reservation centers and airport counters. Its use of automated check-in equipment reduces staffing requirements for terminal check-in.

Dell has created the best, most cost-efficient value chain in the global personal computer industry. Whereas Dell's major rivals (Hewlett-Packard, Lenovo, Sony, and Toshiba) produce their models in volume and sell them through independent resellers and retailers, Dell has elected to market directly to PC users, building its PCs to customer specifications as orders come in and shipping them to customers within a few days of receiving the order. Dell's value chain approach has proved cost-effective in coping with the PC industry's blink-of-an-eye product life cycle. The build-to-order strategy enables the company to avoid misjudging buyer demand for its various models and being saddled with quickly obsolete excess components and finished-goods inventories—all parts and components are obtained on a just-in-time basis from vendors, many of which deliver their items to Dell assembly plants several times a day in volumes matched to the Dell's daily assembly schedule. Also, Dell's sell-direct strategy slices reseller/retailer costs and margins out of the value chain (although some of these savings are offset by the cost of Dell's direct marketing and customer support activities—functions that would otherwise be performed by resellers and retailers). Partnerships with suppliers that facilitate just-in-time deliveries of components and minimize Dell's inventory costs, coupled with Dell's extensive use of e-commerce technologies further reduce Dell's costs. Dell's value chain approach is widely considered to have made it the global low-cost leader in the PC industry.

The Keys to Success in Achieving Low-Cost Leadership

To succeed with a low-cost-provider strategy, company managers have to scrutinize each cost-creating activity and determine what factors cause costs to be high or low. Then they have to use this knowledge to keep the unit costs of each activity low, exhaustively pursuing cost efficiencies throughout the value chain. They have to be proactive in restructuring the value chain to eliminate nonessential work steps and low-value activities. Normally, low-cost producers work diligently to create cost-conscious corporate cultures that feature broad employee participation in continuous cost improvement efforts and limited perks and frills for executives. They strive to operate with exceptionally small corporate staffs to keep administrative costs to a minimum.

Many successful low-cost leaders also use benchmarking to keep close tabs on how their costs compare with rivals and firms performing comparable activities in other industries.

> Success in achieving a low-cost edge over rivals comes from outmanaging rivals in figuring out how to perform value chain activities most cost effectively and eliminating or curbing non essential value chain activities

But while low-cost providers are champions of frugality, they are usually aggressive in investing in resources and capabilities that promise to drive costs out of the business. Wal-Mart, one of the foremost practitioners of low-cost leadership, employs state-of-the-art technology throughout its operations—its distribution facilities are an automated showcase, it uses online systems to order goods from suppliers and manage inventories, it equips its stores with cutting-edge sales-tracking and check-out systems, and it sends daily point-of-sale data to 4,000 vendors. Wal-Mart's information and communications systems and capabilities are more sophisticated than those of virtually any other retail chain in the world.

Other companies noted for their successful use of low-cost provider strategies include Lincoln Electric in arc welding equipment, Briggs & Stratton in small gasoline engines, Bic in ballpoint pens, Black & Decker in power tools, Stride Rite in footwear, Beaird-Poulan in chain saws, and General Electric and Whirlpool in major home appliances.

When a Low-Cost Provider Strategy Works Best

A competitive strategy predicated on low-cost leadership is particularly powerful when:

1. *Price competition among rival sellers is especially vigorous*—Low-cost providers are in the best position to compete offensively on the basis of price, to use the appeal of lower price to grab sales (and market share) from rivals, to win the business of price-sensitive buyers, to remain profitable in the face of strong price competition, and to survive price wars.

2. *The products of rival sellers are essentially identical and supplies are readily available from any of several eager sellers*—Commodity-like products and/or ample supplies set the stage for lively price competition; in such markets, it is less efficient, higher-cost companies whose profits get squeezed the most.

3. *There are few ways to achieve product differentiation that have value to buyers*—When the differences between brands do not matter much to buyers, buyers are nearly always very sensitive to price differences and shop the market for the best price.

4. *Most buyers use the product in the same ways*—With common user requirements, a standardized product can satisfy the needs of buyers, in which case low selling price, not features or quality, becomes the dominant factor in causing buyers to choose one seller's product over another's.

5. *Buyers incur low costs in switching their purchases from one seller to another*—Low switching costs give buyers the flexibility to shift purchases to lower-priced sellers having equally good products or to attractively priced substitute products. A low-cost leader is well positioned to use low price to induce its customers not to switch to rival brands or substitutes.

6. *Buyers are large and have significant power to bargain down prices*—Low-cost providers have partial profit-margin protection in bargaining with high-volume buyers, since powerful buyers are rarely able to bargain price down past the survival level of the next most cost-efficient seller.

7. *Industry newcomers use introductory low prices to attract buyers and build a customer base*—The low-cost leader can use price cuts of its own to make it harder

A low-cost provider is in the best position to win the business of price-sensitive buyers, set the floor on market price, and still earn a profit.

for a new rival to win customers; the pricing power of the low-cost provider acts as a barrier for new entrants.

As a rule, the more price-sensitive buyers are, the more appealing a low-cost strategy becomes. A low-cost company's ability to set the industry's price floor and still earn a profit erects protective barriers around its market position.

The Pitfalls of a Low-Cost Provider Strategy

Perhaps the biggest pitfall of a low-cost provider strategy is getting carried away with overly aggressive price cutting and ending up with lower, rather than higher, profitability. A low-cost/low-price advantage results in superior profitability only if (1) prices are cut by less than the size of the cost advantage or (2) the added gains in unit sales are large enough to bring in a bigger total profit despite lower margins per unit sold. A company with a 5 percent cost advantage cannot cut prices 20 percent, end up with a volume gain of only 10 percent, and still expect to earn higher profits!

A second big pitfall is not emphasizing avenues of cost advantage that can be kept proprietary or that relegate rivals to playing catch-up. The value of a cost advantage depends on its sustainability. Sustainability, in turn, hinges on whether the company achieves its cost advantage in ways difficult for rivals to copy or match.

A low-cost provider's product offering must always contain enough attributes to be attractive to prospective buyers—low price, by itself, is not always appealing to buyers.

A third pitfall is becoming too fixated on cost reduction. Low cost cannot be pursued so zealously that a firm's offering ends up being too features-poor to generate buyer appeal. Furthermore, a company driving hard to push its costs down has to guard against misreading or ignoring increased buyer interest in added features or service, declining buyer sensitivity to price, or new developments that start to alter how buyers use the product. A low-cost zealot risks losing market ground if buyers start opting for more upscale or features-rich products.

Even if these mistakes are avoided, a low-cost competitive approach still carries risk. Cost-saving technological breakthroughs or the emergence of still-lower-cost value chain models can nullify a low-cost leader's hard-won position. The current leader may have difficulty in shifting quickly to the new technologies or value chain approaches because heavy investments lock it in (at least temporarily) to its present value chain approach.

BROAD DIFFERENTIATION STRATEGIES

Core Concept
The essence of a broad differentiation strategy is to be unique in ways that are valuable to a wide range of customers.

Differentiation strategies are attractive whenever buyers' needs and preferences are too diverse to be fully satisfied by a standardized product or by sellers with identical capabilities. A company attempting to succeed through differentiation must study buyers' needs and behavior carefully to learn what buyers consider important, what they think has value, and what they are willing to pay for. Then the company has to incorporate buyer-desired attributes into its product or service offering that will clearly set it apart from rivals. Competitive advantage results once a sufficient number of buyers become strongly attached to the differentiated attributes.

Successful differentiation allows a firm to:

- Command a premium price for its product, and/or
- Increase unit sales (because additional buyers are won over by the differentiating features), and/or

- Gain buyer loyalty to its brand (because some buyers are strongly attracted to the differentiating features and bond with the company and its products).

Differentiation enhances profitability whenever the extra price the product commands outweighs the added costs of achieving the differentiation. Company differentiation strategies fail when buyers don't value the brand's uniqueness and when a company's approach to differentiation is easily copied or matched by its rivals.

Types of Differentiation Themes

Companies can pursue differentiation from many angles: a unique taste (Dr Pepper, Listerine); multiple features (Microsoft Windows, Microsoft Office); wide selection and one-stop shopping (Home Depot, Amazon.com); superior service (FedEx); spare parts availability (Caterpillar); engineering design and performance (Mercedes, BMW); prestige and distinctiveness (Rolex); product reliability (Johnson & Johnson in baby products); quality manufacture (Karastan in carpets, Michelin in tires, Toyota and Honda in automobiles); technological leadership (3M Corporation in bonding and coating products); a full range of services (Charles Schwab in stock brokerage); a complete line of products (Campbell's soups); and top-of-the-line image and reputation (Ralph Lauren and Starbucks).

The most appealing approaches to differentiation are those that are hard or expensive for rivals to duplicate. Indeed, resourceful competitors can, in time, clone almost any product or feature or attribute. If Coca-Cola introduces a vanilla-flavored soft drink, so can Pepsi; if Ford offers a 50,000-mile bumper-to-bumper warranty on its new vehicles, so can Volkswagen and Nissan. If Nokia introduces cell phones with cameras and Internet capability, so can Motorola and Samsung. As a rule, differentiation yields a longer-lasting and more profitable competitive edge when it is based on product innovation, technical superiority, product quality and reliability, comprehensive customer service, and unique competitive capabilities. Such differentiating attributes tend to be tough for rivals to copy or offset profitably, and buyers widely perceive them as having value.

> Easy-to-copy differentiating features cannot produce sustainable competitive advantage; differentiation based on competencies and capabilities tend to be more sustainable.

Where along the Value Chain to Create the Differentiating Attributes

Differentiation is not something hatched in marketing and advertising departments, nor is it limited to the catchalls of quality and service. Differentiation opportunities can exist in activities all along an industry's value chain; possibilities include the following:

- *Supply chain activities* that ultimately spill over to affect the performance or quality of the company's end product. Starbucks gets high ratings on its coffees partly because it has very strict specifications on the coffee beans purchased from suppliers.
- *Product R&D activities* that aim at improved product designs and performance features, expanded end uses and applications, more frequent first-on-the-market victories, wider product variety and selection, added user safety, greater recycling capability, or enhanced environmental protection.
- *Production R&D and technology-related activities* that permit custom-order manufacture at an efficient cost; make production methods safer for the

environment; or improve product quality, reliability, and appearance. Many manufacturers have developed flexible manufacturing systems that allow different models and product versions to be made on the same assembly line. Being able to provide buyers with made-to-order products can be a potent differentiating capability.

- *Manufacturing activities* that reduce product defects, prevent premature product failure, extend product life, allow better warranty coverages, improve economy of use, result in more end-user convenience, or enhance product appearance. The quality edge enjoyed by Japanese automakers stems partly from their distinctive competence in performing assembly-line activities.

- *Distribution and shipping activities* that allow for fewer warehouse and on-the-shelf stockouts, quicker delivery to customers, more accurate order filling, and/or lower shipping costs.

- *Marketing, sales, and customer service activities* that result in superior technical assistance to buyers, faster maintenance and repair services, more and better product information provided to customers, more and better training materials for end users, better credit terms, quicker order processing, or greater customer convenience.

Managers need keen understanding of the sources of differentiation and the activities that drive uniqueness to evaluate various differentiation approaches and design durable ways to set their product offering apart from those of rival brands.

The Four Best Routes to Competitive Advantage via a Broad Differentiation Strategy

While it is easy enough to grasp that a successful differentiation strategy must entail creating buyer value in ways unmatched by rivals, the big issue in crafting a differentiation strategy is which of four basic routes to take in delivering unique buyer value via a broad differentiation strategy. Usually, building a sustainable competitive advantage via differentiation involves pursuing one of four basic routes to delivering superior value to buyers.

One route is to *incorporate product attributes and user features that lower the buyer's overall costs of using the company's product.* Making a company's product more economical for a buyer to use can be done by reducing the buyer's raw materials waste (providing cut-to-size components), reducing a buyer's inventory requirements (providing just-in-time deliveries), increasing maintenance intervals and product reliability so as to lower a buyer's repair and maintenance costs, using online systems to reduce a buyer's procurement and order processing costs, and providing free technical support. Rising costs for gasoline have dramatically spurred the efforts of motor vehicle manufacturers worldwide to introduce models with better fuel economy and reduce operating costs for motor vehicle owners.

A second route is to *incorporate features that raise product performance.*[4] This can be accomplished with attributes that provide buyers greater reliability, ease of use, convenience, or durability. Other performance-enhancing options include making the company's product or service cleaner, safer, quieter, or more maintenance-free than rival brands. Cell phone manufacturrs are in a race to introduce next-generation phones with trendsetting features and options.

A third route to a differentiation-based competitive advantage is to *incorporate features that enhance buyer satisfaction in noneconomic or intangible ways.* Goodyear's Aquatread tire design appeals to safety-conscious motorists wary of slick roads. Rolls Royce, Ralph Lauren, Gucci, Tiffany, Cartier, and Rolex have differentiation-based competitive advantages linked to buyer desires for status, image, prestige, upscale fashion, superior craftsmanship, and the finer things in life. L. L. Bean makes its mail-order customers feel secure in their purchases by providing an unconditional guarantee with no time limit: "All of our products are guaranteed to give 100 percent satisfaction in every way. Return anything purchased from us at any time if it proves otherwise. We will replace it, refund your purchase price, or credit your credit card, as you wish."

> **Core Concept**
> A differentiator's basis for competitive advantage is either a product/service offering whose attributes differ significantly from the offerings of rivals or a set of capabilities for delivering customer value that rivals don't have.

The fourth route is to *deliver value to customers by differentiating on the basis of competencies and competitive capabilities that rivals don't have or can't afford to match.*[5] The importance of cultivating competencies and capabilities that add power to a company's resource strengths and competitiveness comes into play here. Core and/or distinctive competencies not only enhance a company's ability to compete successfully in the marketplace but can also be unique in delivering value to buyers. There are numerous examples of companies that have differentiated themselves on the basis of capabilities. Because Fox News and CNN have the capability to devote more air time to breaking news stories and get reporters on the scene very quickly compared to the major networks, many viewers turn to the cable networks when a major news event occurs. Microsoft has stronger capabilities to design, create, distribute, and advertise an array of software products for PC applications than any of its rivals. Avon and Mary Kay Cosmetics have differentiated themselves from other cosmetics and personal care companies by assembling a sales force numbering in the hundreds of thousands that gives them direct sales capability—their sales associates can demonstrate products to interested buyers, take their orders on the spot, and deliver the items to buyers' homes. Japanese automakers have the capability to satisfy changing consumer preferences for one vehicle style versus another because they can bring new models to market faster than American and European automakers.

The Importance of Perceived Value and Signaling Value

Buyers seldom pay for value they don't perceive, no matter how real the unique extras may be.[6] Thus, the price premium commanded by a differentiation strategy reflects *the value actually delivered* to the buyer and *the value perceived* by the buyer (even if not actually delivered). Actual and perceived value can differ whenever buyers have trouble assessing what their experience with the product will be. Incomplete knowledge on the part of buyers often causes them to judge value based on such signals as price (where price connotes quality), attractive packaging, extensive ad campaigns (i.e., how well-known the product is), ad content and image, the quality of brochures and sales presentations, the seller's facilities, the seller's list of customers, the firm's market share, the length of time the firm has been in business, and the professionalism, appearance, and personality of the seller's employees. Such signals of value may be as important as actual value (1) when the nature of differentiation is subjective or hard to quantify, (2) when buyers are making a first-time purchase, (3) when repurchase is infrequent, and (4) when buyers are unsophisticated.

When a Differentiation Strategy Works Best

Differentiation strategies tend to work best in market circumstances where:

- *Buyer needs and uses of the product are diverse*—Diverse buyer preferences present competitors with a bigger window of opportunity to do things differently and set themselves apart with product attributes that appeal to particular buyers. For instance, the diversity of consumer preferences for menu selection, ambience, pricing, and customer service gives restaurants exceptionally wide latitude in creating a differentiated product offering. Other companies having many ways to strongly differentiate themselves from rivals include the publishers of magazines, the makers of motor vehicles, and the manufacturers of cabinetry and countertops.

- *There are many ways to differentiate the product or service and many buyers perceive these differences as having value*—There is plenty of room for retail apparel competitors to stock different styles and quality of apparel merchandise but very little room for the makers of paper clips, copier paper, or sugar to set their products apart. Likewise, the sellers of different brands of gasoline or orange juice have little differentiation opportunity compared to the sellers of high-definition TVs, patio furniture, or breakfast cereal. Unless different buyers have distinguishably different preferences for certain features and product attributes, profitable differentiation opportunities are very restricted.

- *Few rival firms are following a similar differentiation approach*—The best differentiation approaches involve trying to appeal to buyers on the basis of attributes that rivals are not emphasizing. A differentiator encounters less head-to-head rivalry when it goes its own separate way in creating uniqueness and does not try to outdifferentiate rivals on the very same attributes—when many rivals are all claiming "Ours tastes better than theirs" or "Ours gets your clothes cleaner than theirs," the most likely result is weak brand differentiation and "strategy overcrowding"—a situation in which competitors end up chasing the same buyers with very similar product offerings.

- *Technological change is fast-paced and competition revolves around rapidly evolving product features*—Rapid product innovation and frequent introductions of next-version products not only provide space for companies to pursue separate differentiating paths but also heighten buyer interest. In video game hardware and video games, golf equipment, PCs, cell phones, and MP3 players, competitors are locked into an ongoing battle to set themselves apart by introducing the best next-generation products—companies that fail to come up with new and improved products and distinctive performance features quickly lose out in the marketplace. In network TV broadcasting in the United States, NBC, ABC, CBS, Fox, and several others are always scrambling to develop a lineup of TV shows that will win higher audience ratings and pave the way for charging higher advertising rates and boosting ad revenues.

The Pitfalls of a Differentiation Strategy

Differentiation strategies can fail for any of several reasons. *A differentiation strategy is always doomed when competitors are able to quickly copy most or all of the appealing product attributes a company comes up with.* Rapid imitation means that no rival achieves differentiation, since whenever one firm introduces some aspect of uniqueness that strikes the fancy of buyers, fast-following copycats quickly reestablish similarity. This is why a firm must search out sources of uniqueness that are time-consuming or burdensome for rivals to match if it hopes to use differentiation to win a competitive edge over rivals.

> **Core Concept**
> Any differentiating feature that works well is a magnet for imitators.

*A second pitfall is that the company's differentiation strategy produces a ho-hum market reception because buyers see little value in the unique attributes of a company's produc*t. Thus, even if a company sets the attributes of its brand apart from the brands of rivals, its strategy can fail because of trying to differentiate on the basis of something that does not deliver adequate value to buyers (such as lowering a buyer's cost to use the product or enhancing a buyer's well-being). Anytime many potential buyers look at a company's differentiated product offering and conclude "So what?" the company's differentiation strategy is in deep trouble—buyers will likely decide the product is not worth the extra price, and sales will be disappointingly low.

The third big pitfall of a differentiation strategy is overspending on efforts to differentiate the company's product offering, thus eroding profitability. Company efforts to achieve differentiation nearly always raise costs. The trick to profitable differentiation is either to keep the costs of achieving differentiation below the price premium the differentiating attributes can command in the marketplace (thus increasing the profit margin per unit sold) or to offset thinner profit margins per unit by selling enough additional units to increase total profits. If a company goes overboard in pursuing costly differentiation efforts and then unexpectedly discovers that buyers are unwilling to pay a sufficient price premium to cover the added costs of differentiation, it ends up saddled with unacceptably thin profit margins or even losses. The need to contain differentiation costs is why many companies add little touches of differentiation that add to buyer satisfaction but are inexpensive to institute. Upscale restaurants often provide valet parking. Ski resorts provide skiers with complimentary coffee or hot apple cider at the base of the lifts in the morning and late afternoon. FedEx, UPS, and many catalog and online retailers have installed software capabilities that allow customers to track packages in transit. Some hotels and motels provide free continental breakfasts, exercise facilities, and in-room coffeemaking amenities. Publishers are using their Web sites to deliver supplementary educational materials to the buyers of their textbooks. Laundry detergent and soap manufacturers add pleasing scents to their products.

Other common pitfalls and mistakes in crafting a differentiation strategy include:[7]

- *Overdifferentiating so that product quality or service levels exceed buyers' needs.* Even if buyers like the differentiating extras, they may not find them sufficiently valuable for their purposes to pay extra to get them. Many shoppers shy away from buying top-of-the-line items because they have no particular interest in all the bells and whistles; for them, a less deluxe model or style makes better economic sense.

- *Trying to charge too high a price premium.* Even if buyers view certain extras or deluxe features as nice to have, they may still conclude that the added cost is excessive relative to the value they deliver. A differentiator must guard against turning off would-be buyers with what is perceived as price gouging. Normally, the bigger the price premium for the differentiating extras, the harder it is to keep buyers from switching to the lower-priced offerings of competitors.

- *Being timid and not striving to open up meaningful gaps in quality or service or performance features vis-à-vis the products of rivals.* Tiny differences between rivals' product offerings may not be visible or important to buyers. If a company wants to generate the fiercely loyal customer following needed to earn superior profits and open up a differentiation-based competitive advantage over rivals, then its strategy must result in strong rather than weak product differentiation. In markets where differentiators do no better than achieve weak product differentiation (because the attributes of rival brands are fairly similar in the minds of many buyers), customer loyalty to any one brand is weak, the costs of buyers to switch to rival brands are fairly low, and no one company has enough of a market edge that it can get by with charging a price premium over rival brands.

A low-cost provider strategy can defeat a differentiation strategy when buyers are satisfied with a basic product and don't think extra attributes are worth a higher price.

BEST-COST PROVIDER STRATEGIES

Core Concept
The competitive advantage of a best-cost provider is lower costs than rivals in incorporating upscale attributes, putting the company in a position to underprice rivals whose products have similar upscale attributes.

Best-cost provider strategies aim at giving customers *more value for the money.* The objective is to deliver superior value to buyers by satisfying their expectations on key quality/features/performance/service attributes and beating their expectations on price (given what rivals are charging for much the same attributes). *A company achieves best-cost status from an ability to incorporate attractive or upscale attributes at a lower cost than rivals.* The attractive attributes can take the form of appealing features, good-to-excellent product performance or quality, or attractive customer service. When a company has the resource strengths and competitive capabilities to incorporate these upscale attributes into its product offering *at a lower cost than rivals,* it enjoys best-cost status—it is the low-cost provider *of an upscale product.*

Being a best-cost provider is different from being a low-cost provider because the additional upscale features entail additional costs (that a low-cost provider can avoid by offering buyers a basic product with few frills). As Figure 5.1 indicates, best-cost provider strategies stake out a middle ground between pursuing a low-cost advantage and a differentiation advantage and between appealing to the broad market as a whole and a narrow market niche. From a competitive positioning standpoint, best-cost strategies are thus a *hybrid,* balancing a strategic emphasis on low cost against a strategic emphasis on differentiation (upscale features delivered at a price that constitutes superior value).

The competitive advantage of a best-cost provider is its capability to include upscale attributes at a lower cost than rivals whose products have comparable attributes. A best-cost provider can use its low-cost advantage to underprice rivals whose products have similar upscale attributes—it is usually not difficult to entice customers away from rivals charging a higher price for an item with highly comparable features, quality, performance, and/or customer service attributes. To achieve competitive advantage with a best-cost provider strategy, it is critical that a company have the resources and capabilities to incorporate upscale attributes at a lower cost than rivals. In other words, it must be able to (1) incorporate attractive features at a lower cost than rivals whose products have similar features, (2) manufacture a good-to-excellent quality product at a lower cost than rivals with good-to-excellent product quality, (3) develop a product that delivers good-to-excellent performance at a lower cost than rivals whose products also entail good-to-excellent performance, or (4) provide attractive customer service at a lower cost than rivals who provide comparably attractive customer service.

What makes a best-cost provider strategy so appealing is being able to incorporate upscale attributes at a lower cost than rivals and then using the company's low-cost advantage to underprice rivals whose products have similar upscale attributes.

The target market for a best-cost provider is value-conscious buyers—buyers that are looking for appealing extras at an appealingly low price. Value-hunting buyers (as distinct from buyers looking only for bargain-basement prices) often constitute a very sizable part of the overall market. Normally, value-conscious buyers are willing to pay a fair price for extra features, but they shy away from paying top dollar for items havingall the bells and whistles. It is the desire to cater to *value-conscious buyers* as opposed to *budget-conscious buyers* that sets a best-cost provider apart from a low-cost provider—the two strategies aim at distinguishably different market targets.

When a Best-Cost Provider Strategy Works Best

A best-cost provider strategy works best in markets where buyer diversity makes product differentiation the norm and where many buyers are also sensitive to price and value. This is because a best-cost provider can position itself near the middle of the market with either a medium-quality product at a below-average price or a high-quality product at an average or slightly higher price. Often, substantial numbers of buyers prefer midrange products rather than the cheap, basic products of low-cost producers or the expensive products of top-of-the-line differentiators. But unless a company has the resources, know-how, and capabilities to incorporate upscale product or service attributes at a lower cost than rivals, adopting a best-cost strategy is ill advised—a winning strategy must always be matched to a company's resource strengths and capabilities.

Illustration Capsule 5.3 describes how Toyota has applied the principles of a best-cost provider strategy in producing and marketing its Lexus brand.

The Big Risk of a Best-Cost Provider Strategy

A company's biggest vulnerability in employing a best-cost provider strategy is getting squeezed between the strategies of firms using low-cost and high-end differentiation strategies. Low-cost providers may be able to siphon customers away with the appeal of a lower price (despite their less appealing product attributes). High-end differentiators may be able to steal customers away with the appeal of better product attributes (even though their products carry a higher price tag). Thus, to be successful, a best-cost provider must offer buyers *significantly* better product attributes in order to justify a price above what low-cost leaders are charging. Likewise, it has to achieve *significantly* lower costs in providing upscale features so that it can outcompete high-end differentiators on the basis of a *significantly* lower price.

FOCUSED (OR MARKET NICHE) STRATEGIES

What sets focused strategies apart from low-cost leadership or broad differentiation strategies is concentrated attention on a narrow piece of the total market. The target segment, or niche, can be defined by geographic uniqueness, by specialized requirements in using the product, or by special product attributes that appeal only to niche members. Community Coffee, the largest family-owned specialty coffee retailer in the United States, is a company that focused on a geographic market niche; despite having a national market share of only 1.1 percent, Community has won a 50 percent share of the coffee business in supermarkets in southern Louisiana in competition

Illustration Capsule 5.3

Toyota's Best-Cost Producer Strategy for Its Lexus Line

Toyota Motor Company is widely regarded as a low-cost producer among the world's motor vehicle manufacturers. Despite its emphasis on product quality, Toyota has achieved low-cost leadership because it has developed considerable skills in efficient supply chain management and low-cost assembly capabilities, and because its models are positioned in the low-to-medium end of the price spectrum, where high production volumes are conducive to low unit costs. But when Toyota decided to introduce its new Lexus models to compete in the luxury-car market, it employed a classic best-cost provider strategy. Toyota took the following four steps in crafting and implementing its Lexus strategy:

- Designing an array of high-performance characteristics and upscale features into the Lexus models so as to make them comparable in performance and luxury to other high-end models and attractive to Mercedes, BMW, Audi, Jaguar, Cadillac, and Lincoln buyers.

- Transferring its capabilities in making high-quality Toyota models at low cost to making premium-quality Lexus models at costs below other luxury-car makers. Toyota's supply chain capabilities and low-cost assembly know-how allowed it to incorporate high-tech performance features and upscale quality into Lexus models at substantially less cost than comparable Mercedes and BMW models.

- Using its relatively lower manufacturing costs to underprice comparable Mercedes and BMW models. Toyota believed that with its cost advantage it could price attractively equipped Lexus cars low enough to draw price-conscious buyers away from Mercedes and BMW and perhaps induce dissatisfied Lincoln and Cadillac owners to switch to a Lexus. Lexus's pricing advantage over Mercedes and BMW was sometimes quite significant. For example, in 2006 the Lexus RX 330, a midsized SUV, carried a sticker price in the $36,000–$45,000 range (depending on how it was equipped), whereas variously equipped Mercedes M-class SUVs had price tags in the $50,000–$65,000 range and a BMW X5 SUV could range anywhere from $42,000 to $70,000, depending on the optional equipment chosen.

- Establishing a new network of Lexus dealers, separate from Toyota dealers, dedicated to providing a level of personalized, attentive customer service unmatched in the industry.

Lexus models have consistently ranked first in the widely watched J. D. Power & Associates quality survey, and the prices of Lexus models are typically several thousand dollars below those of comparable Mercedes and BMW models—clear signals that Toyota has succeeded in becoming a best-cost producer with its Lexus brand.

against Starbucks, Folger's, Maxwell House, and asserted specialty coffee retailers. Community Coffee's geographic version of a focus strategy has allowed it to capture sales in excess of $100 million annually by catering to the tastes of coffee drinkers across an 11-state region. Examples of firms that concentrate on a well-defined market niche keyed to a particular product or buyer segment include Animal Planet and the History Channel (in cable TV); Google (in Internet search engines); Porsche (in sports cars); Cannondale (in top-of-the-line mountain bikes); Domino's Pizza (in pizza delivery); Enterprise Rent-a-Car (a specialist in providing rental cars to repair garage customers); Bandag (a specialist in truck tire recapping that promotes its recaps aggressively at over 1,000 truck stops), CGA Inc. (a specialist in providing insurance to cover the cost of lucrative hole-in-one prizes at golf tournaments); Match.com (the world's largest online dating service); and Avid Technology (the world leader in digital technology products to create 3D animation and to edit films, videos, TV broadcasts, video games, and audio recordings). Microbreweries, local bakeries, bed-and-breakfast inns, and local owner-managed retail boutiques are all good examples of enterprises that have scaled their operations to serve narrow or local customer segments.

A Focused Low-Cost Strategy

A focused strategy based on low cost aims at securing a competitive advantage by serving buyers in the target market niche at a lower cost and lower price than rival competitors. This strategy has considerable attraction when a firm can lower costs significantly by limiting its customer base to a well-defined buyer segment. The avenues to achieving a cost advantage over rivals also serving the target market niche are the same as for low-cost leadership—outmanage rivals in keeping the costs of value chain activities contained to a bare minimum and search for innovative ways to reconfigure the firm's value chain and bypass or reduce certain value chain activities. The only real difference between a low-cost provider strategy and a focused low-cost strategy is the size of the buyer group that a company is trying to appeal to—the former involves a product offering that appeals broadly to most all buyer groups and market segments whereas the latter at just meeting the needs of buyers in a narrow market segment.

Focused low-cost strategies are fairly common. Producers of private-label goods are able to achieve low costs in product development, marketing, distribution, and advertising by concentrating on making generic items imitative of name-brand merchandise and selling directly to retail chains wanting a basic house brand to sell to price-sensitive shoppers. Several small printer-supply manufacturers have begun making low-cost clones of the premium-priced replacement ink and toner cartridges sold by Hewlett-Packard, Lexmark, Canon, and Epson; the clone manufacturers dissect the cartridges of the name-brand companies and then reengineer a similar version that won't violate patents. The components for remanufactured replacement cartridges are aquired from various outside sources, and the clones are then marketed at prices as much as 50 percent below the name-brand cartridges. Cartridge remanufacturers have been lured to focus on this market because replacement cartridges constitute a multibillion-dollar business with considerable profit potential given their low costs and the premium pricing of the name-brand companies. Illustration Capsule 5.4 describes how Motel 6 has kept its costs low in catering to budget-conscious travelers.

A Focused Differentiation Strategy

A focused strategy keyed to differentiation aims at securing a competitive advantage with a product offering carefully designed to appeal to the unique preferences and needs of a narrow, well-defined group of buyers (as opposed to a broad differentiation strategy aimed at many buyer groups and market segments). Successful use of a focused differentiation strategy depends on the existence of a buyer segment that is looking for special product attributes or seller capabilities and on a firm's ability to stand apart from rivals competing in the same target market niche.

Companies like Godiva Chocolates, Chanel, Gucci, Rolls-Royce, Häagen-Dazs, and W. L. Gore (the maker of Gore-Tex) employ successful differentiation-based focused strategies targeted at upscale buyers wanting products and services with world-class attributes. Indeed, most markets contain a buyer segment willing to pay a big price premium for the very finest items available, thus opening the strategic window for some competitors to pursue differentiation-based focused strategies aimed at the very top of the market pyramid. Another successful focused differentiator is Trader Joe's, a 150-store East and West Coast "fashion food retailer" that is a combination gourmet deli and grocery warehouse.[8] Customers shop Trader Joe's as much for entertainment as for conventional grocery items—the store stocks out-of-the-ordinary culinary treats like raspberry salsa, salmon burgers, and jasmine fried rice,

Illustration Capsule 5.4
Motel 6's Focused Low-Cost Strategy

Motel 6 caters to price-conscious travelers who want a clean, no-frills place to spend the night. To be a low-cost provider of overnight lodging, Motel 6 (1) selects relatively inexpensive sites on which to construct its units (usually near interstate exits and high-traffic locations but far enough away to avoid paying prime site prices); (2) builds only basic facilities (no restaurant or bar and only rarely a swimming pool); (3) relies on standard architectural designs that incorporate inexpensive materials and low-cost construction techniques; and (4) provides simple room furnishings and decorations. These approaches lower both investment costs and operating costs. Without restaurants, bars, and all kinds of guest services, a Motel 6 unit can be operated with just front-desk personnel, room cleanup crews, and skeleton building-and-grounds maintenance.

To promote the Motel 6 concept with travelers who have simple overnight requirements, the chain uses unique, recognizable radio ads done by nationally syndicated radio personality Tom Bodett; the ads describe Motel 6's clean rooms, no-frills facilities, friendly atmosphere, and dependably low rates (usually under $40 a night).

Motel 6's basis for competitive advantage is lower costs than competitors in providing basic, economical overnight accommodations to price-constrained travelers.

as well as the standard goods normally found in supermarkets. What sets Trader Joe's apart is not just its unique combination of food novelties and competitively priced grocery items but also its capability to turn an otherwise mundane grocery excursion into a whimsical treasure hunt that is just plain fun.

Illustration Capsule 5.5 describes Progressive Insurance's focused differentiation strategy.

When a Focused Low-Cost or Focused Differentiation Strategy Is Attractive

A focused strategy aimed at securing a competitive edge based on either low cost or differentiation becomes increasingly attractive as more of the following conditions are met:

- The target market niche is big enough to be profitable and offers good growth potential.
- Industry leaders do not see that having a presence in the niche is crucial to their own success—in which case focusers can often escape battling head-to-head against some of the industry's biggest and strongest competitors.
- It is costly or difficult for multisegment competitors to put capabilities in place to meet the specialized needs of buyers comprising the target market niche and at the same time satisfy the expectations of their mainstream customers.
- The industry has many different niches and segments, thereby allowing a focuser to pick a competitively attractive niche suited to its resource strengths and capabilities. Also, with more niches, there is more room for focusers to avoid each other in competing for the same customers.

Illustration Capsule 5.5
Progressive Insurance's Focused Differentiation Strategy in Auto Insurance

Progressive Insurance has fashioned a strategy in auto insurance focused on people with a record of traffic violations who drive high-performance cars, drivers with accident histories, motorcyclists, teenagers, and other so-called high-risk categories of drivers that most auto insurance companies steer away from. Progressive discovered that some of these high-risk drivers are affluent and pressed for time, making them less sensitive to paying premium rates for their car insurance. Management learned that it could charge such drivers high enough premiums to cover the added risks, plus it differentiated Progressive from other insurers by expediting the process of obtaining insurance and decreasing the annoyance that such drivers faced in obtaining insurance coverage. Progressive pioneered the low-cost direct sales model of allowing customers to purchase insurance online and over the phone.

Progressive also studied the market segments for insurance carefully enough to discover that some motorcycle owners were not especially risky (middle-aged suburbanites who sometimes commuted to work or used their motorcycles mainly for recreational trips with their friends). Progressive's strategy allowed it to become a leader in the market for luxury-car insurance for customers who appreciated Progressive's streamlined approach to doing business.

In further differentiating and promoting Progressive policies, management created teams of roving claims adjusters who would arrive at accident scenes to assess claims and issue checks for repairs on the spot. Progressive introduced 24-hour claims reporting, now an industry standard. In addition, it developed a sophisticated pricing system so that it could quickly and accurately assess each customer's risk and weed out unprofitable customers.

By being creative and excelling at the nuts and bolts of its business, Progressive has won a 7 percent share of the $150 billion market for auto insurance and has the highest underwriting margins in the auto-insurance industry.

Sources: www.progressiveinsurance.com; Ian C. McMillan, Alexander van Putten, and Rita Gunther McGrath, "Global Gamesmanship," *Harvard Business Review* 81, no. 5 (May 2003), p. 68; and *Fortune,* May 16, 2005, p. 34.

- Few, if any, other rivals are attempting to specialize in the same target segment—a condition that reduces the risk of segment overcrowding.
- The focuser has a reservoir of customer goodwill and loyalty (accumulated from having catered to the specialized needs and preferences of niche members over many years) that it can draw on to help stave off ambitious challengers looking to horn in on its business.

The advantages of focusing a company's entire competitive effort on a single market niche are considerable, especially for smaller and medium-sized companies that may lack the breadth and depth of resources to tackle going after a broad customer base with a "something for everyone" lineup of models, styles, and product selection. eBay has made a huge name for itself and very attractive profits for shareholders by focusing its attention on online auctions—at one time a very small niche in the overall auction business that eBay's focus strategy turned into the dominant piece of the global auction industry. Google has capitalized on its specialized expertise in Internet search engines to become one of the most spectacular growth companies of the past 10 years. Two hippie entrepreneurs, Ben Cohen and Jerry Greenfield, built Ben & Jerry's Homemade into an impressive business by focusing their energies and resources solely on the superpremium segment of the ice cream market.

The Risks of a Focused Low-Cost or Focused Differentiation Strategy

Focusing carries several risks. One is the chance that competitors will find effective ways to match the focused firm's capabilities in serving the target niche—perhaps by coming up with products or brands specifically designed to appeal to buyers in the target niche or by developing expertise and capabilities that offset the focuser's strengths. In the lodging business, large chains like Marriott and Hilton have launched multibrand strategies that allow them to compete effectively in several lodging segments simultaneously. Marriott has flagship hotels with a full complement of services and amenities that allow it to attract travelers and vacationers going to major resorts, it has J. W. Marriot hotels usually located in downtown metropolitan areas that cater to business travelers; the Courtyard by Marriott brand is for business travelers looking for moderately priced lodging; Marriott Residence Inns are designed as a home away from home for travelers staying five or more nights; and the 530 Fairfield Inn locations cater to travelers looking for quality lodging at an affordable price. Similarly, Hilton has a lineup of brands (Conrad Hotels, Doubletree Hotels, Embassy Suite Hotels, Hampton Inns, Hilton Hotels, Hilton Garden Inns, and Homewood Suites) that enable it to operate in multiple segments and compete head-to-head against lodging chains that operate only in a single segment. Multibrand strategies are attractive to large companies like Marriott and Hilton precisely because they enable a company to enter a market niche and siphon business away from companies that employ a focus strategy.

A second risk of employing a focus strategy is the potential for the preferences and needs of niche members to shift over time toward the product attributes desired by the majority of buyers. An erosion of the differences across buyer segments lowers entry barriers into a focuser's market niche and provides an open invitation for rivals in adjacent segments to begin competing for the focuser's customers. A third risk is that the segment may become so attractive it is soon inundated with competitors, intensifying rivalry and splintering segment profits.

THE CONTRASTING FEATURES OF THE FIVE GENERIC COMPETITIVE STRATEGIES: A SUMMARY

Deciding which generic competitive strategy should serve as the framework for hanging the rest of the company's strategy is not a trivial matter. Each of the five generic competitive strategies positions the company differently in its market and competitive environment. Each establishes a central theme for how the company will endeavor to outcompete rivals. Each creates some boundaries or guidelines for maneuvering as market circumstances unfold and as ideas for improving the strategy are debated. Each points to different ways of experimenting and tinkering with the basic strategy—for example, employing a low-cost leadership strategy means experimenting with ways that costs can be cut and value chain activities can be streamlined, whereas a broad differentiation strategy means exploring ways to add new differentiating features or to perform value chain activities differently if the result is to add value for customers in ways they are willing to pay for. Each entails differences in terms of product line, production emphasis, marketing emphasis, and means of sustaining the strategy—as shown in Table 5.1.

Table 5.1 **Distinguishing Features of the Five Generic Competitive Strategies**

	Low-Cost Provider	Broad Differentiation	Best-Cost Provider	Focused Low-Cost Provider	Focused Differentiation
Strategic target	• A broad cross-section of the market	• A broad cross-section of the market	• Value-conscious buyers	• A narrow market niche where buyer needs and preferences are distinctively different	• A narrow market niche where buyer needs and preferences are distinctively different
Basis of competitive advantage	• Lower overall costs than competitors	• Ability to offer buyers something attractively different from competitors	• Ability to give customers more value for the money	• Lower overall cost than rivals in serving niche members	• Attributes that appeal specifically to niche members
Product line	• A good basic product with few frills (acceptable quality and limited selection)	• Many product variations, wide selection; emphasis on differentiating features	• Items with appealing attributes; assorted upscale features	• Features and attributes tailored to the tastes and requirements of niche members	• Features and attributes tailored to the tastes and requirements of niche members
Production emphasis	• A continuous search for cost reduction without sacrificing acceptable quality and essential features	• Build in whatever differentiating features buyers are willing to pay for; strive for product superiority	• Build in upscale features and appealing attributes at lower cost than rivals	• A continuous search for cost reduction while incorporating features and attributes matched to niche member preferences	• Custom-made products that match the tastes and requirements of niche members
Marketing emphasis	• Try to make a virtue out of product features that lead to low cost	• Tout differentiating features • Charge a premium price to cover the extra costs of differentiating features	• Tout delivery of best value • Either deliver comparable features at a lower price than rivals or else match rivals on prices and provide better features	• Communicate attractive features of a budget-priced product offering that fits niche buyers' expectations	• Communicate how product offering does the best job of meeting niche buyers' expectations
Keys to sustaining the strategy	• Economical prices/good value • Strive to manage costs down, year after year, in every area of the business	• Stress constant innovation to stay ahead of imitative competitors • Concentrate on a few key differentiating features	• Unique expertise in simultaneously managing costs down while incorporating upscale features and attributes	• Stay committed to serving the niche at lowest overall cost; don't blur the firm's image by entering other market segments or adding other products to widen market appeal	• Stay committed to serving the niche better than rivals; don't blur the firm's image by entering other market segments or adding other products to widen market appeal

Thus, a choice of which generic strategy to employ spills over to affect several aspects of how the business will be operated and the manner in which value chain activities must be managed. Deciding which generic strategy to employ is perhaps the most important strategic commitment a company makes—it tends to drive the rest of the strategic actions a company decides to undertake.

One of the big dangers in crafting a competitive strategy is that managers, torn between the pros and cons of the various generic strategies, will opt for *stuck-in-the-middle strategies* that represent compromises between lower costs and greater differentiation and between broad and narrow market appeal. Compromise or middle-ground strategies rarely produce sustainable competitive advantage or a distinctive competitive position—a well-executed best-cost producer strategy is the only compromise between low cost and differentiation that succeeds. Usually, companies with compromise strategies end up with a middle-of-the-pack industry ranking—they have average costs, some but not a lot of product differentiation relative to rivals, an average image and reputation, and little prospect of industry leadership. Having a competitive edge over rivals is the single most dependable contributor to above-average company profitability. Hence, only if a company makes a strong and unwavering commitment to one of the five generic competitive strategies does it stand much chance of achieving sustainable competitive advantage that such strategies can deliver if properly executed.

Key Points

Early in the process of crafting a strategy company managers have to decide which of the five basic competitive strategies to employ—overall low-cost, broad differentiation, best-cost, focused low-cost, or focused differentiation.

In employing a low-cost provider strategy and trying to achieve a low-cost advantage over rivals, a company must do a better job than rivals of cost-effectively managing value chain activities and/or find innovative ways to eliminate or bypass cost-producing activities. Low-cost provider strategies work particularly well when the products of rival sellers are virtually identical or very weakly differentiated and supplies are readily available from eager sellers, when there are not many ways to differentiate that have value to buyers, when many buyers are price sensitive and shop the market for the lowest price, and when buyer switching costs are low.

Broad differentiation strategies seek to produce a competitive edge by incorporating attributes and features that set a company's product/service offering apart from rivals in ways that buyers consider valuable and worth paying for. Successful differentiation allows a firm to (1) command a premium price for its product, (2) increase unit sales (because additional buyers are won over by the differentiating features), and/or (3) gain buyer loyalty to its brand (because some buyers are strongly attracted to the differentiating features and bond with the company and its products). Differentiation strategies work best in markets with diverse buyer preferences where there are big windows of opportunity to strongly differentiate a company's product offering from those of rival brands, in situations where few other rivals are pursuing a similar differentiation approach, and in circumstances where companies are racing to bring out the most appealing next-generation product. A differentiation strategy is doomed when competitors are able to quickly copy most or all of the appealing product attributes a company comes up with, when a company's differentiation efforts meet with a ho-hum or so what market reception, or when a company erodes profitability by overspending on efforts to differentiate its product offering.

Best-cost provider strategies combine a strategic emphasis on low cost with a strategic emphasis on more than minimal quality, service, features, or performance. The aim is to create competitive advantage by giving buyers more value for the money—an approach that entails matching close rivals on key quality/service/features/performance attributes and beating them on the costs of incorporating such attributes into the product or service. A best-cost provider strategy works best in markets where buyer diversity makes product differentiation the norm and where many buyers are also sensitive to price and value.

A focus strategy delivers competitive advantage either by achieving lower costs than rivals in serving buyers comprising the target market niche or by developing specialized ability to offer niche buyers an appealingly differentiated offering than meets their needs better than rival brands. A focused strategy based on either low cost or differentiation becomes increasingly attractive when the target market niche is big enough to be profitable and offers good growth potential, when it is costly or difficult for multi-segment competitors to put capabilities in place to meet the specialized needs of the target market niche and at the same time satisfy the expectations of their mainstream customers, when there are one or more niches that present a good match with a focuser's resource strengths and capabilities, and when few other rivals are attempting to specialize in the same target segment.

Deciding which generic strategy to employ is perhaps the most important strategic commitment a company makes—it tends to drive the rest of the strategic actions a company decides to undertake and it sets the whole tone for the pursuit of a competitive advantage over rivals.

Exercises

1. Go to www.google.com and do a search for "low-cost producer." See if you can identify five companies that are pursuing a low-cost strategy in their respective industries.

2. Using the advanced search function at www.google.com, enter "best-cost producer" in the exact-phrase box and see if you can locate three companies that indicate they are employing a best-cost producer strategy.

3. Go to BMW's Web site (www.bmw.com) click on the link for BMW Group. The site you find provides an overview of the company's key functional areas, including R&D and production activities. Explore each of the links on the Research & Development page—People & Networks, Innovation & Technology, and Mobility & Traffic—to better understand the company's approach. Also review the statements under Production focusing on vehicle production and sustainable production. How do these activities contribute to BMW's differentiation strategy and the unique position in the auto industry that BMW has achieved?

4. Which of the five generic competitive strategies do you think the following companies are employing (do whatever research at the various company Web sites might be needed to arrive at and support your answer):
    a. The Saturn division of General Motors
    b. Abercrombie & Fitch
    c. Amazon.com
    d. Home Depot
    e. Mary Kay Cosmetics
    f. *USA Today*

chapter six

Supplementing the Chosen Competitive Strategy

Other Important Strategy Choices

Don't form an alliance to correct a weakness and don't ally with a partner that is trying to correct a weakness of its own. The only result from a marriage of weaknesses is the creation of even more weaknesses.

—**Michel Robert**

Strategies for taking the hill won't necessarily hold it.

—**Amar Bhide**

The sure path to oblivion is to stay where you are.

—**Bernard Fauber**

Successful business strategy is about actively shaping the game you play, not just playing the game you find.

—**Adam M. Brandenburger and Barry J. Nalebuff**

O nce a company has settled on which of the five generic strategies to employ, attention turns to what other *strategic actions* it can take to complement its choice of a basic competitive strategy. Several decisions have to be made:

- What use to make of strategic alliances and collaborative partnerships.
- Whether to bolster the company's market position via merger or acquisitions.
- Whether to integrate backward or forward into more stages of the industry value chain.
- Whether to outsource certain value chain activities or perform them in-house.
- Whether and when to employ offensive and defensive moves.
- Which of several ways to use the Internet as a distribution channel in positioning the company in the marketplace.

This chapter contains sections discussing the pros and cons of each of the above complementary strategic options. The next-to-last section in the chapter discusses the need for strategic choices in each functional area of a company's business (R&D, production, sales and marketing, finance, and so on) to support its basic competitive approach and complementary strategic moves. The chapter concludes with a brief look at the competitive importance of timing strategic moves—when it is advantageous to be a first-mover and when it is better to be a fast-follower or late-mover.

Figure 6.1 shows the menu of strategic options a company has in crafting a strategy and the order in which the choices should generally be made. The portion of Figure 6.1 below the five generic competitive strategy options illustrates the structure of this chapter and the topics that will be covered.

Figure 6.1   **A Company's Menu of Strategy Options**

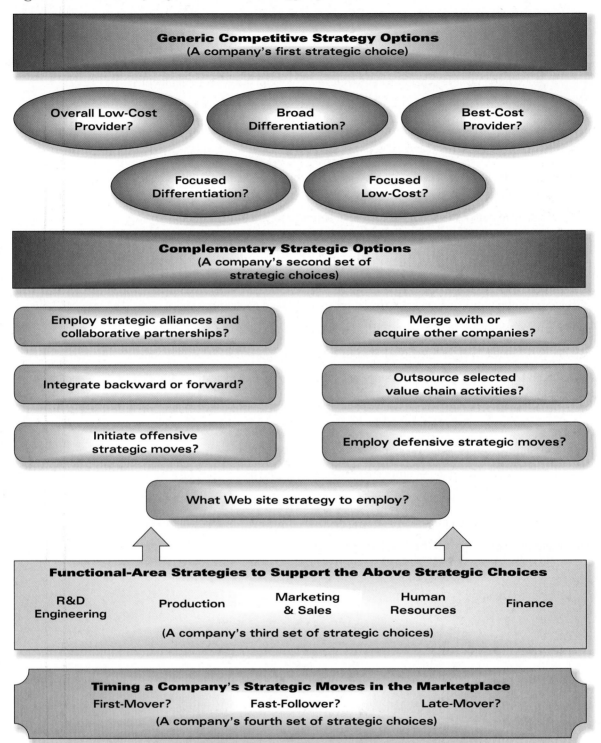

COLLABORATIVE STRATEGIES: ALLIANCES AND PARTNERSHIPS

Companies in all types of industries and in all parts of the world have elected to form strategic alliances and partnerships to complement their own strategic initiatives and strengthen their competitiveness in domestic and international markets. This is an about-face from times past, when the vast majority of companies were content to go it alone, confident that they already had or could independently develop whatever resources and know-how were needed to be successful in their markets. But globalization of the world economy; revolutionary advances in technology across a broad front; and untapped opportunities in Asia, Latin America, and Europe—whose national markets are opening up, deregulating, and/or undergoing privatization—have made strategic partnerships of one kind or another integral to competing on a broad geographic scale.

Many companies now find themselves thrust into two very demanding competitive races: (1) *the global race to build a market presence in many different national markets* and join the ranks of companies recognized as global market leaders, and (2) *the race to seize opportunities on the frontiers of advancing technology* and build the resource strengths and business capabilities to compete successfully in the industries and product markets of the future.[1] Even the largest and most financially sound companies have concluded that simultaneously running the races for global market leadership and for a stake in the industries of the future requires more diverse and expansive skills, resources, technological expertise, and competitive capabilities than they can assemble and manage alone. Such companies, along with others that are missing the resources and competitive capabilities needed to pursue promising opportunities, have determined that the fastest way to fill the gap is often to form alliances with enterprises having the desired strengths. Consequently, these companies form strategic alliances or collaborative partnerships in which two or more companies jointly work to achieve mutually beneficial strategic outcomes. Thus, a **strategic alliance** is a formal agreement between two or more separate companies in which there is strategically relevant collaboration of some sort, joint contribution of resources, shared risk, shared control, and mutual dependence. Often, alliances involve joint marketing, joint sales or distribution, joint production, design collaboration, joint research, or projects to jointly develop new technologies or products. The relationship between the partners may be contractual or merely collaborative; the arrangement commonly stops short of formal ownership ties between the partners (although there are a few strategic alliances where one or more allies have minority ownership in certain of the other alliance members). Five factors make an alliance strategic, as opposed to just a convenient business arrangement:[2]

> **Core Concept**
> **Strategic alliances** are collaborative arrangements where two or more companies join forces to achieve mutually beneficial strategic outcomes.

1. It is critical to the company's achievement of an important objective.
2. It helps build, sustain, or enhance a core competence or competitive advantage.
3. It helps block a competitive threat.
4. It helps open up important new market opportunities.
5. It mitigates a significant risk to a company's business.

Strategic cooperation is a much-favored, indeed necessary, approach in industries where new technological developments are occurring at a furious pace along many different paths and where advances in one technology spill over to affect others (often blurring industry boundaries). Whenever industries are experiencing high-velocity technological advances in many areas simultaneously, firms find it virtually essential to have cooperative relationships with other enterprises to stay on the leading edge of technology and product performance even in their own area of specialization.

Companies in many different industries all across the world have made strategic alliances a core part of their overall strategy; U.S. companies alone announced nearly 68,000 alliances from 1996 through 2003.[3] In the personal computer (PC) industry,

> Company use of alliances is quite widespread.

alliances are pervasive because the different components of PCs and the software to run them are supplied by so many different companies—one set of companies provides the microprocessors, another group makes the motherboards, another the monitors, another the disk drives, another the memory chips, and so on. Moreover, their facilities are scattered across the United States, Japan, Taiwan, Singapore, Malaysia, and parts of Europe. Strategic alliances among companies in the various parts of the PC industry facilitate the close cross-company collaboration required on next-generation product development, logistics, production, and the timing of new product releases.

Toyota has forged long-term strategic partnerships with many of its suppliers of automotive parts and components, both to achieve lower costs and to improve the quality and reliability of its vehicles. Microsoft collaborates very closely with independent software developers to ensure that their programs will run on the next-generation versions of Windows. Genentech, a leader in biotechnology and human genetics, has a partnering strategy to increase its access to novel biotherapeutics products and technologies and has formed alliances with over 30 companies to strengthen its research and development (R&D) pipeline. During the 1998–2004 period, Samsung Electronics, a South Korean corporation with $54 billion in sales, entered into over 50 major strategic alliances involving such companies as Sony, Yahoo, Hewlett-Packard, Nokia, Motorola, Intel, Microsoft, Dell, Mitsubishi, Disney, IBM, Maytag, and Rockwell Automation; the alliances involved joint investments, technology transfer arrangements, joint R&D projects, and agreements to supply parts and components—all of which facilitated Samsung's strategic efforts to transform itself into a global enterprise and establish itself as a leader in the worldwide electronics industry.

Studies indicate that large corporations are commonly involved in 30 to 50 alliances and that some have hundreds of alliances. One recent study estimated that about 35 percent of corporate revenues in 2003 came from activities involving strategic alliances, up from 15 percent in 1995.[4] Another study reported that the typical large corporation relied on alliances for 15 to 20 percent of its revenues, assets, or income.[5] Companies that have formed a host of alliances have a need to manage their alliances like a portfolio—terminating those that no longer serve a useful purpose or that have produced meager results, forming promising new alliances, and restructuring certain existing alliances to correct performance problems and/or redirect the collaborative effort.[6]

Why and How Strategic Alliances Are Advantageous

The most common reasons why companies enter into strategic alliances are to expedite the development of promising new technologies or products, to overcome deficits in their own technical and manufacturing expertise, to bring together the personnel and expertise needed to create desirable new skill sets and capabilities, to improve supply chain efficiency, to gain economies of scale in production and/or marketing, and to acquire or improve market access through joint marketing agreements.[7] In bringing together firms with different skills and knowledge bases, alliances open up learning opportunities that help partner firms better leverage their own resource strengths.[8] In industries where technology is advancing rapidly, alliances are all about fast cycles of learning, staying abreast of the latest developments, and gaining quick access to the latest round of technological know-how and capability.

> The best alliances are highly selective, focusing on particular value chain activities and on obtaining a particular competitive benefit. They tend to enable a firm to build on its strengths and to learn.

There are several other instances in which companies find strategic alliances particularly valuable. A company that is racing for *global market leadership* needs alliances to:

- Get into critical country markets quickly and accelerate the process of building a potent global market presence.
- *Gain inside knowledge about unfamiliar markets and cultures* through alliances with local partners. For example, U.S., European, and Japanese companies wanting to build market footholds in the fast-growing Chinese market have pursued partnership arrangements with Chinese companies to help in getting products through the tedious and typically corrupt customs process, to help guide them through the maze of government regulations, to supply knowledge of local markets, to provide guidance on adapting their products to better match the buying preferences of Chinese consumers, to set up local manufacturing capabilities, and to assist in distribution, marketing, and promotional activities. The Chinese government has long required foreign companies operating in China to have a state-owned Chinese company as a minority or maybe even 50 percent partner—only recently has it backed off this requirement for foreign companies operating in selected parts of the Chinese economy.
- *Access valuable skills and competencies* that are concentrated in particular geographic locations (such as software design competencies in the United States, fashion design skills in Italy, and efficient manufacturing skills in Japan and China).

A company that is racing to *stake out a strong position in an industry of the future* needs alliances to:

- *Establish a stronger beachhead* for participating in the target industry.
- *Master new technologies and build new expertise and competencies* faster than would be possible through internal efforts.
- *Open up broader opportunities* in the target industry by melding the firm's own capabilities with the expertise and resources of partners.

Allies can learn much from one another in performing joint research, sharing technological know-how, and collaborating on complementary new technologies and products—sometimes enough to enable them to pursue other new opportunities on their own.[9] Manufacturers frequently pursue alliances with parts and components suppliers to gain the efficiencies of better supply chain management and to speed new products to market. By joining forces in components production and/or final assembly, companies may be able to realize cost savings not achievable with their own small volumes—German automakers Volkswagen, Audi, and Porsche formed a strategic alliance to spur mutual development of a gasoline-electric hybrid engine and transmission system that they could each then incorporate into their motor vehicle models; BMW, General

> The competitive attraction of alliances is in allowing companies to bundle competencies and resources that are more valuable in a joint effort than when kept separate.

Motors, and DaimlerChrysler formed a similar partnership. Both alliances were aimed at closing the gap on Toyota, generally said to be the world leader in fuel-efficient hybrid engines. Information systems consultant Accenture has developed strategic alliances with such leading technology providers as SAP, Oracle, Siebel, Microsoft, BEA, and Hewlett-Packard to give it greater capabilities in designing and integrating information systems for its corporate clients. Johnson & Johnson and Merck entered into an alliance to market Pepcid AC; Merck developed the stomach distress remedy, and Johnson & Johnson functioned as marketer—the alliance made Pepcid products the best-selling remedies for acid indigestion and heartburn. United Airlines, American Airlines, Continental, Delta, and Northwest created an alliance to form Orbitz, an Internet travel site to compete head-to-head against Expedia and Travelocity, thereby strengthening their access to travelers and vacationers shopping online for airfares, rental cars, lodging, cruises, and vacation packages.

Capturing the Benefits of Strategic Alliances

The extent to which companies benefit from entering into alliances and collaborative partnerships seems to be a function of six factors:[10]

1. *Picking a good partner*—A good partner not only has the desired expertise and capabilities but also shares the company's vision about the purpose of the alliance. Experience indicates that it is generally wise to avoid a partnership in which there is strong potential of direct competition because of overlapping product lines or other conflicting interests—agreements to jointly market each other's products hold much potential for conflict unless the products are complements rather than substitutes and unless there is good chemistry among key personnel. Experience also indicates that alliances between strong and weak companies rarely work because the alliance is unlikely to provide the strong partner with useful resources or skills and because there's a greater chance of the alliance producing mediocre results.

2. *Being sensitive to cultural differences*—Unless the outsider exhibits respect for the local culture and local business practices, productive working relationships are unlikely to emerge.

3. *Recognizing that the alliance must benefit both sides*—Information must be shared as well as gained, and the relationship must remain forthright and trustful. Many alliances fail because one or both partners grow unhappy with what they are learning. Also, if either partner plays games with information or tries to take advantage of the other, the resulting friction can quickly erode the value of further collaboration.

4. *Ensuring that both parties live up to their commitments*—Both parties have to deliver on their commitments for the alliance to produce the intended benefits. The division of work has to be perceived as fairly apportioned, and the caliber of the benefits received on both sides has to be perceived as adequate.

5. *Structuring the decision-making process so that actions can be taken swiftly when needed*—In many instances, the fast pace of technological and competitive changes dictates an equally fast decision-making process. If the parties get bogged down in discussion or in gaining internal approval from higher-ups, the alliance can turn into an anchor of delay and inaction.

6. *Managing the learning process and then adjusting the alliance agreement over time to fit new circumstances*—One of the keys to long-lasting success is adapting the nature and structure of the alliance to be responsive to shifting market conditions, emerging technologies, and changing customer requirements. Wise allies are quick

to recognize the merit of an evolving collaborative arrangement, where adjustments are made to accommodate changing market conditions and to overcome whatever problems arise in establishing an effective working relationship. Most alliances encounter troubles of some kind within a couple of years—those that are flexible enough to evolve are better able to recover.

Most alliances that aim at technology sharing or providing market access turn out to be temporary, fulfilling their purpose after a few years because the benefits of mutual learning have occurred and because the businesses of both partners have developed to the point where they are ready to go their own ways. In such cases, it is important for each partner to learn thoroughly and rapidly about the other partner's technology, business practices, and organizational capabilities and then promptly transfer valuable ideas and practices into its own operations. Although long-term alliances sometimes prove mutually beneficial, most partners don't hesitate to terminate the alliance and go it alone when the payoffs run out.

Alliances are more likely to be long-lasting when (1) they involve collaboration with suppliers or distribution allies and each party's contribution involves activities in different portions of the industry value chain, or (2) both parties conclude that continued collaboration is in their mutual interest, perhaps because new opportunities for learning are emerging or perhaps because further collaboration will allow each partner to extend its market reach beyond what it could accomplish on its own.

Why Many Alliances Are Unstable or Break Apart

The stability of an alliance depends on how well the partners work together, their success in responding and adapting to changing internal and external conditions, and their willingness to renegotiate the bargain if circumstances so warrant. A successful alliance requires real in-the-trenches collaboration, not merely an arm's-length exchange of ideas. Unless partners place a high value on the skills, resources, and contributions each brings to the alliance and the cooperative arrangement results in valuable win–win outcomes, it is doomed. A surprisingly large number of alliances never live up to expectations. A 1999 study by Accenture, a global business consulting organization, revealed that 61 percent of alliances were either outright failures or "limping along." In 2004, McKinsey & Company estimated that the overall success rate of alliances was around 50 percent, based on whether the alliance achieved the stated objectives.[11] Many alliances are dissolved after a few years. The high "divorce rate" among strategic allies has several causes—diverging objectives and priorities, an inability to work well together (an alliance between Disney and Pixar came apart because of clashes between high-level executives—in 2005, after one of the feuding executives retired, Disney acquired Pixar), changing conditions that render the purpose of the alliance obsolete, the emergence of more attractive technological paths, and marketplace rivalry between one or more allies.[12] Experience indicates that *alliances stand a reasonable chance of helping a company reduce competitive disadvantage, but very rarely have they proved a strategic option for gaining a durable competitive edge over rivals.*

The Strategic Dangers of Relying Heavily on Alliances and Collaborative Partnerships

The Achilles heel of alliances and collaborative partnerships is dependence on another company for *essential* expertise and capabilities. To be a market leader (and perhaps even a serious market contender), a company must ultimately develop its own capabilities in areas where internal strategic control is pivotal to protecting its competitiveness and building competitive advantage. Moreover, some alliances hold only limited potential because the partner guards its most valuable skills and expertise; in such instances, acquiring or merging with a company possessing the desired know-how and resources is a better solution.

MERGER AND ACQUISITION STRATEGIES

Mergers and acquisitions are much-used strategic options—for example, U.S. companies alone made 90,000 acquisitions from 1996 through 2003.[13] Mergers and acquisitions are especially suited for situations in which alliances and partnerships do not go far enough in providing a company with access to needed resources and capabilities.[14] Ownership ties are more permanent than partnership ties, allowing the operations of the merger/acquisition participants to be tightly integrated and creating more in-house control and autonomy. A *merger* is a pooling of equals, with the newly created company often taking on a new name. An *acquisition* is a combination in which one company, the acquirer, purchases and absorbs the operations of another, the acquired. The difference between a merger and an acquisition relates more to the details of ownership, management control, and financial arrangements than to strategy and competitive advantage. The resources, competencies, and competitive capabilities of the newly created enterprise end up much the same whether the combination is the result of acquisition or merger.

> Combining the operations of two companies, via merger or acquisition, is an attractive strategic option for achieving operating economies, strengthening the resulting company's competences and competitiveness, and opening up avenues of new market opportunity.

Many mergers and acquisitions are driven by strategies to achieve any of five strategic objectives:[15]

1. *To create a more cost-efficient operation out of the combined companies*—When a company acquires another company in the same industry, there's usually enough overlap in operations that certain inefficient plants can be closed or distribution activities partly combined and downsized (when nearby centers serve some of the same geographic areas), or sales-force and marketing activities combined and downsized (when each company has salespeople calling on the same customer). The combined companies may also be able to reduce supply chain costs because of buying in greater volume from common suppliers and from closer collaboration with supply chain partners. Likewise, it is usually feasible to squeeze out cost savings in administrative activities, again by combining and downsizing such administrative activities as finance and accounting, information technology, and human resources. The merger that formed DaimlerChrysler was motivated in large part by the fact that the motor vehicle industry had far more production capacity worldwide than was needed; top executives at both Daimler-Benz and Chrysler believed that the efficiency of the two companies could be significantly improved by shutting some plants and laying off workers; realigning which models were produced at which plants; and squeezing out efficiencies by combining supply chain activities, product design, and administration. Quite a number of acquisitions are undertaken with the objective of transforming two or more otherwise high-cost companies into one lean competitor with average or below-average costs.

2. *To expand a company's geographic coverage*—One of the best and quickest ways to expand a company's geographic coverage is to acquire rivals with operations in the desired locations. And if there is some geographic overlap, then a side benefit is being able to reduce costs by eliminating duplicate facilities in those geographic areas where undesirable overlap exists. Banks like Wells Fargo, Bank

of America, Wachovia, and Suntrust have pursued geographic expansion by making a series of acquisitions over the years, enabling them to establish a market presence in an ever-growing number of states and localities. Many companies use acquisitions to expand internationally; for example, food products companies like Nestlé, Kraft, Unilever, and Procter & Gamble—all racing for global market leadership—have made acquisitions an integral part of their strategies to widen their geographic reach.

3. *To extend the company's business into new product categories*—Many times a company has gaps in its product line that need to be filled. Acquisition can be a quicker and more potent way to broaden a company's product line than going through the exercise of introducing a company's own new product to fill the gap. PepsiCo acquired Quaker Oats chiefly to bring Gatorade into the Pepsi family of beverages. While Coca-Cola has expanded its beverage lineup by introducing its own new products (like Powerade and Dasani), it has also expanded its lineup by acquiring Fanta (carbonated fruit beverages), Minute Maid (juices and juice drinks), Odwalla (juices), and Hi-C (ready-to-drink fruit beverages).

4. *To gain quick access to new technologies or other resources and competitive capabilities*—Making acquisitions to bolster a company's technological know-how or to fill resource holes is a favorite of companies racing to establish a position in an industry or product category about to be born. Making acquisitions aimed at filling meaningful gaps in technological expertise allows a company to bypass a time-consuming and perhaps expensive R&D effort (which might not succeed). Cisco Systems purchased over 75 technology companies to give it more technological reach and product breadth, thereby buttressing its standing as the world's biggest supplier of systems for building the infrastructure of the Internet. Intel has made over 300 acquisitions in the past five or so years to broaden its technological base, obtain the resource capabilities to produce and market a variety of Internet-related and electronics-related products, and make it less dependent on supplying microprocessors for PCs.

5. *To try to invent a new industry and lead the convergence of industries whose boundaries are being blurred by changing technologies and new market opportunities*—Such acquisitions are the result of a company's management betting that two or more distinct industries are converging into one and deciding to establish a strong position in the consolidating markets by bringing together the resources and products of several different companies. Examples include the merger of AOL and media giant Time Warner—a move predicated on the belief that entertainment content would ultimately converge into a single industry (much of which would be distributed over the Internet)—and News Corporation's purchase of satellite TV companies to complement its media holdings in TV broadcasting (the Fox network and TV stations in various countries); cable TV (Fox News, Fox Sports, and FX); filmed entertainment (Twentieth Century Fox and Fox Studios); and newspaper, magazine, and book publishing.

Numerous companies have employed an acquisition strategy to catapult themselves from the ranks of the unknown into positions of market leadership. During the 1990s, North Carolina National Bank (NCNB) pursued a series of acquisitions to transform itself into a major regional bank in the Southeast. But NCNB's strategic vision was to become a bank with offices across most of the United States, so the company changed its name to NationsBank. In 1998, NationsBank acquired Bank of America for $66 billion and adopted its name. In 2004, Bank of America acquired Fleet Boston Financial for $48 billion. Then in mid-2005, Bank of America spent $35 billion to acquire MBNA,

Illustration Capsule 6.1

Clear Channel Communications: Using Mergers and Acquisitions to Become a Global Market Leader

Going into 2006, Clear Channel Communications was the world's fourth largest media company, behind Disney, Time Warner, and Viacom/CBS. The company, founded in 1972 by Lowry Mays and Billy Joe McCombs, got its start by acquiring an unprofitable country-music radio station in San Antonio, Texas. Over the next 10 years, Mays learned the radio business and slowly bought other radio stations in a variety of states. Going public in 1984 helped the company raise the equity capital needed to continue acquiring radio stations in additional geographic markets.

In the late 1980s, when the Federal Communications Commission loosened the rules regarding the ability of one company to own both radio and TV stations, Clear Channel broadened its strategy and began acquiring small, struggling TV stations. By 1998, Clear Channel had used acquisitions to build a leading position in radio and television stations. Domestically, it owned, programmed, or sold airtime for 69 AM radio stations, 135 FM stations, and 18 TV stations in 48 local markets in 24 states. Clear Channel's big move was to begin expanding internationally, chiefly by acquiring interests in radio station properties in a variety of countries.

In 1997, Clear Channel used acquisitions to establish a major position in outdoor advertising. Its first acquisition was Phoenix-based Eller Media Company, an outdoor advertising company with over 100,000 billboard facings. This was quickly followed by additional acquisitions of outdoor advertising companies, the most important of which were ABC Outdoor in Milwaukee, Wisconsin; Paxton Communications (with operations in Tampa and Orlando, Florida); Universal Outdoor; the More Group, with outdoor operations and 90,000 displays in 24 countries; and the Ackerley Group.

Then in October 1999, Clear Channel made a major move by acquiring AM-FM Inc. and changed its name to

Clear Channel Communications; the AM-FM acquisition gave Clear Channel operations in 32 countries, including 830 radio stations, 19 TV stations, and more than 425,000 outdoor displays.

Additional acquisitions were completed during the 2000–2003 period. The emphasis was on buying radio, TV, and outdoor advertising properties with operations in many of the same local markets, which made it feasible to (1) cut costs by sharing facilities and staffs, (2) improve programming, and (3) sell advertising to customers in packages for all three media simultaneously. Packaging ads for two or three media not only helped Clear Channel's advertising clients distribute their messages more effectively but also allowed the company to combine its sales activities and have a common sales force for all three media, achieving significant cost savings and boosting profit margins. But in 2000 Clear Channel broadened its media strategy by acquiring SFX Entertainment, one of the world's largest promoters, producers, and presenters of live entertainment events.

At year-end 2005, Clear Channel owned radio and television stations, outdoor displays, and entertainment venues in 66 countries around the world. It operated approximately 1,200 radio and 40 television stations in the United States and had equity interests in over 240 radio stations internationally. It also operated a U.S. radio network of syndicated talk shows with about 180 million weekly listeners. In addition, the company owned or operated over 820,000 outdoor advertising displays, including billboards, street furniture, and transit panels around the world. In late 2005, the company spun off its Clear Channel Entertainment division (which was a leading promoter, producer, and marketer of about 32,000 live entertainment events annually and also owned leading athlete management and sports marketing companies) as a separate entity via an initial public offering of stock.

Sources: Information posted at www.clearchannel.com (accessed September 2005), and *BusinessWeek,* October 19, 1999, p. 56.

a leading credit card company. Going into 2006, Bank of America had a network of 5,900 branch banks in 29 states and the District of Columbia, and was managing $140 billion in credit card balances. It was the largest U.S. bank in terms of deposits, the second largest in terms of assets, and the fifth most profitable company in the world (with 2005 profits of about $17 billion).

Illustration Capsule 6.1 describes how Clear Channel Worldwide has used acquisitions to build a leading global position in outdoor advertising and radio and TV broadcasting.

All too frequently, mergers and acquisitions do not produce the hoped-for outcomes.[16] Cost savings may prove smaller than expected. Gains in competitive capabilities may take substantially longer to realize or, worse, may never materialize at all. Efforts to mesh the corporate cultures can stall due to formidable resistance from organization members. Managers and employees at the acquired company may argue forcefully for continuing to do certain things the way they were done prior to the acquisition. Key employees at the acquired company can quickly become disenchanted and leave; morale can drop to disturbingly low levels because personnel who remain disagree with newly instituted changes. Differences in management styles and operating procedures can prove hard to resolve. The managers appointed to oversee the integration of a newly acquired company can make mistakes in deciding what activities to leave alone and what activities to meld into their own operations and systems.

A number of previously applauded mergers/acquisitions have yet to live up to expectations—the merger of America Online (AOL) and Time Warner, the merger of Daimler-Benz and Chrysler, Hewlett-Packard's acquisition of Compaq Computer, Ford's acquisition of Jaguar, and Kmart's acquisition of Sears are prime examples. The AOL–Time Warner merger has proved to be mostly a disaster, partly because AOL's once-rapid growth has evaporated, partly because of a huge clash of corporate cultures, and partly because most of the expected benefits from industry convergence have yet to materialize. Ford paid a handsome price to acquire Jaguar but has yet to make the Jaguar brand a major factor in the luxury-car segment in competition against Mercedes, BMW, and Lexus. Novell acquired WordPerfect for $1.7 billion in stock in 1994, but the combination never generated enough punch to compete against Microsoft Word and Microsoft Office—Novell sold WordPerfect to Corel for $124 million in cash and stock less than two years later. In 2001 electronics retailer Best Buy paid $685 million to acquire Musicland, a struggling 1,300-store music retailer that included stores operating under the names Musicland, Sam Goody, Suncoast, Media Play, and On Cue. But Musicland's sales, already declining, dropped even further. In June 2003, Best Buy "sold" Musicland to a Florida investment firm—no cash changed hands and the "buyer" received shares of stock in Best Buy in return for assuming Musicland's liabilities.

VERTICAL INTEGRATION STRATEGIES: OPERATING ACROSS MORE STAGES OF THE INDUSTRY VALUE CHAIN

Vertical integration extends a firm's competitive and operating scope within the same industry. It involves expanding the firm's range of activities backward into sources of supply and/or forward toward end users. Thus, if a manufacturer invests in facilities to produce certain component parts that it formerly purchased from outside suppliers, it remains in essentially the same industry as before. The only change is that it has operations in two stages of the industry value chain. Similarly, if a paint manufacturer, Sherwin-Williams for example, elects to integrate forward by opening 100 retail stores to market its paint products directly to consumers, it remains in the paint business even though its competitive scope extends from manufacturing to retailing.

Vertical integration strategies can aim at *full integration* (participating in all stages of the industry value chain) or *partial integration* (building positions in selected stages of the industry's total value chain). A firm can pursue vertical integration by starting its own operations in other stages in the industry's activity chain or by acquiring a company already performing the activities it wants to bring in-house.

The Advantages of a Vertical Integration Strategy

Core Concept
A vertical integration strategy has appeal *only* if it significantly strengthens a firm's competitive position.

The two best reasons for investing company resources in vertical integration are to strengthen the firm's competitive position and/or boost its profitability.[17] Vertical integration has no real payoff profitwise or strategywise unless it produces sufficient cost savings or profit increases to justify the extra investment, adds materially to a company's technological and competitive strengths, or helps differentiate the company's product offering.

Integrating Backward to Achieve Greater Competitiveness It is harder than one might think to generate cost savings or boost profitability by integrating backward into activities such as manufacturing parts and components (which could otherwise be purchased from suppliers with specialized expertise in making these parts and components). For backward integration to be a viable and profitable strategy, a company must be able to (1) achieve the same scale economies as outside suppliers and (2) match or beat suppliers' production efficiency with no drop-off in quality. Neither outcome is a slam-dunk. To begin with, a company's in-house requirements are often too small to reach the optimum size for low-cost operation—for instance, if it takes a minimum production volume of 1 million units to achieve mass-production economies and a company's in-house requirements are just 250,000 units, then the company falls way short of being able to capture the scale economies of outside suppliers (which may readily find buyers for 1 million or more units). Furthermore, matching the production efficiency of suppliers is fraught with problems when suppliers have considerable production experience of their own, when the technology they employ has elements that are hard to master, or when substantial R&D expertise is required to develop next-version parts and components or keep pace with advancing technology in parts/components production.

But that being said, there are still occasions when a company can improve its cost position and competitiveness by performing a broad range of value chain activities in-house. The best potential for being able to reduce costs via a backward integration strategy exists in situations where suppliers have outsized profit margins, where the item being supplied is a major cost component, and where the requisite technological skills are easily mastered or can be gained by acquiring a supplier with the desired technological know-how. Furthermore, when a company has proprietary know-how that it is beneficial to keep away from rivals, then in-house performance of value chain activities related to this know-how is beneficial even if such activities could be performed by outsiders. For example, Krispy Kreme Doughnuts has successfully employed a backward vertical integration strategy that involves internally producing both the doughnut-making equipment and ready-mixed doughnut ingredients that company-owned and franchised retail stores used in making Krispy Kreme doughnuts—the company earned substantial profits from producing these items internally rather than having them supplied by outsiders. Furthermore, Krispy Kreme's vertical integration strategy made good competitive sense because both its doughnut-making equipment and its doughnut recipe were proprietary; keeping its equipment manufacturing know-how and its secret recipe out of the hands of outside suppliers helped Krispy Kreme protect its doughnut offering from would-be imitators.

Backward vertical integration can produce a differentiation-based competitive advantage when a company, by performing activities internally rather than using outside suppliers, ends up with a better-quality product/service offering, improves the caliber of its customer service, or in other ways enhances the performance of its final product. On occasion, integrating into more stages along the industry value chain can add to a company's differentiation capabilities by allowing the company to build or strengthen its core competencies, better master key skills or strategy-critical technologies, or add features that deliver greater customer value. Other potential advantages of backward integration include sparing a company the uncertainty of being dependent on suppliers for crucial components or support services and lessening a company's vulnerability to powerful suppliers inclined to raise prices at every opportunity.

Integrating Forward to Enhance Competitiveness   The strategic impetus for forward integration is to gain better access to end users and better market visibility. In many industries, independent sales agents, wholesalers, and retailers handle competing brands of the same product; having no allegiance to any one company's brand, they tend to push whatever sells and earns them the biggest profits. An independent insurance agency, for example, represents a number of different insurance companies—in trying to find the best match between a customer's insurance requirements and the policies of alternative insurance companies, there's plenty of opportunity for independent agents to end up promoting certain insurance companies' policies ahead of others'. An insurance company may therefore conclude that it is better off setting up its own local sales offices with its own local agents to exclusively promote its policies. Likewise, a manufacturer can be frustrated in its attempts to win higher sales and market share or get rid of unwanted inventory or maintain steady, near-capacity production if it must distribute its products through distributors and/or retailers who are only halfheartedly committed to promoting and marketing its brand as opposed to those of rivals. In such cases, it can be advantageous for a manufacturer to integrate forward into wholesaling or retailing via company-owned distributorships or a chain of retail stores. For instance, both Goodyear and Bridgestone opted to integrate forward into tire retailing rather than to use independent distributors and retailers that stocked multiple brands because the independent distributors/retailers stressed selling the tire brands on which they earned the highest profit margins. A number of housewares and apparel manufacturers have integrated forward into retailing so as to move seconds, overstocked items, and slow-selling merchandise through their own branded retail outlet stores located in discount malls. Some producers have opted to integrate forward into retailing by selling directly to customers at the company's Web site. Bypassing regular wholesale/retail channels in favor of direct sales and Internet retailing can have appeal if it lowers distribution costs, produces a relative cost advantage over certain rivals, and results in lower selling prices to end users.

The Disadvantages of a Vertical Integration Strategy

Vertical integration has some substantial drawbacks, however.[18] As it boosts a firm's capital investment in the industry, it increases business risk (what if industry growth and profitability go sour?) and increases the company's vested interests in sticking with its vertically integrated value chain (what if some aspects of its technology and production facilities become obsolete before they are worn out or fully depreciated?). Vertically integrated companies that have invested heavily in a particular technology or in parts/components manufacture are often slow to embrace technological advances or more efficient production methods compared to partially integrated or nonintegrated firms. This is because less integrated firms can pressure suppliers to provide only the latest and best parts and components (even going so far as to shift their purchases from one supplier to another if need be), whereas a vertically integrated firm that is saddled with older technology or facilities that make items it no longer needs is looking at the high costs of premature abandonment. Second, integrating forward or backward locks a firm into relying on its own in-house activities and sources of supply (which later may prove more costly than outsourcing) and potentially results in less flexibility in accommodating shifting buyer preferences or a product design that doesn't include parts and components that it makes in-house. *In today's world of close working relationships with suppliers and efficient supply chain management systems, very few businesses can make a case for integrating backward into the business of suppliers to ensure a reliable supply of materials and components or to reduce production costs.* The best materials and components suppliers stay abreast of advancing technology and are adept in boosting their efficiency and keeping their costs and prices as low as possible. A company that pursues a vertical integration strategy and tries to produce many parts and components in-house is likely to find itself hard-pressed to keep up with technological advances and cutting-edge production practices for each part and component used in making its product.

Third, vertical integration poses all kinds of capacity-matching problems. In motor vehicle manufacturing, for example, the most efficient scale of operation for making axles is different from the most economic volume for radiators, and different yet again for both engines and transmissions. Building the capacity to produce just the right number of axles, radiators, engines, and transmissions in-house—and doing so at the lowest unit cost for each—is much easier said than done. If internal capacity for making transmissions is deficient, the difference has to be bought externally. Where internal capacity for radiators proves excessive, customers need to be found for the surplus. And if by-products are generated—as occurs in the processing of many chemical products—they require arrangements for disposal. Consequently, integrating across several production stages in ways that achieve the lowest feasible costs is not as easy as it might seem.

Fourth, integration forward or backward often calls for radical changes in skills and business capabilities. Parts and components manufacturing, assembly operations, wholesale distribution and retailing, and direct sales via the Internet are different businesses with different key success factors. Managers of a manufacturing company should consider carefully whether it makes good business sense to invest time and money in developing the expertise and merchandising skills to integrate forward into wholesaling and retailing. Many manufacturers learn the hard way that company-owned wholesale/retail networks present many headaches, fit poorly with what they do best, and don't always add the kind of value to their core business they thought they would. Selling to customers via the Internet poses still another set of problems—it is usually easier to use the Internet to sell to business customers than to consumers.

Finally, integrating backward into parts and components manufacture can impair a company's operating flexibility when it comes to changing out the use of certain parts and components. It is one thing to design out a component made by a supplier and another to design out a component being made in-house (which can mean laying off employees and writing off the associated investment in equipment and facilities). Companies that alter designs and models frequently in response to shifting buyer preferences often find that outsourcing the needed parts and components is cheaper and less complicated than producing them in-house. Most of the world's automakers, despite their expertise in automotive technology and manufacturing, have concluded that purchasing many of their key parts and components from manufacturing specialists results in higher quality, lower costs, and greater design flexibility than does the vertical integration option.

Weighing the Pros and Cons of Vertical Integration   All in all, therefore, a strategy of vertical integration can have both important strengths and weaknesses. The tip of the scales depends on (1) whether vertical integration can enhance the performance of strategy-critical activities in ways that lower cost, build expertise, protect proprietary know-how, or increase differentiation; (2) the impact of vertical integration on investment costs, flexibility and response times, and the administrative costs of coordinating operations across more value chain activities; and (3) whether vertical integration substantially enhances a company's competitiveness and profitability. *Vertical integration strategies have merit according to which capabilities and value-chain activities truly need to be performed in-house and which can be performed better or cheaper by outsiders.* Absent solid benefits, integrating forward or backward is not likely to be an attractive strategy option.

OUTSOURCING STRATEGIES: NARROWING THE BOUNDARIES OF THE BUSINESS

Outsourcing involves a conscious decision to abandon or forgo attempts to perform certain value chain activities internally and instead to farm them out to outside specialists and strategic allies. The two big drivers for outsourcing are that (1) outsiders can often perform certain activities better or cheaper and (2) outsourcing allows a firm to focus its entire energies on those activities at the center of its expertise (its core competencies) and that are the most critical to its competitive and financial success.

> **Core Concept**
> *Outsourcing* involves farming out certain value chain activities to outside vendors.

The current interest of many companies in making outsourcing a key component of their overall strategy and their approach to supply chain management represents a big departure from the way that companies used to deal with their suppliers and vendors. In years past, it was common for companies to maintain arm's-length relationships with suppliers and outside vendors, insisting on items being made to precise specifications and negotiating long and hard over price.[19] Although a company might place orders with the same supplier repeatedly, there was no expectation that this would be the case; price usually determined which supplier was awarded an order, and companies used the threat of switching suppliers to get the lowest possible prices. To enhance their bargaining power and, to make the threat of switching credible, it was standard practice for companies to source key parts and components from several suppliers as opposed to dealing with only a single supplier. But today most companies are abandoning such approaches in favor of forging alliances and strategic partnerships with a small number of highly capable suppliers. Collaborative relationships are replacing contractual, purely price-oriented relationships because companies have discovered that many of the advantages of performing value chain activities in-house can be captured and many of the disadvantages avoided by forging close, long-term cooperative partnerships with able suppliers and vendors and tapping into the expertise and capabilities that they have painstakingly developed.

When Outsourcing Strategies Are Advantageous

Outsourcing pieces of the value chain to narrow the boundaries of a firm's business makes strategic sense whenever:

- *An activity can be performed better or more cheaply by outside specialists.* Many PC makers, for example, have shifted from assembling units in-house to using contract assemblers because of the sizable scale economies associated with purchasing PC components in large volumes and assembling PCs. German shoemaker Birkenstock, by outsourcing the distribution of shoes made in its two plants in Germany to UPS, cut the time for delivering orders to U.S. footwear retailers from seven weeks to three weeks.[20]

- *The activity is not crucial to the firm's ability to achieve sustainable competitive advantage and won't hollow out its core competencies, capabilities, or technical know-how.* Outsourcing of maintenance services, data processing and data storage, fringe benefit management, Web site operations, and similar administrative support activities to specialists has become commonplace. American Express, for instance, recently entered into a seven-year, $4 billion deal whereby IBM's Services division would host American Express's Web site, network servers, data storage, and help desk; American Express indicated that it would save several hundred million dollars by paying only for the services it needed when it needed them (as opposed to funding its own full-time staff). A number of companies have begun outsourcing their call center operations to foreign-based contractors who have access to lower-cost labor supplies and can employ lower-paid call center personnel to respond to customer inquiries or requests for technical support.

  - *It reduces the company's risk exposure to changing technology and/ or changing buyer preferences.* When a company outsources certain parts, components, and services, its suppliers must bear the burden of incorporating state-of-the-art technologies and/or undertaking redesigns and upgrades to accommodate a company's plans to introduce next-generation products. If what a supplier provides falls out of favor with buyers or is designed out of next-generation products, it is the supplier's business that suffers rather than a company's own internal operations.

- *It improves a company's ability to innovate.* Collaborative partnerships with world-class suppliers who have cutting-edge intellectual capital and are early adopters of the latest technology give a company access to ever better parts and components—such supplier-driven innovations, when incorporated into a company's own product offering, fuel a company's ability to introduce its own new and improved products.

- *It streamlines company operations in ways that improve organizational flexibility and cuts the time it takes to get new products into the marketplace.* Outsourcing gives a company the flexibility to switch suppliers in the event that its present supplier falls behind competing suppliers. To the extent that its suppliers can speedily get next-generation parts and components into production, then a company can get its own next-generation product offerings into the marketplace quicker. Moreover, seeking out new suppliers with the needed capabilities already in place is frequently quicker, easier, less risky, and cheaper than hurriedly retooling internal operations to replace obsolete capabilities or try to install and master new technologies.

- *It allows a company to assemble diverse kinds of expertise speedily and efficiently.* A company can nearly always gain quicker access to first-rate capabilities and expertise by partnering with suppliers who already have them in place than it can by trying to build them from scratch with its own company personnel.

- *It allows a company to concentrate on its core business, leverage its key resources, and do even better what it already does best.* A company is better able to build and develop its own competitively valuable competencies and capabilities when it concentrates its full resources and energies on performing those activities internally that it can perform better than outsiders and/or that it needs to have under its direct control. Cisco Systems, for example, devotes its energy to designing new generations of switches, routers, and other Internet-related equipment, opting to outsource the more mundane activities of producing and assembling its routers and switching equipment to contract manufacturers that together operate 37 factories, all closely monitored and overseen by Cisco personnel via online systems. Cisco's contract suppliers work so closely with Cisco that they can ship Cisco products to Cisco customers without a Cisco employee ever touching the gear. This system of alliances saves $500 million to $800 million annually.[21]

Dell Computer's partnerships with the suppliers of PC components have allowed it to operate with only three days of inventory (just a couple of hours of inventory in the case of some components), to realize substantial savings in inventory costs, and to get PCs equipped with next-generation components into the marketplace in less than a week after the newly upgraded components start shipping. Hewlett-Packard, IBM, Silicon Graphics (now SGI), and others have sold plants to suppliers and then contracted to purchase the output. Starbucks has found purchasing coffee beans from independent growers far more advantageous than trying to integrate backward into the coffee-growing business.

The Big Risk of an Outsourcing Strategy

The biggest danger of outsourcing is that a company will farm out too many or the wrong types of activities and thereby hollow out its own capabilities.[22] In such cases, a company loses touch with the very activities and expertise that over the long run determine its success. But most companies are alert to this danger and take actions to protect against being held hostage by outside suppliers. Cisco Systems guards against loss of control and protects its manufacturing expertise by designing the production methods that its contract manufacturers must use. Cisco keeps the source code for its designs proprietary, thereby controlling the initiation of all improvements and safeguarding its innovations from imitation. Further, Cisco uses the Internet to monitor the factory operations of contract manufacturers around the clock and can therefore know immediately when problems arise and whether to get involved.

OFFENSIVE STRATEGIES: IMPROVING MARKET POSITION AND BUILDING COMPETITIVE ADVANTAGE

Most every company must at times go on the offensive to improve its market posi tion and try to build a competitive advantage or widen an existing one. Companies like Dell, Wal-Mart, and Toyota play hardball, aggressively pursuing competitive advantage and trying to reap the benefits a competitive edge offers—a leading market share, excellent profit margins and rapid growth (as compared to rivals), and all the intangibles of being known as a company on the move and one that plays to win.[23] The best offensives tend to incorporate several behaviors and principles: (1) focusing relentlessly on building competitive advantage and then striving to convert competitive advantage into decisive advantage, (2) employing the element of surprise as opposed to doing what rivals expect and are prepared for, (3) applying resources where rivals are least able to defend themselves, and (4) being impatient with the status quo and displaying a strong bias for swift, decisive actions to boost a company's competitive position vis-à-vis rivals.[24]

Offensive strategies are also important when a company has no choice but to try to whittle away at a strong rival's competitive advantage and when it is possible to gain profitable market share at the expense of rivals despite whatever resource strengths and capabilities they have. How long it takes for an offensive to yield good results varies with the competitive circumstances.[25] It can be short if buyers respond immediately (as can occur with a dramatic price cut, an imaginative ad campaign, or an especially appealing new product). Securing a competitive edge can take much longer if winning consumer acceptance of an innovative product will take some time or if the firm may need several years to debug a new technology or put new production capacity in place or develop and perfect new competitive capabilities. Ideally, an offensive move will improve a company's market standing or result in a competitive edge fairly quickly; the longer it takes, the more likely it is that rivals will spot the move, see its potential, and begin a counterresponse.

> **Core Concept**
> It takes successful offensive strategies to build competitive advantage—good defensive strategies can help protect competitive advantage but rarely are the basis for creating it.

The principal offensive strategy options include the following:

1. *Offering an equally good or better product at a lower price.* This is the classic offensive for improving a company's market position vis-à-vis rivals. Advanced Micro Devices (AMD), wanting to grow its sales of microprocessors for PCs, has on several occasions elected to attack Intel head-on, offering a faster alternative to Intel's Pentium chips at a lower price. Believing that the company's survival depends on eliminating the performance gap between AMD chips and Intel chips, AMD management has been willing to risk that a head-on offensive might prompt Intel to counter with lower prices of its own and accelerated development of next-generation chips. Lower prices can produce market share gains if competitors don't respond with price cuts of their own and if the challenger convinces buyers that its product is just as good or better. However, such a strategy increases total profits only if the gains in additional unit sales are enough to offset the impact of lower prices and thinner margins per unit sold. Price-cutting offensives generally work best when a company *first achieves a cost advantage and then hits competitors with a lower price.*[26]

2. *Leapfrogging competitors by being the first adopter of next-generation technologies or being first to market with next-generation products.* In 2004–2005, Microsoft waged an offensive to get its next-generation Xbox to market four to six months ahead of Sony's PlayStation 3, anticipating that such a lead time would allow help it convince video gamers to switch to the Xbox rather than wait for the new PlayStation to hit the market in 2006.

3. *Pursuing continuous product innovation to draw sales and market share away from less innovative rivals.* Aggressive and sustained efforts to trump the products of rivals by introducing new or improved products with features calculated to win customers away from rivals can put rivals under tremendous competitive pressure, especially when their new product development capabilities are weak or suspect. But such offensives work only if a company has potent product innovation skills of its own and can keep its pipeline full of ideas that are consistently well received in the marketplace.

4. *Adopting and improving on the good ideas of other companies (rivals or otherwise).*[27] The idea of warehouse-type hardware and home improvement centers did not

originate with Home Depot founders Arthur Blank and Bernie Marcus; they got the big-box concept from their former employer Handy Dan Home Improvement. But they were quick to improve on Handy Dan's business model and strategy and take Home Depot to the next plateau in terms of product line breadth and customer service. Casket maker Hillenbrand greatly improved its market position by adapting Toyota's production methods to casket making. Ryanair has succeeded as a low-cost airline in Europe by imitating many of Southwest Airlines' operating practices and applying them in a different geographic market. Companies that like to play hardball are willing to take any good idea (not nailed down by a patent or other legal protection), make it their own, and then aggressively apply it to create competitive advantage for themselves.[28]

5. *Deliberately attacking those market segments where a key rival makes big profits.*[29] Dell Computer's recent entry into printers and printer cartridges—the market arena where number-two PC maker Hewlett-Packard (HP) enjoys hefty profit margins and makes the majority of its profits—while mainly motivated by Dell's desire to broaden its product line and save its customers money (because of Dell's lower prices), nonetheless represented a hardball offensive calculated to weaken HP's market position in printers. To the extent that Dell might be able to use lower prices to woo away some of HP's printer customers, the move would erode HP's "profit sanctuary," distract HP's attention away from PCs, and reduce the financial resources HP has available for battling Dell in the global market for PCs.

6. *Attacking the competitive weaknesses of rivals.* Offensives aimed at rivals' weaknesses present many options. One is to go after the customers of those rivals whose products lag on quality, features, or product performance. If a company has especially good customer service capabilities, it can make special sales pitches to the customers of those rivals who provide subpar customer service. Aggressors with a recognized brand name and strong marketing skills can launch efforts to win customers away from rivals with weak brand recognition. There is considerable appeal in emphasizing sales to buyers in geographic regions where a rival has a weak market share or is exerting less competitive effort. Likewise, it may be attractive to pay special attention to buyer segments that a rival is neglecting or is weakly equipped to serve.

7. *Maneuvering around competitors and concentrating on capturing unoccupied or less contested market territory.* Examples include launching initiatives to build strong positions in geographic areas where close rivals have little or no market presence and trying to create new market segments by introducing products with different attributes and performance features to better meet the needs of selected buyers.

8. *Using hit-and-run or guerrilla warfare tactics to grab sales and market share from complacent or distracted rivals.* Options for "guerrilla offensives" include occasional lowballing on price (to win a big order or steal a key account from a rival); surprising key rivals with sporadic but intense bursts of promotional activity (offering a 20 percent discount for one week to draw customers away from rival brands); or undertaking special campaigns to attract buyers away from rivals plagued with a strike or problems in meeting buyer demand.[30] Guerrilla offensives are particularly well suited to small challengers who have neither the resources nor the market visibility to mount a full-fledged attack on industry leaders.

9. *Launching a preemptive strike to secure an advantageous position that rivals are prevented or discouraged from duplicating.*[31] What makes a move preemptive

is its one-of-a-kind nature—whoever strikes first stands to acquire competitive assets that rivals can't readily match. Examples of preemptive moves include (1) securing the best distributors in a particular geographic region or country; (2) moving to obtain the most favorable site along a heavily traveled thorough fare, at a new interchange or intersection, in a new shopping mall, in a natural beauty spot, close to cheap transportation or raw material supplies or market outlets, and so on; (3) tying up the most reliable, high-quality suppliers via exclusive partnership, long-term contracts, or even acquisition; and (4) moving swiftly to acquire the assets of distressed rivals at bargain prices. To be successful, a preemptive move doesn't have to totally block rivals from following or copying; it merely needs to give a firm a prime position that is not easily circumvented.

Blue Ocean Strategy: A Special Kind of Offensive

A "blue ocean strategy" seeks to gain a dramatic and durable competitive advantage *by abandoning efforts to beat out competitors in existing markets and, instead, inventing a new industry or distinctive market segment (a wide-open blue ocean of possibility) that renders existing competitors largely irrelevant and allows a company to create and capture altogether new demand.*[32] This strategy views the business universe as consisting of two distinct types of market space. One is where industry boundaries are defined and accepted, the competitive rules of the game are well understood by all industry members, and companies try to outperform rivals by capturing a bigger share of existing demand; in such markets, lively competition constrains a company's prospects for rapid growth and superior profitability since rivals move quickly to either imitate or counter the successes of competitors. In the second type of market space, the industry does not really exist yet, is untainted by competition, and offers wide-open opportunity for profitable and rapid growth if a company can come up with a product offering and strategy that allows it to create new demand rather than fight over existing demand. A terrific example of such a blue ocean market space is the online auction industry that eBay created and now dominates.

Another company that has employed a blue ocean strategy is Cirque du Soleil, which increased its revenues by 22 times during the 1993–2003 period in the circus business, an industry that had been in long-term decline for 20 years. How did Cirque du Soleil pull this off against legendary industry leader Ringling Bros. and Barnum & Bailey? By reinventing the circus, creating a distinctively different market space for its performances (Las Vegas nightclubs and theater-type settings), and pulling in a whole new group of customers—adults and corporate clients—who were noncustomers of traditional circuses and were willing to pay several times more than the price of a conventional circus ticket to have an "entertainment experience" featuring sophisticated clowns and star-quality acrobatic acts in a comfortable big-tent atmosphere. Cirque studiously avoided the use of animals because of costs and because of concerns over their treatment by traditional circus organizations. Cirque's market research led management to conclude that the lasting allure of the traditional circus came down to just three factors: the clowns, classic acrobatic acts, and a tentlike stage. As of 2005, Cirque du Soleil was presenting nine different shows, each with its own theme and story line; was performing before audiences of about 7 million people annually; and had performed 250 engagements in 100 cities before 50 million spectators since its formation in 1984.

Other examples of companies that have achieved competitive advantages by creating blue ocean market spaces include AMC via its pioneering of megaplex movie theaters, The Weather Channel in cable TV, Home Depot in big-box retailing of hardware and building supplies, and FedEx in overnight package delivery. Companies that create blue ocean market spaces can usually sustain their initially won competitive advantage without encountering major competitive challenge for 10 to 15 years because of high barriers to imitation and the strong brand-name awareness that a blue ocean strategy can produce.

Choosing Which Rivals to Attack

Offense-minded firms need to analyze which of their rivals to challenge as well as how to mount that challenge. The following are the best targets for offensive attacks:[33]

- *Market leaders that are vulnerable*—Offensive attacks make good sense when a company that leads in terms of size and market share is not a true leader in terms of serving the market well. Signs of leader vulnerability include unhappy buyers, an inferior product line, a weak competitive strategy with regard to low-cost leadership or differentiation, strong emotional commitment to an aging technology the leader has pioneered, outdated plants and equipment, a preoccupation with diversification into other industries, and mediocre or declining profitability. Offensives to erode the positions of market leaders have real promise when the challenger is able to revamp its value chain or innovate to gain a fresh cost-based or differentiation-based competitive advantage.[34] To be judged successful, attacks on leaders don't have to result in making the aggressor the new leader; a challenger may "win" by simply becoming a stronger runner-up. Caution is well advised in challenging strong market leaders—there's a significant risk of squandering valuable resources in a futile effort or precipitating a fierce and profitless industrywide battle for market share.

- *Runner-up firms with weaknesses in areas where the challenger is strong*—Runner-up firms are an especially attractive target when a challenger's resource strengths and competitive capabilities are well suited to exploiting their weaknesses.

- *Struggling enterprises that are on the verge of going under*—Challenging a hard-pressed rival in ways that further sap its financial strength and competitive position can weaken its resolve and hasten its exit from the market.

- *Small local and regional firms with limited capabilities*—Because small firms typically have limited expertise and resources, a challenger with broader capabilities is well positioned to raid their biggest and best customers—particularly those who are growing rapidly, have increasingly sophisticated requirements, and may already be thinking about switching to a supplier with more full-service capability.

Choosing the Basis for Competitive Attack

As a rule, challenging rivals on competitive grounds where they are strong is an uphill struggle.[35] Offensive initiatives that exploit competitor weaknesses stand a better chance of succeeding than do those that challenge competitor strengths, especially if the weaknesses represent important vulnerabilities and weak rivals can be caught by surprise with no ready defense.[36]

    Strategic offensives should, as a general rule, be grounded in a company's competitive assets and strong points—its core competencies, competitive capabilities, and such resource strengths as a better-known brand name, a cost advantage in manufacturing or distribution, greater technological capability,

Core Concept
The best offensives use a company's resource strengths to attack rivals in those competitive areas where they are weak.

or a superior product. If the attacker's resource strengths give it a competitive advantage over the targeted rivals, so much the better. Ignoring the need to tie a strategic offensive to a company's competitive strengths is like going to war with a popgun—the prospects for success are dim. For instance, it is foolish for a company with relatively high costs to employ a price-cutting offensive—price-cutting offensives are best left to financially strong companies whose costs are relatively low in comparison to those of the companies being attacked. Likewise, it is ill advised to pursue a product innovation offensive without having proven expertise in R&D, new product development, and speeding new or improved products to market.

DEFENSIVE STRATEGIES: PROTECTING MARKET POSITION AND COMPETITIVE ADVANTAGE

It is just as important to discern when to fortify a company's present market position with defensive actions as it is to seize the initiative and launch strategic offensives.

In a competitive market, all firms are subject to offensive challenges from rivals. The purposes of defensive strategies are to lower the risk of being attacked, weaken the impact of any attack that occurs, and influence challengers to aim their efforts at other rivals. While defensive strategies usually don't enhance a firm's competitive advantage, they can definitely help fortify its competitive position, protect its most valuable resources and capabilities from imitation, and defend whatever competitive advantage it might have. Defensive strategies can take either of two forms: actions to block challengers and signaling the likelihood of strong retaliation.

Blocking the Avenues Open to Challengers

There are many ways to throw obstacles in the path of would-be challengers.

The most frequently employed approach to defending a company's present position involves actions that restrict a challenger's options for initiating competitive attack. There are any number of obstacles that can be put in the path of would-be challengers.[37] A defender can participate in alternative technologies as a hedge against rivals attacking with a new or better technology. A defender can introduce new features, add new models, or broaden its product line to close off gaps and vacant niches to opportunity-seeking challengers. It can thwart the efforts of rivals to attack with a lower price by maintaining economy-priced options of its own. It can try to discourage buyers from trying competitors' brands by lengthening warranties, offering free training and support services, developing the capability to deliver spare parts to users faster than rivals can, providing coupons and sample giveaways to buyers most prone to experiment, and making early announcements about impending new products or price changes to induce potential buyers to postpone switching. It can challenge the quality or safety of rivals' products. Finally, a defender can grant volume discounts or better financing terms to dealers and distributors to discourage them from experimenting with other suppliers, or it can convince them to handle its product line *exclusively* and force competitors to use other distribution outlets.

Signaling Challengers that Retaliation Is Likely

The goal of signaling challengers that strong retaliation is likely in the event of an attack is either to dissuade challengers from attacking at all or to divert them to less threatening options. Either goal can be achieved by letting challengers know the battle will cost more than it is worth. Would-be challengers can be signaled by:[38]

- Publicly announcing management's commitment to maintain the firm's present market share.
- Publicly committing the company to a policy of matching competitors' terms or prices.
- Maintaining a war chest of cash and marketable securities.
- Making an occasional strong counterresponse to the moves of weak competitors to enhance the firm's image as a tough defender.

WEB SITE STRATEGIES

One of the biggest strategic issues facing company executives across the world is just what role the company's Web site should play in a company's competitive strategy. In particular, to what degree should a company use the Internet as a distribution channel for accessing buyers? Should a company use its Web site *only as a means of disseminating product information* (with traditional distribution channel partners making all sales to end users), as a *secondary or minor channel* for selling directly to buyers of its product, as *one of several important distribution channels* for accessing customers, as *the primary distribution channel* for accessing customers, or as *the exclusive channel* for transacting sales with customers?[39] Let's look at each of these strategic options in turn.

> Companies today must wrestle with the strategic issue of how to use their Web sites in positioning themselves in the marketplace—whether to use their Web sites just to disseminate product information or whether to operate an e-store to sell direct to online shoppers.

Product Information–Only Web Strategies: Avoiding Channel Conflict

Operating a Web site that contains extensive product information but that relies on click-throughs to the Web sites of distribution channel partners for sales transactions (or that informs site users where nearby retail stores are located) is an attractive market positioning option for manufacturers and/or wholesalers that have invested heavily in building and cultivating retail dealer networks and that face nettlesome channel conflict issues if they try to sell online in direct competition with their dealers. A manufacturer or wholesaler that aggressively pursues online sales to end users is signaling both a weak strategic commitment to its dealers and a willingness to cannibalize dealers' sales and growth potential.

To the extent that strong partnerships with wholesale and/or retail dealers are critical to accessing end users, selling directly to end users via the company's Web site is a very tricky road to negotiate. A manufacturer's efforts to use its Web site to sell around its dealers is certain to anger its wholesale distributors and retail dealers, which may respond by putting more effort into marketing the brands of rival manufacturers that don't sell online. In sum, the manufacturer may stand to lose more sales by offending its dealers than it gains from its own online sales effort. Moreover, dealers may be in better position to employ a brick-and-click strategy than a manufacturer is because dealers have a local presence to complement their online sales approach (which consumers may find appealing). Consequently, in industries where the strong support and goodwill of dealer networks is essential, manufacturers may conclude that their Web site should be designed to partner with dealers rather than compete with them—just as the auto manufacturers are doing with their franchised dealers.

Web Site e-Stores as a Minor Distribution Channel

A second strategic option is to use online sales as a relatively minor distribution channel for achieving incremental sales, gaining online sales experience, and doing marketing research. If channel conflict poses a big obstacle to online sales, or if only a small fraction of buyers can be attracted to make online purchases, then companies are well advised to pursue online sales with the strategic intent of gaining experience, learning more about buyer tastes and preferences, testing reaction to new products, creating added market buzz about their products, and boosting overall sales volume a few percentage points. Sony and Nike, for example, sell most all of their products at their Web sites without provoking resistance from their retail dealers since most buyers of their products prefer to do their buying at retail stores rather than online. They use their Web site not so much to make sales as to glean valuable marketing research data from tracking the browsing patterns of Web site visitors. The behavior and actions of Web surfers are a veritable gold mine of information for companies seeking to keep their finger on the market pulse and respond more precisely to buyer preferences and interests.

Despite the channel conflict that exists when a manufacturer sells directly to end users at its Web site in head-to-head competition with its distribution channel allies, manufacturers might still opt to pursue online sales at their Web sites and try to establish online sales as an important distribution channel because (1) their profit margins from online sales are bigger than they earned from selling to their wholesale/retail customers; (2) encouraging buyers to visit the company's Web site helps educate them to the ease and convenience of purchasing online and, over time, prompts more and more buyers to purchase online (where company profit margins are greater)—which makes incurring channel conflict in the short term and competing against traditional distribution allies potentially worthwhile—and (3) selling directly to end users allows a manufacturer to make greater use of build-to-order manufacturing and assembly, which, if met with growing buyer acceptance of and satisfaction, would increase the rate at which sales migrate from distribution allies to the company's Web site—such migration could lead to streamlining the company's value chain and boosting its profit margins.

Brick-and-Click Strategies

Brick-and-click strategies have two big strategic appeals for wholesale and retail enterprises: They are an economic means of expanding a company's geographic reach, and they give both existing and potential customers another choice of how to communicate with the company, shop for product information, make purchases, or resolve customer service problems. Software developers, for example, have come to rely on the Internet as a highly effective distribution channel to complement sales through brick-and-mortar wholesalers and retailers. Selling online directly to end users has the advantage of eliminating the costs of producing and packaging CDs, as well as cutting out the costs and margins of software wholesalers and retailers (often 35 to 50 percent of the retail price). However, software developers are still strongly motivated to continue to distribute their products through wholesalers and retailers (to maintain broad access to existing and potential users who, for whatever reason, may be reluctant to buy online). Chain retailers like Wal-Mart and Circuit City operate online stores for their products primarily as a convenience to customers who want to buy online rather than making a shopping trip to nearby stores.

Many brick-and-mortar companies can enter online retailing at relatively low cost—all they need is a Web store and systems for filling and delivering individual customer orders. Brick-and-mortar distributors and retailers (as well as manufacturers with company-owned retail stores) can employ brick-and-click strategies by using their current distribution centers and/or retail stores for picking orders from on-hand inventories and making deliveries. Blockbuster, the world's largest chain of video and DVD rental stores, uses the inventories at its stores to fill orders for its online subscribers, who pay a monthly fee for unlimited DVDs delivered by mail carrier; using local stores to fill orders typically allows delivery in 24 hours versus 48 hours for shipments made from a regional shipping center. Walgreen's, a leading drugstore chain, allows customers to order a prescription online and then pick it up at the drive-through window or inside counter of a local store. In banking, a brick-and-click strategy allows customers to use local branches and ATMs for depositing checks and getting cash while using online systems to pay bills, check account balances, and transfer funds. Many industrial distributors are finding it efficient for customers to place their orders over the Web rather than phoning them in or waiting for salespeople to call in person. Illustration Capsule 6.2 describes how office supply chains like Office Depot, Staples, and OfficeMax have successfully migrated from a traditional brick-and-mortar distribution strategy to a combination brick-and-click distribution strategy.

Strategies for Online Enterprises

A company that elects to use the Internet as its exclusive channel for accessing buyers is essentially an online enterprise from the perspective of the customer. The Internet becomes the vehicle for transacting sales and delivering customer services; except for advertising, the Internet is the sole point of all buyer–seller contact. Many so-called pure dot-com enterprises have chosen this strategic approach—prominent examples include eBay, Yahoo, Amazon.com, Buy.com, Overstock.com, and Priceline.com. For a company to succeed in using the Internet as its exclusive distribution channel, its product or service must be one for which buying online holds strong appeal.

A company that decides to use online sales as its exclusive method for sales transactions must address several strategic issues:

- *How it will deliver unique value to buyers*—Online businesses must usually attract buyers on the basis of low price, convenience, superior product information, build-to-order options, or attentive online service.

- *Whether it will pursue competitive advantage based on lower costs, differentiation, or better value for the money*—For an online-only sales strategy to succeed in head-to-head competition with brick-and-mortar and brick-and-click rivals, an online seller's value chain approach must hold potential for a low-cost advantage, competitively valuable differentiating attributes, or a best-cost provider advantage. If an online firm's strategy is to attract customers by selling at cut-rate prices, then it must possess cost advantages in those activities it performs, and it must outsource the remaining activities to low-cost specialists. If an online seller is going to differentiate itself on the basis of a superior buying experience and top-notch customer service, then it needs to concentrate on having an easy-to-navigate Web site, an array of functions and conveniences for customers, Web reps who can answer questions online, and logistical capabilities to deliver products quickly and accommodate returned merchandise. If it is going to deliver more value for the money, then it must manage value chain activities so as to deliver upscale products and services at lower costs than rivals.

Illustration Capsule 6.2
Brick-and-Click Strategies in the Office Supplies Industry

Office Depot was in the first wave of retailers to adopt a combination brick-and-click strategy. Management quickly saw the merits of allowing business customers to use the Internet to place orders instead of having to make a call, generate a purchase order, and pay an invoice—while still getting same-day or next-day delivery from one of Office Depot's local stores.

Office Depot already had an existing network of retail stores, delivery centers and warehouses, delivery trucks, account managers, sales offices, and regional call centers that handled large business customers. In addition, it had a solid brand name and enough purchasing power with its suppliers to counter discount-minded online rivals trying to attract buyers of office supplies on the basis of super-low prices. Office Depot's incremental investment to enter the e-commerce arena was minimal since all it needed to add was a Web site where customers could see pictures and descriptions of the 14,000 items it carried, their prices, and in-stock availability. Marketing costs to make customers aware of its Web store option ran less than $10 million.

Office Depot's online prices were the same as its store prices, the strategy being to promote Web sales on the basis of service, convenience, and lower customer costs for order processing and inventories. Customers reported that doing business with Office Depot online cut their transaction costs by up to 80 percent; plus, Office Depot's same-day or next-day delivery capability allowed them to reduce office supply inventories.

The company set up customized Web pages for 37,000 corporate and educational customers that allowed the customer's employees varying degrees of freedom to buy supplies. A clerk might be able to order only copying paper, toner cartridges, computer disks, and paper clips up to a preset dollar limit per order, while a vice president might have carte blanche to order any item Office Depot sold.

Web site sales cost Office Depot less than $1 per $100 of goods ordered, compared with about $2 for phone and fax orders. And since Web sales eliminate the need to key in transactions, order-entry errors were virtually eliminated and product returns cut by 50 percent. Billing is handled electronically.

In 2005, over 50 percent of Office Depot's major customers were ordering most of their supplies online. Online sales accounted for almost $3 billion in 2004 (about 24 percent of Office Depot's total revenues), up from $982 million in 2000 and making Office Depot the third-largest online retailer. Its online operations were profitable from the start.

Office Depot's successful brick-and-click strategy prompted its two biggest rivals—Staples and OfficeMax—to adopt brick-and-click strategies too. In 2005, all three companies were enjoying increasing success with selling online to business customers and using local stores to fill orders and make deliveries.

Sources: Information posted at www.officedepot.com (accessed September 28, 2005); "Office Depot's e-Diva," *BusinessWeek Online* (www.businessweek.com), August 6, 2001; Laura Lorek, "Office Depot Site Picks Up Speed," *Interactive Week* (www.zdnet.com/intweek), June 25, 2001; "Why Office Depot Loves the Net," *BusinessWeek,* September 27, 1999, pp. EB 66, EB 68; and *Fortune,* November 8, 1999, p. 17.

- *Whether it will have a broad or a narrow product offering*—A one-stop shopping strategy like that employed by Amazon.com (which offers over 30 million items for sale at its Web sites in the United States, Britain, France, Germany, Denmark, and Japan) has the appealing economics of helping spread fixed operating costs over a wide number of items and a large customer base. Other e-tailers, such as E-Loan and Hotel.com, have adopted classic focus strategies and cater to a sharply defined target audience shopping for a particular product or product category.

- *Whether to perform order fulfillment activities internally or to outsource them*—Building central warehouses, stocking them with adequate inventories, and developing systems to pick, pack, and ship individual orders all require substantial start-up capital but may result in lower overall unit costs than would paying the fees of order fulfillment specialists who make a business of providing warehouse space, stocking inventories, and shipping orders for e-tailers. However, outsourcing order fulfillment activities is likely to be more economical unless an e-tailer has high unit volume and the capital to invest in its own order fulfillment capabilities. Buy.com, an online superstore consisting of some 30,000 items, obtains products from name-brand manufacturers and uses outsiders to stock and ship those products; thus, its focus is not on manufacturing or order fulfillment but rather on selling.

- *How it will draw traffic to its Web site and then convert page views into revenues*—Web sites have to be cleverly marketed. Unless Web surfers hear about the site, like what they see on their first visit, and are intrigued enough to return again and again, the site is unlikely to generate adequate revenues. Marketing campaigns that result only in heavy site traffic and lots of page views are seldom sufficient; the best test of effective marketing and the appeal of an online company's product offering is the ratio at which page views are converted into revenues (the "look-to-buy" ratio). For example, in 2001 Yahoo's site traffic averaged 1.2 *billion* page views daily but generated only about $2 million in daily revenues; in contrast, the traffic at brokerage firm Charles Schwab's Web site averaged only 40 *million* page views per day but resulted in an average of $5 million daily in online commission revenues.

CHOOSING APPROPRIATE FUNCTIONAL-AREA STRATEGIES

A company's strategy is not complete until company managers have made strategic choices about how the various functional parts of the business—R&D, production, human resources, sales and marketing, finance, and so on—will be managed in support of its basic competitive strategy approach and the other important competitive moves being taken. Normally, functional-area strategy choices rank third on the menu of choosing among the various strategy options, as shown in Figure 6.1 (see p. 162). But whether commitments to particular functional strategies are made before or after the choices of complementary strategic options shown in Figure 6.1 is beside the point—what's really important is what the functional strategies are and how they mesh to enhance the success of the company's higher-level strategic thrusts.

In many respects, the nature of functional strategies is dictated by the choice of competitive strategy. For example, a manufacturer employing a low-cost provider strategy needs an R&D and product design strategy that emphasizes cheap-to-incorporate features and facilitates economical assembly and a production strategy that stresses capture of scale economies and actions to achieve low-cost manufacture (such as high labor productivity, efficient supply chain management, and automated production processes), and a low-budget marketing strategy. A business pursuing a high-end differentiation strategy needs a production strategy geared to top-notch quality and a marketing strategy aimed at touting differentiating features and using advertising and a trusted brand name to "pull" sales through the chosen distribution channels. A company using a focused differentiation strategy needs a marketing strategy that stresses growing the niche. For example, the Missouri-based franchise Panera Bread has been growing its business by getting more people hooked on fresh-baked specialty breads and patronizing its bakery-cafés, keeping buyer interest in Panera's all-natural specialty breads at a high level, and protecting its specialty bread niche against invasion by outsiders.

Beyond very general prescriptions, it is difficult to say just what the content of the different functional-area strategies should be without first knowing what higher-level strategic choices a company has made, the industry environment in which it operates, the resource strengths that can be leveraged, and so on. Suffice it to say here that company personnel—both managers and employees charged with strategy-making responsibility down through the organizational hierarchy—must be clear about which higher-level strategies top management has chosen and then must tailor the company's functional-area strategies accordingly.

FIRST-MOVER ADVANTAGES AND DISADVANTAGES

Core Concept
Because of first-mover advantages and disadvantages, competitive advantage can spring from *when* a move is made as well as from *what* move is made.

When to make a strategic move is often as crucial as *what* move to make. Timing is especially important when *first-mover advantages* or *disadvantages* exist.[40] Being first to initiate a strategic move can have a high payoff when (1) pioneering helps build a firm's image and reputation with buyers; (2) early commitments to new technologies, new-style components, new or emerging distribution channels, and so on can produce an absolute cost advantage over rivals; (3) first-time customers remain strongly loyal to pioneering firms in making repeat purchases; and (4) moving first constitutes a preemptive strike, making imitation extra hard or unlikely. The bigger the first-mover advantages, the more attractive making the first move becomes.[41] In e-commerce, companies like America Online, Amazon.com, Yahoo, eBay, and Priceline.com that were first with a new technology, network solution, or business model enjoyed lasting first-mover advantages in gaining the visibility and reputation needed to remain market leaders. However, other first-movers such as Xerox in fax machines, eToys (an online toy retailer), Webvan and Peapod (in online groceries), and scores of other dot-com companies never converted their first-mover status into any sort of competitive advantage. Sometimes markets are slow to accept the innovative product offering of a first-mover; sometimes, a fast-follower with greater resources and marketing muscle can easily overtake the first-mover (as Microsoft was able to do when it introduced Internet Explorer against Netscape, the pioneer of Internet browsers with the lion's share of the market); and sometimes furious technological change or product innovation makes a first-mover vulnerable to quickly appearing next-generation technology or products. Hence, just being a first-mover by itself is seldom enough to win a sustainable competitive advantage.[42]

To sustain any advantage that may initially accrue to a pioneer, a first-mover needs to be a fast learner and continue to move aggressively to capitalize on any initial pioneering advantage. It helps immensely if the first-mover has deep financial pockets, important competencies and competitive capabilities, and astute managers. If a first-mover's skills, know-how, and actions are easily copied or even surpassed, then fast-followers and even late-movers can catch or overtake the first-mover in a relatively short period. What makes being a first-mover strategically important is not being the first company to do something but rather being the first competitor to put together the precise combination of features, customer value, and sound revenue/cost/profit economics that gives it an edge over rivals in the battle for market leadership.[43] If the marketplace quickly takes to a first-mover's innovative product offering, a first-mover must have large-scale production, marketing, and distribution capabilities if it is to stave off fast-followers who possess these resources capabilities. If technology is advancing at torrid pace, a first-mover cannot hope to sustain its lead without having strong capabilities in R&D, design, and new product development, along with the financial strength to fund these activities.

The Potential for Late-Mover Advantages or First-Mover Disadvantages

There are instances when there are actually *advantages* to being an adept follower rather than a first-mover. Late-mover advantages (or *first-mover disadvantages*) arise in four instances:

- When pioneering leadership is more costly than imitating followership and only negligible learning/experience curve benefits accrue to the leader—a condition that allows a follower to end up with lower costs than the first-mover.
- When the products of an innovator are somewhat primitive and do not live up to buyer expectations, thus allowing a clever follower to win disenchanted buyers away from the leader with better-performing products.
- When the demand side of the marketplace is skeptical about the benefits of a new technology or product being pioneered by a first-mover.
- When rapid market evolution (due to fast-paced changes in either technology or buyer needs and expectations) gives fast-followers and maybe even cautious late-movers the opening to leapfrog a first-mover's products with more attractive next-version products.

To Be a First-Mover or Not

In weighing the pros and cons of being a first-mover versus a fast-follower versus a slow-mover, it matters whether the race to market leadership in a particular industry is a marathon or a sprint. In marathons, a slow-mover is not unduly penalized—first-mover advantages can be fleeting, and there is ample time for fast-followers and sometimes even late-movers to play catch-up.[44] Thus, the speed at which the pioneering innovation is likely to catch on matters considerably as companies struggle with whether to pursue a particular emerging market opportunity aggressively (as a first-mover or fast-follower) or cautiously (as a late-mover). For instance, it took 18 months for 10 million users to sign up for Hotmail, 5.5 years for worldwide mobile phone use to grow from 10 million to 100 million worldwide, 7 years for videocassette recorders to find their way into 1 million U.S. homes, and close to 10 years for the number of at-home broadband subscribers to grow to 100 million worldwide. The lesson here is that there is a market-penetration curve for every emerging opportunity; typically, the curve has an inflection point at which all the pieces of the business model fall into place, buyer demand explodes, and the market takes off. The inflection point can come early on a fast-rising curve (like use of e-mail) or further up on a slow-rising curve (like the use of broadband). Any company that seeks competitive advantage by being a first-mover thus needs to ask some hard questions:

- Does market takeoff depend on the development of complementary products or services that currently are not available?
- Is new infrastructure required before buyer demand can surge?
- Will buyers need to learn new skills or adopt new behaviors? Will buyers encounter high switching costs?
- Are there influential competitors in a position to delay or derail the efforts of a first-mover?

Illustration Capsule 6.3

The Battle in Consumer Broadband: First-Movers versus Late-Movers

In 1988 an engineer at the Bell companies' research labs figured out how to rush signals along ordinary copper wire at high speed using digital technology, thus creating the digital subscriber line (DSL). But the regional Bells, which dominated the local telephone market in the United States, showed little interest over the next 10 years, believing it was more lucrative to rent T-1 lines to businesses that needed fast data transmission capability and rent second phone lines to households wanting an Internet connection that didn't disrupt their regular telephone service. Furthermore, telephone executives were skeptical about DSL technology—there were a host of technical snarls to overcome, and early users encountered annoying glitches. Many executives doubted that it made good sense to invest billions of dollars in the infrastructure needed to roll out DSL to residential and small business customers, given the success they were having with T-1 and second-line rentals. As a consequence, the Bells didn't seriously begin to market DSL until the late 1990s, two years after the cable TV companies began their push to market cable broadband.

Cable companies were more than happy to be the first-movers in marketing broadband service via their copper cable wires, chiefly because their business was threatened by satellite TV technology and they saw broadband as an innovative service they could provide that the satellite companies could not. (Delivering broadband service via satellite has yet to become a factor in the marketplace, winning only a 1 percent share in 2003.) Cable companies were able to deploy broadband on their copper wire economically because during the 1980s and early 1990s most cable operators had spent about $60 billion to upgrade their systems with fiber-optic technology in order to handle two-way traffic rather than just one-way TV signals and thereby make good on their promises to local governments to develop "interactive" cable systems if they were awarded franchises. Although the early interactive services were duds, technicians discovered in the mid-1990s that the two-way systems enabled high-speed Internet hookups.

With Internet excitement surging in the late 1990s, cable executives saw high-speed Internet service as a no-brainer and began rolling it out to customers in 1998, securing about 362,000 customers by year-end versus only about 41,000 for DSL. Part of the early success of cable broadband was due to a cost advantage in modems—cable executives, seeing the potential of cable broadband several years earlier, had asked CableLabs to standardize the technology for cable modems, a move that lowered costs and made cable modems marketable in consumer electronics stores. DSL modems were substantially more complicated, and it took longer to drive the costs down from several hundred dollars each to under $100—in 2004, both cable and phone companies paid about $50 for modems, but cable modems got there much sooner.

As cable broadband began to attract more and more attention in the 1998–2002 period, the regional Bells continued to move slowly on DSL. The technical problems lingered, and early users were disgruntled by a host of annoying and sometimes horrendous installation difficulties and service glitches. Not only did providing users with convenient and reliable service prove to be a formidable challenge, but some regulatory issues stood in the way as well. Even in 2003 phone company executives found it hard to justify multibillion-dollar investments to install the necessary equipment and support systems to offer, market, manage, and maintain DSL service on the vast scale of a regional Bell company. SBC Communications figured it would cost at least $6 billion to roll out DSL to its customers. Verizon estimated that it would take 3.5 to 4 million customers to make DSL economics work, a number it would probably not reach until the end of 2005.

In 2003–2004, high-speed consumer access to the Internet was a surging business with a bright outlook—the number of U.S. Internet users upgrading to high-speed service increased by close to 500,000 monthly. In 2005, cable broadband was the preferred choice—70 percent of U.S. broadband users had opted for cable modems supplied by cable TV companies, with cable modem subscribers outnumbering DSL subscribers 30 million to 10.6 million. Its late start made it questionable whether DSL would be able to catch cable broadband in the U.S. marketplace, although DSL providers added 1.4 million subscribers in the first three months of 2005 compared to 1.2 million new subscribers for cable. In the rest of the world, however, DSL was the broadband connection of choice—there were an estimated 200 million broadband subscribers worldwide at the end of 2005.

Source: Developed from information in Shawn Young and Peter Grant, "How Phone Firms Lost to Cable in Consumer Broadband Market," *The Wall Street Journal,* March 13, 2003, pp. A1, A6, and Cnet's www.news.com site (accessed September 22, 2005).

When the answers to any of these questions are yes, then a company must be careful not to pour too many resources into getting ahead of the market opportunity—the race is likely going to be more of a 10-year marathon than a 2-year sprint. Being first out of the starting block is competitively important only when pioneering early introduction of a technology or product delivers clear and substantial benefits to early adopters and buyers, thus winning their immediate support, perhaps giving the pioneer a reputational head-start advantage, and forcing competitors to quickly follow the pioneer's lead. In the remaining instances where the race is more of a marathon, the companies that end up capturing and dominating new-to-the-world markets are almost never the pioneers that gave birth to those markets—there is time for a company to marshal the needed resources and to ponder its best time and method of entry.[45] Furthermore, being a late-mover into industries of the future has the advantages of being less risky and skirting the costs of pioneering.

But while a company is right to be cautious about quickly entering virgin territory, where all kinds of risks abound, rarely does a company have much to gain from consistently being a late-mover whose main concern is avoiding the mistakes of first-movers. Companies that are habitual late-movers regardless of the circumstances, while often able to survive, can find themselves and scrambling to keep pace with more progressive and innovative rivals and fighting to retain their customers. For a habitual late-mover to catch up, it must count on first-movers to be slow learners and complacent in letting their lead dwindle. It also has to hope that buyers will be slow to gravitate to the products of first-movers, again giving it time to catch up. And it has to have competencies and capabilities that are sufficiently strong to allow it to close the gap fairly quickly once it makes its move. Counting on all first-movers to stumble or otherwise be easily overtaken is usually a bad bet that puts a late-mover's competitive position at risk.

Illustration Capsule 6.3 describes the challenges that late-moving telephone companies have in winning the battle to supply at-home high-speed Internet access and overcoming the first-mover advantages of cable companies.

Key Points

Once a company has selected which of the five basic competitive strategies to employ in its quest for competitive advantage, then it must decide whether to supplement its choice of a basic competitive strategy approach, as shown in Figure 6.1 (p. 162).

Many companies are using strategic alliances and collaborative partnerships to help them in the race to build a global market presence or be a leader in the industries of the future. Strategic alliances are an attractive, flexible, and often cost-effective means by which companies can gain access to missing technology, expertise, and business capabilities.

Mergers and acquisitions are another attractive strategic option for strengthening a firm's competitiveness. When the operations of two companies are combined via merger or acquisition, the new company's competitiveness can be enhanced in any of several ways—lower costs; stronger technological skills; more or better competitive capabilities; a more attractive lineup of products and services; wider geographic coverage; and/or greater financial resources with which to invest in R&D, add capacity, or expand into new areas.

Vertically integrating forward or backward makes strategic sense only if it strengthens a company's position via either cost reduction or creation of a differentiation-based advantage. Otherwise, the drawbacks of vertical integration (increased investment, greater business risk, increased vulnerability to technological changes, and less flexibility in making product changes) are likely to outweigh any advantages.

Outsourcing pieces of the value chain formerly performed in-house can enhance a company's competitiveness whenever an activity (1) can be performed better or more cheaply by outside specialists; (2) is not crucial to the firm's ability to achieve sustainable competitive advantage and won't hollow out its core competencies, capabilities, or technical know-how; (3) reduces the company's risk exposure to changing technology or changing buyer preferences; (4) streamlines company operations in ways that improve organizational flexibility, cut cycle time, speed decision making, and reduce coordination costs; or (5) allows a company to concentrate on its core business and do what it does best.

One of the most pertinent strategic issues that companies face is how to use the Internet in positioning the company in the marketplace—whether to use the Internet as *only a means of disseminating product information* (with traditional distribution channel partners making all sales to end users), as *a secondary or minor channel*, as *one of several important distribution channels*, as *the company's primary distribution channel,* or as *the company's exclusive channel for accessing customers.*

Companies have a number of offensive strategy options for improving their market positions and trying to secure a competitive advantage: offering an equal or better product at a lower price, leapfrogging competitors by being first to adopt next-generation technologies or the first to introduce next-generation products, pursuing sustained product innovation, attacking competitors weaknesses, going after less contested or unoccupied market territory, using hit-and-run tactics to steal sales away from unsuspecting rivals, and launching preemptive strikes. A blue ocean strategy seeks to gain a dramatic and durable competitive advantage by abandoning efforts to beat out competitors in existing markets and, instead, inventing a new industry or distinctive market segment that renders existing competitors largely irrelevant and allows a company to create and capture altogether new demand.

Defensive strategies to protect a company's position usually take the form of making moves that put obstacles in the path of would-be challengers and fortify the company's present position while undertaking actions to dissuade rivals from even trying to attack (by signaling that the resulting battle will be more costly to the challenger than it is worth).

Once all the higher-level strategic choices have been made, company managers can turn to the task of crafting functional and operating-level strategies to flesh out the details of the company's overall business and competitive strategy.

The timing of strategic moves also has relevance in the quest for competitive advantage. Company managers are obligated to carefully consider the advantages or disadvantages that attach to being a first-mover versus a fast-follower versus a late-mover.

Exercises

1. Go to Google or another Internet search engine and do a search on "strategic alliances." Identify at least two companies in different industries that are making a significant use of strategic alliances as a core part of their strategies. In addition, identify who their alliances are with and describe the purpose of the alliances.

2. Go to Google or another Internet search engine and do a search on "acquisition strategy." Identify at least two companies in different industries that are using

acquisitions to strengthen their market positions. Identify some of the companies that have been acquired, and research the purpose behind the acquisitions.

3. Go to www.goodyear.com/investor and read Goodyear's most recent annual report. To what extent is the company vertically integrated? What segments of the industry value chain has the company chosen to perform? Based on the company's discussion of business unit performance, does it appear the company is becoming more vertically integrated or choosing to narrow its range of internally performed activities?

4. Illustration Capsule 6.3 describes how cable companies used fiber-optic networks to gain a first-mover advantage over telephone companies in providing high-speed Internet access to home subscribers. Telephone companies are attempting to catch up with cable companies in the broadband access market with the widespread rollout of DSL to telephone customers. In addition, phone companies are pursuing fiber-to-the-premises (FTTP) and outdoor wireless networks (outdoor WLAN) technologies to supplement or replace DSL. Conduct Web searches on FTTP and outdoor WLAN, and discuss how use of these technologies by telephone companies might offset the first-mover advantage currently held by cable companies in the high-speed Internet market.

5. Go to the Web sites of various companies (such as those appearing on the Fortune 500) and identify two companies using each of the following Web site strategies and explain why the approach is well matched to the company's business model:

a. Product information only.

b. E-store as a minor distribution strategy.

c. Brick-and-click.

d. Online enterprise.

chapter 7 seven

Competing in Foreign Markets

You have no choice but to operate in a world shaped by globalization and the information revolution. There are two options: Adapt or die.

—Andrew S. Grove

Former Chairman, Intel Corporation

You do not choose to become global. The market chooses for you; it forces your hand.

—Alain Gomez

CEO, Thomson SA

[I]ndustries actually vary a great deal in the pressures they put on a company to sell internationally.

—Niraj Dawar and Tony Frost

Professors, Richard Ivey School of Business

Any company that aspires to industry leadership in the 21st century must think in terms of global, not domestic, market leadership. The world economy is globalizing at an accelerating pace as countries previously closed to foreign companies open up their markets, as the Internet shrinks the importance of geographic distance, and as ambitious growth-minded companies race to build stronger competitive positions in the markets of more and more countries. Companies in industries that are already globally competitive or in the process of becoming so are under the gun to come up with a strategy for competing successfully in foreign markets.

This chapter focuses on strategy options for expanding beyond domestic boundaries and competing in the markets of either a few or a great many countries. The spotlight will be on four strategic issues unique to competing multinationally:

1. Whether to customize the company's offerings in each different country market to match the tastes and preferences of local buyers or to offer a mostly standardized product worldwide.

2. Whether to employ essentially the same basic competitive strategy in all countries or modify the strategy country by country.

3. Where to locate the company's production facilities, distribution centers, and customer service operations so as to realize the greatest location advantages.

4. How to efficiently transfer the company's resource strengths and capabilities from one country to another in an effort to secure competitive advantage.

In the process of exploring these issues, we will introduce a number of core concepts—multicountry competition, global competition, profit sanctuaries, and cross-market subsidization. The chapter includes sections on cross-country differences in cultural, demographic, and market conditions; strategy options for entering and competing in foreign markets; the growing role of alliances with foreign partners; the importance of locating operations in the most advantageous countries; and the special circumstances of competing in such emerging markets as China, India, Brazil, Russia, and Eastern Europe.

WHY COMPANIES EXPAND INTO FOREIGN MARKETS

A company may opt to expand outside its domestic market for any of four major reasons:

1. *To gain access to new customers*—Expanding into foreign markets offers potential for increased revenues, profits, and long-term growth and becomes an especially attractive option when a company's home markets are mature. Firms like Cisco Systems, Dell, Sony, Nokia, Avon, and Toyota, which are racing for global leadership in their respective industries, are moving rapidly and aggressively to extend their market reach into all corners of the world.

2. *To achieve lower costs and enhance the firm's competitiveness*—Many companies are driven to sell in more than one country because domestic sales volume is not large enough to fully capture manufacturing economies of scale or learning/experience curve effects and thereby substantially improve the firm's cost-competitiveness. The relatively small size of country markets in Europe explains why companies like Michelin, BMW, and Nestlé long ago began selling their products all across Europe and then moved into markets in North America and Latin America.

3. *To capitalize on its core competencies*—A company may be able to leverage its competencies and capabilities into a position of competitive advantage in foreign markets as well as just domestic markets. Nokia's competencies and capabilities in mobile phones have propelled it to global market leadership in the wireless telecommunications business. Wal-Mart is capitalizing on its considerable expertise in discount retailing to expand into China, Latin America, and parts of Europe—Wal-Mart executives believe the company has tremendous growth opportunities in China.

4. *To spread its business risk across a wider market base*—A company spreads business risk by operating in a number of different foreign countries rather than depending entirely on operations in its domestic market. Thus, if the economies of certain Asian countries turn down for a period of time, a company with operations across much of the world may be sustained by buoyant sales in Latin America or Europe.

In a few cases, companies in industries based on natural resources (e.g., oil and gas, minerals, rubber, and lumber) often find it necessary to operate in the international arena because attractive raw material supplies are located in foreign countries.

The Difference Between Competing Internationally and Competing Globally

Typically, a company will start to compete internationally by entering just one or maybe a select few foreign markets. Competing on a truly global scale comes later, after the company has established operations on several continents and is racing against rivals for global market leadership. Thus, there is a meaningful distinction between the competitive scope of a company that operates in a few foreign countries (with perhaps modest ambitions to enter several more country markets) and a company that markets its products in 50 to 100 countries and is expanding its operations into additional country markets annually. The former is most accurately termed an *international competitor,* whereas the latter qualifies as a *global competitor.* In the discussion that follows, we'll continue to make a distinction between strategies for competing internationally and strategies for competing globally.

CROSS-COUNTRY DIFFERENCES IN CULTURAL, DEMOGRAPHIC, AND MARKET CONDITIONS

Regardless of a company's motivation for expanding outside its domestic markets, the strategies it uses to compete in foreign markets must be situation-driven. Cultural, demographic, and market conditions vary significantly among the countries of the world.[1] Cultures and lifestyles are the most obvious areas in which countries differ; market demographics and income levels are close behind. Consumers in Spain do not have the same tastes, preferences, and buying habits as consumers in Norway; buyers differ yet again in Greece, Chile, New Zealand, and Taiwan. Less than 20 percent of the populations of Brazil, India, and China have annual purchasing power equivalent to $25,000. Middle-class consumers represent a much smaller portion of the population in these and other emerging countries than in North America, Japan, and much of Western Europe—China's middle class numbers about 125 million out of a population of 1.3 billion.[2]

Sometimes product designs suitable in one country are inappropriate in another—for example, in the United States electrical devices run on 110-volt systems, but in some European countries the standard is a 240-volt system, necessitating the use of different electrical designs and components. In France consumers prefer top-loading washing machines, while in most other European countries consumers prefer front-loading machines. Northern Europeans want large refrigerators because they tend to shop once a week in supermarkets; southern Europeans can get by on small refrigerators because they shop daily. In parts of Asia refrigerators are a status symbol and may be placed in the living room, leading to preferences for stylish designs and colors—in India bright blue and red are popular colors. In other Asian countries household space is constrained and many refrigerators are only four feet high so that the top can be used for storage. In Hong Kong the preference is for compact European-style appliances, but in Taiwan large American-style appliances are more popular. In Italy, most people use automatic washing machines but prefer to hang the clothes out to dry on a clothesline—there is a strongly entrenched tradition and cultural belief that sun-dried clothes are fresher, which virtually shuts down any opportunities for appliance makers to market clothes dryers in Italy. In China, many parents are reluctant to purchase personal computers (PCs) even when they can afford them because of concerns that their children will be distracted from their schoolwork by surfing the Web, playing PC-based video games, and downloading and listening to pop music.

Similarly, market growth varies from country to country. In emerging markets like India, China, Brazil, and Malaysia, market growth potential is far higher than in the more mature economies of Britain, Denmark, Canada, and Japan. In automobiles, for example, the potential for market growth is explosive in China, where 2005 sales of new vehicles amounted to less than 5 million in a country with 1.3 billion people. In India there are efficient, well-developed national channels for distributing trucks, scooters, farm equipment, groceries, personal care items, and other packaged products to the country's 3 million retailers, whereas in China distribution is primarily local and there is no national network for distributing most products. The marketplace is intensely competitive in some countries and only moderately contested in others. Industry driving forces may be one thing in Spain, quite another in Canada, and different yet again in Turkey or Argentina or South Korea.

One of the biggest concerns of companies competing in foreign markets is whether to customize their offerings in each different country market to match the tastes and preferences of local buyers or whether to offer a mostly standardized product worldwide. While making products that are closely matched to local tastes makes them more appealing to local buyers, customizing a company's products country by country may have the effect of raising production and distribution costs due to the greater variety of designs and components, shorter production runs, and the complications of added inventory handling and distribution logistics. Greater standardization of a global company's product offering, however, can lead to scale economies and experience/ learning curve effects, thus contributing to the achievement of a low-cost advantage. *The tension between the market pressures to localize a company's product offerings country by country and the competitive pressures to lower costs is one of the big strategic issues that participants in foreign markets have to resolve.*

Aside from the basic cultural and market differences among countries, a company also has to pay special attention to location advantages that stem from country-to-country variations in manufacturing and distribution costs, the risks of adverse shifts in exchange rates, and the economic and political demands of host governments.

Gaining Competitive Advantage Based on Where Activities Are Located

Differences in wage rates, worker productivity, inflation rates, energy costs, tax rates, government regulations, and the like create sizable variations in manufacturing costs from country to country. Plants in some countries have major manufacturing cost advantages because of lower input costs (especially labor), relaxed government regulations, the proximity of suppliers, or unique natural resources. In such cases, the low-cost countries become principal production sites, with most of the output being exported to markets in other parts of the world. Companies that build production facilities in low-cost countries (or that source their products from contract manufacturers in these countries) have a competitive advantage over rivals with plants in countries where costs are higher. The competitive role of low manufacturing costs is most evident in low-wage countries like China, India, Pakistan, Cambodia, Vietnam, Mexico, Brazil, Guatemala, the Philippines, and several countries in Africa that have become production havens for manufactured goods with high labor content (especially textiles and apparel). Labor costs in China averaged about $0.70 an hour in 2004–2005 versus about $1.50 in Russia, $4.60 in Hungary, $4.90 in Portugal, $16.50 in Canada, $21.00 in the United States, $23.00 in Norway, and $25.00 in Germany.[3] China is fast becoming the manufacturing capital of the world—virtually all of the world's major manufacturing companies now have facilities in China, and China attracted more foreign direct investment in 2002 and 2003 than any other country in the world. Likewise, concerns about short delivery times and low shipping costs make some countries better locations than others for establishing distribution centers.

The quality of a country's business environment also offers locational advantages—the governments of some countries are anxious to attract foreign investments and go all out to create a business climate that outsiders will view as favorable. A good example is Ireland, which has one of the world's most pro-business environments. Ireland offers companies very low corporate tax rates, has a government that is responsive to the needs of industry, and aggressively recruits high-tech manufacturing facilities and multinational companies. Such policies were a significant force in making Ireland the most dynamic, fastest-growing nation in Europe during the 1990s. Ireland's policies were a major factor in Intel's decision to choose Leixlip, County Kildare, as the site for a $2.5 billion chip manufacturing plant that employs over 4,000 people. Another locational advantage is the clustering of suppliers of components and capital equipment; infrastructure suppliers (universities, vocational training providers, research enterprises); trade associations; and makers of complementary products in a geographic area—such clustering can be an important source of cost savings in addition to facilitating close collaboration with key suppliers.

The Risks of Adverse Exchange Rate Shifts

The volatility of exchange rates greatly complicates the issue of geographic cost advantages. Currency exchange rates often move up or down 20 to 40 percent annually. Changes of this magnitude can either totally wipe out a country's low-cost advantage or transform a former high-cost location into a competitive-cost location. For instance, in the mid-1980s, when the dollar was strong relative to the Japanese yen (meaning that $1 would purchase, say, 125 yen as opposed to only 100 yen), Japanese heavy-equipment maker Komatsu was able to undercut U.S.-based Caterpillar's prices by as much as 25 percent, causing Caterpillar to lose sales and market share. But starting in 1985, when exchange rates began to shift and the dollar grew steadily weaker against the yen (meaning that $1 was worth fewer and fewer yen, and that a Komatsu product made in Japan at a cost of 20 million yen translated into costs of many more dollars than before), Komatsu had to raise its prices to U.S. buyers six times over two years. With its competitiveness against Komatsu restored because of the weaker dollar and Komatsu's higher prices, Caterpillar regained sales and market share. *The lesson of fluctuating exchange rates is that companies that export goods to foreign countries always gain in competitiveness when the currency of the country in which the goods are manufactured is weak. Exporters are disadvantaged when the currency of the country where goods are being manufactured grows stronger.* Sizable long-term shifts in exchange rates thus shuffle the global cards of which rivals have the upper hand in the marketplace and which countries represent the low-cost manufacturing location.

> **Core Concept**
> Companies with manufacturing facilities in a particular country are more cost-competitive in exporting goods to world markets when the local currency is weak (or declines in value relative to other currencies); their competitiveness erodes when the local currency grows stronger relative to the currencies of the countries to which the locally made goods are being exported.

As a further illustration of the risks associated with fluctuating exchange rates, consider the case of a U.S. company that has located manufacturing facilities in Brazil (where the currency is reals—pronounced *ray-alls*) and that exports most of the Brazilian-made goods to markets in the European Union (where the currency is euros). To keep the numbers simple, assume that the exchange rate is 4 Brazilian reals for 1 euro and that the product being made in Brazil has a manufacturing cost of 4 Brazilian reals (or 1 euro). Now suppose that for some reason the exchange rate shifts from 4 reals per euro to 5 reals per euro (meaning that the real has declined in value and that the euro is stronger). Making the product in Brazil is now more cost-competitive because a Brazilian good costing 4 reals to produce has fallen to only 0.8 euros at the new exchange rate. If, in contrast, the value of the Brazilian real grows stronger in relation to the euro—resulting in an exchange rate of 3 reals to 1 euro—the same good costing 4 reals to produce now has a cost of 1.33 euros. Clearly, the attraction of manufacturing a good in Brazil and selling it in Europe is far greater when the euro is strong (an exchange rate of 1 euro for 5 Brazilian reals) than when the euro is weak and exchanges for only 3 Brazilian reals.

Insofar as U.S.-based manufacturers are concerned, declines in the value of the U.S. dollar against foreign currencies act to reduce or eliminate whatever cost advantage foreign manufacturers might have over U.S. manufacturers and can even prompt foreign companies to establish production plants in the United States. Likewise, a weak euro enhances the cost competitiveness of companies manufacturing goods in Europe for export to foreign markets; a strong euro versus other currencies weakens the cost competitiveness of European plants that manufacture goods for export.

In 2002, when the Brazilian real declined in value by about 25 percent against the dollar, the euro, and several other currencies, the ability of companies with manufacturing plants in Brazil to compete in world markets was greatly enhanced—of course, in the future years this windfall gain in cost advantage might well be eroded by sustained rises in the value of the Brazilian real against these same currencies. Herein lies the risk: *Currency exchange rates are rather unpredictable, swinging first one way and then another way, so the competitiveness of any company's facilities in any country is partly dependent on whether exchange rate changes over time have a favorable or unfavorable cost impact.* Companies producing goods in one country for export abroad always improve their cost competitiveness when the country's currency grows weaker relative to currencies of the countries where the goods are being exported to, and they find their cost competitiveness eroded when the local currency grows stronger. In contrast, domestic companies that are under pressure from lower-cost imported goods become more cost competitive when their currency grows weaker in relation to the currencies of the countries where the imported goods are made—in other words, a U.S. manufacturer views a weaker U.S. dollar as a *favorable exchange rate shift* because such shifts help make its costs more competitive versus those of foreign rivals.

> **Core Concept**
>
> Fluctuating exchange rates pose significant risks to a company's competitiveness in foreign markets. Exporters win when the currency of the country where goods are being manufactured grows weaker, and they lose when the currency grows stronger. Domestic companies under pressure from lower-cost imports are benefited when their government's currency grows weaker in relation to the countries where the imported goods are being made.

Host Governments' Policies

National governments enact all kinds of measures affecting business conditions and the operation of foreign companies in their markets. Host governments may set local content requirements on goods made inside their borders by foreign-based companies, have rules and policies that protect local companies from foreign competition, put restrictions on exports to ensure adequate local supplies, regulate the prices of imported and locally produced goods, enact deliberately burdensome procedures and requirements for imported goods to pass customs inspection, and impose tariffs or quotas on the imports of certain goods—until 2002, when it joined the World Trade Organization, China imposed a 100 percent tariff on motor vehicle imports. The European Union imposes quotas on textile and apparel imports from China, as a measure to protect European producers in southern Europe. India imposed excise taxes on newly purchased motor vehicles in 2005 ranging from 24 to 40 percent—a policy that has significantly dampened the demand for new vehicles in India (though down from as much as 50 percent in prior years). Governments may or may not have burdensome tax structures, stringent environmental regulations, or strictly enforced worker safety standards. Sometimes outsiders face a web of regulations regarding technical standards, product certification, prior approval of capital spending projects, withdrawal of funds from the country, and required minority (sometimes majority) ownership of foreign company operations by local companies or investors. A few governments may be hostile to or suspicious of foreign companies operating within their borders. Some governments provide subsidies and low-interest loans to domestic companies to help them compete against foreign-based companies. Other governments, anxious to obtain new plants and jobs, offer foreign companies a helping hand in the form of subsidies, privileged market access, and technical assistance. All of these possibilities explain why the managers of companies opting to compete in foreign markets have to take a close look at a country's politics and policies toward business in general, and foreign companies in particular, in deciding which country markets to participate in and which ones to avoid.

THE CONCEPTS OF MULTICOUNTRY COMPETITION AND GLOBAL COMPETITION

There are important differences in the patterns of international competition from industry to industry.[4] At one extreme is **multicountry competition,** in which there's so much cross-country variation in market conditions and in the companies contending for leadership that the market contest among rivals in one country is not closely connected to the market contests in other countries. The standout features of multicountry competition are that (1) buyers in different countries are attracted to different product attributes, (2) sellers vary from country to country, and (3) industry conditions and competitive forces in each national market differ in important respects. Take the banking industry in Italy, Brazil, and Japan as an example—the requirements and expectations of banking customers vary among the three countries, the lead banking competitors in Italy differ from those in Brazil or in Japan, and the competitive battle going on among the leading banks in Italy is unrelated to the rivalry taking place in Brazil or Japan. Thus, with multicountry competition, rival firms battle for national championships, and winning in one country does not necessarily signal the ability to fare well in other countries. In multicountry competition, the power of a company's strategy and resource capabilities in one country may not enhance its competitiveness to the same degree in other countries where it operates. Moreover, any competitive advantage a company secures in one country is largely confined to that country; the spillover effects to other countries are minimal to nonexistent. Industries characterized by multicountry competition include radio and TV broadcasting, consumer banking, life insurance, apparel, metals fabrication, many types of food products (coffee, cereals, breads, canned goods, frozen foods), and retailing.

> **Core Concept**
> *Multicountry competition* exists when competition in one national market is not closely connected to competition in another national market—there is no global or world market, just a collection of self-contained country markets.

At the other extreme is **global competition,** in which prices and competitive conditions across country markets are strongly linked and the term *global market* has true meaning. In a globally competitive industry, much the same group of rival companies competes in many different countries, but especially so in countries where sales volumes are large and where having a competitive presence is strategically important to building a strong global position in the industry. Thus, a company's competitive position in one country both affects and is affected by its position in other countries. In global competition, a firm's overall competitive advantage grows out of its entire worldwide operations; the competitive advantage it creates at its home base is supplemented by advantages growing out of its operations in other countries (having plants in low-wage countries, being able to transfer expertise from country to country, having the capability to serve customers who also have multinational operations, and brand-name recognition in many parts of the world). Rival firms in globally competitive industries vie for worldwide leadership. Global competition exists in motor vehicles, television sets, tires, mobile phones, personal computers, copiers, watches, digital cameras, bicycles, and commercial aircraft.

> **Core Concept**
> *Global competition* exists when competitive conditions across national markets are linked strongly enough to form a true international market and when leading competitors compete head to head in many different countries.

An industry can have segments that are globally competitive and segments in which competition is country by country.[5] In the hotel/motel industry, for example, the low- and medium-priced segments are characterized by multicountry competition—competitors serve travelers mainly within the same country. In the business and luxury segments, however, competition is more globalized. Companies like Nikki, Marriott, Sheraton, and Hilton have hotels at many international locations, use worldwide reservation systems, and establish common quality and service standards to gain marketing advantages in serving businesspeople and other travelers who make frequent international trips. In lubricants, the marine engine segment is globally competitive—ships move from port to port and require the same oil everywhere they stop. Brand reputations in marine lubricants have a global scope, and successful marine engine lubricant producers (Exxon Mobil, BP Amoco, and Shell) operate globally. In automotive motor oil, however, multicountry competition dominates—countries have different weather conditions and driving patterns, production of motor oil is subject to limited scale economies, shipping costs are high, and retail distribution channels differ markedly from country to country. Thus, domestic firms—like Quaker State and Pennzoil in the United States and Castrol in Great Britain—can be leaders in their home markets without competing globally.

It is also important to recognize that an industry can be in transition from multicountry competition to global competition. In a number of today's industries—beer and major home appliances are prime examples—leading domestic competitors have begun expanding into more and more foreign markets, often acquiring local companies or brands and integrating them into their operations. As some industry members start to build global brands and a global presence, other industry members find themselves pressured to follow the same strategic path—especially if establishing multinational operations results in important scale economies and a powerhouse brand name. As the industry consolidates to fewer players, such that many of the same companies find themselves in head-to-head competition in more and more country markets, global competition begins to replace multicountry competition.

At the same time, consumer tastes in a number of important product categories are converging across the world. Less diversity of tastes and preferences opens the way for companies to create global brands and sell essentially the same products in most all countries of the world. Even in industries where consumer tastes remain fairly diverse, companies are learning to use "custom mass production" to economically create different versions of a product and thereby satisfy the tastes of people in different countries.

In addition to taking the obvious cultural and political differences between countries into account, a company has to shape its strategic approach to competing in foreign markets according to whether its industry is characterized by multicountry competition, global competition, or a transition from one to the other.

STRATEGY OPTIONS FOR ENTERING AND COMPETING IN FOREIGN MARKETS

There are a host of generic strategic options for a company that decides to expand outside its domestic market and compete internationally or globally:

1. *Maintain a national (one-country) production base and export goods to foreign markets*, using either company-owned or foreign-controlled forward distribution channels.

2. *License foreign firms to use the company's technology or to produce and distribute the company's products.*

3. *Employ a franchising strategy.*

4. *Follow a multicountry strategy,* varying the company's strategic approach (perhaps a little, perhaps a lot) from country to country in accordance with local conditions and differing buyer tastes and preferences.

5. *Follow a global strategy,* using essentially the same competitive strategy approach in all country markets where the company has a presence.

6. *Use strategic alliances or joint ventures with foreign companies as the primary vehicle for entering foreign markets* and perhaps also using them as an ongoing strategic arrangement aimed at maintaining or strengthening its competitiveness.

The following sections discuss the first five options in more detail; the sixth option is discussed in a separate section later in the chapter.

Export Strategies

Using domestic plants as a production base for exporting goods to foreign markets is an excellent initial strategy for pursuing international sales. It is a conservative way to test the international waters. The amount of capital needed to begin exporting is often quite minimal; existing production capacity may well be sufficient to make goods for export. With an export strategy, a manufacturer can limit its involvement in foreign markets by contracting with foreign wholesalers experienced in importing to handle the entire distribution and marketing function in their countries or regions of the world. If it is more advantageous to maintain control over these functions, however, a manufacturer can establish its own distribution and sales organizations in some or all of the target foreign markets. Either way, a home-based production and export strategy helps the firm minimize its direct investments in foreign countries. Such strategies are commonly favored by Chinese, Korean, and Italian companies—products are designed and manufactured at home and then distributed through local channels in the importing countries; the primary functions performed abroad relate chiefly to establishing a network of distributors and perhaps conducting sales promotion and brand awareness activities.

Whether an export strategy can be pursued successfully over the long run hinges on the relative cost competitiveness of the home-country production base. In some industries, firms gain additional scale economies and experience/learning curve benefits from centralizing production in one or several giant plants whose output capability exceeds demand in any one country market; obviously, a company must export to capture such economies. However, an export strategy is vulnerable when (1) manufacturing costs in the home country are substantially higher than in foreign countries where rivals have plants, (2) the costs of shipping the product to distant foreign markets are relatively high, or (3) adverse shifts occur in currency exchange rates. Unless an exporter can both keep its production and shipping costs competitive with rivals and successfully hedge against unfavorable changes in currency exchange rates, its success will be limited.

Licensing Strategies

Licensing makes sense when a firm with valuable technical know-how or a unique patented product has neither the internal organizational capability nor the resources to enter foreign markets. Licensing also has the advantage of avoiding the risks of committing resources to country markets that are unfamiliar, politically volatile, economically unstable, or otherwise risky. By licensing the technology or the production rights to foreign-based firms, the firm does not have to bear the costs and risks of entering foreign markets on its own, yet it is able to generate income from royalties. The big disadvantage of licensing is the risk of providing valuable technological know-how to foreign companies and thereby losing some degree of control over its use; monitoring licensees and safeguarding the company's proprietary know-how can prove quite difficult in some circumstances. But if the royalty potential is considerable and the companies to whom the licenses are being granted are both trustworthy and reputable, then licensing can be a very attractive option. Many software and pharmaceutical companies use licensing strategies.

Franchising Strategies

While licensing works well for manufacturers and owners of proprietary technology, franchising is often better suited to the global expansion efforts of service and retailing enterprises. McDonald's, Yum! Brands (the parent of Pizza Hut, KFC, and Taco Bell), The UPS Store, Jani-King International (the world's largest commercial cleaning franchisor), Roto-Rooter, 7-Eleven, and Hilton Hotels have all used franchising to build a presence in foreign markets. Franchising has much the same advantages as licensing. The franchisee bears most of the costs and risks of establishing foreign locations; a franchisor has to expend only the resources to recruit, train, support, and monitor franchisees. The big problem a franchisor faces is maintaining quality control; foreign franchisees do not always exhibit strong commitment to consistency and standardization, especially when the local culture does not stress the same kinds of quality concerns. Another problem that can arise is whether to allow foreign franchisees to make modifications in the franchisor's product offering so as to better satisfy the tastes and expectations of local buyers. Should McDonald's allow its franchised units in Japan to modify Big Macs slightly to suit Japanese tastes? Should the franchised KFC units in China be permitted to substitute spices that appeal to Chinese consumers? Or should the same menu offerings be rigorously and unvaryingly required of all franchisees worldwide?

Localized Multicountry Strategies or a Global Strategy?

The issue of whether to vary the company's competitive approach to fit specific market conditions and buyer preferences in each host country or whether to employ essentially the same strategy in all countries is perhaps the foremost strategic issue that companies must address when they operate in two or more foreign markets. Figure 7.1 shows a company's options for resolving this issue.

Core Concept
A *localized* or *multicountry strategy* is one where a company varies its product offering and competitive approach from country to country in an effort to be responsive to differing buyer preferences and market conditions.

Think-Local, Act-Local Approaches to Strategy Making   The bigger the differences in buyer tastes, cultural traditions, and market conditions in different countries, the stronger the case for a think-local, act-local approach to strategy-making, in which a company tailors its product offerings and perhaps its basic competitive strategy to fit buyer tastes and market conditions in each country where it opts to compete. The strength of employing a set of *localized* or *multicountry strategies* is that the company's actions and business approaches are deliberately crafted to accommodate the

Figure 7.1   **A Company's Strategic Options for Dealing with Cross-Country Variations in Buyer Preferences and Market Conditions**

Strategic Posturing Options	Ways to Deal with Cross-Country Variations in Buyer Preferences and Market Conditions
Think Local, Act Local	**Employ localized strategies—one for each country market:** ■ Tailor the company's competitive approach and product offering to fit specific market conditions and buyer preferences in each host country. ■ Delegate strategy making to local managers with firsthand knowledge of local conditions.
Think Global, Act Global	**Employ same strategy worldwide:** ■ Pursue *the same basic competitive strategy theme* (low-cost, differentiation, best-cost, or focused) *in all country markets*—a global strategy. ■ Offer the same products worldwide, with only very minor deviations from one country to another when local market conditions so dictate. ■ Utilize the same capabilities, distribution channels, and marketing approaches worldwide. ■ Coordinate strategic actions from central headquarters
Think Global, Act Local	**Employ a combination global-local strategy:** ■ Employ essentially *the same basic competitive strategy theme* (low-cost, differentiation, best-cost, or focused) in *all country markets*. ■ Develop the capability to customize product offerings and sell different product versions in different countries (perhaps even under different brand names). ■ Give local managers the latitude to adapt the global approach as needed to accommodate local buyer preferences and be responsive to local market and competitive conditions.

differing tastes and expectations of buyers in each country and to stake out the most attractive market positions vis-à-vis local competitors. A think-local, act-local approach means giving local managers considerable strategy-making latitude. It means having plants produce different product versions for different local markets, and adapting marketing and distribution to fit local customs and cultures. The bigger the country-to-country variations, the more that a company's overall strategy is a collection of its localized country strategies rather than a common or global strategy.

A think-local, act-local approach to strategy making is essential when there are significant country-to-country differences in customer preferences and buying habits, when there are significant cross-country differences in distribution channels and marketing methods, when host governments enact regulations requiring that products sold locally meet strict manufacturing specifications or performance standards, and when the trade restrictions of host governments are so diverse and complicated that they preclude a uniform, coordinated worldwide market approach. With localized strategies, a company often has different product versions for different countries and sometimes sells them under different brand names. Sony markets a different Walkman in Norway than in Sweden to better meet the somewhat different preferences and habits of the users in each market. Castrol, a specialist in oil lubricants, has over 3,000 different formulas of lubricants, many of which have been tailored for different climates, vehicle types and uses, and equipment applications that characterize different country markets. In the food products industry, it is common for companies to vary the ingredients in their products and sell the localized versions under local brand names in order to cater to country-specific tastes and eating preferences. Motor vehicle manufacturers routinely produce smaller, more fuel-efficient vehicles for markets in Europe where roads are often narrower and gasoline prices two or three times higher than they produce for the North American market; the models they manufacture for the Asian market are different yet again. DaimlerChrysler, for example, equips all of the Jeep Grand Cherokees and many of its Mercedes cars sold in Europe with fuel-efficient diesel engines. The Buicks that General Motors sells in China are small compacts, whereas those sold in the United States are large family sedans and SUVs.

However, think-local, act-local strategies have two big drawbacks: They hinder transfer of a company's competencies and resources across country boundaries (since the strategies in different host countries can be grounded in varying competencies and capabilities), and they do not promote building a single, unified competitive advantage—especially one based on low cost. Companies employing highly localized or multicountry strategies face big hurdles in achieving low-cost leadership *unless* they find ways to customize their products and *still* be in position to capture scale economies and experience/learning curve effects. Companies like Dell Computer and Toyota, because they have mass customization production capabilities, can cost effectively adapt their product offerings to local buyer tastes.

Think-Global, Act-Global Approaches to Strategy Making   While multicountry or localized strategies are best suited for industries where multicountry competition dominates and a fairly high degree of local responsiveness is competitively imperative, global strategies are best suited for globally competitive industries. A *global strategy* is one in which the company's approach is predominantly the same in all countries—it sells the same products under the same brand names everywhere, uses much the same distribution channels in all countries, and competes on the basis of the same capabilities and marketing approaches worldwide. Although the company's strategy or product offering may be adapted in very minor ways to accommodate specific situations in a few host countries, the company's fundamental competitive approach (low-cost, differentiation, best-cost, or focused) remains very much intact worldwide, and local managers stick close to the global strategy. A think-global, act-global strategic theme prompts company managers to integrate and coordinate the company's strategic moves worldwide and to expand into most if not all nations where there is significant buyer demand. It puts considerable strategic

Core Concept
A *global strategy* is one where a company employs the same basic competitive approach in all countries where it operates, sells much the same products everywhere, strives to build global brands, and coordinates its actions worldwide.

emphasis on building a *global* brand name and aggressively pursuing opportunities to transfer ideas, new products, and capabilities from one country to another.[6] Indeed, with a think global, act global approach to strategy making, a company's operations in each country can be viewed as experiments that result in learning and in capabilities that may merit transfer to other country markets.

Whenever country-to-country differences are small enough to be accommodated within the framework of a global strategy, a global strategy is preferable to localized strategies because a company can more readily unify its operations and focus on establishing a brand image and reputation that is uniform from country to country. Moreover, with a global strategy a company is better able to focus its full resources on building the resource strengths and capabilities to secure a sustainable low-cost or differentiation-based competitive advantage over both domestic rivals and global rivals racing for world market leadership. Figure 7.2 summarizes the basic differences between a localized or multicountry strategy and a global strategy.

Think-Global, Act-Local Approaches to Strategy Making   Often, a company can accommodate cross-country variations in buyer tastes, local customs, and market conditions with a think-global, act-local approach to developing strategy. This middle-ground approach entails using the same basic competitive theme (low-cost, differentiation, best-cost, or focused) in each country but allowing local mangers the latitude to (1) incorporate whatever country-specific variations in product attributes are needed to best satisfy local buyers and (2) make whatever adjustments in production, distribution, and marketing are needed to be responsive to local market conditions and compete successfully against local rivals. Slightly different product versions sold under the same brand name may suffice to satisfy local tastes, and it may be feasible to accommodate these versions rather economically in the course of designing and manufacturing the company's product offerings. The build-to-order component of Dell's strategy in PCs for example, makes it simple for Dell to be responsive to how buyers in different parts of the world want their PCs equipped. However, Dell has not wavered in its strategy to sell directly to customers rather than through local retailers, even though the majority of buyers in countries such as China are concerned about ordering online and prefer to personally inspect PCs at stores before making a purchase.

As a rule, most companies that operate multinationally endeavor to employ as global a strategy as customer needs and market conditions permit. Philips Electronics, the Netherlands-based electronics and consumer products company, operated successfully with localized strategies for many years but has recently begun moving more toward a unified strategy within the European Union and within North America.[7] Whirlpool has been globalizing its low-cost leadership strategy in home appliances for over 15 years, striving to standardize parts and components and move toward worldwide designs for as many of its appliance products as possible. But it has found it necessary to continue producing significantly different versions of refrigerators, washing machines, and cooking appliances for consumers in different regions of the world because the needs and tastes of local buyers for appliances of different sizes and designs have not converged sufficiently to permit standardization of Whirlpool's product offerings worldwide. General Motors began an initiative in 2004 to insist that its worldwide units share basic parts and work together to design vehicles that can be sold, with modest variations, anywhere around the world; by reducing the types of radios used in its cars and trucks from 270 to 50, it expected to save 40 percent in radio costs.

Illustration Capsule 7.1 on page 209 describes how two companies localize their strategies for competing in country markets across the world.

Figure 7.2   **How a Localized or Multicountry Strategy Differs from a Global Strategy**

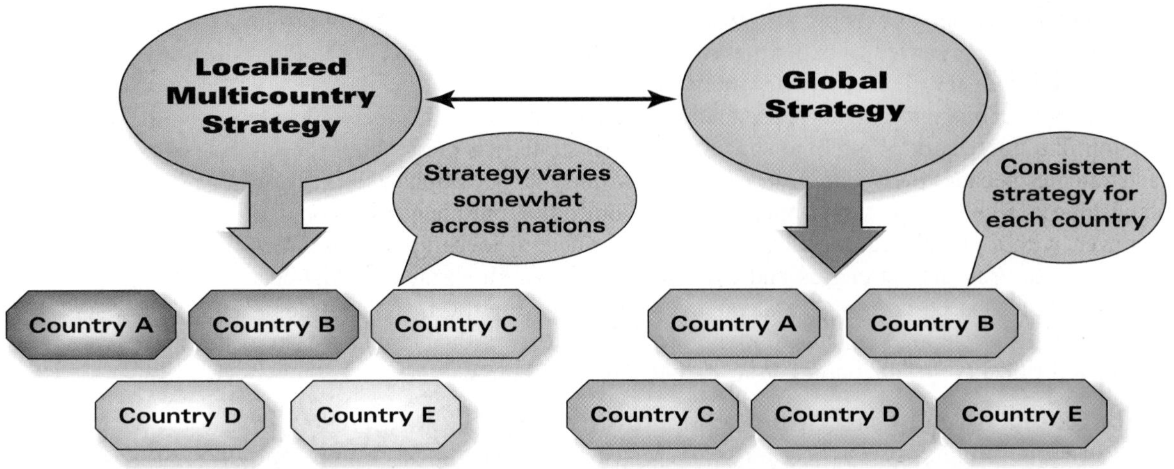

Localized Multicountry Strategy — Strategy varies somewhat across nations

Country A Country B Country C
Country D Country E

- Customize the company's competitive approach as needed to fit market and business circumstances in each host country—strong responsiveness to local conditions.
- Sell different product versions in different countries under different brand names—adapt product attributes to fit buyer tastes and preferences country by country.
- Scatter plants across many host countries, each producing product versions for local markets.
- Preferably use local suppliers (some local sources may be required by host government).
- Adapt marketing and distribution to local customs and culture of each country.
- Transfer competencies and capabilities from country to country where feasible.
- Give country managers fairly wide strategy-making latitude and autonomy over local operations.

Global Strategy — Consistent strategy for each country

Country A Country B
Country C Country D Country E

- Pursue same basic competitive strategy worldwide (low-cost, differentiation, best-cost, focused low-cost, focused differentiation), with minimal responsiveness to local conditions.
- Sell same products under same brand name worldwide; focus efforts on building global brands as opposed to strengthening local/regional brands sold in local/regional markets.
- Locate plants on basis of maximum locational advantage, usually in countries where production costs are lowest but plants may be scattered if shipping costs are high or other locational advantages dominate.
- Use best suppliers from anywhere in world.
- Coordinate marketing and distribution worldwide; make minor adaptation to local countries where needed.
- Compete on basis of same technologies, competencies, and capabilities worldwide; stress rapid transfer of new ideas, products, and capabilities to other countries.
- Coordinate major strategic decisions worldwide; expect local managers to stick close to global strategy.

Illustration Capsule 7.1
Multicountry Strategies at Electronic Arts and Coca-Cola

ELECTRONIC ARTS' MULTICOUNTRY STRATEGY IN VIDEO GAMES

Electronic Arts (EA), the world's largest independent developer and marketer of video games, designs games that are suited to the differing tastes of game players in different countries and also designs games in multiple languages. EA has two major design studios—one in Vancouver, British Columbia, and one in Los Angeles—and smaller design studios in San Francisco, Orlando, London, and Tokyo. This dispersion of design studios helps EA to design games that are specific to different cultures—for example, the London studio took the lead in designing the popular FIFA Soccer game to suit European tastes and to replicate the stadiums, signage, and team rosters; the U.S. studio took the lead in designing games involving NFL football, NBA basketball, and NASCAR racing. No other game software company had EA's ability to localize games or to launch games on multiple platforms in multiple countries in multiple languages. EA's game Harry Potter and the Chamber of Secrets was released simultaneously in 75 countries, in 31 languages, and on seven platforms.

COCA-COLA'S MULTICOUNTRY STRATEGY IN BEVERAGES

Coca-Cola strives to meet the demands of local tastes and cultures, offering 300 brands in some 200 countries. Its network of bottlers and distributors is distinctly local, and the company's products and brands are formulated to cater to local tastes. The ways in which Coca-Cola's local operating units bring products to market, the packaging that is used, and the company's advertising messages are all intended to match the local culture and fit in with local business practices. Many of the ingredients and supplies for Coca-Cola's products are sourced locally.

Sources: Information posted at www.ea.com and www.cocacola.com (accessed September 2004).

THE QUEST FOR COMPETITIVE ADVANTAGE IN FOREIGN MARKETS

There are three important ways in which a firm can gain competitive advantage (or offset domestic disadvantages) by expanding outside its domestic market:[8] One, it can use location to lower costs or achieve greater product differentiation. Two, it can transfer competitively valuable competencies and capabilities from its domestic markets to foreign markets. And three, it can use cross-border coordination in ways that a domestic-only competitor cannot.

Using Location to Build Competitive Advantage

To use location to build competitive advantage, a company must consider two issues: (1) whether to concentrate each activity it performs in a few select countries or to disperse performance of the activity to many nations, and (2) in which countries to locate particular activities.[9]

> Companies that compete multinationally can pursue competitive advantage in world markets by locating their value chain activities in whatever nations prove most advantageous.

When to Concentrate Activities in a Few Locations Companies tend to concentrate their activities in a limited number of locations in the following circumstances:

- *When the costs of manufacturing or other activities are significantly lower in some geographic locations than in others*—For example, much of the world's athletic footwear is manufactured in Asia (China and Korea) because of low labor costs; much of the production of motherboards for PCs is located in Taiwan because of both low costs and the high-caliber technical skills of the Taiwanese labor force.

- *When there are significant scale economies*—The presence of significant economies of scale in components production or final assembly means that a company can gain major cost savings from operating a few superefficient plants as opposed to a host of small plants scattered across the world. Important marketing and distribution economies associated with multinational operations can also yield low-cost leadership. In situations where some competitors are intent on global dominance, being the worldwide low-cost provider is a powerful competitive advantage. Achieving low-cost provider status often requires a company to have the largest worldwide manufacturing share, with production centralized in one or a few world-scale plants in low-cost locations. Some companies even use such plants to manufacture units sold under the brand names of rivals. Manufacturing share (as distinct from brand share or market share) is significant because it provides more certain access to production-related scale economies. Japanese makers of VCRs, microwave ovens, TVs, and DVD players have used their large manufacturing share to establish a low-cost advantage.[10]

- *When there is a steep learning curve associated with performing an activity in a single location*—In some industries experience/learning curve effects in parts manufacture or assembly are so great that a company establishes one or two large plants from which it serves the world market. The key to riding down the learning curve is to concentrate production in a few locations to increase the accumulated volume at a plant (and thus the experience of the plant's workforce) as rapidly as possible.

- *When certain locations have superior resources, allow better coordination of related activities, or offer other valuable advantages*—A research unit or a sophisticated production facility may be situated in a particular nation because of its pool of technically trained personnel. Samsung became a leader in memory chip technology by establishing a major R&D facility in Silicon Valley and transferring the know-how it gained back to headquarters and its plants in South Korea. Where just-in-time inventory practices yield big cost savings and/or where an assembly firm has long-term partnering arrangements with its key suppliers, parts manufacturing plants may be clustered around final assembly plants. An assembly plant may be located in a country in return for the host government's allowing freer import of components from large-scale, centralized parts plants located elsewhere. A customer service center or sales office may be opened in a particular country to help cultivate strong relationships with pivotal customers located nearby.

When to Disperse Activities Across Many Locations   There are several instances when dispersing activities is more advantageous than concentrating them. Buyer-related activities—such as distribution to dealers, sales and advertising, and after-sale service—usually must take place close to buyers. This means physically locating the capability to perform such activities in every country market where a global firm has major customers (unless buyers in several adjoining countries can be served quickly from a nearby central location). For example, firms that make mining and oil-drilling equipment maintain operations in many international locations to support customers' needs for speedy equipment repair and technical assistance. The four biggest public accounting firms have numerous international offices to service the foreign operations of their multinational corporate clients. A global competitor that effectively disperses its buyer-related activities can gain a service-based competitive edge in world markets over rivals whose buyer-related activities are more concentrated—this is one reason the Big Four public accounting firms (PricewaterhouseCoopers, KPMG, Deloitte & Touche, and Ernst & Young) have been so successful relative to regional and national firms. Dispersing activities to many locations is also competitively advantageous when high transportation costs, diseconomies of large size, and trade barriers make it too expensive to operate from a central location. Many companies distribute their products from multiple locations to shorten delivery times to customers. In addition, it is strategically advantageous to disperse activities to hedge against the risks of fluctuating exchange rates; supply interruptions (due to strikes, mechanical failures, and transportation delays); and adverse political developments. Such risks are greater when activities are concentrated in a single location.

The classic reason for locating an activity in a particular country is low cost.[11] Even though multinational and global firms have strong reason to disperse buyer-related activities to many international locations, such activities as materials procurement, parts manufacture, finished goods assembly, technology research, and new product development can frequently be decoupled from buyer locations and performed wherever advantage lies. Components can be made in Mexico; technology research done in Frankfurt; new products developed and tested in Phoenix; and assembly plants located in Spain, Brazil, Taiwan, or South Carolina. Capital can be raised in whatever country it is available on the best terms.

Using Cross-Border Transfers of Competencies and Capabilities to Build Competitive Advantage

One of the best ways for a company with valuable competencies and resource strengths to secure competitive advantage is to use its considerable resource strengths to enter additional country markets. A company whose resource strengths prove particularly potent in competing successfully in newly entered country markets not only grows sales and profits but also may find that its competitiveness is sufficiently enhanced to produce competitive advantage over one or more rivals and contend for global market leadership. Transferring competencies, capabilities, and resource strengths from country to country contributes to the development of broader or deeper competencies and capabilities—ideally helping a company achieve dominating depth in some competitively valuable area. Dominating depth in a competitively valuable capability, resource, or value chain activity is a strong basis for sustainable competitive advantage over other multinational or global competitors, and especially so over domestic-only competitors. A one-country customer base is often too small to support the resource buildup needed to achieve such depth; this is particularly true when the market is just emerging and sophisticated resources have not been required.

Whirlpool, the leading global manufacturer of home appliances, with plants in 14 countries and sales in 170 countries, has used the Internet to create a global information technology platform that allows the company to transfer key product innovations and production processes across regions and brands quickly and effectively. Wal-Mart is slowly but forcefully expanding its operations with a strategy that involves transferring its considerable domestic expertise in distribution and discount retailing to store operations recently established in China, Japan, Latin America, and Europe. Its status as the largest, most resource-deep, and most sophisticated user of distribution/retailing know-how has served it well in building its foreign sales and profitability. But Wal-Mart is not racing madly to position itself in many foreign markets; rather, it is establishing a strong presence in select country markets and learning how to be successful in these before tackling entry into other countries well-suited to its business model.

However, cross-border resource transfers are not a guaranteed recipe for success. Philips Electronics sells more color TVs and DVD recorders in Europe than any other company does; its biggest technological breakthrough was the compact disc, which it invented in 1982. Philips has worldwide sales of about 38 billion euros, but as of 2005 Philips had lost money for 17 consecutive years in its U.S. consumer electronics business. In the United States, the company's color TVs and DVD recorders (sold under the Magnavox and Philips brands) are slow sellers. Philips notoriously lags in introducing new products into the U.S. market and has been struggling to develop an able sales force that can make inroads with U.S. electronics retailers and change its image as a low-end brand.

Using Cross-Border Coordination to Build Competitive Advantage

Coordinating company activities across different countries contributes to sustainable competitive advantage in several different ways.[12] Multinational and global competitors can choose where and how to challenge rivals. They may decide to retaliate against an aggressive rival in the country market where the rival has its biggest sales volume or its best profit margins in order to reduce the rival's financial resources for competing in other country markets. They may also decide to wage a price-cutting offensive against weak rivals in their home markets, capturing greater market share and subsidizing any short-term losses with profits earned in other country markets.

If a firm learns how to assemble its product more efficiently at, say, its Brazilian plant, the accumulated expertise can be quickly communicated via the Internet to assembly plants in other world locations. Knowledge gained in marketing a company's product in Great Britain can readily be exchanged with company personnel in New Zealand or Australia. A global or multinational manufacturer can shift production from a plant in one country to a plant in another to take advantage of exchange rate fluctuations, to enhance its leverage with host-country governments, and to respond to changing wage rates, components shortages, energy costs, or changes in tariffs and quotas. Production schedules can be coordinated worldwide; shipments can be diverted from one distribution center to another if sales rise unexpectedly in one place and fall in another.

Using online systems, companies can readily gather ideas for new and improved products from customers and company personnel all over the world, permitting informed decisions about what can be standardized and what should be customized. Likewise, online systems enable multinational companies to involve their best design and engineering personnel (wherever they are located) in collectively coming up with next-generation products—it is easy for company personnel in one location to use the Internet to collaborate closely with personnel in other locations in performing all sorts of strategically relevant activities. Efficiencies can also be achieved by shifting workloads from where they are unusually heavy to locations where personnel are underutilized. Whirlpool's efforts to link its product R&D and manufacturing operations in North America, Latin America, Europe, and Asia allowed it to accelerate the discovery of innovative appliance features, coordinate the introduction of these features in the appliance products marketed in different countries, and create a cost-efficient worldwide supply chain. Whirlpool's conscious efforts to integrate and coordinate its various operations around the world have helped it become a low-cost producer and also speed product innovations to market, thereby giving Whirlpool an edge over rivals in designing and rapidly introducing innovative and attractively priced appliances worldwide.

Furthermore, a multinational company that consistently incorporates the same differentiating attributes in its products worldwide has enhanced potential to build a global brand name with significant power in the marketplace. The reputation for quality that Honda established worldwide first in motorcycles and then in automobiles gave it competitive advantage in positioning Honda lawn mowers at the upper end of the U.S. outdoor power equipment market—the Honda name gave the company immediate credibility with U.S. buyers of power equipment and enabled it to become an instant market contender without all the fanfare and cost of a multimillion-dollar ad campaign to build brand awareness.

PROFIT SANCTUARIES, CROSS-MARKET SUBSIDIZATION, AND GLOBAL STRATEGIC OFFENSIVES

Profit sanctuaries are country markets (or geographic regions) in which a company derives substantial profits because of its strong or protected market position. McDonald's serves about 50 million customers daily at nearly 32,000 locations in 119 countries on five continents; not surprisingly, its biggest profit sanctuary is the United States, which generated 61.2 percent of 2004 profits, despite accounting for just 34.2 percent of 2004 revenues. Nike, which markets its products in 160 countries, has two big profit sanctuaries: the United States (where it earned 41.5 percent of its operating profits in 2005) and Europe, the Middle East, and Africa (where it earned 34.8 percent of 2005 operating profits). Discount retailer Carrefour, which has stores across much of Europe plus stores in Asia and the Americas, also has two principal profit sanctuaries; its biggest is in France (which in 2004

> **Core Concept**
> Companies with large, protected *profit sanctuaries* have competitive advantage over companies that don't have a protected sanctuary. Companies with multiple profit sanctuaries have a competitive advantage over companies with a single sanctuary.

accounted for 49.2 percent of revenues and 60.8 percent of earnings before interest and taxes), and its second biggest is Europe outside of France (which in 2004 accounted for 37.3 percent of revenues and 33.1 percent of earnings before interest and taxes). Japan is the chief profit sanctuary for most Japanese companies because trade barriers erected by the Japanese government effectively block foreign companies from competing for a large share of Japanese sales. Protected from the threat of foreign competition in their home market, Japanese companies can safely charge somewhat higher prices to their Japanese customers and thus earn attractively large profits on sales made in Japan. In most cases, a company's biggest and most strategically crucial profit sanctuary is its home market, but international and global companies may also enjoy profit sanctuary status in other nations where they have a strong competitive position, big sales volume, and attractive profit margins. Companies that compete globally are likely to have more profit sanctuaries than companies that compete in just a few country markets; a domestic-only competitor, of course, can have only one profit sanctuary (see Figure 7.3).

Figure 7.3   **Profit Sanctuary Potential of Domestic-Only, International, and Global Competitors**

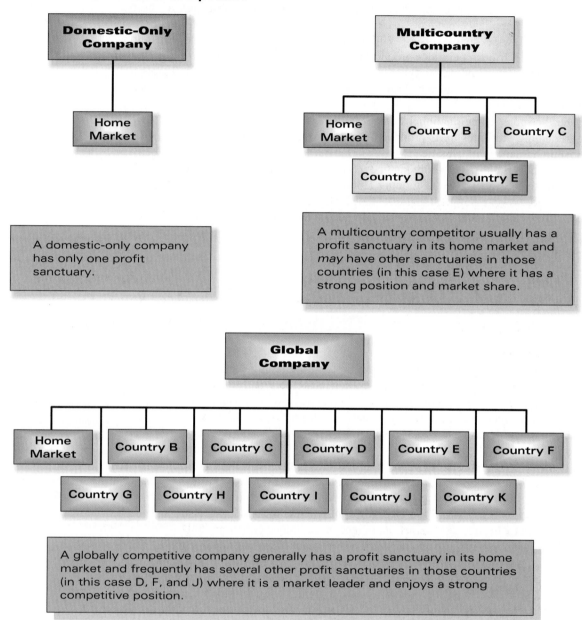

Using Cross-Market Subsidization to Wage a Strategic Offensive

Profit sanctuaries are valuable competitive assets, providing the financial strength to support strategic offensives in selected country markets and fuel a company's race for global market leadership. The added financial capability afforded by multiple profit sanctuaries gives a global or multicountry competitor the financial strength to wage a market offensive against a domestic competitor whose only profit sanctuary is its home market. Consider the case of a purely domestic company in competition with a company that has multiple profit sanctuaries and that is racing for global market leadership. The global company has the flexibility of lowballing its prices in the domestic company's home market and grabbing market share at the domestic company's expense, subsidizing razor-thin margins or even losses with the healthy profits earned in its profit sanctuaries—a practice called **cross-market subsidization.** The global company can adjust the depth of its price cutting to move in and capture market share quickly, or it can shave prices slightly to make gradual market inroads (perhaps over a decade or more) so as not to threaten domestic firms precipitously or trigger protectionist government actions. If the domestic company retaliates with matching price cuts, it exposes its entire revenue and profit base to erosion; its profits can be squeezed substantially and its competitive strength sapped, even if it is the domestic market leader.

> **Core Concept**
> *Cross-market subsidization*—supporting competitive offensives in one market with resources and profits diverted from operations in other markets—is a powerful competitive weapon.

Offensive Strategies Suitable for Competing in Foreign Markets

Companies that compete in multiple foreign markets can, of course, fashion an offensive strategy based on any of the approaches discussed in Chapter 6 (pages 160–193)—these types of offensive strategies are universally applicable and are just as suitable for competing in foreign markets as for domestic markets. But there are three additional types of offensive strategies that are suited to companies competing in foreign markets:[13]

- *Attack a foreign rival's profit sanctuaries.* Launching an offensive in a country market where a rival earns its biggest profits can put the rival on the defensive, forcing it to perhaps spend more on marketing/advertising, trim its prices, boost product innovation efforts, or otherwise undertake actions that raise its costs and erode its profits. If a company's offensive succeeds in eroding a rival's profits in its chief profit sanctuary, the rival's financial resources may be sufficiently weakened to enable the attacker to gain the upper hand and build market momentum. While attacking a rival's profit sanctuary violates the principle of attacking competitor weaknesses instead of competitor strengths, it can nonetheless prove valuable when there is special merit in pursuing actions that cut into a foreign rival's profit margins and force it to defend a market that is important to its competitive well-being. This is especially true when the attacker has important resource strengths and profit sanctuaries of its own that it can draw on to support its offensive.

- *Employ cross-market subsidization to win customers and sales away from select rivals in select country markets.* This can be a particularly attractive offensive strategy for companies that compete in multiple country markets with multiple products (several brands of cigarettes or different brands of food products). Competing in multiple country markets gives a company the luxury of drawing upon the resources, profits, and cash flows derived from particular country markets (especially its profit sanctuaries) to support offensives aimed at winning customers away from select rivals in those country markets that it wants either to enter or to boost its sales and market share. Alternatively, a company whose product lineup consists of different items can shift resources from a product category where it is competitively strong and resource deep (say soft drinks) to add firepower to an offensive in those countries with bright growth prospects in another product category (say bottled water or fruit juices).

- *Dump goods at cut-rate prices in the markets of foreign rivals.* A company is said to be dumping when it sells its goods in foreign markets at prices that are (1) well below the prices at which it normally sells in its home market or (2) well below its full costs per unit. Companies that engage in dumping usually keep their selling prices high enough to cover variable costs per unit, thereby limiting their losses on each unit to some percentage of fixed costs per unit. Dumping can be an appealing offensive strategy in either of two instances. One is when dumping drives down the price so far in the targeted country that domestic firms are quickly put in dire financial straits and end up declaring bankruptcy or being driven out of business—for dumping to pay off in this instance, however, the dumping company needs to have deep enough financial pockets to cover any losses from selling at below-market prices, and the targeted domestic companies need to be financially weak. The second instance in which dumping becomes an attractive strategy is when a company with unused production capacity discovers that it is cheaper to keep producing (as long as the selling prices cover average variable costs per unit) than it is to incur the costs associated with idle plant capacity. By keeping its plants operating at or near capacity, a dumping company not only may be able to cover variable costs and earn a contribution to fixed costs but also may be able to use its below-market prices to draw price-sensitive customers away from foreign rivals, then attentively court these new customers and retain their business when prices later begin a gradual rise back to normal market levels. Thus, dumping may prove useful as a way of entering the market of a particular foreign country and establishing a customer base.

However, dumping strategies run a high risk of host government retaliation on behalf of the adversely affected domestic companies. Indeed, as the trade among nations has mushroomed over the past 10 years, most governments have joined the World Trade Organization (WTO), which promotes fair trade practices among nations and actively polices dumping. The WTO allows member governments to take actions against dumping wherever there is material injury to domestic competitors. In 2002, for example, the U.S. government imposed tariffs of up to 30 percent on selected steel products that Asian and European steel manufacturers were said to be selling at ultra-low prices in the U.S. market. Canada recently investigated charges that companies in Austria, Belgium, France, Germany, Poland and China were dumping supplies of laminate flooring in Canada to the detriment of Canadian producers and concluded that companies in France and China were indeed selling such flooring in Canada at unreasonably low prices.[14] Most all governments can be expected to retaliate against dumping by imposing special tariffs on goods being imported from the countries of the guilty companies. Companies deemed guilty of dumping frequently come under pressure from their government to cease and desist, especially if the tariffs adversely affect innocent companies based in the same country or if the advent of special tariffs raises the specter of a trade war.

A company desirous of employing some type of offensive strategy in foreign markets is well advised to observe the principles for employing offensive strategies in general. For instance, it usually wise to attack foreign rivals on grounds that pit the challenger's competitive strengths against the defender's weaknesses and vulnerabilities. As a rule, trying to steal customers away from foreign rivals with strategies aimed at besting rivals where they are strongest stand a lower chance of succeeding than strategies that attack their competitive weaknesses, especially when the challenger has resource strengths that enable it to exploit rivals' weaknesses and when its attack involves an element of surprise.[15] It nearly always makes good strategic sense to use the challenger's core competencies and best competitive capabilities to spearhead the offensive. Furthermore, strategic offensives in foreign markets should, as a general rule, be predicated on exploiting the challenger's core competencies and best competitive capabilities. The ideal condition for a strategic offensive is when the attacker's resource strengths give it a competitive advantage over the targeted foreign rivals. The only two exceptions to these offensive strategy principles come when a competitively strong company with deep financial pockets sees considerable benefit in attacking a foreign rival's profit sanctuary and/or has the ability to employ cross-market subsidization—both of these offensive strategies can involve attacking a foreign rival's strengths (but they also are grounded in important strengths of the challenger and don't fall into the trap of challenging a competitively strong rival with a strategic offensive based on unproven expertise or inferior technology or a relatively unknown brand name or other resource weaknesses).

STRATEGIC ALLIANCES AND JOINT VENTURES WITH FOREIGN PARTNERS

Strategic alliances, joint ventures, and other cooperative agreements with foreign companies are a favorite and potentially fruitful means for entering a foreign market or strengthening a firm's competitiveness in world markets.[16] Historically, export-minded firms in industrialized nations sought alliances with firms in less-developed countries to import and market their products locally—such arrangements were often necessary to win approval for entry from the host country's government. Both Japanese and American companies are actively forming alliances with European companies to strengthen their ability to compete in the 25-nation European Union (and the five countries that are seeking to become EU members) and to capitalize on the opening up of Eastern European markets. Many U.S. and European companies are allying with Asian companies in their efforts to enter markets in China, India, Malaysia, Thailand, and other Asian countries. Companies in Europe, Latin America, and Asia are using alliances and joint ventures as a means of strengthening their mutual ability to compete across a wider geographical area—for instance, all the countries in the European Union or whole continents or most all country markets where there is sizable demand for the industry's product. Many foreign companies, of course, are particularly interested in strategic partnerships that will strengthen their ability to gain a foothold in the U.S. market.

> Cross-border alliances have proved to be popular and viable vehicles for companies to edge their way into the markets of foreign countries.

However, cooperative arrangements between domestic and foreign companies have strategic appeal for reasons besides gaining better access to attractive country markets.[17] A second big appeal of cross-border alliances is to capture economies of scale in production and/or marketing—cost reduction can be the difference that allows a company to be cost-competitive. By joining forces in producing components, assembling models, and marketing their products, companies can realize cost savings not achievable with their own small volumes. A third motivation for entering into a cross-border alliance is to fill gaps in technical expertise and/or knowledge of local markets (buying habits and product preferences of consumers, local customs, and so on). Allies learn much from one another in performing joint research, sharing technological know-how, studying one another's manufacturing methods, and understanding how to tailor sales and marketing approaches to fit local cultures and traditions. Indeed, one of the win–win benefits of an alliance is to learn from the skills, technological know-how, and capabilities of alliance partners and implant the knowledge and know-how of these partners in personnel throughout the company.

A fourth motivation for cross-border alliances is to share distribution facilities and dealer networks, thus mutually strengthening their access to buyers. A fifth benefit is that cross-border allies can direct their competitive energies more toward mutual rivals and less toward one another; teaming up may help them close the gap on leading companies. A sixth driver of cross-border alliances comes into play when companies desirous of entering a new foreign market conclude that alliances with local companies are an effective way to tap into a partner's local market knowledge and help it establish working relationships with key officials in the host-country government.[18] And, finally, alliances can be a particularly useful way for companies across the world to gain agreement on important technical standards—they have been used to arrive at standards for DVD players, assorted PC devices, Internet-related technologies, high-definition televisions, and mobile phones.

> Cross-border alliances enable a growth-minded company to widen its geographic coverage and strengthen its competitiveness in foreign markets while, at the same time, offering flexibility and allowing a company to retain some degree of autonomy and operating control.

What makes cross-border alliances an attractive strategic means of gaining the above types of benefits (as compared to acquiring or merging with foreign-based companies to gain much the same benefits) is that entering into alliances and strategic partnerships to gain market access and/or expertise of one kind or another allows a company to preserve its independence (which is not the case with a merger), retain veto power over how the alliance operates, and avoid using perhaps scarce financial resources to fund acquisitions. Furthermore, an alliance offers the flexibility to readily disengage once its purpose has been served or if the benefits prove elusive, whereas an acquisition is more permanent sort of arrangement (although the acquired company can, of course, be divested).[19]

Illustration Capsule 7.2 provides six examples of cross-border strategic alliances.

The Risks of Strategic Alliances with Foreign Partners

Alliances and joint ventures with foreign partners have their pitfalls, however. Cross-border allies typically have to overcome language and cultural barriers and figure out how to deal with diverse (or perhaps conflicting) operating practices. The communication, trust-building, and coordination costs are high in terms of management time.[20] It is not unusual for there to be little personal chemistry among some of the key people on whom success or failure of the alliance depends—the rapport such personnel need to work well together may never emerge. And even if allies are able to develop productive personal relationships, they can still have trouble reaching mutually agreeable ways to deal with key issues or resolve differences. There is a natural tendency for allies to struggle to collaborate effectively in competitively sensitive areas, thus spawning suspicions on both sides about forthright exchanges of information and expertise. Occasionally, the egos of corporate executives can clash—an alliance between Northwest Airlines and KLM Royal Dutch Airlines resulted in a bitter feud among both companies' top officials (who, according to some reports, refused to speak to each other).[21] In addition, there is the thorny problem of getting alliance partners to sort through issues and reach decisions fast enough to stay abreast of rapid advances in technology or fast-changing market conditions.

Illustration Capsule 7.2
Six Examples of Cross-Border Strategic Alliances

1. Two auto firms, Renault of France and Nissan of Japan, formed a broad-ranging global partnership in 1999 and then strengthened and expanded the alliance in 2002. The initial objective was to gain sales for new Nissan vehicles introduced in the European market, but the alliance now extends to full cooperation in all major areas, including the use of common platforms, joint development and use of engines and transmissions, fuel cell research, purchasing and use of common suppliers, and exchange of best practices. When the alliance was formed in 1999, Renault acquired a 36.8 percent ownership stake in Nissan; this was extended to 44.4 percent in 2002 when the alliance was expanded. Also, in 2002, the partners formed a jointly and equally owned strategic management company, named Renault-Nissan, to coordinate cooperative efforts.

2. Intel, the world's largest chip maker, has formed strategic alliances with leading software application providers and computer hardware providers to bring more innovativeness and expertise to the architecture underlying Intel's family of microprocessors and semiconductors. Intel's partners in the effort to enhance Intel's next-generation products include SAP, Oracle, SAS, BEA, IBM, Hewlett-Packard, Dell, Microsoft, Cisco Systems, and Alcatel. One of the alliances between Intel and Cisco involves a collaborative effort in Hong Kong to build next-generation infrastructure for Electronic Product Code/Radio Frequency Identification (EPC/RFID) solutions used to link manufacturers and logistics companies in the Hong Kong region with retailers worldwide. Intel and France-based Alcatel (a leading provider of fixed and mobile broadband access products, marketed in 130 countries) formed an alliance in 2004 to advance the definition, standardization, development, integration, and marketing of WiMAX broadband services solutions. WiMAX was seen as a cost-effective wireless or mobile broadband solution for deployment in both emerging markets and developed countries when, for either economic or technical reasons, it was not feasible to provide urban or rural customers with hardwired DSL broadband access.

3. Verio, a subsidiary of Japan-based NTT Communications and one of the leading global providers of Web hosting services and IP data transport, operates with the philosophy that in today's highly competitive and challenging technology market, companies must gain and share skills, information, and technology with technology leaders across the world. Believing that no company can be all things to all customers in the Web hosting industry, Verio executives have developed an alliance-oriented business model that combines the company's core competencies with the skills and products of best-of-breed, technology partners. Verio's strategic partners include Accenture, Cisco Systems, Microsoft, Sun Microsystems, Oracle, Arsenal Digital Solutions (a provider of worry-free tape backup, data restore, and data storage services), Internet Security Systems (a provider of firewall and intrusion detection systems), and Mercantec (a developer of storefront and shopping cart software). Verio management believes that its portfolio of strategic alliances allows it to use innovative, best-of-class technologies in providing its customers with fast, efficient, accurate data transport and a complete set of Web hosting services. An independent panel of 12 judges recently selected Verio as the winner of the Best Technology Foresight Award for its efforts in pioneering new technologies.

4. Toyota and First Automotive Works, China's biggest automaker, entered into an alliance in 2002 to make luxury sedans, sport-utility vehicles (SUVs), and minivehicles for the Chinese market. The intent was to make as many as 400,000 vehicles annually by 2010, an amount equal to the number that Volkswagen, the company with the largest share of the Chinese market, was making as of 2002. The alliance envisioned a joint investment of about $1.2 billion. At the time of the announced alliance, Toyota was lagging behind Honda, General Motors, and Volkswagen in setting up production facilities in China. Capturing a bigger share of the Chinese market was seen as crucial to Toyota's success in achieving its strategic objective of having a 15 percent share of the world's automotive market by 2010.

5. Airbus Industrie was formed by an alliance of aerospace companies from Britain, Spain, Germany, and France that included British Aerospace, Daimler-Benz Aerospace, and Aerospatiale. The objective of the alliance was to create a European aircraft company capable of competing with U.S.-based Boeing Corporation. The alliance has proved highly successful, infusing Airbus with the know-how and resources to compete head-to-head with Boeing for world leadership in large commercial aircraft (over 100 passengers).

6. General Motors, DaimlerChrysler, and BMW have entered into an alliance to develop a hybrid gasoline-electric engine that is simpler and less expensive to produce than the hybrid engine technology being pioneered by Toyota. Toyota, the acknowledged world leader in hybrid engines, is endeavoring to establish its design as the industry standard by signing up other automakers to use it. But the technology favored by the General Motors/DaimlerChrysler/BMW alliance is said to be less costly to produce and easier to configure for large trucks and SUVs than Toyota's (although it is also less fuel efficient). Europe's largest automaker, Volkswagen, has allied with Porsche to pursue the development of hybrid engines. Ford Motor and Honda, so far, have elected to go it alone in developing hybrid engine technology.

Sources: Company Web sites and press releases; Yves L. Doz and Gary Hamel, *Alliance Advantage: The Art of Creating Value through Partnering* (Boston, MA: Harvard Business School Press, 1998); and Norihiko Shirouzu and Jathon Sapsford, "As Hybrid Cars Gain Traction, Industry Battles over Designs," *The Wall Street Journal,* October 19, 2005, pp. A1, A9B.

It requires many meetings of many people working in good faith over time to iron out what is to be shared, what is to remain proprietary, and how the cooperative arrangements will work. Often, once the bloom is off the rose, partners discover they have conflicting objectives and strategies, deep differences of opinion about how to proceed, or important differences in corporate values and ethical standards. Tensions build up, working relationships cool, and the hoped-for benefits never materialize.[22]

Even if the alliance becomes a win–win proposition for both parties, there is the danger of becoming overly dependent on foreign partners for essential expertise and competitive capabilities. If a company is aiming for global market leadership and needs to develop capabilities of its own, then at some juncture cross-border merger or acquisition may have to be substituted for cross-border alliances and joint ventures.

> Strategic alliances are more effective in helping establish a beachhead of new opportunity in world markets than in achieving and sustaining global leadership.

One of the lessons about cross-border alliances is that they are more effective in helping a company establish a beachhead of new opportunity in world markets than they are in enabling a company to achieve and sustain global market leadership. Global market leaders, while benefiting from alliances, usually must guard against becoming overly dependent on the assistance they get from alliance partners—otherwise, they are not masters of their own destiny.

When a Cross-Border Alliance May Be Unnecessary

Experienced multinational companies that market in 50 to 100 or more countries across the world find less need for entering into cross-border alliances than do companies in the early stages of globalizing their operations.[23] Multinational companies make it a point to develop senior managers who understand how "the system" works in different countries; these companies can also avail themselves of local managerial talent and know-how by simply hiring experienced local managers and thereby detouring the hazards of collaborative alliances with local companies. If a multinational enterprise with considerable experience in entering the markets of different countries wants to detour the hazards and hassles of allying with local businesses, it can simply assemble a capable management team consisting of both senior managers with considerable international experience and local managers. The responsibilities of its own in-house managers with international business savvy are (1) to transfer technology, business practices, and the corporate culture into the company's operations in the new country market, and (2) to serve as conduits for the flow of information between the corporate office and local operations. The responsibilities of local managers are (1) to contribute needed understanding of the local market conditions, local buying habits, and local ways of doing business, and (2) in many cases, to head up local operations.

Hence, one cannot automatically presume that a company needs the wisdom and resources of a local partner to guide it through the process of successfully entering the markets of foreign countries. Indeed, experienced multinationals often discover that local partners do not always have adequate local market knowledge—much of the so-called experience of local partners can predate the emergence of current market trends and conditions, and sometimes their operating practices can be archaic.[24]

STRATEGIES THAT FIT THE MARKETS OF EMERGING COUNTRIES

Companies racing for global leadership have to consider competing in emerging markets like China, India, Brazil, Indonesia, and Mexico—countries where the business risks are considerable but where the opportunities for growth are huge, especially as their

Illustration Capsule 7.3

Coca-Cola's Strategy for Growing Its Sales in China and India

In 2004, Coca-Cola developed a strategy to dramatically boost its market penetration in such emerging countries as China and India, where annual growth had recently dropped from about 30 percent in 1994–1998 to 10–12 percent in 2001–2003. Prior to 2003, Coca-Cola had focused its marketing efforts in China and India on making its drinks attractive to status-seeking young people in urbanized areas (cities with populations of 500,000 or more), but as annual sales growth steadily declined in these areas during the 1998–2003 period, Coca-Cola's management decided that the company needed a new, bolder strategy aimed at more rural areas of these countries. It began promoting the sales of 6.5-ounce returnable glass bottles of Coke in smaller cities and outlying towns with populations in the 50,000 to 250,000 range. Returnable bottles (which could be reused about 20 times) were much cheaper than plastic bottles or aluminum cans, and the savings in packaging costs were enough to slash the price of single-serve bottles to one yuan in China and about five rupees in India,

the equivalent in both cases of about 12 cents. Initial results were promising. Despite the fact that annual disposable incomes in these rural areas were often less than $1,000, the one-yuan and five-rupee prices proved attractive. Sales of the small bottles of Coke for one local Coca-Cola distributor in Anning, China, soon accounted for two-thirds of the distributor's total sales; a local distributor in India boosted sales from 9,000 cases in 2002 to 27,000 cases in 2003 and was expecting sales of 45,000 cases in 2004. Coca-Cola management expected that greater emphasis on rural sales would boost its growth rate in Asia to close to 20 percent and help boost worldwide volume growth to the 3–5 percent range as opposed to the paltry 1 percent rate experienced in 2003.

However, Pepsi, which had a market share of about 27 percent in China versus Coca-Cola's 55 percent, was skeptical of Coca-Cola's rural strategy and continued with its all-urban strategy of marketing to consumers in China's 165 cities with populations greater than 1 million people.

Sources: Based on information in Gabriel Kahn and Eric Bellman, "Coke's Big Gamble in Asia: Digging Deeper in China, India," *The Wall Street Journal,* August 11, 2004, pp. A1, A4, plus information at www.cocacola.com (accessed September 20, 2004 and October 6, 2005).

economies develop and living standards climb toward levels in the industrialized world.[25] With the world now comprising more than 6 billion people—fully one-third of whom are in India and China, and hundreds of millions more in other less-developed countries of Asia and in Latin America—a company that aspires to world market leadership (or to sustained rapid growth) cannot ignore the market opportunities or the base of technical and managerial talent such countries offer. For example, in 2003 China's population of 1.3 billion people consumed nearly 33 percent of the world's annual cotton production, 51 percent of the world's pork, 35 percent of all the cigarettes, 31 percent of worldwide coal production, 27 percent of the world's steel production, 19 percent of the aluminum, 23 percent of the TVs, 20 percent of the cell phones, and 18 percent of the washing machines.[26] China is the world's largest consumer of copper, aluminum, and cement and the second largest importer of oil; it is the world's biggest market for mobile phones and the second biggest for PCs, and it is on track to become the second largest market for motor vehicles by 2010.

Illustration Capsule 7.3 describes Coca-Cola's strategy to boost its sales and market share in China.

Tailoring products to fit conditions in an emerging-country market, however, often involves more than making minor product changes and becoming more familiar with local cultures.[27] Ford's attempt to sell a Ford Escort in India at a price of $21,000—a luxury-car price, given that India's best-selling Maruti-Suzuki model sold at the time for $10,000 or less, and that fewer than 10 percent of Indian households have annual purchasing power greater than $20,000—met with a less-than-enthusiastic market response. McDonald's has had to offer vegetable burgers in parts of Asia and to rethink its prices, which are often high by local standards and affordable only by the well-to-do. Kellogg has struggled to introduce its cereals successfully because consumers in many less-developed countries do not eat cereal for breakfast—changing habits is difficult and expensive. In several emerging countries, Coca-Cola has found that advertising its world image does not strike a chord with the local populace in a number of emerging-country markets. Single-serving packages of detergents, shampoos, pickles, cough syrup, and cooking oils are very popular in India because they allow buyers to conserve cash by purchasing only what they need immediately. Thus, many companies find that trying to employ a strategy akin to that used in the markets of developed countries is hazardous.[28] Experimenting with some, perhaps many, local twists is usually necessary to find a strategy combination that works.

Strategy Options

Several strategy options for tailoring a company's strategy to fit the sometimes unusual or challenging circumstances presented in emerging-country markets:

- *Prepare to compete on the basis of low price.* Consumers in emerging markets are often highly focused on price, which can give low-cost local competitors the edge unless a company can find ways to attract buyers with bargain prices as well as better products.[29] For example, when Unilever entered the market for laundry detergents in India, it realized that 80 percent of the population could not afford the brands it was selling to affluent consumers there (or the brands it was selling in wealthier countries). To compete against a low-priced detergent made by a local company, Unilever came up with a low-cost formula that was not harsh to the skin, constructed new low-cost production facilities, packaged the detergent (named Wheel) in single-use amounts so that it could be sold very cheaply, distributed the product to local merchants by handcarts, and crafted an economical marketing campaign that included painted signs on buildings and demonstrations near stores—the new brand quickly captured $100 million in sales and was the number one detergent brand in India in 2004 based on dollar sales. Unilever later replicated the strategy with low-priced packets of shampoos and deodorants in India and in South America with a detergent brand named Ala.

- *Be prepared to modify aspects of the company's business model to accommodate local circumstances (but not so much that the company loses the advantage of global scale and global branding).*[30] For instance when Dell entered China, it discovered that individuals and businesses were not accustomed to placing orders through the Internet (in North America, over 50 percent of Dell's sales in 2002–2005 were online). To adapt, Dell modified its direct sales model to rely more heavily on phone and fax orders and decided to be patient in getting Chinese customers to place Internet orders. Further, because numerous Chinese government departments and state-owned enterprises insisted that hardware vendors make their bids through distributors and systems integrators (as opposed to dealing directly with Dell salespeople as did large enterprises in other countries), Dell opted to use third parties in marketing its products to this buyer segment (although it did sell through its own sales force where it could). But Dell was careful not to abandon those parts of its business model that gave it a competitive edge over rivals. When McDonald's moved into Russia in the 1990s, it was forced to alter its practice of obtaining needed supplies from outside vendors because capable local suppliers were not available; to supply its Russian outlets and stay true to its core principle of serving consistent quality fast food, McDonald's set up its own vertically integrated supply chain (cattle were imported from Holland, russet potatoes were imported from the United States); worked with a select number of Russian bakers for its bread; brought in agricultural specialists from Canada and Europe to improve the management practices of Russian farmers; built its own 100,000-square-foot McComplex to produce hamburgers, French fries, ketchup, mustard, and Big Mac sauce; and set up a trucking fleet to move supplies to restaurants.

- *Try to change the local market to better match the way the company does business elsewhere.*[31] A multinational company often has enough market clout to drive major changes in the way a local country market operates. When Hong Kong–based STAR launched its first satellite TV channel in 1991, it profoundly impacted the TV marketplace in India: The Indian government lost its monopoly on TV broadcasts, several other satellite TV channels aimed at Indian audiences quickly emerged, and the excitement of additional channels triggered a boom in TV manufacturing in India. When Japan's Suzuki entered India in 1981, it triggered a quality revolution among Indian auto parts manufacturers. Local parts and components suppliers teamed up with Suzuki's vendors in Japan and worked with Japanese experts to produce higher-quality products. Over the next two decades, Indian companies became very proficient in making top-notch parts and components for vehicles, won more prizes for quality than companies in any country other than Japan, and broke into the global market as suppliers to many automakers in Asia and other parts of the world.

- *Stay away from those emerging markets where it is impractical or uneconomic to modify the company's business model to accommodate local circumstances.*[32] Home Depot has avoided entry into most Latin American countries because its value proposition of good quality, low prices, and attentive customer service relies on (1) good highways and logistical systems to minimize store inventory costs, (2) employee stock ownership to help motivate store personnel to provide good customer service, and (3) high labor costs for housing construction and home repairs to encourage homeowners to engage in do-it-yourself projects. Relying on these factors in the U.S. market has worked spectacularly for Home Depot, but the company has found that it cannot count on these factors in much of Latin America. Thus, to enter the market in Mexico, Home Depot switched to an acquisition strategy; it has acquired two building supply retailers in Mexico with a total of 40-plus stores. But it has not tried to operate them in the style of its U.S. big-box stores, and it doesn't have retail operations in any other developing nations (although it is exploring entry into China).

Company experiences in entering developing markets like China, India, Russia, and Brazil indicate that profitability seldom comes quickly or easily. Building a market for the company's products can often turn into a long-term process that involves reeducation of consumers, sizable investments in advertising and promotion to alter tastes and buying habits, and upgrades of the local infrastructure (the supplier base, transportation systems, distribution channels, labor markets, and capital markets). In such cases, a company must be patient, work within the system to improve the infrastructure, and lay the foundation for generating sizable revenues and profits once conditions are ripe for market takeoff.

> Profitability in emerging markets rarely comes quickly or easily—new entrants have to adapt their business models and strategies to local conditions and be patient in earning a profit.

Figure 7.4   **Strategy Options for Local Companies in Competing Against Global Companies**

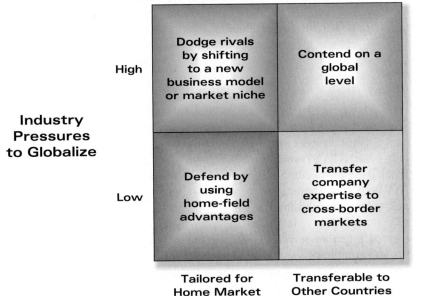

Source: Adapted from Niroj Dawar and Tony Frost, "Competing with Giants: Survival Strategies for Local Companies in Emerging Markets," *Harvard Business Review* 77, no. 1 (January–February 1999), p. 122.

Defending Against Global Giants: Strategies for Local Companies in Emerging Markets

If opportunity-seeking, resource-rich multinational companies are looking to enter emerging markets, what strategy options can local companies use to survive? As it turns out, the prospects for local companies facing global giants are by no means grim. They can employ any of four generic strategic approaches depending on (1) whether their competitive assets are suitable only for the home market or can be transferred abroad, and (2) whether industry pressures to move toward global competition are strong or weak, as shown in Figure 7.4.

Using Home-Field Advantages   When the pressures for competing globally are low and a local firm has competitive strengths well suited to the local market, a good strategy option is to concentrate on the advantages enjoyed in the home market, cater to customers who prefer a local touch, and accept the loss of customers attracted to global brands.[33] A local company may be able to astutely exploit its local orientation—its familiarity with local preferences, its expertise in traditional products, its long-standing customer relationships. In many cases, a local company enjoys a significant cost advantage over global rivals (perhaps because of simpler product design or lower operating and overhead costs), allowing it to compete on the basis of price. Its global competitors often aim their products at upper- and middle-income urban buyers, who tend to be more fashion-conscious, more willing to experiment with new products, and more attracted to global brands.

Another competitive approach is to cater to the local market in ways that pose difficulties for global rivals. A small Middle Eastern cell phone manufacturer competes successfully against industry giants Nokia, Samsung, and Motorola by selling a model designed especially for Muslims—it is loaded with the Koran, alerts people at prayer times, and is equipped with a compass that points them toward Mecca. Several Chinese PC makers have been able to retain customers in competition against global leader Dell because Chinese PC buyers strongly prefer to personally inspect PCs before making a purchase; local PC makers with their extensive retailer networks that allow prospective buyers to check out their offerings in nearby stores have a competitive edge in winning the business of first-time PC buyers vis-à-vis Dell with its build-to-order, sell-direct business strategy (where customers are encouraged to place their orders online or via phone or fax). Bajaj Auto, India's largest producer of scooters, has defended its turf against Honda (which entered the Indian market with local joint venture partner Hero Group to sell scooters, motorcycles, and other vehicles on the basis of its superior technology, quality, and the appeal) by focusing on buyers who wanted low-cost, durable scooters and easy access to maintenance in the countryside. Bajaj designed a rugged, cheap-to-build scooter for India's rough roads, increased its investments in R&D to improve reliability and quality, and created an extensive network of distributors and roadside-mechanic stalls, a strategic approach that allowed it to remain the market leader with a 70–75 percent market share through 2004 despite growing unit sales of Hero Honda motorcycles and scooters.

Transferring the Company's Expertise to Cross-Border Markets When a company has resource strengths and capabilities suitable for competing in other country markets, launching initiatives to transfer its expertise to cross-border markets becomes a viable strategic option.[34] Televisa, Mexico's largest media company, used its expertise in Spanish culture and linguistics to become the world's most prolific producer of Spanish-language soap operas. Jollibee Foods, a family-owned company with 56 percent of the fast-food business in the Philippines, combated McDonald's entry first by upgrading service and delivery standards and then by using its expertise in seasoning hamburgers with garlic and soy sauce and making noodle and rice meals with fish to open outlets catering to Asian residents in Hong Kong, the Middle East, and California.

Shifting to a New Business Model or Market Niche When industry pressures to globalize are high, any of the following three options makes the most sense: (1) shift the business to a piece of the industry value chain where the firm's expertise and resources provide competitive advantage, (2) enter into a joint venture with a globally competitive partner, or (3) sell out to (be acquired by) a global entrant into the home market who concludes the company would be a good entry vehicle.[35] When Microsoft entered China, local software developers shifted from cloning Windows products to developing Windows application software customized to the Chinese market. When the Russian PC market opened to IBM, Compaq, and Hewlett-Packard, local Russian PC maker Vist focused on assembling low-cost models, marketing them through exclusive distribution agreements with selected local retailers, and opening company-owned full-service centers in dozens of Russian cities. Vist focused on providing low-cost PCs, giving lengthy warranties, and catering to buyers who felt the need for local service and support. Vist's strategy allowed it to remain the market leader, with a 20 percent share.

An India-based electronics company has been able to carve out a market niche for itself by developing an all-in-one business machine designed especially for India's 1.2 million small shopkeepers that tolerates heat, dust, and power outages and that sells for a modest $180 for the smallest of its three models.[36]

Contending on a Global Level   If a local company in an emerging market has transferable resources and capabilities, it can sometimes launch successful initiatives to meet the pressures for globalization head-on and start to compete on a global level itself.[37] Lenovo, China's biggest PC maker, recently purchased IBM's PC business, moved its headquarters to New York City, put the Lenovo brand on IBM's PCs, and launched initiative to become a global PC maker alongside leaders Dell and Hewlett-Packard. When General Motors (GM) decided to outsource the production of radiator caps for all of its North American vehicles, Sundaram Fasteners of India pursued the opportunity; it purchased one of GM's radiator cap production lines, moved it to India, and became GM's sole supplier of radiator caps in North America—at 5 million units a year. As a participant in GM's supplier network, Sundaram learned about emerging technical standards, built its capabilities, and became one of the first Indian companies to achieve QS 9000 certification, a quality standard that GM now requires for all suppliers. Sundaram's acquired expertise in quality standards enabled it then to pursue opportunities to supply automotive parts in Japan and Europe. Chinese communications equipment maker Huawei has captured a 16 percent share in the global market for Internet routers because its prices are up to 50 percent lower than those of industry leaders like Cisco Systems; Huawei's success in low-priced Internet networking gear has allowed it to expand aggressively outside China, into such country markets as Russia and Brazil, and achieve the number two worldwide market share in broadband networking gear.[38] In 2005 Chinese automakers were laying plans to begin exporting fuel-efficient small cars to the United States and begin the long-term process of competing internationally against the world's leading automakers.

Key Points

Most issues in competitive strategy that apply to domestic companies apply also to companies that compete internationally. But there are four strategic issues unique to competing across national boundaries:

1. Whether to customize the company's offerings in each different country market to match the tastes and preferences of local buyers or offer a mostly standardized product worldwide.

2. Whether to employ essentially the same basic competitive strategy in all countries or modify the strategy country by country to fit the specific market conditions and competitive circumstances it encounters.

3. Where to locate the company's production facilities, distribution centers, and customer service operations so as to realize the greatest locational advantages.

4. Whether and how to efficiently transfer the company's resource strengths and capabilities from one country to another in an effort to secure competitive advantage.

Multicountry competition refers to situations where competition in one national market is largely independent of competition in another national market—there is no "international market," just a collection of self-contained country (or maybe regional) markets. Global competition exists when competitive conditions across national markets are linked strongly enough to form a true world market and when leading competitors compete head-to-head in many different countries.

In posturing to compete in foreign markets, a company has three basic options: (1) a think-local, act-local approach to crafting a strategy, (2) a think-global, act-global approach to crafting a strategy, and (3) a combination think-global, act-local approach. A think-local, act-local, or multicountry, strategy is appropriate for industries where multicountry competition dominates; a localized approach to strategy making calls for a company to vary its product offering and competitive approach from country to country in order to accommodate differing buyer preferences and market conditions. A think-global, act-global approach (or global strategy) works best in markets that are globally competitive or beginning to globalize; global strategies involve employing the same basic competitive approach (low-cost, differentiation, best-cost, focused) in all country markets and marketing essentially the same products under the same brand names in all countries where the company operates. A think-global, act-local approach can be used when it is feasible for a company to employ essentially the same basic competitive strategy in all markets but still customize its product offering and some aspect of its operations to fit local market circumstances.

Other strategy options for competing in world markets include maintaining a national (one-country) production base and exporting goods to foreign markets, licensing foreign firms to use the company's technology or produce and distribute the company's products, employing a franchising strategy, and using strategic alliances or other collaborative partnerships to enter a foreign market or strengthen a firm's competitiveness in world markets.

Strategic alliances with foreign partners have appeal from several angles: gaining wider access to attractive country markets, allowing capture of economies of scale in production and/or marketing, filling gaps in technical expertise and/or knowledge of local markets, saving on costs by sharing distribution facilities and dealer networks, helping gain agreement on important technical standards, and helping combat the impact of alliances that rivals have formed. Cross-border strategic alliances are fast reshaping competition in world markets, pitting one group of allied global companies against other groups of allied global companies.

There are three ways in which a firm can gain competitive advantage (or offset domestic disadvantages) in global markets. One way involves locating various value chain activities among nations in a manner that lowers costs or achieves greater product differentiation. A second way involves efficient and effective transfer of competitively valuable competencies and capabilities from its domestic markets to foreign markets. A third way draws on a multinational or global competitor's ability to deepen or broaden its resource strengths and capabilities and to coordinate its dispersed activities in ways that a domestic-only competitor cannot.

Profit sanctuaries are country markets in which a company derives substantial profits because of its strong or protected market position. They are valuable competitive assets. A company with multiple profit sanctuaries has the financial strength to support competitive offensives in one market with resources and profits diverted from its operations in other markets—a practice called *cross-market subsidization*. The ability of companies with multiple profit sanctuaries to employ cross-subsidization gives them a powerful offensive weapon and a competitive advantage over companies with a single sanctuary.

Companies racing for global leadership have to consider competing in emerging markets like China, India, Brazil, Indonesia, and Mexico—countries where the business risks are considerable but the opportunities for growth are huge. To succeed in these markets, companies often have to (1) compete on the basis of low price, (2) be prepared to modify aspects of the company's business model to accommodate local circumstances (but not so much that the company loses the advantage of global scale and global branding), and/or (3) try to change the local market to better match the way the company does business elsewhere. Profitability is unlikely to come quickly or easily in emerging markets, typically because of the investments needed to alter buying habits and tastes and/or the need for infrastructure upgrades. And there may be times when a company should simply stay away from certain emerging markets until conditions for entry are better suited to its business model and strategy.

Local companies in emerging country markets can seek to compete against multinational companies by (1) defending on the basis of home-field advantages, (2) transferring their expertise to cross-border markets, (3) dodging large rivals by shifting to a new business model or market niche, or (4) launching initiatives to compete on a global level themselves.

Exercises

1. Go to Caterpillar's Web site (www.caterpillar.com) and search for information about the company's strategy in foreign markets. Is Caterpillar pursuing a global strategy or a localized multicountry strategy? Support your answer.

2. Assume you are in charge of developing the strategy for a multinational company selling products in some 50 different countries around the world. One of the issues you face is whether to employ a multicountry strategy or a global strategy.

   a. If your company's product is personal computers, do you think it would make better strategic sense to employ a multicountry strategy or a global strategy? Why?

   b. If your company's product is dry soup mixes and canned soups, would a multicountry strategy seem to be more advisable than a global strategy? Why?

   c. If your company's product is washing machines, would it seem to make more sense to pursue a multicountry strategy or a global strategy? Why?

   d. If your company's product is basic work tools (hammers, screwdrivers, pliers, wrenches, saws), would a multicountry strategy or a global strategy seem to have more appeal? Why?

3. The Hero Group is among the 10 largest corporations in India, with 19 business segments and annual revenues of $2.75 billion in fiscal 2004–2005. Many of the corporation's business units have used strategic alliances with foreign partners to compete in new product and geographic markets. Review the company's statements concerning its alliances and international business operations at www.herogroup.com and prepare a two-page report that outlines Hero's successful use of international strategic alliances.

4. Using this chapter's discussion of strategies for local companies competing against global rivals and Figure 7.4, develop a strategic approach for a manufacturer or service company in your community that might be forced to compete with a global firm. How might the local company exploit a home-field advantage? Would it make sense for the local company to attempt to transfer its capabilities or expertise to cross-border markets? Or change its business model or market niche? Or join the fight on a global level? Explain.

chapter 8 eight

Tailoring Strategy to Fit Specific Industry and Company Situations

Strategy is all about combining choices of what to do and what not to do into a system that creates the requisite fit between what the environment needs and what the company does.

—**Costas Markides**

Competing in the marketplace is like war. You have injuries and casualties, and the best strategy wins.

—**John Collins**

It is much better to make your own products obsolete than allow a competitor to do it.

—**Michael A. Cusamano and Richard W. Selby**

In a turbulent age, the only dependable advantage is reinventing your business model before circumstances force you to.

—**Gary Hamel and Liisa Välikangas**

P rior chapters have emphasized the analysis and options that go into matching a company's choice of strategy to (1) industry and competitive conditions and (2) its own resource strengths and weaknesses, competitive capabilities, opportunities and threats, and market position. But there's more to be revealed about the hows of matching the choices of strategy to a company's circumstances. This chapter looks at the strategy-making task in 10 commonly encountered situations:

1. Companies competing in emerging industries.
2. Companies competing in rapidly growing markets.
3. Companies competing in maturing industries.
4. Companies competing in stagnant or declining industries.
5. Companies competing in turbulent, high-velocity markets.
6. Companies competing in fragmented industries.
7. Companies striving to sustain rapid growth.
8. Companies in industry leadership positions.
9. Companies in runner-up positions.
10. Companies in competitively weak positions or plagued by crisis conditions.

We selected these situations to shed still more light on the factors that managers need to consider in tailoring a company's strategy. When you finish this chapter, you will have a stronger grasp of the factors that managers have to weigh in choosing a strategy and what the pros and cons are for some of the heretofore unexplored strategic options that are open to a company.

STRATEGIES FOR COMPETING IN EMERGING INDUSTRIES

An emerging industry is one in the formative stage. Examples include Voice over Internet Protocol (VoIP) telephone communications, high-definition TV, assisted living for the elderly, online education, organic food products, e-book publishing, and electronic banking. Many companies striving to establish a strong foothold in an emerging industry are start-up enterprises busily engaged in perfecting technology, gearing up operations, and trying to broaden distribution and gain buyer acceptance. Important product design issues or technological problems may still have to be worked out. The business models and strategies of companies in an emerging industry are unproved—they may look promising but may or may not ever result in attractive profitability.

The Unique Characteristics of an Emerging Industry

Competing in emerging industries presents managers with some unique strategy-making challenges:[1]

- Because the market is in its infancy, there's usually much speculation about how it will function, how fast it will grow, and how big it will get. The little historical information available is virtually useless in making sales and profit projections. There's lots of guesswork about how rapidly buyers will be attracted and how much they will be willing to pay. For example, there is much uncertainty about how many users of traditional telephone service will be inclined to switch over to VoIP telephone technology and how rapidly any such switchovers will occur.

- In many cases, much of the technological know-how underlying the products of emerging industries is proprietary and closely guarded, having been developed in-house by pioneering firms. In such cases, patents and unique technical expertise are key factors in securing competitive advantage. In other cases, numerous companies have access to the requisite technology and may be racing to perfect it, often in collaboration with others. In still other instances, there can be competing technological approaches, with much uncertainty over whether multiple technologies will end up competing alongside one another or whether one approach will ultimately win out because of lower costs or better performance—such a battle is currently under way in the emerging market for gasoline-electric hybrid engines (where demand is mushrooming because of greater fuel efficiency without a loss of power and acceleration). Toyota has pioneered one design; an alliance among General Motors, DaimlerChrysler, and BMW is pursuing another design; a Volkswagen-Porsche alliance is looking at a third technological approach; and Ford and Honda have their own slightly different hybrid engine designs.

- Just as there may be uncertainties surrounding an emerging industry's technology, there may also be no consensus regarding which product attributes will prove decisive in winning buyer favor. Rivalry therefore centers on each firm's efforts to get the market to ratify its own strategic approach to technology, product design, marketing, and distribution. Such rivalry can result in wide differences in product quality and performance from brand to brand.

- Since in an emerging industry all buyers are first-time users, the marketing task is to induce initial purchase and to overcome customer concerns about product features, performance reliability, and conflicting claims of rival firms.

- Many potential buyers expect first-generation products to be rapidly improved, so they delay purchase until technology and product design mature and second- or third-generation products appear on the market.

- Entry barriers tend to be relatively low, even for entrepreneurial start-up companies. Large, well-known, opportunity-seeking companies with ample resources and competitive capabilities are likely to enter if the industry has promise for explosive growth or if its emergence threatens their present business. For instance, many traditional local telephone companies, seeing the potent threat of wireless communications technology and VoIP, have opted to enter the mobile communications business and begin offering landline customers a VoIP option.

- Strong experience/learning curve effects may be present, allowing significant price reductions as volume builds and costs fall.
- Sometimes firms have trouble securing ample supplies of raw materials and components (until suppliers gear up to meet the industry's needs).
- Undercapitalized companies, finding themselves short of funds to support needed R&D and get through several lean years until the product catches on, end up merging with competitors or being acquired by financially strong outsiders looking to invest in a growth market.

Strategy Options for Emerging Industries

The lack of established rules of the game in an emerging industry gives industry participants considerable freedom to experiment with a variety of different strategic approaches. Competitive strategies keyed either to low cost or differentiation are usually viable. Focusing makes good sense when resources and capabilities are limited and the industry has too many technological frontiers or too many buyer segments to pursue at once. Broad or focused differentiation strategies keyed to technological or product superiority typically offer the best chance for early competitive advantage.

> **Core Concept**
> Companies in an emerging industry have wide latitude in experimenting with different strategic approaches.

In addition to choosing a competitive strategy, companies in an emerging industry usually have to fashion a strategy containing one or more of the following actions:[2]

1. Push to perfect the technology, improve product quality, and develop additional attractive performance features. Out-innovating the competition is often one of the best avenues to industry leadership.
2. Consider merging with or acquiring another firm to gain added expertise and pool resource strengths.
3. As technological uncertainty clears and a dominant technology emerges, try to capture any first-mover advantages by adopting it quickly. However, while there's merit in trying to be the industry standard-bearer on technology and to pioneer the dominant product design, firms have to beware of betting too heavily on their own preferred technological approach or product design—especially when there are many competing technologies, R&D is costly, and technological developments can quickly move in surprising new directions.
4. Acquire or form alliances with companies that have related or complementary technological expertise as a means of helping outcompete rivals on the basis of technological superiority.
5. Pursue new customer groups, new user applications, and entry into new geographical areas (perhaps using strategic partnerships or joint ventures if financial resources are constrained).
6. Make it easy and cheap for first-time buyers to try the industry's first-generation product.
7. As the product becomes familiar to a wide portion of the market, shift the advertising emphasis from creating product awareness to increasing frequency of use and building brand loyalty.

8. Use price cuts to attract the next layer of price-sensitive buyers into the market.

9. Form strategic alliances with key suppliers whenever effective supply chain management provides important access to specialized skills, technological capabilities, and critical materials or components.

Young companies in emerging industries face four strategic hurdles: (1) raising the capital to finance initial operations until sales and revenues take off, profits appear, and cash flows turn positive; (2) developing a strategy to ride the wave of industry growth(what market segments and competitive advantages to go after?); (3) managing the rapid expansion of facilities and sales in a manner that positions them to contend for industry leadership; and (4) defending against competitors trying to horn in on their success.[3] Up-and-coming companies can help their cause by selecting knowledgeable members for their boards of directors and by hiring entrepreneurial managers with experience in guiding young businesses through the start-up and takeoff stages. *A firm that develops solid resource capabilities, an appealing business model, and a good strategy has a golden opportunity to shape the rules and establish itself as the recognized industry front-runner.*

But strategic efforts to win the early race for growth and market share leadership in an emerging industry have to be balanced against the longer-range need to build a durable competitive edge and a defendable market position.[4] The initial front-runners in a fast-growing emerging industry that shows signs of good profitability will almost certainly have to defend their positions against ambitious challengers striving to overtake the current market leaders. Well-financed outsiders can be counted on to enter with aggressive offensive strategies once industry sales take off, the perceived risk of investing in the industry lessens, and the success of current industry members becomes apparent. Sometimes a rush of new entrants, attracted by the growth and profit potential, overcrowds the market and forces industry consolidation to a smaller number of players. Resource-rich latecomers, aspiring to industry leadership, may become major players by acquiring and merging the operations of weaker competitors and then using their own perhaps considerable brand name recognition to draw customers and build market share. Hence, the strategies of the early leaders must be aimed at competing for the long haul and making a point of developing the resources, capabilities, and market recognition needed to sustain early successes and stave off competition from capable, ambitious newcomers.

STRATEGIES FOR COMPETING IN RAPIDLY GROWING MARKETS

In a fast-growing market, a company needs a strategy predicated on growing faster than the market average, so that it can boost its market share and improve its competitive standing vis-à-vis rivals.

Companies that have the good fortune to be in an industry growing at double-digit rates have a golden opportunity to achieve double-digit revenues and profit growth. If market demand is expanding 20 percent annually, a company can grow 20 percent annually simply by doing little more than contentedly riding the tide of market growth—it has to simply be aggressive enough to secure enough new customers to realize a 20 percent gain in sales, not a particularly impressive strategic feat. What is more interesting, however, is to craft a strategy that enables sales to grow at 25 or 30 percent when the overall market is growing by 20 percent, such that the company's market share and competitive position improve relative to rivals, on average. Should a company's strategy only deliver sales growth of 12 percent in a market growing at

20 percent, then it is actually losing ground in the marketplace—a condition that signals a weak strategy and an unappealing product offering. The point here is that, in a rapidly growing market, a company must aim its strategy at producing gains in revenue that exceed the market average; otherwise, the best it can hope for is to maintain its market standing (if it is able to boost sales at a rate equal to the market average) and its market standing may indeed erode if its sales rise by less than the market average.

To be able to grow at a pace exceeding the market average, a company generally must have a strategy that incorporates one or more of the following elements:

- *Driving down costs per unit so as to enable price reductions that attract droves of new customers.* Charging a lower price always has strong appeal in markets where customers are price-sensitive, and lower prices can help push up buyers demand by drawing new customers into the marketplace. But since rivals can lower their prices also, a company must really be able to drive its unit costs down *faster than rivals*, such that it can use its low-cost advantage to underprice rivals. The makers of liquid crystal display (LCD) and high-definition TVs are aggressively pursuing cost reduction to bring the prices of their TV sets down under $1,000 and thus make their products more affordable to more consumers.

- *Pursuing rapid product innovation, both to set a company's product offering apart from rivals and to incorporate attributes that appeal to growing numbers of customers.* Differentiation strategies, when keyed to product attributes that draw in large numbers of new customers, help bolster a company's reputation for product superiority and lay the foundation for sales gains in excess of the overall rate of market growth. If the market is one where technology is advancing rapidly and product life cycles are short, then it becomes especially important to be first-to-market with next-generation products. But product innovation strategies require competencies in R&D and new product development and design, plus organizational agility in getting new and improved products to market quickly. At the same time they are pursuing cost reductions, the makers of LCD and high-definition TVs are pursuing all sorts of product improvements to enhance product quality and performance and boost screen sizes, so as to match or beat the picture quality and reliability of conventional TVs (with old-fashioned cathode-ray tubes) and drive up sales at an even faster clip.

- *Gaining access to additional distribution channels and sales outlets.* Pursuing wider distribution access so as to reach more potential buyers is a particularly good strategic approach for realizing above-average sales gains. But usually this requires a company to be a first-mover in positioning itself in new distribution channels and forcing rivals into playing catch-up.

- *Expanding the company's geographic coverage.* Expanding into areas, either domestic or foreign, where the company does not have a market presence can also be an effective way to reach more potential buyers and pave the way for gains in sales that outpace the overall market average.

- *Expanding the product line to add models/styles that appeal to a wider range of buyers.* Offering buyers a wider selection can be an effective way to draw new customers in numbers sufficient to realize above-average sales gains. Makers of MP3 players and cell phones are adding new models to stimulate buyer demand; Starbucks is adding new drinks and other menu selections to build store traffic; and marketers of VoIP technology are rapidly introducing a wider variety of plans to broaden their appeal to customers with different calling habits and needs.

STRATEGIES FOR COMPETING IN MATURING INDUSTRIES

A *maturing industry* is one that is moving from rapid growth to significantly slower growth. An industry is said to be *mature* when nearly all potential buyers are already users of the industry's products and growth in market demand closely parallels that of the population and the economy as a whole. In a mature market, demand consists mainly of replacement sales to existing users, with growth hinging on the industry's abilities to attract the few remaining new buyers and to convince existing buyers to up their usage. Consumer goods industries that are mature typically have a growth rate under 5 percent—roughly equal to the growth of the customer base or economy as a whole.

How Slowing Growth Alters Market Conditions

An industry's transition to maturity does not begin on an easily predicted schedule. Industry maturity can be forestalled by the emergence of new technological advances, product innovations, or other driving forces that keep rejuvenating market demand. Nonetheless, when growth rates do slacken, the onset of market maturity usually produces fundamental changes in the industry's competitive environment:[5]

1. *Slowing growth in buyer demand generates more head-to-head competition for market share.* Firms that want to continue on a rapid-growth track start looking for ways to take customers away from competitors. Outbreaks of price cutting, increased advertising, and other aggressive tactics to gain market share are common.

2. *Buyers become more sophisticated, often driving a harder bargain on repeat purchases.* Since buyers have experience with the product and are familiar with competing brands, they are better able to evaluate different brands and can use their knowledge to negotiate a better deal with sellers.

3. *Competition often produces a greater emphasis on cost and service.* As sellers all begin to offer the product attributes buyers prefer, buyer choices increasingly depend on which seller offers the best combination of price and service.

4. *Firms have a "topping-out" problem in adding new facilities.* Reduced rates of industry growth mean slowdowns in capacity expansion for manufacturers—adding too much plant capacity at a time when growth is slowing can create oversupply conditions that adversely affect manufacturers' profits well into the future. Likewise, retail chains that specialize in the industry's product have to cut back on the number of new stores being opened to keep from saturating localities with too many stores.

5. *Product innovation and new end-use applications are harder to come by.* Producers find it increasingly difficult to create new product features, find further uses for the product, and sustain buyer excitement.

6. *International competition increases.* Growth-minded domestic firms start to seek out sales opportunities in foreign markets. Some companies, looking for ways to cut costs, relocate plants to countries with lower wage rates. Greater product standardization and diffusion of technological know-how reduce entry barriers and make it possible for enterprising foreign companies to become serious market contenders in more countries. Industry leadership passes to companies that succeed in building strong competitive positions in most of the world's major geographic markets and in winning the biggest global market shares.

7. *Industry profitability falls temporarily or permanently.* Slower growth, increased competition, more sophisticated buyers, and occasional periods of overcapacity put pressure on industry profit margins. Weaker, less-efficient firms are usually the hardest hit.

8. *Stiffening competition induces a number of mergers and acquisitions among former competitors, driving industry consolidation to a smaller number of larger players.* Inefficient firms and firms with weak competitive strategies can achieve respectable results in a fast-growing industry with booming sales. But the intensifying competition that accompanies industry maturity exposes competitive weakness and throws second- and third-tier competitors into a survival-of-the-fittest contest.

Strategies that Fit Conditions in Maturing Industries

As the new competitive character of industry maturity begins to hit full force, any of several strategic moves can strengthen a firm's competitive position: pruning the product line, improving value chain efficiency, trimming costs, increasing sales to present customers, acquiring rival firms, expanding internationally, and strengthening capabilities.[6]

Pruning Marginal Products and Models   A wide selection of models, features, and product options sometimes has competitive value during the growth stage, when buyers' needs are still evolving. But such variety can become too costly as price competition stiffens and profit margins are squeezed. Maintaining many product versions works against achieving design, parts inventory, and production economies at the manufacturing levels and can increase inventory stocking costs for distributors and retailers. In addition, the prices of slow-selling versions may not cover their true costs. Pruning marginal products from the line opens the door for cost savings and permits more concentration on items whose margins are highest and/or where a firm has a competitive advantage. General Motors has been cutting slow-selling models and brands from its lineup of offerings—it has eliminated the entire Oldsmobile division and is said to be looking at whether it can eliminate its Saab lineup. Textbook publishers are discontinuing publication of those books that sell only a few thousand copies annually (where profits are marginal at best) and instead focusing their resources on texts that generate sales of at least 5,000 copies per edition.

Improving Value Chain Efficiency   Efforts to reinvent the industry value chain can have a fourfold payoff: lower costs, better product or service quality, greater capability to turn out multiple or customized product versions, and shorter design-to-market cycles. Manufacturers can mechanize high-cost activities, redesign production lines to improve labor efficiency, build flexibility into the assembly process so that customized product versions can be easily produced, and increase use of advanced technology (robotics, computerized controls, and automated assembly). Suppliers of parts and components, manufacturers, and distributors can collaboratively deploy online systems and product coding techniques to streamline activities and achieve cost savings all along the value chain—from supplier-related activities all the way through distribution, retailing, and customer service.

Trimming Costs   Stiffening price competition gives firms extra incentive to drive down unit costs. Company cost-reduction initiatives can cover a broad front. Some of the most frequently pursued options are pushing suppliers for better prices, implementing tighter supply chain management practices, cutting low-value activities out of the value chain, developing more economical product designs, reengineering internal processes using e-commerce technology, and shifting to more economical distribution arrangements.

Increasing Sales to Present Customers   In a mature market, growing by taking customers away from rivals may not be as appealing as expanding sales to existing customers. Strategies to increase purchases by existing customers can involve adding more sales promotions, providing complementary items and ancillary services, and finding more ways for customers to use the product. Convenience stores, for example, have boosted average sales per customer by adding video rentals, automated teller machines, gasoline pumps, and deli counters.

Acquiring Rival Firms at Bargain Prices   Sometimes a firm can acquire the facilities and assets of struggling rivals quite cheaply. Bargain-priced acquisitions can help create a low-cost position if they also present opportunities for greater operating efficiency. In addition, an acquired firm's customer base can provide expanded market coverage and opportunities for greater scale economies. The most desirable acquisitions are those that will significantly enhance the acquiring firm's competitive strength.

Expanding Internationally   As its domestic market matures, a firm may seek to enter foreign markets where attractive growth potential still exists and competitive pressures are not so strong. Many multinational companies are expanding into such emerging markets as China, India, Brazil, Argentina, and the Philippines, where the long-term growth prospects are quite attractive. Strategies to expand internationally also make sense when a domestic firm's skills, reputation, and product are readily transferable to foreign markets. For example, even though the U.S. market for soft drinks is mature, Coca-Cola has remained a growth company by upping its efforts to penetrate emerging markets where soft-drink sales are expanding rapidly.

Building New or More Flexible Capabilities   The stiffening pressures of competition in a maturing or already mature market can often be combated by strengthening the company's resource base and competitive capabilities. This can mean adding new competencies or capabilities, deepening existing competencies to make them harder to imitate, or striving to make core competencies more adaptable to changing customer requirements and expectations. Microsoft has responded to challenges by such competitors as Google and Linux by expanding its competencies in search engine software and revamping its entire approach to programming next-generation operating systems. Chevron has developed a best-practices discovery team and a best-practices resource map to enhance the speed and effectiveness with which it is able to transfer efficiency improvements from one oil refinery to another.

Strategic Pitfalls in Maturing Industries

Perhaps the biggest strategic mistake a company can make as an industry matures is steering a middle course between low cost, differentiation, and focusing—blending efforts to achieve low cost with efforts to incorporate differentiating features and efforts to focus on a limited target market. Such strategic compromises typically leave the firm *stuck in the middle* with a fuzzy strategy, too little commitment to winning a competitive advantage, an average image with buyers, and little chance of springing into the ranks of the industry leaders.

Other strategic pitfalls include being slow to mount a defense against stiffening competitive pressures, concentrating more on protecting short-term profitability than on building or maintaining long-term competitive position, waiting too long to respond to price cutting by rivals, overexpanding in the face of slowing growth, overspending on advertising and sales promotion efforts in a losing effort to combat the growth slow-down, and failing to pursue cost reduction soon enough or aggressively enough.

STRATEGIES FOR COMPETING IN STAGNANT OR DECLINING INDUSTRIES

Many firms operate in industries where demand is growing more slowly than the economy-wide average or is even declining. The demand for an industry's product can decline for any of several reasons: (1) advancing technology gives rise to better-performing substitute products (slim LCD monitors displace bulky CRT monitors; DVD players replace VCRs; wrinkle-free fabrics replace the need for laundry/dry-cleaning services) or lower costs (cheaper synthetics replace expensive leather); (2) the customer group shrinks (baby foods are in less demand when birthrates fall); (3) changing lifestyles and buyer tastes (cigarette smoking and wearing dress hats go out of vogue); (4) the rising costs of complementary products (higher gasoline prices drive down purchases of gas-guzzling vehicles).[7] The most attractive declining industries are those in which sales are eroding only slowly, there are pockets of stable or even growing demand, and some market niches present good profit opportunities. But in some stagnant or declining industries, decaying buyer demand precipitates a desperate competitive battle among industry members for the available business, replete with price discounting, costly sales promotions, growing amounts of idle plant capacity, and fast-eroding profit margins. It matters greatly whether buyer demand falls gradually or sharply and whether competition proves to be fierce or moderate.

Businesses competing in stagnant or declining industries have to make a fundamental strategic choice—whether to remain committed to the industry for the long term despite the industry's dim prospects or whether to pursue an end-game strategy to withdraw gradually or quickly from the market. Deciding to stick with the industry despite eroding market demand can have considerable merit. Stagnant demand by itself is not enough to make an industry unattractive. Market demand may be decaying slowly. Some segments of the market may still present good profit opportunities. Cash flows from operations may still remain strongly positive. Strong competitors may well be able to grow and boost profits by taking market share from weaker competitors.[8] Furthermore, the acquisition or exit of weaker firms creates opportunities for the remaining companies to capture greater market share. On the one hand, striving to become the market leader and be one of the few remaining companies in a declining industry can lead to above-average profitability even though overall market demand is stagnant or eroding. On the other hand, if the market environment of a declining industry is characterized by bitter warfare for customers and lots of overcapacity, such that companies are plagued with heavy operating losses, then an early exit makes much more strategic sense.

If a company decides to stick with a declining industry—because top management is encouraged by the remaining opportunities or sees merit in striving for market share

> It is erroneous to assume that companies in a declining industry are doomed to having declining revenues and profits.

leadership (or even just being one of the few remaining companies in the industry), then its three best strategic alternatives are usually the following:[9]

1. *Pursue a focused strategy aimed at the fastest-growing or slowest-decaying market segments within the industry.* Stagnant or declining markets, like other markets, are composed of numerous segments or niches. Frequently, one or more of these segments is growing rapidly (or at least decaying much more slowly), despite stagnation in the industry as a whole. An astute competitor who zeros in on fast-growing segments and does a first-rate job of meeting the needs of buyers comprising these segments can often escape stagnating sales and profits and even gain decided competitive advantage. For instance, both Ben & Jerry's and Häagen-Dazs have achieved success by focusing on the growing luxury or superpremium segment of the otherwise stagnant market for ice cream; revenue growth and profit margins are substantially higher for high-end ice creams sold in supermarkets and in scoop shops than is the case in other segments of the ice cream market. Companies that focus on the one or two most attractive market segments in a declining business may well decide to ignore the other segments altogether—withdrawing from them entirely or at least gradually or rapidly disinvesting in them. But the key is to *move aggressively* to establish a strong position in the most attractive parts of the stagnant or declining industry.

2. *Stress differentiation based on quality improvement and product innovation.* Either enhanced quality or innovation can rejuvenate demand by creating important new growth segments or inducing buyers to trade up. Successful product innovation opens up an avenue for competing that bypasses meeting or beating rivals' prices. Differentiation based on successful innovation has the additional advantage of being difficult and expensive for rival firms to imitate. New Covent Garden Soup has met with success by introducing packaged fresh soups for sale in major supermarkets, where the typical soup offerings are canned or dry mixes. Procter & Gamble has rejuvenated sales of its toothbrushes with its new line of Crest battery-powered spin toothbrushes, and it has revitalized interest in tooth care products with a series of product innovations related to teeth whitening. Bread makers are fighting declining sales of white breads that use bleached flour by introducing all kinds of whole-grain breads (which have far more nutritional value).

3. *Strive to drive costs down and become the industry's low-cost leader.* Companies in stagnant industries can improve profit margins and return on investment by pursuing innovative cost reduction year after year. Potential cost-saving actions include (*a*) cutting marginally beneficial activities out of the value chain; (*b*) outsourcing functions and activities that can be performed more cheaply by outsiders; (*c*) redesigning internal business processes to exploit cost-reducing e-commerce technologies; (*d*) consolidating underutilized production facilities; (*e*) adding more distribution channels to ensure the unit volume needed for low-cost production; (*f*) closing low-volume, high-cost retail outlets; and (*g*) pruning marginal products from the firm's offerings. Japan-based Asahi Glass (a low-cost producer of flat glass), PotashCorp and IMC Global (two low-cost leaders in potash production), Alcan Aluminum, Nucor Steel, and Safety Components International (a low-cost producer of air bags for motor vehicles) have all been successful in driving costs down in competitively tough and largely stagnant industry environments.

These three strategic themes are not mutually exclusive.[10] Introducing innovative versions of a product can create a fast-growing market segment. Similarly, relentless pursuit of greater operating efficiencies permits price reductions that create price-conscious growth segments. Note that all three themes are spinoffs of the five generic competitive strategies, adjusted to fit the circumstances of a tough industry environment.

End-Game Strategies for Declining Industries

An *end-game strategy* can take either of two paths: (1) a *slow-exit strategy* that involves a gradual phasing down of operations coupled with an objective of getting the most cash flow from the business even if it means sacrificing market position or profitability and (2) a *fast-exit* or *sell-out-quickly strategy* to disengage from the industry during the early stages of the decline and recover as much of the company's investment as possible for deployment elsewhere.[11]

A Slow-Exit Strategy   With a slow-exit strategy, *the key objective is to generate the greatest possible harvest of cash from the business for as long as possible.* Management either eliminates or severely curtails new investment in the business. Capital expenditures for new equipment are put on hold or given low financial priority (unless replacement needs are unusually urgent); instead, efforts are made to stretch the life of existing equipment and make do with present facilities as long as possible. Old plants with high costs may be retired from service. The operating budget is chopped to a rock-bottom level. Promotional expenses may be cut gradually, quality reduced in not-so-visible ways, nonessential customer services curtailed, and maintenance of facilities held to a bare minimum. The resulting increases in cash flow (and perhaps even bottom-line profitability and return on investment) compensate for whatever declines in sales might be experienced. Withering buyer demand is tolerable if sizable amounts of cash can be reaped in the interim. If and when cash flows dwindle to meager levels as sales volumes decay, the business can be sold or, if no buyer can be found, closed down.

A Fast-Exit Strategy   The challenge of a sell-out-quickly strategy is to find a buyer willing to pay an agreeable price for the company's business assets. Buyers may be scarce since there's a tendency for investors to shy away from purchasing a stagnant or dying business. And even if willing buyers appear, they will be in a strong bargaining position once it's clear that the industry's prospects are permanently waning. How much prospective buyers will pay is usually a function of how rapidly they expect the industry to decline, whether they see opportunities to rejuvenate demand (at least temporarily), whether they believe that costs can be cut enough to still produce attractive profit margins or cash flows, whether there are pockets of stable demand where buyers are not especially price sensitive, and whether they believe that fading market demand will weaken competition (which could enhance profitability) or trigger strong competition for the remaining business (which could put pressure on profit margins). Thus, the expectations of prospective buyers will tend to drive the price they are willing to pay for the business assets of a company wanting to sell out quickly.

STRATEGIES FOR COMPETING IN TURBULENT, HIGH-VELOCITY MARKETS

Many companies operate in industries characterized by rapid technological change, short product life cycles, the entry of important new rivals, lots of competitive maneuvering by rivals, and fast-evolving customer requirements and expectations—all occurring in a manner that creates swirling market conditions. Since news of this or that important competitive development arrives daily, it is an imposing task just to monitor and assess developing events. High-velocity change is plainly the prevailing condition in computer/server hardware and software, video games, networking, wireless tele-communications, medical equipment, biotechnology, prescription drugs, and online retailing.

Ways to Cope with Rapid Change

The central strategy-making challenge in a turbulent market environment is managing change.[12] As illustrated in Figure 8.1, a company can assume any of three strategic postures in dealing with high-velocity change:[13]

- *It can react to change.* The company can respond to a rival's new product with a better product. It can counter an unexpected shift in buyer tastes and buyer demand by redesigning or repackaging its product, or shifting its advertising emphasis to different product attributes. Reacting is a defensive strategy and is therefore unlikely to create fresh opportunity, but it is nonetheless a necessary component in a company's arsenal of options.

- *It can anticipate change.* The company can make plans for dealing with the expected changes and follow its plans as changes occur (fine-tuning them as may be needed). Anticipation entails looking ahead to analyze what is likely to occur and then preparing and positioning for that future. It entails studying buyer behavior, buyer needs, and buyer expectations to get insight into how the market will evolve, then lining up the necessary production and distribution capabilities ahead of time. Like reacting to change, anticipating change is still fundamentally defensive in that forces outside the enterprise are in the driver's seat. Anticipation, however, can open up new opportunities and thus is a better way to manage change than just pure reaction.

- *It can lead change.* Leading change entails initiating the market and competitive forces that others must respond to—it is an offensive strategy aimed at putting a company in the driver's seat. Leading change means being first to market with an important new product or service. It means being the technological leader, rushing next-generation products to market ahead of rivals, and having products whose features and attributes shape customer preferences and expectations. It means proactively seeking to shape the rules of the game.

A sound way to deal with turbulent market conditions is to try to lead change with proactive strategic moves while at the same time trying to anticipate and prepare for upcoming changes and being quick to react to unexpected developments.

As a practical matter, a company's approach to managing change should, ideally, incorporate all three postures (though not in the same proportion). The best-performing companies in high-velocity markets consistently seek to lead change with proactive strategies that often entail the flexibility to pursue any of several strategic options, depending on how the market actually evolves. Even so, an environment of relentless change makes it incumbent on any company to anticipate and prepare for the future and to react quickly to unpredictable or uncontrollable new developments.

Strategy Options for Fast-Changing Markets

Competitive success in fast-changing markets tends to hinge on a company's ability to improvise, experiment, adapt, reinvent, and regenerate as market and competitive conditions shift rapidly and sometimes unpredictably.[14] It has to constantly reshape its

Figure 8.1   **Meeting the Challenge of High-Velocity Change**

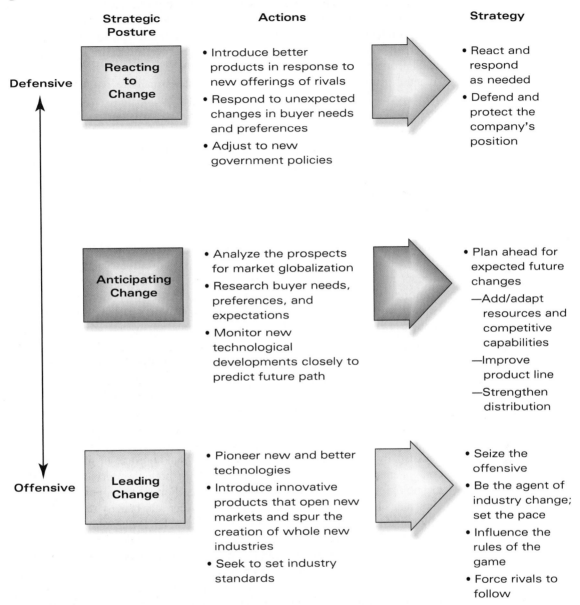

Source: Adapted from Shona L. Brown and Kathleen M. Eisenhardt, *Competing on the Edge: Strategy as Structured Chaos* (Boston, MA: Harvard Business School Press, 1998) p. 5.

strategy and its basis for competitive advantage. While the process of altering offensive and defensive moves every few months or weeks to keep the overall strategy closely matched to changing conditions is inefficient, the alternative—a fast-obsolescing strategy—is worse. The following five strategic moves seem to offer the best payoffs:

1.   *Invest aggressively in R&D to stay on the leading edge of technological know-how.* Translating technological advances into innovative new products (and remaining

close on the heels of whatever advances and features are pioneered by rivals) is a necessity in industries where technology is the primary driver of change. But it is often desirable to focus the R&D effort on a few critical areas, not only to avoid stretching the company's resources too thin but also to deepen the firm's expertise, master the technology, fully capture experience/learning curve effects, and become the dominant leader in a particular technology or product category.[15] When a fast-evolving market environment entails many technological areas and product categories, competitors have little choice but to employ some type of focus strategy and concentrate on being the leader in a particular product/technology category.

2. *Keep the company's products and services fresh and exciting enough to stand out in the midst of all the change that is taking place.* One of the risks of rapid change is that products and even companies can get lost in the shuffle. The marketing challenge here is to keep the firm's products and services in the limelight and, further, to keep them innovative and well matched to the changes that are occurring in the marketplace.

3. *Develop quick-response capability.* Because no company can predict all of the changes that will occur, it is crucial to have the organizational capability to be able to react quickly, improvising if necessary. This means shifting resources internally, adapting existing competencies and capabilities, creating new competencies and capabilities, and not falling far behind rivals. Companies that are habitual late-movers are destined to be industry also-rans.

4. *Rely on strategic partnerships with outside suppliers and with companies making tie-in products.* In many high-velocity industries, technology is branching off to create so many new technological paths and product categories that no company has the resources and competencies to pursue them all. Specialization (to promote the necessary technical depth) and focus (to preserve organizational agility and leverage the firm's expertise) are desirable strategies. Companies build their competitive position not just by strengthening their own internal resource base but also by partnering with those suppliers making state-of-the-art parts and components and by collaborating closely with both the developers of related technologies and the makers of tie-in products. For example, personal computer companies like Gateway, Dell, Compaq, and Acer rely heavily on the developers and manufacturers of chips, monitors, hard drives, DVD players, and software for innovative advances in PCs. None of the PC makers have done much in the way of integrating backward into parts and components because they have learned that the most effective way to provide PC users with a state-of-the-art product is to outsource the latest, most advanced components from technologically sophisticated suppliers who make it their business to stay on the cutting edge of their specialization and who can achieve economies of scale by mass-producing components for many PC assemblers. An outsourcing strategy also allows a company the flexibility to replace suppliers that fall behind on technology or product features or that cease to be competitive on price. The managerial challenge here is to strike a good balance between building a rich internal resource base that, on the one hand, keeps the firm from being at the mercy of its suppliers and allies and, on the other hand, maintains organizational agility by relying on the resources and expertise of capable (and perhaps best-in-world) outsiders.

5. *Initiate fresh actions every few months, not just when a competitive response is needed.* In some sense, change is partly triggered by the passage of time rather

than solely by the occurrence of events. A company can be proactive by making time-paced moves—introducing a new or improved product every four months, rather than when the market tapers off or a rival introduces a next-generation model.[16] Similarly, a company can expand into a new geographic market every six months rather than waiting for a new market opportunity to present itself; it can also refresh existing brands every two years rather than waiting until their popularity wanes. The keys to successfully using time pacing as a strategic weapon are choosing intervals that make sense internally and externally, establishing an internal organizational rhythm for change, and choreographing the transitions. 3M Corporation has long pursued an objective of having 25 percent of its revenues come from products less than four years old, a force that established the rhythm of change and created a relentless push for new products. Recently, the firm's CEO upped the tempo of change at 3M by increasing the goal from 25 to 30 percent.

Cutting-edge know-how and first-to-market capabilities are very valuable competitive assets in fast-evolving markets. Moreover, action-packed competition demands that a company have quick reaction times and flexible, adaptable resources—organizational agility is a huge competitive asset. Even so, companies will make mistakes and take some actions that do not work out well. When a company's strategy doesn't seem to be working well, it has to quickly regroup—probing, experimenting, improvising, and trying again and again until it finds something that strikes the right chord with buyers and that puts it in sync with market and competitive realities.

STRATEGIES FOR COMPETING IN FRAGMENTED INDUSTRIES

A number of industries are populated by hundreds, even thousands, of small and medium-sized companies, many privately held and none with a substantial share of total industry sales.[17] The standout competitive feature of a fragmented industry is the absence of market leaders with king-sized market shares or widespread buyer recognition. Examples of fragmented industries include book publishing, landscaping and plant nurseries, real estate development, convenience stores, banking, health and medical care, mail order catalog sales, computer software development, custom printing, kitchen cabinets, trucking, auto repair, restaurants and fast food, public accounting, apparel manufacture and apparel retailing, paperboard boxes, hotels and motels, and furniture.

Reasons for Supply-Side Fragmentation

Any of several reasons can account for why the supply side of an industry comprises hundreds or even thousands of companies:

- *The product or service is delivered at neighborhood locations so as to be conveniently accessible to local residents.* Retail and service businesses, for example, are inherently local—gas stations and car washes, pharmacies, dry-cleaning services, nursing homes, auto repair firms, furniture stores, flower shops, and lawn care enterprises. Whenever it takes thousands of locations to adequately serve the market, the way is opened for many enterprises to be engaged in providing products/services to local residents and businesses (and such enterprises can operate at just one location or at multiple locations).

- *Buyer preferences and requirements are so diverse that very large numbers of firms can easily coexist trying to accommodate differing buyer tastes, expectations, and pocketbooks.* This is true in the market for apparel, where there are thousands of apparel manufacturers making garments of various styles and price ranges. There's a host of different hotels and restaurants in places like New York City, London, Buenos Aires, Mexico City, and Tokyo. The software development industry is highly fragmented because there are so many types of software applications and because the needs and expectations of software users are so highly diverse—hence, there's ample market space for a software company to concentrate its attention on serving a particular market niche.

- *Low entry barriers allow small firms to enter quickly and cheaply.* Such tends to be the case in many areas of retailing, residential real estate, insurance sales, beauty shops, and the restaurant business.

- *An absence of scale economies permits small companies to compete on an equal cost footing with larger firms.* The markets for business forms, interior design, kitchen cabinets, and picture framing are fragmented because buyers require relatively small quantities of customized products; since demand for any particular product version is small, sales volumes are not adequate to support producing, distributing, or marketing on a scale that yields cost advantages to a large-scale firm. A locally owned pharmacy can be cost competitive with the pharmacy operations of large drugstore chains like Walgreen's or Rite Aid or CVS. Small trucking companies can be cost-competitive with companies that have huge truck fleets. A local pizzeria is not cost-disadvantaged in competing against such chains as Pizza Hut, Domino's, and Papa John's.

- *The scope of the geographic market for the industry's product or service is transitioning from national to global.* A broadening of geographic scope puts companies in more and more countries in the same competitive market arena (as in the apparel industry, where increasing numbers of garment makers across the world are shifting their production operations to low-wage countries and then shipping their goods to retailers in several countries).

- *The technologies embodied in the industry's value chain are exploding into so many new areas and along so many different paths that specialization is essential just to keep abreast in any one area of expertise.* Technology branching accounts for why the manufacture of electronic parts and components is fragmented and why there's fragmentation in prescription drug research.

- *The industry is young and crowded with aspiring contenders.* In most young industries, no firm has yet developed the resource base, competitive capabilities, and market recognition to command a significant market share (as in online e-tailing).

Competitive Conditions in a Fragmented Industry

Competitive rivalry in fragmented industries can vary from moderately strong to fierce. Low barriers tend to make entry of new competitors an ongoing threat. Competition from substitutes may or may not be a major factor. The relatively small size of companies in fragmented industries puts them in a relatively weak position to bargain with powerful suppliers and buyers, although sometimes they can become members of a cooperative formed for the purpose of using their combined leverage to negotiate better sales and purchase terms. In such an environment, the best a firm can expect is to cultivate a loyal customer base and grow a bit faster than the industry average.

Some fragmented industries consolidate over time as growth slows and the market matures. The stiffer competition that accompanies slower growth produces a shake-out of weak, inefficient firms and a greater concentration of larger, more visible sellers. Others remain atomistic because it is inherent in their businesses. And still others remain stuck in a fragmented state because existing firms lack the resources or ingenuity to employ a strategy powerful enough to drive industry consolidation.

Strategy Options for Competing in a Fragmented Industry

In fragmented industries, firms generally have the strategic freedom to pursue broad or narrow market targets and low-cost or differentiation-based competitive advantages. Many different strategic approaches can exist side by side (unless the industry's product is highly standardized or a commodity—like concrete blocks, sand and gravel, or paperboard boxes). Fragmented industry environments are usually ideal for focusing on a well-defined market niche—a particular geographic area or buyer group or product type. In an industry that is fragmented due to highly diverse buyer tastes or requirements, focusing usually offers more competitive advantage potential than trying to come up with a product offering that has broad market appeal.

Some of the most suitable strategy options for competing in a fragmented industry include:

- *Constructing and operating "formula" facilities*—This strategic approach is frequently employed in restaurant and retailing businesses operating at multiple locations. It involves constructing standardized outlets in favorable locations at minimum cost and then operating them cost-effectively. This is a favorite approach for locally owned fast-food enterprises and convenience stores that have multiple locations serving a geographically limited market area. Major fast-food chains like Yum! Brands—the parent of Pizza Hut, Taco Bell, KFC, Long John Silver's, and A&W restaurants—and big convenience store retailers like 7-Eleven have, of course, perfected the formula facilities strategy.

- *Becoming a low-cost operator*—When price competition is intense and profit margins are under constant pressure, companies can stress no-frills operations featuring low overhead, high-productivity/low-cost labor, lean capital budgets, and dedicated pursuit of total operating efficiency. Successful low-cost producers in a fragmented industry can play the price-discounting game and still earn profits above the industry average. Many e-tailers compete on the basis of bargain prices; so do budget motel chains like Econo Lodge, Super 8, and Days Inn.

- *Specializing by product type*—When a fragmented industry's products include a range of styles or services, a strategy to focus on one product or service category can be effective. Some firms in the furniture industry specialize in only one furniture type such as brass beds, rattan and wicker, lawn and garden, or Early American. In auto repair, companies specialize in transmission repair, body work, or speedy oil changes.

- *Specializing by customer type*—A firm can stake out a market niche in a fragmented industry by catering to those customers who are interested in low prices,

Illustration Capsule 8.1

Exertris's Focus Strategy in the Fragmented Exercise Equipment Industry

The exercise equipment industry is largely fragmented from a global perspective—there are hundreds of companies across the world making exercise and fitness products of one kind or another. The window of opportunity for employing a focus strategy is big. In 2001, three fitness enthusiasts in Great Britain came up with a novel way to make exercise more interesting. Their idea was to create an exercise bike equipped with a video game console, a flat-screen display, and an on-board PC that allowed users to play a video game while doing their workout.

After creating a prototype and forming a company called Exertris, the three fitness entrepreneurs approached a product design company for help in turning the prototype into a marketable product. The design company quickly determined that the task was not trivial and required significant additional product development. But the company was enthusiastic about the product and put up the capital to fund the venture as a minority partner. The partners set a goal of having six prototypes ready in time for a major leisure products trade show scheduled to be held in the United Kingdom in several months. The design company assumed responsibility for engineering the product, finding a contract manufacturer, and managing the supply chain; certain other specialty tasks were outsourced. The three cofounders concentrated on developing gaming software where the exerciser's pedaling performance had direct consequences for particular elements of the game; for example, the exerciser had to pedal harder to power a spaceship's weapon systems or move cards around in a game of Solitaire.

The Exertris bike won the "best new product" award at the trade show. It featured four games (Gems, Orbit, Solitaire, and Space Tripper), and new games and features could be added as they were released. Exercisers could play solo or competitively against other people, with the option of handicapping for multiplayer games. The recommended workout included an automatic warm-up and cool-down period. The bike had an armrest, a monitor, and a seat that optimized posture. The LCD display used the latest 3D graphics, and the on-board PC (positioned under the mounting step) used Microsoft Windows XP Embedded and was compatible with Polar heart rate monitors. Earphones were optional, and the game pad and menu control were sweat-proof and easy to clean.

Production by contract manufacturers started soon after the show. In the ensuing months, the Exertris bike was well received by gyms and fitness enthusiasts (for whom the addictive nature of video games broke the monotony and made exercise time fly by). The first interactive fitness arcade featuring 25 linked Exertris Interactive Bikes opened in Great Britain in April 2003. In 2005, the Exertris exercise bike was being marketed online in Great Britain at Amazon's Web site (www.amazon-leisure.co.uk) at a price of £675 (or about $1,150); it could also be purchased at Broadcast Vision Entertainment's online store. Exertris's strategy of focusing on this one niche product in exercise equipment was, however, producing unexpectedly weak results—sales were much slower than initially expected.

Sources: Information posted at www.betterproductdesign.com (accessed October 14, 2005), www.embedded-resources.com (accessed October 14, 2005), and www.broadcastvision.com (accessed December 31, 2005).

unique product attributes, customized features, carefree service, or other extras. A number of restaurants cater to take-out customers; others specialize in fine dining, and still others cater to the sports bar crowd. Bed-and-breakfast inns cater to a particular type of traveler/vacationer (and also focus on a very limited geographic area).

- *Focusing on a limited geographic area*—Even though a firm in a fragmented industry can't win a big share of total industrywide sales, it can still try to dominate a local or regional geographic area. Concentrating company efforts on a limited territory can produce greater operating efficiency, speed delivery and customer services, promote strong brand awareness, and permit saturation advertising, while avoiding the diseconomies of stretching operations out over a much wider area. Several locally owned banks, drugstores, and sporting goods retailers successfully operate multiple locations within a limited geographic area. Numerous local restaurant operators have pursued operating economies by opening anywhere from 4 to 10 restaurants (each with each its own distinctive theme and menu) scattered across a single metropolitan area like Atlanta or Denver or Houston.

Illustration Capsule 8.1 describes how a new start-up company in Great Britain has employed a product niche type of focus strategy in the fragmented exercise equipment industry.

STRATEGIES FOR SUSTAINING RAPID COMPANY GROWTH

Companies that strive to grow their revenues and earnings at double-digit rates year after year (or at rates exceeding the overall market average so that they are growing faster than rivals and gaining market share) generally have to craft *a portfolio of strategic initiatives* covering three horizons:[18]

- *Horizon 1: "Short-jump" strategic initiatives to fortify and extend the company's position in existing businesses*—Short-jump initiatives typically include adding new items to the company's present product line, expanding into new geographic areas where the company does not yet have a market presence, and launching offensives to take market share away from rivals. The objective is to capitalize fully on whatever growth potential exists in the company's present business arenas.

- *Horizon 2: "Medium-jump" strategic initiatives to leverage existing resources and capabilities by entering new businesses with promising growth potential*—Growth companies have to be alert for opportunities to jump into new businesses where there is promise of rapid growth and where their experience, intellectual capital, and technological know-how will prove valuable in gaining rapid market penetration. While Horizon 2 initiatives may take a back seat to Horizon 1 initiatives as long as there is plenty of untapped growth in the company's present businesses, they move to the front as the onset of market maturity dims the company's growth prospects in its present business(es).

- *Horizon 3: "Long-jump" strategic initiatives to plant the seeds for ventures in businesses that do not yet exist*—Long-jump initiatives can entail pumping funds into long-range R&D projects, setting up an internal venture capital fund to invest in promising start-up companies attempting to create the industries of the future, or acquiring a number of small start-up companies experimenting with technologies and product ideas that complement the company's present businesses. Intel, for example, set up a multibillion-dollar venture fund to invest in over 100 different projects and start-up companies, the intent being to plant seeds for Intel's future, broadening its base as a global leader in supplying building blocks for PCs and the worldwide Internet economy. Royal Dutch/ Shell, with over $140 billion in revenues and over 100,000 employees, spent over $20 million on rule-breaking, game-changing ideas put forth by free-thinking employees; the objective was to inject a new spirit of entrepreneurship into the company and sow the seeds of faster growth.[19]

Figure 8.2   **The Three Strategy Horizons for Sustaining Rapid Growth**

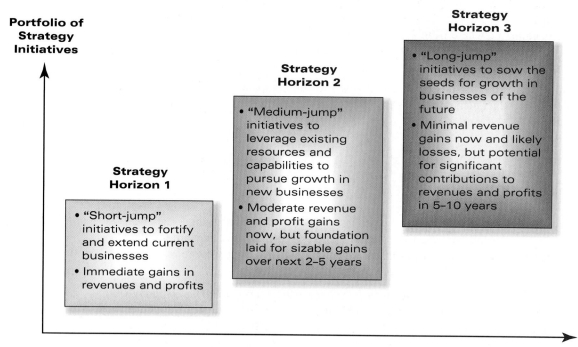

Source: Adapted from Eric D. Beinhocker, "Robust Adaptive Strategies," *Sloan Management Review* 40. No. 3 (Spring 1999), p. 101.

The three strategy horizons are illustrated in Figure 8.2. Managing such a portfolio of strategic initiatives to sustain rapid growth is not easy, however. The tendency of most companies is to focus on Horizon 1 strategies and devote only sporadic and uneven attention to Horizon 2 and 3 strategies. But a recent McKinsey & Company study of 30 of the world's leading growth companies revealed a relatively balanced portfolio of strategic initiatives covering all three horizons. The lesson of successful growth companies is that keeping a company's record of rapid growth intact over the long term entails crafting a diverse population of strategies, ranging from short-jump incremental strategies to grow present businesses to long-jump initiatives with a 5- to 10-year growth payoff horizon.[20] Having a mixture of short-jump, medium-jump, and long-jump initiatives not only increases the odds of hitting a few home runs but also provides some protection against unexpected adversity in present or newly entered businesses.

The Risks of Pursuing Multiple Strategy Horizons

There are, of course, risks to pursuing a diverse strategy portfolio aimed at sustained growth. A company cannot, of course, place bets on every opportunity that appears on its radar screen, lest it stretch its resources too thin. And medium-jump and long-jump initiatives can cause a company to stray far from its core competencies and end up trying to compete in businesses for which it is ill-suited. Moreover, it can be difficult to achieve competitive advantage in medium- and long-jump product families and businesses that prove not to mesh well with a company's present businesses and resource strengths. The payoffs of long-jump initiatives often prove elusive; not all of the seeds a company sows will bear fruit, and only a few may evolve into truly significant contributors to the company's revenue and profit growth. The losses from those long-jump ventures that do not take root may significantly erode the gains from those that do, resulting in disappointingly modest gains in overall profits.

STRATEGIES FOR INDUSTRY LEADERS

The competitive positions of industry leaders normally range from "stronger than average" to "powerful." Leaders typically are well known, and strongly entrenched leaders have proven strategies (keyed either to low-cost leadership or to differentiation). Some of the best-known industry leaders are Anheuser-Busch (beer), Starbucks (coffee drinks), Microsoft (computer software), Callaway (golf clubs), McDonald's (fast food), Procter & Gamble (laundry detergents and soaps), Campbell's (canned soups), Gerber (baby food), Hewlett-Packard (printers), Sony (video game consoles), Black & Decker (power tools), Intel (semiconductors and chip sets), Wal-Mart and Carrefour (discount retailing), Amazon.com (online shopping), eBay (online auctions), Apple (MP3 players), and Ocean Spray (cranberries).

The main strategic concern for a leader revolves around how to defend and strengthen its leadership position, perhaps becoming the dominant leader as opposed to just a leader. However, the pursuit of industry leadership and large market share is primarily important because of the competitive advantage and profitability that accrue to being the industry's biggest company. Three contrasting strategic postures are open to industry leaders:[21]

1. *Stay-on-the-offensive strategy*—The central goal of a stay-on-the-offensive strategy is to be a first-mover and a proactive market leader.[22] It rests on the principle that playing hardball, moving early and frequently, and forcing rivals into a catch-up mode is the surest path to industry prominence and potential market dominance—as the saying goes, the best defense is a good offense. Furthermore, *an offensive-minded industry leader relentlessly concentrates on achieving a competitive advantage over rivals and then widening this advantage over time to achieve extreme competitive advantage.*[23] Being the industry standard setter thus requires being impatient with the status quo, seizing the initiative, and pioneering continuous improvement and innovation—this can mean being first-to-market with technological improvements, new or better products, more attractive performance features, quality enhancements, or customer service improvements. It can mean aggressively seeking out ways to cut operating costs, ways to establish competitive capabilities that rivals cannot match, or ways to make it easier and less costly for potential customers to switch their purchases from runner-up firms to the leader's own products. It can mean aggressively attacking the profit sanctuaries of important rivals, perhaps with bursts of advertising or price-cutting or approaching its customers with special deals.[24]

> The governing principle underlying an industry leader's use of a stay-on-the-offensive strategy is to be an action-oriented first-mover, impatient with the status quo.

A low-cost leader must set the pace for cost reduction, and a differentiator must constantly initiate new ways to keep its product set apart from the brands of imitative rivals in order to be the standard against which rivals' products are judged. The array of options for a potent stay-on-the-offensive strategy can also include initiatives to expand overall industry demand—spurring the creation of new families of products, making the product more suitable for consumers in emerging-country markets, discovering new uses for the product, attracting new users of the product, and promoting more frequent use.

Illustration Capsule 8.2
ESPN's Strategy to Dominate Sports Entertainment

Via a series of offensive initiatives over the past 10 years, ESPN has parlayed its cable TV sports programming franchise into a dominating and pervasive general store of sports entertainment. The thrust of ESPN's strategy has been to stay on the offensive by (1) continually enhancing its program offerings and (2) extending the ESPN brand into a host of cutting-edge sports businesses. Examples of ESPN's enhanced product offering include the ESPY Awards for top achievements in sports, the X Games (an annual extreme sports competition for both winter and summer sports), the addition of *Monday Night Football* (starting in 2006), making new movies to show on ESPN, and producing its own shows (such as *ESPN Hollywood, Cold Pizza,* and *Bound for Glory*). The appeal of ESPN's programming was so powerful that ESPN was able to charge cable operators an estimated $2.80 per subscriber per month—nearly twice as much as the next most popular cable channel (CNN, for instance, was only able to command a monthly fee of roughly $0.40 per subscriber).

But the most important element of ESPN's strategic offensive had been to start up a series of new ESPN-branded businesses—all of which were brainstormed by ESPN's entrepreneurially talented management team. The company's brand extension offensive has produced nine TV channels (the most prominent of which are ESPN, ESPN2, ESPN Classic, ESPNews, and ESPN Desportes); the ESPN radio network, with 700 affiliate stations; ESPN.com (which in 2005 attracted some 16 million unique visitors monthly to view its bazaar of wide-ranging sports stories and information); *ESPN: The Magazine* (with a fast-growing base of 1.8 million subscribers that could in time overtake the barely growing 3.3 million subscriber

base of longtime leader *Sports Illustrated*); ESPN Motion (an online video service); ESPN360 (which offers sports information and video-clip programming tailored for broadband providers—it had 5 million subscribers in 2005 and was available from 14 broadband providers); Mobile ESPN (an ESPN-branded cell phone service provided in partnership with Sprint Nextel); ESPN Zones (nine sports-themed restaurants in various cities); ESPN branded video games (video game developer Electronic Arts has 15-year licensing rights to use the ESPN name for a series of sports-related games), and a business unit that distributes ESPN sports programming in 11 languages in over 180 countries.

In 2005, the empire of ESPN consisted of some 50 different businesses that generated annual revenues in excess of $5 billion and hefty annual operating profits of about $2 billion—about 40 percent of its revenues came from advertising and 60 percent from subscriptions and distribution fees. ESPN, a division of Disney, was one of Disney's most profitable and fastest-growing operations (Disney was also the parent of ABC Broadcasting).

So far, ESPN's stay-a-step-ahead strategy had left lesser rivals in the dust. But Comcast, the largest U.S. cable operator, with 22 million subscribers, was maneuvering to create its own cable TV sports channel; Comcast already owned the Philadelphia 76ers, the Philadelphia Flyers, and a collection of regional sports networks in cities from Philadelphia to Chicago to Los Angeles. And Rupert Murdoch's expansion-minded News Corporation, a worldwide media conglomerate whose many businesses included Fox Broadcasting and DIRECTV, was said to be looking at melding its 15 regional U.S. sports channels into a national sports channel.

Source: Developed from information in Tom Lowry, "ESPN the Zone," *BusinessWeek,* October 17, 2005, pp. 66–78.

A stay-on-the-offensive strategy cannot be considered successful unless it results in growing sales and revenues faster than the industry as a whole and wresting market share from rivals—a leader whose sales growth is only 5 percent in a market growing at 8 percent is losing ground to some of its competitors. Only if an industry's leader's market share is already so dominant that it presents a threat of antitrust action (a market share under 60 percent is usually safe) should an industry leader deliberately back away from aggressively pursuing market share gains.

Illustration Capsule 8.2 describes ESPN's stay-on-the-offensive strategy to dominate the sports entertainment business.

2. *Fortify-and-defend strategy*—The essence of "fortify and defend" is to make it harder for challengers to gain ground and for new firms to enter. The goals of a strong defense are to hold on to the present market share, strengthen current market position, and protect whatever competitive advantage the firm has. Specific defensive actions can include:

- Attempting to raise the competitive ante for challengers and new entrants via increased spending for advertising, higher levels of customer service, and bigger R&D outlays.
- Introducing more product versions or brands to match the product attributes that challenger brands have or to fill vacant niches that competitors could slip into.
- Adding personalized services and other extras that boost customer loyalty and make it harder or more costly for customers to switch to rival products.
- Keeping prices reasonable and quality attractive.
- Building new capacity ahead of market demand to discourage smaller competitors from adding capacity of their own.
- Investing enough to remain cost-competitive and technologically progressive.
- Patenting the feasible alternative technologies.
- Signing exclusive contracts with the best suppliers and dealer/distributors.

A fortify-and-defend strategy best suits firms that have already achieved industry dominance and don't wish to risk antitrust action. It is also well suited to situations where a firm wishes to milk its present position for profits and cash flow because the industry's prospects for growth are low or because further gains in market share do not appear profitable enough to go after. But a fortify-and-defend strategy always entails trying to grow as fast as the market as a whole (to stave off market-share slippage) and requires reinvesting enough capital in the business to protect the leader's ability to compete.

3. *Muscle-flexing strategy*—Here a dominant leader plays competitive hardball (presumably in an ethical and competitively legal manner) when smaller rivals rock the boat with price cuts or mount new market offensives that directly threaten its position. Specific responses can include quickly matching and perhaps exceeding challengers' price cuts, using large promotional campaigns to counter challengers' moves to gain market share, and offering better deals to their major customers. Dominant leaders may also court distributors assiduously to dissuade them from carrying rivals' products, provide salespersons with documented information about the weaknesses of competing products, or try to fill any vacant positions in their own firms by making attractive offers to the better executives of rivals that get out of line.

The leader may also use various arm-twisting tactics to pressure present customers not to use the products of rivals. This can range from simply forcefully communicating its displeasure should customers opt to use the products of rivals to pushing them to agree to exclusive arrangements in return for better prices to charging them a higher price if they use any competitors' products. As a final resort, a leader may grant certain customers special discounts or preferred treatment if they do not use any products of rivals.

The obvious risks of a muscle-flexing strategy are running afoul of laws prohibiting monopoly practices and unfair competition and using bullying tactics that arouse adverse public opinion. Microsoft paid Real Networks $460 million in 2005 to resolve all of Real Network's antitrust complaints and settle a long-standing feud over Microsoft's repeated bullying of PC makers to include Windows Media Player instead of Real's media player as standard installed software on their PCs. In 2005 AMD filed an antitrust suit against Intel, claiming that Intel unfairly and monopolistically coerced 38 named companies on three continents in efforts to get them to use Intel chips instead of AMD chips in the computer products they manufactured or marketed. Consequently, a company that throws its weight around to protect and enhance its market dominance has got to be judicious, lest it cross the line from allowable muscle-flexing to unethical or illegal competitive bullying.

STRATEGIES FOR RUNNER-UP FIRMS

Runner-up, or second-tier, firms have smaller market shares than first-tier industry leaders. Some runner-up firms are often advancing market challengers, employing offensive strategies to gain market share and build a stronger market position. Other runner-up competitors are focusers, seeking to improve their lot by concentrating their attention on serving a limited portion of the market. There are, of course, always a number of firms in any industry that are destined to be perennial runners-up, either because they are content to follow the trendsetting moves of the market leaders or because they lack the resources and competitive strengths to do much better in the marketplace than they are already doing. But it is erroneous to view runner-up firms as inherently less profitable or unable to hold their own against the biggest firms. Many small and medium-sized firms earn healthy profits and enjoy good reputations with customers.

Obstacles for Firms with Small Market Shares

There are times when runner-up companies face significant hurdles in contending for market leadership. In industries where big size is definitely a key success factor, firms with small market shares have four obstacles to overcome: (1) less access to economies of scale in manufacturing, distribution, or marketing and sales promotion; (2) difficulty in gaining customer recognition (since the products and brands of the market leaders are much better known); (3) less money to spend on mass-media advertising; and (4) limited funds for capital expansion or making acquisitions.[25] Some runner-up companies may be able to surmount these obstacles. Others may not. When significant scale economies give large-volume competitors a dominating cost advantage, small-share firms have only two viable strategic options: initiate offensive moves aimed at building sufficient sales volume to approach the scale economies and lower unit costs enjoyed by larger rivals or withdraw from the business (gradually or quickly) because of the inability to achieve low enough costs to compete effectively against the market leaders.

Offensive Strategies to Build Market Share

A runner-up company desirous of closing in on the market leaders has to make some waves in the marketplace if it wants to make big market share gains—this means coming up with distinctive strategy elements that set it apart from rivals and draw buyer attention. If a challenger has a 5 percent market share and needs a 15 to 20 percent share to contend for leadership and earn attractive profits, it requires a more creative approach to competing than just "Try harder" or "Follow in the footsteps of current industry leaders." Rarely can a runner-up significantly improve its competitive position by imitating the strategies of leading firms. A cardinal rule in offensive strategy is to avoid attacking a leader head-on with an imitative strategy, regardless of the resources and staying power an underdog may have.[26] What an aspiring challenger really needs is a strategy aimed at building a competitive advantage of its own (and certainly a strategy capable of quickly eliminating any important competitive disadvantages).

The best "mover-and-shaker" offensives for a second-tier challenger aiming to join the first-tier ranks usually involve one of the following five approaches:

1. Making a series of acquisitions of smaller rivals to greatly expand the company's market reach and market presence. *Growth via acquisition* is perhaps the most frequently used strategy employed by ambitious runner-up companies to form an enterprise that has greater competitive strength and a larger share of the overall market. For an enterprise to succeed with this strategic approach, senior management must be skilled in quickly assimilating the operations of the acquired companies, eliminating duplication and overlap, generating efficiencies and cost savings, and structuring the combined resources in ways that create substantially stronger competitive capabilities. Many banks and public accounting firms owe their growth during the past decade to acquisition of smaller regional and local banks. Likewise, a number of book publishers have grown by acquiring small publishers, and public accounting firms have grown by acquiring lesser-sized accounting firms with attractive client lists.

2. Finding innovative ways to dramatically drive down costs and then using the attraction of lower prices to win customers from higher-cost, higher-priced rivals. This is a necessary offensive move when a runner-up company has higher costs than larger-scale enterprises (either because the latter possess scale economies or have benefited from experience/learning curve effects). A challenger firm can pursue aggressive cost reduction by eliminating marginal activities from its value chain, streamlining supply chain relationships, improving internal operating efficiency, using various e-commerce techniques, and merging with or acquiring rival firms to achieve the size needed to capture greater scale economies.

3. Crafting an attractive differentiation strategy based on premium quality, technological superiority, outstanding customer service, rapid product innovation, or convenient online shopping options.

4. Pioneering a leapfrog technological breakthrough—an attractive option if an important technological breakthrough is within a challenger's reach and rivals are not close behind.

5. Being first-to-market with new or better products and building a reputation for product leadership. A strategy of product innovation has appeal if the runner-up company possesses the necessary resources—cutting-edge R&D capability and organizational agility in speeding new products to market.

Other possible, but likely less effective, offensive strategy options include (1) outmaneuvering slow-to-change market leaders in adapting to evolving market conditions and customer expectations and (2) forging productive strategic alliances with key distributors, dealers, or marketers of complementary products.

Without a potent offensive strategy to capture added market share, runner-up companies have to patiently nibble away at the lead of market leaders and build sales at a moderate pace over time.

Other Strategic Approaches for Runner-Up Companies

There are five other strategies that runner-up companies can employ.[27] While none of the five is likely to move a company from second-tier to first-tier status, all are capable of producing attractive profits and returns for shareholders.

Vacant-Niche Strategy   A version of a focused strategy, the vacant-niche strategy involves concentrating on specific customer groups or end-use applications that market leaders have bypassed or neglected. An ideal vacant niche is of sufficient size and scope to be profitable, has some growth potential, is well suited to a firm's own capabilities, and for one reason or another is hard for leading firms to serve. Two examples where vacant-niche strategies have worked successfully are (1) regional commuter airlines serving cities with too few passengers to fill the large jets flown by major airlines and (2) health-food producers (like Health Valley, Hain, and Tree of Life) that cater to local health-food stores—a market segment that until recently has been given little attention by such leading companies as Kraft, Nestlé, and Unilever.

Specialist Strategy   A specialist firm trains its competitive effort on one technology, product or product family, end use, or market segment (often one in which buyers have special needs). The aim is to train the company's resource strengths and capabilities on building competitive advantage through leadership in a specific area. Smaller companies that successfully use this focused strategy include Formby's (a specialist in stains and finishes for wood furniture, especially refinishing); Blue Diamond (a California-based grower and marketer of almonds); Cuddledown (a specialty producer and retailer of down and synthetic comforters, featherbeds, and other bedding products); and American Tobacco (a leader in chewing tobacco and snuff). Many companies in high-tech industries concentrate their energies on being the clear leader in a particular technological niche; their competitive advantage is superior technological depth, technical expertise that is highly valued by customers, and the capability to consistently beat out rivals in pioneering technological advances.

Superior Product Strategy   The approach here is to use a differentiation-based focused strategy keyed to superior product quality or unique attributes. Sales and marketing efforts are aimed directly at quality-conscious and performance-oriented buyers. Fine craftsmanship, prestige quality, frequent product innovations, and/or close contact with customers to solicit their input in developing a better product usually undergird the superior product approach. Some examples include Samuel Adams in beer, Tiffany in diamonds and jewelry, Chicago Cutlery in premium-quality kitchen knives, Baccarat in fine crystal, Cannondale in mountain bikes, Bally in shoes, and Patagonia in apparel for outdoor recreation enthusiasts.

Distinctive-Image Strategy   Some runner-up companies build their strategies around ways to make themselves stand out from competitors. A variety of distinctive-image strategies can be used: building a reputation for charging the lowest prices (Dollar General), providing high-end quality at a good price (Orvis, Lands' End, and L. L. Bean), going all out to give superior customer service (Four Seasons hotels), incorporating unique product attributes (Omega-3 enriched eggs), making a product with disctinctive styling (General Motors' Hummer), or devising unusually creative advertising (AFLAC's duck ads on TV). Other examples include Dr Pepper's strategy in calling attention to its distinctive taste, Apple Computer's making it easier and more interesting for people to use its Macintosh PCs, and Mary Kay Cosmetics' distinctive use of the color pink.

Content Follower Strategy   Content followers deliberately refrain from initiating trendsetting strategic moves and from aggressive attempts to steal customers away from the leaders. Followers prefer approaches that will not provoke competitive retaliation, often opting for focus and differentiation strategies that keep them out of the leaders' paths. They react and respond rather than initiate and challenge. They prefer defense to offense. And they rarely get out of line with the leaders on price. They are content to simply maintain their market position, albeit sometimes struggling to do so. Followers have no urgent strategic questions to confront beyond "What strategic changes are the leaders initiating and what do we need to do to follow along and maintain our present position?" The marketers of private-label products tend to be followers, imitating many of the newly introduced features of name brand products and content to sell to price-conscious buyers at prices modestly below those of well-known brands.

STRATEGIES FOR WEAK AND CRISIS-RIDDEN BUSINESSES

A firm in an also-ran or declining competitive position has four basic strategic options. If it can come up with the financial resources, it can launch a turnaround strategy keyed either to "low-cost" or "new" differentiation themes, pouring enough money and talent into the effort to move up a notch or two in the industry rankings and become a respectable market contender within five years or so. It can employ a fortify-and-defend strategy, using variations of its present strategy and fighting hard to keep sales, market share, profitability, and competitive position at current levels. It can opt for a fast-exit strategy and get out of the business, either by selling out to another firm or by closing down operations if a buyer cannot be found. Or it can employ an end-game or slow-exit strategy, keeping reinvestment to a bare-bones minimum and taking actions to maximize short-term cash flows in preparation for orderly market withdrawal.

Turnaround Strategies for Businesses in Crisis

Turnaround strategies are needed when a business worth rescuing goes into crisis. The objective is to arrest and reverse the sources of competitive and financial weakness as quickly as possible. Management's first task in formulating a suitable turnaround strategy is to diagnose what lies at the root of poor performance. Is it an unexpected downturn in sales brought on by a weak economy? An ill-chosen competitive strategy? Poor execution of an otherwise viable strategy? High operating costs? Important resource deficiencies? An overload of debt? The next task is to decide whether the business can be saved or whether the situation is hopeless. Understanding what is wrong with the business and how serious its strategic problems are is essential because different diagnoses lead to different turnaround strategies.

Some of the most common causes of business trouble are taking on too much debt, overestimating the potential for sales growth, ignoring the profit-depressing effects of an overly aggressive effort to "buy" market share with deep price cuts, being burdened with heavy fixed costs because weak sales don't permit near-full capacity utilization, betting on R&D efforts but failing to come up with effective innovations, betting on technological long shots, being too optimistic about the ability to penetrate new markets, making frequent changes in strategy (because the previous strategy didn't work out), and being overpowered by more successful rivals. Curing these kinds of problems and achieving a successful business turnaround can involve any of the following actions:

- Selling off assets to raise cash to save the remaining part of the business.
- Revising the existing strategy.
- Launching efforts to boost revenues.

- Pursuing cost reduction.
- Using a combination of these efforts.

Selling Off Assets   Asset-reduction strategies are essential when cash flow is a critical consideration and when the most practical ways to generate cash are (1) through sale of some of the firm's assets (plant and equipment, land, patents, inventories, or profitable subsidiaries) and (2) through retrenchment (pruning of marginal products from the product line, closing or selling older plants, reducing the workforce, withdrawing from outlying markets, cutting back customer service). Sometimes crisis-ridden companies sell off assets not so much to unload losing operations as to raise funds to save and strengthen the remaining business activities. In such cases, the choice is usually to dispose of noncore business assets to support strategy renewal in the firm's core businesses.

Strategy Revision   When weak performance is caused by bad strategy, the task of strategy overhaul can proceed along any of several paths: (1) shifting to a new competitive approach to rebuild the firm's market position; (2) overhauling internal operations and functional-area strategies to better support the same overall business strategy; (3) merging with another firm in the industry and forging a new strategy keyed to the newly merged firm's strengths; and (4) retrenching into a reduced core of products and customers more closely matched to the firm's strengths. The most appealing path depends on prevailing industry conditions, the firm's particular strengths and weaknesses, its competitive capabilities vis-à-vis rival firms, and the severity of the crisis. A situation analysis of the industry, the major competitors, and the firm's own competitive position is a prerequisite for action. As a rule, successful strategy revision must be tied to the ailing firm's strengths and near-term competitive capabilities and directed at its best market opportunities.

Boosting Revenues   Revenue-increasing turnaround efforts aim at generating increased sales volume. The chief revenue-building options include price cuts, increased advertising, a bigger sales force, added customer services, and quickly achieved product improvements. Attempts to increase revenues and sales volumes are necessary (1) when there is little or no room in the operating budget to cut expenses and still break even, and (2) when the key to restoring profitability is increased use of existing capacity. If buyers are not especially price-sensitive (because many are strongly attached to various differentiating features in the company's product offering), the quickest way to boost short-term revenues may be to raise prices rather than opt for volume-building price cuts. A price increase in the 2–4 percent range may well be feasible if the company's prices are already below those of key rivals.

Cutting Costs   Cost-reducing turnaround strategies work best when an ailing firm's value chain and cost structure are flexible enough to permit radical surgery, when operating inefficiencies are identifiable and readily correctable, when the firm's costs are obviously bloated, and when the firm is relatively close to its break-even point. Accompanying a general belt-tightening can be an increased emphasis on paring administrative overheads, elimination of nonessential and low-value-added activities in the firm's value chain, modernization of existing plant and equipment to gain greater productivity, delay of nonessential capital expenditures, and debt restructuring to reduce interest costs and stretch out repayments.

Illustration Capsule 8.3

Sony's Turnaround Strategy—Will It Work?

Electronics was once Sony's star business, but Sony's electronics business was a huge money-loser in 2003–2004, pushing the company's stock price down about 65 percent. Once the clear leader in top-quality TVs, in 2005 Sony lagged miserably behind Samsung, Panasonic, and Sharp in popular flat-panel LCD and plasma TVs, where sales were growing fastest. Apple Computer's iPod players had stolen the limelight in the handheld music market, where Sony's Walkman had long ruled.

In the fall of 2005, Sony management announced a turnaround strategy. Howard Stringer, a dual American and British citizen who was named Sony's CEO in early 2005 and was the first foreigner ever to head Sony, unveiled a plan centered on cutting 10,000 jobs (about 6 percent of Sony's workforce), closing 11 of Sony's 65 manufacturing plants, and shrinking or eliminating 15 unprofitable

electronics operations by March 2008 (the unprofitable operations were not identified). These initiatives were projected to reduce costs by $1.8 billion. In addition to the cost cuts, Sony said it would focus on growing its sales of "champion products" like the next-generation Sony PlayStation 3 video game console, a newly introduced line of Bravia LCD TVs, and Walkman MP3 music players.

Analysts were not impressed by the turnaround plan. Standard & Poor's cut its credit rating for Sony, citing doubts about the company's turnaround strategy and forecasting "substantially" lower profitability and cash flow in fiscal 2005. Moody's put Sony on its watch list for a credit rating downgrade. Other analysts said Stringer's strategy lacked vision and creativity because it was in the same mold as most corporate streamlining efforts.

Sources: Company press releases; Yuri Kageyama, "Sony Announcing Turnaround Strategy," www.yahoo.com (accessed October 20, 2005); *Mainichi Daily News*, October 14, 2005 (accessed on Google News, October 20, 2005); and "Sony to Cut 10,000 Jobs," www.cnn.com (accessed October 20, 2005).

Combination Efforts   Combination turnaround strategies are usually essential in grim situations that require fast action on a broad front. Likewise, combination actions frequently come into play when new managers are brought in and given a free hand to make whatever changes they see fit. The tougher the problems, the more likely it is that the solutions will involve multiple strategic initiatives—see the story of turnaround efforts at Sony in Illustration Capsule 8.3.

The Chances of a Successful Turnaround Are Not High   Turnaround efforts tend to be high-risk undertakings; some return a company to good profitability, but most don't. A landmark study of 64 companies found no successful turnarounds among the most troubled companies in eight basic industries.[28] Many of the troubled businesses waited too long to begin a turnaround. Others found themselves short of both the cash and entrepreneurial talent needed to compete in a slow-growth industry characterized by a fierce battle for market share. Better-positioned rivals simply proved too strong to defeat in a long, head-to-head contest. Even when successful, turnaround may involve numerous attempts and management changes before long-term competitive viability and profitability are finally restored. A recent study found that troubled companies that did nothing and elected to wait out hard times had only a 10 percent chance of recovery.[29] This same study also found that, of the companies studied, the chances of recovery were boosted 190 percent if the turnaround strategy involved buying assets that strengthened the company's business in its core markets; companies that both bought assets or companies in their core markets while selling off noncore assets increased their chances of recovery by 250 percent.

Harvest Strategies for Weak Businesses

When a struggling company's chances of pulling off a successful turnaround are poor, the wisest option may be to forget about trying to restore the company's competitiveness and profitability and, instead employ a *harvesting strategy* that aims at generating the largest possible cash flows from the company's operations for as long as possible. A losing effort to transform a competitively weak company into a viable market contender has little appeal when there are opportunities to generate potentially sizable amounts of cash by running the business in a manner calculated to either maintain the status quo or even let the business slowly deteriorate over a long period.

As is the case with a slow-exit strategy, a harvesting strategy entails trimming operating expenses to the bone and spending the minimum amount on capital projects to keep the business going. Internal cash flow becomes the key measure of how well the company is performing, and top priority is given to cash-generating actions. Thus, advertising and promotional costs are kept at minimal levels; personnel who leave for jobs elsewhere or retire may not be replaced; and maintenance is performed with an eye toward stretching the life of existing facilities and equipment. Even though a harvesting strategy is likely to lead to a gradual decline in the company's business over time, the ability to harvest sizable amounts of cash in the interim makes such an outcome tolerable.

> The overriding objective of a harvesting strategy is to maximize short-term cash flows from operations.

The Conditions That Make a Harvesting Strategy Attractive   A strategy of harvesting the cash flows from a weak business is a reasonable option in the following circumstances:[30]

1. *When industry demand is stagnant or declining and there's little hope that either market conditions will improve*—The growing popularity of digital cameras has forever doomed market demand for camera film.

2. *When rejuvenating the business would be too costly or at best marginally profitable*—A struggling provider of dial-up Internet access is likely to realize more benefit from harvesting than from a losing effort to grow its business in the face of the unstoppable shift to high-speed broadband service.

3. *When trying to maintain or grow the company's present sales is becoming increasingly costly*—A money-losing producer of pipe tobacco and cigars is unlikely to make market headway in gaining sales and market share against the top-tier producers (which have more resources to compete for the business that is still available).

4. *When reduced levels of competitive effort will not trigger an immediate or rapid falloff in sales*—the makers of corded telephones will not likely experience much of a decline in sales if they spend all of their R&D and marketing budgets on wireless phone systems.

5. *When the enterprise can redeploy the freed resources in higher-opportunity areas*—The makers of food products with "bad-for-you" ingredients (saturated fats, high transfats, and sugar) are better off devoting their resources to the development, production, and sale of "good-for-you" products (those with no transfats, more fiber, and good types of carbohydrates).

6. *When the business is not a crucial or core component of a diversified company's overall lineup of businesses*—Harvesting a sideline business and perhaps hastening

its decay is strategically preferable to harvesting a mainline or core business (where even a gradual decline may not be a very attractive outcome).

The more of these six conditions that are present, the more ideal the business is for harvesting.

Liquidation: The Strategy of Last Resort

Sometimes a business in crisis is too far gone to be salvaged and presents insufficient harvesting potential to be interesting. Closing down a crisis-ridden business and liquidating its assets is sometimes the best and wisest strategy. But it is also the most unpleasant and painful strategic alternative due to the hardships of job eliminations and the economic effects of business closings on local communities. Nonetheless, in hopeless situations, an early liquidation effort usually serves owner-stockholder interests better than an inevitable bankruptcy. Prolonging the pursuit of a lost cause further erodes an organization's resources and leaves less to salvage, not to mention the added stress and potential career impairment for all the people involved. The problem, of course, is differentiating between when a turnaround is achievable and when it isn't. It is easy for owners or managers to let their emotions and pride overcome sound judgment when a business gets in such deep trouble that a successful turnaround is remote.

10 COMMANDMENTS FOR CRAFTING SUCCESSFUL BUSINESS STRATEGIES

Company experiences over the years prove again and again that disastrous strategies can be avoided by adhering to good strategy-making principles. We've distilled the lessons learned from the strategic mistakes companies most often make into 10 commandments that serve as useful guides for developing sound strategies:

1. *Place top priority on crafting and executing strategic moves that enhance the company's competitive position for the long term.* The glory of meeting one quarter's or one year's financial performance targets quickly fades, but an ever-stronger competitive position pays off year after year. Shareholders are never well served by managers who let short-term financial performance considerations rule out strategic initiatives that will meaningfully bolster the company's longer-term competitive position and competitive strength. The best way to ensure a company's long-term profitability is with a strategy that strengthens the company's long-term competitiveness and market position.

2. *Be prompt in adapting to changing market conditions, unmet customer needs, buyer wishes for something better, emerging technological alternatives, and new initiatives of competitors.* Responding late or with too little often puts a company in the precarious position of having to play catch-up. While pursuit of a consistent strategy has its virtues, adapting strategy to changing circumstances is normal and necessary. Moreover, long-term strategic commitments to achieve top quality or lowest cost should be interpreted relative to competitors' products as well as customers' needs and expectations; the company should avoid singlemindedly striving to make the absolute highest-quality or lowest-cost product no matter what.

3. *Invest in creating a sustainable competitive advantage.* Having a competitive edge over rivals is the single most dependable contributor to above-average profitability.

As a general rule, a company must play aggressive offense to build competitive advantage and aggressive defense to protect it.

4. *Avoid strategies capable of succeeding only in the most optimistic circumstances.* Expect competitors to employ countermeasures and expect times of unfavorable market conditions. A good strategy works reasonably well and produces tolerable results even in the worst of times.

5. *Consider that attacking competitive weakness is usually more profitable and less risky than attacking competitive strength.* Attacking capable, resourceful rivals is likely to fail unless the attacker has deep financial pockets and a solid basis for competitive advantage despite the strengths of the competitor being attacked.

6. *Strive to open up very meaningful gaps in quality or service or performance features when pursuing a differentiation strategy.* Tiny differences between rivals' product offerings may not be visible or important to buyers.

7. *Be wary of cutting prices without an established cost advantage.* Price cuts run the risk that rivals will retaliate with matching or deeper price cuts of their own. The best chance for remaining profitable if the price-cutting contest turns into a price war is to have lower costs than rivals.

8. *Don't underestimate the reactions and the commitment of rival firms.* Rivals are most dangerous when they are pushed into a corner and their well-being is threatened.

9. *Avoid stuck-in-the-middle strategies that represent compromises between lower costs and greater differentiation and between broad and narrow market appeal.* Compromise strategies rarely produce sustainable competitive advantage or a distinctive competitive position—a well-executed best-cost producer strategy is the only exception in which a compromise between low cost and differentiation succeeds. Companies with compromise strategies most usually end up with average costs, an average product, an average reputation, and *no distinctive image in the marketplace*. Lacking any strategy element that causes them to stand out in the minds of buyers, companies with compromise strategies are destined for a middle-of-the-pack industry ranking, with little prospect of ever becoming an industry leader.

10. *Be judicious in employing aggressive moves to wrest market share away from rivals often provoke retaliation in the form of escalating marketing and sales promotion, a furious race to be first-to-market with next-version products or a price war—to the detriment of everyone's profits.* Aggressive moves to capture a bigger market share invite cutthroat competition, especially when many industry members, plagued with high inventories and excess production capacity, are also scrambling for additional sales.

Key Points

The lessons of this chapter are that (1) some strategic options are better suited to certain specific industry and competitive environments than others and (2) some strategic options are better suited to certain specific company situations than others. Crafting a strategy tightly matched to a company's situation thus involves being alert to which strategy alternatives are likely to work well and which alternatives are unlikely to work well. Specifically:

1. What basic type of industry environment (emerging, rapid-growth, mature/slow-growth, stagnant/declining, high-velocity/turbulent, fragmented) does the company operate in? What strategic options and strategic postures are usually best suited to this generic type of environment?

2. What position does the firm have in the industry (leader, runner-up, or weak/distressed)? Given this position, which strategic options merit strong consideration and which options should definitely be ruled out?

In addition, creating a tight strategy-situation fit entails considering all the external and internal situational factors discussed in Chapters 3 and 4 and then revising the list of strategy options accordingly to take account of competitive conditions, industry driving forces, the expected moves of rivals, and the company's own competitive strengths and weaknesses. Listing the pros and cons of the candidate strategies is nearly always a helpful step. In weeding out the least attractive strategic alternatives and weighing the pros and cons of the most attractive ones, the answers to four questions often help point to the best course of action:

1. What kind of competitive edge can the company realistically achieve, given its resource strengths, competencies, and competitive capabilities? Is the company in a position to lead industry change and set the rules by which rivals must compete?

2. Which strategy alternative best addresses all the issues and problems the firm confronts.

3. Are any rivals particularly vulnerable and, if so, what sort of an offensive will it take to capitalize on these vulnerabilities? Will rivals counterattack? What can be done to blunt their efforts?

4. Are any defensive actions needed to protect against rivals' likely moves or other external threats to the company's future profitability?

In picking and choosing among the menu of strategic options, there are four pitfalls to avoid:

1. Designing an overly ambitious strategic plan—one that overtaxes the company's resources and capabilities.

2. Selecting a strategy that represents a radical departure from or abandonment of the cornerstones of the company's prior success—a radical strategy change need not be rejected automatically, but it should be pursued only after careful risk assessment.

3. Choosing a strategy that goes against the grain of the organization's culture.

4. Being unwilling to commit wholeheartedly to one of the five competitive strategies—picking and choosing features of the different strategies usually produces so many compromises between low cost, best cost, differentiation, and focusing that the company fails to achieve any kind of advantage and ends up stuck in the middle.

Table 8.1 provides a generic format for outlining a strategic action plan for a single-business enterprise. It contains all of the pieces of a comprehensive strategic action plan that we discussed at various places in these first eight chapters.

Table 8.1   **Sample Format for a Strategic Action Plan**

1. Strategic Vision and Mission	**5.** Supporting Functional Strategies • Production
2. Strategic Objectives • Short-term • Long-term	• Marketing/sales • Finance
3. Financial Objectives • Short-term • Long-term	• Personnel/human resources • Other
4. Overall Business Strategy	**6.** Recommended Actions to Improve Company Performance • Immediate • Longer-range

Exercises

1. Listed below are 10 industries. Classify each one as (*a*) emerging, (*b*) rapid-growth, (*c*) mature/slow-growth, (*d*) stagnant/declining, (*e*) high-velocity/turbulent, and (*f*) fragmented. Do research on the Internet, if needed, to locate information on industry conditions and reach a conclusion on what classification to assign each of the following:

   a. Exercise and fitness industry.
   b. Dry-cleaning industry.
   c. Poultry industry.
   d. Camera film and film-developing industry.
   e. Wine, beer, and liquor retailing.
   f. Watch industry.
   g. Cell-phone industry.
   h. Recorded music industry (DVDs, CDs, tapes).
   i. Computer software industry.
   j. Newspaper industry.

2. Toyota overtook Ford Motor Company in 2003 to become the world's second-largest maker of motor vehicles, behind General Motors. Toyota is widely regarded as having aspirations to overtake General Motors as the global leader in motor vehicles within the next 10 years. Do research on the Internet or in the library to determine what strategy General Motors is pursuing to maintain its status as the industry leader. Then research Toyota's strategy to overtake General Motors.

3. Review the discussion in Illustration Capsule 8.1 concerning the focused differentiation strategy that Exertris has employed in the exercise equipment industry. Then answer the following:

   a. What reasons can you give for why sales of the Exertris exercise bike have not taken off?

   b. What strategic actions would you recommend to the cofounders of Exertris to spark substantially greater sales of its innovative exercise bike and overcome the apparent market apathy for its video-game-equipped exercise bike? Should the company consider making any changes in its product offering? What distribution channels should it emphasize? What advertising and promotional approaches should be considered? How can it get gym owners to purchase or at least try its bikes?

   c. Should the company just give up on its product innovation (because the bike is not ever likely to get good reception in the marketplace)? Or should the cofounders try to sell their fledgling business to another exercise equipment company with a more extensive product line and wider geographic coverage?

4. Review the information in Illustration Capsule 8.3 concerning the turnaround strategy Sony launched in the fall of 2005. Go to the company's Web site and check out other Internet sources to see how Sony's strategy to revitalize its electronics business is coming along. Does your research indicate that Sony's turnaround strategy is a success or a failure, or is it still too early to tell? Explain.

5. Yahoo competes in an industry characterized by high-velocity change. Read the company's press releases at http://yhoo.client.shareholder.com/releases.cfm and answer the following questions:

   a. Does it appear that the company has dealt with change in the industry by reacting to change, anticipating change, or leading change? Explain.

   b. What are its key strategies for competing in fast-changing markets? Describe them.

Diversification

Strategies for Managing a Group of Businesses

To acquire or not to acquire: that is the question.

—Robert J. Terry

Fit between a parent and its businesses is a two-edged sword: a good fit can create value; a bad one can destroy it.

—Andrew Campbell, Michael Goold, and Marcus Alexander

Achieving superior performance through diversification is largely based on relatedness.

—Philippe Very

Make winners out of every business in your company. Don't carry losers.

—Jack Welch
Former CEO, General Electric

We measure each of our businesses against strict criteria: growth, margin, and return-on-capital hurdle rate, and does it have the ability to become number one or two in its industry? We are quite pragmatic. If a business does not contribute to our overall vision, it has to go.

—Richard Wambold
CEO, Pactiv

In this chapter, we move up one level in the strategy-making hierarchy, from strategy making in a single-business enterprise to strategy making in a diversified enterprise. Because a diversified company is a collection of individual businesses, the strategy-making task is more complicated. In a one-business company, managers have to come up with a plan for competing successfully in only a single industry environment—the result is what we labeled in Chapter 2 as *business strategy* (or *business-level strategy*). But in a diversified company, the strategy-making challenge involves assessing multiple industry environments and developing a *set* of business strategies, one for each industry arena in which the diversified company operates. And top executives at a diversified company must still go one step further and devise a company-wide or *corporate strategy* for improving the attractiveness and performance of the company's overall business lineup and for making a rational whole out of its diversified collection of individual businesses.

In most diversified companies, corporate-level executives delegate considerable strategy-making authority to the heads of each business, usually giving them the latitude to craft a business strategy suited to their particular industry and competitive circumstances and holding them accountable for producing good results. But the task of crafting a diversified company's overall or corporate strategy falls squarely in the lap of top-level executives and involves four distinct facets:

1. *Picking new industries to enter and deciding on the means of entry*—The first concerns in diversifying are what new industries to get into and whether to enter by starting a new business from the ground up, acquiring a company already in the target industry, or forming a joint venture or strategic alliance with another company. A company can diversify narrowly into a few industries or broadly into many industries. The choice of whether to enter an industry via a start-up operation; a joint venture; or the acquisition of an established leader, an up-and-coming company, or a troubled company with turnaround potential shapes what position the company will initially stake out for itself.

2. *Initiating actions to boost the combined performance of the businesses the firm has entered*—As positions are created in the chosen industries, corporate strategists typically zero in on ways to strengthen the long-term competitive positions and profits of the businesses the firm has invested in. Corporate parents can help their business subsidiaries by providing financial resources, by supplying missing skills or technological know-how or managerial expertise to better perform key value chain activities, and by providing new avenues for cost reduction. They can also acquire another company in the same industry and merge the two operations into a stronger business, or acquire new businesses that strongly complement existing businesses. Typically, a company will pursue rapid-growth strategies in its most promising businesses, initiate turnaround efforts in weak-performing businesses with potential, and divest businesses that are no longer attractive or that don't fit into management's long-range plans.

3. *Pursuing opportunities to leverage cross-business value chain relationships and strategic fits into competitive advantage*—A company that diversifies into businesses with competitively important value chain matchups (pertaining to technology, supply chain logistics, production, overlapping distribution channels, or common customers) gains competitive advantage potential not open to a company that diversifies into businesses whose value chains are totally unrelated. Capturing this competitive advantage potential requires that corporate strategists spend considerable time trying to capitalize on such cross-business opportunities as transferring skills or technology from one business to another, reducing costs via sharing use of common facilities and resources, and using the company's well-known brand names and distribution muscle to grow the sales of newly acquired products.

4. *Establishing investment priorities and steering corporate resources into the most attractive business units*—A diversified company's different businesses are usually not equally attractive from the standpoint of investing additional funds. It is incumbent on corporate management to (*a*) decide on the priorities for investing capital in the company's different businesses, (*b*) channel resources into areas where earnings potentials are higher and away from areas where they are lower, and (*c*) divest business units that are chronically poor performers or are in an increasingly unattractive industry. Divesting poor performers and businesses in unattractive industries frees up unproductive investments either for redeployment to promising business units or for financing attractive new acquisitions.

The demanding and time-consuming nature of these four tasks explains why corporate executives generally refrain from becoming immersed in the details of crafting and implementing business-level strategies, preferring instead to delegate lead responsibility for business strategy to the heads of each business unit.

In the first portion of this chapter we describe the various means a company can use to become diversified and explore the pros and cons of related versus unrelated diversification strategies. The second part of the chapter looks at how to evaluate the attractiveness of a diversified company's business lineup, decide whether it has a good diversification strategy, and identify ways to improve its future performance. In the chapter's concluding section, we survey the strategic options open to already-diversified companies.

WHEN TO DIVERSIFY

So long as a company has its hands full trying to capitalize on profitable growth opportunities in its present industry, there is no urgency to pursue diversification. The big risk of a single-business company, of course, is having all of the firm's eggs in one industry basket. If demand for the industry's product is eroded by the appearance of alternative technologies, substitute products, or fast-shifting buyer preferences, or if the industry becomes competitively unattractive and unprofitable, then a company's prospects can quickly dim. Consider, for example, what digital cameras have done to erode the revenues of companies dependent on making camera film and doing film processing, what CD and DVD technology have done to business outlook for producers of cassette tapes and 3.5-inch disks, and what cell-phone companies with their no-long-distance-charge plans and marketers of Voice over Internet Protocol (VoIP) are doing to the revenues of such once-dominant long-distance providers as AT&T, British Telecommunications, and NTT in Japan.

Thus, diversifying into new industries always merits strong consideration whenever a single-business company encounters diminishing market opportunities and stagnating sales in its principal business—most landline-based telecommunications companies across the world are quickly diversifying their product offerings to include wireless and VoIP services. But there are four other instances in which a company becomes a prime candidate for diversifying:[1]

1. When it spots opportunities for expanding into industries whose technologies and products complement its present business.
2. When it can leverage existing competencies and capabilities by expanding into businesses where these same resource strengths are key success factors and valuable competitive assets.
3. When diversifying into closely related businesses opens new avenues for reducing costs.
4. When it has a powerful and well-known brand name that can be transferred to the products of other businesses and thereby used as a lever for driving up the sales and profits of such businesses.

The decision to diversify presents wide-open possibilities. A company can diversify into closely related businesses or into totally unrelated businesses. It can diversify its present revenue and earning base to a small extent (such that new businesses account for less than 15 percent of companywide revenues and profits) or to a major extent (such that new businesses produce 30 or more percent of revenues and profits). It can move into one or two large new businesses or a greater number of small ones. It can achieve multibusiness/multi-industry status by acquiring an existing company already in a business/industry it wants to enter, starting up a new business subsidiary from scratch, or forming a joint venture with one or more companies to enter new businesses.

BUILDING SHAREHOLDER VALUE: THE ULTIMATE JUSTIFICATION FOR DIVERSIFYING

Diversification must do more for a company than simply spread its business risk across various industries. In principle, diversification cannot be considered a success unless it results in *added shareholder value*—value that shareholders cannot capture on their own by purchasing stock in companies in different industries or investing in mutual funds so as to spread their investments across several industries.

For there to be reasonable expectations that a company's diversification efforts can produce added value, a move to diversify into a new business must pass three tests:[2]

1. *The industry attractiveness test*—The industry to be entered must be attractive enough to yield consistently good returns on investment. Whether an industry is attractive depends chiefly on the presence of industry and competitive conditions that are conducive to earning as good or better profits and return on investment than the company is earning in its present business(es). It is hard to justify diversifying into an industry where profit expectations are *lower* than in the company's present businesses.

2. *The cost-of-entry test*—The cost to enter the target industry must not be so high as to erode the potential for good profitability. A catch-22 can prevail here, however. The more attractive an industry's prospects are for growth and good long-term profitability, the more expensive it can be to get into. Entry barriers for start-up companies are likely to be high in attractive industries; were barriers low, a rush of new entrants would soon erode the potential for high profitability. And buying a well-positioned company in an appealing industry often entails a high acquisition cost that makes passing the cost-of-entry test less likely. For instance, suppose that the price to purchase a company is $3 million and that the company is earning after-tax profits of $200,000 on an equity investment of $1 million (a 20 percent annual return). Simple arithmetic requires that the profits be tripled if the purchaser (paying $3 million) is to earn the same 20 percent return. Building the acquired firm's earnings from $200,000 to $600,000 annually could take several years—and require additional investment on which the purchaser would also have to earn a 20 percent return. Since the owners of a successful and growing company usually demand a price that reflects their business's profit prospects, it's easy for such an acquisition to fail the cost-of-entry test.

3. *The better-off test*—Diversifying into a new business must offer potential for the company's existing businesses and the new business to perform better together under a single corporate umbrella than they would perform operating as independent, stand-alone businesses. For example, let's say that company A diversifies by purchasing company B in another industry. If A and B's consolidated profits in the years to come prove no greater than what each could have earned on its own, then A's diversification won't provide its shareholders with added value. Company A's shareholders could have achieved the same $1 + 1 = 2$ result by merely purchasing stock in company B. Shareholder value is not created by diversification unless it produces a $1 + 1 = 3$ effect where sister businesses *perform better together* as part of the same firm than they could have performed as independent companies.

> **Core Concept**
> Creating added value for shareholders via diversification requires building a multibusiness company where the whole is greater than the sum of its parts.

Diversification moves that satisfy all three tests have the greatest potential to grow shareholder value over the long term. Diversification moves that can pass only one or two tests are suspect.

STRATEGIES FOR ENTERING NEW BUSINESSES

The means of entering new businesses can take any of three forms: acquisition, internal start-up, or joint ventures with other companies.

Acquisition of an Existing Business

Acquisition is the most popular means of diversifying into another industry. Not only is it quicker than trying to launch a brand-new operation, but it also offers an effective way to hurdle such entry barriers as acquiring technological know-how, establishing supplier relationships, becoming big enough to match rivals' efficiency and unit costs, having to spend large sums on introductory advertising and promotions, and securing adequate distribution. Buying an ongoing operation allows the acquirer to move directly to the task of building a strong market position in the target industry, rather than getting bogged down in going the internal start-up route and trying to develop the knowledge, resources, scale of operation, and market reputation necessary to become an effective competitor within a few years.

The big dilemma an acquisition-minded firm faces is whether to pay a premium price for a successful company or to buy a struggling company at a bargain price.[3] If the buying firm has little knowledge of the industry but ample capital, it is often better off purchasing a capable, strongly positioned firm—unless the price of such an acquisition flunks the cost-of-entry test. However, when the acquirer sees promising ways to transform a weak firm into a strong one and has the resources, the know-how, and the patience to do it, a struggling company can be the better long-term investment.

Internal Start-Up

Achieving diversification through *internal start-up* involves building a new business subsidiary from scratch. This entry option takes longer than the ac-quisition option and poses some hurdles. A newly formed business unit not only has to overcome entry barriers but also has to invest in new production capacity, develop sources of supply, hire and train employees, build channels of distribution, grow a customer base, and so on. Generally, forming a start-up subsidiary to enter a new business has appeal only when (1) the parent company already has in-house most or all of the skills and resources it needs to piece together a new business and compete effectively; (2) there is ample time to launch the business; (3) internal entry has lower costs than entry via acquisition; (4) the targeted industry is populated with many relatively small firms such that the new start-up does not have to compete head-to-head against larger, more powerful rivals; (5) adding new production capacity will not adversely impact the supply–demand balance in the industry; and (6) incumbent firms are likely to be slow or ineffective in responding to a new entrant's efforts to crack the market.[4]

> The biggest drawbacks to entering an industry by forming an internal start-up are the costs of overcoming entry barriers and the extra time it takes to build a strong and profitable competitive position.

Joint Ventures

Joint ventures entail forming a new corporate entity owned by two or more companies, where the purpose of the joint venture is to pursue a mutually attractive opportunity. The terms and conditions of a joint venture concern joint operation of a mutually owned business, which tends to make the arrangement more definitive and perhaps more durable than a strategic alliance—in a strategic alliance, the arrangement between the partners is one of limited collaboration for a limited purpose and a partner can choose to simply walk away or reduce its commitment at any time.

A joint venture to enter a new business can be useful in at least three types of situations.[5] First, a joint venture is a good vehicle for pursuing an opportunity that is too complex, uneconomical, or risky for one company to pursue alone. Second, joint ventures make sense when the opportunities in a new industry require a broader range of competencies and know-how than a company can marshal. Many of the opportunities in satellite-based telecommunications, biotechnology, and network-based systems that blend hardware, software, and services call for the coordinated development of complementary innovations and tackling an intricate web of financial, technical, political, and regulatory factors simultaneously. In such cases, pooling the resources and competencies of two or more companies is a wiser and less risky way to proceed.

Third, companies sometimes use joint ventures to diversify into a new industry when the diversification move entails having operations in a foreign country—several governments require foreign companies operating within their borders to have a local partner that has minority, if not majority, ownership in the local operations. Aside from fulfilling host government ownership requirements, companies usually seek out a local partner with expertise and other resources that will aid the success of the newly established local operation.

However, as discussed in Chapters 6 and 7, partnering with another company—in either a joint venture or a collaborative alliance—has significant drawbacks due to the potential for conflicting objectives, disagreements over how to best operate the venture, culture clashes, and so on. Joint ventures are generally the least durable of the entry options, usually lasting only until the partners decide to go their own ways.

CHOOSING THE DIVERSIFICATION PATH: RELATED VERSUS UNRELATED BUSINESSES

Core Concept
Related businesses possess competitively valuable cross-business value chain matchups; ***unrelated businesses*** have dissimilar value chains, containing no competitively useful cross-business relationships.

Once a company decides to diversify, its first big strategy decision is whether to diversify into related businesses, unrelated businesses, or some mix of both (see Figure 9.1). *Businesses are said to be related when their value chains possess competitively valuable cross-business relationships that present opportunities for the businesses to perform better under the same corporate umbrella than they could by operating as stand-alone entities.* The big appeal of related diversification is to build shareholder value by leveraging these cross-business relationships into competitive advantage, thus allowing the company as a whole to perform better than just the sum of its individual businesses. *Businesses are said to be unrelated when the activities comprising their respective value chains are so dissimilar that no competitively valuable cross-business relationships are present.*

The next two sections of this chapter explore the ins and outs of related and unrelated diversification.

THE CASE FOR DIVERSIFYING INTO RELATED BUSINESSES

A related diversification strategy involves building the company around businesses whose value chains possess competitively valuable strategic fits, as shown in Figure 9.2. **Strategic fit** exists whenever one or more activities comprising the value chains of different businesses are sufficiently similar as to present opportunities for:[6]

- Transferring competitively valuable expertise, technological know-how, or other capabilities from one business to another.

Figure 9.1 **Strategy Alternatives for a Company Looking to Diversify**

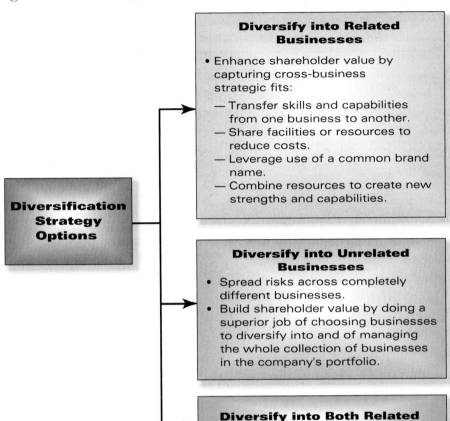

- Combining the related value chain activities of separate businesses into a single operation to achieve lower costs. For instance, it is often feasible to manufacture the products of different businesses in a single plant or use the same warehouses for shipping and distribution or have a single sales force for the products of different businesses (because they are marketed to the same types of customers).

- Exploiting common use of a well-known and potent brand name. For example, Honda's name in motorcycles and automobiles gave it instant credibility and recognition in entering the lawn-mower business, allowing it to achieve a significant market share without spending large sums on advertising to establish a brand identity for its lawn mowers. Canon's reputation in photographic equipment was a competitive asset that facilitated the company's diversification into copying equipment. Sony's name in consumer electronics made it easier and cheaper for Sony to enter the market for video games with its PlayStation console and lineup of PlayStation video games.

- Cross-business collaboration to create competitively valuable resource strengths and capabilities.

Core Concept
Strategic fit exists when the value chains of different businesses present opportunities for cross-business resource transfer, lower costs through combining the performance of related value chain activities, cross-business use of a potent brand name, and cross-business collaboration to build new or stronger competitive capabilities.

Figure 9.2 **Related Businesses Possess Related Value Chain Activities and Competitively Valuable Strategic Fits**

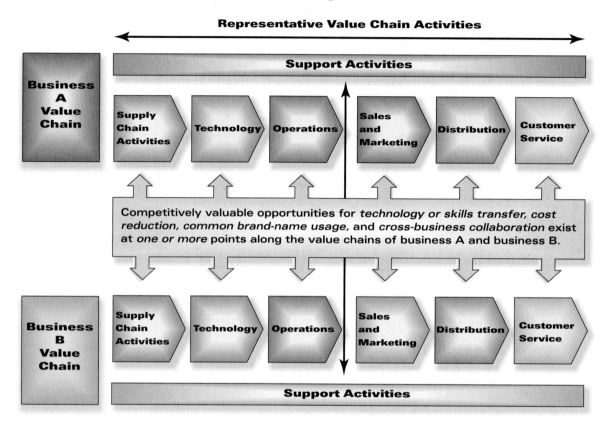

Related diversification thus has strategic appeal from several angles. It allows a firm to reap the competitive advantage benefits of skills transfer, lower costs, a powerful brand name, and/or stronger competitive capabilities and still spread investor risks over a broad business base. Furthermore, the relatedness among the different businesses provides sharper focus for managing diversification and a useful degree of strategic unity across the company's various business activities.

Identifying Cross-Business Strategic Fits along the Value Chain

Cross-business strategic fits can exist anywhere along the value chain—in R&D and technology activities, in supply chain activities and relationships with suppliers, in manufacturing, in sales and marketing, in distribution activities, or in administrative support activities.[7]

Strategic Fits in R&D and Technology Activities   Diversifying into businesses where there is potential for sharing common technology, exploiting the full range of business opportunities associated with a particular technology and its derivatives, or transferring technological know-how from one business to another has considerable appeal. Businesses with technology-sharing benefits can perform better together than apart because of potential cost savings in R&D and potentially shorter times in getting new products to market; also, technological advances in one business can lead to increased sales for both. Technological innovations have been the driver behind the efforts of cable TV companies to diversify into high-speed Internet access (via the use of cable modems) and, further, to explore providing local and long-distance telephone service to residential and commercial customers in either a single wire or using VoIP technology.

Strategic Fits in Supply Chain Activities   Businesses that have supply chain strategic fits can perform better together because of the potential for skills transfer in procuring materials, greater bargaining power in negotiating with common suppliers, the benefits of added collaboration with common supply chain partners, and/or added leverage with shippers in securing volume discounts on incoming parts and components. Dell Computer's strategic partnerships with leading suppliers of microprocessors, motherboards, disk drives, memory chips, flat-panel displays, wireless capabilities, long-life batteries, and other PC-related components have been an important element of the company's strategy to diversify into servers, data storage devices, MP3 players, and LCD TVs—products that include many components common to PCs and that can be sourced from the same strategic partners that provide Dell with PC components.

Manufacturing-Related Strategic Fits   Cross-business strategic fits in manufacturing-related activities can represent an important source of competitive advantage in situations where a diversifier's expertise in quality manufacture and cost-efficient production methods can be transferred to another business. When Emerson Electric diversified into the chain-saw business, it transferred its expertise in low-cost manufacture to its newly acquired Beaird-Poulan business division; the transfer drove Beaird-Poulan's new strategy—to be the low-cost provider of chain-saw products—and fundamentally changed the way Beaird-Poulan chain saws were designed and manufactured. Another benefit of production-related value chain matchups is the ability to consolidate production into a smaller number of plants and significantly reduce overall production costs. When snowmobile maker Bombardier diversified into motorcycles, it was able to set up motorcycle assembly lines in the same manufacturing facility where it was assembling snowmobiles. When Smuckers acquired Procter & Gamble's Jif peanut butter business, it was able to combine the manufacture of its own Smucker's peanut butter products with those of Jif; in addition, it gained greater leverage with vendors in purchasing its peanut supplies.

Distribution-Related Strategic Fits   Businesses with closely related distribution activities can perform better together than apart because of potential cost savings in sharing the same distribution facilities or using many of the same wholesale distributors and retail dealers to access customers. When Sunbeam acquired Mr. Coffee, it was able to consolidate its own distribution centers for small household appliances with those of Mr. Coffee, thereby generating considerable cost savings. Likewise, since Sunbeam products were sold to many of the same retailers as Mr. Coffee products (Wal-Mart, Kmart, Target, department stores, home centers, hardware chains, supermarket chains, and drugstore chains), Sunbeam was able to convince many of the retailers carrying Sunbeam appliances to also take on the Mr. Coffee line and vice versa.

Strategic Fits in Sales and Marketing Activities   Various cost-saving opportunities spring from diversifying into businesses with closely related sales and marketing activities. The same distribution centers can be used for warehousing and shipping the products of different businesses. When the products are sold directly to the same customers, sales costs can often be reduced by using a single sales force and avoiding having two different salespeople call on the same customer. The products of related businesses can be promoted at the same Web site, and included in the same media ads and sales brochures. After-sale service and repair organizations for the products of closely related businesses can often be consolidated into a single operation. There may be opportunities to reduce costs by consolidating order processing and billing and using common promotional tie-ins (cents-off couponing, free samples and trial offers, seasonal specials, and the like). When global power-tool maker Black & Decker acquired General Electric's domestic small household appliance business, it was able to use its own global sales force and distribution facilities to sell and distribute the newly acquired GE line of toasters, irons, mixers, and coffeemakers because the types of customers that carried its power tools (discounters like Wal-Mart and Target, home centers, and hardware stores) also stocked small appliances. The economies Black & Decker achieved for both product lines were substantial.

A second category of benefits arises when different businesses use similar sales and marketing approaches; in such cases, there may be competitively valuable opportunities to transfer selling, merchandising, advertising, and product differentiation skills from one business to another. Procter & Gamble's product lineup includes Folgers coffee, Tide laundry detergent, Crest toothpaste, Ivory soap, Charmin toilet tissue, Gillette razors and blades, Duracell batteries, Oral-B toothbrushes, and Head & Shoulders shampoo. All of these have different competitors and different supply chain and production requirements, but they all move through the same wholesale distribution systems, are sold in common retail settings to the same shoppers, are advertised and promoted in much the same ways, and require the same marketing and merchandising skills.

Strategic Fits in Managerial and Administrative Support Activities
Often, different businesses require comparable types managerial know-how, thereby allowing know-how in one line of business to be transferred to another. At General Electric (GE), managers who were involved in GE's expansion into Russia were able to expedite entry because of information gained from GE managers involved in expansions into other emerging markets. The lessons GE managers learned in China were passed along to GE managers in Russia, allowing them to anticipate that the Russian government would demand that GE build production capacity in the country rather than enter the market through exporting or licensing. In addition, GE's managers in Russia were better able to develop realistic performance expectations and make tough upfront decisions since experience in China and elsewhere warned them (1) that there would likely be increased short-term costs during the early years of start-up and (2) that if GE committed to the Russian market for the long term and aided the country's economic development it could eventually expect to be given the freedom to pursue profitable penetration of the Russian market.[8]

Likewise, different businesses can often use the same administrative and customer service infrastructure. For instance, an electric utility that diversifies into natural gas, water, appliance sales and repair services, and home security services can use the same customer data network, the same customer call centers and local offices, the same

Illustration Capsule 9.1

Related Diversification at L'Oréal, Johnson & Johnson, PepsiCo, and Darden Restaurants

See if you can identify the value chain relationships that make the businesses of the following companies related in competitively relevant ways. In particular, you should consider whether there are cross-business opportunities for (1) transferring skills/technology, (2) combining related value chain activities to achieve lower costs, (3) leveraging use of a well-respected brand name, and/or (4) establishing cross-business collaboration to create new resource strengths and capabilities.

L'ORÉAL

- Maybelline, Lancôme, Helena Rubenstein, Kiehl's, Garner, and Shu Uemura cosmetics.
- L'Oréal and Soft Sheen/Carson hair care products.
- Redken, Matrix, L'Oréal Professional, and Kerastase Paris professional hair care and skin care products.
- Ralph Lauren and Giorgio Armani fragrances.
- Biotherm skin care products.
- La Roche–Posay and Vichy Laboratories dermocosmetics.

JOHNSON & JOHNSON

- Baby products (powder, shampoo, oil, lotion).
- Band-Aids and other first-aid products.
- Women's health and personal care products (Stayfree, Carefree, Sure & Natural).
- Neutrogena and Aveeno skin care products.

- Nonprescription drugs (Tylenol, Motrin, Pepcid AC, Mylanta, Monistat).
- Prescription drugs.
- Prosthetic and other medical devices.
- Surgical and hospital products.
- Accuvue contact lenses.

PEPSICO

- Soft drinks (Pepsi, Diet Pepsi, Pepsi One, Mountain Dew, Mug, Slice).
- Fruit juices (Tropicana and Dole).
- Sports drinks (Gatorade).
- Other beverages (Aquafina bottled water, SoBe, Lipton ready-to-drink tea, Frappucino—in partnership with Starbucks, international sales of 7UP).
- Snack foods (Fritos, Lay's, Ruffles, Doritos, Tostitos, Santitas, Smart Food, Rold Gold pretzels, Chee-tos, Grandma's cookies, Sun Chips, Cracker Jack, Frito-Lay dips and salsas).
- Cereals, rice, and breakfast products (Quaker oatmeal, Cap'n Crunch, Life, Rice-A-Roni, Quaker rice cakes, Aunt Jemima mixes and syrups, Quaker grits).

DARDEN RESTAURANTS

- Olive Garden restaurant chain (Italian-themed).
- Red Lobster restaurant chain (seafood-themed).
- Bahama Breeze restaurant chain (Caribbean-themed).

Source: Company Web sites, annual reports, and 10-K reports.

billing and customer accounting systems, and the same customer service infrastructure to support all of its products and services.

   Illustration Capsule 9.1 lists the businesses of five companies that have pursued a strategy of related diversification.

Strategic Fit, Economies of Scope, and Competitive Advantage

What makes related diversification an attractive strategy is the opportunity to convert cross-business strategic fits into a competitive advantage over business rivals whose operations do not offer comparable strategic-fit benefits. The greater the relatedness among a diversified company's sister businesses, the bigger a company's window for converting strategic fits into competitive advantage via (1) skills transfer, (2) combining related value chain activities to achieve lower costs, (3) leveraging use of a well-respected brand name, and/or (4) cross-business collaboration to create new resource strengths and capabilities.

Economies of Scope: A Path to Competitive Advantage

One of the most important competitive advantages that a related diversification strategy can produce is lower costs than competitors. Related businesses often present opportunities to eliminate or reduce the costs of performing certain value chain activities; such cost savings are termed **economies of scope**—a concept distinct from *economies of scale*. Economies of *scale* are cost savings that accrue directly from a larger-sized operation; for example, unit costs may be lower in a large plant than in a small plant, lower in a large distribution center than in a small one, and lower for large-volume purchases of components than for small-volume purchases. Economies of *scope,* however, stem directly from cost-saving strategic fits along the value chains of related businesses. Such economies are open only to a multibusiness enterprise and are the result of a related diversification strategy that allows sister businesses to share technology, perform R&D together, use common manufacturing or distribution facilities, share a common sales force or distributor/dealer network, use the same established brand name, and/or share the same administrative infrastructure. *The greater the cross-business economies associated with cost-saving strategic fits, the greater the potential for a related diversification strategy to yield a competitive advantage based on lower costs than rivals.*

> **Core Concept**
> ***Economies of scope*** are cost reductions that flow from operating in multiple businesses; such economies stem directly from strategic fit efficiencies along the value chains of related businesses.

From Competitive Advantage to Added Profitability and Gains in Shareholder Value

The competitive advantage potential that flows from economies of scope and the capture of other strategic-fit benefits is what enables a company pursuing related diversification to achieve 1 + 1 = 3 financial performance and the hoped-for gains in shareholder value. The strategic and business logic is compelling: Capturing strategic fits along the value chains of its related businesses gives a diversified company a clear path to achieving competitive advantage over undiversified competitors and competitors whose own diversification efforts don't offer equivalent strategic-fit benefits.[9] Such competitive advantage potential provides a company with a dependable basis for earning profits and a return on investment that exceed what the company's businesses could earn as stand-alone enterprises. Converting the competitive advantage potential into greater profitability is what fuels 1 + 1 = 3 gains in shareholder value—the necessary outcome for satisfying the better-off test and proving the business merit of a company's diversification effort.

> **Core Concept**
> Diversifying into related businesses where competitively valuable strategic fit benefits can be captured puts sister businesses in position to perform better financially as part of the same company than they could have performed as independent enterprises, thus providing a clear avenue for boosting shareholder value.

There are three things to bear in mind here. One, capturing cross-business strategic fits via a strategy of related diversification builds shareholder value in ways that shareholders cannot undertake by simply owning a portfolio of stocks of companies in different industries. Two, the capture of cross-business strategic-fit benefits is possible only via a strategy of related diversification. Three, the benefits of cross-business strategic fits are not automatically realized when a company diversifies into related businesses; *the benefits materialize only after management has successfully pursued internal actions to capture them.*

Figure 9.3   **Unrelated Businesses Have Unrelated Value Chains and No Strategic Fits**

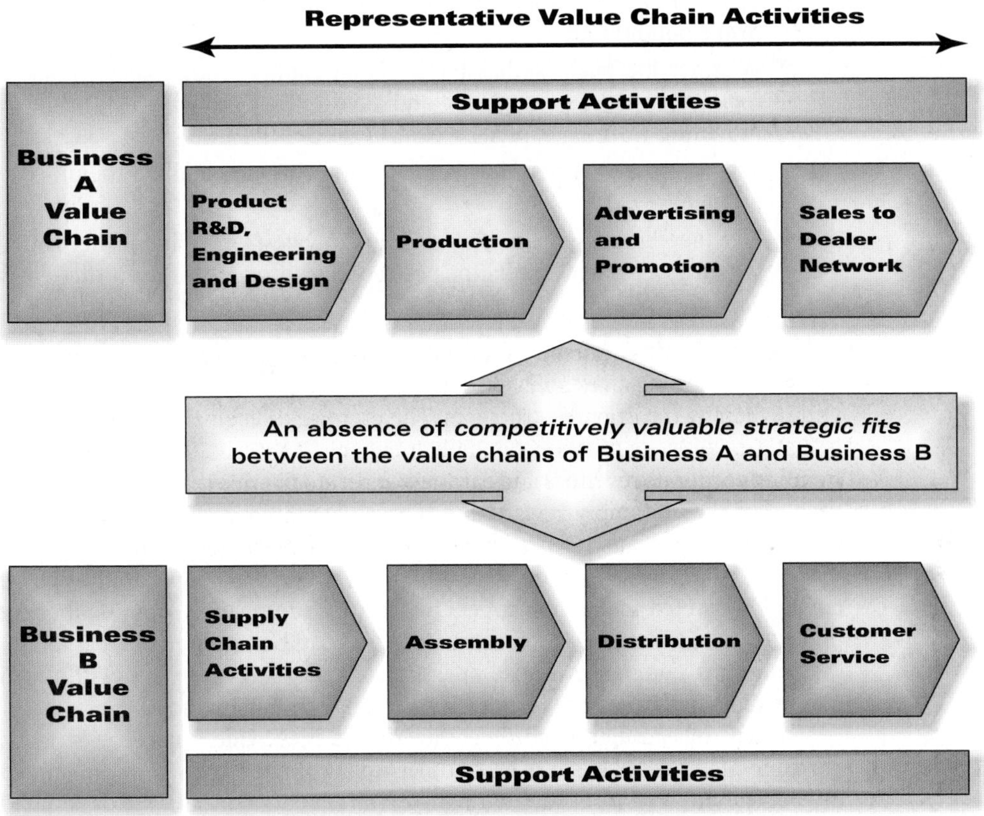

Representative Value Chain Activities

Business A Value Chain				
Support Activities				
	Product R&D, Engineering and Design	**Production**	**Advertising and Promotion**	**Sales to Dealer Network**

An absence of *competitively valuable strategic fits* between the value chains of Business A and Business B

Business B Value Chain				
	Supply Chain Activities	**Assembly**	**Distribution**	**Customer Service**
Support Activities				

THE CASE FOR DIVERSIFYING INTO UNRELATED BUSINESSES

An unrelated diversification strategy discounts the merits of pursuing cross-business strategic fits and, instead, focuses squarely on entering and operating businesses in industries that allow the company as a whole to grow its revenues and earnings. Companies that pursue a strategy of unrelated diversification generally exhibit a willingness to diversify into *any industry* where senior managers see *opportunity* to realize consistently good financial results—*the basic premise of unrelated diversification is that any company or business that can be acquired on good financial terms and that has satisfactory growth and earnings potential represents a good acquisition and a good business opportunity.* With a strategy of unrelated diversification, the emphasis is on satisfying the attractiveness and cost-of-entry tests and each business's prospects for good financial performance. As indicated in Figure 9.3, there's no deliberate effort to satisfy the better-off test in the sense of diversifying only into businesses having strategic fits with the firm's other businesses.

Thus, with an unrelated diversification strategy, company managers spend much time and effort screening acquisition candidates and evaluating the pros and cons or keeping or divesting existing businesses, using such criteria as:

- Whether the business can meet corporate targets for profitability and return on investment.

- Whether the business is in an industry with attractive growth potential.
- Whether the business is big enough to contribute *significantly* to the parent firm's bottom line.
- Whether the business has burdensome capital requirements (associated with replacing out-of-date plants and equipment, growing the business, and/or providing working capital).
- Whether the business is plagued with chronic union difficulties and labor problems.
- Whether there is industry vulnerability to recession, inflation, high interest rates, tough government regulations concerning product safety or the environment, and other potentially negative factors.

Companies that pursue unrelated diversification nearly always enter new businesses by acquiring an established company rather than by forming a start-up subsidiary within their own corporate structures. The premise of acquisition-minded corporations is that growth by acquisition can deliver enhanced shareholder value through upward-trending corporate revenues and earnings and a stock price that *on average* rises enough year after year to amply reward and please shareholders. Three types of acquisition candidates are usually of particular interest: (1) businesses that have bright growth prospects but are short on investment capital—cash-poor, opportunity-rich businesses are highly coveted acquisition targets for cash-rich companies scouting for good market opportunities; (2) undervalued companies that can be acquired at a bargain price; and (3) struggling companies whose operations can be turned around with the aid of the parent company's financial resources and managerial know-how.

A key issue in unrelated diversification is how wide a net to cast in building a portfolio of unrelated businesses. In other words, should a company pursuing unrelated diversification seek to have few or many unrelated businesses? How much business diversity can corporate executives successfully manage? A reasonable way to resolve the issue of how much diversification comes from answering two questions: "What is the least diversification it will take to achieve acceptable growth and profitability?" and "What is the most diversification that can be managed, given the complexity it adds?"[10] The optimal amount of diversification usually lies between these two extremes.

Illustration Capsule 9.2 lists the businesses of three companies that have pursued unrelated diversification. Such companies are frequently labeled *conglomerates* because their business interests range broadly across diverse industries.

The Merits of an Unrelated Diversification Strategy

A strategy of unrelated diversification has appeal from several angles:

1. Business risk is scattered over a set of truly *diverse* industries. In comparison to related diversification, unrelated diversification more closely approximates *pure* diversification of financial and business risk because the company's investments are spread over businesses whose technologies and value chain activities bear no close relationship and whose markets are largely disconnected.[11]

2. The company's financial resources can be employed to maximum advantage by (*a*) investing in *whatever industries* offer the best profit prospects (as opposed to considering only opportunities in industries with related value chain activities) and (*b*) diverting cash flows from company businesses with lower growth and profit prospects to acquiring and expanding businesses with higher growth and profit potentials.

Illustration Capsule 9.2

Unrelated Diversification at General Electric, United Technologies, American Standard, and Lancaster Colony

The defining characteristic of unrelated diversification is few competitively valuable cross-business relationships. Peruse the business group listings for General Electric, United Technologies, American Standard, and Lancaster Colony and see if you can confirm why these four companies have unrelated diversification strategies.

GENERAL ELECTRIC

- Advanced materials (engineering thermoplastics, silicon-based products and technology platforms, and fused quartz and ceramics)—revenues of $8.3 billion in 2004.
- Commercial and consumer finance (loans, operating leases, financing programs and financial services provided to corporations, retailers, and consumers in 38 countries)—revenues of $39.2 billion in 2004.
- Major appliances, lighting, and integrated industrial equipment, systems and services—revenues of $13.8 billion in 2004.
- Commercial insurance and reinsurance products and services for insurance companies, Fortune 1000 companies, self-insurers, health care providers and other groups—revenues of $23.1 billion in 2004.
- Jet engines for military and civil aircraft, freight and passenger locomotives, motorized systems for mining trucks and drills, and gas turbines for marine and industrial applications—revenues of $15.6 billion in 2004.
- Electric power generation equipment, power transformers, high-voltage breakers, distribution transformers and breakers, capacitors, relays, regulators, substation equipment, metering products—revenues of $17.3 billion in 2004.
- Medical imaging and information technologies, medical diagnostics, patient monitoring systems, disease research, drug discovery and biopharmaceuticals—revenues of $13.5 billion in 2004.
- NBC Universal—owns and operates the NBC television network, a Spanish-language network (Telemundo), several news and entertainment networks (CNBC, MSNBC, Bravo, Sci-Fi Channel, USA Network), Universal Studios, various television production operations, a group of television stations, and theme parks—revenues of $12.9 billion in 2004.
- Chemical treatment programs for water and industrial process systems; precision sensors; security and safety systems for intrusion and fire detection, access and

building control, video surveillance, explosives and drug detection; and real estate services—revenues of $3.4 billion in 2004.
- Equipment services, including Penske truck leasing; operating leases, loans, sales, and asset management services for owners of computer networks, trucks, trailers, railcars, construction equipment, and shipping containers—revenues of $8.5 billion in 2004.

UNITED TECHNOLOGIES

- Pratt & Whitney aircraft engines—2005 revenues of $9.3 billion.
- Carrier heating and air-conditioning equipment—2005 revenues of $12.5 billion.
- Otis elevators and escalators—2005 revenues of $9.6 billion.
- Sikorsky helicopters and Hamilton Sunstrand aerospace systems—2005 revenues of $7.2 billion.
- Chubb fire detection and security systems—2005 revenues of $4.3 billion.

AMERICAN STANDARD

- Trane and American Standard furnaces, heat pumps, and air conditioners—2005 revenues of $6.0 billion.
- American Standard, Ideal Standard, Standard, and Porcher lavatories, toilets, bath tubs, faucets, whirlpool baths, and shower basins—2005 revenues of $2.4 billion.
- Commercial and utility vehicle braking and control systems—2005 revenues of $1.8 billion.

LANCASTER COLONY

- Specialty food products: Cardini, Marzetti, Girard's, and Pheiffer salad dressings; Chatham Village croutons; New York Brand, Sister Schubert, and Mamma Bella frozen breads and rolls; Reames and Aunt Vi's frozen noodles and pastas; Inn Maid and Amish dry egg noodles; and Romanoff caviar—fiscal 2005 revenues of $674 million.
- Candles and glassware: Candle-lite candles; Indiana Glass and Fostoria drinkware and tabletop items; Colony giftware; and Brody floral containers—fiscal 2005 revenues of $234 million.
- Automotive products: Rubber Queen automotive floor mats; Dee Zee aluminum accessories and running boards for light trucks; Protecta truck bed mats; and assorted other truck accessories—fiscal 2005 revenues of $224 million.

Source: Company Web sites, annual reports, and 10-K reports.

3. To the extent that corporate managers are exceptionally astute at spotting bargain-priced companies with big upside profit potential, shareholder wealth can be enhanced by buying distressed businesses at a low price, turning their operations around fairly quickly with infusions of cash and managerial know-how supplied by the parent company, and then riding the crest of the profit increases generated by the newly acquired businesses.

4. Company profitability may prove somewhat more stable over the course of economic upswings and downswings because market conditions in all industries don't move upward or downward simultaneously—in a broadly diversified company, there's a chance that market downtrends in some of the company's businesses will be partially offset by cyclical upswings in its other businesses, thus producing somewhat less earnings volatility. (In actual practice, however, there's no convincing evidence that the consolidated profits of firms with unrelated diversification strategies are more stable or less subject to reversal in periods of recession and economic stress than the profits of firms with related diversification strategies.)

Unrelated diversification certainly merits consideration when a firm is trapped in or overly dependent on an endangered or unattractive industry, especially when it has no competitively valuable resources or capabilities it can transfer to an adjacent industry. A case can also be made for unrelated diversification when a company has a strong preference for spreading business risks widely and not restricting itself to investing in a family of closely related businesses.

Building Shareholder Value via Unrelated Diversification   Given the absence of cross-business strategic fits with which to capture added competitive advantage, the task of building shareholder value via unrelated diversification ultimately hinges on the business acumen of corporate executives. To succeed in using a strategy of unrelated diversification to produce companywide financial results above and beyond what the businesses could generate operating as stand-alone entities, corporate executives must:

- Do a superior job of diversifying into new businesses that can produce consistently good earnings and returns on investment (thereby satisfying the attractiveness test).

- Do an excellent job of negotiating favorable acquisition prices (thereby satisfying the cost-of-entry test).

- Do such a good job overseeing the firm's business subsidiaries and contributing to how they are managed—by providing expert problem-solving skills, creative strategy suggestions, and high caliber decision-making guidance to the heads of the various business subsidiaries—that the subsidiaries perform at a higher level than they would otherwise be able to do through the efforts of the business-unit heads alone (a possible way to satisfy the better-off test).

- Be shrewd in identifying when to shift resources out of businesses with dim profit prospects and into businesses with above-average prospects for growth and profitability.

- Be good at discerning when a business needs to be sold (because it is on the verge of confronting adverse industry and competitive conditions and probable declines in long-term profitability) and also finding buyers who will pay a price higher than the company's net investment in the business (so that the sale of divested businesses will result in capital gains for shareholders rather than capital losses).

To the extent that corporate executives are able to craft and execute a strategy of unrelated diversification that produces enough of the above outcomes to result in a stream of dividends and capital gains for stockholders greater than a 1 + 1 = 2 outcome, a case can be made that shareholder value has truly been enhanced.

The Drawbacks of Unrelated Diversification

Unrelated diversification strategies have two important negatives that undercut the pluses: demanding managerial requirements and limited competitive advantage potential.

Demanding Managerial Requirements Successfully managing a set of fundamentally different businesses operating in fundamentally different industry and competitive environments is an exceptionally challenging proposition for corporate-level managers. It is difficult because key executives at the corporate level, while perhaps having personally worked in one or two of the company's businesses, rarely have the time and expertise to be sufficiently familiar with all the circumstances surrounding each of the company's businesses to be in a position to give high-caliber guidance to business-level managers. Indeed, the greater the number of businesses a company is in and the more diverse they are, the harder it is for corporate managers to (1) stay abreast of what's happening in each industry and each subsidiary and thus judge whether a particular business has bright prospects or is headed for trouble, (2) know enough about the issues and problems facing each subsidiary to pick business-unit heads having the requisite combination of managerial skills and know-how, (3) be able to tell the difference between those strategic proposals of business-unit managers that are prudent and those that are risky or unlikely to succeed, and (4) know what to do if a business unit stumbles and its results suddenly head downhill.[12]

> **Core Concept**
> The two biggest drawbacks to unrelated diversification are the difficulties of competently managing many different businesses and being without the added source of competitive advantage that cross-business strategic fit provides.

In a company like General Electric (see Illustration Capsule 9.2) or Tyco International (which acquired over 1,000 companies during the 1990–2001 period), corporate executives are constantly scrambling to stay on top of fresh industry developments and the strategic progress and plans of each subsidiary, often depending on briefings by business-level managers for many of the details. As a rule, the more unrelated businesses that a company has diversified into, the more corporate executives are dependent on briefings from business unit heads and "managing by the numbers"—that is, keeping a close track on the financial and operating results of each subsidiary and assuming that the heads of the various subsidiaries have most everything under control so long as the latest key financial and operating measures look good. Managing by the numbers works if the heads of the various business units are quite capable and consistently meet their numbers. But the problem comes when things start to go awry in a business despite the best effort of business-unit managers and corporate management has to get deeply involved in turning around a business it does not know all that much about—as the former chairman of a Fortune 500 company advised, "Never acquire a business you don't know how to run." Because every business tends to encounter rough sledding, a good way to gauge the merits of acquiring a company in an unrelated industry is to ask, "If the business got into trouble, is corporate management likely to know how to bail it out?" When the answer is no (or even a qualified yes or maybe), growth via acquisition into unrelated businesses is a chancy strategy.[13] Just one or two unforeseen declines or big strategic mistakes (misjudging the importance of certain competitive forces or the impact of driving forces or key success factors, encountering unexpected problems in a newly acquired business, or being too optimistic about turning around a struggling subsidiary) can cause a precipitous drop in corporate earnings and crash the parent company's stock price.

Hence, competently overseeing a set of widely diverse businesses can turn out to be much harder than it sounds. In practice, comparatively few companies have proved up to the task. There are far more companies whose corporate executives have failed at delivering consistently good financial results with an unrelated diversification strategy than there are companies with corporate executives who have been successful.[14] It is simply very difficult for corporate executives to achieve $1 + 1 = 3$ gains in shareholder value based on their expertise in (*a*) picking which industries to diversify into and which companies in these industries to acquire, (*b*) shifting resources from low-performing businesses into high-performing businesses, and (*c*) giving high-caliber decision-making guidance to the general managers of their business subsidiaries. The odds are that the result of unrelated diversification will be $1 + 1 = 2$ or less.

> Relying solely on the expertise of corporate executives to wisely manage a set of unrelated businesses is *a much weaker foundation for enhancing shareholder value* than is a strategy of related diversification where corporate performance can be boosted by competitively valuable cross-business strategic fits.

Limited Competitive Advantage Potential   The second big negative is that *unrelated diversification offers no potential for competitive advantage beyond what each individual business can generate on its own.* Unlike a related diversification strategy, there are no cross-business strategic fits to draw on for reducing costs, beneficially transferring skills and technology, leveraging use of a powerful brand name, or collaborating to build mutually beneficial competitive capabilities and thereby *adding to any competitive advantage possessed by individual businesses.* Yes, a cash-rich corporate parent pursuing unrelated diversification can provide its subsidiaries with much-needed capital and maybe even the managerial know-how to help resolve problems in particular business units, but otherwise it has little to offer in the way of enhancing the competitive strength of its individual business units. *Without the competitive advantage potential of strategic fits, consolidated performance of an unrelated group of businesses stands to be little or no better than the sum of what the individual business units could achieve if they were independent.*

COMBINATION RELATED–UNRELATED DIVERSIFICATION STRATEGIES

There's nothing to preclude a company from diversifying into both related and unrelated businesses. Indeed, in actual practice the business makeup of diversified companies varies considerably. Some diversified companies are really *dominant-business enterprises*—one major "core" business accounts for 50 to 80 percent of total revenues and a collection of small related or unrelated businesses accounts for the remainder. Some diversified companies are *narrowly diversified* around a few (two to five) related or unrelated businesses. Others are *broadly diversified* around a wide-ranging collection of related businesses, unrelated businesses, or a mixture of both. And a number of multibusiness enterprises have diversified into unrelated areas but have a collection of related businesses within each area—thus giving them a business portfolio consisting of *several unrelated groups of related businesses.* There's ample room for companies to customize their diversification strategies to incorporate elements of both related and unrelated diversification, as may suit their own risk preferences and strategic vision.

Figure 9.4   **Identifying a Diversified Company's Strategy**

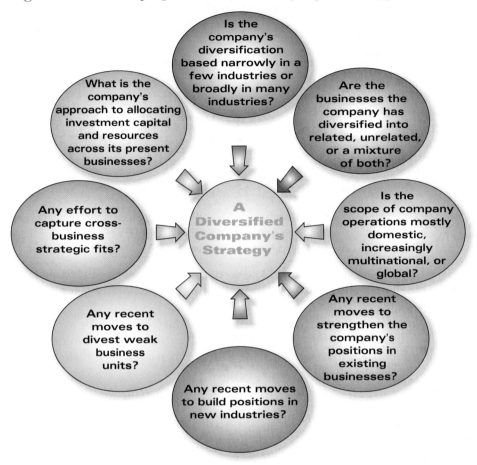

Figure 9.4 indicates what to look for in identifying the main elements of a company's diversification strategy. Having a clear fix on the company's current corporate strategy sets the stage for evaluating how good the strategy is and proposing strategic moves to boost the company's performance.

EVALUATING THE STRATEGY OF A DIVERSIFIED COMPANY

Strategic analysis of diversified companies builds on the concepts and methods used for single-business companies. But there are some additional aspects to consider and a couple of new analytical tools to master. The procedure for evaluating the pluses and minuses of a diversified company's strategy and deciding what actions to take to improve the company's performance involves six steps:

1. Assessing the attractiveness of the industries the company has diversified into, both individually and as a group.
2. Assessing the competitive strength of the company's business units and determining how many are strong contenders in their respective industries.

3. Checking the competitive advantage potential of cross-business strategic fits among the company's various business units.

4. Checking whether the firm's resources fit the requirements of its present business lineup.

5. Ranking the performance prospects of the businesses from best to worst and determining what the corporate parent's priority should be in allocating resources to its various businesses.

6. Crafting new strategic moves to improve overall corporate performance.

The core concepts and analytical techniques underlying each of these steps merit further discussion.

Step 1: Evaluating Industry Attractiveness

A principal consideration in evaluating a diversified company's business makeup and the caliber of its strategy is the attractiveness of the industries in which it has business operations. Answers to several questions are required:

1. *Does each industry the company has diversified into represent a good business for the company to be in?* Ideally, each industry in which the firm operates will pass the attractiveness test.

2. *Which of the company's industries are most attractive and which are least attractive?* Comparing the attractiveness of the industries and ranking them from most to least attractive is a prerequisite to wise allocation of corporate resources across the various businesses.

3. *How appealing is the whole group of industries in which the company has invested?* The answer to this question points to whether the group of industries holds promise for attractive growth and profitability. A company whose revenues and profits come chiefly from businesses in relatively unattractive industries probably needs to look at divesting businesses in unattractive industries and entering industries that qualify as highly attractive.

The more attractive the industries (both individually and as a group) a diversified company is in, the better its prospects for good long-term performance.

Calculating Industry Attractiveness Scores for Each Industry into Which the Company Has Diversified   A simple and reliable analytical tool involves calculating quantitative industry attractiveness scores, which can then be used to gauge each industry's attractiveness, rank the industries from most to least attractive, and make judgments about the attractiveness of all the industries as a group.

The following measures are typically used to gauge an industry's attractiveness:

- *Market size and projected growth rate*—Big industries are more attractive than small industries, and fast-growing industries tend to be more attractive than slow-growing industries, other things being equal.

- *The intensity of competition*—Industries where competitive pressures are relatively weak are more attractive than industries where competitive pressures are strong.

- *Emerging opportunities and threats*—Industries with promising opportunities and minimal threats on the near horizon are more attractive than industries with modest opportunities and imposing threats.

- *The presence of cross-industry strategic fits*—The more the industry's value chain and resource requirements match up well with the value chain activities of other industries in which the company has operations, the more attractive the industry is to a firm pursuing related diversification. However, cross-industry strategic fits may be of no consequence to a company committed to a strategy of unrelated diversification.

- *Resource requirements*—Industries having resource requirements within the company's reach are more attractive than industries where capital and other resource requirements could strain corporate financial resources and organizational capabilities.

- *Seasonal and cyclical factors*—Industries where buyer demand is relatively steady year-round and not unduly vulnerable to economic ups and downs tend to be more attractive than industries where there are wide swings in buyer demand within or across years. However, seasonality may be a plus for a company that is in several seasonal industries, if the seasonal highs in one industry correspond to the lows in another industry, thus helping even out monthly sales levels. Likewise, cyclical market demand in one industry can be attractive if its up-cycle runs counter to the market down-cycles in another industry where the company operates, thus helping reduce revenue and earnings volatility.

- *Social, political, regulatory, and environmental factors*—Industries with significant problems in such areas as consumer health, safety, or environmental pollution or that are subject to intense regulation are less attractive than industries where such problems are not burning issues.

- *Industry profitability*—Industries with healthy profit margins and high rates of return on investment are generally more attractive than industries where profits have historically been low or unstable.

- *Industry uncertainty and business risk*—Industries with less uncertainty on the horizon and lower overall business risk are more attractive than industries whose prospects for one reason or another are quite uncertain, especially when the industry has formidable resource requirements.

After settling on a set of attractiveness measures that suit a diversified company's circumstances, each attractiveness measure is assigned a weight reflecting its relative importance in determining an industry's attractiveness—it is weak methodology to assume that the various attractiveness measures are equally important. The intensity of competition in an industry should nearly always carry a high weight (say, 0.20 to 0.30). Strategic-fit considerations should be assigned a high weight in the case of companies with related diversification strategies; but, for companies with an unrelated diversification strategy, strategic fits with other industries may be given a low weight or even dropped from the list of attractiveness measures altogether. Seasonal and cyclical factors generally are assigned a low weight (or maybe even eliminated from the analysis) unless a company has diversified into industries strongly characterized by seasonal demand and/or heavy vulnerability to cyclical upswings and downswings. The importance weights must add up to 1.0.

Next, each industry is rated on each of the chosen industry attractiveness measures, using a rating scale of 1 to 10 (where a *high* rating signifies *high* attractiveness and a *low* rating signifies *low* attractiveness). *Keep in mind here that the more intensely competitive an industry is, the lower the attractiveness rating for that industry.* Likewise, the higher the capital and resource requirements associated with being in a particular industry, the lower the attractiveness rating. And an industry that is subject

Table 9.1   **Calculating Weighted Industry Attractiveness Scores**

Industry Attractiveness Measure	Importance Weight	Industry A Rating/ Score	Industry B Rating/ Score	Industry C Rating/ Score	Industry D Rating/ Score
Market size and projected growth rate	0.10	8/0.80	5/0.50	7/0.70	3/0.30
Intensity of competition	0.25	8/2.00	7/1.75	3/0.75	2/0.50
Emerging opportunities and threats	0.10	2/0.20	9/0.90	4/0.40	5/0.50
Cross-industry strategic fits	0.20	8/1.60	4/0.80	8/1.60	2/0.40
Resource requirements	0.10	9/0.90	7/0.70	10/1.00	5/0.50
Seasonal and cyclical influences	0.05	9/0.45	8/0.40	10/0.50	5/0.25
Societal, political, regulatory, and environmental factors	0.05	10/1.00	7/0.70	7/0.70	3/0.30
Industry profitability	0.10	5/0.50	10/1.00	3/0.30	3/0.30
Industry uncertainty and business risk	0.05	5/0.25	7/0.35	10/0.50	1/0.05
Sum of the assigned weights	1.00				
Overall industry attractiveness scores		**7.70**	**7.10**	**5.45**	**3.10**

Rating scale: 1 = Very unattractive to company; 10 = Very attractive to company.

to stringent pollution control regulations or that causes societal problems (like cigarettes or alcoholic beverages) should usually be given a low attractiveness rating. Weighted attractiveness scores are then calculated by multiplying the industry's rating on each measure by the corresponding weight. For example, a rating of 8 times a weight of 0.25 gives a weighted attractiveness score of 2.00. The sum of the weighted scores for all the attractiveness measures provides an overall industry attractiveness score. This procedure is illustrated in Table 9.1.

Interpreting the Industry Attractiveness Scores   Industries with a score much below 5.0 probably do not pass the attractiveness test. If a company's industry attractiveness scores are all above 5.0, it is probably fair to conclude that the group of industries the company operates in is attractive as a whole. But the group of industries takes on a decidedly lower degree of attractiveness as the number of industries with scores below 5.0 increases, especially if industries with low scores account for a sizable fraction of the company's revenues.

For a diversified company to be a strong performer, a substantial portion of its revenues and profits must come from business units with relatively high attractiveness scores. It is particularly important that a diversified company's principal businesses be in industries with a good outlook for growth and above-average profitability. Having a big fraction of the company's revenues and profits come from industries with slow growth, low profitability, or intense competition tends to drag overall company performance down. Business units in the least attractive industries are potential candidates for divestiture, unless they are positioned strongly enough to overcome the unattractive aspects of their industry environments or they are a strategically important component of the company's business makeup.

The Difficulties of Calculating Industry Attractiveness Scores   There are two hurdles to calculating industry attractiveness scores. One is deciding on appropriate weights for the industry attractiveness measures. Not only may different analysts have different views about which weights are appropriate for the different attractiveness measures but also different weightings may be appropriate for different companies—based on their strategies, performance targets, and financial circumstances. For instance, placing a low weight on industry resource requirements may be justifiable for a cash-rich company, whereas a high weight may be more appropriate for a financially strapped company. The second hurdle is gaining sufficient command of the industry to assign accurate and objective ratings. Generally, a company can come up with the statistical data needed to compare its industries on such factors as market size, growth rate, seasonal and cyclical influences, and industry profitability. Cross-industry fits and resource requirements are also fairly easy to judge. But the attractiveness measure where judgment weighs most heavily is that of intensity of competition. It is not always easy to conclude whether competition in one industry is stronger or weaker than in another industry because of the different types of competitive influences that prevail and the differences in their relative importance. In the event that the available information is too skimpy to confidently assign a rating value to an industry on a particular attractiveness measure, then it is usually best to use a score of 5, which avoids biasing the overall attractiveness score either up or down.

But despite the hurdles, calculating industry attractiveness scores is a systematic and reasonably reliable method for ranking a diversified company's industries from most to least attractive—numbers like those shown for the four industries in Table 9.1 help pin down the basis for judging which industries are more attractive and to what degree.

Step 2: Evaluating Business-Unit Competitive Strength

The second step in evaluating a diversified company is to appraise how strongly positioned each of its business units are in their respective industry. Doing an appraisal of each business unit's strength and competitive position in its industry not only reveals its chances for industry success but also provides a basis for ranking the units from competitively strongest to competitively weakest and sizing up the competitive strength of all the business units as a group.

Calculating Competitive Strength Scores for Each Business Unit   Quantitative measures of each business unit's competitive strength can be calculated using a procedure similar to that for measuring industry attractiveness. The following factors are using in quantifying the competitive strengths of a diversified company's business subsidiaries:

- *Relative market share*—A business unit's *relative market share* is defined as the ratio of its market share to the market share held by the largest rival firm in the industry, with market share measured in unit volume, not dollars. For instance, if business A has a market-leading share of 40 percent and its largest rival has 30 percent, A's relative market share is 1.33. (Note that only business units that are market share leaders in their respective industries can have relative market shares greater then 1.0.) If business B has a 15 percent market share and B's largest rival has 30 percent, B's relative market share is 0.5. *The further below 1.0 a business unit's relative market share is, the weaker its competitive strength and market position vis-à-vis rivals.* A 10 percent market share, for example, does not signal much competitive strength if the leader's share is 50 percent

> Using relative market share to measure competitive strength is analytically superior to using straight-percentage market share.

(a 0.20 relative market share), but a 10 percent share is actually quite strong if the leader's share is only 12 percent (a 0.83 relative market share)—this is why a company's relative market share is a better measure of competitive strength than a company's market share based on either dollars or unit volume.

- *Costs relative to competitors' costs*—Business units that have low costs relative to key competitors' costs tend to be more strongly positioned in their industries than business units struggling to maintain cost parity with major rivals. Assuming that the prices charged by industry rivals are about the same, there's reason to expect that business units with higher relative market shares have lower unit costs than competitors with lower relative market shares because their greater unit sales volumes offer the possibility of economies from larger-scale operations and the benefits of any experience/learning curve effects. Another indicator of low cost can be a business unit's supply chain management capabilities. The only time when a business unit's competitive strength may not be undermined by having higher costs than rivals is when it has incurred the higher costs to strongly differentiate its product offering and its customers are willing to pay premium prices for the differentiating features.

- *Ability to match or beat rivals on key product attributes*—A company's competitiveness depends in part on being able to satisfy buyer expectations with regard to features, product performance, reliability, service, and other important attributes.

- *Ability to benefit from strategic fits with sister businesses*—Strategic fits with other businesses within the company enhance a business unit's competitive strength and may provide a competitive edge.

- *Ability to exercise bargaining leverage with key suppliers or customers*—Having bargaining leverage signals competitive strength and can be a source of competitive advantage.

- *Caliber of alliances and collaborative partnerships with suppliers and/or buyers*—Well-functioning alliances and partnerships may signal a potential competitive advantage vis-à-vis rivals and thus add to a business's competitive strength. Alliances with key suppliers are often the basis for competitive strength in supply chain management.

- *Brand image and reputation*—A strong brand name is a valuable competitive asset in most industries.

- *Competitively valuable capabilities*—Business units recognized for their technological leadership, product innovation, or marketing prowess are usually strong competitors in their industry. Skills in supply chain management can generate valuable cost or product differentiation advantages. So can unique production capabilities. Sometimes a company's business units gain competitive strength because of their knowledge of customers and markets and/or their proven managerial capabilities. *An important thing to look for here is how well a business unit's competitive assets match industry key success factors.* The more a business unit's resource strengths and competitive capabilities match the industry's key success factors, the stronger its competitive position tends to be.

- *Profitability relative to competitors*—Business units that consistently earn above-average returns on investment and have bigger profit margins than their rivals usually have stronger competitive positions. Moreover, above-average profitability signals competitive advantage, while below-average profitability usually denotes competitive disadvantage.

Table 9.2   **Calculating Weighted Competitive Strength Scores for a Diversified Company's Business Units**

Competitive Strength Measure	Importance Weight	Business A in Industry A Rating/ Score	Business B in Industry B Rating/ Score	Business C in Industry C Rating/ Score	Business D in Industry D Rating/ Score
Relative market share	0.15	10/1.50	1/0.15	6/0.90	2/0.30
Costs relative to competitors' costs	0.20	7/1.40	2/0.40	5/1.00	3/0.60
Ability to match or beat rivals on key product attributes	0.05	9/0.45	4/0.20	8/0.40	4/0.20
Ability to benefit from strategic fits with sister businesses	0.20	8/1.60	4/0.80	8/0.80	2/0.60
Bargaining leverage with suppliers/ buyers; caliber of alliances	0.05	9/0.90	3/0.30	6/0.30	2/0.10
Brand image and reputation	0.10	9/0.90	2/0.20	7/0.70	5/0.50
Competitively valuable capabilities	0.15	7/1.05	2/0.20	5/0.75	3/0.45
Profitability relative to competitors	0.10	5/0.50	1/0.10	4/0.40	4/0.40
Sum of the assigned weights	1.00				
Overall industry attractiveness scores		**8.30**	**2.35**	**5.25**	**3.15**

Rating scale: 1 = Very weak; 10 = Very strong.

After settling on a set of competitive strength measures that are well matched to the circumstances of the various business units, weights indicating each measure's importance need to be assigned. A case can be made for using different weights for different business units whenever the importance of the strength measures differs significantly from business to business, but otherwise it is simpler just to go with a single set of weights and avoid the added complication of multiple weights. As before, the importance weights must add up to 1.0. Each business unit is then rated on each of the chosen strength measures, using a rating scale of 1 to 10 (where a *high* rating signifies competitive *strength* and a *low* rating signifies competitive *weakness*). In the event that the available information is too skimpy to confidently assign a rating value to a business unit on a particular strength measure, then it is usually best to use a score of 5, which avoids biasing the overall score either up or down. Weighted strength ratings are calculated by multiplying the business unit's rating on each strength measure by the assigned weight. For example, a strength score of 6 times a weight of 0.15 gives a weighted strength rating of 0.90. The sum of weighted ratings across all the strength measures provides a quantitative measure of a business unit's overall market strength and competitive standing. Table 9.2 provides sample calculations of competitive strength ratings for four businesses.

Interpreting the Competitive Strength Scores   Business units with competitive strength ratings above 6.7 (on a scale of 1 to 10) are strong market contenders in their industries. Businesses with ratings in the 3.3 to 6.7 range have moderate competitive strength vis-à-vis rivals. Businesses with ratings below 3.3 are in competitively weak market positions. If a diversified company's business units all have competitive strength scores above 5.0, it is fair to conclude that its business units are all fairly strong market contenders in their respective industries. But as the number of business units with scores below 5.0 increases, there's reason to question whether the company can perform well with so many businesses in relatively weak competitive positions. This concern takes on even more importance when business units with low scores account for a sizable fraction of the company's revenues.

Using a Nine-Cell Matrix to Simultaneously Portray Industry Attractiveness and Competitive Strength   The industry attractiveness and competitive strength scores can be used to portray the strategic positions of each business in a diversified company. Industry attractiveness is plotted on the vertical axis, and competitive strength on the horizontal axis. A nine-cell grid emerges from dividing the vertical axis into three regions (high, medium, and low attractiveness) and the horizontal axis into three regions (strong, average, and weak competitive strength). As shown in Figure 9.5, high attractiveness is associated with scores of 6.7 or greater on a rating scale of 1 to 10, medium attractiveness to scores of 3.3 to 6.7, and low attractiveness to scores below 3.3. Likewise, high competitive strength is defined as a score greater than 6.7, average strength as scores of 3.3 to 6.7, and low strength as scores below 3.3. *Each business unit is plotted on the nine-cell matrix according to its overall attractiveness score and strength score, and then shown as a bubble.* The size of each bubble is scaled to what percentage of revenues the business generates relative to total corporate revenues. The bubbles in Figure 9.5 were located on the grid using the four industry attractiveness scores from Table 9.1 and the strength scores for the four business units in Table 9.2.

The locations of the business units on the attractiveness–strength matrix provide valuable guidance in deploying corporate resources to the various business units. In general, *a diversified company's prospects for good overall performance are enhanced by concentrating corporate resources and strategic attention on those business units having the greatest competitive strength and positioned in highly attractive industries*—specifically, businesses in the three cells in the upper left portion of the attractiveness–strength matrix, where industry attractiveness and competitive strength/market position are both favorable. The general strategic prescription for businesses falling in these three cells (for instance, business A in Figure 9.5) is "grow and build," with businesses in the high–strong cell standing first in line for resource allocations by the corporate parent.

Next in priority come businesses positioned in the three diagonal cells stretching from the lower left to the upper right (businesses B and C in Figure 9.5). Such businesses usually merit medium or intermediate priority in the parent's resource allocation ranking. However, some businesses in the medium-priority diagonal cells may have brighter or dimmer prospects than others. For example, a small business in the upper right cell of the matrix (like business B), despite being in a highly attractive industry, may occupy too weak a competitive position in its industry to justify the investment and resources needed to turn it into a strong market contender and shift its position leftward in the matrix over time. If, however, a business in the upper right cell has attractive opportunities for rapid growth and a good potential for winning a much stronger market position over time, it may merit a high claim on the corporate parent's resource allocation ranking and be given the capital it needs to pursue a grow-and-build strategy–the strategic objective here would be to move the business leftward in the attractiveness–strength matrix over time.

Businesses in the three cells in the lower right corner of the matrix (like business D in Figure 9.5) typically are weak performers and have the lowest claim on corporate resources. Most such businesses are good candidates for being divested (sold to other companies) or else managed in a manner calculated to squeeze out the maximum cash flows from operations—the cash flows from low-performing/low-potential businesses

Figure 9.5   **A Nine-Cell Industry Attractiveness–Competitive Strength Matrix**

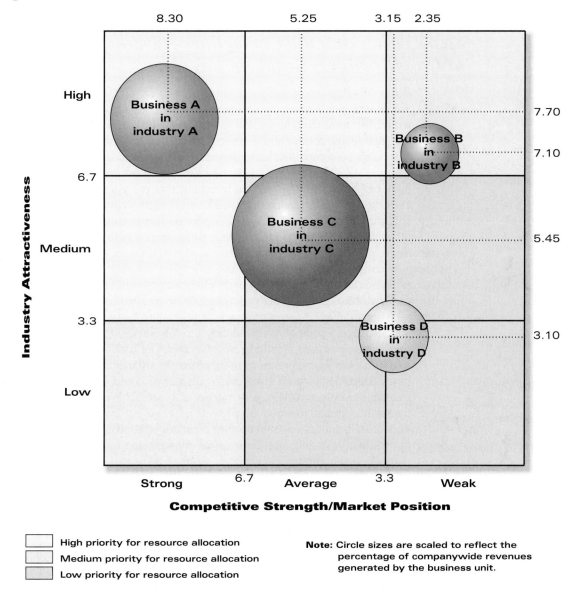

can then be diverted to financing expansion of business units with greater market opportunities. In exceptional cases where a business located in the three lower right cells is nonetheless fairly profitable (which it might be if it is in the low–average cell) or has the potential for good earnings and return on investment, the business merits retention and the allocation of sufficient resources to achieve better performance.

The nine-cell attractiveness–strength matrix provides clear, strong logic for why a diversified company needs to consider both industry attractiveness and business strength in allocating resources and investment capital to its different businesses. A good case can be made for concentrating resources in those businesses that enjoy higher degrees of attractiveness and competitive strength, being very selective in making investments in businesses with intermediate positions on the grid, and withdrawing resources from businesses that are lower in attractiveness and strength unless they offer exceptional profit or cash flow potential.

Step 3: Checking the Competitive Advantage Potential of Cross-Business Strategic Fits

Core Concept
A company's related diversification strategy derives its power in large part from the presence of competitively valuable strategic fits among its businesses.

While this step can be bypassed for diversified companies whose businesses are all unrelated (since, by design, no strategic fits are present), a high potential for converting strategic fits into competitive advantage is central to concluding just how good a company's related diversification strategy is. Checking the competitive advantage potential of cross-business strategic fits involves searching for and evaluating how much benefit a diversified company can gain from value chain matchups that present (1) opportunities to combine the performance of certain activities, thereby reducing costs and capturing economies of scope; (2) opportunities to transfer skills, technology, or intellectual capital from one business to another, thereby leveraging use of existing resources; (3) opportunities to share use of a well-respected brand name; and (4) opportunities for sister businesses to collaborate in creating valuable new competitive capabilities (such as enhanced supply chain management capabilities, quicker first-to-market capabilities, or greater product innovation capabilities).

Figure 9.6 illustrates the process of comparing the value chains of sister businesses and identifying competitively valuable cross-business strategic fits. *But more than just strategic fit identification is needed. The real test is what competitive value can be generated from these fits.* To what extent can cost savings be realized? How much competitive value will come from cross-business transfer of skills, technology, or intellectual capital? Will transferring a potent brand name to the products of sister businesses grow sales significantly? Will cross-business collaboration to create or strengthen competitive capabilities lead to significant gains in the marketplace or in financial performance? Absent significant strategic fits and dedicated company efforts to capture the benefits, one has to be skeptical about the potential for a diversified company's businesses to perform better together than apart.

Core Concept
The greater the value of cross-business strategic fits in enhancing a company's performance in the marketplace or on the bottom line, the more competitively powerful is its strategy of related diversification.

Step 4: Checking for Resource Fit

Core Concept
Sister businesses possess *resource fit* when they add to a company's overall resource strengths and when a company has adequate resources to support their requirements.

The businesses in a diversified company's lineup need to exhibit good **resource fit.** Resource fit exists when (1) businesses add to a company's overall resource strengths and (2) a company has adequate resources to support its entire group of businesses without spreading itself too thin. One important dimension of resource fit concerns whether a diversified company can generate the internal cash flows sufficient to fund the capital requirements of its businesses, pay its dividends, meet its debt obligations, and otherwise remain financially healthy.

Financial Resource Fits: Cash Cows versus Cash Hogs   Different businesses have different cash flow and investment characteristics. For example, business units in rapidly growing industries are often **cash hogs**—so labeled because the cash flows they are able to generate from internal operations aren't big enough to fund their expansion. To keep pace with rising buyer demand, rapid-growth businesses frequently need sizable annual capital investments—for new facilities and equipment, for

Figure 9.6 **Identifying the Competitive Advantage Potential of Cross-Business Strategic Fits**

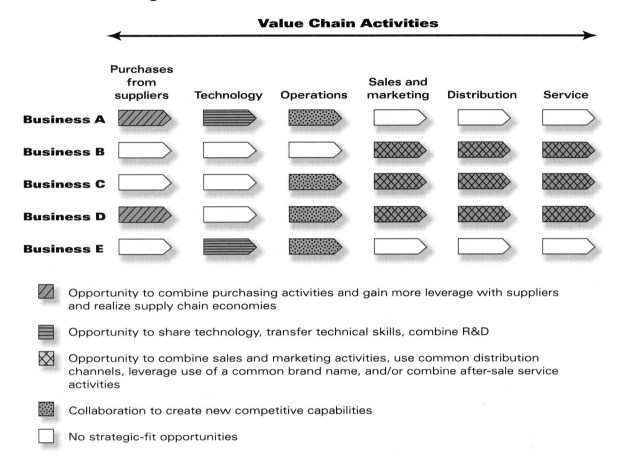

Opportunity to combine purchasing activities and gain more leverage with suppliers and realize supply chain economies

Opportunity to share technology, transfer technical skills, combine R&D

Opportunity to combine sales and marketing activities, use common distribution channels, leverage use of a common brand name, and/or combine after-sale service activities

Collaboration to create new competitive capabilities

No strategic-fit opportunities

new product development or technology improvements, and for additional working capital to support inventory expansion and a larger base of operations. A business in a fast-growing industry becomes an even bigger cash hog when it has a relatively low market share and is pursuing a strategy to become an industry leader. Because a cash hog's financial resources must be provided by the corporate parent, corporate managers have to decide whether it makes good financial and strategic sense to keep pouring new money into a business that continually needs cash infusions.

In contrast, business units with leading market positions in mature industries may, however, be **cash cows**—businesses that generate substantial cash surpluses over what is needed to adequately fund their operations. Market leaders in slow-growth industries often generate sizable positive cash flows *over and above what is needed for growth and reinvestment* because their industry-leading positions tend to give them the sales volumes and reputation to earn attractive profits and because the slow-growth nature of their industry often entails relatively modest annual investment requirements. Cash cows, though not always attractive from a growth standpoint, are valuable businesses from a financial resource perspective. The surplus cash flows they generate can be used to pay corporate dividends, finance acquisitions, and provide

> **Core Concept**
> A *cash hog* generates cash flows that are too small to fully fund its operations and growth; a cash hog requires cash infusions to provide additional working capital and finance new capital investment.

funds for investing in the company's promising cash hogs. It makes good financial and strategic sense for diversified companies to keep cash cows in healthy condition, fortifying and defending their market position so as to preserve their cash-generating capability over the long term and thereby have an ongoing source of financial resources to deploy elsewhere. The cigarette business is one of the world's biggest cash cows. General Electric, whose business lineup is shown in Illustration Capsule 9.2, considers that its advanced materials, equipment services, and appliance and lighting businesses are cash cows.

Viewing a diversified group of businesses as a collection of cash flows and cash requirements (present and future) is a major step forward in understanding what the financial ramifications of diversification are and why having businesses with good financial resource fit is so important. For instance, *a diversified company's businesses exhibit good financial resource fit when the excess cash generated by its cash cows is sufficient to fund the investment requirements of promising cash hogs.* Ideally, investing in promising cash hog businesses over time results in growing the hogs into self-supporting *star businesses* that have strong or market-leading competitive positions in attractive, high-growth markets and high levels of profitability. Star businesses are often the cash cows of the future—when the markets of star businesses begin to mature and their growth slows, their competitive strength should produce self-generated cash flows more than sufficient to cover their investment needs. The "success sequence" is thus cash hog to young star (but perhaps still a cash hog) to self-supporting star to cash cow.

If, however, a cash hog has questionable promise (either because of low industry attractiveness or a weak competitive position), then it becomes a logical candidate for divestiture. Pursuing an aggressive invest-and-expand strategy for a cash hog with an uncertain future seldom makes sense because it requires the corporate parent to keep pumping more capital into the business with only a dim hope of eventually turning the cash hog into a future star and realizing a good return on its investments. Such financially draining businesses fail the resource fit test because they strain the corporate parent's ability to adequately fund its other businesses. Divesting a cash hog is usually the best alternative unless (1) it has valuable strategic fits with other business units or (2) the capital infusions needed from the corporate parent are modest relative to the funds available and there's a decent chance of growing the business into a solid bottom-line contributor yielding a good return on invested capital.

Other Tests of Resource Fit   Aside from cash flow considerations, there are four other factors to consider in determining whether the businesses comprising a diversified company's portfolio exhibit good resource fit:

- *Does the business adequately contribute to achieving companywide performance targets?* A business has good financial fit when it contributes to the achievement of corporate performance objectives (growth in earnings per share, above-average return on investment, recognition as an industry leader, etc.) and when it materially enhances shareholder value via helping drive increases in the company's stock price. A business exhibits poor financial fit if it soaks up a disproportionate share of the company's financial resources, makes subpar or inconsistent bottom-line contributions, is unduly risky and failure would jeopardize the entire enterprise, or remains too small to make a material earnings contribution even though it performs well.

- *Does the company have adequate financial strength to fund its different businesses and maintain a healthy credit rating?* A diversified company's strategy fails the resource fit test when its financial resources are stretched across so many businesses that its credit rating is impaired. Severe financial strain sometimes occurs when a company borrows so heavily to finance new acquisitions that it has to trim way back on capital expenditures for existing businesses and use the big majority of its financial resources to meet interest obligations and to pay down debt. Time Warner, Royal Ahold, and AT&T, for example, have found themselves so financially overextended that they have had to sell off some of their business units to raise the money to pay down burdensome debt obligations and continue to fund essential capital expenditures for the remaining businesses.

- *Does the company have or can it develop the specific resource strengths and competitive capabilities needed to be successful in each of its businesses?*[15] Sometimes the resource strengths a company has accumulated in its core or mainstay business prove to be a poor match with the key success factors and competitive capabilities needed to succeed in one or more businesses it has diversified into. For instance, BTR, a multibusiness company in Great Britain, discovered that the company's resources and managerial skills were quite well suited for parenting industrial manufacturing businesses but not for parenting its distribution businesses (National Tyre Services and Texas-based Summers Group); as a consequence, BTR decided to divest its distribution businesses and focus exclusively on diversifying around small industrial manufacturing.[16] One company with businesses in restaurants and retailing decided that its resource capabilities in site selection, controlling operating costs, management selection and training, and supply chain logistics would enable it to succeed in the hotel business and in property management; but what management missed was that these businesses had some significantly different key success factors—namely, skills in controlling property development costs, maintaining low overheads, product branding (hotels), and ability to recruit a sufficient volume of business to maintain high levels of facility use.[17] Thus, a mismatch between the company's resource strengths and the key success factors in a particular business can be serious enough to warrant divesting an existing business or not acquiring a new business. In contrast, when a company's resources and capabilities are a good match with the key success factors of industries it is not presently in, it makes sense to take a hard look at acquiring companies in these industries and expanding the company's business lineup.

- *Are recently acquired businesses acting to strengthen a company's resource base and competitive capabilities or are they causing its competitive and managerial resources to be stretched too thin?* A diversified company has to guard against overtaxing its resource strengths, a condition that can arise when (1) it goes on an acquisition spree and management is called on to assimilate and oversee many new businesses very quickly or (2) when it lacks sufficient resource depth to do a creditable job of transferring skills and competences from one of its businesses to another (especially, a large acquisition or several lesser ones). The broader the diversification, the greater the concern about whether the company has sufficient managerial depth to cope with the diverse range of operating problems its wide business lineup presents. And the more a company's diversification strategy is tied to transferring its existing know-how or technologies to new businesses, the more it has to develop a big enough and deep enough resource pool to supply these businesses with sufficient capability to create competitive advantage.[18] Otherwise its strengths end up being thinly spread across many businesses and the opportunity for competitive advantage slips through the cracks.

A Cautionary Note About Transferring Resources from One Business to Another   Just because a company has hit a home run in one business doesn't mean it can easily enter a new business with similar resource requirements and hit a second home run.[19] Noted British retailer Marks & Spencer, despite possessing a range of impressive resource capabilities (ability to choose excellent store locations, having a supply chain that gives it both low costs and high merchandise quality, loyal employees, an excellent reputation with consumers, and strong management expertise) that have made it one of Britain's premier retailers for 100 years, has failed repeatedly in its efforts to diversify into department store retailing in the United States. Even though Philip Morris (now named Altria) had built powerful consumer marketing capabilities in its cigarette and beer businesses, it floundered in soft drinks and ended up divesting its acquisition of 7UP after several frustrating years of competing against strongly entrenched and resource-capable rivals like Coca-Cola and PepsiCo. Then in 2002 it decided to divest its Miller Brewing business—despite its long-standing marketing successes in cigarettes and in its Kraft Foods subsidiary—because it was unable to grow Miller's market share in head-to-head competition against the considerable marketing prowess of Anheuser-Busch.

Step 5: Ranking the Performance Prospects of Business Units and Assigning a Priority for Resource Allocation

Once a diversified company's strategy has been evaluated from the perspective of industry attractiveness, competitive strength, strategic fit, and resource fit, the next step is to rank the performance prospects of the businesses from best to worst and determine which businesses merit top priority for resource support and new capital investments by the corporate parent.

The most important considerations in judging business-unit performance are sales growth, profit growth, contribution to company earnings, and return on capital invested in the business. Sometimes cash flow is a big consideration. Information on each business's past performance can be gleaned from a company's financial records. While past performance is not necessarily a good predictor of future performance, it does signal whether a business already has good-to-excellent performance or has problems to overcome.

Furthermore, the industry attractiveness/business strength evaluations provide a solid basis for judging a business's prospects. Normally, strong business units in attractive industries have significantly better prospects than weak businesses in unattractive industries. And, normally, the revenue and earnings outlook for businesses in fast-growing industries is better than for businesses in slow-growing industries—one important exception is when a business in a slow-growing industry has the competitive strength to draw sales and market share away from its rivals and thus achieve much faster growth than the industry as whole. As a rule, the prior analyses, taken together, signal which business units are likely to be strong performers on the road ahead and which are likely to be laggards. And it is a short step from ranking the prospects of business units to drawing conclusions about whether the company as a whole is capable of strong, mediocre, or weak performance in upcoming years.

Figure 9.7   **The Chief Strategic and Financial Options for Allocating a Diversified Company's Financial Resources**

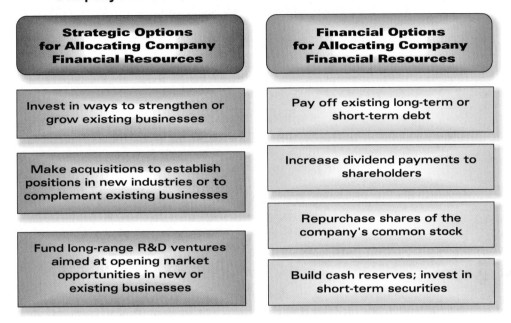

The rankings of future performance generally determine what priority the corporate parent should give to each business in terms of resource allocation. The task here is to decide which business units should have top priority for corporate resource support and new capital investment and which should carry the lowest priority. *Business subsidiaries with the brightest profit and growth prospects and solid strategic and resource fits generally should head the list for corporate resource support.* More specifically, corporate executives need to consider whether and how corporate resources can be used to enhance the competitiveness of particular business units. And they must be diligent in steering resources out of low-opportunity areas and into high-opportunity areas. Divesting marginal businesses is one of the best ways of freeing unproductive assets for redeployment. Surplus funds from cash cows also add to the corporate treasury.

Figure 9.7 shows the chief strategic and financial options for allocating a diversified company's financial resources. Ideally, a company will have enough funds to do what is needed, both strategically and financially. If not, strategic uses of corporate resources should usually take precedence unless there is a compelling reason to strengthen the firm's balance sheet or divert financial resources to pacify shareholders.

Step 6: Crafting New Strategic Moves to Improve Overall Corporate Performance

The diagnosis and conclusions flowing from the five preceding analytical steps set the agenda for crafting strategic moves to improve a diversified company's overall performance. The strategic options boil down to five broad categories of actions:

1. Sticking closely with the existing business lineup and pursuing the opportunities these businesses present.

2. Broadening the company's business scope by making new acquisitions in new industries.

3. Divesting certain businesses and retrenching to a narrower base of business operations.

4. Restructuring the company's business lineup and putting a whole new face on the company's business makeup.

5. Pursuing multinational diversification and striving to globalize the operations of several of the company's business units.

The option of sticking with the current business lineup makes sense when the company's present businesses offer attractive growth opportunities and can be counted on to generate good earnings and cash flows. As long as the company's set of existing businesses puts it in good position for the future and these businesses have good strategic and/or resource fits, then rocking the boat with major changes in the company's business mix is usually unnecessary. Corporate executives can concentrate their attention on getting the best performance from each of its businesses, steering corporate resources into those areas of greatest potential and profitability. The specifics of "what to do" to wring better performance from the present business lineup have to be dictated by each business's circumstances and the preceding analysis of the corporate parent's diversification strategy.

However, in the event that corporate executives are not entirely satisfied with the opportunities they see in the company's present set of businesses and conclude that changes in the company's direction and business makeup are in order, they can opt for any of the four other strategic alternatives listed above. These options are discussed in the following section.

AFTER A COMPANY DIVERSIFIES: THE FOUR MAIN STRATEGY ALTERNATIVES

Diversifying is by no means the final chapter in the evolution of a company's strategy. Once a company has diversified into a collection of related or unrelated businesses and concludes that some overhaul is needed in the company's present lineup and diversification strategy, there are four main strategic paths it can pursue (see Figure 9.8). To more fully understand the strategic issues corporate managers face in the ongoing process of managing a diversified group of businesses, we need to take a brief look at the central thrust of each of the four postdiversification strategy alternatives.

Strategies to Broaden a Diversified Company's Business Base

Diversified companies sometimes find it desirable to build positions in new industries, whether related or unrelated. There are several motivating factors. One is sluggish growth that makes the potential revenue and profit boost of a newly acquired business look attractive. A second is vulnerability to seasonal or recessionary influences or to threats from emerging new technologies. A third is the potential for transferring resources and capabilities to other related or complementary businesses. A fourth is rapidly changing conditions in one or more of a company's core businesses brought on by technological, legislative, or new product innovations that alter buyer requirements and preferences. For instance, the passage of legislation in the United States allowing

Figure 9.8 **A Company's Four Main Strategic Alternatives After It Diversifies**

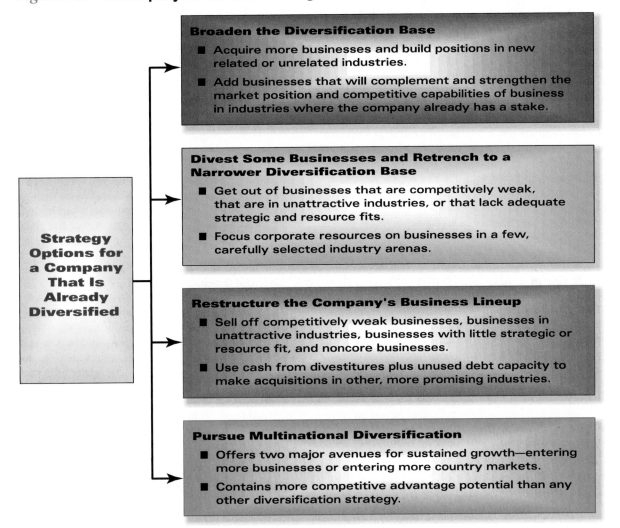

banks, insurance companies, and stock brokerages to enter each other's businesses spurred a raft of acquisitions and mergers to create full-service financial enterprises capable of meeting the multiple financial needs of customers. Citigroup, already the largest U.S. bank, with a global banking franchise, acquired Salomon Smith Barney to position itself in the investment banking and brokerage business and acquired insurance giant Travelers Group to enable it to offer customers insurance products.

A fifth, and often very important, motivating factor for adding new businesses is to complement and strengthen the market position and competitive capabilities of one or more of its present businesses. Procter & Gamble's recent acquisition of Gillette strengthened and extended P&G's reach into personal care and household products—Gillette's businesses included Oral-B toothbrushes, Gillette razors and razor blades, Duracell batteries, Braun shavers and small appliances (coffeemakers, mixers, hair dryers, and electric toothbrushes), and toiletries (Right Guard, Foamy, Soft & Dry, White Rain, and Dry Idea). Unilever, a leading maker of food and personal care products, expanded its business lineup by acquiring SlimFast, Ben & Jerry's Homemade,

Illustration Capsule 9.3

Managing Diversification at Johnson & Johnson: The Benefits of Cross-Business Strategic Fits

Johnson & Johnson (J&J), once a consumer products company known for its Band-Aid line and its baby care products, has evolved into a $42 billion diversified enterprise consisting of some 200-plus operating companies organized into three divisions: drugs, medical devices and diagnostics, and consumer products. Over the past decade J&J has acquired 56 businesses at a cost of about $30 billion; about 10 to 15 percent of J&J's annual growth in revenues has come from acquisitions. Much of the company's recent growth has been in the pharmaceutical division, which in 2004 accounted for 47 percent of J&J's revenues and 57 percent of its operating profits.

While each of J&J's business units sets its own strategies and operates with its own finance and human resource departments, corporate management strongly encourages cross-business cooperation and collaboration, believing that many of the advances in 21st century medicine will come from applying advances in one discipline to another. J&J had 9,300 scientists working in 40 research labs in 2003, and the frequency of cross-disciplinary collaboration was increasing. One of J&J's new drug-coated stents grew out of a discussion between a drug researcher and a

researcher in the company's stent business. (When stents are inserted to prop open arteries following angioplasty, the drug coating helps prevent infection.) A gene technology database compiled by the company's gene research lab was shared with personnel from the diagnostics division, who developed a test that the drug R&D people could use to predict which patients would most benefit from an experimental cancer therapy. J&J experts in various diseases have been meeting quarterly for the past five years to share information, and top management is setting up cross-disciplinary groups to focus on new treatments for particular diseases. J&J's new liquid Band-Aid product (a liquid coating applied to hard-to-cover places like fingers and knuckles) is based on a material used in a wound-closing product sold by the company's hospital products company.

J&J's corporate management maintains that close collaboration among people in its diagnostics, medical devices, and pharmaceuticals businesses—where numerous cross-business strategic fits exist—gives J&J an edge on competitors, most of whom cannot match the company's breadth and depth of expertise.

Sources: Amy Barrett, "Staying on Top," *BusinessWeek,* May 5, 2003, pp. 60–68, and www.jnj.com (accessed October 19, 2005).

and Bestfoods (whose brands included Knorr's soups, Hellman's mayonnaise, Skippy peanut butter, and Mazola cooking oils). Unilever saw these businesses as giving it more clout in competing against such other diversified food and household products companies as Nestlé, Kraft, Procter & Gamble, Campbell Soup, and General Mills.

Usually, expansion into new businesses is undertaken by acquiring companies already in the target industry. Some companies depend on new acquisitions to drive a major portion of their growth in revenues and earnings, and thus are always on the acquisition trail. Cisco Systems built itself into a worldwide leader in networking systems for the Internet by making 95 technology-based acquisitions during 1993–2005 to extend its market reach from routing and switching into Internet Protocol (IP) telephony, home networking, wireless local-area networking (LAN), storage networking, network security, broadband, and optical and broadband systems. Tyco International, now recovering from charges of looting on the part of several top executives, transformed itself from an obscure company in the early 1990s into a $40 billion global manufacturing enterprise with operations in over 100 countries as of 2005 by making over 1,000 acquisitions; the company's far-flung diversification includes businesses in electronics, electrical components, fire and security systems, health care products, valves, undersea telecommunications systems, plastics, and adhesives. Tyco made over 700 acquisitions of small companies in the 1999–2001 period alone. As a group, Tyco's businesses were cash cows, generating a combined free cash flow in 2005 of around $4.4 billion.

Illustration Capsule 9.3 describes how Johnson & Johnson has used acquisitions to diversify far beyond its well-known Band-Aid and baby care businesses and become a major player in pharmaceuticals, medical devices, and medical diagnostics.

Divestiture Strategies Aimed at Retrenching to a Narrower Diversification Base

A number of diversified firms have had difficulty managing a diverse group of businesses and have elected to get out of some of them. Retrenching to a narrower diversification base is usually undertaken when top management concludes that its diversification strategy has ranged too far afield and that the company can improve long-term performance by concentrating on building stronger positions in a smaller number of core businesses and industries. Hewlett-Packard spun off its testing and measurement businesses into a stand-alone company called Agilent Technologies so that it could better concentrate on its PC, workstation, server, printer and peripherals, and electronics businesses. PepsiCo divested its cash-hog group of restaurant businesses, consisting of KFC, Pizza Hut, Taco Bell, and California Pizza Kitchens, to provide more resources for strengthening its soft-drink business (which was losing market share to Coca-Cola) and growing its more profitable Frito-Lay snack foods business. Kmart divested OfficeMax, Sports Authority, and Borders Bookstores in order to refocus management attention and all of the company's resources on restoring luster to its distressed discount retailing business, which was (and still is) being totally outclassed in the marketplace by Wal-Mart and Target. In 2003–2004, Tyco International began a program to divest itself of some 50 businesses, including its entire undersea fiber-optics telecommunications network and an assortment of businesses in its fire and security division; the initiative also involved consolidating 219 manufacturing, sales, distribution, and other facilities and reducing its workforce of some 260,000 people by 7,200. Lucent Technology's retrenchment strategy is described in Illustration Capsule 9.4.

> Focusing corporate resources on a few core and mostly related businesses avoids the mistake of diversifying so broadly that resources and management attention are stretched too thin.

But there are other important reasons for divesting one or more of a company's present businesses. Sometimes divesting a business has to be considered because market conditions in a once-attractive industry have badly deteriorated. A business can become a prime candidate for divestiture because it lacks adequate strategic or resource fit, because it is a cash hog with questionable long-term potential, or because it is weakly positioned in its industry with little prospect the corporate parent can realize a decent return on its investment in the business. Sometimes a company acquires businesses that, down the road, just do not work out as expected even though management has tried all it can think of to make them profitable—mistakes cannot be completely avoided because it is hard to foresee how getting into a new line of business will actually work out. Subpar performance by some business units is bound to occur, thereby raising questions of whether to divest them or keep them and attempt a turnaround. Other business units, despite adequate financial performance, may not mesh as well with the rest of the firm as was originally thought.

Illustration Capsule 9.4
Lucent Technology's Retrenchment Strategy

At the height of the telecommunications boom in 1999–2000, Lucent Technology was a company with $38.3 billion in revenues and 157,000 employees; it was the biggest maker of telecommunications equipment in the United States and a recognized leader worldwide. The company's strategy was to build positions in a number of blossoming technologies and industry arenas and achieve 20 percent annual revenue growth in each of 11 different business groups. But when customers' orders for new equipment began to evaporate in 2000–2001, Lucent's profits vanished and the once-growing company found itself battling to overcome bloated costs, deep price discounting, and customer defaults on the $7.5 billion in loans Lucent had made to finance their purchases. As it became clear that equipment sales and prices would never return to former levels, Lucent executives concluded that the company had overextended itself trying to do too many things and needed to pare its lineup of businesses.

Alongside efforts to curtail lavish spending at the company's fabled Bell Labs research unit, make deep workforce cutbacks, streamline order-taking and billing systems, shore up the balance sheet, and conserve cash by ending dividend payments, management launched a series of retrenchment initiatives:

- Of the 40 businesses Lucent acquired since 1996, 27 were sold, closed, or spun off.
- Lucent ceased all manufacturing operations, opting to outsource everything.
- It stopped making gear for wireless phone networks based on global system for mobile communication (GSM) technology (the dominant technology used in Europe and much of the world) in order to focus more fully on wireless gear using code division multiple

access (CDMA) technology (a technology prevalent in the United States and some developing nations). As of 2004 Lucent had an estimated 45 percent share in the CDMA market and the CDMA gear division was the company's chief revenue and profit producer.

- The wireline and wireless business units were combined to form a single, unified organization called Network Solutions.
- All the remaining businesses were grouped into a unit called Lucent Worldwide Services that was engaged in designing, implementing, integrating, and managing sophisticated voice and data networks for service providers in 45 countries.
- The role of Bell Labs was narrowed to supporting the efforts of both the Network Solutions group and the Worldwide Services group.

Lucent's strategic moves to retrench stemmed a string of 13 straight money-losing quarters. In fiscal 2004 Lucent reported profits of $2 billion from continuing operations (equal to EPS of $0.47 but still far below the levels of $0.93 in 2000 and $1.12 in 1999). In May 2004, Lucent announced its first acquisition in four years, buying a maker of Internet transmission technology for $300 million to help it become a leader in Internet telephony technology. Going into 2006, Lucent was a company with sales of about $9 billion (versus $38 billion in 1999) and a workforce of about 30,000 (versus 157,000 in 1999). The company's stock price, which reached a high of $62 in 1999 before crashing to below $1 in 2002, languished in the $3–$4 range for most of 2004–2005, indicating continuing investor skepticism about Lucent's prospects despite its having retreated to businesses where it was strongest.

Sources: Shawn Young, "Less May Be More," *The Wall Street Journal,* October 23, 2004, p. R10, and www.lucent.com (accessed October 19, 2005).

On occasion, a diversification move that seems sensible from a strategic-fit stand point turns out to be a poor *cultural fit.*[20] Several pharmaceutical companies had just this experience. When they diversified into cosmetics and perfume, they discovered their personnel had little respect for the "frivolous" nature of such products compared to the far nobler task of developing miracle drugs to cure the ill. The absence of shared values and cultural compatibility between the medical research and chemical-compounding expertise of the pharmaceutical companies and the fashion/marketing orientation of the cosmetics business was the undoing of what otherwise was diversification into businesses with technology-sharing potential, product-development fit, and some overlap in distribution channels.

There's evidence indicating that pruning businesses and narrowing a firm's diversification base improves corporate performance.[21] Corporate parents often end up selling off businesses too late and at too low a price, sacrificing shareholder value.[22] A useful guide to determine whether or when to divest a business subsidiary is to ask, "If we were not in this business today, would we want to get into it now?"[23] When the answer is no or probably not, divestiture should be considered. Another signal that a business should become a divestiture candidate is whether it is worth more to another company than to the present parent; in such cases, shareholders would be well served if the company sells the business and collects a premium price from the buyer for whom the business is a valuable fit.[24]

> Diversified companies need to divest low-performing businesses or businesses that don't fit in order to concentrate on expanding existing businesses and entering new ones where opportunities are more promising.

The Two Options for Divesting a Business: Selling It or Spinning It Off as an Independent Company

Selling a business outright to another company is far and away the most frequently used option for divesting a business. But sometimes a business selected for divestiture has ample resource strengths to compete successfully on its own. In such cases, a corporate parent may elect to spin the unwanted business off as a financially and managerially independent company, either by selling shares to the investing public via an initial public offering or by distributing shares in the new company to existing shareholders of the corporate parent. When a corporate parent decides to spin off one of its businesses as a separate company, it must decide whether or not to retain partial ownership. Retaining partial ownership makes sense when the business to be divested has a hot product or technological capabilities that give it good profit prospects. When 3Com elected to divest its PalmPilot business, which investors then saw as having very promising profit potential, it elected to retain a substantial ownership interest so as to provide 3Com shareholders a way of participating in whatever future market success that PalmPilot (now Palm Inc.) might have on its own. In 2001, when Philip Morris (now Altria) became concerned that its popular Kraft Foods subsidiary was suffering because of its affiliation with Philip Morris's cigarette business (antismoking groups were leading a national boycott of Kraft macaroni and cheese, and a Harris poll revealed that about 16 percent of people familiar with Philip Morris had boycotted its products), Philip Morris executives opted to spin Kraft Foods off as an independent public company but retained a controlling ownership interest. R. J. Reynolds Tobacco was also spun off from Nabisco Foods in 1999 in an effort to distance the tobacco operations part of the company from the food operations part. (Nabisco was then acquired by Philip Morris in 2000 and integrated into Kraft Foods.) In 2005, Cendant announced it would split its diversified businesses into four separate publicly traded companies—one for vehicle rental services (which consisted of Avis and Budget car rental companies); one for real estate and mortgage services (which included Century 21, Coldwell Banker, ERA, Sotheby's International Realty, and NRT—a residential real estate brokerage company); one for hospitality and lodging (consisting of such hotels and motel chains as Wyndam, Ramada, Days Inn, Howard Johnson, Travelodge, AmeriHost Inn, and Knights Inn, plus an assortment of time-share resort properties); and one for travel (consisting of various travel agencies, online ticket and vacation travel sites like Orbitz and Cheap Tickets, and vacation rental operations handling some 55,000 villas and condos). Cendant said the reason for the split-up was that shareholders would realize more value from operating the businesses independently—a clear sign that Cendant's diversification strategy had failed to deliver added shareholder value and that the parts were worth more than the whole.

Selling a business outright requires finding a buyer. This can prove hard or easy, depending on the business. As a rule, a company selling a troubled business should not ask, "How can we pawn this business off on someone, and what is the most we can get for it?"[25] Instead, it is wiser to ask, "For what sort of company would this business be a good fit, and under what conditions would it be viewed as a good deal?" Enterprises for which the business is a good fit are likely to pay the highest price. Of course, if a buyer willing to pay an acceptable price cannot be found, then a company must decide whether to keep the business until a buyer appears; spin it off as a separate company; or, in the case of a crisis-ridden business that is losing substantial sums, simply close it down and liquidate the remaining assets. Liquidation is obviously a last resort.

Strategies to Restructure a Company's Business Lineup

> **Core Concept**
> **Restructuring** involves divesting some businesses and acquiring others so as to put a whole new face on the company's business lineup.

Restructuring strategies involve divesting some businesses and acquiring others so as to put a whole new face on the company's business lineup. Performing radical surgery on a company's group of businesses is an appealing strategy alternative when its financial performance is being squeezed or eroded by:

- Too many businesses in slow-growth, declining, low-margin, or otherwise unattractive industries (a condition indicated by the number and size of businesses with industry attractiveness ratings below 5 and located on the bottom half of the attractiveness–strength matrix—see Figure 9.5).
- Too many competitively weak businesses (a condition indicated by the number and size of businesses with competitive strength ratings below 5 and located on the right half of the attractiveness–strength matrix).
- Ongoing declines in the market shares of one or more major business units that are falling prey to more market-savvy competitors.
- An excessive debt burden with interest costs that eat deeply into profitability.
- Ill-chosen acquisitions that haven't lived up to expectations.

Restructuring can also be mandated by the emergence of new technologies that threaten the survival of one or more of a diversified company's important businesses or by the appointment of a new CEO who decides to redirect the company. On occasion, restructuring can be prompted by special circumstances—as when a firm has a unique opportunity to make an acquisition so big and important that it has to sell several existing business units to finance the new acquisition, or when a company needs to sell off some businesses in order to raise the cash for entering a potentially big industry with wave-of-the-future technologies or products.

Candidates for divestiture in a corporate restructuring effort typically include not only weak or up-and-down performers or those in unattractive industries but also business units that lack strategic fit with the businesses to be retained, businesses that are cash hogs or that lack other types of resource fit, and businesses incompatible with the company's revised diversification strategy (even though they may be profitable or in an attractive industry). As businesses are divested, corporate restructuring generally involves aligning the remaining business units into groups with the best strategic fits and then redeploying the cash flows from the divested business to either pay down debt or make new acquisitions to strengthen the parent company's business position in the industries it has chosen to emphasize.[26]

Over the past decade, corporate restructuring has become a popular strategy at many diversified companies, especially those that had diversified broadly into many different industries and lines of business. For instance, one struggling diversified company over a two-year period divested four business units, closed down the operations of four others, and added 25 new lines of business to its portfolio (16 through acquisition and 9 through internal start-up). PerkinElmer used a series of divestitures and new acquisitions to transform itself from a supplier of low-margin services sold to the government agencies into an innovative high-tech company with operations in over 125 countries and businesses in four industry groups—life sciences (drug research and clinical screening), optoelectronics, medical instruments, and fluid control and containment services (for customers in aerospace, power generation, and semiconductors). In 2005, PerkinElmer took a second restructuring step by divesting its entire fluid control and containment business group so that it could concentrate on its higher-growth health sciences and optoelectronics businesses; the company's CEO said, "While fluid services is an excellent business, it does not fit with our long-term strategy."[27] Before beginning a restructuring effort in 1995, British-based Hanson PLC owned companies with more than $20 billion in revenues in industries as diverse as beer, exercise equipment, tools, construction cranes, tobacco, cement, chemicals, coal mining, electricity, hot tubs and whirlpools, cookware, rock and gravel, bricks, and asphalt. By early 1997, Hanson had restructured itself into a $3.8 billion enterprise focused more narrowly on gravel, crushed rock, cement, asphalt, bricks, and construction cranes; the remaining businesses were divided into four groups and divested.

During Jack Welch's first four years as CEO of General Electric (GE), the company divested 117 business units, accounting for about 20 percent of GE's assets; these divestitures, coupled with several important acquisitions, provided GE with 14 major business divisions and led to Welch's challenge to the managers of GE's divisions to become number one or number two in their industry. Ten years after Welch became CEO, GE was a different company, having divested operations worth $9 billion, made new acquisitions totaling $24 billion, and cut its workforce by 100,000 people. Then, during the 1990–2001 period, GE continued to reshuffle its business lineup, acquiring over 600 new companies, including 108 in 1998 and 64 during a 90-day period in 1999. Most of the new acquisitions were in Europe, Asia, and Latin America and were aimed at transforming GE into a truly global enterprise. In 2003, GE's new CEO, Jeffrey Immelt, began a further restructuring of GE's business lineup with three initiatives: (1) spending $10 billion to acquire British-based Amersham and extend GE's Medical Systems business into diagnostic pharmaceuticals and biosciences, thereby creating a $15 billion business designated as GE Healthcare; (2) acquiring the entertainment assets of debt-ridden French media conglomerate Vivendi Universal Entertainment (Universal Studios, five Universal theme parks, USA Network, Sci-Fi Channel, the Trio cable channel, and Spanish-language broadcaster Telemundo) and integrate its operations into GE's NBC division (the owner of NBC, 29 television stations, and cable networks CNBC, MSNBC, and Bravo), thereby creating a broad-based $13 billion media business positioned to compete against Walt Disney, Time Warner, Fox, and Viacom; and (3) beginning a withdrawal from the insurance business by divesting several companies in its insurance division and preparing to spin off its remaining life and mortgage insurance businesses through an initial public offering of stock for a new company called Genworth Financial.

In a study of the performance of the 200 largest U.S. corporations from 1990 to 2000, McKinsey & Company found that those companies that actively managed their business portfolios through acquisitions and divestitures created substantially more shareholder value than those that kept a fixed lineup of businesses.[28]

Multinational Diversification Strategies

The distinguishing characteristics of a multinational diversification strategy are a *diversity of businesses* and a *diversity of national markets.*[29] Such diversity makes multinational diversification a particularly challenging and complex strategy to conceive and execute. Managers have to develop business strategies for each industry (with as many multinational variations as conditions in each country market dictate). Then they have to pursue and manage opportunities for cross-business and cross-country collaboration and strategic coordination in ways calculated to result in competitive advantage and enhanced profitability.

Moreover, the geographic operating scope of individual businesses within a diversified multinational corporation (DMNC) can range from one country only to several countries to many countries to global. Thus, each business unit within a DMNC often competes in a somewhat different combination of geographic markets than the other businesses do—adding another element of strategic complexity, and perhaps an element of opportunity.

Illustration Capsule 9.5 shows the scope of four prominent DMNCs.

The Appeal of Multinational Diversification: More Opportunities for Sustained Growth and Maximum Competitive Advantage Potential

Despite their complexity, multinational diversification strategies have great appeal. They contain *two major avenues* for growing revenues and profits: One is to grow by entering additional businesses, and the other is to grow by extending the operations of existing businesses into additional country markets. Moreover, a strategy of multinational diversification also contains six attractive paths to competitive advantage, *all of which can be pursued simultaneously:*

1. *Full capture of economies of scale and experience/learning curve effects.* In some businesses, the volume of sales needed to realize full economies of scale and/or benefit fully from experience/learning curve effects is rather sizable, often exceeding the volume that can be achieved operating within the boundaries of a single country market, especially a small one. *The ability to drive down unit costs by expanding sales to additional country markets is one reason why a diversified multinational may seek to acquire a business and then rapidly expand its operations into more and more foreign markets.*

2. *Opportunities to capitalize on cross-business economies of scope.* Diversifying into related businesses offering economies of scope can drive the development of a low-cost advantage over less diversified rivals. For example, a DMNC that uses mostly the same distributors and retail dealers worldwide can diversify into new businesses using these same worldwide distribution channels at relatively little incremental expense. The cost savings of piggybacking distribution activities can be substantial. Moreover, with more business selling more products in more countries, a DMNC acquires more bargaining leverage in its purchases from suppliers and more bargaining leverage with retailers in securing attractive display space for its products. Consider, for example, the competitive power that Sony derived

Illustration Capsule 9.5

The Global Scope of Four Prominent Diversified Multinational Corporations

Company	Global Scope	Businesses into Which the Company Has Diversified
Sony	Operations in more than 100 countries and sales offices in more than 200 countries	• Televisions, VCRs, DVD players, Walkman MP3 players, radios, digital cameras and video equipment, Vaio PCs, and Trinitron computer monitors; PlayStation game consoles and video game software; Columbia, Epic, and Sony Classical pre-recorded music; Columbia TriStar motion pictures; syndicated television programs; entertainment complexes, and insurance
Nestlé	Operations in 70 countries and sales offices in more than 200 countries	• Beverages (Nescafé and Taster's Choice coffees, Nestea, Perrier, Arrowhead, & Calistoga mineral and bottled waters); milk products (Carnation, Gloria, Neslac, Coffee Mate, Nestlé ice cream and yogurt); pet foods (Friskies, Alpo, Fancy Feast, Mighty Dog); Contadina, Libby's, and Stouffer's food products and prepared dishes; chocolate and confectionery products (Nestlé Crunch, Smarties, Baby Ruth, Butterfinger, KitKat); and pharmaceuticals (Alcon opthalmic products, Galderma dermatological products)
Siemens	Operations in 160 countries and sales offices in more than 190 countries	• Electrical power generation, transmission, and distribution equipment and products; manufacturing automation systems; industrial motors, machinery, and tools; plant construction and maintenance; corporate communication networks; telephones; PCs, mainframes, computer network products, consulting services; mass transit and light rail systems, rail cars, locomotives, lighting products (bulbs, lamps, theater and television lighting systems); semiconductors; home appliances; vacuum cleaners; and financial, procurement, and logistics services
Samsung	Operations in more than 60 countries and sales in more than 200 countries	• Notebook computers, hard disk drives, CD/DVD-ROM drives, monitors, printers, and fax machines; televisions (big-screen TVs, plasma-screen TVs, and LCD-screen TVs); DVD and MP3 players; Cell phones and various other telecommunications products; compressors; home appliances; DRAM chips, flash memory chips, and graphics memory chips; and optical fibers, fiber-optic cables, and fiber-optic connectors

Source: Company annual reports and Web sites.

from these very sorts of economies of scope when it decided to diversify into the video game business with its PlayStation product line. Sony had in place capability to go after video game sales in all country markets where it presently did business in other electronics product categories (TVs, computers, DVD players, VCRs, radios, CD players, and camcorders). And it had the marketing clout and brand-name credibility to persuade retailers to give Sony's PlayStation products prime shelf space and visibility. These strategic-fit benefits helped Sony quickly overtake long-time industry leaders Nintendo and Sega and defend its market leadership against Microsoft's new Xbox.

3. *Opportunities to transfer competitively valuable resources both from one business to another and from one country to another.* A company pursuing related diversification can gain a competitive edge over less diversified rivals by transferring competitively valuable resources from one business to another; a multinational company can gain competitive advantage over rivals with narrower geographic coverage by transferring competitively valuable resources from one country to another. But a strategy of multinational diversification enables simultaneous pursuit of both sources of competitive advantage.

4. *Ability to leverage use of a well-known and competitively powerful brand name.* Diversified multinational companies whose businesses have brand names that are well known and respected across the world possess a valuable strategic asset with competitive advantage potential. For example, Sony's well-established global brand-name recognition gives it an important marketing and advertising advantage over rivals with lesser-known brands. When Sony goes into a new marketplace with the stamp of the Sony brand on its product families, it can command prominent display space with retailers. It can expect to win sales and market share simply on the confidence that buyers place in products carrying the Sony name. While Sony may spend money to make consumers aware of the availability of its new products, it does not have to spend nearly as much on achieving brand recognition and market acceptance as would a lesser-known competitor looking at the marketing and advertising costs of entering the same new product/business/country markets and trying to go head-to-head against Sony. Further, if Sony moves into a new country market for the first time and does well selling Sony PlayStations and video games, it is easier to sell consumers in that country Sony TVs, digital cameras, PCs, MP3 players, and so on—plus, the related advertising costs are likely to be less than they would be without having already established the Sony brand strongly in the minds of buyers.

5. *Ability to capitalize on opportunities for cross-business and cross-country collaboration and strategic coordination.*[30] A multinational diversification strategy allows competitively valuable cross-business and cross-country coordination of certain value chain activities. For instance, by channeling corporate resources directly into a combined R&D/technology effort for all related businesses, as opposed to letting each business unit fund and direct its own R&D effort however it sees fit, a DMNC can merge its expertise and efforts *worldwide* to advance core technologies, expedite cross-business and cross-country product improvements, speed the development of new products that complement existing products, and pursue promising technological avenues to create altogether new businesses—all significant contributors to competitive advantage and better corporate performance.[31] Honda has been very successful in building R&D expertise in gasoline engines and transferring the resulting technological advances to its businesses in automobiles, motorcycles, outboard engines, snow blowers, lawn mowers, garden tillers, and portable power generators. Further, a DMNC can reduce costs through cross-business and cross-country coordination of purchasing and procurement from suppliers, from collaborative introduction and shared use of e-commerce technologies and online sales efforts, and from coordinated product introductions and promotional campaigns. Firms that are less diversified and less global in scope have less such cross-business and cross-country collaborative opportunities.

6. *Opportunities to use cross-business or cross-country subsidization to outcompete rivals.* A financially successful DMNC has potentially valuable organizational resources and multiple profit sanctuaries in both certain country markets and certain businesses that it can draw on to wage a market offensive. In comparison, a one-business domestic company has only one profit sanctuary—its home market. A diversified one-country competitor may have profit sanctuaries in several businesses, but all are in the same country market. A one-business multinational company may have profit sanctuaries in several country markets, but all are in the same business. All three are vulnerable to an offensive in their more limited profit sanctuaries by an aggressive DMNC willing to lowball its prices or spend extravagantly on advertising to win market share at their expense. A DMNC's ability to keep hammering away at competitors with low prices year after year may reflect either a cost advantage growing out of its related diversification strategy or a willingness to accept low profits or even losses in the market being attacked because it has ample earnings from its other profit sanctuaries. For example, Sony's global-scale diversification strategy gives it unique competitive strengths in outcompeting Nintendo and Sega, neither of which are diversified. If need be, Sony can maintain low prices on its PlayStations or fund high-profile promotions for its latest video game products, using earnings from its other business lines to fund its offensive to wrest market share away from Nintendo and Sega in video games. At the same time, Sony can draw on its considerable resources in R&D, its ability to transfer electronics technology from one electronics product family to another, and its expertise in product innovation to introduce better and better video game players, perhaps players that are multifunctional and do more than just play video games. Such competitive actions not only enhance Sony's own brand image but also make it very tough for Nintendo and Sega to match Sony's prices, advertising, and product development efforts and still earn acceptable profits.

The Combined Effects of These Advantages Is Potent

A strategy of diversifying into *related* industries and then competing *globally* in each of these industries thus has great potential for being a winner in the marketplace because of the long-term growth opportunities it offers and the multiple corporate-level competitive advantage opportunities it contains. Indeed, *a strategy of multinational diversification contains more competitive advantage potential* (above and beyond what is achievable through a particular business's own competitive strategy) *than any other diversification strategy.* The strategic key to maximum competitive advantage is for a DMNC to concentrate its diversification efforts in those industries where there are resource-sharing and resource-transfer opportunities and where there are important economies of scope and brand-name benefits. The more a company's diversification strategy yields these kinds of strategic-fit benefits, the more powerful a competitor it becomes and the better its profit and growth performance is likely to be.

> **Core Concept**
> A strategy of multinational diversification has more built-in potential for competitive advantage than any other diversification strategy.

However, it is important to recognize that while, in theory, a DMNC's cross-subsidization capabilities are a potent competitive weapon, cross-subsidization can, in actual practice, be used only sparingly. It is one thing to *occasionally* divert a portion of the profits and cash flows from existing businesses to help fund entry into a new business or country market or wage a competitive offensive against select rivals. It is quite another thing to *regularly* use cross-subsidization tactics and thereby weaken

Core Concept
Although cross-subsidization is a potent competitive weapon, it must be used sparingly to prevent eroding a DMNC's overall profitability.

overall company performance. A DMNC is under the same pressures as any other company to demonstrate consistently acceptable profitability across its whole operation.[32] At some juncture, every business and every country market needs to make a profit contribution or become a candidate for abandonment. As a general rule, *cross-subsidization tactics are justified only when there is a good prospect that the short-term impairment to corporate profitability will be offset by stronger competitiveness and better overall profitability over the long term.*

Key Points

The purpose of diversification is to build shareholder value. Diversification builds shareholder value when a diversified group of businesses can perform better under the auspices of a single corporate parent than they would as independent, stand-alone businesses—the goal is not to achieve just a 1 + 1 = 2 result, but rather to realize important 1 + 1 = 3 performance benefits. Whether getting into a new business has potential to enhance shareholder value hinges on whether a company's entry into that business can pass the attractiveness test, the cost-of-entry test, and the better-off test.

Entry into new businesses can take any of three forms: acquisition, internal start-up, or joint venture/strategic partnership. Each has its pros and cons, but acquisition is the most frequently used; internal start-up takes the longest to produce home-run results, and joint venture/strategic partnership, though used second most frequently, is the least durable.

There are two fundamental approaches to diversification—into related businesses and into unrelated businesses. The rationale for *related* diversification is *strategic*: Diversify into businesses with strategic fits along their respective value chains, capitalize on strategic-fit relationships to gain competitive advantage, and then use competitive advantage to achieve the desired 1 + 1 = 3 impact on shareholder value.

The basic premise of unrelated diversification is that any business that has good profit prospects and can be acquired on good financial terms is a good business to diversify into. Unrelated diversification strategies surrender the competitive advantage potential of strategic fit in return for such advantages as (1) spreading business risk over a variety of industries and (2) providing opportunities for financial gain (if candidate acquisitions have undervalued assets, are bargain priced and have good upside potential given the right management, or need the backing of a financially strong parent to capitalize on attractive opportunities). However, the greater the number of businesses a company has diversified into and the more diverse these businesses are, the harder it is for corporate executives to select capable managers to run each business, know when the major strategic proposals of business units are sound, or decide on a wise course of recovery when a business unit stumbles.

Analyzing how good a company's diversification strategy is a six-step process:

1. *Evaluate the long-term attractiveness of the industries into which the firm has diversified.* Industry attractiveness needs to be evaluated from three angles: the attractiveness of each industry on its own, the attractiveness of each industry relative to the others, and the attractiveness of all the industries as a group.

2. *Evaluate the relative competitive strength of each of the company's business units.* Again, quantitative ratings of competitive strength are preferable to subjective

judgments. The purpose of rating the competitive strength of each business is to gain clear understanding of which businesses are strong contenders in their industries, which are weak contenders, and the underlying reasons for their strength or weakness. The conclusions about industry attractiveness can be joined with the conclusions about competitive strength by drawing an industry attractiveness–competitive strength matrix that helps identify the prospects of each business and what priority each business should be given in allocating corporate resources and investment capital.

3. *Check for cross-business strategic fits.* A business is more attractive strategically when it has value chain relationships with sister business units that offer potential to (*a*) realize economies of scope or cost-saving efficiencies; (*b*) transfer technology, skills, know-how, or other resource capabilities from one business to another; (*c*) leverage use of a well-known and trusted brand name; and (*d*) to build new or stronger resource strengths and competitive capabilities via cross-business collaboration. Cross-business strategic fits represent a significant avenue for producing competitive advantage beyond what any one business can achieve on its own.

4. *Check whether the firm's resource strengths fit the resource requirements of its present business lineup.* Resource fit exists when (*a*) businesses add to a company's resource strengths, either financially or strategically; (*b*) a company has the resources to adequately support the resource requirements of its businesses as a group without spreading itself too thin; and (*c*) there are close matches between a company's resources and industry key success factors. One important test of financial resource fit involves determining whether a company has ample cash cows and not too many cash hogs.

5. *Rank the performance prospects of the businesses from best to worst and determine what the corporate parent's priority should be in allocating resources to its various businesses.* The most important considerations in judging business-unit performance are sales growth, profit growth, contribution to company earnings, and the return on capital invested in the business. Sometimes, cash flow generation is a big consideration. Normally, strong business units in attractive industries have significantly better performance prospects than weak businesses or businesses in unattractive industries. Business subsidiaries with the brightest profit and growth prospects and solid strategic and resource fits generally should head the list for corporate resource support.

6. *Crafting new strategic moves to improve overall corporate performance.* This step entails using the results of the preceding analysis as the basis for devising actions to strengthen existing businesses, make new acquisitions, divest weak-performing and unattractive businesses, restructure the company's business lineup, expand the scope of the company's geographic reach multinationally or globally, and otherwise steer corporate resources into the areas of greatest opportunity.

Once a company has diversified, corporate management's task is to manage the collection of businesses for maximum long-term performance. There are four different strategic paths for improving a diversified company's performance: (1) broadening the firm's business base by diversifying into additional businesses, (2) retrenching to a narrower diversification base by divesting some of its present businesses, (3) restructuring the company, and (4) diversifying multinationally.

Exercises

1. Consider the business lineup of General Electric (GE) shown in Illustration Capsule 9.2. What problems do you think the top executives at GE encounter in trying to stay on top of all the businesses the company is in? How might they decide the merits of adding new businesses or divesting poorly performing businesses? What types of advice might they be in a position to give to the general managers of each of GE's business units?

2. The Walt Disney Company is in the following businesses:
   - Theme parks.
   - Disney Cruise Line.
   - Resort properties.
   - Movie, video, and theatrical productions (for both children and adults).
   - Television broadcasting (ABC, Disney Channel, Toon Disney, Classic Sports Network, ESPN and ESPN2, E!, Lifetime, and A&E networks).
   - Radio broadcasting (Disney Radio).
   - Musical recordings and sales of animation art.
   - Anaheim Mighty Ducks NHL franchise.
   - Anaheim Angels major league baseball franchise (25 percent ownership).
   - Books and magazine publishing.
   - Interactive software and Internet sites.
   - The Disney Store retail shops.

   Given the above listing, would you say that Walt Disney's business lineup reflects a strategy of related or unrelated diversification? Explain your answer in terms of the extent to which the value chains of Disney's different businesses seem to have competitively valuable cross-business relationships.

3. Newell Rubbermaid is in the following businesses:
   - Cleaning and organizations businesses: Rubbermaid storage, organization, and cleaning products; Blue Ice ice substitute; Roughneck storage itemmms; Stain Shield and TakeAlongs food storage containers; and Brute commercial-grade storage and cleaning products (25 percent of annual revenues).
   - Home and family businesses: Calphalon cookware and bakeware, Cookware Europe, Graco strollers, Little Tikes children's toys and furniture, and Goody hair accessories (20 percent of annual sales).
   - Home fashions: Levolor and Kirsch window blinds, shades, and hardware in the United States; Swish, Gardinia and Harrison Drape home furnishings in Europe (15 percent of annual revenues).
   - Office products businesses: Sharpie markers, Sanford highlighters, Eberhard Faber and Berol ballpoint pens, Paper Mate pens and pencils, Waterman and Parker fine writing instruments, and Liquid Paper (25 percent of annual revenues).

   Would you say that Newell Rubbermaid's strategy is one of related diversification, unrelated diversification or a mixture of both? Explain.

4. Explore the Web sites of the following companies and determine whether the company is pursuing a strategy of related diversification, unrelated diversification, or a mixture of both:

- Berkshire Hathaway
- News Corporation
- Dow Jones & Company
- Kimberly Clark

chapter ten

Strategy, Ethics, and Social Responsibility

When morality comes up against profit, it is seldom profit that loses.

—Shirley Chisholm
Former Congresswoman

But I'd shut my eyes in the sentry box so I didn't see nothing wrong.

—Rudyard Kipling
Author

Values can't just be words on a page. To be effective, they must shape action.

—Jeffrey R. Immelt
CEO, General Electric

Leaders must be more than individuals of high character. They must "lead" others to behave ethically.

**—Linda K. Treviño
and Michael E. Brown**
Professors

Integrity violations are no-brainers. In such cases, you don't need to hesitate for a moment before firing someone or fret about it either. Just do it, and make sure the organization knows why, so that the consequences of breaking the rules are not lost on anyone.

—Jack Welch
Former CEO, General Electric

There is one and only one social responsibility of business—to use its resources and engage in activities designed to increase its profits so long as it stays within the rules of the game, which is to say engages in free and open competition, without deception or fraud.

—Milton Friedman
Nobel Prize–winning economist

Corporations are economic entities, to be sure, but they are also social institutions that must justify their existence by their overall contribution to society.

—Henry Mintzberg, Robert Simons, and Kunal Basu
Professors

Clearly, a company has a responsibility to make a profit and grow the business—in capitalistic, or market, economies, management's fiduciary duty to create value for shareholders is not a matter for serious debate. Just as clearly, a company and its personnel also have a duty to obey the law and play by the rules of fair competition. But does a company have a duty to operate according to the ethical norms of the societies in which it operates—should it be held to some standard of ethical conduct? And does it have a duty or obligation to contribute to the betterment of society independent of the needs and preferences of the customers it serves? Should a company display a social conscience and devote a portion of its resources to bettering society?

The focus of this chapter is to examine what link, if any, there should be between a company's efforts to craft and execute a winning strategy and its duties to (1) conduct its activities ethically and (2) demonstrate socially responsible behavior by being a committed corporate citizen and directing corporate resources to the betterment of employees, the communities in which it operates, and society as a whole.

WHAT DO WE MEAN BY *BUSINESS ETHICS?*

Business ethics is the application of ethical principles and standards to business behavior.[1] Business ethics does not really involve a special set of ethical standards applicable only to business situations. Ethical principles in business are not materially different from ethical principles in general. Why? Because business actions have to be judged in the context of society's standards of right and wrong, not by a special set of rules that businesspeople decide to apply to their own conduct. If dishonesty is considered to be unethical and immoral, then dishonest behavior in business—whether it relates to customers, suppliers, employees or shareholders—qualifies as equally unethical and immoral. If being ethical entails not deliberately harming others, then recalling a defective or unsafe product is ethically necessary and failing to undertake such a recall or correct the problem in future shipments of the product is likewise unethical. If society deems bribery to be unethical, then it is unethical for company personnel to make payoffs to government officials to facilitate business transactions or bestow gifts and other favors on prospective customers to win or retain their business.

Core Concept
Business ethics concerns the application of general ethical principles and standards to the actions and decisions of companies and the conduct of company personnel.

WHERE DO ETHICAL STANDARDS COME FROM—ARE THEY UNIVERSAL OR DEPENDENT ON LOCAL NORMS AND SITUATIONAL CIRCUMSTANCES?

Notions of right and wrong, fair and unfair, moral and immoral, ethical and unethical are present in all societies, organizations, and individuals. But there are three schools of thought about the extent to which the ethical standards travel across cultures and whether multinational companies can apply the same set of ethical standards in any and all of the locations where they operate.

The School of Ethical Universalism

> **Core Concept**
> According to the school of *ethical universalism,* the same standards of what's ethical and what's unethical resonate with peoples of most societies regardless of local traditions and cultural norms; hence, common ethical standards can be used to judge the conduct of personnel at companies operating in a variety of country markets and cultural circumstances.

According to the school of **ethical universalism,** some concepts of what is right and what is wrong are *universal*; that is, they transcend all cultures, societies, and religions.[2] For instance, being truthful (or not lying, or not being deliberately deceitful) is considered right by the peoples of all nations. Likewise, demonstrating integrity of character, not cheating, and treating people with dignity and respect are concepts that resonate with people of most cultures and religions. In most societies, people believe that companies should not pillage or degrade the environment in the course of conducting their operations. In most societies, people would concur that it is unethical to knowingly expose workers to toxic chemicals and hazardous materials or to sell products known to be unsafe or harmful to the users. *To the extent that there is common moral agreement about right and wrong actions and behaviors across multiple cultures and countries, there exists a set of universal ethical standards to which all societies, all companies, and all individuals can be held accountable*. These universal ethical principles or norms put limits on what actions and behaviors fall inside the boundaries of what is right and which ones fall outside. They set forth the traits and behaviors that are considered virtuous and that a good person is supposed to believe in and to display.

Many ethicists believe that the most important moral standards travel well across countries and cultures and thus are *universal*—universal norms include honesty or trustworthiness, respecting the rights of others, practicing the Golden Rule, avoiding unnecessary harm to workers or to the users of the company's product or service, and respect for the environment.[3] In all such instances where there is cross-cultural agreement as to what actions and behaviors are inside and outside ethical and moral boundaries, adherents of the school of ethical universalism maintain that the conduct of personnel at companies operating in a variety of country markets and cultural circumstances can be judged against the resulting set of common ethical standards.

The strength of ethical universalism is that it draws on the collective views of multiple societies and cultures to put some clear boundaries on what constitutes ethical business behavior and what constitutes unethical business behavior no matter what country market or culture a company or its personnel are operating in. This means that whenever basic moral standards really do not vary significantly according to local cultural beliefs, traditions, religious convictions, or time and circumstance, a multinational company can apply a code of ethics more or less evenly across its worldwide operations.[4] It can avoid the slippery slope that comes from having different ethical standards for different company personnel depending on where in the world they are working.

The School of Ethical Relativism

Apart from select universal basics—honesty, trustworthiness, fairness, a regard for worker safety, and respect for the environment—there are meaningful variations in what societies generally agree to be right and wrong in the conduct of business activities. Divergent religious beliefs, historic traditions, social customs, and prevailing political and economic doctrines (whether a country leans more toward a capitalistic market economy or one heavily dominated by socialistic or communistic principles) frequently produce ethical norms that vary from one country to another. The school of **ethical relativism** holds that when there are cross-country or cross-cultural differences in what is deemed fair or unfair, what constitutes proper regard for human rights, and what is considered ethical or unethical in business situations, it is appropriate for local moral standards to take precedence over what the ethical standards may be elsewhere—for instance, in a company's home market. The thesis is that whatever a culture thinks is right or wrong really is right or wrong for that culture.[5] Hence, the school of ethical relativism contends that there are important occasions when cultural norms and the circumstances of the situation determine whether certain actions or behaviors are right or wrong. Consider the following examples.

> **Core Concept**
>
> According to the school of *ethical relativism* different societal cultures and customs have divergent values and standards of right and wrong—thus what is ethical or unethical must be judged in the light of local customs and social mores and can vary from culture or nation to another.

The Use of Underage Labor In industrialized nations, the use of underage workers is considered taboo; social activists are adamant that child labor is unethical and that companies should neither employ children under the age of 18 as full-time employees nor source any products from foreign suppliers that employ underage workers. Many countries have passed legislation forbidding the use of underage labor or, at a minimum, regulating the employment of people under the age of 18. However, in India, Bangladesh, Botswana, Sri Lanka, Ghana, Somalia, Turkey, and 100-plus other countries, it is customary to view children as potential, even necessary, workers.[6] Many poverty-stricken families cannot subsist without the income earned by young family members, and sending their children to school instead of having them participate in the workforce is not a realistic option. In 2000, the International Labor Organization estimated that 211 million children ages 5 to 14 were working around the world.[7] If such children are not permitted to work—due to pressures imposed by activist groups in industrialized nations—they may be forced to seek work in lower-wage jobs in "hidden" parts of the economy of their countries, beg on the street, or even traffic in drugs or engage in prostitution.[8] So if all businesses succumb to the protests of activist groups and government organizations that, based on their values and beliefs, loudly proclaim that underage labor is unethical, then have either businesses or the protesting groups really done something good on behalf of society in general?

The Payment of Bribes and Kickbacks A particularly thorny area facing multinational companies is the degree of cross-country variability in paying bribes.[9] In many countries in Eastern Europe, Africa, Latin America, and Asia, it is customary to pay bribes to government officials in order to win a government contract, obtain a license or permit, or facilitate an administrative ruling.[10] Senior managers in China often use their power to obtain kickbacks and offer bribes when they purchase materials or other products for their companies.[11] In some developing nations, it is difficult for any company, foreign or domestic, to move goods through customs without paying off low-level officials.[12] Likewise, in many countries it is normal to make payments to prospective customers in order to win or retain their business. A *Wall Street Journal* article reported that 30 to 60 percent of all business transactions in Eastern Europe involved paying bribes, and the costs of bribe payments averaged 2 to 8 percent of revenues.[13] Three recent annual issues of the *Global Corruption Report,* sponsored by Berlin-based Transparency International, provide credible evidence that corruption among public officials and in business transactions is widespread across the world.[14] Some people stretch to justify the payment of bribes and kickbacks on grounds that bribing government officials to get goods through customs or giving kickbacks to customers to retail their business or win an order is simply a payment for services rendered, in the same way that people tip for service at restaurants.[15] But this argument rests on moral quicksand, even though it is a clever and pragmatic way to rationalize why such facilitating payments should be viewed as a normal and maybe unavoidable cost of doing business in some countries.

Companies that forbid the payment of bribes and kickbacks in their codes of ethical conduct and that are serious about enforcing this prohibition face a particularly vexing problem in those countries where bribery and kickback payments have been entrenched as a local custom for decades and are not considered unethical by the local population.[16] Refusing to pay bribes or kickbacks (so as to comply with the company's code of ethical conduct) is very often tantamount to losing business. Frequently, the sales and profits are lost to more unscrupulous companies, with the result that both ethical companies and ethical individuals are penalized. However, winking at the code of ethical conduct and going along with the payment of bribes or kickbacks not only undercuts enforcement of and adherence to the company's code of ethics but can also risk breaking the law. U.S. companies are prohibited by the Foreign Corrupt Practices Act (FCPA) from paying bribes to government officials, political parties, political candidates, or others in all countries where they do business; the FCPA requires U.S. companies with foreign operations to adopt accounting practices that ensure full disclosure of a company's transactions so that illegal payments can be detected. The 35 member countries of the Organization for Economic Cooperation and Development (OECD) in 1997 adopted a convention to combat bribery in international business transactions; the Anti-Bribery Convention obligated the countries to criminalize the bribery of foreign public officials, including payments made to political parties and party officials. So far, however, there has been only token enforcement of the OECD convention and the payment of bribes in global business transactions remains a common practice in many countries.

Ethical Relativism Equates to Multiple Sets of Ethical Standards   The existence of varying ethical norms such as those cited above explains why the adherents of ethical relativism maintain that there are few absolutes when it comes to business ethics and thus few ethical absolutes for consistently judging a company's conduct in various countries and markets. Indeed, the thesis of ethical relativists is that while there are sometimes general moral prescriptions that apply in most every society and business circumstance there are plenty of situations where ethical norms must be contoured to fit the local customs, traditions, and the notions of fairness shared by the parties involved. They argue that a one-size-fits-all template for judging the ethical appropriateness of business actions and the behaviors of company personnel simply does not exist—in other words, ethical problems in business cannot be fully resolved without appealing to the shared convictions of the parties in question.[17] European and American managers may want to impose standards of business conduct that give heavy weight to such core human rights as personal freedom, individual security, political participation, the ownership of property, and the right to subsistence as well as the obligation to respect the dignity of each human person, adequate health and safety standards for all employees, and respect for the environment; managers in China have a much weaker commitment to these kinds of human rights. Japanese managers may prefer ethical standards that show respect for the collective good of society. Muslim managers may wish to apply ethical standards compatible with the teachings of Mohammed. Individual companies may want to give explicit recognition to the importance of company personnel living up to the company's own espoused values and business principles. Clearly, there is merit in the school of ethical relativism's view that what is deemed right or wrong, fair or unfair, moral or immoral, ethical or unethical in business situations depends partly on the context of each country's local customs, religious traditions, and societal norms. Hence, there is a kernel of truth in the argument that businesses need some room to tailor their ethical standards to fit local situations. A company has to be very cautious about exporting its home-country values and ethics to foreign countries where it operates—"photocopying" ethics is disrespectful of other cultures and neglects the important role of moral free space.

> Under ethical relativism, there can be no one-size-fits-all set of authentic ethical norms against which to gauge the conduct of company personnel.

Pushed to Extreme, Ethical Relativism Breaks Down While the relativistic rule of "When in Rome, do as the Romans do" appears reasonable, it nonetheless presents a big problem—when the envelope starts to be pushed, as will inevitably be the case, *it is tantamount to rudderless ethical standards.* Consider, for instance, the following example: In 1992, the owners of the SS *United States,* an aging luxury ocean liner constructed with asbestos in the 1940s, had the liner towed to Turkey, where a contractor had agreed to remove the asbestos for $2 million (versus a far higher cost in the United States, where asbestos removal safety standards were much more stringent).[18] When Turkish officials blocked the asbestos removal because of the dangers to workers of contracting cancer, the owners had the liner towed to the Black Sea port of Sevastopol, in the Crimean Republic, where the asbestos removal standards were quite lax and where a contractor had agreed to remove more than 500,000 square feet of carcinogenic asbestos for less than $2 million. There are no moral grounds for arguing that exposing workers to carcinogenic asbestos is ethically correct, irrespective of what a country's law allows or the value the country places on worker safety.

A company that adopts the principle of ethical relativism and holds company personnel to local ethical standards necessarily assumes that what prevails as local morality is an adequate guide to ethical behavior. This can be ethically dangerous—it leads to the conclusion that if a country's culture is accepting of bribery or environmental degradation or exposing workers to dangerous conditions (toxic chemicals or bodily harm), then so much the worse for honest people and protection of the environment and safe working conditions. Such a position is morally unacceptable. Even though bribery of government officials in China is a common practice, when Lucent Technologies found that managers in its Chinese operations had bribed government officials, it fired the entire senior management team.[19]

> Managers in multinational enterprises have to figure out how to navigate the gray zone that arises when operating in two cultures with two sets of ethics.

Moreover, from a global markets perspective, ethical relativism results in a maze of conflicting ethical standards for multinational companies wanting to address the very real issue of what ethical standards to enforce companywide. On the one hand, multinational companies need to educate and motivate their employees worldwide to respect the customs and traditions of other nations, and, on the other hand, they must enforce compliance with the company's own particular code of ethical behavior. It is a slippery slope indeed to resolve such ethical diversity without any kind of higher-order moral compass. Imagine, for example, that a multinational company in the name of ethical relativism takes the position that it is okay for company personnel to pay bribes and kickbacks in countries where such payments are customary but forbids company personnel from making such payments in those countries where bribes and kickbacks are considered unethical or illegal. Or that the company says it is ethically fine to use underage labor in its plants in those countries where underage labor is acceptable and ethically inappropriate to employ underage labor at the remainder of its plants. Having thus adopted conflicting ethical standards for operating in different countries, company managers have little moral basis for enforcing ethical standards companywide—rather, the clear message to employees would be that the company has no ethical standards or principles of its own, preferring to let its practices be governed by the countries in which it operates. This is scarcely strong moral ground to stand on.

Ethics and Integrative Social Contracts Theory

Core Concept
According to *integrated social contracts theory,* universal ethical principles or norms based on the collective views of multiple cultures and societies combine to form a "social contract" that all individuals in all situations have a duty to observe. Within the boundaries of this social contract, local cultures or groups can specify other impermissible actions; however, universal ethical norms always take precedence over local ethical norms.

Social contract theory provides a middle position between the opposing views of universalism (that the same set of ethical standards should apply everywhere) and relativism (that ethical standards vary according to local custom).[20] According to **integrative social contracts theory,** the ethical standards a company should try to uphold are governed both by (1) a limited number of universal ethical principles that are widely recognized as putting legitimate ethical boundaries on actions and behavior in *all* situations and (2) the circumstances of local cultures, traditions, and shared values that further prescribe what constitutes ethically permissible behavior and what does not. However, *universal ethical norms take precedence over local ethical norms.* In other words, universal ethical principles apply in those situations where most all societies—endowed with rationality and moral knowledge—have common moral agreement on what is wrong and thereby put limits on what actions and behaviors fall inside the boundaries of what is right and which ones fall outside. *These mostly uniform agreements about what is morally right and wrong form a "social contract" or contract with society that is binding on all individuals, groups, organizations, and businesses in terms of establishing right and wrong and in drawing the line between ethical and unethical behaviors.* But these universal ethical principles or norms nonetheless still leave some moral free space for the people in a particular country (or local culture or even a company) to make specific interpretations of what other actions may or may not be permissible within the bounds defined by universal ethical principles. Hence, while firms, industries, professional associations, and other business-relevant groups are contractually obligated to society to observe universal ethical norms, they have the discretion to go beyond these universal norms and specify other behaviors that are out of bounds and place further limitations on what is considered ethical. Both the legal and medical professions have standards regarding what kinds of advertising are ethically permissible and what kinds are not. Food products companies are beginning to establish ethical guidelines for judging what is and is not appropriate advertising for food products that are inherently unhealthy and may cause dietary or obesity problems for people who eat them regularly or consume them in large quantities.

The strength of integrated social contracts theory is that it accommodates the best parts of ethical universalism and ethical relativism. It is indisputable that cultural differences impact how business is conducted in various parts of the world and that these cultural differences sometimes give rise to different ethical norms. But it is just as indisputable that some ethical norms are more authentic or universally applicable than others, meaning that, in many instances of cross-country differences, one side may be more "ethically correct" or "more right" than another. In such instances, resolving cross-cultural differences entails applying universal, or first-order, ethical norms and overriding the local, or second-order, ethical norms. A good example is the payment of bribes and kickbacks. Yes, bribes and kickbacks seem to be common in some countries, but does this justify paying them? Just because bribery flourishes in a country does not mean that it is an authentic or legitimate ethical norm. Virtually all of the world's major religions (Buddhism, Christianity, Confucianism, Hinduism, Islam, Judaism, Sikhism, and Taoism) and all moral schools of thought condemn bribery and corruption.[21] Bribery is commonplace in India but interviews with Indian CEOs whose companies constantly engaged in payoffs indicated disgust for the practice and they expressed no illusions about its impropriety.[22] Therefore, a multinational company might reasonably conclude that the right ethical standard is one of refusing to condone bribery and kickbacks on the part of company personnel no matter what the local custom is and no matter what the sales consequences are.

Granting an automatic preference to local country ethical norms presents vexing problems to multinational company managers when the ethical standards followed in a foreign country are lower than those in its home country or are in conflict with the company's code of ethics. Sometimes there can be no compromise on what is ethically permissible and what is not. *This is precisely what integrated social contracts theory maintains—universal or first-order ethical norms should always take precedence over local or second-order norms.* Integrated social contracts theory offers managers in multinational companies clear guidance in resolving cross-country ethical differences: Those parts of the company's code of ethics that involve universal ethical norms must be enforced worldwide, but within these boundaries there is room for ethical diversity and opportunity for host country cultures to exert *some* influence in setting their own moral and ethical standards. Such an approach detours the somewhat scary case of a self-righteous multinational company trying to operate as the standard-bearer of moral truth and imposing its interpretation of its code of ethics worldwide no matter what. And it avoids the equally scary case for a company's ethical conduct to be no higher than local ethical norms in situations where local ethical norms permit practices that are generally considered immoral or when local norms clearly conflict with a company's code of ethical conduct. But even with the guidance provided by integrated social contracts theory, there are many instances where cross-country differences in ethical norms create gray areas in which it is tough to draw a line in the sand between right and wrong decisions, actions, and business practices.

THE THREE CATEGORIES OF MANAGEMENT MORALITY

Three categories of managers stand out with regard to ethical and moral principles in business affairs:[23]

- *The moral manager*—Moral managers are dedicated to high standards of ethical behavior, both in their own actions and in their expectations of how the company's business is to be conducted. They see themselves as stewards of ethical behavior and believe it is important to exercise ethical leadership. Moral managers may well be ambitious and have a powerful urge to succeed, but they pursue success in business within the confines of both the letter and the spirit of what is ethical and legal—they typically regard the law as an ethical minimum and have a habit of operating well above what the law requires.

- *The immoral manager*—Immoral managers have no regard for so-called ethical standards in business and pay no attention to ethical principles in making decisions and conducting the company's business. Their philosophy is that good businesspeople cannot spend time watching out for the interests of others and agonizing over "the right thing to do." In the minds of immoral managers, nice guys come in second and the competitive nature of business requires that you either trample on others or get trampled yourself. They believe what really matters is single-minded pursuit of their own best interests—they are living examples of capitalistic greed, caring only about their own or their organization's gains and successes. Immoral managers may even be willing to short-circuit legal and regulatory requirements if they think they can escape detection. And they are always on the lookout for legal loopholes and creative ways to get around rules and regulations that block or constrain actions they deem in their own or their company's self-interest. Immoral managers are thus the bad guys—they have few scruples, little or no integrity, and are willing to do most anything they believe they can get away with. It doesn't bother them much to be seen by others as wearing the black hats.

- *The amoral manager*—Amoral managers appear in two forms: the intentionally amoral manager and the unintentionally amoral manager. Intentionally amoral managers are of the strong opinion that business and ethics are not to be mixed. They are not troubled by failing to factor ethical considerations into their decisions and actions because it is perfectly legitimate for businesses to do anything they wish so long as they stay within legal and regulatory bounds—in other words, if particular actions and behaviors are legal and comply with existing regulations, then they qualify as permissible and should not be seen as unethical. Intentionally amoral managers view the observance of high ethical standards (doing more than what is required by law) as too Sunday-schoolish for the tough competitive world of business, even though observing some higher ethical considerations may be appropriate in life outside of business. Their concept of right and wrong tends to be lawyer-driven—how much can we get by with and can we go ahead even if it is borderline? Thus intentionally amoral managers hold firmly to the view that anything goes, so long as actions and behaviors are not clearly ruled out by prevailing legal and regulatory requirements.

  Unintentionally amoral managers do not pay much attention to the concept of business ethics either, but for different reasons. They are simply casual about, careless about, or inattentive to the fact that certain kinds of business decisions or company activities are unsavory or may have deleterious effects on others—in short, they go about their jobs as best they can without giving serious thought to the ethical dimension of decisions and business actions. They are ethically unconscious when it comes to business matters, partly or mainly because they have just never stopped to consider whether and to what extent business decisions or company actions sometimes spill over to create adverse impacts on others. Unintentionally amoral managers may even see themselves as people of integrity and as personally ethical. But, like intentionally amoral managers, they are of the firm view that businesses ought to be able to do whatever the current legal and regulatory framework allows them to do without being shackled by ethical considerations.

Core Concept

Amoral managers believe that businesses ought to be able to do whatever current laws and regulations allow them to do without being shackled by ethical considerations—they think that what is permissible and what is not is governed entirely by prevailing laws and regulations, not by societal concepts of right and wrong.

By some accounts, the population of managers is said to be distributed among all three types in a bell-shaped curve, with immoral managers and moral managers occupying the two tails of the curve, and the amoral managers (especially the intentionally amoral managers) occupying the broad middle ground.[24] Furthermore, within the population of managers, there is experiential evidence to support that while the average manager may be amoral most of the time, he or she may slip into a moral or immoral mode on occasion, based on a variety of impinging factors and circumstances.

Evidence of Managerial Immorality in the Global Business Community

There is considerable evidence that a sizable majority of managers are either amoral or immoral. The *2005 Global Corruption Report,* sponsored by Transparency International, found that corruption among public officials and in business transactions is widespread across the world. Table 10.1 shows some of the countries where corruption is believed to be lowest and highest—even in the countries where business practices are deemed to be least corrupt, there is considerable room for improvement in the extent to which managers observe ethical business practices. Table 10.2 presents data showing the perceived likelihood that companies in the 21 largest exporting countries are paying bribes to win business in the markets of 15 emerging-country markets—Argentina, Brazil, Colombia, Hungary, India, Indonesia, Mexico, Morocco, Nigeria, the Philippines, Poland, Russia, South Africa, South Korea, and Thailand.

Table 10.1   **Corruption Perceptions Index, Selected Countries, 2004**

Country	2004 CPI Score*	High–Low Range	Number of Surveys Used	Country	2004 CPI Score*	High–Low Range	Number of Surveys Used
Finland	9.7	9.2–10.0	9	Taiwan	5.6	4.7–6.0	15
New Zealand	9.6	9.2–9.7	9	Italy	4.8	3.4–5.6	10
Denmark	9.5	8.7–9.8	10	South Africa	4.6	3.4–5.8	11
Sweden	9.2	8.7–9.5	11	South Korea	4.5	2.2–5.8	14
Switzerland	9.1	8.6–9.4	10	Brazil	3.9	3.5–4.8	11
Norway	8.9	8.0–9.5	9	Mexico	3.6	2.6–4.5	11
Australia	8.8	6.7–9.5	15	Thailand	3.6	2.5–4.5	14
Netherlands	8.7	8.3–9.4	10	China	3.4	2.1–5.6	16
United Kingdom	8.6	7.8–9.2	12	Saudi Arabia	3.4	2.0–4.5	5
Canada	8.5	6.5–9.4	12	Turkey	3.2	1.9–5.4	13
Germany	8.2	7.5–9.2	11	India	2.8	2.2–3.7	15
Hong Kong	8.0	3.5–9.4	13	Russia	2.8	2.0–5.0	15
United States	7.5	5.0–8.7	14	Philippines	2.6	1.4–3.7	14
Chile	7.4	6.3–8.7	11	Vietnam	2.6	1.6–3.7	11
France	7.1	5.0–9.0	12	Argentina	2.5	1.7–3.7	11
Spain	7.1	5.6–8.0	11	Venezuela	2.3	2.0–3.0	11
Japan	6.9	3.5–9.0	15	Pakistan	2.1	1.2–3.3	7
Israel	6.4	3.5–8.1	10	Nigeria	1.6	0.9–2.1	9
Uruguay	6.2	5.6–7.3	6	Bangladesh	1.5	0.3–2.4	5

* The CPI scores range between 10 (highly clean) and 0 (highly corrupt); the data were collected between 2002 and 2004 and reflects a composite of 18 data sources from 12 institutions, as indicated in the number of surveys used. The CPI score represents the perceptions of the degree of corruption as seen by businesspeople, academics, and risk analysts. CPI scores were reported for 146 countries.

Source: Transparency International, *2005 Global Corruption Report,* www.globalcorruptionreport.org (accessed October 31, 2005), pp. 235–38.

Table 10.2 **The Degree to Which Companies in Major Exporting Countries Are Perceived to Be Paying Bribes in Doing Business Abroad**

Rank/Country	Bribe-Payer Index (10 = Low; 0 = High)	Rank/Country	Bribe-Payer Index (10 = Low; 0 = High)
1. Australia	8.5	12. France	5.5
2. Sweden	8.4	13. United States	5.3
3. Switzerland	8.4	14. Japan	5.3
4. Austria	8.2	15. Malaysia	4.3
5. Canada	8.1	16. Hong Kong	4.3
6. Netherlands	7.8	17. Italy	4.1
7. Belgium	7.8	18. South Korea	3.9
8. Britain	6.9	19. Taiwan	3.8
9. Singapore	6.3	20. China (excluding Hong Kong)	3.5
10. Germany	6.3	21. Russia	3.2
11. Spain	5.8		

Note: The bribe-payer index is based on a questionnaire developed by Transparency International and a survey of some 835 private-sector leaders in 15 emerging countries accounting for 60 percent of all imports into non-Organization for Economic Cooperation and Development countries—actual polling was conducted by Gallup International.

Source: Transparency International, *2003 Global Corruption Report*, www.globalcorruptionreport.org (accessed November 1, 2005), p. 267.

The *2003 Global Corruption Report* cited data indicating that bribery occurred most often in (1) public works contracts and construction, (2) the arms and defense industry, and (3) the oil and gas industry. On a scale of 1 to 10, where 10 indicates negligible bribery, even the "cleanest" industry sectors—agriculture, light manufacturing, and fisheries—only had "passable" scores of 5.9, indicating that bribes are quite likely a common occurrence in these sectors as well (see Table 10.3).

The corruption, of course, extends beyond just bribes and kickbacks. For example, in 2005, four global chip makers (Samsung and Hynix Semiconductor in South Korea, Infineon Technologies in Germany, and Micron Technology in the United States) pleaded guilty to conspiring to fix the prices of dynamic random access memory (DRAM) chips sold to such companies as Dell, Apple Computer, and Hewlett-Packard—DRAM chips generate annual worldwide sales of around $26 billion and are used in computers, electronics products, and motor vehicles.[25] So far, the probe has resulted in fines of $730 million, jail terms for nine executives, and pending criminal charges for three more employees for their role in the global cartel; the guilty companies face hundreds of millions of dollars more in damage claims from customers and from consumer class-action lawsuits.

A global business community that is apparently so populated with unethical business practices and managerial immorality does not bode well for concluding that many companies ground their strategies on exemplary ethical principles or for the vigor with which company managers try to ingrain ethical behavior into company personnel. And, as many business school professors have noted, there are considerable numbers of amoral business students in our classrooms. So efforts to root out shady and corrupt business practices and implant high ethical principles into the managerial process of crafting and executing strategy is unlikely to produce an ethically strong global business climate anytime in the near future, barring major effort to address and correct the ethical laxness of company managers.

Table 10.3   **Bribery in Different Industries**

Business Sector	Bribery Score (10 = Low; 0 = High)
Agriculture	5.9
Light manufacturing	5.9
Fisheries	5.9
Information technology	5.1
Forestry	5.1
Civilian aerospace	4.9
Banking and finance	4.7
Heavy manufacturing	4.5
Pharmaceuticals/medical care	4.3
Transportation/storage	4.3
Mining	4.0
Power generation/transmission	3.7
Telecommunications	3.7
Real estate/property	3.5
Oil and gas	2.7
Arms and defense	1.9
Public works/construction	1.3

Note: The bribery scores for each industry are based on a questionnaire developed by Transparency International and a survey of some 835 private sector leaders in 15 emerging countries accounting for 60 percent of all imports into non-Organization for Economic Cooperation and Development countries—actual polling was conducted by Gallup International.

Source: Transparency International, *2003 Global Corruption Report,* www.globalcorruption report.org (accessed November 1, 2005), p. 268.

DO COMPANY STRATEGIES NEED TO BE ETHICAL?

Company managers may formulate strategies that are ethical in all respects, or they may decide to employ strategies that, for one reason or another, have unethical or at least gray-area components. While most company managers are usually careful to ensure that a company's strategy is within the bounds of what is legal, the available evidence indicates they are not always so careful to ensure that all elements of their strategies are within the bounds of what is generally deemed ethical. Senior executives with strong ethical convictions are normally proactive in insisting that all aspects of company strategy fall within ethical boundaries. In contrast, senior executives who are either immoral or amoral may use shady strategies and unethical or borderline business practices, especially if they are clever at devising schemes to keep ethically questionable actions hidden from view.

During the past five years, there has been an ongoing series of revelations about managers who have ignored ethical standards, deliberately stepped out of bounds, and been called to account by the media, regulators, and the legal system. Ethical misconduct has occurred at Enron, Tyco International, HealthSouth, Rite Aid, Citicorp, Bristol-Myers, Squibb, Adelphia, Royal Dutch/Shell, Parmalat (an Italy-based food products company), Mexican oil giant Pemex, Marsh & McLennan and other insurance brokers, several leading brokerage houses and investment banking firms, and a host of mutual fund companies. The consequences of crafting strategies that cannot pass the test of moral scrutiny are manifested in the sharp drops in the stock prices of the guilty companies that have cost shareholders billions of dollars; the frequently devastating public relations hits that the accused companies have taken, the sizes of the fines that have been levied (often amounting to several hundred million dollars); the growing legion of criminal indictments and convictions of company executives; and the numbers of executives who have either been dismissed from their jobs, shoved into early retirement, and/or suffered immense public embarrassment. The fallout from all these scandals has resulted in heightened management attention to legal and ethical considerations in crafting strategy. Illustration Capsule 10.1 details the ethically flawed strategy at the world's leading insurance broker, and the consequences to those concerned.

What Are the Drivers of Unethical Strategies and Business Behavior?

The apparent pervasiveness of immoral and amoral businesspeople is one obvious reason why ethical principles are an ineffective moral compass in business dealings and why companies may resort to unethical strategic behavior. But apart from thinking that maintains "The business of business is business, not ethics," three other main drivers of unethical business behavior also stand out:[26]

- Faulty oversight such that overzealous or obsessive pursuit of personal gain, wealth, and other selfish interests is overlooked by or escapes the attention of higher-ups (most usually the board of directors).
- Heavy pressures on company managers to meet or beat performance targets.
- A company culture that puts the profitability and good business performance ahead of ethical behavior.

Overzealous Pursuit of Personal Gain, Wealth, and Selfish Interests
People who are obsessed with wealth accumulation, greed, power, status, and other selfish interests often push ethical principles aside in their quest for self-gain. Driven by their ambitions, they exhibit few qualms in skirting the rules or doing whatever is necessary to achieve their goals. The first and only priority of such corporate bad apples is to look out for their own best interests and if climbing the ladder of success means having few scruples and ignoring the welfare of others, so be it. A general disregard for business ethics can prompt all kinds of unethical strategic maneuvers and behaviors at companies. Top executives, directors, and majority shareholders at cable-TV company Adelphia Communications ripped off the company for amounts totaling well over $1 billion, diverting hundreds of millions of dollars to fund their Buffalo Sabres hockey team, build a private golf course, and buy timber rights—among other things—and driving the company into bankruptcy. Their actions, which represent one of the biggest instances of corporate looting and self-dealing in American business, took place despite the company's public pontifications about the principles it would observe in trying to care for customers, employees, stockholders, and the local communities where it operated. Andrew Fastow, Enron's chief financial officer (CFO), set himself up as the manager of one of Enron's off-the-books partnerships and as the part-owner of another, allegedly earning extra compensation of $30 million for his owner-manager roles in the two partnerships; Enron's board of directors agreed to suspend the company's conflict-of-interest rules designed to protect the company from this very kind of executive self-dealing (but directors and perhaps Fastow's superiors were kept in the dark about how much Fastow was earning on the side).

Marsh & McLennan's Ethically Flawed Strategy

In October 2004, *Wall Street Journal* headlines trumpeted that a cartel among insurance brokers had been busted. Among the ringleaders was worldwide industry leader Marsh & McLennan Companies Inc., with 2003 revenues of $11.5 billion and a U.S. market share of close to 20 percent. The gist of the brokers' plan was to cheat corporate clients by rigging the bids brokers solicited for insurance policies and thereby collecting big fees (called contingent commissions) from major insurance companies for steering business their way. Two family members of Marsh & McLennan CEO Jeffery Greenberg were CEOs of major insurance companies to which Marsh sometimes steered business. Greenberg's father was CEO of insurance giant AIG (which had total revenues of $81 billion and insurance premium revenues of $28 billion in 2003), and Greenberg's younger brother was CEO of ACE Ltd., the 24th biggest property-casualty insurer in the United States, with 2003 revenues of $10.7 billion and insurance premium revenues of more than $5 billion worldwide. Prior to joining ACE, Greenberg's younger brother had been president and chief operating officer of AIG, headed by his father.

Several months prior to the cartel bust, a Marsh subsidiary, Putnam Investments, had paid a $110 million fine for securities fraud and another Marsh subsidiary, Mercer Consulting, was placed under Securities and Exchange Commission (SEC) investigation for engaging in pay-to-play practices that forced investment managers to pay fees in order to secure Mercer's endorsement of their services when making recommendations to Mercer's pension fund clients.

The cartel scheme arose from the practice of large corporations to hire the services of such brokers as Marsh & McLennan, Aon Corporation, A. J. Gallaher & Company, Wells Fargo, or BB&T Insurance Services to manage their risks and take out appropriate property and casualty insurance on their behalf. The broker's job was to solicit bids from several insurers and obtain the best policies at the lowest prices for the client.

Marsh's insurance brokerage strategy was to solicit artificially high bids from some insurance companies so that it could guarantee that the bid of a preferred insurer on a given deal would win the bid. Marsh brokers called underwriters at various insurers, often including AIG and ACE, and asked for "B" quotes—bids that were deliberately high. Insurers asked for B quotes knew that Marsh wanted another insurer to win the business, but they were willing to participate because on other policy solicitations Marsh could end up steering the business to them via Marsh's same strategy. Sometimes Marsh even asked underwriters that were providing B quotes to attend a meeting with Marsh's client and make a presentation regarding their policy to help bolster the credibility of their inflated bid.

Since it was widespread practice among insurers to pay brokers contingent commissions based on the volume or profitability of the business the broker directed to them, Marsh's B-quote solicitation strategy allowed it to steer business to those insurers paying the largest contingent commissions—these contingent commissions were in addition to the fees the broker earned from the corporate client for services rendered in conducting the bidding process for the client. A substantial fraction of the policies that Marsh unlawfully steered were to two Bermuda-based insurance companies that it helped start up and in which it also had ownership interests (some Marsh executives also indirectly owned shares of stock in one of the companies); indeed, these two insurance companies received 30–40 percent of their total business from policies steered to them by Marsh.

At Marsh, steering business to insurers paying the highest contingent commission was a key component of the company's overall strategy. Marsh's contingent commissions generated revenues of close to $1.5 billion over the 2001–2003 period, including $845 million in 2003. Without these commission revenues, Marsh's $1.5 billion in net profits would have been close to 40 percent lower in 2003.

Within days of headlines about the cartel bust, Marsh's stock price had fallen by 48 percent (costing shareholders about $11.5 billion in market value) and the company was looking down the barrel of a criminal indictment. To stave off the criminal indictment (something no insurance company had ever survived), board members forced Jeffrey Greenberg to resign as CEO. Another top executive was suspended. Criminal charges against several Marsh executives for their roles in the bid-rigging scheme were filed several weeks thereafter.

In an attempt to lead industry reform, Greenberg's successor quickly announced a new business model for Marsh that included not accepting any contingent commissions from insurers. Marsh's new strategy and business model involved charging fees only to its corporate clients for soliciting bids, placing their insurance, and otherwise managing clients' risks and crises. This eliminated Marsh's conflict of interest in earning fees from both sides of the transactions it made on behalf of its corporate clients. Marsh also committed to provide up-front disclosure to clients of the fees it would earn on their business (in the past such fees had been murky and incomplete). Even so, there were indications that close to 10 lawsuits, some involving class action, would soon be filed against the company.

Meanwhile, all major commercial property-casualty insurers were scrambling to determine whether their payment of contingent commissions was ethical, since such arrangements clearly gave insurance brokers a financial incentive to place insurance with companies paying the biggest contingent commissions, not those with the best prices or terms. Prosecutors of the cartel had referred to the contingent commissions as kickbacks.

Sources: Monica Langley and Theo Francis, "Insurers Reel from Bust of a 'Cartel,'" *The Wall Street Journal,* October 18, 2004, pp. A1, A14; Monica Langley and Ian McDonald, "Marsh Averts Criminal Case with New CEO," *The Wall Street Journal,* October 26, 2004, pp. A1, A10; Christopher Oster and Theo Francis, "Marsh and Aon Have Holdings in Two Insurers," *The Wall Street Journal,* November 1, 2004, p. C1; and Marcia Vickers, "The Secret World of Marsh Mac," *BusinessWeek,* November 1, 2004, pp. 78–89.

According to a civil complaint filed by the Securities and Exchange Commission, the CEO of Tyco International, a well-known $35.6 billion manufacturing and services company, conspired with the company's CFO to steal more than $170 million, including a company-paid $2 million birthday party for the CEO's wife held on Sardinia, an island off the coast of Italy; a $7 million Park Avenue apartment for his wife; and secret low-interest and interest-free loans to fund private businesses and investments and purchase lavish artwork, yachts, estate jewelry, and vacation homes in New Hampshire, Connecticut, Massachusetts, and Utah. The CEO allegedly lived rent-free in a $31 million Fifth Avenue apartment that Tyco purchased in his name, directed millions of dollars of charitable contributions in his own name using Tyco funds, diverted company funds to finance his personal businesses and investments, and sold millions of dollars of Tyco stock back to Tyco itself through Tyco subsidiaries located in offshore bank-secrecy jurisdictions. Tyco's CEO and CFO were further charged with conspiring to reap more than $430 million from sales of stock, using questionable accounting to hide their actions, and engaging in deceptive accounting practices to distort the company's financial condition from 1995 to 2002. At the trial on the charges filed by the SEC, the prosecutor told the jury in his opening statement, "This case is about lying, cheating and stealing. These people didn't win the jackpot—they stole it." Defense lawyers countered that "every single transaction . . . was set down in detail in Tyco's books and records" and that the authorized and disclosed multimillion-dollar compensation packages were merited by the company's financial performance and stock price gains. The two Tyco executives were convicted and sentenced to jail.

Prudential Securities paid a total of about $2 billion in the 1990s to settle misconduct charges relating to practices that misled investors on the risks and rewards of limited-partnership investments. Providian Financial Corporation, despite an otherwise glowing record of social responsibility and corporate citizenship, paid $150 million in 2001 to settle claims that its strategy included systematic attempts to cheat credit card holders. Ten prominent Wall Street securities firms in 2003 paid $1.4 billion to settle charges that they knowingly issued misleading stock research to investors in an effort to prop up the stock prices of client corporations. A host of mutual-fund firms made under-the-table arrangements to regularly buy and sell stock for their accounts at special after-hours trading prices that disadvantaged long-term investors and had to pay nearly $2.0 billion in fines and restitution when their unethical practices were discovered by authorities during 2002–2003. Salomon Smith Barney, Goldman Sachs, Credit Suisse First Boston, and several other financial firms were assessed close to $2 billion in fines and restitution for the unethical manner in which they contributed to the scandals at Enron and WorldCom and for the shady practice of allocating shares of hot initial public offering stocks to a select list of corporate executives who either steered or were in a position to steer investment banking business their way.

Heavy Pressures on Company Managers to Meet or Beat Earnings Targets   When companies find themselves scrambling to achieve ambitious earnings growth and meet the quarterly and annual performance expectations of Wall Street analysts and investors, managers often feel enormous pressure to do whatever it takes to sustain the company's reputation for delivering good financial performance. Executives at high-performing companies know that investors will see the slightest sign of a slowdown in earnings growth as a red flag and drive down the company's stock price. The company's credit rating could be downgraded if it has used lots of debt to finance its growth. The pressure to watch the scoreboard and never miss a quarter—so as not to upset the expectations of Wall Street analysts and fickle stock market investors—prompts managers to cut costs wherever savings show up immediately, squeeze extra sales out of early deliveries, and engage in other short-term maneuvers to make the numbers. As the pressure builds to keep performance numbers looking good, company personnel start stretching the rules further and further, until the limits of ethical conduct are overlooked.[27] Once ethical boundaries are crossed in efforts to "meet or beat the numbers," the threshold for making more extreme ethical compromises becomes lower.

Several top executives at WorldCom (the remains of which is now part of Verizon Communications), a company built with scores of acquisitions in exchange for WorldCom stock, allegedly concocted a fraudulent $11 billion accounting scheme to hide costs and inflate revenues and profit over several years; the scheme was said to have helped the company keep its stock price propped up high enough to make additional acquisitions, support its nearly $30 billion debt load, and allow executives to cash in on their lucrative stock options. At Qwest Communications, a company created by the merger of a go-go telecom start-up and U.S. West (one of the regional Bell companies), management was charged with scheming to improperly book $2.4 billion in revenues from a variety of sources and deals, thereby inflating the company's profits and making it appear that the company's strategy to create a telecommunications company of the future was on track when, in fact, it was faltering badly behind the scenes. Top-level Qwest executives were dismissed, and in 2004 new management agreed to $250 million in fines for all the misdeeds.

At Bristol-Myers Squibb, the world's fifth-largest drug maker, management apparently engaged in a series of numbers-game maneuvers to meet earnings targets, including such actions as:

- Offering special end-of-quarter discounts to induce distributors and local pharmacies to stock up on certain prescription drugs—a practice known as channel stuffing.
- Issuing last-minute price increase alerts to spur purchases and beef up operating profits.
- Setting up excessive reserves for restructuring charges and then reversing some of the charges as needed to bolster operating profits.
- Making repeated asset sales small enough that the gains could be reported as additions to operating profit rather than being flagged as one-time gains. (Some accountants have long used a rule of thumb that says a transaction that alters quarterly profits by less than 5 percent is "immaterial" and need not be disclosed in the company's financial reports.)

Such numbers games were said to be a common "earnings management" practice at Bristol-Myers and, according to one former executive, "sent a huge message across the organization that you make your numbers at all costs."[28]

Company executives often feel pressured to hit financial performance targets because their compensation depends heavily on the company's performance. During the late 1990s, it became fashionable for boards of directors to grant lavish bonuses, stock option awards, and other compensation benefits to executives for meeting specified performance targets. So outlandishly large were these rewards that executives had strong personal incentives to bend the rules and engage in behaviors the allowed the targets to be met. Much of the accounting hocus-pocus at the root of recent corporate scandals has entailed situations in which executives benefited enormously from misleading accounting or other shady activities that allowed them to hit the numbers and receive incentive awards ranging from $10 million to $100 million. At Bristol-Myers Squibb, for example, the pay-for-performance link spawned strong rules-bending incentives. About 94 percent of one top executive's $18.5 million in total compensation in 2001 came from stock-option grants, a bonus, and long-term incentive payments linked to corporate performance; about 92 percent of a second executive's $12.9 million of compensation was incentive-based.[29]

The fundamental problem with a "make the numbers and move on" syndrome is that a company doesn't really serve its customers or its shareholders by going overboard in pursuing bottom-line profitability. In the final analysis, shareholder interests are best served by doing a really good job of serving customers (observing the rule that customers are king) and by improving the company's competitiveness in the marketplace—these outcomes are the most reliable drivers of higher profits and added shareholder value. Cutting ethical corners or stooping to downright illegal actions in the name of profits first carries exceptionally high risk for shareholders—the steep stock-price decline and tarnished brand image that accompany the discovery of scurrilous behavior leaves shareholders with a company worth much less than before—and the rebuilding task can be arduous, taking both considerable time and resources.

Company Cultures That Put the Bottom Line Ahead of Ethical Behavior

When a company's culture spawns an ethically corrupt or amoral work climate, people have a company-approved license to ignore what's right and engage in most any behavior or employ most any strategy they think they can get away with. Such cultural norms as "No one expects strict adherence to ethical standards," "Everyone else does it," and "It is politic to bend the rules to get the job done" permeate the work environment.[30] At such companies, ethically immoral or amoral people play down observance of ethical strategic actions and business conduct. Moreover, the pressures to conform to cultural norms can prompt otherwise honorable people to make ethical mistakes and succumb to the many opportunities around them to engage in unethical practices.

A perfect example of a company culture gone awry on ethics is Enron.[31] Enron's leaders encouraged company personnel to focus on the current bottom line and to be innovative and aggressive in figuring out what could be done to grow current revenues and earnings. Employees were expected to pursue opportunities to the utmost. Enron executives viewed the company as a laboratory for innovation; the company hired the best and brightest people and pushed them to be creative, look at problems and opportunities in new ways, and exhibit a sense of urgency in making things happen. Employees were encouraged to make a difference and do their part in creating an entrepreneurial environment in which creativity flourished, people could achieve their full potential, and everyone had a stake in the outcome. Enron employees got the message—pushing the limits and meeting one's numbers were viewed as survival skills. Enron's annual "rank and yank" formal evaluation process, in which the 15 to 20 percent lowest-ranking employees were let go or encouraged to seek other employment, made it abundantly clear that hitting earnings targets and being *the* mover and shaker -in the marketplace were what counted. The name of the game at Enron became devising clever ways to boost revenues and earnings, even if it sometimes meant operating outside established policies and without the knowledge of superiors. In fact, outside-the-lines behavior was celebrated if it generated profitable new business. Enron's energy contracts and its trading and hedging activities grew increasingly more complex and diverse as employees pursued first this avenue and then another to help keep Enron's financial performance looking good.

As a consequence of Enron's well-publicized successes in creating new products and businesses and leveraging the company's trading and hedging expertise into new market arenas, Enron came to be regarded as exceptionally innovative. It was ranked by its corporate peers as the most innovative U.S. company for three consecutive years in *Fortune* magazine's annual surveys of the most-admired companies. A high-performance/high-rewards climate came to pervade the Enron culture, as the best workers (determined by who produced the best bottom-line results) received impressively large incentives and bonuses (amounting to as much as $1 million for traders and even more for senior executives). On Car Day at Enron, an array of luxury sports cars arrived for presentation to the most successful employees. Understandably, employees wanted to be seen as part of Enron's star team and partake in the benefits that being one of Enron's best and smartest employees entailed. The high monetary rewards, the ambitious and hard-driving people that the company hired and promoted, and the competitive, results-oriented culture combined to give Enron a reputation not only for trampling competitors at every opportunity but also for practicing internal ruthlessness. The company's super-aggressiveness and win-at-all-costs mind-set nurtured a culture that gradually and then more rapidly fostered the erosion of ethical standards, eventually making a mockery of the company's stated values of integrity and respect. When it became evident in the fall of 2001 that Enron was a house of cards propped up by deceitful accounting and a myriad of unsavory practices, the company imploded in a matter of weeks—the biggest bankruptcy of all time cost investors $64 billion in losses (between August 2000, when the stock price was at its five-year high, and November 2001), and Enron employees lost their retirement assets, which were almost totally invested in Enron stock.

More recently, a team investigating an ethical scandal at oil giant Royal Dutch/Shell Group that resulted in the payment of $150 million in fines found that an ethically flawed culture was a major contributor to why managers made rosy forecasts that they couldn't meet and why top executives engaged in maneuvers to mislead investors by overstating Shell's oil and gas reserves by 25 percent (equal to 4.5 billion barrels of oil). The investigation revealed that top Shell executives knew that a variety of internal practices, together with unrealistic and unsupportable estimates submitted by overzealous, bonus-conscious managers in Shell's exploration and production group, were being used to overstate reserves. An e-mail written by Shell's top executive for exploration and production (who was caught up in the ethical misdeeds and later forced to resign) said, "I am becoming sick and tired about lying about the extent of our reserves issues and the downward revisions that need to be done because of our far too aggressive/optimistic bookings."[32]

Illustration Capsule 10.2 describes Philip Morris USA's new strategy for growing the sales of its leading Marlboro cigarette brand—judge for yourself whether the strategy is ethical or shady in light of the undisputed medical links between smoking and lung cancer.

Approaches to Managing a Company's Ethical Conduct

The stance a company takes in dealing with or managing ethical conduct at any given point can take any of four basic forms:[33]

- The unconcerned, or nonissue, approach.
- The damage control approach.
- The compliance approach.
- The ethical culture approach.

The differences in these four approaches are discussed briefly below and summarized in Table 10.4 on page 335.

Illustration Capsule 10.2

Philip Morris USA's Strategy for Marlboro Cigarettes: Ethical or Unethical?

In late 2005, Philip Morris USA and its corporate parent, Altria Group Inc., wrapped up a year of promotions and parties to celebrate the 50th year of selling Marlboro cigarettes. Marlboro commanded a 40 percent share of the U.S. market for cigarettes and was also one of the world's top cigarette brands. Despite sharp advertising restrictions agreed to by cigarette marketers in 1998 and a big jump in state excise taxes on cigarettes since 2002, Marlboro's sales and market share were climbing, thanks to a new trailblazing marketing strategy.

Marlboro had become a major brand in the 1960s and 1970s via a classic mass-marketing strategy anchored by annual ad budgets in the millions of dollars. The company's TV, magazine, and billboard ads for Marlboros always featured a rugged cowboy wearing a Stetson, riding a horse in a mountainous area, and smoking a Marlboro—closely connecting the brand with the American West gave Marlboro a distinctive and instantly recognized brand image. The Marlboro ad campaign was a gigantic success, making Marlboro one of the world's best-known and valuable brands.

But following the ad restrictions in 1998, Philip Morris had to shift to a different marketing strategy to grow Marlboro's sales. It opted for an approach aimed at generating all kinds of marketing buzz for the Marlboro brand and creating a larger cadre of loyal Marlboro smokers (who often felt persecuted by social pressures and antismoking ordinances). Philip Morris directed company field reps to set up promotions at local bars where smokers could sign up for promotional offers like price discounts on Marlboro purchases, a Marlboro Miles program that awarded points for each pack purchased, and sweepstakes prizes that included cash, trips, and Marlboro apparel; some prizes could be purchased with Marlboro Miles points. It also began to sponsor live concerts and other events to generate additional sign-ups among attendees. A Web site was created to spur Internet chatter among the Marlboro faithful and to encourage still more sign-ups

for special deals and contests (some with prizes up to a $1 million)—an online community quickly sprang up around the brand. Via all the sign-ups and calls to an 800 number, Philip Morris created a database of Marlboro smokers that by 2005 had grown to 26 million names. Using direct mail and e-mail, the company sent the members of its database a steady stream of messages and offers, ranging from birthday coupons for free breakfasts to price discounts to chances to attend local concerts, enjoy a day at nearby horse tracks, or win a trip to the company's ranch in Montana (where winners got gifts, five-course meals, massages, and free drinks and could go snowmobiling, fly fishing, or horseback riding).

Meanwhile, Philip Morris also became considerably more aggressive in retail stores, launching an offensive initiative to give discounts and incentives to retailers who utilized special aisle displays and signage for its cigarette brands. One 22-store retail chain reported that, by agreeing to a deal to give Philip Morris brands about 66 percent of its cigarette shelf space, it ended up paying about $5.50 per carton less for its Marlboro purchases than it paid for cartons of Camels supplied by rival R. J. Reynolds. Some Wal-Mart stores were said to have awarded Philip Morris as much as 80 percent of its cigarette shelf space.

Thus, despite being besieged by the costs of defending lawsuits and paying out billions to governments as compensation for the increased health care costs associated with smoking, Philip Morris and other cigarette makers were making very healthy profits: operating margins of nearly 28 percent in 2005 (up from 26 percent in 2004) and net income of about $11.4 billion on sales of $66.3 billion in the United States and abroad.

However, health care officials were highly critical of Philip Morris's marketing tactics for Marlboro, and the U.S. Department of Justice had filed a lawsuit claiming, among other things, that the company knowingly marketed Marlboros to underage people in its database, a charge denied by the company.

Source: Based largely on information in Nanette Byrnes, "Leader of the Packs," *BusinessWeek,* October 31, 2005, pp. 56, 58.

The Unconcerned, or Nonissue, Approach   The unconcerned approach is prevalent at companies whose executives are immoral and unintentionally amoral. Senior executives at companies using this approach ascribe to the view that notions of right and wrong in matters of business are defined entirely by government via the prevailing laws and regulations. They maintain that trying to enforce ethical standards above and beyond what is legally required is a nonissue because businesses are entitled to conduct their affairs in whatever

Table 10.4   **Four Approaches to Managing Business Ethics**

	Unconcerned, or Nonissue Approach	Damage Control Approach	Compliance Approach	Ethical Culture Approach
Underlying beliefs	• The business of business is business, not ethics. • All that matters is whether an action is legal. • Ethics has no place in the conduct of business. • Companies should not be morally accountable for their actions.	• The company needs to make a token gesture in the direction of ethical standards (a code of ethics).	• The company must be committed to ethical standards and monitoring ethics performance. • Unethical behavior must be prevented and punished if discovered. • It is important to have a reputation for high ethical standards.	• Ethics is basic to the culture. • Behaving ethically must be a deeply held corporate value and become a way of life. • Everyone is expected to walk the talk.
Ethics management approaches	• There's no need to make decisions concerning business ethics—if its legal, it is okay. • No intervention regarding the ethical component of decisions is needed.	• The company must act to protect against the dangers of unethical strategies and behavior. • Ignore unethical behavior or allow it to go unpunished unless the situation is extreme and requires action.	• The company must establish a clear, comprehensive code of ethics. • The company must provide ethics training for all personnel. • Have formal ethics compliance procedures, an ethics compliance office, and a chief ethics officer.	• Ethical behavior is ingrained and reinforced as part of the culture. • Much reliance on co-worker peer pressure—"That's not how we do things here." • Everyone is an ethics watchdog—whistle-blowing is required. • Ethics heroes are celebrated; ethics stories are told.
Challenges	• Financial consequences can become unaffordable. • Some stakeholders are alienated.	• Credibility problems with stakeholders can arise. • The company is susceptible to ethical scandal. • The company has a subpar ethical reputation—executives and company personnel don't walk the talk.	• Organizational members come to rely on the existing rules for moral guidance—fosters a mentality of what is not forbidden is allowed. • Rules and guidelines proliferate. • The locus of moral control resides in the code and in the ethics compliance system rather than in an individual's own moral responsibility for ethical behavior.	• New employees must go through strong ethics induction program. • Formal ethics management systems can be underutilized. • Relying on peer pressures and cultural norms to enforce ethical standards can result in eliminating some or many of the compliance trappings and, over time, induce moral laxness.

Source: Adapted from Gedeon J. Rossouw and Leon J. van Vuuren, "Modes of Managing Morality: A Descriptive Model of Strategies for Managing Ethics," *Journal of Business Ethics* 46, no. 4 (September 2003), pp. 392–93.

manner they wish so long as they comply with the letter of what is legally required. Hence, there is no need to spend valuable management time trying to prescribe and enforce standards of conduct that go above and beyond legal and regulatory requirements. In companies where senior managers are immoral, the prevailing view may well be that under-the-table dealing can be good business if it can be kept hidden or if it can be justified on grounds that others are doing it too. Companies in this mode usually engage in most any business practices they believe they can get away with, and the strategies they employ may well embrace elements that are either borderline from a legal perspective or ethically shady and unsavory.

The Damage Control Approach   Damage control is favored at companies whose managers are intentionally amoral but who are wary of scandal and adverse public relations fallout that could cost them their jobs of tarnish their careers. Companies using this approach, not wanting to risk tarnishing the reputations of key personnel or the company, usually make some concession to window-dressing ethics, going so far as to adopt a code of ethics—so that their executives can point to it as evidence of good-faith efforts to prevent unethical strategy making or unethical conduct on the part of company personnel. But the code of ethics exists mainly as nice words on paper, and company personnel do not operate within a strong ethical context—there's a notable gap between talking ethics and walking ethics. Employees quickly get the message that rule bending is tolerated and may even be rewarded if the company benefits from their actions.

> The main objective of the damage control approach is to protect against adverse publicity and any damaging consequences brought on by headlines in the media, outside investigation, threats of litigation, punitive government action, or angry or vocal stakeholders.

Company executives that practice the damage control approach are prone to look the other way when shady or borderline behavior occurs—adopting a kind of "See no evil, hear no evil, speak no evil" stance (except when exposure of the company's actions put executives under great pressure to redress any wrongs that have been done). They may even condone questionable actions that help the company reach earnings targets or bolster its market standing—such as pressuring customers to stock up on the company's product (channel stuffing), making under-the-table payments to win new business, stonewalling the recall of products claimed to be unsafe, bad-mouthing the products of rivals, or trying to keep prices low by sourcing goods from disreputable suppliers in low-wage countries that run sweatshop operations or use child labor. But they are usually careful to do such things in a manner that lessens the risks of exposure or damaging consequences. This generally includes making token gestures to police compliance with codes of ethics and relying heavily on spin to help extricate the company or themselves from claims that the company's strategy has unethical components or that company personnel have engaged in unethical practices.

The Compliance Approach   Anywhere from light to forceful compliance is favored at companies whose managers (1) lean toward being somewhat amoral but are highly concerned about having ethically upstanding reputations or (2) are moral and see strong compliance methods as the best way to impose and enforce ethical rules and high ethical standards. Companies that adopt a compliance mode usually do some or all of the following to display their commitment to ethical conduct: make the code of ethics a visible and regular part of communications with employees, implement ethics training programs, appoint a chief ethics officer or ethics ombudsperson, have ethics committees to give guidance on ethics matters, institute formal procedures for investigating alleged ethics violations, conduct ethics audits to measure and document compliance, give ethics awards to employees for outstanding efforts to create an ethical climate and improve ethical performance, and/or try to deter violations by setting up ethics hotlines for anonymous callers to use in reporting possible violations.

Emphasis here is usually on securing broad compliance and measuring the degree to which ethical standards are upheld and observed. However, violators are disciplined and sometimes subjected to public reprimand and punishment (including dismissal), thereby sending a clear signal to company personnel that complying with ethical standards needs to be taken seriously. The driving force behind the company's commitment to eradicate unethical behavior normally stems from a desire to avoid the cost and damage associated with unethical conduct or else a quest to gain favor from stakeholders (especially ethically conscious customers, employees, and investors) for having a highly regarded reputation for ethical behavior. One of the weaknesses of the compliance approach is that moral control resides in the company's code of ethics and in the ethics compliance system rather than in (1) the strong peer pressures for ethical behavior that come from ingraining a highly ethical corporate culture and (2) an individual's own moral responsibility for ethical behavior.[34]

The Ethical Culture Approach   At some companies, top executives believe that high ethical principles must be deeply ingrained in the corporate culture and function as guides for "how we do things around here." A company using the ethical culture approach seeks to gain employee buy-in to the company's ethical standards, business principles, and corporate values. The ethical principles embraced in the company's code of ethics and/or in its statement of corporate values are seen as integral to the company's identity and ways of operating—they are at the core of the company's soul and are promoted as part of business as usual. The integrity of the ethical culture approach depends heavily on the ethical integrity of the executives who create and nurture the culture—it is incumbent on them to determine how high the bar is to be set and to exemplify ethical standards in their own decisions and behavior. Further, it is essential that the strategy be ethical in all respects and that ethical behavior be ingrained in the means that company personnel employ to execute the strategy. Such insistence on observing ethical standards is what creates an ethical work climate and a workplace where displaying integrity is the norm.

Many of the trappings used in the compliance approach are also manifest in the ethical culture mode, but one other is added—strong peer pressure from coworkers to observe ethical norms. Thus, responsibility for ethics compliance is widely dispersed throughout all levels of management and the rank-and-file. Stories of former and current moral heroes are kept in circulation, and the deeds of company personnel who display ethical values and are dedicated to walking the talk are celebrated at internal company events. The message that ethics matters—and matters a lot—resounds loudly and clearly throughout the organization and in its strategy and decisions. However, one of the challenges to overcome in the ethical culture approach is relying too heavily on peer pressures and cultural norms to enforce ethics compliance rather than on an individual's own moral responsibility for ethical behavior—absent unrelenting peer pressure or strong internal compliance systems, there is a danger that over time company personnel may become lax about its ethical standards. Compliance procedures need to be an integral part of the ethical culture approach to help send the message that management takes the observance of ethical norms seriously and that behavior that falls outside ethical boundaries will have negative consequences.

Why a Company Can Change Its Ethics Management Approach
Regardless of the approach they have used to managing ethical conduct, a company's executives may sense that they have exhausted a particular mode's potential for managing ethics and that they need to become more forceful in their approach to ethics management. Such changes typically occur when the company's ethical failures have made the headlines and created an embarrassing situation for company officials or when the business climate changes. For example, the recent raft of corporate scandals, coupled with aggressive enforcement of anticorruption legislation such as the Sarbanes-Oxley Act of 2002 (which addresses corporate governance and accounting practices), has prompted numerous executives and boards of directors to clean up their acts in accounting and financial reporting, review their ethical standards, and tighten up ethics compliance procedures. Intentionally amoral managers using the unconcerned approach to ethics management may see less risk in shifting to the damage control approach (or, for appearance's sake, maybe a "light" compliance mode). Senior managers who have employed the damage control mode may be motivated by bad experiences to mend their ways and shift to a compliance mode. In the wake of so many corporate scandals, companies in the compliance mode may move closer to the ethical culture approach.

WHY SHOULD COMPANY STRATEGIES BE ETHICAL?

There are two reasons why a company's strategy should be ethical: (1) because a strategy that is unethical in whole or in part is morally wrong and reflects badly on the character of the company personnel involved and (2) because an ethical strategy is good business and in the self-interest of shareholders.

The Moral Case for an Ethical Strategy

Managers do not dispassionately assess what strategic course to steer. Ethical strategy making generally begins with managers who themselves have strong character (i.e., who are honest, have integrity, are ethical, and truly care about how they conduct the company's business). Managers with high ethical principles and standards are usually advocates of a corporate code of ethics and strong ethics compliance, and they are typically genuinely committed to certain corporate values and business principles. They walk the talk in displaying the company's stated values and living up to its business principles and ethical standards. They understand that there is a big difference between adopting values statements and codes of ethics that serve merely as window dressing and those that truly paint the white lines for a company's actual strategy and business conduct. As a consequence, ethically strong managers consciously opt for strategic actions that can pass moral scrutiny—they display no tolerance for strategies with ethically controversial components.

The Business Case for an Ethical Strategy

There are solid business reasons to adopt ethical strategies even if most company managers are not of strong moral character and personally committed to high ethical standards. Pursuing unethical strategies not only damages a company's reputation but can also have costly, wide-ranging consequences. Some of the costs are readily visible; others are hidden and difficult to track down—as shown in Figure 10.1. The costs of

Figure 10.1   **The Business Costs of Ethical Failures**

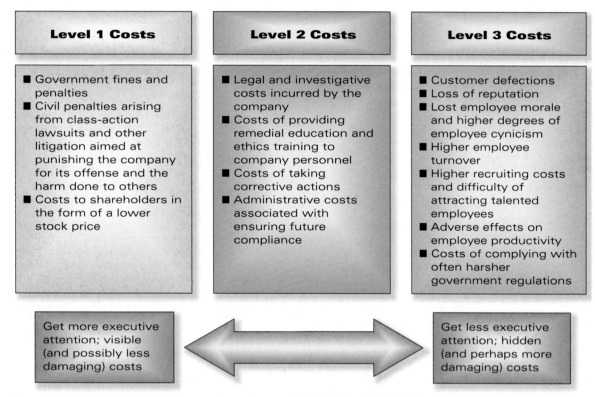

Source: Adapted from Terry Thomas, John R. Schermerhorn, and John W. Dienhart, "Strategic Leadership of Ethical Behavior," *Academy of Management Executive* 18, no. 2 (May 2004), p. 58.

fines and penalties and any declines in the stock price are easy enough to calculate. The administrative cleanup (or Level 2) costs are usually buried in the general costs of doing business and can be difficult to ascribe to any one ethical misdeed. Level 3 costs can be quite difficult to quantify but can sometimes be the most devastating—the aftermath of the Enron debacle left Arthur Andersen's reputation in shreds and led to the once-revered accounting firm's almost immediate demise, and it remains to be seen whether Marsh & McLennan can overcome the problems described in Illustration Capsule 10.1. Merck, once one of the world's most respected pharmaceutical firms, has been struggling against the revelation that senior management deliberately concealed that its Vioxx painkiller, which the company pulled off the market in September 2004, was tied to much greater risk of heart attack and strokes—some 20 million people in the United States had taken Vioxx over the years, and Merck executives had reason to suspect as early as 2000 (and perhaps earlier) that Vioxx had dangerous side effects.[35]

Rehabilitating a company's shattered reputation is time-consuming and costly. Customers shun companies known for their shady behavior. Companies with reputations for unethical conduct have considerable difficulty in recruiting and retaining talented employees. Most hardworking, ethically upstanding people are repulsed by a work environment where unethical behavior is condoned; they don't want to get entrapped in a compromising

> Conducting business in an ethical fashion is in a company's enlightened self-interest.

A Test of Your Business Ethics

As a gauge of your own ethical and moral standards, take the following quiz and see how you stack up against other members of your class. For the test to be valid, you need to answer the questions candidly, not on the basis of what you think the ethically correct answer is.

1. Do you think that it would be unethical for you to give two Super Bowl tickets to an important customer? Would your answer be different if the customer is likely to place a large order that would qualify you for a large year-end sales bonus?

_____Yes _____No _____Unsure (it depends)

_____Need more information

2. Would it be wrong to accept a case of fine wine from an important customer? Would your answer be different if you have just convinced your superiors to authorize a special price discount on a big order that the customer has just placed?

_____Yes _____No _____Unsure (it depends)

_____Need more information

3. Is it unethical for a high school or college coach to accept a "talent fee" or similar type of payment from a maker of sports apparel or sports equipment when the coach has authority to determine which brand of apparel or equipment to use for his or her team and subsequently chooses the brand of the company making the payment? Is it unethical for the maker of the sports apparel or equipment to make such payments in expectation that the coach will reciprocate by selecting the company's brand? (Would you answer be different if everybody else is doing it?)

_____Yes _____No _____Unsure (it depends)

_____Need more information

4. Is it unethical to accept an invitation from a supplier to spend a holiday weekend skiing at the supplier company's resort home in Colorado? (Would your answer be different if you were presently considering a proposal from that supplier to purchase $1 million worth of components?)

_____Yes _____No _____Unsure (it depends)

_____Need more information

5. Is it unethical for a food products company to incorporate ingredients that have trans fats in its products, given that trans fats are known to be very unhealthy for consumers and that alternative ingredients (which might be somewhat more expensive) can be used in producing the product?

_____Yes _____No _____Unsure (it depends)

_____Need more information

6. Would it be wrong to keep quiet if you, as a junior financial analyst, had just calculated that the projected return on a possible project was 18 percent and your boss (a) informed you that no project could be approved without the prospect of a 25 percent return and (b) told you to go back and redo the numbers and "get them right"?

_____Yes _____No _____Unsure (it depends)

_____Need more information

7. Would it be unethical to allow your supervisor to believe that you were chiefly responsible for the success of a new company initiative if it actually resulted from a team effort or major contributions by a co-worker?

_____Yes _____No _____Unsure (it depends)

_____Need more information

8. Would it be unethical for you, as the chief company official in India to (a) authorize a $25,000 payment to a local government official to facilitate governmental approval to construct a $200 million petrochemical plant and (b) disguise this payment by instructing accounting personnel to classify the payment as part of the cost of obtaining a building permit? (As you can see from Table 10.1, corruption is the norm in India, and bribes and kickbacks are often a "necessary" cost of doing business there.)

_____Yes _____No _____Unsure (it depends)

_____Need more information

9. Is it unethical for a motor vehicle manufacturer to resist recalling some of its vehicles when governmental authorities present it with credible evidence that the vehicles have safety defects?

_____Yes _____No _____Unsure (it depends)

_____Need more information

10. Is it unethical for a credit card company to aggressively try to sign up new accounts when, after an introductory period of interest-free or low-interest charges on unpaid monthly balances, the interest rate on unpaid balances jumps to 1.5 percent or more monthly (even though such high rates of 18 percent or more annually are disclosed in fine print)?

_____Yes _____No _____Unsure (it depends)

_____Need more information

11. Is it unethical to bolster your résumé with exaggerated claims of your credentials and prior job accomplishments in hopes of improving your chances of gaining employment at another company?

_____Yes _____No _____Unsure (it depends)

_____Need more information

12. Is it unethical for a company to spend as little as possible on pollution control when, with some extra effort and expenditures, it could substantially reduce the amount of pollution caused by its operations?

_____Yes _____No _____Unsure (it depends)

_____Need more information

Answers: The answers to questions 1, 2, and 4 probably shift from no/unsure to a definite yes when the second part of the circumstance comes into play. We think a strong case can be made that the answers to the remaining 9 questions are yes, although it can be argued that more information about the circumstances might be needed in responding to questions 5, 7, 9, and 12.

situation, nor do they want their personal reputations tarnished by the actions of an unsavory employer. A 1997 survey revealed that 42 percent of the respondents took into account a company's ethics when deciding whether to accept a job.[36] Creditors are usually unnerved by the unethical actions of a borrower because of the potential business fallout and subsequent risk of default on any loans. To some significant degree, therefore, companies recognize that ethical strategies and ethical conduct are good business. Most companies have strategies that pass the test of being ethical, and most companies are aware that both their reputations and their long-term well-being are tied to conducting their business in a manner that wins the approval of suppliers, employees, investors, and society at large.

As a test your own business ethics and where you stand on the importance of companies having an ethical strategy, take the test on page 340.

LINKING A COMPANY'S STRATEGY TO ITS ETHICAL PRINCIPLES AND CORE VALUES

Many companies have officially adopted a code of ethical conduct and a statement of company values—in the United States, the Sarbannes-Oxley Act, passed in 2002, requires that companies whose stock is publicly traded have a code of ethics or else explain in writing to the Securities and Exchange Commission why they do not. But there's a big difference between having a code of ethics and a values statement that serve merely as a public window dressing and having ethical standards and corporate values that truly paint the white lines for a company's actual strategy and business conduct. If ethical standards and statements of core values are to have more than a cosmetic role, boards of directors and top executives must work diligently to see that they are scrupulously observed in crafting the company's strategy and conducting every facet of the company's business. In other words, living up to the ethical principles and displaying the core values in actions and decisions must become a way of life at the company.

Indeed, the litmus test of whether a company's code of ethics and statement of core values are cosmetic is the extent to which they are embraced in crafting strategy and in operating the business day to day. It is up to senior executives to walk the talk and make a point of considering two sets of questions whenever a new strategic initiative is under review:

- Is what we are proposing to do fully compliant with our code of ethical conduct? Is there anything here that could be considered ethically objectionable?

- Is it apparent that this proposed action is in harmony with our core values? Are any conflicts or concerns evident?

Unless questions of this nature are posed—either in open discussion or by force of habit in the minds of strategy makers, then there's room for strategic initiatives to become disconnected from the company's code of ethics and stated core values. If a company's executives are ethically principled and believe strongly in living up to the company's stated core values, there's a good chance they will pose these types of questions and reject strategic initiatives that don't measure up. There's also a good chance that strategic actions will be scrutinized for their compatibility with ethical standards and core values when the latter are so deeply ingrained in a company's culture and in the

Core Concept
More attention is paid to linking strategy with ethical principles and core values in companies headed by moral executives and in companies where ethical principles and core values are a way of life.

everyday conduct of company personnel that they are automatically taken into account in all that the company does. However, in companies with window-dressing ethics and core values or in companies headed by immoral or amoral managers, any strategy-ethics-values link stems mainly from a desire to avoid the risk of embarrassment, scandal, and possible disciplinary action should strategy makers get called on the carpet and held accountable for approving an unethical strategic initiative.

STRATEGY AND SOCIAL RESPONSIBILITY

The idea that businesses have an obligation to foster social betterment, a much-debated topic in the past 40 years, took root in the 19th century when progressive companies in the aftermath of the industrial revolution began to provide workers with housing and other amenities. The notion that corporate executives should balance the interests of all stakeholders—shareholders, employees, customers, suppliers, the communities in which they operated, and society at large—began to blossom in the 1960s. A group of chief executives of America's 200 largest corporations, calling themselves the Business Roundtable, promoted the concept of corporate social responsibility. In 1981, the Roundtable's "Statement on Corporate Responsibility" said:[37]

> Balancing the shareholder's expectations of maximum return against other priorities is one of the fundamental problems confronting corporate management. The shareholder must receive a good return but the legitimate concerns of other constituencies (customers, employees, communities, suppliers and society at large) also must have the appropriate attention . . . [Leading managers] believe that by giving enlightened consideration to balancing the legitimate claims of all its constituents, a corporation will best serve the interest of its shareholders.

Today, corporate social responsibility is a concept that resonates in Western Europe, the United States, Canada, and such developing nations as Brazil and India.

What Do We Mean by Social Responsibility?

Core Concept

The notion of *social responsibility* as it applies to businesses concerns a company's *duty* to operate in an honorable manner, provide good working conditions for employees, be a good steward of the environment, and actively work to better the quality of life in the local communities where it operates and in society at large.

The essence of socially responsible business behavior is that a company should balance strategic actions to benefit shareholders against the *duty* to be a good corporate citizen. The thesis is that company managers are obligated to display a *social conscience* in operating the business and specifically take into account how management decisions and company actions affect the well-being of employees, local communities, the environment, and society at large. Acting in a socially responsible manner thus encompasses more than just participating in community service projects and donating money to charities and other worthy social causes. Demonstrating social responsibility also entails undertaking actions that earn trust and respect from all stakeholders—operating in an honorable and ethical manner, striving to make the company a great place to work, demonstrating genuine respect for the environment, and trying to make a difference in bettering society. As depicted in Figure 10.2, the menu for demonstrating a social conscience and choosing specific ways to exercise social responsibility includes:

- *Efforts to employ an ethical strategy and observe ethical principles in operating the business*—A sincere commitment to observing ethical principles is

Figure 10.2   **Demonstrating a Social Conscience: The Five Components of Socially Responsible Business Behavior**

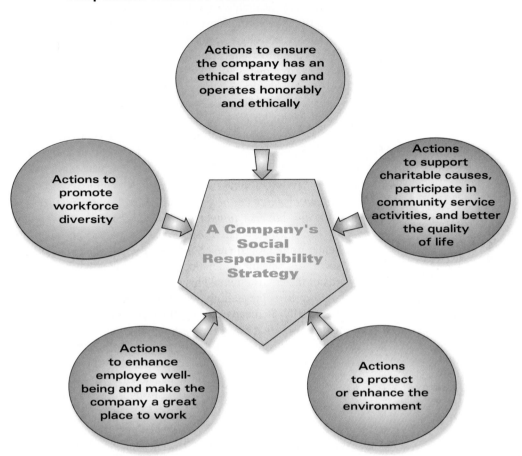

Source: Adapted from material in Ronald Paul Hill, Debra Stephens, and Iain Smith, "Corporate Social Responsibility: An Examination of Individual Firm Behavior," *Business and Society Review* 108, no. 3 (September 2003), p. 348.

necessary here simply because unethical strategies and conduct are incompatible with the concept of good corporate citizenship and socially responsible business behavior.

- *Making charitable contributions, donating money and the time of company personnel to community service endeavors, supporting various worthy organizational causes, and reaching out to make a difference in the lives of the disadvantaged*—Some companies fulfill their corporate citizenship and community outreach obligations by spreading their efforts over a multitude of charitable and community activities; for instance, Microsoft and Johnson & Johnson support a broad variety of community art, social welfare, and environmental programs. Others prefer to focus their energies more narrowly. McDonald's, for example, concentrates on sponsoring the Ronald McDonald House program (which provides a home away from home for the families of seriously ill children receiving treatment at nearby hospitals), preventing child abuse and neglect, and participating in local community service activities; in 2004, there were 240 Ronald McDonald Houses in 25 countries and more than 6,000 bedrooms available nightly. British Telecom gives 1 percent of its profits directly to communities, largely for education—teacher training, in-school workshops, and digital technology. Leading prescription drug maker GlaxoSmithKline and other pharmaceutical companies either donate or heavily discount medicines for distribution in the least-developed nations. Numerous health-related businesses take a leading role in community activities that promote effective health care. Many companies work closely with community officials to minimize the impact of hiring large numbers of new employees (which could put a strain on local schools and utility services) and to provide outplacement services for laid-off workers. Companies frequently reinforce their philanthropic efforts by encouraging employees to support charitable causes and participate in community affairs, often through programs to match employee contributions.

- *Actions to protect or enhance the environment and, in particular, to minimize or eliminate any adverse impact on the environment stemming from the company's own business activities*—Social responsibility as it applies to environmental protection means doing more than what is legally required. From a social responsibility perspective, companies have an obligation to be stewards of the environment. This means using the best available science and technology to achieve higher-than-required environmental standards. Even more ideally, it means putting time and money into improving the environment in ways that extend past a company's own industry boundaries—such as participating in recycling projects, adopting energy conservation practices, and supporting efforts to clean up local water supplies. Retailers such as Home Depot in the United States and B&Q in the United Kingdom have pressured their suppliers to adopt stronger environmental protection practices.[38]

> Business leaders who want their companies to be regarded as exemplary corporate citizens must not only see that their companies operate ethically but they must personally display a social conscience in making decisions that affect employees, the environment, the communities in which they operate, and society at large.

- *Actions to create a work environment that enhances the quality of life for employees and makes the company a great place to work*—Numerous companies go beyond providing the ordinary kinds of compensation and exert extra efforts to enhance the quality of life for their employees, both at work and at home. This can include varied and engaging job assignments, career development programs and mentoring, rapid career advancement, appealing compensation incentives, ongoing training to ensure future employability, added decision-making authority, onsite day care, flexible work schedules for single parents, workplace exercise facilities, special leaves to care for sick family members, work-at-home opportunities, gender pay equity, showcase plants and offices, special safety programs, and the like.

- *Actions to build a workforce that is diverse with respect to gender, race, national origin, and perhaps other aspects that different people bring to the workplace*—Most large companies in the United States have established workforce diversity programs, and some go the extra mile to ensure that their workplaces are attractive to ethnic minorities and inclusive of all groups and perspectives. The pursuit of workforce diversity can be good business—Johnson & Johnson, Pfizer, and Coca-Cola believe that a reputation for workforce diversity makes recruiting employees easier (talented employees from diverse backgrounds often seek out such companies). And at Coca-Cola, where strategic success depends on getting people all over the world to become loyal consumers of the company's beverages, efforts to build a public persona of inclusiveness for people of all races, religions, nationalities, interests, and talents has considerable strategic value. Multinational companies are particularly inclined to make workforce diversity a visible strategic component; they recognize that respecting individual differences and promoting inclusiveness resonate well with people all around the world. At a few companies the diversity initiative extends to suppliers—sourcing items from small businesses owned by women or ethnic minorities.

Crafting a Social Responsibility Strategy: The Starting Point for Demonstrating a Social Conscience

While striving to be socially responsible entails choosing from the menu outlined in the preceding section, there's plenty of room for every company to make its own statement about what charitable contributions to make, what kinds of community service projects to emphasize, what environmental actions to support, how to make the company a good place to work, where and how workforce diversity fits into the picture, and what else it will do to support worthy causes and projects that benefit society. The particular combination of socially responsible endeavors a company elects to pursue defines its **social responsibility strategy.** However, unless a company's social responsibility initiatives become part of the way it operates its business every day, the initiatives are unlikely to catch fire and be fully effective. As an executive at Royal Dutch/Shell put it, corporate social responsibility "is not a cosmetic; it must be rooted in our values. It must make a difference to the way we do business."[39] Thus some companies are integrating social responsibility objectives into their missions and overall performance targets—they see social performance and environmental metrics as an essential component of judging the company's overall future performance. Some 2,500 companies around the world are not only articulating their social responsibility strategies and commitments but they are also issuing annual social responsibility reports (much like an annual report) that set forth their commitments and the progress they are making for all the world to see and evaluate.[40]

> **Core Concept**
> A company's **social responsibility strategy** is defined by the specific combination of socially beneficial activities it opts to support with its contributions of time, money, and other resources.

At Starbucks, the commitment to social responsibility is linked to the company's strategy and operating practices via the tag line "Giving back to our communities is the way we do business"; top management makes the theme come alive via the company's extensive community-building activities, efforts to protect the welfare of coffee growers and their families (in particular, making sure they receive a fair price), a variety of recycling and environmental conservation practices, and the financial support it provides to charities and the disadvantaged through the Starbucks Foundation. At Green Mountain Coffee Roasters, social responsibility includes fair dealing with suppliers and trying to do something about the poverty of small coffee growers; in its dealings with suppliers at small farmer cooperatives in Peru, Mexico, and Sumatra, Green Mountain pays "fair trade" prices for coffee beans (in 2002, the fair trade prices were a minimum of $1.26 per pound for conventional coffee and $1.41 for organically grown versus market prices of 24 to 50 cents per pound). Green Mountain also purchases about 25 percent of its coffee direct from farmers so as to cut out intermediaries and see that farmers realize a higher price for their efforts—coffee is the world's second most heavily traded commodity after oil, requiring the labor of some 20 million people, most of whom live at the poverty level.[41] At Whole Foods Market, a $5 billion supermarket chain specializing in organic and natural foods, the social responsibility emphasis is on supporting organic farming and

> Many companies tailor their strategic efforts to operate in a socially responsible manner to fit their core values and business mission, thereby making their own statement about "how we do business and how we intend to fulfill our duties to all stakeholders and society at large."

sustainable agriculture, recycling, sustainable seafood practices, giving employees paid time off to participate in worthy community service endeavors, and donating 5 percent of after-tax profits in cash or products to charitable causes. At General Mills the social responsibility focus is on service to the community and bettering the employment opportunities for minorities and women. Stonyfield Farm, a producer of yogurt and ice cream products, employs a social responsibility strategy focused on wellness, good nutrition, and earth-friendly actions (10 percent of profits are donated to help protect and restore the earth, and yogurt lids are used as miniature billboards to help educate people about environmental issues); in addition, it is stressing the development of an environmentally friendly supply chain, sourcing from farmers that grow organic products and refrain from using artificial hormones in milk production. Chick-Fil-A, an Atlanta-based fast-food chain with over 1,200 outlets in 38 states, has a charitable foundation; supports 14 foster homes and a summer camp (for some 1,600 campers from 22 states and several foreign countries); funds two scholarship programs (including one for employees that has awarded more than $20 million in scholarships); and maintains a closed-on-Sunday policy to ensure that every Chick-Fil-A employee and restaurant operator has an opportunity to worship, spend time with family and friends, or just plain rest from the workweek.[42] Toys "R" Us supports initiatives addressing the issues of child labor and fair labor practices around the world. Community Pride Food Stores is assisting in revitalizing the inner city of Richmond, Virginia, where the company is based.

It is common for companies engaged in natural resource extraction, electric power production, forestry and paper products, motor vehicles, and chemicals production to place more emphasis on addressing environmental concerns than, say, software and electronics firms or apparel manufacturers. Companies whose business success is heavily dependent on high employee morale or attracting and retaining the best and brightest employees are somewhat more prone to stress the well-being of their employees and foster a positive, high-energy workplace environment that elicits the dedication and enthusiastic commitment of employees, thus putting real meaning behind the claim "Our people are our greatest asset." Ernst & Young, one of the four largest global accounting firms, stresses its "People First" workforce diversity strategy, which focuses on respecting differences, fostering individuality, and promoting inclusiveness so that its 105,000 employees in 140 countries can feel valued, engaged, and empowered in developing creative ways to serve the firm's clients.

Thus, while the strategies and actions of all socially responsible companies have a sameness in the sense of drawing on the five categories of socially responsible behavior shown in Figure 10.2, each company's version of being socially responsible is unique.

The Moral Case for Corporate Social Responsibility

Every action a company takes can be interpreted as a statement of what it stands for.

The moral case for why businesses should actively promote the betterment of society and act in a manner that benefits all of the company's stakeholders—not just the interests of shareholders—boils down to the fact that it's the right thing to do. Ordinary decency, civic-mindedness, and contributing to the well-being of society should be expected of any business. In today's social and political climate, most business leaders can be expected to acknowledge that socially responsible actions are important and that businesses have a duty to be good corporate citizens. But there is a complementary school of thought that business operates on the basis of an implied social contract with the members of society. According to this contract, society grants a business the right to conduct its business affairs and agrees not to unreasonably restrain its pursuit of a fair profit for the goods or services it sells; in return for this "license to operate," a business is obligated to act as a responsible citizen and do its fair share to promote the general welfare. Such a view clearly puts a moral burden on a company to take corporate citizenship into consideration and to do what's best for shareholders within the confines of discharging its duties to operate honorably, provide good working conditions to employees, be a good environmental steward, and display good corporate citizenship.

The Business Case for Socially Responsible Behavior

Whatever the merits of the moral case for socially responsible business behavior, it has long been recognized that it is in the enlightened self-interest of companies to be good citizens and devote some of their energies and resources to the betterment of employees, the communities in which they operate, and society in general. In short, there are several reasons why the exercise of social responsibility is good business:

- *It generates internal benefits (particularly as concerns employee recruiting, workforce retention, and training costs)*—Companies with deservedly good reputations for contributing time and money to the betterment of society are better able to attract and retain employees compared to companies with tarnished reputations. Some employees just feel better about working for a company committed to improving society.[43] This can contribute to lower turnover and better worker productivity. Other direct and indirect economic benefits include lower costs for staff recruitment and training. For example, Starbucks is said to enjoy much lower rates of employee turnover because of its full benefits package for both full-time and part-time employees, management efforts to make Starbucks a great place to work, and the company's socially responsible practices. When a U.S. manufacturer of recycled paper, taking eco-efficiency to heart, discovered how to increase its fiber recovery rate, it saved the equivalent of 20,000 tons of waste paper—a factor that helped the company become the industry's lowest-cost producer.[44] Various benchmarking and measurement mechanisms have shown that workforce diversity initiatives promote the success of companies that stay behind them. Making a company a great place to work pays dividends in recruiting talented workers, more creativity and energy on the part of workers, higher worker productivity, and greater employee commitment to the company's business mission/vision and success in the marketplace.

- *It reduces the risk of reputation-damaging incidents and can lead to increased buyer patronage*—Firms may well be penalized by employees, consumers, and shareholders for actions that are not considered socially responsible. When a major oil company suffered damage to its reputation on environmental and social grounds, the CEO repeatedly said that the most negative impact the company suffered—and the one that made him fear for the future of the company—was that bright young graduates were no longer attracted to work for the company.[45] Consumer, environmental, and human rights activist groups are quick to criticize businesses whose behavior they consider to be out of line, and they are adept at getting their message into the media and onto the Internet. Pressure groups can generate widespread adverse publicity, promote boycotts, and influence like-minded or sympathetic buyers to avoid an offender's products.

> The higher the public profile of a company or brand, the greater the scrutiny of its activities and the higher the potential for it to become a target for pressure-group action.

Research has shown that product boycott announcements are associated with a decline in a company's stock price.[46] Outspoken criticism of Royal Dutch/Shell by environmental and human rights groups and associated boycotts were said to be major factors in the company's decision to tune in to its social responsibilities. For many years, Nike received stinging criticism for not policing sweatshop conditions in the Asian factories of its contractors, causing Nike CEO Phil Knight to observe that "Nike has become synonymous with slave wages, forced overtime, and arbitrary abuse."[47] In 1997, Nike began an extensive effort to monitor conditions in the 800 overseas factories from which it outsourced its shoes; Knight said, "Good shoes come from good factories, and good factories have good labor relations." Nonetheless, Nike has continually been plagued by complaints from human rights activists that its monitoring procedures are flawed and that it is not doing enough to correct the plight of factory workers. In contrast, to the extent that a company's socially responsible behavior wins applause from consumers and fortifies its reputation, the company may win additional patronage; Ben & Jerry's, Whole Foods Market, Stonyfield Farm, and the Body Shop have definitely expanded their customer bases because of their visible and well-publicized activities as socially conscious companies. More and more companies are recognizing the strategic value of social responsibility strategies that reach out to people of all cultures and demographics—in the United States, women are said to having buying power of $3.7 trillion, retired and disabled people close to $4.1 trillion, Hispanics nearly $600 billion, African Americans some $500 billion, and Asian Americans about $255 billion.[48] So reaching out in ways that appeal to such groups can pay off at the cash register. Some observers and executives are convinced that a strong, visible social responsibility strategy gives a company an edge in differentiating itself from rivals and in appealing to those consumers who prefer to do business with companies that are solid corporate citizens. Yet there is only limited evidence that consumers go out of their way to patronize socially responsible companies if it means paying a higher price or purchasing an inferior product.[49]

- *It is in the best interest of shareholders*—Well-conceived social responsibility strategies work to the advantage of shareholders in several ways. Socially responsible business behavior helps avoid or preempt legal and regulatory actions that could prove costly and otherwise burdensome. Increasing numbers of mutual funds and pension benefit managers are restricting their stock purchases to companies that meet social responsibility criteria. According to one survey, one out of every eight dollars under professional management in the United States involved socially responsible investing.[50] Moreover, the growth in socially responsible investing and identifying socially responsible companies has led to a substantial increase in the number of companies that publish formal reports on their social and environmental activities.[51] The stock prices of companies that rate high on social and environmental performance criteria have been found to perform 35 to 45 percent better than the average of the 2,500 companies comprising the Dow Jones Global Index.[52] A two-year study of leading companies found that improving environmental compliance and developing environmentally friendly products can enhance earnings per share, profitability, and the likelihood of winning contracts.[53] Nearly 100 studies have examined the relationship between corporate citizenship and corporate financial performance over the past 30 years; the majority point to a positive relationship. Of the 80 studies that examined whether a company's social performance is a good predictor of its financial performance, 42 concluded yes, 4 concluded

There's little hard evidence indicating shareholders are disadvantaged in any meaningful way by a company's actions to be socially responsible.

no, and the remainder reported mixed or inconclusive findings.[54] To the extent that socially responsible behavior is good business, then, a social responsibility strategy that packs some punch and is more than rhetorical flourish turns out to be in the best interest of shareholders.

In sum, companies that take social responsibility seriously can improve their business reputations and operational efficiency while also reducing their risk exposure and encouraging loyalty and innovation. Overall, companies that take special pains to protect the environment (beyond what is required by law), are active in community affairs, and are generous supporters of charitable causes and projects that benefit society are more likely to be seen as good investments and as good companies to work for or do business with. Shareholders are likely to view the business case for social responsibility as a strong one, even though they certainly have a right to be concerned whether the time and money their company spends to carry out its social responsibility strategy outweighs the benefits and reduces the bottom line by an unjustified amount.

Companies are, of course, sometimes rewarded for bad behavior—a company that is able to shift environmental and other social costs associated with its activities onto society as a whole can reap large short-term profits. The major cigarette producers for many years were able to earn greatly inflated profits by shifting the health-related costs of smoking onto others and escaping any responsibility for the harm their products caused to consumers and the general public. Most companies will, of course, try to evade paying for the social harms of their operations for as long as they can. Calling a halt to such actions usually hinges upon (1) the effectiveness of activist social groups in publicizing the adverse consequences of a company's social irresponsibility and marshaling public opinion for something to be done, (2) the enactment of legislation or regulations to correct the inequity, and (3) widespread actions on the part of socially conscious buyers to take their business elsewhere.

The Well-Intentioned Efforts of Do-Good Executives Can Be Controversial

While there is substantial agreement that businesses have obligations to non-owner stakeholders and to society at large, and that these must be factored into a company's overall strategy and into the conduct of its business operations, there is much less agreement about the extent to which "do-good" executives should pursue their personal vision of a better world using company funds. One view holds that any money executives authorize for so-called social responsibility initiatives is effectively theft from a company's shareholders who can, after all, decide for themselves what and how much to give to charity and other causes they deem worthy. A related school of thought says that companies should be wary of taking on an assortment of societal obligations because doing so diverts valuable resources and weakens a company's competitiveness. Many academics and businesspeople believe that businesses best satisfy their social responsibilities through conventional business activities, primarily producing needed goods and services at prices that people can afford. They further argue that spending shareholders' or customers' money for social causes not only muddies decision making by diluting the focus on the company's business mission but also thrusts business executives into the role of social engineers—a role more appropriately performed by charitable and nonprofit organizations and duly elected government officials. Do we really want corporate executives deciding how to best balance the different interests of stakeholders and functioning as social engineers? Are they competent to make such judgments?

Take the case of Coca-Cola and Pepsi bottlers. Local bottlers of both brands have signed contracts with public school districts that provide millions of dollars of support for local schools in exchange for vending-machine distribution rights in the schools.[55] While such contracts would seem to be a win–win proposition, protests from parents concerned about children's sugar-laden diets and commercialism in the schools make such contracts questionable. Opponents of these contracts claim that it is the role of government to provide adequate school funding and that the learning environment in local schools should be free of commercialism and the self-serving efforts of businesses to hide behind providing support for education.

In September 1997, the Business Roundtable changed its stance from one of support for social responsibility and balanced consideration of stakeholder interests to one of skepticism with regard to such actions:

> The notion that the board must somehow balance the interests of stockholders against the interests of other stakeholders fundamentally misconstrues the role of directors. It is, moreover, an unworkable notion because it would leave the board with no criteria for resolving conflicts between the interest of stockholders and of other stakeholders or among different groups of stakeholders.[56]

The new Business Roundtable view implied that the paramount duty of management and of boards of directors is to the corporation's stockholders. Customers may be "king," and employees may be the corporation's "greatest asset" (at least in the rhetoric), but the interests of shareholders rule.[57]

However, there are real problems with disconnecting business behavior from the well-being of non-owner stakeholders and the well-being of society at large.[58] Isolating business from the rest of society when the two are inextricably intertwined is unrealistic. Many business decisions spill over to impact non-owner stakeholders and society. Furthermore, the notion that businesses must be managed solely to serve the interests of shareholders is something of a stretch. Clearly, a business's first priority must be to deliver value to customers. Unless a company does a creditable job of satisfying buyer needs and expectations of reliable and attractively priced goods and services, it cannot survive. While shareholders provide capital and are certainly entitled to a return on their investment, fewer and fewer shareholders are truly committed to the companies whose stock they own. Shareholders can dispose of their holdings in a moment's whim or at the first sign of a downturn in the stock price. Mutual funds buy and sell shares daily, adding and dropping companies whenever they see fit. Day traders buy and sell within hours. Such buying and selling of shares is nothing more than a financial transaction and results in no capital being provided to the company to fund operations except when it entails the purchase of newly issued shares of stock. So why should shareholders—a group distant from the company's operations and adding little to its operations except when new shares of stock are purchased—lay such a large claim on how a company should be managed? Are most shareholders really interested in or knowledgeable about the companies they own? Or do they just own a stock for whatever financial returns it is expected to provide?

While there is legitimate concern about the use of company resources for do-good purposes and the motives and competencies of business executives in functioning as social engineers, it is tough to argue that businesses have no obligations to nonowner stakeholders or to society at large. If one looks at the category of activities that fall under the umbrella of socially responsible behavior (Figure 10.2), there's really very little for shareholders or others concerned about the do-good attempts of executives to object to in principle. Certainly, it is legitimate for companies to minimize or eliminate any adverse impacts of their operations on the environment. It is hard to argue against efforts to make the company a great place to work or to promote workforce diversity. And with regard to charitable contributions, community service projects, and the like, it would be hard to find a company where spending on such activities is so out of control that shareholders might rightfully complain or that the company's competitiveness is being eroded. What is likely to prove most objectionable in the social responsibility arena are the specific activities a company elects to engage in and/or the manner in which a company carries out its attempts to behave in a socially responsible manner.

How Much Attention to Social Responsibility Is Enough?

What is an appropriate balance between the imperative to create value for shareholders and the obligation to proactively contribute to the larger social good? What fraction of a company's resources ought to be aimed at addressing social concerns and bettering the well-being of society and the environment? A few companies have a policy of setting aside a specified percentage of their profits (typically 5 percent or maybe 10 percent) to fund their social responsibility strategy; they view such percentages as a fair amount to return to the community as a kind of thank-you or a tithe to the betterment of society. Other companies shy away from a specified percentage of profits or revenues because it entails upping the commitment in good times and cutting back on social responsibility initiatives in hard times (even cutting out social responsibility initiatives entirely if profits temporarily turn into losses). If social responsibility is an ongoing commitment rooted in the corporate culture and enlists broad participation on the part of company personnel, then a sizable portion of the funding for the company's social responsibility strategy has to be viewed as simply a regular and ongoing cost of doing business.

But judging how far a particular company should go in pursuing particular social causes is a tough issue. Consider, for example, Nike's commitment to monitoring the workplace conditions of its contract suppliers.[59] The scale of this monitoring task is significant: in 2005, Nike had over 800 contract suppliers employing over 600,000 people in 50 countries. How frequently should sites be monitored? How should it respond to the use of underage labor? If only children above a set age are to be employed by suppliers, should suppliers still be required to provide schooling opportunities? At last count, Nike had some 80 people engaged in site monitoring. Should Nike's monitoring budget be $2 million, $5 million, $10 million, or whatever it takes?

Consider another example: If pharmaceutical manufacturers donate or discount their drugs for distribution to low-income people in less-developed nations, what safeguards should they put in place to see that the drugs reach the intended recipients and are not diverted by corrupt local officials for reexport to markets in other countries? Should drug manufacturers also assist in drug distribution and administration in these less-developed countries? How much should a drug company invest in R&D to develop medicines for tropical diseases commonly occurring in less-developed countries when it is unlikely to recover its costs in the foreseeable future?

And how much should a company allocate to charitable contributions? Is it falling short of its responsibilities if its donations are less than 1 percent of profits? Is a company going too far if it allocates 5 percent or even 10 percent of its profits to worthy causes of one kind or another? The point here is that there is no simple or widely accepted standard for judging when a company has or has not gone far enough in fulfilling its citizenship responsibilities.

Linking Social Performance Targets to Executive Compensation

Perhaps the most surefire way to enlist a genuine commitment to corporate social responsibility initiatives is to link the achievement of social performance targets to executive compensation. If a company's board of directors is serious about corporate citizenship, then it will incorporate measures of the company's social and environmental performance into its evaluation of top executives, especially the CEO. And if the CEO uses compensation incentives to further enlist the support of down-the-line company personnel in effectively crafting and executing a social responsibility strategy, the company will over time build a culture rooted in social responsible and ethical behavior. According to one survey, 80 percent of surveyed CEOs believe that environmental and social performance metrics are a valid part of measuring a company's overall performance. At Verizon Communications, 10 percent of the annual bonus of the company's top 2,500 managers is tied directly to the achievement of social responsibility targets; for the rest of the staff, there are corporate recognition awards in the form of cash for employees who have made big contributions towards social causes. The corporate social responsibility reports being issued annually by 2,500 companies across the world that detail social responsibility initiatives and the results achieved are a good basis for compensating executives and judging the effectiveness of their commitment to social responsibility.

Key Points

Ethics involves concepts of right and wrong, fair and unfair, moral and immoral. Beliefs about what is ethical serve as a moral compass in guiding the actions and behaviors of individuals and organizations. Ethical principles in business are not materially different from ethical principles in general.

There are three schools of thought about ethical standards:

1. According to the *school of ethical universalism*, the same standards of what's ethical and what's unethical resonate with peoples of most societies regardless of local traditions and cultural norms; hence, common ethical standards can be used to judge the conduct of personnel at companies operating in a variety of country markets and cultural circumstances.

2. According to the *school of ethical relativism* different societal cultures and customs have divergent values and standards of right and wrong—thus, what is ethical or unethical must be judged in the light of local customs and social mores and can vary from culture or nation to another.

3. According to *integrated social contracts theory*, universal ethical principles or norms based on the collective views of multiple cultures and societies combine to form a "social contract" that all individuals in all situations have a duty to observe. Within the boundaries of this social contract, local cultures can specify other impermissible actions; however, universal ethical norms always take precedence over local ethical norms.

Three categories of managers stand out as concerns their prevailing beliefs in and commitments to ethical and moral principles in business affairs: the moral manager; the immoral manager, and the amoral manager. By some accounts, the population of managers is said to be distributed among all three types in a bell-shaped curve, with immoral managers and moral managers occupying the two tails of the curve, and the amoral managers, especially the intentionally amoral managers, occupying the broad middle ground.

The apparently large numbers of immoral and amoral businesspeople are one obvious reason why some companies resort to unethical strategic behavior. Three other main drivers of unethical business behavior also stand out:

1. Overzealous or obsessive pursuit of personal gain, wealth, and other selfish interests.
2. Heavy pressures on company managers to meet or beat earnings targets.
3. A company culture that puts the profitability and good business performance ahead of ethical behavior.

The stance a company takes in dealing with or managing ethical conduct at any given time can take any of four basic forms:

1. The unconcerned, or nonissue, approach.
2. The damage control approach.
3. The compliance approach.
4. The ethical culture approach.

There are two reasons why a company's strategy should be ethical: (1) because a strategy that is unethical in whole or in part is morally wrong and reflects badly on the character of the company personnel involved, and (2) because an ethical strategy is good business and in the self-interest of shareholders.

The term *corporate social responsibility* concerns a company's *duty* to operate in an honorable manner, provide good working conditions for employees, be a good steward of the environment, and actively work to better the quality of life in the local communities where it operates and in society at large. The menu of actions and behavior for demonstrating social responsibility includes:

1. Employing an ethical strategy and observing ethical principles in operating the business.
2. Making charitable contributions, donating money and the time of company personnel to community service endeavors, supporting various worthy organizational causes, and making a difference in the lives of the disadvantaged. Corporate commitments are further reinforced by encouraging employees to support charitable and community activities.
3. Protecting or enhancing the environment and, in particular, striving to minimize or eliminate any adverse impact on the environment stemming from the company's own business activities.
4. Creating a work environment that makes the company a great place to work.
5. Employing a workforce that is diverse with respect to gender, race, national origin, and perhaps other aspects that different people bring to the workplace.

There is ample room for every company to tailor its social responsibility strategy to fit its core values and business mission, thereby making their own statement about "how we do business and how we intend to fulfill our duties to all stakeholders and society at large."

The moral case for social responsibility boils down to a simple concept: It's the right thing to do. The business case for social responsibility holds that it is in the enlightened self-interest of companies to be good citizens and devote some of their energies and resources to the betterment of such stakeholders as employees, the communities in which it operates, and society in general.

Exercises

1. Given the description of Marsh & McLennan's strategy presented in Illustration Capsule 10.1, would it be fair to characterize the payment of contingent commissions by property-casualty insurers as nothing more than thinly disguised kickbacks? Why or why not? If you were the manager of a company that hired Marsh & McLennan to provide risk management services, would you see that Marsh had a conflict of interest in steering your company's insurance policies to insurers in which it has an ownership interest? Given Marsh's unethical and illegal foray into rigging the bids on insurance policies for its corporate clients, what sort of fines and penalties would you impose on the company for its misdeeds (assuming you were asked to recommend appropriate penalties by the prosecuting authorities). In arriving at a figure, bear in mind that Prudential Securities paid a total of about $2 billion in the 1990s to settle civil regulatory charges and private lawsuits alleging that it misled investors on the risks and rewards of limited-partnership investments. Ten Wall Street securities firms in 2003 paid $1.4 billion to settle civil charges for issuing misleading stock research to investors. Prominent mutual-fund firms were assessed nearly $2 billion in fines and restitution for engaging in after-hours stock trading at prearranged prices that were contrary to the interests of long-term shareholders. And several well-known financial institutions, including Citigroup, Merrill Lynch, Goldmans Sachs, and Credit Suisse First Boston agreed to pay several billion dollars in fines and restitution for their role in scandals at Enron and WorldCom and for improperly allocating initial public offerings of stock. Using Internet research tools, determine what Marsh & McLennan ended up paying in fines and restitution for its unethical and illegal strategic behavior and assess the extent to which the conduct of company personnel damaged shareholders.

2. Consider the following portrayal of strategies employed by major recording studios:[60]

> Some recording artists and the Recording Artists' Coalition claim that the world's five major music recording studios—Universal, Sony, Time Warner, EMI/Virgin, and Bertelsmann—deliberately employ strategies calculated to take advantage of musicians who record for them. One practice to which they strenuously object is that the major-label record companies frequently require artists to sign contracts committing them to do six to eight albums, an obligation that some artists say can entail an indefinite term of indentured servitude. Further, it is claimed that audits routinely detect unpaid royalties to musicians under contract; according to one music industry attorney, record companies misreport and underpay artist royalties by 10 to 40 percent and are "intentionally fraudulent." One music writer was recently quoted as saying the process was "an entrenched system whose prowess and conniving makes Enron look like amateur hour." Royalty calculations are based on complex formulas that are paid only after artists pay for recording costs and other expenses and after any advances are covered by royalty earnings.
>
> A *Baffler* magazine article outlined a hypothetical but typical record deal in which a promising young band is given a $250,000 royalty advance on a new album. The album subsequently sells 250,000 copies, earning $710,000 for the

record company; but the band, after repaying the record company for $264,000 in expenses ranging from recording fees and video budgets to catering, wardrobe, and bus tour costs for promotional events related to the album, ends up $14,000 in the hole, owes the record company money, and is thus paid no royalties on any of the $710,000 in revenues the recording company receives from the sale of the band's music. It is also standard practice in the music industry for recording studios to sidestep payola laws by hiring independent promoters to lobby and compensate radio stations for playing certain records. Record companies are often entitled to damages for undelivered albums if an artist leaves a recording studio for another label after seven years. Record companies also retain the copyrights in perpetuity on all music recorded under contract, a practice that artists claim is unfair. The Dixie Chicks, after a year-long feud with Sony over contract terms, ended up refusing to do another album; Sony sued for breach of contract, prompting a countersuit by the Dixie Chicks charging "systematic thievery" to cheat them out of royalties. The suits were settled out of court. One artist said, "The record companies are like cartels."

Recording studios defend their strategic practices by pointing out that fewer than 5 percent of the signed artists ever deliver a hit and that they lose money on albums that sell poorly. According to one study, only 1 of 244 contracts signed during 1994–1996 was negotiated without the artists being represented by legal counsel, and virtually all contracts renegotiated after a hit album added terms more favorable to the artist.

a.   If you were a recording artist, would you be happy with some of the strategic practices of the recording studios? Would you feel comfortable signing a recording contract with studios engaging in any of the practices?

b.   Which, if any, of the practices of the recording studios do you view as unethical?

3.   Recently, it came to light that three of the world's four biggest public accounting firms may have overbilled clients for travel-related expenses. Pricewaterhouse Coopers, KPMG, and Ernst & Young were sued for systematically charging their clients full price for airline tickets, hotel rooms and car-rental expenses, even though they received volume discounts and rebates of up to 40 percent under their contracts with various travel companies. Large accounting firms, law firms, and medical practices have in recent years used their size and purchasing volumes to negotiate sizable discounts and rebates on up-front travel costs; some of these contracts apparently required that the discounts not be disclosed to other parties, which seemingly included clients.

However, it has long been the custom for accounting and law firms to bill their clients for actual out-of-pocket expenses. The three accounting firms, so the lawsuit alleges, billed clients for the so-called full prices of the airline tickets, hotel rooms, and car-rental expenses rather than for the out-of-pocket discounted amounts. They pocketed the differences to the tune of several million dollars annually in additional profits. Several clients, upon learning of the full-price billing practices, claimed fraud and sued.

Do you consider the accounting firms' billing practice to be unethical? Why or why not?

4.   Suppose you found yourself in the following situation: In preparing a bid for a multimillion-dollar contract in a foreign country, you are introduced to a "consultant" who offers to help you in submitting the bid and negotiating with the customer company. You learn in conversing with the consultant that she is well connected in local government and business circles and knows key personnel in the customer company extremely well. The consultant quotes you a six-figure fee.

Later, your local co-workers tell you that the use of such consultants is normal in this country—and that a large fraction of the fee will go directly to people working for the customer company. They further inform you that bidders who reject the help of such consultants have lost contracts to competitors who employed them. What would you do, assuming your company's code of ethics expressly forbids the payments of bribes or kickbacks in any form?

5. Assume that you are the sales manager at a European company that makes sleepwear products for children. Company personnel discover that the chemicals used to flameproof the company's line of children's pajamas might cause cancer if absorbed through the skin. Following this discovery, the pajamas are then banned from sale in the European Union and the United States, but senior executives of your company learn that the children's pajamas in inventory and the remaining flameproof material can be sold to sleepwear distributors in certain East European countries where there are no restrictions against the material's use. Your superiors instruct you to make the necessary arrangements to sell the inventories of banned pajamas and flameproof materials to East European distributors. Would you comply if you felt that your job would be in jeopardy if you didn't?

6. At Salomon Smith Barney (a subsidiary of Citigroup), Credit Suisse First Boston (CSFB), and Goldman Sachs (three of the world's most prominent investment banking companies), part of the strategy for securing the investment banking business of large corporate clients (to handle the sale of new stock issues or new bond issues or advise on mergers and acquisitions) involved (a) hyping the stocks of companies that were actual or prospective customers of their investment banking services, and (b) allocating hard-to-get shares of hot new initial public offerings (IPOs) to select executives and directors of existing and potential client companies, who then made millions of dollars in profits when the stocks went up once public trading began.[61] Former WorldCom CEO Bernard Ebbers reportedly made more than $11 million in trading profits over a four-year period on shares of IPOs received from Salomon Smith Barney; Salomon served as WorldCom's investment banker on a variety of deals during this period. Jack Grubman, Salomon's top-paid research analyst at the time, enthusiastically touted WorldCom stock and was regarded as the company's biggest cheerleader on Wall Street.

To help draw in business from new or existing corporate clients, CSFB established brokerage accounts for corporate executives who steered their company's investment banking business to CSFB. Apparently, CSFB's strategy for acquiring more business involved promising the CEO and/or CFO of companies about to go public for the first time or needing to issue new long-term bonds that if CSFB was chosen to handle their company's IPO of common stock or a new bond issue, then CSFB would ensure they would be allocated shares at the initial offering price of all subsequent IPOs in which CSFB was a participant. During 1999–2000, it was common for the stock of a hot new IPO to rise 100 to 500 percent above the initial offering price in the first few days or weeks of public trading; the shares allocated to these executives were then sold for a tidy profit over the initial offering price. According to investigative sources, CSFB increased the number of companies whose executives were allowed to participate in its IPO offerings from 26 companies in January 1999 to 160 companies in early 2000; executives received anywhere from 200 to 1,000 shares each of every IPO in which CSFB was a participant in 2000. CSFB's accounts for these executives reportedly generated profits of about $80 million for the participants. Apparently, it was CSFB's practice to curtail access to IPOs for some executives if their companies didn't come through with additional securities business for CSFB or if CSFB concluded that other securities offerings by these companies would be unlikely.

Goldman Sachs also used an IPO-allocation scheme to attract investment banking business, giving shares to executives at 21 companies—among the participants were the CEOs of eBay, Yahoo, and Ford Motor Company. eBay's CEO was a participant in over 100 IPOs managed by Goldman during the 1996–2000 period and was on Goldman's board of directors part of this time; eBay paid Goldman Sachs $8 million in fees for services during the 1996–2001 period.

a. If you were a top executive at Salomon Smith Barney, CSFB, or Goldman Sachs, would you be proud to defend your company's actions?

b. Would you want to step forward and take credit for having been a part of the group who designed or approved of the strategy for gaining new business at any of these three firms?

c. Is it accurate to characterize the allocations of IPO shares to "favored" corporate executives as bribes or kickbacks?

chapter eleven

Building an Organization Capable of Good Strategy Execution

The best game plan in the world never blocked or tackled anybody.

—Vince Lombardi
Hall of Fame football coach

Strategies most often fail because they aren't executed well.

—Larry Bossidy and Ram Charan
CEO Honeywell International; author and consultant

A second-rate strategy perfectly executed will beat a first-rate strategy poorly executed every time.

—Richard M. Kovacevich
Chairman and CEO, Wells Fargo

Any strategy, however brilliant, needs to be implemented properly if it is to deliver the desired results.

—Costas Markides
Professor

People are *not* your most important asset. The right people are.

—Jim Collins
Professor and author

Organizing is what you do before you do something, so that when you do it, it is not all mixed up.

—A. A. Milne
Author

Once managers have decided on a strategy, the emphasis turns to converting it into actions and good results. Putting the strategy into place and getting the organization to execute it well call for different sets of managerial skills. Whereas crafting strategy is largely a market-driven activity, implementing and executing strategy is primarily an operations-driven activity revolving around the management of people and business processes. Whereas successful strategy making depends on business vision, solid industry and competitive analysis, and shrewd market positioning, successful strategy execution depends on doing a good job of working with and through others, building and strengthening competitive capabilities, motivating and rewarding people in a strategy-supportive manner, and instilling a discipline of getting things done. Executing strategy is an action-oriented, make-things-happen task that tests a manager's ability to direct organizational change, achieve continuous improvement in operations and business processes, create and nurture a strategy-supportive culture, and consistently meet or beat performance targets.

Experienced managers are emphatic in declaring that it is a whole lot easier to develop a sound strategic plan than it is to execute the plan and achieve the desired outcomes. According to one executive, "It's been rather easy for us to decide where we wanted to go. The hard part is to get the organization to act on the new priorities."[1] *Just because senior managers announce a new strategy doesn't mean that organizational members will agree with it or enthusiastically move forward in implementing it.* Senior executives cannot simply direct immediate subordinates to abandon old ways and take up new ways, and they certainly cannot expect the needed actions and changes to occur in rapid-fire fashion and lead to the desired outcomes. Some managers and employees may be skeptical about the merits of the strategy, seeing it as contrary to the organization's best interests, unlikely to succeed, or threatening to their departments or careers. Moreover, different employees may interpret the new strategy differently or have different ideas about what internal changes are needed to execute it. Long-standing attitudes, vested interests, inertia, and ingrained organizational practices don't melt away when managers decide on a new strategy and begin efforts to implement it—especially when only comparatively few people have been involved in crafting the strategy and when the rationale for strategic change has to be sold to enough organizational members to root out the status quo.

It takes adept managerial leadership to convincingly communicate the new strategy and the reasons for it, overcome pockets of doubt and disagreement, secure the commitment and enthusiasm of concerned parties, identify and build consensus on all the hows of implementation and execution, and move forward to get all the pieces into place. Company personnel have to understand—in their heads and in their hearts—why a new strategic direction is necessary and where the new strategy is taking them.[2] Instituting change is, of course, easier when the problems with the old strategy have become obvious and/or the company has spiraled into a financial crisis.

But the challenge of successfully implementing new strategic initiatives goes well beyond managerial adeptness in overcoming resistance to change. What really makes executing strategy a tougher, more time-consuming management challenge than crafting strategy are the wide array of managerial activities that have to be attended to, the many ways that managers can proceed, and the number of bedeviling issues that must be worked out. It takes first-rate "managerial smarts" to zero in on what exactly needs to be done to put new strategic initiatives in place and, further, how best to get these things done in a timely fashion and in a manner that yields good results. Demanding people-management skills are required. Plus, it takes follow-through and perseverance to get a variety of initiatives launched and moving and to integrate the efforts of many different work groups into a smoothly functioning whole. Depending on how much consensus building and organizational change is involved, the process of implementing strategy changes can take several months to several years. And it takes still longer to achieve *real proficiency* in executing the strategy.

Like crafting strategy, *executing strategy is a job for the whole management team, not just a few senior managers.* While an organization's chief executive officer and the heads of major units (business divisions, functional departments, and key operating units) are ultimately responsible for seeing that strategy is executed successfully, the process typically affects every part of the firm, from the biggest operating unit to the smallest frontline work group. Top-level managers have to rely on the active support and cooperation of middle and lower managers to push strategy changes into functional areas and operating units and to see that the organization actually operates in accordance with the strategy on a daily basis. Middle and lower-level managers not only are responsible for initiating and supervising the execution process in their areas of authority but also are instrumental in getting subordinates to continuously improve on how strategy-critical value chain activities are being performed and in producing the operating results that allow company performance targets to be met—their role on the company's strategy execution team is by no means minimal.

Core Concept

Good strategy execution requires a *team effort.* All managers have strategy-executing responsibility in their areas of authority, and all employees are participants in the strategy execution process.

Strategy execution thus requires every manager to think through the answer to "What does my area have to do to implement its part of the strategic plan, and what should I do to get these things accomplished effectively and efficiently?" The bigger the organization or the more geographically scattered its operating units, the more that successful strategy execution depends on the cooperation and implementing skills of operating managers who can push the needed changes at the lowest organizational levels and, in the process, deliver good results. Only in small organizations can top-level managers get around the need for a team effort on the part of management and personally orchestrate the actions steps required for good strategy execution and operating excellence.

A FRAMEWORK FOR EXECUTING STRATEGY

Implementing and executing strategy entails figuring out all the hows—the specific techniques, actions, and behaviors that are needed for a smooth strategy-supportive operation—and then following through to get things done and deliver results. The idea is to make things happen and make them happen right. The first step in implementing strategic changes is for management to communicate the case for organizational change so clearly and persuasively to organizational members that a determined commitment takes hold throughout the ranks to find ways to put the strategy into place, make it work, and meet performance targets. The ideal condition is for managers to arouse enough enthusiasm for the strategy to turn the implementation process into a companywide crusade. *Management's handling of the strategy implementation process can be considered successful if and when the company achieves the targeted strategic and financial performance and shows good progress in making its strategic vision a reality.*

The specific hows of executing a strategy—the exact items that need to be placed on management's action agenda—always have to be customized to fit the particulars of a company's situation. Making minor changes in an existing strategy differs from implementing radical strategy changes. The hot buttons for successfully executing a low-cost provider strategy are different from those in executing a high-end differentiation strategy. Implementing and executing a new strategy for a struggling company in the midst of a financial crisis is a different job from that of improving strategy execution in a company where the execution is already pretty good. Moreover, some managers are more adept than others at using this or that approach to achieving the desired kinds of organizational changes. Hence, there's no definitive managerial recipe for successful strategy execution that cuts across all company situations and all types of strategies or that works for all types of managers. Rather, the specific hows of implementing and executing a strategy—the to-do list that constitutes management's agenda for action—must always be custom-tailored to fit an individual company's own circumstances and represents management's judgment about how best to proceed.

THE PRINCIPAL MANAGERIAL COMPONENTS OF THE STRATEGY EXECUTION PROCESS

Despite the need to tailor a company's strategy-executing approaches to the particulars of its situation, certain managerial bases have to be covered no matter what the circumstances. Eight managerial tasks crop up repeatedly in company efforts to execute strategy (see Figure 11.1):

1. Building an organization with the competencies, capabilities, and resource strengths to execute strategy successfully.
2. Marshaling sufficient money and people behind the drive for strategy execution.
3. Instituting policies and procedures that facilitate rather than impede strategy execution.
4. Adopting best practices and pushing for continuous improvement in how value chain activities are performed.
5. Installing information and operating systems that enable company personnel to carry out their strategic roles proficiently.

Figure 11.1   **The Eight Components of the Strategy Execution Process**

6.   Tying rewards directly to the achievement of strategic and financial targets and to good strategy execution.

7.   Instilling a corporate culture that promotes good strategy execution.

8.   Exercising strong leadership to drive execution forward, keep improving on the details of execution, and achieve operating excellence as rapidly as feasible.

How well managers perform these eight tasks has a decisive impact on whether the outcome is a spectacular success, a colossal failure, or something in between.

In devising an action agenda for implementing and executing strategy, the place for managers to start is with *a probing assessment of what the organization must do differently and better to carry out the strategy successfully.* They should then consider *precisely how to make the necessary internal changes* as rapidly as possible. Successful strategy implementers have a knack for diagnosing what their organizations need to do to execute the chosen strategy well and figuring out how to get things done—they are

When strategies fail, it is often because of poor execution— things that were supposed to get done slip through the cracks.

masters in promoting results-oriented behaviors on the part of company personnel and following through on making the right things happen in a timely fashion.[3]

In big organizations with geographically scattered operating units, the action agenda of senior executives mostly involves communicating the case for change to others, building consensus for how to proceed, installing strong allies in positions where they can push implementation along in key organizational units, urging and empowering subordinates to keep the process moving, establishing measures of progress and deadlines, recognizing and rewarding those who achieve implementation milestones, directing resources to the right places, and personally leading the strategic change process. Thus, the bigger the organization, the more successful strategy execution depends on the cooperation and implementing skills of operating managers who can push needed changes at the lowest organizational levels and deliver results. In small organizations, top managers can deal directly with frontline managers and employees, personally orchestrating the action steps and implementation sequence, observing firsthand how implementation is progressing, and deciding how hard and how fast to push the process along. Regardless of the organization's size and whether implementation involves sweeping or minor changes, the most important leadership traits are a strong, confident sense of what to do and how to do it. Having a strong grip on these two things comes from understanding the circumstances of the organization and the requirements for effective strategy execution. Then it remains for those managers and company personnel in strategy-critical areas to step up to the plate and produce the desired results.

What's Covered in Chapters 11, 12, and 13   In the remainder of this chapter and the next two chapters, we will discuss what is involved in performing the eight key managerial tasks (shown in Figure 11.1) that shape the process of implementing and executing strategy. This chapter explores building an organization with the competencies, capabilities, and resource strengths to execute the strategy successfully. Chapter 12 looks at marshaling resources, instituting strategy-facilitating policies and procedures, adopting best practices, installing operating systems, and tying rewards to the achievement of good results. Chapter 13 deals with creating a strategy-supportive corporate culture and exercising the leadership needed to drive the execution process forward.

BUILDING AN ORGANIZATION CAPABLE OF GOOD STRATEGY EXECUTION

Proficient strategy execution depends heavily on competent personnel, better-than-adequate competitive capabilities, and effective internal organization. Building a capable organization is thus always a top priority in strategy execution. As shown in Figure 11.2, three types of organization-building actions are paramount:

1. *Staffing the organization*—putting together a strong management team, and recruiting and retaining employees with the needed experience, technical skills, and intellectual capital.

2. *Building core competencies and competitive capabilities*—developing proficiencies in performing strategy-critical value chain activities and updating them to match changing market conditions and customer expectations.

3. *Structuring the organization and work effort*—organizing value chain activities and business processes and deciding how much decision-making authority to push down to lower-level managers and frontline employees.

Figure 11.2   **The Three Components of Building an Organization Capable of Proficient Strategy Execution**

Staffing the Organization

- ■ Putting together a strong management team
- ■ Recruiting and retaining talented employees

Building Core Competencies and Competitive Capabilities

- ■ Developing a set of competencies and capabilities suited to the current strategy
- ■ Updating and revising this set as external conditions and strategy change
- ■ Training and retraining employees as needed to maintain skills-based competencies

Matching the Organization Structure to Strategy

- ■ Instituting organizational arrangements that facilitate good strategy execution
- ■ Deciding how much decision-making authority to push down to lower-level managers and front line employees

A Company with the Competencies and Capabilities Needed for Proficient Strategy Execution

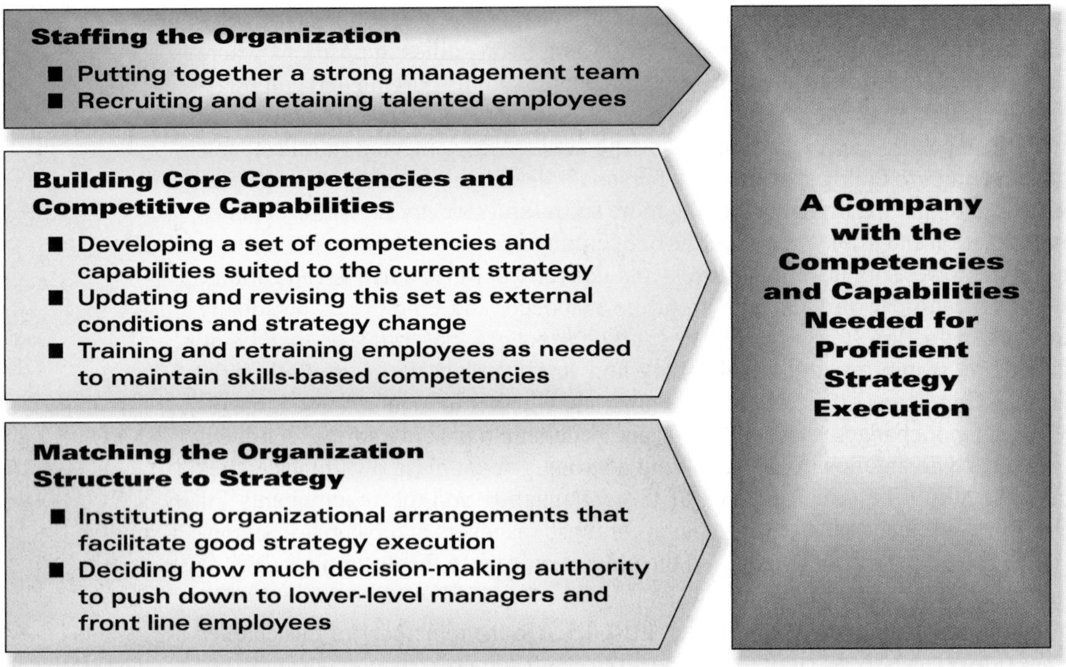

STAFFING THE ORGANIZATION

No company can hope to perform the activities required for successful strategy execution without attracting and retaining talented managers and employees with suitable skills and *intellectual capital.*

Putting Together a Strong Management Team

Assembling a capable management team is a cornerstone of the organization-building task.[4] While different strategies and company circumstances sometimes call for different mixes of backgrounds, experiences, values, beliefs, management styles, and know-how, *the most important consideration is to fill key managerial slots with smart people who are clear thinkers, good at figuring out what needs to be done, and skilled in "making it happen" and delivering good results.*[5] The task of implementing and executing challenging strategic initiatives must be assigned to executives who have the skills and talents to handle them and who can be counted on to turn their decisions and actions into results that meet or beat the established performance targets. It helps enormously when a company's top management team has several people who are particularly good change agents—true believers who champion change, know how to make it happen, and love every second of the process.[6] Without a smart, capable, results-oriented management team, the implementation-execution process ends up being hampered by missed deadlines, misdirected or wasteful efforts, and/or managerial ineptness.[7] Weak executives are serious impediments to getting

Core Concept

Putting together a talented management team with the right mix of experiences, skills, and abilities to get things done is one of the first strategy-implementing steps.

optimal results because they are unable to differentiate between ideas and approaches that have merit and those that are misguided—the caliber of work done under their supervision suffers.[8] In contrast, managers with strong strategy-implementing capabilities have a talent for asking tough, incisive questions. They know enough about the details of the business to be able to challenge and ensure the soundness of the approaches and decisions of the people around them, and they can discern whether the resources people are asking for to put the strategy in place make sense. They are good at getting things done through others, typically by making sure they have the right people under them and that these people are put in the right jobs.[9] They consistently follow through on issues, monitor progress carefully, make adjustments when needed, and not let important details slip through the cracks. In short, they understand how to drive organizational change, and they have the managerial discipline requisite for first-rate strategy execution.

Sometimes a company's existing management team is suitable; at other times it may need to be strengthened or expanded by promoting qualified people from within or by bringing in outsiders whose experiences, talents, and leadership styles better suit the situation. In turnaround and rapid-growth situations, and in instances when a company doesn't have insiders with the requisite know-how, filling key management slots from the outside is a fairly standard organization-building approach. In addition, it is important to ferret out and replace managers who, for whatever reasons, prefer the status quo and who either do not buy into the case for making organizational changes or do not see ways to make things better.[10] For a top management team to be truly effective, it has got to consist of "true believers" who recognize that organizational changes are needed and are ready to get on with the process. Weak executives and diehard resisters have to be replaced or sidelined (by shifting them to positions of lesser influence where they cannot hamper or derail new strategy execution initiatives).

The overriding aim in building a management team should be to assemble a *critical mass* of talented managers who can function as agents of change and further the cause of first-rate strategy execution—every manager's success is enhanced (or limited) by the quality of their managerial colleagues and the degree to which they freely exchange ideas, debate how to improve approaches that have merit, and join forces to tackle issues and solve problems.[11] When a first-rate manager enjoys the help and support of other first-rate managers, it's possible to create a managerial whole that is greater than the sum of individual efforts—talented managers who work well together as a team can produce organizational results that are dramatically better than what one or two star managers acting individually can achieve. The chief lesson here is that *a company needs to get the right executives on the bus—and the wrong executives off the bus—before trying to drive the bus in the desired direction.*[12]

Illustration Capsule 11.1 describes General Electric's widely acclaimed approach to developing a top-caliber management team.

Recruiting and Retaining Capable Employees

Assembling a capable management team is not enough. Staffing the organization with the right kinds of people must go much deeper than managerial jobs in order for value chain activities to be performed competently. *The quality of an organization's people is always an essential ingredient of successful strategy execution—knowledgeable, engaged employees are a company's best source of creative ideas for the nuts-and-bolts operating improvements that lead to operating excellence.* Companies

> **Core Concept**
> In many industries, adding to a company's talent base and building intellectual capital is more important to good strategy execution than additional investments in plants, equipment, and capital projects.

Illustration Capsule 11.1

How General Electric Develops a Talented and Deep Management Team

General Electric (GE) is widely considered to be one of the best-managed companies in the world, partly because of its concerted effort to develop outstanding managers. For starters, GE strives to hire talented people with high potential for executive leadership; it then goes to great lengths to expand the leadership, business, and decision-making capabilities of all its managers. Four key elements undergird GE's efforts to build a talent-rich stable of managers:

- GE makes a practice of transferring managers across divisional, business, or functional lines for sustained periods of time. Such transfers allow managers to develop relationships with colleagues in other parts of the company, help break down insular thinking in business "silos," and promote the sharing of cross-business ideas and best practices. There is an enormous emphasis at GE on transferring ideas and best practices from business to business and making GE a "boundaryless" company.

- In selecting executives for key positions, GE is strongly disposed to candidates who exhibit what are called the four E's—enormous personal *energy,* the ability to motivate and *energize* others, *edge* (a GE code word for instinctive competitiveness and the ability to make tough decisions in a timely fashion, saying yes or no, and not maybe), and *execution* (the ability to carry things through to fruition). Considerable attention is also paid to problem-solving ability, experience in multiple functions or businesses, and experience in driving business growth (as indicated by good market instincts, in-depth knowledge of particular markets, customer touch, and technical understanding).

- All managers are expected to be proficient at what GE calls *workout*—a process in which managers and employees come together to confront issues as soon as they come up, pinpoint the root cause of the issues, and bring about quick resolutions so the business can move forward. Workout is GE's way of training its managers to diagnose what to do and how to do it.

- Each year GE sends about 10,000 newly hired and long-time managers to its Leadership Development Center (generally regarded as one of the best corporate training centers in the world), for a three-week course on the company's Six Sigma quality initiative. Close to 10,000 "master black belt" and "black belt" Six Sigma experts have graduated from the program to drive forward thousands of quality initiatives throughout GE. Six Sigma training is an ironclad requirement for promotion to any professional and managerial position and any stock option award. GE's Leadership Development Center also offers advanced courses for senior managers that may focus on a single management topic for a month. All classes involve managers from different GE businesses and different parts of the world. Some of the most valuable learning comes in between formal class sessions when GE managers from different businesses trade ideas about how to improve processes and better serve the customer. This knowledge sharing not only spreads best practices throughout the organization but also improves each GE manager's knowledge.

All of GE's 85,000 managers and professionals are graded in an annual process that divides them into five tiers: the top 10 percent, the next 15 percent, the middle 50 percent, the next 15 percent, and the bottom 10 percent. Everyone in the top tier gets stock awards, nobody in the fourth tier gets shares of stock, and most of those in the fifth tier become candidates for being weeded out. Business heads are pressured to wean out "C" players. GE's CEO personally reviews the performance of the top 3,000 managers. Senior executive compensation is heavily weighted toward Six Sigma commitment and successful business results.

According to Jack Welch, GE's CEO from 1980 to 2001, "The reality is, we simply cannot afford to field anything but teams of 'A' players."

Sources: General Electric's 1998 and 2003 annual reports; www.ge.com; John A. Byrne, "How Jack Welch Runs GE," *BusinessWeek,* June 8, 1998, p. 90; Miriam Leuchter, "Management Farm Teams," *Journal of Business Strategy,* May 1998, pp. 29–32; and "The House That Jack Built, *The Economist,* September 18, 1999.

like Microsoft, McKinsey & Company, Southwest Airlines, Cisco Systems, Amazon.com, Procter & Gamble, PepsiCo, Nike, Electronic Data Systems, Google, and Intel make a concerted effort to recruit the best and brightest people they can find and then retain them with excellent compensation packages, opportunities for rapid advancement and professional growth, and challenging and interesting assignments. Having a pool of "A players" with strong skill sets and lots of brainpower is essential to their business. Microsoft makes a point of hiring the very brightest and most talented programmers it can find and motivating them with both good monetary incentives and the challenge of working on cutting-edge software design projects. McKinsey & Company, one of the world's premier management consulting companies, recruits only cream-of-the-crop MBAs at the nation's top 10 business schools; such talent is essential to McKinsey's strategy of performing high-level consulting for the world's top corporations. The leading global accounting firms screen candidates not only on the basis of their accounting expertise but also on whether they possess the people skills needed to relate well with clients and colleagues. Southwest Airlines goes to considerable lengths to hire people who can have fun and be fun on the job; it uses special interviewing and screening methods to gauge whether applicants for customer-contact jobs have outgoing personality traits that match its strategy of creating a high-spirited, fun-loving, in-flight atmosphere for passengers; it is so selective that only about 3 percent of the people who apply are offered jobs.

In high-tech companies, the challenge is to staff work groups with gifted, imaginative, and energetic people who can bring life to new ideas quickly and inject into the organization what one Dell Inc. executive calls "hum."[13] The saying "People are our most important asset" may seem hollow, but it fits high-technology companies dead-on. Besides checking closely for functional and technical skills, Dell tests applicants for their tolerance of ambiguity and change, their capacity to work in teams, and their ability to learn on the fly. Companies like Amazon.com, Google, Yahoo, and Cisco Systems have broken new ground in recruiting, hiring, cultivating, developing, and retaining talented employees—most of whom are in their 20s and 30s. Cisco goes after the top 10 percent, raiding other companies and endeavoring to retain key people at the companies it acquires so as to maintain a cadre of star engineers, programmers, managers, salespeople, and support personnel in executing its strategy to remain the world's leading provider of Internet infrastructure products and technology.

In instances where intellectual capital greatly aids good strategy execution, companies have instituted a number of practices aimed at staffing jobs with the best people they can find:

1. Spending considerable effort in screening and evaluating job applicants, selecting only those with suitable skill sets, energy, initiative, judgment, and aptitudes for learning and adaptability to the company's work environment and culture.

2. Putting employees through training programs that continue throughout their careers.

3. Providing promising employees with challenging, interesting, and skill-stretching assignments.

4. Rotating people through jobs that not only have great content but also span functional and geographic boundaries. Providing people with opportunities to gain experience in a variety of international settings is increasingly considered an essential part of career development in multinational or global companies.

5. Encouraging employees to challenge existing ways of doing things, to be creative and innovative in proposing better ways of operating, and to push their ideas for new products or businesses. Progressive companies work hard at creating an environment in which ideas and suggestions bubble up from below and employees are made to feel that their views and suggestions count.

6. Making the work environment stimulating and engaging such that employees will consider the company a great place to work.

7. Striving to retain talented, high-performing employees via promotions, salary increases, performance bonuses, stock options and equity ownership, fringe benefit packages, and other perks.

> The best companies make a point of recruiting and retaining talented employees—the objective is to make the company's entire workforce (managers and rank-and-file employees) a genuine resource strength

8. Coaching average performers to improve their skills and capabilities, while weeding out underperformers and benchwarmers.

It is very difficult for a company to competently execute its strategy and achieve operating excellence without a large band of capable employees who are actively engaged in the process of making ongoing operating improvements.

BUILDING CORE COMPETENCIES AND COMPETITIVE CAPABILITIES

High among the organization-building priorities in the strategy implementing/executing process is the need to build and strengthen competitively valuable core competencies and organizational capabilities. Whereas managers identify the desired competencies and capabilities in the course of crafting strategy, good strategy execution requires putting the desired competencies and capabilities in place, upgrading them as needed, and then modifying them as market conditions evolve. Sometimes a company already has some semblance of the needed competencies and capabilities, in which case managers can concentrate on strengthening and nurturing them to promote better strategy execution. More usually, however, company managers have to significantly broaden or deepen certain capabilities or even add entirely new competencies in order to put strategic initiatives in place and execute them proficiently.

A number of prominent companies have succeeded in establishing core competencies and capabilities that have been instrumental in making them winners in the marketplace. Intel's core competence is in the design and mass production of complex chips for personal computers, servers, and other electronic products. Procter & Gamble's core competencies reside in its superb marketing/distribution skills and its R&D capabilities in five core technologies—fats, oils, skin chemistry, surfactants, and emulsifiers. Ciba Specialty Chemicals has technology-based competencies that allow it to quickly manufacture products for customers wanting customized products relating to coloration, brightening and whitening, water treatment and paper processing, freshness, and cleaning. General Electric has a core competence in developing professional managers with broad problem-solving skills and proven ability to grow global businesses. Disney has core competencies in theme park operation and family entertainment. Dell Inc. has the capabilities to deliver state-of-the-art products to its customers within days of next-generation components coming available—and to do so at attractively low costs (it has leveraged its collection of competencies and capabilities into being the global low-cost leader in PCs). Toyota's success in motor vehicles is due, in large part, to its legendary "production system," which it has honed and perfected and which gives it the capability to produce high-quality vehicles at relatively low costs.

The Three-Stage Process of Developing and Strengthening Competencies and Capabilities

Building core competencies and competitive capabilities is a time-consuming, managerially challenging exercise. While some organization-building assist can be gotten from discovering how best-in-industry or best-in-world companies perform a particular activity, trying to replicate and then improve on the competencies and capabilities of others is, however, much easier said than done—for the same reasons that one is unlikely to ever become a good golfer just by studying what Tiger Woods does. Putting a new capability in place is more complicated than just forming a new team or department and charging it with becoming highly competent in performing the desired activity, using whatever it can learn from other companies having similar competencies or capabilities. Rather, it takes a series of deliberate and well orchestrated organizational steps to achieve mounting proficiency in performing an activity. The capability-building process has three stages:

> **Core Concept**
> Building competencies and capabilities is a multistage process that occurs over a period of months and years, not something that is accomplished overnight.

> *Stage 1*—First, the organization must develop the *ability* to do something, however imperfectly or inefficiently. This entails selecting people with the requisite skills and experience, upgrading or expanding individual abilities as needed, and then molding the efforts and work products of individuals into a collaborative effort to create organizational ability.

> *Stage 2*—As experience grows and company personnel learn how to perform the activity *consistently well and at an acceptable cost,* the ability evolves into a tried-and-true *competence* or *capability.*

> *Stage 3*—Should company personnel continue to polish and refine their know-how and otherwise sharpen their performance of an activity such that the company eventually becomes *better than rivals* at performing the activity, the core competence rises to the rank of a *distinctive competence* (or the capability becomes a competitively superior capability), thus providing a path to competitive advantage.

Many companies are able to get through stages 1 and 2 in performing a strategy-critical activity, but comparatively few achieve sufficient proficiency in performing strategy-critical activities to qualify for the third stage.

Managing the Process   Four traits concerning core competencies and competitive capabilities are important in successfully managing the organization-building process:[14]

1. *Core competencies and competitive capabilities are bundles of skills and know-how that most often grow out of the combined efforts of cross-functional work groups and departments performing complementary activities at different locations in the firm's value chain.* Rarely does a core competence or capability consist of narrow skills attached to the work efforts of a single department. For instance, a core competence in speeding new products to market involves the collaborative efforts of personnel in research and development (R&D), engineering and design, purchasing, production, marketing, and distribution. Similarly, the capability to provide superior customer service is a team effort among people in customer call centers (where orders are taken and inquiries are answered), shipping and delivery, billing and accounts receivable, and after-sale support. Complex activities (like designing and manufacturing a sports-utility vehicle or creating the capability for secure credit card transactions over the Internet) usually involve a number of component skills, technological disciplines, competencies, and capabilities— some performed in-house and some provided by suppliers/allies. An important part of the organization-building function is to think about which activities of which groups need to be linked and made mutually reinforcing and then to forge the necessary collaboration both internally and with outside resource providers.

2. *Normally, a core competence or capability emerges incrementally out of company efforts either to bolster skills that contributed to earlier successes or to respond to customer problems, new technological and market opportunities, and the*

competitive maneuverings of rivals. Migrating from the one-time ability to do something up the ladder to a core competence or competitively valuable capability is usually an organization-building process that takes months and often years to accomplish—it is definitely not an overnight event.

3. *The key to leveraging a core competence into a distinctive competence (or a capability into a competitively superior capability) is concentrating more effort and more talent than rivals on deepening and strengthening the competence or capability, so as to achieve the dominance needed for competitive advantage.* This does not necessarily mean spending more money on such activities than competitors, but it does mean consciously focusing more talent on them and striving for best-in-industry, if not best-in-world, status. To achieve dominance on lean financial resources, companies like Cray in large computers and Honda in gasoline engines have leveraged the expertise of their talent pool by frequently re-forming high-intensity teams and reusing key people on special projects. The experiences of these and other companies indicate that the usual keys to successfully building core competencies and valuable capabilities are superior employee selection, thorough training and retraining, powerful cultural influences, effective cross-functional collaboration, empowerment, motivating incentives, short deadlines, and good databases—not big operating budgets.

4. *Evolving changes in customers' needs and competitive conditions often require tweaking and adjusting a company's portfolio of competencies and intellectual capital to keep its capabilities freshly honed and on the cutting edge.* This is particularly important in high-tech industries and fast-paced markets where important developments occur weekly. As a consequence, wise company managers work at anticipating changes in customer-market requirements and staying ahead of the curve in proactively building a package of competencies and capabilities that can win out over rivals.

Managerial actions to develop core competencies and competitive capabilities generally take one of two forms: either strengthening the company's base of skills, knowledge, and intellect, or coordinating and networking the efforts of the various work groups and departments. Actions of the first sort can be undertaken at all managerial levels, but actions of the second sort are best orchestrated by senior managers who not only appreciate the strategy-executing significance of strong competencies/capabilities but also have the clout to enforce the necessary networking and cooperation among individuals, groups, departments, and external allies.

One organization-building question is whether to develop the desired competencies and capabilities internally or to outsource them by partnering with key suppliers or forming strategic alliances. The answer depends on what can be safely delegated to outside suppliers or allies versus what internal capabilities are key to the company's long-term success. Either way, though, calls for action. Outsourcing means launching initiatives to identify the most attractive providers and to establish collaborative relationships. Developing the capabilities in-house means marshaling personnel with relevant skills and experience, collaboratively networking the individual skills and related cross-functional activities to form organizational capability, and building the desired levels of proficiency through repetition (practice makes perfect).[15]

Sometimes the tediousness of internal organization building can be shortcut by buying a company that has the requisite capability and integrating its competencies into the firm's value chain. Indeed, a pressing need to acquire certain capabilities quickly is one reason to acquire another company—an acquisition aimed at building greater capability can be every bit as competitively valuable as an acquisition aimed at adding new products or services to the company's business lineup. Capabilities-motivated acquisitions are essential (1) when a market opportunity can slip by faster than a needed capability can be created internally, and (2) when industry conditions, technology, or competitors are moving at such a rapid clip that time is of the essence. But usually there's no good substitute for ongoing internal efforts to build and strengthen the company's competencies and capabilities in performing strategy-critical value chain activities.

Updating and Remodeling Competencies and Capabilities as External Conditions and Company Strategy Change   Even after core competencies and competitive capabilities are in place and functioning, company managers can't relax. Competencies and capabilities that grow stale can impair competitiveness unless they are refreshed, modified, or even phased out and replaced in response to ongoing market changes and shifts in company strategy. Indeed, the buildup of knowledge and experience over time, coupled with the imperatives of keeping capabilities in step with ongoing strategy and market changes, makes it appropriate to view a company as *a bundle of evolving competencies and capabilities.* Management's organization-building challenge is one of deciding when and how to recalibrate existing com petencies and capabilities, and when and how to develop new ones. Although the task is formidable, ideally it produces a dynamic organization with "hum" and momentum as well as a distinctive competence. Toyota, aspiring to overtake General Motors as the global leader in motor vehicles, has been aggressively upgrading its capabilities in fuel-efficient hybrid engine technology and is constantly fine-tuning its famed Toyota Production System to enhance its already proficient capabilities in manufacturing top-quality vehicles at relatively low costs—see Illustration Capsule 11.2. Likewise, Honda, which has long had a core competence in gasoline engine technology and small engine design, has accelerated its efforts to broaden its expertise and capabilities in hybrid engines so as to stay close behind Toyota. TV broadcasters are upgrading their capabilities in digital broadcasting technology in readiness for the upcoming switchover from analog to digital signal transmission. Microsoft has totally retooled the manner in which its programmers attack the task of writing code for its new operating systems for PCs and servers (the first wave of which was due out in 2006).

The Strategic Role of Employee Training

Training and retraining are important when a company shifts to a strategy requiring different skills, competitive capabilities, managerial approaches, and operating methods. Training is also strategically important in organizational efforts to build skills-based competencies. And it is a key activity in businesses where technical know-how is changing so rapidly that a company loses its ability to compete unless its skilled people have cutting-edge knowledge and expertise. Successful strategy implementers see to it that the training function is both adequately funded and effective. If the chosen strategy calls for new skills, deeper technological capability, or building and using new capabilities, training should be placed near the top of the action agenda.

The strategic importance of training has not gone unnoticed. Over 600 companies have established internal "universities" to lead the training effort, facilitate continuous organizational learning, and help upgrade company competencies and capabilities. Many companies conduct orientation sessions for new employees, fund an assortment

Illustration Capsule 11.2

Toyota's Legendary Production System: A Capability That Translates into Competitive Advantage

The heart of Toyota's strategy in motor vehicles is to outcompete rivals by manufacturing world-class, quality vehicles at lower costs and selling them at competitive price levels. Executing this strategy requires top-notch manufacturing capability and super-efficient management of people, equipment, and materials. Toyota began conscious efforts to improve its manufacturing competence more than 50 years ago. Through tireless trial and error, the company gradually took what started as a loose collection of techniques and practices and integrated them into a full-fledged process that has come to be known as the Toyota Production System (TPS). The TPS drives all plant operations and the company's supply chain management practices. TPS is grounded in the following principles, practices, and techniques:

- *Deliver parts and components just-in-time to the point of vehicle assembly.* The idea here is to cut out all the bits and pieces of transferring materials from place to place and to discontinue all activities on the part of workers that don't add value (particularly activities where nothing ends up being made or assembled).

- *Develop people who can come up with unique ideas for production improvements.*

- *Emphasize continuous improvement.* Workers are expected to use their heads and develop better ways of doing things, rather than mechanically follow instructions. Toyota managers tell workers that the *T* in TPS also stands for "Thinking." The thesis is that a work environment where people have to think generates the wisdom to spot opportunities for making tasks simpler and easier to perform, increasing the speed and efficiency with which activities are performed, and constantly improving product quality.

- *Empower workers to stop the assembly line when there's a problem or a defect is spotted.* Toyota views worker efforts to purge defects and sort out the problem immediately as critical to the whole concept of building quality

into the production process. According to TPS, "If the line doesn't stop, useless defective items will move on to the next stage. If you don't know where the problem occurred, you can't do anything to fix it." The tool for halting the assembly line is the *andon* electric light board, which is visible to everyone on the production floor.

- *Deal with defects only when they occur.* TPS philosophy holds that when things are running smoothly, they should not be subject to control; if attention is directed to fixing problems that are found, quality control along the assembly line can be handled with fewer personnel.

- *Ask yourself "Why?" five times.* While errors need to be fixed whenever they occur, the value of asking "Why?" five times enables identifying the root cause of the error and correcting it so that the error won't recur.

- *Organize all jobs around human motion to create a production/assembly system with no wasted effort.* Work organized in this fashion is called standardized work, and people are trained to observe standardized work procedures (which include supplying parts to each process on the assembly line at the proper time, sequencing the work in an optimal manner, and allowing workers to do their jobs continuously in a set sequence of subprocesses).

- *Find where a part is made cheaply and use that price as a benchmark.*

The TPS uses unique terms (such as *kanban, takt time, jikoda, kaizen, heijunka, monozukuri, poka yoke,* and *muda*) that facilitate precise discussion of specific TPS elements. In 2003, Toyota established a Global Production Center to efficiently train large numbers of shop-floor experts in the latest TPS methods and better operate an increasing number of production sites worldwide. There's widespread agreement that Toyota's ongoing effort to refine and improve on its renowned TPS gives it important manufacturing capabilities that are the envy of other motor vehicle manufacturers.

Sources: Information posted at www.toyotageorgetown.com, and Taiichi Ohno, *Toyota Production System: Beyond Large-Scale Production* (New York: Sheridan, 1988).

of competence-building training programs, and reimburse employees for tuition and other expenses associated with obtaining additional college education, attending professional development courses, and earning professional certification of one kind or another. A number of companies offer online, just-in-time training courses to employees around the clock. Increasingly, employees at all levels are expected to take an active role in their own professional development, assuming responsibility for keeping their skills and expertise up-to-date and in sync with the company's needs.

From Competencies and Capabilities to Competitive Advantage

While strong core competencies and competitive capabilities are a major assist in executing strategy, they are an equally important avenue for securing a competitive edge over rivals in situations where it is relatively easy for rivals to copy smart strategies. Any time rivals can readily duplicate successful strategy features, making it difficult or impossible to outstrategize rivals and beat them in the marketplace with a superior strategy, the chief way to achieve lasting competitive advantage is to outexecute them (beat them by performing certain value chain activities in a superior fashion). *Building core competencies and competitive capabilities that are very difficult or costly for rivals to emulate and that push a company closer to true operating excellence promotes very proficient strategy execution.* Moreover, because cutting-edge core competencies and competitive capabilities represent resource strengths that are often time-consuming and expensive for rivals to match or trump, any competitive edge they produce tends to be sustainable and pave the way for above-average company performance.

> **Core Concept**
> Building competencies and capabilities that are very difficult or costly for rivals to emulate has a huge payoff—improved strategy execution and a potential for competitive advantage.

It is easy to cite instances where companies have gained a competitive edge based on superior competencies and capabilities. Toyota's production capabilities (see Illustration Capsule 11.2) have given it a decided market edge over such rivals as General Motors, Ford, DaimlerChrysler, and Volkswagen. Dell's competitors have spent years and millions of dollars in what so far is a futile effort to match Dell's cost-efficient supply chain management capabilities. FedEx has unmatched capabilities in reliable overnight delivery of documents and small parcels. Various business news media have been unable to match the competence of Dow-Jones in gathering and reporting business news via *The Wall Street Journal.*

EXECUTION-RELATED ASPECTS OF ORGANIZING THE WORK EFFORT

There are few hard-and-fast rules for organizing the work effort to support good strategy execution. Every firm's organization chart is partly a product of its particular situation, reflecting prior organizational patterns, varying internal circumstances, executive judgments about reporting relationships, and the politics of who gets which assignments. Moreover, every strategy is grounded in its own set of key success factors and value chain activities. But some organizational considerations are common to all companies. These are summarized in Figure 11.3 and discussed in turn in the following sections.

Deciding Which Value Chain Activities to Perform Internally and Which to Outsource

The advantages of a company having an outsourcing component in its strategy were discussed in Chapter 6 (pp. 160–193), but there is also a need to consider the role of outsourcing in executing the strategy. Aside from the fact than an outsider, because of

Figure 11.3   **Structuring the Work Effort to Promote Successful Strategy Execution**

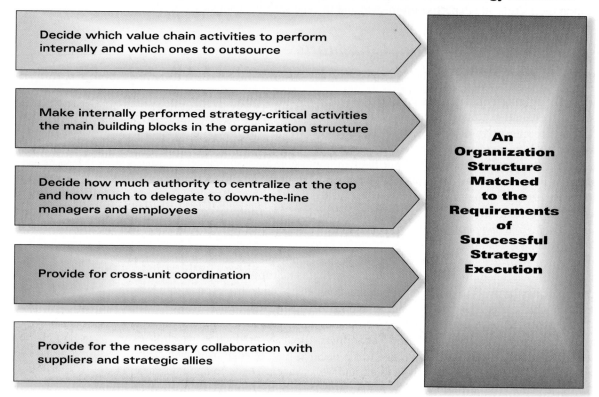

its expertise and specialized know-how, may be able to perform certain value chain activities better or cheaper than a company can perform them internally, outsourcing can also have several organization-related benefits. Managers too often spend inordinate amounts of time, mental energy, and resources haggling with functional support groups and other internal bureaucracies over needed services, leaving less time for them to devote to performing strategy-critical activities in the most proficient manner. One way to reduce such distractions is to outsource the performance of assorted administrative support functions and perhaps even selected core or primary value chain activities to outside vendors, thereby enabling the company to *heighten its strategic focus and concentrate its full energies and resources on even more competently performing those value chain activities that are at the core of its strategy and for which it can create unique value.* For example, E. & J. Gallo Winery outsources 95 percent of its grape production, letting farmers take on the weather and other grape-growing risks while it concentrates its full energies on wine production and sales.[16] A number of personal computer (PC) makers outsource the mundane and highly specialized task of PC assembly, concentrating their energies instead on product design, sales and marketing, and distribution.

When a company uses outsourcing to zero in on ever better performance of those truly strategy-critical activities where its expertise is most needed, then it may be able to realize three very positive benefits:

1. The company improves its chances for outclassing rivals in the performance of strategy-critical activities and turning a core competence into a distinctive competence. At the very least, the heightened focus on performing a select few value chain activities should meaningfully strengthen the company's existing core competences and promote more innovative performance of those activities—either of which could lower costs or materially improve competitive capabilities. Eastman Kodak, Ford, Exxon Mobil, Merrill Lynch, and Chevron have outsourced their data processing activities to computer service firms, believing that outside specialists can perform the needed services at lower costs and equal or better quality. A relatively large number of companies outsource the operation of their Web sites to Web design and hosting enterprises. Many business that get a lot of inquiries from customers or that have to provide 24/7 technical support to users of their products across the world have found that it is considerably less expensive to outsource these functions to specialists (often located in foreign countries where skilled personnel are readily available and worker compensation costs are much lower) than to operate their own call centers.

2. *The streamlining of internal operations that flows from outsourcing often acts to decrease internal bureaucracies, flatten the organization structure, speed internal decision making, and shorten the time it takes to respond to changing market conditions.*[17] In consumer electronics, where advancing technology drives new product innovation, organizing the work effort in a manner that expedites getting next-generation products to market ahead of rivals is a critical competitive capability. Motor vehicle manufacturers have found that they can shorten the cycle time for new models, improve the quality and performance of those models, and lower overall production costs by outsourcing the big majority of their parts and components from independent suppliers and then working closely with their vendors to advance the design and functioning of the items being supplied, to swiftly incorporate new technology, and to better integrate individual parts and components to form engine cooling systems, transmission systems, and electrical systems.

3. *Outsourcing the performance of certain value chain activities to able suppliers can add to a company's arsenal of capabilities and contribute to better strategy execution.* By building, continually improving, and then leveraging its partnerships with able suppliers, a company enhances its overall organizational capabilities and builds resource strengths—strengths that deliver value to customers and consequently pave the way for competitive success. Soft-drink and beer manufacturers all cultivate their relationships with their bottlers and distributors to strengthen access to local markets and build the loyalty, support, and commitment for corporate marketing programs, without which their own sales and growth are weakened. Similarly, fast-food enterprises like McDonald's and Taco Bell find it essential to work hand-in-hand with franchisees on outlet cleanliness, consistency of product quality, in-store ambience, courtesy and friendliness of store personnel, and other aspects of store operations. Unless franchisees continuously deliver sufficient customer satisfaction to attract repeat business, a fast-food chain's sales and competitive standing will suffer quickly. Companies like Boeing, Aerospatiale, Verizon Communications, and Dell have learned that their central R&D groups cannot begin to match the innovative capabilities of a well-managed network of supply chain partners having the ability to advance the technology, lead the development of next-generation parts and components, and supply them at a relatively low price.[18]

As a general rule, companies refrain from outsourcing those value chain activities over which they need direct strategic and operating control in order to build core competencies, achieve competitive advantage, and effectively manage key customer–supplier–distributor relationships. It is the strategically less important activities—like handling customer inquiries and providing technical support, doing the payroll, administering employee benefit programs, providing corporate security, managing stockholder relations, maintaining fleet vehicles, operating the company's Web site, conducting employee training, and managing an assortment of information and data processing functions—where outsourcing is most used.

Even so, a number of companies have found ways to successfully rely on outside vendors to perform strategically significant value chain activities.[19] Broadcom, a global leader in chips for broadband communications systems, outsources the manufacture of its chips to Taiwan Semiconductor, thus freeing company personnel to focus their full energies on R&D, new chip design, and marketing. For years Polaroid Corporation bought its film from Eastman Kodak, its electronics from Texas Instruments, and its cameras from Timex and others, while it concentrated on producing its unique self-developing film packets and designing its next-generation cameras and films. Nike concentrates on design, marketing, and distribution to retailers, while outsourcing virtually all production of its shoes and sporting apparel. Cisco Systems outsources virtually all manufacturing of its routers, switches, and other Internet gear, yet it protects its market position by retaining tight internal control over product design and closely monitors the daily operations of its manufacturing vendors. Large numbers of electronics companies outsource the design, engineering, manufacturing, and shipping of their products to such companies as Flextronics and Solectron, both of which have built huge businesses as providers of such services to companies worldwide. So while performing *core* value chain activities in-house normally makes good sense, there can be times when outsourcing some of them works to good advantage.

The Dangers of Excessive Outsourcing   Critics contend that a company can go overboard on outsourcing and so hollow out its knowledge base and capabilities as to leave itself at the mercy of outside suppliers and short of the resource strengths to be a master of its own destiny.[20] The point is well taken, but most companies appear alert to the danger of taking outsourcing to an extreme or failing to maintain control of the work performed by specialist vendors or offshore suppliers. Many companies refuse to source key components from a single supplier, opting to use two or three suppliers as a way of avoiding single supplier dependence or giving one supplier too much bargaining power. Moreover, they regularly evaluate their suppliers, looking not only at the supplier's overall performance but also at whether they should switch to another supplier or even bring the activity back in-house. To avoid loss of control, companies typically work closely with key suppliers, meeting often and setting up online systems to share data and information, collaborate on work in progress, monitor performance, and otherwise document that suppliers' activities are closely integrated with their own requirements and expectations. Indeed, sophisticated online systems permit companies to work in "real time" with suppliers 10,000 miles away, making rapid response possible whenever concerns or problems arise. Hence *the real debate surrounding outsourcing is not about whether too much outsourcing risks loss of control, but about how to use outsourcing in a manner that produces greater competitiveness.*

Making Strategy-Critical Activities the Main Building Blocks of the Organization Structure

In any business, some activities in the value chain are always more critical to strategic success and competitive advantage than others. For instance, hotel/motel enterprises have to be good at fast check-in/check-out, housekeeping and facilities maintenance, food service, and the creation of a pleasant ambience. For a manufacturer of chocolate bars, buying quality cocoa beans at low prices is vital and reducing production costs by a fraction of a cent per bar can mean a seven-figure improvement in the bottom line. In discount stock brokerage, the strategy-critical activities are fast access to information, accurate order execution, efficient record keeping and transactions processing, and good customer service. In specialty chemicals, the critical activities are R&D, product innovation, getting new products onto the market quickly, effective marketing, and expertise in assisting customers. Where such is the case, it is important for management to build its organization structure around proficient performance of these activities, making them the centerpieces or main building blocks on the organization chart.

The rationale for making strategy-critical activities the main building blocks in structuring a business is compelling: If activities crucial to strategic success are to have the resources, decision-making influence, and organizational impact they need, they have to be centerpieces in the organizational scheme. Plainly, implementing a new or changed strategy is likely to entail new or different key activities, competencies, or capabilities and therefore to require new or different organizational arrangements. If workable organizational adjustments are not forthcoming, the resulting mismatch between strategy and structure can open the door to execution and performance problems.[21] Hence, attempting to carry out a new strategy with an old organization structure is usually unwise.

What Types of Organization Structures Fit Which Strategies?   It is generally agreed that some type of functional structure is the best organizational arrangement when a company is in just one particular business (irrespective of which of the five competitive strategies it opts to pursue). The primary organizational building blocks within a business are usually *traditional functional departments* (R&D, engineering and design, production and operations, sales and marketing, information technology, finance and accounting, and human resources) and *process departments* (where people in a single work unit have responsibility for all the aspects of a certain process like supply chain management, new product development, customer service, quality control, or selling direct to customers via the company's Web site). For instance, a technical instruments manufacturer may be organized around research and development, engineering, supply chain management, assembly, quality control, marketing, technical services, and corporate administration. A hotel may have a functional organization based on front-desk operations, housekeeping, building maintenance, food service, convention services and special events, guest services, personnel and training, and accounting. A discount retailer may organize around such functional units as purchasing, warehousing and distribution, store operations, advertising, merchandising and promotion, customer service, and corporate administrative services.

In enterprises with operations in various countries around the world (or with geographically scattered organizational units within a country), the basic building blocks may also include *geographic organizational units,* each of which has profit/loss responsibility for its assigned geographic area. In vertically integrated firms, the major building blocks are *divisional units performing one or more of the major processing steps along the value chain* (raw materials production, components manufacture, assembly, wholesale distribution, retail store operations); each division in the value chain may operate as a profit center for performance measurement purposes. The typical building blocks of a diversified company are its *individual businesses,* with each business unit usually operating as an independent profit center and with corporate headquarters performing assorted support functions for all of its business units. But a divisional business-unit structure can present problems to a company pursuing related diversification.

Determining the Degree of Authority and Independence to Give Each Unit and Each Employee

In executing the strategy and conducting daily operations, companies must decide how much authority to delegate to the managers of each organization unit—especially the heads of business subsidiaries; functional and process departments; and plants, sales offices, distribution centers, and other operating units—and how much decision-making latitude to give individual employees in performing their jobs. The two extremes are to *centralize decision making* at the top (the CEO and a few close lieutenants) or to *decentralize decision making* by giving managers and employees considerable decision-making latitude in their areas of responsibility. As shown in Table 11.1, the two approaches are based on sharply different underlying principles and beliefs, with each having its pros and cons.

Centralized Decision Making: Pros and Cons *In a highly centralized organization structure, top executives retain authority for most strategic and operating decisions and keep a tight rein on business-unit heads, department heads, and the*

Table 11.1   **Advantages and Disadvantages of Centralized versus Decentralized Decision Making**

Centralized Organizational Structures	Decentralized Organizational Structures
Basic tenets • Decisions on most matters of importance should be pushed to managers up the line who have the experience, expertise, and judgment to decide what is the wisest or best course of action. • Frontline supervisors and rank-and-file employees can't be relied on to make the right decisions—because they seldom know what is best for the organization and because they do not have the time or the inclination to properly manage the tasks they are performing (letting them decide "what to do" is thus risky).	**Basic tenets** • Decision-making authority should be put in the hands of the people closest to and most familiar with the situation and these people should be trained to exercise good judgment. • A company that draws on the combined intellectual capital of all its employees can outperform a command-and-control company.
Chief advantage • Fixes accountability.	**Chief advantages** • Encourages lower level managers and rank-and-file employees to exercise initiative and act responsibly. • Promotes greater motivation and involvement in the business on the part of more company personnel. • Spurs new ideas and creative thinking. • Allows fast response times. • Entails fewer layers of management.
Primary disadvantages • Lengthens response times because management bureaucracy must decide on a course of action. • Does not encourage responsibility among lower level managers and rank-and-file employees. • Discourages lower level managers and rank-and-file employees from exercising any initiative—they are expected to wait to be told what to do.	**Primary disadvantages** • Puts the organization at risk if many bad decisions are made at lower levels—top management lacks full control. • Impedes cross-business coordination and capture of strategic fits in diversified companies.

managers of key operating units; comparatively little discretionary authority is granted to frontline supervisors and rank-and-file employees. The command-and-control paradigm of centralized structures is based on the underlying assumption that frontline personnel have neither the time nor the inclination to direct and properly control the work they are performing, and that they lack the knowledge and judgment to make wise decisions about how best to do it—hence the need for managerially prescribed policies and procedures, close supervision, and tight control. The thesis underlying authoritarian structures is that strict enforcement of detailed procedures backed by rigorous managerial oversight is the most reliable way to keep the daily execution of strategy on track.

The big advantage of an authoritarian structure is tight control by the manager in charge—it is easy to know who is accountable when things do not go well. But there are some serious disadvantages. Hierarchical command-and-control structures make an organization sluggish in responding to changing conditions because of the time it takes for the review/approval process to run up all the layers of the management bureaucracy. Furthermore, to work well, centralized decision making requires top-level managers to gather and process whatever information is relevant to the decision. When the relevant knowledge resides at lower organizational levels (or is technical, detailed, or hard to express in words), it is difficult and time-consuming to get all of the facts and nuances in front of a high-level executive located far from the scene of the action—full understanding of the situation cannot be readily copied from one mind to another. Hence, centralized decision making is often impractical—the larger the company and the more scattered its operations, the more that decision-making authority has to be delegated to managers closer to the scene of the action.

> There are disadvantages to having a small number of top-level managers micromanage the business either by personally making decisions or by requiring lower-level subordinates to gain approval before taking action.

Decentralized Decision Making: Pros and Cons   *In a highly decentralized organization, decision-making authority is pushed down to the lowest organizational level capable of making timely, informed, competent decisions.* The objective is to put adequate decision-making authority in the hands of the people closest to and most familiar with the situation and train them to weigh all the factors and exercise good judgment. Decentralized decision making means that the managers of each organizational unit are delegated lead responsibility for deciding how best to execute strategy (as well as some role in shaping the strategy for the units they head). Decentralization thus requires selecting strong managers to head each organizational unit and holding them accountable for crafting and executing appropriate strategies for their units. Managers who consistently produce unsatisfactory results have to be weeded out.

The case for empowering down-the-line managers and employees to make decisions related to daily operations and executing the strategy is based on the belief that a company that draws on the combined intellectual capital of all its employees can outperform a command-and-control company.[22] Decentralized decision making means, for example, that in a diversified company the various business-unit heads have broad authority to execute the agreed-on business strategy with comparatively little interference from corporate headquarters; moreover, the business-unit heads delegate considerable decision-making latitude to functional and process department heads and the heads of the various operating units (plants, distribution centers, sales offices) in implementing and executing their pieces of the strategy. In turn, work teams may be empowered to manage and improve their assigned value chain activity, and employees with customer contact may be empowered to do what it takes to please customers.

The ultimate goal of decentralized decision making is to put decision-making authority in the hands of those persons or teams closest to and most knowledgeable about the situation.

At Starbucks, for example, employees are encouraged to exercise initiative in promoting customer satisfaction—there's the story of a store employee who, when the computerized cash register system went offline, enthusiastically offered free coffee to waiting customers.[23] *With decentralized decision making, top management maintains control by limiting empowered managers' and employees' discretionary authority and holding people accountable for the decisions they make.*

Decentralized organization structures have much to recommend them. Delegating greater authority to subordinate managers and employees creates a more horizontal organization structure with fewer management layers. Whereas in a centralized vertical structure managers and workers have to go up the ladder of authority for an answer, in a decentralized horizontal structure they develop their own answers and action plans—making decisions in their areas of responsibility and being accountable for results is an integral part of their job. Pushing decision-making authority down to middle and lower-level managers and then further on to work teams and individual employees shortens organizational response times and spurs new ideas, creative thinking, innovation, and greater involvement on the part of subordinate managers and employees. In worker-empowered structures, jobs can be defined more broadly, several tasks can be integrated into a single job, and people can direct their own work. Fewer managers are needed because deciding how to do things becomes part of each person's or team's job. Further, today's online communication systems make it easy and relatively inexpensive for people at all organizational levels to have direct access to data, other employees, managers, suppliers, and customers. They can access information quickly (via the Internet or company intranet), readily check with superiors or coworkers as needed, and take responsible action. Typically, there are genuine gains in morale and productivity when people are provided with the tools and information they need to operate in a self-directed way. Decentralized decision making not only can shorten organizational response times but also can spur new ideas, creative thinking, innovation, and greater involvement on the part of subordinate managers and employees.

The past decade has seen a growing shift from authoritarian, multilayered hierarchical structures to flatter, more decentralized structures that stress employee empowerment. There's strong and growing consensus that authoritarian, hierarchical organization structures are not well suited to implementing and executing strategies in an era when extensive information and instant communication are the norm and when a big fraction of the organization's most valuable assets consists of intellectual capital and resides in the knowledge and capabilities of its employees. Many companies have therefore begun empowering lower-level managers and employees throughout their organizations, giving them greater discretionary authority to make strategic adjustments in their areas of responsibility and to decide what needs to be done to put new strategic initiatives into place and execute them proficiently.

Maintaining Control in a Decentralized Organization Structure

Pushing decision-making authority deep down into the organization structure and empowering employees presents its own organizing challenge: *how to exercise adequate control over the actions of empowered employees so that the business is not put at risk at the same time that the benefits of empowerment are realized.*[24] Maintaining adequate organizational control over empowered employees is generally accomplished by placing limits on the authority that empowered personnel can exercise, holding people accountable for their decisions, instituting compensation incentives that reward people for doing their jobs in a manner that contributes to good company performance, and creating a corporate culture where there's strong peer pressure on individuals to act responsibly.

Capturing Strategic Fits in a Decentralized Structure   Diversified companies striving to capture cross-business strategic fits have to beware of giving business heads full rein to operate independently when cross-business collaboration is essential in order to gain strategic fit benefits. Cross-business strategic fits typically have to be captured either by enforcing close cross-business collaboration or by centralizing performance of functions having strategic fits at the corporate level.[25] For example, if businesses with overlapping process and product technologies have their own independent R&D departments—each pursuing their own priorities, projects, and strategic agendas—it's hard for the corporate parent to prevent duplication of effort, capture either economies of scale or economies of scope, or broaden the company's R&D efforts to embrace new technological paths, product families, end-use applications, and customer groups. Where cross-business R&D fits exist, the best solution is usually to centralize the R&D function and have a coordinated corporate R&D effort that serves both the interests of individual businesses and the company as a whole. Likewise, centralizing the related activities of separate businesses makes sense when there are opportunities to share a common sales force, use common distribution channels, rely on a common field service organization to handle customer requests or provide maintenance and repair services, use common e-commerce systems and approaches, and so on.

The point here is that efforts to decentralize decision making and give organizational units leeway in conducting operations have to be tempered with the need to maintain adequate control and cross-unit coordination—decentralization doesn't mean delegating authority in ways that allow organization units and individuals to do their own thing. There are numerous instances when decision-making authority must be retained at high levels in the organization and ample cross-unit coordination strictly enforced.

Providing for Internal Cross-Unit Coordination

The classic way to coordinate the activities of organizational units is to position them in the hierarchy so that the most closely related ones report to a single person (a functional department head, a process manager, a geographic area head, a senior executive). Managers higher up in the ranks generally have the clout to coordinate, integrate, and arrange for the cooperation of units under their supervision. In such structures, the chief executive officer, chief operating officer, and business-level managers end up as central points of coordination because of their positions of authority over the whole unit. When a firm is pursuing a related diversification strategy, coordinating the related activities of independent business units often requires the centralizing authority of a single corporate-level officer. Also, diversified companies commonly centralize such staff support functions as public relations, finance and accounting, employee benefits, and information technology at the corporate level both to contain the costs of support activities and to facilitate uniform and coordinated performance of such functions within each business unit.

However, close cross-unit collaboration is usually needed to build core competencies and competitive capabilities in strategically important activities—such as speeding new products to market and providing superior customer service—that involve employees scattered across several internal organization units (and perhaps the employees of outside strategic partners or specialty vendors). A big weakness of traditional functionally organized structures is that pieces of strategically relevant activities and capabilities often end up scattered across many departments, with the result that no one group or manager is accountable. Consider, for example, how the following strategy-critical activities cut across different functions:

- *Filling customer orders accurately and promptly*—a process that involves personnel from sales (which wins the order); finance (which may have to check credit terms or approve special financing); production (which must produce the goods and replenish warehouse inventories as needed); warehousing (which has to verify whether the items are in stock, pick the order from the warehouse, and package it for shipping); and shipping (which has to choose a carrier to deliver the goods and release the goods to the carrier).[26]

- *Fast, ongoing introduction of new products*—a cross-functional process involving personnel in R&D, design and engineering, purchasing, manufacturing, and sales and marketing.

- *Improving product quality*—a process that entails the collaboration of personnel in R&D, design and engineering, purchasing, in-house components production, manufacturing, and assembly.

- *Supply chain management*—a collaborative process that cuts across such functional areas as purchasing, inventory management, manufacturing and assembly, and warehousing and shipping.

- *Building the capability to conduct business via the Internet*—a process that involves personnel in information technology, supply chain management, production, sales and marketing, warehousing and shipping, customer service, finance, and accounting.

- *Obtaining feedback from customers and making product modifications to meet their needs*—a process that involves personnel in customer service and after-sale support, R&D, design and engineering, purchasing, manufacturing and assembly, and marketing research.

Handoffs from one department to another lengthen completion time and frequently drive up administrative costs, since coordinating the fragmented pieces can soak up hours of effort on the parts of many people.[27] This is not a fatal flaw of functional organization—organizing around specific functions normally works to good advantage in support activities like finance and accounting, human resource management, and engineering, and in such primary activities as R&D, manufacturing, and marketing. But the tendency for pieces of a strategy-critical activity to be scattered across several functional departments is an important weakness of functional organization and accounts for why a company's competencies and capabilities are typically cross-functional.

Many companies have found that rather than continuing to scatter related pieces of a strategy-critical business process across several functional departments and scrambling to integrate their efforts, it is better to reengineer the work effort and pull the people who performed the pieces in functional departments into a group that works together to perform the whole process, thus creating *process departments* (like customer service or new product development or supply chain management). And sometimes the coordinating mechanisms involve the use of cross-functional task forces, dual reporting relationships, informal organizational networking, voluntary cooperation, incentive compensation tied to measures of group performance, and strong executive-level insistence on teamwork and cross-department cooperation (including removal of recalcitrant managers who stonewall collaborative efforts). At one European-based company, a top executive promptly replaced the managers of several plants who were not fully committed to collaborating closely on eliminating duplication in product development and production efforts among plants in several different countries. Earlier, the executive, noting that negotiations among the managers had stalled on which labs and plants to close, had met with all the managers, asked them to cooperate to find a solution, discussed with them which options were unacceptable, and given them a deadline to find a solution. When the asked-for teamwork wasn't forthcoming, several managers were replaced.

Providing for Collaboration with Outside Suppliers and Strategic Allies

Someone or some group must be authorized to collaborate as needed with each major outside constituency involved in strategy execution. Forming alliances and cooperative relationships presents immediate opportunities and opens the door to future possibilities, but nothing valuable is realized until the relationship grows, develops, and blossoms. Unless top management sees that constructive organizational bridge building with strategic partners occurs and that productive working relationships emerge, the value of alliances is lost and the company's power to execute its strategy is weakened. If close working relationships with suppliers are crucial, then supply chain management must be given formal status on the company's organization chart and a significant position in the pecking order. If distributor/dealer/franchisee relationships are important, someone must be assigned the task of nurturing the relationships with forward channel allies. If working in parallel with providers of complementary products and services contributes to enhanced organizational capability, then cooperative organizational arrangements have to be put in place and managed to good effect.

Building organizational bridges with external allies can be accomplished by appointing "relationship managers" with responsibility for making particular strategic partnerships or alliances generate the intended benefits. Relationship managers have many roles and functions: getting the right people together, promoting good rapport, seeing that plans for specific activities are developed and carried out, helping adjust internal organizational procedures and communication systems, ironing out operating dissimilarities, and nurturing interpersonal cooperation. Multiple cross-organization ties have to be established and kept open to ensure proper communication and coordination.[28] There has to be enough information sharing to make the relationship work and periodic frank discussions of conflicts, trouble spots, and changing situations.[29]

CURRENT ORGANIZATIONAL TRENDS

Many of today's companies are winding up the task of remodeling their traditional hierarchical structures once built around functional specialization and centralized authority. Much of the corporate downsizing movement in the late 1980s and early 1990s was aimed at recasting authoritarian, pyramidal organizational structures into flatter, decentralized structures. The change was driven by growing realization that command-and-control hierarchies were proving a liability in businesses where customer preferences were shifting from standardized products to custom orders and special features, product life cycles were growing shorter, custom mass-production methods were replacing standardized mass-production techniques, customers wanted to be treated as individuals, technological change was ongoing, and market conditions were fluid. Layered management hierarchies with lots of checks and controls that required people to look upward in the organizational structure for answers and approval were failing to deliver responsive customer service and timely adaptations to changing conditions.

The organizational adjustments and downsizing of companies in 2001–2005 brought further refinements and changes to streamline organizational activities and shake out inefficiencies. The goals have been to make companies leaner, flatter, and more responsive to change. Many companies are drawing on five tools of organizational design: (1) managers and workers empowered to act on their own judgments, (2) work process redesign (to achieve greater streamlining and tighter cohesion), (3) self-directed work teams, (4) rapid incorporation of Internet technology applications, and (5) networking with outsiders to improve existing organization capabilities and create new ones. Considerable management attention is being devoted to building a company capable of outcompeting rivals on the basis of superior resource strengths and competitive capabilities—capabilities that are increasingly based on intellectual capital and cross-unit collaboration.

Several other organizational characteristics are emerging:

- Extensive use of Internet technology and e-commerce business practices—real-time data and information systems; greater reliance on online systems for transacting business with suppliers and customers; and Internet-based communication and collaboration with suppliers, customers, and strategic partners.
- Fewer barriers between different vertical ranks, between functions and disciplines, between units in different geographic locations, and between the company and its suppliers, distributors/dealers, strategic allies, and customers—an outcome partly due to pervasive use of online systems.
- Rapid dissemination of information, rapid learning, and rapid response times—also an outcome partly due to pervasive use of online systems.
- Collaborative efforts among people in different functional specialties and geographic locations—essential to create organization competencies and capabilities.

Key Points

Implementing and executing strategy is an operation-driven activity revolving around the management of people and business processes. The managerial emphasis is on converting strategic plans into actions and good results. *Management's handling of the process of implementing and executing the chosen strategy can be considered successful if and when the company achieves the targeted strategic and financial performance and shows good progress in making its strategic vision a reality.* Shortfalls in performance signal weak strategy, weak execution, or both.

The place for managers to start in implementing and executing a new or different strategy is with *a probing assessment of what the organization must do differently and better to carry out the strategy successfully.* They should then consider *precisely how to make the necessary internal changes* as rapidly as possible.

Like crafting strategy, executing strategy is a job for a company's whole management team, not just a few senior managers. Top-level managers have to rely on the active support and cooperation of middle and lower managers to push strategy changes into functional areas and operating units and to see that the organization actually operates in accordance with the strategy on a daily basis.

Eight managerial tasks crop up repeatedly in company efforts to execute strategy:

1. Building an organization with the competencies, capabilities, and resource strengths to execute strategy successfully.

2. Marshaling sufficient money and people behind the drive for strategy execution.

3. Instituting policies and procedures that facilitate rather than impede strategy execution.

4. Adopting best practices and pushing for continuous improvement in how value chain activities are performed.

5. Installing information and operating systems that enable company personnel to carry out their strategic roles proficiently.

6. Tying rewards directly to the achievement of strategic and financial targets and to good strategy execution.

7. Shaping the work environment and corporate culture to fit the strategy.

8. Exercising strong leadership to drive execution forward, keep improving on the details of execution, and achieve operating excellence as rapidly as feasible.

Building an organization capable of good strategy execution entails three types of organization-building actions: (1) *staffing the organization*—assembling a talented, can-do management team, and recruiting and retaining employees with the needed experience, technical skills, and intellectual capital; (2) *building core competencies and competitive capabilities* that will enable good strategy execution and updating them as strategy and external conditions change; and (3) *structuring the organization and work effort*—organizing value chain activities and business processes and deciding how much decision-making authority to push down to lower-level managers and frontline employees.

Building core competencies and competitive capabilities is a time-consuming, managerially challenging exercise that involves three stages: (1) developing the *ability* to do something, however imperfectly or inefficiently, by selecting people with the requisite skills and experience, upgrading or expanding individual abilities as needed, and then molding the efforts and work products of individuals into a collaborative group effort; (2) coordinating group efforts to learn how to perform the activity *consistently well and at an acceptable cost,* thereby transforming the ability into a tried-and-true *competence or capability;* and (3) continuing to polish and refine the organization's know-how and otherwise sharpen performance such that it becomes *better than rivals* at performing the activity, thus raising the core competence (or capability) to the rank of a *distinctive competence* (or competitively superior capability) and opening an avenue to competitive advantage. Many companies manage to get through stages 1 and 2 in performing a strategy-critical activity but comparatively few achieve sufficient proficiency in performing strategy-critical activities to qualify for the third stage.

Strong core competencies and competitive capabilities are an important avenue for securing a competitive edge over rivals in situations where it is relatively easy for rivals to copy smart strategies. Any time rivals can readily duplicate successful strategy features, making it difficult or impossible to *outstrategize* rivals and beat them in the marketplace with a superior strategy, the chief way to achieve lasting competitive advantage is to *outexecute* them (beat them by performing certain value chain activities in superior fashion). *Building core competencies and competitive capabilities that are very difficult or costly for rivals to emulate and that push a company closer to true operating excellence is one of the best and most reliable ways to achieve a durable competitive edge.*

Structuring the organization and organizing the work effort in a strategy-supportive fashion has five aspects: (1) deciding which value chain activities to perform internally and which ones to outsource; (2) making internally performed strategy-critical activities the main building blocks in the organization structure; (3) deciding how much authority to centralize at the top and how much to delegate to down-the-line managers and employees; (4) providing for internal cross-unit coordination and collaboration to build and strengthen internal competencies/capabilities; and (5) providing for the necessary collaboration and coordination with suppliers and strategic allies.

Exercises

1. As the new owner of a local ice cream store located in a strip mall adjacent to a university campus, you are contemplating how to organize your business—whether to make your ice cream in-house or outsource its production to a nearby ice cream manufacturer whose brand is in most of the local supermarkets, and how much authority to delegate to the two assistant store managers and to employees working the counter and the cash register. You plan to sell 20 flavors of ice cream.

   a. What are the pros and cons of contracting with the local company to custom-produce your product line?

   b. Since you do not plan to be in the store during all of the hours it is open, what specific decision-making authority would you delegate to the two assistant store managers?

   c. To what extent, if any, should store employees—many of whom will be university students working part-time—be empowered to make decisions relating to store operations (opening and closing, keeping the premises clean and attractive, keeping the work area behind the counter stocked with adequate supplies of cups, cones, napkins, and so on)?

   d. Should you create a policies and procedures manual for the assistant managers and employees, or should you just give oral instructions and have them learn their duties and responsibilities on the job?

   e. How can you maintain control during the times you are not in the store?

2. Go to Home Depot's corporate home page (www.homedepot.com/corporate) and review the information under the headings About The Home Depot, Investor Relations, and Careers. How does Home Depot go about building core competencies and competitive capabilities? Would any of Home Depot's competencies qualify as a distinctive competence? Please use the chapter's discussion of building core competencies and competitive capabilities as a guide for preparing your answer.

3. Using Google Scholar or your access to EBSCO, InfoTrac, or other online database of journal articles and research in your university's library, do a search for recent writings on self-directed or empowered work teams. According to the articles you found in the various management journals, what are the conditions for the effective use of such teams? Also, how should such teams be organized or structured to better ensure their success?

chapter twelve

Managing Internal Operations

Actions That Promote Good Strategy Execution

Winning companies know how to do their work better.

—Michael Hammer and James Champy

Companies that make best practices a priority are thriving, thirsty, learning organizations. They believe that everyone should always be searching for a better way. Those kinds of companies are filled with energy and curiosity and a spirit of can-do.

—Jack Welch
Former CEO, General Electric

If you want people motivated to do a good job, give them a good job to do.

—Frederick Herzberg

You ought to pay big bonuses for premier performance . . . Be a top payer, not in the middle or low end of the pack.

—Lawrence Bossidy
CEO, Honeywell International

I n Chapter 11 we emphasized the importance of building organization capabilities and structuring the work effort so as to perform strategy-critical activities in a coordinated and highly competent manner. In this chapter we discuss five additional managerial actions that promote the success of a company's strategy execution efforts:

1. Marshaling resources behind the drive for good strategy execution.

2. Instituting policies and procedures that facilitate strategy execution.

3. Adopting best practices and striving for continuous improvement in how value chain activities are performed.

4. Installing information and operating systems that enable company personnel to carry out their strategic roles proficiently.

5. Tying rewards and incentives directly to the achievement of strategic and financial targets and to good strategy execution.

MARSHALING RESOURCES BEHIND THE DRIVE FOR GOOD STRATEGY EXECUTION

Early in the process of implementing and executing a new or different strategy, managers need to determine what resources will be needed and then consider whether the current budgets of organizational units are suitable. Plainly, organizational units must have the budgets and resources for executing their parts of the strategic plan effectively and efficiently. Developing a strategy-driven budget requires top management to determine what funding is needed to execute new strategic initiatives and to strengthen or modify the company's competencies and capabilities. This includes careful screening of requests for more people and more or better facilities and equipment, approving those that hold promise for making a cost-justified contribution to strategy execution, and turning down those that don't. Should internal cash flows prove insufficient to fund the planned strategic initiatives, then management must raise additional funds through borrowing or selling additional shares of stock to willing investors.

A company's ability to marshal the resources needed to support new strategic initiatives and steer them to the appropriate organizational units has a major impact on the strategy execution process. Too little funding (stemming either from constrained financial resources or from sluggish management action to adequately increase the budgets of strategy-critical organizational units) slows progress and impedes the efforts of organizational units to execute their pieces of the strategic plan proficiently. Too much funding wastes organizational resources and reduces financial performance. Both outcomes argue for managers to be deeply involved in reviewing budget proposals and directing the proper kinds and amounts of resources to strategy-critical organization units.

A change in strategy nearly always calls for budget reallocations and resource shifting. Units important in the prior strategy but having a lesser role in the new strategy may need downsizing. Units that now have a bigger and more critical strategic role may need more people, new equipment, additional facilities, and above-average increases in their operating budgets. More resources may have to be devoted to quality control or to adding new product features or to building a better brand image or to cutting costs or to employee retraining. Strategy implementers need to be active and forceful in shifting resources, downsizing some functions and upsizing others, not only to amply fund activities with a critical role in the new strategy but also to avoid inefficiency and achieve profit projections. They have to exercise their power to put enough resources behind new strategic initiatives to make things happen, and they have to make the tough decisions to kill projects and activities that are no longer justified.

Visible actions to reallocate operating funds and move people into new organizational units signal a determined commitment to strategic change and frequently are needed to catalyze the implementation process and give it credibility. Microsoft has made a practice of regularly shifting hundreds of programmers to new high-priority programming initiatives within a matter of weeks or even days. At Harris Corporation, where the strategy was to diffuse research ideas into areas that were commercially viable, top management regularly shifted groups of engineers out of government projects and into new commercial venture divisions. Fast-moving developments in many markets are prompting companies to abandon traditional annual or semiannual budgeting and resource allocation cycles in favor of cycles that match the strategy changes a company makes in response to newly developing events.

The bigger the change in strategy (or the more obstacles that lie in the path of good strategy execution), the bigger the resource shifts that will likely be required. Merely fine-tuning the execution of a company's existing strategy seldom requires big movements of people and money from one area to another. The desired improvements can usually be accomplished through above-average budget increases to organizational units launching new initiatives and below-average increases (or even small cuts) for the remaining organizational units. The chief exception occurs where all the strategy changes or new execution initiatives need to be made without adding to total expenses. Then managers have to work their way through the existing budget line-by-line and activity-by-activity, looking for ways to trim costs in some areas and shift the resources to higher priority activities where new execution initiatives are needed.

INSTITUTING POLICIES AND PROCEDURES THAT FACILITATE GOOD STRATEGY EXECUTION

A company's policies and procedures can either assist the cause of good strategy execution or be a barrier. Anytime a company moves to put new strategy elements in place or improve its strategy execution capabilities, managers are well advised to undertake a careful review of existing policies and procedures, proactively revising or discarding those that are out of sync. A change in strategy or a push for better strategy execution generally requires some changes in work practices and the behavior of company personnel. One way of promoting such changes is by instituting a select set of new policies and procedures deliberately aimed at steering the actions and behavior of company personnel in a direction more conducive to good strategy execution and operating excellence.

Figure 12.1   **How Prescribed Policies and Procedures Facilitate Strategy Execution**

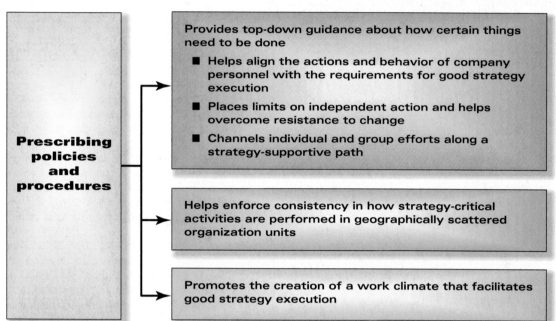

As shown in Figure 12.1, prescribing new policies and operating procedures acts to facilitate strategy execution in three ways:

1. *Instituting new policies and procedures provides top-down guidance regarding how certain things now need to be done.* Asking people to alter established habits and procedures, of course, always upsets the internal order of things. It is normal for pockets of resistance to develop and for people to exhibit some degree of stress and anxiety about how the changes will affect them, especially when the changes may eliminate jobs. But when existing ways of doing things pose a barrier to improving strategy execution, actions and behaviors have to be changed. The managerial role of establishing and enforcing new policies and operating practices is to paint a different set of white lines, place limits on independent behavior, and channel individual and group efforts along a path more conducive to executing the strategy. Policies are a particularly useful way to counteract tendencies for some people to resist change—most people refrain from violating company policy or going against recommended practices and procedures without first gaining clearance or having strong justification.

2. *Policies and procedures help enforce needed consistency in how particular strategy-critical activities are performed in geographically scattered operating units.* Standardization and strict conformity are sometimes desirable components of good strategy execution. Eliminating significant differences in the operating practices of different plants, sales regions, customer service centers, or the individual outlets in a chain operation helps a company deliver consistent product quality and service to customers. Good strategy execution nearly always entails an ability to replicate product quality and the caliber of customer service at every location where the company does business—anything less blurs the company's image and fails to meet customer expectations.

Illustration Capsule 12.1

Granite Construction's Short-Pay Policy: An Innovative Way to Drive Better Strategy Execution

In 1987, the owners of Granite Construction, a 100-plus-year-old supplier of crushed gravel, sand, concrete, and asphalt in Watsonville, California, decided to pursue two strategic targets: total customer satisfaction and a reputation for superior service. To drive the internal efforts to achieve these two objectives and signal both employees and customers that it was deadly serious about these two strategic commitments, top management instituted a short-pay policy that appeared on the bottom of every Granite Construction invoice:

If you are not satisfied for any reason, don't pay us for it. Simply scratch out the line item, write a brief note about the problem, and return a copy of this invoice along with your check for the balance.

Customers did not have to call and complain and were not expected to return the product. They were given complete discretionary power to decide whether and how much to pay based on their satisfaction level. Management believed that empowering customers not to pay for items or service they found lacking would provide unmistakable feedback and spur company personnel to correct any problems quickly in order to avoid repeated short payments.

The short-pay policy had the desired impact, focusing the attention of company personnel on avoiding short payments by customers and boosting customer satisfaction

significantly. Granite has enjoyed compound annual sales gains of 12.2 percent since 2000, while charging a 6 percent price premium for its commodity products in competition against larger rivals.

In addition to its short-pay policy, Granite employs two other policies to help induce company personnel to do their very best to satisfy the company's customers. It has a no-layoff policy (no employees have been laid off in over 80 years), and it sends positive customer comments about employees home for families to read. To make sure its workforce force is properly trained, company employees go through training programs averaging 43 hours per employee annually. And compensation is attractive: Entry-level employees, called job owners, start at $16 an hour and progress to such positions as "accomplished job owner" and "improvement champion" (base pay of $26 an hour); all employees are entitled to 12 company-paid massages annually.

Granite won the prestigious Malcolm Baldrige National Quality Award in 1992, about five years after instituting the short-pay policy. *Fortune* rated Granite as one of the 100 best companies to work for in America in eight of the nine years from 1998 to 2006 (its highest ranking was 16th in 2002, and its lowest was 90th in 2004). The company was on *Fortune's* "Most Admired Companies" list in 2005 and 2006.

Source: Based on information in Jim Collins, "Turning Goals into Results: The Power of Catalytic Mechanisms," *Harvard Business Review* 77, no. 4 (July–August 1999), pp. 72–73; Robert Levering and Milton Moskowitz, "The 100 Best Companies to Work For," *Fortune,* February 4, 2004, p. 73; Robert Levering and Milton Moskowitz, "The 100 Best Companies to Work For," *Fortune,* January 12, 2005, p. 78; and www.fortune.com (accessed November 11, 2005).

3. *Well-conceived policies and procedures promote the creation of a work climate that facilitates good strategy execution.* Because discarding old policies and procedures in favor of new ones invariably alters the internal work climate, managers can use the policy-changing process as a powerful lever for changing the corporate culture in ways that produce a stronger fit with the new strategy. The trick here, obviously, is to hit upon a new policy that will catch the immediate attention of the whole organization, quickly shift their actions and behavior, and then become embedded in how things are done—as with Granite Construction's short-pay policy discussed in Illustration Capsule 12.1.

In an attempt to steer "crew members" into stronger quality and service behavior patterns, McDonald's policy manual spells out detailed procedures that personnel in each McDonald's unit are expected to observe; for example, "Cooks must turn, never flip, hamburgers," "If they haven't been purchased, Big Macs must be discarded in 10 minutes after being cooked and French fries in 7 minutes," and "Cashiers must make eye contact with and smile at every customer."

Nordstrom's strategic objective is to make sure that each customer has a pleasing shopping experience in its department stores and returns time and again; to get store personnel to dedicate themselves to outstanding customer service, Nordstrom has a policy of promoting only those people whose personnel records contain evidence of "heroic acts" to please customers—especially customers who may have made "unreasonable requests" that require special efforts. To keep its R&D activities responsive to customer needs and expectations, Hewlett-Packard (HP) requires R&D people to make regular visits to customers to learn about their problems and learn their reactions to HP's latest new products.

One of the big policymaking issues concerns what activities need to be rigidly prescribed and what activities ought to allow room for independent action on the part of empowered personnel. Few companies need thick policy manuals to direct the strategy execution process or prescribe exactly how daily operations are to be conducted. Too much policy can erect as many obstacles as wrong policy or be as confusing as no policy. There is wisdom in a middle approach: *Prescribe enough policies to give organization members clear direction in implementing strategy and to place desirable boundaries on their actions; then empower them to act within these boundaries however they think makes sense.* Allowing company personnel to act anywhere between the "white lines" is especially appropriate when individual creativity and initiative are more essential to good strategy execution than standardization and strict conformity. Instituting strategy-facilitating policies can therefore mean more policies, fewer policies, or different policies. It can mean policies that require things to be done a certain way or policies that give employees leeway to do activities the way they think best.

ADOPTING BEST PRACTICES AND STRIVING FOR CONTINUOUS IMPROVEMENT

Company managers can significantly advance the cause of competent strategy execution by pushing organization units and company personnel to identify and adopt the best practices for performing value chain activities and, further, insisting on continuous improvement in how internal operations are conducted. One of the most widely used and effective tools for gauging how well a company is executing pieces of its strategy entails benchmarking the company's performance of particular activities and business processes against best-in-industry and best-in-world performers.[1] It can also be useful to look at best-in-company performers of an activity if a company has a number of different organizational units performing much the same function at different locations. Identifying, analyzing, and understanding how top companies or individuals perform particular value chain activities and business processes provides useful yardsticks for judging the effectiveness and efficiency of internal operations and setting performance standards for organization units to meet or beat.

> **Core Concept**
> Managerial efforts to identify and adopt best practices are a powerful tool for promoting operating excellence and better strategy execution.

How the Process of Identifying and Incorporating Best Practices Works

A **best practice** is a technique for performing an activity or business process that at least one company has demonstrated works particularly well. To qualify as a legitimate best practice, the technique must have a proven record in significantly lowering costs, improving quality or performance, shortening time requirements, enhancing safety, or

Core Concept

A **best practice** is any practice that at least one company has proved works particularly well.

delivering some other highly positive operating outcome. Best practices thus identify a path to operating excellence. For a best practice to be valuable and transferable, it must demonstrate success over time, deliver quantifiable and highly positive results, and be repeatable.

Benchmarking is the backbone of the process of identifying, studying, and implementing outstanding practices. A company's benchmarking effort looks outward to find best practices and then proceeds to develop the data for measuring how well a company's own performance of an activity stacks up against the best-practice standard. Informally, benchmarking involves being humble enough to admit that others have come up with world-class ways to perform particular activities yet wise enough to try to learn how to match, and even surpass, them. But, as shown in Figure 12.2, the payoff of benchmarking comes from adapting the top-notch approaches pioneered by other companies in the company's own operation and thereby boosting, perhaps dramatically, the proficiency with which value chain tasks are performed.

However, benchmarking is more complicated than simply identifying which companies are the best performers of an activity and then trying to imitate their approaches—especially if these companies are in other industries. Normally, the outstanding practices of other organizations have to be *adapted* to fit the specific circumstances of a company's own business and operating requirements. Since most companies believe their work is unique, the telling part of any best-practice initiative is how well the company puts its own version of the best practice into place and makes it work.

Indeed, a best practice remains little more than another company's interesting success story unless company personnel buy into the task of translating what can be learned from other companies into real action and results. The agents of change must be frontline employees who are convinced of the need to abandon the old ways of doing things and switch to a best-practice mind-set. *The more that organizational units use best practices in performing their work, the closer a company moves toward performing its value chain activities as effectively and efficiently as possible.* This is what operational excellence is all about.

Legions of companies across the world now engage in benchmarking to improve their strategy execution efforts and, ideally, gain a strategic, operational, and financial advantage over rivals. Scores of trade associations and special interest organizations have undertaken efforts to collect best-practice data relevant to a particular industry or business function and make their databases available online to members—good

Figure 12.2 **From Benchmarking and Best-Practice Implementation to Operating Excellence**

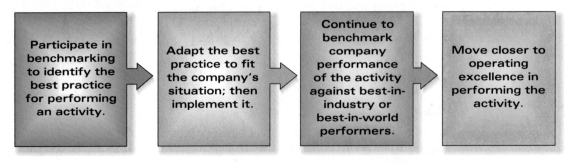

examples include The Benchmarking Exchange's BenchNet (www.benchnet.com), Best Practices LLC (www.best-in-class.com), and the American Productivity and Quality Center (www.apqc.org). Benchmarking and best-practice implementation have clearly emerged as legitimate and valuable managerial tools for promoting operational excellence.

Business Process Reengineering, Six Sigma Quality Programs, and TQM: Tools for Promoting Operating Excellence

In striving for operating excellence, many companies have also come to rely on three other potent management tools: business process reengineering, Six Sigma quality control techniques, and total quality management (TQM) programs. Indeed, these three tools have become globally pervasive techniques for implementing strategies keyed to cost reduction, defect-free manufacture, superior product quality, superior customer service, and total customer satisfaction. The following sections describe how business process reengineering, Six Sigma, and TQM can contribute to operating excellence and better strategy execution.

Business Process Reengineering   Companies scouring for ways to improve their operations have sometimes discovered that the execution of strategy-critical activities is hindered by an organizational arrangement where pieces of the activity are performed in several different functional departments, with no one manager or group being accountable for optimum performance of the entire activity. This can easily occur in such inherently cross-functional activities as customer service (which can involve personnel in order filling, warehousing and shipping, invoicing, accounts receivable, after-sale repair, and technical support), new product development (which can typically involve personnel in R&D, design and engineering, purchasing, manufacturing, and sales and marketing), and supply chain management (which cuts across such areas as purchasing, inventory management, manufacturing and assembly, warehousing, and shipping). Even if personnel in all the different departments and functional areas are inclined to collaborate closely, the activity may not end up being performed optimally or cost-efficiently, such that performance is adversely affected.

To address such shortcomings in strategy execution, many companies during the past decade have opted to *reengineer the work effort* by pulling the pieces of strategy-critical activities out of different departments and unifying their performance in a single department or cross-functional work group. Reorganizing the people who performed the pieces in functional departments into a close-knit group that has charge over the whole process and that can be held accountable for performing the activity in a cheaper, better, and/or more strategy-supportive fashion is called *business process reengineering.*[2]

When done properly, business process reengineering can produce dramatic operating benefits. In the order-processing section of General Electric's circuit breaker division, elapsed time from order receipt to delivery was cut from three weeks to three days by consolidating six production units into one, reducing a variety of former inventory and handling steps, automating the design system to replace a human custom-design process, and cutting the organizational layers between managers and workers from three to one. Productivity rose 20 percent in one year, and unit manufacturing costs dropped 30 percent. Northwest Water, a British utility, used business process reengineering to eliminate 45 work depots that served as home bases to crews who installed and repaired water and sewage lines and equipment. Now crews work directly from their vehicles, receiving assignments and reporting work completion from computer terminals in their trucks. Crew members are no longer employees but rather contractors to Northwest Water. These reengineering efforts not only eliminated the need for the work depots but also allowed Northwest Water to eliminate a big percentage of the bureaucratic personnel and supervisory organization that managed the crews.[3]

Since the early 1990s, reengineering of value chain activities has been undertaken at many companies in many industries all over the world, with excellent results being achieved at some companies.[4] While reengineering has produced only modest results in some instances, usually because of ineptness or lack of wholehearted commitment, reengineering has nonetheless proved itself as a useful tool for streamlining a company's work effort and moving closer to operational excellence.

Total Quality Management Programs   Total quality management (TQM) is a philosophy of managing a set of business practices that emphasizes continuous improvement in all phases of operations, 100 percent accuracy in performing tasks, involvement and empowerment of employees at all levels, team-based work design, benchmarking, and total customer satisfaction.[5] While TQM concentrates on the production of quality goods and fully satisfying customer expectations, it achieves its biggest successes when it is also extended to employee efforts in *all departments*— human resources, billing, R&D, engineering, accounting and records, and information systems—that may lack pressing, customer-driven incentives to improve. It involves reforming the corporate culture and shifting to a total quality/continuous improvement business philosophy that permeates every facet of the organization.[6] TQM aims at

Core Concept
TQM entails creating a total quality culture bent on continuously improving the performance of every task and value chain activity.

instilling enthusiasm and commitment to doing things right from the top to the bottom of the organization. Management's job is to kindle an companywide search for ways to improve, a search that involves all company personnel exercising initiative and using their ingenuity. TQM doctrine preaches that there's no such thing as "good enough" and that everyone has a responsibility to participate in continuous improvement. TQM is thus a race without a finish. Success comes from making little steps forward each day, a process that the Japanese call *kaizen*.

TQM takes a fairly long time to show significant results—very little benefit emerges within the first six months. The long-term payoff of TQM, if it comes, depends heavily on management's success in implanting a culture within which TQM philosophies and practices can thrive. TQM is a managerial tool that has attracted numerous users and advocates over several decades, and it can deliver good results when used properly.

Six Sigma Quality Control   Six Sigma quality control consists of a disciplined, statistics-based system aimed at producing not more than 3.4 defects per million iterations for any business process—from manufacturing to customer transactions.[7] The Six Sigma process of define, measure, analyze, improve, and control (DMAIC) is an improvement system for existing processes falling below specification and needing incremental improvement. The Six Sigma process of define, measure, analyze, design, and verify (DMADV) is used to develop *new* processes or products at Six Sigma quality levels. Both Six Sigma processes are executed by personnel who have earned Six Sigma "green belts" and Six Sigma "black belts," and are overseen by personnel who have completed Six Sigma "master black belt" training. According to the Six Sigma Academy, personnel with black belts can save companies approximately $230,000 per project and can complete four to six projects a year.[8]

The statistical thinking underlying Six Sigma is based on the following three principles: All work is a process, all processes have variability, and all processes create data that explains variability.[9] To illustrate how these three principles drive the metrics of DMAIC, consider the case of a janitorial company that wants to improve the caliber of work done by its cleaning crews and thereby boost customer satisfaction. The janitorial company's Six Sigma team can pursue quality enhancement and continuous improvement via the DMAIC process as follows:

- *Define.* Because Six Sigma is aimed at reducing defects, the first step is to define what constitutes a defect. Six Sigma team members might decide that leaving streaks on windows is a defect because it is a source of customer dissatisfaction.

- *Measure.* The next step is to collect data to find out why, how, and how often this defect occurs. This might include a process flow map of the specific ways that cleaning crews go about the task of cleaning a commercial customer's windows. Other metrics may include recording what tools and cleaning products the crews use to clean windows.

- *Analyze.* After the data are gathered and the statistics analyzed, the company's Six Sigma team discovers that the tools and window-cleaning techniques of certain employees are better than those of other employees because their tools and procedures leave no streaked windows—a "best practice" for avoiding window streaking is thus identified and documented.

- *Improve.* The Six Sigma team implements the documented best practice as a standard way of cleaning windows.

- *Control.* The company teaches new and existing employees the best practice technique for window cleaning. Over time, there's significant improvement in customer satisfaction and increased business.

Six Sigma's DMAIC process is a particularly good vehicle for improving performance when there are *wide variations* in how well an activity is performed.[10] For instance, airlines striving to improve the on-time performance of their flights have more to gain from actions to curtail the number of flights that are late by more then 30 minutes than from actions to reduce the number of flights that are late by less than 5 minutes. Likewise, an overnight delivery service might have a 16-hour average delivery time, but if the actual delivery time varies around the 16-hour average from a low of 12 hours to a high of 26 hours such that 10 percent of its packages are delivered more than 6 hours late, then the company has a huge *reliability* problem.

Since the mid-1990s, thousands of companies and nonprofit organizations around the world have begun using Six Sigma programs to promote operating excellence. Such manufacturers as Motorola, Allied Signal, Caterpillar, DuPont, Xerox, Alcan Aluminum, BMW, Volkswagen, Nokia, Owens Corning, and Emerson Electric have employed Six Sigma techniques to good advantage in improving production quality. General Electric (GE), one of the most successful companies implementing Six Sigma training and pursuing Six Sigma perfection, estimated benefits on the order of $10 billion during the first five years of implementation. GE first began Six Sigma in 1995 after Motorola and Allied Signal blazed the Six Sigma trail. One of GE's successes was in its Lighting division, where Six Sigma was used to cut invoice defects and disputes by 98 percent, a particular benefit to Wal-Mart, the division's largest customer. GE Capital Mortgage improved the chances of a caller reaching a "live" GE person from 76 to 99 percent.[11] Illustration Capsule 12.2 describes Whirlpool's use of Six Sigma in its appliance business.

Illustration Capsule 12.2

Whirlpool's Use of Six Sigma to Promote Operating Excellence

Top management at Whirlpool Corporation, the leading global manufacturer and marketer of home appliances in 2005 with 50 manufacturing and technology centers aound the globe and sales in some 170 countries, has a vision of Whirlpool appliances in "Every Home, Everywhere." One of management's chief objectives in pursuing this vision is to build unmatched customer loyalty to the Whirlpool brand. Whirlpool's strategy to win the hearts and minds of appliance buyers the world over has been to produce and market appliances with top-notch quality and innovative features that users will find appealing. In addition, Whirlpool's strategy has been to offer a wide selection of models (recognizing that buyer tastes and needs differ) and to strive for low-cost production efficiency, thereby enabling Whirlpool to price its products competitively. Executing this strategy at Whirlpool's operations in North America (where it is the market leader), Latin America (where it is also the market leader), Europe (where it is ranks third), and Asia (where it is number one in India and has a foothold with huge growth opportunities elsewhere) has involved a strong focus on continuous improvement, lean manufacturing capabilities, and a drive for operating excellence. To marshal the efforts of Whirlpool's 68,000 employees in executing the strategy successfully, management developed a comprehensive Operational Excellence program with Six Sigma as one of the centerpieces.

The Operational Excellence initiative, which began in the 1990s, incorporated Six Sigma techniques to improve the quality of Whirlpool products, while at the same time lowering costs and trimming the time it took to get product innovations into the marketplace. The Six Sigma program helped Whirlpool save $175 million in manufacturing costs in its first three years.

To sustain the productivity gains and cost savings, Whirlpool embedded Six Sigma practices within each of its manufacturing facilities worldwide and instilled a culture based on Six Sigma and lean manufacturing skills and capabilities. Beginning in 2002, each of Whirlpool's operating units began taking the Six Sigma initiative to a higher level by first placing the needs of the customer at the center of every function—R&D, technology, manufacturing, marketing, and administrative support—and then striving to consistently improve quality levels while eliminating all unnecessary costs. The company systematically went through every aspect of its business with the view that company personnel should perform every activity at every level in a manner that delivers value to the customer and that leads to continuous improvement on how things are done.

Whirlpool management believes that the company's Operational Excellence process has been a major contributor in sustaining the company's global leadership in appliances.

Source: Information posted at www.whirlpool.com (accessed September 25, 2003, and November 15, 2005).

Six Sigma is, however, not just a quality-enhancing tool for manufacturers. At one company, product sales personnel typically wined and dined customers to close their deals.[12] But the costs of such entertaining were viewed as excessively high in many instances. A Six Sigma project that examined sales data found that although face time with customers was important, wining, dining, and other types of entertainment were not. The data showed that regular face time helped close sales, but that time could be spent over a cup of coffee instead of golfing at a resort or taking clients to expensive restaurants. In addition, analysis showed that too much face time with customers was counterproductive. A regularly scheduled customer picnic was found to be detrimental to closing sales because it was held at a busy time of year, when customers preferred not to be away from their offices. Changing the manner in which prospective customers were wooed resulted in a 10 percent increase in sales.

A Milwaukee hospital used Six Sigma to map the process as prescriptions originated with a doctor's writeup, were filled by the hospital pharmacy, and then administered by nurses. DMAIC analysis revealed that most mistakes came from misreading the doctor's handwriting.[13] The hospital implemented a program requiring doctors to type the prescription into a computer, which slashed the number of errors dramatically.

A problem tailor-made for Six Sigma occurs in the insurance industry, where it is common for top agents to outsell poor agents by a factor of 10 to 1 or more. If insurance executives offer a trip to Hawaii in a monthly contest to motivate low-performing agents, the typical result is to motivate top agents to be even more productive and make the performance gap even wider. A DMAIC Six Sigma project to reduce the variation in the performance of agents and correct the problem of so many low-performing agents would begin by measuring the performance of all agents, perhaps discovering that the top 20 percent sell 7 times more policies than the bottom 40 percent. Six Sigma analysis would then consider such steps as mapping how top agents spend their day, investigating the factors that distinguish top performers from low performers, learning what techniques training specialists have employed in converting low-performing agents into high performers, and examining how the hiring process could be improved to avoid hiring underperformers in the first place. The next step would be to *test* proposed solutions—better training methods or psychological profiling to identify and weed out candidates likely to be poor performers—to identify and measure which alternative solutions really work, which don't, and why. Only those actions that prove statistically beneficial are then introduced on a wide scale. The DMAIC method thus entails empirical analysis to diagnose the problem (*design, measure, analyze*), test alternative solutions (*improve*) and then *control* the variability in how well the activity is performed by implementing actions shown to truly fix the problem.

A company that systematically applies Six Sigma methods to its value chain, activity by activity, can make major strides in improving the proficiency with which its strategy is executed. As is the case with TQM, obtaining managerial commitment, establishing a quality culture, and fully involving employees are the three most intractable challenges encountered in the implementation of Six Sigma quality programs.[14]

The Difference between Business Process Reengineering and Continuous Improvement Programs Like Six Sigma and TQM   Business process reengineering and continuous improvement efforts like TQM and Six Sigma both aim at improved efficiency and reduced costs, better product quality, and greater customer satisfaction. The essential difference between business process reengineering and continuous improvement programs is that reengineering aims at *quantum gains* on the order of 30 to 50 percent or more whereas total quality programs stress *incremental progress,* striving for inch-by-inch gains again and again in a never-ending stream. The two approaches to improved performance of value chain activities and operating excellence are not mutually exclusive; it makes sense to use them in tandem. Reengineering can be used first to produce a good basic design that yields quick, dramatic improvements in performing a business process. Total quality programs can then be used as a follow-on to reengineering and/or best-practice implementation, delivering gradual improvements. Such a two-pronged approach to implementing operational excellence is like a marathon race in which you run the first four miles as fast as you can, then gradually pick up speed the remainder of the way.

> Business process reengineering aims at one-time quantum improvement; continuous improvement programs like TQM and Six Sigma aim at ongoing incremental improvements.

Capturing the Benefits of Initiatives to Improve Operations

Usually, the biggest beneficiaries of benchmarking and best-practice initiatives, reengineering, TQM, and Six Sigma are companies that view such programs not as ends in themselves but as tools for implementing and executing company strategy more effectively. The skimpiest payoffs occur when company managers seize them as something worth trying—novel ideas that could improve things. In most such instances, they result in strategy-blind efforts to simply manage better. There's an important lesson here. Best practices, TQM, Six Sigma quality, and reengineering all need to be seen and used as part of a bigger-picture effort to execute strategy proficiently. Only strategy can point to which value chain activities matter and what performance targets make the most sense. Absent a strategic framework, managers lack the context in which to fix things that really matter to business-unit performance and competitive success.

> **Core Concept**
> The purpose of using benchmarking, best practices, business process reengineering, TQM, Six Sigma, or other operational improvement programs is to improve the performance of strategy-critical activities and enhance strategy execution.

To get the most from initiative to better execute strategy, managers must have a clear idea of what specific outcomes really matter. Is it a Six Sigma or lower defect rate, high on-time delivery percentages, low overall costs relative to rivals, high percentages of pleased customers and few customer complaints, shorter cycle times, a higher percentage of revenues coming from recently introduced products, or what? Benchmarking best-in-industry and best-in-world performance of most or all value chain activities provides a realistic basis for setting internal performance milestones and longer-range targets.

Then comes the managerial task of building a total quality culture genuinely committed to achieving the performance outcomes that strategic success requires.[15] Managers can take the following action steps to realize full value from TQM or Six Sigma initiatives:[16]

1. Visible, unequivocal, and unyielding commitment to total quality and continuous improvement, including a quality vision and specific, measurable objectives for boosting quality and making continuous improvement.

2. Nudging people toward quality-supportive behaviors by:

   a. Screening job applicants rigorously and hiring only those with attitudes and aptitudes right for quality-based performance.

   b. Providing quality training for most employees.

   c. Using teams and team-building exercises to reinforce and nurture individual effort (the creation of a quality culture is facilitated when teams become more cross-functional, multitask-oriented, and increasingly self-managed).

   d. Recognizing and rewarding individual and team efforts regularly and systematically.

   e. Stressing prevention (doing it right the first time), not inspection (instituting ways to correct mistakes).

3. Empowering employees so that authority for delivering great service or improving products is in the hands of the doers rather than the overseers—*improving quality has to be seen as part of everyone's job.*

4. Using online systems to provide all relevant parties with the latest best practices and actual experiences with them, thereby speeding the diffusion and adoption of best practices throughout the organization and also allowing them to exchange data and opinions about how to upgrade the prevailing best practices.

5. Preaching that performance can, and must, be improved because competitors are not resting on their laurels and customers are always looking for something better.

If the targeted performance measures are appropriate to the strategy and if all organizational members (top executives, middle managers, professional staff, and line employees) buy into a culture of operating excellence, then a company's work climate becomes decidedly more conducive to proficient strategy execution. Benchmarking, best-practice implementation, reengineering, TQM, and Six Sigma initiatives can greatly enhance a company's product design, cycle time, production costs, product quality, service, customer satisfaction, and other operating capabilities—and they can even deliver competitive advantage.[17] Not only do improvements from such initiatives add up over time and strengthen organizational capabilities, but the benefits they produce have hard-to-imitate aspects. While it is relatively easy for rivals to undertake benchmarking, process improvement, and quality training, it is much more difficult and time-consuming for them to instill a deeply ingrained culture of operating excellence (as occurs when such techniques are religiously employed) and top management exhibits lasting commitment to operational excellence throughout the organization.

INSTALLING INFORMATION AND OPERATING SYSTEMS

Company strategies can't be executed well without a number of internal systems for business operations. Southwest, American, Northwest, Delta, and other major airlines cannot hope to provide passenger-pleasing service without a user-friendly online reservation system, an accurate and speedy baggage handling system, and a strict aircraft maintenance program that minimizes equipment failures requiring at-the-gate service and delaying plane departures. FedEx has internal communication systems that allow it to coordinate its over 70,000 vehicles in handling an average of 5.5 million packages a day. Its leading-edge flight operations systems allow a single controller to direct as many as 200 of FedEx's 650 aircraft simultaneously, overriding their flight plans should weather or other special emergencies arise. In addition, FedEx has created a series of e-business tools for customers that allow them to ship and track packages online (either at FedEx's Web site or on their own company intranets or Web sites), create address books, review shipping history, generate custom reports, simplify customer billing, reduce internal warehousing and inventory management costs, purchase goods and services from suppliers, and respond quickly to changing customer demands. All of FedEx's systems support the company's strategy of providing businesses and individuals with a broad array of package delivery services (from premium next-day to economical five-day deliveries) and boosting its competitiveness against United Parcel Service, Airborne Express, and the U.S. Postal Service.

Otis Elevator, the world's largest manufacturer of elevators, has 24-hour communications service centers for customers called OtisLine to coordinate its maintenance efforts for some 1.5 million elevators and escalators it has installed worldwide.[18] Electronic monitors installed on each user's site can detect when an elevator or escalator has any of 325 problems and will automatically place a service call to the nearest service center location. Trained operators take all trouble calls, input critical information on a computer screen, and can dispatch trained mechanics from 325 locations across the world to the local trouble spot when needed. All customers have online access to performance data on each of their Otis elevators. More than 80 percent of mechanics in North America carry Web-enabled phones connected to e*Service that transport needed information quickly and allow mechanics to update data in Otis computers for future reference. The OtisLine system helps keep outage times to less than two and a half hours. All the trouble-call data is relayed to design and manufacturing personnel, allowing them to quickly alter design specifications or manufacturing procedures when needed to correct recurring problems.

Amazon.com ships customer orders from fully computerized, 1,300-by-600-foot warehouses containing about 3 million books, CDs, toys, and houseware items.[19] The warehouses are so technologically sophisticated that they require about as many lines of code to run as Amazon's Web site does. Using complex picking algorithms, computers initiate the order-picking process by sending signals to workers' wireless receivers, telling them which items to pick off the shelves in which order. Computers also generate data on misboxed items, chute backup times, line speed, worker productivity, and shipping weights on orders. Systems are upgraded regularly, and productivity improvements are aggressively pursued. In 2003 Amazon's six warehouses were able to handle three times the volume handled in 1999 at costs averaging 10 percent of revenues (versus 20 percent in 1999); in addition, they turned their inventory over 20 times annually in an industry whose average was 15 turns. Amazon's warehouse efficiency and cost per order filled was so low that one of the fastest-growing and most profitable parts of Amazon's business was using its warehouses to run the e-commerce operations of Toys "R" Us and Target.

Most telephone companies, electric utilities, and TV broadcasting systems have online monitoring systems to spot transmission problems within seconds and increase the reliability of their services. At eBay, there are systems for real-time monitoring of new listings, bidding activity, Web site traffic, and page views. Kaiser Permanente spent $3 billion to digitize the medical records of its 8.2 million members so that it could manage patient care more efficiently.[20] IBM has created a database of 36,000 employee profiles that enable it to better assign the most qualified IBM consultant to the projects it is doing for clients. In businesses such as public accounting and management consulting, where large numbers of professional staff need cutting-edge technical know-how, companies have developed systems that identify when it is time for certain employees to attend training programs to update their skills and know-how. Many companies have cataloged best-practice information on their intranets to promote faster transfer and implementation throughout the organization.[21]

Well-conceived state-of-the-art operating systems not only enable better strategy execution but also strengthen organizational capabilities—perhaps enough to provide a competitive edge over rivals. For example, a company with a differentiation strategy based on superior quality has added capability if it has systems for training personnel in quality techniques, tracking product quality at each production step, and ensuring that all goods shipped meet quality standards. A company striving to be a low-cost provider is competitively stronger if it has a benchmarking system that identifies opportunities to implement best practices and drive costs out of the business. Fast-growing companies get an important assist from having capabilities in place to recruit and train new employees in large numbers and from investing in infrastructure that gives them the capability to handle rapid growth as it occurs. It is nearly always better to put infrastructure and support systems in place before they are actually needed than to have to scramble to catch up to customer demand.

> **Core Concept**
> State-of-the-art support systems can be a basis for competitive advantage if they give a firm capabilities that rivals can't match.

Instituting Adequate Information Systems, Performance Tracking, and Controls

Accurate and timely information about daily operations is essential if managers are to gauge how well the strategy execution process is proceeding. Information systems need to cover five broad areas: (1) customer data, (2) operations data, (3) employee data, (4) supplier/partner/collaborative ally data, and (5) financial performance data. All key strategic performance indicators have to be tracked and reported as often as practical. Monthly profit-and-loss statements and monthly statistical summaries, long the norm, are fast being replaced by daily statistical updates and even up-to-the-minute performance monitoring that online technology makes possible. Many retail companies have automated online systems that generate daily sales reports for each store and maintain up-to-the-minute inventory and sales records on each item. Manufacturing plants typically generate daily production reports and track labor productivity on every shift. Many retailers and manufacturers have online data systems connecting them with their suppliers that monitor the status of inventories, track shipments and deliveries, and measure defect rates.

Real-time information systems permit company managers to stay on top of implementation initiatives and daily operations, and to intervene if things seem to be drifting off course. Tracking key performance indicators, gathering information from operating personnel, quickly identifying and diagnosing problems, and taking corrective actions are all integral pieces of the process of managing strategy implementation and execution and exercising adequate organization control. A number of companies have recently begun creating "electronic scorecards" for senior managers that gather daily or weekly statistics from different databases about inventory, sales, costs, and sales trends; such information enables these managers to easily stay abreast of what's happening and make better decisions on a real-time basis.[22] Telephone companies have elaborate information systems to measure signal quality, connection times, interrupts, wrong connections, billing errors, and other measures of reliability that affect customer service and satisfaction. To track and manage the quality of passenger service, airlines have information systems to monitor gate delays, on-time departures and arrivals, baggage handling times, lost baggage complaints, stockouts on meals and drinks, overbookings, and maintenance delays and failures. Continental Airlines has an online system that alerts the company when planes arrive late and assesses whether connecting flights needs to be delayed slightly for late-arriving passengers and carts sent to the gate to shorten the time it will take for passengers to reach their connecting flight. British Petroleum (BP) has outfitted rail cars carrying hazardous materials with sensors and global positioning system (GPS) devices so that it can track the status, location, and other information about these shipments via satellite and relay the data to its corporate intranet. Companies that rely on empowered customer-contact personnel to act promptly and creatively in pleasing customers have installed online information systems that put essential customer data on their computer monitors with a few keystrokes so that they can respond effectively to customer inquiries and deliver personalized customer service.

Statistical information gives managers a feel for the numbers, briefings and meetings provide a feel for the latest developments and emerging issues, and personal contacts add a feel for the people dimension. All are good barometers. Managers have to identify problem areas and deviations from plan before they can take actions to get the organization back on course, by either improving the approaches to strategy execution or fine-tuning the strategy. Jeff Bezos, Amazon's CEO, is an ardent proponent of managing by the numbers—as he puts it, "Math-based decisions always trump opinion and judgment. The trouble with most corporations is that they make judgment-based decisions when data-based decisions could be made."[23]

Core Concept
Having good information systems and operating data are integral to competent strategy execution and operating excellence.

Exercising Adequate Controls over Empowered Employees

Another important aspect of effectively managing and controlling the strategy execution process is monitoring the performance of empowered workers to see that they are acting within the specified limits.[24] Leaving empowered employees to their own devices in meeting performance standards without appropriate checks and balances can expose an organization to excessive risk.[25] Instances abound of employees' decisions or behavior having gone awry, sometimes costing a company huge sums or producing lawsuits aside from just generating embarrassing publicity.

Managers shouldn't have to devote big chunks of their time to making sure that the decisions and behavior of empowered employees stay between the white lines—this would defeat the major purpose of empowerment and, in effect, lead to the reinstatement of a managerial bureaucracy engaged in constant over-the-shoulder supervision. Yet managers have a clear responsibility to exercise sufficient control over empowered employees to protect the company against out-of-bounds behavior and unwelcome surprises. Scrutinizing daily and weekly operating statistics is one of the important ways in which managers can monitor the results that flow from the actions of empowered subordinates—if the operating results flowing from the actions of empowered employees look good, then it is reasonable to assume that empowerment is working.

But close monitoring of real-time or daily operating performance is only one of the control tools at management's disposal. Another valuable lever of control in companies that rely on empowered employees, especially in those that use self-managed work groups or other such teams, is peer-based control. Most team members feel responsible for the success of the whole team and tend to be relatively intolerant of any team member's behavior that weakens team performance or puts team accomplishments at risk (especially when team performance has a big impact on each team member's compensation). Because peer evaluation is such a powerful control device, companies organized into teams can remove some layers of the management hierarchy and rely on strong peer pressure to keep team members operating between the white lines. This is especially true when a company has the information systems capability to monitor team performance daily or in real time.

TYING REWARDS AND INCENTIVES TO GOOD STRATEGY EXECUTION

It is important for both organization units and individuals to be enthusiastically committed to executing strategy and achieving performance targets. Managers typically use an assortment of motivational techniques and rewards to enlist companywide commitment to executing the strategic plan. A manager has to do more than just talk to everyone about how important new strategic practices and performance targets are to the organization's well-being. No matter how inspiring, talk seldom commands people's best efforts for long. *To get employees' sustained, energetic commitment, management has to be resourceful in designing and using motivational incentives—both monetary and nonmonetary.* The more a manager understands what motivates subordinates and the more he or she relies on motivational incentives as a tool for achieving the targeted strategic and financial results, the greater will be employees' commitment to good day-in, day-out strategy execution and achievement of performance targets.[26]

Core Concept
A properly designed reward structure is management's most powerful tool for mobilizing organizational commitment to successful strategy execution.

Strategy-Facilitating Motivational Practices

Financial incentives generally head the list of motivating tools for trying to gain whole-hearted employee commitment to good strategy execution and operating excellence. Monetary rewards generally include some combination of base pay increases, performance bonuses, profit-sharing plans, stock awards, company contributions to employee

401(k) or retirement plans, and piecework incentives (in the case of production workers). But successful companies and managers normally make extensive use of such nonmonetary carrot-and-stick incentives as frequent words of praise (or constructive criticism), special recognition at company gatherings or in the company newsletter, more (or less) job security, stimulating assignments, opportunities to transfer to attractive locations, increased (or decreased) autonomy, and rapid promotion (or the risk of being sidelined in a routine or dead-end job). In addition, companies use a host of other motivational approaches to make their workplaces more appealing and spur stronger employee commitment to the strategy execution process; the following are some of the most important:[27]

> **Core Concept**
> One of management's biggest strategy-executing challenges is to employ motivational techniques that build wholehearted commitment to operating excellence and winning attitudes among employees.

- *Providing attractive perks and fringe benefits*—The various options here include full coverage of health insurance premiums; full tuition reimbursement for work on college degrees; paid vacation time of three or four weeks; on-site child care at major facilities; on-site gym facilities and massage therapists; getaway opportunities at company-owned recreational facilities (beach houses, ranches, resort condos); personal concierge services; subsidized cafeterias and free lunches; casual dress every day; personal travel services; paid sabbaticals; maternity leaves; paid leaves to care for ill family members; telecommuting; compressed workweeks (four 10-hour days instead of five 8-hour days); reduced summer hours; college scholarships for children; on-the-spot bonuses for exceptional performance; and relocation services.

- *Relying on promotion from within whenever possible*—This practice helps bind workers to their employer and employers to their workers; plus, it is an incentive for good performance. Promotion from within also helps ensure that people in positions of responsibility actually know something about the business, technology, and operations they are managing.

- *Making sure that the ideas and suggestions of employees are valued and that those with merit are promptly acted on*—Many companies find that their best ideas for nuts-and-bolts operating improvements come from the suggestions of employees. Moreover, research indicates that the moves of many companies to push decision making down the line and empower employees increases employee motivation and satisfaction, as well as boosting their productivity. The use of self-managed teams has much the same effect.

- *Creating a work atmosphere in which there is genuine sincerity, caring, and mutual respect among workers and between management and employees*—A "family" work environment in which people are on a first-name basis and there is strong camaraderie promotes teamwork and cross-unit collaboration.

- *Stating the strategic vision in inspirational terms that make employees feel they are a part of doing something very worthwhile in a larger social sense*—There's strong motivating power associated with giving people a chance to be part of something exciting and personally satisfying. Jobs with noble purpose tend to turn employees on. At Pfizer, Merck, and most other pharmaceutical companies, it is the notion of helping sick people get well and restoring patients to full life. At Whole Foods Market (a natural foods grocery chain), it is helping customers discover good eating habits and thus improving human health and nutrition.

- *Sharing information with employees about financial performance, strategy, operational measures, market conditions, and competitors' actions*—Broad disclosure and prompt communication send the message that managers trust their workers. Keeping employees in the dark denies them information useful to performing their job, prevents them from being "students of the business," and usually turns them off.

- *Having knockout facilities*—A workplace with appealing features and amenities usually has decidedly positive effects on employee morale and productivity.

- *Being flexible in how the company approaches people management (motivation, compensation, recognition, recruitment) in multinational, multicultural environments*—There is usually some merit in giving local managers in foreign operations to adapt their motivation, compensation, recognition, and recruitment practices to fit local customs, habits, values, and business practices rather than insisting on consistent people-management practices worldwide. But the one area where consistency is essential is conveying the message that the organization values people of all races and cultural backgrounds and that discrimination of any sort will not be tolerated.

For specific examples of the motivational tactics employed by several prominent companies (many of which appear on *Fortune*'s list of "The 100 Best Companies to Work for in America"), see Illustration Capsule 12.3.

Striking the Right Balance between Rewards and Punishment

While most approaches to motivation, compensation, and people management accentuate the positive, companies also embellish positive rewards with the risk of punishment. At General Electric, McKinsey & Company, several global public accounting firms, and other companies that look for and expect top-notch individual performance, there's an "up-or-out" policy—managers and professionals whose performance is not good enough to warrant promotion are first denied bonuses and stock awards and eventually weeded out. A number of companies deliberately give employees heavy workloads and tight deadlines—personnel are pushed hard to achieve "stretch" objectives and expected to put in long hours (nights and weekends if need be). At most companies, senior executives and key personnel in underperforming units are pressured to boost performance to acceptable levels and keep it there or risk being replaced.

As a general rule, it is unwise to take off the pressure for good individual and group performance or play down the stress, anxiety, and adverse consequences of shortfalls in performance. There is no evidence that a no-pressure/no-adverse-consequences work environment leads to superior strategy execution or operating excellence. As the CEO of a major bank put it, "There's a deliberate policy here to create a level of anxiety. Winners usually play like they're one touchdown behind."[28] *High-performing organizations nearly always have a cadre of ambitious people who relish the opportunity to climb the ladder of success, love a challenge, thrive in a performance-oriented environment, and find some competition and pressure useful to satisfy their own drives for personal recognition, accomplishment, and self-satisfaction.*

However, if an organization's motivational approaches and reward structure induce too much stress, internal competitiveness, job insecurity, and unpleasant consequences, the impact on workforce morale and strategy execution can be counterproductive. Evidence shows that managerial initiatives to improve strategy execution should incorporate more positive than negative motivational elements because when cooperation is

Illustration Capsule 12.3

What Companies Do to Motivate and Reward Employees

Companies have come up with an impressive variety of motivational and reward practices to help create a work environment that energizes employees and promotes better strategy execution. Here's a sampling of what companies are doing:

- Google has a sprawling four-building complex known as the Googleplex where the company's roughly 1,000 employees are provided with free food, unlimited ice cream, pool and Ping-Pong tables, and complimentary massages—management built the Googleplex to be "a dream environment." Moreover, the company gives its employees the ability to spend 20 percent of their work time on any outside activity.

- Lincoln Electric, widely known for its piecework pay scheme and incentive bonus plan, rewards individual productivity by paying workers for each nondefective piece produced. Workers have to correct quality problems on their own time—defects in products used by customers can be traced back to the worker who caused them. Lincoln's piecework plan motivates workers to pay attention to both quality and volume produced. In addition, the company sets aside a substantial portion of its profits above a specified base for worker bonuses. To determine bonus size, Lincoln Electric rates each worker on four equally important performance measures: dependability, quality, output, and ideas and cooperation. The higher a worker's merit rating, the higher the incentive bonus earned; the most highly rated workers in good profit years receive bonuses of as much as 110 percent of their piecework compensation.

- At JM Family Enterprises, a Toyota distributor in Florida, employees get a great lease on new Toyotas and are flown to the Bahamas for cruises on the 172-foot company yacht. The company's office facility has such amenities as a heated lap pool, a fitness center, and a free nail salon. Employees get free prescriptions delivered by a "pharmacy concierge" and professionally made take-home dinners.

- Amazon.com hands out Just Do It awards to employees who do something they think will help Amazon *without*

getting their boss's permission. The action has to be well thought through but doesn't have to succeed.

- Nordstrom, widely regarded for its superior in-house customer service experience, typically pays its retail salespeople an hourly wage higher than the prevailing rates paid by other department store chains plus a commission on each sale. Spurred by a culture that encourages salespeople to go all out to satisfy customers and to seek out and promote new fashion ideas, Nordstrom salespeople often earn twice the average incomes of sales employees at competing stores. Nordstrom's rules for employees are simple: "Rule #1: Use your good judgment in all situations. There will be no additional rules."

- At W. L. Gore (the maker of Gore-Tex), employees get to choose what project/team they work on and each team member's compensation is based on other team members' rankings of his or her contribution to the enterprise.

- At Ukrop's Super Markets, a family-owned chain, stores stay closed on Sunday; the company pays out 20 percent of pretax profits to employees in the form of quarterly bonuses; and the company picks up the membership tab for employees if they visit their health club 30 times a quarter.

- At biotech leader Amgen, employees get 16 paid holidays, generous vacation time, tuition reimbursements up to $10,000, on-site massages, a discounted car wash, and the convenience of shopping at on-site farmers' markets.

- At Synovus, a financial services and credit card company, the company adds as much as 20 percent annually to each employee's compensation via a "wealth-building" program that includes a 401(k) and profit sharing; plus, it holds an annual bass fishing tournament.

- At specialty chipmaker Xilinx, new hires receive stock option grants; the CEO responds promptly to employee e-mails, and during hard times management takes a 20 percent pay cut instead of laying off employees.

Sources: Fortune's lists of the 100 best companies to work for in America, 2002, 2004, and 2005 (accessed November 14, 2005); Jefferson Graham, "The Search Engine that Could," *USA Today,* August 26, 2003, p. B3; and Fred Vogelstein, "Winning the Amazon Way," *Fortune* (May 26, 2003), p. 73.

positively enlisted and rewarded, rather than strong-armed by orders and threats (implicit or explicit), people tend to respond with more enthusiasm, dedication, creativity, and initiative. Something of a middle ground is generally optimal—not only handing out decidedly positive rewards for meeting or beating performance targets but also imposing sufficiently negative consequences (if only withholding rewards) when actual performance falls short of the target. But the negative consequences of underachievement should never be so severe or demoralizing as to impede a renewed and determined effort to overcome existing obstacles and hit the targets in upcoming periods.

Linking the Reward System to Strategically Relevant Performance Outcomes

The most dependable way to keep people focused on strategy execution and the achievement of performance targets is to *generously* reward and recognize individuals and groups who meet or beat performance targets and deny rewards and recognition to those who don't. *The use of incentives and rewards is the single most powerful tool management has to win strong employee commitment to diligent, competent strategy execution and operating excellence.* Decisions on salary increases, incentive compensation, promotions, key assignments, and the ways and means of awarding praise and recognition are potent attention-getting, commitment-generating devices.

Core Concept

A properly designed reward system aligns the well-being of organization members with their contributions to competent strategy execution and the achievement of performance targets.

Such decisions seldom escape the closest employee scrutiny, saying more about what is expected and who is considered to be doing a good job than about any other factor. Hence, when meeting or beating strategic and financial targets become *the dominating basis* for designing incentives, evaluating individual and group efforts, and handing out rewards, company personnel quickly grasp that it is in their own self-interest to do their best in executing the strategy competently and achieving key performance targets.[29] Indeed, it is usually through the company's system of incentives and rewards that workforce members emotionally ratify their commitment to the company's strategy execution effort.

Ideally, performance targets should be set for every organization unit, every manager, every team or work group, and perhaps every employee—targets that measure whether strategy execution is progressing satisfactorily. If the company's strategy is to be a low-cost provider, the incentive system must reward actions and achievements that result in lower costs. If the company has a differentiation strategy predicated on superior quality and service, the incentive system must reward such outcomes as Six Sigma defect rates, infrequent need for product repair, low numbers of customer complaints, speedy order processing and delivery, and high levels of customer satisfaction. If a company's growth is predicated on a strategy of new product innovation, incentives should be tied to factors such as the percentages of revenues and profits coming from newly introduced products.

Illustration Capsule 12.4 provides two vivid examples of how companies have designed incentives linked directly to outcomes reflecting good strategy execution.

The Importance of Basing Incentives on Achieving Results, Not on Performing Assigned Duties

To create a strategy-supportive system of rewards and incentives, a company must emphasize rewarding people for accomplishing results, not for just dutifully performing assigned tasks. Focusing jobholders' attention and energy on what to *achieve* as opposed to what to *do* makes the work

Illustration Capsule 12.4

Nucor and Bank One: Two Companies that Tie Incentives Directly to Strategy Execution

The strategy at Nucor Corporation, now the biggest steel producer in the United States, is to be *the* low-cost producer of steel products. Because labor costs are a significant fraction of total cost in the steel business, successful implementation of Nucor's low-cost leadership strategy entails achieving lower labor costs per ton of steel than competitors' costs. Nucor management uses an incentive system to promote high worker productivity and drive labor costs per ton below rivals'. Each plant's workforce is organized into production teams (each assigned to perform particular functions), and weekly production targets are established for each team. Base pay scales are set at levels comparable to wages for similar manufacturing jobs in the local areas where Nucor has plants, but workers can earn a 1 percent bonus for each 1 percent that their output exceeds target levels. If a production team exceeds its weekly production target by 10 percent, team members receive a 10 percent bonus in their next paycheck; if a team exceeds its quota by 20 percent, team members earn a 20 percent bonus. Bonuses, paid every two weeks, are based on the prior two weeks' actual production levels measured against the targets.

Nucor's piece-rate incentive plan has produced impressive results. The production teams put forth exceptional effort; it is not uncommon for most teams to beat their weekly production targets anywhere from 20 to 50 percent. When added to their base pay, the bonuses earned by Nucor workers make Nucor's workforce among the highest-paid in the U.S. steel industry. From a management perspective, the incentive system has resulted in Nucor having labor productivity levels 10 to 20 percent above the average of the unionized workforces at several of its largest rivals, which in turn has given Nucor a significant labor cost advantage over most rivals.

At Bank One (recently acquired by JP Morgan Chase), management believed it was strategically important to boost its customer satisfaction ratings in order to enhance its competitiveness vis-à-vis rivals. Targets were set for customer satisfaction and monitoring systems for measuring customer satisfaction at each branch office were put in place. Then, to motivate branch office personnel to be more attentive in trying to please customers and also to signal that top management was truly committed to achieving higher levels of overall customer satisfaction, top management opted to tie pay scales in each branch office to that branch's customer satisfaction rating—the higher the branch's ratings, the higher that branch's pay scales. Management believed its shift from a theme of equal pay for equal work to one of equal pay for equal performance contributed significantly to its customer satisfaction priority.

environment results-oriented. It is flawed management to tie incentives and rewards to satisfactory performance of duties and activities in hopes that the by-products will be the desired business outcomes and company achievements.[30] In any job, performing assigned tasks is not equivalent to achieving intended outcomes. Diligently showing up for work and attending to one's job assignment does not, by itself, guarantee results. As any student knows, the fact that an instructor teaches and students go to class doesn't necessarily mean that the students are learning. The enterprise of education would no doubt take on a different character if teachers were rewarded for the result of student learning rather than for the activity of teaching.

> It is folly to reward one outcome in hopes of getting another outcome.

Incentive compensation for top executives is typically tied to such financial measures as revenue and earnings growth, stock price performance, return on investment, and creditworthiness and perhaps such strategic measures as market share, product quality, or customer satisfaction. However, incentives for department heads, teams, and individual workers may be tied to performance outcomes more closely related to their strategic area of responsibility. In manufacturing, incentive compensation may be tied to unit manufacturing costs, on-time production and shipping, defect rates, the number and extent of work stoppages due to labor disagreements and equipment breakdowns, and so on. In sales and marketing, there may be incentives for achieving dollar sales or unit volume targets, market share, sales penetration of each target customer group, the fate of newly introduced products, the frequency of customer complaints, the number of new accounts acquired, and customer satisfaction. Which performance measures to base incentive compensation on depends on the situation—the priority placed on various financial and strategic objectives, the requirements for strategic and competitive success, and what specific results are needed in different facets of the business to keep strategy execution on track.

Guidelines for Designing Incentive Compensation Systems

The concepts and company experiences discussed above yield the following prescriptive guidelines for creating an incentive compensation system to help drive successful strategy execution:

1. *Make the performance payoff a major, not minor, piece of the total compensation package.* Payoffs must be at least 10 to 12 percent of base salary to have much impact. Incentives that amount to 20 percent or more of total compensation are big attention-getters, likely to really drive individual or team effort; incentives amounting to less than 5 percent of total compensation have comparatively weak motivational impact. Moreover, the payoff for high-performing individuals and teams must be meaningfully greater than the payoff for average performers, and the payoff for average performers meaningfully bigger than for below-average performers.

2. *Have incentives that extend to all managers and all workers, not just top management.* It is a gross miscalculation to expect that lower-level managers and employees will work their hardest to hit performance targets just so a few senior executives can get lucrative rewards.

3. *Administer the reward system with scrupulous objectivity and fairness.* If performance standards are set unrealistically high or if individual/group performance evaluations are not accurate and well documented, dissatisfaction with the system will overcome any positive benefits.

4. *Tie incentives to performance outcomes directly linked to good strategy execution and financial performance.* Incentives should never be paid just because people are thought to be "doing a good job" or because they "work hard." Performance evaluation based on factors not tightly related to good strategy execution signal that either the strategic plan is incomplete (because important performance targets were left out) or management's real agenda is something other than the stated strategic and financial objectives.

5. *Make sure that the performance targets each individual or team is expected to achieve involve outcomes that the individual or team can personally affect.* The role of incentives is to enhance individual commitment and channel behavior in beneficial directions. This role is not well served when the performance measures by which company personnel are judged are outside their arena of influence.

6. *Keep the time between achieving the target performance outcome and the payment of the reward as short as possible.* Companies like Nucor and Continental Airlines have discovered that weekly or monthly payments for good performance work much better than annual payments. Nucor pays weekly bonuses based on

prior-week production levels; Continental awards employees a monthly bonus for each month that on-time flight performance meets or beats a specified percentage companywide. Annual bonus payouts work best for higher-level managers and for situations where target outcome relates to overall company profitability or stock price performance.

7. *Make liberal use of nonmonetary rewards; don't rely solely on monetary rewards.* When used properly, money is a great motivator, but there are also potent advantages to be gained from praise, special recognition, handing out plum assignments, and so on.

8. *Absolutely avoid skirting the system to find ways to reward effort rather than results.* Whenever actual performance falls short of targeted performance, there's merit in determining whether the causes are attributable to subpar individual/group performance or to circumstances beyond the control of those responsible. An argument can be made that exceptions should be made in giving rewards to people who've tried hard, gone the extra mile, yet still come up short because of circumstances beyond their control. The problem with making exceptions for unknowable, uncontrollable, or unforeseeable circumstances is that once good excuses start to creep into justifying rewards for subpar results, the door is open for all kinds of reasons why actual performance failed to match targeted performance. A "no excuses" standard is more evenhanded and certainly easier to administer.

Once the incentives are designed, they have to be communicated and explained. Everybody needs to understand how their incentive compensation is calculated and how individual/group performance targets contribute to organizational performance targets. The pressure to achieve the targeted strategic and financial performance and continuously improve on strategy execution should be unrelenting, with few (if any) loopholes for rewarding shortfalls in performance. People at all levels have to be held accountable for carrying out their assigned parts of the strategic plan, and they have to understand their rewards are based on the caliber of results that are achieved. But with the pressure to perform should come meaningful rewards. Without an ample payoff, the system breaks down, and managers are left with the less workable options of barking orders, trying to enforce compliance, and depending on the goodwill of employees.

> **Core Concept**
> The unwavering standard for judging whether individuals, teams, and organizational units have done a good job must be whether they meet or beat performance targets that reflect good strategy execution.

Performance-Based Incentives and Rewards in Multinational Enterprises   In some foreign countries, incentive pay runs counter to local customs and cultural norms. Professor Steven Kerr cites the time he lectured an executive education class on the need for more performance-based pay and a Japanese manager protested, "You shouldn't bribe your children to do their homework, you shouldn't bribe your wife to prepare dinner, and you shouldn't bribe your employees to work for the company."[31] Singling out individuals and commending them for unusually good effort can also be a problem; Japanese culture considers public praise of an individual an affront to the harmony of the group. In some countries, employees have a preference for nonmonetary rewards—more leisure time, important titles, access to vacation villages, and nontaxable perks. Thus, multinational companies have to build some degree of flexibility into the design of incentives and rewards in order to accommodate cross-cultural traditions and preferences.

Key Points

Managers implementing and executing a new or different strategy must identify the resource requirements of each new strategic initiative and then consider whether the current pattern of resource allocation and the budgets of the various subunits are suitable.

Anytime a company alters its strategy, managers should review existing policies and operating procedures, proactively revise or discard those that are out of sync, and formulate new ones to facilitate execution of new strategic initiatives. Prescribing new or freshly revised policies and operating procedures aids the task of strategy execution (1) by providing top-down guidance to operating managers, supervisory personnel, and employees regarding how certain things need to be done and what the boundaries are on independent actions and decisions; (2) by enforcing consistency in how particular strategy-critical activities are performed in geographically scattered operating units; and (3) by promoting the creation of a work climate and corporate culture that promotes good strategy execution.

Competent strategy execution entails visible, unyielding managerial commitment to best practices and continuous improvement. Benchmarking, the discovery and adoption of best practices, reengineering core business processes, and continuous improvement initiatives like total quality management (TQM) or Six Sigma programs, all aim at improved efficiency, lower costs, better product quality, and greater customer satisfaction. *These initiatives are important tools for learning how to execute a strategy more proficiently.*

Company strategies can't be implemented or executed well without a number of support systems to carry on business operations. Well-conceived state-of-the-art support systems not only facilitate better strategy execution but also strengthen organizational capabilities enough to provide a competitive edge over rivals. Real-time information and control systems further aid the cause of good strategy execution.

Strategy-supportive motivational practices and reward systems are powerful management tools for gaining employee commitment. The key to creating a reward system that promotes good strategy execution is to make strategically relevant measures of performance *the dominating basis* for designing incentives, evaluating individual and group efforts, and handing out rewards. Positive motivational practices generally work better than negative ones, but there is a place for both. There's also a place for both monetary and nonmonetary incentives.

For an incentive compensation system to work well (1) the monetary payoff should be a major percentage of the compensation package, (2) the use of incentives should extend to all managers and workers, (3) the system should be administered with care and fairness, (4) the incentives should be linked to performance targets spelled out in the strategic plan, (5) each individual's performance targets should involve outcomes the person can personally affect, (6) rewards should promptly follow the determination of good performance, (7) monetary rewards should be supplemented with liberal use of nonmonetary rewards, and (8) skirting the system to reward nonperformers or subpar results should be scrupulously avoided. Companies with operations in multiple countries often have to build some degree of flexibility into the design of incentives and rewards in order to accommodate cross-cultural traditions and preferences.

Exercises

1. Go to Google or another Internet search engine and, using the advanced search feature, enter "best practices." Browse through the search results to identify at least five organizations that have gathered a set of best practices and are making the best-practice library they have assembled available to members. Explore at least one of the sites to get an idea of the kind of best-practice information that is available.

2. Do an Internet search on "Six Sigma" quality programs. Browse through the search results and (*a*) identify at least three companies that offer Six Sigma training and (*b*) find lists of companies that have implemented Six Sigma programs in their pursuit of operational excellence—you should be able to cite at least 25 companies that are Six Sigma users. Prepare a one-page report to your instructor detailing the experiences and benefits that one company has realized from employing Six Sigma methods in its operations. To learn more about how Six Sigma works, go to www.isixsigma.com and explore the Q&A menu option.

3. Do an Internet search on "total quality management." Browse through the search results and (*a*) identify 10 companies that offer TQM training, (*b*) identify 5 books on TQM programs, and (*c*) find lists of companies that have implemented TQM programs in their pursuit of operational excellence—you should be able to name at least 20 companies that are TQM users.

4. Consult the latest issue of *Fortune* containing the annual "100 Best Companies to Work For" (usually a late-January or early-February issue, or else use a search engine to locate the list online) and identify at least five compensation incentives and work practices that these companies use to enhance employee motivation and reward them for good strategic and financial performance. Choose compensation methods and work practices that are different from those cited in Illustration Capsule 12.3.

5. Review the profiles and applications of the latest Malcolm Baldrige National Quality Award recipients at www.quality.nist.gov. What are the standout features of the companies' approaches to managing operations? What do you find impressive about the companies' policies and procedures, use of best practices, emphasis on continuous improvement, and use of rewards and incentives?

6. Using Google Scholar or your access to online business periodicals in your university's library, search for the term "incentive compensation" and prepare a report of one to two pages to your instructor discussing the successful (or unsuccessful) use of incentive compensation plans by various companies. According to your research, what factors seem to determine whether incentive compensation plans succeed or fail?

13

Corporate Culture and Leadership

Keys to Good Strategy Execution

The biggest levers you've got to change a company are strategy, structure, and culture. If I could pick two, I'd pick strategy and culture.

—Wayne Leonard
CEO, Entergy

An organization's capacity to execute its strategy depends on its "hard" infrastructure—its organizational structure and systems—and on its "soft" infrastructure—its culture and norms.

—Amar Bhide

Weak leadership can wreck the soundest strategy; forceful execution of even a poor plan can often bring victory.

—Sun Zi

Leadership is accomplishing something through other people that wouldn't have happened if you weren't there . . . Leadership is being able to mobilize ideas and values that energize other people . . . Leaders develop a story line that engages other people.

—Noel Tichy

Seeing people in person is a big part of how you drive any change process. You have to show people a positive view of the future and say "we can do it."

—Jeffrey R. Immelt
CEO, General Electric

In the previous two chapters we examined six of the managerial tasks important to good strategy execution and operating excellence—building a capable organization, marshaling the needed resources and steering them to strategy-critical operating units, establishing policies and procedures that facilitate good strategy execution, adopting best practices and pushing for continuous improvement in how value chain activities are performed, creating internal operating systems that enable better execution, and employing motivational practices and compensation incentives that gain wholehearted employee commitment to the strategy execution process. In this chapter we explore the two remaining managerial tasks that shape the outcome of efforts to execute a company's strategy: creating a strategy-supportive corporate culture and exerting the internal leadership needed to drive the implementation of strategic initiatives forward and achieve higher plateaus of operating excellence.

INSTILLING A CORPORATE CULTURE THAT PROMOTES GOOD STRATEGY EXECUTION

Every company has its own unique culture. The character of a company's culture or work climate is a product of the core values and business principles that executives espouse, the standards of what is ethically acceptable and what is not, the work practices and behaviors that define "how we do things around here," the approach to people management and style of operating, the "chemistry" and the "personality" that permeates the work environment, and the stories that get told over and over to illustrate and reinforce the company's values, business practices, and traditions. The meshing together of stated beliefs, business principles, styles of operating, ingrained behaviors and attitudes, and work climate define a company's **corporate culture.** A company's culture is important because it influences the organization's actions and approaches to conducting business—in a very real sense, the culture is the company's "operating system" or organizational DNA.[1]

> **Core Concept**
> ***Corporate culture*** refers to the character of a company's internal work climate and personality—as shaped by its core values, beliefs, business principles, traditions, ingrained behaviors, work practices, and styles of operating.

The psyche of corporate cultures varies widely. For instance, the bedrock of Wal-Mart's culture is dedication to customer satisfaction, zealous pursuit of low costs and frugal operating practices, a strong work ethic, ritualistic Saturday-morning headquarters meetings to exchange ideas and review problems, and company executives' commitment to visiting stores, listening to customers, and soliciting suggestions from employees. General Electric's culture is founded on a hard-driving, results-oriented atmosphere (where all of the company's business divisions are held to a standard of being number one or two in their industries as well as achieving good business results); extensive cross-business sharing of ideas, best practices, and learning; the reliance on "workout sessions" to identify, debate, and resolve burning issues; a commitment to Six Sigma quality; and globalization of the company. At Occidental Petroleum, the culture is grounded in entrepreneurship on the part of employees; the company's empowered employees are encouraged to be innovative, excel in their fields of specialization, respond quickly to strategic opportunities, and creatively apply state-of-the-art technology in a manner that promotes operating excellence and sets Occidental apart from its competitors. At Nordstrom, the corporate culture is centered on delivering exceptional service to customers; the company's motto is "Respond to unreasonable customer requests"—each out-of-the-ordinary request is seen as an opportunity for a "heroic" act by an employee that can further the company's reputation for a customer-pleasing shopping environment. Nordstrom makes a point of promoting employees noted for their heroic acts and dedication to outstanding service; the company motivates its salespeople with a commission-based compensation system that enables Nordstrom's best salespeople to earn more than double what other department stores pay.

Illustration Capsule 13.1 relates how Google and Alberto-Culver describe their corporate cultures.

Identifying the Key Features of a Company's Corporate Culture

A company's corporate culture is mirrored in the character or "personality" of its work environment—the factors that underlie how the company tries to conduct its business and the behaviors that are held in high esteem. The chief things to look for include the following:

- *The values, business principles, and ethical standards that management preaches and practices.* Actions speak much louder than words here.
- *The company's approach to people management* and the official policies, procedures, and operating practices that paint the white lines for the behavior of company personnel.
- *The spirit and character that pervade the work climate.* Is the workplace vibrant and fun, methodical and all-business, tense and harried, or highly competitive and politicized? Are people excited about their work and emotionally connected to the company's business or are they just there to draw a paycheck? Is there an emphasis on empowered worker creativity or do people have little discretion in how jobs are done?
- *How managers and employees interact and relate to each other.* How much reliance is there on teamwork and open communication? To what extent is there good camaraderie? Are people called by their first names? Do coworkers spend little or lots of time together outside the workplace? What are the dress codes (the accepted styles of attire and whether there are casual days)?
- *The strength of peer pressure to do things in particular ways and conform to expected norms.* What actions and behaviors are approved (and rewarded by management in the form of compensation and promotion) and which ones are frowned on?

Illustration Capsule 13.1

The Corporate Cultures at Google and Alberto-Culver

GOOGLE

Founded in 1998 by Larry Page and Sergey Brin, two Ph.D. students in computer science at Stanford University, Google has beome world-renowned for its search engine technology. Google.com is one of the five most popular sites on the Internet, attracting over 380 million unique visitors monthly from around the world. Google has some unique ways of operating, and its culture is rather quirky. The company describes its culture as follows:

> Though growing rapidly, Google still maintains a small company feel. At the Googleplex headquarters almost everyone eats in the Google café (known as "Charlie's Place"), sitting at whatever table has an opening and enjoying conversations with Googlers from all different departments. Topics range from the trivial to the technical, and whether the discussion is about computer games or encryption or ad serving software, it's not surprising to hear someone say, "That's a product I helped develop before I came to Google."
>
> Google's emphasis on innovation and commitment to cost containment means each employee is a hands-on contributor. There's little in the way of corporate hierarchy and everyone wears several hats. The international webmaster who creates Google's holiday logos spent a week translating the entire site into Korean. The chief operations engineer is also a licensed neurosurgeon. Because everyone realizes they are an equally important part of Google's success, no one hesitates to skate over a corporate officer during roller hockey.
>
> Google's hiring policy is aggressively non-discriminatory and favors ability over experience. The result is a staff that reflects the global audience the search engine serves. Google has offices around the globe and Google engineering centers are recruiting local talent in locations from Zurich to Bangalore. Dozens of languages are spoken by Google staffers, from Turkish to Telugu. When not at work, Googlers pursue interests from cross-country cycling to wine tasting, from flying to Frisbee. As Google expands its development team, it continues to look for those who share an obsessive commitment to creating search perfection and having a great time doing it.

ALBERTO-CULVER

The Alberto-Culver Company, with fiscal 2005 revenues of about $3.5 billion, is the producer and marketer of Alberto VO5, TRESemmé, Consort, and Just for Me hair care products; St. Ives skin care, hair care, and facial care products; and such brands as Molly McButter, Mrs. Dash, Sugar Twin, and Static Guard. Alberto-Culver brands are sold in 120 countries. Its Sally Beauty Company, with over 3,250 stores and 1,250 professional sales consultants, is the largest marketer of professional beauty care products in the world.

At the careers section of its Web site, the company described its culture in the following words:

> Building careers is as important to us as building brands. We believe that passionate people create powerful growth. We believe in a workplace built on values and believe our best people display those same values in their families and their communities. We believe in recognizing and rewarding accomplishment and celebrating our victories.
>
> We believe the best ideas work their way—quickly—up an organization, not down. We believe that we should take advantage of every ounce of your talent on teams and cross-functional activities, not just assign you to a box.
>
> We believe in open communication. We believe that you can improve what you measure, so we survey and spot check all the time. For that same reason, every one has specific goals so that their expectations are in line with their managers' and the company's.
>
> We believe that victory is a team accomplishment. We believe in personal development. We believe if you talk with us you will catch our enthusiasm and want to be a part of the Alberto-Culver team.

Sources: Information posted at www.google.com and www.alberto.com (accessed November 16, 2005).

- *The company's revered traditions and oft-repeated stories.* Do people talk a lot about "heroic acts" and "how we do things around here"?
- *The manner in which the company deals with external stakeholders (particularly vendors and local communities where it has operations).* Does it treat suppliers as business partners or does it prefer

hardnosed, arm's-length business arrangements? How strong and genuine is its commitment to corporate citizenship?

Some of these sociological forces are readily apparent, and others operate quite subtly.

The values, beliefs, and practices that undergird a company's culture can come from anywhere in the organization hierarchy, most often representing the business philosophy and managerial style of influential executives but also resulting from exemplary actions on the part of company personnel and consensus agreement about "how we ought to do things around here."[2] Typically, key elements of the culture originate with a founder or certain strong leaders who articulated them as a set of business principles, company policies, operating approaches, and ways of dealing with employees, customers, vendors, shareholders, and local communities where the company has operations. Over time, these cultural underpinnings take root, become embedded in how the company conducts its business, come to be accepted by company managers and employees alike, and then persist as new employees are encouraged to adopt and follow the professed values, behaviors, and work practices.

The Role of Stories   Frequently, a significant part of a company's culture is captured in the stories that get told over and over again to illustrate to newcomers the importance of certain values and the depth of commitment that various company personnel have displayed. One of the folktales at FedEx, world renowned for the reliability of its next-day package delivery guarantee, is about a deliveryman who had been given the wrong key to a FedEx drop box. Rather than leave the packages in the drop box until the next day when the right key was available, the deliveryman unbolted the drop box from its base, loaded it into the truck, and took it back to the station. There, the box was pried open and the contents removed and sped on their way to their destination the next day. Nordstrom keeps a scrapbook commemorating the heroic acts of its employees and uses it as a regular reminder of the beyond-the-call-of-duty behaviors that employees are encouraged to display. At Frito-Lay, there are dozens of stories about truck drivers who went to extraordinary lengths in overcoming adverse weather conditions in order to make scheduled deliveries to retail customers and keep store shelves stocked with Frito-Lay products. At Microsoft, there are stories of the long hours programmers put in, the emotional peaks and valleys in encountering and overcoming coding problems, the exhilaration of completing a complex program on schedule, the satisfaction of working on cutting-edge projects, the rewards of being part of a team responsible for a popular new software program, and the tradition of competing aggressively. Such stories serve the valuable purpose of illustrating the kinds of behavior the company encourages and reveres. Moreover, each retelling of a legendary story puts a bit more peer pressure on company personnel to display core values and do their part in keeping the company's traditions alive.

Perpetuating the Culture   Once established, company cultures are perpetuated in six important ways: (1) by screening and selecting new employees that will mesh well with the culture, (2) by systematic indoctrination of new members in the culture's fundamentals, (3) by the efforts of senior group members to reiterate core values in daily conversations and pronouncements, (4) by the telling and retelling of company legends, (5) by regular ceremonies honoring members who display desired cultural behaviors, and (6) by visibly rewarding those who display cultural norms and penalizing those who don't.[3] *The more new employees a company is hiring, the more important it becomes to screen job applicants every bit as much for how well their values, beliefs, and personalities match up with the culture as for their technical skills and experience.*

For example, a company that stresses operating with integrity and fairness has to hire people who themselves have integrity and place a high value on fair play. A company whose culture revolves around creativity, product innovation, and leading change has to screen new hires for their ability to think outside the box, generate new ideas, and thrive in a climate of rapid change and ambiguity. Southwest Airlines—whose two core values, "LUV" and fun, permeate the work environment and whose objective is to ensure that passengers have a positive and enjoyable flying experience—goes to considerable lengths to hire flight attendants and gate personnel who are witty, cheery, and outgoing and who display whistle-while-you-work attitudes. Fast-growing companies risk creating a culture by chance rather than by design if they rush to hire employees mainly for their talents and credentials and neglect to screen out candidates whose values, philosophies, and personalities aren't a good fit with the organizational character, vision, and strategy being articulated by the company's senior executives.

As a rule, companies are attentive to the task of hiring people who will fit in and who will embrace the prevailing culture. And, usually, job seekers lean toward accepting jobs at companies where they feel comfortable with the atmosphere and the people they will be working with. Employees who don't hit it off at a company tend to leave quickly, while employees who thrive and are pleased with the work environment stay on, eventually moving up the ranks to positions of greater responsibility. The longer people stay at an organization, the more they come to embrace and mirror the corporate culture—their values and beliefs tend to be molded by mentors, fellow workers, company training programs, and the reward structure. Normally, employees who have worked at a company for a long time play a major role in indoctrinating new employees into the culture.

Forces That Cause a Company's Culture to Evolve   However, even stable cultures aren't static; just like strategy and organization structure, they evolve. New challenges in the marketplace, revolutionary technologies, and shifting internal conditions—especially eroding business prospects, an internal crisis, or top executive turnover—tend to breed new ways of doing things and, in turn, cultural evolution. An incoming CEO who decides to shake up the existing business and take it in new directions often triggers a cultural shift, perhaps one of major proportions. Likewise, diversification into new businesses, expansion into foreign countries, rapid growth, an influx of new employees, and merger with or acquisition of another company can all precipitate cultural changes of one kind or another.

Company Subcultures: The Problems Posed by New Acquisitions and Multinational Operations   Although it is common to speak about corporate culture in the singular, it is not uncommon for companies to have multiple cultures (or subcultures).[4] Values, beliefs, and practices within a company sometimes vary significantly by department, geographic location, division, or business unit. A company's subcultures can clash, or at least not mesh well, if they embrace conflicting business philosophies or operating approaches, if key executives employ different approaches to people management, or if important differences between a company's culture and those of recently acquired companies have not yet been ironed out. *Global and multinational companies tend to be at least partly multicultural* because cross-country organization units have different operating histories and work climates, as well as members who have grown up under different social customs and traditions and who have different sets of values and beliefs. The human resources manager of a global pharmaceutical company who took on an assignment in the Far East discovered, to his surprise, that one of his biggest challenges was to persuade his company's managers in China,

Korea, Malaysia, and Taiwan to accept promotions—their cultural values were such that they did not believe in competing with their peers for career rewards or personal gain, nor did they relish breaking ties to their local communities to assume cross-national responsibilities.[5] Many companies that have merged with or acquired foreign companies have to deal with language- and custom-based cultural differences.

Nonetheless, the existence of subcultures does not preclude important areas of commonality and compatibility. For example, General Electric's cultural traits of boundarylessness, workout, and Six Sigma quality can be implanted and practiced successfully in different countries. AES, a global power company with operations in over 25 countries, has found that the four core values of integrity, fairness, fun, and social responsibility underlying its culture are readily embraced by people in most countries. Moreover, AES tries to define and practice its cultural values the same way in all of its locations while still being sensitive to differences that exist among various people groups across the world; top managers at AES express the views that people across the world are more similar than different and that the company's culture is as meaningful in Buenos Aires or Kazakhstan as in Virginia.

In today's globalizing world, multinational companies are learning how to make strategy-critical cultural traits travel across country boundaries and create a workably uniform culture worldwide. Likewise, company managements are quite alert to the importance of cultural compatibility in making acquisitions and the need to address how to merge and integrate the cultures of newly acquired companies—cultural due diligence is often as important as financial due diligence in deciding whether to go forward on an acquisition or merger. On a number of occasions, companies have decided to pass on acquiring particular companies because of culture conflicts that they believed would be hard to resolve.

Strong versus Weak Cultures

Company cultures vary widely in strength and influence. Some are strongly embedded and have a big impact on a company's practices and behavioral norms. Others are weak and have comparatively little influence on company operations.

Strong-Culture Companies   The hallmark of a strong-culture company is the dominating presence of certain deeply rooted values and operating approaches that

Core Concept
In a strong-culture company, culturally-approved behaviors and ways of doing things are nurtured while culturally-disapproved behaviors and work practices get squashed.

"regulate" the conduct of a company's business and the climate of its workplace.[6] Strong cultures emerge over a period of years (sometimes decades) and are never an overnight phenomenon. In strong culture companies, senior managers make a point of reiterating these principles and values to organization members and explaining how they relate to its business environment. But, more important, they make a conscious effort to display these principles in their own actions and behavior—they walk the talk, and they *insist that company values and business principles be reflected in the decisions and actions taken by all company personnel.* An unequivocal expectation that company personnel will act and behave in accordance with the adopted values and ways of doing business leads to two important outcomes: (1) Over time, the values come to be widely shared by rank-and-file employees—people who dislike the culture tend to leave—and (2) individuals encounter strong peer pressure from coworkers to observe the culturally approved norms and behaviors. Hence, a strongly implanted corporate culture ends up having a powerful influence on "how we do things around here" because so many company personnel are accepting of cultural traditions and because this acceptance is reinforced both by management expectations and coworker peer pressure to conform to cultural norms. Since cultural traditions and norms have such a dominating influence in strong-culture companies, the character of the culture becomes the the company's soul or psyche.

Three factors contribute to the development of strong cultures: (1) a founder or strong leader who establishes values, principles, and practices that are consistent and sensible in light of customer needs, competitive conditions, and strategic requirements; (2) a sincere, long-standing company commitment to operating the business according to these established traditions, thereby creating an internal environment that supports decision making and strategies based on cultural norms; and (3) a genuine concern for the well-being of the organization's three biggest constituencies—customers, employees, and shareholders. Continuity of leadership, small group size, stable group membership, geographic concentration, and considerable organizational success all contribute to the emergence and sustainability of a strong culture.[7]

During the time a strong culture is being implanted, there's nearly always a good strategy–culture fit (which partially accounts for the organization's success). Mismatches between strategy and culture in a strong-culture company tend to occur when a company's business environment undergoes significant change, prompting a drastic strategy revision that clashes with the entrenched culture. A strategy–culture clash can also occur in a strong-culture company whose business has gradually eroded; when a new leader is brought in to revitalize the company's operations, he or she may push the company in a strategic direction that requires substantially different cultural and behavioral norms. In such cases, a major culture-changing effort has to be launched.

In strong-culture companies, values and behavioral norms are so ingrained that they can endure leadership changes at the top—although their strength can erode over time if new CEOs cease to nurture them or move aggressively to institute cultural adjustments. And the cultural norms in a strong-culture company may not change much as strategy evolves and the organization acts to make strategy adjustments, either because the new strategies are compatible with the present culture or because the dominant traits of the culture are somewhat strategy-neutral and compatible with evolving versions of the company's strategy.

> In a strong-culture company, values and behavioral norms are like crabgrass: deeply rooted and hard to weed out.

Weak-Culture Companies   In direct contrast to strong-culture companies, weak-culture companies lack values and principles that are consistently preached or widely shared (usually because the company has had a series of CEOs with differing values and differing views about how the company's business ought to be conducted). As a consequence, the company has few widely revered traditions and few culture-induced norms are evident in operating practices. Because top executives at a weak-culture company don't repeatedly espouse any particular business philosophy, exhibit long-standing commitment to particular values, or extol particular operating practices and behavioral norms, individuals encounter little coworker peer pressure to do things in particular ways. Moreover, a weak company culture breeds no strong employee allegiance to what the company stands for or to operating the business in well-defined ways. While individual employees may well have some bonds of identification with and loyalty toward their department, their colleagues, their union, or their boss, there is neither passion about the company nor emotional commitment to what it is trying to accomplish—a condition that often results in many employees viewing their company as just a place to work and their job as just a way to make a living. Very often, cultural weakness stems from moderately entrenched subcultures that block the emergence of a well-defined companywide work climate.

As a consequence, *weak cultures provide little or no assistance in executing strategy* because there are no traditions, beliefs, values, common bonds, or behavioral norms that management can use as levers to mobilize commitment to executing the chosen strategy. The only plus of a weak culture is that it does not usually pose a strong barrier to strategy execution, but the negative of not providing any support means that culture-building has to be high on management's action agenda. Absent a work climate that channels organizational energy in the direction of good strategy execution, managers are left with the options of either using compensation incentives and other motivational devices to mobilize employee commitment or trying to establish cultural roots that will in time start to nurture the strategy execution process.

Unhealthy Cultures

The distinctive characteristic of an unhealthy corporate culture is the presence of counterproductive cultural traits that adversely impact the work climate and company performance.[8] The following four traits are particularly unhealthy:

1. A highly politicized internal environment in which many issues get resolved and decisions made on the basis of which individuals or groups have the most political clout to carry the day.
2. Hostility to change and a general wariness of people who champion new ways of doing things.
3. An insular "not-invented-here" mind-set that makes company personnel averse to looking outside the company for best practices, new managerial approaches, and innovative ideas.
4. A disregard for high ethical standards and overzealous pursuit of wealth and status on the part of key executives.

Politicized Cultures   What makes a politicized internal environment so unhealthy is that political infighting consumes a great deal of organizational energy, often with the result that what's best for the company takes a backseat to political maneuvering. In companies where internal politics pervades the work climate, empire-building managers jealously guard their decision-making prerogatives. They have their own agendas and operate the work units under their supervision as autonomous "fiefdoms," and the positions they take on issues is usually aimed at protecting or expanding their turf. Collaboration with other organizational units is viewed with suspicion (What are "they" up to? How can "we" protect "our" flanks?), and cross-unit cooperation occurs grudgingly. When an important proposal moves to the front burner, advocates try to ram it through and opponents try to alter it in significant ways or else kill it altogether. The support or opposition of politically influential executives and/or coalitions among departments with vested interests in a particular outcome typically weigh heavily in deciding what actions the company takes. All this maneuvering takes away from efforts to execute strategy with real proficiency and frustrates company personnel who are less political and more inclined to do what is in the company's best interests.

Change-Resistant Cultures   In less-adaptive cultures where skepticism about the importance of new developments and resistance to change are the norm, managers prefer waiting until the fog of uncertainty clears before steering a new course, making fundamental adjustments to their product line, or embracing a major new technology. They believe in moving cautiously and conservatively, preferring to follow others rather than taking decisive action to be in the forefront of change. Change-resistant cultures place a premium on not making mistakes, prompting managers to lean toward safe, don't-rock-the-boat options that will have only a ripple effect on the status quo, protect or advance their own careers, and guard the interests of their immediate work groups.

Change-resistant cultures encourage a number of undesirable or unhealthy behaviors—avoiding risks, not making bold proposals to pursue emerging opportunities, a lax approach to both product innovation and continuous improvement in performing value chain activities, and following rather than leading market change. In change-resistant cultures, word quickly gets around that proposals to do things differently face an uphill battle and that people who champion them may be seen as either something of a nuisance or a troublemaker. Executives who don't value managers or employees with initiative and new ideas put a damper on product innovation, experimentation, and efforts to improve. At the same time, change-resistant companies have little appetite for being first-movers or fast-followers, believing that being in the forefront of change is too risky and that acting too quickly increases vulnerability to costly mistakes. They are more inclined to adopt a wait-and-see posture, carefully analyze several alternative responses, learn from the missteps of early movers, and then move forward cautiously and conservatively with initiatives that are deemed safe. Hostility to change is most often found in companies with multilayered management bureaucracies that have enjoyed considerable market success in years past and that are wedded to the "We have done it this way for years" syndrome.

When such companies encounter business environments with accelerating change, going slow on altering traditional ways of doing things can be become a liability rather than an asset. General Motors, IBM, Sears, and Eastman Kodak are classic examples of companies whose change-resistant bureaucracies were slow to respond to fundamental changes in their markets; clinging to the cultures and traditions that made them successful, they were reluctant to alter operating practices and modify their business approaches. As strategies of gradual change won out over bold innovation and being an early mover, all four lost market share to rivals that quickly moved to institute changes more in tune with evolving market conditions and buyer preferences. These companies are now struggling to recoup lost ground with cultures and behaviors more suited to market success—the kinds of fit that caused them to succeed in the first place.

Insular, Inwardly Focused Cultures   Sometimes a company reigns as an industry leader or enjoys great market success for so long that its personnel start to believe they have all the answers or can develop them on their own. There is a strong tendency to neglect what customers are saying and how their needs and expectations are changing. Such confidence in the correctness of how it does things and in the company's skills and capabilities breeds arrogance—company personnel discount the merits of what outsiders are doing and what can be learned by studying best-in-class performers. Benchmarking and a search for the best practices of outsiders are seen as offering little payoff. Any market share gains on the part of up-and-coming rivals are regarded as temporary setbacks, soon to be reversed by the company's own forthcoming initiatives (which, it is confidently predicted, will be an instant market hit with customers).

Insular thinking, internally driven solutions, and a must-be-invented-here mindset come to permeate the corporate culture. An inwardly focused corporate culture gives rise to managerial inbreeding and a failure to recruit people who can offer fresh thinking and outside perspectives. The big risk of insular cultural thinking is that the company can underestimate the competencies and accomplishments of rival companies and overestimate its own progress—with a resulting loss of competitive advantage over time.

Unethical and Greed-Driven Cultures   Companies that have little regard for ethical standards or that are run by executives driven by greed and ego gratification are scandals waiting to happen. Enron's collapse in 2001 was largely the product of an ethically dysfunctional corporate culture—while the culture embraced the positives of product innovation, aggressive risk taking, and a driving ambition to lead global change in the energy business, its executives exuded the negatives of arrogance, ego, greed, and an ends-justify-the-means mentality in pursuing stretched revenue and profitability targets.[9] A number of Enron's senior managers were all too willing to wink at unethical behavior, to cross over the line to unethical (and sometimes criminal) behavior themselves, and to deliberately stretch generally accepted accounting principles to make Enron's financial performance look far better than it really was. In the end, Enron came unglued because a few top executives chose unethical and illegal paths to pursue corporate revenue and profitability targets—in a company that publicly preached integrity and other notable corporate values but was lax in making sure that key executives walked the talk. Unethical cultures and executive greed have also produced scandals at WorldCom, Qwest, HealthSouth, Adelphia, Tyco, McWane, Parmalat, Rite Aid, Hollinger International, Refco, and Marsh & McLennan, with executives being indicted and/or convicted of criminal behavior. The U.S. Attorney's office elected not to prosecute the accounting firm KPMG with "systematic" criminal acts to market illegal tax shelters to wealthy clients (which KPMG tried mightily to cover up) because a criminal indictment would have resulted in the immediate collapse of KPMG and cut the number of global public accounting firms from four to just three; instead, criminal charges were filed against the company officials deemed most responsible. In 2005, U.S. prosecutors elected not to press criminal charges against Royal Dutch Petroleum (Shell Oil) for repeatedly and knowingly reporting inflated oil reserves to the U.S. Securities and Exchange Commission and not to indict Tommy Hilfiger USA for multiple tax law violations—but both companies agreed to sign nonprosecution agreements, the terms of which were not made public but which almost certainly involved fines and a long-term company commitment to cease and desist.

High-Performance Cultures

Some companies have high-performance cultures, in which the standout cultural traits are a can-do spirit, pride in doing things right, no-excuses accountability, and a pervasive results-oriented work climate in which people go the extra mile to meet or beat stretch objectives. In high-performance cultures, there is a strong sense of involvement on the part of company personnel and emphasis on individual initiative and creativity. Performance expectations are clearly delineated for the company as a whole, for each organizational unit, and for each individual. Issues and problems are promptly addressed—a strong bias exists for being proactive instead of reactive. There is a razor-sharp focus on what needs to be done. The clear and unyielding expectation is that all company personnel, from senior executives to frontline employees will display high-performance behaviors and a passion for making the company successful. There is respect for the contributions of individuals and groups.

A high-performance culture is a valuable contributor to good strategy execution and operating excellence. High performance, results-oriented cultures are permeated with a spirit of achievement and have a good track record in meeting or beating performance targets.

The challenge in creating a high-performance culture is to inspire high loyalty and dedication on the part of employees, such that they are both energized and preoccupied with putting forth their very best efforts to do things right and be unusually productive. Managers have to reinforce constructive behavior, reward top performers, and purge habits and behaviors that stand in the way of high productivity and good results. They must work at knowing the strengths and weaknesses of their subordinates, so as to better match talent with task and enable people to make meaningful contributions by doing what they do best.[10] They have to stress correcting and learning from mistakes, and they must put an unrelenting emphasis on moving forward and making good progress—in effect, there has to be a disciplined, performance-focused approach to managing the organization.

Adaptive Cultures

The hallmark of adaptive corporate cultures is willingness on the part of organizational members to accept change and take on the challenge of introducing and executing new strategies.[11] Company personnel share a feeling of confidence that the organization can deal with whatever threats and opportunities come down the pike; they are receptive to risk taking, experimentation, and innovation. In direct contrast to change-resistant cultures, adaptive cultures are very supportive of managers and employees at all ranks who propose or help initiate useful change. Internal entrepreneurship on the part of individuals and groups is encouraged and rewarded. Senior executives seek out, support, and promote individuals who exercise initiative, spot opportunities for improvement, and display the skills to implement them. Managers openly evaluate ideas and suggestions, fund initiatives to develop new or better products, and take prudent risks to pursue emerging market opportunities. As in high-performance cultures, the adaptive company exhibits a proactive approach to identifying issues, evaluating the implications and options, and quickly moving ahead with workable solutions. Strategies and traditional operating practices are modified as needed to adjust to or take advantage of changes in the business environment.

> **Core Concept**
> In adaptive cultures, there is a spirit of doing what's necessary to ensure long-term organizational success provided the new behaviors and operating practices that management is calling for are seen as legitimate and consistent with the core values and business principles underpinning the culture.

But why is change so willingly embraced in an adaptive culture? Why are organization members not fearful of how change will affect them? Why does an adaptive culture not become unglued with ongoing changes in strategy, operating practices, and behavioral norms? The answers lie in two distinctive and dominant traits of an adaptive culture: (1) Any changes in operating practices and behaviors must *not* compromise core values and long-standing business principles, and (2) the changes that are instituted must satisfy the legitimate interests of stakeholders—customers, employees, shareowners, suppliers, and the communities in which the company operates.[12] In other words, what sustains an adaptive culture is that organization members perceive the changes that management is trying to institute as legitimate and in keeping with the core values and business principles that form the heart and soul of the culture.

Thus, for an adaptive culture to remain intact over time, top management must orchestrate organizational changes in a manner that (1) demonstrates genuine care for the well-being of all key constituencies and (2) tries to satisfy all their legitimate interests simultaneously. Unless fairness to all constituencies is a decision-making principle and a commitment to doing the right thing is evident to organization members, the changes are not likely to be seen as legitimate and thus be readily accepted and implemented wholeheartedly.[13] Making changes that will please customers and that protect, if not enhance, the company's long-term well-being are generally seen as legitimate and are often seen as the best way of looking out for the interests of employees, stockholders, suppliers, and communities where the company operates. At companies with adaptive cultures, management concern for the well-being of employees is nearly always a big factor in gaining employee support for change—company personnel are usually receptive to change as long as employees understand that changes in their job assignments are part of the process of adapting to new conditions and that their employment security will not be threatened unless the company's business unexpectedly reverses direction. In cases where workforce downsizing becomes necessary, management concern for employees dictates that separation be handled humanely, making employee departure as painless as possible. Management efforts to make the process of adapting to change fair and equitable for customers, employees, stockholders, suppliers, and communities where the company operates, keeping adverse impacts to a minimum insofar as possible, breeds acceptance of and support for change among all organization stakeholders.

> Adaptive cultures are exceptionally well suited to companies with fast-changing strategies and market environments.

Technology companies, software companies, and today's dot-com companies are good illustrations of organizations with adaptive cultures. Such companies thrive on change—driving it, leading it, and capitalizing on it (but sometimes also succumbing to change when they make the wrong move or are swamped by better technologies or the superior business models of rivals). Companies like Google, Intel, Cisco Systems, eBay, Nokia, Amazon.com, and Dell cultivate the capability to act and react rapidly. They are avid practitioners of entrepreneurship and innovation, with a demonstrated willingness to take bold risks to create altogether new products, new businesses, and new industries. To create and nurture a culture that can adapt rapidly to changing to shifting business conditions, they make a point of staffing their organizations with people who are proactive, who rise to the challenge of change, and who have an aptitude for adapting.

In fast-changing business environments, a corporate culture that is receptive to altering organizational practices and behaviors is a virtual necessity. However, adaptive cultures work to the advantage of all companies, not just those in rapid-change environments. Every company operates in a market and business climate that is changing to one degree or another and that, in turn, requires internal operating responses and new behaviors on the part of organization members. *As a company's strategy evolves, an adaptive culture is a definite ally in the strategy-implementing, strategy-executing process as compared to cultures that have to be coaxed and cajoled to change.*

Culture: Ally or Obstacle to Strategy Execution?

A company's present culture and work climate may or may not be compatible with what is needed for effective implementation and execution of the chosen strategy. *When a company's present work climate promotes attitudes and behaviors that are well suited to first-rate strategy execution, its culture functions as a valuable ally in the strategy execution process.* When the culture is in conflict with some aspect of the company's direction, performance targets, or strategy, the culture becomes a stumbling block.[14]

How a Company's Culture Can Promote Better Strategy Execution   A culture grounded in strategy-supportive values, practices, and behavioral norms adds significantly to the power and effectiveness of a company's strategy execution effort.

For example, a culture where frugality and thrift are values widely shared by organizational members nurtures employee actions to identify cost-saving opportunities—the very behavior needed for successful execution of a low-cost leadership strategy. A culture built around such business principles as pleasing customers, fair treatment, operating excellence, and employee empowerment promotes employee behaviors and an esprit de corps that facilitate execution of strategies keyed to high product quality and superior customer service. A culture in which taking initiative, challenging the status quo, exhibiting creativity, embracing change, and collaborating with team members pervade the work climate promotes a company's drive to lead market change—outcomes that are conducive to successful execution of product innovation and technological leadership strategies.[15] Good alignment between ingrained cultural norms and the behaviors needed for good strategy execution makes the culture a valuable ally in the strategy-execution process. In a company where strategy and culture are misaligned, some of the very behaviors needed to execute strategy successfully run contrary to the behaviors and values imbedded in the prevailing culture. Such a clash nearly always produces a roadblock from employees whose actions and behaviors are strongly linked to the present culture. Culture-bred resistance to the actions and behaviors needed for good execution, if strong and widespread, poses a formidable hurdle that has to be cleared for strategy execution to get very far.

> **Core Concept**
> The tighter the culture–strategy fit, the more that the culture steers company personnel into displaying behaviors and adopting operating practices that promote good strategy execution.

A tight culture–strategy matchup furthers a company's strategy execution effort in three ways:[16]

1. *A culture that encourages actions, behaviors, and work practices supportive of good strategy execution not only provides company personnel with clear guidance regarding "how we do things around here" but also produces significant peer pressure from coworkers to conform to culturally acceptable norms.* The stronger the admonishments from top executives about "how we need to do things around here" and the stronger the peer pressure from coworkers, the more the culture influences people to display behaviors and observe operating practices that support good strategy execution.

2. *A deeply embedded culture tightly matched to the strategy aids the cause of competent strategy execution by steering company personnel to culturally approved behaviors and work practices and thus makes it far simpler to root out any operating practice that is a misfit.* This is why it is very much in management's best interests to build and nurture a deeply rooted culture where ingrained behaviors and operating practices marshal organizational energy behind the drive for good strategy execution.

3. *A culture imbedded with values and behaviors that facilitate strategy execution promotes strong employee identification with and commitment to the company's vision, performance targets, and strategy.* When a company's culture is grounded in many of the needed strategy-executing behaviors, employees feel genuinely better about their jobs, the company they work for, and the merits of what the company is trying to accomplish. As a consequence, greater numbers of company personnel exhibit some passion about their work and exert their best efforts to execute the strategy and achieve performance targets. All this helps move the company closer to realizing its strategic vision and, from employees' standpoint, makes the company a more engaging place to work.

These aspects of culture–strategy alignment say something important about the task of managing the strategy executing process: *Closely aligning corporate culture with the requirements for proficient strategy execution merits the full attention of senior executives.* The culture-building objective is to create a work climate and style of operating that mobilize the energy and behavior of company personnel squarely behind efforts to execute strategy competently. The more deeply that management can embed strategy-supportive ways of doing things, the more that management can rely on the culture to automatically steer company personnel toward behaviors and work practices that aid good strategy execution and away from ways of doing things that impede it.

Furthermore, culturally astute managers understand that nourishing the right cultural environment not only adds power to their push for proficient strategy execution but also promotes strong employee identification with and commitment to the company's vision, performance targets, and strategy. A culture–strategy fit prompts employees with emotional allegiance to the culture to feel genuinely better about their jobs, the company they work for, and the merits of what the company is trying to accomplish. As a consequence, their morale is higher and their productivity is higher. In addition, greater numbers of company personnel exhibit passion for their work and exert their best efforts to make the strategy succeed and achieve performance targets. All this helps move the company closer to realizing its strategic vision and, from the employees' standpoint, makes the company a more engaging place to work.

The Perils of Strategy–Culture Conflict   Conflicts between behaviors approved by the culture and behaviors needed for good strategy execution pose a real dilemma for company personnel. Should they be loyal to the culture and company traditions (to which they are likely to be emotionally attached) and thus resist or be indifferent to actions and behaviors that will promote better strategy execution—a choice that will certainly weaken the drive for good strategy execution? Or should they go along with the strategy execution effort and engage in actions and behaviors that run counter to the culture—a choice that will likely impair morale and lead to less-than-wholehearted commitment to management's strategy execution efforts? Neither choice leads to desirable outcomes, and the solution is obvious: eliminate the conflict.

When a company's culture is out of sync with the actions and behaviors needed to execute the strategy successfully, the culture has to be changed as rapidly as can be managed—this, of course, presumes that it is one or more aspects of the culture that are out of whack rather than the strategy executions approaches management wishes to institute. While correcting a strategy–culture conflict can occasionally mean revamping a company's approach to executing the strategy to produce good cultural fit, more usually it means altering aspects of the mismatched culture to ingrain new behaviors and work practices that will enable first-rate strategy execution. The more entrenched the mismatched aspects of the culture, the greater the difficulty of implementing and executing new or different strategies until better strategy–culture alignment emerges. A sizable and prolonged strategy–culture conflict weakens and may even defeat managerial efforts to make the strategy work.

Changing a Problem Culture

Changing a company culture that impedes proficient strategy execution is among the toughest management tasks because of the heavy anchor of ingrained behaviors and ways of doing things. It is natural for company personnel to cling to familiar practices and to be wary, if not hostile, to new approaches of how things are to be done. Consequently, it takes concerted management action over a period of time to root out certain unwanted behaviors and replace an out-of-sync culture with different behaviors and ways of doing things deemed more conducive to executing the strategy. *The single most visible factor that distinguishes successful culture-change efforts from failed attempts is competent leadership at the top.* Great power is needed to force major cultural change and overcome the springback resistance of entrenched cultures—and great power is possessed only by the most senior executives, especially the CEO. However, while top management must be out front leading the effort, marshaling support for a new culture and, more important, instilling new cultural behaviors are tasks for the whole management team. Middle managers and frontline supervisors play a key role in implementing the new work practices and operating approaches, helping win rank-and-file acceptance of and support for the changes, and instilling the desired behavioral norms.

As shown in Figure 13.1, the first step in fixing a problem culture is for top management to identify those facets of the present culture that are dysfunctional and pose obstacles to executing new strategic initiatives and meeting or beating company performance targets. Second, managers have to clearly define the desired new behaviors and features of the culture they want to create. Third, managers have to convince company personnel why the present culture poses problems and why and how new behaviors and operating approaches will improve company performance—the case for cultural change and the benefits of a reformed culture have to be persuasive. Finally, and most important, all the talk about remodeling the present culture has to be followed swiftly by visible, forceful actions to promote the desired new behaviors and work practices—actions that company personnel will interpret as a determined top management commitment to alter the culture and instill a different work climate and different ways of operating.

Making a Compelling Case for Culture Change   The place for management to begin a major remodeling of the corporate culture is by selling company personnel on

Figure 13.1   **Changing a Problem Culture**

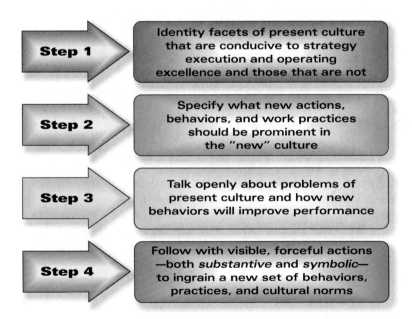

Step 1 — Identity facets of present culture that are conducive to strategy execution and operating excellence and those that are not

Step 2 — Specify what new actions, behaviors, and work practices should be prominent in the "new" culture

Step 3 — Talk openly about problems of present culture and how new behaviors will improve performance

Step 4 — Follow with visible, forceful actions —both *substantive* and *symbolic*— to ingrain a new set of behaviors, practices, and cultural norms

the need for new-style behaviors and work practices. This means making a compelling case for why the company's new strategic direction and culture-remodeling efforts are in the organization's best interests and why company personnel should wholeheartedly join the effort to doing things somewhat differently. Skeptics and opinion leaders have to be convinced that all is not well with the status quo. This can be done by:

- Citing reasons why the current strategy has to be modified and why new strategic initiatives that are being undertaken will bolster the company's competitiveness and performance. The case for altering the old strategy usually needs to be predicated on its shortcomings—why sales are growing slowly, why rivals are doing so much better, why too many customers are opting to go with the products of rivals, why costs are too high, why the company's price has to be lowered, and so on. There may be merit in holding events where managers and other key personnel are forced to listen to dissatisfied customers, the complaints of strategic allies, alienated employees, or disenchanted stockholders
- Citing why and how certain behavioral norms and work practices in the current culture pose obstacles to good execution of new strategic initiatives.
- Explaining how certain new behaviors and work practices that are to be introduced and have important roles in the new culture will be more advantageous and produce better results.

It is essential for the CEO and other top executives to personally talk to company personnel all across the company about the reasons for modifying work practices and culture-related behaviors. Senior officers and department heads have to play the lead role in explaining the behaviors, practices, and operating approaches that are to be introduced and why they are beneficial—and the explanations will likely have to be repeated many times. For the culture-change effort to be successful, frontline supervisors and employee opinion leaders must be won over to the cause, which means convincing them of the merits of *practicing* and *enforcing* cultural norms at the lowest levels in the organization. Until a big majority of employees accept the need for a new culture and agree that different work practices and behaviors are called for, there's more work to be done in selling company personnel on the whys and wherefores of culture change. Building widespread organizational support requires taking every opportunity to repeat the messages of why the new work practices, operating approaches, and behaviors are good for company stakeholders (particularly customers, employees, and shareholders). Effective culture-change leaders are good at telling stories to describe the new values and desired behaviors and connect them to everyday practices.

Management's efforts to make a persuasive case for changing what is deemed to be a problem culture must be *quickly followed* by forceful, high-profile actions across several fronts. The actions to implant the new culture must be both substantive and symbolic.

Substantive Culture-Changing Actions   No culture change effort can get very far with just talk about the need for different actions, behaviors, and work practices. Company executives have to give the culture-change effort some teeth by initiating *a series of actions* that company personnel will see as credible and unmistakably indicative of the seriousness of management's commitment to new strategic initiatives and the associated cultural changes. The strongest signs that management is truly committed to instilling a new culture include:

1. Replacing key executives who are strongly associated with the old culture and are stonewalling needed organizational and cultural changes.

2. Promoting individuals who are known to possess the desired cultural traits, who have stepped forward to advocate the shift to a different culture, and who can serve as role models for the desired cultural behavior.

3. Appointing outsiders with the desired cultural attributes to high-profile positions—bringing in new-breed managers to serve as role models and help drive the culture-change movement sends an unmistakable message that a new era is dawning and acts to reinforce company personnel who have already gotten on board the culture-change effort.

4. Screening all candidates for new positions carefully, hiring only those who appear to fit in with the new culture—this helps build a critical mass of people to help turn the tide in favor of the new culture.

5. Mandating that all company personnel attend culture-training programs to learn more about the new work practices and operating approaches and to better understand the cultured-related actions and behaviors that are expected.

6. Pushing hard to implement new-style work practices and operating procedures.

7. Designing compensation incentives that boost the pay of teams and individuals who display the desired cultural behaviors and hit change resisters in the pocketbook—company personnel are much more inclined to exhibit the desired kinds of actions and behaviors when it is in their financial best interest to do so.

8. Granting generous pay raises to individuals who step out front, lead the adoption of the desired work practices, display the new-style behaviors, and achieve pacesetting results.

9. Revising policies and procedures in ways that will help drive cultural change.

Executives must take care to launch enough companywide culture-change actions at the outset to leave no room for doubt that management is dead serious about changing the present culture and that a cultural transformation is inevitable. To convince doubters and skeptics that they cannot just wait in hopes the culture-change initiative will soon die out, the series of actions initiated by top management must create lots of hallway talk across the whole company, get the change process off to a fast start, and be followed by unrelenting efforts to firmly establish the new work practices and style of operating as standard.

Symbolic Culture-Changing Actions   Symbolic managerial actions are necessary to alter a problem culture and tighten the strategy–culture fit. The most important symbolic actions are those that top executives take to *lead by example.* For instance, if the organization's strategy involves a drive to become the industry's low-cost producer, senior managers must display frugality in their own actions and decisions: inexpensive decorations in the executive suite, conservative expense accounts and entertainment allowances, a lean staff in the corporate office, scrutiny of budget requests, few executive perks, and so on. At Wal-Mart, all the executive offices are simply decorated; executives are habitually frugal in their own actions, and they are zealous in their own efforts to control costs and promote greater efficiency. At Nucor, one of the world's low-cost producers of steel products, executives fly coach class and use taxis at airports rather than limousines. If the culture change imperative is to be more responsive to customers' needs and to pleasing customers, the CEO can instill greater customer awareness by requiring all officers and executives to spend a significant portion of each week talking with customers about their needs. Top executives must be alert to the fact that company personnel will be watching their actions and decisions to see if they are walking the talk. Hence, they need to make sure that their current decisions will be construed as consistent with new-culture values and behaviors.[17]

Another category of symbolic actions includes holding ceremonial events to single out and honor people whose actions and performance exemplify what is called for in the new culture. A point is made of holding events to celebrate each culture-change success (and any other outcome that management would like to see happen again). Executives sensitive to their role in promoting strategy–culture fits make a habit of appearing at ceremonial functions to praise individuals and groups that get with the program. They show up at employee training programs to stress strategic priorities, values, ethical principles, and cultural norms. Every group gathering is seen as an opportunity to repeat and ingrain values, praise good deeds, expound on the merits of the new culture, and cite instances of how the new work practices and operating approaches have worked to good advantage.

The use of symbols in culture building is widespread. Many universities give outstanding teacher awards each year to symbolize their commitment to good teaching and their esteem for instructors who display exceptional classroom talents. Numerous businesses have employee-of-the-month awards. The military has a long-standing custom of awarding ribbons and medals for exemplary actions. Mary Kay Cosmetics awards an array of prizes—from ribbons to pink automobiles—to its beauty consultants for reaching various sales plateaus.

How Long Does It Take to Change a Problem Culture?   Planting and growing the seeds of a new culture require a determined effort by the chief executive and other senior managers. Neither charisma nor personal magnetism is essential. But a sustained and persistent effort to reinforce the culture at every opportunity through both word and deed is very definitely required. Changing a problem culture is never a short-term exercise. It takes time for a new culture to emerge and prevail. Overnight transformations simply don't occur. And it takes even longer for a new culture to become deeply embedded The bigger the organization and the greater the cultural shift needed to produce a strategy–culture fit, the longer it takes. In large companies, fixing a problem culture and instilling a new set of attitudes and behaviors can take two to five years. In fact, it is usually tougher to reform an entrenched problematic culture than it is to instill a strategy-supportive culture from scratch in a brand-new organization. Sometimes executives succeed in changing the values and behaviors of small groups of managers and even whole departments or divisions, only to find the changes eroded over time by the actions of the rest of the organization—what is communicated, praised, supported, and penalized by an entrenched majority undermines the new emergent culture and halts its progress. Executives, despite a series of well-intended actions to reform a problem culture, are likely to fail at weeding out embedded cultural traits when widespread employee skepticism about the company's new directions and culture-change effort spawns covert resistance to the cultural behaviors and operating practices advocated by top management. This is why management must take every opportunity to convince employees of the need for culture change and communicate to them how new attitudes, behaviors, and operating practices will benefit the interests of organizational stakeholders.

A company that succeeded in fixing a problem culture is Alberto-Culver— see Illustration Capsule 13.2.

Illustration Capsule 13.2

Changing the Culture in Alberto-Culver's North American Division

In 1993, Carol Bernick—vice chairperson of Alberto-Culver, president of its North American division, and daughter of the company's founders—concluded that her division's existing culture had four problems: Employees dutifully waited for marching orders from their bosses, workers put pleasing their bosses ahead of pleasing customers, some company policies were not family-friendly, and there was too much bureaucracy and paperwork. What was needed, in Bernick's opinion, was a culture in which company employees had a sense of ownership and an urgency to get things done, welcomed innovation, and were willing to taking risks.

Alberto-Culver's management undertook a series of actions to introduce and ingrain the desired cultural attributes:

- In 1993, a new position, called growth development leader (GDL), was created to help orchestrate the task of fixing the culture deep in the ranks (there were 70 GDLs in Alberto-Culver's North American division). GDLs came from all ranks of the company's managerial ladder and were handpicked for such qualities as empathy, communication skills, positive attitude, and ability to let their hair down and have fun. GDLs performed their regular jobs in addition to taking on the GDL roles; it was considered an honor to be chosen. Each GDL mentored about 12 people from both a career and a family standpoint. GDLs met with senior executives weekly, bringing forward people's questions and issues and then, afterward, sharing with their groups the topics and solutions that were discussed. GDLs brought a group member as a guest to each meeting. One meeting each year is devoted to identifying "macros and irritations"—attendees are divided into four subgroups and given 15 minutes to identify the company's four biggest challenges (the macros) and the four most annoying aspects of life at the company (the irritations); the whole group votes on which four deserve the company's attention. Those selected are then addressed, and assignments made for follow-up and results.

- Changing the culture was made an issue across the company, starting in 1995 with a two-hour State of the Company presentation to employees covering where the company was and where it wanted to be. The State of the Company address then became an annual event.

- Management created ways to measure the gains in changing the culture. One involved an annual all-employee survey to assess progress against cultural goals and to get 360-degree feedback—the 2000 survey had 180 questions, including 33 relating to the performance of each respondent's GDL. A bonfire celebration was held in the company parking lot to announce that paperwork would be cut by 30 percent.

- A list of 10 cultural imperatives was formalized in 1998—honesty, ownership, trust, customer orientation, commitment, fun, innovation, risk taking, speed and urgency, and teamwork. These imperatives came to be known internally as HOT CC FIRST.

- Numerous celebrations and awards programs were instituted. Most celebrations are scheduled, but some are spontaneous (an impromptu thank-you party for a good fiscal year). Business Builder Awards (initiated in 1997) are given to individuals and teams that make a significant impact on the company's growth and profitability. The best-scoring GDLs on the annual employee surveys are awarded shares of company stock. The company notes all work anniversaries and personal milestones with "Alberto-appropriate" gifts; appreciative company employees sometimes give thank-you gifts to their GDLs. According to Carol Bernick, "If you want something to grow, pour champagne on it. We've made a huge effort—maybe even an over-the-top effort—to celebrate our successes and, indeed, just about everything we'd like to see happen again."

The culture change effort at Alberto-Culver North America was viewed as a major contributor to improved performance. From 1993 (when the effort first began) to 2001, the division's sales increased from just under $350 million to over $600 million and pretax profits rose from $20 million to almost $50 million. Carol Bernick was elevated to chairman of Alberto-Culver's board of directors in 2004.

Source: Based on information in Carol Lavin Bernick, "When Your Culture Needs a Makeover," *Harvard Business Review* 79, no. 6 (June 2001), p. 61 and information posted at the company's Web site, www.alberto.com (accessed November 10, 2005).

Grounding the Culture in Core Values and Ethics

The foundation of a company's corporate culture nearly always resides in its dedication to certain core values and the bar it sets for ethical behavior. The culture-shaping significance of core values and ethical behaviors accounts for why so many companies have developed a formal values statement and a code of ethics—see Table 13.1 for representative core values and the ground usually covered in codes of ethics. Many companies today convey their values and codes of ethics to stakeholders and interested parties in their annual reports and on their Web sites. The trend of making stakeholders aware of a company's commitment to core values and ethical business conduct is attributable to three factors: (1) greater management understanding of the role these statements play in culture building, (2) a renewed focus on ethical standards stemming from the numerous corporate scandals that hit the headlines during 2001–2005, and (3) the sizable fraction of consumers and suppliers who prefer doing business with ethical companies.

Core Concept

A company's culture is grounded in and shaped by its core values and the bar it sets for ethical behavior.

At Darden Restaurants—the world's largest casual dining company, which employs more than 150,000 people and serves 300 million meals annually at 1,400 Red Lobster, Olive Garden, Bahama Breeze, Smokey Bones Barbeque & Grill, and Seasons 52 restaurants in North America—the core values are operating with integrity and fairness, caring and respect, being of service, teamwork, excellence, always learning and teaching, and welcoming and celebrating workforce diversity. Top executives at

Table 13.1   **Representative Content of Company Values Statements and Codes of Ethics**

Typical Core Values	Areas Covered by Codes of Ethics
• Satisfying and delighting customers	• Expecting all company personnel to display honesty and integrity in their actions and avoid conflicts of interest
• Dedication to superior customer service, top-notch quality, product innovation, and/or technological leadership	• Mandating full compliance with all laws and regulations, specifically:
• A commitment to excellence and results	—Antitrust laws prohibiting anticompetitive practices, conspiracies to fix prices, or attempts to monopolize
• Exhibiting such qualities as integrity, fairness, trustworthiness, pride of workmanship, Golden Rule behavior, respect for coworkers, and ethical behavior	—Foreign Corrupt Practices Act
• Creativity, exercising initiative, and accepting responsibility	—Securities laws and prohibitions against insider trading
• Teamwork and cooperative attitudes	—Environmental and workplace safety regulations
• Fair treatment of suppliers	—Discrimination and sexual harassment regulations
• Making the company a great place to work	—Political contributions and lobbying activities
• A commitment to having fun and creating a fun work environment	• Prohibiting giving or accepting bribes, kickbacks, or gifts
• Being stewards of shareholders' investments and remaining committed to profits and growth	• Engaging in fair selling and marketing practices
• Exercising social responsibility and being a good community citizen	• Not dealing with suppliers that employ child labor or engage in other unsavory practices
• Caring about protecting the environment	• Being above-board in acquiring and using competitively sensitive information about rivals and others
• Having a diverse workforce	• Avoiding use of company assets, resources, and property for personal or other inappropriate purposes
	• Responsibility to protect proprietary information and not divulge trade secrets

Darden believe the company's practice of these values has been instrumental in creating a culture characterized by trust, exciting jobs and career opportunities for employees, and a passion to provide "a terrific dining experience to every guest, every time, in every one of our restaurants."[18]

Of course, sometimes a company's stated core values and codes of ethics are cosmetic, existing mainly to impress outsiders and help create a positive company image. But more usually they have been developed to shape the culture. Many executives want the work climate at their companies to mirror certain values and ethical standards, partly because they are personally committed to these values and ethical standards but mainly because they are convinced that adherence to such values and ethical principles will make the company a much better performer *and* improve its image. As discussed earlier, values-related cultural norms promote better strategy execution and mobilize company personnel behind the drive to achieve stretch objectives and the company's strategic vision. Hence, a corporate culture grounded in well-chosen core values and high ethical standards contributes mightily to a company's long-term strategic success.[19] And, not incidentally, strongly ingrained values and ethical standards reduce the likelihood of lapses in ethical and socially-approved behavior that mar a company's reputation and put its financial performance and market standing at risk.

> A company's values statement and code of ethics communicate expectations of how employees should conduct themselves in the workplace.

The Culture-Building Role of Values and Codes of Ethics   At companies where executives believe in the merits of practicing the values and ethical standards that have been espoused, *the stated core values and ethical principles are the cornerstones of the corporate culture.* As depicted in Figure 13.2, a company's stated core values and ethical principles have two roles in the culture-building process. One, a company that works hard at putting its stated core values and ethical principles into practice fosters a work climate where company personnel share common and strongly held convictions about how the company's business is to be conducted. Second, the stated values and ethical principles provide company personnel with guidance about the manner in which

Figure 13.2   **The Two Culture-Building Roles of a Company's Core Values and Ethical Standards**

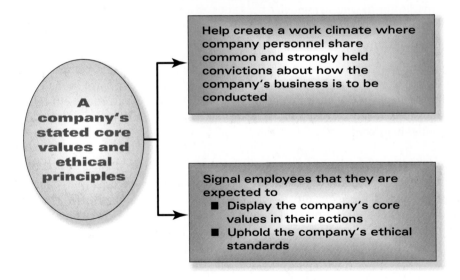

they are to do their jobs—which behaviors and ways of doing things are approved (and expected) and which are out-of-bounds.

Transforming Core Values and Ethical Standards into Cultural Norms

Once values and ethical standards have been formally adopted, they must be institutionalized in the company's policies and practices and embedded in the conduct of company personnel. This can be done in a number of different ways.[20] Tradition-steeped companies with a rich folklore rely heavily on word-of-mouth indoctrination and the power of tradition to instill values and enforce ethical conduct. But most companies employ a variety of techniques to hammer in core values and ethical standards, using some or all of the following:

1. Giving explicit attention to values and ethics in recruiting and hiring to screen out applicants who do not exhibit compatible character traits.
2. Incorporating the statement of values and the code of ethics into orientation programs for new employees and training courses for managers and employees.
3. Having senior executives frequently reiterate the importance and role of company values and ethical principles at company events and internal communications to employees.
4. Using values statements and codes of ethical conduct as benchmarks for judging the appropriateness of company policies and operating practices.
5. Making the display of core values and ethical principles a big factor in evaluating each person's job performance—there's no better way to win the attention and commitment of company personnel than by using the degree to which individuals observe core values and ethical standards as a basis for compensation increases and promotion.
6. Making sure that managers, from the CEO down to frontline supervisors, are diligent in stressing the importance of ethical conduct and observance of core values. Line managers at all levels must give serious and continuous attention to the task of explaining how the values and ethical code apply in their areas.
7. Encouraging everyone to use their influence in helping enforce observance of core values and ethical standards—strong peer pressures to exhibit core values and ethical standards are a deterrent to outside-the-lines behavior.
8. Periodically having ceremonial occasions to recognize individuals and groups who display the values and ethical principles.
9. Instituting ethics enforcement procedures.

To deeply ingrain the stated core values and to high ethical standards, companies must turn them into *strictly enforced cultural norms*. They must put a stake in the ground, making it unequivocally clear that living up to the company's values and ethical standards has to be a way of life at the company and that there will be little toleration of outside-the-lines behavior.

The Benefits of Cultural Norms Grounded in Core Values and Ethical Principles

The more that managers succeed in making the espoused values and ethical principles the main drivers of "how we do things around here," the more that the values and ethical principles function as cultural norms. Over time, a strong culture grounded in the display of core values and ethics may emerge. As shown in Figure 13.3, *cultural norms* rooted in core values and ethical behavior are highly beneficial in three respects.[21] One, the advocated core values and ethical standards accurately

Figure 13.3   **The Benefits of Cultural Norms Strongly Grounded in Core Values and Ethical Principles**

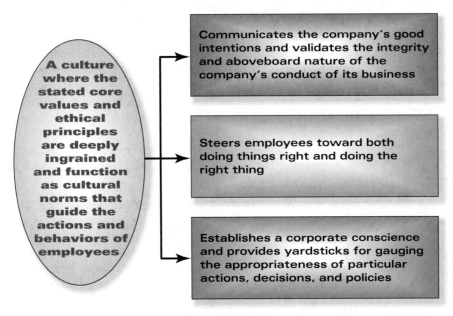

communicate the company's good intentions and validate the integrity and above-board character of its business principles and operating methods. There's nothing cosmetic or fake about the company's values statement and code of ethics—company personnel actually strive to practice what is being preached. Second, the values-based and ethics-based cultural norms steer company personnel toward both doing things right and doing the right thing. Third, they establish a "corporate conscience" and provide yardsticks for gauging the appropriateness of particular actions, decisions, and policies.

Establishing a Strategy–Culture Fit in Multinational and Global Companies

In multinational and global companies, establishing a tight strategy–culture fit is complicated by the diverse societal circumstances surrounding the company's operations in different countries. The nature of the local economies, living conditions, per capita incomes, and lifestyles can give rise to considerable cross-border diversity in a company's workforce and to subcultures within the corporate culture. Leading cross-border culture-change initiatives requires sensitivity to prevailing differences in local circumstances; company managers must discern when local subcultures have to be accommodated and when cross-border differences in the company's corporate culture can be and should be narrowed.[22] Cross-border diversity in a multinational enterprise's corporate culture is more tolerable if the company is pursuing a multicountry strategy and if the company's culture in each country is well aligned with its strategy in that country. But significant cross-country differences in a company's culture are likely to impede execution of a global strategy and have to be addressed.

As discussed earlier in this chapter, *the trick to establishing a workable strategy–culture fit in multinational companies is to ground the culture in strategy-supportive values and operating practices that travel well across country borders* and strike a

Core Concept
A multinational company needs to build its corporate culture around values and operating practices that travel well across borders.

chord with managers and workers in many different areas of the world, despite varying local customs and traditions. A multinational enterprise with a misfit between its strategy and culture in certain countries where it operates can attack the problem by rewording its values statement so as to express core values in ways that have universal appeal. The alternative is to allow *some leeway* for certain core values to be reinterpreted or de-emphasized or applied somewhat differently from country to country whenever local customs and traditions in a few countries really need to be accommodated. But such accommodation needs to be done in ways that do not impede good strategy execution. Sometimes certain offending operating styles can be modified to good advantage in all locations where the company operates.

Aside from trying to build the corporate culture around a set of core values that have universal appeal, management can seek to minimize the existence of subcultures and promote greater cross-country cultural uniformity by:

- *Instituting culture training in each country.* The goals of this training should be to (1) communicate the meaning of core values in language that resonates with company personnel in that country and (2) explain the case for common operating approaches and work practices. The use of uniform work practices becomes particularly important when the company's work practices are efficient and aid good strategy execution—in such instances, local managers have to find ways to skirt local preferences and win support for "how we do things around here."

- *Creating a cultural climate where the norm is to adopt best practices, use common work procedures, and pursue operating excellence.* Companies may find that a values-based corporate culture is less crucial to good strategy execution that an operations-based, results-oriented culture in which the dominant cultural norm is an all-out effort to do things in the best possible manner, achieve continuous improvement, and meet or beat performance targets. A results-oriented culture keyed to operating excellence and meeting stretch objectives sidesteps many of the problems with trying to get people from different societies and traditions to embrace common values.

- *Giving local managers the flexibility to modify people management approaches or operating styles.* In some situations, adherence to companywide cultural traditions simply doesn't work well. However, local modifications have to be infrequent and done in a manner that doesn't undermine the establishment of a mostly uniform corporate culture.

- *Giving local managers discretionary authority to use somewhat different motivational and compensation incentives to induce local personnel to adopt and practice the desired cultural behaviors.* Personnel in different countries may respond better to some compensation structures and reward systems than to others.

Generally, a high degree of cross-country homogeneity in a multinational company's corporate culture is desirable and has to be pursued, particularly when it comes to ingraining universal core values and companywide enforcement of such ethical standards as the payment of bribes and kickbacks, the use of underage labor, and environmental stewardship. Having too much variation in the culture from country to country not only makes it difficult to use the culture in helping drive the strategy execution process but also works against the establishment of a one-company mind-set and a consistent corporate identity.

LEADING THE STRATEGY EXECUTION PROCESS

The litany of managing the strategy process is simple enough: Craft a sound strategic plan, implement it, execute it to the fullest, adjust it as needed, and win! But the leadership challenges are significant and diverse. Exerting take-charge leadership, being a "spark plug," ramrodding things through, and achieving results thrusts a manager into a variety of leadership roles in managing the strategy execution process: resource acquirer and allocator, capabilities builder, motivator, policymaker, policy enforcer, head cheerleader, crisis solver, decision maker, and taskmaster, to mention a few. There are times when leading the strategy execution process entails being hard-nosed and authoritarian, times when it is best to be a perceptive listener and a compromising decision maker, times when matters are best delegated to people closest to the scene of the action, and times when mentoring or coaching is appropriate. Many occasions call for the manager in charge to assume a highly visible role and put in long hours guiding the process, while others entail only a brief ceremonial performance with the details delegated to subordinates.

For the most part, leading the strategy execution process is a top-down responsibility driven by mandates to get things on the right track and show good results. It must start with a perceptive diagnosis of the requirements for good strategy execution, given the company's circumstances. Then comes diagnosis of the organization's capabilities and preparedness to execute the necessary strategic initiatives and decisions as to which of several ways to proceed to get things done and achieve the targeted results.[23] In general, leading the drive for good strategy execution and operating excellence calls for five actions on the part of the manager-in-charge:

1. Staying on top of what is happening, closely monitoring progress, ferreting out issues, and learning what obstacles lie in the path of good execution.
2. Putting constructive pressure on the organization to achieve good results and operating excellence.
3. Leading the development of stronger core competencies and competitive capabilities.
4. Displaying ethical integrity and leading social responsibility initiatives.
5. Pushing corrective actions to improve strategy execution and achieve the targeted results.

Staying on Top of How Well Things Are Going

To stay on top of how well the strategy execution process is going, a manager needs to develop a broad network of contacts and sources of information, both formal and informal. The regular channels include talking with key subordinates, attending meetings and quizzing the presenters, reading reviews of the latest operating results, talking to customers, watching the competitive reactions of rival firms, exchanging e-mail and holding telephone conversations with people in outlying locations, making on-site visits, and listening to rank-and-file employees. However, some information is more trustworthy than the rest, and the views and perspectives offered by different people can vary widely. Presentations and briefings by subordinates may be colored by wishful thinking or shoddy analysis rather than representing the unvarnished truth. Bad news is sometimes filtered, minimized, or distorted by people pursuing their own agendas, and in some cases not reported at all as subordinates delay conveying failures and problems in hopes that they can turn things around in time. Hence, managers have to decide which information is trustworthy and get an accurate feel for the existing situation. They have to confirm whether things are on track, identify problems, learn what obstacles lie in the path of good strategy execution, ruthlessly assess whether the organization has the talent and attitude needed to drive the required changes, and develop a basis for determining what, if anything, they can personally do to move the process along.[24]

One of the best ways for executives to stay on top of the strategy execution process is by making regular visits to the field and talking with many different people at many different levels—a technique often labeled **managing by walking around (MBWA).** Wal-Mart executives have had a long-standing practice of spending two to three days every week visiting Wal-Mart's stores and talking with store managers and employees. Sam Walton, Wal-Mart's founder, insisted, "The key is to get out into the store and listen to what the associates have to say." Jack Welch, the highly effective CEO of General Electric (GE) from 1980 to 2001, not only spent several days each month personally visiting GE operations and talking with major customers but also arranged his schedule so that he could spend time exchanging information and ideas with GE managers from all over the world who were attending classes at the company's leadership development center near GE's headquarters.

> **Core Concept**
> *Management by walking around (MBWA)* is one of the techniques that effective leaders use to stay informed about how well the strategy execution process is progressing.

Often, customers and suppliers can provide valuable perspectives on how well a company's strategy execution process is going. Joe Tucci, chief operating officer at data-storage leader EMC, when confronted with an unexpected dropoff in EMC's sales in 2001 and not sure whether the downturn represented a temporary slump or a structural market change went straight to the source for hard information: the chief executive officers and chief financial officers to whom chief information officers at customer companies reported and to the consultants who advised them. The information he got was eye-opening—fundamental market shifts were occurring, and the rules of market engagement now called for major strategy changes at EMC followed by quick implementation.

To keep their fingers on the company's pulse, managers at some companies host weekly get-togethers (often on Friday afternoons) to create a regular opportunity for tidbits of information to flow freely between down-the-line employees and executives. Many manufacturing executives make a point of strolling the factory floor to talk with workers and meeting regularly with union officials. Some managers operate out of open cubicles in big spaces so that they can interact easily and frequently with coworkers. Jeff Bezos, Amazon.com's CEO, is noted for his practice of MBWA, firing off a battery of questions when he tours facilities and insisting that Amazon managers spend time in the trenches with their people to avoid abstract thinking and getting disconnected from the reality of what's happening.[25]

Most managers practice MBWA, attaching great importance to spending time with people at various company facilities and gathering information and opinions firsthand from diverse sources about how well various aspects of the strategy execution process are going. They believe facilities visits and face-to-face contacts give them a good feel for what progress is being made, what problems are being encountered, and whether additional resources or different approaches may be needed. Just as important, MBWA provides opportunities to talk informally to many different people at different organizational levels, give encouragement, lift spirits, shift attention from the old to the new priorities, and create some excitement—all of which generate positive energy and help mobilize organizational efforts behind strategy execution.

Putting Constructive Pressure on the Organization to Achieve Good Results and Operating Excellence

Managers have to be out front in mobilizing organizational energy behind the drive for good strategy execution and operating excellence. Part of the leadership requirement here entails nurturing a results-oriented work climate, where performance standards are high and a spirit of achievement is pervasive. The intended outcome is an organization with a good track record in meeting or beating stretch performance targets. A high-performance culture in which there is constructive pressure to achieve good results is a valuable contributor to good strategy execution and operating excellence. If management wants to drive the strategy execution effort by instilling a results-oriented work climate, then senior executives have to take the lead in promoting certain enabling cultural drivers: a strong sense of involvement on the part of company personnel, emphasis on individual initiative and creativity, respect for the contribution of individuals and groups, and pride in doing things right.

Organizational leaders who succeed in creating a results-oriented work climate typically are intensely people-oriented, and they are skilled users of people-management practices that win the emotional commitment of company personnel and inspire them to do their best.[26] They understand that treating employees well generally leads to increased teamwork, higher morale, greater loyalty, and increased employee commitment to making a contribution. All of these foster an esprit de corps that energizes organizational members to contribute to the drive for operating excellence and proficient strategy execution.

Successfully leading the effort to instill a spirit of high achievement into the culture generally entails such leadership actions and managerial practices as:

- *Treating employees with dignity and respect.* This often includes a strong company commitment to training each employee thoroughly, providing attractive career opportunities, emphasizing promotion from within, and providing a high degree of job security. Some companies symbolize the value of individual employees and the importance of their contributions by referring to them as cast members (Disney), crew members (McDonald's), coworkers (Kinko's and CDW Computer Centers), job owners (Granite Construction), partners (Starbucks), or associates (Wal-Mart, Lenscrafters, W. L. Gore, Edward Jones, Publix Supermarkets, and Marriott International). At a number of companies, managers at every level are held responsible for developing the people who report to them.

- *Making champions out of the people who turn in winning performances.* This must be done in ways that promote teamwork and cross-unit collaboration as opposed to spurring an unhealthy footrace among employees to best one another. Would-be champions who advocate radical or different ideas must not be looked on as disruptive or troublesome. The best champions and change agents are persistent, competitive, tenacious, committed, and fanatic about seeing their idea through to success. It is particularly important that people who champion an unsuccessful idea not be punished or sidelined but rather encouraged to try again—encouraging lots of "tries" is important since many ideas won't pan out.

- *Encouraging employees to use initiative and creativity in performing their work.* Operating excellence requires that everybody be expected to contribute ideas, exercise initiative, and pursue continuous improvement. The leadership trick is to keep a sense of urgency alive in the business so that people see change and innovation as necessities. Moreover, people with maverick ideas or out-of-the-ordinary proposals have to be tolerated and given room to operate; anything less tends to squelch creativity and initiative.

- *Setting stretch objectives.* Managers must clearly communicate an expectation that company personnel are to give their best in achieving performance targets.

- *Using the tools of benchmarking, best practices, business process reengineering, TQM, and Six Sigma quality to focus attention on operating excellence.* These are proven approaches to getting better operating results and facilitating better strategy execution.

- *Using the full range of motivational techniques and compensation incentives to inspire company personnel, nurture a results-oriented work climate, and enforce high-performance standards.* Managers cannot mandate innovative improvements by simply exhorting people to "be creative," nor can they make continuous progress toward operating excellence with directives to "try harder." Rather, they have to foster a culture where innovative ideas and experimentation with new ways of doing things can blossom and thrive. Individuals and groups need to be strongly encouraged to brainstorm, let their imaginations fly in all directions, and come up with proposals for improving how things are done. This means giving company personnel enough autonomy to stand out, excel, and contribute. And it means that the rewards for successful champions of new ideas and operating improvements should be large and visible.

- *Celebrating individual, group, and company successes.* Top management should miss no opportunity to express respect for individual employees and their appreciation of extraordinary individual and group effort.[27] Companies like Mary Kay Cosmetics, Tupperware, and McDonald's actively seek out reasons and opportunities to give pins, buttons, badges, and medals for good showings by average performers—the idea being to express appreciation and give a motivational boost to people who stand out in doing ordinary jobs. General Electric and 3M Corporation make a point of ceremoniously honoring individuals who believe so strongly in their ideas that they take it on themselves to hurdle the bureaucracy, maneuver their projects through the system, and turn them into improved services, new products, or even new businesses.

While leadership efforts to instill a results-oriented, high performance culture usually accentuate the positive, there are negative reinforcers too. Managers whose units consistently perform poorly have to be replaced. Low-performing workers and people who reject the results-oriented cultural emphasis have to be weeded out or at least moved to out-of-the-way positions. Average performers have to be candidly counseled that they have limited career potential unless they show more progress in the form of additional effort, better skills, and improved ability to deliver good results.

Leading the Development of Better Competencies and Capabilities

A third avenue to better strategy execution and operating excellence is proactively strengthening core competencies and competitive capabilities to better perform value chain activities and pave the way for better bottom-line results. This often requires top management intervention for two reasons. One, senior managers are more likely to recognize and appreciate the strategy-executing significance of stronger capabilities; this is especially true in multinational companies where it is top executives are in the best position to spot opportunities to leverage existing competencies and competitive capabilities across geographical borders. Two, senior managers usually have to *lead* the strengthening effort because core competencies and competitive capabilities typically reside in the combined efforts of different work groups, departments, and strategic allies and only senior managers have the organizational clout to enforce the necessary networking and collaboration.

Aside from leading efforts to strengthen *existing* competencies and capabilities, effective strategy leaders try to anticipate changes in customer-market requirements and proactively build *new* competencies and capabilities that offer a competitive edge over rivals. Again, senior managers are in the best position to see the need and potential of new capabilities and then to play a lead role in the capability-building, resource-enhancing process. Proactively building new competencies and capabilities ahead of rivals to gain a competitive edge is strategic leadership of the best kind, but strengthening the company's resource base in reaction to newly developed capabilities of pioneering rivals occurs more frequently.

Displaying Ethical Integrity and Leading Social Responsibility Initiatives

For an organization to avoid the pitfalls of scandal and disgrace and consistently display the intent to conduct its business in a principled manner, the CEO and those around the CEO must be openly and unswervingly committed to ethical conduct and socially redeeming business principles and core values. Leading the effort to operate the company's business in an ethically principled fashion has three pieces. First and foremost, the CEO and other senior executives must set an excellent example in their own ethical behavior, demonstrating character and personal integrity in their actions and decisions. The behavior of senior executives sends a clear message to company personnel regarding what the "real" standards of personal conduct are. Moreover, the company's strategy and operating decisions have to be seen as ethical—actions always speak far louder than the words in a company's code of ethics. Second, top management must declare unequivocal support of the company's ethical code and take an uncompromising stand on expecting all company personnel to conduct themselves in an ethical fashion at all times. This means iterating and reiterating to employees that it is their duty to observe the company's ethical codes. Third, top management must be prepared to act as the final arbiter on hard calls; this means removing people from key positions or terminating them when they are guilty of a violation. It also means reprimanding those who have been lax in monitoring and enforcing ethical compliance. Failure to act swiftly and decisively in punishing ethical misconduct is interpreted as a lack of real commitment.

Establishing an Effective Ethics Compliance and Enforcement Process
If a company's executives truly aspire for company personnel to behave ethically, they must personally see to it that strong and effective procedures for enforcing ethical standards and handling potential violations are put in place. Even in an ethically strong company, there can be bad apples—and some of the bad apples may be executives. So it is rarely enough to rely on either the exhortations of senior executives or an ethically principled culture to produce ethics compliance.

Executive action to institute formal ethics compliance and enforcement mechanisms can entail forming an ethics committee to give guidance on ethics matters, appointing an ethics officers to head the compliance effort, establishing an ethics hotline or Web site that employees can use to either anonymously report a possible violation or get confidential advice on a troubling ethics-related situation, and having an annual ethics audit to measure the extent of ethical behavior and identify problem areas. If senior executives are really serious about enforcing ethical behavior, they probably need to do five things:[28]

1. Have mandatory ethics training programs for employees. Company personnel have to be educated about what is ethical and what is not and given guidance about the gray areas. Special training programs probably are needed for personnel in such ethically vulnerable areas as procurement, sales, and lobbying. Company personnel assigned to subsidiaries in foreign countries can find themselves trapped in ethical dilemmas if bribery and corruption of public officials are common practices or if suppliers or customers are accustomed to kickbacks of one kind or another.

2. Openly encourage company personnel to report possible infractions via anonymous calls to a hotline or e-mails sent to a designated address. Ideally, the company's culture will be sufficiently ethically principled that most company personnel will feel it is their obligation and duty to report possible ethical violations (not so much to get someone in trouble but to prevent further damage and help the company avoid the dire consequences of a debilitating scandal. Furthermore, everyone must be encouraged to raise issues about ethically gray areas and to get confidential advice from the company's ethics specialists.

3. Conduct an annual audit of each manager's efforts to uphold ethical standards and require formal reports on the actions taken by managers to remedy deficient conduct.

4. Require all employees to sign a statement annually certifying that they have complied with the company's code of ethics.

5. Make sure that ethical violations carry appropriate punishment, including dismissal if the violation is sufficiently egregious.

While these actions may seem extreme, they leave little room to doubt the seriousness of executive commitment to ethics compliance. Openly encouraging people to report possible ethical violations heightens awareness of operating within ethical bounds. And while violators have to be disciplined, *the main purpose of the various means of enforcement is to encourage compliance rather than administer punishment.* Most company personnel will think twice about knowingly engaging in unethical conduct when their actions could be reported by watchful coworkers. The same is true when they know their actions will be audited and/or when they have to sign statements certifying compliance with the company's code of ethics.

Top executives in multinational companies face big challenges in enforcing strict ethical standards companywide because what is considered ethical often varies substantially or subtly from country to country. There are shades and variations in what societies generally agree to be right and wrong based on the prevailing circumstances, local customs, and predominant religious convictions. And certainly there are cross-country variations in the *degree* to which certain behaviors are considered unethical.[29] Thus, transnational companies have to make a fundamental decision regarding whether to try to enforce common ethical standards across their operations in all countries or whether to allow some rules to be bent in some cases.

Leading Social Responsibility Initiatives The exercise of social responsibility, just as with observance of ethical principles, requires top executive leadership. *What separates companies that make a sincere effort to carry their weight in being good corporate citizens from companies that are content to do only what is legally required of them are company leaders who believe strongly that just making a profit is not good enough. Such leaders are committed to a higher standard of performance that includes social and environmental metrics as well as financial and strategic metrics.* Thus, it is up to the CEO and other senior executives to insist that the company go past the rhetoric and cosmetics of corporate citizenship and implement social responsibility initiatives.

> CEOs who are committed to a core value of corporate social responsibility move beyond the rhetorical flourishes and enlist the full support of company personnel behind the execution of social responsibility initiatives.

Among the leadership responsibilities of the CEO and other senior managers, therefore, are to *step out front,* to wave the flag of socially responsible behavior for all to see, to marshal the support of company personnel, and to make social responsibility initiatives an everyday part of how the company conducts its business affairs. Top executives have to use social and environmental metrics in evaluating performance and, ideally, the company's board of directors will elect to tie the company's social and environmental performance to executive compensation—a surefire way to make sure that social responsibility efforts are more than window dressing. To help ensure that it has commitment from senior managers, Verizon Communications ties 10 percent of the annual bonus of the company's top 2,500 managers directly to the achievement of social responsibility targets. One survey found over 60 percent of senior managers believed that a portion of executive compensation should be linked to a company's performance on social and environmental measures. The strength of the commitment from the top—typically a company's CEO and board of directors—ultimately determines whether a company will implement and execute a full-fledged strategy of social responsibility that embraces some customized combination of actions to protect the environment (beyond what is required by law), actively participate in community affairs, be a generous supporter of charitable causes and projects that benefit society, and have a positive impact on workforce diversity and the overall well-being of employees. One of the most reliable signs that company executives are leading an authentic effort to carry out fruitful social responsibility initiatives is whether the company issues an annual report on its social responsibility efforts that cites quantitative and qualitative evidence of the company accomplishments.

Leading the Process of Making Corrective Adjustments

The leadership challenge of making corrective adjustments is twofold: deciding when adjustments are needed and deciding what adjustments to make. Both decisions are a normal and necessary part of managing the strategy execution process, since no scheme for implementing and executing strategy can foresee all the events and problems that will arise. There comes a time at every company when managers have to fine-tune or overhaul the approaches to strategy execution and push for better results. Clearly, when a company's strategy execution effort is not delivering good results and making measurable progress toward operating excellence, it is the leader's responsibility to step forward and push corrective actions.

The *process* of making corrective adjustments varies according to the situation. In a crisis, it is typical for leaders to have key subordinates gather information, identify and evaluate options (crunching whatever numbers may be appropriate), and perhaps prepare a preliminary set of recommended actions for consideration. The organizational leader then usually meets with key subordinates and personally presides over extended discussions of the proposed responses, trying to build a quick consensus among members of the executive inner circle. If no consensus emerges and action is required immediately, the burden falls on the manager in charge to choose the response and urge its support.

When the situation allows managers to proceed more deliberately in deciding when to make changes and what changes to make, most managers seem to prefer a process of incrementally solidifying commitment to a particular course of action.[30] The process that managers go through in deciding on corrective adjustments is essentially the same for both proactive and reactive changes: They sense needs, gather information, broaden and deepen their understanding of the situation, develop options and explore their pros and cons, put forth action proposals, generate partial (comfort-level) solutions, strive for a consensus, and finally formally adopt an agreed-on course of action.[31] Deciding what corrective changes to initiate can take a few hours, a few days, a few weeks, or even a few months if the situation is particularly complicated.

Success in initiating corrective actions usually hinges on thorough analysis of the situation, the exercise of good business judgment in deciding what actions to take, and good implementation of the corrective actions that are initiated. Successful managers are skilled in getting an organization back on track rather quickly; they (and their staffs) are good at discerning what actions to take and in ramrodding them through to a successful conclusion. Managers that struggle to show measurable progress in generating good results and improving the performance of strategy-critical value chain activities are candidates for being replaced.

The challenges of leading a successful strategy execution effort are, without question, substantial.[32] But the job is definitely doable. Because each instance of executing strategy occurs under different organizational circumstances, the managerial agenda for executing strategy always needs to be situation-specific—there's no neat generic procedure to follow. And, as we said at the beginning of Chapter 11, executing strategy is an action-oriented, make-the-right-things-happen task that challenges a manager's ability to lead and direct organizational change, create or reinvent business processes, manage and motivate people, and achieve performance targets. If you now better understand what the challenges are, what approaches are available, which issues need to be considered, and why the action agenda for implementing and executing strategy sweeps across so many aspects of administrative and managerial work, then we will look on our discussion in Chapters 11, 12, and 13 as a success.

A Final Word on Managing the Process of Crafting and Executing Strategy   In practice, it is hard to separate the leadership requirements of executing strategy from the other pieces of the strategy process. As we emphasized in Chapter 1, the job of crafting, implementing, and executing strategy is a five-phase process with much looping and recycling to fine-tune and adjust strategic visions, objectives, strategies, capabilities, implementation approaches, and cultures to fit one another and to fit changing circumstances. The process is continuous, and the conceptually separate acts of crafting and executing strategy blur together in real-world situations. The best tests of good strategic leadership are whether the company has a good strategy and whether the strategy execution effort is delivering the hoped-for results. If these two conditions exist, the chances are excellent that the company has good strategic leadership.

Key Points

The character of a company's culture is a product of the core values and business principles that executives espouse, the standards of what is ethically acceptable and what is not, the work practices and behaviors that define "how we do things around here," its approach to people management and style of operating, the "chemistry" and the "personality" that permeates its work environment, and the stories that get told over and over to illustrate and reinforce the company's values, business practices, and traditions. A company's culture is important because it influences the organization's actions and approaches to conducting business—in a very real sense, the culture is the company's "operating system" or organizational DNA.

The psyche of corporate cultures varies widely. Moreover, company cultures vary widely in strength and influence. Some are strongly embedded and have a big impact on a company's practices and behavioral norms. Others are weak and have comparatively little influence on company operations. There are four types of unhealthy cultures: (1) those that are highly political and characterized by empire building, (2) those that are change resistant, (3) those that are insular and inwardly focused, and (4) those that are ethically unprincipled and are driven by greed. High-performance cultures and adaptive cultures both have positive features that are conducive to good strategy execution.

A culture grounded in values, practices, and behavioral norms that match what is needed for good strategy execution helps energize people throughout the company to do their jobs in a strategy-supportive manner, adding significantly to the power of a company's strategy execution effort and the chances of achieving the targeted results. But when the culture is in conflict with some aspect of the company's direction, performance targets, or strategy, the culture becomes a stumbling block. Thus, an important part of the managing the strategy execution process is establishing and nurturing a good fit between culture and strategy.

A company's present culture and work climate may or may not be compatible with what is needed for effective implementation and execution of the chosen strategy. *When a company's present work climate promotes attitudes and behaviors that are well suited to first-rate strategy execution, its culture functions as a valuable ally in the strategy execution process.* When the culture is in conflict with some aspect of the company's direction, performance targets, or strategy, the culture becomes a stumbling block.

Changing a company's culture, especially a strong one with traits that don't fit a new strategy's requirements, is a tough and often time-consuming challenge. Changing a culture requires competent leadership at the top. It requires symbolic actions and substantive actions that unmistakably indicate serious commitment on the part of top management. The more that culture-driven actions and behaviors fit what's needed for good strategy execution, the less managers have to depend on policies, rules, procedures, and supervision to enforce what people should and should not do.

The taproot of a company's corporate culture nearly always is its dedication to certain core values and the bar it sets for ethical behavior. Of course, sometimes a company's stated core values and codes of ethics are cosmetic, existing mainly to impress outsiders and help create a positive company image. But more usually they have been developed to shape the culture. If management practices what it preaches, a company's core values and ethical standards nurture the corporate culture in three highly positive ways: (1) They communicate the company's good intentions and validate the integrity and above-board character of its business principles and operating methods; (2) they steer company personnel toward both doing the right thing and doing things right; and (3) they establish a corporate conscience that gauges the appropriateness of particular actions, decisions, and policies. Companies that really care about how they conduct their business put a stake in the ground, making it unequivocally clear that company personnel are expected to live up to the company's values and ethical standards—how well individuals display core values and adhere to ethical standards is often part of the job performance evaluations. Peer pressures to conform to cultural norms are quite strong, acting as an important deterrent to outside-the-lines behavior.

Leading the drive for good strategy execution and operating excellence calls for five actions on the part of the manager-in-charge:

1. Staying on top of what is happening, closely monitoring progress, ferreting out issues, and learning what obstacles lie in the path of good execution.

2. Putting constructive pressure on the organization to achieve good results and operating excellence.

3. Leading the development of stronger core competencies and competitive capabilities.

4. Displaying ethical integrity and leading social responsibility initiatives.

5. Pushing corrective actions to improve strategy execution and achieve the targeted results.

Exercises

1. Go to Herman Miller's Web site (www.hermanmiller.com) and read what the company has to say about its corporate culture in its careers sections. Do you think this statement is just public relations, or, based on what else you can learn about the Herman Miller Company from browsing this Web site, is there reason to believe that management has truly built a culture that makes the stated values and principles come alive?

2. Go to the careers section at Qualcomm's Web site (www.qualcomm.com) and see what this company, one of the most prominent companies in mobile communications technology, has to say about life at Qualcomm. Is what's on this Web site just recruiting propaganda, or does it convey the type of work climate that management is actually trying to create? If you were a senior executive at Qualcomm, would you see merit in building and nurturing a culture like what is described in the section "Life at Qualcomm"? Would such a culture represent a tight fit with Qualcomm's high-tech business and strategy? (You can get an overview of the Qualcomm's strategy by exploring the section for investors and some of the recent press releases.) Is your answer consistent with what is presented in the "Awards and Honors" menu selection in the "About Qualcomm" portion of the Web site?

3. Go to the Web site of Johnson & Johnson (www.jnj.com) and read the "J&J Credo," which sets forth the company's responsibilities to customers, employees, the community, and shareholders. Then read the "Our Company" section. Why do you think the credo has resulted in numerous awards and accolades that recognize the company as a good corporate citizen?

4. Do an Internet search or use the resources of your university's library to identify at least five companies that have experienced a failure of strategic leadership on the part of the CEO since 2000. Three candidate companies you might want to research are Adelphia Communications, AIG, and HealthSouth. Then determine which, if any, of the five factors discussed in this chapter's section titled "Leading the Strategy Execution Process" came into play in the CEOs' failure.

5. Dell Inc. has been listed as one of *Fortune*'s most admired companies for several years. Click on the "About Dell" link at www.dell.com. What is your assessment of the company's extensive discussion of accountability, concern for the environment, and community involvement? Does it appear these programs have the support of upper-level management? Is there evidence that this is more than a public relations initiative?

6. Review the material in Illustration Capsule 13.1 on Google's corporate culture; then go to the company's Web site, click on the "About Google" link, then on the "Corporate Info" link and read the "Ten things Google has found to be true" in the "Our Philosophy" section. What relationships do you see between these 10 things and Google's description of its culture? Are the two closely connected? Why or why not? Explain.

part two
2

Cases in Crafting and
Executing Strategy

Whole Foods Market in 2006: Mission, Core Values, and Strategy

Arthur A. Thompson
The University of Alabama

Founded in 1980 as a local supermarket for natural and health foods in Austin, Texas, Whole Foods Market had by 2006 evolved into the world's largest retail chain of natural and organic foods supermarkets. The company had 180 stores in the United States, Canada, and Great Britain and 2005 sales of $4.7 billion; revenues had grown at a compound annual rate of 20 percent since 1998. John Mackey, the company's cofounder and CEO, believed that Whole Foods' rapid growth and market success had much to do with having "remained a uniquely mission-driven company—highly selective about what we sell, dedicated to our core values and stringent quality standards and committed to sustainable agriculture." The company's stated mission was to promote vitality and well-being for all individuals by offering the highest quality, least processed, most flavorful natural and naturally preserved foods available. But as the company's motto—"Whole Foods, Whole People, Whole Planet"—implied, its core mission extended well beyond food retailing (see Exhibit 1).

John Mackey's vision was for Whole Foods to become a national brand synonymous not just with natural and organic foods but also with being the best food retailer in every community it served. In pursuit of this vision, the company's strategic plan aimed at expanding its retail operations to offer the highest quality and most nutritious foods to more and more customers and promoting organically grown foods, food safety concern, and sustainability of the entire

ecosystem. During its 25-year history, Whole Foods Market had been a leader in the natural and organic foods movement across the United States, helping the industry gain acceptance among growing numbers of consumers. The company's long-term objectives were to have 400 stores and sales of $12 billion by 2010.

THE NATURAL AND ORGANIC FOODS INDUSTRY

The combined sales of natural and organic foods—about $43 billion in 2003—represented 5.5 percent of the roughly $775 billion in total U.S. grocery store sales. *Natural foods* are defined as foods that are minimally processed; largely or completely free of artificial ingredients, preservatives, and other non–naturally occurring chemicals; and as near to their whole, natural state as possible. The U.S. Department of Agriculture's Food and Safety Inspection Service defines *natural food* as "a product containing no artificial ingredient or added color and that is minimally processed." While sales of natural foods products had increased at double-digit rates in the 1990s, growth had slowed to the 7–9 percent range in 2001–2005.

Organic foods were a special subset of the natural foods category and had to be grown and processed without the use of pesticides, antibiotics, hormones,

Exhibit 1   **Whole Foods Market's Motto: Whole Foods,**
Whole People, Whole Planet

Whole Foods

We obtain our products locally and from all over the world, often from small, uniquely dedicated food artisans. We strive to offer the highest quality, least processed, most flavorful and naturally preserved foods. Why? Because food in its purest state—unadulterated by artificial additives, sweeteners, colorings and preservatives—is the best tasting and most nutritious food available.

Whole People

We recruit the best people we can to become part of our team. We empower them to make their own decisions, creating a respectful workplace where people are treated fairly and are highly motivated to succeed. We look for people who are passionate about food. Our team members are also well-rounded human beings. They play a critical role in helping build the store into a profitable and beneficial part of its community.

Whole Planet

We believe companies, like individuals, must assume their share of responsibility as tenants of Planet Earth. On a global basis we actively support organic farming—the best method for promoting sustainable agriculture and protecting the environment and the farm workers. On a local basis, we are actively involved in our communities by supporting food banks, sponsoring neighborhood events, compensating our team members for community service work, and contributing at least five percent of total net profits to not-for-profit organizations.

Source: Information posted at www.wholefoodsmarket.com (accessed November 28, 2005).

synthetic chemicals, artificial fertilizers, preservatives, dyes or additives, or genetic engineering. Organic foods included fresh fruits and vegetables, meats, and processed foods that had been produced using:

1. Agricultural management practices that promoted a healthy and renewable ecosystem that used no genetically engineered seeds or crops, sewage sludge, long-lasting pesticides, herbicides, or fungicides.

2. Livestock management practices that involved organically grown feed, fresh air and outdoor access for the animals, and no use of antibiotics or growth hormones.

3. Food processing practices that protected the integrity of the organic product and did not involve the use of radiation, genetically modified organisms, or synthetic preservatives.

In 1990, passage of the Organic Food Production Act started the process of establishing national standards for organically grown products in the United States, a movement that included farmers, food activists, conventional food producers, and consumer groups. In October 2002, the U.S. Department of Agriculture (USDA) officially established labeling standards for organic products, overriding both the patchwork of inconsistent state regulations for what could be labeled as organic and the different rules of some

43 agencies for certifying organic products. The new USDA regulations established four categories of food with organic ingredients and varying levels of organic purity:

1. *100 percent organic products:* Such products were usually whole foods, such as fresh fruits and vegetables, grown by organic methods—which meant that the product had been grown without the use of synthetic pesticides or sewage-based fertilizers, had not been subjected to irradiation, and had not been genetically modified or injected with bioengineered organisms, growth hormones, or antibiotics. Products that were 100 percent organic could carry the green USDA organic certification seal, provided the merchant could document that the food product had been organically grown (usually by a certified organic producer).

2. *Organic products:* Such products, often processed, had to have at least 95 percent organically certified ingredients. These could also carry the green USDA organic certification seal.

3. *Made with organic ingredients:* Such products had to have at least 70 percent organic ingredients; they could be labeled "made with organic ingredients" but could not display the USDA seal.

4. *All other products with organic ingredients:* Products with less than 70 percent organic ingredients could not use the word *organic* on the front of a package, but organic ingredients could be listed among other ingredients in a less prominent part of the package.

An official with the National Organic Program, commenting on the appropriateness and need for the new USDA regulations, said, "For the first time, when consumers see the word *organic* on a package, it will have consistent meaning."[1] The new labeling program was not intended as a health or safety program (organic products have not been shown to be more nutritious than conventionally grown products, according to the American Dietetic Association), but rather as a marketing solution. An organic label has long been a selling point for shoppers wanting to avoid pesticides or to support environmentally friendly agricultural practices. However, the new regulations required additional documentation on the part of growers, processors, exporters, importers, shippers, and merchants to verify that they were certified to grow, process, or handle organic products carrying the USDA's organic seal. In 2003, Whole Foods was designated as the first national "Certified Organic" grocer by Quality Assurance International, a federally recognized independent third-party certification organization. In 2005, major food processors were lobbying to make the definition of organic foods less restrictive and permit the use of synthetics in so-called 100 percent organic products.

Organic farmland in the United States was estimated at close to 3 million acres, with an estimated 14,000 mostly small-scale farmers growing organic products in 2004. The amount of certified organic cropland had doubled between 1997 and 2001, and livestock pastures increased at an even faster rate. However, less than 1 percent of U.S. farmland was certified organic in 2004. The Rodale Institute, a Pennsylvania-based advocate of organic farming, had set a goal of 100,000 certified organic U.S. farmers by 2013, a number equal to 5 percent of the 2 million U.S. farmers.[2]

A 2004 survey conducted by the Organic Trade Association found that U.S. manufacturers' sales of organic food products hit $10.4 billion in 2003, up from $1 billion in 1990; sales were expected to reach $30 billion in 2007.[3] In 2005, organic products were sold in about 14,500 natural foods stores in the United States and over 75 percent of the nation's conventional grocery stores and supermarkets. Organic foods and beverages were available in nearly every food category in 2005.

RETAILING OF NATURAL AND ORGANIC FOODS

According to the USDA, 2000 was the first year in which more organic food was sold in conventional U.S. supermarkets than in the nation's 14,500 natural foods stores. Since 2002, most mainstream supermarkets had been expanding their selections of natural and organic products, which ranged from potato chips to fresh produce to wines, cereals, pastas, cheeses, yogurt, vinegars, beef, chicken, and canned and frozen fruits and vegetables. Fresh produce was the most popular organic product—lettuce, broccoli, cauliflower, celery, carrots, and apples were the biggest sellers. Meat, dairy, bread, and snack foods were among the fastest-growing organic product categories. Most supermarket chains stocked a selection of natural and organic food items, and the number and variety of items they carried was growing. Leading supermarket chains like Wal-Mart, Kroger, Publix, Safeway, Albertson's, and Supervalu/Save-a-Lot had created special organic and health food sections for nonperishable foods in most of their stores. Kroger, Publix, and several other chains also had special sections for fresh organic fruits and vegetables in their produce cases in many of their stores in 2005. Kroger had reopened several of its supermarkets as Fresh Fare stores, offering shoppers items such as sushi, gourmet takeout food, organic produce, and an extensive selection of fine wines and cheeses; in 2004–2005, there were 20 Fresh Fare stores in California operating under the Ralph's Fresh Fare name and the Fresh Fare concept was being tested in five Michigan locations. A Kroger official indicated that Fresh Fare was not aimed at the customer who shopped exclusively at upscale, natural foods chains like Whole Foods, but rather at the customer who already shopped Kroger but might travel to Whole Foods for things like vegetables, meats, and prepared foods. Two chains—upscale Harris Teeter in the southeastern United States and Whole Foods Market—had launched their own private-label brands of organics. Exhibit 2 shows 2004–2005 data for the leading supermarket retailers in North America.

Exhibit 2   **Leading North American Supermarket Chains, 2004–2005 (ranked by sales revenues)**

Rank/Company	Number of Stores	2004–2005 Sales Revenues (in billions)	Share of Total U.S. Grocery Sales ($775 billion)
1. Wal-Mart Supercenters	1,713	$70.8	9.1%
2. Kroger	2,530	56.2	7.3
3. Albertson's	1,810	39.7	5.1
4. Safeway	1,817	35.8	4.6
5. Costco	434	29.3	3.8
6. Ahold USA*	1,489	27.4	3.5
7. Sam's Clubs	551	22.3	2.9
8. Loblaw	1,050	21.7	n.a.‡
9. Supervalu/Save-a-Lot	1,544	19.5	2.5
10. Publix Super Markets	847	18.6	2.4
11. Delhaize†	1,494	15.8	2.0
27. Whole Foods Market	171	4.7	0.6

Note: Sales revenue numbers represent estimated sales of supermarket items only in the case of Wal-Mart, Sam's Club, and Costco. Sales data for Kroger's (whose supermarket brands also include City Market, King Sooper, Ralph's, and 11 smaller chains) and Albertson's include revenues from company-owned retail outlets (fuel centers, drugstores, apparel, and jewelry) that are not supermarket related.

*Ahold USA , the U.S. division of Netherlands-based Ahold, includes 339 Stop & Shops, 197 Giant Foods (Landover, Maryland), 180 Bruno's units, 292 Bi-Los, 116 Giant Foods (Carlisle, Pennsylvania), and 365 Tops Friendly Markets.

†Delhaize includes 1,214 Food Lion stores, 123 Hannaford Bros. stores, 103 Kash 'n Karry stores, and 54 Harvey's stores.

‡**n.a.** = Not applicable. Loblaw is a Canadian chain, and market shares are based on U.S. supermarket sales.

Sources: Top 75, www.supermarketnews.com (accessed November 28, 2005); www.walmartstores.com (accessed November 28, 2005); and Whole Foods Market press release, November 9, 2005.

Most industry observers expected that conventional supermarkets would continue to expand their offerings and selection as demand for natural and organic foods expanded. Supermarkets were attracted to merchandising natural and organic foods for two reasons: Consumer demand for natural and organic foods was growing at 7–9 percent annually and was expected to accelerate; meanwhile, retail sales of general food products were growing slowly because of intense price pressures and because more and more consumers were eating out rather than cooking at home.

Leading food processors were showing greater interest in organics as well. Heinz had introduced an organic ketchup and owned a 19 percent stake in Hain Celestial Group, one of the largest organic and natural foods producers. Campbell Soup had introduced organic tomato juice. Starbucks, Green Mountain Coffee, and several other premium coffee

marketers were marketing organically grown coffees; Coca-Cola's Odwalla juices were organic; and Tyson Foods and several other chicken producers had introduced organic chicken products. Producers of organically grown beef were selling all they could produce, and sales were expected to grow 30 percent annually through 2008. Safeway, Publix, and Kroger were stocking organic beef and chicken in a number of their stores. Whole Foods was struggling to find organic beef and chicken suppliers big enough to supply all its stores. Lite House organic salad dressings had recently been added to the shelves of several mainstream supermarkets. Major food-processing companies like Kraft, General Mills, Groupe Danone (the parent of Dannon Yogurt), Dean Foods, and Kellogg had all purchased organic food producers in an effort to capitalize on sales-growth opportunities for healthy foods that taste good. In the fall of 2005, McDonald's began marketing organic coffee in

650 units in New England. Most observers saw the trend toward organics as in its infancy, believing that organic products had staying power in the marketplace and were not a fad marching by in the night.

Several factors had combined to transform natural and organic foods retailing, once a niche market, into the fastest-growing segment of U.S. food sales:

- Healthier eating patterns on the part of a populace that was becoming better educated about foods, nutrition, and good eating habits. Among those most interested in organic products were aging affluent people concerned about health and better-for-you foods.

- Increasing consumer concerns over the purity and safety of food due to the presence of pesticide residues, growth hormones, artificial ingredients and other chemicals, and genetically engineered ingredients.

- Environmental concerns due to the degradation of water and soil quality.

- A wellness, or health-consciousness, trend among people of many ages and ethnic groups.

An August 2004 report by Mintel indicated that 10 percent of consumers purchased organic products frequently enough to be "organically obsessed" and another 34 percent purchased them "at least occasionally." All age groups were at least as likely to buy organics in 2004 as they were in 2002, but the largest increases were among young adults, ages 18 to 24 (49 percent versus 34 percent in 2002), and 55- to 64-year-olds (45 percent, up from 25 percent in 2002).[4]

A 2005 survey commissioned by Whole Foods found that 65 percent of U.S. consumers had tried organic foods and beverages, up from 54 percent in both 2003 and 2004; 27 percent of respondents indicated they consumed more organic foods and beverages than they did one year ago.[5] Ten percent consumed organic foods several times per week, up from just 7 percent in 2004. The top three reasons why consumers were buying organic foods and beverages were avoidance of pesticides (70.3 percent), freshness (68.3 percent), and health and nutrition (67.1 percent); 55 percent reported buying organic to avoid genetically modified foods. Also, many respondents agreed that organic foods and beverages were "better for my health" (52.8 percent) and better for the environment (52.4 percent). The

categories of organic foods and beverages that were purchased most frequently by those participating in the Whole Foods survey were fresh fruits and vegetables (73 percent), nondairy beverages (32 percent), bread or baked goods (32 percent), dairy items (24.6 percent), packaged goods such as soup or pasta (22.2 percent), meat (22.2 percent), snack foods (22.1 percent), frozen foods (16.6 percent), prepared and ready-to-eat meals (12.2 percent), and baby food (3.2 percent).

The higher prices of organic products were the primary barrier for most consumers in trying or using organic products—75 percent of those participating in the 2005 Whole Foods survey believed organics were too expensive. Other reasons for not consuming more organics were availability (46.1 percent) and loyalty to non-organic brands (36.7 percent).

WHOLE FOODS MARKET

Whole Foods Market was founded in Austin, Texas, when John Mackey, the current CEO, and two other local natural foods grocers in Austin decided the natural foods industry was ready for a supermarket format. The original Whole Foods Market opened in 1980 with a staff of only 19. It was an immediate success. At the time, there were less than half a dozen natural foods supermarkets in the United States. By 1991, the company had 10 stores, revenues of $92.5 million, and net income of $1.6 million. Whole Foods became a public company in 1992, with its stock trading on the Nasdaq; Whole Foods stock was added to the Standard & Poor's (S&P) Mid-Cap 400 Index in May 2002 and to the Nasdaq-100 Index in December 2002. The company had 32,000 employees in 2005 and expected sales of around $5.6 billion in 2006; Mackey believed the company's cash flow from operations in upcoming years would prove more than sufficient to cover the capital costs of the company's aggressive store expansion plan. In November 2005, the company announced a 20 percent increase in its quarterly dividend to $0.30, a special dividend of $4.00 per share, a 2-for-1 stock split, and a $200 million four-year stock buyback program.

Core Values

In 1997, when Whole Foods developed the "Whole Foods, Whole People, Whole Planet" slogan, John

Mackey, known as a go-getter with a "cowboy way of doing things," said:

> This slogan taps into perhaps the deepest purpose of Whole Foods Market. It's a purpose we seldom talk about because it seems pretentious, but a purpose nevertheless felt by many of our Team Members and by many of our customers (and hopefully many of our shareholders too). Our deepest purpose as an organization is helping support the health, well-being, and healing of both people (customers and Team Members) and of the planet (sustainable agriculture, organic production and environmental sensitivity). When I peel away the onion of my personal consciousness down to its core in trying to understand what has driven me to create and grow this company, I come to my desire to promote the general well-being of everyone on earth as well as the earth itself. This is my personal greater purpose with the company and the slogan perfectly reflects it.

Complementing the slogan were five core values shared by both top management and company personnel (see Exhibit 3 on page C-8). In the company's 2003 annual report, John Mackey said:

> Our core values reflect the sense of collective fate among our stakeholders and are the soul of our company. Our Team Members, shareholders, vendors, community and environment must flourish together through their affiliation with us or we are not succeeding as a business. It is leadership's role to balance the needs and desires of all our stakeholders and increase the productivity of Whole Foods Market. By growing the collective pie, we create larger slices for all of our shareholders.

Growth Strategy

Prior to 2002, Whole Foods' growth strategy had been to expand via a combination of opening its own new stores and acquiring small, owner-managed chains. About 35 percent of the company's store base had come from acquisitions; since 1991, the company had acquired 14 chains with 67 stores (see Exhibit 4 on page C-9). Since the natural foods industry was highly fragmented, consisting of close to 20,000 mostly one-store operations and small and regional chains, Whole Foods' management had continued to explore acquisitions that provided access to desirable locations and markets and that had capable personnel that would fit in with Whole Foods. However, since 2002 the company's growth strategy had shifted markedly to opening its own large stores

(50,000 square feet and larger) rather than be acquiring small chains having stores in the range of 5,000 to 20,000 square feet—very few natural foods competitors had stores bigger than 20,000 square feet.

Store Sizes and Locations

Whole Foods' 180 stores (as of January 2006) had an open format and generated average annual sales of about $26 million. Stores opened in fiscal 2004–2005 were averaging sales of over $30 million annually. Stores more than eight years old averaged about 30,000 square feet, stores less than eight years old averaged about 36,000 square feet, and the company's newest stores ranged between 25,000 and 80,000 square feet. The three Harry's Farmers Market stores in Atlanta that Whole Foods acquired in 2001 each measured 75,000–80,000 square feet. Whole Foods' newly opened 58,000-square-foot store on Columbus Circle in New York City was the largest grocery in Manhattan and the company's biggest revenue producer in 2005; Whole Foods opened a three-story 48,500-square-foot store in the Union Square area of Manhattan in March 2005. Whole Foods had a new 74,500-square-foot store in Columbus, Ohio; a flagship 78,000-square-foot store in Austin, Texas; a 62,500-square-foot store in Princeton, New Jersey; a 62,200-square-foot store in Plano, Texas; a 61,000-square-foot store in Omaha, Nebraska; a 56,000-square-foot store in Bellevue, Washington; and a 53,000-square-foot store in Torrance, California. The company was on the verge of opening a 75,000-square-foot store in London, England; a 60,000-square-foot store in Chandler (outside Phoenix); and a 65,000-square-foot store in Plymouth Meeting (a suburb of Philadelphia). In early 2006, 113 of the company's 180 stores were 30,000 square feet or larger. It was the company's practice each year to relocate some of its smaller stores to larger sites with improved visibility and parking. Exhibit 5 on page C-10 provides store-related statistics.

Whole Foods sought to locate its new stores in the upscale areas of urban metropolitan centers—86 percent of the U.S. stores were in the top 50 statistical metropolitan areas. In 2005, Whole Foods had stores in 31 states and 38 of the top 50 U.S. metropolitan areas. In 2002, the company entered Toronto, Canada, and expanded into London and Bristol, England, in 2004. In November 2005, the company had 64 stores averaging 55,000 square feet

Exhibit 3   **Whole Foods Market's Core Values**

Our Core Values

The following list of core values reflects what is truly important to us as an organization. These are not values that change from time to time, situation to situation or person to person, but rather they are the underpinning of our company culture. Many people feel Whole Foods is an exciting company of which to be a part and a very special place to work. These core values are the primary reasons for this feeling, and they transcend our size and our growth rate. By maintaining these core values, regardless of how large a company Whole Foods becomes, we can preserve what has always been special about our company. These core values are the soul of our company.

Selling the Highest Quality Natural and Organic Products Available

- **Passion for Food**—We appreciate and celebrate the difference natural and organic products can make in the quality of one's life.
- **Quality Standards**—We have high standards and our goal is to sell the highest quality products we possibly can. We define quality by evaluating the ingredients, freshness, safety, taste, nutritive value and appearance of all of the products we carry. We are buying agents for our customers and not the selling agents for the manufacturers.

Satisfying and Delighting Our Customers

- **Our Customers**—They are our most important stakeholders in our business and the lifeblood of our business. Only by satisfying our customers first do we have the opportunity to satisfy the needs of our other stakeholders.
- **Extraordinary Customer Service**—We go to extraordinary lengths to satisfy and delight our customers. We want to meet or exceed their expectations on every shopping trip. We know that by doing so we turn customers into advocates for our business. Advocates do more than shop with us, they talk about Whole Foods to their friends and others. We want to serve our customers competently, efficiently, knowledgeably and with flair.
- **Education**—We can generate greater appreciation and loyalty from all of our stakeholders by educating them about natural and organic foods, health, nutrition and the environment.
- **Meaningful Value**—We offer value to our customers by providing them with high quality products, extraordinary service and a competitive price. We are constantly challenged to improve the value proposition to our customers.
- **Retail Innovation**—We value retail experiments. Friendly competition within the company helps us to continually improve our stores. We constantly innovate and raise our retail standards and are not afraid to try new ideas and concepts.
- **Inviting Store Environments**—We create store environments that are inviting and fun, and reflect the communities they serve. We want our stores to become community meeting places where our customers meet their friends and make new ones.

Team Member Happiness and Excellence

- **Empowering Work Environments**—Our success is dependent upon the collective energy and intelligence of all of our Team Members. We strive to create a work environment where motivated Team Members can flourish and succeed to their highest potential. We appreciate effort and reward results.
- **Self-Responsibility**—We take responsibility for our own success and failures. We celebrate success and see failures as opportunities for growth. We recognize that we are responsible for our own happiness and success.
- **Self-Directed Teams**—The fundamental work unit of the company is the self-directed Team. Teams meet regularly to discuss issues, solve problems and appreciate each others' contributions. Every Team Member belongs to a Team.
- **Open & Timely Information**—We believe knowledge is power and we support our Team Members' right to access information that impacts their jobs. Our books are open to our Team Members, including our annual individual compensation report. We also recognize everyone's right to be listened to and heard regardless of their point of view.
- **Incremental Progress**—Our company continually improves through unleashing the collective creativity and intelligence of all of our Team Members. We recognize that everyone has a contribution to make. We keep getting better at what we do.
- **Shared Fate**—We recognize there is a community of interest among all of our stakeholders. There are no entitlements; we share together in our collective fate. To that end we have a salary cap that limits the compensation (wages plus profit incentive bonuses) of any Team Member to fourteen times the average total compensation of all full-time Team Members in the company.

(Continued)

Exhibit 3   **Continued**

Creating Wealth Through Profits & Growth

- **Stewardship**—We are stewards of our shareholders' investments and we take that responsibility very seriously. We are committed to increasing long term shareholder value.
- **Profits**—We earn our profits everyday through voluntary exchange with our customers. We recognize that profits are essential to creating capital for growth, prosperity, opportunity, job satisfaction and job security.

Caring About Our Communities & Our Environment

- **Sustainable Agriculture**—We support organic farmers, growers and the environment through our commitment to sustainable agriculture and by expanding the market for organic products.
- **Wise Environmental Practices**—We respect our environment and recycle, reuse, and reduce our waste wherever and whenever we can.
- **Community Citizenship**—We recognize our responsibility to be active participants in our local communities. We give a minimum of 5% of our profits every year to a wide variety of community and non-profit organizations. In addition, we pay our Team Members to give of their time to community and service organizations.
- **Integrity in All Business Dealings**—Our trade partners are our allies in serving our stakeholders. We treat them with respect, fairness and integrity at all times and expect the same in return.

Source: Information posted at www.wholefoodsmarket.com (accessed November 29, 2005).

in varying stages of development (the new stores of supermarket chains like Safeway and Kroger averaged around 55,000 square feet).

Most stores were in high-traffic shopping locations, some were freestanding, and some were in strip centers. Whole Foods had its own internally developed model to analyze potential markets according to education levels, population density, and income. After picking a target metropolitan area, the company's site consultant did a comprehensive site study and developed sales projections; potential sites had to pass certain financial hurdles. New stores opened 12 to 24 months after a lease was signed.

The cash investment needed to ready a new Whole Foods Market for opening varied with the metropolitan area, site characteristics, store size, and amount of work performed by the landlord; totals ranged from as little as $2 million to as much as $16 million—the average for the past five years was $8.6 million. In addition to the cost of readying a

Exhibit 4   **Major Acquisitions by Whole Foods Market**

Year	Company Acquired	Location	Number of Stores	Acquisition Costs
1992	Bread & Circus	Northeast United States	6	$20 million plus $6.2 million in common stock
1993	Mrs. Gooch's	Southern California	7	2,970,596 shares of common stock
1996	Fresh Fields Markets	East Coast and Chicago area	22	4.8 million shares of stock plus options for 549,000 additional shares
1997	Merchant of Vino	Detroit area	6	Approximately 1 million shares of common stock
1997	Bread of Life	South Florida	2	200,000 shares of common stock
1999	Nature's Heartland	Boston area	4	$24.5 million in cash
2000	Food 4 Thought (Natural Abilities Inc.)	Sonoma County, California	3	$25.7 million in cash, plus assumption of certain liabilities
2001	Harry's Farmer's Market	Atlanta	3	Approximately $35 million in cash
2004	Fresh & Wild	Great Britain	7	$20 million in cash plus 239,000 shares of common stock

Source: Investor relations section of www.wholefoodsmarket.com (accessed November 18, 2004).

Exhibit 5   **Number of Stores in the Whole Foods Markets Chain, 1991–2005, and Selected Store Operating Statistics, 2000–2005**

Year	Number of Stores at End of Fiscal Year
1991	10
1992	25
1993	42
1994	49
1995	61
1996	68
1997	75
1998	87
1999	100
2000	117
2001	126
2002	135
2003	145
2004	163
2005	178

Store Counts	1998	1999	2000	2001	2002	2003	2004	2005
Beginning of fiscal year	75	87	100	117	126	135	145	163
New stores opened	9	9	17	12	11	12	12	15
Stores acquired	6	5	3	0	3	0	7	0
Relocations and closures	(2)	(3)	(1)	(3)	(3)	(5)	(2)	(1)
End of fiscal year	87	100	117	126	135	145	163	178

	Fiscal Year					
	2000	2001	2002	2003	2004	2005
Store sales (000s)	$1,838,630	$2,272,231	$2,690,475	$3,148,593	$3,864,950	$4,701,289
Average weekly sales	$324,710	$353,024	$392,837	$424,095	$482,061	$536,986
Comparable store sales growth	8.6%	9.2%	10.0%	8.6%	14.9%	12.8%
Total square footage of all stores, end of year	3,180,207	3,598,469	4,098,492	4,545,433	5,145,261	5,819,843
Average store size, end of year, in square feet	27,181	28,559	30,359	31,348	31,566	33,200
Gross margin, all-store average	34.5%	34.7%	34.6%	34.2%	34.2%	35.1%
Store contribution, all-store average*	9.4%	9.5%	9.6%	9.2%	9.3%	9.6%

*Defined as gross profit minus direct store expenses, where gross profit equals store revenues less cost of goods sold.

Source: Information posted at www.wholefoodsmarket.com (accessed November 18, 2004, and November 29, 2005).

store for operation, it took approximately $750,000 to stock the store with inventory, a portion of which was financed by vendors. Preopening expenses had averaged approximately $600,000 per store over the past five years.

Product Line

While product and brand selections varied from store to store (because of differing store sizes and clientele), Whole Foods' product line included some 30,000 natural, organic, and gourmet food and non-food items:

- Fresh produce—fruits and vegetables; displays of fresh-cut fruits; and a selection of seasonal, exotic, and specialty products like cactus pears and cippolini onions.

- Meat and poultry—natural and organic meats, house-made sausages, and poultry products from animals raised on wholesome grains, pastureland, and well water (and not grown with the use of by-products, hormones, or steroids).

- Fresh seafood—a selection of fresh fish; shrimp; oysters; clams; mussels; homemade marinades; and exotic items like octopus, sushi, and black-tip shark. A portion of the fresh fish selections at the seafood station came from the company's Pigeon Cove and Select Fish seafood processing subsidiaries. Seafood items coming from distant supply sources were flown in to stores to ensure maximum freshness.

- A selection of daily baked goods—breads, cakes, pies, cookies, bagels, muffins, and scones.

- Prepared foods—soups, canned and packaged goods, oven-ready meals, rotisserie meats, hearth-fired pizza, pastas, patés, salad bars, a sandwich station, and a selection of entrées and side foods prepared daily.

- Fine-quality cheeses, olives (up to 40 varieties in some stores), and chocolates and confections.

- Frozen foods, juices, yogurt and dairy products, smoothies, and bottled waters.

- A wide selection of bulk items in bins.

- Beer and wines—the selection of domestic and imported wines varied from store to store; organic wines were among those available.

- A body care and nutrition department containing a wide selection of natural and organic body care and cosmetics products, along with assorted vitamin supplements, homeopathic remedies, yoga supplies, and aromatherapy products. All items entailed the use of non-animal testing methods and contained no artificial ingredients.

- Natural and organic pet foods (including the company's own private-label line), treats, toys, and pest control remedies.

- Grocery and household products—canned and packaged goods, pastas, soaps, cleaning products, and other conventional household items. Whole Foods' larger stores stocked conventional household products in order to make Whole Foods a one-stop grocery-shopping destination.

- A floral department with sophisticated flower bouquets.

- A 365 Every Day Value line of private-label products that included over 440 items at very competitive price points, a 365 Organic line consisting of 200 items, a 29-item Whole X line of best-of-class premium and superpremium organic products, and a 50-item organic food product line developed for children under the Whole Kids label. Most recently, the company had begun using four other private brands—Whole Catch (for frozen seafood selections), Whole Ranch (for frozen meats), Whole Treats (for candies, cookies, and frozen desserts), and Whole Kitchen (a wide selection of frozen entrées and appetizers).

- Educational products (information on alternative health care) and books relating to healing, cookery, diet, and lifestyle. In some stores, there were cooking classes and nutrition sessions.

Whole Foods was the world's biggest seller of organic produce. Perishables accounted for about 65 percent of Whole Foods' sales, considerably higher than the 40–50 percent that perishables represented at conventional supermarkets. The acquisition of the three 75,000-plus-square-foot Harry's Market superstores in Atlanta, where 75 percent of sales were perishables, had provided the company with personnel having valuable intellectual capital in creatively merchandising all major perishables categories. Management believed that the company's emphasis on fresh fruits and vegetables, bakery goods, meats, seafood, and other perishables differentiated Whole Foods stores from other supermarkets and attracted a broader customer base. According to John Mackey:

First-time visitors to Whole Foods Market are often awed by our perishables. We devote more space to fresh fruits and vegetables, including an extensive selection of organics, than most of our competitors. Our meat and poultry products are natural—no artificial ingredients, minimal processing, and raised without the use of artificial growth hormones, antibiotics or animal by-products in their feed. Our seafood is either wild-caught or sourced from aquaculture farms where environmental concerns are a priority. Also, our seafood is never treated with chlorine or other chemicals, as is common practice in the food retailing industry. With each new store or renovation, we challenge ourselves to create more entertaining, theatrical, and scintillatingly appetizing prepared foods areas. We bake daily, using whole grains and unbleached, unbromated flour and feature European-style loaves, pastries, cookies and cakes as well as gluten-free baked goods for those allergic to wheat. We also offer many vegetarian and vegan products for our customers seeking to avoid all animal products. Our cheeses are free of artificial flavors, colors, and synthetic preservatives, and we offer an outstanding variety of both organic cheeses and cheeses made using traditional methods.[6]

Whole Foods' three-story showcase Union Square store in Manhattan carried locally made New York offerings, seasonal items from the nearby Greenmarket farmers' market, and numerous exotic and gourmet items. A 28-foot international section featured such items as Lebanese fig jam, preserved lemons from Morocco, Indian curries, Thai rice, stuffed grape leaves from Greece, and goulash from Hungary. The prepared foods section had a Grilling Station where shoppers could get grilled-to-order dishes such as swordfish in red pepper Romesco sauce and steak with a mushroom demi-glace.

One of Whole Foods Market's foremost commitments to its customers was to sell foods that met strict standards and that were of high quality in terms of nutrition, freshness, appearance, and taste. (Exhibit 6 shows the company's quality standards.) Whole Foods guaranteed 100 percent satisfaction on all items purchased and went to great lengths to live up to its core value of satisfying and delighting customers. Buyers personally visited the facilities of many of the company's suppliers and were very picky about the items they chose and the ingredients they contained. For the benefit of prospective food suppliers, the company maintained a list of ingredients it considered unacceptable in food products (see Exhibit 6).

Pricing

Because the costs of growing and marketing organic foods ran 25 to 75 percent more than those of conventionally grown items, prices at Whole Foods were higher than at conventional supermarkets. For the most part, Whole Foods sold premium products at premium prices. Because the prices for price-sensitive consumers and some media critics had dubbed Whole Foods as "Whole Paycheck," chiefly because some of its exotic items had eye-popping price tags—for example, Graffitti eggplants grown in Holland were $4 per pound, lobster mushrooms from Oregon were $25 per pound, and a three-ounce can of organic pearl jasmine tea was $14.[7] Its earth-friendly detergents, toilet papers, and other household items frequently were priced higher than the name brands of comparable products found in traditional supermarkets. However, as one analyst noted, "If people believe that the food is healthier and they are doing something good for themselves, they are willing to invest a bit more, particularly as they get older. It's not a fad."[8] Another grocery industry analyst noted that while Whole Foods served a growing niche, it had managed to attract a new kind of customer, one who was willing to pay a premium to dabble in health food without being totally committed to vegetarianism or an organic lifestyle.[9]

Store Description and Merchandising

Whole Foods Market did not have a standard store design. Instead, each store's layout was customized to fit the particular site and building configuration and to best show off the particular product mix for the store's target clientele. For instance, the new 78,000-square-foot Austin store opened in March 2005 was already a top Central Texas tourist destination and downtown Austin landmark; it had an intimate village-style layout; six mini-restaurants within the store; a raw food and juice bar; more than 600 varieties of cheese and 40 varieties of olives; a selection of 1,800 wines; a Candy Island with handmade lollipops and popcorn balls; a hot nut bar with an in-house nut roaster; a World Foods section; a walk-in beer cooler with 800 selections; 14 pastry chefs making a variety of items; a Natural Home

Exhibit 6   **Whole Foods Market's Product Quality Standards
and Customer Commitments**

Our business is to sell the highest quality foods we can find at the most competitive prices possible. We evaluate quality in terms of nutrition, freshness, appearance, and taste. Our search for quality is a never-ending process involving the careful judgment of buyers throughout the company.

- We carefully evaluate each and every product we sell.
- We feature foods that are free from artificial preservatives, colors, flavors and sweeteners.
- We are passionate about great tasting food and the pleasure of sharing it with each other.
- We are committed to foods that are fresh, wholesome and safe to eat.
- We seek out and promote organically grown foods.
- We provide food and nutritional products that support health and well-being.

Whole Foods Market's Quality Standards team maintains an extensive list of unacceptable ingredients (see below). However, creating a product with no unacceptable ingredients does not guarantee that Whole Foods Market will sell it. Our buyers are passionate about seeking out the freshest, most healthful, minimally processed products available.

As of December 2005, the following 83 chemicals were on Whole Foods' list of unacceptable ingredients:

- acesulfame-K (acesulfame potassium)
- acetylated esters of mono- and diglycerides
- ammonium chloride
- artificial colors
- artificial flavors
- aspartame
- azodicarbonamide
- benzoates in food
- benzoyl peroxide
- BHA (butylated hydroxyanisole)
- BHT (butylated hydroxytoluene)
- bleached flour
- bromated flour
- brominated vegetable oil (BVO)
- calcium bromate
- calcium disodium EDTA
- calcium peroxide
- calcium propionate
- calcium saccharin
- calcium sorbate
- calcium stearoyl-2-lactylate
- caprocaprylobehenin
- carmine (see cochineal)
- certified colors
- cochineal (carmine)
- cyclamates
- cysteine (l-cysteine), as an additive for bread products
- DATEM (diacetyl tartaric and fatty acid esters of mono and diglycerides)
- dimethylpolysiloxane

- dioctyl sodium sulfosuccinate (DSS)
- disodium calcium EDTA
- disodium dihydrogen EDTA
- disodium guanylate
- disodium inosinate
- EDTA
- ethyl vanillin
- ethylene oxide
- ethyoxyquin
- FD & C colors
- fois gras
- GMP (disodium guanylate)
- hexa-, hepta- and octa-esters of sucrose
- hydrogenated oil
- IMP (disodium inosinate)
- irradiated foods
- lactylated esters of mono- and diglycerides
- lead soldered cans
- methyl silicon
- methylparaben
- microparticularized whey protein derived fat substitute
- monosodium glutamate (MSG)
- natamyacin
- nitrates/nitrites
- partially hydrogenated oil
- polydextrose
- potassium benzoate

- potassium bisulfite
- potassium bromate
- potassium metabisulfite
- potassium sorbate
- propionates
- propyl gallate
- propylparaben
- saccharin
- sodium aluminum phosphate
- sodium aluminum sulfate
- sodium benzoate
- sodium bisulfite
- sodium diacetate
- sodium glutamate
- sodium metabisulfite
- sodium nitrate/nitrite
- sodium propionate
- sodium stearoyl-2-lactylate
- sodium sulfite
- solvent extracted oils, as standalone single-ingredient oils (except grapeseed oil)
- sorbic acid
- sucralose
- sucroglycerides
- sucrose polyester
- sulfites (sulfur dioxide)
- TBHQ (tertiary butylhydroquinone)
- tetrasodium EDTA
- vanillin

Whole Foods reserved the right to alter its list of unacceptable ingredients at any time.

Source: Information posted at www.wholefoodsmarket.com (accessed November 29, 2005).

section with organic cotton apparel and household linens; an extensive meat department with an in-house smoker and 50 oven-ready items prepared by in-house chefs; and a theater-like seafood department with more than 150 fresh seafood items and on-the-spot shucking, cooking, smoking, slicing, and frying to order. The Columbus Circle store in Manhattan had a 248-seat café where shoppers could enjoy restaurant-quality prepared foods while relaxing in a comfortable community setting; a Jamba Juice smoothie station that served freshly blended-to-order fruit smoothies and juices; a full-service sushi bar by Genji Express where customers sat on bar stools wrapped in nori enjoying fresh-cut sushi wrapped in organic seaweed; a walk-in greenhouse showcasing fresh-cut and exotic flowers; a wine shop with more than 700 varieties of wine from both large and small vineyards and family estates; and a chocolate enrobing station in the bakery where customers could request just about anything covered in chocolate.

The driving concept of Whole Foods' merchandising strategy was to create an inviting and interactive store atmosphere that turned shopping for food into a fun, pleasurable experience. Management at Whole Foods wanted customers to view company stores as a "third place" (besides home and office) where people could gather, learn, and interact while at the same time enjoying an intriguing food-shopping and eating experience. Stores had a colorful decor, and products were attractively merchandised (see Exhibit 7). According to one industry analyst, Whole Foods had "put together the ideal model for the foodie who's a premium gourmet and the natural foods buyer. When you walk into a Whole Foods store, you're overwhelmed by a desire to look at everything you see."[10]

Most stores featured hand-stacked produce, in-store chefs and open kitchens, scratch bakeries, prepared foods stations, European-style charcuterie departments, Whole Body departments with a wide selection of natural cosmetics (as well as a makeup station) and personal care items, salad bars, sit-down dining areas, gourmet food sections with items from around the world, and ever-changing selections and merchandise displays. Many stores had recipe cards at the end of key aisles. A few stores offered valet parking, home delivery, and massages. Management believed that the extensive and attractive displays of fresh produce, seafood, meats and house-made sausages (up to 40 varieties), baked goods, and prepared foods in its larger stores appealed to a broader customer base and were responsible for the stores bigger than 30,000 square feet showing higher performance than the smaller stores.

Whole Foods got very high marks from merchandising experts and customers for its presentation—from the bright colors of the produce displays, to the quality of the foods and customer service, to the wide aisles and cleanliness. Management was continually experimenting with new merchandising concepts to keep stores fresh and exciting for customers. According to a Whole Foods regional manager, "We take the best ideas from each of our stores and try to incorporate them in all our other stores. We're constantly making our stores better."[11] Whole Foods' merchandising skills were said to be a prime factor in its success in luring shoppers back time and again—Whole Foods stores had annual sales averaging more than $800 per square foot of space about double the sales per square foot of Kroger and Safeway.

To further a sense of community and interaction with customers, stores typically included customer comment boards and Take Action centers for customers who wanted information on such topics as sustainable agriculture, organics, the sustainability of seafood supplies and overfishing problems, and the environment in general. The Toronto store had biographies of farmers suspended from the ceiling on placards and a board calling attention to Whole Foods' Sustainable Seafood Policy hung above the seafood station.

Marketing and Customer Service

Whole Foods spent about 0.5 percent of its revenues on advertising, a much smaller percentage than conventional supermarkets spent, preferring instead to rely primarily on word-of-mouth recommendations from customers. The corporate marketing budget was allocated to regionwide programs, marketing efforts for individual stores, a national brand awareness initiative, and consumer research. Stores spent most of their marketing budgets on in-store signage and store events such as taste fairs, classes, and product samplings. Store personnel were encouraged to extend company efforts to encourage the adoption of a natural and organic lifestyle by going out into the community and conducting a proactive public relations campaign. Each store also had a separate

Exhibit 7   **Scenes from Whole Foods Stores**

budget for making contributions to philanthropic activities and community outreach programs.

Since one of its core values was to satisfy and delight customers (see Exhibit 3), Whole Foods Market strove to meet or exceed customer expectations on every shopping trip. Competent, knowledgeable, and friendly service was a hallmark of shopping at a Whole Foods Market. The aim was to turn highly satisfied customers into advocates for Whole Foods who talked to close friends and acquaintances about their positive experiences with the company. Store personnel were personable and chatty with shoppers. Customers could get personal attention in every department of the store. When customers asked where an item was located, team members often took them to the spot, making conversation along the way and offering to answer any questions. Team members were quite knowledgeable and enthusiastic about the products in their particular department and tried to take advantage of opportunities to inform and educate customers about natural foods, organics, healthy eating, and food-related environmental issues. They took pride in helping customers navigate the extensive variety to make the best choices. Meat department personnel provided customers with custom cuts, cooking instructions, and personal recommendations.

Store Operations

Depending on store size and traffic volume, Whole Foods stores employed between 80 and 500 team members, who were organized into up to 11 teams, each led by a team leader. Each team within a store was responsible for a different product category or aspect of store operations such as customer service and customer check-out stations. Team leaders screened candidates for job openings on their team, but a two-thirds majority of the team had to approve a new hire—approval came only after a 30-day trial for the candidate.

Whole Foods practiced a decentralized team approach to store operations, with many personnel, merchandising, and operating decisions made by teams at the individual store level. Management believed that the decentralized structure made it critical to have an effective store team leader. The store team leader worked with one or more associate store team leaders, as well as with all the department team leaders, to operate the store as efficiently and profitably as possible. Store team leaders were paid a salary plus a bonus based on the store's economic value added

(EVA) contribution; they were also eligible to receive stock options.[12] Store team leaders reported directly to one of the 10 regional presidents.

Management believed its team members were inspired by the company's mission because it complemented their own views about the benefits of a natural and organic foods diet. In management's view, many Whole Foods team members felt good about their jobs because they saw themselves as contributing to the welfare of society and to the company's customers by selling clean and nutritious foods, by helping advance the cause of long-term sustainable agriculture methods, and by promoting a healthy, pesticide-free environment.

In December 2005, the company had some 32,000 team members, of which approximately 86 percent were full-time. None were represented by unions, although there had been a couple of unionization attempts. John Mackey was viewed as fiercely anti-union and had once said: "The union is like having herpes. It doesn't kill you, but it's unpleasant and inconvenient and it stops a lot of people from becoming your lover."[13] Union leaders were critical of the company's anti-union stance and a Web site (www.wholeworkersunite.org) was devoted to criticizing Mackey, explaining why unionization was good for Whole Foods employees, and compiling instances of the company's anti-union actions. A second Web site (www.michaelbluejay.com) touted so-called scandals at Whole Foods; the material consisted of two articles from publications that criticized Whole Foods' wage rates and Mackey's anti-union stance.

Whole Foods had been ranked by *Fortune* magazine for eight consecutive years (1998–2006) as one of the top 100 companies to work for in America—Whole Foods was one of only 22 companies to make the list every year since its inception. Whole Foods was the only national supermarket chain to ever make the list, although the regional supermarket chain Wegman's was the top-ranked company on the 2005 list. (In scoring companies, *Fortune* places a two-thirds weight on responses to a random survey of employees and a one-third weight on its evaluation of a company's benefits and practices.) A team member at Whole Foods' store in Austin, Texas, said, "I really feel like we're a part of making the world a better place. When I joined the company 17 years ago, we only had four stores. I have always loved—as a customer and now as a Team Member—the camaraderie, support for others, and progressive atmosphere at Whole Foods Market."[14] According to the company's vice president of human resources, "Team members who love to take initiative, while enjoying working as part of a team and being rewarded through shared fate, thrive here."

During 2002, team members across the company actively contributed ideas about the benefits they would like the company to offer; the suggestions were compiled and, through three subsequent votes, put into package form. The benefits plan that was adopted for three years was approved by 83 percent of the 79 percent of the team members participating in the benefits vote. Under the adopted plan, each team member could select his or her own benefits package. The resulting health insurance plan that the company put in place in January 2003 involved the company paying 100 percent of the premium for full-time employees and the establishment of company-funded "personal wellness accounts" that team members could use to pay the higher deductibles; any unused balances in a team member's account could roll over and accumulate for future expenses. Whole Foods expected to repeat its benefits vote every three years.

Every year, management gave team members an opportunity to complete a morale survey covering job satisfaction, opportunity and empowerment, pay, training, and benefits. In 2004, the overall participation rate was 63 percent (versus 71 percent in 2003). Of the team members responding in 2004, 86 percent said they almost always or frequently enjoyed their job (the same percentage as in 2003), and 82 percent said they almost always or frequently felt empowered to do their best work at Whole Foods Market (up slightly from 81 percent in 2003). In response to the question "What is the best thing about working at Whole Foods Market?" common responses included coworkers, customers, flexibility, work environment, growth and learning opportunities, the products Whole Foods sold, benefits, the team concept, and the culture of empowerment.

Compensation and Incentives

Whole Foods' management strove to create a "shared-fate consciousness" on the part of team members by uniting the self-interests of team members with those of shareholders. One way management reinforced this concept was through a gain-sharing program that rewarded a store's team members according to their store's contribution to operating profit (store sales less

cost of goods sold less store operating expenses)—gain-sharing distributions added 5–7 percent to team member wages. The company also encouraged stock ownership on the part of team members through three other programs:

1. *A team member stock option plan*—Team members were eligible for stock options based on seniority, promotion, or the discretion of regional or national executives. Roughly 85 percent of the company's stock options in 2004 were held by non-executives.

2. *A team member stock purchase plan*—Team members could purchase a restricted number of shares at a discount from the market price through payroll deductions.

3. *A team member 401(k) plan*—Whole Foods Market stock was one of the investment options in the 401(k) plan.

All the teams at each store were continuously evaluated on measures relating to sales, operations, and morale; the results were made available to team members and to headquarters personnel.[15] Teams competed not only against the goals they had set for themselves but also against other teams at their stores or in their region—competition among teams was encouraged. In addition, stores went through two review processes—a store tour and a "customer snapshot." Each store was toured periodically and subjected to a rigorous evaluation by a group of 40 personnel from another region; the group included region heads, store team leaders, associate team leaders, and leaders from two operating teams. Customer snapshots involved a surprise inspection by a headquarters official or regional president who rated the store on 300 items; each store had 10 surprise inspections annually, with the results distributed to every store and included in the reward system. Rewards were team-based and tied to performance metrics—all compensation was publicly disclosed.

Whole Foods had a salary cap that limited the compensation (wages plus profit incentive bonuses) of any team member to 14 times the average total compensation of all full-time team members in the company—a policy mandated in the company's core values (see Exhibit 3). The salary cap was raised from 10 to 14 times the average total compensation in 2005—it had been 8 times in 2003; the increases stemmed from the need to attract and retain key executives. For example, if the average total compensation was $50,000, then a cap of

10 times the average meant that an executive could not be paid more than $500,000. Such an amount was below top-level salaries at companies of comparable size and growing as rapidly as Whole Foods. In 2005, the average annual compensation was $73,061 for salaried workers and $25,451 for hourly workers. Any employee could look up anyone else's pay.

Promotions were primarily from within, with people often moving up to assume positions at stores soon to be opened or at stores in other regions.

The Use of Economic Value Added   In 1999, Whole Foods adopted an economic value added (EVA) management and incentive system. EVA is defined as net operating profits after taxes minus a charge for the cost of capital necessary to generate that profit. EVA at the store level was based on store contribution (store revenues minus cost of goods sold minus store operating expenses) relative to store investment over and above the cost of capital—see Exhibit 5 for average store contribution percentages. Senior executives managed the company with the goal of *improving* EVA at the store level and companywide; they believed that an EVA-based bonus system was the best financial framework for team members to use in helping make decisions that created sustainable shareholder value. The teams in all stores were challenged to find ways to boost store contribution and EVA—the team member bonuses paid on EVA improvement averaged 6 percent in 2003.

In 2005, over 500 senior executives, regional managers, and the store leaders were on EVA-based incentive compensation plans. The primary measure for payout was EVA improvement. In fiscal year 2001, the company's overall EVA was a negative $30.4 million, but companywide EVA was $2.6 million in fiscal 2003, $15.6 million in fiscal 2004, and a record $25.8 million in 2005.

In addition, management used EVA calculations to determine whether the sales and profit projections for new stores would yield a positive and large enough EVA to justify the investment; EVA was also used to guide decisions on store closings and to evaluate new acquisitions.

Purchasing and Distribution

Whole Foods' buyers purchased most of the items retailed in the company's stores from local, regional, and national wholesale suppliers and vendors. In recent years, the company had shifted much of the buying responsibility from the store level to the regional and national levels in order to put the company in a better position to negotiate volume discounts with major vendors and distributors. Whole Foods Market was the largest account for many suppliers of natural and organic foods. United Natural Foods was the company's biggest supplier, accounting for about 20 percent of Whole Foods' purchases.

Whole Foods owned two produce procurement centers and procured and distributed the majority of its produce itself. However, where feasible, local store personnel sourced produce items from local organic farmers as part of the company's commitment to promote and support organic farming methods. Two subsidiaries, the Pigeon Cove seafood processing facility in Massachusetts and Select Fish, a West Coast seafood processing facility, supplied a portion of the company's seafood requirements. A regional seafood distribution facility had recently been established in Atlanta.

The company operated eight regional distribution centers to supply its stores. The largest distribution center in Austin supplied a full range of natural products to the company's stores in Texas, Louisiana, Colorado, Kansas, and New Mexico; the other seven regional centers distributed mainly produce and private-label goods to area stores. Twelve regional bake houses and five regional commissary kitchens supplied area stores with various prepared foods. A central coffee-roasting operation supplied stores with the company's Allegro brand of coffees.

Community Citizenship and Social Activism

Whole Foods demonstrated its social conscience and community citizenship in two ways: (1) by donating at least 5 percent of its after-tax profits in cash or products to nonprofit or educational organizations and (2) by giving each team member 20 hours of paid community service hours to use for volunteer work for every 2,000 hours worked. Team members at every store were heavily involved in such community citizenship activities as sponsoring blood donation drives, preparing meals for seniors and the homeless, holding fund-raisers to help the disadvantaged, growing vegetables for a domestic violence shelter, participating in housing renovation projects, and working as deliverypeople for Meals on Wheels.

Further, John Mackey indicated the company was sincere in living up to its core values as they related to healthy eating habits and protection of environmental ecosystems. In an effort to "walk the talk," Mackey had initiated the gathering of information about key issues that could affect people's health and well-being—the genetic engineering of food supplies, food irradiation practices, and the organic standards process; Whole Foods disseminated this information via in-store brochures, presentations to groups, and postings on its Web site. Mackey had also charged company personnel with developing position statements on sustainable seafood practices (see Exhibit 8), the merits of organic farming, and wise environmental practices. Whole Foods regularly publicized its position statements in its stores and on its Web site, along with the company's commitment to selling only those meats that had been raised without the use of growth hormones, antibiotics, and animal by-products. Company personnel were conscientious in identifying and implementing "green" actions on Whole Foods' part that enhanced the health of the planet's ecosystems. The company's Web site had a legislative action center that alerted people to pending legislation on these types of issues and made it easy for them to send their comments and opinions to legislators and government officials.

In 2004, *Business Ethics* named Whole Foods Market to its list "100 Best Corporate Citizens."

Whole Foods Market's Financial Performance

From 1991 to 2005, Whole Foods Market's net income rose at a compound average rate of 37.4 percent. The company had been profitable every year except one since 1991, when it became a public company. The one money-losing year in 2000, which involved a net loss of $8.5 million, stemmed from a decision to divest a nutritional supplement business and losses in two affiliated dot-com enterprises (Gaiam.com and WholePeople.com) in which Whole Foods owned a minority interest. The company's stock price had jumped from $30 in December 2000 to $152.50 as of December 1, 2005, and was set for a 2-for-1 stock split in January 2006.

Whole Foods paid its first quarterly dividend of $0.15 per share in January 2004; the quarterly dividend was increased to $0.19 per share in January 2005, to $0.25 per share in April 2005, and to $0.30 per share starting in January 2006 (before the scheduled stock split). The company's business was generating strong, positive cash flows. In fiscal 2004, for instance, cash flow from operations was $330 million, allowing Whole Foods to self-fund $265 million in capital expenditures (of which $155 million was for new stores) and cover cash outlays of $28 million for dividends. In fiscal 2005, Whole Foods realized $411 million in cash flow from operations, which more than covered $324 million

Exhibit 8 **Whole Foods' Position on Seafood Sustainability**

The simple fact is our oceans are soon to be in trouble. Our world's fish stocks are disappearing from our seas because they have been overfished or harvested using damaging fishing practices. To keep our favorite seafood plentiful for us to enjoy and to keep it around for future generations, we must act now.

As a shopper, you have the power to turn the tide. When you purchase seafood from fisheries using ocean-friendly methods, you reward their actions and encourage other fisheries to operate responsibly.

At Whole Foods Market, we demonstrate our long-term commitment to seafood preservation by:

- Supporting fishing practices that ensure the ecological health of the ocean and the abundance of marine life.
- Partnering with groups who encourage responsible practices and provide the public with accurate information about the issue.
- Operating our own well-managed seafood facility and processing plant, Pigeon Cove Seafood, located in Gloucester, Massachusetts.
- Helping educate our customers on the importance of practices that can make a difference now and well into the future.
- Promoting and selling the products of well-managed fisheries.

Source: Information posted at www.wholefoodsmarket.com (accessed November 26, 2004).

Exhibit 9   **Whole Foods Market, Statement of Operations, Fiscal Years 2002–2005 (in thousands)**

	Fiscal Year 2005	Fiscal Year 2004	Fiscal Year 2003	Fiscal Year 2002
Sales	$4,701,289	$3,864,950	$3,148,593	$2,690,475
Cost of goods sold and occupancy costs	3,048,870	2,523,816	2,070,334	1,758,281
Gross profit	1,652,419	1,341,134	1,078,259	932,194
Direct store expenses	1,199,870	986,040	794,422	677,704
Store contribution	452,549	355,094	283,837	254,490
General and administrative expenses	149,364	119,800	100,693	95,871
Share-based compensation*	19,896			
Pre-opening and relocation costs	37,035	18,648	15,765	17,934
Natural disaster costs†	16,521	—	—	—
Operating income	229,733	216,646	167,379	140,985
Interest expense, net	2,223	7,249	8,114	10,384
Investment and other income (loss)	9,623	6,456	5,593	2,056
Income before income taxes	237,133	215,853	164,858	132,657
Provision for income taxes	100,782	86,341	65,943	53,063
Net income	$ 136,351	$ 129,512	$ 98,915	$ 79,594
Basic earnings per share	$2.10	$2.11	$1.68	$1.41
Weighted average shares outstanding	65,045	61,324	59,035	56,385
Diluted earnings per share	$1.98	$1.98	$1.58	$1.32
Weighted average shares outstanding, diluted basis	69,975	67,727	65,330	63,340

*The company began expensing the costs of stock option compensation in 2005.

†Costs associated with damage to two stores in New Orleans resulting from Hurricane Katrina.

Sources: Company press release, November 9, 2005, and 2004 10K/A report.

in capital expenditures (of which $208 million was related to opening new stores) and dividend payments of $55 million. During fiscal 2005, Whole Foods also reduced its long-term debt from $164.7 million to $12.9 million. Exhibits 9 and 10 present the company's recent statements of operations and consolidated balance sheets.

COMPETITORS

The food retailing business was intensely competitive. The degree of competition Whole Foods faced varied from locality to locality, and to some extent from store location to store location within a given locale. Competitors included local, regional, and national supermarkets, along with specialty grocery stores and health and natural foods stores. Most supermarkets had offered at least a limited selection of natural and organic foods and some had chosen to expand their offerings aggressively. Whole Foods' executives had said it was to the company's benefit for conventional supermarkets to offer natural and organic foods for two reasons: First, it helped fulfill the company's mission of improving the health and well-being of people and the planet, and, second, it helped create new customers for Whole Foods by providing a gateway experience. They contended that as more

Exhibit 10   **Whole Foods Market, Consolidated Balance Sheet, Fiscal Years 2004–2005 (in thousands)**

	September 25, 2005	September 26, 2004
Assets		
Current assets:		
Cash and cash equivalents	$ 308,524	$ 194,747
Restricted cash	36,922	26,790
Trade accounts receivable	66,682	64,972
Merchandise inventories	174,848	152,912
Deferred income taxes	39,588	29,974
Prepaid expenses and other current assets	45,965	16,702
Total current assets	$ 672,529	$ 486,097
Property and equipment, net of accumulated depreciation and amortization	1,054,605	873,397
Goodwill	112,476	112,186
Intangible assets, net of accumulated amortization	21,990	24,831
Deferred income taxes	22,452	4,193
Other assets	5,244	20,302
Total assets	$1,889,296	$1,521,006
Liabilities and shareholders' equity		
Current liabilities:		
Current installments of long-term debt and capital lease obligations	$ 5,932	$ 5,973
Trade accounts payable	103,348	90,751
Accrued payroll, bonus and other benefits due team members	126,981	100,536
Dividends payable	17,208	9,361
Other current liabilities	164,914	128,329
Total current liabilities	$ 418,383	$ 334,950
Long-term debt and capital lease obligations, less current installments	12,932	164,770
Deferred rent liability	91,775	70,067
Other long-term liabilities	530	1,581
Total liabilities	$ 523,620	$ 571,368
Shareholders' equity:		
Common stock, no par value, 300,000 and 150,000 shares authorized; 68,009 and 62,771 shares issued; 67,954 and 62,407 shares outstanding in 2005 and 2004, respectively	874,972	535,107
Accumulated other comprehensive income	4,405	2,053
Retained earnings	486,299	412,478
Total shareholders' equity	$1,365,676	$ 949,638
Commitments and contingencies		
Total liabilities and shareholders' equity	$1,889,296	$1,521,006

Source: Company press release, November 9, 2005.

people were exposed to natural and organic products, they were more likely to become a Whole Foods customer because Whole Foods was the category leader for natural and organic products, offered the largest selection at competitive prices, and provided the most well-informed customer service.

Whole Foods Market's two biggest competitors in the natural foods and organics segment of the food retailing industry were Wild Oats Markets and Fresh Market. Another competitor with some overlap in products and shopping ambience was Trader Joe's. Supervalu/Save-a-Lot, the ninth largest supermarket chain in North America (see Exhibit 2), had begun an initiative to launch a chain of small natural and organic foods stores called Sunflower Markets.

Wild Oats Markets

Wild Oats Markets—a 113-store natural foods chain based in Boulder, Colorado—ranked second behind Whole Foods in the natural foods and organics segment. The company's stores were in 24 states and British Columbia, Canada; stores were operated under four names: Wild Oats Natural Marketplace, Henry's Marketplace, Sun Harvest, and Capers Community Markets. Founded in 1987, Wild Oats had sales of $1.05 billion in 2004, up from $969 million in 2003. In 1993 and 1994, Wild Oats was named one of the "500 Fastest-Growing Private Companies in America" by *Inc.* magazine. Interest quickly spread to Wall Street, and in 1996 Wild Oats became a public company traded on the Nasdaq under the symbol OATS. Grocery analysts believed that Wild Oats had close to a 3 percent market share of the natural and organic foods market in 2000, compared to about 14 percent for Whole Foods.

Wild Oats' CEO, Perry Odak, formerly the CEO of Ben & Jerry's Homemade until it was acquired by Unilever in 2000, joined the company in 2001 and had launched a turnaround strategy, which was still in progress in 2005. The company's prior CEO and founder, Mike Gilliland, had gone on an aggressive acquisition streak during the late 1990s to expand Wild Oats' geographic coverage; store growth peaked in 1999 with the acquisition of 47 stores. But Gilliland's acquisition binge piled up extensive debt and dropped the company into a money-losing position with too many stores, a dozen different store names, and a dozen different ways of operating. Product selection

and customer service were inconsistent from one location to another.

When Odak arrived in March 2001, he streamlined operations, closed 28 unprofitable stores, cut prices, trimmed store staffing by 100 employees, and launched a new, smaller prototype store with a heavier emphasis on fresh food. Merchandising and marketing were revamped. The strategy was to draw in more "crossover" shoppers with lower-priced produce, meat, and seafood, along with a Fresh Look program stressing freshness and affordability to increase store traffic and raise the average purchase above the current $19 level. While the lower prices cut into the company's gross profit margin, management had tried to restore margins by concentrating purchases with fewer vendors and getting better discounts. An agreement was reached in September 2002 for Wild Oats to obtain a substantial part of its store inventories from Tree of Life, one of the leading natural foods distributors. Another of Odak's strategic thrusts was to drive a customer service mindset throughout the organization via training programs and enhanced employee communication. Odak wanted to position Wild Oats as a resource for value-added services and education about health and well-being. In 2002 Wild Oats sold close to 4.45 million shares at $11.50 to raise capital for opening 58 stores in the next three years (13 in 2003, 20 in 2004, and 25 in 2005) and remodeling a number of existing stores. While both Whole Foods and Wild Oats had stores in some of the same urban areas and were targeting some of the same areas for expansion, Wild Oats was targeting city and metropolitan neighborhoods for its new stores where there were no Whole Foods stores.

Wild Oats' new prototype stores were 22,000 to 24,000 square feet and featured a grocery-store layout where produce, dairy, meat, seafood, and baked goods were around the perimeters of the store), an expanded produce section at the front of the store, a deli, a sushi bar, a juice and java bar, a reduced selection of canned and packaged items, and store-within-a-store sections for supplements and specialty personal care products. Wild Oats had completed the remodeling of six stores (as part of its overall store remodeling initiative begun in 2003); it opened 12 new stores in 2004 and closed, sold, or relocated 7 others; it was planning to open 12 stores and remodel 10 others in 2005—both new store numbers were below the original target set when new shareholder capital had been raised in 2002. Wild Oats ended 2004 with 2.45 million square feet of floor space in its 113 stores (versus 5.8 million for Whole Foods); its expansion plans called for a total of 2.6 million square feet of floor space by year-end 2006. Also, in 2004, Wild Oats (1) completed a transition to using United Natural Foods as its primary distributor; (2) consolidated its smaller produce warehouse facilities into a single, 240,000-square-foot, state-of-the-art perishables distribution center in Riverside, California; and (3) completed the centralization and reorganization of its operations to improve efficiency. Like Whole Foods, Wild Oats was expanding its private-label offerings—400 Wild Oats and Henry's products were scheduled for introduction in 2005.

As was the case at Whole Foods, Perry Odak believed that while conventional supermarkets would continue to expand their offerings of natural and organic products, the competitive threat posed by conventional supermarkets was only moderate because their selection was more limited than what Wild Oats stores offered and because they lacked the knowledge and high level of service provided by a natural foods supermarket. In his view, "They are introducing conventional shoppers to natural brands, which will benefit us in the long run."

Wild Oats' sales in 2004 were adversely affected by conventional grocers' overly aggressive promotional activity in Southern California and by intense competition in Texas. This competition resulted in negative comparable store sales throughout the third quarter in approximately one-third of the company's store base. As a result, comparable store customer traffic in the third quarter of 2004 was a negative 4.1 percent. Wild Oats management took "aggressive action" in the form of lower prices and additional promotions to rebuild its customer traffic and sales in regions affected by intense competitive activity. But despite all of the moves that had been made under Perry Odak's leadership, the company was still struggling. After reporting losses of $15.0 million in 2000 before Odak became CEO, Wild Oats recorded losses of $43.9 million in 2001, net income of $5.1 million in 2002, net income of $1.6 million in 2003, and a loss of $40.0 million in 2004. It was expecting a small profit for 2005—through the first nine months of fiscal 2005, Wild Oats reported a small net loss of $148,000 on sales of $841.2 million

(compared to sales of $766.2 million in the first nine months of 2004). Gross margins (sales minus cost of goods sold) at Wild Oats averaged about 28.5 percent in 2002–2005, compared to 34.5 percent at Whole Foods (see Exhibit 5). Wild Oats stores averaged sales per square foot of about $440 annually versus just over $800 for Whole Foods.

Odak's latest initiatives to improve Wild Oats Markets' performance were to offer Wild Oats branded products in other retail environments. The company had reached agreement to test two alternative retail concepts. The first—a test in the Chicago market with Peapod, the country's leading Internet grocer—began in October 2004 and involved offering more than 200 private-label products on the Peapod site to consumers in the greater Chicago metropolitan area. The second, which began in June 2005, was a three-to-five store test of a Wild Oats branded store-within-a-store concept with Stop & Shop, the largest food retailer in the northeastern United States.

In a June 2004 financial move, Wild Oats sold $100 million in 3.25 percent convertible debentures to private investors; the debentures were convertible into Wild Oats common stock, at the option of the holders, at an initial price of $17.70 per share and could be redeemed starting in May 2011. Management intended to use proceeds of the offering to accelerate its growth plans, fund the repurchase of $25 million in common stock, and finance other "general corporate purposes." Wild Oats stock had traded in the $6–$16 range since 2002 and in December 2005 was trading in the $11–$13 range.

Fresh Market

Fresh Market, headquartered in Greensboro, North Carolina, was a 50-store chain operating in 12 southeastern and midwestern states (Alabama, Florida, Georgia, North Carolina, South Carolina, Tennessee, Virginia, Louisiana, Indiana, Illinois, Ohio, and Kentucky).[16] The company was founded by Ray Berry, a former vice president with Southland Corporation who had responsibility over some 3,600 7-Eleven stores. The first Fresh Market store opened in 1982 in Greensboro. Berry borrowed ideas from stores he had seen all over the United States and, as the chain expanded, used his convenience-store experience to replicate the store format and shape the product lines. During the 1982–2000 period, Fresh Market's sales revenues grew at a 25.2 percent compound rate, reaching $193 million in 2000; revenues were an estimated $280 million in 2004. Fresh Market's goal was to be the food destination store for people who enjoy cooking and good eating. The company was founded on the premise of getting customers to return again and again by offering quality products at reasonable prices and providing top-notch customer service.

Fresh Market's product line included meats, seafood, fresh produce, fresh-baked goods, prepared foods, 40 varieties of coffees, a selection of grocery and dairy items, bulk products, cheeses and deli meats, wine and beer, and floral and gift items. Fresh Market stores averaged 18,000 square feet and were located in neighborhoods near educated, high-income residents. Fresh Market differentiated itself with "upscale grocery boutique" items such as free-range chicken; pick-and-pack spices; gourmet coffees; chocolates; hard-to-get H&H bagels from New York City; Ferrara's New York cheesecake; fresh Orsini parmesan cheese; Acqua della Madonna bottled water; and an extended selection of olive oils, mustards, bulk products (granolas, nuts, beans, dried fruits, spices, and snack mixes), wine, and beer. Stores also stocked a small assortment of floral items and gifts (cookbooks, gift cards, cutting boards, and gift baskets) and a bare lineup of general grocery products. None of the meats and seafood and few of the deli products were prepackaged, and each department had at least one employee in the area constantly to help shoppers—the idea was to force interaction between store employees and shoppers. Fresh Market's warm lights, classical background music and terra-cotta-colored tiles made it a cozier place to shop than a typical grocery store. From time to time, stores had cooking classes, wine tastings, and food-sampling events. Fresh Market sponsored an annual fund-raiser for the Juvenile Diabetes Research Foundation called the Root Beer Float. The average store had 75 employees, resulting in labor costs about double those of typical supermarkets.

Merchandisers at Fresh Market's headquarters selected the stores' products, but store managers placed orders directly from third-party distributors. According to Berry, Fresh Market didn't have the concentration of stores that would make running its own warehouses profitable; Berry believed some grocers' distribution operations had grown so big that they drove the retail business, rather than the other way around.

Since 2000, the company had opened 3 to 5 new stores each year, but going forward the company planned to open 8 to 10 new stores annually. Expansion was funded by internal cash flows and bank debt. Financial data was not available because the company was privately owned, but Fresh Market's profitability was believed to be above the industry average. Several public companies had shown interest in buying the chain. In 2001 Ray Berry, then age 60, had said, "If I can get what I think the company's worth three years from now, I'll sell it. But I won't sell it for what it's worth today because I'm having too much fun."

Trader Joe's

Based in Pasadena, California, Trader Joe's was a specialty supermarket chain with over 200 stores in Arizona, California, Connecticut, Delaware, Illinois, Indiana, Maryland, Massachusetts, Michigan, Missouri, Nevada, New Jersey, New Mexico, New York, Ohio, Oregon, Pennsylvania, Virginia, and Washington. Management described the company's mission and business as follows:

At Trader Joe's, our mission is to bring our customers the best food and beverage values and the information to make informed buying decisions. There are more than 2000 unique grocery items in our label, all at honest everyday low prices. We work hard at buying things right: Our buyers travel the world searching for new items and we work with a variety of suppliers who make interesting products for us, many of them exclusive to Trader Joe's. All our private label products have their own "angle," i.e., vegetarian, Kosher, organic or just plain decadent, and all have minimally processed ingredients.

Customers tell us, "I never knew food shopping could be so much fun!" Some even call us "The home of cheap thrills!" We like to be part of our neighborhoods and get to know our customers. And where else do you shop that even the CEO, Dan Bane, wears a loud Hawaiian shirt.

Our tasting panel tastes every product before we buy it. If we don't like it, we don't buy it. If customers don't like it, they can bring it back for a no-hassle refund.

We stick to the business we know: good food at the best prices! Whenever possible we buy direct from our suppliers, in large volume. We bargain hard and manage our costs carefully. We pay in cash, and on time, so our suppliers like to do business with us.

Trader Joe's Crew Members are friendly, knowledgeable and happy to see their customers. They taste our items too, so they can discuss them with their customers. All our stores regularly cook up new and interesting products for our customers to sample.[17]

Plans called for ongoing development and introduction of new, one-of-a-kind food items at value prices, and continued expansion of store locations across the country.

Prices and product offerings varied somewhat by region and state. Customers could choose from a variety of baked goods, organic foods, fresh fruits and vegetables, imported and domestic cheeses, gourmet chocolates and candies, coffees, fresh salads, meatless entrées and other vegan products, low-fat and low-carbohydrate foods, frozen fish and seafood, heat-and-serve entrées, packaged meats, juices, wine and beer, snack foods, energy bars, vitamins, nuts and trail mixes, and whatever other exotic items the company's buyers had come upon. About 10–15 new, seasonal, or one-time-buy items were introduced each week. Products that weren't selling well were dropped. Trader Joe's had recently worked with its vendors to remove genetically modified ingredients from all of its private-label products. It had also discontinued sale of duck meat because of the cruel conditions under which ducks were grown.

Stores were open, with wide aisles, appealing displays, cedar plank walls, a nautical decor, and crew members wearing colorful Hawaiian shirts. Because of its combination of low prices, emporium-like atmosphere, intriguing selections, and friendly service, customers viewed shopping at Trader Joe's as an enjoyable experience. The company was able to keep the prices of its unique products attractively low (relative to those at Whole Foods, Fresh Market, and Wild Oats) partly because its buyers were always on the lookout for exotic items they could buy at a discount (all products had to pass a taste test and a cost test) and partly because most items were sold under the Trader Joe's label.

Sunflower Markets

Sunflower Markets, out to establish a discount niche in organic and natural foods, entered the market in 2003 with four stores—two in Phoenix, one in Albuquerque, and one in Denver.[18] As of November 2004 the company had opened three additional stores in Arizona and one in Colorado. Based in Longmont, Colorado, Sunflower's strategy borrowed from concepts employed by Trader Joe's and

small farmers' market–type stores. The company's mission statement described its four-pronged strategic approach:

- We Will Always Offer the Best Quality Food at the Lowest Prices in Town. "Better-than-supermarket quality at better-than-supermarket prices" is our motto.
- We Keep Our Overhead Low. No fancy fixtures or high rent. No corporate headquarters . . . just regular people, like you, looking for the best deals we can find.
- We Buy Big. We source directly, we pay our vendors quickly and we buy almost everything by the pallet or truckload. That buying power means big savings for you!
- We Keep It Simple. We don't charge our vendors "slotting allowances" or shelf space fees. Just honest-to-goodness negotiating for the lowest possible price and we pass the savings on to you.

The company's tag line was "Serious Food . . . Silly Prices." According to founding partner Mark Gilliland, "The last thing we want to be is another wanna-be Whole Foods." Gilliland was formerly the founder and president of Wild Oats but was forced out when his aggressive expansion strategy put Wild Oats in a financial bind.

Each Sunflower Market was about 40,000 square feet and had a warehouse-like atmosphere, with no customer service except for check-out personnel. Stores featured many one-of-a-kind items purchased in large lots from brokers. Pallets of goods were placed wherever floor space was available.

In late 2005, Sunflower had begun downsizing some of its stores to the 30,000-square-foot range and reducing the number of sections within each category—for instance, it was decreasing its selections of capers from 19 to 2 varieties.

Supervalu/Save-a-Lot

In early 2006, Minneapolis-based Supervalu, a Fortune 500 company with 2005 sales of $19.5 billion that operated 649 corporate stores (under eight brands) and 841 licensed Save-A-Lot stores in 40 states, was on the front end of launching a new 12,000- to 15,000-square-foot grocery format called Sunflower Market. The first Sunflower Market opened in January 2006 in Indianapolis as a value-priced organic and natural food store. The stores were modeled after Supervalu's Save-A-Lot small-box, limited-assortment format but had a focus on natural and organic products. Sunflower's offerings consisted of 8,000 to 12,000 stock-keeping units (SKUs) of grocery, frozen and dairy items, produce, deli and cheese, bakery, café, hormone- and antibiotic-free meat and seafood, beer and wine, and wellness products. All Sunflower Market stores were to be operated by Supervalu. Supervalu's venture had no connection to Mike Gilliland's Sunflower Market chain; Supervalu had trademarked the Sunflower name some years earlier and had licensed it to Gilliland for use in the Southwest. It was expected that the first wave of Supervalu's Sunflower Market stores would be opened in the Midwest, where Wild Oats and Whole Foods had comparatively few stores.

Jeff Noddle, Supervalu's chairman and CEO, said, "Across the nation, we are seeing a growing demand for affordable organic foods with exceptional taste and nutritional quality. Sunflower Market draws on our expertise in small-box formats, and leverages our supply chain expertise, which enables us to deliver outstanding natural and organic products at a price point consistent with consumer expectations."[19] Supervalu decided to enter the natural and organics market because the 17 to 21 percent annual growth in sales of natural and organic products was eight times higher than the growth of the conventional food market and because of the success of Whole Foods and Wild Oats. Supervalu's research indicated that 96 percent of consumers purchased organic products occasionally and 27 percent of grocery shoppers bought organics weekly. Another Supervalu executive noted, "Organics is not a fad. It is fast becoming a constant in consumers' lives. By offering these items in a convenient neighborhood market at a value price point, we create a compelling proposition for the middle-market consumer." Supervalu management believed that the company's ownership of specialty produce company W. Newell & Co. would enable Sunflower's prices to run 10 to 15 percent below that of conventional and natural food stores. Supervalu was also launching a new 100-plus-item line of private-label organic and natural products under the Nature's Best brand at Sunflower Market and planned to also make the brand available to Supervalu's 2,200 distribution customers.

Independent Natural and Health Food Grocers

In 2005 there were approximately 14,000 small, independent retailers of natural and organic foods, vitamins/supplements, and beauty and personal care products. Most were single-store, owner-managed enterprises. Combined sales of the 14,000 independents were in the $15 billion range in 2004. Two other vitamin/supplement chains, General Nutrition and Vitamin World, dominated the vitamin/supplement segment with about 7,500 store locations. Most of the independent stores had less than 2,500 square feet of retail sales space and generated revenues of less than $1 million annually, but there were roughly 850 natural foods and organic retailers with store sizes exceeding 6,000 square feet and sales of between $1 million and $5 million annually.

Product lines and range of selection at the stores of independent natural and health foods retailers varied from narrow to moderately broad, depending on a store's market focus and the shopper traffic it was able to generate. Inventories at stores under 1,000 square feet could run as little as $10,000, while those at stores of 6,000 square feet or more often ranged from $400,000 to $1.2 million. Many of the independents had some sort of deli or beverage bar, and some even had a small dine-in area with a limited health food menu. Revenues and customer traffic at most independent stores were trending upward, reflecting growing buyer interest in natural and organic products. Most independent retailers had average annual sales per square foot of store space of $200 (for stores under 2,000 square feet) to as much as $470 (for stores greater than 6,000 square feet)—Whole Foods' average was over $800 per square foot in 2005.[20]

Endnotes

[1]As quoted in Elizabeth Lee, "National Standards Now Define Organic Food," *Atlanta Journal and Constitution,* October 21, 2002.

[2]Press release, May 22, 2003, www.newfarm.org (accessed November 24, 2004).

[3]Organic Trade Association, "2004 Manufacturer Survey," www.ota.com (accessed November 28, 2005).

[4]Cited in the Trendspotting section of *Natural Foods Buyer,* Fall 2004, www.newhope.com (accessed November 26, 2004).

[5]Company press release, November 18, 2005.

[6]Letter to shareholders, 2003 annual report.

[7]Prices cited in "Eating Too Fast at Whole Foods," *BusinessWeek,* October 24, 2005, p. 84.

[8]Hollie Shaw, "Retail-Savvy Whole Foods Opens in Canada," *National Post,* May 1, 2002, p. FP9.

[9]See Karin Schill Rives, "Texas-Based Whole Foods Market Makes Changes to Cary, N.C., Grocery Store," *News and Observer,* March 7, 2002.

[10]As quoted in Marilyn Much, "Whole Foods Markets: Austin, Texas Green Grocer Relishes Atypical Sales," *Investors Business Daily,* September 10, 2002.

[11]As quoted in "Whole Foods Market to Open in Albuquerque, N.M.," *Santa Fe New Mexican,* September 10, 2002.

[12]EVA at the store level was based on store contribution (store revenues minus cost of goods sold minus store operating expenses) relative to store investment over and above the cost of capital.

[13]As quoted in John K. Wilson, "Going Whole Hog with Whole Foods," Bankrate.com, December 23, 1999. Mackey made the statement in 1991 when efforts were being made to unionize the company's store in Berkeley, California.

[14]Company press release, January 21, 2003.

[15]Information contained in John R. Wells and Travis Haglock, "Whole Foods Market, Inc." Harvard Business School case study 9-705-476.

[16]Much of the information in this section is based on M. E. Lloyd, "Specialty-Grocer Fresh Market Cultivates Upscale Consumers, Reaps Big Returns," *The Wall Street Journal,* February 20, 2001, p. B11, and information posted at www. freshmarket.com (accessed December 1, 2005).

[17]Information posted at www.traderjoes.com (accessed December 1, 2005).

[18]This section is based on information posted at www.sunflowermarkets.com and in Joe Lewandowski, "Naturals Stores Freshen Their Strategies," *Natural Foods Merchandiser,* January 1, 2004 (accessed November 19, 2004, at www.naturalfoodsmerchandiser.com).

[19] Company press release, October 19, 2005.

[20]*Natural Foods Merchandiser,* June 2004, p. 27.

Oliver's Markets

Armand Gilinsky Jr.
Sonoma State University

John Moore
Sonoma State University

Richard L. McCline
San Francisco State University

In September 2005, Oliver's Markets was nearing completion of an estimated $500,000 remodel of its original Cotati, California, store when its top management team, consisting of Steve Maass (owner) and Tom Scott (general manager), quickly had to decide whether or not to bid on an expansion opportunity. Oliver's Markets consisted of two supermarkets in Sonoma County, one in Cotati and the other in nearby Santa Rosa, which together generated about $40 million in sales per year. Sonoma County was situated at the northern fringe of the San Francisco Bay Area, about an hour's driving time from the Golden Gate Bridge. Oliver's had just been informed by its grocery wholesaler that Kroger's, a national chain, was selling 20 supermarkets in the San Francisco Bay Area. Within a week of receiving the list of Kroger's locations for sale, Steve and Tom narrowed the choice to two stores—Ralph's Supermarket in Santa Rosa and Bell's Market in Novato. Novato was in Marin County, about 30 minutes south of Santa Rosa. Oliver's had one week to tender a bid on one or both of the Kroger stores, either of which could cost an estimated $2 million to retrofit, in addition to the ongoing lease and operating costs.

In deciding whether or not to purchase and retrofit the new site(s), Steve and Tom were primarily guided by logistics, that is, proximity to existing stores, and by expected leasehold costs. Of greater concern, perhaps, was how to continue to differentiate Oliver's Markets from other supermarket chains. Prominent among these rivals, Trader Joe's,

Costco, and Whole Foods had recently entered Oliver's Markets' sales territory with brand-new stores; Wal-Mart and Target had also announced plans to develop regional supercenters, that is, large-format discount supermarkets, in California. See Exhibit 1 for an explanation of supermarket terms.

OLIVER'S HISTORY

In 1988, Steve Oliver Maass purchased the then bankrupt Cotati Farmer's Market. He recalled:

> We came in here and it was just the worst store I'd ever seen. I looked at it and I said I know I can do a better job than this store has been doing. There's just no way I'd do this bad a job. But I had absolutely no grocery experience, none. I worked in the produce department of a grocery store, which isn't the same. We went to bankruptcy court and bought it for $200,000, I mortgaged my house. There wasn't a lot of money so we painted, and cleaned, and cleaned. What Farmer's had done is they had eliminated things that didn't work, instead of trying to figure out how to make them work. They wouldn't carry lamb because they wouldn't sell it. They had very little to offer. The first question I asked was, "Why would anyone want to shop here?"

Steve named his new store Oliver's Market, using his middle name because he thought that would sound more upscale than Steve's Market. His wife, Ruth, worked in the store for about the first four years, much of the time as a self-trained bookkeeper. Oliver's was organized as a Subchapter S corporation. Steve Maass was president, and Ruth Maass was vice president and secretary. They were co-owners.

Exhibit 1   **Glossary of Supermarket Terms**

Grocery store—Any retail store selling a line of dry grocery, canned goods, or nonfood items as well as some perishable items.

Supermarket—Any full-line self-service grocery store generating a sales volume of $2 million or more annually.

Convenience store—Any full-line, self-service grocery store that is open long hours, is easy to access, and offers limited line of high-convenience items. The majority sell gasoline with an annual sales of $2 million or more.

Independent—An operator of fewer than 11 retail stores.

Chain—An operator of 11 or more retail stores.

Wholesale club—A membership retail/wholesale hybrid with a varied selection and limited variety of products presented in a warehouse-type environment. These 120,000-square-foot stores have 60 percent to 70 percent general merchandise/health and beauty care and a grocery line dedicated to large sizes and bulk sales. Memberships include both business accounts and consumer groups. Examples are Sam's Club, Costco, and BJ's.

Supercenter—A large food/drug combination store and mass merchandiser under a single roof. The supercenters offer a wide variety of food, as well as nonfood merchandise. These stores average more than 170,000 square feet and typically devote as much as 40 percent of the space to grocery items. Examples are Wal-Mart, Kmart, Super Target, Meijer, and Fred Meyer.

Sources: *Progressive Grocer's 2003 Marketing Guidebook* and Bishop Consulting, 2003.

Oliver's added a deli in 1990, and an aisle of health foods in 1991. In 1994, the city of Cotati offered Steve and Ruth Maass a low-interest redevelopment loan of $500,000. They used the money to expand by taking over the adjacent space and adding an additional 11,000 square feet, for a total of 36,000 square feet with about 28,000 square feet of selling space. Steve recalled:

At that time I decided that, in every aisle, we would have the same things that Whole Foods did. We would give people a choice in all their health foods and we would integrate it throughout the store. There isn't a section you can go to where you won't have a good selection of organic or health foods and conventional. We didn't mirror Whole Foods so much as Whole Foods did a wonderful job on health foods, and people were going in there and buying it. But we couldn't sell health foods. The only reason we couldn't sell it was because we weren't doing it well enough. So, we learned how to do it well enough, and we did it everywhere.

Oliver's opened a second store in Santa Rosa on April 4, 2000, and thenceforth changed its name to Oliver's Markets. Steve recalled:

The landlord came to us. I wasn't really that interested in expanding at the time. It was a good deal, as we didn't have to pay anything for the store. We considered hiring a nationally known retail architect, but decided that was too costly, so we just sort of designed it ourselves. We picked the colors out and figured out what we wanted for a deli. I think the deli was to a large degree fashioned after Woodlands Market, the best little market I've seen.[1]

In 2005, Oliver's began a remodel of its Cotati store. Steve had hoped to invest $2 million in the remodel, but uncertainty over the future of the lease forced him to scale back his plans. He recounted, "Our landlords wouldn't talk to us. I couldn't even get a meeting going with them. I wanted to get another ten years on the lease so we could put a couple million dollars in here and do a really good job. Even with nine years left on this lease we're putting in $500,000, because otherwise we'll get down to the sixth or seventh year and be in trouble."

Steve himself was now 59 years old and had been in the business since 1988. Ruth was ill with cancer. Steve and Ruth's only child, Eva, 40, had worked full-time for Oliver's for about four years, primarily as the scan coordinator at the Cotati store. She had worked part-time as needed, doing an assortment of jobs—such as bookkeeper and gift buyer. Steve reflected that Eva was extremely smart and quite capable, but as a musician and painter she was more interested in Oliver's design and decor than in the business side. She had, for example, designed and purchased new fixtures for a remodeled gift department. Steve and Tom were both working to involve her more in various aspects of the operation.

Exhibit 2 presents milestones in Oliver's Markets' history. Oliver's recent track record is shown

Exhibit 2   **Oliver's Markets' Milestones**

1988	Oliver's in Cotati opened
1990	Service deli added
1991	Health foods added
1994	Cotati store enlarged with an additional 11,000 square feet; natural and organic products added in every category throughout store
2000	Oliver's in Santa Rosa opened
2004	5,000-square-foot warehouse opened adjacent to the Santa Rosa store
2005	Cotati store remodeling started in May
2005	Oliver's named one of six Outstanding Retailers of 2005 by the National Association for the Specialty Food Trade.

Source: Oliver's Markets Inc.

in Exhibits 3 and 4, containing 2000–2004 income statements for the two Oliver's Markets. The financial condition of Oliver's as a consolidated entity is shown in Exhibit 5, presenting 2003 and 2004 consolidated balance sheets. Exhibit 6 provides a comparison of Oliver's performance to selected industry standards. Exhibit 7 provides comparisons of Oliver's performance to industrywide statistics on cost items, including labor and rent.

FOOD RETAILING IN THE UNITED STATES

Supermarkets had become the dominant form of food retailer in the United States throughout the second half of the 20th century, but by the early 2000s, that dominance was being challenged by five major trends: (1) the increasing dominance of warehouse club stores and discount supercenters such as Costco and Wal-Mart's Sam's Clubs, (2) increased purchases of prepared foods away from home in restaurants and fast-food outlets, (3) chronic overcapacity in the supermarket industry, (4) changing shopping patterns due to the emergence of "lifestyle" food operators and Internet delivery services, and (5) higher labor costs, particularly for chains that had a unionized labor force.

Discount Supermarkets

Owing to a growing number of price-sensitive and time-pressed customers, traditional supermarkets struggled to protect their market share against discount supercenters or "hypermarkets," warehouse club stores, dollar stores, and drugstores. Such nontraditional retail outlets increased their share of consumers' food-at-home expenditures from 17.7 percent in 1998 to 30.8 percent in 2003. According to the U.S. Department of Agriculture (USDA), traditional retailers' market share declined from 82.3 percent to 69.2 percent over the same period.[2] Wal-Mart was both a driver and a beneficiary of this change in shopping patterns: its share of U.S. supermarket sales reached 15.2 percent by 2003.[3] In 2004, Wal-Mart opened its first California supercenter, marking the format's entry into the country's most populous state. By 2007, the number of Wal-Mart supercenters nationwide was forecast by *Progressive Grocer* to approach 2,000, translating into a 35 percent share of food store industry sales.[4] Union Bank of Switzerland (UBS) predicted that traditional supermarkets' share of food sales would drop to 63 percent by 2006, as shown in Exhibit 8.[5]

Food Prepared Away from Home

Food-service operators—including restaurants and fast-food outlets—were increasing their share of consumers' total food dollars. Long-term trends showed that increases in household incomes, due in part to the growth of dual-income households, had raised the share of food spending devoted to prepared foods and meals. By 2002, food-service outlets accounted for 46.1 percent of all food spending, up from 45.4 percent in 1990 and 39 percent in 1980.[6] According to *American Demographics,* from 1996 to 2001, married couples with children reduced the fraction of their food budget spent on food to

(Continued on page C-35)

Exhibit 3   Oliver's Markets' Five-Year Income Statements, 2000–2004—Cotati Store (in thousands)

	2000	2001	2002	2003	2004
Sales					
Grocery	$ 5,929.2	$ 6,192.4	$ 6,154.9	$ 5,835.4	$ 5,658.2
Floral	211.8	236.2	249.4	223.3	196.8
Liquor	2,016.0	2,038.2	2,090.8	1,902.7	1,823.3
Meat	1,696.6	1,761.4	1,795.1	1,745.1	1,678.9
Natural foods	3,051.8	3,296.7	3,692.1	3,743.3	3,788.6
Produce	1,886.5	2,059.9	2,235.9	2,205.3	2,254.0
Deli	1,806.1	2,041.1	2,537.8	2,725.6	2,619.4
Bakery	1,007.4	1,086.8	1,158.8	1,149.2	1,046.8
Sushi bar	274.8	260.4	270.4	270.5	232.6
Billbacks	108.0	78.1	45.5	51.8	56.4
Total sales	$ 17,988.3	$ 19,051.4	$ 20,230.8	$ 19,852.2	$ 19,355.3
Cost of sales					
Grocery	$ 4,150.9	4,294.4	4,249.1	4,008.1	3,961.1
Floral	153.3	172.5	174.9	143.4	135.4
Liquor	1,415.1	1,440.8	1,480.0	1,379.6	1,374.0
Meat	1,177.3	1,142.5	1,202.6	1,209.4	1,141.4
Natural foods	1,942.0	2,099.9	2,394.3	2,465.6	2,487.5
Produce	1,159.7	1,244.6	1,325.0	1,317.8	1,364.5
Deli	877.7	1,006.4	1,198.5	1,348.9	1,295.5
Bakery	579.9	643.5	656.0	628.8	595.5
Sushi bar	208.6	195.4	202.8	202.9	174.7
Total cost of sales	$ 11,664.5	$ 12,240.0	$ 12,883.2	$ 12,704.5	$ 12,529.6
Gross profit	$ 6,323.8	$ 6,811.3	$ 7,347.6	$ 7,147.7	$ 6,825.7
Operating expenses					
Wages	$ 2,640.4	$ 2,925.3	$ 3,137.1	$ 3,298.7	$ 214.8
Benefits	593.5	684.7	1,014.7	1,163.7	1,256.3
Supplies	324.1	304.7	295.2	314.1	300.1
Rent	320.8	334.0	364.1	350.1	378.3
Telephone	10.9	12.7	7.4	6.6	6.9
Utilities	172.8	291.9	264.1	259.3	256.7
Garbage	32.3	34.5	42.1	46.2	49.0
Repair	179.1	144.5	165.2	149.9	167.4
Customer refunds	0.4	0.4	0.2	0.4	0.2
Depreciation	111.8	60.0	93.0	162.0	165.0
Taxes and licenses	27.9	19.1	32.9	23.5	23.4
Administrative	456.4	476.1	467.7	496.3	503.7
Other costs	108.0	131.9	179.2	209.1	224.6
Total operating expense	$ 4,978.5	$ 5,419.8	$ 6,062.9	$ 6,479.9	$ 6,546.3
Income from operations	$ 1,345.3	$ 1,391.5	$ 1,284.8	$ 667.8	$ 279.4
Other income and expense					
Interest expense	12.2	11.6	11.3	11.1	10.8
Other income	—	(11.0)	(15.9)	(14.9)	(12.7)
Total other income (expense)	12.2	0.6	(4.6)	(3.9)	(1.9)
Pretax income (loss)	$ 1,357.4	$ 1,392.1	$ 1,280.2	$ 664.0	$ 277.5

Note: Fiscal year is same as calendar year.
Source: Oliver's Markets Inc.

Exhibit 4 Oliver's Markets' Five-Year Income Statements, 2000–2004 —Santa Rosa Store (in thousands)

	2000	2001	2002	2003	2004
Sales					
Grocery	$ 2,988.9	$ 4,287.1	$ 4,569.0	$ 4,935.7	$ 5,090.3
Floral	58.9	200.5	223.8	251.9	248.6
Liquor	962.1	1,389.1	1,548.5	1,576.7	1,647.2
Meat	1,206.6	1,766.9	1,933.9	2,226.5	2,318.2
Natural foods	1,278.6	2,112.5	2,503.5	2,930.0	3,252.8
Produce	1,056.7	1,651.7	2,037.0	2,400.5	2,544.1
Deli	1,310.4	2,177.3	2,640.7	3,200.7	3,546.4
Bakery	493.9	786.5	924.5	990.1	981.0
Sushi bar	146.5	200.8	226.6	235.3	229.9
Billbacks	24.8	55.7	29.5	28.1	43.7
Total sales	$ 9,527.4	$ 14,628.0	$ 16,636.9	$ 18,775.4	$ 19,902.1
Cost of sales					
Grocery	$ 2,193.5	$ 2,984.1	$ 3,162.7	$ 3,365.5	$ 3,470.5
Floral	50.2	171.5	171.9	162.6	161.3
Liquor	732.5	1,003.6	1,080.5	1,154.3	1,252.9
Meat	856.7	1,167.6	1,211.5	1,498.1	1,558.8
Natural foods	802.6	1,383.6	1,605.5	1,958.6	2,142.1
Produce	722.9	1,055.4	1,252.4	1,472.3	1,517.8
Deli	714.7	1,096.8	1,187.0	1,505.1	1,656.6
Bakery	304.0	473.3	542.1	583.0	570.7
Sushi bar	107.4	152.3	168.1	176.5	172.3
Total cost of sales	$ 6,484.7	$ 9,488.3	$ 10,381.6	$ 11,876.0	$ 12,503.0
Gross profit	$ 3,042.7	$ 5,139.7	$ 6,255.2	$ 6,899.3	$ 7,399.1
Operating expenses					
Wages	$ 1,890.4	$ 2,527.0	$ 2,764.5	$ 3,128.3	$ 3,320.1
Benefits	321.7	574.8	898.7	1,118.5	1,309.3
Supplies	245.2	242.0	246.4	286.6	292.8
Rent	196.5	288.5	337.0	377.4	410.0
Telephone	5.9	5.8	6.9	5.9	6.2
Utilities	119.1	185.1	181.0	213.0	200.2
Garbage	21.9	35.0	28.1	33.1	44.2
Repair	74.7	106.4	103.0	113.6	127.4
Customer refunds	0.3	0.2	0.3	0.6	0.2
Depreciation	266.0	144.0	197.0	250.0	279.0
Taxes and licenses	17.8	28.7	22.3	25.8	28.3
Administrative	287.2	356.9	386.0	468.7	517.6
Other costs	64.1	91.9	108.7	165.3	207.7
Total operating expense	$ 3,510.8	$ 4,586.5	$ 5,279.8	$ 6,186.9	$ 6,742.8
Income from operations	$ (468.1)	$ 553.3	$ 975.5	$ 712.4	$ 656.3
Other income and expense					
Interest expense	$ 126.0	$ 157.5	$ 144.2	$ 103.1	$ 85.8
Other income	3.2	—	(7.6)	(7.9)	(7.9)
Total other income (expense)	$ 129.2	$ 157.5	$ 136.5	$ 95.2	$ 77.9
Pretax income (loss)	$ (338.9)	$ 710.7	$ 1,112.0	$ 807.6	$ 734.2

Source: Oliver's Markets Inc.

Exhibit 5   **Oliver's Markets, Consolidated Balance Sheets, 2003–2004**

	Fiscal Year Ending 12/31	
	2003	2004
Assets		
Current assets		
Cash and marketable securities	$2,411,598	$2,310,120
Inventory	2,276,374	2,461,271
Note receivable		100,000
Prepaid expenses	534,718	345,883
Other current assets	742	5,673
Total current assets	$5,223,433	$5,222,948
Fixed assets		
Equipment	$3,218,389	$3,568,810
Less accumulated amortization	(2,482,489)	(2,861,360)
Total fixed assets	$ 735,900	$ 707,450
Other assets		
Goodwill and intangible assets	$ 71,441	$ 71,441
Less accumulated amortization	(11,730)	(11,730)
Total other assets	59,711	59,711
Total assets	$6,019,043	$5,990,109
Liabilities and stockholders' equity		
Current liabilities		
Accounts payable	$1,135,870	$1,144,713
Accrued payroll	211,522	124,076
Other accrued liabilities	620,746	597,420
Total current liabilities	$1,968,138	$1,866,209
Long-term debt		
Note payable	$1,000,331	$ 809,585
Stockholder loans	121,841	118,669
Total long-term debt	$1,122,172	$ 928,254
Stockholders' equity		
Common stock	$ 200,000	$ 200,000
Retained earnings	2,424,774	2,728,733
Accumulated adjustments	(703,976)	(624,929)
Current-year income	1,007,935	891,842
Total equity	$2,928,733	$3,195,646
Total liabiities and stockholders' equity	$6,019,043	$5,990,109

Source: Oliver's Markets Inc.

Exhibit 6   **Oliver's Markets Versus National Average Supermarket Performance, 2004**

	National Average	Oliver's Cotati	Oliver's Santa Rosa
Average supermarket:			
Selling area in square feet	31,245	28,000	17,500
Volume in millions	$ 13.35	$ 19.36	$ 19.90
Number of check-outs	9	8	6
Number of full-time equivalent employees	69	110	115
Weekly sales per:			
Store	$256,730	$372,217	$382,733
Check-out line	$ 28,414	$ 46,527	$ 63,789
Full-time equivalent employee	$ 3,730	$ 3,384	$ 3,328
Employee hour	$ 93.25	$ 84.59	$ 83.21
Square foot	$ 8.22	$ 13.29	$ 21.87

Source: Progressive Grocer, April 2004, p. 32. Oliver's Markets figures: supplied by Oliver's, for fiscal year 2004.

Exhibit 7   **Oliver's Markets Versus National Average Supermarket Operating Costs, 2003**

	National Average % of Sales	Oliver's Markets, Consolidated 2003
Gross margin	27.6%	36.4%
Expenses		
Payroll	11.4	16.6
Employee benefits	3.5	5.9
Utilities	1.3	1.2
Property rentals	1.8	1.9
Taxes and licenses	0.4	0.1
Insurance	0.3	0.2
Depreciation and amortization	1.3	1.1
Maintenance and repairs	0.7	0.7
Supplies	1.1	1.6
Other operating costs	3.8	3.5
Total expenses	25.7	36.4
Operating profit	1.6	3.6
Other income (expense)	0.1	0.1
Income before taxes	2.0	3.8

Sources: FMI Speaks 2004 Key Industry Facts—Prepared by FMI Information Service, July 2004, p. 16.

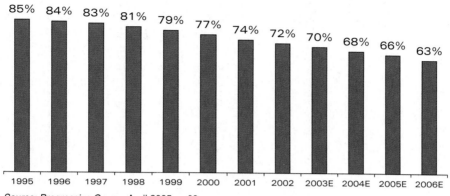

Exhibit 8 **Traditional Supermarket Share of U.S. Retail Food Dollars 1995–2006 (estimated)**

Source: *Progressive Grocer,* April 2005, p. 62.

be prepared at home from 62 percent to 59 percent, translating into a reduction of over $7 billion a year in food spending at retail outlets.[7]

Industry Overcapacity

Declining market share combined with growing store counts contributed to poor year-on-year comparable store sales growth results for the major supermarket chains. Many food retailers struggled with comparable store sales that had, at best, increased by 1 to 2 percent and, in some cases, decreased. Exhibit 9 presents 2000–2004 financial results for several national chains. With a net increase of 411 supermarkets in 2004, many industry analysts considered the industry to be at overcapacity.[8]

Changing Shopping Patterns

Nearly one-third (31 percent) of households shopped in 29 or more retailers or retail channels per year.[9] Due to increased competition from nontraditional food retailers, supermarkets suffered from a decline in shopping trips. In 1999, the average household made 83 trips to supermarkets; by 2004, that statistic had fallen to 69 trips, as shown in Exhibit 10.

Early in 2005, household penetration of supermarkets was below 100 percent for the first time in recent memory. One percent of shoppers, over a

period of a year, had found that they could live without visiting a supermarket. That is, a tiny minority of consumers acquired all their food for home preparation without visiting a traditional supermarket. They did this by shopping at warehouse club stores, supercenters, dollar stores, and niche operators such as Trader Joe's. Some also shopped over the Internet, but the demise of Webvan and the sale of Peapod had largely left this market to traditional retailers, with perhaps the sole exception of FreshDirect, a rapidly growing Internet-based delivery service in New York City. Although many chains offered Internet shopping, Albertson's advertisements proclaimed that it was the largest Internet grocery provider in terms of geographic reach.

Labor Costs

Many traditional supermarkets faced another obstacle—higher labor costs—in their attempts to compete with Wal-Mart, Costco, and other nontraditional food retailers. The higher labor costs were due to the fact that traditional retailers were predominantly union shops. Three major Southern California supermarket chains, Safeway, Albertson's, and Kroger's settled a prolonged costly dispute with unionized workers in March 2004.[10]

The food retailing industry in Sonoma County and throughout northern California prior to 2005

Exhibit 9 **Food Retail Chain Store Financial Statistics, 2000–2004**

(\$ figures are in millions and include international operations)

	2000	2001	2002	2003	2004
Safeway[1]					
Comp store sales growth (%)	2.8%	2.3%	−0.7%	−2.4%	0.9%
Revenue	\$ 32,103	\$ 34,434	\$ 34,917	\$ 35,727	\$ 35,823
Gross profit	\$ 9,666	\$ 10,776	\$ 10,996	\$ 10,724	\$ 10,595
Gross margin %	30.11%	31.30%	31.49%	30.02%	29.58%
EBIT	\$ 2,282	\$ 2,589	\$ 948	\$ 574	\$ 1,173
Net income	\$ 1,092	\$ 1,254	\$ (828)	\$ (170)	\$ 560
Kroger[2]					
Comp store sales growth (%)	1.9%	1.5%	0.8%	0.3%	1.7%
Revenue	\$ 49,000	\$ 50,098	\$ 51,760	\$ 53,791	\$ 56,434
Gross profit	\$ 13,196	\$ 13,700	\$ 13,950	\$ 14,154	\$ 14,294
Gross margin %	26.93%	27.35%	26.95%	26.31%	25.33%
EBIT	\$ 2,183	\$ 2,359	\$ 2,569	\$ 1,370	\$ 847
Net Income	\$ 874	\$ 1,040	\$ 1,202	\$ 312	−\$ 100
Albertson's[3]					
Comp store sales growth (%)	0.6%	1.3%	−0.4%	−2.4%	0.2%
Revenue	\$ 35,221	\$ 36,294	\$ 35,316	\$ 35,107	\$ 39,897
Gross profit	\$ 9,989	\$ 10,337	\$ 10,298	\$ 10,048	\$ 11,187
Gross margin %	28.36%	28.48%	29.16%	28.62%	28.04%
EBIT	\$ 1,588	\$ 1,248	\$ 1,801	\$ 1,316	\$ 1,229
Net Income	\$ 765	\$ 501	\$ 485	\$ 556	\$ 444
Costco[4]					
Comp store sales growth (%)	11.0%	4.0%	6.0%	5.0%	10.0%
Revenue	\$ 32,169	\$ 34,797	\$ 38,762	\$ 42,456	\$ 48,107
Gross profit	\$ 3,847	\$ 4,199	\$ 4,779	\$ 5,221	\$ 6,015
Gross margin %	11.96%	12.07%	12.33%	12.30%	12.50%
EBIT	\$ 1,037	\$ 992	\$ 1,132	\$ 1,157	\$ 1,385
Net Income	\$ 631	\$ 602	\$ 700	\$ 721	\$ 882
Whole Foods[5]					
Comp store sales growth (%)	8.6%	9.2%	10.0%	8.6%	14.9%
Revenue	\$ 1,839	\$ 2,272	\$ 2,698	\$ 3,149	\$ 3,865
Gross profit	\$ 633	\$ 789	\$ 932	\$ 1,078	\$ 1,341
Gross margin %	34.42%	34.73%	34.54%	34.23%	34.70%
EBIT	\$ 94	\$ 104	\$ 141	\$ 167	\$ 216
Net Income	−\$ 5	\$ 65	\$ 82	\$ 100	\$ 132
Wal-Mart[6]					
Comp store sales growth (%)	5.0%	6.0%	5.0%	4.0%	3.0%
Revenue	\$180,787	\$204,011	\$229,616	\$256,320	\$285,222
Gross profit	\$ 40,067	\$ 44,914	\$ 51,317	\$ 57,573	\$ 65,249
Gross margin %	22.16%	22.02%	22.35%	22.46%	22.88%
EBIT	\$ 9,245	\$ 9,767	\$ 11,334	\$ 12,664	\$ 14,144
Net Income	\$ 6,235	\$ 6,592	\$ 7,955	\$ 9,054	\$ 10,267

[1] Safeway opened 34 "Lifestyle" stores in 2003 and remodeled 108 stores to the format by the end of that year.

[2] Kroger Co. includes advertising expense in cost of goods sold.

[3] Comp store sales for 2003 were down 0.1% for stores not affected by southern CA strike.

[4] Costco includes membership sales in total revenue; data also includes all products, not just supermarket items.

[5] Whole Foods includes occupancy expense in cost of goods sold.

[6] Comp store sales figures are for U.S. stores only; other figures include all products, not just supermarket items.

Sources: Annual reports as found on company Web sites and the U.S. Securities and Exchange Commission's Web site.

Exhibit 10 **Shopping Trip and Basket Size Statistics**

	1999	2000	2001	2002	2003	2004	Five-Year Change (%)
Percent of Households That Shop at Selected Retail Outlets							
Supermarkets	100%	100%	100%	100%	100%	99%	−1%
Mass merchants	95	94	95	93	91	89	−6
Drugstores	87	86	86	86	85	84	−3
Supercenters*	52	51	51	54	54	54	2
Dollar stores	52	55	59	62	66	67	15
Warehouse	50	49	50	52	51	51	1
Convenience/gas	50	48	45	46	45	44	−6
Annual Trips Made per Household							
Supermarkets	83	78	75	73	72	69	−14%
Mass merchants	26	25	24	23	21	20	−6
Drugstores	15	15	15	15	15	15	0
Supercenters*	15	17	20	22	25	27	12
Dollar stores	10	10	11	12	13	13	3
Warehouse	9	10	10	11	11	11	2
Convenience/gas	13	14	15	14	15	15	2
Total	171	169	170	169	172	170	−1%
Basket $ Size							
Supermarkets	$31	$32	$32	$33	$33	$34	3%
Mass merchants	36	38	39	41	41	42	6
Drugstores	18	19	19	20	20	20	2
Supercenters*	45	49	51	53	55	56	11
Dollar stores	10	11	11	11	11	11	1
Warehouse	82	83	82	83	83	83	1
Convenience/gas	9	10	10	10	11	12	3

* Includes Kmart, Target, and Wal-Mart supercenters.
Source: Progressive Grocer, April 2005, p. 60.

appeared to mirror the national scene with one major exception—the absence of Wal-Mart supercenters. Exhibit 11 shows store counts and estimated sales for selected retailers. In 2003, Safeway was the number one food retailer in Sonoma County; Oliver's ranked ninth in sales (Exhibit 12).

OLIVER'S STORE OPERATIONS

Oliver's flagship operation in Cotati was one part traditional supermarket, one part natural foods store, and one part gourmet foods store. The main entrance led directly into the health and beauty aids (HABA) area of the store, which featured vitamins, homeopathic treatments, essential oils, and other natural HABA products. The department hired an in-store therapist four evenings a week to do massages. The placement and size of the department gave the store its predominant feel as a natural foods retailer. In virtually every area of the store, shoppers could find natural products, including organic baby food, organic spices, and organic pet food.

Gourmet foods were also in abundance. In June 2005, Oliver's was one of just six retailers to be honored with an Outstanding Retailer Award by the National Association for the Specialty Food Trade. Oliver's had 108 stock-keeping units of olive oil, ranging from a 17-ounce bottle of Star Extra Virgin for $3.79, to a 101-ounce tin of Spectrum Naturals

Exhibit 11   **Store Counts and Estimated Grocery Sales, Northern California Food Retailers, 2004**

	Number of Stores	Estimated Grocery Sales ($ millions)
Safeway	251	$4,688
Albertson's	158	3,230
Raley's	113	2,320
Costco	35	2,250
Trader Joe's	44	340
Whole Foods	18	320
Ralph's (Kroger's)	17	363

Sources: Sales estimated using figures from *Progressive Grocer*'s annual list of the 50 largest food retailers (May 2005) and from information found on company Web sites.

Organic Spanish that retailed for $35.89. The store's cheese department featured cheeses imported from England, Italy, France, and Spain that sold for as much as $26.99 per pound. Steve stated, "Nobody has good cheese in this area and we're doing a phenomenal business in good cheese. I mean $21, $22 a pound, and we can hire someone for $50 an hour that's going to double our cheese business, because she's unique enough and *we're* unique enough." The cheese department in Cotati did $15,000–$20,000

Exhibit 12   **Sonoma County Retail Food Sales, 2003**

Rank*		Number of Stores	Total Sales ($ millions)	Estimated Grocery Sales ($ millions)
1	Safeway	12	$ 240	$ 240
2	Costco†	2	340	211
3	Albertson's	7	108	108
4	FoodMaxx	2	78	78
5	Raley's	3	73	73
6	Whole Foods	3	65	65
7	Ralph's (Kroger)	3	61	61
8	G&G	2	50	50
9	Oliver's	2	40	40
10	Wal-Mart‡	2	121	36
11	Fiesta	2	20	20
12	Petaluma	1	13	13
13	Andy's Produce	1	11	11
14	Molsberry	1	10	10
15	Big John's	1	8	8
16	Berry's	6	8	8

† Estimated grocery sales for Costco were determined using *Supermarket News*' estimate that 62% of Costco's sales are derived from traditional grocery categories.

‡ Estimated grocery sales for Wal-Mart were derived using *Supermarket News*' estimate that 30% of Wal-Mart's discount store sales are derived from traditional grocery categories.

Source: Figures derived from the *Santa Rosa Press Democrat's Outlook 2004* survey of Sonoma County businesses, www.pressdemo.com. The businesses listed above all made the paper's list of the 350 largest companies in Sonoma County.

in sales per week. The store also featured a 3,000-square-foot wine department staffed with two full-time employees every day and a biweekly wine tasting. Wine buyer Renay Santero said,

> On a good day, we'll do $16,000 in wine. The wine tasting is most beneficial to the customer. Because I have an on-site license, I get every restaurant wine. What makes me a little different is that I get wines that other places cannot get.

The deli included a taqueria, a salad bar, and an inside seating area. Tom said, "When Safeway took out their salad bar, we put one in." The deli benefited from a front-end cold case used to sell Oliver's branded take-and-heat entrées, such as beef stroganoff and vegetarian lasagna, which were produced in the kitchen of the deli in the Santa Rosa store.

Deli manager Roxanne "Rocky" Abruzzo said, "It's the closest to homemade you're going to get without takeout . . . We do an easy $1,000 a day." The sushi bar located next to the deli was contracted to an outside vendor, AFC, and Oliver's received 25 percent of the gross sales as profit. The bakery featured gourmet store-baked desserts and a coffee bar that served mochas and lattes in addition to brewed organic coffees. Produce included a large organics section, and the department tried to source as much local produce as possible. The full-service meat department carried lamb, veal, and buffalo in addition to three grades of beef. Tom stated, "We feel that we need to have a better quality of meat . . . It's the same in produce. They're told to buy the best and charge what they have to get for it . . . So, having a steak that's twice the price of our competition is kind of a way of doing business in the summer here. This is a secondary shop for a lot of people in this neighborhood. They'll do their pantry loading at Costco or FoodMaxx and come here and buy their perishables." As evidence of this, Oliver's experienced a significant increase in sales during the 2004 holidays, jumping from an average of about $369,000 per week to $525,000 the week before Christmas.

Oliver's Santa Rosa

While the layout of the Cotati store provided an "organic, health foods store" feel, the size and design of the Santa Rosa store provided more of an upscale, gourmet market ambience. The most significant difference between the two stores was size, as the Santa Rosa store occupied only 22,000 square feet with 17,500 in selling space. In 2004, Oliver's opened a 5,000-square-foot warehouse to alleviate space constraints in Santa Rosa. The other significant difference was the focus on food service, bakery, deli, and taqueria, which ran almost the entire length of the left-hand wall. Tom stated, "The customers at the Santa Rosa store have the disposable income to just basically ask us to cook for them."

Marketing Strategy

Pricing   In 2002, Oliver's changed its pricing strategy to a program that involved setting its merchandise at prices relative to Safeway's, chosen because it was the dominant supermarket retailer in Sonoma County. Safeway was a traditional "hi-lo" retailer, meaning that low ad prices were used to offset high regular prices. For example, in early May 2005, Safeway advertised Clorox bleach for $1.00 when the regular retail was $2.59. Safeway was able to do this by negotiating special deals with its suppliers for ad periods. Oliver's set its everyday prices on traditional grocery items approximately 8 to 10 percent below Safeway's prices, having determined that being below Safeway by that amount provided acceptable margins while providing value to customers. Similarly, pricing in the natural foods department was maintained at just below the prices found at Whole Foods. Oliver's management considered the Whole Foods store in Santa Rosa to be its primary competitor in that market. Point-of-sale (POS) coordinator Laurie Tuxhorn reflected, "[Our pricing strategy] has proven to be really good to us. When I first took over this department and started doing printouts, we were so out of line. It was incredible how much lower we were." Department managers were responsible for setting prices in perishables departments such as deli, bakery, meat and produce. They were given a gross margin goal as part of the budget process and priced products to attain that goal. In line with Oliver's overall strategy, they tended to focus more on uniqueness and quality than on price.

Wine department manager Renay Santero said, "We've considered adjusting our margins to be more competitive. What makes sense to me is to turn people on to something that maybe nobody else can get a hold of."

Tom stated that Oliver's price strategy was "to try to communicate value amidst the perception of quality. We don't have a problem selling the idea that our product is better. We try to do that in a way that allows customers to feel that they're getting value." Tom admitted that his pricing strategy was not communicated well to customers and that Oliver's was perceived to have higher prices than Safeway. He opined that typical consumers could not believe that an apparently upscale two-store independent could have lower prices than a major chain store given the chain store's clear advantages in economies of scale.

Promotion   Oliver's also offered a weekly ad, an in-store flyer featuring items at no more than 10 percent above cost and temporary price reductions provided by vendors. Tom stated, "We pass through virtually everything we get . . . The one big price impact program is the 'Direct to You' program that's geared at . . . the kind of thing you'd buy at Trader Joes's." Oliver's offered a 10 percent discount to seniors on Wednesdays before 4:00 p.m. The Santa Rosa store was quite successful with this program due to its proximity to an affluent senior community, Oakmont. In 2004, Oliver's began experimenting with an everyday-low-price program on key items. Laurie, the POS coordinator, recalled,

> We have a program that Tom started a while back called the "staples program" where he compares our prices to Safeway for everyday items such as Tide, Nabisco crackers, things like that. We just want to show the customer that even with the Safeway Club card going on, we're still cheaper than them on everyday items.

Steve expressed his concerns about the mixed messages Oliver's might be sending to customers: "We have all these pricing programs like 'Direct to You' and 'staples,' which we stopped temporarily while we try and figure out whether we are price or quality focused."

Oliver's Private Label   Oliver's had a small private-label program that included vitamins, spices, and juices. The take-and-heat entrées from the deli also carried the Oliver's label. The private-label program was generally used as a way to provide value to their customers rather than as a way to build the Oliver's brand; there were no plans to significantly expand the private-label line.

Customer Service   Oliver's prided itself on its willingness to try to get any product a customer requested. According to Steve:

Most stores look at how many turns they get on an item to determine if the product is worth carrying. We almost do the opposite. If somebody wants it, we're going to have it . . . so we become the place that people call and say, "Somebody said if anybody would have it, you would." It's not the item we look at, it's the overall picture . . . It's not whether that one item sells well, it's what it adds to the rest of the store.

Stores had a special-request kiosk against the front wall near the check-out counters. Tom noted:

> We were the first store around here to carry Glaceau Vitamin Water. We're always looking for something new to add to the mix. If a customer wants us to carry something, we'll at least slot one case and see how it goes, and it only falls off the shelf due to competition from other items.

Mission and Culture

Oliver's mission statement, written by Tom, was printed on the back of the stores' item locator maps; thus, it was readily available to employees and customers. It read:

> Our mission is to provide the communities we serve with the finest grocery store in the marketplace. To this end we seek out our customer's specific needs and tailor our products and services to meet those needs. We carry the largest possible selection of natural, conventional and gourmet products. We carry only the highest quality meat, produce and deli products, buying locally whenever possible. We also strive to provide merchandise at the lowest possible cost so that we can offer value to our customers and maintain fair price. We treat each customer like a guest in our own home and we strive to exceed our customer's expectations every time they shop with us.
>
> We believe that our employees work to live, not live to work. We believe that each employee's talents and creativity contribute to making Oliver's successful. We also support employees in their life goals by offering competitive wage and benefit packages and special scheduling whenever possible.
>
> Oliver's is committed to playing an active role in the communities we serve. We support local schools and civic groups. Whenever possible, we fill staffing needs from the local neighborhood.

Oliver's offered a casual, relaxed shopping environment. Most employees, including management, wore blue jeans and company-supplied T-shirts or baseball caps with the Oliver's logo. Male employees were allowed to wear earrings and facial hair.

Employees played classic rock-and-roll on the in-store compact disc system.

Human Resources

Department managers ran their departments as if they were independent businesses. Tom stated that the performance of the individual departments, and of the company as a whole, was driven very much by the managers' individual personalities. Each was given the autonomy to decide what products to carry and how to price them. Each was expected to look for innovative ways to grow his or her department and to enhance the store's position in the market. Renay, formerly a Lucky's manager, said, "There's a lot of autonomy. They allow us to do what we think is best for the store. We negotiate price. We set our own prices. We have our own business plans. It's not like working in a chain where I was told what to do."

Rocky, a veteran of 22 years as a deli manager with Safeway, agreed: "There, I was just the most experienced clerk in the department. Here, it's like the Safeway corporate job and the deli manager job all tied into one. It enables me to use my brain, and still get behind the counter and help customers."

Oliver's maintained department-level fiscal accountability by requiring department managers to turn in financial statements every week. The department managers reported figures on cost of sales, labor, gross margin, and supplies to their store managers. The accounting department generated monthly statements, which were compared to the departments' weekly statements. All departments that sold perishable products were inventoried twice per year, as opposed to the industry standard of monthly inventories. Early in 2005, Tom put the cheese department in Cotati on a monthly inventory schedule and reiterated his preference that all departments selling perishable items conduct inventory as often.

Tom, 46, in addition to being general manager, was the manager of the Cotati Oliver's. Eric Meuse, 32, had started with Oliver's as a courtesy clerk in 1989. He had worked his way up through grocery management; Steve had promoted him to store manager when Oliver's expanded into Santa Rosa. Tom and Eric functioned as business coaches for the department managers. This was a role that had evolved over time, and it had been facilitated by the development of the employment contracts for department managers. Tom and Eric were able to approach issues as mentors, sharing their observations in terms that related to the manager's contract and potential bonus. They helped them to reach goals, rather than ordering them to do specific things. The coaching role was considered successful, first of all, to the extent that financial goals were achieved. The second measure was the professional growth of the department managers in terms of their business acumen and their leadership of their own crews. Renay commented, "It's like family. They're dedicated to helping me with my career."

Rocky amplified this view, stating with a grin, "I always tell Tom, my worst day here is better than my best day at Safeway."

Eric noted, "The fun part about Oliver's is that we all set the standards. Everyone works as a team in creating the vision for Oliver's. Together, we decide which road we're going to take. Everybody has a little bit of say in it."

Tom agreed: "Ultimately, I think, we find good places in that tension, in that sort of give and take between all of us here."

As store managers, Tom and Eric had responsibility for tracking financial performance and for maintaining Oliver's standards in such areas as merchandising, customer service and cleanliness. In conjunction with their department heads, the two store managers oversaw all human resource functions. They were responsible for recruiting, training, and evaluating all employees. Whenever possible, Oliver's promoted from within. According to Tom, "There's a certain cultural learning curve in coming to work for us. Guys who come from the chain stores have a real problem with the entrepreneurial nature." Tom stated that all department managers in Santa Rosa had been promoted from within, and he estimated that this was also true of over 70 percent of the managers in Cotati.

The key component of Oliver's human resource program was its use of an employment contract with all department managers. Oliver's had been using these contracts since about 1998. Tom said, "It's one thing to say, 'If you hit this number, I'll give you this much money,' but the ritual of signing the contract has power to it." The contracts spelled out required hours, personal time off, holidays, and bonuses. Company management structured the bonuses so as to address the needs of the individual departments as they fit in with overall strategy. The primary factor in the bonus calculation was net profit percentage, defined as sales minus cost of goods and minus all operating expenses, including labor. Other factors, such as inventory control, were also included in the bonus calculations for particular managers.

Of her contract, Renay said, "You're on contract to make *this.* If you don't, you don't bonus, and potentially, you don't have a job."

Being a non-union operator gave Oliver's flexibility in pay structure. In a typical unionized Northern California supermarket, deli clerks reached top scale at about $13.50 per hour while journeyman grocery clerks, including checkers, made over $19.00. Union stores were also required to provide benefits to all courtesy clerks who worked over 16 hours per week and to all other clerks who worked more than 24 hours. At Oliver's top level, deli clerks made about the same amount as cashiers, $14 to $15 per hour. Oliver's benefited from additional cost savings as only employees who worked over 32 hours per week were eligible for benefits.

Eric felt that he needed more help with human resource issues: "I think if we had a dedicated professional, just one for the two stores, they could take care of a lot of issues we have, such as hiring people we shouldn't have." Tom agreed with Eric that more help was needed and that poor hiring practices and ignorance about the details of worker's compensation laws had cost Oliver's dearly. It had suffered a number of injuries in the year the Santa Rosa store opened and the change in their accident rate contributed to an increase in their premiums from $200,000 to $1.2 million in one year's time. The rates had since come down, but they were still at a 30 percent premium over industry standards. Tom also cited the need to improve Oliver's training program, especially in the meat department, where Oliver's needed to develop its own apprentice program if it was to remain non-union throughout the store. Most butchers were trained either in family shops or through the apprentice program at the local union meat hall. However, Steve did not feel that there was enough work for a 40-hour professional and instead outsourced training to a consulting firm.

The General Manager's Role

Tom's role as general manager required him to do tasks beyond that of store manager. With input from Eric and the department managers, Tom was responsible for writing all department budgets and

for negotiating them with Steve. Tom also wrote the ad budget and ran Oliver's advertising program, coordinating newsprint and radio ads with respective agencies on a weekly basis. He was responsible for the quarterly "Direct to You" mailer. He actively pursued co-op money from vendors to support additional radio advertising during the holidays, and spent an additional $25,000–$30,000 during that period. Tom was also responsible for maintaining all training materials. He spoke about his background:

> I began working at Alpha Beta (the ancestor of the current Albertson's Chain) in 1975 as a bagger in high school. I worked my way through my undergraduate studies at Cal-State San Bernardino (BA in political science 1982) at Alpha Beta. In 1985, while working as an assistant store manager, I enrolled at Sonoma State University and took a sufficient number of accounting courses to sit for and pass the CPA exam. I then went to work for Eckhoff Accountancy Corp. in San Rafael in 1988. I never received certification due to lack of audit experience. In 1989, I became a minority owner and controller for Montecito Markets. We opened a store in Rincon Valley and shortly thereafter one in Lakeport. In 1991, I sold my shares and went to work for Steve as the general manager in Cotati. When we opened the Santa Rosa store, I moved up there and ran it for the first five years. I was brought down to Cotati in October of 2004, to shore up some management problems and coordinate the limited remodeling we've been doing. Eric was promoted to store manager in Cotati and transferred to Santa Rosa when I came down here.

A recent graduate with an MBA degree from a local state university, Tom had been directly involved in all aspects of opening the Santa Rosa store, in the Cotati store remodel, and performing the financial analysis for the potential new store acquisitions.

Tom assumed that if a second Oliver's in Santa Rosa were opened, he would be replaced as Cotati store manager and be freed up to function solely as general manager. Due to the time-consuming nature of his duties as store manager, Tom had had little opportunity to coach Eric and the other managers in the Santa Rosa store. He felt that he was successful in his role as store manager but that his general manager duties suffered from the demands put on a store manager. Additionally, Tom's entire salary was charged to the Cotati store and his bonus was based solely on that store.

Nevertheless, Tom expressed some frustration stemming from his uncertainty about what direction Steve wanted to take Oliver's for the long term. If Steve wanted to own Oliver's for 20 more years, then Tom thought he was doing the right things. If he wanted to sell in five years, they needed to make some changes. At the same time, Tom was comfortable with the level of supervision he received, noting that "Steve is very generous . . . He knows when to be involved and when not to."

THE EXPANSION DECISION

In weighing the decision to bid on one or both Kroger-owned supermarkets, Steve and Tom compiled demographic data and financial data for each location. Tom explained Oliver's site-selection criteria:

> We are looking for existing buildings with older leases that are renting below current market value. We look for an area that is growing in population with at least 10,000 households making over $75,000 per year, with at least 25 percent of the population having had college educations, all within a three-mile radius. An important criterion is the absence of Whole Foods within the trade area as they appeal directly to the same demographic. We do not currently cater to Hispanic shoppers, which could be an issue for the proposed Stony Point Road (Santa Rosa) location.

Tom estimated that they would need to invest approximately $2 million in each store to make it an Oliver's Market. Exhibit 13 presents selected demographic data for the Oliver's Markets in Cotati and Santa Rosa, Exhibit 14 presents comparative demographic data for the Santa Rosa Ralph's supermarket and Novato Bell Market, and Exhibit 15 summarizes information about existing and potential competitors in each location.

Kroger's Santa Rosa supermarket, Ralph's, was a traditional market, with deli, bakery, dry and frozen grocery, produce, meat, and liquor sections. Tom thought that he could run the store in its current condition, incorporating natural and organic items, and be profitable. He estimated that the market rate rent for this site would be about $360,000 per year. Ralph's was located in a center that was fully occupied and that had more than 20 other businesses, including a Longs' Drugs, Radio Shack, Carl's Jr., KFC, Subway

and Domino's Pizza. There was also a Chinese restaurant, a Mexican restaurant, a hair salon, a mail center, and a bank.

Kroger's had decided to put two Bell Markets in Novato up for sale. Oliver's management was interested in the South Novato Boulevard site because it had a very favorable lease and because it was the southernmost store in central Novato, meaning that approximately half the population would have to go past that store to get to its competitors. Estimated market rate rent for this location was about $460,000 per year. This Bell Market was located in a center considered tiny by comparison to the Vintage Oaks Mall that housed Costco across the freeway; still, the site housed the only post office in Novato. It also featured an Ace hardware, a bicycle shop, and a couple of small restaurants.

Oliver's Future

Steve and Tom had previously considered expanding to three stores, even making an offer on one, but nothing had come of these bids. Steve stated unequivocally that he would not open a third store on his own. He was interested in the possibility, however, because it would provide the opportunity to explore some sort of ownership position for Tom. Tom's future was a concern to Steve. He was comfortable with Tom's leadership style and with his decision making. He felt that he and Tom were very much alike and that Tom ran Oliver's Markets the way he, Steve, would run it. That allowed Steve to be as involved as he wanted to be, with no particular day-to-day responsibility.

Steve felt that his days of working 60 to 80 hours per week were past and admitted that he was uncertain what he would do if Tom left to pursue something else. He stated that perhaps then it would be time to sell. If Oliver's expanded, however, Tom could buy into the company and become a minority partner; Tom would also relinquish his position as store manager and function solely as general manager. Steve was nervous about the decision to bid on either (or both) supermarkets, and debated whether or not Oliver's should expand at all. Also, as his wife was ill and his daughter was not actively involved in running the family business, Steve wondered if perhaps a new expansion initiative might provide the impetus for him to begin to step aside and thereby allow his trusted general manager, Tom, to buy into and eventually take over the business. Steve said,

(Continued on page C-47)

Exhibit 13   **Selected Demographic Data for Oliver's Markets, Cotati and Santa Rosa**

	Cotati	Santa Rosa
Population	50,458	34,966
Number of households	15,867	14,777
Average household size	3.18	2.37
Under 14	20.8%	16.6%
15 to 24 years	18.7	9.7
25 to 44 years	32.3	21.5
45 to 64 years	20.2	28.1
Over 65	8.0	24.1
	100.0%	100.0%
Race		
White	80.9%	90.1%
Black	2.0	0.9
Asian	5.2	2.5
Other	11.9	6.5
Hispanic or Latino of any race	13.3	6.4
Educational Attainment for Population 25 Years and Over		
Less than high school grad	12.3%	7.3%
High school grad	23.3	17.9
Some college	30.0	26.9
Associate degree	9.8	8.8
Bachelor's degree	17.8	23.8
Graduate or professional degree	6.7	15.2
Percent high school graduate or higher	87.7	92.7
Percent bachelor's degree or higher	24.5	39.0
Household Income		
Less than $10,000	6.0%	3.3%
$10,000 to $14,999	4.2	3.5
$15,000 to $24,999	8.9	7.7
$25,000 to $34,999	11.3	10.8
$35,000 to $49,999	16.5	15.0
$50,000 to $74,999	25.1	20.1
$75,000 to $99,999	14.3	13.1
$100,000 to $149,999	10.1	15.2
$150,000 to $199,999	1.9	5.3
$200,000 or more	1.7	6.0
	100.0%	100.0%
Median household income (dollars)	$52,010	$62,067

Source: American Fact Finder on www.census.gov.

Exhibit 14   **Demographic Data: Ralph's Santa Rosa and Bell Markets, Novato**

	Ralph's Market, 461 Stony Point Rd., Santa Rosa, CA (0–3 mile radius)	Bell Market, 1535 S. Novato Blvd. Novato, CA (0–3 mile radius)
Population		
2010 projection	122,986	47,700
2005 estimate	114,839	46,905
2000 census	106,307	46,114
Growth 2005–2010	7.09%	1.69%
Growth 2000–2005	8.03%	1.72%
2005 Estimated Population by Race Classification		
White alone	75,395	38,393
Black or African American alone	3,042	852
American Indian and Alaska Native alone	2,269	229
Asian alone	5,489	2,553
Hispanic or Latino	38,236	6,676
2005 Estimated Population by Age		
Age 0–14 (%)	21.46%	17.87%
Age 15–24 (%)	14.28	11.49
Age 25–44 (%)	31.95	24.54
Age 45–64 (%)	22.93	32.09
Age 65 and over (%)	9.38	14.01
2005 estimated median age	33.72	42.39
2005 estimated average age	35.17	40.63
2005 Estimated Population Age 25+ by Educational Attainment		
Less than high school graduate	16,886	3,093
High school graduate (or GED)	16,705	5,953
Some college, no degree	19,490	9,092
Associate degree	6,487	2,688
Bachelor's degree	10,159	8,150
Master's degree	2,476	2,611
Professional school degree or doctorate	1,584	1,545
Households		
2010 projection	41,870	18,686
2005 estimate	39,745	18,238
2000 census	37,534	17,824
Growth, 2005–2010	5.35%	2.46%
Growth, 2000–2005	5.89%	2.32%
2005 Estimated Households by Household Income	39,745	18,238
Income less than $15,000	4,154	1,043
Income, $15,000–$24,999	3,917	1,039
Income, $25,000–$34,999	3,971	1,119
Income, $35,000–$49,999	6,367	2,133
Income, $50,000–$74,999	8,880	3,446

(*Continued*)

Exhibit 14 **Continued**

	Ralph's Market, 461 Stony Point Rd., Santa Rosa, CA (0–3 mile radius)	Bell Market, 1535 S. Novato Blvd. Novato, CA (0–3 mile radius)
Income, $75,000–$99,999	5,598	2,763
Income, $100,000–$149,999	5,050	3,500
Income, $150,000 and more	1,809	3,193
2005 estimated average household income	$64,736	$102,150
2005 estimated median household income	$54,123	$78,062
2005 estimated per capita income	$22,942	$40,153
2005 estimated average household size	2.80	2.52

Source: Claritas online demographics database, www.claritas.com, supplied by Oliver's Markets.

Exhibit 15 **Competitor Stores Near Proposed Locations for Oliver's Markets**

Store	Estimated Square Feet of Selling Space	Estimated Weekly Sales (in thousands)	Estimated Distance in Miles	Notes
Santa Rosa Location				
Ralph's/proposed Oliver's	20,848	n/a	—	Could run as is and remodel while open. Estimated $1–$2 million to remodel.
FoodMaxx	50,000	$840	0.5	Former Food 4 Less
G&G	53,000	750	1.0	Plus 25,000 square feet of warehouse
Lola's	6,000	220	1.2	Hispanic market, originally a carniceria
Safeway	35,000	500	1.4	Marketplace format
Raley's	38,000	500	2.3	Includes pharmacy
Novato Location				
Bell Market/proposed Oliver's	16,917	n/a	—	Some cases need to be replaced. Could remodel while open.
Whole Foods	39,000	n/a	0.6	Anticipated opening—early 2007
Trader Joe's	10,000	n/a	1.0	Scheduled to open November 2005
Safeway				
900 Diablo Ave	60,000	900	0.1	One block north
470 Ignacio Blvd	25,000	500	3.5	South off Highway 101
Albertson's	45,000	300	1.2	North on same major road
Bell Market	20,000	131		Also for sale
Apple Market	26,000	230	3.2	Out-of-state ownership
Costco	137,000	2,028	1.5	South off U.S. 101 on opposite side of freeway

n/a = Not available.
Source: Oliver's Markets.

"We have grown every year except the last two years. I attribute it to us not doing as good a job as we could do. I can't do anything about Costco, but I can do something about the job we're doing here. I don't think the age of smaller stores like ours is gone."

Bibliography

American Factfinder. Available at www.census.gov (accessed May to July 2005).

"Consumers Continue to Shift Shopping Away from Grocery Stores." Available at http://retailindustry.about.com/library/bl/03q1/bl_acn030403a.htm (accessed April 10, 2005).

Currie, Neil. "UBS Q-Series Report: Do Supermarkets Have a Future?" *Progressive Grocer* 84, no. 6 (2005), pp. 62–79.

D'Aveni, Richard A. *Hypercompetition: Managing the Dynamics of Strategic Maneuvering.* New York: The Free Press, 1994.

Economic Research Service of the U.S. Department of Agriculture. "Food Market Structures: Food Retailing." Available at www.ers.usda.gov/briefing.htm (accessed June 15, 2005).

FMI Speaks 2004 Key Industry Facts. Prepared by FMI Information Service, July 2004, p. 16. Available at www.fmi.org (accessed June 2005).

Food Marketing Institute. "Facts and Figures." Available at www.fmi.org (accessed June and July 2005).

Francese, Peter. "Trend Ticker: Trouble in Store." *American Demographics* 25, no. 10 (December 2003–January 2004), p. 36.

Goll, David. "Grocers, Union Reach Tentative Agreement." *East Bay Business Times,* February 27, 2004. Available at www.bizjournals.com/eastbay/stories/2004/02/23/daily36.html (accessed October 20, 2005).

Heller, Walter, and Jenny McTaggart. "The Search for Growth: 71st Annual Report of the Grocery Industry." *Progressive Grocer* 83, no. 6 (2004), pp. 31–41.

Lasher, William. *Process to Profits: Strategic Planning for a Growing Business.* Mason, OH: Texere, 2005.

McTaggart, Jenny, and Walter Heller. "Forces of Change: 72nd Annual Report of the Grocery Industry." *Progressive Grocer* 84, no. 6 (2005), pp. 48–60.

Naumes, William, and Margaret J. Naumes. *The Art & Craft of Case Writing.* Thousand Oaks, California: Sage, 1999.

"Outlook 2004." *Santa Rosa Press Democrat.* Available at www1.pressdemocrat.com/apps/pbcs.dll/section?Category=BUSINESS06 (accessed May 2005).

Porter, Michael E. *Competitive Strategy: Techniques for Analyzing Industries and Competitors.* New York: Free Press, 1980.

"SN's Top 75." *Supermarket News.* Available at www.supermarketnews.com/sntop752004.htm (accessed March 21, 2005).

"Store Definitions." *Progressive Grocer's 2003 Marketing Guidebook and Bishop Consulting, 2003.* Available at www.fmi.org/facts_figs/superfact.htm (accessed June 2005).

"The Super 50: Views from the Top." *Progressive Grocer* 84, no. 7 (2005), pp. 74–84.

Tarnowski, Joseph, and Walter Heller. "The Super 50." *Progressive Grocer* 83, no. 7 (2004), pp. 59–66.

Turock, Art. "Alternative Formats: Teflon Retailing." *Progressive Grocer* 84, no. 7 (2005), pp. 22–24.

Endnotes

[1] Woodlands Market was located in Kentfield, a town with upscale demographics in affluent Marin County, approximately 40 miles south of Santa Rosa.
[2] Economic Research Service of the U.S. Department of Agriculture, www.ers.usda.gov/briefing.
[3] *Progressive Grocer* 83, no. 7 (May 1, 2004), p. 59.
[4] *Progressive Grocer* 83, no. 6 (April 15, 2004), pp. 31–32.
[5] Neil Currie, analyst for UBS, advised against opening stores solely for the pursuit of market share. In a report published in *Progressive Grocer,* he wrote, "There's too much capacity in the marketplace, leading to poor sales densities. While short-term sacrifices may have to be made to take out weaker competition, stores will be much more efficient if there are less around." *Progressive Grocer* 84, no. 6 (April 15, 2005), p. 70.
[6] www.ers.usda.gov.
[7] *American Demographics* 25, no. 10 (December 2003–January 2004), p. 36.
[8] *Progressive Grocer,* 84(6), April 15, 2005, p. 70.
[9] Report found on www.retailindustryabout.com on April 10, 2005.
[10] The bitter dispute, which affected 852 stores from San Diego in the south to Mammoth Lakes in the north, had begun on October 11, 2003, when 21,000 union workers walked off their jobs at Safeway's 329 Vons and Pavilions supermarkets. Later the same day, it expanded to include a total of 70,000 grocery employees throughout the region when Albertson's and Kroger, which owned the Ralph's chain, locked out their union workers. The standoff centered on reductions in employee health care benefits proposed by the grocers, as well as a two-tiered compensation package that would result in lower pay and benefits for newly hired workers. Union leaders characterized the health care cuts as excessive. Safeway CEO Steve Burd told industry analysts that major cuts in expenses were necessary for his and other traditional grocery companies to compete with nonunion rivals such as Wal-Mart Stores Inc. Losses suffered by the grocers as a result of the strike were estimated at $2.5 billion. D. Goll, "Grocers, Union Reach Tentative Settlement," *East Bay Business Times,* February 27, 2004, www.bizjournals.com/eastbay/stories/2004/02/23/daily36.html (accessed October 20, 2005).

JetBlue Airways: Can It Survive in a Turbulent Industry?

Janet Rovenpor
Manhattan College

It was the night of February 17, 2005. Snowfall in the Boston area had already reached 55 inches for the season, with several more major storms on the way. People started to line up at the Prudential Center's Terrace Food Court on Boylston Street. One woman was dressed in a Winnie-the-Pooh costume. A man a few steps behind her wore a straw hat and a colorful lei. Still others carried donations of canned food intended for the Greater Boston Food Bank. What brought these Bostonians out on such a cold winter night? Dressed to represent a JetBlue Airways travel destination, they arrived early for a chance to win the free airline tickets that had been promised to the first 250 people. In all, 1,000 people showed up for the event. JetBlue rose to the occasion and rewarded them with double the number of tickets originally planned. JetBlue tickets were especially coveted at this time of year, providing travelers with an opportunity to fly to such sunny destinations as Tampa and West Palm Beach.

The JetBlue giveaway program in Boston was meant to demonstrate the airline's commitment to expanding its operations at Logan Airport. More significantly, it was part of the company's fifth anniversary celebration. JetBlue had a lot to celebrate. Annual revenues in 2004 surpassed $1 billion. The company thus met the U.S. Transportation Department's definition of a major airline carrier

and became the youngest airline ever to achieve such status. JetBlue organized other celebratory promotions, including one in which passengers could win a variety of prizes by logging on to the company's Web site. Prizes included 12 XM satellite radio systems (to feature the airline's new XM digital radio in-flight service) and five La-Z-Boy recliners (in honor of the airline's leather seats and extra leg room). Here was one of the company's strategies for success—a dedicated effort to make air travel fun and comfortable.

COMPANY BACKGROUND

David Neeleman, a Salt Lake City entrepreneur, founded JetBlue Airways when he was 39 years old. His vision was to "bring humanity back to air travel."[1] He had raised $130 million in capital—a record high for an airline industry start-up—to do just that. In its first full year in business, JetBlue operated 64 flights a day and served 12 destinations in four states. It had 11 Airbus A320 aircraft and employed 1,028 employees. By late 2005, JetBlue was operating 318 flights a day and serving 33 destinations in 14 states, Puerto Rico, the Dominican Republic, and the Bahamas. It had a fleet of 82 Airbus A320 aircraft and employed approximately 8,600 employees. It won several awards, including "Best U.S. Airline" by *Conde Nast Traveler* readers and "Best Overall Airline" for onboard service.

David Neeleman's Entrepreneurial Spirit

Using his wristwatch calculator, David Neeleman (pronounced Neel-uh-man), the CEO of JetBlue, could punch in some numbers and predict to his colleagues that a competitor was not going to break even because it operated too many flights in and out of small markets.[2] He might have been found once a week on a JetBlue flight serving biscotti, animal crackers, or Terra-Blue potato chips to passengers. Passengers were surprised when they learned that the crew member nicknamed "Snack Boy" was actually the CEO.[3] Neeleman would ask passengers if they were comfortable and jot down their suggestions for improvement on a cocktail napkin. He also loved giving interviews and explaining how JetBlue got its start.

Contrary to popular notions, JetBlue did not enter the airline industry as an overnight sensation that simply benefited from the good fortune of having the right strategy at the right time. The company's success took years of planning and preparation on the part of its founder. Some of Neeleman's insights came from careful study of the airline industry; others came in a roundabout way as he tried to find a suitable occupation that would hold his interest. Over the course of his career, Neeleman would develop skills in accounting, salesmanship, and technology. He would use his own air travel experiences as lessons regarding how to provide superior customer service. He would learn that he suffered from attention deficit disorder (ADD), a situation that had its advantages and disadvantages. Neeleman attributed his creativity and high levels of energy to ADD, yet he also recognized that he had difficulty writing memos and keeping track of his belongings. He knew he needed to work with other individuals who could handle details.

Neeleman was born in São Paulo, Brazil, in 1959. His father worked there as a foreign correspondent for United Press International. The family moved to Sandy, Utah, when Neeleman was five years old. One of Neeleman's first jobs was in his grandfather's grocery store in downtown Salt Lake City.[4] As a teenager he would order items, cut the meat, and stack the beer. He learned from his grandfather never to disappoint customers. Satisfied customers would return. Neeleman even pushed elderly customers'

shopping carts home for them. Later, when Neeleman became CEO of JetBlue, he performed similar good deeds. He once drove an elderly couple from New York's JFK Airport to their home in Connecticut (to where he had relocated) to save them $200 for a taxi. His customer service message was communicated throughout the company. It was common, for example, for a pilot to buy dozens of McDonald's Happy Meals for children whose flight was delayed.[5]

As a young man, Neeleman studied accounting at the University of Utah. He did not complete four consecutive years of study. After his freshman year, he spent time in Brazil as a Mormon missionary. There, he learned to be frugal, saving $1,300 out of the $3,000 his parents had given him.[6] Neeleman dropped out of college for good in his junior year and opened up his own travel agency near Salt Lake City. He sold vacation packages to Hawaii that included airfare and a stay in a time-share. His company grew to 20 employees and brought in $8 million in business.[7] Unfortunately, the air charter company with which he had an agreement to transport his customers, Pineapple Express, went bankrupt. Neeleman was forced to close his business in 1983, but he took away with him two lessons: (1) Never rely on someone who could put you out of business, and (2) use funds wisely so that they will be available during tough times.[8]

In 1984, Neeleman joined Morris Air, a small local carrier based in Salt Lake City. Working there for about eight years, he held the titles of executive vice president and later president. The carrier's most popular routes provided service from Salt Lake City to Los Angeles, from Salt Lake City to Hawaii, and from Salt Lake City to Cancun, Mexico. Neeleman solicited business from shoppers in malls and sold honeymoon packages to couples during weddings he attended. He convinced venture capitalists to invest $15 million and expanded Morris Air's operations to 300 flights a day with a fleet of 22 Boeing 737 airplanes. He introduced electronic ticketing and allowed reservation agents to work from home.

Neeleman's early ideas at Morris Air were later implemented at JetBlue Airways. Take, for example, the unconventional way in which he sold airline tickets at shopping malls and weddings. When JetBlue started service out of Long Beach, California, in 2001, paid college interns rode local streets in nine Volkswagen Beatles painted in the airline's logo and colors. For a month, they handed out bumper stickers, buttons, and tote bags to potential passengers in hotels, movie studios, and restaurants. It was especially important to talk to bartenders and hotel concierges—people whom vacationers sought out for all kinds of advice.[9] Off-beat guerrilla advertising was always part of the company's approach to marketing.

Like Morris Air, JetBlue also issued electronic tickets. Travelers printed boarding passes at check-in kiosks at the airport. This was convenient for people like Neeleman who often forgot their paper tickets at home. Reservation agents worked from home, serving six-hour shifts with two 15-minute breaks. By February 2005, 900 agents worked from their homes in the Salt Lake City area. The company thus saved money on paper tickets, on postage needed to mail out paper tickets, and on rent for office space. Neeleman raised capital for JetBlue from some of the same investors in Morris Air.

In 1993, Southwest Airlines purchased Morris Air for $129 million. The deal made Neeleman $20 million wealthier. Investors got back two and a half times their investment. Southwest hired Neeleman, but his tenure as a member of the executive planning committee was very brief. Unable to get used to the company's policies and procedures, he was fired. At Southwest Airlines, though, Neeleman learned that it was important to treat employees with respect and that it was better to purchase new airplanes instead of leasing them.[10]

Because he had signed a five-year noncompete agreement with Southwest Airlines, Neeleman had to wait before he could start up another airline company. He kept himself busy in the meantime. With a college student, he developed a computerized system called "Open Skies" that could handle electronic ticketing, Internet bookings, and revenue management. He sold the system to Hewlett-Packard in 1999 for $22 million. Neeleman also served as a consultant to a low-fare Canadian carrier, WestJet.

By 1998, Neeleman was ready to move on and start JetBlue. He contributed $5 million of his own money and raised $130 million from investors, including George Soros, Weston Presidio, and Chase Manhattan Bank's venture capital group. When he began JetBlue, Neeleman and his wife moved to New Canaan, Connecticut, with their nine children. His salary in 2004 was $200,000, with a bonus of $90,000. He owned 7.3 million JetBlue shares, worth about $150 million as of December 2005.[11]

THE JETBLUE CONCEPT

Neeleman envisioned that JetBlue would combine the low fares of a discount airline carrier with the comforts of a cozy den in people's homes. Passengers would be able to save money while they sat in leather seats, munched on gourmet snacks, and watched television. Individual monitors were installed in all seats so that passengers had access to 24-channel live television via satellite—for free. Neeleman wanted leather seats because they were more durable and easier to clean (he had once had the unfortunate personal experience of having been assigned a fabric seat soaked with urine). Having been on a flight forced to land because of engine failure, and not receiving any information or compensation afterward, Neeleman also made sure that inconvenienced JetBlue travelers would get discount coupons for future flights as well as food and accommodations.

Neeleman's customer service philosophy fit in well with the sociocultural and political environment of the times. In 1999, the House Transportation Committee held hearings in which passengers told horror stories of being kept on a Northwest Airlines plane during a blizzard in Detroit for hours as toilets overflowed, hungry infants cried, and chronically ill travelers went without medication. One woman complained that her six-year-old son, who was traveling as a unaccompanied minor, was put in a hotel room with a sexually abusive teenager.[12] As a result of such complaints, the Clinton administration tried to enact a passenger "bill of rights" that would have doubled the minimum payment for lost baggage to $2,500, doubled the maximum compensation for being bumped from an overbooked flight to $800, required airlines to tell customers whether they must change planes during a trip, and required airlines to hire an ombudsman.

Airline companies were opposed to the bill but voluntarily agreed to make improvements to customer service on their own. Their 12-point plan included a pledge to quote the lowest available fare on their telephone reservation systems; to notify passengers of delays, cancellations, and diversions; and to make an effort to provide food, water, restrooms, and medical attention to on-board passengers held on the tarmac for extended periods.[13] Following the terrorist attacks of September 11, 2001, however, the nation's attention shifted from issues related to customer satisfaction to issues related to airline security.

BUILDING A STRONG TOP MANAGEMENT TEAM

Neeleman took the staffing of his senior management team very seriously. He did not hesitate to recruit top talent from other airline companies. As Ann Roades, executive vice president of human resources, said, "He realized that if you hire A-players, you don't have to sit on them and tell them what to do."[14] David Barger was hired as president and chief operating officer. With 10 years' experience in the airline industry, Barger had been the vice president at Continental Airlines and was responsible for running its Newark, New Jersey, hub. Barger helped Neeleman make the decision to purchase all new aircraft of a single body type and to eventually operate point-to-point service instead of the more costly hub and spoke system.[15]

John Owen was hired as executive vice president and chief financial officer. His career began as a financial analyst at American Airlines. He later worked at Southwest Airlines as vice president of operations/ planning and analysis, and then as treasurer. Every morning, Owen received the previous day's financial and operating statistics. He evaluated such information as the number of seats sold, revenues generated from every passenger mile flown, take-off and landing times, and the length of time it took to unload baggage. He traveled to Europe in an attempt to raise capital to finance the purchase of new jets. He was opposed to installing live television in airplanes, viewing it as an expense that would never be recovered. He realized, however, that sometimes financial officers needed to see the big picture. He learned that service was an essential part of the JetBlue experience and that it contributed to "loyalty and passenger buzz that will result in higher demand."[16]

Neeleman's longtime business partner Thomas Kelly became JetBlue's executive vice president and general counsel. Kelly had left private law practice to join Morris Air in 1990. Ann Rhoades was hired as executive vice president to handle human resources. She had been the head of the people department at Southwest Airlines and was the one who had fired Neeleman from the carrier back in 1993. She implemented many of the company's highly successful human resource strategies to hire, retain, and motivate high quality employees. Out of all five original members of the top management team, she was the only one to leave JetBlue, doing so in 2005 to devote time to her own consulting company, People Ink,

in Arizona. She remained, however, a member of JetBlue's board of directors.

JETBLUE'S NEW YORK CITY ROOTS

On February 11, 2000, JetBlue launched its first ceremonial flight between Buffalo and New York City, making John F. Kennedy International Airport (JFK) its hub. The one-way fare for the first month was set at $25, which would then go up to $98 round-trip. Fares available from other carriers at that time were as high as $600 round-trip.[17] Although the flight was delayed for three hours because of heavy fog, David Neeleman was exuberant. His vision was about to become a reality. Senator Charles Schumer, who had been instrumental in helping the airline obtain its 75 take-off and landing slots at JFK, and Mayor Rudolph Guiliani were among the celebrity passengers. Schumer wanted to make good on a campaign promise that he would help stimulate the stagnant economy in upper New York State. Given low-fare accessibility to such cities as Buffalo and Syracuse, outside employers might be encouraged to open up new businesses.

Later that day, JetBlue introduced its first commercial flight from JFK to Fort Lauderdale, Florida, with 152 passengers aboard. The fare was $159 one-way, which was 70 percent less than the fares of other carriers. JetBlue would soon fly to Tampa, Orlando, West Palm Beach, and Fort Myers, Florida. David Barger viewed Florida as "the sixth borough of New York."[18] It became JetBlue's most popular destination.

The decision to start up service at JFK was a risky one. The airport was called the "black sheep of New York airports" because of its crowded skies, high costs, and inevitable hassles.[19] Even Southwest Airlines had entered the region by choosing to fly in and out of a secondary airport, MacArthur Airport in Islip, Long Island, instead of JFK. Yet Neeleman saw an opportunity at JFK that no one else saw. While airlines faced heavy delays during the 3:00–8:00 p.m. time period (when most international flights arrived and departed), the morning hours were relatively free. Neeleman noted that only 15 flights left JFK between the hours of 8:00 and 9:00 a.m.[20] JFK had an average gate utilization of 2.7 flights a day, much lower than La Guardia's 5.5 flights a day.[21]

In addition, the demographics were great. Neeleman originally thought that JetBlue's target market consisted of the 8 million people in a five-mile radius around JFK. He later found that his service also appealed to young, affluent professionals with Manhattan zip codes. "You have this large population that makes a lot of money per capita, and everyone in New York would like to get out. At the same time, everyone outside New York would like to get in. It's truly the nirvana of all markets," said Neeleman.[22] New York City travelers had not had access to a low-fare carrier since People Express folded in 1986.

JETBLUE'S RAPID EXPANSION

From the beginning, JetBlue introduced a simple fare structure. All passengers flew coach and purchased one-way, nonrefundable tickets. The average one-way fare in 2000 was $88.84; in 2004, it was $103.61. No Saturday stay was required. A $25 fee was charged to passengers who wanted to change their departure times.

Exhibit 1 shows JetBlue's rapid growth. By the end of 2000, JetBlue was flying to 12 cities and had boarded its millionth passenger. It had 1,174 employees and a fleet of 10 Airbus A320 airplanes. In addition to its Florida destinations, JetBlue provided service from JFK to Buffalo and Rochester, New York; to Burlington, Vermont; to Salt Lake City, Utah; and to Oakland and Ontario, California. One of its goals was to balance out short-haul routes with transcontinental routes.

In April 2001, JetBlue boarded its 2 millionth passenger. It had more than doubled the number

of its aircraft from the previous year. It also added service from JFK to Syracuse, New York; to Seattle, Washington; to Denver, Colorado; to Long Beach, California; and to New Orleans, Louisiana. More important, it started direct service between Washington, D.C. (Dulles International Airport), and Fort Lauderdale, Florida—on the first flight, 133 out of 162 seats were full. Fares ranged from $79 to $199 one-way. This marked the beginning of the company's plans to operate as a point-to-point carrier. JetBlue wanted be the preferred carrier for Washington-area businesses. Executives mailed letters, along with free round-trip tickets, to corporate travel managers and chief financial officers of the top 100 local companies.[23]

On March 7, 2002, JetBlue flew its 5 millionth passenger. On April 12, JetBlue raised $182 million from its first public offering of stock, selling 5.87 million shares at a starting price of $27 a share. In September, JetBlue acquired LiveTV LLC, its provider of in-flight satellite entertainment systems. JetBlue added service from Washington, D.C., to Oakland and Long Beach, California. It significantly expanded its operations out of Long Beach by offering nine flights to Oakland, California; five daily flights to Las Vegas, Nevada; and one daily flight to Salt Lake City, Utah. This brought JetBlue into close competition with Southwest Airlines, which had dominated the California market for many years. JetBlue opportunistically launched its service between JFK and Las Vegas two months ahead of schedule, filling a void left by National Airlines, a Las Vegas–based discount carrier, which had halted all flights as part of its liquidation efforts.

On January 1, 2003, JetBlue flew its 10 millionth passenger. It also launched service that year between JFK and San Diego, Long Beach, Fort Lauderdale,

Exhibit 1 *JetBlue Airways' Expansion from 2000 to 2004*

	2000	2001	2002	2003	2004
Number of cities served	12	18	20	21	30
Number of departures	10,265	26,334	44,144	66,920	90,532
Number of aircraft (owned and leased)	10	21	37	53	69
Number of full-time and part-time employees	1,174	2,361	4,011	5,433	7,211
Percentage of sales through JetBlue.com	28.7%	44.1%	63%	73%	75.4%

Source: 2005 10-K report, JetBlue Web site.

and it ordered a new type of plane, the Embraer 190, and started construction on a new hangar complex at JFK. It pulled out of Atlanta, Georgia, because of competition from Delta and AirTran on its transcontinental routes to Oakland and Long Beach.

In 2004, JetBlue added satellite radio and movie channels to its in-flight entertainment systems. It had 7,211 employees and 69 airplanes. It was a big year for route expansion. JetBlue started service out of Boston (with flights to Long Beach, Denver, Fort Lauderdale, Orlando, and Tampa) and out of New York's LaGuardia Airport (with flights to Fort Lauderdale). It launched service out of JFK to seven new cities, including Aguadillo, Puerto Rico; Santiago, Dominican Republic; and Nassau, the Bahamas.

In 2005, JetBlue added flights from Boston to San Jose, California; Las Vegas, Nevada; and Seattle, Washington. It started a new service between Washington's Dulles Airport and San Diego, California. In the New York area, it added flights out of JFK to Burbank, California; to Portland, Oregon; and to Ponce, Puerto Rico; and out of La Guardia to West Palm Beach, Florida, and to San Juan, Puerto Rico. In September, people were glued to their television sets as they watched the pilot of JetBlue flight 292 successfully make an emergency landing at Los Angeles International airport (with the wheel of the aircraft's front landing gear skewed sideways). In a first in aviation history, passengers on the airplane watched their own predicament on live television. In November, JetBlue started service between New York's JFK Airport and Boston's Logan Airport with its Embraer 190 airplanes. To celebrate the introduction of a new type of airplane into its fleet, JetBlue employees randomly distributed free tickets to pedestrians walking in Manhattan who were wearing the color blue. On the first day of service, most of the Embraer flights were delayed due to minor maintenance issues.

JETBLUE'S COMMITMENT TO LOW COSTS AND SERVICE QUALITY

Over the years, JetBlue had developed an excellent reputation for on-time performance, few reports from passengers about mishandled baggage, and a low number of passenger complaints (see Exhibit 2). For the 12 months ending in January 2004, 84 percent of JetBlue's flights arrived within 15 minutes of their scheduled times (earning JetBlue third place for this measure among major U.S. airlines). For the 12 months ending in January 2005, 80.3 percent of JetBlue's flights arrived within 15 minutes of their scheduled times (fourth place). In 2003, JetBlue received 3.21 reports of mishandled baggage (baggage that was lost or damaged) per 1,000 passengers, putting it in fourth place among 18 other carriers. In 2004, that number went down to 2.99 (third place). In 2003, JetBlue had 0.31 complaints per 100,000 passengers (for such things as cancelled flights, poor customer service, discrimination); in 2004 it had 0.27, which moved it from fourth place to third place among the major airlines.

JetBlue modeled itself after the pioneering discount carrier Southwest Airlines. Managers at Southwest had figured out how to operate an airline company successfully by keeping its costs down. Both carriers offered passengers low fares and operated point-to-point systems. Flight attendants wore casual uniforms and created a relaxed atmosphere for passengers. The carriers became highly efficient by using one type of aircraft, serving only snacks and maintaining quick turnaround times. Exhibit 3 displays comparative operating cost statistics for 10 major airline carriers.

Southwest Airlines flew only Boeing 737s; JetBlue flew only Airbus A320s. The Airbus model had 30 additional seats and was more fuel efficient and less costly to operate than a Boeing 737.[24] Costs were kept down since pilots and maintenance technicians were trained for only one aircraft. The same spare parts could be stored in inventory. Delta, in comparison, operated 16 different kinds of aircraft. It needed larger and more expensive planes to fly on its international routes. Eight weeks of extra training were required to transfer a pilot from one type of aircraft to another. In addition, Delta had to pay another pilot to cover the pilot-in-training's existing route.[25] This got expensive since pilots earned more than $100 an hour.

Most large airlines required an hour on the ground to service their aircraft and board passengers before taking off again. JetBlue's turnaround time ranged from 20 to 30 minutes. Because no meals were served, JetBlue did not have to wait for catering services to replenish the aircraft. To save time, flight attendants themselves stowed carry-on bags

Exhibit 2 **On-Time Flights, Mishandled Baggage, and Passenger Complaints of Major U.S. Airlines, 2003–2005**

Percentage of Flights Arriving within 15 Minutes of the Scheduled Time, and Carrier Rank

| Airline | 12 Months Ending January 2005 | | 12 Months Ending January 2004 | |
	%	Rank	%	Rank
AirTran	77.4	(10)	77.4	(15)
Alaska	76.7	(12)	79.9	(10)
America West	75.4	(17)	81.9	(6)
American	76.9	(11)	80.3	(9)
American Eagle	73.1	(19)	77.4	(14)
ATA	80.4	(3)	79.3	(13)
Atlantic Southeast	75.2	(18)	75.7	(16)
Comair	76.7	(13)		
Continental	78.7	(8)	81.6	(8)
Delta	75.9	(15)	81.6	(7)
Express Jet	76.5	(14)	79.3	(12)
Hawaiian	94.3	(1)		
Independence Air	75.6	(16)	74.4	(17)
JetBlue	**80.3**	**(4)**	**84.0**	**(3)**
Northwest	79.0	(7)	82.0	(4)
Skywest	82.5	(2)	86.6	(1)
Southwest	79.4	(6)	86.0	(2)
United	79.6	(5)	81.9	(5)
US Airways	78.2	(9)	79.5	(1)
Average	77.8		81.2	

Mishandled Baggage Reports Filed by Passengers

| Airline | January–December 2004 | | January–December 2003 | |
	Reports per 1,000 Passengers	Rank	Reports per 1,000 Passengers	Rank
AirTran	2.82	(1)	2.84	(2)
Alaska	3.51	(5)	2.56	(1)
America West	3.98	(9)	3.30	(5)
American	4.73	(11)	4.45	(12)
American Eagle	8.95	(15)	8.42	(14)
ATA	3.82	(7)	4.06	(11)
Atlantic Southeast	14.49	(19)	15.41	(17)
Comair	10.66	(17)		
Continental	3.58	(6)	3.11	(3)
Delta	5.17	(12)	3.84	(9)
Express Jet	5.70	(14)	4.51	(13)
Hawaiian	2.85	(2)		
Independence Air	10.68	(18)	9.23	(16)
JetBlue	**2.99**	**(3)**	**3.21**	**(4)**
Northwest	4.22	(10)	3.42	(7)
Skywest	10.00	(16)	8.62	(15)
Southwest	3.35	(4)	3.35	(6)
United	3.93	(8)	3.93	(10)
US Airways	5.33	(13)	3.55	(8)
Average	4.91		4.19	

(*Continued*)

Exhibit 2   **Continued**

Passenger Complaints				
	January–December 2004		January–December 2003	
Airline	Complaints per 100,000 Passengers Boarded	**Rank**	Complaints per 100,000 Passengers Boarded	**Rank**
AirTran	0.89	(13)	0.83	(12)
Alaska	3.51	(5)	0.52	(6)
America West	3.98	(9)	0.84	(13)
American	0.88	(12)	0.88	(14)
American Eagle	0.54	(6)	0.51	(5)
ATA	0.79	(10)	0.66	(8)
Atlantic Southeast	0.40	(4)	0.59	(7)
Comair	1.10	(18)		
Continental	0.82	(11)	0.95	(3)
Delta	0.79	(9)	0.78	(17)
Express Jet	0.16	(1)	0.21	(2)
Hawaiian	0.46	(5)		
Independence Air	0.95	(17)	0.76	(9)
JetBlue	**0.27**	**(3)**	**0.31**	**(4)**
Northwest	0.89	(15)	3.42	(7)
Skywest	0.56	(7)	0.30	(3)
Southwest	0.18	(2)	0.14	(1)
United	0.88	(12)	0.83	(11)
US Airways	1.21	(19)	3.55	(8)
Average	0.74		0.71	

Source: U.S. Department of Transportation, Air Travel Consumer Report, www.airconsumer.ost.dot.gov/reports, February 2005.

and coats in the overhead bins. Everyone—pilots, flight attendants, and passengers—helped throw away the trash after each flight. JetBlue's aircraft were the most productive of all U.S. fleets and operated almost 14 hours per day.[26]

There were some differences between JetBlue and Southwest. JetBlue exhibited a stronger commitment to service quality than Southwest. JetBlue offered assigned seats to make boarding a more orderly process. It equipped its planes with leather seats at an additional cost of $15,000 per airplane before Southwest did. The live television was another unique benefit. Southwest did not even offer in-flight movies. JetBlue wanted to ensure that its flights arrived at their destinations on time. It spent extra funds for emergency equipment—life rafts and beacons—so that it could fly over water and avoid traffic along its East Coast routes. It flew at 10,000 feet instead of 18,000 feet to avoid congestion in upstate New York. This added $400 to the cost of operating the flight.[27]

JetBlue paid attention to the little details customers found special. It added amenities while other airlines were cutting back. Delta Air Lines stopped providing hot meals to passengers in 2003. It announced that it would not even sell food on board starting in 2005, nor would it continue to provide pillows. American Airlines also eliminated pillows on its domestic and Caribbean flights to save over $300,000 a year.[28] It reversed its "More Room Throughout Coach" program by adding 12,000 seats back into its fleet of jets in 2005. JetBlue, in contrast, kept its promise to give passengers more legroom. In 2003, it removed a row of seats from its planes, increasing legroom by two inches.[29] Exhibit 4 shows that JetBlue's aircraft "seat pitch" (a measure of the distance from one point on a seat to the same point on the seat in front) was favorable compared to that of other carriers. JetBlue worked with a unit of Bally Total Fitness to offer in-flight yoga cards in seat pockets. Passengers received instruction on how they could hold four yoga poses without removing

(*Continued on page C-58*)

Exhibit 3 **Comparative Operating Cost Statistics, JetBlue versus Major U.S. Airlines, 1995, 2000–2004 (in cents per available seat mile)***

Carrier	Year	Food	Salaries & Benefits	Aircraft Fuel & Oil	Commissions	Landing Fees	Advertising	Other Operating & Maintenance Expenses	Total Operating Expenses	Rent & Leasing Fees
JetBlue	2003	0.06¢	2.12¢	1.08¢	0.00¢	0.22¢	0.18¢	1.90¢	6.06¢	0.72¢
	2004	0.05	1.95	1.35	0.00	0.22	0.13	2.38	6.08	0.63
American	1995	0.41¢	3.70¢	1.01¢	0.80¢	0.15¢	0.15¢	3.23¢	9.45¢	0.73¢
	2000	0.44	4.18	1.48	0.60	0.17	0.13	3.49	10.49	0.74
	2001	0.44	4.55	1.57	0.47	0.19	0.13	4.53	11.89	0.78
	2002	0.40	4.97	1.33	0.35	0.22	0.11	3.75	11.12	0.87
	2003	0.37	4.31	1.57	0.25	0.23	0.09	4.24	11.41	0.83
	2004	0.32	3.72	2.10	0.25	0.23	0.08	4.23	10.94	0.72
Alaska	1995	0.31¢	2.60¢	1.07¢	0.55¢	0.15¢	0.12¢	3.10¢	7.89¢	1.17¢
	2000	0.29	3.53	1.76	0.38	0.18	0.38	3.72	10.25	1.08
	2001	0.31	3.81	1.45	0.35	0.25	0.21	3.78	10.17	1.07
	2002	0.32	3.83	1.21	0.30	0.21	0.10	3.98	9.95	1.02
	2003	0.28	3.94	1.42	0.24	0.25	0.10	3.10	9.79	0.96
	2004	0.21	3.65	1.94	0.12	0.19	0.19	3.30	9.61	0.89
Continental	1995	0.22¢	2.45¢	1.11¢	0.74¢	0.18¢	0.16¢	3.82¢	8.67¢	1.20¢
	2000	0.28	3.30	1.62	0.54	0.18	0.07	4.21	10.20	1.23
	2001	0.27	3.44	1.39	0.37	0.21	0.02	4.52	10.23	1.32
	2002	0.26	3.52	1.10	0.28	0.25	0.00	5.18	10.57	1.42
	2003	0.24	3.63	1.46	0.16	0.23	0.00	3.04	9.60	1.29
	2004	0.23	3.34	1.83	0.14	0.27	0.00	4.50	10.15	1.18
Delta	1995	0.26¢	3.25¢	1.11¢	0.85¢	0.20¢	0.13¢	3.06¢	8.86¢	0.81¢
	2000	0.27	3.73	1.27	0.42	0.16	0.08	3.51	9.43	0.72
	2001	0.28	4.10	1.20	0.36	0.16	0.11	3.81	10.02	0.76
	2002	0.25	4.37	1.10	0.28	0.18	0.10	4.03	10.30	0.81
	2003	0.23	4.79	1.44	0.17	0.19	0.11	5.28	12.75	0.90
	2004	0.23	4.38	1.98	0.16	0.18	0.11	5.87	12.91	0.82

Airline	Year									
America West	1995	0.19¢	2.08¢	0.96¢	0.64¢	0.16¢	0.19¢	3.07¢	7.29¢	1.30¢
	2000	0.12	2.21	1.54	0.32	0.13	0.09	4.17	8.57	1.58
	2001	0.10	2.42	1.35	0.28	0.15	0.06	4.50	8.86	1.72
	2002	0.06	2.36	1.09	0.19	0.16	0.08	4.67	8.61	1.56
	2003	0.05	2.47	1.44	0.08	0.16	0.03	2.44	7.89	1.46
	2004	0.04	2.30	1.94	0.06	0.17	0.03	3.37	8.31	1.40
Northwest	1995	0.28¢	3.47¢	1.24¢	0.93¢	0.27¢	0.16¢	2.80¢	9.15¢	0.70¢
	2000	0.29	3.65	1.80	0.61	0.24	0.13	3.24	9.96	0.67
	2001	0.27	4.15	1.73	0.45	0.27	0.11	3.55	10.52	0.70
	2002	0.24	4.18	1.40	0.36	0.27	0.10	3.60	10.15	0.77
	2003	0.24	4.45	1.68	0.27	0.31	0.08	3.38	10.62	0.80
	2004	0.24	4.27	2.37	0.30	0.32	0.18	5.11	12.79	0.82
Southwest	1995	0.02¢	2.56¢	1.01¢	0.39¢	0.23¢	0.27¢	2.61¢	7.09¢	0.71¢
	2000	0.03	2.99	1.38	0.30	0.22	0.26	2.55	7.72	0.55
	2001	0.03	3.01	1.29	0.18	0.22	0.24	2.51	7.48	0.54
	2002	0.03	3.02	1.17	0.10	0.24	0.22	2.58	7.36	0.55
	2003	0.02	3.25	1.28	0.08	0.23	0.23	2.28	7.59	0.54
	2004	0.02	3.34	1.44	0.02	0.24	0.21	2.50	7.76	0.52
United	1995	0.37¢	3.34¢	1.06¢	0.93¢	0.21¢	0.13¢	2.84¢	8.89¢	0.94¢
	2000	0.38	4.16	1.43	0.59	0.20	0.20	3.64	10.60	0.88
	2001	0.37	4.73	1.50	0.43	0.22	0.13	4.64	12.02	0.90
	2002	0.35	4.87	1.21	0.32	0.22	0.11	4.27	11.35	1.07
	2003	0.30	4.07	1.52	0.22	0.26	0.12	4.06	10.95	0.87
	2004	0.30	3.60	2.03	0.23	0.26	0.15	5.04	11.61	0.77
US Airways	1995	0.25¢	4.93¢	1.04¢	0.90¢	0.19¢	0.11¢	4.18¢	11.61¢	1.16¢
	2000	0.28	5.35	1.72	0.51	0.20	0.08	5.73	13.88	1.11
	2001	0.28	5.62	1.56	0.39	0.20	0.08	6.00	14.13	1.31
	2002	0.21	5.93	1.20	0.25	0.23	0.06	6.57	14.45	1.30
	2003	0.17	4.76	1.50	0.23	0.24	0.03	6.18	13.94	1.31
	2004	0.15	4.17	1.87	0.18	0.23	0.04	7.11	13.75	1.27

*The airline industry statistic "available seat miles" is calculated by multiplying the number of seats on each aircraft by the number of miles flown by each aircraft.

Source: U.S. Department of Transportation, Bureau of Transportation Statistics, Office of Airline Information, Form 41B, Form 41P, Form T100.

Exhibit 4   **Airline Seat Pitch as of April 2005**

Airline Company	Type of Aircraft	Seat Pitch
AirTran	Boeing 717	31"
Alaska	Boeing 737-400	31
America West	Airbus A320	31
American	McDonald Douglas MD80	31
Continental	Boeing 737-800	31
Delta	Boeing 757-200	31
Delta Song	Boeing 757	33
Frontier	Airbus A319	33
JetBlue—rear rows	**Airbus A320**	**34**
JetBlue—front rows		**32**
Midwest	Boeing 717	33
Northwest	DC9-30	30
Southwest	Boeing 737-700	32
United—regular coach	Airbus A320, Boeing 757	31
United—economy plus*		36
US Airways	Boeing 737-300	31

*Offers roomier coach seats with limited availability.

Source: Scott McCartney, "The Middle Seat: Discounters Win the Legroom Wars," *The Wall Street Journal*, April 5, 2005, p. D1.

their seatbelts. JetBlue wanted to avoid the "cattle-car image of discount flying."[30]

Even JetBlue's terminals had several unique features. The company used a simple queue program at its check-in counters so that the next person in line knew which agent was available. Average check-in times were under a minute.[31] In 2005, JetBlue partnered with Oasis Day Spa to offer private massages, manicures, and hair styling to travelers at JetBlue's JFK Terminal 6. It was "just another way we look to take the stress and hassle out of traveling," said JetBlue's spokesperson, Gareth Edmondson-Jones.[32] A children's play area and a big-screen television could be found near its gates. Free wireless Internet access was also available.

JETBLUE'S INNOVATIVE USE OF TECHNOLOGY

JetBlue's operating costs per seat mile were historically low. In the first quarter of 2005, for example, it spent only 6.74 cents to fly one seat one mile. This compared to 7.70 cents for Southwest, 9.80 cents for American, 10.12 cents for United, 10.56 cents for Continental, 10.89 cents for US Airways,

and 11.62 cents for Delta.[33] Jet Blue used technology to help improve efficiency and minimize costs.

JetBlue operated "Open Skies" software to handle electronic ticketing, Internet bookings, and revenue management. It cost 25 cents to process an e-ticket compared to $25 for a paper ticket.[34] JetBlue's Web site was responsible for 75 percent of ticket sales. Since it did not sell its tickets through such online reservation systems as Expedia, it saved money on booking fees.

JetBlue hired reservation agents to sell tickets over the telephone. They worked at home with company-supplied computers and second telephone lines. The home offices had certain advantages. During a blizzard one winter, for example., the agents of a competing carrier found it difficult to reach their call centers in the Northeast; such events did not affect JetBlue's agents. JetBlue needed to operate only a small office in Salt Lake City for training. Average pay for the agents was $8.25 per hour.[35] Southwest Airlines, in contrast, operated 10 call centers across the country, but three were closed in 2004 because of the growing popularity of Internet reservations. Call centers cost about $10 more per employee hour to operate than a network of home-based operators. Agents who worked at home were more satisfied and had much lower rates of turnover than call center agents. Turnover was as low as 4 percent at JetBlue.[36]

JetBlue pilots did not have to carry heavy flight manuals with them into the cockpit. All instruction books were computerized and loaded onto laptop computers. Before a flight, pilots used their laptops in an airport lounge to log on to the Internet wirelessly or via a high-speed connection. They could also download the latest manual updates and technical notices. Pilots at other carriers had flight manuals in three- or five-ring binders; they inserted paper updates and removed the old pages manually. The electronic system saved JetBlue $600,000 a year in printing and distribution costs.[37]

Once in the cockpit, JetBlue pilots read from a printout from the airline's dispatch department and entered basic information, including the outside temperature, destination, weight of the aircraft, fuel load, and number of passengers. The takeoff-calculation software program determined how much engine thrust the pilot should apply and which runways could be used. Pilots did not have to rely on dispatchers at headquarters for the calculations, saving 4,800 worker-hours a year.[38] If an air traffic controller changed a runway at the last minute, the pilot could redo the calculations in 15 seconds, often jumping ahead of other planes still waiting for their numbers. The program detected human errors; if a grossly wrong number was entered, a warning flashed on the screen. The program also helped save on fuel and engine wear. With a paper system, pilots used rules of thumb and thus had to add extra thrust and speed to widen the safety margin.[39]

JETBLUE'S CORPORATE CULTURE

JetBlue had a delicate balancing act to perform. The most significant cost for airlines was labor, which accounted for 36 to 40 percent of total operating expenses.[40] Historically, relations between unions and management were contentious. Unions could shut down an airline if they told their members to go out on strike. JetBlue had to find ways to keep costs down and make employees happy. It wanted to prevent unionization of its employees by offering attractive working conditions. By keeping employees happy, JetBlue managers could then motivate them

to take the next crucial step, which was to provide extraordinary service to passengers. The following are some excerpts from David Neeleman's letter to shareholders in JetBlue's 2003 annual report:

> JetBlue has turned the airline industry upside-down. We set out with the revolutionary idea to create an airline that would treat customers with humanity and provide everyone with high-quality service at affordable fares. We also aspired to build a company with a positive environment where crewmembers would feel respected and excited to come to work every day . . .
>
> At JetBlue, we live by our belief in the 3 P's: great **people** drive solid **performance** which generates **prosperity** for all . . .
>
> At the heart of our company is a conviction that the airline business is fundamentally one of customer service. As such, our crewmembers work hard to exceed expectations on every flight. Our job is to "get it right" every step of the way, from the initial reservation booking with our friendly home-based Reservation team or via www.jetblue.com, to the efficient delivery of the last bag at the customer's destination by our Customer Service team. Our Inflight Crew, Pilots, Technicians and everyone else working to support our front-line crewmembers are central to delivering "the JetBlue experience."

David Neeleman served as a role model to JetBlue employees in a myriad of ways. He constantly strove to make flying a safe, memorable, and satisfying experience for passengers. His goal was for JetBlue to be the best "customer service" company, not necessarily the best "airline" company. He felt that it was too easy to outperform major industry competitors because most of them, including Southwest Airlines, were run in a mediocre fashion. During a speech at an executive breakfast at the Graduate Center of the City University of New York in May 2005, Neeleman said that the foundations for excellent customer service were rooted in (1) crew members who were ambassadors of a brand; (2) flawless execution in which reservation agents who worked from home got what they wanted (e.g., a uniform consisting of JetBlue logo slippers) and in which passengers were told the truth and were compensated for air-travel hassles; and (3) a leader who made sure that his or her company mattered (that customers cared about it and would be distraught if it one day disappeared).

Neeleman tried to create an egalitarian culture at JetBlue. When he went on business trips, he rented a standard midsized automobile, not a limousine. There was no reserved parking, and there were no special perquisites for managers at JetBlue's corporate offices. Passengers were also on an equal footing with one another. There was only one class of airplanes, and the same types of gourmet snacks were offered to all passengers. Neeleman attributed his personal value system, and its subsequent impact on JetBlue's culture, to the time he spent in his youth in the slums of Brazil. He was keenly aware of the differences between the "haves" and the "have-nots"; he did not feel that wealthy people were entitled to consider themselves better than those who were poor. As Neeleman liked to tell his pilots, "There are people who make more money at this company than others, but that doesn't mean you should flaunt it."[41]

Neeleman flew on a JetBlue flight once a week so that he could talk to passengers about what they liked and did not like about the airline. He proudly reported that it once took him as long as three and a half hours to walk through the entire cabin. He never had time to watch the live television broadcasts on board. Neeleman also remembered how he felt on September 11, 2001, after the attacks on the World Trade Center and the Pentagon. Since he himself no longer wanted to fly on an airplane, how could he expect his passengers to want to fly? He acted quickly and made sure that six weeks after the attacks, Kevlar® bulletproof cockpit doors (with titanium bolts that could be opened only from the inside) were installed in all JetBlue airplanes. Camera surveillance devices were connected to the onboard DIRECTV system so that the captain and co-pilot could monitor the activities of passengers in the cabin.

Teamwork was important too. It was JetBlue's vice president for marketing, Amy Curtis-McIntyre, who came up with the company name. Her help was important because a series of proposals from outside agencies had been rejected and discussions among senior executives were stalled. While the name Blue was popular because it suggested something airy, futuristic, and vague; and it was in the public domain and could not be protected by a trademark. Curtis-McIntyre thought of the name JetBlue during a conversation with Neeleman.

Often, Neeleman was overruled by his managers. After the September 11 attacks, JetBlue managers faced the difficult task of developing an appropriate marketing message for its customers, many of whom were based in New York City. Neeleman drafted a personal letter that would appear as a full-page advertisement, but his team criticized it for being too "self-conscious." Instead, the carrier ran an ad that suggested understanding and patience: "We know you need time to heal. JetBlue will be here when you're ready to fly again."[42]

Ann Rhoades, JetBlue's first executive vice president of human resources, helped Neeleman put in place a strong organizational culture. She believed that "people can accomplish the extraordinary when they are give the authority and responsibility to succeed."[43] She helped the company achieve extraordinary results from its employees by implementing five steps.

The first step for the company was to determine its values. At JetBlue, these values were safety, caring, integrity, fun, and passion. Safety was the company's number one priority, with the other four values being approximately equal in importance.[44] The values guided employees in the decision-making process.

- The carrier's concern over safety was exhibited early on when it signed an agreement with Medaire Inc. that enabled crew members to immediately consult with land-based emergency physicians anytime a passenger fell ill during a flight. JetBlue's Web site featured a link called "inflight health," which offered tips on such topics as what to do if flying caused ear pain and how to prevent deep-vein thrombosis, a rare condition that occurred when blood clots formed in the leg and pelvic veins.

- Caring, according to Rhoades, was exhibited after the September 11 terrorist attacks when the company did not lay off anyone and continued paying salaries and benefits.[45] Both the CEO and the president/chief operating officer donated part of their salaries to a "crisis fund." It might pay the medical bills of an employee's wife who was sick with cancer or replace the personal belongings of an employee whose home was destroyed by a fire.[46] Neeleman once helped a widowed employee make a down payment on a house.[47]

- CEO Neeleman responded with integrity when JetBlue's security department violated company policy and released passenger data to a U.S. Defense Department contractor. Neeleman took personal responsibility for the incident. He either e-mailed, called, or wrote letters to passengers whose information had been released, and he sent out free airline tickets. He hired Deloitte & Touche to analyze and further develop the carrier's privacy policies.

- Fun was apparent at JetBlue's JFK terminal. Employees used George Foreman grills for barbecues. Passengers could hit yellow punching bags to relieve stress. The bags were tagged with such humorous sayings as "Forget where you parked?" and "Left the iron on?"

- The company demonstrated a passion for many things. Employees were passionate about providing excellent service to customers. Once, a passenger who had landed at JFK could not board a connecting flight to Italy because she had left her passport at home in Buffalo. A JetBlue customer service agent telephoned a colleague in Buffalo who went to the woman's home, collected her passport, and put it on a flight to JFK. The passenger was able to depart for Italy.[48] Managers were passionate about showing that they cared about employees. When employees in Burlington, Vermont, complained that there were not enough health care providers in their area, the company added a second health insurance plan. The company was passionate about the larger community; it distributed information about the American Red Cross to its customers during the month of March 2003.

The second step was for managers to hire employees who mirrored company values. An example of an outstanding flight attendant who embodied the values of safety and caring was a 63-year-old former firefighter who had rescued people during the 1993 World Trade Center bombing. An example of someone who was not hired was a pilot who promoted himself by saying that he had 15,000 hours of experience in the cockpit and could fly a plane anywhere, anytime. Yet when asked by the recruiter what else he had done, he could not provide an answer. JetBlue wanted to hear that a candidate had done something special for someone else.

Rhoades encouraged managers to be creative during the hiring process. Instead of asking, "How should we do a better job of screening flight attendants?" one might ask, "Why don't people want to be flight attendants?" College graduates did not want to commit themselves to a long-term contract, so Rhoades agreed to hire them for a year. That way, they could meet people and visit places. Parents with children did not want to be away from home for long periods of time. She created the Friends Crew Program, which allowed two people to train and share a job. This was perfect for a mother and daughter.

When the daughter worked, the mother cared for her grandchild. Rhoades developed three different paths: one for traditional flight attendants, one for college students, and one for friends.

The third and fourth steps were for the company to continually exceed employee expectations and to listen to its customers. JetBlue pilots received immediate benefits and profit-sharing opportunities in their first year of service. Passengers told JetBlue that they wanted television shows free of charge and low-carb snacks such as almonds. They indicated that there was no need for separate restrooms for men and women. The fifth step was for the company to create a "disciplined culture of excellence." It had to continually improve its services and differentiate itself from its competitors.

JETBLUE'S HUMAN RESOURCE MANAGEMENT PRACTICES

Rhoades laid the foundations for JetBlue's focus on people. Employees were called "crew members"; passengers were referred to as "customers"; vendors were addressed as "business partners." Vincent Stabile, who replaced Rhoades as executive vice president of human resources, made sure the company values became an integral part of JetBlue's human resource management practices. His first day at JetBlue was September 11, 2001. He witnessed firsthand how JetBlue employees put their values into action. Soon after the attacks on the World Trade Center, crew members realized that the airports would be closing. At the company's expense, they booked blocks of hotel rooms and reserved buses to transport passengers to their accommodations. They extended the same courtesy to stranded passengers who were booked on the flights of their competitors.[49]

Hiring

According to Stabile, JetBlue received over 100,000 applications and hired between 2,400 and 2,500 employees a year. To screen applicants, JetBlue used a guide created by Development Dimensions International. Every candidate was interviewed by a recruiter, a line manager, and a person from the unit (e.g., customer service) in which he or she might work. The interviewers kept notes, scored the interview, and then met as a group to decide whether the candidate should be hired.

The company looked for employees who were energetic, had a positive attitude, and showed a breadth of skills. For some jobs, candidates did not need experience in the airline industry. If an employee were to have direct contact with customers, he or she needed to have a minimum of two years in a similar service environment. Candidates could have worked at a Ritz-Carlton Hotel or a Nordstrom's department store.[50] In a flight attendant class, one could find a woman in her 50s with a law degree or with a background in the financing of exotic cars. There might be a man in his early 20s who had worked part-time as an emergency medical technician or a man in his 40s who had been an elementary school physical education teacher.[51]

Pilots were encouraged to do more than just fly a plane skillfully. One created diagrams to help orient colleagues to an airport's physical layout, another performed financial analyses, and yet another developed an inventory of pilot skills to screen job applicants.[52] Every executive was assigned to one of the JetBlue's destinations and was expected to tour the airport, visit with JetBlue's staff, and thoroughly check out how well things were going. This was a way for managers at headquarters to learn the names of their subordinates, show that they cared, and develop good working relationships with employees in the field.

Training

JetBlue's director of training was Mike Barger (whose brother David was the president). Initially, Mike Barger ran his program as most airline companies did: Training was tailored to each specific discipline. Worried that the system was fragmented, he proposed bringing all of JetBlue's resources together so that a common philosophy could be developed and standardized. This led to the creation of JetBlue University, which was responsible for the orientation and training of new hires, annual refresher sessions, and leadership courses. The company spent $30 million a year (or 3 percent of its operating budget) on training.[53]

During the new-hire orientation, Mike Barger discussed JetBlue's brand, Neeleman indicated how airline companies made money, and Stabile focused on the company's culture and its values. New hires also learned about the company's informal and formal communication processes. The need for leadership courses arose in 2002 after the company conducted its annual "Speak-Up" survey of all its crew members. One-third of the respondents said they were unhappy with their supervisors, who were abrasive and showed favoritism. The company realized it had promoted people without proper training. It developed a five-day program called "Principles of Leadership," taught by its senior executives. The program emphasized that effective managers were expected to inspire greatness in others.

In 2004, JetBlue formed an educational partnership with New York University (NYU) to teach its trainers at JetBlue University. NYU faculty developed a customized curriculum for JetBlue. It taught trainers how to write a lesson plan, how to conduct assessments, how to design systems, and how to develop facilitation skills. It offered opportunities for trainers to apply their newly acquired knowledge to practical situations. The curriculum was also designed to include specialized training.

In 2005, JetBlue completed construction on a 107,000-square-foot building at Orlando International Airport that became the new home for the airline's training center. It had the capacity for eight flight simulators, two cabin simulators, classrooms, a training pool, a firefighting training station, and a cafeteria. Pilots and in-flight crew would receive all their training there. JetBlue planned to phase out its training with Airbus in Miami in two years. The new facility was situated 2,000 feet away from a LiveTV hangar completed earlier in the year. The firm planned to add a lodge to the location with 300 rooms to house crew members during their training. Total costs for the related projects were estimated at $160 million.

Compensation

JetBlue paid employees lower base salaries than its competitors. Flight attendants started at $25 an hour, mechanics at $26 an hour, and pilots at $108 an hour. US Airways, after implementing cuts, paid its flight attendants $39.95 an hour, its mechanics $28 an hour, and its pilots $134 an hour.[54] JetBlue also had a health coverage plan for employees, as well as profit-sharing and 401(k) retirement plans. Employees who participated in profit sharing received payouts equivalent to seven weeks of pay in 2000 and

2001, eight weeks of pay in 2002, and nine weeks of pay in 2003; 84 percent of the company's employees were JetBlue shareholders. The company had a no-layoff policy.[55]

JETBLUE'S FINANCIAL AND OPERATING PERFORMANCE

Was it too good to be true? The JetBlue story was amazing. It had a CEO who admitted he had ADD but who worked hard to run a company with a caring attitude toward employees and customers. It had a great set of values, including integrity and passion. Passengers liked its hip image and expressed enthusiasm for its service. Nonetheless, JetBlue needed to demonstrate that it was profitable too. It needed to assure shareholders that its long-term prospects were good, not an easy thing to do in an industry where Chapter 11 bankruptcy filings had become common and industrywide losses had totaled over $20 billion during 2001–2005.

Among the major airlines, only Southwest had established that it could remain profitable in tough and turbulent times. JetBlue's performance was encouraging, but scarcely comforting (see Exhibit 5). Sharply rising fuel prices were a particular concern to all the airlines. Eclat Consulting estimated that an increase of one cent per gallon of fuel meant an increase of approximately $2.6 million a year in operating expenses for JetBlue.[56] The summer hurricanes in the Gulf Coast—Katrina and Rita—had further disrupted the jet fuel market. Crude oil prices surged to $70 a barrel, while jet fuel prices rose to $109 a barrel (from $48.82 a barrel in January 2005). The increased fuel costs prompted Neeleman to issue a "grave warning" in October 2005 that the company would report a fourth-quarter loss and a loss for the entire year. Standard & Poor's Rating Services placed JetBlue Airways on a credit watch. In November, the company issued 7 million new shares of its common stock to raise equity.

In 2000, airlines sold tickets for 73.2 percent of the available seats on all flights. Due to flight cutbacks, grounding of some planes, assorted bankruptcy filings, and growing passenger traffic, the number of empty seats on flights in 2004 was down substantially, thus producing a load factor of 83.2 percent.

JetBlue did a good job filling its planes to near capacity, thus helping to lower its operating costs per available seat mile from 9.17 cents to 6.10 cents (refer back to Exhibit 3).

JetBlue's load factors and operating costs (if fuel costs were excluded) were good for most of 2005. JetBlue did, however, encounter a significant problem with delays. Its on-time performance during the months starting from December 2004 and ending in July 2005 put it into 14th place among 19 U.S. carriers. In July 2005, for example, only 61.5 percent of its flights arrived on time. The delays were attributed to bad weather, runway construction at both JFK and Boston's Logan airports; and the firm's preference to proceed with a delayed flight instead of canceling it.[57]

JETBLUE'S POSITION IN THE AIRLINE INDUSTRY

For two consecutive years, a seat at the Phoenix Sky Harbor International Airport Aviation Symposium was left empty.[58] In 2004, the seat was intended for David Siegel, the CEO of US Airways, who resigned under pressure two days before the conference began. US Airways was undergoing Chapter 11 restructuring, and Siegel was unpopular with labor because he had pushed for further employee wage and benefit concessions. In 2005, the seat was vacant because Doug Parker, CEO of America West, was negotiating a merger with US Airways. His attorneys advised him not to attend. The unfilled seats were symbolic of the significant challenges facing the U.S. airline industry, which was said to be at a tipping point.[59]

Several of the so-called legacy carriers (United, Delta, and US Airways) had sustained financial losses over a period of four years and were struggling to survive. In addition to US Airways, UAL Corporation, the parent company of United Airlines, was in bankruptcy. Delta Air Lines and Northwest Airlines filed for bankruptcy protection in September 2005. Restructuring efforts entailed salary cuts, benefits trimming, layoffs, and heavier workloads for remaining employees. The human toll was evident. Employees experienced job-related stresses and frustrations. In 2004, a large flight attendant's union considered an industrywide strike. The FBI investigated employees at US Airways for possibly sabotaging airplanes by punching small

Exhibit 5   **Summary of JetBlue Airways' Financial and Operating Performance, 2000–2004 (in thousands, except per share data)**

	2004	2003	2002	2001	2000
Operating revenues	$1,265,972	$998,351	$635,191	$320,414	$104,618
Operating expenses	1,153,029	829,518	530,204	293,607	125,806
Operating income (loss)	112,943	168,833	104,987	26,807	(21,188)
Government compensation	—	22,761	407	18,706	—
Other income (expense)	(36,121)	(16,155)	(10,370)	(3,598)	(381)
Income (loss) before income taxes	76,822	175,439	95,024	41,915	(21,569)
Income tax expense (benefit)	29,355	71,541	40,116	3,378	(239)
Net income	47,467	103,898	54,908	38,537	(21,330)
Earnings (loss) per share, basic	0.46	1.07	0.73	4.39	(11.85)
Earnings (loss) per share, diluted	0.43	0.96	0.56	0.51	(11.85)
Cash, cash equivalents and investment securities	449,162	607,305	257,853	117,522	34,403
Total assets	2,798,644	2,185,757	1,378,923	673,773	344,128
Total debt	1,544,812	1,108,595	711,931	374,431	177,048
Common stockholders' equity (deficit)	$ 756,200	$671,136	$414,673	$ (32,167)	$ (54,153)
Revenue passengers	11,782,625	9,011,552	5,752,105	3,116,817	1,144,421
Revenue passenger miles (000)	15,730,302	11,526,945	6,835,828	3,281,835	1,004,496
Available seat miles (ASMs) (000)	18,911,051	13,639,488	8,239,938	4,208,267	1,371,836
Load factor	83.2%	84.5%	83.0%	78.0%	73.2%
Aircraft utilization (hours per day)	13.4	13.0	12.9	12.6	12.0
Average fare	$ 103.61	$ 107.09	$ 106.95	$ 99.62	$ 88.84
Passenger revenue per ASM	6.46¢	7.08¢	7.47¢	7.38¢	7.41¢
Operating revenue per ASM	6.69¢	7.32¢	7.71¢	7.61¢	7.63¢
Operating expense per ASM	6.10¢	6.08¢	6.43¢	6.98¢	9.17¢
Fuel gallons consumed (000)	241,087	173,157	105,515	55,095	18,340

Source: 2005 10-K report.

holes into three jets. ComPysch, an employee assistance provider, received 20 percent more calls for help from baggage handlers, flight attendants, and pilots in 2004 compared to 2003. Demoralized employees tended to be less pleasant to passengers. Not surprisingly, customer satisfaction with service provided by the major carriers, went down.[60]

Small carriers were in trouble too. Hawaiian Airlines, a unit of Hawaiian Holdings, had been in bankruptcy since March 2003. As part of its restructuring under Chapter 11, ATA Airlines sold the leasing rights to 6 of its 14 gates at Midway Airport to Southwest Airlines; it also announced plans to sell its Chicago Express regional airline. In June 2004, Flyi Incorporated, the parent of Independence Air, tried to transform itself from a regional feeder for larger airlines into a low-cost carrier. It lost millions of dollars every quarter, its stock price on the Nasdaq fell to $0.07, and it finally filed for bankruptcy protection in November 2005.

Meanwhile, three of the better-positioned low-cost carriers—Southwest Airlines, JetBlue Airways, and AirTran Holdings—were able to increase their market shares and seemed strong enough to expand their operations into new cities. The future seemed promising—until crude oil prices surged to an all-time high of $70 a barrel in September 2005. In October and November, as the refineries shut down by the Gulf hurricanes went back into service and as the East Coast experienced warmer-than-expected temperatures, crude oil prices fell into a more reasonable price range of between $56 to $60 per barrel. Nonetheless, airlines were expected to pay a total of $30 billion on fuel in 2005 (up from $21 billion in 2004 and $15 billion in 2003).[61]

Southwest Airlines employed the best hedging strategy to lock in lower jet fuel prices (see Exhibit 6). During 2005, it paid $26 a barrel for 85 percent of its fuel and it would pay $32 a barrel for 65 percent of its fuel in 2006. JetBlue, in contrast, had contracts to purchase only 22 percent of its fuel at $30 a barrel for 2005. It did not have any hedges in place for subsequent years. It did the next best thing. It purchased "caps" to ensure that it would not pay more than $65 a barrel for 20 percent of its fuel needs in August and $66 a barrel for 15 percent of its fuel

Exhibit 6 **Fuel Hedge Positions of Major U.S. Air Carriers (crude-equivalent prices)**

	2005		2006		2007		2008		2009	
	% Hedged	Price/ Barrel	% Hedged	Price/ Barrel	% Hedged	Price/ Barrel	% Hedged	Price/ Barrel	% Hedged	Price/ Barrel
AirTran Airways	74%	$50	23%	$55	16%	$31	0%		0%	
Alaska Airways	50	30	43	40	20	45	7	$49	0	
American Airlines	6	40	0		0		0		0	
America West	57	55	12	60	0		0		0	
Continental Airlines	0		0		0		0		0	
Delta Air Lines	0		0		0		0		0	
Frontier Airlines	17	51	0		0		0		0	
JetBlue Airways	22	30	0		0		0		0	
Northwest Airlines	6	42	0		0		0		0	
Southwest Airlines	85	26	65	32	45	31	30	33	25	$35
United Airlines	0		0		0		0		0	

Source: Bear Stearns as Reported to Subcommittee on Aviation, Hearing on Current Situation and Future Outlook of US Commercial Airline Industry (www.house.gov/transportation/aviation/09-28-05/09-28-05memo.html).

needs in September.[62] Some carriers—Continental, Delta, and United—had no hedges. It was not just a lack of foresight. Even if carriers could have gone back in time to purchase hedging contracts with reasonable prices for crude oil, most of them would not have had the funds to afford them.

Energy conservation became crucial. To save fuel, airlines used one engine instead of two to taxi on runways, installed wing fins to minimize drag, flew at slower speeds to reduce the burn rate, and carried less fuel on long flights to decrease weight. Other strategies included flying at higher altitudes, where the air was thinner (and there was less resistance so planes used less fuel), and "tankering" (filling up with more fuel than needed at locations where fuel was less expensive). Many carriers imposed fuel surcharges—between $10 to $50—on one-way fares. Others resorted to canceling flights. American Airlines eliminated 15 daily flights from its hubs in Chicago and Dallas. JetBlue eliminated one round-trip flight from New York to seven Florida destinations on Tuesdays and Thursdays during the month of December. In September 2005, airline industry executives asked Congress to suspend a federal fuel tax for just one year. Suspension of the tax—4.3 cents per gallon—would help the industry save $600 million.

Besides the volatility of jet fuel prices, airline companies faced the prospects of increased competition from new entrants. The British entrepreneur Richard Branson prepared to launch a low-fare carrier, Virgin America, with a hub in San Francisco and administrative offices in New York City. Since foreign ownership of a U.S. airline was limited by law to 25 percent, Branson was in the process of raising funds and finding American investors. David Spurlock, a former executive at British Airways, filed a Department of Transportation application to offer low-fare international service from JFK to Europe on Atlantic Express. Mark Morris, former head of DHL Air Group, formed a plan to start Primaris Airlines, which would offer first-class service in and out of Las Vegas.

Would JetBlue be able to compete? In 2005, JetBlue was still considered a relatively small airline company. Domestically, it ranked 10th in terms of the number of passengers transported per mile and 10th in terms of its 2003 operating revenues. Worldwide, it held the 62nd place for its 2003 revenues.[63] JetBlue faced significant challenges. What would it do if jet fuel prices rose sharply again in 2006? Would it be able to integrate its fleet of smaller Embraer jetliners smoothly into its existing operations? Could it continue to afford investments in the construction of new facilities at the airports in Orlando and New York (JFK)? JetBlue's managers spoke confidently of the future and outlined an aggressive growth strategy. Efforts were under way to recruit 3,500 new employees in 2006. Route expansion was announced for 2006 that would start service between such destinations as New York and Cancun, Mexico; New York and Richmond, Virginia; and New York and Austin, Texas. Airline consultant, Julius Maldutis, however, issued the following warning to airline executives: "You'd better have a very unique business plan that will give you sufficient financial leverage to survive the Armageddon that is already underway in the airline business."[64]

Endnotes

[1] R. Newman, "Loyal Clients Key, JetBlue CEO Says," *Knight Ridder Tribune Business News*, November, 2003, p. 1. Retrieved May 5, 2005, from ABI/INFORM (Proquest) database.
[2] R. Newman, "Preaching JetBlue," *Chief Executive* 202 (October 2004), pp. 26–29. Retrieved March 5, 2005, from ABI/INFORM (Proquest) database.
[3] S. Prasso, "Piloting JetBlue and eBay," *BusinessWeek*, March 17, 2003, p. 16. Retrieved March 24, 2003, from ABI/INFORM (Proquest) database.
[4] D. Neeleman, "From Milk Crates to High Altitudes," *New York Times*, November 5, 2000, p. 3. Retrieved March 12, 2005, from ABI/INFORM (Proquest) database.
[5] C. Salter, "And Now the Hard Part," *Fast Company* 82 (May 2004), p. 67. Retrieved March 12, 2005, from ABI/INFORM (Proquest) database.
[6] S. B. Donnelly, "Blue Skies," *Time*, July 30, 2001, pp. 24–26. Retrieved March 13, 2005, from ABI/INFORM (Proquest) database.
[7] "On the Record: David Neeleman," *San Francisco Chronicle*, September 12, 2004, p. J1. Retrieved March 6, 2005, from ABI/INFORM (Proquest) database.
[8] Newman, "Preaching Jet Blue."
[9] C. Woodyard, "JetBlue Turns to Beetles, Beaches, Bars," *USA Today*, August 22, 2001, p. B3. Retrieved March 6, 2005, from ABI/INFORM (Proquest) database.
[10] Newman, "Preaching JetBlue."
[11] W. Zellner, "Is JetBlue's Flight Plan Flawed?" *BusinessWeek*, February 16, 2004, p. 72. Retrieved March 5, 2005, from ABI/INFORM (Proquest) database.
[12] R. Alonso-Zaldivar, "Frustrated Air Travelers May Get 'Bill of Rights,'" *Los Angeles Times*, March 11, 1999, p. 10. Retrieved March 1, 2005, from ABI/INFORM (Proquest) database.
[13] P. Mann, "Passenger Bill of Rights Loses Luster in Congress," *Aviation Week & Space Technology*, September 27, 1999, p. 41. Retrieved March 1, 2005, from ABI/INFORM (Proquest) database.
[14] Salter, "And Now the Hard Part."
[15] S. Overby, "JetBlue Skies Ahead," *CIO*, July 1, 2002, pp. 72–78. Retrieved January 22, 2003, from ABI/INFORM (Proquest) database.
[16] R. Harris, "The Long Haul," *CIO*, February 1, 2005, p. 1. Retrieved May 5, 2005, from ABI/INFORM (Proquest) database.

[17]R. Smothers, "New Airline to Emphasize More Flights for Upstate," *New York Times*, February 11, 2000, p. B8. Retrieved March 2, 2005, from ABI/INFORM (Proquest) database.

[18]J. M. Feldman, "JetBlue Loves New York," *Air Transport World* 38 (June 2001), pp. 78–80. Retrieved March 3, 2005, from ABI/INFORM (Proquest) database.

[19]E. Brown, "A Smokeless Herb," *Fortune*, May 28, 2001, pp. 78–79. Retrieved May 5, 2005, from ABI/INFORM (Proquest) database.

[20]A. Williams, "SuperFly," *New York Magazine On the Web,* January 31, 2000. Retrieved March 2, 2005, from www.newyorkmetro.com/nymetro/news/bizfinance/biz/features/1879.

[21]R. Dwyer, "Blue Skies," *AirFinance Journal*, 227 (April 2000), p. 26. Retrieved March 15, 2005, from ABI/INFORM (Proquest) database.

[22]Williams, "SuperFly."

[23]K. L. Alexander, "It's Advantage JetBlue in Race for California," *Washington Post*, November 6, 2002, p. F1. Retrieved April 1, 2003, from ABI/INFORM (Proquest) database.

[24]D. Armstrong, "David Neeleman, Founder and CEO of JetBlue Airways, Has a Successful Flight Plan," *San Francisco Chronicle*, December 28, 2002, p. B1. Retrieved January 20, 2003, from ABI/INFORM (Proquest) database.

[25] K. L. Alexander, "The Math Flies," *Washington Post*, February 29, 2004, p. F1. Retrieved March 17, 2005, from ABI/INFORM (Proquest) database.

[26]S. Lott and A. Taylor, "Arrivals: As Planes Go Up, Costs Come Down," *Aviation Daily,* November 16, 2005, p. 5. Retrieved November 25, 2005, from ABI/INFORM (Proquest) database.

[27]Donnelly, "Blue Skies."

[28]K. L. Alexander, "In-Flight Perks Are Steadily Disappearing," *Washington Post*, March 1, 2005, p. E01. Retrieved March 18, 2005, from ABI/INFORM (Proquest) database.

[29]E. Wong, "JetBlue Gives More Passengers 2 Inches More Legroom," *New York Times*, November 14, 2003, p. C3. Retrieved February 28, 2005, from ABI/INFORM (Proquest) database.

[30]R. Smothers, "New Airline to Emphasize More Flights for Upstate," *New York Times*, February 11, 2000, p. B8. Retrieved March 2, 2005, from ABI/INFORM (Proquest) database.

[31]Overby, "JetBlue Skies Ahead."

[32]W. Woodberry, "JFK's Spa Has Riders on Cloud 9," *New York Daily News*, February 8, 2005. Retrieved March 5, 2005, from www.nydailynews.com.

[33]S. Carey, "UAL Hopes Latest Cost Cuts Will Yield Needed Efficiencies," *The Wall Street Journal*, May 12, 2005, p. A10. Retrieved May 26, 2005, from ABI/INFORM (Proquest) database.

[34]M. Walker, "The Thrill Is Gone," *Los Angeles Times*, December 14, 2003, p. I22. Retrieved March 20, 2005, from ABI/INFORM (Proquest) database.

[35]Alexander, "The Math Flies."

[36]D. Whelan, "The Slipper Solution," *Forbes*, May 24, 2004, p. 64. Retrieved March 17, 2005, from ABI/INFORM (Proquest) database.

[37]C. J. Dickinson, "JetBlue CIO Shares Secrets at Technology 2003," *Business Journal—Central New York*, May 9, 2003, p. A2. Retrieved March 17, 2005, from ABI/INFORM (Proquest) database.

[38]Overby, "JetBlue Skies Ahead."

[39]S. Carey and D. Michaels, "At Some Airlines, Laptops Replace Pilots' 'Brain Bags,'" *The Wall Street Journal*, March 26, 2002, p. B1. Retrieved March 20, 2005, from ABI/INFORM (Proquest) database.

[40]*Standard & Poor's Industry Surveys: Airlines*, November 25, 2004.

[41]D. Wademan, "Lessons from the Slums of Brazil," *Harvard Business Review* 83 (March 2005), p. 24.

[42]P. Judge, "How Will Your Company Adapt?" *Fast Company*, December 2001, pp. 128–138. Retrieved March 17, 2005, from ABI/INFORM (Proquest) database.

[43]J. Ginovsky, "Corporate Excellence," *ABA Bankers News* 12 (March 16, 2004), pp 1–2. Retrieved March 17, 2005, from ABI/INFORM (Proquest) database.

[44]"Corporate Culture," *Air Safety Week*, November 12, 2001, p. 1. Retrieved March 17, 2005, from ABI/INFORM (Proquest) database.

[45]"Find a Way to Yes! SLA Keynoter's Tips," *Information Outlook* 8 (March 2004). Retrieved March 17, 2005, from ABI/INFORM (Proquest) database.

[46]B. Finn and D. Neeleman, "How to Turn Managers into Leaders," *Business 2.0* 5 (September 2004), p. 70. Retrieved March 17, 2005, from ABI/INFORM (Proquest) database.

[47]M. Wells, "Lord of the Skies," *Forbes*, October 14, 2002, pp. 130–136. Retrieved April 1, 2003, from ABI/INFORM (Proquest) database.

[48]E. Sanger, "JetBlue Flying High with Service," *New York Newsday*, June 14, 2004. Retrieved March 18, 2005, from www.nynewsday.com.

[49]E. Tahmincioglu, "True Blue," *Workforce Management* 84 (February 2005), pp. 47–50. Retrieved March 17, 2005, from ABI/INFORM (Proquest) database.

[50]P. Flint, "It's a Blue World After All," *Air Transport World* 40 (June 2003), p. 36. Retrieved March 15, 2005, from ABI/INFORM (Proquest) database.

[51]R. Kennedy, "The Skies Are Blue and the Chips Are, Too," *New York Times*, March 18, 2001, p. 9.1. Retrieved March 17, 2005, from ABI/INFORM (Proquest) database.

[52]Salter, "And Now the Hard Part."

[53]Sanger, "JetBlue Flying High."

[54]M. Maynard, "Coffee, Tea or Job?" *New York Times*, September 3, 2004, p. C1.

[55]F. Campailla, "JetBlue Founder Believes Happy Employees Make Successful Companies," *QU Daily*, November 17, 2004. Retrieved March 19, 2005, from www.quinnipiac.edu/x13967.xml.

[56]J. W. Peters, "Rougher Times Amid Higher Costs at JetBlue," *New York Times*, November 11, 2004, p. C1. Retrieved March 5, 2005, from ABI/INFORM (Proquest) database.

[57]S. Lott, "JetBlue Plans Operational Changes to Recover from Chronic Delays," *Aviation Daily*, August 25, 2005, p. 1. Retrieved November 3, 2005, from ABI/INFORM (Proquest) database.

[58]C. Daniel, "Aviation Needs More Than Mergers to Rise Again," *Financial Times*, May 3, 2005, p. 27. Retrieved May 21, 2005, from LexisNexis Academic.

[59]*Standard & Poor's Industry Surveys*, p. 1.

[60]B. De Lollis, "Job Stress Beginning to Take Toll on Some Airline Workers," *USA Today*, November 30, 2004, p. B1. Retrieved November 3, 2005, from ABI/INFORM (Proquest) database.

[61]J. Mouawad and M. Maynard, "On Wall and Main, Worries about Oil," *New York Times*, October 6, 2005, p. C1. Retrieved November 25, 2005, from ABI/INFORM (Proquest) database.

[62]D. McDonald, "A Hard Landing," *New York Magazine*, October 17, 2005, p. 38. Retrieved November 3, 2005, from ABI/INFORM (Proquest) database.

[63]C. Baker, "Challenges Ahead," *Airline Business* 20 (August 2004), pp. 50–58.

[64]D. Reed, "Start-ups Risk It All to Be the Next Southwest," *USA Today*, March 1, 2005, p. B1. Retrieved March 5, 2005, from ABI/INFORM (Proquest) database.

Competition in the Golf Equipment Industry in 2005

John E. Gamble
University of South Alabama

It is not known with certainty when the game of golf originated, but historians believe it evolved from ball-and-stick games played throughout Europe in the Middle Ages. The first known reference to golf in historical documents was a 1452 decree by King James II of Scotland banning the game. The ban was instituted because King James believed his archers were spending too much time playing golf and not enough time practicing archery. King James III and King James IV reaffirmed the ban in 1471 and 1491, respectively, but King James IV ultimately repealed the ban in 1502 after he himself became hooked on the game. The game became very popular with royalty and commoners alike, with the Archbishop of Saint Andrews decreeing in 1553 that the local citizenry had the right to play on the links of Saint Andrews and King James VI declaring in 1603 that his subjects had the right to play golf on Sundays.

The first known international golf tournament was played in Leith, Scotland, in 1682 when Scotsmen George Patterson and James VII prevailed over two Englishmen. By the 1700s golf had become an established sport in the British Isles, complete with golfing societies, published official rules, regularly held tournaments, full-time equipment manufacturers, and equipment exports from Scotland to the American colonies. The course at Saint Andrews became a private golf society in 1754 and was bestowed the title of Royal & Ancient Golf Club of Saint Andrews by King William IV in 1834. The first golf society in the United States was founded in Charleston, South Carolina, in 1786.

By 2000, the U.S. golf economy accounted for approximately $62 billion worth of goods and services. The golf economy involved core industries such as golf equipment manufacturers, course designers, turf maintenance services, and club management services. The golf economy also included such enabled industries as residential golf communities and hospitality and tourism. In 2000, the size of golf-enabled industries was estimated at approximately $23 billion. The overall size of core golf industries was estimated at nearly $39 billion, with retail sales of golfing supplies totaling nearly $6 billion. The largest segment of the golfing supply industry was golf equipment, at approximately $4 billion in retail sales, followed by golf apparel, at $989 million; golf magazines, at $737 million; and golf books, at $160 million in retail sales.

Even though golf had grown to have a greater total effect on the U.S. economy than, for example, the motion picture industry or the mining industry, at $57.8 billion and $51.6 billion, respectively, the golf equipment industry was faced with serious troubles in 2005. The retail value of the golf equipment industry had declined from approximately $4 billion in 2000 to $3.2 billion projected for 2005. In addition, the number of golfers in the United States playing eight or more times per year had declined by 3 percent between 2000 and 2004. Industry sales were keyed to the number of core golfers playing eight or more times per year since these frequent golfers accounted for the majority of equipment sales. In addition, equipment manufacturers were finding it more difficult to develop technological innovations that would encourage occasional and core golfers to purchase new equipment. Golf's governing body in North America, the United States Golf Association (USGA), had ruled in 1998 that some clubs planned for introduction at that time were too technologically advanced and posed a threat to the game. The primary concern of the USGA was that technologically advanced driving clubs might produce a spring-like effect to help launch the ball as it was struck by a golfer. As a result of its concern, the USGA established a coefficient of restitution (COR) club face performance limitation that created a technology ceiling; all major manufacturers had reached this ceiling by 2005. Once the USGA felt comfortable that it was able to hold golf club innovation in check, it turned its attention to golf balls. In June 2005, the USGA asked all golf ball manufacturers to develop prototypes of golf balls that would fly 25 yards shorter than current models. USGA officials asked that these prototypes be submitted for evaluation by golf's governing body.

The combined effect of technological limitations imposed by the USGA, slowing growth in the number of new golfers, a decline in the number of core golfers, and blurred differentiation between golf equipment brands had set off some notable price competition in the industry and had led to significant declines in industry profitability and market value. Industry leader Callaway Golf Company, which had earned a record $132 million when it enjoyed a large technology-based competitive advantage over rivals in 1997, experienced a $10.1 million loss in 2004. The company's share price declined from a peak of $35 in 1997 to approximately $15 in late 2005. The company's shares had traded as low as $10 before the company was rumored to be an acquisition target during mid-2005. TaylorMade Golf, which was an adidas-Salomon business unit and another technological leader in the industry, suffered a 1 percent decline in sales and an 11 percent decline in operating profits between 2003 and 2004. Industry rivals with less-developed technological capabilities had actually benefited from the USGA COR limitation, since it provided those companies with an opportunity to catch up to TaylorMade and Callaway Golf from a technology standpoint. Revenues for Adams Golf, which had been a niche seller with limited technological capabilities, increased from $41.7 million in 2000 to $56.8 million in 2004 after its products eventually matched the COR of those offered by such industry leaders as Callaway Golf and TaylorMade. The sizable increase in revenues allowed Adams Golf to swing from a $37 million loss in 2000 to a $3.1 million profit in 2004.

Even though the equalization of technological capabilities and market shares had resulted in increased profits for some golf equipment manufacturers, the overall slim operating profit margins in the industry and emergence of price competition were troubling signs for investors seeking growth and preservation of principal. Golf equipment retail sales, units sold, and average selling price by product category for 1997–2004 are presented in Exhibit 1.

INDUSTRY CONDITIONS IN 2005

In 2005, approximately 27.5 million Americans played golf at least once per year. About one-third of golfers were considered core golfers—those playing at least eight times per year and averaging 37 rounds per year. In 2004, there were 10.2 million adult male core golfers and 2.5 million adult female core golfers in the United States. One million of the 2.9 million junior golfers in the United States played eight or more rounds per year. Minority participation was relatively low in the United States, with only 1.3 million African American golfers, 1.1 million Asian American golfers, and 1.0 million Hispanic American golfers participating in 2003. Ninety-one percent of rounds played per year were accounted for by core golfers. Core golfers also accounted for 87 percent of the industry equipment sales, membership fees, and greens fees.

A large percentage of the sales of gloves, shoes, and bags were replacement purchases by existing golfers since those products tended to wear out over time. Similarly, golf balls needed to be replaced regularly because they were frequently lost. However, the sales of new golf clubs were usually dependent on whether existing golfers believed new clubs would improve their games. Many golfers new to the game tended either to purchase used clubs or to borrow a set, but it was not uncommon for core golfers to spend considerable amounts of money on new equipment in anticipation of lower scores. Even though core golfers might play once a week or more, only a small fraction of golfers might be confused for Professional Golfers' Association (PGA) touring professionals while on the course. The average score for adult male golfers on an 18-hole course was 95, with only 8 percent of adult male golfers regularly

(Continued on page C-72)

Exhibit 1 **Retail Value, Units Sold, and Average Selling Price of Golf Equipment in the United States, 1997–2004 (dollar amounts and units in millions)**

Drivers and Woods

Year	Retail Value	Drivers/Woods Sold	Average Selling Price
1997	$676.8	2.93 million	$231
1998	601.1	2.81	214
1999	583.8	2.91	201
2000	599.1	2.94	204
2001	626.6	2.99	210
2002	608.7	3.09	197
2003	660.4	3.28	201
2004	654.1	3.56	184
2004 vs. 2003	−1.0%	8.5%	−8.7%

Irons

Year	Retail Value	Irons Sold	Average Selling Price
1997	$533.4	7.12 million	$74.90
1998	485.4	6.87	70.71
1999	447.9	6.97	64.28
2000	475.3	7.14	66.57
2001	459.3	7.17	64.06
2002	456.4	7.42	61.50
2003	461.4	7.66	60.23
2004	482.6	8.06	59.88
2004 vs. 2003	4.6%	4.6%	−0.6%

Putters

Year	Retail Value	Putters Sold	Average Selling Price
1997	$142.1	1.70 million	$83.49
1998	150.3	1.68	89.20
1999	160.1	1.68	95.13
2000	161.5	1.67	96.52
2001	167.2	1.65	101.44
2002	184.3	1.65	111.38
2003	195.2	1.60	121.92
2004	188.6	1.58	119.67
2004 vs. 2003	−3.4%	−1.6%	−1.8%

Wedges

Year	Retail Value	Wedges Sold	Average Selling Price
1997	$67.6	0.78 million	$86.17
1998	64.3	0.79	81.79
1999	65.0	0.81	80.45
2000	68.3	0.82	82.88
2001	69.4	0.82	84.78
2002	71.2	0.83	85.24
2003	77.0	0.88	86.99
2004	79.3	0.93	85.58
2004 vs. 2003	3.1%	4.8%	−1.6%

(*Continued*)

Exhibit 1 **Continued**

Golf Balls

Year	Retail Value	Golf Balls Sold	Average Selling Price per Dozen
1997	$458.7	19.97 million	$22.97
1998	487.4	20.06	24.30
1999	518.1	20.46	25.32
2000	530.8	20.80	25.52
2001	555.6	21.32	26.06
2002	529.9	20.81	25.46
2003	496.4	19.85	25.01
2004	506.3	19.98	25.34
2004 vs. 2003	2.0%	0.7%	1.3%

Footwear

Year	Retail Value	Pairs Sold	Average Selling Price
1997	$214.3	2.48 million	$86.49
1998	204.3	2.43	84.13
1999	206.9	2.47	83.77
2000	220.8	2.52	87.68
2001	217.8	2.57	84.62
2002	211.7	2.68	78.95
2003	217.1	2.82	76.97
2004	234.4	3.00	78.22
2004 vs. 2003	8.0%	6.2%	1.6%

Gloves

Year	Retail Value	Gloves Sold	Average Selling Price
1997	$156.7	12.81 million	$12.23
1998	160.6	12.79	12.56
1999	161.6	12.98	12.46
2000	165.4	13.20	12.53
2001	169.2	13.42	12.61
2002	163.7	13.36	12.26
2003	157.1	12.92	12.16
2004	159.3	13.15	12.11
2004 vs. 2003	1.4%	1.8%	−0.4%

Golf Bags

Year	Retail Value	Golf Bags Sold	Average Selling Price
1997	$171.8	1.37 million	$125.82
1998	165.6	1.32	125.13
1999	165.4	1.32	125.22
2000	165.1	1.31	125.56
2001	163.2	1.32	124.02
2002	153.4	1.32	116.27
2003	145.5	1.32	110.58
2004	146.8	1.34	109.55
2004 vs. 2003	0.9%	1.8%	−0.9%

Source: Golf Datatech

breaking a score of 80. The average score for adult female golfers was 106. Throughout the 1990s, it was very common for core golfers to purchase a new driver at $400–$500 at least every other year as clubs with new technological advances were introduced. Most core golfers seemed to believe it was worth the cost of new drivers, putters, and irons if technology could help offset their modest skill levels.

Key Competitive Capabilities in the Golf Equipment Industry

Competitive rivalry in the industry centered on technological innovation in clubhead and shaft design, product performance, company image, and tour exposure. The pace of technological innovation had increased rapidly during the late 1990s as industry leaders Callaway Golf, Ping Golf, TaylorMade Golf, and Titleist each attempted to beat the other to market with clubs touting unique performance characteristics. The breakneck pace of technological change caused product life cycles to decline from about three to four years during the early 1990s to about 12–18 months by 2000. Similarly, the manufacturers of golf balls introduced new products at intervals of 12–18 months to keep the interest of golfers who were looking for products that included innovations and improved performance.

The innovations in clubhead design focused on the use of lightweight metal or carbon composite materials to increase clubhead size without adding weight, to improve weight distribution within the clubhead, and to create a larger club face. After Callaway Golf Company's 1991 launch of the oversized Big Bertha driver, golf equipment manufacturers began to search for materials that would allow the clubhead to increase further in size and have a thinner face. The larger clubhead size and thinness of the club face created a larger "sweet spot," which reduced the negative effects of mis-hit shots. Beginning in the early 2000s, clubhead designers began to reposition weight in the clubhead to produce higher launch angles and to create a draw bias. Higher launch angles tended to help golfers achieve greater distance, while a draw bias helped many golfers hit straighter shots.

A golf club manufacturer's image was based in large part on its reputation for innovation and on endorsements from touring professionals. Most recreational golfers who watched televised golf tournaments or read golf magazines were very aware of what brands of clubs and golf balls their favorite touring professionals used. Also, it was not unusual for recreational golfers to base purchase decisions on the equipment choices of successful golfers on the PGA Tour. All leading golf equipment companies had long-term endorsement agreements with well-known touring professionals and also went to great lengths to make sure their products were used by lesser-known golfers as well.

The Darrell Survey counted and recorded the brand and model of each club in every golfer's bag during every professional tournament. Many golf equipment companies would pay tournament entrants a "tee-up fee" of $1,000 to $2,000 to put a club in their bag during the day of the Darrell Survey count. The tee-up fees allowed some golf club manufacturers to make factual, although misleading, claims in upcoming ads in golf magazines that their products were "number one on the PGA Tour." Endorsements paid to professional golfers totaled nearly $255 million in 2000. The best players in the game commanded multimillion-dollar contracts. Ernie Els's contract with Titleist was worth $3 million per year, while Callaway Golf paid Phil Mickelson a reported $8 million per year to use its clubs in PGA tournaments. Tiger Woods's $125 million five-year contract inked with Nike in 2003 far exceeded that provided to any other PGA touring professional in 2005. Woods's total endorsements were estimated to be worth more than $50 million per year.

Golf equipment companies also relied on personalized service in addition to lucrative endorsement fees to retain endorsements from key touring professionals. All golf equipment companies supported their touring staff members with equipment trailers during tournaments that could make adjustments to clubs prior to and during a tournament or make club substitutions at the pro's request. Some professionals' requests during the tournament might be as simple as asking the manufacturer's support staff to substitute a long iron for an additional fairway wood, while others, who might have struggled during the day, might ask that the shafts be replaced in all of their clubs before the next day's round. Touring staff members also frequented the manufacturer's headquarters to give designers feedback during the development process and to have their equipment customized to their preference. For example, when Tiger Woods became a Nike Golf staff player in 1999, his Nike irons were so highly customized they did not even resemble Nike irons offered to consumers.

Suppliers to the Industry

Most club makers' manufacturing activities were restricted to club assembly since clubhead production was contracted out to investment casting houses located in Asia and shafts and grips were usually purchased from third-party suppliers. Casting houses, such as Advanced International Multitech Company in Taiwan, produced clubheads to manufacturers' specifications and shipped the clubheads to the United States for assembly. Manufacturers were quite selective in establishing contracts with offshore casting houses since the quality of clubhead greatly affected consumers' perception of overall golf club quality and performance. Poor casting could result in clubheads that could easily break or fail to perform to the developers' expectations. Ping Golf was the only golf club producer vertically integrated into clubhead casting.

Differentiation based on shaft performance became more important to golf club manufacturers as technological differences between brands of golf clubs decreased after the USGA enacted its limitation on clubhead size and performance. Most golf club manufacturers developed modestly sized lines of proprietary shafts, which were also produced by outside suppliers. The relatively narrow line of shafts bearing the club manufacturer's name was supplemented with branded shafts produced and marketed by companies such as UST, Fujikura, or Graffaloy. Even though third-party branded shafts were equally available to all manufacturers, they were important in attracting sales to highly discriminating consumers, since these golfers might have as strong a preference for a particular shaft as for a clubhead design. For example, the purchase decision made by a low-handicap golfer considering two drivers might come down to which club could be ordered with a specific shaft.

The USGA limitation on clubhead size and club face performance had helped shaft manufacturers record higher revenues and profits. Like many shaft manufacturers, Aldila had struggled during years when consumers' greatest interest was on clubhead innovations, but a shifting consumer focus on shafts had allowed the company to swing from a $1.7 million loss in 2003 to a $9.3 million profit in 2004. At the end of the company's second quarter 2005, its net profit margins had soared to nearly 19 percent, its current ratio was nearly 4.0, and its stock price had improved to $25 per share from $1 per share in late

2002. Grips had yet to prove to be a point of differentiation, and few golfers showed a strong preference for one brand of grip over another.

Golf Equipment Retailers and the Distribution and Sale of Golf Equipment

Leading golf equipment manufacturers distributed their products through on-course pro shops, off-course pro shops such as Edwin Watts and Nevada Bob's, and online golf retailers such as Golfsmith.com and TGW.com. Most on-course pro shops sold only to members and carried few clubs since their members purchased golf clubs infrequently. Off-course pro shops accounted for the largest portion of retail golf club sales because they carried a wider variety of brands and marketed more aggressively than on-course shops. Off-course pro shops held an advantage over online retailers as well, since golf equipment consumers could inspect clubs and try out demo models before committing to a purchase. Also, both on-course and off-course pro shops were able to offer consumers custom fitting and advice from a PGA member or other individual with the training necessary to properly match equipment to the customer. Most consumers making online purchases had already decided on a brand and model, choosing to buy online to get a lower price or to avoid sales taxes. However, most of the top brands required online retailers to sell their equipment at the same prices as those offered by traditional retailers.

Custom fitting was offered by most manufacturers and large off-course pro shops with the use of specialized computer equipment. Common swing variables recorded and evaluated in determining the proper clubs for golfers included clubhead speed and path, club face angle at impact, ball position, the golfer's weight distribution, ball flight pattern, and ball flight distance. Custom fitting had become very important as golf equipment companies expanded shaft flex options during the early 2000s. In 2005, most iron sets could be equipped with shafts in senior, regular, stiff, or extra-stiff flex. Manufacturers offered drivers with dozens of different shaft configurations. For example, the Callaway Golf Big Bertha Fusion FT-3 Driver could be ordered with Aldila, Fujikura, Graffaloy, UST, or Graphite Design shafts. There were 20 different Aldila shafts available for the Fusion FT-3, each with a unique flex, weight, torque, and kick point. A wide variety of shafts from UST, Graphite Design, Fujikura, and Graffaloy were also available on the Fusion FT-3 driver.

Pro shops generally chose to stock only equipment produced by leading manufacturers and did not carry less expensive, less technologically advanced equipment. Low-end manufacturers sold their products mainly through discounters, mass merchandisers, and large sporting goods stores. These retailers had no custom fitting capabilities and rarely had sales personnel knowledgeable about the performance features of the different brands and models of golf equipment carried in the store. Such retail outlets offered the appeal of low price; they mainly attracted beginning golfers and occasional golfers who were unwilling to invest in more expensive equipment.

RECENT TRENDS IN THE GOLF EQUIPMENT INDUSTRY

Limited Opportunities for Innovation in Clubface Design

Not long after Callaway Golf Company's introduction of the Great Big Bertha titanium driver in 1995, the United States Golf Association (USGA) began to show concern that technologically advanced golf equipment might change the game of golf. The driving distance of John Daly, Tiger Woods, and other PGA members had overwhelmed some golf courses designed in the age of persimmon woods, and it was not unusual for the average driving distance of professional tournament golfers to exceed 300 yards. Many golfers playing on the Champions Tour claimed that new, technologically advanced drivers had helped them hit the longest drives of their careers even though they might be age 60 or over. The USGA believed that the added distance was a product of ultra-thin driver clubfaces that produced a springlike or trampoline effect that could help propel the ball forward.

Beginning in 1998, the USGA limited the coefficient of restitution (COR) for drivers to 0.83 to prevent manufacturers from developing clubs with a so-called springlike effect. The COR—the ratio of incoming to outgoing velocity—was calculated by firing a golf ball at a driver out of a cannonlike

machine at 109 miles per hour. The speed that the ball returned to the cannon could not exceed 83 percent of its initial speed (90.47 miles per hour). Drivers that did not conform to the USGA 0.83 COR threshold were barred from use by recreational or professional golfers in the United States, Canada, and Mexico who intended to play by the USGA's Rules of Golf. The USGA refused to calculate handicaps for golfers who had used nonconforming equipment, but it did not attempt to restrict the club's usage among players who did not choose to establish or maintain handicaps.

A discrepancy existed between the USGA's limitation on driver performance and the Rules of Golf as published by the Royal and Ancient (R&A) Golf Club of Saint Andrews, Scotland, which governed play in most countries outside of North America. The R&A did not measure the COR for driving clubs at the time of the USGA's ruling and did not have a COR limitation for clubhead performance. The two organizations agreed to develop a common worldwide standard for clubhead performance in May 2002, but the USGA unexpectedly withdrew its support from the compromise standard in August 2002. In December 2003, the R&A announced its policy regarding driver performance that would become effective in January 2004. The R&A developed a less complex test for a springlike or trampoline effect that used a pendulum to drop a weight onto the clubface of the driver. The R&A pendulum test required that the clubface and the weight remain in contact for 239 microseconds, with a tolerance of 18 microseconds. The pendulum test was applied only to drivers used in elite professional tournaments. The R&A ruled that recreational golfers and those competing in lesser tournaments were not subject to its Driving Club Condition of Competition. The USGA developed a similar pendulum test to replace its test for COR after the R&A made its December 2003 announcement. However, the USGA's use of a pendulum test did not change its specifications for drivers or make nonconforming drivers available to recreational golfers wishing to maintain a handicap.

Golf club manufacturers disagreed that a springlike effect could be produced by a metal golf club and believed that the USGA's ruling, which affected recreational as well as professional tournament golfers, would discourage new golfers from taking up the game. During the 2000 Masters Tournament in Augusta, Georgia, Callaway Golf's chief engineer, Richard Helmstetter, challenged the suggestion that clubs with a high COR could produce a springlike effect:

> We do a great deal of research at Callaway Golf and I think we are the most technologically advanced golf company in the world. We have been unable to find any evidence at all that a club face, no matter how thin, plays a role like a trampoline in striking the ball. We do think that certain kinds of construction and materials will reduce the loss of energy in the golf ball at impact and give the golfer longer drives, but this is quite different from a trampoline. The club face vibrates during impact at a speed so high that it cannot be timed, we believe, to the compression and release of a golf ball. Consequently, we think that trampoline effect is a misnomer, if not a myth entirely.[1]

Callaway Golf challenged the USGA's COR limitation in 2000 when it introduced for sale in the United States the ERC II driver with a COR of 0.86. The company's management believed that the 6–10 additional yards of carry achieved by recreational golfers using the ERC II posed no threat to the game of golf. Callaway Golf executives did concede that equipment limitations might be set for professional golfers, but saw no need to limit the performance of equipment used by recreational golfers who might gain more pleasure from hitting longer drives. Callaway Golf founder Ely Callaway suggested there were "two games of golf—tournament golf and recreational golf, and the two games differ in many respects . . . We believe that recreational golfers should not be denied the benefits of modern technology that can bring them added enjoyment that comes from occasionally hitting the ball a little bit further."[2]

Upon the announcement that Callaway Golf would make the club available to golfers in the United States, Arnold Palmer supported the company's decision by saying, "I think what Callaway is doing is just right. I have given a lot of thought to conforming and nonconforming clubs. If my daughter, who is a 100s shooter can shoot 90 with a nonconforming driver, I can't imagine that there would be anything wrong with that."[3]

The ERC II was a failure in the United States since the USGA did not agree with Callaway Golf's arguments and recreational golfers were hesitant to purchase a nonconforming club. The club did sell in large numbers in markets where the R&A Rules of Golf governed play. In 2005, all major golf club producers produced two versions of their drivers—high-COR drivers for markets outside North America and a version with a COR of 0.83 for the United States, Mexico, and Canada.

Slowing Growth in the Number of New Golfers and Rounds Played

Golf was the 12th most popular form of recreation in the United States, with approximately 27.5 million participants. In 2003, there were approximately 6.3 million golfers in Europe and 16.7 million golfers in Asia. The industry had seemingly reached maturity as a sport, with the number of new participants each year barely exceeding the number who were giving up the sport. Asia's 2–3 percent annual growth in the number of new golfers made it the only geographic region to experience growth between 1999 and 2003. Poor economic conditions in the United States during 2000 caused many frequent golfers to scale back their participation levels that year, but the number of core and avid core golfers rebounded in 2001 through 2004. However, the overall number of rounds played by golfers declined until 2004, when the number of rounds played increased by nearly 7 percent. Exhibits 2 and 3 present trends in frequency of play and rounds played for the U.S. golf market for various years between 1991 and 2004.

A survey of golfers conducted in June 2003 by the National Golf Foundation found that golfers of all types were finding it more difficult to play golf often. Golfers who were married with children were most likely to comment that job responsibilities, lack of free time, and family responsibilities prohibited them from playing golf on a more regular basis. Job responsibilities and lack of free time were also barriers to playing golf more frequently for married or single golfers who had no children. Older golfers who were either retired or who were working less than 40 hours per week had fewer job and family responsibilities and had ample free time, but were frequently troubled with heath concerns or injuries. About 30 percent of golfers said that high golf fees prevented them from playing golf more often. In fact, a different study on golf participation conducted by the National Golf Foundation in 2003 found that income was the primary predictor of golf participation.

The 2003 National Golf Foundation study on minority golf participation in the United States found there were differences in participation rates

Exhibit 2 **Number of U.S. Golfers by Frequency of Play, 1991, 1994, 1997, 2000–2003 (in thousands)**

Year	Occasional Golfers (1–7 rounds/year)	Core Golfers (8–24 rounds/year)	Avid Core Golfers (25+ rounds per year)	Total Golfers
1991	11,480	6,133	5,348	22,961
1994	11,463	6,058	5,113	22,634
1997	10,619	7,897	5,602	24,118
2000	10,961	7,399	6,276	24,636
2001	14,190	5,676	5,934	25,800
2002	13,624	6,812	5,764	26,200
2003	14,184	7,083	6,133	27,400

Source: National Golf Foundation

among races, but income tended to reduce those differences. For golfers with household incomes lower than $100,000, white non-Hispanics and Asians were nearly twice as likely to play golf as African Americans or Hispanic Americans. Nearly 15 percent of white non-Hispanic Americans and 12.4 percent of Asian Americans with household incomes of less than $100,000 per year played golf, whereas only 8.4 percent of African Americans and 8.0 percent of Hispanic Americans with incomes under $100,000 played golf. However, the percentage of individuals with household incomes less than $100,000 interested in playing golf did not vary to a great degree among U.S. citizens of different races. White non-Hispanic Americans were most interested in golf (29.6 percent), but 23.8 percent of African Americans, 24.2 percent of Asian Americans, and 20.2 percent of Hispanic Americans were also interested in playing golf. About 28 percent of adults with household incomes exceeding $100,000 played golf, regardless of race. At household incomes exceeding $150,000, the National Golf Foundation

study found that Hispanic Americans had the highest golf participation rate, at 32 percent.

Foretelling the findings of the National Golf Foundation's studies on golf participation, former Callaway Golf CEO Ron Drapeau said in a 2002 interview with *Smart Money*, "The cost of golf is a concern: We need to see more affordable municipal-type golf courses, including alternative facilities; 9-hole courses, pitch-and-putt, and par 3 courses. The time it takes to play is also an issue."[4]

The Rise of Counterfeiting in the Golf Equipment Industry

Knockoffs of branded golf equipment had been produced by Chinese manufacturers and sold in the United States since the early 1990s, but they weren't a serious threat to the industry because knockoffs only appeared similar to legitimate products. For example, knockoffs like the Canterbury Big Bursar looked similar to the Callaway Big Bertha driver but

Exhibit 3 **Total Rounds of Golf Played in the United States, 2001–2004 (in millions)**

Year	Rounds Played (in millions)	Percent Change
2001	518.1	—
2002	502.4	−3.0%
2003	494.9	−1.5
2004	528.6	6.8

Source: National Golf Foundation

would never pass for a Big Bertha upon close inspection. Beginning golfers were most likely to purchase knockoffs since they looked similar to brand-name clubs but sold for as much as 75 percent less than clubs made by Callaway Golf, Cobra, TaylorMade, Ping, or Titleist. Serious golfers tended not to purchase knockoff clubs since they were made from poor-quality alloy metals, did not perform as well as branded clubs, and were prone to breaking.

Counterfeit clubs were a much greater threat to the industry since good counterfeits were nearly exact copies of legitimate products and could only be identified as counterfeits by very knowledgeable golfers, trained personnel of golf equipment retailers, or golf equipment producers. Like knockoffs, counterfeits were made from inferior materials, were not produced to the standards of legitimate equipment manufacturers, and were not very durable. However, the extraordinarily low prices that counterfeit clubs were offered at were too great a temptation for many bargain-hunter golfers. In 2005, it was not unusual to see complete sets of new Callaway Golf, TaylorMade, Ping, Titleist, Nike, or Cobra clubs that would retail for more than $2,000 sell on eBay or similar auction Web sites for $150 to $400. Sellers who dealt in counterfeit merchandise could purchase counterfeit sets complete with eight irons, a driver, two or three fairway woods, a putter, a golf bag, and a travel bag for as little as $100 in China. Callaway Golf Company alerted visitors to its Web site to counterfeit clubs sold on eBay or other Internet sites with the following warning: "A full set of authentic Callaway Golf clubs, depending on the models, will retail for $2,500–$3,000 or more. If the deal looks too good to be true, it probably is."[5]

The rise in counterfeiting was attributable to the improved manufacturing capabilities of companies in China and the decision by golf equipment companies to source components from Chinese manufacturers. In 2005, about 60 percent of all golf equipment was produced in China and more than 90 percent of counterfeits came from China. Counterfeiters were able to make very accurate copies of branded golf clubs through reverse engineering or by enticing employees of contract manufacturers to steal clubhead molds that could be used to produce counterfeit clubheads. Similarly, counterfeit shafts and grips could be fabricated to produce complete sets of counterfeit golf clubs. Counterfeiters even copied the details of the packaging golf clubs were shipped in to better disguise the fakes. It was

estimated that counterfeiters in China could produce golf clubs for less than $3 per club.

The golf equipment industry's six leading manufacturers created an alliance in December 2003 to identify and pursue counterfeiters and sellers of counterfeit clubs. TaylorMade Golf, Fortune Brands (parent of Titleist and Cobra Golf), Callaway Golf, Ping Golf, Cleveland Golf, and Nike Golf had successfully shut down many Internet auction sellers in the United States and Canada that listed counterfeit clubs and had gained cooperation from the Chinese government to confiscate counterfeit goods produced in that country. The Chinese government conducted two raids in 2004 that netted approximately $3 million worth of counterfeit golf equipment and the Chinese seized more than $1 million worth of counterfeit clubs in 2005. However, the efforts to shut down Internet sellers of counterfeits and manufacturers of counterfeits had achieved limited success. A Nike executive explained, "Often these aren't legitimate businesses, so you can't take the case to a court of law, you have to hunt them down. Many times it isn't even worth the effort. They simply create a new company and move. It's really frustrating."[6]

PROFILES OF THE LEADING MANUFACTURERS AND MARKETERS OF GOLF EQUIPMENT

Callaway Golf Company

Callaway Golf Company began to take form in 1983 when Ely Reeves Callaway Jr. purchased a 50 percent interest in a Temecula, California, manufacturer and marketer of hickory-shafted wedges and putters for $400,000. Upon acquiring an interest in Hickory Stick USA, Callaway became the company's president and CEO and soon began to transform the little-known maker of reproductions of antique clubs into the world's largest producer of golf clubs. Callaway knew from the outset that the company's prospects for outstanding profits were limited as long as its product line was restricted to hickory-shafted clubs. Callaway noticed that most golf equipment had changed very little since the 1920s and believed that, due to the difficulty of the game of golf (there was so much room for variation in *each* swing of the club and for off-center contact with the ball), recreational golfers would be willing to invest in high-tech, premium-priced equipment if such clubs could improve their game by being more forgiving of a less-than-optimum swing. Ely Callaway's vision was at odds with that of the company's founders and eventually resulted in Callaway's outright purchase of the company. In 1985 Ely Callaway hired Richard C. Helmstetter as the company's chief club designer, who was aided by a team of five aerospace and metallurgical engineers, to develop what Callaway termed a "demonstrably superior and pleasingly different" line of clubs that was set apart from competing brands by its technological innovation. Helmstetter and his team introduced the company's S2H2 (short, straight, hollow hosel) line of irons in 1988 and an S2H2 line of metal woods in 1989. The 1988 S2H2 launch was accompanied by a name change from Callaway Hickory Stick USA to Callaway Golf Company. The S2H2 line of clubs was well received by professional and recreational golfers alike and became the number one driver on the Senior PGA Tour by year-end 1989.

The company's engineers followed up the successful S2H2 line with the Big Bertha—named by Callaway after the World War I German long-distance cannon—which was launched in 1991. The Big Bertha was revolutionary in that it was much larger than conventional woods and lacked a hosel so that the weight could be better distributed throughout the clubhead. This innovative design gave the clubhead a larger sweet spot, which allowed a player to mis-hit or strike the golf ball off-center and not suffer much loss of distance or accuracy. By 1992 Big Bertha drivers were number one on the Senior PGA, LPGA, and Hogan Tours. Callaway Golf Company became a public company on February 28, 1992. By year-end 1992 its annual revenues had doubled to $132 million, and by 1996 Callaway Golf had become the world's largest manufacturer and marketer of golf clubs, with annual sales of more than $683 million.

The company's technological leadership and financial performance eroded during a brief retirement by Ely Callaway between 1996 and 1998, but rebounded soon after Ely Callaway returned as CEO in October 1998. The founder's first efforts upon his return to active management at Callaway Golf were to "direct [the company's] resources—talent,

energy, and money—in an ever-increasing degree toward the creation, design, production, sale and service of new and better products."[7] As part of his turnaround strategy Ely Callaway also initiated a $54.2 million restructuring program that involved a number of cost-reduction actions and operational improvements. Ely's strategies allowed the company to regain its technological leadership with the introduction of Callaway Golf Company's low center-of-gravity Steelhead line of metal woods in 1998, the ERC Forged Titanium Driver in 1999, and variable face thickness X-14 irons and the ERC II Forged Titanium Driver in 2000. Also, the company acquired Odyssey, a leading brand of putters, in 1996 and began manufacturing and marketing golf balls in 2000. Ely Callaway believed that golf balls were a natural product-line extension for the company, pointing out, "We have 7 million people out there playing our products, and 80% of them think they're the best clubs in the world—we have almost a guaranteed 'try' on our new products."[8]

In February 2000 a survey of golf equipment company executives voted Callaway's Big Bertha driver the best golf product of the century by a 2-to-1 margin. The same group of executives called Ely Callaway the most influential golf trade person of the 1990s. Ely Callaway stepped down as president and CEO of the company on May 15, 2001, after being diagnosed with pancreatic cancer. He was replaced by the company's senior executive vice president of manufacturing, Ron Drapeau, and passed away at his home in Rancho Santa Fe, California, on July 5, 2001. Drapeau began his employment with Callaway Golf in late 1996 and had headed the company's Odyssey Golf unit for 18 months before becoming responsible for all of the company's manufacturing operations as vice president of manufacturing in February 1999.

As it had during Ely Callaway's 1996 retirement, the company's performance declined soon after his death in 2001. Callaway's share of drivers began to decline after the USGA instituted its 0.83 COR limitation in 1998, but the company's share of the driver market fell at a faster rate under Drapeau. The 0.83 limitation left Callaway with fewer innovation options since the company had already met the 0.83 threshold at the time the rule went into effect. The key innovation of Callaway's highly successful Great Big Bertha driver launched in 1995 was its titanium construction. Titanium was a much lighter metal than stainless steel, which allowed Callaway

Golf's engineers to create a larger clubhead featuring an expanded sweet spot. After competitors had matched Callaway Golf Company's titanium construction, the company's research and development efforts steered toward identifying materials lighter than titanium. In 2002, Callaway Golf introduced the C4 driver—a 360-cubic-centimeter (cc) driver made from a carbon composite material. The carbon composite material performed exceptionally well and was 75 percent lighter than titanium, which allowed golfers to generate more clubhead speed than with heavier titanium clubs.

Even though the C4 performed up to the R&D staff's expectations, the driver was a failure in the marketplace. The driver met the 0.83 COR limit, as did competing drivers, but golfers were much more impressed with the drivers offered by Titleist, Ping, Cobra, and TaylorMade. The C4 had two shortcomings in the minds of many golfers. First, most of Callaway's rivals chose to push the size of their drivers toward the USGA size limit of 460 cc rather than experiment with lighter materials. The larger clubhead tended to give some golfers more confidence at the tee and produced a higher launch angle, which equated to greater distance. Also, golfers were dissatisfied with the sound of the carbon composite driver, which was rather muffled when it struck a ball. The extra-large, hollow titanium drivers produced by Callaway Golf's rivals tended to produce an exceptionally loud noise when they made contact with the ball. Golf retailers found that many customers that tried C4 and competing demo drivers returned the C4 to their stores stating that "even though they hit the club very well, it didn't sound like they hit it well."

The company also misjudged the importance of a new type of club introduced by rivals that was a substitute for low-lofted, long irons. Hybrid clubs had a clubhead smaller than, but similar to, a fairway wood with a shaft the length of that used in a midlength iron. Golfers of all abilities (even touring professionals) found the hybrid clubs much easier to hit than long irons. TaylorMade's Rescue was the first hybrid to gain a widespread appeal, but almost all manufacturers raced to quickly get hybrid clubs to the market. Callaway Golf's inability to get its hybrid club to market before 2005 caused it to lose significant sales as many golfers purchased TaylorMade, Nike Golf, Adams Golf, and Cobra hybrid clubs to replace 2-, 3-, and 4-irons from their bags. Some golfers replaced fairway woods with hybrids as well.

As Callaway Golf struggled with its golf club business, its golf ball operations also failed to perform to management's expectations. When Ely Callaway announced that the company would enter the golf ball business, the company expected to gain a 10 percent market share within two years and eventually become one of the two top brands of golf balls. The company missed its projections, with its sales growing to just $66 million and its share reaching only 5.7 percent in 2002. In addition, Callaway Golf's golf ball business had lost $90 million between 2000 and 2002 and showed little hope of providing a return on its $170 million investment in golf ball development and plant and equipment. In 2003, the company acquired Top-Flite Golf for $125 million to give it the volume necessary to achieve economies of scale in golf ball production. At the time of its acquisition by Callaway Golf, the maker of Top-Flite golf balls, Strata golf balls, and Ben Hogan golf clubs had sales of $250 million and was in bankruptcy. About $175 million of the company's 2002 revenues were generated from the sale of golf balls.

Even though the Top-Flite acquisition made Callaway Golf the number two golf ball producer behind Titleist, the acquisition led to further financial problems for the company. Integrating Top-Flite's operations into Callaway's golf ball business was more troublesome than expected. Callaway Golf's golf balls were the most technologically advanced in the industry in 2003 and were produced at its state-of-the-art production facility in Carlsbad, California. Top-Flite primarily produced lower-end golf balls for mass merchandisers using an older golf ball production facility with few technological capabilities. Callaway was unable to use Top-Flite's production facility to produce Callaway Golf golf balls until 2005 because Callaway's high-tech golf balls were too complex to be produced in the older Top-Flite plant. In addition, the integration of Top-Flite and Callaway personnel was a challenge because the two companies had dramatically different cultures. Ely Callaway had developed a professional, technology-based culture that encouraged employees to exhibit the highest levels of gentlemanly behavior, while some retailers had likened Top-Flite's freewheeling sales force to carnival barkers.

With Callaway's growing problems in its golf club operations and golf ball business, pressure began to mount on Ron Drapeau to produce results acceptable to investors. Under Drapeau, the company did introduce the highly successful Odyssey 2-Ball putter, which allowed the company to increase its share of the putter market from 30.7 percent in 1999 to 40.2 percent in 2002. In fact, the sales of 2-Ball putters alone were greater than the total revenues for any golf company except Titleist/Cobra, TaylorMade, and Ping in 2003. Callaway Golf had also achieved acceptable results in the irons category of the golf equipment industry, where its share grew from 14.4 percent in 1999 to 16.1 percent in 2002, but its inventory of fairway woods and drivers grew to unacceptable levels as its share of those products declined from 30.9 percent in 1999 to 21.6 percent in 2002. In 2003 and 2004, Drapeau dropped retail prices on its drivers by as much as $100 and even gave some products away to retailers. The price cut on current models was a first in the company's history. Typically, the company did not discount products until a new generation was launched and available in retail stores.

Ron Drapeau stepped down as Callaway Golf CEO in August 2004 to be replaced on an interim basis by longtime board member 71-year-old William Baker. The company did not name a permanent replacement until August 2005, when it hired former Revlon CEO George Fellows to lead the company. While at Revlon as CEO between 1997 and 1999, Fellows had been credited for producing a turnaround year in 1997 after years of losses. However, the company returned to a loss in 1998 and recorded its worst-ever loss in 1999. Some analysts suggested that Fellows did "not [have] a strong résumé" for the job, and others claimed that while Fellows was at Revlon, he "was handed a deck that didn't have 52 cards."[9]

During William Baker's tenure as interim CEO, Callaway Golf continued to struggle with excessive inventory and integration of Top-Flite and Ben Hogan Golf operations. However, the company was able to develop some of its most innovative products prior to George Fellows's arrival. The company's titanium-faced Big Bertha Fusion irons were unlike any made by other golf equipment manufacturers at the time and were said by some retailers to be the best product Callaway Golf had ever developed. The company had also launched new X-18 and X-Tour irons, which contributed to a 28 percent increase in the sales of its irons between the second quarter of 2004 and the second quarter of 2005. The two-piece X-Tour iron was Callaway Golf's first forged iron, which was the preference of touring professionals and some low-handicap golfers. The company also

developed new versions of its 2-Ball putter that produced a 16 percent increase in putter sales between the second quarter of 2004 and the second quarter of 2005 and had created a 460-cc replacement to its ERC Fusion driver. The Fusion FT-3, like the original Big Bertha Fusion featured a titanium clubface and carbon composite shell, but also featured prepositioned weights to produce a draw, fade, or neutral ball path. The success of the FT-3 in the marketplace was critical to Callaway's turnaround since its Big Bertha 454 had met with limited success—leading to a 32 percent decline in net sales of woods for the six months ending June 30, 2005, when compared to the months ending June 30, 2004.

Callaway Golf also added the state-of-the-art HX Tour 56 golf ball to its lineup of Top-Flite and Callaway golf balls in June 2005. The HX Tour 56 was Callaway Golf's most technologically advanced golf ball and accounted for nine victories across all six professional tours since it was released to touring professionals in early 2005. The Tour 56 also was used in three of Phil Mickelson's lowest career 18-hole scores. In addition to the HX Tour 56's nine pro tour wins in 2005, the company's HX Tour golf ball had accounted for 46 global tour wins between 2003 and 2005. Callaway Golf expected the HX Tour 56 to help the golf ball division reverse an 11 percent decline in sales during the first six months of 2005. However, in mid-2005 the company was unable to get large quantities of its HX Tour 56 golf ball to retailers because of production problems in its Top-Flite plant. The company was also unable to ship sufficient quantities of its Fusion FT-3 drivers to retailers due to production problems at supplier foundries. As of late 2005, it was unknown how successful the FT-3 would be in allowing Callaway to recapture lost market share in the driver segment of the golf equipment industry since Callaway had not made the driver available to many retailers.

Even though Callaway Golf had significant hurdles to clear to return to its late-1990s glory, the company's stock price rose by nearly 50 percent in mid-2005 amid talks of a possible takeover. At least two separate groups of investors were pursuing the company with offers as high as $1.2 billion, or $16.25 per share. Prior to the hiring of George Fellows as Callaway Golf's CEO, its board had hired an investment bank to evaluate strategic alternatives for the company. However, upon his acceptance of the job, Fellows commented that the company was worth substantially more than the amounts of the two buyout bids and that he had been hired to turn around the company, not to prepare it for sale. At the end of the company's third quarter in 2005, Fellows announced a broad restructuring plan that would reduce expenses by $70 million by year-end 2006 by consolidating all golf ball operations; integrating sales functions of Callaway, Odyssey, Top-Flite, and Ben Hogan brands; and eliminating an unspecified number of jobs. The restructuring program would result in charges against 2005 and 2006 earnings of $12 million. A financial summary for Callaway Golf Company is presented in Exhibit 4. Exhibit 5 provides the company's revenues by product group for the period 1999 to 2004.

TaylorMade-adidas Golf

TaylorMade was founded in 1979 when Gary Adams mortgaged his home and began production of his "metalwoods" in an abandoned car dealership building in McHenry, Illinois. Both touring pros and golf retailers alike were skeptical of the new club design until they found that the metal woods actually hit the ball higher and farther than persimmon woods. By 1984, TaylorMade metalwoods were the number one wood on the PGA Tour and the company had grown to be the third-largest golf equipment company in the United States. The company was acquired by France-based Salomon SA in 1984, which provided the capital necessary for the company to continue to develop innovative new lines of metal woods. The company also produced irons and putters, but most of TaylorMade's sales were derived from high-margin drivers and fairway woods.

TaylorMade's metalwood drivers were the most technologically advanced in the industry until Callaway Golf's 1991 introduction of the oversized Big Bertha metalwood. During the entire decade of the 1990s, TaylorMade was unable to leapfrog Callaway Golf's innovations and remained a runner-up in the driver segment. Even though TaylorMade was unable to beat Callaway to the market with latest technology, the company was always able to launch drivers nearing the performance of Callaway products within months of a Callaway product introduction. TaylorMade and its parent were acquired by athletic footwear and apparel company adidas in 1997.

TaylorMade's introduction of a 400-cc driver in 2003 gave it the innovation it had long sought to become the largest seller of drivers and fairway woods. The company's R580 driver was 40 cc larger than Callaway's competing Great Big Bertha II driver and matched consumers' preference for the largest possible driver. TaylorMade expanded its lead over Callaway Golf in drivers with its 2004 introduction of its r5 series and r7 Quad drivers. The r5 was a 450 cc driver that came in three varieties and used prepositioned weights to produce a draw, slight fade, or straight shots. The r5 was one of the best-selling drivers in the marketplace but was less technologically advanced (and lower-priced) than TaylorMade's r7 Quad driver. The r7's movable weight technology allowed users to use a special tool move four tungsten weights with a total weight of 48 grams to ports in various positions in the clubhead to produce whatever bias the golfer found necessary on a given day. For example, a golfer who was struggling with a low fade could move the heaviest of the four weights to the toe of the clubhead favor a high draw. The golfer could later move the weights to a different position if he or she experienced a different ball flight on a different day. The movable weight system allowed golfers to have a single driver that could produce six ball flight paths.

TaylorMade was also the leading seller of hybrid clubs. TaylorMade introduced its Rescue line of hybrid clubs in 1999, but the clubs did not become a huge success in the marketplace until 2002. In 2005, TaylorMade extended its Rescue line by adding models that featured its movable weight technology. Retailers were uncertain that movable weights would be a strong selling point in hybrids, since hybrids were already marketed as clubs that were easier to hit with than woods or long irons.

TaylorMade had traded positions with Titleist and Ping as the second-largest brand of irons, but it had never challenged Callaway Golf for market share leadership in the category. In late 2005, the company introduced its r7 irons in hopes of repeating the success of the r7 driver. The r7 irons were designed much like Callaway Golf's Fusion irons, with a titanium face mounted to a stainless-steel perimeter-weighted frame. The r7 irons also featured prepositioned tungsten cartridges imbedded into the stainless-steel clubhead to improve launch angles.

TaylorMade was a relatively weak competitor in the putter segment. Its Maxfli golf ball business produced successful models such as the Noodle—which sold more than 2 million dozen per year—but the division had yet to post a profit since its acquisition by adidas-Salomon in 2002. In 2005, the Maxfli brand accounted for less than 5 percent golf ball sales worldwide.

Exhibit 4 **Callaway Golf Company, Financial Summary, 1992–2004 (in thousands, except per share amounts)**

	2004	2003	2002	2001	2000	1999	1998	1997	1996	1995	1994	1993	1992
Net sales	$934,564	$514,032	$792,064	$816,163	$837,627	$719,038	$703,060	$848,941	$683,536	$557,048	$451,779	$256,376	$132,956
Pretax income	(23,713)	67,883	111,671	98,192	128,365	85,497	(38,899)	213,765	195,595	158,401	129,405	69,600	33,175
Pretax income as a percent of sales	–3%	13%	14%	12%	15%	12%	–6%	25%	29%	29%	29%	27%	25%
Net income	$ 10,103	$ 45,523	$ 69,446	$ 58,375	$ 80,999	$ 55,322	($25,564)	$13 2,704	$122,337	$ 97,736	$ 78,022	$ 42,862	$ 19,280
Net income as a percent of sales	1%	9%	9%	7%	10%	8%	–4%	16%	18%	18%	17%	17%*	15%
Fully diluted earnings per share	($0.15)	$0.68	$1.03	$0.82	$1.13	$0.78	($0.38)	$1.85	$1.73	$1.40	$1.07	$0.62	$0.32
Shareholders' equity	$586,317	$589,383	$543,387	$514,349	$511,744	$499,934	$453,096	$481,425	$362,267	$224,934	$186,414	$116,577	$ 49,750

Source: Callaway Golf Company annual reports.

Exhibit 5   **Callaway Golf Company's Net Sales by Product Group, 1999–2004 (in thousands)**

Product Group	2004	2003	2002	2001	2000	1999
Woods	$238.6	$252.4	$310.00	$392.90	$403.00	$429.00
Irons	259.1	280.7	243.5	248.9	299.9	221.3
Balls	231.3	78.4	66.0	54.9	34.0	—
Putters, accessories and other	205.6	202.5	172.6	119.5	100.8	68.7
Net sales	$934.6	$814.0	$792.10	$816.20	$837.60	$719.00

Source: Callaway Golf Company annual reports.

TaylorMade's net sales on a currency-neutral basis grew by 5 percent between 2003 and 2004, but declined by 1 percent after the effects of exchange rates were taken into account. The company's growth in sales was attributable to the popularity of its r7 Quad driver, which recorded wins in the U.S. Open and the PGA Championship. Growth in adidas golf footwear and apparel also contributed to the 5 percent revenue increase. In 2004, the company's Asian sourcing allowed its gross margins to improve to 47.0 percent, from 45.5 percent in 2003, but its operating margins declined from 10.5 percent in 2003 to 9.5 percent in 2004 because of increased marketing expenses. Exhibit 6 presents net sales and operating profit between 2001 and 2004 for TaylorMade-adidas Golf. The table also presents the adidas-Salomon golf division's sales by product category in 2004. Market shares for the leading sellers of drivers and fairway woods, irons, and golf shoes between January 2002 and July 2004 are presented in Exhibit 7.

Titleist/Cobra

The Acushnet Company was a rubber deresinating company founded in 1910 in Acushnet, Massachusetts. The company opened a golf ball division in 1932 when founder Phil Young believed that a bad putt during a round of golf he was playing was a result of a faulty ball rather than his poor putting. Young took the ball to a dentist's office to have it X-rayed and found that the core of the ball was indeed off-center. Believing that Acushnet could develop and manufacture high-quality golf balls, Young teamed with a fellow Massachusetts Institute of Technology graduate, Fred Bommer, to create the Titleist line of balls. Young and Bommer introduced their first Titleist golf ball in 1935, and by 1949 Titleist had become the most played ball on the PGA Tour.

Acushnet's acquisition of John Reuter Jr. Inc. in 1958 and Golfcraft Inc. in 1969 put Titleist into the golf club business. Titleist's Reuter Bulls Eye

Exhibit 6   **Selected Data for Taylor Made-adidas Golf**

	2004	2003	2002	2001
Net sales (in millions)	€633	€637	€707	€545
Operating profit (in millions)	60	67	74	63
Sales by Product				
Metalwoods	48%			
Irons	19			
Apparel	11			
Footwear	7			
Golf balls	6			
Accessories	6			
Putters	3			

Source: adidas-Salomon annual reports.

Exhibit 7   **Market Shares of Leading Sellers of Golf Equipment for Drivers and Fairway Woods, Irons, and Footwear, January 2002–July 2004**

Drivers and fairway woods

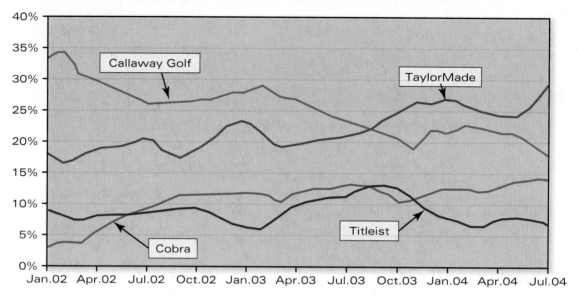

Irons

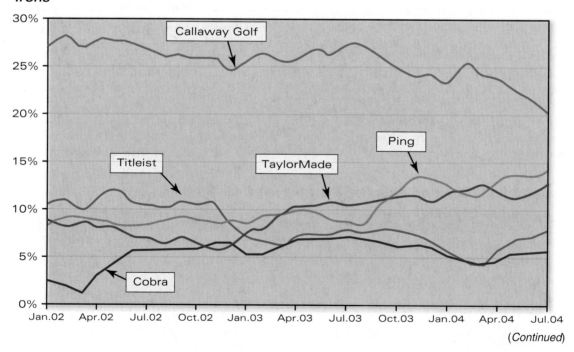

(*Continued*)

Exhibit 7 **Continued**

Footwear

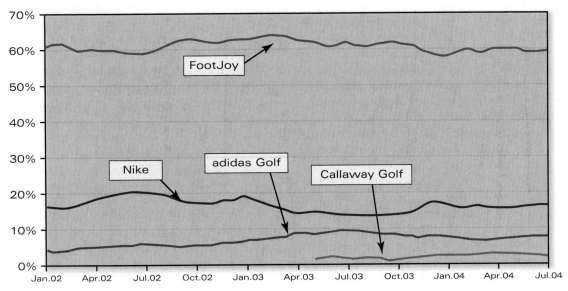

Source: Adidas-Salomon AG Investor Day 2004 Presentation, October 5, 2004.

putter became a favorite on the PGA Tour during the 1960s, and its AC-108 heel-toe weighted irons were among the most popular brands of irons during the early 1970s. The company's Pinnacle line of golf balls was developed in 1980 as a lower-priced alternative to Titleist-branded golf balls. In 1996, The Acushnet Company was acquired by tobacco and spirits producer and marketer American Brands. American Brands increased its presence in the golf equipment industry in 1985 when it acquired Foot-Joy, the number one seller of golf gloves and shoes. In 1996 American Brands acquired Cobra Golf for $715 million. The company changed its name to Fortune Brands in 1997 when it completed the divestiture of tobacco businesses begun in 1994. Fortune Brands' golf and leisure products division had an operating profit of $154 million on sales of $1.2 billion in 2004.

At year-end 2004, Titleist and Cobra were ranked third and fourth, respectively, in total equipment sales, with the sales of each brand totaling nearly $200 million. The sales of Titlist and Pinnacle golf balls amounted to approximately $485 million and accounted for more than 70 percent of industry sales. In addition, FootJoy led the industry in the sale of golf shoes, golf gloves, and golf outerwear, with revenues of $363 million.

Most golfers considered Titleist golf balls to be technologically superior to other brands, although industry analysts and golf retailers considered Callaway Golf's HX technology equally impressive. Titleist's Pro V1 golf ball was the company's most advanced and expensive golf ball and was able to offer maximum distance along with spin rates that allowed low-handicap golfers to stop approach shots near the pin. Lower-grade golf balls were able to offer golfers distance off the tee but were likely to roll across the green on approach shots to the hole. Titleist's line of golf clubs was targeted toward low-handicap golfers. Titleist produced only forged irons, which were difficult for all but the best recreational golfers to hit with since they had a small sweet spot and were very unforgiving of mis-hits. Titleist offered one driver model—the 905, which was a 400-cc driver and a popular choice with professionals and better recreational golfers.

Titleist offered only one hybrid club, which was more ironlike in its design than hybrids offered by Callaway or TaylorMade. Titleist's Vokey forged wedges were frequently used on the PGA Tour and were favorites of many low-handicap golfers. The Titleist Scotty Cameron putter line sold at the highest price points in the industry. Scotty Cameron putter models sold between $270 and $300 and were status symbols at country clubs and golf resorts throughout North America and Asia.

Fortune Brands' Cobra line of golf clubs was targeted to golfers of an average skill level. The brand's drivers pushed the regulatory limits in terms of clubhead size. In 2005, Cobra offered a 460-cc driver with the largest clubface among all major brands, a 454-cc driver, and 414-cc driver. All of the company's King Cobra drivers featured carbon composite top plates and milled titanium clubfaces. Cobra emphasized distance and forgiveness in its advertisements and fielded a long-drive team, which competed in various long-drive competitions held throughout the United States. King Cobra irons sold at slight lower price points than competing brands and were mostly perimeter-weighted models. The Cobra Baffler hybrid club was similar in design to the TaylorMade Rescue and Callaway Golf Heavenwood and sold at a slightly lower price point than models offered by key rivals. The company's wedges and putters were not widely used on the PGA Tour or among recreational golfers.

Titleist management's biggest concern in late 2005 centered on the USGA's interest in lesser-performing golf balls. In a special equipment issue of *Inside the USGA* published in October 2005, the editors worried openly that technology might endanger some of golf's most historic courses. The editors recalled how the wound, rubber-cored Haskell ball developed in 1898 and popularized during the early 1900s eventually "removed for consideration the Myopia Hunt Club, which hosted four U.S. Opens between 1898 and 1908."[10] The USGA editorial staff continued to speculate that the "confluence of golf science and commercial investment . . . accelerated by the injection of large amounts of capital" might possibly have the same effect on such championship courses as Merion or Oakland Hills.[11] The USGA believed it had a responsibility to the protect the game of golf and pointed out in its special issue that the average driving distance of touring professionals had increased by 26 yards between 1990 and 2005. In addition, the USGA commented that improvements in golf clubs and golf balls had contributed to a 1.5 stroke improvement in average handicaps between 1994 and 2005. Titleist management responded to such concerns by pointing out that the average score per round during PGA tournaments had improved by only one stroke between 1980 and 1997. In addition, Titleist management also disagreed with the contention that historic courses were likely to become obsolete because of technology. Titleist noted on its Web site that the average score during the 2005 PGA Championship at Baltusrol—the site of three U.S Opens dating back to 1967—was .345 higher than the average score posted during when the Springfield, New Jersey, course hosted the 1993 U.S. Open.

Titleist's CEO, Wally Uihlein, attributed the overall scoring improvement among recreational and tournament golfers to "six contributing factors: 1) the introduction of low-spinning high performance golf balls, 2) the introduction of oversize, thin-faced drivers, 3) improved golf course conditioning and agronomy; 4) player physiology—they're bigger and stronger; 5) improved techniques and instruction; and 6) launch monitors and the customization of equipment."[12] In a tit-for-tat reply, the USGA quoted famous golf course designer Pete Dye, who commented, "It's not the strength of the players. My good friend John Daly hits the ball 30 yards farther in 2005 than he did in 1991. Now John will be the first one to tell you he hasn't done too many push-ups in the last 15 years."[13]

Ping Golf

Perimeter weighting came about due to the poor putting of Karsten Solheim, a General Electric mechanical engineer, who took up golf at the age of 47 in 1954. Solheim designed a putter for himself that he found provided more "feel" when he struck the ball. Solheim moved much of the clubhead weight to the heel and toe, leaving a cavity at the rear and center of the club. Perimeter-weighted, or cavity-back, clubs had a larger sweet spot because of a higher moment of inertia or resistance to twisting. The resistance to twisting reduced the gear effect of the clubhead and resulted in straighter, longer shots with irons. In addition to perimeter weighting, Solheim also developed the investment-casting manufacturing process. This process allowed clubheads to be formed from molds rather than forged from steel—the traditional manufacturing process.

Solheim made his putters by hand from 1959 until 1967, when he left GE and founded Karsten Manufacturing. By the 1970s, Karsten manufactured a full line of perimeter-weighted putters and irons that carried the Ping brand. Solheim named the brand Ping because of the sound the perimeter-weighted clubhead made when it struck the ball. Karsten Manufacturing's Ping putters and irons were thought to be among the most technologically advanced throughout the 1980s and reigned as the market leaders. Karsten Manufacturing was renamed Ping Inc. in 1999.

Karsten Solheim was also the pioneer of custom fitting, with his fitting activities predating the official founding of the company. During the 1960s, touring professionals would meet with Solheim to have him custom-fit putters to their body measurements, and by the 1970s Solheim had developed a fitting system for irons. His system used the golfer's physical measurements, stance and swing, and ball flight to select irons with the optimal lie. The company's irons were sold in 10 color-coded lie configurations to best match recreational golfers' unique fit conditions. In a 2005 golf consumer survey, Ping was rated as the industry leader in custom fitting by a 3-to-1 margin. In addition to producing 10 configurations of iron models, Ping invited retailers to three-day training programs in its plant in Phoenix to become better skilled at custom fitting. By 2005, Ping had trained thousands of retailers.

Ping remained an industry leader in the iron segment in 2005, with a number two position in irons behind Callaway Golf. The company offered three lines of irons—the traditional blade S59 irons, which featured minimal perimeter weighting; the i5 line, with a medium degree of perimeter weighting; and the G5 line, which had expanded perimeter weighting. The S59 line was suitable for professionals and low-handicap recreational golfers, while the i5 was designed for average players looking for a lower ball flight. The G5 produced a higher ball flight than other models and was intended for average golfers who were able to produce only modest amounts of clubhead speed. The company produced a broad line of putters and regularly traded positions with Odyssey as the number one brand of putters.

Even though Ping had been known at one time for only its irons and putters, in late 2005 the privately owned company had become the maker of the most sought-after driver in the industry. The company's 460-cc G5 titanium driver had become the best-selling driver in late 2005 as golfers began to question the merit of the r7's movable weight system and found it difficult to locate Callaway Golf's FT-3 Fusion on retailer shelves. The company had failed to develop a hybrid until late 2005, but retailers expected Ping's G5 hybrid to become one of the best-selling hybrid clubs during equipment upgrades in the spring of 2006. The company's wedges were not big sellers in the market.

Nike Golf

Nike management believed that Tiger Woods could not only generate interest in golf but also help generate substantial revenues for a golf equipment company. Nike seized on the instant popularity of Tiger Woods in 1996 by signing the young star to a five-year, $40 million contract to endorse Nike shoes and apparel. In 1999 Woods extended the contract for an additional five years for $90 million to endorse Nike's new golf ball and forthcoming golf clubs. As with its athletic and apparel and footwear, Nike outsourced the production of its golf balls (in this instance to Bridgestone), while it hired a custom-club designer to design and lead its new golf club business. Nike's new driver, irons, and wedges were introduced during the 2002 PGA Merchandise Show. The company's 2002 line of golf clubs achieved only modest success and an improved line, including a 400-cc forged titanium driver, was introduced during the 2003 PGA Merchandise Show. Tiger Woods began endorsing the company's golf ball in 2000 and began using its driver and irons in 2002. Woods again extended his contract to endorse Nike's golf equipment, golf balls, apparel, and footwear in 2003 for $25 million per year for five years.

Nike management's 1996 assessment of Tiger Woods's enduring worldwide popularity was on the mark with PGA tournament viewership doubling when Woods was in contention for a Sunday win. However, Woods's appeal with television viewers did not translate into equipment sales. Nike's entry into the golf equipment industry had proved successful in terms of apparel and footwear sales, where it was the second leading seller of golf shoes behind FootJoy, but Nike Golf held only a 2.6 percent share of the golf club market in 2004. Nike Golf had achieved nearly a 10 percent market share in golf balls in 2004 and might likely benefit from Tiger Woods's miracle chip shot on the 16th hole of the 2005 Masters that put him in a playoff with Chris DiMarco and led to an eventual win. While an estimated television audience of 15 million watched, Woods's Nike Platinum One golf ball slowly rolled across the 16th green, where it clung to the edge of the hole for what seemed like eternity. As the ball perched at the edge of the cup, the Nike logo could not have been aligned with the camera more perfectly if it had been placed there by the company's advertising agency. After being tracked by CBS's cameras for 17 seconds, the ball fell into the cup.

Nike also boasted after the 2005 Masters Tournament that its brand of irons was the most widely used during the tournament. However, with the exception of those used by Woods, all Nike irons were used by former champions who were not expected to be in contention for a win at the Masters, including Billy Casper, who withdrew from the tournament after shooting a first-round score of 106. Casper's withdrawal from the tournament prevented his score from being recorded as an official statistic. It was reported that Nike paid $20,000 tee-up fees during the Masters practice rounds to those willing to use the company's irons during the day. As of late

2005, Nike's 460-cc SasQuatch and Ignite drivers; Slingshot, NDS, Forged, and Combo irons; and CPR hybrids remained poor sellers. Demand for the company's putters and wedges was also low. Nike had more recently signed 13 additional professional golfers to endorsement contracts, including 15-year-old Michelle Wie. Nike's October 2005 agreement with Wie would pay the teenager, who had yet to win a tournament competing against professionals in her 30 attempts, $20 million over four years. Nike did not disclose in its financial statements what percentage of its 2004 revenues of $12.3 billion was made up of golf equipment and apparel sales.

End notes

[1] As quoted in *The Callaway Connection*, Spring 2000, p. 7.
[2] As quoted in "Callaway Golf Introduced ERC II Forged Titanium Driver—Its Hottest and Most Forgiving Driver Ever," *PR Newswire*, October 24, 2000.
[3] Ibid.
[4] As quoted in *Smart Money*, August 2002, p. 34.
[5] Posted at www.callawaygolf.com/EN/customerservice.aspx?pid=9ways.
[6] As quoted in "Teed Off: Counterfeiters Are Cashing In on Big-Name Clubs by Hawking Bogus Merchandise on the Internet," *St. Louis Post-Dispatch*, May 18, 2005, p. C1.
[7] Callaway Golf Company 1998 annual report.
[8] "Callaway Enters the Ball Game," *Show News*, February 5, 2000.
[9] As quoted in "Looking for the Sweet Spot: Prospects Are Rosier for Carlsbad's Callaway Golf, but Some Wonder If New CEO Can Complete the Turnaround," *San Diego Union-Tribune*, August 28, 2005, p. H-1.
[10] As quoted in "Keeping Our Eye on the Ball," *Inside the USGA, Special Issue: Equipment*, October 2005, p. 1.
[11] Ibid, p. 9.
[12] As quoted in a reprint of "Mr. Titleist Talks," *Travel & Leisure Golf*, posted at www.titleist.com, 2005.
[13] As quoted in "Keeping Our Eye on the Ball," p. 16.

Case 5

Dell Inc. in 2006: Can Rivals Beat Its Strategy?

Arthur A. Thompson
The University of Alabama

John E. Gamble
University of South Alabama

In 1984, at the age of 19, Michael Dell invested $1,000 of his own money and founded Dell Computer with a simple vision and business concept—that personal computers (PCs) could be built to order and sold directly to customers. Michael Dell believed his approach to the PC business had two advantages: (1) bypassing distributors and retail dealers eliminated the markups of resellers, and (2) building to order greatly reduced the costs and risks associated with carrying large stocks of parts, components, and finished goods. Between 1986 and 1993 the company worked to refine its strategy, build an adequate infrastructure, and establish market credibility against better-known rivals. In the mid- and late 1990s, Dell's strategy started to click into full gear. By 2003, Dell's sell-direct and build-to-order business model and strategy had provided the company with the most efficient procurement, manufacturing, and distribution capabilities in the global PC industry and given Dell a substantial cost and profit margin advantage over rival PC vendors. During 2004–2005, the company solidified its position as the global market leader in PCs.

Dell had a commanding 33.9 percent share of PC sales in the United States in the first nine months of 2005, comfortably ahead of Hewlett-Packard (19.1 percent), Gateway (6.0 percent), and IBM/Lenovo (4.3 percent)—and its lead over rivals was increasing. Dell had moved ahead of IBM into second place during 1998 and then overtaken Compaq Computer as the U.S. sales leader in the third quarter of 1999. Its market share leadership in the United States had widened every year since 2000. Dell had

eclipsed Compaq as the global market leader in 2001. But when Hewlett-Packard (HP), the third-ranking PC seller in the world, acquired Compaq, the second-ranking PC vendor in 2002, Dell found itself in a tight battle with HP for the top spot globally. Dell was the world leader in unit sales in the first and third quarters of 2002, and HP was the sales leader in the second and fourth quarters. However, Dell opened a clear market share gap over HP in 2003–2005. Nonetheless, Dell trailed HP in PC sales outside the United States; HP's non-U.S. share had been in the 12.5 to 14.1 percent range since late 2001, with Dell's overall share of sales outside the United States climbing from about 7.5 percent in late 2001 to 11.6 percent in 2005. Exhibit 1 shows the shifting domestic and global sales and market share rankings in PCs during 1998–2005.

Since the late 1990s, Dell had also been driving for industry leadership in servers. In 2004 Dell was the number one domestic seller of servers, with close to a 33 percent market share (up from about 3–4 percent in the mid-1990s). It was number two in the world in server shipments, with a 24.5 percent share in the third quarter of 2004, within striking distance of global market leadership. Dell was the leader in servers (based on unit volume) in the three largest server markets—the United States, Japan, and China. In the mid- to late-1990s, a big fraction of the servers sold were proprietary machines running on customized Unix operating systems and carrying price tags ranging from $30,000 to $1 million or more. But a seismic shift in server technology, coupled with growing cost-consciousness on the part of server users, produced a radical shift away from more costly, proprietary, Unix-based servers during

Exhibit 1 **U.S. and Global Market Shares of Leading PC Vendors, 1998–2005**

A. U.S. Market Shares of the Leading PC Vendors, 1998–2005

2003 Rank	Vendor	First Nine Months of 2005		2004		2003		2002		2001		2000		1998	
		Shipments (in 000s)	Market Share	Shipments (in 000s)	Market Share	Shipments (in 000s)	Market Share	Shipments (in 000s)	Market Share	Shipments (in 000s)	Market Share	Shipments (in 000s)	Market Share	Shipments (in 000s)	Market Share
1	Dell	15,725	33.1%	19,296	33.1%	16,319	30.9%	13,324	27.9%	10,817	23.5%	9,645	19.7%	4,799	13.2%
	Compaq*	—	—	—	—	—	—	—	—	5,341	11.6	7,761	15.9	6,052	16.7
2	Hewlett-Packard*	8,869	19.1	11,600	19.9	10,851	20.6	8,052	16.8	4,374	9.5	5,630	11.5	2,832	7.8
3	Gateway	2,802	6.0	2,945	5.1	1,987	3.8	2,725	5.7	3,219	7.0	4,237	8.7	3,039	8.4
4	IBM/ Lenovo	1,995	4.3	2,932	5.0	2,748	5.2	2,531	5.3	2,461	5.3	2,668	5.5	2,983	8.2
5	Apple	n.a.	n.a.	1,935	3.3	1,675	3.2	1,693	3.5	1,665	3.6	n.a	n.a.	n.a.	n.a.
	Others	n.a.	n.a.	19,548	33.6	19,158	36.3	19,514	40.8	23,509	51.0	18,959	38.8	16,549	45.6
	All vendors	46,337	100.0%	58,256	100.0%	52,739	100.0%	47,839	100.0%	46,051	100.0%	48,900	100.0%	36,254	100.0%

B. Worldwide Market Shares of the Leading PC Vendors, 1998–2005

2003 Rank	Vendor	First Nine Months of 2005		2004		2003		2002		2001		2000		1998	
		Shipments (in 000s)	Market Share	Shipments (in 000s)	Market Share	Shipments (in 000s)	Market Share	Shipments (in 000s)	Market Share	Shipments (in 000s)	Market Share	Shipments (in 000s)	Market Share	Shipments (in 000s)	Market Share
1	Dell	27,192	18.7%	31,771	17.9%	25,833	16.9%	20,672	15.2%	17,231	12.9%	14,801	10.6%	7,770	8.5%
	Compaq*	—	—	—	—	—	—	—	—	14,673	11	17,399	12.5	13,266	14.5
2	Hewlett-Packard*	22,825	15.7	28,063	15.8	25,009	16.4	18,432	13.6	9,309	7	10,327	7.4	5,743	6.3
3	IBM/ Lenovo	9,942	6.8	10,492	5.9	9,000	5.9	7,996	5.9	8,292	6.2	9,308	6.7	7,946	8.7
4	Fujitsu Siemens	—	—	7,182	4.0	6,375	4.2	5,822	4.3	6,022	4.5	6,582	4.7	n.a.	n.a.
5	Acer	—	—	6,461	3.6	n.a.	n.a.	n.a	n.a.	n.a	n.a	n.a.	n.a	n.a	n.a.
	Others	—	—	93,511	52.7	81,271	53.3	78,567	57.8	73,237	54.9	80,640	58	50,741	55.5
	All vendors	145,542	100.0%	177,480	100.0%	152,568	100.0%	136,022	100.0%	133,466	100.0%	139,057	100.0%	91,442	100.0%

n.a. = Not available.

*Compaq was acquired by Hewlett-Packard in May 2002. The 2002 data for Hewlett-Packard includes both Compaq-branded and Hewlett-Packard-branded PCs for the last three quarters of 2002 plus only Hewlett-Packard-branded PCs for Q1 2002.

1999–2004. In 2003–2004, about 8 out of 10 servers sold carried price tags below $10,000, were based on standardized components and technology, and ran on either Windows or Linux operating systems. The overall share of Unix-based servers shipped in 2003–2004 was under 10 percent, down from about 18 percent in 1997. Dell's rise to prominence in servers came from its focus on low- and midrange servers that used standard technology.

In addition, Dell was making market inroads in other product categories. Its sales of data storage devices had grown to over $2 billion annually, aided by a strategic alliance with EMC, a leader in data storage. In 2001–2002, Dell began selling low-cost, data-routing switches—a product category in which Cisco Systems was the dominant global leader. In late 2002, Dell introduced a new line of handheld PCs— the Axim X5—to compete against the higher-priced products of Palm, HP, and others; the Axim offered a solid but not trendsetting design, was packed with features, and was priced roughly 50 percent below the best-selling models of rivals. Starting in 2003, Dell began marketing Dell-branded printers and printer cartridges, product categories that provided global leader HP with the lion's share of its profits—the company was on track to sell over 5 million printers and generate more than $1 billion in imaging and printing revenues in 2004. Also in 2003, Dell began selling flat-screen LCD TVs and retail-store systems, including electronic cash registers, specialized software, services, and peripherals required to link retail-store check-out lanes to corporate information systems. Dell's MP3 player, the Dell DJ, was number two behind the Apple iPod. Dell added plasma-screen TVs to its TV product line in 2004. Since the late 1990s, Dell had been marketing CD and DVD drives, printers, scanners, modems, monitors, digital cameras, memory cards, data storage devices, and speakers made by a variety of manufacturers.

So far, Dell's foray into new products and businesses had proved profitable. According to Michael Dell, "We believe that all our businesses should make money. If a business doesn't make money, if you can't figure out how to make money in that business, you shouldn't be in that business."[1] In 2003 and 2004, Dell earned a profit in each of its product categories, customer segments, and geographic markets. Dell products were sold in more than 170 countries, but sales in 60 countries accounted for about 95 percent of total revenues.

COMPANY BACKGROUND

At age 12, Michael Dell was running a mail order stamp-trading business, complete with a national catalog, and grossing $2,000 a month. At 16 he was selling subscriptions to the *Houston Post,* and at 17 he bought his first BMW with money he had earned. He enrolled at the University of Texas in 1983 as a premed student (his parents wanted him to become a doctor), but he soon became immersed in computers and started selling PC components out of his college dormitory room. He bought random-access memory (RAM) chips and disk drives for IBM PCs at cost from IBM dealers, who at the time often had excess supplies on hand because they were required to order large monthly quotas from IBM. Dell resold the components through newspaper ads (and later through ads in national computer magazines) at 10–15 percent below the regular retail price.

By April 1984 sales were running about $80,000 per month. Michael decided to drop out of college and form a company, PCs Ltd., to sell both PC components and PCs under the brand name PCs Limited. He obtained his PCs by buying retailers' surplus stocks at cost, then powering them up with graphics cards, hard disks, and memory before reselling them. His strategy was to sell directly to end users; by eliminating the retail markup, Dell's new company was able to sell IBM clones (machines that copied the functioning of IBM PCs using the same or similar components) about 40 percent below the price of IBM's best-selling PCs. The discounting strategy was successful, attracting price-conscious buyers and generating rapid revenue growth. By 1985, the company was assembling its own PC designs with a few people working on six-foot tables. The company had 40 employees, and Michael Dell worked 18-hour days, often sleeping on a cot in his office. By the end of fiscal 1986, sales had reached $33 million.

During the next several years, however, PCs Limited was hampered by growing pains—specifically, a lack of money, people, and resources. Michael Dell sought to refine the company's business model; add needed production capacity; and build a bigger, deeper management staff and corporate infrastructure while at the same time keeping costs low. The company was renamed Dell Computer in 1987, and the first international offices were opened that same year. In 1988 Dell added a sales force to serve large customers, began selling to government agencies, and became a public company—raising $34.2 million in its first offering of common stock. Sales to large customers quickly became the dominant part of Dell's business. By 1990 Dell Computer had sales of $388 million, a market share of 2–3 percent, and a research and development (R&D) staff of over 150 people. Michael Dell's vision was for Dell Computer to become one of the top three PC companies.

Thinking its direct sales business would not grow fast enough, in 1990–93 the company began distributing its computer products through Soft Warehouse Superstores (now CompUSA), Staples (a leading office products chain), Wal-Mart, Sam's Club, and Price Club (now Price/Costco). Dell also sold PCs through Best Buy stores in 16 states and through Xerox in 19 Latin American countries. But when the company learned how thin its margins were in selling through such distribution channels, it realized it had made a mistake and withdrew from selling to retailers and other intermediaries in 1994 to refocus on direct sales. At the time, sales through retailers accounted for only about 2 percent of Dell's revenues.

In 1993, further problems emerged: Dell reportedly lost $38 million in a risky foreign-currency hedging, quality difficulties arose with certain PC lines made by the company's contract manufacturers, profit margins declined, and buyers were turned off by the company's laptop PC models. To get laptop sales back on track, the company took a charge of $40 million to write off its laptop line and suspended sales of laptops until it could get redesigned models into the marketplace.

Because of higher costs and unacceptably low profit margins in selling to individuals and households, Dell did not pursue the consumer market aggressively until sales to individuals at the company's Internet site took off in 1996 and 1997. It became clear that PC-savvy individuals, who were buying their second and third computers, wanted powerful computers with multiple features; did not need much technical support; and liked the convenience of buying direct from Dell, ordering exactly what they wanted, and having it delivered to their door within a matter of days. In early 1997, Dell created an internal sales and marketing group dedicated to serving the individual consumer segment and introduced a product line designed especially for individual users. In 2005, sales to consumers accounted for 15 percent of Dell's worldwide PC business, with sales to business, government, and educational institutions accounting for 85 percent.

By late 1997, Dell had become a low-cost leader among PC vendors by wringing greater and greater efficiency out of its direct sales and build-to-order business model. Since then, the company had continued driving hard to reduce its costs and, in 2003–2005, was considered the lowest-cost producer among all the leading vendors of PCs and servers. The company was a pioneer and an acknowledged world leader in incorporating e-commerce technology and use of the Internet into its everyday business practices. Michael Dell's goal was to stitch Dell's business together with its supply partners and customers in real time such that all three appeared to be part of the same organizational team.[3]

In its 2005 fiscal year, Dell posted revenues of $49.2 billion and profits of $3.0 billion. Since fiscal 1995, revenues had grown at a compound average growth rate of 30.6 percent and profits had grown at 36.0 percent compound rate. Dell reported close to $56 billion in sales in its fiscal year ending January 2006. A $100 investment in Dell's stock at its initial public offering in June 1988 would have been worth close to $40,000 in December 2005. Based on 2004 data, Dell ranked number 28 on the Fortune 500, number 84 on the Fortune Global 500, and number 3 on the Fortune Global "most admired" list. In February 2006, Dell Computer had 65,200 employees worldwide, up from 16,000 at year-end 1997; over 60 percent of Dell's employees were located in countries outside the United States, and this percentage was growing. The company's headquarters and main office complex was in Round Rock, Texas (an Austin suburb). The company changed its name from Dell Computer to Dell Inc. in 2003 to reflect the company's growing business base outside of PCs. Exhibits 2 and 3 provide information about Dell's financial performance and geographic operations.

Michael Dell

In the company's early days Michael Dell hung around mostly with the company's engineers. He was so shy that some employees thought he was stuck up because he never talked to them. But people who worked with him closely described him as a likable young man who was slow to warm up to strangers.[4] He was a terrible public speaker and wasn't good at running meetings. But Lee Walker, a 51-year-old venture capitalist brought in by Michael Dell to provide much-needed managerial and financial experience during the

Exhibit 2   **Selected Financial Statement Data for Dell Inc., Fiscal Years 1998–2006 (in millions, except per share data)**

	Fiscal Year Ended						
	February 3, 2006	January 28, 2005	January 30, 2004	January 31, 2003	February 1, 2002	January 28, 2000	February 1, 1998
Results of operations:							
Net revenue	$55,908	$49,205	$41,444	$35,404	$31,168	$25,265	$12,327
Cost of revenue	45,958	40,190	33,892	29,055	25,661	20,047	9,605
Gross margin	9,950	9,015	7,552	6,349	5,507	5,218	2,722
Operating expenses:							
Selling, general and administrative	5,140	4,298	3,544	3,050	2,784	2,387	1,202
Research, development and engineering	463	463	464	455	452	374	204
Special charges	—	—	—	—	482	194	—
Total operating expenses	5,603	4,761	4,008	3,505	3,718	2,955	1,406
Operating income	4,347	4,254	3,544	2,844	1,789	2,263	1,316
Investment and other income (loss), net	227	191	180	183	(58)	188	52
Income before income taxes, extraordinary loss, and cumulative effect of change in accounting principle	4,574	4,445	3,724	3,027	1,731	2,451	1,368
Provision for income taxes	1,002	1,402	1,079	905	485	785	424
Net income	$ 3,572	$ 3,043	$ 2,645	$ 2,122	$ 1,246	$ 1,666	$ 944
Earnings per common share:							
Basic	$1,49	$1.21	$1.03	$0.82	$0.48	$0.66	$0.36
Diluted	$1,46	$1.18	$1.01	$0.80	$0.46	$0.61	$0.32
Weighted average shares outstanding:							
Basic	2,403	2,509	2,565	2,584	2,602	2,536	2,631
Diluted	2,449	2,568	2,619	2,644	2,726	2,728	2,952
Cash flow and balance sheet data							
Net cash provided by operating activities	$ 4,839	$ 5,310	$ 3,670	$ 3,538	$ 3,797	$ 3,926	$ 1,592
Cash, cash equivalents, and investments	11,749	14,101	11,922	9.905	8,287	6,853	1,844
Total assets	23,109	23,215	19,311	15,470	13,535	11,560	4,268
Long-term debt	504	505	505	506	520	508	17
Total stockholders' equity	$ 4,129	$ 6,485	$ 6,280	$ 4,873	$ 4,694	$ 5,308	$ 1,293

*Includes effect of $59 million adjustment due to the cumulative effect of a change in accounting principle.

Source: Dell Inc. 2005 10-K report, 1999 annual report, and press release on February 16, 2006.

Exhibit 3   **Dell's Geographic Area Performance, Fiscal Years 2000–2006 (in millions of dollars)**

	February 3, 2006	January 28, 2005	January 30, 2004	January 31, 2003	February 1, 2002	January 28, 2000
Net revenues						
Americas						
Business	$28,481	$25,339	$21,888	$19,394	$17,275	$15,160
U.S. consumer	7,930	7,601	6,715	5,653	4,485	2,719
Total Americas	36,411	32,940	28,603	25,047	21,760	17,879
Europe*	12,873	10,787	8,495	6,912	6,429	5,590
Asia Pacific-Japan	6,624	5,478	4,436	3,445	2,979	1,796
Total net revenues	$55,908	$49,205	$41,444	$35,404	$31,168	$25,265
Operating income						
Americas						
Business	$ 3,015	$ 2,579	$ 2,124	$ 1,945	$ 1,482	$ 1,800
U.S. consumer	414	399	400	308	260	204
Total Americas	3,429	2,978	2,594	2,253	1,742	2,004
Europe*	857	818	637	388	377	359
Asia Pacific-Japan	503	458	313	203	152	94
Special charges	—	—	—	—	(482)	(194)
Total operating income	$ 4,789	$ 4,254	$ 3,544	$ 2,844	$ 1,789	$ 2,263

*Includes Africa and the Middle East.
Source: Dell Inc. 10-K reports 2006, 2005, and 2002.

company's organization-building years, became Michael Dell's mentor, built up his confidence, and was instrumental in turning him into a polished executive.[5] Walker served as the company's president and chief operating officer during the 1986–1990 period; he had a fatherly image, knew everyone by name, and played a key role in implementing Michael Dell's marketing ideas. Under Walker's tutelage, Michael Dell became intimately familiar with all parts of the business, overcame his shyness, learned to control his ego, and turned into a charismatic leader with an instinct for motivating people and winning their loyalty and respect.

When Walker had to leave the company in 1990 for health reasons, Dell turned to Morton Meyerson, former CEO and president of Electronic Data Systems, for advice and guidance on how to transform Dell Computer from a fast-growing medium-sized company into a billion-dollar enterprise. Though sometimes given to displays of impatience, Michael Dell usually spoke in a quiet, reflective manner and came across as a person with maturity and seasoned

judgment far beyond his age. His prowess was based more on an astute combination of technical knowledge and marketing know-how than on being a technological wizard. In 1992, at the age of 27, Michael Dell became the youngest CEO ever to head a Fortune 500 company; he was a billionaire at the age of 31.

By the late 1990s, Michael Dell had become one of the most respected executives in the PC industry. Media journalists had described him as "the quintessential American entrepreneur" and "the most innovative guy for marketing computers." He was a much-sought-after speaker at industry and company conferences. His views and opinions about the future of PCs, the Internet, and e-commerce practices carried considerable weight both in the PC industry and among executives worldwide. In early 2005, the once pudgy and bespectacled 40-year-old Michael Dell was physically fit, considered good-looking, wore contact lenses, ate only health foods, and lived in a three-story 33,000-square-foot home on a 60-acre estate in Austin, Texas, with his wife and four children. In 2005, he owned about 9 percent of Dell's common stock, worth about $8.7 billion.

Michael Dell was considered a very accessible CEO and a role model for young executives because he had done what many of them were trying to do. He delegated authority to subordinates, believing that the best results came from turning loose "talented people who can be relied upon to do what they're supposed to do." Business associates viewed Michael Dell as an aggressive personality, an extremely competitive risk taker who had always played close to the edge. He spent about 30 percent of his time traveling to company operations and meeting with customers. In a typical year, he would make two or three trips to Europe and two trips to Asia.

In mid-2004, Michael Dell, the company's first and only CEO, transferred his title of CEO to Kevin Rollins, the company's president and chief operating officer. Dell remained as chairman of the board. Dell and Rollins had run the company for the past seven years under a shared leadership structure. The changes were primarily ones of title, not of roles or responsibilities.

DELL'S STRATEGY AND BUSINESS MODEL

In orchestrating Dell's rise to global prominence, company executives had come to believe strongly that five tenets were the key to delivering superior customer value:[6]

1. A direct relationship is the most efficient path to the customer because it eliminates wholesale and retail dealers that impede Dell's understanding of customer needs and expectations and that add unnecessary time and cost.

2. Allowing customers to purchase custom-built products and custom-tailored services is the most effective way to meet customer needs.

3. Nonproprietary, standardized technologies deliver the best value to customers.

4. A highly efficient supply chain and manufacturing organization, grounded in the use of standardized technologies and selling direct, paves the way for a low-cost structure where cost-savings can be passed along to customers in the form of lower prices.

5. Dell should endeavor to deliver added value to customers by (*a*) researching all the technological options, (*b*) trying to determine which ones are "optimal" in the sense of delivering the best combination of performance and efficiency, and (*c*) being accountable to customers for helping them obtain the highest return on their investment in information technology (IT) products and services.

In accordance with these tenets, Dell's strategy during the 2002–2005 period had seven core elements: a cost-efficient approach to build-to-order manufacturing, partnerships with suppliers aimed at squeezing cost savings out of the supply chain, direct sales to customers, award-winning customer service and technical support, customer-driven R&D, emphasis on using standardized technologies, and product-line expansion aimed at capturing a bigger share of the dollars its customers spent for IT products and services.

The business model on which the strategy was predicated was powerful: Use the company's strong capabilities in supply chain management, low-cost manufacturing, and direct sales capabilities to expand into product categories where Dell could provide added value to its customers in the form of lower prices. The standard pattern of attack was to identify an IT product with good margins; figure out how to build it (or else have it built by others) cheaply enough to be able to significantly underprice competitive products; and then market the new product to Dell's steadily growing customer base and watch the market share points, incremental revenues, and incremental profits pile up.

Cost-Efficient Build-to-Order Manufacturing

Dell built its computers, workstations, and servers to order; none were produced for inventory. Dell customers could order custom-equipped servers and workstations according to the needs of their applications. Desktop and laptop customers ordered whatever configuration of microprocessor speed, random-access memory, hard disk capacity, CD or DVD drives, fax/modem/wireless capabilities, graphics cards, monitor size, speakers, and other accessories they preferred. The orders were directed to the nearest factory. In 2005 Dell had assembly plants in Austin, Texas; Nashville, Tennessee; Limerick,

Ireland; Xiamen, China; Penang, Malaysia; and El Dorado do Sul, Brazil. A seventh manufacturing plant with capacity to make 15,000 to 20,000 desktops per day opened outside Winston-Salem, North Carolina, in late 2005—it was Dell's largest plant to date and could turn out a new PC every five seconds. Dell opened a second plant in Xiamen in January 2006, and an additional plant in Europe was in the planning stages. At all locations, the company had the capability to assemble PCs, workstations, and servers; Dell assembled its data storage products at its Austin, Limerick, and Penang plants. All plants used the same production systems and procedures. In 2002–2005, typical orders were built and delivered in three to five days; however, the new North Carolina plant was expected to be able to deliver orders to customers on the eastern coast of the United States in one to three days. Dell believed in building its plants close to customers because the labor costs to assemble a PC were about $10, whereas the logistics costs to move parts and ship a finished PC were about $40 per unit.[7]

Until 1997, Dell operated its assembly lines in traditional fashion, with workers performing a single operation. An order form accompanied each metal chassis across the production floor; drives, chips, and ancillary items were installed to match customer specifications. As a partly assembled PC arrived at a new workstation, the operator, standing beside a tall steel rack with drawers full of components, was instructed what to do by little red and green lights flashing beside the drawers. When the operator was finished, the drawers containing the used components were automatically replenished from the other side, and the PC chassis glided down the line to the next workstation. However, Dell had reorganized its plants in 1997, shifting to "cell manufacturing" techniques whereby a team of workers operating at a group workstation (or cell) assembled an entire PC according to customer specifications. The shift to cell manufacturing reduced Dell's assembly times by 75 percent and doubled productivity per square foot of assembly space. Assembled computers were first tested and then loaded with the desired software, shipped, and typically delivered five to six business days after the order was placed.

At Dell's newest plant in Austin, the cell manufacturing approach had been abandoned in favor of an even more efficient assembly-line approach. Workers at the new plant in 2004 could turn out close to 800 desktop PCs per hour on three assembly lines that took half the floor space of the older cell manufacturing process, where production had run

about 120 units per hour. Although the new Austin plant was originally designed for production of 400 units per hour (1 PC every 9 seconds), management expected to boost hourly production to 1,000 units per hour. The gains in productivity were being achieved partly by redesigning the PCs to permit easier and faster assembly, partly by innovations in the assembly process, and partly by reducing the number of times a computer was touched by workers during assembly and shipping by 50 percent. In 2005 it took about 66 minutes to assemble and test a PC. Moreover, just-in-time inventory practices that left pallets of parts sitting around everywhere had been tweaked to just-in-the-nick-of-time delivery by suppliers of the exact parts needed every couple of hours; double-decker conveyor belts moved parts and components to designated assembly points. Newly assembled PCs were routed on conveyors to shipping, where they were boxed and shipped to customers the same day.

Dell's new 750,000-square-foot plant in North Carolina featured a production layout that allowed computers to be tested as its components and software were installed. This "instantaneous build and test" operation permitted team members to identify and correct any problems on the spot, rather than waiting until the PC was fully assembled. The assembly innovations pioneered in the Austin and North Carolina plants were in the process of being instituted in Dell's other plants. Workers at all Dell plants competed with each other to come up with more efficient assembly methods. New cost-saving ideas at one plant were quickly implemented worldwide.

Dell was regarded as a world-class manufacturing innovator and a pioneer in how to mass-produce a customized product—its methods were routinely studied in business schools worldwide. Most of Dell's PC rivals—notably, IBM and HP/Compaq—had given up on trying to produce their own PCs as cheaply as Dell and shifted to outsourcing their PCs from contract manufacturers. Dell management believed that its in-house manufacturing delivered about a 6 percent cost advantage versus outsourcing. Dell's build-to-order strategy meant that the company had no in-house stock of finished goods inventories and that, unlike competitors using the traditional value chain model, it did not have to wait for resellers to clear out their own inventories before it could push new models into the marketplace—resellers typically operated with 30 to 60 days inventory of prebuilt models (see Exhibit 4). Equally important was the fact that customers who bought from Dell got the satisfaction

Exhibit 4   **Comparative Value Chain Models of PC Vendors**

| Traditional Build-to-Stock Value Chain Used by Hewlett-Packard, IBM/Lenovo, Apple, Sony, and most others |

| Manufacture and delivery of PC parts and components by suppliers | Assembly of PCs as needed to fill orders from distributors and retailers | Sales and marketing activities of PC vendors to build a brand image and establish a network of resellers | Sales and marketing activities of resellers | Purchases by PC users | Service and support activities provided to PC users by resellers (and some PC vendors) |

| Dell's Build-to-Order, Sell-Direct Value Chain |

| Manufacture and delivery of PC parts and components by supply partners | Custom assembly of PCs as orders are received from PC buyers | Sales and marketing activities of PC vendor to build brand image and secure orders from PC buyers | Purchases by PC users | Service and support activities provided to PC users by Dell or contract providers |

Close collaboration and real-time data-sharing to drive down costs of supply chain activities, minimize inventories, keep assembly costs low, and respond quickly to changes in the makeup of customer orders

of having their computers customized to their particular liking and pocketbook.

Quality Control

All assembly plants had the capability to run testing and quality control processes on components, parts, and subassemblies obtained from suppliers, as well as on the finished products Dell assembled. Suppliers were urged to participate in a quality certification program that committed them to achieving defined quality specifications. Quality control activities were undertaken at various stages in the assembly process. In addition, Dell's quality control program included testing of completed units after assembly, ongoing production reliability audits, failure tracking for early identification of problems associated with new models shipped to customers,

and information obtained from customers through its service and technical support programs. All of the company's plants had been certified as meeting ISO 9002 quality standards.

Partnerships with Suppliers

Michael Dell believed that it made much better sense for the company to partner with reputable suppliers of PC parts and components than to integrate backward and get into parts and components manufacturing on its own. He explained why:

> If you've got a race with 20 players all vying to make the fastest graphics chip in the world, do you want to be the twenty-first horse, or do you want to evaluate the field of 20 and pick the best one?[8]

Dell management evaluated the various makers of each component; picked the best one or two as suppliers; and then stuck with them as long as they maintained their leadership in technology, performance, quality, and cost. Management believed that long-term partnerships with reputable suppliers had at least five advantages. First, using name-brand processors, disk drives, modems, speakers, and multimedia components enhanced the quality and performance of Dell's PCs. Because of varying performance among different brands of components, the brand of the components was quite important to customers concerned about performance and reliability. Second, because Dell partnered with suppliers for the long term and because it committed to purchase a specified percentage of its requirements from each supplier, Dell was assured of getting the volume of components it needed on a timely basis even when overall market demand for a particular component temporarily exceeded the overall market supply. Third, Dell's long-run commitment to its suppliers made it feasible for suppliers to locate their plants or distribution centers within a few miles of Dell assembly plants, putting them in position to make deliveries daily or every few hours, as needed. Dell supplied data on inventories and replenishment needs to its suppliers at least once a day—hourly in the case of components being delivered several times daily from nearby sources.

Fourth, long-term supply partnerships facilitated having some of the supplier's engineers assigned to Dell's product design teams and being treated as part of Dell. When new products were launched, suppliers' engineers were stationed in Dell's plants; if early buyers called with a problem related to design, further assembly and shipments were halted while the supplier's engineers and Dell personnel corrected the flaw on the spot.[9] Fifth, long-term partnerships enlisted greater cooperation on the part of suppliers to seek new ways to drive costs out of the supply chain. Dell openly shared its daily production schedules, sales forecasts, and new model introduction plans with vendors. Dell also did a three-year plan with each of its key suppliers and worked with suppliers to minimize the number of different stock-keeping units of parts and components in its products and to identify ways to drive costs down.

Commitment to Just-in-Time Inventory Practices

Dell's just-in-time inventory emphasis yielded major cost advantages and shortened the time it took for

Dell to get new generations of its computer models into the marketplace. New advances were coming so fast in certain computer parts and components (particularly microprocessors, disk drives, and wireless devices) that any given item in inventory was obsolete in a matter of months, sometimes quicker. Moreover, rapid-fire reductions in the prices of components were not unusual—for example, Intel regularly cut the prices on its older chips when it introduced newer chips, and it introduced new chip generations about every three months. In 2003–2004, component costs declined an average of 0.5 percent weekly.[10] Michael Dell explained the competitive and economic advantages of minimal component inventories:

> If I've got 11 days of inventory and my competitor has 80 and Intel comes out with a new chip, that means I'm going to get to market 69 days sooner. In the computer industry, inventory can be a pretty massive risk because if the cost of materials is going down 50 percent a year and you have two or three months of inventory versus eleven days, you've got a big cost disadvantage. And you're vulnerable to product transitions, when you can get stuck with obsolete inventory.[11]

For a growing number of parts and components, Dell's close partnership with suppliers was allowing it to operate with no more than two hours of inventory.

Dell's supplier of CRT monitors was Sony. Because the monitors Sony supplied with the Dell name already imprinted were of dependably high quality (a defect rate of fewer than 1,000 per million), Dell didn't even open up the monitor boxes to test them at its Reno, Nevada, monitor distribution center.[12] Using sophisticated data exchange systems, Dell arranged for its shippers (Airborne Express and United Parcel Service) to pick up computers at U.S. assembly plants, then pick up the accompanying monitors at its Reno distribution center and deliver both to the customer simultaneously. The savings in time and cost were significant. Dell had been working hard for the past several years to refine and improve its relationships with suppliers and its procedures for operating with smaller inventories.

In fiscal year 1995, Dell averaged an inventory turn cycle of 32 days. By the end of fiscal 1997 (January 1997), the average was down to 13 days. In fiscal 1998 Dell's inventory averaged 7 days, which compared very favorably with Gateway's 14-day average, Compaq's 23-day average, and the estimated industrywide average of over 50 days. In fiscal years

1999 and 2000, Dell operated with an average of six days' supply in inventory; the average dropped to 5 days' supply in fiscal year 2001, 4 days' supply in 2002, and 3 to 4 days' supply in 2003–2006.

Dell's Direct Sales Strategy and Marketing Efforts

With thousands of phone, fax, and Internet orders daily and ongoing field sales force contact with customers, the company kept its finger on the market pulse, quickly detecting shifts in sales trends, design problems, and quality glitches. If the company got more than a few of the same complaints, the information was relayed immediately to design engineers who checked out the problem. When design flaws or components defects were found, the factory was notified and the problem corrected within a few days. Management believed Dell's ability to respond quickly gave it a significant advantage over PC makers that operated on the basis of large production runs of variously configured and equipped PCs and sold them through retail channels. Dell saw its direct sales approach as a totally customer-driven system, with the flexibility to transition quickly to new generations of components and PC models.

Dell's Customer-Based Sales and Marketing Focus Whereas many technology companies organized their sales and marketing efforts around product lines, Dell was organized around customer groups. Dell had placed managers in charge of developing sales and service programs appropriate to the needs and expectations of each customer group. Up until the early 1990s, Dell operated with sales and service programs aimed at just two market segments—high-volume corporate and governmental buyers and low-volume business and individual buyers. But as sales took off in 1995–97, these segments were subdivided into finer, more homogeneous categories that by 2000 included global enterprise accounts, large and midsize companies (over 400 employees), small companies (under 400 employees), health care businesses (over 400 employees), federal government agencies, state and local government agencies, educational institutions, and individual consumers. Many of these customer segments were further subdivided—for instance, in education, there were separate sales and marketing programs for K–12 schools; higher education institutions; and personal-use purchases by faculty, staff, and students.

Dell had a field sales force that called on large business and institutional customers throughout the world. Dell's largest global enterprise accounts were assigned their own dedicated sales force—for example, Dell had a sales force of 150 people dedicated to meeting the needs of General Electric's facilities and personnel scattered across the world. Individuals and small businesses could place orders by telephone or at Dell's Web site. Dell had call centers in the United States, Canada, Europe, and Asia with toll-free lines; customers could talk with a sales representative about specific models, get information faxed or mailed to them, place an order, and pay by credit card. The Asian and European call centers were equipped with technology that routed calls from a particular country to a particular call center. Thus, for example, a customer calling from Lisbon, Portugal, was automatically directed to a Portuguese-speaking sales rep at the call center in Montpelier, France.

Dell in Japan Dell's share in Japan had climbed steadily from 1.0 percent in 1995 to 7.7 percent in 2002 to close to 12 percent in 2005, making it the number three provider of computer systems in Japan (behind NEC and Toshiba). Other competitors in Japan included Sony, Fujitsu, Hitachi, IBM/Lenovo, Sharp, and Matshusita. Based on units sold, however, Dell was number one in business desktop computers and number two in entry-level and midrange servers. Dell's 2004 sales in Japan were up about 30 percent, in a market where overall sales were flat, and its sales in 2005 were up around 20 percent. Dell's technical and customer support for PCs, servers, and network storage devices was ranked the best in Japan in 2002 and 2003. Dell had 1,100 personnel in Japan and was tracking Japanese buying habits and preferences with its proprietary software. The head of Dell's consumer PC sales group in Japan had installed 34 kiosks in leading electronics stores around Japan, allowing shoppers to test Dell computers, ask questions of staff, and place orders—close to half the sales were to people who did not know about Dell prior to visiting the kiosk. The kiosks proved quite popular and were boosting Dell's share of PC sales to consumers in Japan. Dell believed that it was more profitable than any other PC-server vendor selling in the Japanese market. Dell's profit margins in Japan were higher than those in the U.S. market.

Dell in China Dell Computer entered China in 1998 and achieved faster growth there than in any other foreign market it had entered. The market for PCs in China was the third largest in the world, behind the United States and Japan, and was on the verge of being the second largest. PC sales in China were growing 20–30 percent annually and, with a population of 1.4 billion people (of which some 400 million lived in metropolitan areas where computer use was growing rapidly), the Chinese market for PCs was expected to become the largest in the world by 2010. Dell's shipments in China rose 60 percent in fiscal 2004 (four times the rest of the industry) and its revenues were up 40 percent, making China Dell's fourth largest market. Sales growth in 2005 was almost as strong—unit sales rose 46 percent in the third quarter of 2005 and revenues were up 29 percent, with the strongest gains coming in the home and small business segment.

The market leader in China was Lenovo with a 25.0 percent share in 2005; Lenovo was a company on the move, having acquired the PC business of IBM in 2004 to become the third largest PC maker in the world. Other major local PC producers were Founder (with about a 10 percent share) and Great Wall (with about a 9.0 percent share). Dell had close to a 10 percent share in 2005. Other competitors in China included Hewlett-Packard, Toshiba, Acer, and NEC Japan. All of the major contenders except Dell relied on resellers to handle sales and service; in 2005, Lenovo had more than 4,800 retail outlets carrying its PCs in China. Dell sold directly to customers in China just as it did elsewhere.

Dell's primary target market in China consisted of large corporate accounts. Management believed that many Chinese companies would find the savings from direct sales appealing, that they would like the idea of having Dell build PCs and servers to their requirements and specifications, and that—once they became a Dell customer—they would like the convenience of Internet purchases and the company's growing array of products and services. In 2005, Dell had 5,000 employees in China. It operated a call center in Xiamen, a city of over 1 million people on China's southeast coast, where sales representatives took most of Dell's orders via telephone. In nine other cities in China, Dell had sales representatives who called on large business and government customers, relaying orders back to their colleagues in Xiamen. Dell had contracted with service providers in 40 cities in China to provide onsite service in no more than four hours.

Dell recognized that its direct sales approach put it at a short-term disadvantage in appealing to small business customers and individual consumers, since most of these customers were reluctant to place orders by phone or over the Internet. According to an executive from rival Lenovo, "It takes two years of a person's savings to buy a PC in China. And when two years of savings is at stake, the whole family wants to come out to a store to touch and try the machine."[13] But Dell believed that over time, as Chinese consumers became more familiar with PCs and more comfortable with making online purchases, growing numbers of small business customers and consumers would become comfortable with placing Internet and telephone orders. In 2005, more than 100 million Chinese consumers had access to the Internet at home or at work and the numbers were growing rapidly. In 2005, about 6 percent of Dell's sales in China were over the Internet. Dell believed its business in China was two to three times more profitable than Lenovo's business in China.

Dell in Latin America   In 2002, PC sales in Latin America exceeded 5 million units. Latin America had a population of 450 million people. Dell management believed that in the next few years PC use in Latin America would reach 1 for every 30 people (one-tenth the penetration in the United States), pushing annual sales up to 15 million units. The company's plant in Brazil, the largest market in Latin America, was opened to produce, sell, and provide service and technical support for customers in Brazil, Argentina, Chile, Uruguay, and Paraguay.

Using Dell Direct Store Kiosks to Access Individual Consumers   Inspired by the success of kiosks in Japan, Dell began installing Dell Direct Store kiosks in a variety of U.S. retail settings as a hands-on complement to Internet and phone sales in 2002. The stores showcased Dell's newest notebook and desktop computers, plasma and LCD TVs, printers, and music players. The kiosks did not carry inventory, but customers could talk face-to-face with a knowledgeable Dell sales representative, inspect Dell's products, and place an order via the Internet while at the kiosk. The kiosks were considered a success in getting consumers to try Dell products, and more kiosks had been added. In December 2005, Dell had 145 Dell Direct Store kiosks in 20 states, within reach of more than 50 percent of the U.S. population.

Customer Service and Technical Support

Service became a feature of Dell's strategy in 1986 when the company began providing a year's free onsite service with most of its PCs after users complained about having to ship their PCs back to Austin for repairs. Dell contracted with local service providers to handle customer requests for repairs; onsite service was provided on a four-hour basis to large customers and on a next-day basis to small customers. In 2005, Dell had five Enterprise Command Centers (ECCs) coordinating around-the-clock service globally for large customers; 350 hubs in cities around the world with four-hour service capability; 52,000 people worldwide who were trained to service Dell products; and 81 million active contracts to service PCs, servers, and other equipment it had sold to customers. Dell used the ECCs to monitor and manage the repair service and support effectiveness of Dell's field engineers and contract service personnel. If business or institutional customers preferred to work with their own service provider, Dell supplied the provider of choice with training and spare parts needed to service customers' equipment. When individuals or small businesses purchased their PCs, they could obtain a service contract for At Home service (usually the next day). Dell also offered Complete-Care accidental damage service, had a help desk for all software and peripherals support, and Gold Technical Support for advanced technical service. Dell's online training programs featured over 1,200 courses for consumer, business, and IT professionals.

Customers needing technical support could contact Dell via a toll-free phone number or e-mail. Dell received 6 to 8 million phone calls and 500,000 to 600,000 e-mail messages annually requesting service and support. Dell was aggressively pursuing initiatives to enhance its online technical support tools and reduce the number and cost of telephone support calls. The company was adding Web-based customer service and support tools to make customers' online experiences pleasant and satisfying. In 2003–2005, over 50 percent of Dell's technical support activities were conducted via the Internet. Dell had instituted a First Call Resolution initiative to strengthen its capabilities to resolve customer inquiries or difficulties on the first call; First Call Resolution percentages were made an important measure in evaluating the company's technical support performance. Dell had recently opened new customer contact and distribution facilities in Oklahoma and Ohio.

Value-Added Services   Dell kept close track of the purchases of its large global customers, country by country and department by department—and customers themselves found this purchase information valuable. Dell's sales and support personnel used their knowledge about a particular customer's needs to help that customer plan PC purchases, to configure the customer's PC networks, and to provide value-added services. For example, for its large customers Dell loaded software and placed ID tags on newly ordered PCs at the factory, thereby eliminating the need for the customer's IT personnel to unpack the PC, deliver it to an employee's desk, hook it up, place asset tags on the PC, and load the needed software from an assortment of CD-ROMs and diskettes—a process that could take several hours and cost $200–$300.[14] While Dell charged an extra $15 or $20 for the software-loading and asset-tagging services, the savings to customers were still considerable—one large customer reported savings of $500,000 annually from this service.[15]

Premier Pages   Dell had developed customized, password-protected Web sites called Premier Pages for over 50,000 corporate, governmental, and institutional customers worldwide. These Premier Pages gave customers' personnel online access to information about all Dell products and configurations the company had purchased or that were currently authorized for purchase. Employees could use Premier Pages to (1) obtain customer-specific pricing for whatever machines and options the employee wanted to consider, (2) place an order online that would be electronically routed to higher-level managers for approval and then on to Dell for assembly and delivery, and (3) seek advanced help desk support. Customers could also search and sort all invoices and obtain purchase histories. These features eliminated paper invoices, cut ordering time, and reduced the internal labor customers needed to staff corporate purchasing and accounting functions. Customer use of Premier Pages had boosted the productivity of Dell salespeople assigned to these accounts by 50 percent. Dell was providing Premier Page service to thousands of additional customers annually and adding more features to further improve functionality.

www.dell.com   Dell operated one of the world's highest-volume Internet commerce sites, with nearly 8 billion page requests annually at 81 country sites in 28 languages/dialects and 26 currencies. Dell began Internet sales at its Web site (www.dell.com) in 1995, achieving sales of $1 million a day almost overnight. By early 2003, over 50 percent of Dell's sales were Web-enabled—and the percentage was increasing, especially for sales to small businesses and consumers. Dell's Web site sales exceeded $60 million a day in 2004, up from $35 million daily in early 2000 and $5 million daily in early 1998. The revenues generated at Dell.com were greater than those of Yahoo, Google, eBay, and Amazon.com combined.[16] Its Web site was averaging 300 million visits by some 100 million unique visitors per quarter in 2005.

At the company's Web site, prospective buyers could review Dell's entire product line in detail, configure and price customized PCs, place orders, and track orders from manufacturing through shipping. The closing rate on sales at Dell's Web site was 20 percent higher than that on sales inquiries received via telephone. Management believed that enhancing Dell.com to shrink transaction and order fulfillment times, increase accuracy, and provide more personalized content resulted in a higher degree of "e-loyalty" than traditional attributes like price and product selection.

On-Site Services   Corporate customers paid Dell fees to provide technical support, on-site service, and help with migrating to new IT technologies. Services were one of the fastest-growing part of Dell, with revenues climbing from $1.7 billion in 2002 to about $5 billion in 2005. Dell's service business was split about 50–50 between what Michael Dell called close-to-the-box services and management and professional services—but the latter were growing faster, at close to 25 percent annually. Dell estimated that close-to-the-box support services for Dell products represented about a $50 billion market, whereas the market for management and professional services (IT life-cycle services, deployment of new technology, and solutions for greater IT productivity) was about $90 billion. IT consulting services were becoming more standardized, driven primarily by growing hardware and software standardization, reduction in on-site service requirements (partly because of online diagnostic and support tools, growing ease of repair and maintenance, increased customer knowledge, and increased remote management

capabilities), and declines in the skills and know-how that were required to perform service tasks on standardized equipment and install new, more standardized systems.

Dell's strategy in services, like its strategy in hardware products, was to bring down the cost of IT consulting services for its large enterprise customers. The providers of on-site service, technical support, and other types of IT consulting typically charged premium prices and realized hefty profits for their efforts. According to Michael Dell, customers who bought the services being provided by Dell saved 40 to 50 percent over what they would have paid other providers of IT services.

Top management expected services to play an expanding role in the company's growth. Kevin Rollins, Dell's president and CEO, indicated the company's business model "isn't just about making cheap boxes, it's also about freeing customers from overpriced relationships" with such vendors as IBM, Sun Microsystems, and Hewlett-Packard.[17] While a number of Dell's corporate accounts were large enough to justify dedicated on-site teams of Dell support personnel, Dell generally contracted with third-party providers to make the necessary on-site service calls. Customers notified Dell when they had problems; such notices triggered two electronic dispatches—one to ship replacement parts from Dell's factory to the customer sites, and one to notify the contract service provider to prepare to make the needed repairs as soon as the parts arrived.[18] Bad parts were returned so that Dell could determine what went wrong and how to prevent such problems from happening again. Problems relating to faulty components or flawed components design were promptly passed along to the relevant supplier for correction.

Customer Forums   In addition to using its sales and support mechanisms to stay close to customers, Dell periodically held regional forums for its best customers. The company formed Platinum and Gold Councils composed of its largest customers in the United States, Europe, Japan, and the Asia-Pacific region; regional meetings were held every six to nine months.[19] Some regions had two meetings—one for chief information officers and one for technical personnel. At the meetings, which frequently included a presentation by Michael Dell, Dell's senior technologists shared their views on the direction of the latest technological developments, what the flow of technology really meant for customers, and Dell's plans for introducing new and upgraded products over the next two years. There were also breakout sessions on topics of current interest. Dell found that the information gleaned from customers at these meetings assisted the company in forecasting demand for its products.

In a 2005 survey of IT executives by *CIO Magazine,* Dell was rated number one among leading vendors for providing "impeccable customer service."

Customer-Driven Research and Development and Standardized Technology

Dell's R&D focus was to track and test new developments in components and software, ascertain which ones would prove most useful and cost-effective for customers, and then design them into Dell products. Management's philosophy was that it was Dell's job on behalf of its customers to sort out all the new technology coming into the marketplace and help steer customers to options and solutions most relevant to their needs. The company talked to its customers frequently about "relevant technology," listening carefully to customers' needs and problems and endeavoring to identify the most cost-effective solutions.

Dell was a strong advocate of incorporating standardized components in its products so as not to tie either it or its customers to one company's proprietary technology and components, which almost always carried a price premium and increased costs for its customers. Dell actively promoted the use of industrywide standards and regularly pressed its suppliers of a particular part or component to agree on common standards. Dell executives saw standardized technology as beginning to take over the largest part of the $800 billion spent annually on IT—standardization was particularly evident in servers, storage, networking, and high-performance computing. One example of the impact of standardized technology was at the University of Buffalo, where Dell had installed a 5.6 teraflop cluster of about 2,000 Dell servers containing 4,000 microprocessors that was being used to decode the human genome. The cluster of servers, which were the same as those Dell sold to its business customers, had been installed in about 60 days at a cost of a few million dollars and represented the third most powerful supercomputer in the world. High-performance clusters of PCs and servers were replacing mainframe computers

and custom-designed supercomputers because of their much lower cost. Amerada Hess, attracted by Dell's use of standardized and upgradable parts and components, installed a cluster of several hundred Dell workstations and allocated about $300,000 a year to upgrade and maintain it; the cluster had replaced an IBM supercomputer that cost $1.5 million a year to lease and operate. Studies conducted by Dell indicated that, over time, products incorporating standardized technology delivered about twice the performance per dollar of cost as products based on proprietary technology.

Dell's R&D group included about 4,000 engineers, and its annual R&D budget had been in the $450 to $465 million range for the past four years (see Exhibit 2). The company's R&D unit also studied and implemented ways to control quality and to streamline the assembly process. In 2005, Dell had a portfolio of 1,128 U.S. patents and another 719 patent applications were pending—at least 10 percent of Dell's U.S. patents were ranked "elite."

Expansion into New Products

Dell's recent expansion into data storage hardware, switches, handheld PCs, printers, and printer cartridges represented an effort to diversify the company's product base and to use its competitive capabilities in PCs and servers to pursue revenue growth opportunities. Michael Dell explained why Dell had decided to expand into products and services that complemented its sales of PCs and servers:

> We tend to look at what is the next big opportunity all the time. We can't take on too many of these at once, because it kind of overloads the system. But we believe fundamentally that if you think about the whole market, it's about an $800 billion market, all areas of technology over time go through a process of standardization or commoditization. And we try to look at those, anticipate what's happening, and develop strategies that will allow us to get into those markets. In the server market in 1995 we had a 2 percent market share, today we have over a 30 percent share, we're number 1 in the U.S. How did that happen? Well, first of all it happened because we started to have a high market share for desktops and notebooks. Then customers said, oh yes, we know Dell, those are the guys who have really good desktops and notebooks. So they have servers, yes, we'll test those, we'll test them around the periphery, maybe not in the most critical applications at first, but we'll test them here.

[Then they discover] these are really good and Dell provides great support . . . and I think to some extent we've benefited from the fact that our competitors have underestimated the importance of value, and the power of the relationship and the service that we can create with the customer.

And, also, as a product tends to standardize there's not an elimination of the requirement for custom services, there's a reduction of it. So by offering some services, but not the services of the traditional proprietary computer company, we've been able to increase our share. And, in fact, what tends to happen is customers embrace the standards, because they know that's going to save them costs. Let me give you an example . . . about a year ago we entered into the data networking market. So we have Ethernet switches, layer 2 switches. So if you have PCs and servers, you need switches; every PC attaches to a switch, every server attaches to a switch. It's a pretty easy sale, switches go along with computer systems. We looked at this market and were able to come up with products that are priced about 2½ times less than the market leader today, Cisco, and as a result the business has grown very, very quickly. We shipped 1.8 million switch ports in a period of about a year, when most people would have said that's not going to work and come up with all kinds of reasons why we can't succeed.[20]

As Dell's sales of data-routing switches accelerated in 2001–2002 and Dell management mulled whether to expand into other networking products and Internet gear, Cisco elected to discontinue supplying its switches to Dell for resale as of October 2002. Dell's family of PowerConnect switches—simple commodity-like products generally referred to as layer 2 switches in the industry—carried a price of $20 per port, versus $70–$100 for comparable Cisco switches and $38 for comparable 3Com switches.

Michael Dell and Kevin Rollins saw external storage devices as a growth opportunity because the company's corporate and institutional customers were making increasing use of high-speed data storage and retrieval devices. Dell's PowerVault line of storage products had data protection and recovery features that made it easy for customers to add and manage storage and simplify consolidation. The PowerVault products used standardized technology and components (which were considerably cheaper than customized ones), allowing Dell to underprice rivals and drive down storage costs for its customers

by about 50 percent. Dell's competitors in storage devices included Hewlett-Packard and IBM.

Some observers saw Dell's 2003 entry into the printer market as a calculated effort to go after Hewlett-Packard's biggest and most profitable business segment and believed the Dell offensive was deliberately timed to throw a wrench into HP's efforts to resolve the many challenges of successfully merging its operations with those of Compaq. One of the reasons that Dell had entered the market for servers back in 1995 was that Compaq Computer, then its biggest rival in PCs, had been using its lucrative profits on server sales to subsidize charging lower prices on Compaq computers and thus be more price competitive against Dell's PCs—at the time Compaq was losing money on its desktop and notebook PC business. According to Michael Dell:

> Compaq had this enormous profit pool that they were using to fight against us in the desktop and notebook business. That was not an acceptable situation. Our product teams knew that the servers weren't that complicated or expensive to produce, and customers were being charged unfair prices.[21]

Dell management believed that HP was doing much the same thing in printers and printer products, where it had a dominant market share worldwide and generated about 75 percent of its operating profits. Dell believed HP was using its big margins on printer products to subsidize selling its PCs at prices comparable to Dell's, even though Dell had costs that were about 8 percent lower than HP. HP's PC operations were either in the red or barely in the black during most of 2003–2004, while Dell consistently had profit margins of 8 percent or more on PCs. Dell management believed the company's entry into the printer market would add value for its customers. Michael Dell explained:

> We think we can drive down the entire cost of owning and using printing products. If you look at any other market Dell has gone into, we have been able to significantly save money for customers. We know we can do that in printers; we have looked at the supply chain all the way through its various cycles and we know there are inefficiencies there. I think the price of the total offering when we include the printer and the supplies . . . can come down quite considerably.[22]

Dell's entry and market success in printer products had put pricing pressure on HP in the printer market and had helped erode HP's share of the printer market worldwide from just under 50 percent to around 46 percent. Kevin Rollins believed that Dell's decision to enter the printer market as as a head-to-head rival of HP served two purposes: "Any strategist is going to try to develop a strategy that is going to help them and hurt competitors. Our whole vision here was to do both: improve the revenues and profits of our own business, and at the same time put our competitors at a disadvantage."[23] As of the fall of 2005, Dell had sold over 10 million printers and had an estimated 20 percent of the market for color network lasers and color inkjet printers in the United States.[24]

When Dell announced it had contracted with Lexmark to make printers and printer and toner cartridges for sale under the Dell label beginning in 2003, HP immediately discontinued supplying HP printers to Dell for resale at Dell's Web site. Dell had been selling Lexmark printers for two years and since 2000 had resold about 4 million printers made by such vendors as HP, Lexmark, and other vendors to its customers. Lexmark designed and made critical parts for its printers but used offshore contract manufacturers for assembly. Gross profit margins on printers (sales minus cost of goods sold) were said to be in single digits in 2002–2004, but the gross margins on printer supplies were in the 50–60 percent range—brand-name ink cartridges for printers typically ran $25 to $35.

To further keep the pricing pressure on HP in 2003, Dell had priced its new Axim line of handheld PCs at about 50 percent less than HP's popular iPaq line of handhelds, and Dell's storage and networking products also carried lower prices than comparable HP products.

Exhibit 5 shows a breakdown of Dell's sales by product type. Exhibit 6 shows trends in Dell's market shares in various categories.

Other Elements of Dell's Business Strategy

Dell's strategy had three other elements that assisted the company's drive for industry leadership: the use of the Internet and e-commerce technologies, entry into the white-box segment of the PC industry, and advertising.

Pioneering Leadership in Use of the Internet and E-Commerce Technology   Dell was a leader in using the Internet and e-commerce technologies to squeeze greater efficiency out of its supply chain activities, to streamline the order-to-delivery process, to encourage greater customer use of its Web site, and to gather and use all types of information. In a 1999 speech to 1,200 customers, Michael Dell said:

Exhibit 5   **Dell's Revenues by Product Category, First Nine Months, Fiscal 2006 versus Fiscal 2005**

	Nine Months Ended			
	October 28, 2005		October 29, 2004	
Product Category	Revenues (in billions)	% of Total Revenues	Revenues (in billions)	% of Total Revenues
Desktop PCs	$15.5	38%	$15.2	43%
Mobility products (notebook PCs, Dell DJ, Axim)	10.3	25	8.7	24
Printers, monitors, TVs, projectors, ink and toner cartridges	6.1	15	4.7	13
Servers and networking hardware	4.0	10	3.6	10
Professional consulting and support services	3.5	9	2.6	7
Storage products	1.3	3	0.9	3
Totals	$40.7	100%	$35.7	100%

Source: Dell's 10-Q report, third quarter, fiscal 2006.

Exhibit 6 **Trends in Dell's Market Shares in PCs, 1994–2005**

Market Segment	Dell's Market Share						
	2005*	2004	2002	2000	1998	1996	1994
Worldwide share	18.7%	17.7%	14.9%	10.5%	8.0%	4.1%	2.7%
United States	33.1	33.1	28.0	18.4	12.0	6.4	4.2
Europe/Middle East/Africa	13.0	11.5	9.6	7.8	7.0	3.8	2.4
Asia-Pacific	8.0	7.0	4.8	3.4	2.4	1.3	0.3
Japan	12.1	11.3	7.7	4.0	3.0	1.6	1.1
Desktop PCs	18.5%	18.0%	14.8%	10.1%	7.8%	4.3%	3.0%
Notebook PCs	17.6	16.2	14.4	11.3	8.5	3.4	1.1
x86 Servers	26.8	24.8	21.7	15.4	9.7	3.4	3.1
U.S segment share	33.1%	33.1%	28.0%	18.4%	12.0%	6.4%	4.2%
Education	45.2	44.3	34.9	26.2	11.0	3.9	1.1
Government	34.8	32.9	33.7	22.9	14.6	6.5	7.1
Home	28.8	29.7	22.7	6.5	3.5	2.1	1.2
Large business	44.9	44.2	39.9	31.3	21.6	11.2	6.9
Small/medium business	29.1	28.5	24.2	22.6	14.3	7.9	5.4

*First nine months.

Source: Information posted at www.dell.com (accessed December 12, 2005).

The world will be changed forever by the Internet . . . The Internet will be your business. If your business isn't enabled by providing customers and suppliers with more information, you're probably already in trouble. The Internet provides a dramatic reduction in the cost of transactions and the cost of interaction among people and businesses, and it creates dramatic new opportunities and destroys old competitive advantages. The Internet is like a weapon sitting on a table ready to be picked up by either you or your competitors.[25]

Dell's use of its Web site and various Internet technology applications had proved instrumental in helping the company become the industry's low-cost provider and drive costs out of its business. Internet technology applications were a cornerstone of Dell's collaborative efforts with suppliers. The company provided order-status information quickly and conveniently over the Internet, thereby eliminating tens of thousands of order-status inquiries coming in by phone. It used its Web site as a powerful sales and technical support tool. Few companies could match Dell's competencies and capabilities in the use of Internet technology to improve operating efficiency and gain new sales in a cost-efficient manner.

Dell's Entry into the White-Box PC Segment   In 2002 Dell announced it would begin making so-called white-box (i.e., unbranded) PCs for resale under the private labels of retailers. PC dealers that supplied white-box PCs to small businesses and price-conscious individuals under the dealer's own brand name accounted for about one-third of total PC sales and about 50 percent of sales to small businesses. According to one industry analyst, "Increasingly, Dell's biggest competitor these days isn't big brand-name companies like IBM or HP, it's white-box vendors." Dell's thinking in entering the white-box PC segment was that it was cheaper to reach many small businesses through the white-box dealers that already served them than by using its own sales force and support groups to sell and service businesses with fewer than 100 employees. Dell believed its low-cost supply chain and assembly capabilities would allow it to build generic machines cheaper than white-box resellers could buy components and assemble a customized machine. Management forecasted that Dell would achieve $380 million in sales of white-box PCs in 2003 and would generate profit margins equal to those on Dell-branded PCs. Some industry analysts were skeptical of Dell's move into white-box PCs because they expected white-box dealers to be reluctant to buy their PCs from a company that had a history of taking their clients. Others believed this was a test effort by Dell to develop the capabilities to take on white-box dealers in Asia and especially in China, where the sellers of generic PCs were particularly strong.

Advertising   Michael Dell was a strong believer in the power of advertising and frequently espoused its importance in the company's strategy. He insisted that the company's ads be communicative and forceful, not soft and fuzzy. The company regularly had prominent ads describing its products and prices in such leading computer publications as *PC Magazine* and *PC World,* as well as in *USA Today, The Wall Street Journal,* and other business publications. From time to time, the company ran ads on TV to promote its products to consumers and small businesses. Catalogs of about 25–30 pages describing Dell's latest desktop and laptop PCs, along with its printers, TVs, MP3 players, handheld PCs, and other related products were periodically mailed to consumers who had bought Dell products. Other direct marketing initiatives included sending their newsletters and promotional pieces to customers via the Internet.

DELL'S PERFORMANCE IN 2005

Dell shipped about 27 million units during the first nine months of 2005, and it had a record shipment of 9.2 million units in the third quarter of fiscal 2006. Despite steadily eroding average selling prices— $1,540 in fiscal 2004, down from $1,640 in 2003, $1,700 in 2002, $2,050 in 2001, $2,250 in 2000, and $2,600 in 1998—Dell's revenues were climbing as the company gained volume and market share in virtually all product categories and geographic areas where it competed.

Worldwide revenues, which reached $40.7 billion in the first nine months of fiscal 2006, were expected to run 10–12 percent higher than fiscal 2005 levels and total about $55 billion for the full year. Dell's sales increases were strongest in outside the United States (non-U.S. sales were up 20 percent), in servers (where shipments were up 21 percent), storage products (where sales were up 35 percent, three times the industrywide rate). Unit sales of "mobility" products (laptop PC and work-stations, Dell DJ MP3 players, and Axim handheld computers) were up 41 percent and produced revenues gains of 18 percent (the lower growth rate for revenues was due to falling prices industrywide for virtually all types of mobile devices). Dell's shipments of printers were up 8 percent and sales of replacement ink and toner cartridges doubled.

Dell ended fiscal 2006 with $11.7 billion in cash and investments. The company had invested about $500 million in property, plant, and equipment in fiscal 2005 and expected that total capital expenditures for all of fiscal 2006 would approximate $700 million.

MARKET CONDITIONS IN THE INFORMATION TECHNOLOGY INDUSTRY IN LATE 2005

Analysts expected the $800 billion worldwide IT industry to grow roughly 6–9 percent in 2005, following nearly a 10 percent increase in 2004, a single-digit increase in 2003, a 2.3 percent decline in 2002, and close to a 1 percent decline in 2001— corporate spending for IT products accounted for about 45 percent of all capital expenditures of U.S. businesses. From 1980 to 2000, IT spending had grown at an average annual rate of 12 percent and then flattened. The slowdown in IT spending reflected a combination of factors: sluggish economic growth worldwide that was prompting businesses to delay IT upgrades and hold on to aging equipment longer, overinvestment in IT in the 1995–99 period, declining unit prices for many IT products (especially PCs and servers), and a growing preference for lower-priced, standard-component hardware that was good enough to perform a variety of functions using off-the-shelf Windows or Linux operating systems (as opposed to relying on proprietary hardware and customized Unix software). The selling points that appealed most to IT customers were standardization, flexibility, modularity, simplicity, economy of use, and value.

Exhibit 7 shows actual and projected PC sales for 1980–2009 as compiled by industry researcher International Data Corporation (IDC). According to Gartner Research, the billionth PC was shipped sometime in July 2002; of the billion, an estimated

Exhibit 7 **Worldwide Shipments of PCs, Actual and Forecasted, 1980–2009**

Year	PCs Shipped (millions)	Year	PCs Shipped (millions)
1980	1	2001	133
1985	11	2002	136
1990	24	2003	153
1995	58	2004	177
1996	69	2005*	205
1997	80	2006*	223
1998	91	2007*	243
1999	113	2008*	265
2000	139	2009*	286

*Forecasted.

Source: International Data Corporation.

550 million were still in use. Nearly 82 percent of the 1 billion PCs that had been shipped were desktops, and 75 percent were sold to businesses. With a world population of 6 billion, most industry participants believed there was ample opportunity for further growth in the PC market. Computer usage in Europe was half of that in the United States, even though the combined economies of the European countries were a bit larger than the U.S. economy. Growth potential for PCs was particularly strong in China, India, several other Asian countries, and portions of Latin America. Forrester Research estimated that the numbers of PCs in use worldwide would approach 1.3 billion by 2010, up from 575 million in 2004, with the growth being driven by the emerging markets in China, India, and Russia. IDC had predicted that notebook PC sales would grow from 26.9 percent of PC shipments in 2003 to 37.3 percent in 2007.

Currently, there was growing interest in notebook computers equipped wireless capability; many businesses were turning to notebooks equipped with wireless data communications devices to improve worker productivity and keep workers connected to important information. The emergence of Wireless Fidelity (Wi-Fi) networking technology, along with the installation of wireless home and office networks, was fueling the trend. Wi-Fi systems were being used in businesses, on college campuses, in airports, and other locations to link users to the Internet and to private networks. Three other devices—flat-panel LCD monitors, DVD recorders, and portable music players like Apple's iPod—were also stimulating sales of new PCs.

At the same time, forecasters expected full global build-out of the Internet to continue, which would require the installation of millions of servers. But since 2000 IT customers had been switching from the use of expensive high-end servers running customized Unix operating systems to the use of low-cost servers running on standardized Intel/Windows/Linux technologies; the switch to stands-based servers had caused a slowdown in dollar revenues from server sales despite rapidly increasing unit volume. A number of industry observers believed that the days of using expensive, proprietary Unix-based servers were numbered. The Unix share of the server operating system market (based on unit shipments) was said to have decreased by nearly 50 percent over the past five years, whereas Windows and Linux servers had tripled in use.

HOW DELL'S STRATEGY PUTS RIVALS IN A COMPETITIVE BIND

When the personal computer industry first began to take shape in the early 1980s, the founding companies manufactured many of the components themselves—disk drives, memory chips, graphics chips, microprocessors, motherboards, and software. Subscribing to a philosophy that mandated in-house development of key components, they built expertise in a variety of PC-related technologies and created organizational units to produce components as well as handle final assembly. While certain noncritical items were typically outsourced, if a computer maker was not at least partially vertically integrated and produced some components for its PCs, then it was not taken seriously as a manufacturer. But as the industry grew, technology advanced quickly in so many directions on so many parts and components that the early personal computer manufacturers could not keep pace as experts on all fronts. There were too many technologies and manufacturing intricacies to master for a vertically integrated manufacturer to keep its products on the cutting edge.

As a consequence, companies emerged that specialized in making particular components. Specialists could marshal enough R&D capability and resources to either lead the technological developments in their area of specialization or else quickly match the advances made by their competitors.

Moreover, specialist firms could mass-produce the component and supply it to several computer manufacturers far cheaper than any one manufacturer could fund the needed component R&D and then make only whatever smaller volume of components it needed for assembling its own brand of PCs. Thus, in the early 1990s, such computer makers as Compaq Computer, IBM, Hewlett-Packard, Sony, Toshiba, and Fujitsu-Siemens began to abandon vertical integration in favor of a strategy of outsourcing most components from specialists and concentrating on efficient assembly and marketing their brand of computers. They adopted the build-to-stock value chain model (shown in the top section of Exhibit 4). It featured arm's-length transactions between specialist suppliers, manufacturer/assemblers, distributors and retailers, and end users. However, a few others, most notably Dell and Gateway, employed a shorter value chain model, selling directly to customers and eliminating the time and costs associated with distributing through independent resellers. Building to order avoided (1) having to keep many differently equipped models on retailers' shelves to fill buyer requests for one or another configuration of options and components, and (2) having to clear out slow-selling models at a discount before introducing new generations of PCs (for instance, Hewlett-Packard's retail dealers had an average of 43 days of HP products in stock as of October 2004). Direct sales eliminated retailer costs and markups (retail dealer margins were typically in the range of 4 to 10 percent).

Because of Dell's success in using its business model and strategy to become the low-cost leader, most other PC makers in 2002–2005 were endeavoring to emulate various aspects of Dell's strategy, but with only limited success. Nearly all vendors were trying to cut days of inventory out of their supply chains and reduce their costs of goods sold and operating expenses to levels that would make them more cost competitive with Dell. In an effort to cut their assembly costs, Hewlett-Packard, IBM, and several others had begun outsourcing assembly to contract manufacturers and refocused their internal efforts on product design and marketing. Virtually all vendors were trying to minimize the amount of finished goods in dealer/distributor inventories and shorten the time it took to replenish dealer stocks. Collaboration with contract manufacturers was increasing to develop the capabilities to build and deliver PCs equipped to customer specifications within 7 to 14 days, but these efforts were hampered by the use of Asia-based contract manufacturers—delivering built-to-order PCs to North American and European customers within a two-week time frame required the use of costly air freight from Asia-based assembly plants.

While most PC vendors would have liked to adopt Dell's sell-direct strategy for at least some of their sales, they confronted big channel conflict problems: if they started to push direct sales hard, they would almost certainly alienate the independent dealers on whom they depended for the bulk of their sales and service to customers. Dealers saw sell-direct efforts on the part of a manufacturer whose brand they represented as a move to cannibalize their business and to compete against them. However, Dell's success in gaining large enterprise customers with its direct sales force had forced growing numbers of PC vendors to supplement the efforts of their independent dealers with direct sales and service efforts of their own. During 2003–2005 several of Dell's rivals were selling 15 to 25 percent of their products direct.

PROFILES OF SELECTED COMPETITORS IN THE PC INDUSTRY

This section presents brief profiles of three of Dell's principal competitors. Exhibit 8 summarizes Dell's principal competitors in the various product categories where it competed and the sizes of these product markets.

Hewlett-Packard

In one of the most contentious and controversial acquisitions in U.S. history, Hewlett-Packard shareholders voted by a narrow margin in early 2002 to approve the company's acquisition of Compaq Computer, the world's second largest full-service global computing company (behind IBM) and a company with 2001 revenues of $33.6 billion and a net loss of $785 million. Compaq had passed IBM to become the world leader in PCs in 1995 and remained in first place until it was overtaken by Dell in late 1999. Compaq had acquired Tandem Computer in 1997 and Digital Equipment Corporation in 1998 to give it capabilities, products, and service offerings that allowed it to compete in every sector of the computer industry—PCs, servers, workstations, mainframes, peripherals, and such services as business and e-commerce solutions, hardware and software support, systems integration, and technology consulting.[26] In 2000, Compaq spent $370 million to acquire certain assets of Inacom Corporation that management believed would help Compaq reduce inventories, speed cycle time, and enhance its capabilities to do business with customers via the Internet. Nonetheless, at the time of its acquisition by HP, Compaq was struggling to compete successfully in all of its many product and service arenas where it operated.

Carly Fiorina, who became HP's CEO in 1999, explained why the acquisition of Compaq was strategically sound:

> With Compaq, we become No. 1 in Windows, No. 1 in Linux and No. 1 in Unix . . . With Compaq, we become the No. 1 player in storage, and the leader in the fastest growing segment of the storage market—storage area networks. With Compaq, we double our service and support capacity in the area of mission-critical infrastructure design, outsourcing and support . . . Let's talk about PCs . . . Compaq has been

able to improve their turns in that business from 23 turns of inventory per year to 62—100 percent improvement year over year—and they are coming close to doing as well as Dell does. They've reduced operating expenses by $130 million, improved gross margins by three points, reduced channel inventory by more than $800 million. They ship about 70 percent of their commercial volume through their direct channel, comparable to Dell. We will combine our successful retail PC business model with their commercial business model and achieve much more together than we could alone. With Compaq, we will double the size of our sales force to 15,000 strong. We will build our R&D budget to more than $4 billion a year, and add important capabilities to HP Labs. We will become the No. 1 player in a whole host of countries around the world—HP operates in more than 160 countries, with well over 60 percent of our revenues coming from outside the U.S. The new HP will be the No. 1 player in the consumer and small- and medium-business segments . . . We have estimated cost synergies of $2.5 billion by 2004 . . . It is a rare opportunity when a technology company can advance its market position substantially and reduce its cost structure substantially at the same time. And this is possible because Compaq and HP are in the same

Exhibit 8   **Dell's Principal Competitors and Dell's Estimated Market Shares by Product Category, 2004–2005**

Product Category	Dell's Principal Competitors	Estimated Size of Worldwide Market, 2003–2004 (in billions)	Dell's Estimated Worldwide Share, 2004–2005
PCs	Hewlett-Packard (maker of both Compaq and HP brands); IBM/Lenovo, Gateway, Apple, Acer, Sony, Fujitsu-Siemens (in Europe and Japan)	$175	18.5%
Servers	Hewlett-Packard, IBM, Sun Microsystems, Fujitsu	$50	≈11%
Data storage devices	Hewlett-Packard, IBM, EMC, Hitachi	$40	≈5%
Networking switches and related equipment	Cisco Systems, Enterasys, Nortel, 3Com	$58	2–3%
Handheld PCs	Palm, Sony, Hewlett-Packard, Toshiba, Casio	$4	≈2–3%
Printers and printer cartridges	Hewlett-Packard, Lexmark, Canon, Epson	≈$50	≈6%
Cash register systems	IBM, NCR, Wincor Nixdorf, Hewlett-Packard, Sun Microsystems	$4 (in North America)	≈1–2%
Services	Accenture, IBM, Hewlett-Packard, many others	$350	≈2%

Source: Compiled by the case authors from a variety of sources, including International Data Corporation and www.dell.com.

businesses, pursuing the same strategies, in the same markets, with complementary capabilities.

However, going into 2005 the jury was still out on whether HP's acquisition of Compaq was the success that Carly Fiorina had claimed it would be. The company's only real bright spot was its $24 billion crown jewel printer business, which still reigned as the unchallenged world leader (largely because of a highly productive $1 billion investment in printer R&D). But the rest of HP's businesses were underachievers. Its PC and server businesses were struggling, losing money in most quarters and barely breaking even in others—and HP was definitely losing ground to Dell in PCs and low-priced servers. In servers, HP was being squeezed on the low end by Dell's low prices and on the high end by strong competition from IBM. Most observers saw IBM as overshadowing HP in corporate computing—high-end servers and IT services. In data storage and technical support services, HP had been able to grow revenues but profit margins and total operating profits were declining. While HP had successfully cut annual operating costs by $3.5 billion—beating the $2.5 billion target set at the time of the Compaq acquisition—the company had missed its earnings forecasts in 7 of the past 20 quarters.

With the company's stock price stuck in the $18–$23 price range, impatient investors in 2004 began clamoring for the company to break itself up and create two separate companies, one for its printer business and one for all the rest of the businesses (PCs, servers, storage devices, digital cameras, calculators, and IT services). While HP's board of directors had looked at breaking up the company into smaller pieces, Carly Fiorina had been opposed, arguing that HP's broad product/business lineup paid off in the form of added sales and lower costs.

HP reported total revenues of $79.9 billion and net profits of $3.5 billion for fiscal 2004, versus total revenues of $73.1 billion and earnings of $2.5 billion in 2003. However, a substantial portion of the increase in net earnings in 2004 was due to cutbacks in R&D spending and a lower effective tax rate. Moreover, the company's EPS of $1.16 in 2004 was substantially below the EPS of $1.80 reported in 2000. In February 2005, with HP's financial performance continuing to lag and mounting differences with HP's board of directors, Carly Fiorina resigned her post as HP's CEO.

Mark Hurd, president and CEO of NCR (formerly National Cash Resister Systems), was brought in to replace Fiorina, effective April 1, 2005; Hurd had been at NCR for 25 years in a variety of management positions and was regarded as a no-nonsense executive who underpromised and overdelivered on results.[27] Hurd immediately sought to bolster HP's competitiveness and financial performance by bringing in new managers and attacking bloated costs. In his first seven months as CEO, the results were somewhat encouraging. HP posted revenues of $86.7 billion and net profits of $2.4 billion for the fiscal year ending October 31, 2005. HP had the number one ranking worldwide for server shipments (a position it had held for 14 consecutive quarters) and disk storage systems; plus, it was the world leader in server revenues for Unix, Windows, and Linux systems. Since Hurd had taken over, the company's stock price had risen about 25 percent.

Exhibit 9 shows the performance of HP's four major business groups for the 2001–2005 period.

IBM/Lenovo

IBM was seen as a "computer solutions" company and had the broadest and deepest capabilities in customer service, technical support, and systems integration of any company in the world. IBM's Global Services business group was the world's largest information technology services provider, with sales of $46.2 billion in 2004. In addition to its IT services business, IBM had 2004 hardware sales of $31.3 billion and software sales of $15.1 billion. IBM conducted business in 170 countries and had total sales of $96.3 billion and earnings of $8.4 billion in 2004. Once the world's undisputed king of computing and information processing, IBM was struggling to remain a potent contender in PCs, servers, storage products, and other hardware-related products. In 2003–2005, IBM's only remaining strength in IT hardware was in high-end servers.

IBM's Troubles in PCs   Formerly the dominant global and U.S. market leader, with a market share exceeding 50 percent in the late 1980s and early 1990s, IBM had become an also-ran in PCs, with a global market share of only 5.9 percent in 2004 (see Exhibit 1). IBM had lost about $750 million in PCs in the last three years. Its last stronghold in PCs was in laptop computers, where its ThinkPad line was a

Exhibit 9   **Performance of Hewlett-Packard's Four Major Business Groups, Fiscal Years 2001–2005 (in billions of dollars)**

	Printing and Imaging	Personal Computing Systems*	Enterprise Systems*	HP Services
2005 (fiscal year ending October 31)				
Net revenue	$25,155	$26,741	$17,778	$15,536
Operating income (loss)	3,413	657	751	1,151
2004 (fiscal year ending October 31)				
Net revenue	$24,199	$24,622	$16,074	$13,778
Operating income (loss)	3,847	210	28	1,263
2003 (fiscal year ending October 31)				
Net revenue	$22,569	$21,210	$15,367	$12,357
Operating income (loss)	3,596	22	(48)	1,362
2002 (fiscal year ending October 31)*				
Net revenue	$20,358	$21,895	$11,105	$12,326
Operating income (loss)	3,365	(372)	(656)	1,369
2001 (fiscal year ending October 31)*				
Net revenue	$19,602	$26,710	$20,205	$12,802
Operating income (loss)	2,103	(728)	(579)	1,617

*Results for 2001 and 2002 represent the combined results of both HP and Compaq Computer.

Source: 2004 10-K report, 2003 10-K report, and company press release, November 17, 2005.

consistent award winner on performance, features, and reliability—but it was losing money on ThinkPad sales as well. The vast majority of IBM's laptop and desktop sales were to long-standing IBM customers that had IBM mainframe computers. IBM's PC group had higher costs than rivals, making it virtually impossible to match rivals on price and make a profit. IBM distributed its PCs, workstations, and servers through reseller partners, but used its own sales force to market to large enterprises. IBM competed against rival hardware vendors by emphasizing confidence in the IBM brand and the company's long-standing strengths in software applications, IT services and support, and systems integration capabilities. IBM had responded to the direct sales inroads Dell had made in the corporate market by allowing some of its resellers to economize on costs by custom-assembling IBM PCs to buyer specifications.

The Sale of IBM's PC Business to Lenovo in Late 2004   In December 2004, IBM agreed to

sell its money-losing PC business to Lenovo Group Ltd., the number one computer maker in China, in a $1.75 billion business deal that made Lenovo the world's third-biggest PC maker, with a global market share of close to 7 percent. As part of the deal, IBM had an 18.9 percent ownership interest in Lenovo. The head of IBM's PC operations became CEO of Lenovo, with Lenovo's current CEO (who did not speak English) assuming the role of chairman. Shortly after the transaction was finalized, Lenovo moved its corporate headquarters from Beijing to New York City.

The new company had about $10 billion in annual sales and 20,000 employees, including about 10,000 IBM employees that would be a part of the new company—about 2,500 of the IBM employees that became part of Lenovo were in North Carolina, about half were in China, and the rest were scattered around the world. The new company had the rights to use the IBM name on its PCs for a maximum of five years, but in the months following the acquisition

Lenovo began co-branding efforts. The new company planned to continue to sell its PCs through the efforts of an internal sales force for large accounts and its network of distributors and retail outlets.

Prior to the acquisition of IBM's PC business, Lenovo had little reputation for innovation, and it usually followed the technology lead of Intel and Microsoft, the PC industry's standard setters. It was regarded as a made-in-China-for-China producer of PCs. It had previously tried to enter the PC market outside China without success and was under competitive pressure in its home market, particularly from Dell (which was said to have lower costs). However, the company's original parent, the government's Chinese Academy of Sciences, was still a major shareholder, which gave Lenovo access to loans from state banks.

Some observers believed that one of management's major challenges would be integrating the cultures of the operations. Twice daily at Lenovo's headquarters, the sound system broadcast "Number Six Broadcast Exercises," a set of stretches and knee bends—participation was voluntary but highly encouraged.[28] The company song was played every morning at 8:00 a.m. and sung by workers at the start of widely attended meetings. Lenovo employees who were late to meetings had to stand behind their chairs for a minute (as an attempt to humiliate them into being punctual). Employees' activities were strictly monitored; time spent outside the work area during work hours had to be accounted for, and deductions were made from employees' paychecks if the explanations were unsatisfactory. Most employees were young and had worked at Lenovo since graduating from college; few spoke English and most had never met a foreigner.

Lenovo's new management team had its sights set on using the acquisition of IBM's PC business as the platform for becoming a global competitor in PCs and for making Lenovo a recognized international brand. The company was pursuing initiatives to cut its costs closer to Dell's level. It was experimenting with selling directly to a few of its largest customers in China. It had opened a telephone sales center in China to handle orders from small customers and was trying to match Dell's speedy four-hour service capability. Lenovo had implemented new processes and systems that cut its inventory levels from about 30 days in 2000–2002 to about 16–19 days in 2004–2005. Although Lenovo reported earnings of $47 million for the 2005 fourth quarter

on revenue of about $4 billion, in 2006 the company announced it was cutting 1,000 jobs, taking a $100 million restructuring charge to pay for restructuring, moving its headquarters from New York City to North Carolina to reduce expenses. A new president took over in late 2005.

Gateway

Founded in 1985, Gateway had grown from a two-person start-up into a Fortune 500 company with $3.6 billion in revenues in 2004. It was battling with IBM/Lenovo for third place in the U.S. market and was one of the top 10 sellers of PCs worldwide. However, as shown in Exhibit 1, its unit sales and market share had been sliding since 2000. Gateway's all-time peak revenues were $9.6 billion in 2000, and its peak-year profits were $428 million; the company reported a loss every year during the 2001–2004 period.

After a series of failed turnaround efforts during 2001–2003, Gateway acquired eMachines, one of the world's fastest-growing and most efficient PC makers, in early 2004, for 50 million shares of Gateway stock and $30 million in cash. eMachines was a $1.1 billion producer of low-end computers and had distribution capabilities in Japan, Great Britain, and parts of Western Europe. The two companies had combined sales of $4.5 billion in 2003. Gateway management believed the eMachines acquisition would allow it to better compete in the low end of the PC market and also give it the resources and competitive strength to reenter markets outside the United States. As part of the deal, the founder and CEO of eMachines, Wayne Inouye, became the CEO of Gateway, with Ted Waitt, Gateway's founder and former CEO, functioning as chairman. The company moved its headquarters from South Dakota to Irvine, California, in September 2004.

Inouye immediately refocused the company's efforts on its core PC business and products like Media Center PCs, MP3 players, and digital displays. As of 2005, the company's value-based eMachines PC brand was sold exclusively by leading retailers worldwide, while the premium Gateway line was available at major retailers, over the phone and Web, and through the company's direct sales force. In 2004–2005, Gateway made several moves to restore the company to profitability:

- All 188 company-owned Gateway stores were closed, and distribution of Gateway PCs was shifted to selling through some 3,000 retailers, including Best Buy, Circuit City, Comp USA, Costco, Micro Center, and Office Depot in the United States as well as Best Buy and Future Shop in Canada. In total, Gateway and eMachines products were sold in more than 6,300 retail locations in North America alone in 2005.

- A new, more efficient manufacturing model was instituted.
- The company began expanding internationally, reentering the Japanese market with the Gateway brand and introducing eMachines in the Mexican retail market.
- The workforce was cut to about 1,900 (compared with 7,400 at the start of 2004).
- The company's supply base and service and support relationships were consolidated to further drive business efficiencies, ensure quality, and optimize the overall customer experience.
- Product development and sales operations were consolidated in centers in North Sioux City, South Dakota, and Kansas City, Missouri.
- Selling, general, and administrative (SG&A) costs were reduced significantly—fourth-quarter 2004 SG&A costs were 57 percent lower than the 2003 quarterly average. SG&A expenses for the first nine months of 2005 were $252.5 million versus $803.3 million in the comparable period for 2004.

The results of Inouye's turnaround strategy were encouraging. In the fourth quarter of 2004, unit sales were 128 percent higher than during the fourth quarter of 2003. During the first nine months of 2005, the company sold about 3.2 million units and had become profitable—Gateway reported sales of $2.7 billion and net income of $27.1 million (compared to sales of $2.6 billion and a loss of $576 million for the first nine months of 2004). Gateway expected that full-year revenues for 2005 would approach $4 billion and that net earnings would be about $45 million.

DELL'S FUTURE PROSPECTS

In a February 2003 article in *Business 2.0,* Michael Dell said, "The best way to describe us now is as a broad computer systems and services company. We

have a pretty simple system. The most important thing is to satisfy our customers. The second most important thing is to be profitable. If we don't do the first one well, the second one won't happen."[29] For the most part, Michael Dell was not particularly concerned about the efforts of competitors to copy many aspects of Dell's build-to-order, sell-direct strategy. He explained why:

The competition started copying us seven years ago. That's when we were a $1 billion business . . . And they haven't made much progress to be honest with you. The learning curve for them is difficult. It's like going from baseball to soccer.[30]

I think a lot of people have analyzed our business model, a lot of people have written about it and tried to understand it. This is an 18½ year process . . . It comes from many, many cycles of learning . . . It's very, very different than designing products to be built to stock . . . Our whole company is oriented around a very different way of operating . . . I don't, for any second, believe that they are not trying to catch up. But it is also safe to assume that Dell is not staying in the same place. You know, this past year we've driven a billion dollars of cost out of our supply chain, and certainly next year we plan to drive quite a bit of cost out as well.[31]

On other occasions, Michael Dell spoke about the size of the company's future opportunities:

When technologies begin to standardize or commoditize, the game starts to change. Markets open up to be volume markets and this is very much where Dell has made its mark—first in the PC market in desktops and notebooks and then in the server market and the storage market and services and data networking. We continue to expand the array of products that we sell, the array of services and, of course, expand on a geographic basis. The way we think about it is that there are all of these various technologies out there . . . What we have been able to do is build a business system that takes those technological ingredients, translates them into products and services and gets them to the customer more efficiently than any company around.[32]

We have only seven percent market share in an $800 billion market. There are enormous opportunities for us to grow across multiple dimensions in terms of products, with servers, storage, printing and services, representing a huge realm of expansion for us. There's geographic expansion and market share expansion back in the core business. The primary focus for us is picking those opportunities, seizing on them, and making sure we have the talent and the leadership growing inside the company to support all that growth. And there's also a network effect here. As we grow our product lines and enter new markets, we see a faster ability to gain share in new markets versus ones we've previously entered.[33]

A great portion of our growth will come from key markets outside the U.S. We have about 10 percent market share outside the United States, so

there's definitely room to grow. We'll grow in the enterprise with servers, storage, and services. Our growth will come from new areas like printing. And, quite frankly, those are really enough. There are other things that I could mention, other things we do, but those opportunities I mentioned can drive us to $80 billion and beyond.[34]

Endnotes

[1]As quoted in "Dell Puts Happy Customers First," *Nikkei Weekly,* December 16, 2002.

[3]Joan Magretta, "The Power of Virtual Integration: An Interview with Dell Computer's Michael Dell, *Harvard Business Review,* March–April 1998, p. 75.

[4]"Michael Dell: On Managing Growth," *MIS Week,* September 5, 1988, p. 1.

[5]"The Education of Michael Dell," *BusinessWeek,* March 22, 1993, p. 86.

[6]Dell's 2005 10-K report, pp. 1–2.

[7]Remarks by Kevin Rollins in a speech at Peking University, November 2, 2005, and posted at www.dell.com.

[8]As quoted in Magretta, "The Power of Virtual Integration," p. 74.

[9]Magretta, "The Power of Virtual Integration," p. 75.

[10]Speech by Michael Dell at University of Toronto, September 21, 2004, posted at www.dell.com (accessed December 15, 2004).

[11]Ibid., p. 76.

[12]Ibid.

[13]Quoted in Neel Chowdhury, "Dell Cracks China," *Fortune,* June 21, 1999, p. 121.

[14]Magretta, "The Power of Virtual Integration," p. 79.

[15]"Michael Dell Rocks," *Fortune,* May 11, 1998, p. 61.

[16]Remarks by Michael Dell, Gartner Symposium, Orlando, Florida, October 20, 2005, and posted at www.dell.com.

[17]Quoted in Kathryn Jones, "The Dell Way," *Business 2.0,* February 2003.

[18]Kevin Rollins, "Using Information to Speed Execution," *Harvard Business Review,* March–April, 1998, p. 81.v

[19]Magretta, "The Power of Virtual Integration," p. 80.

[20]Remarks by Michael Dell, Gartner Fall Symposium, Orlando, Florida, October 9, 2002; posted at www.dell.com.

[21]Remarks by Michael Dell at the University of Toronto, September 21, 2004; posted at www.dell.com.

[22]Quoted in the *Financial Times* Global News Wire, October 10, 2002

[23]Quoted in Adam Lashinsky, "Where Dell Is Going Next," *Fortune,* October 18, 2004, p. 116.

[24]Remarks by Michael Dell, Gartner Symposium, Orlando, Florida, October 20, 2005; posted at www.dell.com.

[25]Keynote speech given on August 25, 1999, in Austin, Texas, at Dell's DirectConnect Conference and posted at www.dell.com.

[26]"Can Compaq Catch Up?" *BusinessWeek,* May 3, 1999, p. 163.

[27]Louise Lee and Peter Burrows, "What's Dogging Dell's Stock," *BusinessWeek,* September 5, 2005, p. 90.

[28]Julie Chao, "Chinese Computer Maker Lenovo Shoots for Leadership in the World," *Atlanta Journal-Constitution,* December 14, 2004, pp. F1, F8.

[29]*Business 2.0,* February 2003; posted at www.business2.com.

[30]Comments made to students at the University of North Carolina and reported in the *Raleigh News & Observer,* November 16, 1999.

[31]Remarks by Michael Dell, Gartner Fall Symposium, Orlando, Florida, October 9, 2002; posted at www.dell.com.

[32]Remarks by Michael Dell, MIT Sloan School of Management, September 26, 2002; posted at www.dell.com.

[33]Remarks by Michael Dell, University of Toronto, September 21, 2004; posted at www.dell.com.

[34]Remarks by Michael Dell, Gartner Symposium, Orlando, Florida, October 20, 2005; posted at www.dell.com.

Case 6

Competition in the MP3 Player Industry in 2005

Louis D. Marino
The University of Alabama

Katy Beth Jackson
The University of Alabama

The earliest portable music players were transistor radios introduced by Regency in 1954. While these radios allowed their owners to listen to broadcasts on the go, they generally suffered from relatively weak signal reception, poor sound quality, and the ability to only receive AM stations. It was not until the mid-1970s that consumers had access to portable personal stereos; the smallest of these were slightly larger than a shoebox and allowed users not only to listen to both AM and FM radio but also to carry their personal music collections, recorded on cassette tapes, with them. However, it was not until 1979 that consumers could purchase the first truly portable personal music player, the Sony Walkman, which only played cassettes and did not offer radio reception. By 1984, the cassette tape was beginning to be supplanted by the compact disc (CD), and Sony led the way again with the development of the portable CD player, the CD Walkman or the Discman.

The portable CD player, and its more advanced cousin the minidisc player, were the mechanical precursors to the modern digital music players. These were referred to as mechanical players since they had moving parts that were involved in playing the music. The main drawbacks to these players were that they could hold only a relatively limited amount of music and were subject to skipping if the player was bumped or jostled. In an effort to overcome these weaknesses, and to capitalize on the growing popularity of digitally encoded music that individuals were storing on their computers in the form of MP3s, in 1997 SaeHan information systems developed the MPMan F10, the world's first nonmechanical digital audio player.[1]

The MPMan player was introduced to the U.S. market in the summer of 1998 as the Eiger Labs MPMan F10, a 32-megabyte digital audio player (DAP) that could only be expanded by returning it to the manufacturer. The second DAP (also known as an MP3 player) introduced in the U.S. market was the Rio PMP300, which was brought to market by Diamond Multimedia in September 1998. The Rio was so successful in the 1998 Christmas season that it led to significant investment in the MP3 player industry by other players and to a lawsuit by the Recording Industry Association of America for enabling the illegal copying of music. This suit was resolved in Diamond's favor; thus, digital music players were ruled legal. By the end of 1999, Remote Solutions had introduced the first hard-drive-based player, the Personal Jukebox, which had a 4.8-gigabyte (GB) internal hard drive and could hold about 1,200 songs consumers could choose from flash memory, hard drive, and in-dash digital audio players from a variety of manufacturers.[2]

Growth in the MP3 player market continued fairly slowly until Apple released its legendary iPod in the latter half of 2001. Apple's original hard-drive player virtually revolutionized the MP3 market single-handedly, spurring the development of many look-alike models from competing manufacturers. By 2004, sales of portable audio players had reached 27.8 million units. Just over the Christmas season of 2004 (a five-week period), MP3 player sales reached $270 million, up 147.5 percent from Christmas 2003, and most analysts predicted continued rapid growth in the industry for the foreseeable future. The research firm Gartner predicted that over 150 million units would be shipped in 2010 (see Exhibit 1).[3] With only 11 percent of the U.S. population owning

Exhibit 1   **MP3 Player Forecast (millions of units shipped)**

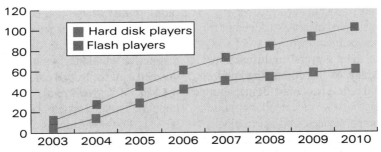

Gartner expects sales of MP3 players to remain strong for several years before slowing by the end of the decade.

Source: Gartner.

an MP3 player in 2004, and much lower penetration rates worldwide, normally conservative analysts were using descriptors such as *boom* and *explosive* to describe growth in MP3 player industry. While sales were expected to grow in each of the main categories of players (flash-based and hard-drive players), the clear winners, in terms of millions of units shipped, were expected to be flash memory players such as the iPod Nano and the iRiver U10.

TRENDS IN THE MP3 PLAYER INDUSTRY

One important factor that had remained fairly constant in the MP3 industry since its beginnings was the pace of technological innovation. MP3 player manufacturers were continuously working to develop players that were physically smaller, with larger storage capacity, a longer battery life, and a simpler user interface. In developing their offerings, MP3 player manufacturers typically purchased component pieces from various computer hardware vendors and assembled them into the end product. There was not a significant differentiation between the types of batteries used, and many firms developed their user interfaces in-house. However, the key element of a player that influenced the unit's size and weight was the memory used in the player. Firms such as Toshiba, Samsung, and Hitachi that supplied the hard drives and flash memory to the MP3 player manufacturers were constantly trying to cut down the size of their

hardware component so that MP3 player manufacturers could ultimately make their product as small and lightweight as possible. Likewise, memory card manufacturers were continuously investigating ways to make their flash cards smaller while maintaining a fairly high level of capacity. While there were numerous manufacturers of hard drives and flash memory, the leading MP3 player manufacturers preferred to partner with the leading memory manufacturers so that they could use the newest and most innovative memory in their players.

Another important trend in the industry was increasing convergence between consumer electronics devices. In response to consumers' changing lifestyles and increasing frustration at having to carry multiple devices, manufacturers of electronic devices, including MP3 players, had recently begun to combine as many features as possible into a single, portable unit. Combinations of cameras, MP3s, Personal digital assistants (PDAs), and even cell phones were becoming abundantly popular. Consumers were leading increasingly busy lives, and with more people constantly on the go—spending more time in the car, exercising, or waiting in line to accomplish some other task—there was an increasing demand for products that would let people carry their music with them so they could essentially "listen while they live." By 2005, MP3 players had evolved into another piece of technology that many busy consumers could hardly live without; that box the size of a deck of cards could hold their entire record collection and allow them to listen to it anytime, anywhere. With the boom of the cell phone industry, many MP3 companies were scrambling to partner with the successful phone brands to incorporate MP3 players into new cell phones that were already able to act as cameras and camcorders as well.

In response to consumers' increasing demands for convergence, MP3 player manufacturers were seeking ways to increase their players' multifunctional usage capabilities. Many of the competing models available in 2005 could be used not only for managing and listening to music but also as calendar/appointment books, data storage devices, and alarm clocks, as well as other functions similar to those found on PDAs. For example, hard-drive-based iPods could be used as an external hard drive when attached to a computer and also had photo storage capabilities; the ability to be used as an alarm clock, a calendar, an appointment book, and a gaming device; and voice-recording abilities (with the purchase of an accessory). Other attributes that MP3 player manufacturers were adding included a built-in radio tuner and sound-manipulating hardware. Some of the MP3 players also had the ability to store and display videos.

The growing size of, access to, and comfort of consumers with the Internet was also fueling the MP3 player boom. Not every electronics company had access to retail outlets, and the Internet allowed consumers to shop for just about any MP3 player on the market at the lowest price, no matter where the unit was physically located. After purchasing the player itself online, users could then go online to shop for brand-new songs to load onto the unit. Hordes of legitimate subscription and pay-as-you-go online music stores had begun appearing on the Internet. Between January and July 2005, over 184 million tracks were sold online, more than twice the sales in January–July 2004. Growth of the online digital music market not only facilitated but also was facilitated by the increasing popularity of MP3 players. Some MP3 manufacturers operated their own online music stores. This was especially important for Apple, which used a proprietary audio format in programming its MP3 players so that only music purchased from its online store would work on an Apple player. A host of other online music stores were owned by various industry players, including RealNetworks and Wal-Mart.

As MP3 players increasingly became a part of everyday life, they were also changing from being mere music players to becoming fashion statements and status symbols. MP3 players were being seen as the new toy for the young and old alike to sport in their daily lives, and generally, the smaller, lighter, and "prettier" models were the most popular. Apple's product design and color schemes were nearly famous for their elegance and simplicity; the original iPod (about the size of a box of cigarettes) had distinctive white headphones that were easily distinguished, and the Mini's colorful pastel models (about the size of a credit card) were equally unique and popular. Said one article, "iPod has become so popular it is now a fashion statement."[4] The popularity of those players was due partly to Apple's excellent marketing scheme and partly to the many very famous celebrities who had been photographed or seen with an Apple player or happened to mention their iPod during interviews.[5] Additionally, other players were literally being incorporated as fashion. For example, Oakley, a sunglasses maker, had introduced a line of sunglasses called Oakley Thump, which had tiny MP3 players built into them and were priced between $395 and $495.[6] As another example of these tiny wearable players, Virgin had one so small that it could be worn as a necklace. There were a few reasons why MP3 players were becoming more fashion-oriented, including the fact that they were actually worn on the body, which made their appearance important, and that MP3 players were extremely popular with younger consumers, a group that often demanded that the products they bought look just as good as they function.

Finally, with the increasing competition in the MP3 player industry, some major producers were deciding to exit the market. Specifically, Rio, the company that brought the second MP3 player to the U.S. market, closed its doors in September 2005. Rio was owned by Digital Networks North America (a subsidiary of D&M Holdings U.S.). In the fiscal year ended in March 2005, D&M reported an increase in revenues of almost 5 percent over the previous year and an increase in net income of 123 percent over the same year (it reported a large net loss in 2004). However, in July 2005, D&M sold the technology underlying its Rio MP3 players in an effort to recoup some of the losses the Rio subsidiary had generated but the parent corporation had not yet decided whether to completely terminate the Rio division.[7] At that point, the company was still manufacturing its current-generation players and shipping them out while making final decisions about Rio's future in the MP3 industry. Early in September 2005,

D&M decided to discontinue all Rio products by the end of the month. The company's reason for exiting the MP3 industry was that management felt any investment would be eroded by the high level of competition facing the market.[8]

COMPETITION IN THE MP3 PLAYER INDUSTRY

Although well over 100 companies manufactured MP3 players by the end of 2005, only about 7 could legitimately claim real importance in this market: Apple, Archos, Creative, Dell, iRiver, SanDisk, and Sony. However, the market was clearly dominated by Apple, with estimates of the company's market share ranging from 65 to 80 percent and each of the other manufacturers having less than 6 percent of the market. All MP3 manufacturers, however, realized that their continued success depended, in large part, on how well they could satisfy their current customers as well as their ability to attract new ones. Research showed that most buyers shopped for players on the basis of song capacity (some users required significantly more capacity than the average user), availability of and compatibility with online music stores, unit battery life, physical size and weight specifications, and ease of use. While price was factor in some consumer purchases, Apple's success had proved that many consumers were willing to pay a premium for some perceived benefit, whether it was higher quality, more technological sophistication, or greater ease of use. However, industry experts predicted that as competition and rivalry became tougher, price would be likely to play a more central role in the buyer's decision. Exhibit 2 provides information on the MP3 players offered by the major players in the industry and consumer satisfaction with the players.

Apple

In fiscal year 2005 (ended in September 2005), Apple reported net revenues of $13.9 billion, a 68 percent increase over 2004. Net income over the same period increased from $276 million to $1.34 billion, a whopping 384 percent increase over the span of a year. For much of the company's history, Apple had been very good at being the first company to introduce a concept or a new product but had then struggled to maintain control of its market share for that product line. Although Apple didn't introduce the first portable MP3 player, it did introduce the first one that gained widespread attention and widespread popularity—the iPod, which came on the market in October 2001. At first, many critics did not give the iPod much of a chance for success, as its launch came about one month after the September 11 terrorist attacks and carried a fairly hefty price tag of $399. However, the success of the iPod had reached phenomenal proportions, such that "it is now a fashion statement, and any other digital music player is considered 'Brand X' for many consumers."[9] What Sony did for portable cassette devices with the Walkman in the 1980s, Apple was doing for the digital music industry with the iPod line.

The iPod accounted for over $4.5 billion, or 32.3 percent, of Apple's total sales in 2005. Unit sales of the iPods had increased by 410 percent since 2004, to almost 22.5 million units in 2005 alone (total unit sales since the product's introduction were 28 million units). Apple's strategy with regard to its iPods centered largely on quick product innovation and marketing. By July 2004, the regular iPod was in its fourth-generation model. The Mini had been introduced in January of that year; by mid-2005, it no longer existed, but the iPod Nano and iPod Shuffle did. Each successive product or model improved on previous ones, in terms of both features and price. Apple had used unique and creative television and magazine ads as well as several brand alliances—with BMW, Hewlett-Packard, Motorola, and U2—in an effort to make the iPod *the* choice for buyers in this industry. After the company's success skyrocketed, the MP3 player industry exploded and competition became widespread and intense. Both computer industry regulars and newcomers solely devoted to the MP3 player product moved into the market, quickly making competition intense. As the technology continued to evolve, even traditional cellular phone manufacturers had become potential rivals in this fast-paced market.

Some analysts felt that Apple was merely "making a careful gamble" with regard to the company's tentative entry into the MP3 player/cell phone market by teaming with Motorola to offer a phone that could hold 100 songs.[10] That judgment was based on the fact that other cell phone companies like Nokia and Samsung had introduced phones that could

Exhibit 2   **Customer Satisfaction with MP3 Players**

	Customer Satisfaction (out of 10)	Quality of Sound (out of 10)	Ease of Use (out of 10)	Reliability (out of 10)	Percent Needing Repair
All MP3 Players					
Apple	8.6	8.8	8.8	8.5	9%
Archos	7.5	8.0	7.1	7.5	3
Creative	7.6	8.2	7.5	7.9	5
Dell	7.7	8.1	7.9	7.9	7
iRiver	7.9	8.6	7.2	8.3	3
RCA	6.8	7.4	7.0	7.3	1
Rio	7.1	7.8	7.5	7.5	6
SanDisk	7.1	7,7	6.9	7.7	4
Sony	7.3	8.0	7.4	7.7	1
Average	7.6	8.1	7.5	7.9	5%
MP3 Players with Flash Drives (1 GB or Less)					
Apple	8.2	8.6	8.4	8.4	3%
Creative	7.3	7.8	7.4	7.8	2
iRiver	7.7	8.3	7.2	8.2	2
Rio	6.8	7.5	7.3	7.3	4
SanDisk	7.0	7.6	6.8	7.6	3
Sony	7.1	7.9	7.2	7.6	1
Average	7.3	7.9	7.3	7.8	3%
MP3 Players with Micro Drives (More than 1 GB but Less Than 10 GB)					
Apple	8.5	8.7	8.6	8.4	9%
Creative	8.0	8.6	7.7	8.0	9
Rio	7.9	8.4	8.2	8.1	8
Sony	7.6	8.0	7.6	7.9	2
Average	8.0	8.4	8.0	8.1	7%
MP3 Players with 10 GB or Larger Hard Drives					
Apple	8.8	9.0	9.0	8.6	11
Archos	7.7	8.2	7.2	7.7	2
Creative	7.8	8.6	7.4	7.9	7
Dell	8.1	8.5	8.3	8.3	9
iRiver	8.3	9.2	7.2	8.6	5
Average	8.2	8.7	7.8	8.2	7%

Source: Developed by the case authors from infromation in a *PC Magazine* customer survey, *PC Magazine*, November 8, 2005, available at www.pcmag.com.

hold up to 3,000 songs and were meant to replace the user's regular MP3 player. The last thing Apple wanted was Motorola users, or any others for that matter, to use their cell phones as a replacement for the iPod. However, the possibilities offered by the huge and booming cell phone market were too big to be ignored by any MP3 company. Only time would tell whether users would prefer to carry an all-in-one unit or would opt to keep their phones and music players separate. However, other analysts felt these new cell phone company additions to the industry and the copycat products would soon break Apple's stride with the iPod and cut deeply into the product's astounding success.[11]

Archos

For the six months ended in June 2004, Archos, headquartered in France, reported net revenues of 17.9 million euros (€), a 14.7 percent decrease over the same period in 2003. Net income for that time period was a net loss of € 3.5 million, a 4.3 percent decrease over the same six months during 2003. The company's U.S. and German subsidiaries also reported net losses for the year, while the UK subsidiary posted a modest net income. Also during 2004, the company had laid off 25 percent of its employees in its U.S. subsidiary and began work on restructuring management and sales and marketing.

Archos had paired with a broadband video service that would allow users of its portable players to access the movies and other video files they would want to store on the player. In addition, with the Gmini XS 100 player, the company had offered support for a subscription-based online music store as part of what users get in the box when they bought that particular player. For that last initiative, Archos teamed with Microsoft's subscription-based download service called Janus to allow users to transfer any available video and audio files to their portable players as long as they continued to pay the subscription fee. The company's wide product line and reputation for offering players with many features made the company stand apart from others. Most players offered by Archos had audio, video, radio, and numerous recording abilities built in to the unit. One drawback was that many of the company's products were priced at a premium. However, Archos was very quick to get a foot into emerging technologies and incorporate as many of those as possible into single units to appeal to consumers who demanded the convenience offered by multifunction media products.

Creative

Creative Technology, founded in 1981 in Singapore, reported fiscal year 2005 (ending June 2005) revenues of $1.2 billion (up 50 percent from fiscal 2004) and net income of $588 million (down 99 percent from 2004). Creative first gained success and fame with its Sound Blaster audio cards for computers and was the first Singapore company listed on the Nasdaq. Since that time, the company had expanded its product lines to include audio as well as graphics, video, and music products. Several of the company's MP3 players had won industry awards—including the Zen Portable Media Center, the Zen Micro, and the Zen Micro Photo—and Creative introduced the world's first MP3 player with a hard drive.

Creative had announced early that it would play tough in the MP3 market, specifically referencing competition with Apple. During Christmas 2004, the company sold 2 million units; during the first quarter of 2005, it sold another 2 million (the iPod sold about 4.5 million and 5.3 million over the same periods, respectively). Creative had announced plans for aggressive advertising campaigns and had focused on offering an extremely extensive product line in the MP3 player market. Many of its portable players had been designed to appeal to consumers' demand for a fashionable and easy-to-use music player. Many analysts felt that Creative's biggest problems were not its wide product line, but its brand appeal, brand image, and other marketing issues. One said, "The biggest lesson learnt is that no matter how good your product is, if it's not branded properly, it's going to fail. Especially with the style-conscious audience it's targeted at."[12]

Dell

Headquartered in Round Rock, Texas, Dell had become famous for its successful direct business model in the personal computer industry. In fiscal year 2006 (ending February 3, 2006), Dell reported net revenues of $55.9 billion (a 14 percent increase from 2004) and net income of $3.6 billion (up 17 percent from the year before). A longtime supplier of customized PCs, Dell was a relatively new entry to the personal electronics market. In October 2003, Dell entered the digital music market in direct competition with a host of rivals by offering its Dell Digital Jukebox (Dell DJ), a personal, portable MP3 player. With the DJ, users could either download music from the Internet to the device or "rip" tracks from the CD collection they already owned.

Although later than some to enter the MP3 player market, Dell had long recognized consumers' interest in and demand for electronics that catered to digital music fans. As early as 1999, it began offering PC customization features such as a CD-recordable disk drive, specialized software for managing a digital music library, and, of course, the jukebox software necessary to play all the digital music on the PC. So with Dell's recent forays into computer peripherals and other electronics, the Dell DJ was a natural extension of the company's product line, and one that placed Dell in a market with a perhaps more constant and steady stream of income than personal computers, which most consumers only purchased once every few years.

In a recent press release, an executive at Dell mentioned that the company had not yet established plans to enter the market for portable entertainment units that included MP3 players as well as video capabilities.[13] However, Dell had established other advantages in the MP3 market that stemmed primarily from the company's pared-down players that afforded consumers a price advantage on the rather expensive hard-drive players by cutting out a lot of the extra features offered in other players. With few or no exceptions, Dell offered a fairly significant price savings in their 30 GB model. Most players with that much capacity cost at least $50 to $100 more than Dell's price. That, of course, stemmed from Dell's direct-sales strategy, which cut out retail intermediaries entirely.

When Dell did decide to enter the already very competitive MP3 market in late 2003, it realized that style was a very important selling point for these players, but rather than focusing on just making an aesthetically pleasing product, it examined the way customers used a variety of preexisting MP3 players and noted the good points and problem areas encountered with each player.[14] During this research, Dell discovered that a prominent button for volume control was lacking in many competitors' players, so it made that a more dominant feature of the DJ. Dell also found customers to be easily annoyed by fingerprints on their MP3 player, so it chose to use aluminum for the body of the DJ in hopes that that material would resist smudges easier than other players did. This approach to entering the market reinforced Dell's history of commitment to customer service and to discovering what product features its customers valued and which were considered unnecessary.

Overall, Dell's product stacked up well against other competitors, especially given the size and strength of the company and its success in other electronics areas. Although some critics would argue that the Dell DJ just was not as aesthetically

pleasing or quite as easy to use as others, it was generally considered a solid contender in the MP3 player market.

iRiver

The manufacturer iRiver Inc. was owned by Reigncom Ltd. (based in South Korea), which reported in 2003 sales growth of over 182 percent from 2002. The company had been involved in many portable device products and had at one time released the world's thinnest MP3-compatible portable CD player. More recently, its large product line had offered flash-based and hard-drive MP3 players as well as multifunction players with video and audio capabilities. iRiver had partnered with many important players in the computer and electronics industries, including Microsoft, Samsung, Philips, Hitachi, and Texas Instruments.

In a survey of Asian consumers, iRiver won in Korea, with over 46 percent of respondents preferring the brand above all others.[15] The company also saw the increasing necessity of competing head-to-head with Apple as executives specifically named that company in announcements about future plans for competing in the MP3 player industry. To achieve that, at the beginning of 2005, the company initiated greater spending on marketing—one ad even featured a person listening to music on an iRiver player while eating an Apple, perhaps a deliberate stab at Apple. The company had also underestimated prices for component parts at the beginning of 2005 and had some issues with lower-than-expected profitability at that time. The underestimates of budget were partly the failure of company executives to correctly assess the popularity of the iPod Shuffle and the ensuing increase in demand for flash-based component parts, demand that would not allow component prices to fall as low as iRiver had expected.[16]

Recently, the company had teamed up with Soundbuzz, an online music provider based in Singapore. Following the alliance, iRiver purchasers would also receive the software that would allow them to load Soundbuzz's music database onto their computers and search for songs to download for a fee. The company's catalog of songs ranged above 300,000 and had selections from American, Mandarin, and Canto pop music. In addition, Reigncom had planned to license Soundbuzz the rights to any Korean music that it already owned.[17]

SanDisk

SanDisk was founded in 1988 and had become one of the world's leading suppliers of flash memory data storage products such as USB storage drives, flash storage cards, and memory sticks for use in digital cameras and digital music players. SanDisk designed, developed, and manufactured its products and sold them to consumers and to manufacturers of electronic products. SanDisk also licensed its technology to other memory manufacturers. On January 6, 2005, SanDisk announced that it would leverage its experience in manufacturing flash-based memory and memory products to vertically integrate into the flash memory segment of the MP3 player market. SanDisk designed its MP3 players to be small and light, and to be expandable through Secure Digital (SD) cards, a form of flash-based memory manufactured by SanDisk and other flash memory manufacturers. To provide software for its products, SanDisk partnered with Rhapsody, AudioFeast, and Audible. Rhapsody provided SanDisk MP3 player users with a digital jukebox that allowed them to manage their music on their MP3 players and purchase music from Rhapsody's library of over 850,000 songs. AudioFeat was a commercial-free digital radio service that allowed users to update music, news, sports, and entertainment programs and news on their MP3 players and to listen to the content on the go. Finally, Audible was a provider of digital audiobooks, radio programs, and newspapers that users could download to their MP3 players for listening on the go. Analysts applauded SanDisk's expansion into the MP3 player market as a natural extension for the company. The first SanDisk MP3 players were shipped in May 2005, and by June 2005 the company had captured 8.9 percent of the flash memory digital music player market.

Sony

In fiscal year 2005 (ending in March), Sony Corporation brought in $66.9 billion in revenue (down 4.5 percent from fiscal 2004) and $1.5 billion in net income (up 85 percent from 2004). The company's net revenues specifically from the electronics segment had fallen every year since fiscal year 2002; from 2004 to 2005, sales in the electronics segment fell by a little less than 0.5 percent. In the 1980s, Sony revolutionized mobile music technology when it introduced the Walkman, a portable cassette tape player that spawned dozens of imitations and look-alikes. Unfortunately, Sony was relatively late to enter the new digital music/MP3 player revolution and was forced to be one of the look-alikes in that market. The Sony Network Walkman was released in August 2004—nearly three years after the iPod, and the iPod was not even the first MP3 player out on the market.

According to some critics, the Network Walkman's user interface was confusing and difficult to use and the accompanying computer software for unloading and managing the music was weaker than the competition. One other point that could potentially work against Sony was that the Network Walkman could not play MP3 files or any other standard music format files like WMA. The Walkman would only play a special format unique to Sony called ATRAC3. Therefore, when the user transferred MP3 or any other type of files to the device, the software had to painstakingly convert each file into the ATRAC format so that it could play on the Network Walkman. Sony claimed to use this unusual format because it improved sound quality and helped extend battery life.

In March 2005, the chairman, the CEO, and the chief operating officer resigned from the company. At the same time, other officers were shuffled, with some demoted. The head of the company was replaced with Sir Howard Stringer, the first non-Japanese person ever placed in the position (he does not speak Japanese). Sony had opted for these drastic measures because it faced intense competition in many of its market segments, including MP3 players, video game equipment, DVD players, and because other electronics companies had gained market share. Sony walkman devices had dominated the portable music player market for more than a decade. However, while the company was not looking, MP3 technology took over the portable music industry and Sony had been late to join in. Now the huge conglomerate was forced to compete with significantly smaller companies just to regain some amount of market share in this fast-growing market. One analyst stated, "Sony's failure to recognize the digital music revolution is classic big-company myopia. As the leading manufacturer of portable CD players and boom boxes, it's easy to see how it could reflexively dismiss MP3 players as a passing fad."[18] In most of Sony's product lines, other Asian electronics manufacturers had forced the company to cut prices since the other companies were making the same electronics for much cheaper. The only product line where Sony was still able to charge a premium price was in the video game segment, with its PlayStation products.

Types of MP3 Payers

Most of the major players in the industry offered products in both of the industry's major segments: hard-drive players and flash memory players. While some analysts included other types of MP3 players in the market—CD players; hard-drive players, which could be separated into microdrive or minidrive players (those with less than 10 GB of storage); and larger players sometimes referred to as digital jukeboxes—flash memory players comprised over 99 percent of the MP3 player market.

Hard-Drive Players

MP3 players with very large levels of capacity typically contained internal hard drives that could be as small as 1.5 GB or as large as 100 GB. These players behaved similarly to real computers in the way they stored and retrieved files from their hard drives. In fact, some players (such as the iPod) would actually function as an external computer hard drive when connected to a computer. Literally thousands of songs as well as other types of files could be stored in players no larger than a deck of cards—for the average user, that meant an entire record collection could be carried in a pocket or purse. Most MP3 manufacturers' product lines included at least one hard-drive player, and many of them had at least one option at the microdrive level and one at a higher-capacity level. This segment of the market also included portable video players (PVPs), which worked much like MP3 players but could store and display video and photo files in addition to audio files. At the end of 2004, Apple controlled 83.7 percent of the hard-drive MP3 player market, followed by Hewlett-Packard (HP), whose device had 3.6 percent of the market. Rio controlled 2.8 percent of the hard-drive MP3 player market at this time, with Creative controlling 2.6 percent and iRiver with 1.5 percent of the market.

Apple   Since the legendary Apple iPod's October 2001 introduction, Apple had altered the product several times, always adding some new feature while consistently lowering the price to keep up with heavy competition. In early 2006, the iPod was available in black or white and in two hard-drive capacities: 30 GB (7,500 songs) and 60 GB (15,000 songs). The smaller model could last for up to 14 hours of playback time, while the larger model boasted up to 20 hours of playback time. The iPods supported several audio formats, including MP3, Apple Lossless, WAV, and Apple's own AAC. All iPods other than the Shuffle included Apple's unique "click wheel" for navigation through the simple interface. With a single finger, the user could adjust volume and move along the intuitive menus, tapping at the center of the wheel to select an option. The color screen displayed a picture of the album cover of whatever song was currently playing. In the newest-generation iPod, Apple had built in up to 150 hours of video capability. That allowed the user to purchase music videos at the online iTunes store for $1.99 each and watch them on the go. Users could also buy ad-free ABC and Disney television shows to watch at any time, and the store also offered a selection of audio books for users to purchase and listen to on the iPod. Whenever they finished listening for the day, they could set a "book marker" at that location and pick up there later. Another feature on the iPod was the Podcast—radio talk shows to which buyers could subscribe from the iPod interface. The iPod could also hold up to 25,000 photos, which could be viewed in thumbnail or full-screen size or in a slide show, on the iPod itself or on any television. Extra features offered by Apple included a calendar, a contact list, a world clock (which included a sleep timer and an alarm clock), a stopwatch, password protection, four games, and the ability to create custom playlists from the unit itself (users did not have to wait until they could connect to a computer). The 30 GB and 60 GB iPods retailed for $299 and $399, respectively. Users could purchase music for the iPod, iPod Nano, and iPod shuffle only at iTunes, Apple's online music store.

Archos   The Gmini XS 202 was a 20 GB hard-drive MP3 player that could store about 10,000 songs. The unit could play back WMA, MP3, and WAV audio files for up to 17 hours. The XS 202 had an internal battery that could be charged though an included AC adapter. When connected with a computer, the product could automatically sync with Windows Media Player to allow the user to transfer songs or playlists from the PC to the player. This player used a double browser to help the user organize music files without a computer—a sort of split screen appeared that had files and folders on one side and playlists and songs on the other. That feature facilitated the user in moving, copying, deleting, renaming, and creating new files and folders. Any online music stores that sold songs in the previously mentioned formats could be used to buy new songs for the XS 202. In addition, Archos had the Gmini 400, a combination video, photo, game, and music player. Its 20 GB hard drive could hold 80 hours of video, 200,000 photos, or 10,000 songs. The 400 supported the same audio formats as the XS 202 and could play up to 10 hours of music or 4 hours of video. In addition, users could record audio directly into the device at stereo quality. For photo viewing, users could download their pictures directly to the player from a compact flash reader. An optional adapter could be purchased to allow the unit the ability to read all types of flash memory cards. The company boasted near-DVD-quality video storage and viewing capability. The XS 202 retailed for about $249, while the Gmini 400 sold for $329.

In the microdrive segment of the market, Archos offered the XS 100 model. This 3 GB hard-drive player could hold up to 1,500 songs and was the lightest and smallest model offered by Archos. The product was available in pink, blue, gray, and black and offered features similar to the larger hard-drive models. The XS 100 automatically synced with Windows Media Player, used the split-screen feature, and allowed the user to connect the player to his or her home stereo for playback purposes. This smaller player retailed for $169.

Creative   Creative Labs offered a vast product selection in both the hard-drive and microdrive segments. The Zen Vision had a 30 GB hard drive with the ability to store and view thousands of photos, 120 hours of video, or 15,000 songs. Its wide array of features included photo slide-show abilities, direct transfer of photos through the compact flash reader (optional adapter for other types of flash cards), an FM tuner and live radio recording ability, a voice recorder, and a personal organizer. The battery supported 13 hours of music listening and 4.5 hours of video playback. The Vision was available in black or white and sold for $399. Another player was the Zen Sleek, a 20 GB hard-drive player that held up to 10,000 WMA-formatted songs or 5,000 MP3 songs. With an 18-hour battery and a built-in FM tuner and recording ability, the Sleek was similar to other Creative products. The player also offered a

vertical touchpad that allowed users to select options with their fingertips. Creative's Zen Sleek sold for $269. Next, Creative's Zen Touch took the idea of the touchpad and made an entirely new product line out of it. The Touch is a model that reduced the size of the regular Play, Stop, Rewind, and Fast Forward buttons and made the touchpad a more predominant feature on the front of the player. The streamlined Touch was offered in a 20 GB model (10,000 WMA songs/5,000 MP3 songs) or a 40 GB model (16,000 WMA songs/10,000 MP3 songs). The battery could last for up to 32 hours of play time. Playlists could be created on the go, without a computer, and the unique search function allowed users to locate a specific artist, song, or album. The 20 GB and 40 GB Zen Touch models sold for $229 and $299, respectively.

Creative's primary microdrive players were the Zen Micro and Zen Micro Photo. The Micro was offered in a 4, 5, or 6 GB model (holding 1,000, 1,250, and 1,500 MP3 songs, respectively). This model had a contoured shape, designed with portability and pocketability in mind. Available in 10 fashionable colors, the Micro could appeal to many consumers. Like Creative's many other models, the Micro had an FM tuner, a voice and radio recorder, a vertical touchpad, a personal organizer, a sleep timer, an alarm clock, a customizable menu, and various song shuffling features. In order of size, this model's variations sold for $179, $199, and $229. The only significant changes made to the Zen Micro Photo were the size upgrade (to 8 GB) and, of course, the ability to view still images or slide shows. The increased capacity allowed 4,000 songs to be stored, and the model was still offered in 10 colors and sold for $249.

Dell   The Dell Digital Jukebox (DJ) was offered in a 30 GB size (15,000 songs). The DJ was in its second generation and lasted for about 12 hours of listening. Very few additional features were offered; the model had a backlit blue screen just under two inches wide and navigational buttons on the front. The model sold for $239.

The Dell Pocket DJ offered a microdrive alternative with 5 GB of capacity, or 2,500 songs. With battery life of 10 hours and a small, sleek design, the Pocket DJ was a slightly shrunken version of the Dell DJ and sold for $169. Both the DJ and Pocket DJ could be customized with accessories such as jackets, premium headphones, armbands or other carrying cases, and various auto accessories.

iRiver   The 20 GB iRiver H10 model played up to 600 hours of music and had a color screen display. In a feature similar to Apple's Click Wheel, the H10 had a touch strip that allowed the user's finger to move up and down to navigate the menu options. Young Se Kim, the designer of the H10, got the idea for the vertical touch strip by watching people use the iPod in a coffee shop. He noticed that most people only used about one-fourth of the circular wheel on the front of the iPod, so he though a short vertical strip made more sense.[19] Battery life claimed to be 16 hours (it was rechargeable) and the player could also display digital photos on the screen. Supported files included WMA, MP3, TXT, and JPEG files. Two extra, unique features were an FM radio tuner and a built-in voice recorder. The iRiver H10 sold for about $299. In addition, iRiver offered the PMC-120, a 20 GB multimedia portable unit that could play video, music, and photos. This model had a 3.5-inch color widescreen and played up to 600 hours of music or 80 hours of video, but it did not offer the FM tuner or voice-recording ability of the H10. The removable, rechargeable battery could last for 14 hours of audio use or 5 hours of video use. It retailed for $499.

Among its H10 products, iRiver also offered two microdrive models, either a 5 GB or a 6 GB option. The former played up to 150 hours of music; the latter, up to 180 hours. Both supported WMA, MP3, and ASF audio files as well as JPEG and TXT data files and had built-in FM radio tuners and voice recorders. The smaller model sold for around $249, while the larger was priced at $279.

Rio   The Rio Karma was a 20 GB player that could hold about 10,000 songs (5,000 if in WMA format). Special features included Cross-Fader, which blended the end of one song seamlessly with the beginning of the next, an Ogg Vorbis audio format (different from either MP3 or WMA), and a large display screen that had animated menus and visualizations. The auto-synchronization function meant that whenever the unit was connected to the user's computer, it would automatically update its playlist with any missing songs. The Karma also had a DJ capability that let it find the user's 10 most-played songs, rarely played songs, or songs downloaded to the unit in a certain time period. Rio's Karma sold for about $199.

Rio's microdrive offerings included the ce2100, a small 2.5 GB player. In addition, the Rio Carbon was sold in a 5 GB or 6 GB capacity. This model's tapered design had won awards; the unit was about the size of a business card. Extra features included voice recording through a built-in microphone. All Rio players included software called Rio Music Manager, which could play MP3 files and manage playlists. In order of size, Rio's three microdrive players retailed for approximately $125, $149, and $179.

Sony   Sony's hard-drive player, the Network Walkman, was offered in a single capacity: 20 GB, or 13,000 songs, according to Sony. The unit could store audio and data files and supported MP3, WMA, WAV, and ATRAC3 (Sony's own format) audio formats. The Network Walkman could last for up to 40 hours of playback time, and the removable battery could charge through a USB cable or an AC adapter, both provided with the unit. The newest model offered the user a choice for the viewing screen—it could be switched between horizontal or vertical viewing. Another unique feature of the Network Walkman was G-Sensor Shock Protection, a system that could react quickly to changes in gravity and velocity to protect the hard drive's surface. The product also had built-in technology to help prevent music skipping caused by forceful impact. Songs for the unit could only be purchased through Sony's online Connect music store. The Network Walkman was available in black, silver, or red and retailed for $279.

Flash-Based Players

Flash-based MP3 players used either an internal or external source of memory to store and retrieve audio files. The most common type of storage media used was a memory card, available in a wide variety of sizes and capacities, usually ranging from 128 MB to 1 GB for portable music players. However, some manufacturers had players with as much as 4 GB of flash memory. The players could be as large as some of the smaller hard-drive players or as small as a pack of gum. Although flash players stored fewer songs than hard-drive players, their primary advantage over the larger-capacity players was that they had no moving parts, which made them ideal for physical activity. Even with jostling and shaking, they were less likely to skip during songs. All of the manufacturers previously discussed in this case had at least one flash-based player in their product lines. According to the market research firm NPD Group, the top manufacturers of flash memory players in June 2005, were Apple, which had captured 46.3 percent of the market; SanDisk, which controlled 8.9 percent of the market; Rio, with 2.9 percent of the market; and Creative Labs, with 2.4 percent of the total market.

Apple   Apple had recently stopped making the iPod Mini, a micro drive player, and replaced it with the 62 percent smaller iPod Nano, which used a built-in USB flash drive and was available in sizes of 2 GB (500 songs in AAC format) and 4 GB (1,000 songs). The Nano was also able to store and display up to 25,000 photos on its color screen. Apple incorporated its click wheel into the design of the Nano, which made navigation simple and easy. The player could play songs in shuffle mode, or the user could browse for a specific song by title, artist, composer, genre, album, or playlist. In addition, for whatever song was currently playing, the cover art of song's album was displayed on the Nano's screen. Like the larger iPods, the Nano also had the capability to allow the user to subscribe to Podcasts. Other features included the ability to purchase and listen to audio books from the iTunes store, to display photos individually, as thumbnails, or in a slideshow, and to maintain a calendar with appointments and an address book. The Nano also had games, a world clock, a stopwatch, and password protection, and it allowed the user to create custom playlists without a computer. The 2 GB model retailed for $199, while the 4 GB model sold for $249.

Apple also offered one other flash player, the tiny Shuffle, about the size of a pack of chewing gum. The Shuffle came in 512 MB (120 songs) or 1 GB (240 songs) capacities. With this player, Apple eliminated the screen altogether and offered users two options: play the songs in order or shuffle the songs to play randomly. The songs stored on the player could be changed as often as the user liked, and the user could choose a specific playlist to load for the day from his or her purchased collection at the iTunes store. Any Podcasts the user had purchased could also be loaded onto the player. The only thing on the front of the Shuffle was a small circular control pad that had buttons for play/pause, fast forward, rewind, and volume up and down. The back side of the player contained a simple switch that moved vertically to turn the power off, to choose in-order playing mode, or to choose shuffle mode. The 512 MB model sold for $99, while the 1 GB Shuffle sold for $129.

Creative   Creative also offered an extremely extensive product line; the MuVo players were Creative's flash-based MP3 players. The MuVo Vidz was offered in 512 MB or 1 GB models but was not yet available in North America. Small enough to wear around the neck, the Vidz could hold music, photos, or video and had a 1.8-inch widescreen color display. The player could hold up to 500 songs (WMA or MP3 format), eight hours of video, or 999 photos in its largest capacity. With a 10-hour battery life, the Vidz offered extra features such as an FM radio and recorder, a voice recorder, and the ability to store any other type of computer file (Word documents, spreadsheets, etc.).

The MuVo Chameleon was also unavailable in North America but came in a 1 GB model that could hold 500 songs. The Chameleon's special feature was that it came with 10 interchangeable color pieces that snapped onto the front of the player and allowed the user to coordinate "every outfit, every occasion, and every mood," according to Creative's Web site. The Chameleon, like the Vidz, had an FM tuner and recorder, a voice recorder, and the ability to function as a flash memory drive for storage of all types of computer files. With an 18-hour battery life, this player also offered some other unique features, such as random playback mode and a reversible LCD screen that could adapt to a left- or right-handed user.

For the sports enthusiast, the MuVo Sport C100 was a small flash-based player that could stand physical jostling and moderate exposure to moisture. The player came in 128 MB or 256 MB ($99) models and included three sport timers: a lap timer, a split timer, and a countdown timer. The player also had an FM radio tuner and an expansion slot for an optional memory card that could hold up to an additional 1 GB of memory. The player came with a carrying case and an armband and ran on a AAA battery.

Dell   Dell offered one flash-based player, the DJ Ditty, the size of a pack of gum and available in a 512 MB capacity (220 songs in WMA format) for $99. With a small LCD screen, the Ditty had an FM tuner and a built-in rechargeable battery that lasted up to 14 hours. Like all of Dell's players, the Ditty was compatible with several online music stores and operated in regular or random playback mode. One end of the Ditty was a USB port that facilitated the player's connection to a computer, and Dell had recently started selling colorful caps for the port (the player came with a black cap). Like other manufacturers' tiny flash players, the Ditty was ideal for physical activity because of its size, light weight, and lack of moving parts.

iRiver The extensive iRiver collection of flash-based MP3 players included the U10 player, which came in 512 MB ($199) or 1 GB ($249) sizes and featured a two-inch color screen. The U10 could play music, video, or photo files for up to 28 hours of battery life (according to iRiver). This player supported WMA and MP3 formatted files, among others. Extra features the iRiver incorporated into the U10 included an FM tuner, a voice recorder, and an alarm clock.

Another flash-based player offered by iRiver was the T10, also in 512 MB ($149) and 1 GB ($199) sizes. The company claimed a whopping 45 hours of battery life, and music could be purchased for any of iRiver's players from almost any online music store including subscription-based and pay-as-you-go stores (excluding the iTunes and Connect stores). The T10 also had an FM tuner, an FM recorder, and a color screen. Made for physical activity, the U10 had a sport clip that allowed the user to attach the player to his or her clothing and also featured skip-free song play. Finally, iRiver also included a voice recorder with the U10 players.

The company's N10 flash-based series came in three sizes: 512 MB ($239), 256 MB ($169), and 128 MB ($139). A tiny player about the size of a pack of gum, the N10 was meant to be worn either around the neck or on the arm or wrist. With up to 11 hours of battery life, the N10 series had a small display screen that provided song titles and the artist's name. Finally, iRiver was able to incorporate its voice recorder into this player as well. Although iRiver's product line included several other flash-based players, those mentioned were representative of the types of capacities, prices, and features the company offered in its players.

Rio Rio had two flash-based players. The first was the Rio Forge Sport, available in 128, 256 (about $150), or 512 MB (about $189) capacities. With a unique circular design, the Forge Sport had a rubber grip around its perimeter to allow the user to get a better hold on it. Features included an FM radio, 20 hours of battery life, and a stopwatch and lap timer. The player also had a slot for memory card expansion, which meant the user could buy up to 1 GB of

additional song capacity for this player. The player came boxed with sport clip earphones, a carrying case, and an armband. Like Rio's hard-drive players, the Forge also came with Rio Music Manager software for managing a music library.

Rio's other flash player was the se510 sport player, which had a similar design to the Forge. This player was only available in the 512 MB capacity and sold for $129. Like the Forge, the se510 lasted up to 20 hours and included a sports armband and stopwatch and lap timer. The primary difference between Rio's flash-based players was that the se510 did not offer an expandable memory card slot.

SanDisk In May 2005 SanDisk shipped its first flash MP3 players, the 512 MB Sansa e130 (up to 240 songs in WMA format) and the 1GB Sansa e140 (up to 480 songs in WMA format). Each of these players had an SD slot for additional storage; supported MP3, WMA, and audible files; had a digital FM radio receiver; and could purportedly last up to 17 hours on a single AAA battery. The front of each unit offered a multiline backlit LCD that provided the title, artists, and album of the song currently being played. In September 2005, SanDisk began offering a car transmitter that would allow the user to play MP3 music through a car radio, and a portable speaker dock for Sansa MP3 players.

Sony Sony offered two flash-based MP3 players. The first was the Network Walkman NW-E407, available in 512 MB (345 songs in ATRAC3 format) and 1 GB (695 songs) capacities. About the size of a pack of chewing gum, the player had built-in flash memory and could serve as an MP3 player or as an FM tuner. The front of the unit had a small, three-line display screen that revealed information like the song title. Sony claimed that the internal battery on the flash Network Walkman could last up to 50 hours and could be charged for just three minutes to provide 3 hours of playback time (under certain playing conditions, such as when the unit was in super-power-saving mode). The 512 MB Network Walkman sold for $119; the 1 GB model sold for $179.

Sony's other flash player was the Walkman Bean, also available in a 512 MB or 1 GB model (song capacities were the same as for the flash Network Walkman). Similar in overall size to Sony's other flash player, the Walkman Bean had a curved shape, like a kidney bean. The Bean also had an FM tuner with preset station capability and a one-line display screen. The battery power and charging ability of the Bean was the same as for the flash Network Walkman. While the smaller Bean player sold for $119, the larger sold for $149. Music for all of Sony's MP3 players (including the hard-drive players) could only be purchased through Sony's online music store, Sony Connect.

Endnotes

[1]http://en.wikipedia.org/wiki/MP3_player (accessed December 23, 2005).

[2] Ibid.

[3] Russ Arensman, "MP3 Leaders Face Off," *Electronic Business*, June 1, 2005, www.reed-electronics.com/eb-mag/article/CA603499.html?industryid-43314 (accessed December 16, 2005).

[4] Steve Smith, "iPod's Lessons," *Twice*, July 26, 2004, p. 12.

[5] Steven Levy, "iPod Nation." *Newsweek*, July 26, 2004, pp. 42–50.

[6] Paul Hansell, "Battle of Form (and Function) in MP3 Players," *New York Times*, October 4, 2004.

[7] Joseph Palenchar, "Rio Foresees Delay for Next Generation Devices," *Twice*, August 8, 2005, p. 6.

[8] Antony Bruno, "No More Rio," *Billboard*, September 10, 2005, p. 6.

[9] Smith, "iPod's Lessons."

[10] Peter Burrows and Roger O. Crockett, "Apple's Phones Isn't Ringing Any Chimes," *BusinessWeek*, September 19, 2005, p. 58.

[11]Steve Maich, "Nowhere to Go but Down," *Maclean's*, May 9, 2005, p. 32.

[12]Arun Sudhaman, "Bid to Beat Apple Has Creative Striking Out," *Media Asia*, June 17, 2005, p. 18.

[13]Mark Hachman, "Dell Brings Bling to Gaming Notebook," *ExtremeTech.com*, February 24, 2005, p. 1.

[14]Jennifer Vilaga, "Fast Talk," *Fast Company*, June 2005, p. 43.

[15]Aki Tsukioka, "Info Plant Announces Results of Survey of Youth in East Asia on MP3 Players," *JCN Newswire*, October 3, 2005, p. 1.

[16]Evan Ramstad, "An iPod Casualty: The Rio Digital Music Player," *The Wall Street Journal*, September 1, 2005, p. B3.

[17]"Soundbuzz Seals iRiver Music Deal," *Media*, August 12, 2005, p. 8.

[18]"Executive Shake-Up at Sony," *Knight Ridder Tribune Business News*, March 8, 2005, p. 1.

[19]Jennifer Vilaga, "Fast Talk," *Fast Company*, June 2005, p. 43.

Apple Computer in 2006

Lou Marino
The University of Alabama

John Hattaway
The University of Alabama

Katy Beth Jackson
The University of Alabama

When Steve Jobs unveiled the fifth-generation iPod on October 12, 2005, he called it the "evolution of a revolution." In this statement, Jobs perfectly described the progress of Apple's flagship iPod line, and the progress of Apple itself. Adding video playback to its popular music player was a natural step in Apple's transformation from an innovative computer manufacturer to a state-of-the-art consumer electronics company. Entering the video sector signaled that Apple would not be content to stop with music and that the company intended to further its penetration into the vast consumer electronics market. With this step, analysts and Apple enthusiasts agreed that the company had come a long way from its personal computing history.

HISTORY OF APPLE

Steven Wozniak and Steven Jobs founded Apple Computer in 1976 by introducing the initial version of what was to become the first highly successful mass-produced personal computer, the Apple I. Alth-ough the original Apple I needed some refinement (it lacked a monitor, a keyboard, or even a case), it eventually influenced the computer industry immeasurably. Wozniak and Jobs had attended high school together and maintained contact after graduation despite taking jobs with different companies in Silicon Valley (at Hewlett-Packard and Atari, respectively). Wozniak was the true designer of the Apple I, but Jobs recognized its commercial potential and insisted that they sell the computer. Although the original model was certainly no rousing success, Wozniak was already designing the Apple II, which was introduced at a local trade show in 1977 and launched in April 1978. This second machine was instantly much more popular than its predecessor and included a plastic case and color graphics. Apple's president, Michael Scott, and chairman of the board, Mike Markkula, were happy with the computer's sales; by the end of 1980, Apple had sold more than 10,000 Apple IIs.

While the Apple II was relatively successful, the next revision of the product line, which was code-named Macintosh (or Mac), was already in the works by 1979 under the direction of Jeff Raskin, a former professor at the University of California at San Diego and a researcher at Xerox's Palo Alto Research Center (PARC) who had proposed the project to Mike Markkula. Raskin's ambitious goal was to design a user-friendly computer that would feature a graphical user interface (GUI) and would cost less than $500. At Raskin's urging, in the same year, Jobs visited PARC, where he saw researchers using a GUI to simplify their computing. Jobs immediately recognized the importance of the interface and decided to use it in the project he was spearheading with project manager Ken Rothmuller, the Apple Lisa, named after Jobs's daughter. However, Jobs's constant drive for innovation and demands for refinements of, and additional features for, the Lisa drove up costs for the system, delayed the shipping date, and resulted in Jobs's frustration with the process. Apple's president, Michael Scott, eventually removed Jobs from the project when Jobs tried to take it over. Due to excessive cost, the Lisa never performed up to Apple's expectations and was retired from the market soon after it was introduced.

Undeterred, Jobs took his passion for the GUI to Raskin's Macintosh project. Jobs's 11 percent share of Apple's equity helped convince Scott to allow him to take over the Macintosh project, and personality conflicts between Jobs and Raskin eventually forced Raskin to leave Apple in 1981. In the same year, Scott resigned as president of Apple and became the vice chairman of the board. Scott was replaced by Mike Markkula, who became president and CEO, while Jobs became the chairman of the board. Under Jobs, the Macintosh team was challenged to make something "insanely great," and by many accounts they succeeded. The Macintosh, introduced in 1984, was hailed as a breakthrough in user-friendly computing. It was also the first computer to use a 3.5-inch disk drive. Unfortunately, the Macintosh did not have the speed, power, or software availability to compete with the personal computer (PC) that had been introduced by IBM in 1981. One of the reasons the Macintosh lacked the necessary software was that Apple put strict restrictions on the Apple Certified Developer Program, which made it difficult for software developers to obtain Macs at a discount and receive informational materials about the operating system that they could use to develop software for the Macintosh.

Back in 1981, Jobs had begun actively working to replace Mike Markkula with John Sculley, then president of Pepsi-Cola, as president and CEO of Apple. In April 1983, Sculley assumed the head position at Apple Computer and Markkula became the associate chairman. In 1984, when Apple introduced the Macintosh and it was not as well received as initially expected, Jobs (a volatile individual) and Sculley began to have personal disputes. Finally, in 1985, Jobs staged an unsuccessful "boardroom coup" to replace Sculley as Sculley was planning a trip to China. Sculley found out about the coup and canceled his trip. After Apple's board voted unanimously to keep Sculley in his position, Jobs, who was retained as chairman of the company but stripped of all decision-making authority, resigned. During the remainder of 1985, Apple continued to encounter problems and laid off one-fifth of its employees while posting its first-ever quarterly loss. In addition, Sculley entered a legal battle with Microsoft's Bill Gates over the introduction of Windows 1.0, which used technology similar to the Mac's GUI. Gates eventually signed a document that in effect ensured that Microsoft would not use

Mac technology in Windows 1.0, but he made no such promises for any later versions of Windows. Essentially, Apple had lost the exclusive right to use its own GUI.

Despite these setbacks, Apple kept bringing innovative products to the market, realizing that innovation would have to be its strategy against big companies like IBM and Microsoft, especially since Microsoft had made its technology available to any PC company that wanted to incorporate that software into its own hardware components. However, Apple had always been famous for closely guarding the secrets behind its technology. In 1987, Apple released the second version of the unsuccessful Macintosh computer, but this machine, like the Apple II, was a phenomenal success. The Mac II was easy to use, making it a favorite at schools and in homes. In addition, it had excellent graphics capabilities. However, by 1990, PCs with Microsoft software had flooded the marketplace and Windows technology was far more prevalent than Mac because Microsoft had licensed its software for use on computers built by many different companies.

In 1991, Apple released the first generation of its notebook computers, the PowerBook, which was successful. In the meantime, Sculley began to push for the completion of a project that was under way to develop a new type of computer system called the personal digital assistant (PDA). Apple's version of the PDA was called the Newton, and under Sculley's persistence the product was completed and released to the market in August 1993. However, the machines did not sell well, partly because they failed to successfully recognize handwriting. Also in 1993, Sculley began to lose interest in Apple's daily operations; in June, the board of directors opted to remove Sculley from the position of CEO. The board chose to place the chief operating officer, Michael Spindler, in the vacated spot. Sculley was allowed to keep his position as chairman, but he chose to resign from the company altogether a few months later.

Although Spindler was not a personable, accessible leader, he did oversee the development of several important Apple products. First, in 1994, Apple released the PowerMac family of PCs, the first Macs to incorporate the PowerPC chip, a very fast processor co-developed with Motorola and IBM. For the first time since Intel technology had become prevalent, Apple could compete with, and sometimes even surpass, the speed of Intel's processors in its computers. Spindler also made a somewhat half-hearted attempt to license the Mac operating system (OS) to other companies. However, few companies ever chose to license the Mac OS because many felt the licensing agreements were far too restrictive. By 1995, Apple had bigger problems than selling computers: It had $1 billion in back orders and insufficient parts to build those machines. And worse, in the late summer of 1995, Microsoft released its Windows 95 OS, which was well suited to compete with the strengths of the Mac OS. During the winter between 1995 and 1996, Apple made some misguided judgments concerning its product line and as a result posted a loss for that quarter. In January 1996, Apple asked Spindler to resign and chose Gil Amelio, former president of National Semiconductor, to take his place.

During his first 100 days in office, Amelio announced many sweeping changes for the company. He split Apple into seven distinct divisions, each responsible for its own profit or loss, and he tried to better inform software developers and consumers of Apple's products and projects. Although Apple announced a staggering first-quarter loss of $740 million in 1996, it brought that down to a $33 million loss for the second quarter, an achievement the financial experts had not imagined the company could accomplish. And in the third quarter, Apple again beat the best estimates, reporting a $30 million profit for that period. At the end of 1996, the company astonished the industry when it announced that it planned to acquire Steve Jobs's new venture, NeXT Software Inc., and rehire Jobs. The acquisition was chosen in order to control NeXTstep, a software design Apple planned to use for its next-generation operating system, Rhapsody. During the summer of 1997, after announcing another multimillion-dollar quarterly loss, Apple determined that Gil Amelio had made many significant improvements in Apple's operations but that he had done all he could. No permanent replacement was announced, but Fred Anderson, chief financial officer, was placed in charge of daily operations; Jobs was also given an expanded role in the company.

Jobs's "expanded role" soon became more clear in terms of his responsibilities—Apple had no CEO, stock prices were at a five-year low, and important decisions needed to be made. Jobs soon began to be referred to as interim CEO, and 1997 proved to be a landmark year for his company. A conference called MacWorld Boston was held in August of that

year, and Jobs was the keynote speaker. He used that event to make several significant announcements that would turn Apple around. An almost entirely new board of directors was announced, an aggressive advertising campaign was planned, and an alliance with Microsoft was revealed. Microsoft received $150 million in Apple stock, Apple received a five-year patent cross-license, and the long legal battle between the two companies started to taper off. As part of the legal dispute resolution, Microsoft paid an undisclosed amount to Apple to quiet the allegations that it had stolen Apple's intellectual property (the Mac GUI). By year's end, Microsoft's Windows 1998 was available for Mac users. Jobs also effectively ended Apple's licensing agreements with other companies, buying out all but one, with the understanding that company would only serve the low-end market for computers (under $1,000). At a late 1997 press conference, Jobs announced that Apple would begin selling direct to consumers over the Web and by phone. Within a week, the Apple e-store was the third-largest e-commerce site on the Web.

Jobs continued to make several changes during 1998, a year in which Apple reported four quarters of profitable earnings, a full year of profitability. Apple's stock price was on the rise, and Apple had released the iMac, an all-new design for the Macintosh that was meant to serve the lower-end consumer market. The iMac had more processing capabilities than most consumers would ever need and was priced affordably. In the fall of that year, the iMac was the best-selling computer in the country. Apple followed up that success by introducing the iBook in 1999, the portable counterpart to the iMac, a laptop meant to be stylish, affordable, and powerful. Throughout 1999, Apple's stock continued to soar, and in the fall was as high as the upper $70s.

In early 2000, Jobs announced that he was now permanent CEO of Apple. The remainder of that year was a slow one for Apple and for the rest of the computer industry. As a result, Apple reported its first quarterly loss in three years. In late 2000 the company cut prices across the board, and in early 2001 it released a new set of PowerMacs with optical drives that let consumers choose whether to burn or listen to CDs or read or write DVDs as well. In May 2001, Jobs announced that Apple would open several retail stores that would sell Apple products as well as third-party products, including MP3 players, digital cameras, and digital video cameras. In October

2001, Apple released its first noncomputer product in years, the iPod. This small machine was a portable MP3 player that stored songs on a hard drive and could be taken anywhere. Apple took quite a risk in pricing the small machine at a premium, but it felt that consumers would be willing to pay more for the unique style, design, and technology.

Over the next few years, Apple made adjustments and additions to its product line, both on the software side and on the hardware side. Although the latter half of 2002 was a poor time for the entire economy as a whole, Apple did well, with net earnings of $65 million. The company's other products sold well and also enjoyed success, but it was the iPod that would revolutionize the company and the industry. In 2003, when the company released iTunes, the online retail store where consumers could purchase individual songs legally, the success of the venture skyrocketed. The iTunes technology was available only for Macs at first, but has since become available for PC users as well. By July 2004, 100 million songs had been sold and iTunes had a 70 percent market share among all legal online music download services.

APPLE'S CURRENT SITUATION

By 2005, Jobs's leadership had placed Apple at the forefront of the MP3 player industry and had established the company as a player once again in the computer industry. Jobs had idea after idea for how to improve the company and turn its performance around. He not only consistently pushed for innovative ideas and products but also enforced several structural changes, including ridding the company of unprofitable segments and divisions. His leadership style, which epitomized the spirit and standards upon which Apple was founded, blended with the business discipline that was lacking in the younger Jobs. Jobs also credited Apple's success to its skill management team, which included Peter Oppenheimer and Timothy Cook.

Peter Oppenheimer started with Apple in 1996 as controller for the Americas and was senior vice president and chief financial officer for the company. He was promoted to these positions after less than two years with the company, due to his extensive experience in business and financial

areas. Oppenheimer, who reported to the CEO, was responsible for the supervision of the controller, treasury, investor relations, tax, information systems, internal audit, corporate development, and human resources departments, and he helped return a healthy fiscal discipline to the company. Timothy D. Cook, Apple's executive vice president of worldwide sales and operations, also reported to the CEO. Cook was responsible for managing Apple's supply chain, sales activities, and service and support in all markets and countries. His position was accountable for maintaining Apple's flexibility in serving more-demanding consumers. Cook had extensive experience in technological industries and had worked previously for IBM and then for Compaq. The skill management team, along with the other members of the executive staff and the board of directors, was responsible for ensuring that all operations of Apple ran efficiently and smoothly, while Jobs provided the vision for the organization. Together they worked to ensure that Apple could continue to be a vital, innovative company in a competitive environment.

In February 2005, Apple's stock prices reached record highs (prices were in the $80s, though just a year before a record low of $21.89 had been hit) and the company announced a 2-for-1 stock split. Investor confidence in the company was rewarded as, during Apple's fiscal fourth quarter of 2005, which ended September 24, 2005, Apple reported the highest revenue and earnings in the company's history, with revenues of $3.68 billion and a net quarterly profit of $430 million, up from revenues of $2.35 billion and a net profit of $106 million, or $.13 per diluted share, in the same quarter of the previous year. In the fourth quarter of 2005, Apple shipped 1,236,000 Macintosh units (up 48 percent from the same quarter the previous year) and 6,451,000 iPods (up 48 percent from the same quarter the previous year). As of October 2005, the price of a share of Apple stock was above $55. Apple's financial performance is shown in Exhibit 1.

Jobs reported that these figures represented the company's highest-ever quarterly revenue and income. With 10 million iPod units already sold by 2005, and with Apple's plans to continue to grow and design innovative products in the iPod line, the enormous success of the iPod line really could not be overstated. As a result of the introduction of the iPod, Apple's sales and financial information had consistently surpassed expectations since 2001.

Exhibit 1   **Apple Computer's Financial Performance, Fiscal Years 2001–2005 (in millions, except share amounts)**

Results of Operations	2005	2004	2003	2002	2001
Net sales					
Domestic	$ 8,334	$4,893	$3,626	$3,272	$2,936
International	5,597	3,386	2,581	2,470	2,427
Total net sales	13,931	8,279	6,207	5,742	5,363
Costs and expenses					
Cost of sales	9,888	6,020	4,499	4,139	4,128
Research and development (R&D)	534	489	471	446	430
Selling, general and administrative (SG&A)	1,859	1,421	1,212	1,111	1,138
Operating expenses before special charges	2,393	1,910	1,683	1,557	1,568
Special charges					
Executive bonus	—	—	—	−2	—
In-process research and development	—	—	—	1	11
Restructuring costs and other	—	23	26	30	—
Total operating expenses	2,393	1,933	1,709	1,586	1,579
Operating income (loss)	1,650	326	−1	17	−344
Interest and other income (expense) net	165	57	93	70	292
Income (loss) before provision (benefit) for income taxes	1,815	383	92	87	−52
Provision (benefit) for income taxes	480	107	24	22	−15
Cumulative income of accounting change, net of income taxes of	5	0	0	1	12
Net earnings (loss)	$ 1,335	$ 276	$ 69	$ 65	$ (25)
Diluted earnings (loss) per common and common equivalent share	$1.56	$0.36	$0.09	$0.09	$(0.04)
Diluted common and common equivalent shares used in the calculations of earnings (loss) per share (in thousands)	856,780	774,622	726,932	723,570	691,226
Financial position					
Cash, cash equivalents and short-term investments	$8,261	$5,464	$4,566	$4,337	$4,336
Accounts receivable, net	895	774	766	565	466
Inventories	165	101	56	45	11
Net property, plant and equipment	817	707	669	621	564
Total assets	11,551	8,050	6,815	6,298	6,021
Current liabilities	3,484	2,680	2,357	1,658	1,518
Long-term debt	—	—	—	316	317
Deferred tax liabilities and other noncurrent liabilities	601	294	235	229	266
Shareholders' equity	$7,466	$5,076	$4,223	$4,095	$3,920

Source: Company 2005 10-K report.

Further, some analysts believed that sales of iPods would create permanent consumer converts to the entire line of Apple products, including PCs. While a few analysts believed that interest in a portable MP3 player could not possibly generate a significant amount of interest in Apple's computers, at least one source reported that as many as 11 percent of iPod users intended to purchase an Apple Mac, and "in a November [2004] survey, money managers Piper Jaffray & Co., found that 6 percent of iPod users had switched from a standard personal computer running Microsoft Corp.'s Windows operating software to an Apple Mac, and another 7 percent planned to switch in the coming year."[1]

Most of the actions Apple had taken over its history were consistent with its underlying philosophy that innovation and improvement of existing products was essential for the growth and development of the company and its continued success. Since 2002, Apple had determined that the digital electronics market was converging with the computer market and that consumers would begin to demand more synchronization and harmony between the two. That belief had led Apple to release the iPod and iTunes, as well as to improve the software and available options on its computers to incorporate more closely the two areas of demand.

In Apple's fiscal-year 2005, the company had $13.93 billion in sales, with about $6 billion of that from sales of all Macintosh computers and approximately $4.5 billion from iPod sales (see Exhibit 2). Apple's unit sales for the same fiscal year, broken down by product, revealed that approximately 4.5 million Mac units were sold in 2005, while approximately 22.5 million iPods, including all types of iPods, were sold over the same time period.

One other impressive feature of Apple's financial statements was that although the company had some minimal long-term debt in recent years, in February 2004, the company retired $300 million of outstanding debt and reduced long-term liabilities to $0. In retiring this debt, Apple did not deprive key operating areas of the necessary levels of funding and additional funds were allocated to research and development (see Exhibit 2). Spending more on R&D was consistent with the company's philosophy that its continued achievement would depend heavily on its ability to improve existing products, introduce new products, offer the items at competitive prices to achieve widespread popularity,

and perhaps even more importantly, to convince investors and consumers that Apple products were better than those of competitors in the two main industries in which it competed, personal computers and MP3 players.

PERSONAL COMPUTER INDUSTRY

In the third quarter of 2005, the worldwide PC market experienced its 10th consecutive quarter of double-digit growth. The PC industry was relatively consolidated. The U.S. market was dominated by five main players (see Exhibit 3), who controlled 64.2 percent of the market. Internationally, the top five controlled over 40 percent of the market, and Apple only accounted for 2 percent of international volume. While the market had experienced substantial growth, experts predicted that the market in the United States, as well as the market throughout the world with the exception of Asia, would experience a slowdown to 8 percent unit sales growth from 2006 to 2009, with flat revenue growth. In the face of these flat margins, it was predicted that the marginal players were likely to be forced out of the market.

Apple's Computer Operations

Even though Apple's revenues were increasingly coming from noncomputer products, primarily the iPod, Apple still remained a company with computers at its core. Apple's approach of handling every facet of the computer in-house differentiated it from its primary competitors in the PC market but left out many of the synergies that Windows/Intel (Wintel) PC makers benefited from. Many analysts still projected that Apple's greatest opportunity for growth would come from the projected halo effect of iPods (i.e., consumers switching to Apple computers after being exposed to the iPod/iTunes combination), rather than from just iPod sales.

Apple's computer product line consisted of several models in various configurations. Its desktop lines included the Power Mac (aimed at professional users), the iMac (home and educational use), and the eMac (made specifically for educational use). Apple had two notebook product lines as well: PowerBook (for professional and business users) and iBook (for

Exhibit 2   Apple's Net Sales by Operating Segment, Fiscal Years 2003–2005

	September 24, 2005	Percent Change	September 25, 2004	Percent Change	September 27, 2003
Net sales by operating segment:					
Americas	$ 6,950	64%	$4,019	26%	$3,181
Europe	3,073	71	1,799	37	1,309
Japan	920	36	677	−3	698
Retail	2,350	98	1,185	91	621
Other segments[a]	998	67	599	51	398
Total net sales	$13,931	68%	$8,279	33%	$6,207
Net sales by product:					
Desktops[b]	$ 3,436	45%	$2,373	−4%	$2,475
Portables[c]	2,839	11	2,550	26	2,016
Total Macintosh sales	$ 6,275	27%	$4,923	10%	$4,491
iPod	4,540	248	1,306	279	345
Other music-related products and services[d]	899	223	278	672	36
Peripherals and other hardware[e]	1,126	18	951	38	691
Software, service, and other products[f]	1,091	33	821	27	644
Total	$13,931	68%	$8,279	33%	$6,207
Unit sales by product:					
Desktops[b]	$ 2,520	55%	$1,625	−8%	$1,761
Portables[c]	2,014	21	1,665	33	1,251
Total Macintosh unit sales	$ 4,534	38%	$3,290	9%	$3,012
Net sales per Macintosh unit sold[g]	$1,384	−7%	$1,496	0%	$1,491
iPod unit sales(in 000s)	22,497	409%	4,416	370%	939
Net revenue per iPod unit sold[h]	$202	−32%	$296	−19%	$367

Notes:
[a]Other Segments include Asia Pacific and FileMaker.
[b]Includes iMac, eMac, Mac mini, Power Mac and Xserve product lines.
[c]Includes iBook and PowerBook product lines.
[d]Consists of iTunes Music Store sales, iPod services, and Apple-branded and third-party iPod accessories.
[e]Includes sales of Apple-branded and third-party displays, wireless connectivity and networking solutions, and other hardware accessories.
[f]Includes sales of Apple-branded operating system, application software, third-party software, AppleCare, and Internet services.
[g]Derived by dividing total Macintosh net sales by total Macintosh unit sales.
[h]Derived by dividing total iPod net sales by total iPod unit sales.
Source: 2005 10-K report.

consumers and students). In both cases, the Power products were higher-end and offered more computing power at a premium price. The other models were lower on the price scale but still high relative to Wintel sellers, but had less power and fewer features.

To help drive customers toward its products, Apple released its first truly low-end computer in January 2005, the Mac Mini. This small computer, about the size of five CD cases, started at $499, but came without a keyboard or monitor. Sales of the Mini took off and lifted Apple's share of the U.S. PC market almost overnight. However, even with the large increase in sales, Apple remained a small player in the PC market as a whole (see Exhibit 3).

Exhibit 3 **U.S. Market Shares of Leading Personal Computer Manufacturers, Third-Quarter 2005 versus Third-Quarter 2004**

Company	Q3 2005	Q3 2004
Dell Inc.	30.7%	30.3%
Hewlett-Packard	19.1	19.1
Gateway	6.0	4.9
Lenovo/IBM	4.2	4.4
Apple Computer	4.2	3.2

Source: www.gartner.com (accessed October 25, 2005).

COMPETITORS IN THE PC MARKET

Dell

Dell, the industry leader in PC sales, recorded net revenues of almost $50 billion for the fiscal year ending in January 2005. Dell's revenues had been consistently growing, and this trend would continue into 2005. Of this revenue, about 40 percent came from sales of desktop PCs (see Exhibit 4). These PCs ranged from low-end bargain desktops to high-end gaming setups with the latest hardware and software. However, competition in the desktop market was lowering the profitability of desktop sales. Dell, a company that attempted to be a low-cost provider through supply chain and distribution logistics, was beginning to see a shift in consumer demand toward mobility products: laptops, MP3 players, and PDAs. Dell's notebook computers, like its desktops, ranged from low-end and low-priced to state-of-the-art and high-priced. The notebook segment showed promising revenue growth for Dell. The company also offered peripherals such as LCD televisions as it attempted to move into a role as a consumer electronics provider along with its role as a PC manufacturer.

Hewlett-Packard

Hewlett-Packard's Personal Systems Group, which included sales of PCs, accounted for about one-third

Exhibit 4 **Dell's Revenues by Product Category, First Nine Months, Fiscal 2006 versus Fiscal 2005**

Product Category	Percentage of Total Revenues for Nine Months Ended	
	October 28, 2005	October 29, 2004
Desktop PCs	38%	43%
Mobility products (notebook PCs, Dell DJ, Axim)	25	24
Printers, monitors, TVs, projectors, ink and toner cartridges	15	13
Servers and networking hardware	10	10
Professional consulting and support services	9	7
Storage products	3	3
Total	100%	100%

Source: Dell's 10-Q report for the third quarter of 2005.

of the company's revenues in fiscal year 2004. HP's biggest revenue producers were printers, printer supplies, other imaging products, servers, and information systems consulting services. The Personal Systems Group provided half of the company's net revenue growth from 2003 to 2004, however. Earnings from the division were only 0.9 percent of net revenues, though ($210 million in earnings on $24.6 billion in net revenues). Overall revenue growth in the Personal Systems Group broke down as shown in Exhibit 5.

The desktop and notebook lines were the key growth areas for HP. At one point, HP offered a branded version of Apple's iPod, but that relationship ended because the partnership wasn't helping HP as much as had been hoped. HP then moved to Microsoft-compatible devices but did not develop its own product for this market. Like Dell, HP offered desktops and notebooks in various configurations, with prices determined by the features offered and hardware contained in the systems. HP also offered peripherals such as televisions and related media devices.

Gateway

Gateway initially set itself apart from Dell, HP, and other PC brands by selling its wares through proprietary stores designed to give consumers a chance to test the systems they were considering purchasing. While this tactic worked for a time, by 2004 the stores were losing money for the company. Because of this, the company closed its stores and began focusing on selling through third-party retailers and online. Gateway also purchased eMachines in early 2004, acquiring a company that had a cost structure comparable to Dell's. This was important to Gateway, as the

company was not profitable, with a net loss of $568 million during fiscal 2004. Much of the increase in desktop sales during 2004 (see Exhibit 6) was due to the acquisition of eMachines. However, unlike many of its competitors, Gateway was not showing strong growth in the mobile (laptop) market.

Like its competitors, Gateway included high- and low-priced desktops and notebooks in its product line. Gateway also made a strong effort to sell its computers as media centers, using Microsoft's Media Center version of Windows XP. Gateway was one of the first computer manufacturers to venture into the consumer electronics side of the business, selling TVs and related peripherals to tie in to the media-center hub. Gateway, like HP, sold MP3 players from companies like Creative rather than developing its own product for the category.

MP3 PLAYER INDUSTRY

The personal electronics industry existed long before the iPod was popular. However, much of the history of the industry was related to the iPod's ancestors: portable music devices. Sony, with its Walkman product line, was one of the early giants in this sector of the personal electronics industry. The first Walkman appeared in 1979 in Japan. This device was a tape player that, notably, did not have a record function and was an innovative gamble by Sony's management. After a slow start, sales skyrocketed and music history was made. By 1995, over 150 million Walkman products had been sold worldwide. The Walkman line eventually included CD-playing devices.

The history of personal digital assistants (PDAs) reaches back almost as far as the history of portable

Exhibit 5   **Weighted Average Revenue Growth, Hewlett-Packard's Personal Systems Group, 2003–2004**

Product	Weighted Average Growth	
	2004	2003
Desktop PCs	7.9%	21.9%
Notebook PCs	7.1	19.6
Handhelds	0.7	2.0
Workstations	0.4	1.1
Other	—	(0.1)
Total Personal Systems Group growth	16.1%	44.5%

Source: Company records.

Exhibit 6   **Gateway's Sales of Personal Computer Products, 2002–2004 (in millions of $)**

Product Line	2004 Sales Revenues	2004 % of Revenues	2003 Sales Revenues	2003 % of Revenues	2002 Sales Revenues	2002 % of Revenues
Desktop PCs	$1,982	54.3%	$1,649	48.4%	$2,600	62.3%
Mobile PCs	790	21.7	755	22.2	731	17.5
Servers	54	1.5	53	1.6	52	1.3
Non-PC products	823	22.5	946	27.8	788	18.9
Total	$3,650	100.0%	$3,402	100.0%	$4,171	100.0%

Source: Company financial reports.

music players. While Apple is often credited with making and distributing the first true PDA, there were many forerunners to Apple's Newton. Sharp, Toshiba, and Casio, among others, had products that mimicked the functions of PDAs. However, Apple's Newton was the first product to successfully bring the functionality into a package for mass marketing.[2]

As PDAs have become more and more functional in recent years, the line between them and portable computers has blurred. Microsoft's specialized edition of Windows for PDAs has further blurred this line. PDAs can sync with PC software and hold calendar events, task lists, and even documents. However, despite this increase in functionality, pure PDA sales declined leading up to 2005 and were expected to continue to fall. This decline was due not to a lack of demand for portable devices, but to a convergence between PDAs and other devices—particularly the cell phone.

The other major consumer electronics product of the past 25 years sector was the cellular telephone. The first public testing of cell phones was in Chicago in 1977, although a successful demonstration of cell phone technology had occurred as early as 1973. In 1982, the U.S. Federal Communications Commission (FCC) authorized commercial cellular service in the United States. By 1987, demand was so high (over 1 million users) that the original allocations for bandwidth were no longer sufficient. Changes and improvements were made to the technology, and the FCC allowed broader innovation in the industry. By 2000, there were over 100 million cell phone users in the United States.[3] The market for cell phones was expected to near 800 million units worldwide in 2005.[4]

The last 30 years of consumer electronics history were filled with companies expanding functionality

and portability in products. At the same time, personal computers were getting smaller and creeping toward the market that these consumer electronics products historically filled. Apple's foray into the consumer electronics market with its iPod was a perfect example of this movement. The iPod had the functionality of a Walkman and many of the features found in PDAs: calendar, calculator, address book, and more. Microsoft's partnership with PDA market leader Palm, which put Windows in Palm's products, was another example of this convergence. Apple even moved toward the cell phone market through a partnership with Cingular and Motorola. The Motorola ROKR, though not the first phone to play music, was the first to have a portable version of Apple's iTunes built in.

While a number of the major computer manufacturers had entered the MP3 player industry, there were over 100 manufacturers offering MP3 players in the United States in 2006. Apple was the undisputed leader of the young market. In fact, it was the introduction of the user-friendly iPod in 2001 that spurred growth in the MP3 industry. By 2004, sales of portable audio players had reached 27.8 million units and Gartner, a U.S.-based research firm, predicted that over 150 million units would be shipped in 2010.

It was estimated that by the end of 2004, Apple had captured 83.7 percent of the hard-drive MP3 player market. HP, selling its own version of the iPod, followed with 3.6 percent of the market. Rio had 2.8 percent of the hard-drive MP3 player market, while Creative and iRiver had 2.6 percent and 1.5 percent of the market, respectively. In the flash-based segment, the top manufacturers of flash memory players were Apple (which controlled 46.3 percent of the market), SanDisk (which had captured 8.9 percent of the market), Rio (with 2.9 percent of the market), and Creative Labs (with 2.4 percent of the market).

The substantial growth in the market was fueled by (1) the increasing availability of digital music, both paid and pirated; (2) consumers' increasing familiarity with MP3 technology; and (3) the fact that in 2004 only 11 percent of the U.S. population owned an MP3 player. While the phenomenal growth in the MP3 player industry was expected to favor both of the main categories of players (flash-based and hard-drive players), flash-based players such as the iPod Nano were expected to disproportionately benefit from the growth.

IPOD AND ITUNES

Aside from the iPod's ease of use, one of the primary factors that contributed to the popularity of the iPod was Apple's iPod/iTunes combination. In fact, some analysts believed that, despite the acclaim that had been heaped on the iPod, the device would not achieved its dominant position without iTunes.

Apple first released the iTunes digital music management software for Macintosh computers in 2001. It was innovative, but not alone. Originally, the software was intended to allow users to store music from their compact discs (CDs) to their computer hard drives and make the content easily accessible. As features such as the ability to burn custom CDs were added to the software, iTunes became more and more useful to consumers.

When the iPod was released in 2001, iTunes was quickly adjusted to allow for syncing between the music management software and the new music player. This interface made it easy for consumers to move content from their computer to their iPod, an essential part of the product value of the iPod. While the iTunes software was a key component in Apple's strategy, it did not have a significant impact on iPod sales until the iTune's fourth edition was released in April 2003.

With the release of iTunes' fourth edition, Steve Jobs announced that he had reached a deal with the music industry's five major recording labels to sell their content in a copy-protected form via the iTunes online music store—and the world took notice. This announcement marked the first time that such a large library of popular music was available in one place via a simple method. Jobs was able to negotiate the agreement with the music companies for two main

reasons: First, the recording labels were eager to offer a legitimate online source for their music that would reduce the flow of pirated music. Second, the music Apple provided at iTunes was compressed using Apple's proprietary Advanced Audio Coding (AAC) and was protected with Apple's Fairplay Digital Rights Management system, one of the strongest in the country.

In October 2003, a version of the iTunes software, including the iTunes music store, was released for Windows users. This immediately opened up Apple's music store to millions of users who had previously been shut out. By October 2005, Apple had introduced a new version of iTunes that sold not only music but video as well. This version of iTunes was released in conjunction with Apple's video iPods. As with the original launch of iTunes, Apple formed partnerships with major networks such as ABC, NBC, ESPN, and Disney to make content such as television shows, sports programming, newscasts, and children's shows available in a secure, encoded format. In the first 20 days of offering video, Apple reported that it sold over 1 million videos. Most important, Apple's innovative iTunes was again the first company to really enter the digital music market, and the digital video industry, in a big way. When Apple's iTunes became a major hit in 2003, it ushered in the digital music era for mainstream computer users and encouraged new competitors to enter the market. There was little doubt that competition for the digital video segment would be significant as well.

Apple: The iPod and the iPod Mini

In fiscal year 2003, Apple Computer Inc. reported net revenues of $6.2 billion (up 8.1 percent from 2002) and net income of $69 million. For much of the company's history, Apple had excelled at being the first company to introduce a concept or a new product but had then struggled to maintain its market share in that product line. Although Apple didn't introduce the first portable MP3 player (EigerLabs did in 1998), its iPod, introduced in October 2001, was the first such device to gain widespread attention and popularity.

Many critics did not give the iPod much of a chance for success, because its launch came about one month after the September 11 terrorist attacks and because it carried a fairly hefty price tag of

$399. However, the success of the iPod reached phenomenal proportions, leading one analyst to say that "it is now a fashion statement, and any other MP3 player is considered 'Brand X' for many consumers."[5] Industry experts agreed that the iPod's success revolutionized the portable music industry as the Sony Walkman had in 1980.

By June 2005, Apple's iPod models accounted for well over 70 percent of the hard-drive MP3 player market and more than 40 percent of the flash-based player market. In December 2005, the iPod was available in many models:

- The iPod Shuffle, a flash memory player with no screen that was about the size of a pack of chewing gum, was offered in either a 512 megabyte (MB) model with the capacity for about 120 songs ($99), and in a 1 gigabyte (GB) model that could hold 240 songs ($149).

- The iPod Nano, a flash-based player that was about the size of a credit card, but thicker, was offered in a 2GB model that held 500 songs ($199) and a 4GB model that held 100 songs ($249). The Nano also had games, a calendar with an appointment scheduler, a contact manager, a world clock, a stopwatch, and password protection. It allowed the user to create custom playlists without a computer and could hold up to 25,000 photos.

- The iPod, a hard-drive player, was offered in a 30GB version that could hold 7,500 songs, 25,000 photos, or 75 hours of video ($299) and in a 60GB version that could hold 15,000 songs, 25,000 photos, or over 150 hours of video. Like the Nano, the iPod had games, a calendar with an appointment scheduler, a contact manager, a world clock, a stopwatch, and password protection, and it allowed the user to create custom playlists without a computer. However, the iPod also allowed users to play video.

All of Apple's iPods featured a thumb wheel, a concept that Apple first introduced in MP3 players, which served as the tool for scrolling through playlists and other menus on the iPod interfaces. When comparing the iPod with other competing products, most critics agreed that Apple's simple and elegant interface was superior to most competitors' and made the product especially attractive to consumers who were new to the MP3 player industry and were willing to pay a premium for the simplicity. Another fairly unique feature was that the iPod included a calendar, a contact list, and a to-do list. These features allowed the iPods to meet both the music and PDA needs of their owners, who thus did not have to carry two separate units to accomplish both tasks. The iPod also featured some unique antipiracy software: If the iPod was connected to a foreign computer (one that it did not recognize) and the user tried to transfer music files either to or from the computer, the software would give the user a choice—either stop the transfer or proceed with it and the newly transferred music would delete every file that was on the iPod, essentially overwriting it and replacing it.

While each new version of the iPod offered innovative technology, the introductions were not without their challenges. The original iPods were criticized for poor battery life, and eventually users brought a class-action lawsuit against Apple claiming that Apple had misrepresented the life of the rechargeable battery used in the iPod. Although Apple denied this claim, it offered a battery replacement service for $99 and offered to settle the suit in June 2005, offering purchasers of first-, second-, and third-generation iPods an extended warranty and a $50 voucher. Apple also experienced problems with the launch of the Nano in 2005, with customer complaints related to the tendency of the device to freeze and to the ease with the device, especially the screen, scratched or stopped functioning. Apple offered a repair and replacement service for these devices, but it expected to face a class-action suit similar to the one filed over the battery-life problem.

Regardless of these challenges, a 2005 customer survey by *PC Magazine* showed that Apple iPods ranked significantly higher than other brands of MP3 players in terms of overall quality, sound quality, ease of use, and overall reliability (see Exhibit 7). By the end of 2005, many iPod fans were eagerly awaiting the next version of the iPod, and the competition was working diligently to take a bite out of Apple's market share.

COMPETITION IN THE MP3 PLAYER INDUSTRY

Creative Labs

Creative Labs first became famous for its Sound Blaster sound cards, which set the standard in PC audio in 1989. Since that time, Creative had been an

Exhibit 7   **Customer Satisfaction with MP3 Players, Based on a Reader Survey by *PC Magazine*, 2005 (Scale: 10 = High; 1 = Low)**

Brand of MP3 Players	Sound Quality	Ease of Use	Reliability	Overall Satisfaction
Apple	8.8	8.8	8.5	8.6
Creative	8.2	7.5	7.9	7.6
Dell	8.1	7.9	7.9	7.7
iRiver	8.6	7.2	8.3	7.9
RCA	7.4	7.0	7.3	6.8
Rio	7.8	7.5	7.5	7.1
SanDisk	7.7	6.9	7.7	7.1
Sony	8.0	7.4	7.7	7.3
Average	8.1	7.5	7.9	7.6

Source: Compiled by the case authors from information in *PC Magazine* November 8, 2005, www.pcmag.com (accessed January 8, 2006).

industry leader in PC audio technology and had built a large user base and strong brand name in this area. Leveraging this position, Creative offered the broadest and most diverse product line of MP3 players. Additionally, Creative had won the prestigious Best of CES (Consumer Electronics Show) Award three years in a row with its Zen Portable Media Center in 2004, the Zen Microphoto in 2005, and the Zen Vision:M in 2006. The 30GB Zen Vision:M ($299), which also was named the best overall product at CES in 2006, was about the same size as an iPod 30GB, although twice as thick, and could play back music, video, and photos; it also included a personal organizer that would sync with Microsoft Outlook to transfer the user's calendar, contacts, and task list. This player was viewed as the first real competition to the iPod video, as it would hold about as much content as the iPod but had a superior screen, a battery that lasted twice as long as the iPod's, an FM tuner, and a voice recorder.

Creative's product line also included:

- The 30GB Zen Vision ($399) multimedia player, which used Windows Media Center Edition software and allowed users to listen to, record, and play back WMAs and MP3s (up to 16,000 songs) and movies and television shows (up to 120 hours of video), to view photos (over 20,000), and to listen to and record FM radio.
- The 20GB Zen Sleek ($230) photo player, which held up to 10,000 songs or thousands of photos and featured a 19-hour rechargeable battery, a voice recorder, an FM radio tuner, and an organizer that would sync with Microsoft Outlook.

- The 8GB Zen Microphoto ($249), which featured a 15-hour rechargeable battery, a color screen, 10 different colors, an FM radio and recorder, a personal organizer that synced with Microsoft Outlook, a sleep timer, and a capacity of 4,000 songs
- The 5GB Zen Neeon ($199), which was offered in six colors and had an LED that had seven color options. This player held 2,500 songs, included a 16-hour rechargeable battery, an FM tuner and recorder, a voice recorder, and a line-in port that allowed users to recorder directly from a CD player, a record player, or a mixing turntable.
- The flash-based 512MB ($109) or 1GB ($139.99) Zen Nano Plus, which was about the size of the iPod shuffle, was offered in 10 colors, used a single AAA battery (for up to 18 hours of playback), and held up to 500 songs. The Zen Nano offered a monochrome LED, an FM tuner, a voice recorder, and a line-in recorder.

Like the other hard-drive models, the Nomad Zen Xtra players doubled as external hard drives and could carry any type of files, not just music or MP3 files. Creative's players also allowed users to slow down a song while it was playing without ruining the pitch or to speed up an audio file (such as a book) without making it sound nonsensical.[6] Downsides to the Creative products were that the car adapter kit had to be purchased separately and that the user had to purchase online music from other sources.

Creative also offered nine MP3 players under the MuVo brand, ranging from the Creative MuVo Micro, which was offered in eight colors, claimed a

15-hour battery life from a single AAA battery, and included an FM tuner and the ability to record from the tuner, to the MuVo Sport ($99), which was a splash-proof 256MB player that offered memory expansion through SD or MMC cards and included a stopwatch, an armband, and a case as well as an FM tuner.

In Creative's fiscal year ending June 30, 2005, the company experienced an operating loss of $68.5 million on a net sales of $1.2 billion, as compared to an operating income of $44.2 million on net sales of $814 million in 2004. However, the company had strongly reinforced its dedication to the MP3 player market in 2006 and beyond, and had declared its intention to be a leader in this dynamic market.

Dell

Dell was best known for its direct business model in the personal computer industry and had the leading market share in the United States and worldwide in 2005. In fiscal year 2006, Dell reported a net income of approximately $3.6 billion on net revenues of $55.9 billion (a 14 percent increase in net revenue from 2005). A longtime supplier of customized PCs, Dell was a relatively new entry to the personal electronics market, introducing the Dell Digital Jukebox (Dell DJ), a personal MP3 player that was a direct competitor to Apple's hard-drive players, in October 2003.

As with most other MP3 players, Dell DJ users could either download music from the Internet to the device or "rip" tracks from their CD collection and load them onto the device. The Dell DJ was both physically and technically similar to the iPod and, in early 2005, was available in three hard-drive models. The 5GB Pocket DJ (similar to the iPod Mini) held 2,500 songs ($179); the 20GB DJ held about 9,900 songs (128-bit rate) and sold for $179; and the 30GB model held up to 15,000 songs compressed at the same bit rate and sold regularly for $299 (but was occasionally sold by Dell for as low as $254). The Dell DJ also claimed 12 hours of battery life with continuous play, although some consumers found that the device could last for up to 23 hours of play.[7] Additionally, the Dell DJ, like any other voice recorder, allowed the user to record sound, while the iPod users had to purchase a kit that allowed external sound recording.

Although a relatively late entrant to the MP3 player market, Dell had long recognized consumers' interest in, and demand for, electronics that catered to digital music fans. As early as 1999, Dell had begun offering PC customization features such as a CD-recordable disk drive, specialized software for managing a digital music library, and of course the jukebox software necessary to play all the digital music on a PC. Dell saw its recent forays into computer peripherals and other electronics such as the Digital Jukebox as a natural extension of its product line. Dell was committed to building a relatively diversified product line to afford the company a more constant and steady stream of income than it realized on personal computers alone. Overall, Dell's product rated well against Apple and other competitors, especially given the size and strength of the company and its success in other electronics areas. Although some critics argued that it was not as aesthetically pleasing or quite as easy to use as the iPod, the Dell DJ was considered a very solid contender in the MP3 player market. With Dell's price advantage and much more flexibility concerning where users could shop for their digital music, it was suggested that many consumers might decide the iPod was not worth the extra cash and lack of options.

In September 2005, Dell introduced the DJ Ditty, a 512MB flash player that was about the size of an iPod shuffle but included a screen and an integrated FM tuner. The Ditty weighed only 1.29 ounces, held 220 songs, and would play for up to 14 hours. In October 2005, Dell announced that in 2006 it would offer a third-generation Dell DJ and Pocket DJ that would be capable of receiving XM radio, with the appropriate docking equipment, and would be able to play recorded XM radio streams. It was expected that the third-generation DJs would offer a color screen, as opposed to the second-generation's monochrome blue display. However, in January 2006, the only Dell-branded MP3 player offered at the company's Web site was the Ditty, but customers could purchase a variety of 5GB, 8GB, 20GB, and 30GB Creative Labs MP3 players from Dell's site. While Dell had announced a 2006 launch of its third generation of players in October 2005, the lack of any Dell micro-drive or hard-drive players on the company's site left its future in the MP3 player industry unclear.

iRiver

In 2005, iRiver produced multimedia players, hard-drive-based players, flash-based players, and CD players. The company's 20GB multimedia player, the PMC-120 ($499.99), offered a widescreen color display (3.5 inches) and used Microsoft's Media Center interface to connect with Windows Media Player. The PMC-120 held 80 hours of video or

600 hours of music and offered a rechargeable battery that provided 5 hours of video playback or up to 14 hours of audio playback. The iRiver H10 audio jukebox players included two 20GB ($299) models, as well as a 6GB ($279) and a 5GB ($229) player. The H10 MP3 players were the first to be fully compatible with Microsoft's PlaysForSure platform and allowed users to play music or view photos; they also included an integrated FM tuner and recorder, an integrated voice recorder, and a rechargeable battery that lasted approximately 16 hours. Furthermore, the user interface of the iRiver models was versatile, allowing users to customize the buttons and the method of scrolling through the music. Like RCA, Rio, and Creative, iRiver users could shop for music at almost any online store other than Sony's or Apple's. Additionally, the screens of iRiver's players included a significant amount of information about the song currently playing, as well as the status of the machine, such as volume and battery levels.

In its Ultra Portable Players category, iRiver also offered seven flash players, ranging from the u10 multimedia player, offered in 1GB and 512MB models, to the 100 series, offered in 256MB and 128MB models. All of the players in this category played WMA and MP3 music and offered an integrated FM tuner and recorder, and a voice recorder. The 1GB u10 ($249) played music (up to 34 hours of WMA or MP3) and video, displayed photos, and included some limited games, an ultrabright 2.2-inch screen, and a rechargeable battery that would last up to 28 hours. The T30 series, offered in 1GB ($149.99) and 512MB ($99.99) models, offered up to 24 hours of battery life on a single AAA battery and could record music from any source, with no PC required. The T10 series, offered in 1GB ($199.99) and 512MB models ($149.99), had a color display and played for up to 45 hours on a single AA battery. The 700 series ranged in size from 1GB ($179.99) to 128MB ($79.99), but also offered a waterproof case ($99.99) that allowed users to take their iRiver player swimming or surfing. At the low end, iRiver offered its 100 series in 256MB ($99.99) and 128MB ($79.99) models. Even these low-end players offered a screen, an FM tuner, an integrated voice and FM recorder, and long battery life from a single AA battery.

At the end of 2005, iRiver had a dominant position in Korea's MP3 player market. The Korea-based ReignCom, iRiver's parent company, estimated that the company controlled 50 percent of the Korean market. In the U.S. market, ReignCom acknowledged that it was having a more difficult time, but it intended for iRiver to capture 15 percent of the North American and global hard-drive MP3 player market. Additionally, ReignCom intended future iRiver portable media players to be Wi-Fi enabled and to include more portable Internet and gaming applications.

RCA

RCA was owned and manufactured by Thomson Worldwide, which earned a net income of 373 million euros in 2004, up from 26 million euros in 2003. Thompson's RCA division released its first portable MP3 player, called the Lyra, in 1999. In 2005, RCA offered a relatively broad range of players, including the Lyra.2780 portable multimedia player, flash players (ranging from 128MB to 1GB, some with secure digital expansion slots), hard-drive players (with 5GB or less of capacity except the Lyra 2780, with 20GB capacity), and the Lyra CD player with MP3 playback. RCA's Lyra players supported either MP3 or WMA music files, which allow users to shop for music from any online music store or subscription service.

Similar to other MP3 players with internal hard drives, the Lyra players could be used for file or data storage, similar to a computer hard drive. The Lyra 2780 ($399.99) featured a 20B hard drive that could store up to 80 hours of video and a compact flash slot to allow users to easily transfer audio or video to the player, or to view pictures from a digital camera. Lyra's other three models of hard-drive players were similar to other industry offerings and included the 5GB RD2763 ($179.99), which featured a built-in FM transmitter for playing music in a car; the 4GB RD2762 ($199.99), which featured a color screen; and the 5GB RD2765 ($229.99), which offered a color screen with icons, a JPG viewer for album art, and upgraded earphones.

RCA's line of flash-based players offered more variety than its hard-drive players. The flash-based Lyras included:

- The M100 ($119.99) series, which was a 1GB player that had a screen and plugged directly into a computer like a thumb drive.
- The RD 22 series, which ranged in size from 256MB ($99.99) to 1GB ($169.99) and featured an LCD screen, a 50-hour battery life, a digital FM tuner with FM record, a stopwatch, a calorie counter, and a pulse rate monitor.
- The RD10 series, which ranged in size from 128MB ($89.99) to 256MB ($149.99) and in-

cluded a digital FM turner and an expansion card slot for external SD/MMC memory.

- The RD 23 series, which featured a dual orientation backlit LCD screen that allowed users to view the LCD from multiple angles, and ranged in size from 256MB ($99.99) to 1GB ($169.99). These players also included a digital FM tuner with FM record and allowed for voice recording and line-in recording form multiple sources.

RCA's Lyras shipped with MusicMatch Jukebox software, which users could install on their computer to allow music to be loaded and unloaded from their MP3 player. The MusicMatch software also played the music on the PC itself and allowed users to convert and transfer music from their own CDs to their MP3 players.

Rio

Rio was the second company to introduce an MP3 player in the United States when it launched the Rio in 1998, but by 2005 the company was fighting to survive in the dynamic industry. Recognizing Rio's position, its parent company D&M Holdings Inc. decided to exit the business and sold Rio's assets to SigmaTel Inc., a leading supplier of integrated circuits for the portable digital audio player market. With this acquisition, one of the founders of the MP3 player industry was out of the game. SigmaTel believed that it could leverage its production efficiencies and Rio's brand name to revive the struggling MP3 player manufacturer, and by January 2006 the company listed four models of MP3 players on its site. However, these models were not available from major online retailers such as Amazon.com. The models listed on Rio's site, all MP3 and WMA compatible, included:

- The 5GB Rio Carbon ($130), a 5GB player (competitive with the iPod Mini) that held about 1,250 songs compressed at 128 Kbps. The unit could be charged through an electrical outlet or through a computer's USB port, and the rechargeable battery's life was claimed to be 20 hours. The Carbon also allowed voice recordings, like the Dell, and was supported on either PC or Mac operating systems. The carbon was available in a pearl-colored casing.
- The 2.5GB Rio ce2100, a hard-drive model that held about 625 songs. Its 20-hour rechargeable battery could be charged either from a computer or an electrical wall outlet.

- The Rio Forge, a flash-based player ranging from 128MB to 512MB and included a memory expansion slot, a stopwatch and lap timer, an FM tuner, and a battery life of up to 20 hours.
- Rio's se510, was basically the same as the Forge. While it did not offer an FM tuner, it did include an armband for wearing the unit while working out.

SanDisk

A new entrant in the flash-based MP3 player market, SanDisk, a leader in digital memory manufacturing, shipped its first players in May 2005. SanDisk's original offerings included the 512MB Sansa e130 (240 songs in WMA format) and the 1GB Sansa e140 (up to 480 songs in WMA format). SanDisk's players featured an SD slot for additional storage and a digital FM radio receiver, and they were claimed to be able to last up to 17 hours on a single AAA battery. SanDisk's players also offered a multiline backlit LCD that provided the title, artists, and album of the song currently being played. In September 2005, SanDisk began offering a car transmitter that would allow users to play MP3 music through a car radio, and a portable speaker dock for Sansa MP3 players. In 2006, SanDisk planned aggressively expand its product line to include:

- The SanDisk Sansa e200, which would be offered in 2GB (480 songs), 4GB (960 songs), and 6GB (1,440 songs) capacities. The e200 series would feature a metal case, a color screen, a removable rechargeable battery, a microSD memory expansion slot, and a digital FM tuner and recorder.
- The SanDisk Sansa c10, which SanDisk planned to offer in 1GB (240 songs) and 2B (480 songs) capacities. The c10 models featured a color screen, a digital FM tuner and recorder, and one AAA battery.
- The Sansa m200, which became available in January 2006 and was offered in 512MB ($79.99, 120 songs), 1GB ($119.99, 240 songs) and 2GB ($159.99, 480 songs) capacities. The m200 series featured 19 hours of play from a single AAA battery, an FM tuner and recorder, a voice recorder with a built-in microphone, and a backlit LCD display.
- The SanDisk Sansa e100 series, which was introduced in January 2006 and was offered in 512MB ($79.99, 120 songs) and 1GB ($119.99,

240 songs) capacities. The e10 players featured a backlit multiline LCD display, a digital FM tuner, and up to 17 hours of play from a single AAA battery.

- The SanDisk digital audio player, which was introduced in January 2006 in 256MB ($49.99, 60 songs), 512MB ($79.99, 120 songs), and 1GB ($119.99, 240 songs) capacities. The digital audio players featured 15 hours of play from a single AAA battery, a digital FM tuner, a voice recorder with a built-in microphone, and a backlit multiline display.

While SanDisk operated only in the flash-based seg-ment, there was little doubt that the company intended to leverage its expertise in flash-based manufacturing and distribution to compete vigorously in the MP3 player industry.

Sony

In fiscal-year 2005, Sony Corporation earned $1.5 billion in net income (up 85 percent from 2004) on revenues of $66.9 billion in revenue (down 4.5 percent from 2004). Sony became the original pioneer in the portable music industry when it introduced the Walkman portable cassette tape player in the 1980s. That product spawned dozens of imitations and look-alikes. Prior to 2004, Sony had been active in the digital music industry but had resisted selling portable players that were MP3-compatible, arguing that its proprietary compression technology, Acoustic TRansform Adaptive Coding (ATRAC3), was superior to MP3. However, in the face of declining sales, Sony relented in August 2004 and released its first hard-drive-based MP3-compatible player, the 20GB Sony Network Walkman, and released an MP3-compatible flash player by year's end. Additionally, Sony allowed users of some earlier hard-drive-based players to upgrade to MP3 compatibility for a fee of $20. However, by this time roles were reversed and Sony was viewed as one of the imitators in the digital music industry.

In 2004 and 2005, Sony expanded its line of MP3 players. New offerings included 40GB Vaio Pocket Digital Music Player ($399), which allowed users to download photos as well as music, and the Psyc Network Walkman, which was intended to be a direct competitor to Apple's Shuffle. The Psyc had the option to shuffle songs and was available in a

256MB model ($89), a 512MB model ($99), and a 1GB model ($149).

This move meant Sony was finally competing on a more level playing field with Apple in terms of the price of the models and their capacities. In terms of physical characteristics, the 20GB Walkman was about 10 percent smaller than the iPod in total volume, was about one-third lighter than the iPod, and had a much better battery life (up to 30 hours).[8] However, critics generally viewed the Network Walkman as somewhat inferior to other MP3 players. The user interface on the machine was found by some to be confusing and difficult to use, and the accompanying computer software for unloading and managing the music was thought to be weaker than the competition. Critics believed that these perceived weaknesses coupled with the company's late entry to the digital music market indicated that the company would encounter significant trouble in overcoming the competition.

In the face of competitive pressures, by January 2006, Sony no longer offered a hard-drive-based MP3 player, but did offer three models of flash-based players, a CD player, a minidisc player, and a boom box that were all MP3 and ATRAC compatible and that were compatible with Sony's Connect online music store. Sony's flash-based models included the Walkman Core, the Walkman Bean, and the Walkman Circ. The Walkman Core was available in 512MB ($129.95, 345 songs) and 1GB models ($149.95, 695 songs) and included a three-line display and a rechargeable battery that lasted up to 50 hours and could be quick-charged in 3 minutes for 3 hours of play. The Walkman Bean was a small, ergonomic player that was shaped like a bean and came in white, pink, black, and blue. This model was offered in 512MB ($109.95, 345 songs) and 1GB ($139.95, 695 songs) options and featured a one-line display, a built-in FM tuner and a rechargeable battery that lasted 50 hours and could be quick-charged in 3 minutes for 3 hours of play. The Walkman Circ was a round player that had a diameter about twice the size of a quarter. The Circ was powered by an AA battery that would last up to 70 hours and was offered in both 512MB ($89.95, 345 songs) and 1GB ($119.95, 695 songs) sizes, which both included a two-line display.

Sony's CD-based MP3 players included a portable CD player, a minidisc player, and a boom box. Sony's MP3 CD Walkman ($39.95) featured a compact full-circle design and MP3 playback of prerecorded tracks or user-recorded CD-R/RW media. The Hi-MD Walkman Digital Music Player ($299.95) offered a six-line display, a remote control, the ability to record from multiple sources using the line-in, mic-in capabilities, a digital amplifier, and a rechargeable battery that would last up to 33 hours. The Psyc ($79.95) MP3/ATRAC3 CD/Tuner Boom-box included a two-line display, a remote control with 10-key direct access, an AM/FM digital tuner, and AC/DC power; it could hold 490 songs (compressed with Sony's proprietary ATRAC3plus) on a single CD.

THE FUTURE

Heading into 2006, Apple had much to be excited about. During the 2005 holiday season, the company had sold 14 million digital media players, up from 4.5 million in the same period of 2004, and reported record revenues for the quarter of $5.7 billion compared to $3.5 billion in the same quarter of 2004. In the digital music segment, Apple had also expanded its agreements with automobile manufacturers to build iPod accessories, such as iPod docks, into new cars. Additionally, Apple introduced a new line of Apple computers that were based on Intel chips six months ahead of schedule. Apple also announced that, in February 2006, it would ship its new MacBook Pro, which was four times faster than the company's current PowerBooks and was designed in a manner consistent with the company's dedication to products that were powerful, easy to use, and aesthetically pleasing. These new Macs included a program named iLife '06, which included tools to enable users to edit movies, digital photographs, and homegrown music, as well as iWeb, which allowed users to easily create and upload Web sites, blogs, and podcasts. Additionally, the new MacBooks were expected to have a new piece of software named Front Row, which was targeted squarely at Microsoft's Media Center. This software served as a simple user interface for accessing digital media on the computer.

However, Apple also faced some significant challenges. Microsoft planned on releasing its new operating system, Vista, late in 2006. Vista was designed to enhance the ease of use of Windows-based computers and to make multimedia content development and editing easier. Additionally, in the rush to provide digital entertainment to the living room, competitors were becoming more diverse. Microsoft's new gaming console, the Xbox 360, integrated the gaming console and the PC and was set to become even more widely available. Sony's and Nintendo's counters to the new Xbox 360 were expected sometime early in 2006. In the digital music market, Microsoft partnered with MTV to announce a new online media service named Urge, which was targeted directly at Apple's iTunes. Microsoft planned, upon Urge's launch, to have 2 million songs available for purchase, and to offer video clips. Unlike iTunes, Urge was expected to offer a subscription service as well as allowing customers to purchase individual songs.

In assessing Apple's future, most analysts agreed that Apple would undoubtedly continue its well-established track record of introducing innovative, high-quality consumer electronics to the masses. However, many believed that it would be very difficult for Apple to maintain its substantial market share indefinitely, recognizing that it was much easier to control 60 percent of the digital music player market when only 11 percent of the U.S. population owned the devices than it would be when they were more common. Additionally, analysts acknowledged that Apple had once lost a big lead in the operating systems market because it refused to license to others and it appeared that Apple was making the same gamble in the MP3 player and digital music industries. The question was whether Apple had enough of a lead to maintain its status as the market leader. Would the company's refusal to license its technology to others eventually relegate it to the same niche position in the MP3 player industry that the company occupied in computers?

Endnotes

[1]Peter J. Howe, "Powered by iPod, Apple Splits Stock," *Knight Ridder Tribune Business News*, February 12, 2005, p. 1.
[2]www.snarc.net/pda/pda-treatise.htm.
[3]www.inventors.about.com.
[4]www.redherring.com.
[5]Steve Smith, "iPod's Lessons," *Twice New York* 19, no. 5 (July 26, 2004), p. 12.

[6]Bill Machrone, "New Music Players Gun for the iPod," *PC Magazine*, August 17, 2004, pp. 34–35.
[7]Peter Rojas, "Feeding Power-Hungry Gadgets," *Money* 33, no. 5 (May 2004), pp. 131–32.
[8]Walter S. Mossberg, "The Mossberg Solution: Sony's iPod Killer," *The Wall Street Journal (Eastern Ed.)*, July 28, 2004, p. D1.

Case 8

Netflix versus Blockbuster versus Video-on-Demand

Braxton Maddox
The University of Alabama

Arthur A. Thompson
The University of Alabama

Heading into 2006, Netflix had convinced most skeptics that its pioneering business model for renting DVDs online could be profitable. Netflix had attracted some 3.6 million subscribers who paid monthly fees ranging from $9.99 to $47.99; subscribers went to Netflix's Web site, selected one or more movies from its library of 55,000 titles, and received the DVDs by first-class mail within one to three business days. Subscribers could keep a DVD for as long as they wished, with no due dates or late fees, although they were limited to having a certain number of DVDs in their possession at any one time (the number depended on which fee plan they had chosen). A unique aspect of Netflix's business model was that it provided subscribers with all the benefits of a typical movie rental store but without the hassle of having to drive to the store, pick out DVDs, and return the rentals by a specified time.

However, Netflix's rapid growth and profit outlook had a major downside—they had induced movie rental leader Blockbuster to enter the online movie rental segment and try to horn in on the market opportunity that Netflix was exploiting. Amazon.com was also looking at entering the market. Wal-Mart had pursued online movie rentals for a short time, but in May 2005 it decided to enter into an arrangement with Netflix whereby Wal-Mart would refer customers interested in online DVD rentals to Netflix while Netflix would steer customers wanting to purchase a movie DVD to www.walmart.com. Wal-Mart's existing DVD rental customers were

offered the option of becoming Netflix subscribers at the current Wal-Mart rate for one year from their sign-up date. Wal-Mart was motivated to team up with Netflix because its own online movie rental business presented an assortment of troublesome operating problems and was unprofitable, and because it saw more opportunity in focusing on the growing numbers of customers who were buying movie DVDs at www.walmart.com. Entry barriers into online DVD rentals were relatively low, but the barriers to profitability were considered rather high because of the need to attract a subscriber base of 2 to 4 million in order to operate at a profit.

Reed Hastings, founder and CEO of Netflix, was concerned about how to outcompete Blockbuster, and he was also concerned about the competitive threat posed by video-on-demand (VOD). Several new competitors were gearing up to offer movies on a pay-per-view basis to Internet customers with high-speed broadband connections. Providing VOD had been technically possible for a number of years, but VOD had not garnered substantial usage because movie studios were leery of the potential for movie pirating and doubtful of whether they could profit from a VOD business model. Nonetheless, the major Hollywood studios had formed a joint venture called MovieLink to offer VOD to the public. And several ambitious start-up companies, like San Francisco–based GreenCine, were offering online movie viewing to consumers who had Microsoft's Windows Media Player installed on their PCs and a broadband Internet connection. Once they downloaded a movie, consumers could play it on their desktop or laptop PCs or connect the PC to a TV.

Hastings's challenge was how to sustain Netflix's growth and put together a strategy that would protect Netflix's industry-leading position against mounting competition. In Hastings's view, "No one is going to out-hare Netflix. Our danger is in a tortoise attack."

COMPANY BACKGROUND AND STRATEGY

After successfully founding his first company, Pure Software, in 1991, Reed Hastings engineered several acquisitions and grew Pure Software into one of the 50 largest software companies in the world—the company's principal product was a debugging tool for engineers. When Pure Software was acquired by Rational Software in 1997 for $750 million, Hastings used the money from selling his shares of Pure Software to help fund his pursuit of another, entirely different business venture. Sensing the opportunity for online movie rentals in a climate where

the popularity of the Interet was mushrooming, he founded Netflix in 1997, launched the online subscription service in 1999, and attracted a subscriber base of over 2 million in just four years (America Online took six years to acquire the same number of subscribers). Exhibit 1 shows trends in Netflix's subscriber growth.

By 2005, in what proved to be a rapidly evolving marketplace, Netflix had made a name for itself. It was the world's largest online DVD movie rental service, with 2005 revenues approaching $700 million and a selection of movie titles that far exceeded those available in local brick-and-mortar movie rental stores. Its strategy and market success were predicated on providing an expansive selection of DVDs, an easy way to choose movies, and fast, free delivery—the goal was to deliver customer value by eliminating the hassle involved in choosing, renting, and returning movies. Netflix's DVD lineup included everything from the latest big Hollywood releases to hard-to-locate documentaries to independent films to TV shows and how-to videos.

Exhibit 1   **Subscriber Data for Netflix, 2000–2005**

	1999	2000	2001	2002	2003	2004	First Nine Months, 2005
Total subscribers at beginning of period	0	107,000	292,000	456,000	857,000	1,487,000	2,610,000
Gross subscriber additions during period	127,000	515,000	566,000	1,140,000	1,571,000	2,716,000	2,573,000
Subscriber cancellations during the period	20,000	330,000	402,000	739,000	941,000	1,593,000	1,591,000
Total subscribers at end of period	107,000	292,000	456,000	857,000	1,487,000	2,610,000	3,592,000
Net subscriber additions during the period	107,000	185,000	164,000	401,000	630,000	1,123,000	982,000
Free trial subscribers*	n.a.	n.a.	56,000	61,000	71,000	124,000	169,000
Subscriber acquisition cost	$110.79	$49.96	$37.16	$31.39	$31.79	$36.09	$36.92

n.a. = Not available.

*First-time subscribers automatically were eligible for a free two-week trial; membership fees began after the two-week trial expired (unless the membership was canceled).

Members had the choice of eight subscription plans:

- $9.99, unlimited DVDs, one title out at a time.
- $11.99, four DVDs a month, two titles out at a time.
- $14.99, unlimited DVDs, two titles out at a time.
- $17.99, unlimited DVDs, three titles out at a time.
- $23.99, unlimited DVDs, four titles out at a time.
- $29.99, unlimited DVDs, five titles out at a time.
- $35.99, unlimited DVDs, six titles out at a time.
- $41.99, unlimited DVDs, seven titles out at a time.
- $47.99, unlimited DVDs, eight titles out at a time.

The most popular plan in 2005 was $17.99 a month. Subscribers could cancel anytime. Subscribers were drawn to Netflix's policies of no late fees and no due dates (which eliminated the hassle of getting DVDs back to local rental stores by the designated due date), and the convenience of being provided a postage-paid return envelope for mailing the DVDs back to Netflix. Netflix provided subscribers extensive information about DVD movies, including critic reviews, member reviews, online trailers, ratings, and personalized movie recommendations. Subscribers could create a "wish list" of all the movies they wanted to see, change the list at any time, and use the list to order their next round of movies.

Netflix's Cinematch Software Technology

Netflix had developed proprietary software technology, called Cinematch, which enabled it to provide subscribers with personalized movie recommendations every time they visited the Netflix Web site. These personalized recommendations were based on a subscriber's individual likes and dislikes (determined by their wish list, rental history, and movie ratings). Cinematch was an Oracle database that organized Netflix's library of movies into clusters of similar movies and analyzed how customers rated them after they rented them. Those customers who rated similar movies in similar clusters were then matched as like-minded viewers. When a customer was online, Cinematch looked at the clusters the subscriber had rented from in the past, determined which movies the customer had yet to rent in that cluster, and recommended only those movies in the cluster that had been highly rated by viewers. The recommendations helped subscribers quickly identify films they might like to rent and allowed Netflix to promote lesser-known, high-quality films to subscribers who otherwise might have missed spotting them in the company's massive 55,000-film library (to which new titles were continuously being added).

In December 2005 Netflix had more than 1 billion movie ratings from customers in its database, and the average subscriber had rated more than 200 movies. On average, more than 85 percent of the movie titles in the Netflix library of offerings were rented each quarter, an indication of the effectiveness of the company's Cinematch software in steering subscribers to movies of interest. Netflix management believed that over 50 percent of its rentals came from the recommendations generated by Cinematch.

Shipping

Netflix had 37 regional shipping centers scattered across the United States, giving it one-business-day delivery capability for 90 percent of its subscribers. Additional shipping centers were on the drawing board.

Netflix had developed sophisticated software to track its inventory and minimize delivery times. Netflix's system allowed the distribution centers to communicate to determine the fastest way of getting DVDs to customers. When a customer placed an order for a specific DVD, the system first looked for that DVD at the shipping center closest to the customer. If that center didn't have the DVD in stock, the system then moved the next closest center and checked there. The search continued until the DVD was found, at which point the shipping center was provided with the information needed to initiate the order fulfillment and shipping process. If the DVD was unavailable anywhere in the system, it was waitlisted. The system then moved to the customer's next choice and the process started all over. And no matter where the DVD was sent from, the system knew to print the return label on the prepaid envelope to send the DVDs to the shipping center closest to the customer to reduce return mail times and permit more efficient use of the company's DVD inventory.

In 2005, Netflix was shipping more than 1 million DVDs a day. It had an inventory of around 20 million DVDs (which was growing as the subscriber base increased). In the first nine months of 2005, Netflix spent $84.2 million on the acquisition of new DVDs; it had an arrangement with movie studios to purchase new-release DVDs for an upfront fee plus a percentage of revenue earned from rentals for a defined period. The company's September 30, 2005, balance sheet indicated that its DVD holdings had a net value of $52.7 million (after depreciation). New-release DVDs were amortized over one year; the useful life of back-library titles (some of which qualified as classics) were amortized over periods of one to three years (since they continued to be rented from time to time because of the Cinematch recommendations). DVDs that the company expected to sell at the end of their useful lives carried a salvage value of $3 per DVD; DVDs that the company did not expect to sell were assigned a salvage value of zero.

Target Customers and Customer Satisfaction

The company's subscriber base consisted of three types of customers: those who liked the convenience of home delivery, bargain hunters who were enthused about being able to watch 10 or more movies a month at an economical price (on the $17.99 plan, 12 movies a month equated to a rental fee of $1.50 per movie), and movie buffs who wanted access to a wide selection of films.

In a survey by Netflix, customers said they rented twice as many movies per month as they did prior to joining Netflix. New Netflix customers also said they were immediately more satisfied with their home-entertainment experience than they were prior to joining Netflix. And 9 out of 10 customers said they were so satisfied with the service that they recommended the service to family and friends. Netflix was the top-rated Web site for customer satisfaction according to a spring 2005 survey by ForeSee Results and FGI Research. In the fall of 2005, *Fast Company* magazine named Netflix the winner of its annual Customers First Award.

Growth Strategy

Netflix's growth strategy had three primary components:

- Continue to innovate and enhance the consumer experience.
- Use Netflix's market-leading position to lead the transition to high-definition DVDs and eventually digital downloading.
- Focus on rapid subscriber growth in order to
  —Maintain market leadership.
  —Realize economies of scale.

Netflix's strategic intent was to be the world's largest and most influential movie supplier.

Netflix's Performance

The company's recent operating statistics and financial statement data are shown in Exhibits 2 and 3. Netflix's decline in profit in 2005 reflected the adverse effects of lower subscription prices that had been instituted in late 2004. Concerned about mounting competitive pressures—particularly from Blockbuster, which announced its entry into the online rental segment in August 2004—Netflix had halted expansion into Britain and Canada and dropped the monthly subscription price on its most popular plan from $21.99 to $17.99 starting November 1, 2004. At the lower $17.99 price, Netflix believed it could continue to grow its subscriber base but would only be able to break even (given the $48 per year revenue loss for many of its subscribers). Blockbuster responded in December 2004 with a price drop from $19.99 to $14.99 per month on its most popular plan, which allowed three DVDs out at a time.

Following Blockbuster's announced entry into online movie rentals and Netflix's November price cut, investors immediately grew nervous about Netflix's profitability and competitive staying power—the company's stock price dropped sharply from around $35 per share in late July 2004 to $10 to $12 per share in the November 2004–February 2005 period. Starting March 2005, the stock began a climb back to the $25 to $30 range, as investors took comfort in Netflix's continued growth in subscribers, the partnership arrangement with Wal-Mart (which had eliminated a prime competitive threat), the company's return to profitability in the second and third quarters of 2005, and upbeat management forecasts for 2006.

Exhibit 2   **Netflix's Statement of Operations, 2000–2005 (in thousands of $, except per share data)**

| | Year Ended December 31, | | | | | |
Statement of Operations Data	2000	2001	2002	2003	2004	First Nine Months, 2005
Revenues:						
Subscriptions	$ 35,894	$ 74,255	$150,818	$270,410	$500,611	$489,213
Sales	—	1,657	1,988	1,833	5,617	3,741
Total revenues	35,894	75,912	152,806	272,243	506,228	492,954
Cost of revenues:						
Subscriptions	24,861	49,088	77,044	147,736	273,401	291,821
Sales	—	819	1,092	624	3,057	2,542
Total cost of revenues	24,861	49,907	78,136	148,360	276,458	294,363
Gross profit	11,033	26,005	74,670	123,883	229,770	198,591
Operating expenses:						
Fulfillment	10,247	13,452	19,366	31,274	56,609	51,798
Technology and development	16,823	17,734	14,625	17,884	22,906	22,674
Marketing	25,727	21,031	35,783	49,949	98,027	95,008
General and administrative	6,990	4,658	6,737	9,585	16,287	17,925
Restructuring charges	—	671	—	—	—	—
Stock-based compensation	9,714	6,250	8,832	10,719	16,587	10,995
Total operating expenses	69,501	63,796	85,343	119,411	210,416	198,400
Operating income (loss)	(58,468)	(37,791)	(10,673)	4,472	19,354	191
Other income (expense):						
Interest and other income	1,645	461	1,697	2,457	2,592	3,788
Interest and other expense	(1,451)	(1,852)	(11,972)	(417)	(170)	(54)
Net income before income taxes	(58,274)	(39,182)	(20,948)	6,512	21,776	3,925
Provision for income taxes	—	—	—	—	181	109
Net income (loss)	$(58,274)	$(39,182)	$ (20,948)	$ 6,512	$ 21,595	$ 3,816
Net income (loss) per share:						
Basic	$ (20.61)	$ (10.73)	$ (0.74)	$ 0.14	$ 0.42	$ 0.07
Diluted	(20.61)	(10.73)	(0.74)	0.10	0.33	0.06
Weighted-average shares outstanding:						
Basic	2,828	3,652	28,204	47,786	51,988	53,237
Diluted	2,828	3,652	28,204	62,884	64,713	64,928

Source: Netflix's 2004 10-K Report and company press release, October 19, 2005.

Netflix expected to end 2005 with about 4 million subscribers, revenues of close to $685 million (versus $506 million in 2004), and net income of $5 to $10 million (versus $21.6 million in 2004); the lower profits in 2005 were a direct result of having lowered subscription fees in November 2004.

Netflix reported a loss of $8.8 million in the first quarter of 2005, a profit of $5.7 million in the second quarter, and a profit of $6.9 million in the third quarter. Management's latest forecast for 2006 called for 5.65 million subscribers at year-end, revenues of at least $940 million, and pretax income

Exhibit 3 **Selected Balance Sheet and Cash Flow Data for Netflix, 2000–2005 (in thousands of $)**

	2000	2001	2002	2003	2004	September 30, 2005
Selected Balance Sheet Data						
Cash and cash equivalents	$ 14,895	$ 16,131	$ 59,814	$ 89,894	$174,461	$181,886
Short-term investments	—	—	43,796	45,297	—	—
Current assets	n.a.	19,552	107,075	138,946	187,346	191,198
Net investment in DVD library	n.a.	3,633	9,972	22,238	42,158	52,735
Total assets	52,488	41,630	130,530	176,012	251,793	278,302
Current liabilities	n.a.	26,208	40,426	63,019	94,910	98,755
Working capital*	(1,655)	(6,656)	66,649	75,927	92,436	93,163
Notes payable, less current portion	1,843	—	—	—	—	—
Subordinated notes payable	—	2,799	—	—	—	—
Redeemable convertible preferred stock	101,830	101,830	—	—	—	—
Stockholders' equity	(73,267)	(90,504)	89,356	112,708	156,283	178,672
Cash flow data						
Net cash provided by operating activities	$(22,706)	$ 4,847	$ 40,114	$ 89,792	$147,571	$ 99,245
Net cash used in investing activities	(24,972)	(12,670)	(67,301)	(64,677)	(68,381)	(99,307)
Net cash provided by financing activities	48,375	9,059	70,870	4,965	5,599	7,487

*Defined as current assets minus current liabilities.

Sources: 2002 10-K report, 2004 10-K report, and company press release October 19, 2005.

of $50 to $60 million. One Wall Street analyst had recently forecast that Netflix could have 7 million subscribers by the end of 2007. Adams Media Research and Netflix had projected that there would be more than 20 million online subscribers for DVD movie rentals within the next five to seven years.

MARKET TRENDS IN MOVIE DVDs

The digital video disc (DVD) player was one of the most successful consumer electronic products of all time. As of December 2005, more than 160 million DVD players had been sold since launch and more than 80 million U.S. households had DVD players (many had more than one). DVD playback had worked its way into a number of electronic devices, and DVD recording was expected to be an essential driver of the DVD market. DVD recorders were forecast to surpass sales of play-only DVD players by 2007, with an expected compound annual growth rate of 126 percent.

Consumers could obtain movie DVDs through a wide variety of channels:

- Retail outlets such as Wal-Mart, Target, Circuit City, Best Buy, Office Depot, and Staples.
- Rental outlets such as Blockbuster and Movie Gallery.
- Web sites of both brick-and-mortar retailers (Wal-Mart) and Internet-only retailers such as Amazon.com.
- Online rental services such as Netflix and GreenCine.

- PC downloads from Web sites such as Movielink or file-sharing programs such as Kazaa.

According to Kagan Research, consumer spending for in-home movie viewing increased from about $22.6 billion in 2003 to about $25.1 billion in 2004 and was projected to increase to about $33.8 billion by 2009.[1] These numbers represented rental fees and household purchases of videocassettes and DVDs. According to Adams Media Research, DVD sales and rentals amounted to a $23.4 billion market in the United States in 2005, up from $22.0 billion in 2004.[2]

But despite growing sales of DVD players, there were some other factors at work in the marketplace:[3]

- Growth in the sales of DVDs was slowing from double-digit growth to forecasts of single-digit growth in 2006. Online rentals of movie DVDs, computer downloads of music and movie files, video-on-demand (VOD) services, and growing popularity of high-definition TV programs were cited as factors.

- The flood of new and old TV shows on DVDs that had recently hit the marketplace had cut into the sales of movie DVDs—the multidisc sets of TVs shows were more expensive than many new releases of movie DVDs.

- A growing number of households were purchasing digital video recorders (DVRs), which made it simple to record a TV program or movie and then replay it at a convenient time. Many DVR owners were highly attracted to recording movies (and other programs) shown in high definition and then watching them at their convenience.

- Cable companies like Comcast were offering VOD options for many of their premium movie channels. The Starz Entertainment Group claimed that its research showed that Comcast customers who were using the Starz on Demand VOD service tended to reduce their purchases and rentals of movie DVDs due to the ease of using the VOD service.

- Cable and satellite TV companies were expected to expand their VOD services over the next several years and make many more movie titles available to their customers.

- Cable customers with DVRs could readily substitute use of VOD movie offerings from their cable TV provider for purchasing or renting movie DVDs.

- Online rentals and VOD services were not only cutting into sales of movie DVDs but also taking business away from video rental stores. Just as Netflix posed a competitive threat to Blockbuster and Movie Gallery in the United States, market research in Great Britain indicated that one out of every five DVDs rented was rented online.

- Hollywood movie producers were hoping that next-generation, high-definition optical-disc-format DVDs would rejuvenate sales of movie DVDs, but it remained to be seen whether such hopes were well founded, given the growing popularity of DVRs, VOD, and online rentals.

Another factor acting to spur watching movies at home was rapidly growing sales of wide-screen TVs with a 16:9 scale as opposed to the old-style 4:3 scale. Most TV manufacturers had introduced a variety of high-tech TV models with screen sizes up to 72 inches. Prices for wide-screen TVs were dropping rapidly, and picture quality was exceptionally good, if not stunning, on increasing numbers of models. Consumers with wide-screen TVs typically found watching movies at home much more appealing, as compared to those having TVs with 27-inch to 36-inch screens.

BLOCKBUSTER INC.

Blockbuster was the world leader in the videocassette, DVD, and video game rental market, with an estimated 40 percent share of the roughly $13 billion rental market. Founded in Dallas, Texas, in 1985, Blockbuster had grown to over 9,000 company-operated and franchised stores worldwide—in 2005, it had 4,660 company-operated stores in the United States, 2,585 company-operated stores outside the United States, and 1,831 franchised stores (400 of which were in the United States). The company's revenues were derived from rentals of videocassettes for VCRs (11.4 percent of 2004 revenues), DVDs (53.5 percent), video games (8.2 percent), and sales of videotapes, DVDs, and video games (25.3 percent). Revenue from rentals and sales of tapes for VCRs was falling sharply, mainly because more and more households were converting from VCRs to DVD players. Blockbuster's rental revenues from tapes for VCRs had fallen from $1.43 billion in 2003 to $692 million in 2004 to just $150 million in the first nine months of 2005. Its DVD rental revenues had risen from $2.6 billion in 2003 to $3.24 billion in 2004 and accounted for 61.8 percent of rental revenues in first nine months of 2005 (up from 54.9 percent for the comparable period in 2004).

Recent Strategic Moves at Blockbuster's Retail Stores

In September 2000, Blockbuster began marketing DIRECTV system equipment in its U.S. stores; in June 2001, the partnership with DIRECTV was extended to marketing a co-branded pay-per-view movie service that made Blockbuster one of the early entrants into the pay-per-view segment of the home entertainment industry.

In 2002, Blockbuster announced a strategic vision of becoming the complete source for movies and games—rental and retail. Already the leader in movie and game rental market, the company set its sights on increasing its share of the growing retail market by launching a variety promotional programs and expanding its in-store selection of movies and gaming equipment, including hardware, software and accessories. In 2003, it began offering an in-store movie rental subscription program, the Blockbuster Freedom Pass, in approximately 25 percent of its stores. For a flat monthly fee, the Freedom Pass allowed members to rent an unlimited supply of movies without due dates or extended viewing fees for as long as they subscribed to the pass. The Freedom Pass program was rolled out to all U.S. company-operated stores in 2004, and the name was changed to Blockbuster Movie Pass. For $24.99 per month, members could take up to two movies out at a time; for $29.99 per month, they could choose the three-movies-at-a-time option. Both plans entitled customers to watch all the movies they wanted, with no specified return dates and no extended viewing fees. Once customers purchased the pass, their credit card or check card was automatically charged the monthly fee; subscriptions could be cancelled at any time.

To expand its presence in the gaming marketplace, in 2002 Blockbuster purchased the U.K.-based video game retailer Gamestation and proceeded to grow the chain from 64 to more than 150 stores. In the United States, the company began offering a Game

Freedom Pass rental subscription program in all of its U.S. company-operated stores. Customers could purchase a single-month pass for just $19.99 and get unlimited game rentals for 30 consecutive days with a maximum of one game rented at any given time, and no extended viewing fees during the 30 days; a gamer could keep one game for the entire 30 consecutive days or change out the game daily—or even multiple times a day.

Several other initiatives in video games were launched in 2004–2005. Blockbuster began carrying PlayStation portable handheld games for rent in all stores. And it had boosted its games offering by creating a special "Game Rush" section within certain high-traffic Blockbuster stores where customers could rent, sell, and buy new and used game software and hardware. During peak hours, Game Rush sections were staffed by trained game specialists. Blockbuster believed that about half its U.S. stores were suited to having a Game Rush section.

However, despite all these and other strategic initiatives, Blockbuster was a troubled company in 2005. Sales revenues were stagnant at around $6 billion annually (see Exhibit 4), and the company had lost money in five of the past six years. Blockbuster reported net losses of $1.62 billion in 2002, $979 million in 2003, $1.25 billion in 2004, and $606 million through the first nine months of 2005. It had split off from media conglomerate Viacom in October 2004; part of the split-off arrangement involved paying a special one-time $5 dividend (totaling $905 million) to all shareholders, including Viacom (which owned 81.5 percent of Blockbuster's shares prior to the divestiture deal).

Blockbuster's Online Rental Business

Blockbuster entered the online rental segment in August 2004, offering customers a choice of three monthly plans (all with unlimited rentals and no due dates or late fees): (1) a $19.99 plan with three DVDs out at a time, (2) a $29.99 plan with five DVDs out at a time, and (3) a $39.99 plan with eight DVDs out at a time. Customers could choose from 25,000 titles, ranging from classics to new releases. In addition, subscribers were e-mailed two "e-coupons" each month for two free in-store rentals; all Blockbuster Online members were eligible for exclusive deals and discounts at participating Blockbuster stores.

Exhibit 4 Selected Financial and Operating Statistics for Blockbuster Inc., 2002–2005 ($ in millions, except for per share data)

	First Nine Months, 2005	2004	2003	2002
Selected statement of operations data				
Revenues				
Rentals	$3,165.2	$ 4,428.6	$4,533.5	$4,460.4
Merchandise sales	1,114.0	1,532.6	1,281.6	1,019.7
Other	54.6	92.0	96.6	85.8
Total	4,333.8	6,053.2	5,911.7	5,565.9
Cost of rental revenues	1,046.8	1,250.7	1,362.1	1,513.8
Gross margin on rentals	66.9%	71.8%	70.0%	66.1%
Cost of merchandise sold	861.9	1,190.7	1,027.7	844.9
Gross margin on merchandise sales	22.6%	22.3%	19.8%	17.1%
Gross profit	2,425.1	3,611.8	3,521.9	3,207.2
Gross profit margin	56.0%	59.7%	59.6%	57.6%
Operating expenses				
General and administrative	2,147.4	2,835.2	2,605.9	2,369.5
Share-based compensation	—	18.3		
Advertising	227.1	257.4	179.4	249.2
Depreciation	173.0	247.4	266.0	239.1
Impairment of goodwill and other long-lived assets	356.8	1,504.4	1,304.9	—
Amortization of intangibles	1.8	2.3	2.4	1.7
Total	2,906.1	4,865.0	4,358.6	2,859.5
Operating income	(481.0)	(1,253.2)	(836.7)	347.7
Interest expense	(70.0)	(38.1)	(33.1)	(49.5)
Interest income	2.8	3.6	3.1	4.1
Income (loss) before income taxes	(551.0)	(1,286.1)	(867.1)	305.2
Net profit (loss)	$ (606.1)	$(1,248.8)	$ (978.7)	$ 195.9
Earnings per share (diluted)	$(3.30)	$(6.89)	$(5.41)	$1.08
Dividends per share	$0.04	$5.08	$0.08	$0.08
Selected balance sheet data				
Cash and cash equivalents	$ 190.2	$ 330.3	$ 233.4	$ 152.5
Merchandise inventories	352.2	516.6	415.1	452.1
Current assets	866.5	1,217.7	960.3	958.9
Total assets	3,030.4	3,863.4	4,822.0	6,243.8
Current liabilities	1,989.5	1,449.4	1,323.4	1,477.6
Long-term debt, less current portion	300.0	1,044.9	0.7	328.9
Stockholders' equity	465.9	1,062.9	3,188.4	4,100.9
Selected cash flow data				
Net cash flow provided by operations	$ 492.4	$ 1,215.4	$1,430.3	$ 1,462.3
Net cash flow (used for)/provided by investing activities	(741.2)	(1,112.3)	(1,024.6)	(1,314.6)
Net cash flow (used for)/provided by financing activities	112.8	(18.8)	(335.5)	(199.2)
Worldwide Store Data				
Same-store revenue increase (decrease)	(2.9)%	(3.2)%	(2.2)%	5.1%
Company-owned stores, end-of-year	7,245	7,265	7,105	6,907
Franchised stores, end-of-year	1,831	1,829	1,762	1,638
Total stores, end-of-year	9,076	9,094	8,867	8,545

Source: Blockbuster's 2003 10-K report, 2004 10-K report, and third-quarter 2005 10-Q report.

Rentals were shipped from 11 distribution centers to subscribers via first-class mail and usually arrived in one to three business days. Subscribers were provided with a postage-paid envelope for returning the DVDs. Subscribers could create and maintain a personal queue of movies they wished to rent at Blockbuster's Web site. When Blockbuster received return DVDs from subscribers, it automatically shipped the next available titles in the subscriber's rental queue. Management said the online rental service was the latest in a series of initiatives being implemented by Blockbuster to transform itself from a neighborhood movie rental store into an "anywhere, anytime" entertainment destination that eventually would enable customers to rent, buy, or trade movies and games, new or used, in-store and online. The initial response to Blockbuster Online was promising; John Antonico, Blockbuster's CEO, said, "After six weeks, we had more subscribers than Netflix had in a year and a half of existence."

On December 22, 2004, Blockbuster cut the price on its most popular subscription plan from $19.99 per month to $14.99 and announced it was expanding the copy-depth of new-release movies, boosting the number of titles available for online rental to 30,000, and expanding the selection of TV shows, anime, Hollywood classics, Asian cinema, music performance, documentaries, fitness, and how-to categories among others. It also announced that it was increasing the number of shipping centers to 23 and implementing new technology with the U.S. Postal Service that would shorten delivery times.

Developments at Blockbuster in 2005

In a move to revitalize stagnant store sales (see the worldwide store data section of Exhibit 4) and combat the attractiveness of the no-due-dates/no-late-fees policies of Netflix, Blockbuster in January 2005 discontinued its practice of charging late fees on DVD rental returns at its retail stores. However, it held on to the practice of specified due dates—one week for games and two days or one week for movies. If customers kept the rental beyond the due date, they were automatically granted an extra one-week goodwill period at no additional charge. If a customer chose to keep his or her rental past the end of the seventh day after the due date per the posted rental terms, Blockbuster converted the rental to

a sale and charged the customer for the movie or game, minus the original rental fee. If the customer later decided he or she did not want to own the movie or game and returned the product within 30 days, Blockbuster reversed the sale and charged a minimal restocking fee of $1.25 (some franchise stores charged a higher restocking fee).

Blockbuster ran extensive ads in December 2004 and January 2005 touting its new no-late-fee policy. To help compensate for the estimated $250 to $300 million that late fees were expected to contribute to Blockbuster's revenues in 2005, management planned to lower its ongoing marketing, operating, and promotional costs. Nonetheless, John Antioco, CEO of Blockbuster, was under fire from shareholders and some members of the company's board of directors for instituting the no-late-fee policy, given the big revenue erosion impact, Blockbuster's string of huge losses, and the need to increase store inventories of DVDs to compensate for the extra time that customers were keeping the DVDs. Investors and board members were also skeptical about Blockbuster's move in the online rental market segment because of the heavy costs (estimated at $100 to $200 million) and what some considered as dim prospects for profitability. About 160 Blockbuster franchisees decided to discontinue the no-late-fees policy in 2005, even though the program was popular with customers, because of the extra expenses involved in stocking additional copies of popular titles.

In May 2005, disgruntled Blockbuster shareholders ignored management's recommendations and elected an opposing slate of three new directors to the company's board, one of whom was running against CEO John Antioco. When Antioco indicated that he would leave his position as CEO as a consequence of being defeated in his reelection bid, the newly constituted board opted to expand from six to eight members, appointed Antioco to one of the two newly created seats, and made him chairman. It was understood, however, that Antioco would not continue on as CEO past 2005 if the board was not satisfied with the progress being made to restore Blockbuster to profitability.

During his contentious campaign against the opposing slate of directors, Antonico had defended his strategy for Blockbuster:

> A key feature of our growth strategy is the recently introduced "End of Late Fees" program, which directly addresses the major problem customers had

with their movie rental experience. The program also positions us better to compete with home entertainment options that do not have late fees, including retail DVD, pay-per-view and VOD. To date, the "End of Late Fees" program is producing the desired results. Since the first of January when we introduced the program, we have had positive growth in active membership for the first time in nearly two years.

Another critically important initiative—and the only significant investment we intend to make this year—is our online rental business. Blockbuster is uniquely positioned to compete in this fast growing business. Given the views of leading industry experts that within three years online rental could represent 20% to 30% of movie rental revenues, it is imperative that we pursue this opportunity, which we believe will mean hundreds of millions of dollars in future operating income for our company.

We are prioritizing new initiatives, investing wisely for the future and cutting costs aggressively. We have cut 2005 capital spending by over $100 million from last year and reduced corporate overhead by $70 million on an annualized basis. Additionally, to reduce costs further and better focus our resources, we have put our game initiative, as well as the marketing of our movie trading business, on hold until 2006.

Regarding our dividend policy, during 2004 Blockbuster paid a one-time dividend of $5 per share in addition to its normal quarterly dividends. As a result, our shareholders received a total of $920 million in dividends in 2004. We have consistently said that once we have successfully executed our business initiatives and delivered on our strategic plan, we would consider paying increased quarterly dividends or repurchasing stock.[4]

In characterizing the company's direction, Antonico said, "Our mission right now is to transform Blockbuster from a place you go to rent movies to a place you go to rent or buy movies or games new or used, pay by the day, pay by the month, online or in-store." In August 2005, Blockbuster Online's pricing was raised. Customers could choose from among three plans:

- $9.99, unlimited DVDs, one title out at a time.
- $14.99, unlimited DVDs, two titles out at a time.
- $17.99, unlimited DVDs, three titles out at a time.

The $17.99 plan was the most popular; all plans included a free two-week trial. The company said it had 1 million online subscribers and during 2005 had added about as many net new subscribers as Netflix. As of mid-2005, online subscribers could choose from over 40,000 titles, with new titles added weekly. Blockbuster had 30 distribution centers, and more than 200 local Blockbuster stores were fulfilling online orders for nearby customers (to help shorten delivery times). More local stores were being added daily to fulfill online orders.

Also in 2005, Blockbuster integrated its in-store and online subscription programs—members paid the same fees and had the same privileges. To conserve cash and bolster Blockbuster's lackluster balance sheet, the company's board of directors elected not to pay the $0.02 per share dividend for the third quarter of 2005. Blockbuster management had plans to reduce costs by over $100 million in 2006 and an additional $50 million in 2007 through a combination of overhead reductions, lower marketing expenditures, and operational savings from divesting a subsidiary that acquired and distributed products for the theatrical, home entertainment, and television markets. Management further planned to cut capital expenditures from $140 million in 2005 to $90 million in 2006, principally because of fewer new store openings.

MOVIE GALLERY INC.

In 2005, Movie Gallery was the second-largest North American home video retailer, with more than 4,700 stores located in all 50 U.S. states, Mexico, and Canada. It specialized in the rental and sale of DVD and VHS movies and video games. Since the company's initial public offering in August 1994, Movie Gallery had grown from 97 stores in 1994 to nearly 2,500 stores at year-end 2004 via new store openings and a series of acquisitions. It had revenues of $791 million in 2004 and earnings of $49.5 million. In April 2005, Movie Gallery beat out Blockbuster in a bidding war to acquire Hollywood Entertainment, which had 2004 revenues of $1.78 billion and operated 2,000 Hollywood Video stores and 700 Game Crazy stores.

The company's stores operating under the Movie Gallery brand primarily targeted small towns and suburban areas. Movie Gallery's scale of operations and resource capabilities enabled it to compete effectively against the independently owned stores and small regional chains in these areas; it was regarded as the industry's lowest-cost operator. The strategy of the Movie Gallery stores was to take advantage of purchasing economics, effective labor strategies, and a strong, proven business model to generate cash flow and continued growth.

The stores operating under the Hollywood Video and Game Crazy brands primarily targeted urban centers and surrounding suburban neighborhoods—much the same places that Blockbuster targeted. The strategy of these stores was predicated on exceptional customer service, innovative marketing and merchandising programs, a strong brand image, and solid in-store execution.

Movie Gallery was formed in 1985 by Joe Malugen and Harrison Parrish in Dothan, Alabama. Through its wholly owned subsidiary M.G.A., the company's founders began operating video specialty stores in southern Alabama and the Florida panhandle, and franchising the Movie Gallery store concept. By June 1987 the company owned five stores and had a franchise operation of 45 stores. In 1988, Movie Gallery began to consolidate the franchisees into company-owned stores; by 1992, it had a total of 37 stores and annual revenues of $6 million.

In August 1994, Movie Gallery completed an initial public offering of its stock and used the proceeds to acquire small video chains, primarily in the Southeast. Additional shares were issued in 1995 to open new stores and continue making acquisitions. By mid-1996 Movie Gallery had made over 100 separate acquisitions and built a chain of over 850 stores. In 1999, Movie Gallery announced plans to build 100 new stores and completed an 88-store acquisition of Blowout Entertainment; it went into 2000 with more than 950 locations in 31 states.

In 2000, Movie Gallery again set its goal at opening 100 new stores and relocating 25. This goal was met and surpassed. In late 2001, Movie Gallery expanded its store base by 30 percent by acquiring Video Update, its largest single-chain acquisition to date. The Video Update acquisition, which included 100 retail locations in Canada, marked Movie Gallery's emergence as a leader in video rentals in North America. Movie Gallery continued to execute an aggressive growth strategy, reaching the 2,000-store mark in 2003.

Following the April 2005 acquisition of Hollywood Entertainment, Movie Gallery strengthened its presence in Western Canada by acquiring the 61-store VHQ Entertainment chain. VHQ also operated VHQ Online (www.VHQonline.ca), a flat-fee, direct-to-home movie delivery service.

Movie Gallery had not launched an online DVD rental service, but its large and diverse geographic spread and its ambitions to be "the dominant entertainment source for video and video game rental and sale in rural and secondary markets in the United States" made it a likely entry candidate.

In the first nine months of 2005, Movie Gallery reported revenues of $1.31 billion and a net loss of $6.3 million. Movie Gallery anticipated fourth-quarter 2005 revenues of $675 to $705 million and same-store revenues in the range of −5 to −9 percent, as compared to the fourth quarter of 2004. In June 2005, management revised the new store development plan for the Movie Gallery and Hollywood Entertainment, cutting the plans for 500 new stores in 2005 to 300 stores; in the fall of 2005 it was on track to meet the target of 300 new store openings. Movie Gallery intended to further reduce its annual capital expenditures for new store development and open approximately 150 new stores in 2006, primarily in rural and secondary markets. It was also exploring various strategic alternatives for its Game Crazy business, including a potential sale, strategic partnership, or joint venture.

VIDEO-ON-DEMAND

Some analysts saw video-on-demand as a huge threat to Netflix because it could kill the market for DVD rentals. Growing numbers of households had high-speed Internet access, thus allowing technologically-savvy consumers to download movies to their PCs and then use the capabilities of Windows Media Center (which was standard on many newly purchased PCs shipped in 2005) to show the downloaded movies on their TVs. Alternatively, they could simply use a credit card to pay a fee to online movie suppliers to watch the movie on their PCs via streaming video.

However, VOD was materializing more slowly than expected because of wrangles with getting movie studios to license more movies for digital downloads—most movie studios feared that any contribution on their part to wider digital downloading of movies would facilitate even greater movie pirating (via file-sharing software) and cause them to lose significant revenues from both declining movie attendance and movie DVD sales. The file-sharing software used to pirate music files over the Internet also allowed people to pirate movies—in 2004, an estimated 400,000 to 600,000 movies were being illegally downloaded each day, costing film companies hundreds of millions in lost sales. More than half of the college-educated adults 35 and under in the United States had broadband connections at home, making it easy to trade copyrighted music and movie files. To try to deter illegal movie downloading, the Motion Picture Association of America in 2004 launched a major ad campaign in daily newspapers and consumer magazines across the country, as well as in more than 100 college newspapers, explaining why movie piracy was illegal, how it impacted jobs and the economy, and what the consequences were for engaging in illegal trafficking. Additionally, antipiracy messages appeared in motion picture theaters across the country.

Movielink's VOD Service

In 2005, Movielink (www.movielink.com), headquartered in Santa Monica, California, was the leading broadband video-on-demand (VOD) service. It offered an extensive selection of new and classic hit movies, foreign films, and other hard-to-find content. The business was a joint venture of Metro-Goldwyn-Mayer Studios, Paramount Pictures, Sony Pictures Entertainment, Universal Studios, and Warner Bros. Studios. Movielink drew its content offerings from the vast libraries of those studios, as well as Walt Disney Pictures, Twentieth Century Fox, Miramax, Artisan, and others on a non-exclusive basis.

After browsing the selection of movies, customers registered and rented movies using a valid credit card. There were no late fees or return times, and Movielink did not require a subscription or membership. Instead, each movie was independently priced by the content provider and charged per rental—fees were as low as $1.99 per movie. "We're excited about the opportunity to work with Movielink and its growing customer base of broadband households," said Peter Levinsohn, Fox's president of worldwide pay television and digital media.

Movielink was available to U.S. Internet users with broadband connections. Consumers could browse Movielink's site and view trailers of available titles without charge. Once customers were ready to rent a title, they registered with Movielink and paid for their rental via credit card. Movielink's Movies in Minutes software let customers either begin watching titles within 2–10 minutes after beginning the download or store them on their hard drives for up to 30 days and experience unlimited viewing for any 24-hour period on a PC, a television connected to the PC, or a laptop computer. Customers could also use Movielink's MultiPlay software feature to re-rent titles for additional 24-hour viewing periods for up to 30 days after the initial rental. Thirty days after the download, movie files were automatically deleted from the customer's hard drive.

Movielink had partnered with Verizon to launch a co-branded movie downloading service for Verizon Online's consumer broadband subscribers. Verizon Online's consumer DSL and FiOS Internet Service customers could purchase and download movies to watch at home or rent movies through Verizon's special agreement with Movielink.

GreenCine's Combination Online Rental-VOD Movie Offering

GreenCine was an online DVD rental company that also offered its subscribers two other options for watching movies—VOD and DivX downloads, both priced at $4.99 per movie and both allowing customers to watch the movie as many times as they wished over a 10-day period (GreenCine's adult movies had a 30-day use period). GreenCine had 10,000 on-demand movie titles that included independent, international, documentary, classic, and adult movies covering 32 genres.

GreenCine's online rental customers could select from a library of 25,000 titles and choose from among seven plans:

- $9.95, unlimited DVDs, 1 title out at a time.
- $14.95, unlimited DVDs, 2 titles out at a time.
- $21.95, unlimited DVDs, 3 titles out at a time.
- $27.95, unlimited DVDs, 4 titles out at a time.
- $33.95, unlimited DVDs, 5 titles out at a time.
- $49.95, unlimited DVDs, 8 titles out at a time.
- $59.95, unlimited DVDs, 10 titles out at a time.

Like Netflix, GreenCine offered a free two-week trial period. It had one distribution center and delivery could run two to three days. GreenCine sent members an e-mail alert when a movie was mailed out and when it received a movie that the member had returned.

Headquartered in the San Francisco Bay area, GreenCine touted itself as a movie source for people who liked the arts and were fond of off-the-wall, offbeat, eclectic, and unusual movies. Its collection featured independent, foreign, anime, and art house movies, as well as HK action and classic titles. The company's Web site said, "If what you like to see is off-center, or dead center, in terms of taste, Green-Cine is for you."

NETFLIX'S OUTLOOK

Reed Hastings believed that Netflix's prospects were exceptionally bright. In a December 2005 interview with *Inc.* magazine, he said:

> Netflix has at least another decade of dominance ahead of it. But movies over the Internet are coming, and at some point it will become big business. We started investing 1% to 2% of revenue every year in downloading, and I think it's tremendously exciting because it will fundamentally lower our mailing costs. We want to be ready when video-on-demand happens. That's why the company is called Netflix, not DVD-by-Mail.[5]

But two new developments cast shadows on this prognosis. In January 2006, *The Wall Street Journal* reported that cable TV companies and major movie studios were considering strategies to release movies through VOD cable services the same day that the DVDs were available in retail stores and rental outlets.[6] The move was precipitated by deals that Walt Disney and NBC Universal had recently made to make television shows available on Apple Computer's video-capable iPod. With movie box-office attendance and revenues lagging, movie studios were anxious to pursue highly lucrative sales of movie DVDs and prevent that revenue stream from eroding. Historically, movie studios had released new movies first to theaters and then several weeks or months later made them available on DVD, cable video-on-demand services, and other platforms (each a few weeks apart)—a strategy that they believed maximized revenue.

Also in January 2006, Google announced that it would begin allowing consumers to buy videos from major content partners through the Google site.[7] Consumers would be able to pay to download and view videos, such as television shows, on their computers from Google content partners that included CBS Corporation, the National Basketball Association, and other partners soon to be named.

Endnotes

[1] As cited in Blockbuster's 2004 10-K report, p. 1.
[2] As cited in Sarah McBride, Peter Grant, and Merissa Marr, "Movies May Hit DVD Cable Simultaneously," *The Wall Street Journal,* January 4, 2006, p. B1.
[3] Based on information in Shane C. Buettner, "DVD Sales Peaking," posted at Ultimate AV, www.guidetohometheater.com (accessed December 29, 2005).
[4] Excerpt from company press release, April 18, 2005.

[5] Interview with *Inc.* magazine's Patrick J. Sauer, posted at www.inc.com (accessed December 29, 2005).
[6] McBride, Grant, and Marr, "Movies May Hit DVD Cable Simultaneously," p. B1.
[7] Kevin J. Delaney and Nick Wingfield, "Google to Offer Video, Software That Rivals Microsoft's," *The Wall Street Journal,* January 5, 2006, p. A9.

easyCar.com

John J. Lawrence
University of Idaho

Luis Solis
Instituto de Empresa

In 2003 easyCar.com had become the fastest-growing rental car company in Europe by offering a minimal selection of cars that could be booked at low daily rates via the company's Web site. Its mission was "to offer you outstanding value for money. To us value for money means a reliable service at a low price. We achieve this by simplifying the product we offer, and passing on the benefits to you in the form of lower prices."[1]

EasyCar was a member of the easyGroup family of companies, founded by the flamboyant Greek entrepreneur Stelios Haji-Ioannou, who was known simply as Stelios to most. Stelios founded low-cost air carrier easyJet.com in 1995 after convincing his father, a Greek shipping billionaire, to loan him the £5 million to start the business.[2] (Note: In January 2003, £1 = €1.52 = U.S.$1.61.) EasyJet was one of the early low-cost, no-frills air carriers in the European market and was built on a foundation of simple point-to-point flights, Internet-only flight reservations, and the aggressive use of yield management policies. The company proved highly successful, and as a result Stelios expanded the easyJet business model to industries with characteristics similar to the airline industry. One such business was easyCar, which was founded in 2000 with a £10 million initial investment.

EasyCar's business model was quite different than that of traditional rental car companies. EasyCar rented only a single vehicle type at each location it operated, while most of its competitors rented a wide variety of vehicle types. EasyCar did not work

with agents—over 95 percent of its bookings were made through the company's Web site, with the remainder of bookings being made directly through the company's phone reservation system (at a cost to the customer of €0.95/minute for the call). Most rental car companies worked with a variety of intermediaries, with their own Web sites accounting for less than 10 percent of their total booking.[3] And like easyJet, easyCar managed rental rates in an attempt to have its fleet rented out 100 percent of the time and to generate the maximum revenue from its rentals. EasyCar's information system constantly evaluated projected demand and expected utilization at each site, and adjusted price accordingly. Because of its aggressive pricing, easyCar was able to achieve a fleet utilization rate in excess of 90 percent[4]—much higher than other major rental car companies. Industry leader Avis Europe, for example, had a fleet utilization rate of 68 percent.[5]

EasyCar's business model was showing signs of success by fiscal year-end 2002, when it broke even on revenues of £27 million[6] after losing £7.5 million on revenues of £18.5 million in 2001.[7] Pleased with the company's early performance, Stelios announced the company would open an average of two new sites a week through 2003 and 2004 to reach a total of 180 sites by the end of 2004.[8] Stelios expected new locations would allow easyCar to quadruple revenues to £100 million in revenue and earn profits of £10 million by year-end 2004 in preparation for a planned initial public offering (IPO) that same year. The company's management and financial advisers projected the IPO might yield as much as £250 million to fund future growth in the European rental car market.[9]

THE RENTAL CAR INDUSTRY IN WESTERN EUROPE

The western European rental car industry consisted of many different national markets that were only semi-integrated. While there were many companies that competed within this industry, a handful of companies held dominant positions, either across a number of national markets or within one or a few national markets. Industry experts saw the sector as ripe for consolidation.[10] Several international companies—notably Avis, Europcar, and Hertz—had strong positions across most major European markets. Within most countries, there was also a primarily national or regional company that had a strong position in its home market and perhaps moderate market share in neighboring markets. Sixt was the market leader in Germany, for example, while Atesa (in partnership with National) was the market leader in Spain. Generally these major players accounted for more than half of the market. In Germany, for example, Sixt, Europcar, Avis, and Hertz had a combined 60 percent of the €2.5 billion German rental car market.[11] In Spain, the top five firms accounted for

60 percent of the €920 million Spanish rental car market. Generally, these top firms targeted both business and vacation travelers and offered a wide range of vehicles for rent. Exhibit 1 provides basic information on these market-leading companies.

In addition to these major companies in each market, there were many smaller rental companies operating in each market. In Germany, for example, there were over 700 smaller companies,[12] while in Spain there were more than 1,600 smaller companies. Many of these smaller companies operated at only one or a few locations and were particularly prevalent in tourist locations. Also operating in the sector were a number of brokers, like Holiday Autos. Brokerage companies did not own their own fleet of cars but instead managed the excess inventory of other companies and matched customers with rental companies with excess fleet capacity.

Overall, the rental car market could be thought of as composed of two broad segments, a business segment and a tourist/leisure segment. Depending on the market, the leisure segment represented somewhere between 45 and 65 percent of the overall market, and a large part of this segment was very price-conscious. The business segment made up the remaining 35 to 55 percent of the market. It was less price-sensitive than the tourist segment and more

Exhibit 1   **Information on easyCar's Major European Competitors, 2002**

	easyCar	Avis Europe	Europcar	Hertz	Sixt
Number of rental outlets	46	3,100	2,650	7,000	1,250
2002 fleet size	7,000	120,000	220,000	700,000	(46,700)
Number of countries	5	107	118	150	50
Largest market	United Kingdom	France	France	United States	Germany
Who owns company	EasyGroup/ Stelios Haji-Ioannou	D'Ieteren (Belgium) is majority shareholder	Volkswagen AG	Ford Motor Company	Publicly traded
European revenues	€41 million	€1.25 billion	€1.12 billion	€910 million	€600 million
Company Web site	www.easycar.com	www.avis-europe.com	www.europcar.com	www.hertz.com	ag.sixt.com

Source: Information in this table came from each company's Web site and online annual reports. European revenues are for vehicle rental in Europe and are estimated on the basis of market share estimates for 2001 from Avis Europe's Web site.

concerned about service quality, convenience, and flexibility.

THE GROWTH OF EASYCAR

EasyCar opened its first location in London, in April 2000, under the name easyRentacar. In the same week, easyCar opened locations in Glasgow and Barcelona. All three locations were popular easyJet destinations. Vehicles initially could be rented for as low as €15 a day plus a one-time car preparation fee of €8. Each of these locations had a fleet consisting entirely of Mercedes A-class vehicles, which was the smallest car manufactured by the German automaker. It was the only vehicle that easyCar rented at the time. Exhibit 2 presents images of easyCar's Spanish home page, an A-class model, and its Mercedes MPV rental fleet.

Exhibit 2 **Images of easyCar's Spanish Home Page, A-Class Mercedes Rental Car, and Its Mercedes MPV Rental Fleet**

Source: easyCar.com's Web site (accessed October and November 2004).

EasyCar had signed a deal with Mercedes, amid much fanfare, at the Geneva Motor Show earlier in the year to purchase a total of 5,000 A-class vehicles. The vehicles, which came with guaranteed buy-back terms, cost easyCar's parent company a little over £6 million.[13] Many in the car rental industry were surprised by the choice, expecting easyCar to rely on less expensive compact models.[14] In describing the acquisition of the 5,000 Mercedes vehicles, Stelios had said:

> The choice of Mercedes reflects the easyGroup brand. EasyRentacar will use brand new Mercedes cars in the same way that easyJet uses brand new Boeing aircraft. We do not compromise on the hardware, we just use innovation to substantially reduce costs. The car hire industry is where the airline industry was five years ago, a cartel feeding off the corporate client. EasyRentacar will provide a choice for consumers who pay out of their own pockets and who will not be ripped off for traveling mid-week.[15]

EasyCar quickly expanded to other locations, focusing first on those locations popular with easy-Jet customers, including Amsterdam, Geneva, Nice, and Malagra. By July 2001, a little over a year after its initial launch, easyCar had fleets of Mercedes A-class vehicles in 14 locations in the United Kingdom, Spain, France, and the Netherlands. At this point, EasyCar secured £27 million from a consortium of Bank of Scotland Corporate Banking and NBGI Private Equity to further expand its operations. The package consisted of a combination of equity and loan stock.

While easyCar added a few sites in the second half of 2001 and early 2002, volatile demand in the wake of the September 11, 2001, terrorist attacks forced easyCar to roll out new rental locations somewhat slower than originally expected.[16] Growth accelerated, however, in the spring of 2002. Between May 2002 and January 2003, EasyCar opened 30 new locations, going from 18 to 48 sites. This acceleration in growth also coincided with a change in easyCar's policy regarding the makeup of its fleet. By May 2002, easyCar's fleet consisted of 6,000 Mercedes A-class vehicles across 18 sites. Beginning in May, however, easyCar began to stock its fleet with other types of vehicles. It still maintained its policy of offering only a single type of vehicle at each location, but now the vehicle the customer received depended on the location. The first new vehicle easyCar introduced was the Vauxhall Corsa. According to Stelios,

> Vauxhall Corsas cost easyCar £2 a day less than Mercedes A-Class so we can pass this saving on to customers. Customers themselves will decide if they want to pay a premium for a Mercedes. EasyGroup companies benefit from economies of scale where relevant but we also want to create contestable markets among our suppliers so that we can keep the cost to our customers as low as possible.[17]

By January 2003, EasyCar was also using Ford Focuses (4 locations), Renault Clios (3 locations), Toyota Yarises (3 locations), and Smart cars (2 locations) in addition to the Vauxhall Corsas (7 locations) and the Mercedes A-Class vehicles (28 locations). Plans called for a further expansion of the fleet, from the 7,000 vehicles that easyCar had in January to 24,000 vehicles across 180 rental sites by the end of 2004.[18]

In addition to making vehicles available at more locations, easyCar had also changed its policies for 2003 to allow rentals for as little as one hour, and with as little as one hour's notice of rental. By making this change, Stelios felt that easyCar could be a serious competitor to local taxis, buses, trains, and even car ownership. EasyCar expected that if it made car rental simple enough and cheap enough, that some people living in traffic-congested European cities who only used their car occasionally would give up the costs and hassles of car ownership and simply hire an easyCar when they needed a vehicle. Tapping into this broader transportation market would help the company reach its ambitious future sales goals.

FACILITIES

In January 2003 easyCar had facilities in a total of 17 cities in five European countries, as shown in Exhibit 3. It primarily located its facilities near bus and train stations in the major European cities, seeking out sites that offered lower lease costs. It generally avoided prime airport locations, as the cost for space at, and in some cases near, airports was significantly higher than most other locations. When easyCar did locate near an airport, it generally chose sites off the airport, in order to reduce the cost of the lease. Airport locations also tended to require longer hours to satisfy customers arriving on late flights or departing on very early flights. EasyCar kept its airport locations open 24 hours a day, whereas its other locations were generally only open from 7:00 a.m. to 11:00 p.m.

Exhibit 3   **easyCar Locations in January 2003**

Country	City	Number	Number Near an Airport
France	Nice	1	1
France	Paris	8	0
Netherlands	Amsterdam	3	1
Spain	Barcelona	2	0
Spain	Madrid	2	0
Spain	Majorca	1	1
Spain	Malagra	1	1
Switzerland	Geneva	1	1
United Kingdom	Birmingham	2	0
United Kingdom	Bromley	1	0
United Kingdom	Croydon	1	1
United Kingdom	Glasgow	2	1
United Kingdom	Kingston-upon-Thames	1	0
United Kingdom	Liverpool	2	1
United Kingdom	London	15	0
United Kingdom	Manchester	2	1
United Kingdom	Waterford	1	0
Total	**5 Countries, 17 Cities**	**46**	**9**

Source: www.easyCar.com, January 2003.

The physical facilities at all locations were kept to a minimum. In many locations, easyCar leased space in an existing parking garage. Employees worked out of a small, self-contained cubicle within the garage. The cubicle, depending on the location, might be no more than 15 square meters and included little more than a small counter and a couple of computers at which staff processed customers as they came to pick up or return their vehicles. EasyCar also leased a number of spaces within the garage for its fleet of cars. However, because easyCar's vehicles were rented 90 percent of the time, only 15 to 20 spaces were required at an average site, which had a fleet of about 150 cars.[19] To speed up the opening of new sites, easyCar had equipped a number of vans with all the needed computer and telephone equipment to run a site.[20] From an operational perspective, it could open a new location by simply leasing 20 or so spaces in a parking garage, hiring a small staff, driving a van to the location, and adding the location to the company's Web site. Depending on the fleet size at a location, easyCar typically had only one or two people working at a site at a time.

VEHICLE PICKUP AND RETURN PROCESSES

Customers arrived to a site to pick up a vehicle within a prearranged one-hour period. They selected this time slot when they booked the vehicles. EasyCar adjusted the first day's rental price according to the pickup time. Customers who picked their cars up earlier in the day or at popular times were charged more than were customers picking up their cars later in the day or at less busy times. Customers were required to bring a printed copy of their contract, along with the credit card they used to make the booking and identification. Given the low staffing levels, customers occasionally had to wait 30 minutes or more to be processed and receive their vehicles, particularly at peak times of the day. Processing a customer began with the employee accessing the customer's contract online. If the customer was new to the site, the basic policies and possible additional charges were briefly explained. The employee then made copies of the customer's identification and credit card and took a digital photo of the customer. The customer put down an €80 refundable deposit, signed the contract, and drove the car away.

All vehicles were rented with more or less empty fuel tanks, with the exact level dependent on how much gasoline was left in the vehicle when the previous renter returned it. Customers were provided with a small map of the immediate area around the rental site, showing the locations and hours of nearby gas stations. Customers could return vehicles with any amount of gas in them as long as the low-fuel indicator light in the vehicle was not on. Customers who returned vehicles with the low-fuel indicator light on were charged a fueling fee of €16.

Customers were also expected to return the vehicle within a prearranged one-hour period, which they also selected at the time of booking. While customers did not have to worry about refueling the car before returning it, they were expected to thoroughly clean the car. This clean car policy was implemented in May 2002 as a way to further reduce the price customers could pay for their vehicle. Prior to this change, all customers paid a fixed preparation fee of €11 each time they rented a vehicle (up from the €8 preparation fee when the company started operations in 2000). The new policy reduced this up-front preparation fee to €4 but required customers to either return the vehicle clean or pay an additional cleaning fee of €16. In order to avoid any misunderstanding, easyCar provided customers with an explicit description of what constituted a clean car, both for the interior and the exterior. It had to be apparent, for example, that the exterior of the car had been washed. The maps showing nearby gas stations also showed nearby car washes. While easyCar had received some bad press in relation to the policy,[21] 85 percent of customers returned their vehicles clean as a result of it.

When a customer returned the vehicle, an easyCar employee would check to make sure that the vehicle was clean and undamaged and that the low-fuel indicator light was not on. The employee would also check the kilometers driven. The customer would then be notified of any additional charges. These charges would be subtracted from the €80 deposit and the difference refunded to the customer's credit card (or, if additional charges exceeded the €80 deposit, the customer's credit card would be charged the difference).

PRICING

EasyCar's low pricing was a major point of distinction from rival car rental companies. EasyCar advertised prices as low as €5 a day plus a per rental preparation fee of €4. Prices, however, varied by the location and dates of the rental, by when the booking was made, and by what time the car was to be picked up and returned. EasyCar's systems constantly evaluated projected demand and expected use at each site, and adjusted price accordingly. Achieving the €5 a day rate usually required customers to book well in advance, and these rates were typically available only on weekdays. Weekend rates, when booked well in advance, typically started a few euros higher than the weekday rates. As a given rental date approached, however, the price typically went up significantly as easyCar approached 100 percent fleet use for that day. Rates could triple overnight if there was sufficient booking activity. Generally, however, easyCar's price was less than half that of its major competitors. EasyCar, unlike most other rental car companies, required customers to pay in full at the time of booking, and once a booking was made, it was nonrefundable.

EasyCar's base price covered only the core rental of the vehicle—the total price customers paid was in many cases much higher and depended on how the customer reserved, paid for, used, and returned the vehicle. EasyCar's price was based on customers booking through the company's Web site and paying for their rental with their easyMoney credit card. EasyMoney was the easyGroup's credit and financial services company. Customers who chose to book through the company's phone reservation system were charged an additional €0.95 a minute for the call, and those who used other credit cards were charged €5 extra. All vehicles had to be paid for by a credit or debit card—cash was not accepted. The base rental price allowed customers to drive vehicles 100 kilometers per day—additional kilometers were charged at a rate of €0.12 per kilometer. In addition, customers were expected to return their cars clean and on time. Customers who returned cars that did not meet easyCar's standards for clean were charged a €16 cleaning fee. Those who returned their cars late were immediately charged €120 and subsequently charged an additional €120 for each subsequent

24-hour period in which the car was not returned. EasyCar explained the high late fee as representing the cost that the company would likely incur in providing another vehicle to the next customer. Customers wishing to make any changes to their bookings were also charged a change fee of €16. Changes could be made either before the rental started or during the rental period, but were limited to changing the dates, times, and location of the rental, and were subject to the prices and vehicle availability at the time the change was made. If the change resulted in an overall lower price for the rental, however, no refund was provided for the difference.

Beginning in 2003, for an additional charge of €4 a day, all customers were also required to purchase loss/damage insurance that eliminated the customer's liability for loss or damage to the vehicle (excluding damage to the tires or windshield of the vehicle). Through 2002, customers were able to choose whether or not to purchase additional insurance from easyCar to eliminate any financial liability in the event that the rental vehicle was damaged. The cost of this optional insurance had been €6 a day, and approximately 60 percent of easyCar's customers had purchased it. Those not purchasing this insurance either had assumed the liability for the first €800 in damages personally or had had their own insurance through some other means (e.g., some credit card companies provide this insurance to their cardholders at no additional charge for short-term rentals paid for with the credit card).

EasyCar's Web site attempted to make all of these additional charges clear to customers at the time of the booking. EasyCar had received a fair amount of bad press when it first opened for business after many renters complained about having to pay undisclosed charges when they returned their cars.[22] In response, easyCar had revamped its Web site in an effort to make these charges more transparent to customers and to explain the logic behind many of them.

PROMOTION

EasyCar's promotional efforts through 2002 had focused primarily on posters and press advertising. Posters were particularly prevalent in metro systems and bus and train stations in cities where easyCar

had operations. All of this advertising focused on easyCar's low price. According to founder Stelios:

> You will never see an advert for an easy company offering an experience—it's about price. If you create expectations you can't live up to, then you will ultimately suffer as a result.[23]

The company allocated £1.43 million to advertising in 2002.[24]

EasyCar also promoted itself by displaying its name, phone number, and Web address prominently on the doors and rear window of its entire fleet of vehicles, and took advantage of free publicity when the opportunity presented itself. An example of seeking out such publicity occurred when Hertz complained that easyCar's comparative advertising campaign in the Netherlands that featured the line "The best reason to use easyCar.com can be found at hertz.nl" violated Dutch law that required comparative advertising to be exact, not general. In response, Stelios and a group of easyCar employees, dressed in orange boiler suits and with a fleet of easyCar vehicles, protested outside the Hertz Amsterdam office with signs asking "What is Hertz frightened of?"[25]

In an effort to help reach its goal of quadrupling sales in the next two years, easyCar had recently hired Jennifer Mowat into the new position of commercial director to take over responsibility for easyCar's European marketing. Mowat had previously been eBay's UK country manager and had recently completed an MBA in Switzerland. Previously, Stelios and easyCar's managing director, Andrew Fitzmaurice, had handled the marketing function themselves.[26] As part of this stepped-up marketing effort, easyCar also planned to double its advertising budget for 2003, to £3 million, and to begin to advertise on television. The television advertising campaign was to feature easyCar's founder, Stelios.[27]

LEGAL CHALLENGES

EasyCar faced several challenges to its approaches. The most significant dealt with a November 2002 ruling made by the Office of Fair Trading (OFT) that easyCar had to grant customers seven days from the time they made a booking to cancel their booking and receive a full refund. The OFT was a

UK governmental agency responsible for protecting UK consumers from unfair and/or anticompetitive business practices. The ruling against easyCar was based on the 2000 Consumer Protection Distance Selling Regulations. These regulations stipulated that companies that sell at a distance (e.g., by Internet or phone) must provide customers with a seven-day cooling-off period, during which time customers can cancel their contracts with the company and receive a full refund. The law exempted accommodation, transportation, catering, and leisure service companies from this requirement. The OFT's ruling concluded that easyCar did not qualify as a transportation service company because the consumer had to drive themselves, and therefore they were not receiving a transport service, just a car.[28]

EasyCar had appealed the OFT's decision to the UK High Court on the grounds that it was indeed a transportation service company and was entitled to an exemption from this requirement. EasyCar was hopeful that it would eventually win this legal challenge. EasyCar had argued that this ruling would destroy the company's book-early-pay-less philosophy and could lead to a tripling of prices.[29] Chairman Stelios was quoted as saying:

> It is very serious. My fear is that as soon as we put in the seven-day cooling off periods our utilization-rate will fall from 90% to 65%. That's the difference between a profitable company and an unprofitable one.[30]

EasyCar was also concerned that prolonged legal action on this point could interfere with its plans for a 2004 IPO.

The OFT, for its part, had also applied to the UK High Court for an injunction to make the company comply with the ruling. Other rental car companies were generally unconcerned about the ruling, because few offered big discounts for early bookings or nonrefundable bookings.[31]

EasyCar's new policy of posting the pictures of customers whose cars were 15 days or more overdue was also drawing legal criticism. EasyCar had recently received public warnings from lawyers that this new policy might violate data protection, libel, privacy, confidentiality, and human rights laws.[32] Of particular concern to some lawyers was the possibility that easyCar might post the wrong person's picture, given the large number of customers the company dealt with.[33] Such a mistake could open the company to costly libel suits. The policy of posting the pictures of overdue customers on the easyCar Web site, initiated in November 2002, was designed to reduce the losses associated with customers renting a vehicle and never returning it. The costs were significant, according to Stelios:

> These cars are expensive, £15,000 each, and we have 6,000 of them. At any given time we are looking for as many as several tens which are overdue. If we don't get one back, it's a write-off. We are writing off an entire car, and it's uninsurable.[34]

Stelios was also convinced of the legality of the new policy. In a letter to the editor responding to the legal concerns raised in the press, Stelios said:

> From a legal perspective, we have been entirely factual and objective and are merely reporting the details of the overdue car and the person who collected it. In addition, our policy is made very clear in our terms and conditions and the photo is taken both overtly and with the consent of the customer . . . I estimate the total cost of overdue cars to be 5 percent of total easyCar costs, or 50p on every car rental day for all customers. In 2004, when I intend to float easyCar, this cost will amount to £5 million unless we can reduce our quantity of overdue cars.[35]

In the past, easyCar had simply provided pictures to police when a rental was 15 or more days overdue. It was hoped that posting the picture would both discourage drivers from not returning vehicles and shame those drivers who currently had overdue cars into returning them. In fact, the first person whose photo was posted on the easyCar Web site did indeed return his car two days later. The vehicle was 29 days late.[36]

THE FUTURE

At the end of 2002, Stelios had stepped down as the CEO of easyJet so that he could devote more of his time to the other easyGroup companies, including easyCar. He had three priorities for the new year. One was to turn around the money-losing easyInternetCafe business, which Stelios had described as "the worst mistake of my career."[37] The 22-store chain had lost £80 million in the last two years. Stelios's second priority was to oversee the planned launch of another new easyGroup business, easy-Cinema, in the spring of 2003. And the third was to oversee the rapid expansion of the easyCar chain so that it would be ready for an initial public offering by year-end 2004.

Endnotes

[1] www.easyCar.com

[2] "The Big Picture—an Interview with Stelios," *Sunday Herald* (UK), March 16, 2003.

[3] "Click to Fly," *The Economist,* May 13, 2004.

[4] E. Simpkins, "Stelios Isn't Taking It Easy," *Sunday Telegraph* (UK), December 15, 2002.

[5] Avis Europe plc 2002 annual report, p. 10, http://ir.avis-europe.com/avis/reports, accessed August 16, 2004.

[6] "Marketing: Former eBay UK Chief Lands Top easyCar Position," *Financial Times* Information Limited, January 9, 2003.

[7] T. Burt, "EasyCar Agrees Deal with Vauxhall," *Financial Times,* April 30, 2002, p. 24.

[8] Simpkins, "Stelios Isn't Taking It Easy."

[9] N. Hodgson, "Stelios Plans easyCar Float," *Liverpool Echo,* September 24, 2002.

[10] "Marketing Week: Don't Write Off the Car Rental Industry," *Financial Times* Information Limited, September 26, 2002.

[11] "EasyCar Set to Shake Up German Car Rental Market," European Intelligence Wire, February 22, 2002.

[12] Ibid.

[13] Hodgson, "Stelios Plans easyCar Float."

[14] A. Felsted, "EasyCar Courts Clio for Rental Fleet," *Financial Times,* February 11, 2002, p. 26.

[15] EasyCar.com news release, March 1, 2000, www.easyCar.com.

[16] T. Burt, "EasyCar Agrees Deal with Vauxhall."

[17] EasyCar.com news release, May 2, 2002, www.easyCar.com.

[18] "Marketing Week: EasyCar Appoints Head of European Marketing," *Financial Times* Information Limited, January 9, 2003.

[19] Simpkins, "Stelios Isn't Taking It Easy."

[20] Ibid.

[21] J. Hyde, "Travel View: Clearing Up on the Extras," *The Observer* (UK), July 7, 2002.

[22] J. Stanton, "The Empire That's Easy Money," *Edinburgh Evening News,* November 26, 2002.

[23] "The Big Picture."

[24] "EasyCar Appoints Head of European Marketing."

[25] EasyCar.com news release, April 22, 2002, www.easyCar.com.

[26] "EasyCar Appoints Head of European Marketing."

[27] "Campaigning: EasyGroup Appoints Publicist for easyCar TV Advertising Brief," *Financial Times* Information Limited, January 31, 2003.

[28] J. Macintosh, "EasyCar Sues OFT amid Threat to Planned Flotation," *Financial Times,* November 22, 2002, p. 4.

[29] "EasyCar Appoints Head of European Marketing."

[30] Mackintosh, "EasyCar Sues OFT amid Threat.

[31] Ibid.

[32] B. Sherwood & A. Wendlandt, "EasyCar May Be in Difficulty over Naming Ploy," *Financial Times,* November 14, 2002, p. 2.

[33] Ibid.

[34] "E-Business: Internet Fraudsters Fail to Steal Potter Movie's Magic & Other News," *Financial Times* Information Limited, November 19, 2002.

[35] S. Haji-Ioannou, "Letters to the Editor: Costly Effect of Late Car Return," *Financial Times,* November 16, 2002, p. 10.

[36] M. Hookham, "How Stelios Nets Return of His Cars," *Daily Post* (Liverpool, UK), November 14, 2002.

[37] S. Bentley, "The Worst Mistake of My Career, by Stelios" *Financial Times,* December 24, 2002.

Smithfield Foods' Vertical Integration Strategy

LaRue T. Hosmer
The University of Michigan

In 2005 Smithfield Foods was the largest hog producer and pork processor in the world. The company raised 14 million hogs domestically (a 14 percent U.S. share) and processed 27 million hogs annually (a 27 percent U.S. share). Smithfield marketed chops, roasts, ribs, loins, ground pork, bacon, hams, sausages, and sliced deli meats under such brands as Smithfield, Smithfield Lean Generation, John Morrell, Gwaltney, Patrick Cudahy, Stefano's, Farmland, Quick-n-Easy, and Jean Caby (France), plus it had the two best-known meat brands in Poland—Krakus and Morliny. Smithfield specialized in producing exceptionally lean hogs; the company had exclusive U.S. franchise rights to a proprietary breed of SPG sows that accounted for about 55 percent of its herd and provided live hogs for its best-selling Smithfield Lean Generation Pork products. In 2005 Smithfield operated 52 pork processing plants and 7 beef processing plants. A new state-of-the-art ham processing plant opened in 2005.

Since 1981, the company had made some 32 acquisitions to expand geographically, diversify into new product segments, and vertically integrate its pork business. Smithfield's acquisitions of Moyer Packing Company and Packerland Holdings in 2002 made it the fifth largest beef producer in the United States. In 1998, Smithfield began expanding into foreign markets, making acquisitions in Canada, France, Romania, and Poland and establishing joint ventures in Mexico, Spain, and China. Two meat processors in Poland and Romania were acquired in 2004, along with a Romanian hog farming operation with 15,000 sows producing 200,000 market hogs

annually. Management believed its acquisitions and joint ventures gave the company strong market positions, high-quality manufacturing facilities, and excellent growth and exporting potential to serve regions that already had high pork consumption levels and that were emerging as major meat consumers. Executives were particularly excited about the company's opportunities in the European Union.

In pork, Smithfield had pursued a vertical integration strategy, establishing operations in hog farming, feed mills, meat packing plants, and distribution. Smithfield's hog processing group, the chief subsidiary of which was Murphy-Brown LLC, owned and operated hog farms with close to 900,000 sows in North Carolina, South Carolina, Virginia, Utah, Colorado, Texas, Oklahoma, South Dakota, Iowa, Missouri, Illinois, Mexico, Romania, and Poland.

Smithfield Foods was headquartered in Smithfield, Virginia, where it operated two large hog processing plants. But large parts of the company's operations were in North Carolina—Smithfield's biggest pork processing plant was in Bladen County, North Carolina, and the company's Murphy-Brown hog production subsidiary had a very sizable hog farming operation in eastern North Carolina. Smithfield opened a new state-of-the-art ham processing plant in Kinston, North Carolina, in 2005 that employed 206 workers; the Kinston plant was expected to be the most efficient premier-cooked-ham plant in the United States, employing the newest technologies available and meeting the highest food standards in the industry. Smithfield's large southern base provided low wages and relatively low operating costs across much of its integrated operations, factors that helped pave the

Exhibit 1 **Financial and Operating Summary, Smithfield Foods, 1995–2004 (in millions, except per share amounts)**

	2004	2003	2001	1999	1995
Operations					
Sales revenues	$9,267.0	$7,135.4	$5,123.7	$3,550.0	$1,526.5
Gross profit	938.9	602.2	762.3	448.6	126.9
Selling, general, and administrative expenses	570.8	497.9	416.2	280.4	62.4
Depreciation expense	167.5	151.5	114.5	59.3	19.7
Interest expenses	121.3	87.8	81.5	38.4	14.1
Income from continuing operations	162.7	11.9	214.3	89.6	31.9
Net income	$ 227.1	$ 26.3	$ 223.5	$ 94.9	$ 27.8
Earnings per share	$2.03	$0.24	$2.03	$1.16	$0.40
Financial position					
Working capital	$1,056.6	$ 833.0	$ 635.4	$ 215.9	$ 60.9
Total assets	4,813.7	4,410.6	3,250.9	1,771.6	550.2
Total debt	1,801.5	1,642.3	1,188.7	610.3	234.7
Shareholders' equity	1,617.2	1,299.2	1,053.1	542.2	184.0
Current ratio	2.09	2.02	2.01	1.46	1.35
Total debt to total capitalization	52.7%	55.8%	53.0%	53.0%	58.4%
Other statistics					
Capital expenditures	$151.4	$172.0	$113.3	$92.0	$90.6
Number of employees	46,400	44,100	34,000	33,000	9,000

Source: 2004 annual report.

way for Smithfield's competitive prices and strong growth.

The company's longtime chairman and CEO, Joseph W. Luter III, continually emphasized the need to drive down costs and push up sales. Top executives at Smithfield Foods wanted to continue the company's rapid and profitable expansion and were constantly on the lookout for opportunities to grow the company's business. Going into 2006, Smithfield had annualized sales of close to $11 billion, up from $1.5 billion in 1995; revenues had grown at a compound average rate of close to 24 percent during the past decade. Exhibit 1 provides historical financial data.

OPPOSITION TO SMITHFIELD'S EXPANSION

Over the last decade, Smithfield Foods had met with mounting opposition to expansion of its business,

particularly in hog farming. The chief pockets of opposition to Smithfield's hog farming activities came from rural residents in eastern North Carolina, where there were some 8,000 hog farms. Neighboring residents complained that commercial hog farming had essentially been imposed on them and that it entailed substantial adverse impacts in the form of low wages and environmental discharges.

Eastern North Carolina and Smithfield's Hog Farming Operations

Eastern North Carolina, essentially the area extending about 150 miles from Raleigh (the state capital) to the Atlantic coast, is a region of flat land, sandy soil, and ample rainfall. At one time it was a relatively prosperous region, with thousands of small family farms, each of which had a tobacco allotment. During the 1930s far more tobacco had been grown than was needed, and the price plummeted. One of the government initiatives of the Depression era was a restriction on the total amount of tobacco that could be grown, and this total amount was divided up among the existing growers by restricting each to a set percentage of the amount of their land that had been devoted to the crop during a given base year. These restrictions on growth first stabilized and later increased the price, and the possession of an allotment almost guaranteed the financial prosperity of the farm.

The typical family farm would have 150 to 200 acres. Perhaps 15 acres would be devoted to tobacco, and the balance would be sown in corn, wheat, rye, or soybeans, or left as pasture for cattle or—more frequently—hogs. The grains grown locally would be trucked to the nearest town within the region to be milled into feed and then returned to the farm for the livestock. The cattle and hogs produced locally would be trucked to the nearest town to be sold at auction, and then slaughtered and processed at a nearby packing plant. These towns were also relatively prosperous, as the farmers and their families purchased clothing and household goods at local stores and automobiles and farm machinery at local dealers.

This prosperity started downhill in the 1970s as the national campaigns against smoking led to continual reductions in the size, and consequently the profitability, of the tobacco allotments, which eventually came almost to an end. Local prosperity continued to decline in the 1980s as very large feed lots in Nebraska, Iowa, and Kansas developed a much less costly means of raising hogs prior to slaughter; the piglets spent only the first 12 to 15 months of their lives on the farms where they were bred before being brought to fenced open-air corrals where they were closely confined but fed continuously to gain weight. Farmers in eastern North Carolina had to compete against this new and far more efficient production process. Prices for the hogs raised in eastern North Carolina declined sharply, and many of the local packing plants went out of business.

Local prosperity stabilized to some extent in the 1990s, though with a greatly changed distribution of income, as Smithfield Foods introduced the concept of the factory farm. Large metal sheds with concrete floors were built, each designed to hold up to 1,000 hogs. Feeding was by means of a mechanized conveyor that carried food alongside both walls. Waste was removed by hosing it off the floors to a central trough that carried it to a storage lagoon. Temperature was controlled by huge fans at each end of each shed. Every effort was made to reduce costs. Feed grains were no longer grown, purchased, and milled locally; instead most grains were grown, purchased, and milled in the Midwest and transported to eastern North Carolina by unit feed trains, which were strings of covered hopper cars that moved as a unit, without switching, from the feed mill in Nebraska or Iowa directly to one of the company's distribution centers in North Carolina. Some feed grains were grown and purchased even more cheaply abroad, primarily in Australia and Argentina, and then carried by ship to a company-leased milling facility and distribution center in Wilmington (a port in southeastern North Carolina, near the South Carolina border).

Limited farm machinery was needed for this new method of raising hogs, given that few feed grains were grown locally, but the little that was needed was purchased by the Smithfield headquarters office directly from the manufacturer. Many farm equipment dealers within the region were forced to close. Even diesel fuel, needed for the trucks that transported the feed grains to the farms and the mature hogs to the packing plants, was purchased from the refinery, transported by railway tank cars to large storage tanks at the distribution centers, and pumped directly into the trucks. Local fuel dealers got little or none of this business. All truck purchases were arranged by bid from national dealers located in Detroit (auto companies had refused to sell outside their dealer chains, but they allegedly gave favored prices to very large dealers near their corporate headquarters) at very low prices, and all subsequent truck repairs were done at company-owned repair shops located at the company-owned distribution centers. Some truck dealers in the region were forced to close.

Executives at Smithfield Foods did not apologize for the business model that they had created. Their attitude could be summed up as follows: "This is the way the world is going and this is what the market demands. All we have done is to create a competitive system that works. Moreover, we have saved farms and brought jobs to the eastern North Carolina region through this system, and we have provided better (leaner) pork products at lower prices to our customers." Smithfield's development of a "competitive system that works" had won Joseph Luter an award as Master Entrepreneur of the Year in 2002;

a Smithfield news release dated December 21, 2002, said:

> Joseph W. Luter III has been named the Ernst & Young 2002 Virginia Master Entrepreneur of the Year. The Ernst & Young program recognizes entrepreneurs who have demonstrated excellence and extraordinary success in such areas as innovation, financial performance and personal commitment to their businesses and communities . . .
>
> Since becoming chairman and chief executive officer of Smithfield Foods, Inc. in 1975, Mr. Luter transformed the company from a small, regional meat packer with sales of $125 million and net worth of $1 million to an international concern with annual sales of $8 billion and a net worth of $1.4 billion.

Smithfield Foods did not own the farms that raised the hogs. Instead, company representatives would select a reasonably large farm, one that had been successful in the past and therefore was financially solvent now, and negotiate a contract with the owning family to raise hogs at a set price per animal. The farm family would frequently use a loan provided through the Smithfield Corporation and a contractor licensed by the Smithfield Corporation to build metal barns with concrete floors, feed conveyors, ventilation fans, and waste systems; connect the waste systems to storage lagoons (five to eight acres in size); construct feed bins and loading ramps; and be ready for business. Smithfield Corporation would then deliver the hogs at piglet stage, provide a constant supply of feed grains mixed with antibiotics (to prevent disease in the crowded conditions of the metal barns), and offer free veterinarian service. The responsibility of the farm family was to raise those hogs to marketable weight as quickly and as efficiently as possible. This was termed *contract farming*; it was described in the following terms in a five-part investigative series that ran February 19–26, 1995, in the *Raleigh News and Observer*:

> Greg Stephens is the 1995 version of the North Carolina hog farmer. He owns no hogs. Stephens carries a mortgage on four new confinement barns that cost him $300,000 to build. The 4,000 hogs inside belong to a company called Prestage Farms, Inc. (one of the larger suppliers of Smithfield Foods). Prestage simply pays Stephens a fee to raise them . . .
>
> This arrangement is called contract farming, and it's hardly risk-free. But for anyone wanting to

break into the swine business these days, it's the only game in town. "Without a contract, there's no way I'd be raising hogs," says Stephens, "and even if I had somehow gotten in, my pockets aren't nearly deep enough to let me stay in."

Welcome to corporate livestock production, the force behind the swine industry's explosive growth in North Carolina. The backbone of the new system is a network of hundreds of contractors like Stephens, the franchise owners in a system that more closely resembles a fast-food chain than traditional agriculture.

Nowhere in the nation has this change been as dramatic, or as officially embraced, as in North Carolina. As a result, the hog population has more than doubled in four years, and nearly all of that growth has occurred on farms controlled by the big companies. Meanwhile, independent farmers have left the business by the thousands.

In 1998 Smithfield Foods reportedly had a two-year waiting list of farmers wishing to obtain hog farming contracts. Industry observers, however, worried about the practice of saddling hundreds of small farmers with thousands of dollars of debt. As one elected state representative said, "Why invest your capital when you can get a farmer to take the risk? Why own the farm when you can own the farmer?"[1]

The problem foreseen by industry observers was the possibility that a company could cancel its contract with only 30 days' notice, leaving the farmer with the debt and no income to repay it, or could threaten to cancel and then renew the contract only with a sharply lower price per animal. Both sudden cancellations and lower prices were said to have happened frequently in the poultry industry:

> The changes that are sweeping the swine industry today were pioneered by chicken and turkey growers in the 1960s and '70s. Total confinement housing, vertical integration, and contract farming are all standard practices in the feather world. As a result, you need only look at chickens to see where pork is headed.
>
> The poultry industry today is fully integrated—meaning a handful of companies control all phases of production—and the labor is performed by an army of contract growers, some of them decidedly unhappy. "It's sharecropping, that's what it is," said Larry Holder, a chicken farmer and president of the Contract Poultry Growers Association.

The *Raleigh News and Observer* interviewed a number of farmers with hog-growing contracts in

North Carolina. One farmer with 10 years of experience growing for Carroll Farms (another large supplier of Smithfield Foods), said, "They've been nothing but good to me."[2] Greg Stephens, the farmer quoted earlier, told the *News and Observer* that in his case the biggest selling point had been his freedom from market risk: "If hog prices go south, as they did two months ago, the contract farmer is barely affected. The company that owns the pigs takes on more risk than you do."[3]

The survival of over 1,000 family farms as contract hog growers is cited as one of the major benefits of the industrialization of agriculture in eastern North Carolina. Another is the creation of new agricultural jobs. Each of the contract farms averages 7,500 animals. The owning families cannot care for all those animals, even though the hogs are closely confined and automatically fed and watered. The typical farm will employ five people from the community at wages of $7 to $8 an hour; working conditions are hard and unpleasant. Most of the people filling such jobs are untrained and poorly educated area residents.

Smithfield's three newest slaughterhouses in North Carolina employed about 3,200 people. Many of the jobs at these plants were regarded as hard and unpleasant; some involved killing and disemboweling the hogs. The killing was said to be painless, and much of the early processing (scraping the carcass to remove the hair, and dealing with the internal organs) was automated. One of the more labor-intensive tasks involved preparing cuts of meat for packaged sale at grocery chains. Most grocery chains, to reduce their internal costs, had eliminated the position of store butchers, opting instead to buy their fresh meats cut, wrapped, packaged, and ready for sale. The cutting at meatpacking facilities was done on a high-speed assembly line, using very sharp laser-guided knives; workers were under continual pressure to perform and were exposed to dangers of injury. Workers who became skilled at this cutting and were able to endure the stress earned $10 to $12 an hour; turnover was relatively high because of the strenuous job demands. Many of the workers at the high-volume packing plants in eastern North Carolina were immigrants from Central or South America. The jobs were described in the following terms by an undercover reporter for the *New York Times* who worked at one of the Smithfield packing plants for three weeks on what was termed the picnic line:

One o'clock means it is getting near the end of the workday [for the first shift]. Quota has to be met, and the workload doubles. The conveyor belt always overflows with meat around 1 o'clock. So the workers redouble their pace, hacking pork from shoulder bones with a driven single-mindedness. They stare blankly, like mules in wooden blinders, as the butchered slabs pass by.

It is called the picnic line: 18 workers lined up on both sides of a belt, carving meat from bone. Up to 16 million shoulders a year come down that line here at Smithfield Packing Co., the largest pork production plant in the world. That works out to about 32,000 per shift, 63 a minute, one every 17 seconds for each worker for eight and a half hours a day. The first time you stare down at that belt you know your body is going to give in way before the machine ever will.[4]

Smithfield's vertical integration strategy, which had resulted in very limited purchasing of feed, machinery, and fuel from local sources; the debt-laden nature of the farm contracts, which fueled concerns about the possibility of future contract cancellations or price reductions; and the low-pay/low-quality nature of the jobs that had been created at both the farms and the packing plants had combined to create strong, often vocal, opposition on the part of many local residents to any planned expansion of Smithfield Foods within eastern North Carolina.

A much bigger and far more intense issue, however, was the alleged impact of a concentrated cluster of hog farms on the environment:

Imagine a city as big as New York suddenly grafted onto North Carolina's Coastal Plain. Double it. Now imagine that this city has no sewage treatment plants. All the wastes from 15 million inhabitants are simply flushed into open pits and sprayed onto fields.

Turn those humans into hogs, and you don't have to imagine at all. It's already here. A vast city of swine has risen practically overnight in the counties east of Interstate 95. It's a megalopolis of 7 million animals that live in metal confinement barns and produce two to four times as much waste, per hog, as the average human.

All that manure—about 9.5 million tons a year—is stored in thousands of earthen pits called lagoons, where it is decomposed and sprayed or spread on crop lands. The lagoon system is the source of most hog farm odor, but industry officials say it's a proven and effective way to keep harmful chemicals and bacteria out of water supplies. New evidence says otherwise:

- The *News and Observer* has obtained new scientific studies showing that contaminants from hog lagoons are getting into groundwater. One N.C. State University report estimates that as many as half of existing lagoons—perhaps hundreds— are leaking badly enough to contaminate ground water.

- The industry also is running out of places to spread or spray the waste from lagoons. On paper, the state's biggest swine counties already are producing more phosphorous-rich manure than available land can absorb, state Agriculture Department records show.

- Scientists are discovering that hog farms emit large amounts of ammonia gas, which returns to earth in rain. The ammonia is believed to be contributing to an explosion of algae growth that's choking many of the state's rivers and estuaries.[5]

Raising hogs is admitted even by farm families to be a messy and smelly business. Hogs eat more than other farm animals, and they excrete more. And those excretions smell far, far worse. Having 50 to 100 hogs running free in a fenced pasture is one thing. The odor is clearly noticeable, but that sharp and pungent smell is felt to be part of rural living. Having 5,000 to 10,000 hogs closely confined in metal barns, with large ventilation fans moving the air continually from each barn, and the wastes from those hogs collected in huge open-air lagoons is something else. People who live near one of the large hog farms say that, unless you've experienced it, you just can't know what it is like:

> At 11 o'clock sharp on a Sunday morning the choir marched into the sanctuary of New Brown's Chapel Baptist Church. And the stench of 4,800 hogs rolled right in with them.
>
> The odor hung oppressively in the vestibule, clinging to church robes, winter coats and fancy hats. It sent stragglers scurrying indoors from the parking lot, some holding their noses. Sherry Leveston, 4, pulled her fancy white sweater over her face as she ran. "It stinks," she cried.
>
> It was another Sunday morning in Brownsville, a Greene County North Carolina hamlet that's home to 200 people and one hog farm. Like many of its counterparts throughout the eastern portion of the state, the town hasn't been the same since the hogs moved in a couple of years ago.

> To some, each new gust from the south [the direction of the farm] is a reminder of serious wrongs committed for which there has been no redress. "We've basically given up," said the Rev. Charles White, pastor at New Brown's Chapel.
>
> In scores of rural neighborhoods down east [the eastern portion of North Carolina] the talk is the same. There's something new in the air, and people are furious about it.
>
> Hog odor is by far the most emotional issue facing the pork industry—and the most divisive. Growers assert their right to earn a living; neighbors say they have a right to odor-free air. Hog company officials, meanwhile, accuse activists of exaggerating the problem to stir up opposition . . .
>
> For other residents [of Brownsville, close to New Brown's Chapel] hog odor has simply become an inescapable part of their daily routine. It's usually heaviest about 5 a.m., when Lisa Hines leaves the house for her factory job. It seeps into her car and follows her on her commute to work. It clings to her hair and clothes during the day. And it awaits her when she returns home in the afternoon.
>
> "It makes me so mad," she said. "The owner lives miles away from here, and he can go home and smell apples and cinnamon if he wants to. But we have no choice."[6]

The 7 million hogs in eastern North Carolina currently generate about 9.5 million tons of manure each year. This waste was stored in large earthen pits called lagoons. These pits were open so that sunlight would decompose the wastes and kill the harmful bacteria; the manure was then spread on farm fields as organic fertilizer. This had been the accepted means for disposing of animal wastes on small family farms for centuries. It was a method fully protected by federal, state, and local laws; a hog farmer—whether a small family or large contract farm—could not be sued for any inconveniences brought about by the hogs, unless those inconveniences were the result of clear negligence in caring for the hogs.

The difference now, of course, comes from the huge expansion of scale. Again, the wastes of 50 to 100 animals were easily accommodated. There was a noticeable effect on air quality, but that was felt to be a natural consequence of living in the country, and the smell came from your own farm, or that of your neighbor, or that of a person who had been there for years. There was a probable effect on water quality, but farm wells were always located uphill and a substantial distance from manure piles, and it was thought that neighbors would be protected by natural filtration through the clay subsoils of the region. No one worried very much about possible public health effects of small numbers of farm animals.

The wastes from 5,000 to 10,000 animals could not be so easily accommodated, and people did worry about the possible public health effects of very large numbers of farm animals. Debilitating asthma had become a much more frequent condition among young children who lived near large hog farms, and there was concern that waste was leaking from the lagoons and contaminating the groundwater. The conventional wisdom about the lagoons was that the heavier sludge was supposed to settle on the bottom and form a seal that would prevent the escape of harmful bacteria or destructive chemicals:

> As recently as two years ago, the U.S. Division of Environmental Management told state lawmakers in a briefing that lagoons effectively self-seal within months with "little or no groundwater contamination." Wendell H. Murphy, a former state senator who was also [in partnership with Smithfield Corporation] the nation's largest producer of hogs, said in an interview this month that "lagoons will seal themselves" and that "there is not one shred, not one piece of evidence anywhere in this nation that any groundwater is being contaminated by any hog lagoon."
>
> What Murphy didn't know was that a series of brand-new studies, conducted among Eastern North Carolina hog farms, showed that large numbers of lagoons are leaking, some of them severely.[7]

The *Raleigh News and Observer* had reported that researchers at North Carolina State University had dug test wells near 11 lagoons that were at least seven years old. They found that more than half of the lagoons were leaking moderately to severely; even those lagoons that were described as leaking only moderately still produced groundwater nitrate levels up to three times the allowable limit. The researchers also found that lagoons were not the only source of groundwater contamination. They dug test wells and examined water quality in fields where hog waste had been sprayed as fertilizer, and found evidence of widespread bacterial and chemical contamination. It was felt that fully as much water contamination came from the practice of attempting to dispose of the decomposed waste through spraying on crops as from the earlier storage of decomposing waste in the lagoons. According to the *Raleigh*

News and Observer reporter, too much waste was being sprayed on too few fields, even though almost all farmers in the region now accepted this natural fertilizer in lieu of buying commercial products.

The researchers from North Carolina State University, however, did not urge rural residents to rush out to buy bottled water. In most of the cases they concluded that the contaminants appeared to be migrating laterally toward the nearest ditch or stream, and they found no evidence that a private well had been contaminated. But they did find evidence that numerous streams had been contaminated, partially from leakage but primarily from spills and overflows:

> Frequently major spills are cleaned up quickly so that the public never hears about them. That's what happened in May 1995 when a 10-acre lagoon ruptured on Murphy's Farms' 8,000-hog facility in Magnolia, North Carolina. A limestone layer beneath the lagoon collapsed, sending tons of waste cascading into nearby Millers Creek in an accident that was never reported to state water-quality officials.
>
> An employee of the town's water department discovered the problem when he saw corn kernels and hog waste floating by in the creek that runs through the center of town. He alerted the company, and within hours a task force had been assembled to plug the leak.
>
> It took four days to find the source and fix the problem. But neither Magnolia town officials nor Murphy Farms executives ever notified the state about the spill.
>
> "In retrospect, maybe we should have," Wendell Murphy said, "but I would also say that to my knowledge no harm has ever come of it."
>
> Former employees of hog companies, however, told *News and Observer* reporters that spills were a common occurrence. "Hardly a week goes by," said a former manager for one of the largest hog farms in the state, "that there isn't some sort of leak or overflow. Almost any heavy rain will bring an overflow. When that happens, workers do the best they can to clean it up. After that it's just pray no one notices and keep your mouth shut," he explained.[8]

The waste lagoons could not be covered with a roof to prevent overflows associated with heavy rains, or enclosed with a building to prevent the escape of odors; They were simply too large—five to eight acres—and it was necessary to have direct sunlight to create the natural conditions that would break down the toxic chemicals and kill the harmful bacteria in the wastes. Company officials seemed to believe that there was no possible solution to the problem of the extremely bad odors; essentially they said it would just be necessary for people to learn to live with the smell, which extends up to two miles from the open lagoons and the sprayed fields. According to the *Raleigh News and Observer,*

> Wendell Murphy, chairman of Murphy Family Farms [part of the Murphy Brown hog farming subsidiary of Smithfield Foods] said that while the hog industry is extremely sensitive to the odor problem, he thinks the industry's economic importance should be considered in the equation. "Should we expect the odor to never drift off the site to a neighbor's house? If so, then we're out of business. We all have to have some inconvenience once in a while for the benefits that come with it."[9]

As the *Raleigh News and Observer* reported, feelings ran high among eastern North Carolina residents in opposing further expansion of hog farming in the region:

> Three weeks ago, the tiny town of Faison held a referendum of sorts on whether its residents wanted a new industrial plant, with 1,500 new jobs, built in their community. The jobs lost.
>
> Because the industry in question was a hog-processing plant, people packed the local fire station an hour early to blast the idea. They jeered and hissed every time the county's industrial recruiter mentioned pigs or the plant. "I want to know two things," thundered one burly speaker thrusting a finger at that much smaller industrial recruiter, Woody Brinson. "How can we stop this thing, and how can we get you fired?"
>
> The town council's eventual 3–0 vote against the proposed IBP [a subsidiary of Smithfield Foods] hog slaughterhouse may have little effect on whether the plant is built. [Zoning within rural North Carolina is controlled by the county, not the municipality, and agriculturally related zoning has always been very loosely applied, to benefit local farmers.] What was striking about this meeting, and this vote, was that both occurred in the heart of Duplin County, an economic showcase for the hog industry.
>
> With a pigs-per-person ratio of 32-to-1, Duplin has seen big payoffs from eastern North Carolina's hog revolution in the past decade. The county's revenues from sales and property taxes have soared, and Duplin's per capita income has risen from the lowest 25 percent statewide to about the middle.

Pork production also has spawned jobs in support businesses in Duplin and neighboring counties. People in the hog business say farm odor—"the smell of money"—is a small price to pay for a big benefit. "These hog farms are putting money in people's pockets," says Woody Brinston [the county's director of industrial development]. "Duplin County is booming."

But even here, some bitterly resent the way the industry has transformed the way the countryside looks and smells. Some say that their property has gone down in value. Others note the contrasts in the economic picture. In Duplin County, just 70 miles east of the booming Research Triangle [an area located between Raleigh, Durham, and Chapel Hill with a large number of advanced electronic and biotechnology firms], the population hasn't grown in 10 years. Farm jobs are dwindling despite the rise in hog production.

Daryl Walker, a newly elected Duplin County commissioner, says he hears these arguments all the time. "If this is prosperity," he says, "many of my constituents would just as soon do without it. They are scared to death that there are just going to be more and more hogs, and more and more of the problems that come with those hogs.[10]

A subsequent letter to the editor of the *Raleigh News and Observer* said:

> Last Sunday, returning from a weekend at Wrightsville Beach, we stopped at an Interstate 40 rest area near Clinton. When we stepped from our car the stench brought tears to our eyes. So add to the ever-mounting environment damage the poor image our state now leaves with tourists heading towards our beautiful coast. We'll never know how many big tourism bucks are now and soon will be going elsewhere.[11]

SMITHFIELD'S EFFORTS TO ADDRESS CONCERNS ABOUT THE ENVIRONMENTAL IMPACT OF ITS VERTICAL INTEGRATION STRATEGY

Smithfield management was endeavoring to combat opposition to its operations in eastern North Carolina and elsewhere and to respond to the environmental challenges that its pork business presented.

Exhibit 2   **Examples of Smithfield Foods' Environmental Projects, 2000–2004**

- In 2000, Smithfield signed an agreement with the Office of the North Carolina Attorney General to contribute $2 million per year for 25 years to a fund used for such environmental enhancement projects as constructing and maintaining wetlands, preserving environmentally sensitive lands, and promoting similar projects. In 2003, the attorney general used Smithfield's contributions for grants to five recipients: the Cape Fear River Assembly, Save Our State, the Green Trust Alliance, the North Carolina Coastal Land Trust, and the North Carolina Foundation for Soil and Water Conservation Districts.

- Smithfield had funded a $15 million research project at North Carolina State University to investigate 18 different technologies to modify or replace current methods of swine waste removal at hog farms. A major goal of the project was to achieve cleaner air by finding ways to reduce methane and ammonia emissions of the swine waste lagoons. Smithfield had agreed to implement the recommended technologies, if they were commercially feasible, at all of its hog farms.

- In 2001, all of Murphy-Brown's company-owned swine production farms in North Carolina, South Carolina, and Virginia implemented "environmental management systems" (EMSs) to identify and manage parts of Smithfield's activities that have, or could have, an impact on the environment—the objective was to monitor environmental performance, pinpoint problem areas, and implement any needed preventive and corrective action. These farms then went an extra step and achieved ISO 14001 certification, making Murphy-Brown the first livestock operation in the world to do so—ISO 14001 certification was considered the gold standard for environmental excellence in implementing methods to monitor and measure the environmental impact of production operations and pinpoint problem areas. Since that time, Murphy-Brown has completed EMS implementation and achieved ISO 14001 certification for all company-owned farms in the United States.

- Smithfield was investing up to $20 million in a majority-owned subsidiary, BEST BioFuels, to build a waste collection system and a central treatment facility in southwestern Utah that used proprietary technology to convert livestock waste (which contained methane, a greenhouse gas) into biomethanol. Biomethanol could be processed with a variety of vegetable- or animal-based oils to create biodiesel, an environmentally friendly alternative to petroleum diesel. The waste-to-biomethanol treatment facility in Utah, which began operations in 2004, was connected by an underground sewage network to 23 area farms and received waste from approximately 257,000 hogs over the course of a year. The Utah plant shipped much of its 2.7 million gallons of biomethanol to a newly constructed BEST Biofuels plant in Texas, where it was processed with used cooking oil, rendered animal fat, or other oil feedstock to create biodiesel, an environmentally friendly alternative to petroleum diesel that emitted nearly 50 percent less carbon monoxide and hazardous particulate matter than regular petroleum diesel. Fuel distributors then blended biodiesel with conventional petroleum diesel in a 20/80 ratio to create a cleaner diesel fuel.

- Cooling towers were installed at four of Smithfield's company processing plants to recirculate water needed in operating the plants; these water conservation measures reduced use of groundwater and relieved stresses on local water tables.

- Smithfield had partnered with its primary corrugated packaging suppliers to pursue cardboard recycling in its operations. Since 2002, close to 50,000 tons of cardboard had been recycled rather than being sent to landfills.

- Several Smithfield plants had modified their facilities to allow biogas—a fuel source derived from plant wastewater—to be used as an energy source. Most all Smithfield plants were pursuing projects to conserve on the use of electric energy.

Source: Information contained in Smithfield's 2003 Stewardship Report and information posted at www.smithfieldfoods.com (accessed December 26, 2002, and November 23, 2004).

Exhibit 2 describes examples of Smithfield's environmental improvement projects during 2000–2004. Exhibit 3 presents Smithfield Foods' environmental policy statement. Exhibit 4 presents senior management's statement regarding the company's "Strategy for Responsible Growth." Exhibit 5 presents excerpts from the company's Code of Business Conduct.

During the spring of 2003, the highest seasonal rainfall in North Carolina's recorded history caused elevated lagoon levels at many eastern North Carolina hog farms. Farmers reported the levels to the state agency, as was the standard practice, but officials at North Carolina's Department of Environment and Natural Resources nonetheless sent out hundreds of notices of violations (NOVs), 55 of which were

Exhibit 3   Smithfield Foods' Environmental Policy Statement, 2004

It is the corporate policy of Smithfield Foods, Inc., and its subsidiaries to conduct business in a manner consistent with continual improvement in regard to protecting the environment.

- Smithfield Foods, Inc., is committed to protecting the environment through pollution prevention and continual improvement of our environmental practices.
- Smithfield Foods, Inc., seeks to demonstrate its responsible corporate citizenship by complying with relevant environmental legislation and regulations, and with other requirements to which we subscribe. We will create, implement, and periodically review appropriate environmental objectives and targets.
- Protection of the environment is the responsibility of all Smithfield Foods, Inc., employees.

Source: www.smithfieldfoods.com (accessed November 23, 2004).

to farms operated by Smithfield's Murphy-Brown subsidiary. While elevated lagoon levels did not compromise the structural integrity of the lagoons, they did decrease the reserve designated for storage

of rainfall accumulated over a 24-hour period from intense storms. Many farmers and legislative leaders protested the number of NOVs issued, prompting the Department of Environment and Natural Resources

Exhibit 4   Statement of Smithfield Foods' Management Regarding the Company's Strategy for Responsible Growth

Over the past few years, our company has set the foundations for continuous improvement in our stewardship responsibilities, which include our environmental, employee safety and animal welfare–related performance. We have firmly established the necessary policies, organizations, management systems, programs, funding, and expertise.

This foundation is now in place within the majority of our U.S. operations. We continue to move forward guided by the principles of accountability, transparency, and sustainability, and by our primary objectives:

- Achieve 100 percent regulatory compliance, 100 percent of the time.
- Move well beyond compliance in stewardship responsibilities.
- Reduce the frequency and severity of injuries to employees.
- Enhance communications and transparency with external stakeholders.
- Continue to expand community involvement.

We also have a more ambitious vision, and that is to be recognized as the industry leader for stewardship. To do this, we will continue to explore approaches to the issues that are unique to our industry. We will continue to find ways to participate productively in key industry and multi-stakeholder groups where we can help facilitate win–win solutions. We will share our experiences and best practices with our peers and other interested parties. We will also work toward policy changes that promote industry innovation and enable our company to better deliver financial, environmental, and social value.

In 2003, Smithfield embarked on a major project, committing to invest $20 million to implement technology beneficial to the environment and that will also play a key role in the solution for our global energy needs. We are using the untapped energy stored in livestock waste to create a fully renewable motor fuel—biodiesel. Our renewable fuel project at Circle Four Farms in Utah will produce in excess of 7,000 gallons of biomethanol per day. Blended with rendered fats, this biomethanol is converted to biodiesel that would meet the daily fuel requirements for about 300 over-the-road trucks, offsetting the need to import crude oil to produce that quantity of traditional diesel fuel. The project is highlighted in more detail in other sections of this report and is expected to be in full operation in late spring 2004.

We are very encouraged by the results we have seen over the past few years. Moving forward, Smithfield's strategy for responsible growth can be summed up as follows: more of the same. And by that we mean more management systems, more measurement and target setting, more innovative thinking and partnering, further support of environmentally superior waste management technologies, more communication, transparency and relationship building, more improvement—and more listening. This is what Smithfield will strive to accomplish.

Source: Smithfield Foods, *2003 Stewardship Report,* pp. 11–12.

Exhibit 5   **Excerpts from Smithfield Foods' Code of Business Conduct, 2004**

Smithfield is committed to compliance with the laws, rules, and regulations applicable to the conduct of our business wherever we operate. Our ultimate goal is 100% compliance, 100% of the time. Employees must avoid activities that could involve or lead to involvement of Smithfield or its personnel in any unlawful practice.

Employee awareness of Smithfield operating practices must include knowledge of the environmental laws and Smithfield policies governing their operations. Employees must immediately control and report all spills and releases as required by applicable regulations and facility rules.

The nature of Smithfield's business requires it to conduct various monitoring, inspecting, and testing to ensure compliance with applicable laws and regulations. Such monitoring, inspecting, and testing must be performed, and accurate records thereof made and retained, in compliance with all applicable legal requirements. Employees who have questions about legal requirements applicable to such areas should consult their supervisor or a member of the Smithfield Law Department.

Smithfield employees are expected to comply with all federal, state, local, and foreign environmental laws and all Smithfield policies related to environmental affairs. We expect 100% compliance 100% of the time. It is each employee's responsibility to know and understand the legal, policy, and operating practice requirements applicable to his or her job and to notify management when the employee believes that a violation of law or Smithfield policies has occurred. Any employee who has concerns regarding compliance in this area should immediately consult with the environmental contact for his or her facility or subsidiary, a senior environmental officer, or the Smithfield Law Department. The Smithfield Foods, Inc. Employee Hotline (1-877-237-5270) is available for reporting employee concerns anonymously.

Compliance with environmental laws and all Smithfield policies is the single highest priority for the company's environmental program. Our employees' job performance is important to us, and is evaluated not only on business results achieved, but also on whether our employees, and particularly our management team, operate within our expectations for environmental performance. We hold all of our employees to a high standard of conduct and accountability for environmental performance.

Compliance with the Smithfield Foods, Inc., Code of Business Conduct and Ethics is a condition of employment. Failure to comply may result in a range of disciplinary actions, including termination. Failure by any Smithfield employee to disclose violations of these standards and practices by other Smithfield employees or contract workers is also grounds for disciplinary action.

Source: Smithfield Foods' Code of Business Conduct, www.smithfieldfoods.com (accessed November 23, 2004).

to reconsider their having issued so many NOVs; a substantial number were subsequently reclassified as notices of deficiency (NODs). Following the severe weather, Smithfield moved swiftly to get its lagoon levels back to compliance levels and no further regulatory actions were taken. All told, Smithfield received 77 notices of violations or noncompliance in 2003, resulting in fines of $124,204. The biggest fine ($77,000) was for a wastewater incident at its Moyer beef processing plant in Pennsylvania, and a $17,875 fine was imposed for an ammonia release at a Georgia plant.

Endnotes

[1] Quoted in the five-part series by Joby Warrick and Pat Stith, "Boss Hog: North Carolina's Pork Revolution—Hog Waste Is Polluting the Ground Water," *Raleigh News and Observer,* February 19, 1995. This series, based on a seven-month investigation and run in the *News and Observer,* February 19–26, 1995, was awarded the Pulitzer Prize for Public Service Journalism in 1996.
[2] Ibid.
[3] Ibid.
[4] Charlie LeDuff, "At a Slaughterhouse, Some Things Never Die," *New York Times,* June 16, 2000, p. A1.
[5] *Raleigh News and Observer,* February 19, 1995.
[6] Joby Warrick and Pat Stith, "Boss Hog: North Carolina's Pork Revolution—Money Talks," *Raleigh News and Observer,* February 24, 1995, p. A9.
[7] Ibid.
[8] Ibid.
[9] Ibid.
[10] Joby Warrick and Pat Stith, "Boss Hog: North Carolina's Pork Revolution—Pork Barrels," *Raleigh News and Observer,* February 26, 1995.
[11] *Raleigh News and Observer,* March 4, 1995, p. A10.

Zoës Kitchen: Making Cents of the Fast-Casual Dining Industry

Braxton Maddox
The University of Alabama

Jennifer Traywick
The University of Alabama

As the globed lights illuminated the glass storefront of the newest Zoës Kitchen in Brentwood, Tennessee, curious passers-by could see a multitude of activities late that night. John Cassimus, president and CEO of Zoës Kitchen, knew every detail had to be perfect for opening day. Required were sweeping, mopping, cleaning, prepping food, and double-checking every inch of the store. The success of the entire Zoës Kitchen brand depended on how well the next few restaurants performed. As Cassimus carefully placed T-shirts, hats, and "Zoës Life" booklets, on the merchandising racks, his thoughts wandered from the cheerful, inviting store that was now almost complete to the challenges on the road ahead.

Zoës Kitchen was the natural extension of Zoë Cassimus's own kitchen—a place livened by her love of family and warm hospitality. Zoë had carefully created all the recipes from scratch, producing fresh food that also promoted good health. Her son John had carefully grown Zoës Kitchen from a single family restaurant into what could soon be one of the leading concepts in the fast-casual restaurant industry.

The fast-casual dining classification was the newest segment to emerge in the maturing restaurant industry. Year after year of double-digit sales growth was proving that fast-casual was not just a fad, and many of the major food companies had begun to take notice. With new, larger competitors looking to enter the market, John Cassimus was convinced that now was the time for Zoës Kitchen to make its strategic move.

ZOËS STORY

Marcus and Zoë Cassimus opened the first Zoës Kitchen in Homewood, Alabama, in 1995, serving lunch five days a week. Zoës Kitchen quickly became a favorite spot for both mothers with children and primarily white-collar employees in the area. As of December 2005, Zoës Kitchen operated 16 locations in five states, and each store had helped build a brand synonymous with fresh ingredients, family recipes, and homemade food. Zoës menu included a healthy selection of chicken sandwiches, rollups, pitas, dinner plates, and an assortment of salads including chicken, potato, pasta, and egg (see Exhibit 1). Customers could also purchase many salads and sides by the pound to take home. Most menu items had a Greek influence, reflecting the heritage of the Cassimus family.

John Cassimus graduated from the University of Alabama in 1990 as a four-time football letterman. After graduation, he began work with Pittman Financial Partners in Birmingham, Alabama, and honed his marketing and sales skills. Cassimus was often described as a hard worker, optimist, excellent salesman, true entrepreneur, and visionary—attributes that contributed much to his success in the business arena. His first start-up, launched in

Exhibit 1   **Zoës Kitchen Menu**

the fall of 1993, was an apparel company named J-Rag Inc. After J-Rag became the leader in imprinted sportswear to cycling manufacturers, Cassimus sold the company in 1996. He spent the next two years traveling extensively in his efforts to direct a new venture called Compensation Management Associates, and during that time he successfully tripled the company's sales. Recognizing national trends and the success of the first Zoës Kitchen, Cassimus turned his attention to growing his family's restaurant business.

Under Cassimus's leadership, Zoës Kitchen quickly expanded from its original location, adding three more Zoës Kitchen locations in Birmingham;

one in Tuscaloosa; and two in Nashville, Tennessee. Franchises were also developed successfully in Memphis, Tennessee; Destin, Florida; and Phoenix, Arizona. Zoës Kitchen was quickly gaining brand awareness and a loyal customer base. Cassimus decided that to continue the pace of growth he would need his pilot's license. The Zoës Kitchen Sirrus plane allowed Cassimus and his team to quickly and easily visit stores in disparate locations and facilitated the process of making site-selection decisions.

Cassimus knew from the beginning that he wanted to operate Zoës Kitchen like a world-class company, even when there was only one unit. He also wanted to develop a company that could one day be sold, if he so desired. With the goal of a steady, predictable cash flow, Cassimus invested heavily in people, brand image, and systems. Zoës Kitchen generally compensated its hourly employees and managers at rates above the market average, which allowed the company to recruit good candidates and reduce turnover. A bonus system tied managers' compensation to their performance based on key metrics. Morale was high in stores, and many employees had been with the company for much of its existence.

In 2001, as Cassimus was speaking to a class at the University of Alabama, a student suggested redesigning the original logo to enhance the Zoës Kitchen brand image. Cassimus was initially opposed to the idea, primarily because the logo had been designed by his mother Zoë and because the cost to effect widespread image change would be high. However, after Cassimus's mentor from Chick-Fil-A made the same recommendation, he reconsidered.

A marketing survey the University of Alabama conducted for Zoës Kitchen indicated that customer loyalty to Zoës Kitchen was strong. Customers surveyed most often selected four words to describe Zoës Kitchen: fresh, healthy, tasty, and unique. Respondents also indicated that those who ate at Zoës Kitchen more than once a week told their friends and family about their experience. Of the 242 customers surveyed, nearly 50 percent of the respondents had discovered the restaurant through friends and family, 21 percent were enticed by seeing the store, 9 percent had been recommended by coworkers, and only 3 percent were influenced by advertising. Customers also placed the highest value on service and quality of menu offerings, so Zoës Kitchen did not compete primarily on price. After analyzing the survey results, Zoës Kitchen underwent an extensive brand redesign

in 2002. Cassimus hired an architectural design company to create an identity for Zoës Kitchen. After many brainstorming sessions, the new Zoës Kitchen look and feel emerged. Simple decor, bright colors, vivid stripes, a trademarked logo, and Zoës Kitchen merchandise became crucial elements of all locations. Customers noticed, and sales improved immediately.

By 2006, Zoës Kitchen had strong systems in place to manage food costs, inventory, and labor. Tight food ordering processes and cash controls helped Zoës Kitchen mitigate risk. Zoës Kitchen used a point-of-sale (POS) system that featured a biometric thumbprint employees used to clock in, clock out, and take orders. Managers were assisted throughout the day by a "dashboard" in the POS system that allowed them to easily monitor sales and labor costs. A defined training program and job duties helped hourly employees succeed every day.

Zoës Kitchen remained close to what Zoë Cassimus pictured, with approximately 70 percent of its sales occurring during lunch. Most stores were open seven days a week from 10:00 a.m. to 8:00 p.m. While nearly half of the food purchased was consumed off premises, there were still significant growth opportunities available in developing the catering and dinner business.

THE RESTAURANT INDUSTRY IN THE UNITED STATES

In 2005, the United States restaurant industry included over 870,000 restaurants and employed 11.6 million workers. According to an article by Lori Dahm titled "Fast-Casual: Positioned for Growth" in *Stagnito's New Products Magazine,* fast-casual chains in the United States grew by 13 percent in 2004, while overall the restaurant industry grew by 4.5 percent. Fast-casual restaurants brought in $7.5 billion in sales in 2004, or 2.5 percent of the $300 billion restaurant industry (see Exhibit 2). Despite being dominated by giant fast-food chains, most restaurants in the industry were small operations. More than 70 percent were independent, single-unit businesses with fewer than 20 employees. One out of every three was owned by a sole proprietor or a partnership. While the restaurant industry had grown

Exhibit 2   **Share of Restaurant Meal Occasions by Segment**

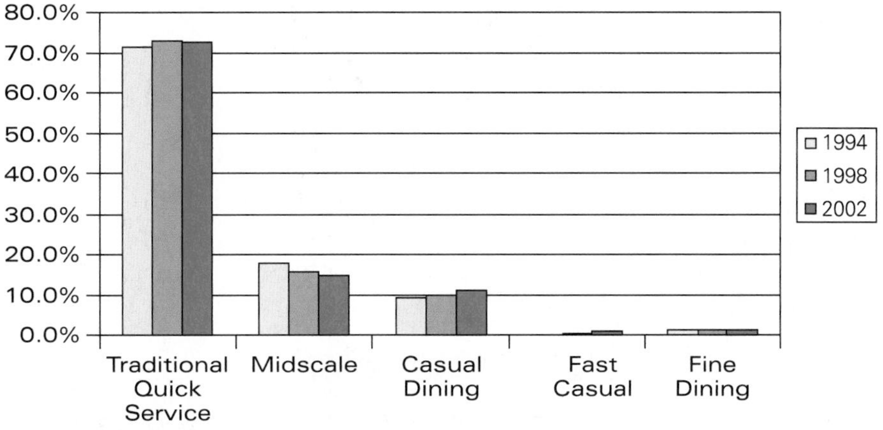

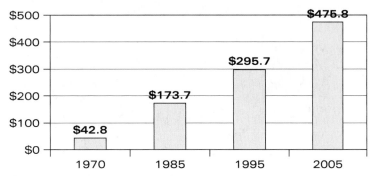

Source: Zoës Kitchen.

rapidly from 1970 to 2005 (see Exhibit 3), it was now regarded as mature, and unfortunately the outlook for overall restaurant industry growth had become rather bleak. A report in the *McKinsey Quarterly* projected annual growth of only 2 percent until 2010. Many large players were suffering because they could not profitably offer what consumers desired: fresh food served quickly in a distinctive, casual environment. The growth in the industry was expected to come from the middle ground—a segment with strong potential called fast-casual.

The fast-casual segment of the restaurant industry emerged in the mid-1990s, beginning with high-end bakeries and cafés including Panera Bread and Corner Bakery. There was no exact, agreed-on definition of fast-casual in the industry, typically because each chain is so distinctive. However, there were some characteristics that most chains shared: high quality, fresh food, and a wide variety of menu items. Many innovative menu items could be rotated seasonally and tailored to customers' requests, which helped preserve the "fresh" connotation. Customers usually ordered at a counter, and a server brought food to their table. The restaurants often focused on dining-room ambiance, creating a warm environment for customers. Even though fast-casual was a small part of the overall restaurant industry, the fast-casual chains were able to grow by adapting their offerings to consumer demands. Most consumers had time-starved lifestyles, leaving little time to visit a sit-down restaurant (see Exhibit 4). However, consumers did want to eat healthy, high-quality foods. Fast-casual chains overcame this dilemma by offering quality food in a unique environment at a speed close to that of fast-food restaurants.

Exhibit 3   **Restaurant Industry Sales (billions of dollars)**

Source: National Restaurant Association.

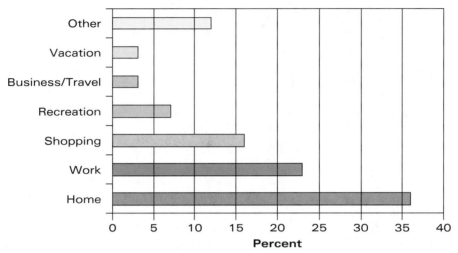

Exhibit 4 **Distribution of Fast-Casual Visits (where consumers came from), 2004**

Source: "The Casual Dining Evolution and the Rise of Fast Casual," presentation prepared by Dan White, Coca-Cola Fountain Marketing.

Therefore, many consumers frequented fast-casual restaurants several times each week because they saw the experience as a valuable use of time and money (see Exhibit 5). The fast-casual segment was expected to be worth approximately $35 billion by the end of the decade and to account for more than half of all food-service growth.

Consumers welcomed fast-casual with open arms because it met their lifestyle demands by providing an alternative to traditional fast food and offering more choices. "They woke up the industry to what consumers want when they eat out," said Michele Schmal, vice president of product management for

NPD Foodworld. Each fast-casual restaurant had a personality all its own and a menu to match. Before fast-casual, there were two ends of the dining-out spectrum: fast food and sit-down casual dining. Fast-casual brought the two together and essentially bridged the gap in quality, taste, ambiance, price, and convenience for quick service (see Exhibit 6).

According the NPD Group's latest "Fast-Casual Report", fast-casual restaurants were continuing to see increases in units (locations), traffic, and sales. Unit expansion increased by 17 percent in 2003, while the total number of restaurants nationally remained constant. The segment's expansion slowed to 13 percent

Exhibit 5 **Average Income of Fast-Casual Customers, 2004**

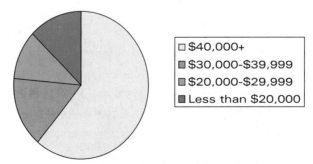

Source: "The Casual Dining Evolution and the Rise of Fast-Casual," presentation prepared by Dan White, Coca-Cola Fountain Marketing.

Exhibit 6 **Fast-Casual Consumer Demographics Compared with Other Food-Service Providers, 2004**

	Quick-Service Restaurant	Fast-Casual	Casual Dining
Ages 35–64	40%	47%	47%
Professional/white collar	39	54	48
Female	52	54	52

Source: "The Casual Dining Evolution and the Rise of Fast Casual," presentation prepared by Dan White, Coca-Cola Fountain Marketing.

in 2004, but customer traffic rose 7 percent in 2004 versus 5 percent in 2003.

This change in the industry resulted from changing lifestyles and subsequent demands those lifestyles placed on consumers. The typical consumer was strapped for time, especially during meals, and valued control, personality, and healthy choices from food providers. Kasey Burleson, chief financial officer of Zoës Kitchen, said, "People are more educated than ever on health and global cuisine, and their acumen of quality, freshness, and value is becoming more precise. People demand extremely high levels of quality, service, and speed, and the fast-casual dining segment is poised to grow and change with consumers." A fast-paced society valued quick service and increasingly more health-conscious meals. Consumers were also increasingly unwilling or unable to cook, a factor that had the most profound effect on dinner (see Exhibit 7). In the last 10 years, consumers had increasingly shifted from home-prepared dinners to restaurant-prepared meals either served at the restaurant or consumed off-premises (see Exhibit 8).

These factors naturally left a gap with regard to both speed and quality of food, giving rise to fast-casual providers. Since most of the large quick-service food providers were struggling to reach this segment,

most of the unit supply was expected to come from small, specialized food establishments. Naturally, the biggest challenge for these small competitors was reaching a critical mass of customers that would enable fast-casual restaurants to enjoy the economies of scale of mass fast-food chains while maintaining the quality consumers wanted.

The atmosphere of fast-casual stores often attempted to reflect the brand. For instance, Corner Bakery Café aimed for a comfortable, old-fashioned bistro feel, while Panera Bread strategically positioned fireplaces in the middle of the restaurant to project coziness. The fluorescent lights and plastic utensils often seen in fast-food restaurants were considered taboo. Customers were often served on high-end plastic plates with metal silverware, even though they were expected to bus their own tables.

Offering fresh food instead of frozen, hiring talented labor, and constructing each restaurant with character could be very expensive. While fast-casual chains offered high-quality products at relatively low prices compared to sit-down restaurants, expenses could quickly erode profit margins. Even the best service would fail if it lacked the scale or operational efficiency. For example, Cosi, a New York–based bread and coffee chain, generated $70 million

Exhibit 7 **Total Meal Occasions for Meals Prepared Outside the Home (in percent)**

Meal Occasion	1987	1999	2005
Breakfast	14%	12%	11%
Lunch	41	39	38
Dinner	45	49	51
Total	100%	100%	100%

Source: Technomic; McKinsey analysis.

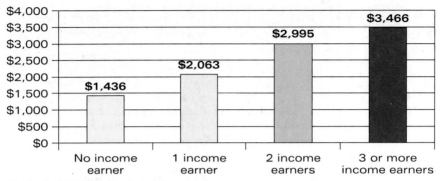

Exhibit 8   **Average Expenditures for Food Away from Home by Households with Two or More Persons, 2003**

Source: National Restaurant Association.

in sales in 2001 from more than 60 restaurants but recorded a net loss of $35 million. Therefore, fast-casual restaurants sought growth in number of units to capitalize quickly on economies of scale.

Fast-food companies, also known as quick-service restaurants (QSRs), seemed likely to move into the fast-casual segment because their operations were streamlined and operationally efficient. They possessed strong distribution networks, and most carried heavy purchasing clout. However, they had scant experience beyond their current offerings, and their supplier network was not tuned for the shipment of fresh products. Moreover, their image and value proposition of fast food was seen as a liability as far as consumers were concerned. To compete, fast-food chains were likely to find it more beneficial to enter the market through a buyout or other form of a merger. Full-service restaurants offered similar products, but their service was slower than consumers desired.

COMPETITION

For Zoës Kitchen, trying to identify close competitors was somewhat challenging because of the number and variety of choices consumers had for dining out. Zoës Kitchen experienced the most direct competition with other restaurants in a five-minute radius of each location. On a national scale, Zoës Kitchen did not have any competitors that emulated its format and menu. However, several fast-food chains had added more healthful offerings to their menus—a move that might prove trendsetting for the entire fast-casual dining segment.

The recent success of the fast-casual segment had turned heads in the quick-service segment (see Exhibit 9). Various fast-casual brands had popped up around the nation, most with strong regional appeal (see Exhibit 10). The fast-food giants found it very difficult to break into this market with their existing operations. The features consumers wanted—including

Exhibit 9   **Top Fast-Casual Restaurants (ranked by 2004 sales)**

Rank	Chain	Sales (in $ millions)	% Change 2003 to 2004
1	Panera Bread	$1,241	+23%
2	Chipotle Mexican Grill	430	+34
3	Baja Fresh Mexican Grill	348	+11
4	Atlanta Bread	220	+22
5	Qdoba Mexican Grill	133	+53

Source: Technomic; figures for year-end 2004.

Exhibit 10   **Comparisons of Select Restaurant Industry Competitors**

Competitor	Menu Options	Decor/Target Customers	Growth and Growth Potential	Geographic Placement
Panera Bread	Baked breads, sandwiches, paninis, salads, soups, bagels	Mimicked Starbucks (bold colors, varied seating options, contemporary fixtures, young professionals)	478 current locations and 346 franchised in 30 states	Locations were in high-traffic areas with visibility
Qdoba Mexican Grill	Generous portions of Mexican food; all food prepared in front of customer	Slightly industrial decor (deep reds and dark woods and aluminum tabletops)/targeted the trend-seeking consumer	100 locations in 15 states; 301 locations in development (due to acquisition of Jack in the Box)	Tuscaloosa, Alabama, location had high visibility near university of Alabama campus
Baja Fresh	Fresh Mexican food	Contemporary decor with black-and-white theme lends itself to attracting the modern consumer	210 locations in 18 states (acquired by Wendy's in 2002)	None in Alabama, on the West Coast, or in the Midwest
Moe's Southwestern Grill	Restaurant claimed to not even own a freezer, supporting its claim that all food was fresh and made to order; all food was prepared in front of customer	Muted tones covered the walls, icons from the 1960s and 70s were featured throughout	115 locations	Birmingham locations were in strip malls and usually surrounded by other restaurants

Source: Zoës Kitchen.

healthy, wide-ranging product offerings and an up-scale atmosphere—could not be replicated profitably by most of the larger quick-service companies. In response, companies such as Wendy's, McDonald's, and Jack in the Box acquired smaller companies in hopes of fueling growth in this illusive segment with their strong financial resources (see Exhibit 11).

Wendy's spent $9 million to purchase a 45 percent stake in Café Express, a fast-casual chain owned by the Schiller Del Grande Restaurant Group in Houston. Wendy's was planning to expand the current 13 Café Express locations in Houston, Dallas, and Phoenix to 50 units nationwide. In 2002, Wendy's acquired Baja Fresh, which still operated as a wholly owned subsidiary and remained loyal to the vision of becoming the leading name and defining standard in fresh Mexican food. Wendy's also changed its own menu in response to fast-casual by adding a choice of sides including salad, fruit, baked potato, and yogurt, in addition to the traditional fries.

McDonald's was also trying to break into fast-casual. Looking for relief from its sliding sales and profit margins, it purchased a minority interest in Chipotle Mexican Grill, headquartered in Denver, in 1998. In 2004, McDonald's expanded its stake in Chipotle to a majority interest. Chipotle showed phenomenal success with its 150 units in more than 20 markets. Same-store sales growth had increased annually by 15 percent for the last three years, with an average unit volume estimated to be $1.05 million per unit. In the fourth quarter of 2005, McDonald's filed with the Securities Exchange Commission to spin off Chipotle into a separate, publicly held company.

Subway was the only company experimenting with completely refashioning itself as a fast-casual brand. Subway had recently opened its own

Exhibit 11   **The 10 Fastest-Growing Restaurant Chains (ranked by sales increase)**

Rank	Chain	Sales Increase 2002–2003 ($000)	% Sales Change	2003 U.S. Sales ($000)
1	McDonald's	$1,816,100	8.9%	$22,121,800
2	Starbucks	759,694	25.8	3,699,972
3	Wendy's	525,000	7.7	7,350,000
4	Subway	499,000	9.6	5,699,000
5	Applebee's	336,404	10.6	3,518,961
6	Dunkin' Donuts	300,000	11.1	3,000,000
7	Chili's Grill	246,553	11.4	2,402,517
8	Panera Bread	221,689	29.3	977,099
9	International House of Pancakes	212,459	14.5	1,676,026
10	Krispy Kreme	207,708	26.3	997,708
	Total top 10	$5,124,607	11.1%	$51,443,083

Source: Technomic.

Tuscan-themed restaurant, which was the first major brand overhaul in a decade. The new restaurant, located in Chicago, sported soft gold tones, instead of the company's trademark bright yellow, and earth-toned tiles instead of linoleum floors. Since making these changes, Subway had noticed a new wave of customer traffic, including more suits and ties for lunch.

Panera Bread

Panera Bread was founded as Au Bon Pain in 1981 by Louis Kane and Ron Shaich. The company prospered along the East Coast and internationally during the 1980s and 1990s and became the dominant operator in the bakery-café segment. In 1993, Au Bon Pain purchased Saint Louis Bread Company, then a chain of 20 bakery-cafés located in the Saint Louis area. The management conducted a restaging of Saint Louis Bread, and ultimately the name was changed to Panera Bread. In May 1999, Au Bon Pain was renamed Panera Bread, and it sold all its business units with the exception of its namesake. As of 2006 the company was publicly held, with numerous locations across the country, and had a market capitalization of $1.8 billion.

Panera Bread had seen strong growth, and it planned to expand into New York and California. Of its 741 bakery-cafés in 35 states, 226 were company-owned; the rest were franchised. There were 155 Panera bakery-cafés projected to open in 2005.

The primary basis of Panera's product offering was, simply, bread. The company claimed that it baked more bread from scratch each day than any other restaurant chain and operated with the goal of making quality bread broadly available to everyone in the United States. Panera was highly recognized nationwide for its specialty breads and had among the highest rankings in terms of customer loyalty and quality food.

Qdoba Mexican Grill

In 1995, Anthony Miller and Robert Hauser opened the first Qdoba Mexican Grill restaurant in Denver, Colorado. Since its beginning, Qdoba had won over both customers and critics with its big portions and big flavors. The *Denver Post* and *Westward* named Qdoba's the "best burrito," and *Gabby Gourmet* recognized Qdoba as one of the top 15 inexpensive restaurants in Colorado. In just a few years, Qdoba grew to over 100 locations in more than 30 states. In 2003, Qdoba was acquired by Jack in the Box Inc., the first major drive-through hamburger chain. Jack in the Box has more than 1,900 franchised restaurants.

Baja Fresh

Jim and Linda Magglos introduced the first all-fresh, fire-grilled, fast-casual concept as Baja Fresh in August 1990. The product offering included fresh flavors and generous portions that quickly drew a loyal following of customers. The idea was a restaurant that catered to the more mature tastes for healthy, vibrant, flavorful foods in a festive atmosphere. The restaurants were designed to involve many senses with bright, contemporary decor, artistic lighting, and clean, crisp design. The resulting customer following helped Baja Fresh expand rapidly from a regional to a national scope, with a high volume of requests for franchises resulting in over 288 locations. In an effort to take full advantage of this new concept, Greg Dollarhyde and Pete Siracusa, with over 60 collective years of restaurant experience, were hired to help manage the growth.

Moe's Southwestern Grill

Emphasizing simplicity, Moe's Southwestern Grill was the fastest-growing fast-casual concept in the country. The founder wanted to create a place that combined his favorite flavors from road trips through the Southwest with the music of days gone by. Moe's stressed freshness; it even claimed not to own a freezer. It made every menu item on the day that a customer ordered it. The atmosphere paid tribute to Moe's musical heroes with relics from the 1960s and 70s.

Moe's recently announced that it had signed a 20-store deal for the northern Virginia/greater Washington, D.C., territory. The company had over 800 franchise deals in development and was on pace to open 150 additional units in 2005. Moe's was part of Raving Brands, which also franchised Mama Fu's Asian House, Planet Smoothie, PJ's Coffee, Shane's Rib Shack, Doc Green's Gourmet Salads, and Bonehead's Seafood.

FRANCHISES

Offering franchises allowed many companies to rapidly expand after their start-up stage. Most of the fast-casual concepts had seen such strong growth due to franchising that they continued to increase the number of franchises planned to open each year. In a market when numbers of units counted, franchising had become a catalyst for growth.

Franchisees were able to run their own business, gaining instant brand recognition, training, and other support as needed to succeed. The franchisee typically paid a franchising fee, which could cost several thousand dollars. The franchisor provides the franchisee with the format to use in operating the business, the right to use the company's name for a limited amount of time, and other assistance that

varied greatly. Company systems for cash control, inventory management, labor, and technology were usually included as well. The franchisee could reduce investment risk by associating with an established company. Only 2 percent of franchises discontinued operations within three years of opening. However, franchising could have high intangible costs. A franchisor could require franchisees to relinquish significant control over operations and take on contractual obligations. Other payments often included continued royalties and advertising fees.

Zoës Kitchen had expanded primarily through company-owned stores and had not yet tapped too deeply into the franchising aspect of the business. With systems in place to control food costs, inventory costs, labor, and cash, Zoës was positioned well to take advantage of franchise opportunities in the future.

ZOËS GROWTH

This was an exciting time for fast-casual and even more so for Zoës Kitchen. With the industry still young and scale economies a core aspect of gaining fast-casual supremacy, strategic growth was Zoës main priority. "Zoës Kitchen is positioned in the fastest growing sector of the food service industry. Offering a fresh, tasty, healthy, and unique menu, more profitable business model, and differentiation from any of our peers allows us to replicate our menu for success in strategically planned markets," said John Cassimus.

Whether operating as company-owned stores or franchises, Zoës Kitchen had to have a sound, executable plan for entering new markets, focusing first on excellent site selection (see Exhibit 12). The desire to grow and achieve economies of scale had to be balanced with the desire to find outstanding locations, and growth had to be deferred if only subpar sites were available. When looking for new sites, Zoës Kitchen primarily considered the following criteria:

- Well-located space in dense, affluent markets.
- Average household income above $75,000 in a three-mile radius.
- Premier end-cap or similar positions.
- Minimum of 25 feet of storefront footage.
- Parking ratio of 10 per 1,000 square feet.
- Excellent visibility and signage to primary traffic corridors.

Exhibit 12   **Zoës Kitchen Locations, as of December 2005, and Scheduled 2006 Openings**

Locations as of December 2005
Birmingham, AL—Crestline
Birmingham, AL—Downtown
Birmingham, AL—Summit
Homewood, AL
Montgomery, AL
Hoover, AL
Spanish Fort, AL
Tuscaloosa, AL
Phoenix, AZ—Central Avenue
Phoenix, AZ—West McDowell
Destin, FL
Ponte Vedra Beach, FL
Baton Rouge, LA
Brentwood, TN
Nashville, TN
Memphis, TN
2006 Scheduled Openings
Mobile, AL
Phoenix, AZ—Camelback
Dallas, TX

- Daytime population within two miles above 50,000.
- Co-tenancy that generated daily traffic (i.e., groceries, gyms, schools).
- Real estate projects that promoted the quality and uniqueness of the Zoës Kitchen brand.

In the restaurant industry, sales were often measured in average unit volumes (AUV), with company value often based on a multiple of its AUV. To increase the AUV of each restaurant, Zoës Kitchen had to increase its dinner sales by further developing its dinner dine-in and dinner take-out business. In 2005, Zoës Kitchen added three new menu items targeted at this segment: chicken kabobs, a red chicken sandwich, and a red chicken plate. Zoës Kitchen also developed "Dinners for Four," which allowed customers to take home a meal that could be served on family-style platters with no preparation time. While Zoës Kitchen offered its entire menu for catering, a menu specifically designed to increase catering sales was expected to be introduced in the first quarter of 2006. Zoës Catering was to feature more platters, trays, and new menu items aimed directly at the catering segment of the industry.

The year 2006 was expected to be a year for concept validation, and success would largely determine Zoës ability to continue to grow. Zoës Kitchen sought to position itself to best capitalize on market opportunities. Expansion in the fast-casual segment had remained strong, but growth had already seen a decline while the industry was still seemingly in its infancy. Even so, fast-casual had made such a dramatic impact on current and new quick-service providers that everyone wanted to be poised to take advantage of growth opportunities.

As John Cassimus flew over the Brentwood, Tennessee, location after a successful grand opening, he believed that the newest Zoës restaurant was positioned for success. His employees, brand image, and systems gave him confidence that everything would run smoothly. A true visionary at heart, Cassimus focused his attention on the future of Zoës Kitchen. When would he be ready and able to sell the company? How much growth needed to occur, and when? What was the best mechanism for growth, and how could the value of the company continue to increase?

Case 12

Krispy Kreme Doughnuts in 2006: Is a Turnaround Possible?

Arthur A. Thompson
The University of Alabama

Amit J. Shah
Frostburg State University

We think we're the Stradivarius of doughnuts.
—*Scott Livengood, former president, chairman, and CEO*

How can a company firing on all cylinders until 2003, with revenue and earnings growth running at 20–25 percent per year and the stock price more than tripling since its initial public offering, go so wrong so quickly? In 2004–2005 Krispy Kreme Doughnuts was besieged with declining doughnut sales, falling revenues, the prospect of store closings and failed franchises, problems with the U.S. Securities and Exchange Commission over false and misleading financial statements, and lawsuits from shareholders and franchisees. The stock price in late 2005 was trading at around $6 per share, down 88 percent from its all-time high of close to $50 per share.

Until May 2004, Krispy Kreme's prospects appeared bright. With 357 Krispy Kreme stores in 45 states, Canada, Great Britain, Australia, and Mexico, the company was riding the crest of customer enthusiasm for its light, warm, melt-in-your-mouth doughnuts. During the past four years, consumer purchases of Krispy Kreme's doughnut products had taken off, with sales reaching 7.5 million doughnuts a day. Considerable customer excitement—approaching a cult-like frenzy—often surrounded the opening of the first store in an area. When a new Krispy Kreme opened in Rochester, New York, in 2000, more than 100 people

lined up in a snowstorm before 5:00 a.m. to get some of the first hot doughnuts coming off the conveyor line; within an hour there were 75 cars in the drive-through lane. Three TV stations and a radio station broadcast live from the store site. The first Krispy Kreme store in Denver, Colorado, opened in 2001, grossed $1 million in revenues in its first 22 days of operation, commonly had lines running out the door with a one-hour wait for doughnuts, and, according to local newspaper reports, one night had 150 cars in line for the drive-through window at 1:30 a.m.—opening day was covered by local TV and radio stations, and off-duty sheriff's deputies were brought in to help with traffic jams for a week following the grand opening.

The first Minnesota store, just outside of Minneapolis, had opening-week sales of $480,693—the company record for fiscal 2002. In July 2003, the first store to open in the Massachusetts market—in Medford, outside Boston—had a record opening-day revenue of $73,813 and a record opening-week sales volume of $506,917; sales at the Medford store exceeded $2 million in the first seven weeks. At the June 2003 opening of the company's first store in Australia, in the outskirts of Sydney, customers camped overnight in anticipation of the opening and others waited in line for hours to experience their first Krispy Kreme hot doughnut—the store, about an hour from downtown Sydney, attracted more than 500,000 customers from Sydney in its first six months of operations. In South Bend, Indiana, one exuberant customer camped out in the parking lot for 17 days to be the first in line for the Krispy Kreme Store's grand opening.

To capitalize on all the buzz and customer excitement, Krispy Kreme had been adding new stores at a record pace throughout 2002–2003. The company's strategy and business model were aimed at opening a sufficient number of new stores and boosting sales at existing stores to achieve 20 percent annual revenue growth and 25 percent annual growth in earnings per share. In the just-completed 2004 fiscal year, total company revenues rose by 35.4 percent, to $665.6 million compared with $491.5 million in the fiscal 2003. Net income in fiscal 2004 increased by 70.4 percent, from $33.5 million to $57.1 million. Krispy Kreme's stock price had increased eightfold since it went public in April 2000, giving the company a high profile with investors and Wall Street analysts. In February 2004, Krispy Kreme stock was trading at 30 times the consensus earnings estimates for fiscal 2005, a price/earnings ratio that was "justified" only if the company continued to grow 20–25 percent annually.

A number of securities analysts doubted whether Krispy Kreme's strategy and growth potential would continue to push the company's stock price upward. According to one analyst, "The odds are against this stock for long-term success." Another commented, "I think the market is overly optimistic about the long-term opportunities of the growth of the doughnut business." A third said, "Single-product concepts only have so many years to run." Indeed, restaurants with quick-service products presently had the slowest revenue growth of any restaurant type. The Krispy Kreme bears were particularly concerned about reports from franchisees that, as the number of Krispy Kreme stores expanded in choice markets, average-store sales were slowing and newly opened stores were not performing as well as the first one or two stores. After the initial buying frenzy at high-profile store openings in a major market, the buzz tended to fade as the fourth, fifth, and sixth outlets opened; moreover, new stores started to cannibalize sales from existing stores, thus moderating the potential for new stores to boost overall sales. Several franchisees in California, Michigan, New York, Canada and a few other places were said to be in

financial difficulty because of overexpansion and disappointing sales at newly opened stores.

COMPANY BACKGROUND

In 1933, Vernon Rudolph bought a doughnut shop in Paducah, Kentucky, from Joe LeBeau. His purchase included the company's assets, goodwill, the Krispy Kreme name, and rights to a secret yeast-raised doughnut recipe that LeBeau had created in New Orleans years earlier. Several years thereafter, Rudolph and his partner, looking for a larger market, moved their operations to Nashville, Tennessee; other members of the Rudolph family joined the enterprise, opening doughnut shops in Charleston, West Virginia, and Atlanta, Georgia. The business consisted of producing, marketing, and delivering fresh-made doughnuts to local grocery stores. Then, during the summer of 1937, Rudolph decided to quit the family business and left Nashville, taking with him a 1936 Pontiac, $200 in cash, doughnut-making equipment, and the secret recipe; after some disappointing efforts to find another location, he settled on opening the first Krispy Kreme Doughnuts shop in Winston-Salem, North Carolina. Rudolph was drawn to Winston-Salem because the city was developing into a tobacco and textiles hub in the Southeast, and he thought a doughnut shop would make a good addition to the thriving local economy. Rudolph and his two partners, who accompanied him from Nashville, used their last $25 to rent a building across from Salem College and Academy. With no money left to buy ingredients, Rudolph convinced a local grocer to lend them what they needed, promising payment once the first doughnuts were sold. To deliver the doughnuts, he took the backseat out of the 1936 Pontiac and installed a delivery rack. On July 13, 1937, the first Krispy Kreme doughnuts were made at Rudolph's new Winston-Salem shop and delivered to grocery retailers.

Soon afterward, people began stopping by the shop to ask if they could buy hot doughnuts. There were so many requests that Rudolph decided to cut a hole in the shop's wall so that he could sell doughnuts at retail to passersby. Krispy Kreme doughnuts proved highly popular in Winston-Salem, and Rudolph's shop prospered. By the late 1950s, Krispy Kreme had 29 shops in 12 states, with each shop having the capacity to produce 500 dozen doughnuts per hour.

In the early 1950s, Vernon Rudolph met Mike Harding, who was then selling powdered milk to bakeries. Rudolph was looking for someone to help grow the business, and Harding joined the company as a partner in 1954. Starting with six employees, the two began building an equipment department and a plant for blending doughnut mixes. They believed the key to Krispy Kreme's expansion was to have control over each step of the doughnut-making process and to be able to deliver hot doughnuts to customers as soon as they emerged from the frying and sugar-glazing process. In 1960, they decided to standardize all Krispy Kreme shops with a green roof, a red-glazed brick exterior, a viewing window inside, an overhead conveyor for doughnut production, and bar stools—creating a look that became Krispy Kreme's trademark during that era.

Harding focused on operations, while Rudolph concentrated on finding promising locations for new stores and getting bank financing to support expansion into other southeastern cities and towns. Harding became Krispy Kreme's president in 1958, and he became chief executive officer when Rudolph died in 1973. Under Rudolph and then Harding, Krispy Kreme's revenues grew from less than $1 million in 1954 to $58 million by the time Harding retired in 1974. Corporate headquarters remained in Winston-Salem.

In 1976, Beatrice Foods bought Krispy Kreme and proceeded to make a series of changes. The recipe was changed, and the company's script-lettered signs were altered to produce a more modern look. As customers reacted negatively to Beatrice's changes, business declined. A group of franchisees, led by Joseph McAleer, bought the company from Beatrice in 1982 in a $22 million leveraged buyout. The new owners quickly reinstated the original recipe and the original script-lettered signs. Sales rebounded, but with double-digit interest rates in the early 1980s, it took years to pay off the buyout debt, leaving little for expansion.

To grow revenues, the company relied mainly on franchising "associate" stores, opening a few new company-owned stores—all in the southeastern United States—and boosting store volume through off-premises sales. Associate stores operated under a 15-year licensing agreement that permitted them to use the Krispy Kreme system within a specific geographic territory. They paid royalties of 3 percent of on-premises sales and 1 percent of all other branded sales (to supermarkets, convenience stores, charitable organizations selling doughnuts for fund-raising projects, and other wholesale buyers); no royalties were paid on sales of unbranded or private-label doughnuts. The primary emphasis of the associate stores and many of the company stores was on wholesaling both Krispy Kreme doughnuts and private-label doughnuts to local groceries and supermarkets. Corporate revenues rose gradually to $117 million in 1989 and then flattened for the next six years.

New Leadership and a New Strategy

In the early 1990s, with interest rates falling and much of the buyout debt paid down, the company began experimenting cautiously with expanding under Scott Livengood, the company's newly appointed president and chief operating officer. Livengood, 48, joined Krispy Kreme's human relations department in 1978 three years after graduating from the University of North Carolina at Chapel Hill with a degree in industrial relations and a minor in psychology. Believing strongly in the company's product and long-term growth potential, he rose through the management ranks, becoming president and chief operating officer in 1992, a member of the board of directors in 1994, president and CEO in 1998, and president, CEO, and chairman of the board in 1999.

Shortly after becoming president in 1992, Livengood became increasingly concerned about stagnant sales and shortcomings in the company's strategy: "The model wasn't working for us. It was more about selling in wholesale channels and less about the brand." He and other Krispy Kreme executives, mindful of the thousands of "Krispy Kreme stories" told by passionate customers over the years, concluded that the emphasis on off-premises sales did not adequately capitalize on the enthusiasm and loyalty of customers for Krispy Kreme's doughnuts. A second shortcoming was that the company's exclusive focus on southeastern U.S. markets unnecessarily handcuffed efforts to leverage the company's brand equity and product quality in the rest of the U.S. doughnut market. The available data also indicated that the standard 7,000-plus-square-foot stores were uneconomic to operate in all but very high-volume locations.

By the mid-1990s, with fewer than 100 franchised and company-owned stores and corporate sales stuck in the $110–$120 million range for six years, company executives determined that it was time for a new strategy and aggressive expansion outside the Southeast. Beginning in 1996, Krispy Kreme began implementing a new strategy to reposition the company, shifting the focus from a wholesale bakery strategy to a specialty retail strategy that promoted sales at the company's own retail outlets and emphasized the "hot doughnut experience" so often stressed in customers' Krispy Kreme stories. Doughnut sizes were also increased. The second major part of the new strategy was to expand the number of stores nationally using both area franchisees and company-owned stores. In preparing to launch the strategy, the company tested several different store sizes, eventually concluding that stores in the 2,400- to 4,200-square-foot range were better suited for the company's market repositioning and expansion plans.

The franchising part of the strategy called for the company to license territories, usually defined by metropolitan statistical areas, to select franchisees with proven experience in multi-unit food operations. Franchisees were expected to be thoroughly familiar with the local area market they were to develop and also to have the capital and organizational capability to open a prescribed number of stores in their territory within a specified period. The minimum net worth requirement for franchise area developers was $750,000 per store or $5 million, whichever was greater. Area developers paid Krispy Kreme a franchise fee of $20,000 to $40,000 for each store they opened. They also were required to pay a 4.5 percent royalty fee on all sales and to contribute 1.0 percent of revenues to a company-administered advertising and public relations fund. Franchisees were expected to strictly adhere to high standards of quality and service.

By early 2000, the company had signed on 13 area developers operating 33 Krispy Kreme stores and committed to open another 130 stores in their territories within five years. In addition, the company was operating 61 stores under its own management. Sales had zoomed to $220 million, and profits were a record $6 million.

After a decision was made to take the company public in April 2000, Krispy Kreme spent much of late 1999 and early 2000 preparing for an initial public offering (IPO) of the company's stock. The old corporate structure, Krispy Kreme Doughnut Corporation, was merged into a new company, Krispy Kreme Doughnuts Inc. The new company planned to use the proceeds from its IPO to remodel or relocate older company-owned stores, to repay debt, to make joint venture investments in franchised stores, and to expand its capacity to make doughnut mix.

The IPO of 3.45 million shares was oversubscribed at $21 per share, and when the stock began trading in April under the ticker symbol KREM, the price quickly rose. Krispy Kreme was the second-best-performing stock among all IPO offerings in the United States in 2000. The company's stock began trading on the New York Stock Exchange in May 2001 under the symbol KKD.

Between early 2000 and early 2004, the company increased the number of Krispy Kreme stores from 144 to 357, boosted doughnut sales from an average of 3 million a day to an average of 7.5 million a day, and began the process of expanding internationally—opening its first factory store in Europe, located in the world-renowned department store Harrods of Knightsbridge, London (with plans for another 25 stores in Britain and Ireland by 2008), and continuing expansion in Australia, Canada, and Mexico. In fiscal 2004, Krispy Kreme captured an estimated 30.6 percent of the market for packaged doughnut sales, compared with 23.9 percent in fiscal 2003 and 6.4 percent in fiscal 2002. In December 2005, the total number of company stores domestically stood at 349.

Exhibit 1 presents a summary of Krispy Kreme's financial performance and operations for fiscal years 2000–2004.

KRISPY KREME'S BUSINESS MODEL AND STRATEGY

Krispy Kreme's business model involved generating revenues and profits from three sources:

- Sales at company-owned stores.
- Royalties from franchised stores and franchise fees from new store openings.
- Sales of doughnut mixes, customized doughnut-making equipment, and coffees to franchised stores.

Exhibit 1   **Financial Statement Data for Krispy Kreme Doughnuts, Fiscal Years 2000–2004 (dollar amounts in thousands, except per share)**

	Fiscal Years Ending				
	Jan. 30, 2000	Jan. 28, 2001	Feb. 3, 2002	Feb. 2, 2003	Feb. 1, 2004
Statement of operations data					
Total revenues	$220,243	$300,715	$394,354	$491,549	$665,592
Operating expenses	190,003	250,690	316,946	381,489	507,396
General and administrative expenses	14,856	20,061	27,562	28,897	36,912
Depreciation and amortization expenses	4,546	6,457	7,959	12,271	19,723
Arbitration award	—	—	—	9,075	(575)
Income from operations	$ 10,838	$ 23,507	$ 41,887	$ 59,817	$102,086
Interest expense, (income), net, and other adjustments	1,232	(276)	(659)	5,044	7,409
Income (loss) before income taxes	9,606	23,783	42,546	54,773	94,677
Provision for income taxes	3,650	9,058	16,168	21,295	37,590
Net income	$ 5,956	$ 14,725	$ 26,378	$ 33,478	$ 57,087
Net income per share:					
Basic	$0.16	$0.30	$0.49	$0.61	$0.96
Diluted	0.15	0.27	0.45	0.56	0.92
Shares used in calculation of net income per share (in 000s):					
Basic	37,360	49,184	53,703	55,093	59,188
Diluted	39,280	53,656	58,443	59,492	62,388
Balance sheet data					
Current assets	$ 41,038	$ 67,611	$101,769	$141,128	$138,644
Current liabilities	29,586	38,168	52,533	59,687	53,493
Working capital	11,452	29,443	49,236	81,441	85,151
Total assets	104,958	171,493	255,376	410,487	660,664
Long-term debt, including current maturities	22,902	—	4,643	60,489	137,917
Total shareholders' equity	$ 47,755	$125,679	$187,667	$273,352	$452,207
Cash flow data					
Net cash provided by operating activities	$ 8,498	$ 32,112	$ 36,210	$ 51,036	$ 95,553
Net cash used for investing activities	(11,826)	(67,288)	(52,263)	(94,574)	(186,241)
Net cash provided by (used for) financing activities	(398)	39,019	30,931	53,837	79,514
Cash and cash equivalents at end of year	3,183	7,026	21,904	32,203	21,029

Source: Company SEC filings and annual reports.

Exhibit 2 shows revenues, operating expenses, and operating income by business segment.

The company was drawn to franchising because it minimized capital requirements, provided an attractive royalty stream, and put responsibility for local store operations in the hands of successful franchisees who knew the ins and outs of operating multi-unit chains efficiently. Krispy Kreme had little trouble attracting top-quality franchisees because of the attractive economics of its new stores (see Exhibit 3).

Krispy Kreme had developed a vertically integrated supply chain whereby it manufactured the mixes for its doughnuts at company plants in North Carolina and Illinois and also manufactured proprietary

Exhibit 2   **Krispy Kreme's Performance by Business Segment, Fiscal Years 2000–2004 (in thousands)**

	Fiscal Years Ending				
	Jan. 30, 2000	Jan. 20, 2001	Feb. 3, 2002	Feb. 2, 2003	Feb. 1, 2004
Revenues by business segment					
Company store operations	$164,230	$213,677	$266,209	$319,592	$ 441,868
Franchise operations	5,529	9,445	14,008	19,304	23,848
KK manufacturing & distribution	50,484	77,593	114,137	152,653	193,129
Total	$220,243	$300,715	$394,354	$491,549	$ 665,592*
Operating income by business segment (before depreciation and amortization)					
Company store operations	$ 18,246	$ 27,370	$ 42,932	$ 58,214	$ 83,724
Franchise operations	1,445	5,730	9,040	14,319	19,043
KK manufacturing & distribution	7,182	11,712	18,999	26,843	39,345
Total	$ 10,838	$ 23,507	$ 41,887	$ 59,817	$ 102,086*
Unallocated general and administrative expenses	$ (16,035)	$ (21,305)	$ (29,084)	$ (30,484)	$ (38,564)
Depreciation and amortization expenses					
Company store operations	$3,059	$4,838	$5,859	$ 8,854	$14,392
Franchise operations	72	72	72	108	173
KK manufacturing & distribution	236	303	507	1,723	3,006
Corporate administration	1,179	1,244	1,521	1,586	1,653
Total	$4,546	$6,457	$7,959	$12,271	$19,723*

*Totals include operations of Montana Mills, a business which was acquired in April 2003 and divested during fiscal 2005.
Source: Company SEC filings and annual reports.

doughnut-making equipment for use in both company-owned and franchised stores. The sale of mixes and equipment, referred to as "KK manufacturing & distribution" by the company, generated a substantial fraction of both revenues and earnings (Exhibit 2).

Many of the stores built prior to 1997 were designed primarily as wholesale bakeries, and their formats and site locations differed considerably from the newer stores being located in high-density areas where there were lots of people and high traffic counts. In order to improve on-premises sales at these older stores, the company was implementing a program to either remodel them or close and relocate them to sites that could better attract on-premises sales. In new markets, the company's strategy was to focus initial efforts on on-premises sales at its stores and then leverage the interest generated in Krispy Kreme products to secure supermarket and convenience store accounts and grow packaged sales.

So far, the company had spent very little on advertising to introduce its product to new markets, relying instead on local media publicity, product giveaways, and word of mouth. In almost every instance, local newspapers had run big features headlining the opening of the first Krispy Kreme stores

Exhibit 3   **Estimated Krispy Kreme Store Economics as of 2001**

Store revenues	$3,600,000
Cash flow (after operating expenses)	960,000
Cash flow margin	27%
Owner's equity investment to construct store	$1,050,000
Cash flow return on equity investment	91%

Source: As estimated by Deutsche Banc Alex. Brown.

in their area; in some cases, local radio and TV stations had sent news crews to cover the opening and conduct on-the-scene interviews. The grand opening in Austin, Texas, was covered live by five TV crews and four radio station crews (there were 50 people in line at 11:30 p.m. the night before the 5:30 a.m. store opening). At the first San Diego store opening, there were five remote TV trucks on the scene; radio reporters were out interviewing customers camped out in their pickup trucks in the parking lot; and a nationally syndicated radio show broadcast "live" at the site. It was common for customers to form lines at the door and at the drive-through window well before the initial day's 5:30 a.m. grand opening, when the HOT DOUGHNUTS NOW sign was first turned on. In a number of instances, there were traffic jams at the turn in to the store—a Buffalo, New York, traffic cop said, "I've never seen anything like this . . . and I mean it." As part of the grassroots marketing effort surrounding new-store openings, Krispy Kremes were typically given away at public events as a treat for participants—then, as one franchisee said, "the Krispy Kremes seem to work their own magic and people start to talk about them."

Krispy Kreme had originally financed its expansion strategy with the aid of long-term debt. However, the April 2000 IPO raised enough equity capital to completely pay off the long-term debt outstanding as of fiscal 2001. Since then the company had borrowed about $50 million on a long-term basis to help fund Its rapid growth during 2002–2004. When the company went public, it ceased paying dividends to shareholders; currently all earnings were being retained and reinvested in growing the business.

COMPANY OPERATIONS

Products and Product Quality

Krispy Kreme produced nearly 50 varieties of doughnuts, including specialty doughnuts offered at limited times and locations. By far the biggest seller was the company's signature "hot original glazed" doughnut made from Joe LeBeau's original yeast-based recipe. Exhibit 4 shows the company's doughnut varieties as of December 2005. Exhibit 5 indicates the nutritional content for a representative selection of Krispy Kreme doughnuts.

Company research indicated that Krispy Kreme's appeal extended across all major demographic groups, including age and income. Many customers purchased doughnuts by the dozen for their office, clubs, and family. According to one enthusiastic franchisee:

> We happen to think this is a very, very unique product which has what I can only describe as a one-of-a-kind taste. They are extremely light in weight and texture. They have this incredible glaze. When you have one of the hot original doughnuts as they come off the line, there's just nothing like it.

In 2003, Krispy Kreme ranked number one in Restaurants and Institutions' Choice in Chains category, beating number-two-ranked Starbucks.

The company received several thousand e-mails and letters monthly from customers. By all accounts, most were from customers who were passionate about Krispy Kreme products, and there were always some from people pleading for stores to be opened in their area. Exhibit 6 presents sample comments

---

Exhibit 4   **Varieties of Krispy Kreme Doughnuts, 2005**

• Original Glazed	• Chocolate Iced Custard Filled	• Glazed Cruller
• Glazed Cinnamon	• Raspberry Filled	• Powdered Cake
• Chocolate Iced	• Lemon Filled	• Glazed Chocolate Cake
• Chocolate Iced with Sprinkles	• Cinnamon Apple Filled	• Chocolate Iced Cruller
• Maple Iced	• Powdered Blueberry Filled	• Cinnamon Bun
• Chocolate Iced Kreme Filled	• Chocolate Iced Cake	• Glazed Blueberry
• Glazed Kreme Filled	• Dulce de Leche	• Glazed Sour Kream
• Traditional Cake	• Sugar Coated	• Caramel Kreme Crunch
• Apple Fritter	• New York Cheesecake	• Cinnamon Twist
• Powdered Strawberry Filled		
• Key Lime Pie		

Source: www.krispykreme.com, December 7, 2005.

Exhibit 5   **Nutritional Content of Selected Varieties of Krispy Kreme Doughnuts, 2005**

Product	Calories	Calories from Fat	Total Fat Grams	Total Fat % Daily Value*	Saturated Fat Grams	Saturated Fat % Daily Value*	Carbohydrates Grams	Carbohydrates % Daily Value*	Sugars
Original Glazed	200	100	12g	18%	3g	15%	22g	7%	10g
Chocolate Iced Glazed	250	110	12	19	3	15	33	11	21
Maple Iced Glazed	240	100	12	18	3	15	32	11	20
Powdered Blueberry Filled	290	150	16	25	4	20	33	11	14
Chocolate Iced Kreme Filled	350	180	20	32	5	25	38	13	23
Glazed Kreme Filled	340	180	20	31	5	24	38	13	23
Traditional Cake	230	120	13	20	3	15	25	8	9
Glazed Cruller	240	130	14	22	3.5	17	26	9	14
Cinnamon Bun	260	140	16	24	4	20	28	9	13
Glazed Chocolate Cake	340	140	15	23	3.5	18	41	14	26

*Based on a 2,000-calorie diet.

Source: www.Krispykreme.com, December 7, 2005.

from customers and franchisees. According to Scott Livengood:

> You have to possess nothing less than a passion for your product and your business because that's where you draw your energy. We have a great product . . . We have loyal customers, and we have great brand equity. When we meet people with a Krispy Kreme story, they always do it with a smile on their faces.

Coffee   Krispy Kreme had recently launched strategic initiatives to improve the caliber and appeal of its on-premises coffee and beverage offerings, aligning them more closely with the hot doughnut experience in its stores. The first move came in early 2001 when Krispy Kreme acquired Digital Java Inc., a small Chicago-based coffee company that sourced and roasted premium quality coffees and that marketed a broad line of coffee-based and noncoffee beverages. Scott Livengood explained the reasons for the acquisition:

> We believe the Krispy Kreme brand naturally extends to a coffee and beverage offering that is more closely aligned with the hot doughnut experience in our stores. Vertical integration of our coffee business provides the capability to control the sourcing and

roasting of our coffee. Increasing control of our supply chain will help ensure quality standards, recipe formulation, and roast consistency. With this capability, one of our first priorities will be the research and benchmarking necessary to develop premier blends and roasts of coffee which will help make Krispy Kreme a coffee destination for a broader audience. Beyond coffee, we intend to offer a full line of beverages including espresso-based drinks and frozen beverages. We believe we can substantially increase the proportion of our business devoted to coffee specifically and beverages generally by upgrading and broadening our beverage offering.

Since the acquisition of Digital Java, coffee sales at Krispy Kreme stores had increased nearly 40 percent due to expanded product offerings and upgraded quality. In 2003, Krispy Kreme was marketing four types of coffee: Smooth, Rich, Bold, and Robust Decaf—all using coffee beans from the top 5 percent of the world's growing regions. Beverage sales accounted for about 10 percent of store sales, with coffee accounting for about half of the beverage total and the other half divided among milk, juices, soft drinks, and bottled water. In the years ahead, Krispy Kreme hoped to increase beverage sales to about 20 percent of store sales.

Exhibit 6   **Sample Comments from Krispy Kreme Customers and Franchisees**

Customer Comments

- "I ate one and literally it brought a tear to my eye. I kid you not."
- "Oh my gosh, this is awesome. I wasn't even hungry, but now I'm going to get two dozen."
- "We got up at 3 o'clock this morning. I told them I would be late for work. I was going to the grand opening."
- "They melt in your mouth. They really do."
- "Krispy Kreme rocks."
- It's hot, good and hot. The way a doughnut should be."
- "The doughnut's magnificent. A touch of genius."
- "I love doughnuts, but these are different. It's terrible for your weight because when you eat just one, you feel like you've barely tasted it. You want more. It's like popcorn."*
- When you bite into one it's like biting into a sugary cloud. It's really fun to give one to someone who hasn't had one before. They bite into one and just exclaim."†

Franchisee Comments

- "Krispy Kreme is a 'feel good' business as much as it is a doughnut business. Customers come in for an experience which makes them feel good—they enjoy our doughnuts and they enjoy the time they spend in our stores watching the doughnuts being made."
- "We're not selling doughnuts as much as we are creating an experience. The viewing window into the production room is a theater our customers can never get enough of. It's fun to watch doughnuts being made and even more fun to eat them when they're hot off the line."
- "Southern California customers have responded enthusiastically to Krispy Kreme. Many of our fans first came to Krispy Kreme not because of a previous taste experience but rather because of the "buzz" around the brand. It was more word of mouth and publicity that brought them in to sample our doughnuts. Once they tried them, they became loyal fans who spread the word that Krispy Kreme is something special . . . We witness the excitement every day, especially when we're away from the store and wearing a hat or shirt with the Krispy Kreme logo. When people see the logo, we get the big smile and are always asked. 'When will we get one in our neighborhood?' . . . The tremendous local publicity coupled with the amazing brand awareness nationwide has helped us make the community aware of our commitment to support local charities. Our fund-raising program, along with product donations to schools, churches, and other charitable organizations have demonstrated our real desire to give back. This commitment also impacts our employees who understand firsthand the value of supporting the needy as well as the worthy causes in our neighborhoods."
- "In all my many years of owning and operating multiple food franchise businesses, we have never been able to please—until Krispy Kreme—such a wide range of customers in the community. Its like an old friend has come to town when we open our doors: we're welcomed with open arms . . . Quite frankly, in my experience, publicity for Krispy Kreme is like nothing I have ever seen. It is truly unprecedented."
- We happen to think this is a very, very unique product which has what I can only describe as a one-of-a-kind taste. They are extremely light in weight and texture. They have this incredible glaze. When you have one of the hot original doughnuts as they come off the line, there's just nothing like it.

*As quoted in "Winchell's Scrambles to Meet Krispy Kreme Challenge," *Los Angeles Times,* September 30, 1999, p. C1.
†As quoted in Greg Sukiennik, "Will Dunkin' Donuts Territory Take to Krispy Kreme?" Associated Press State & Local Wire, April 8, 2001.
Source: Krispy Kreme's 2000 and 2001 annual reports, except for the two quotes noted above.

Store Operations

Each store was designed as a "doughnut theater" where customers could watch the doughnuts being made through a 40-foot glass window (see Exhibit 7). New stores ranged in size between 2,400 and 4,200 square feet. Stores had a drive-through window and a dining area that would seat 50 or more people—a few of the newer and larger stores had special rooms for hosting Krispy Kreme parties. Store decor was a vintage 1950s look with mint green walls and smooth metal chairs; some of the newest stores had booths (see Exhibit 8). A typical store employed about 125 people, including about 65 full-time positions. Approximately half of on-premises sales occurred in the morning hours and half in the afternoon and

Exhibit 7   **Making the Doughnuts**

Mixing Ingredients

Rising

Frying and Flipping

Inspection and Draining

Drying and Entering Glazing

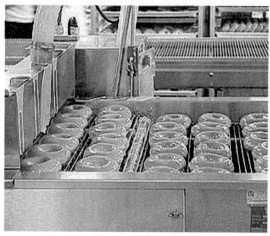

Exiting Glazing

Packaging

Exhibit 8   **Representative Krispy Kreme Stores and Store Scenes**

evening. Many stores were open 24 hours a day, with much of the doughnut making for off-premises sales being done between 6:00 p.m. and 6:00 a.m. Production was nearly always under way during peak in-store traffic times. In several large metropolitan areas, however, the doughnut making for off-premises sales was done in a central commissary specially equipped for large-volume production, packaging, and local-area distribution.

Each doughnut took about one hour to make. After the ingredients were mixed into dough, the dough was rolled and cut. The pieces went into a 12-foot-tall machine where each piece rotated on a wire rack for 33 minutes under high humidity and a low heat of 126 degrees to allow the dough to rise. When the rising process was complete, the doughnuts moved along a conveyor to be fried on one side, flipped, fried on the other side, and drained. Following all this came inspection. Doughnuts destined to be glazed were directed through a waterfall of warm, sugary topping; the others were directed to another part of the baking section to be filled and/or frosted. Exhibit 8 depicts the mixing, rising, frying, draining, and glazing parts of the process. Depending on store size and location, a typical day's production ranged between 4,000 and 10,000 dozen doughnuts.

Each producing store featured a prominent HOT DOUGHNUTS NOW neon sign (Exhibit 8) signaling customers that freshly made original glazed doughnuts were coming off the bakery conveyor belt and were available for immediate purchase. Generally, the signs glowed from 6:00 to 11:00 a.m. and then came on again during the late afternoon into the late-night hours.

Depending on the store location, Krispy Kreme's original glazed doughnuts sold for 60 to 75 cents each, or $4.50 to $7.50 per dozen; a mixed dozen usually sold for about 50 cents extra. Some stores charged a small premium for hot doughnuts coming right off the production line. Customers typically got a $1.00 per dozen discount on purchases of two or more dozen.

Stores generated revenues in three ways:

- On-premise sales of doughnuts.
- Sales of coffee and other beverages.
- Off-premise sales of branded and private-label doughnuts to local supermarkets, convenience stores, and fund-raising groups. Krispy Kreme stores actively promoted sales to schools, churches, and civic groups for fund-raising drives.

The company had developed a highly effective system for delivering fresh doughnuts, both packaged and unpackaged, to area supermarket chains and convenience stores. Route drivers had the capability to take customer orders and deliver products directly to retail accounts, where they were typically merchandised either from Krispy Kreme branded displays or from bakery cases (as unbranded doughnuts). The popularity of Krispy Kreme's stores had prompted many area supermarkets to begin stocking a selection of Krispy Kreme products in either branded display cases or in dozen and half-dozen packages.

The franchisee for Krispy Kreme stores in San Francisco had arranged to sell a four-pack of Krispy Kremes for $5 at San Francisco Giant baseball games at Pacific Bell Park—Krispy Kreme sold out of 2,100 packs by the third inning of the first game and, despite increasing supplies, sold out again after the fourth and sixth innings of the next two games; stadium vendors were supplied with 3,450 four-packs for the fourth game. The franchisee of the Las Vegas stores had a Web site that allowed customers to place orders online before 2:00 p.m. and have them delivered to their place of work by a courier service.

A Texas franchisee built a new 18,000-square-foot production and distribution center to supply Metroplex supermarkets, convenience stores, and other area retailers with Krispy Kreme 12-packs because newly opened Krispy Kreme stores did not have the baking capacity to keep up with both on-premises and off-premises demand; there were similar franchiser-operated wholesale baking and distribution centers in Nashville, Cincinnati, Atlanta, Chicago, and Philadelphia. Several of these centers had established delivery capability to supply Krispy Kremes to retailers in outlying areas deemed too small to justify a stand-alone Krispy Kreme store.

In 2004, about 20,000 supermarkets, convenience stores, truck stops, and other outside locations sold Krispy Kreme doughnuts. A growing number of these locations had special Krispy Kreme display cases, stocked daily with trays of different varieties for shoppers to choose from; these stand-alone cases could be placed in high-traffic locations at the end of an aisle or close to the check-out register.

The cost of opening a new store was around $2 million (including the standard package of equipment purchased from Krispy Kreme), but new store construction could range as high as $2.5 million in locations with high land and/or building costs. The initial franchise fee per unit was $40,000. Site selection was based on household density, proximity to both daytime employment and residential centers, and proximity to other retail traffic generators. A record number of new stores were opened in fiscal 2004—28 company-owned stores and 58 franchised stores (the net gain in stores was only 81 because 5 older stores were closed). Plans were in place to open 75 new stores in the upcoming fiscal 2005 year.

Weekly sales at newly opened stores could run anywhere from $100,000 to $500,000 the first couple of weeks a new store was open. Weekly sales tended to moderate to around $40,000 to $50,000 after several months of operation, but Krispy Kreme management expected new stores to have annual sales averaging more than $3 million in their first year of operation. In fiscal 2003, sales at all of the company's 276 stores (which included those open less than a year) averaged $2.82 million. In fiscal 2004, sales at all 357 stores averaged $2.76 million—slightly lower than in 2003, chiefly because of the larger number of new store openings (roughly half of the 86 new stores were open less than six months). Exhibit 9 provides data on store operations.

Krispy Kreme Manufacturing and Distribution

All the doughnut mix and equipment used in Krispy Kreme stores was manufactured and supplied by the company, partly as a means of ensuring consistent recipe quality and doughnut making throughout the chain and partly as a means of generating sales and profits from franchise operations. Revenues of the Krispy Kreme Manufacturing and Distribution (KKM&D) unit had averaged about 30 percent of total Krispy Kreme revenues for the past three years and contributed 38 to 45 percent of annual operating income (see Exhibit 2). The company's line of custom stainless-steel doughnut-making machines ranged in capacity from 230 to 600 dozen doughnuts per hour. Franchisees paid Krispy Kreme about $770,000 for the standard doughnut-making equipment package in 2003–2004 (up from about $500,000 in the late 1990s); the price increase was due partly to increased equipment capacity and partly to longer equipment durability. Increased doughnut sales at franchised stores also translated into increased revenues for KKM&D from sales of mixes, sugar, and other supplies to franchisees.

Krispy Kreme had recently opened a state-of-the-art 187,000-square-foot manufacturing and distribution facility in Effingham, Illinois, dedicated to the blending and packaging of prepared doughnut mixes and to distributing mixes, equipment, and other supplies to stores in the Midwest and the western half of North America. This facility had significantly lowered Krispy Kreme's unit costs and provided triple the production capacity of the older plant in Winston-Salem.

Exhibit 9   **Store Operations Data, Krispy Kreme Doughnuts, Fiscal Years 1998–2004**

	1998	2000	2001	2002	2003	2004
Systemwide sales	$203,439	$318,854	$448,129	$621,665	$778,573	$984,895
Number of stores at end of period:						
Company-owned	58	58	63	75	99	141
Franchised	62	86	111	143	177	216
Systemwide total	120	144	174	218	276	357
Increase in comparable store sales						
Company-owned	11.5%	12.0%	22.9%	11.7%	12.8%	13.6%
Franchised	12.7%	14.1%	17.1%	12.8%	11.8%	10.2%
Average weekly sales per store:						
Company-owned (000s)	$42	$54	$69	$72	$76	$73
Franchised (000s)	23	38	43	53	58	56

Source: Company annual reports and 10-K reports.

Training

Since mid-1999, Krispy Kreme had invested in the creation of a multimedia management and employee training curriculum. The program included classroom instruction, computer-based and video training modules, and in-store training experiences. The online part of the training program made full use of graphics, video, and animation, as well as seven different types of test questions. Every Krispy Kreme store had access to the training over the company's intranet and the Internet; employees who registered for the course could access the modules from home using their Internet connection. Learners' test results were transferred directly to a Krispy Kreme human resources database; learners were automatically redirected to lessons where their test scores indicated that they had not absorbed the material well on the first attempt. The online course was designed to achieve 90 percent mastery from 90 percent of the participants and could be updated as needed.

KKD'S BRIGHT GROWTH PROSPECTS

In 2003 and continuing into early 2004, Krispy Kreme management expressed confidence that the company was still in its infancy. The company's highest priority was on expanding into markets with over 100,000 households; management believed these markets were attractive because the dense population characteristics offered opportunities for multiple store locations, gave greater exposure to brand-building efforts, and afforded multi-unit operating economies. However, the company believed that secondary markets with fewer than 100,000 households held significant sales and profit potential—it was exploring smaller-sized store designs suitable for secondary markets. In 2002, Krispy Kreme CEO Scott Livengood stated, "We are totally committed to putting full factory stores in every town in the U.S." Krispy Kreme's management further believed the food-service and institutional channel of sales offered significant opportunity to extend the brand into colleges and universities, business and industry facilities, and sports and entertainment complexes. Management had stated that the company's strong brand name, highly differentiated product, high-volume production capability, and multichannel market penetration strategy put the company in a position to become the recognized leader in every market it entered.

Expansion into Foreign Markets

In December 2000, the company hired Donald Henshall, 38, to fill the newly created position of president of international development; Henshall was formerly managing director of new business development with the London-based Overland Group, a maker and marketer of branded footwear and apparel. Henshall's job was to refine the company's global strategy, develop the capabilities and infrastructure to support expansion outside the United States, and consider inquiries from qualified parties wanting to open Krispy Kreme stores in foreign markets. Outside of the United States, Krispy Kreme stores had opened in Canada, Australia, Mexico, the United Kingdom, and the Republic of South Korea. Krispy Kreme and its franchisees planned to open 39 new stores in Canada, 30 in Australia and New Zealand, 20 in Mexico, and 25 in Great Britain and Ireland in the coming years. So far, sales had been very promising at the foreign locations that had been opened, and franchise agreements were in the works for further global expansion.

As of May 2001, the company had stopped accepting franchise applications for U.S. locations, indicating that there were no open territories. By 2003, it had stopped accepting franchise applications in Canada, Mexico, Western Europe, and Australia, indicating that franchise contracts were already under way and that Krispy Kreme would be opening in these areas soon. According to Scott Livengood, "Krispy Kreme is a natural to become a global brand. Looking at our demographics, we appeal to a very broad customer base. We receive lots of interest on a weekly basis to expand into international locations and we are confident our brand will be received extremely well outside the U.S."

THE MONTANA MILLS ACQUISITION

Krispy Kreme's chief strategic move in 2003 was to acquire Montana Mills Bread Company, a bakery operation based in Rochester, New York, with 11 retail locations. The acquisition price was 1.2 million shares of Krispy Kreme stock (worth roughly $50 million). The Montana Mills chain of neighborhood bakeries featured fresh stone-ground flour, a highly visual presentation of the baking process in full view of the customer, and customer sampling with large slices of a variety of fresh-baked breads. In explaining why the acquisition was made, Scott Livengood said:

> This acquisition is a natural outgrowth of the development of Krispy Kreme over the past five years. As I have indicated previously, we view Krispy Kreme Doughnuts, Inc., first and foremost as a set of unique capabilities which include the abilities to explore and nurture our customers' passion for and connection to a brand, create an effective franchise network, vertically integrate to provide a complete range of products and services to a system-wide store network serving flour-based, short shelf life products, and deliver these products daily across multiple channels. Applying these core organizational competencies to the development of a second concept has the potential to create significant leverage.
>
> The opportunity to create a wholesome, fresh-baked bakery and cafe concept the 'Krispy Kreme way' is obviously unique to Krispy Kreme. I have long considered how to capitalize on this opportunity. In Montana Mills, we found the perfect foundation for this new concept—passionate bread bakers who have created a fiercely loyal customer following around a wide variety of fresh-baked goods, bread-baking theater and sampling of large slices of bread. I have personally observed this passion that each Montana Mills employee carries for their customers and their breads. This is a great platform on which to build. We will work closely with the Montana Mills team as we try to add value to an already outstanding concept.
>
> I expect we will spend in the range of two years fully developing the concept I described. As we have indicated regarding our international expansion, we will always try to prepare for any type of expansion well before we need the growth. We want the time to do it right. For this concept, I think that time is now.

In fiscal 2004, Montana Mills generated revenues of $6.7 million and had operating expenses of $8.7 million, thus resulting in an operating loss of $2.0 million.

INDUSTRY ENVIRONMENT

By some estimates, the U.S. doughnut industry was a $5 to $6 billion market in 2003–2005. Americans consumed an estimated 10 to 12 billion doughnuts annually—over three dozen per capita. In 2002, doughnut industry sales rose by about 13 percent. According to a study done by Technomic, a marketing research specialist in foods, doughnut shops were the fastest-growing dining category in the country in 2002–2003.

Prior to the excitement over Krispy Kreme's doughnuts, growth in packaged doughnut sales at supermarkets, convenience stores, and other retail outlets had been quite small. The proliferation of bakery departments in supermarkets had squeezed out many locally owned doughnut shops and, to some extent, had constrained the growth of doughnut chains. Doughnuts were a popular item in supermarket bakeries, with many customers finding it more convenient to buy them when doing their regular supermarket shopping as opposed to making a special trip to local bakeries. Doughnut aficionados, however, tended to pass up doughnuts in the grocery store, preferring the freshness, quality, and variety offered by doughnut specialty shops. Most patrons of doughnut shops frequented those in their neighborhoods or normal shopping area; it was unusual for them to make a special trip of more than a mile or two for doughnuts.

Small independent doughnut shops usually had a devoted clientele, drawn from neighborhood residents and regular commuters passing by on their way to and from work. A longtime employee at a family-owned shop in Denver said, "Our customers are very loyal to us. Probably 80 percent are regulars."[1] Owners of independent shops seemed to believe that new entry by popular chains like Krispy Kreme posed little competitive threat, arguing that the market was big enough to support both independents and franchisers, that the Krispy Kreme novelty was likely to wear off, and that unless a doughnut franchiser located a store close to their present location the impact would be minimal at worst. A store owner in Omaha said, "Our doughnut sales increased when Krispy Kreme came to town. We benefit every time they advertise because doughnuts are as popular as ever."[2]

As of early 2004, there was little indication that the low-carbohydrate weight-watching craze that had swept the United States and other countries in recent years had cut much into sales. Industry observers and company officials attributed this in part to doughnuts being an affordable indulgence, easy to eat on the run, and in part to the tendency of many people to treat themselves occasionally. Doughnuts were readily available almost anywhere.

KRISPY KREME'S CHIEF COMPETITORS

The three leading doughnut chains in North America were Krispy Kreme, Dunkin' Donuts, and Tim Hortons.

Dunkin' Donuts

Dunkin' Donuts was the largest coffee and baked-goods chain in the world, selling 4.4 million donuts and 1.8 million cups of coffee daily. The quick-service restaurant chain was owned by British-based Allied Domecq PLC, a diversified enterprise whose other businesses included the Baskin-Robbins ice cream chain, ToGo's Eateries (sandwiches), and an assortment of alcoholic beverage brands (Kahla, Beefeater's, Maker's Mark, Courvoisier, Tia Maria, and a host of wines). Allied Domecq traded on the London Stock Exchange under the symbol ALLD. In 2004, Allied Domecq's Dunkin' Donuts chain had total sales approaching $4 billion, almost 6,200 franchised outlets in 40 countries (including 4,418 in the United States), and comparable store sales growth of 4.4 percent in the United States. About 83 percent of the chain's total sales were in the United States. In New England alone, Dunkin' Donuts operated 1,200 stores, including 600 in the Greater Boston area, where the chain was founded in 1950. Starting in 2000, Dunkin' Donuts franchisees could open co-branded stores that included Baskin Robbins and ToGo. Dunkin' Donuts ranked 9th in *Entrepreneur* magazine's annual Franchise Top 500 for 2005.

The key thrust of Dunkin' Donuts' strategy was to expand into those geographic areas in the United States where it was underrepresented. In areas where there were clusters of Dunkin' Donuts outlets, most baked items were supplied from centrally located kitchens rather than being made on-site. Despite its name, Dunkin' Donuts put more emphasis on coffee and convenience than on doughnuts. According to one company executive, "People talk about our coffee first. We're food you eat on the go. We're part of your day. We're not necessarily a destination store." Roughly half of all purchases at Dunkin' Donuts included coffee without a doughnut.[3] Dunkin' Donuts menu included doughnuts (50 varieties), muffins, bagels, cinnamon buns, cookies, brownies, Munchkins doughnut holes, cream cheese sandwiches, nine flavors of fresh coffee, iced coffees, and a lemonade Coolatta.

In 2004, Coolatta was being promoted in collaboration with MTV in a campaign called "Route to Cool." Dunkin' Donuts also had a new "Express Donuts" campaign to promote the sale of boxed donuts—12-packs containing the top six flavors. This campaign was being supported by advertising based on the theme "Who brought the donuts?" In addition, the chain was emphasizing coffee sales by the pound and had recently broadened its coffee offerings to include cappuccino, latte, espresso, and iced coffees.

With regard to nutritional content, Dunkin' Donuts' 50 doughnut varieties ranged between 200 and 340 calories, between 8 and 19 grams of fat, between 1.5 and 6 grams of saturated fat, and between 9 and 31 grams of sugars; its cinnamon buns had 540 calories, 15 grams of fat, 4 grams of saturated fat, and 42 grams of sugars. Whereas Krispy Kreme's best-selling original glazed doughnuts had 200 calories, 12 grams of fat, 3 grams of saturated fat, and 10 grams of sugar, the comparable item at Dunkin' Donuts had 180 calories, 8 grams of fat, 1.5 grams of saturated fat, and 6 grams of sugar. Several Dunkin' Donuts customers in the Boston area who had recently tried Krispy Kreme doughnuts reported that Krispy Kremes had more flavor and were lighter.[4]

Dunkin' Donuts had successfully fended off competition from national bagel chains and Starbucks. When national bagel chains, promoting bagels as a healthful alternative to doughnuts, opened new stores in areas where Dunkin' Donuts had stores, the company responded by adding bagels and cream cheese sandwiches to its menu offerings. Dunkin' Donuts had countered threats from Starbucks by adding a wider variety of hot-and-cold coffee beverages—and whereas coffee drinkers had to wait for a Starbucks barista to properly craft a $3 latte, they could get coffee and a doughnut on the fly at Dunkin' Donuts for less money. Quick and consistent service was a Dunkin' Donuts forte. Management further believed that the broader awareness of coffee created by the market presence of Starbucks stores had actually helped boost coffee sales at Dunkin' Donuts. In markets such as New York City and Chicago where there were both Dunkin' Donuts and Krispy Kreme stores, sales at Dunkin' Donuts had continued to rise.

In commenting on the competitive threat from Krispy Kreme, a Dunkin' Donuts vice president said:

> We have a tremendous number of varieties, a tremendous level of convenience, tremendous coffee and other baked goods. I think the differentiation that Dunkin' enjoys is clear. We're not pretentious and don't take ourselves too seriously, but we know how important a cup of coffee and a donut or bagel in the morning is. Being able to deliver a great cup of coffee when someone is on their way to something else is a great advantage.[5]

In 2003, Couche-Tard, Canada's largest convenience store operator, bought control of the Dunkin' Donuts name in Quebec as well as the 104 Dunkin' Donuts outlets located there. Couche-Tard planned to double the number of outlets within five years to better compete with Tim Hortons and Krispy Kreme.

Tim Hortons

Tim Hortons, a subsidiary of Wendy's International, was one of North America's largest coffee and fresh-baked-goods chains, with almost 2,400 restaurants across Canada and a steadily growing base of 200 locations in key markets within the United States. In April 2004, Tim Hortons acquired 42 Bess Eaton coffee and doughnut restaurants throughout Rhode Island, Connecticut, and Massachusetts, which it planned to convert to the Tim Hortons brand and format. Tim Hortons had systemwide sales of around $3 billion in 2003, equal to annual sales of about $1.3 million per store. Same store sales were up about 4.7 percent in 2003 and, during the first nine months of 2004, were up 10.1 percent in the United States and 7.7 percent in Canada. In Canada, the Tim Hortons chain was regarded as something of an icon—it was named for a popular Canadian-born professional hockey player who played for the Toronto Maple Leafs, Pittsburgh Penguins, and Buffalo Sabers; Horton was born in 1930, started playing hockey when he was five years old, and died in an auto accident while playing for the Buffalo Sabers. A recent survey of Canadian consumers rated Tim Hortons as the best-managed brand in Canada.

The Tim Hortons division of Wendy's relied heavily on franchising—only 57 of the 2,527 Tim Hortons outlets at year-end 2003 were company owned. Franchisees paid a royalty of 3 to 6 percent of weekly sales to the parent company, depending on whether they leased the land and/or buildings from Tim Hortons and on certain other conditions; in addition, franchisees paid fees equal to 4 percent of monthly gross sales to fund advertising and promotional activities undertaken at the corporate level. Franchisees were also required to purchase such products as coffee, sugar, flour, and shortening from a Tim Hortons subsidiary; these products were distributed from five warehouses located across Canada and were delivered to the company's Canadian restaurants primarily by its fleet of trucks and trailers. In the United States, both company and franchised stores purchased ingredients from a supplier approved by the parent company.

Tim Hortons used outside contractors to construct its restaurants. The restaurants were built to company specifications as to exterior style and interior decor. The standard Hortons restaurant being built in 2003–2004 consisted of a freestanding production unit ranging from 1,150 to 3,030 square feet. Each included a bakery capable of supplying fresh baked goods throughout the day to several satellite Tim Hortons within a defined area. Tim Hortons locations ranged from full-standard stores with in-store baking facilities; to combo units with Wendy's and Tim Hortons under one roof; to carts and kiosks in shopping malls, highway outlets, universities, airports, and hospitals. Most full-standard Tim Hortons locations offered 24-hour drive-through service. Tim Hortons promoted its full-standard stores as neighborhood meeting places and was active in promoting its products for group fund-raisers and community events.

The menu at each Tim Hortons unit consisted of coffee, cappuccino, teas, hot chocolate, soft drinks, soups, sandwiches, and fresh baked goods such as doughnuts, muffins, pies, croissants, tarts, cookies, cakes, and bagels. In recent years, the chain had expanded its lunch menu to include a bigger variety of offerings. One of the chain's biggest drawing cards was its special blend of fresh-brewed coffee, which was also sold in cans for customers' use at home. About half of the purchases at Tim Hortons included coffee without a doughnut. Tim Hortons was number one in market share in Canada during breakfast, was number one in the afternoon/early-evening snack category, and had a strong number two position at lunch with a menu featuring six sandwiches.

Executives at Tim Hortons did not feel threatened by Krispy Kreme's expansion into Canada and those parts of the United States where it had stores (Michigan, New York, Ohio, Kentucky, Maine, and West Virginia). According to David House, Tim Horton's president, "We really welcome them. Anyone who draws attention to doughnuts can only help us. It is a big market and a big marketplace. I would put our doughnut up against theirs any day."[6] A Canadian retailing consultant familiar with Tim Hortons and Krispy Kreme said, "This is the Canadian elephant and the U.S. mouse. Listen, if there's anything where Canadians can kick American butt, it is in doughnuts."[7] Another Canadian retailing consultant said, "It [Krispy Kreme] is an American phenomenon. These things are sickeningly sweet."[8]

Canada was reputed to have more doughnut shops per capita than any other country in the world. Aside from Tim Hortons, other chains in Canada featuring doughnuts included Dunkin' Donuts, Robin's Donuts, Country Style, and Coffee Time. Tim Hortons management had a goal of opening 500 Tim Hortons stores in the United States over the next three years, mostly in the Northeast and Great Lakes regions, and a longer-term goal of growing to about 3,500 outlets in Canada.

Winchell's Donut House

Winchell's, founded by Verne Winchell in 1948, was owned by Shato Holdings Ltd., of Vancouver, Canada. In 2000, there were approximately 600 Winchell's units located in 10 states west of the Mississippi River, along with international franchises in Guam, Saipan, Korea, Egypt, Saudi Arabia, and New Zealand. Since then, Winchell's Doughnut House had lost steam and closed two-thirds of its locations. In 2003, there were 200 units in 12 states, plus locations in Guam, Saipan, New Zealand, and Saudi Arabia. Winchell's was the largest doughnut chain on the West Coast. To combat Krispy Kreme's entry into Southern California, where Winchell's had a brand awareness of 97 percent, Winchell's had launched a Warm 'n Fresh program for all outlets in 2000. The program entailed having display cases full of fresh glazed doughnuts that were replaced every 15 to 20 minutes between 6:00 and 9:00 a.m. daily. A flashing red light on display cases signaled that a fresh batch of glazed doughnuts was available. Winchell's was offering customers a Warm 'n Fresh doughnut between 6:00 and 11:00 a.m. daily.

As of September 2003, a "Winchell's dozen" of 14 doughnuts sold for $5.99 and a double dozen (28) sold for $9.99—a single donut sold for about 60 cents, and many stores regularly ran a special of two donuts and a cup of coffee for $1.99. Winchell's bakery offerings included 20 varieties of doughnuts and 14 flavors of muffins, as well as croissants, bagels (breakfast bagel sandwiches were available at select locations), éclairs, tarts, apple fritters, and bear claws. It served three varieties of its "Legendary" coffees—Dark Roast Supreme, Legendary Blend, and Legendary Decaf—all using only 100 percent arabica beans (considered by many to be the finest coffee beans in the world). Other beverages included regular and frozen cappuccino, soft drinks, milk, and juices.

Winchell's corporate goal for the next five years was to triple its sales. In 2003–2004 it was actively seeking franchisees in 14 western and midwestern states. Winchell's charged a franchise fee of $7,500 and required franchisee to be able to invest $75,000 of unborrowed funds; the cost of new stores depended on such factors as store size, location, style of decor, and landscaping. A 5 percent royalty and a 3 percent advertising fee were charged on net sales.

LaMar's Donuts

Headquartered in Englewood, Colorado, LaMar's was a small, privately held chain that had 32 corporate-owned and franchised doughnut shops open or under development in 10 states; 8 stores were in the Denver area. Ray LaMar opened the original LaMar's Donuts in 1960 on Linwood Avenue in Kansas City and quickly turned the shop into a local institution. On a typical day, lines started forming before 6:00 a.m., and by closing time about 11,000 donuts would be sold. Based on the doughnut shop's success and reputation, Ray and his wife, Shannon, decided in the early 1990s to franchise LaMar's. Hundreds of LaMar's devotees applied for the limited number of franchises made available in the Kansas City area; 15 were granted over a few months. But little became of the initial franchising effort, and, in 1997, Franchise Consortium International, headed by Joseph J. Field, purchased a majority interest in LaMar's Franchising, renamed the company LaMar's Donuts International, moved the company's headquarters to a Denver suburb, and began laying the groundwork for a national expansion program.

LaMar's stores were typically located along neighborhood traffic routes. Average unit sales were $500,000 in 2003, and management expected the average to increase to $750,000 in a few years.

At one point, Fields expressed an objective of having 1,200 stores in operation by 2013, but so far LaMar's expansion was far slower than had been anticipated.

LaMar's used a secret recipe to produce "artisan-quality" doughnuts that were handmade daily with all-natural ingredients and no preservatives. Day-old doughnuts were never sold at the shops but were donated at day's end to the needy. In addition to 75 varieties of doughnuts, LaMar's menu included gourmet coffee and cappuccino. LaMar's had recently partnered with Dazbog Coffee Company in Denver, Colorado, and created over a dozen customized specialty coffee blends under the LaMar's Old World Roast label. Beans were handpicked from Costa Rica and then slow-roasted in an authentic Italian brick oven. Coffee products at LaMar's shops included cappuccinos, espressos, lattes, iced coffee drinks, and chai teas.

The company used the tag line "Simply a better doughnut." Joe Fields said, "People come in and try the product and they are surprised. They are wowed, in a very different way than Krispy Kreme. They say, 'Oh my God, this is the best doughnut I've had in my life.' " The Zagat Survey, a well-known rater of premier dining spots nationwide, described LaMar's Donuts as "extraordinary; fit for kings." *Gourmet* magazine, in search of the country's favorite doughnut, conducted a nationwide poll; the winner was a LaMar's doughnut. LaMar's Donuts has been named Best in the Country by the *John Walsh Show,* a one-hour daily nationally syndicated television program. Several newspapers had named LaMar's doughnuts as tops in their market area.

UNEXPECTED DEVELOPMENTS AT KRISPY KREME IN 2004

In March 2004, KKD management announced that it expected the company to have diluted earnings per share of $1.16 to $1.18 for fiscal 2005 (up from $0.92 in fiscal 2004) and systemwide comparable store sales growth in the mid-to-high single digits. Executives estimated that systemwide sales would increase approximately 25 percent in fiscal 2005 (ending January 29, 2005) and that approximately 120 new stores would be opened systemwide, including 20 to 25 smaller doughnut-and-coffee-shop stores, during the next 12 months. But as 2004 progressed, Krispy Kreme's business prospects went from rosy to stark within a matter of months.

Developments at Krispy Kreme in May 2004

In a May 7, 2004, press release that caught investors by surprise, CEO Scott Livengood said:

> For several months, there has been increasing consumer interest in low-carbohydrate diets, which has adversely impacted several flour-based food categories, including bread, cereal and pasta. This trend had little discernable effect on our business last year. However, recent market data suggests consumer interest in reduced carbohydrate consumption has heightened significantly following the beginning of the year and has accelerated in the last two to three months. This phenomenon has affected us most heavily in our off-premises sales channels, in particular sales of packaged doughnuts to grocery store customers.

Sales at Krispy Kreme's franchised stores were approximately evenly split between on-premises and off-premises sales, while approximately 60 percent of company-owned store sales were off-premises. As a consequence of the falloff in sales at external outlets, sales at Krispy Kreme stores open at least 18 months grew by only 4 percent, well below the 9 percent realized in preceding quarter. Due to the lower than expected off-premises sales at company stores, Livengood said the company was lowering its earnings guidance for the first quarter of fiscal 2005 to about $0.23 per share, down from about $0.26 per share. The company went on to announce in the same press release that it was:

- Divesting its recently acquired Montana Mills operation. The plan was to close the majority of the Montana Mills store locations, which were underperforming, and pursue a sale of the remaining Montana Mills stores. Management indicated the Montana Mills divesture would entail write-offs of approximately $35–$40 million in the first quarter on its Montana Mills investment and would likely involve further write-offs of $2–$4 million in subsequent quarters.

- Closing six underperforming factory stores—four in older retail locations in below-average retail trade areas and two commissaries.

- Lowering its guidance for fiscal 2005 diluted earnings per share from continuing operations, excluding asset impairment and other charges described below, to between $1.04 and $1.06, approximately 10 percent lower than prior forecasts. Including the Montana Mills charges, diluted earnings per share from continuing operations were estimated to be between $0.93 and $0.95 for fiscal 2005.

In the hours following the announcement, the company's stock price was hammered in trading—dropping by about 20 percent.

On May 25, 2004, Krispy Kreme reported a $24.4 million loss for the first quarter of fiscal 2005, blaming (1) trendy low-carb diets such as Atkins and South Beach for a decline in its sales in grocery stores and (2) a $34 million write-off of its investment in Montana Mills. The stock price was down 37 percent since the May 7 lower earnings announcement and was trading at about $20.

At the company's annual stockholders' meeting on May 26, 2004, executives said the company was slowing down expansion plans and had plans to counter consumer interest in low-carbohydrate foods by adding a sugar-free doughnut to its product lineup. Management also announced that the company would soon (1) introduce a chocolate-flavored glazed doughnut, mini rings that were 40 percent smaller, and crushed-ice drinks in raspberry, latte, and double chocolate flavors and (2) begin selling bags of the company's own brand of coffee in whole-bean and ground form in grocery stores alongside Krispy Kreme doughnut displays. The company said it planned to go forward with overseas expansion. The overseas expansion was concentrated in Asia; 25 new stores were being planned for South Korea and on the horizon were stores in Japan, China, Indonesia, the Philippines, and the Persian Gulf.

Developments at Krispy Kreme in July–August 2004

In late July 2004, the company announced that the Securities and Exchange Commission was launching an inquiry into the company's accounting practices regarding certain franchise buybacks. A *Wall Street Journal* article in May had detailed questionable accounting in the $32.1 million repurchase of a

struggling seven-unit franchise in Michigan that was behind on its payments for equipment, ingredients, and franchise fees, along with questionable accounting for another reacquired franchise in southern California.

In late August 2004, Krispy Kreme reported its second-quarter fiscal 2005 results:

- Systemwide sales increases of 14.8 percent as compared with the prior year's second quarter.

- An 11.5 percent increase in company revenue to $177.4 million (versus $159.2 million in the second quarter of the prior year)—company store sales increased by 18.7 percent to $123.8 million, revenues from franchise operations grew by 13.7 percent to $6.8 million, and KKM&D revenues decreased by 4.1 percent to $46.9 million (principally because of lower equipment sales to franchisees opening new stores).

- Very small comparable store sales increases—sales at company-owned stores increased by 0.6 percent and systemwide sales (at both company-owned and franchised stores) increased by only 0.1 percent.

- A decline in operating income from continuing operations for the second quarter of fiscal 2005 to $6.2 million, or $0.10 per diluted share, versus $13.4 million, or $0.22 per diluted share, in the second quarter of fiscal 2004.

- The opening of 22 new Krispy Kreme factory/retail stores in 12 new markets, and 10 doughnut-and-coffee-shop stores. Six company-owned factory/retail stores and three doughnut-and-coffee shops were closed during the quarter.

Commenting on the Krispy Kreme's second-quarter performance, Scott Livengood, said:

> Although we are disappointed with the second-quarter financial results, we are optimistic about the long-term growth potential of the business. We are focusing our efforts and resources on initiatives that improve long-term business prospects. We have core strategies with supporting initiatives, a leading consumer brand and great people to address the current challenges. Krispy Kreme has proven over its 67-year history an ability to overcome challenges, and I am confident in our ability to restore our business momentum.[9]

Top management indicated that systemwide sales should grow by approximately 15 percent for fiscal 2005 and approximately 10 percent in the last two quarters of the year but declined to provide updated earnings estimates. The company said it had scaled back expansion plans and would only open approximately 75 new stores systemwide (60 factory/retail stores and 15 doughnut-and-coffee shops) during fiscal 2005.

Developments at Krispy Kreme in November–December 2004

In November 2004, Krispy Kreme reported that the company lost $3 million in the third quarter of fiscal 2005. Total revenues for the quarter, which included sales from company stores, franchise operations, and KKM&D, were up by only 1.4 percent to $170.1 million (versus $167.8 million in the third quarter of fiscal 2004). Third-quarter systemwide sales at both company-owned and franchised stores were up by 4.7 percent over the third quarter of fiscal 2004. The sales increases were well below the 10 percent gains that management had forecast in August.

During the quarter, 13 company-owned factory/retail stores and two doughnut-and-coffee shop stores were opened, and 7 company-owned factory/retail stores and two doughnut-and-coffee shop stores were closed. There were 429 Krispy Kreme stores systemwide at the end of October 2004, consisting of 393 factory/retail stores and 36 doughnut-and-coffee shops. There were plans to open approximately 10 new stores systemwide in the fourth quarter of fiscal 2005.

Exhibit 10 shows the declining performance of Krispy Kreme's stores during the first three quarters of fiscal 2005. Exhibits 11 and 12 show selected financial statistics for Krispy Kreme Doughnuts during the first nine months of fiscal 2005 compared to the first nine months of fiscal 2004.

Management declined to provide systemwide sales and earnings guidance for the fourth quarter of fiscal 2005 and withdrew its previous estimates of 10 percent systemwide sales growth made in August. Commenting on the company's performance, Scott Livengood said, "Clearly we are disappointed with our third-quarter results. We are focused on addressing the challenges facing the Company and regaining our business momentum." Early in the fourth fiscal quarter, Krispy Kreme sold its remaining Montana Mills assets for what management described as "a modest amount."

In December 2004, Krispy Kreme announced that it had identified accounting errors related to its acquisition of two franchises that could reduce net income for fiscal 2004 by 2.7 percent to 8.6 percent. It was, as yet, unclear whether it would have to restate its results for fiscal year 2004. A special committee of the company's board of directors was investigating the accounting problems. The company's outside auditor, PricewaterhouseCoopers LLP, said it refused to complete reviews of Krispy Kreme's financial performance for the first six months of 2005 until the special committee completed its probe of the bookkeeping problems. In late December 2004, Krispy Kreme's stock

Exhibit 10   **Quarterly Operating Performance of Krispy Kreme Stores, Fiscal Years 2004–2005**

	Fiscal Year 2004				Fiscal Year 2005		
	Q1	Q2	Q3	Q4	Q1	Q2	Q3
Average sales per week							
Company stores	$77.4	$74.4	$73.0	$69.1	$67.9	$63.1	$58.4
Area developer stores	58.0	61.2	60.3	58.7	59.2	54.3	49.9
Associate stores	52.4	48.7	45.9	42.6	46.7	43.9	41.7
Franchised store average	56.2	57.3	56.3	54.3	56.0	51.6	47.9
Systemwide average	64.1	63.7	62.7	60.1	60.7	56.3	52.2
Change in comparable store sales							
Company stores	15.4%	15.6%	13.3%	10.7%	5.2%	0.6%	−6.2%
Systemwide	11.2	11.3	9.5	9.1	4.0	0.1	−6.4
Increase in systemwide sales	24.4%	27.6%	28.6%	25.5%	24.2%	14.8%	4.7%

Source: Company press releases of quarterly earnings results.

Exhibit 11   **Financial Statement Data for Krispy Kreme Doughnuts, First Nine Months of Fiscal 2004 Versus First Nine Months of Fiscal 2005 (dollar amounts in thousands, except per share)**

	Nine Months Ending November 2, 2003	Nine Months Ending October 31, 2004
Statement of operations data		
Total revenues	$475,598	$531,941
Operating expenses	359,820	430,613
General and administrative expenses	27,362	34,928
Depreciation and amortization expenses	13,473	19,496
Arbitration award	(525)	—
Impairment charge and store closing costs	—	14,865
Income from operations	$ 75,468	$ 32,039
Interest expense, (income), net, and other expenses and adjustments	6,410	5,424
Income (loss) from continuing operations before income taxes	69,058	26,615
Provision for income taxes	27,488	11,543
Income from continuing operations	41,570	15,072
Discontinued operations	(907)	(36,741)
Net income (loss)	$ 40,663	$ (21,669)
Diluted earnings (loss) per share		
Income (loss) from continuing operations	$ 0.67	$0.24
Discontinued operations	(0.01)	(0.58)
Net income (loss) per share	0.66	(0.34)
Diluted shares outstanding (in 000s)	61,975	63,441
Balance sheet data		
Cash and cash equivalents	$ 39,287	$ 17,213
Receivables	62,454	73,416
Inventories	29,717	32,287
Payables and accrued expenses	52,101	67,820
Long-term debt and other long-term obligations, including current maturities	149,142	170,509
Total assets	629,431	675,897
Total shareholders' equity	$428,188	$437,568

Source: Company press releases, November 21, 2003, and November 22, 2004.

was trading in the $10–$13 range, well below the $40 high attained in March 2004.

KRISPY KREME IN 2005

In mid-January 2005, Krispy Kreme's board of directors took steps indicating that the company's deteriorating sales and financial problems were worse than expected. The company's board of directors forced Scott Livengood to retire. The board hired two outsiders with noted expertise in turning around troubled companies; Stephen Cooper was named CEO, and Steven Panagos was named president and chief operating officer. Both executives came to KKD from Kroll Zolfo Cooper (KZC), a company best known for presiding over the remains of Enron and rejuvenating Sunbeam and Polaroid; Cooper was chairman of KZC, and Panagos was a managing director. The two new executives were assisted by a team of professionals from KZC. Along with the management changes, Krispy Kreme also announced that average

Exhibit 12   **Krispy Kreme's Performance by Business Segment, First Nine Months of Fiscal 2004 Versus First Nine Months of Fiscal 2005 (in thousands)**

	Nine Months Ending November 2, 2003	Nine Months Ending October 31, 2004
Revenues by business segment		
Company store operations	$317,158	$369,593
Franchise operations	17,555	20,060
KK manufacturing & distribution	140,885	142,288
Total	$475,598*	$531,941
Operating income by business segment (before depreciation and amortization)		
Company store operations	$ 61,969	$ 41,797
Franchise operations	13,721	14,694
KK manufacturing & distribution	27,824	26,706
Total	$103,514*	$ 83,197
Unallocated general and administrative expenses	$ (28,571)	$ (36,293)

*Totals do not include operations of Montana Mills, a business which was acquired in April 2004 and divested during fiscal 2005; nine month revenues for Montana Mills were $4,481,000 and the operating loss at Montana Mills was $1,408,000.
Source: Company press releases, November 21, 2003, and November 22, 2004.

weekly sales per factory store were down 18 percent systemwide and down 25 percent at company stores for the eight weeks ended December 26, 2004 (compared to the corresponding weeks of 2003).

In early 2005, Krispy Kreme announced workforce reductions of about 25 percent; it was estimated that the reduced employment levels would result in annual pretax savings of about $7.4 million The company also divested its corporate airplane, realizing annual pretax savings of $3 million. In an unrelated development, employees of Krispy Kreme filed a class action lawsuit accusing Krispy Kreme of not sharing information that resulted in losses in employees' retirement accounts. The lawsuit, if won by the employees, asked that the money lost on the investments be repaid personally by four of the board members, including former CEO Scott Livengood, who allegedly withheld the needed information from the employees.

In April 2005, Krispy Kreme completed a deal that provided $225 million in new financing. The proceeds were used to repay $90 million in debt and to provide cash for operations. Management believed the move greatly strengthened the company's balance sheet and provided the cash needed to turn the company's operations around.

Also in April, Krispy Kreme asked the Securities and Exchange Commission for permission to delay submitting its 10-K report for 2005 since it was still analyzing the need to restate its financial results for fiscal years 2001, 2002, 2003, and the first nine months of 2005; the company had recently discovered further need to revise its fiscal 2004 financials by $5.2 to $6.2 million (apart from adjustments previously announced in December 2004) and determined that its financial statements for 2001 through the first nine months of fiscal 2005 should no longer be relied on. On a positive note, management said that it expected to report fiscal 2005 revenues of approximately $685 million (up about 4 percent over the $665.6 million reported in fiscal 2004). However, a big portion of the sales gains came from store sales of reacquired franchisees that were financially distressed, and management said that it expected to report a loss for the fourth quarter of fiscal 2005.

In June 2005, Krispy Kreme announced that its special committee of independent directors had concluded that six of the company's officers—including four senior vice presidents—should be discharged. The six executives were in the areas of operations, finance, business development, and manufacturing and distribution—five of the executives resigned and one retired. A new chief accounting officer, who had been a consultant with the company since December 2004 and had spent 17 years at Pricewaterhouse-Coopers, was appointed in July.

In August, Krispy Kreme and Kroll Zolfo Cooper agreed to the terms of the success fee under which KZC was providing management services. The success fee entitled KZC to purchase 1.2 million shares of Krispy Kreme's common stock at a cash exercise price of $7.75 per share. KZC monthly fees had averaged $800,000 per month since being hired in January.

The Report of the Special Committee of the Board of Directors

In August 2005, the Special Committee of Krispy Kreme's board of directors completed its studies and issued the following statement:

> The Krispy Kreme story is one of a newly-public company, experiencing rapid growth, that failed to meet its accounting and financial reporting obligations to its shareholders and the public. While some may see the accounting errors . . . as relatively small in magnitude, they were critical in a corporate culture driven by a narrowly focused goal of exceeding projected earnings by a penny each quarter.
>
> In our view, Scott A. Livengood, former Chairman of the Board and Chief Executive Officer, and John W. Tate, former Chief Operating Officer, bear primary responsibility for the failure to establish the management tone, environment and controls essential for meeting the Company's responsibilities as a public company. Krispy Kreme and its shareholders have paid dearly for those failures, as measured by the loss in market value of the Company's shares, a loss in confidence in the credibility and integrity of the Company's management and the considerable costs required to address those failures.
>
> The number, nature and timing of the accounting errors strongly suggest that they resulted from an intent to manage earnings. All those we interviewed have repeatedly and firmly denied having any intent to manage earnings or having given or received any instruction (explicit or otherwise) to do so. But we never received credible explanations for transactions that appear to have been structured or timed to allow for the improper recognition of revenue or improper reduction of expense . . .
>
> All officers or employees who we believe had any substantial involvement in or responsibility for the accounting errors have left the Company . . .
>
> Also . . . the Special Committee has concluded that it is in the best interests of the Company (i) to reject the demands by shareholders that the Company commence litigation against present and former directors and officers of the Company and the sellers of certain franchises to the Company, (ii) to seek dismissal of shareholder derivative litigation against the outside directors, the sellers of certain franchises and current and former officers other than Scott Livengood, John Tate and Randy S. Casstevens, the Company's former Chief Financial Officer, and (iii) not to seek dismissal of shareholder derivative litigation against Messrs. Livengood, Tate and Casstevens, although the Company will not assist or participate in such litigation.[10]

At the same time, top management announced that its investigation of the company's internal controls over financial reporting under Livengood, Tate, and Casstevens revealed four material weaknesses:

- The Company failed to maintain an effective control environment, including failure of former senior management to set the appropriate tone at the top of the organization and to ensure adequate controls were designed and operating effectively.

- The Company failed to maintain a sufficient complement of personnel with a level of accounting knowledge, experience and training in the application of generally accepted accounting principles [GAAP] commensurate with the Company's financial reporting requirements and the complexity of the Company's operations and transactions.

- The Company failed to maintain effective controls over the documentation and analysis of acquisitions to ensure they were accounted for in accordance with GAAP.

- The Company failed to maintain effective controls over the selection and application of accounting policies related to leases and leasehold improvements to ensure they were accounted for in accordance with GAAP.

It was as yet unclear whether the company's outside auditors, PricewaterhouseCoopers, shared any responsibility for the numerous accounting and financial reporting deficiencies discovered at Krispy Kreme during the 2001–2005 period.

Financial Statement Adjustments

In August 2005, Krispy Kreme announced that it expected to make adjustments to its prior financial statements for fiscal years 2001–2005 that would have the effect of decreasing pretax income through the third quarter of fiscal 2005 by an estimated $25.6 million. In December 2005, these adjustments were increased to an estimated $35.1 million. The latest adjustments called for decreases in pretax income of $1.6 million, $3.7 million, $4.0 million, $16.5 million, and $5.4 million for fiscal 2001, 2002, 2003, and 2004 and the first nine months of fiscal 2005, respectively, plus decreases of $3.9 million for periods prior to fiscal 2001. However, the estimates were subject to further revision and the results of the audit of the company's annual financial statements. Management said that the results of operations for both fiscal 2005 and 2006 would be adversely affected by adjustments to recognize the financial difficulties faced by certain franchisees.

In mid-December 2005, the company indicated that it would be unable to provide restated financial statements much before a recently extended deadline of April 2006.

The Latest Available Operating Results

Despite not issuing financial statements, Krispy Kreme indicated that the company lost money in the fourth quarter of fiscal 2005 and the first three quarters of fiscal 2006 (through October 31, 2005). Average weekly sales at company-owned and franchised stores, however, appeared to have stabilized at around $45,000 to $50,000 weekly (see Exhibit 13).

The company expected to report revenues of approximately $130 million for the third quarter of fiscal 2006 (which ended October 30, 2005), compared to revenues of approximately $170 million previously reported for the third quarter of fiscal 2005.

Stephen Cooper, the company's CEO, believed the company's prospects for a turnaround were good:

> While a number of challenges remain, I am pleased to report that we continue to make progress with the Company's turnaround. We have closed approximately 30 underperforming Company stores, significantly reduced overhead costs, made progress in strengthening the senior management team and are taking steps to deal with certain troubled franchisees.
>
> Our plan is simple. We are focusing on excellence in Company and franchise operations and on what makes Krispy Kreme a great brand: delivering the highest quality doughnuts and coffee and other beverages to our retail and wholesale customers. While the Company still faces serious challenges, we believe we are addressing the critical issues.[11]

Following the lead of Krispy Kreme's new management team to weed out unproductive stores, several franchisees had closed some of their worst-performing stores. And some factory stores had been converted into "satellite" stores that emphasized retail sales of doughnuts and coffee (satellite stores made few, if any, doughnuts for off-premises sales). Cooper believed that Krispy Kreme needed urban stores that were smaller on average and that focused on increasing sales of coffee and other beverages as well as doughnuts. Krispy Kreme had also restructured the

Exhibit 13   **Selected Operating Results for Krispy Kreme, Fourth Quarter 2005 Through Third Quarter 2006**

	Q4, FY 2005	Q1, FY 2006	Q2, FY 2006	Q3, FY 2006
Krispy Kreme's revenues	$153 million	n.a.	n.a.	$130 million
Decrease from prior year quarter	17.5%	n.a	n.a.	23.5%
Number of Krispy Kreme factory stores systemwide	400	400	400	360
Number of associate and/or satellite stores	n.a.	n.a.	50	50
Average weekly sales, systemwide	$48,000	$48,000	$46,000	$43,000
Decrease from prior year	20%	21%	18%	14%
Average weekly sales, company-owned stores	$50,000	$50,000	$49,000	$47,000
Decrease from prior year	27%	26%	20%	19%

n.a. = Not announced.

Source: Company press releases.

operations of its Canadian subsidiary, KremeKo, and was working with troubled franchisees—in some cases reacquiring their operations. In October 2005, Krispy Kreme's Philadelphia franchisee, Freedom Rings, filed for Chapter 11 bankruptcy. Krispy Kreme owned 70 percent of Freedom Rings and acquired the remaining 30 percent, prior to filing, for a nominal price; Freedom Rings owed Krispy Kreme approximately $24.1 million.[12] In November, the company announced the approval of restructuring of KremeKo. KremeKo and Krispy Kreme announced in November 2005 that KremeKo would become a wholly owned subsidiary. In December, Krispy Kreme completed the acquisition of KremeKo Inc., which had six factory stores in eastern and central Canada. KremeKo had been operating under Chapter 11 since April 2005.[13]

Going into 2006, there were 330 Krispy Kreme factory stores and 80 satellites operating systemwide in 44 U.S. states, Australia, Canada, Mexico, the Republic of South Korea, and the United Kingdom. The only new Krispy Kreme factory store in calendar year 2005 was opened in November in Missoula, Montana, by a franchisee that had 14 stores in Idaho, Nevada, Montana, and Utah.

In late 2005 Krispy Kreme named Jeff Jervik as executive vice president of operations, responsible for all company-owned operations, franchisee operations, and wholesale operations. Jervik had been national vice president of operations for Pizza Hut, with responsibility for the operations of over 1,000 Pizza Hut restaurants, having sales of approximately $800 million and over 25,000 employees. Krispy Kreme had hired an executive search firm with experience placing top executives in companies such as Starbucks, Sara Lee, Dean Foods, and Gillette, to assist in the search for a permanent chief executive officer. The company's board wanted to identify and retain a CEO as soon as possible. Krispy Kreme's stock traded in the $5–$9 range for most of 2005 and was trading around $6 in late December 2005.

Sometime in April 2006, Krispy Kreme expected to issue its first financial statements since November 2004 (at which time the financials for the third quarter of fiscal year 2005 were released).

Endnotes

[1]As quoted in "Dough-Down at the Mile High Corral," *Rocky Mountain News,* March 25, 2001, p. 1G.
[2]As quoted in "Hole-ly War: Omaha to Be Battleground for Duel of Titans," *Omaha World Herald,* September 7, 1999, p. 14.
[3]According to information in Hermione Malone, "Krispy Kreme to Offer Better Coffee as It Tackles New England," *Charlotte Observer,* March 16, 2001.
[4]"Time to Rate the Doughnuts: Krispy Kreme Readies to Roll into N.E. to Challenge Dunkin' Donuts," *Boston Globe,* February 21, 2001, p. D1.
[5]As quoted in Malone, "Krispy Kreme to Offer Better Coffee."
[6]As quoted in "Can Krispy Kreme Cut It in Canada?" *Ottawa Citizen,* December 30, 2000, p. H1.
[7]As quoted in ibid.
[8]As quoted in ibid.
[9]Company press release, August 26, 2004.
[10]Company press release, August 10, 2005.
[11]Company press releases, August 10, 2005, and December 13, 2005.
[12]Company press release, October 17, 2005.
[13]Company press release, November 14, 2005, and December 19, 2005.

Case 13

Kodak at a Crossroads: The Transition from Film-Based to Digital Photography

Boris Morozov
University of Nebraska at Omaha

Rebecca J. Morris
University of Nebraska at Omaha

It's not clear with Kodak if they can successfully compete in the digital world. Are they a buggy whip manufacturer?[1] —**David Winters, chief investment officer, Franklin Mutual Advisers, Inc.**

It's a challenging strategy, there's no question about it. This is about our belief in where the company can go, and in our ability to bring growth back to the company in the next three or four years.[2] —**Daniel Carp, CEO, Eastman Kodak Company**

On September 25, 2003, Eastman Kodak Company's CEO, Daniel Carp, announced to investors that, after a three-year decline in sales, the company would stop making major investments in its consumer film business and devote its resources to becoming a "digital-oriented growth company." By the end of trading on the day of the announcement, Kodak's stock fell to an 18-year low. Institutional investors criticized Kodak's announced strategy, expressing annoyance at the company's intention to invest in ink-jet printing, a business dominated by Hewlett-Packard.[3] People at the company's meeting said that Carp did not provide enough detail on how the strategy would affect earnings before 2006.[4] Investment analyst Shannon Cross expressed the concerns of many investors, saying, "There are so many questions with regard to Kodak's future

strategy . . . The track record we've seen out of management in terms of being able to hit targets and implement a strategy has been pretty spotty."[5]

Since January 1, 2000, when Carp took over as chief executive of Kodak, the company's revenues and net income had declined, its shares had dropped by 66 percent, and Standard & Poor's (S&P) had cut Kodak's credit rating by five grades.[6] Kodak had reduced its workforce by 49 percent since 1989, cutting 7,300 employees in 2002.[7] Plans were announced to eliminate up to 6,000 jobs in 2003 to stem future losses, cutting Kodak's traditional photography divisions in Rochester, New York, to fewer workers than the firm had employed during the Great Depression.[8] Kodak's income statements for 1993 through 2003 are presented in Exhibit 1. The company's balance sheets for the 11-year period ending 2003 are presented in Exhibit 2.

Despite investing over $4 billion in digital research and related technologies since the early 1990s, Kodak was characterized as a firm struggling to find its footing in the world of digital photography. Analysts gave Kodak only two to three years to find its way or find itself fading into history. "The question is, can Kodak come up with the new products, the new insights that make sense out of digital?" asked a marketing professor from the Rochester Institute of Technology. "They have to be able to execute fast. They've got to differentiate themselves because they're going very heavily into a commodity market."[9]

An earlier version of this case was anonymously peer reviewed and accepted by the North American Case Research Association (NACRA) for presentation at its annual meeting, October 7–9, 2004, Sedona, Arizona. Copyright © 2004 by Boris Morozov and Rebecca J. Morris. All rights reserved.

Exhibit 1 **Eastman Kodak's Income Statement, 1993–2003 ($ in millions except per share data)**

	2003	2002	2001	2000	1999	1998	1997	1996	1995	1994	1993
Sales	$13,317	$12,835	$13,234	$13,994	$14,089	$13,406	$14,538	$15,968	$14,980	$13,557	$16,364
Cost of goods sold	8,130	7,391	7,749	7,105	6,731	6,372	6,986	7,423	7,046	6,442	6,952
Gross profit	5,187	5,444	5,485	6,889	7,358	7,034	7,552	8,545	7,934	7,115	9,412
SG&A expense	3,339	3,260	3,333	3,747	3,986	4,119	4,956	5,438	5,039	4,570	6,290
Operating income before depreciation	1,848	2,184	2,152	3,142	3,372	2,915	2,596	3,107	2,895	2,545	3,122
Depreciation and amortization	830	818	919	889	918	853	828	903	916	883	1,111
Operating profit	1,018	1,366	1,233	2,253	2,454	2,062	1,768	2,204	1,979	1,662	2,011
Interest expense	148	173	219	178	142	110	131	112	108	177	635
Nonoperating income (expense)	(23)	(66)	(29)	96	141	210	57	209	109	(143)	18
Special Items	(651)	(164)	(888)	(39)	(344)	(56)	(1,641)	(745)	(54)	(340)	(538)
Pretax income	196	963	97	2,132	2,109	2,106	53	1,556	1,926	1,002	856
Total income taxes	(66)	153	32	725	717	716	48	545	674	448	381
Minority interest	24	17	(11)	—	—	—	—	—	—	—	—
Income before extraordinary items	238	793	76	1,407	1,392	1,390	5	1,011	1,252	554	475
Extraordinary items	0	0	0	0	0	0	0	0	0	(266)	(2,182)
Discontinued operations	27	(23)	0	0	0	0	0	277	0	269	192
Adjusted net income	$ 265	$ 770	$ 76	$ 1,407	$ 1,392	$ 1,390	$ 5	$ 1,288	$ 1,252	$ 557	($1,515)
EPS excluding extraordinary items and discontinued operations	$0.83	$2.72	$0.26	$4.62	$4.38	$4.30	$0.01	$3.00	$3.67	$1.65	$1.44
EPS including extraordinary items and discontinued operations	0.92	2.64	0.26	4.62	4.38	4.30	0.01	3.82	3.67	1.66	(4.62)
EPS diluted; excluding extraordinary items and discontinued operations	0.83	2.72	0.26	4.59	4.33	4.24	0.01	3.00	3.58	1.63	1.44
EPS diluted; including extraordinary items and discontinued operations	0.92	2.64	0.26	4.59	4.33	4.24	0.01	3.82	3.58	1.63	(4.62)
EPS basic from operations	2.37	2.77	2.37	4.73	5.09	4.42	3.52	4.50	3.77	2.40	2.60
EPS diluted from operations	2.37	2.77	2.37	4.70	5.03	4.37	3.46	n.a.	n.a.	n.a.	n.a.
Dividends per share	$1.15	$1.80	$1.77	$1.76	$1.76	$1.76	$1.76	$1.60	$1.60	$1.60	$2.00
Common shares for basic EPS (in millions)	286.5	291.5	290.6	304.9	318.0	323.3	327.4	337.4	341.5	335.7	328.3
Common shares for diluted EPS (in millions)	286.6	291.7	291.0	306.6	321.5	327.8	331.9	n.a.	n.a.	n.a.	n.a.

Source: Eastman Kodak 2003 annual report.

Exhibit 2 **Eastman Kodak's Balance Sheet, 1993–2003 ($ in millions)**

	2003	2002	2001	2000	1999	1998	1997	1996	1995	1994	1993
Assets											
Cash and equivalents	$ 1,261	$ 578	$ 451	$ 251	$ 393	$ 500	$ 752	$1,796	$ 1,811	$ 2,068	$ 1,966
Net receivables	2,389	2,234	2,337	2,653	2,537	2,527	2,271	2,738	3,145	3,064	3,463
Inventories	1,075	1,062	1,137	1,718	1,519	1,424	1,252	1,575	1,660	1,480	1,913
Other current assets	730	660	758	869	995	1,148	1,200	856	693	1,071	679
Total current assets	5,455	4,534	4,683	5,491	5,444	5,599	5,475	6,965	7,309	7,683	8,021
Gross property and equipment	13,277	13,288	12,982	12,963	13,289	13,482	12,824	12,585	12,652	12,299	13,311
Accumulated depreciation	8,183	7,868	7,323	7,044	7,342	7,568	7,315	7,163	7,275	7,007	6,945
Net property and equipment	5,094	5,420	5,659	5,919	5,947	5,914	5,509	5,422	5,377	5,292	6,366
Investments at equity	426	382	360	0	2	3	25	31	74	@CF	@CF
Other investments	310	53	85	—	—	—	—	—	—	338	187
Intangibles	1,678	981	948	947	982	1,232	548	581	536	616	4,312
Deferred charges	1,147	972	482	0	0	0	0	0	0	0	0
Other assets	708	1,027	1,145	1,855	1,995	1,985	1,588	1,439	1,181	1,039	1,439
Total assets	$14,818	$13,369	$13,362	$14,212	$14,370	$14,733	$13,145	$14,438	$14,477	$14,968	$20,325
Liabilities and shareholder equity											
Long-term debt due in one year	$ 457	$ 387	$ 156	$ 150	$ 2	$ 78	$ 3	$ 245	$ 0	$ 0	$ 350
Notes payable	489	1,055	1,378	2,056	1,161	1,440	608	296	586	371	305
Accounts payable	834	720	674	817	940	947	943	966	799	703	737
Taxes payable	654	584	544	572	612	593	567	603	567	1,701	420
Accrued expenses	1,696	1,739	1,635	1,358	1,460	1,289	1,080	1,160	731	616	609
Other current liabilities	1,177	892	967	1,262	1,594	1,831	1,976	2,147	1,960	2,344	2,489
Total current liabilities	5,307	5,377	5,354	6,215	5,769	6,178	5,177	5,417	4,643	5,735	4,910
Long-term debt	2,302	1,164	1,666	1,166	936	504	585	559	665	660	6,853
Deferred taxes	81	52	81	61	59	69	64	102	97	95	79
Minority interest	45	70	84	93	98	128	24				
Other liabilities	3,819	3,929	3,283	3,249	3,596	3,866	4,134	3,626	3,951	4,461	5,127
Total liabilities	$11,554	$10,592	$10,468	$10,784	$10,458	$10,745	$ 9,984	$ 9,704	$ 9,356	$10,951	$16,969
Common stock, at per value	$ 978	$ 978	$ 978	$ 978	$ 978	$ 978	$ 978	$ 978	$ 974	$ 966	$ 948
Additional paid in capital	842	849	849	871	889	902	914	910	803	515	213
Retained earnings	7,296	6,840	6,834	7,387	6,850	6,052	5,141	6,006	5,277	4,493	4,234
Less: treasury stock	(5,852)	(5,890)	(5,767)	(5,808)	(4,805)	(3,944)	(3,872)	(3,160)	(1,933)	(1,957)	(2,039)
Total shareholders' equity	3,264	2,777	2,894	3,428	3,912	3,988	3,161	4,734	5,121	4,017	3,356
Total liabilities and equity	$14,818	$13,369	$13,362	$14,212	$14,370	$14,733	$13,145	$14,438	$14,477	$14,968	$20,325

Source: Eastman Kodak 2003 annual report.

The switch by consumers to digital photography was coming much faster than expected, and Kodak's traditional film, papers, and photofinishing businesses were declining. By the end of 2003, analysts expected that digital cameras would begin to outsell film cameras for the first time in the United States. The digital photography industry was fast-paced and crowded, offering razor-thin profit margins. Kodak was clearly at a crossroads. Would the strategy announced on September 25, 2003, position the company for growth, or would the company continue to decline?

KODAK'S CHALLENGES IN 2003

With the slogan "You press the button, we do the rest," George Eastman put the first simple camera into the hands of consumers in 1888. In so doing, he changed an awkward and intricate process into something easy to use and accessible to nearly everyone. Since that time, the Eastman Kodak Company had led the way with an abundance of new products and processes to make photography simpler, more useful, and more enjoyable. However, in 2003, Kodak's CEO, Daniel Carp, faced challenges similar to those George Eastman faced over a century before: How to make the process of printing the picture even easier in an era of digital technologies.

The economy was in a recession in 2003, major market indexes were still at a low level, and investors were cautious. As a result of an unfavorable economic situation, shareholder wealth had been cut to a portion of what it was during the phenomenal technology-based run-up of the market in the late 1990s. The bursting of the technology bubble proved that the absence of a strong profit-generating business model could not be replaced with information technology solutions.

Kodak's moves paralleled those at many companies whose comfortable business models were threatened by rapid changes in information technology. When asked whether Kodak had moved into digital photography soon enough, Carp replied, "I saw my first digital camera inside Kodak in 1982. Today, we're arguably one of the top three providers of digital cameras in the U.S. So we did the right thing. At the same time, we shouldn't have walked away from the

historical film businesses before they turned down, because it would have destroyed value."[10]

Under slumping economic and competitive market conditions, Kodak faced tough pressure from its existing competitors as well as from new rivals in the area of digital photography. Kodak coined the term *infoimaging* to describe the use of technology to combine images and information—a development that held the potential to profoundly change how people and businesses communicated.[11] Infoimaging was a $385 billion industry composed of devices (digital cameras and personal data assistants); infrastructure (online networks and delivery systems for images); services; and media (software, film, and paper) that enabled people to access, analyze, and print images.

Although the company had invested $4 billion in digital research and related technologies and spent many years perfecting its digital cameras,[12] Kodak's status as an iconic brand was threatened by the technological shift away from its cash-cow business of traditional film and film processing. In July 2003, Kodak reported flat sales and a 60 percent drop in second-quarter profits.

When announcing the latest rounds of workforce reductions in July 2003, Carp expressed his perspective on Kodak's challenges: "I think we're at the point where we have to get on with reality. The consumer traditional business is going to begin a slow decline, though it's not going to fall off a cliff." Was Kodak closer to the edge of the cliff than Carp thought? Could Kodak survive and thrive in the digital shift? Or would Kodak fade from history like a piece of film exposed to the light?

GROWTH IN DIGITAL PHOTOGRAPHY

Three years into the 21st century, the digital camera market was expanding at a fast pace. This was a major transfer from the previous decade of consumer photography as a largely mature market. Color film photography (also known as traditional photography) was a technology rich in history and closely tied to the art world. Eastman Kodak popularized color photography after the introduction of Kodachrome slide film in 1935.[13] Color print photography using 35-millimeter film grew rapidly in 1961 after the introduction of Kodacolor II print film.[14]

Exhibit 3   **Number of Households Owning Cameras, 1996–2003 (in millions)**

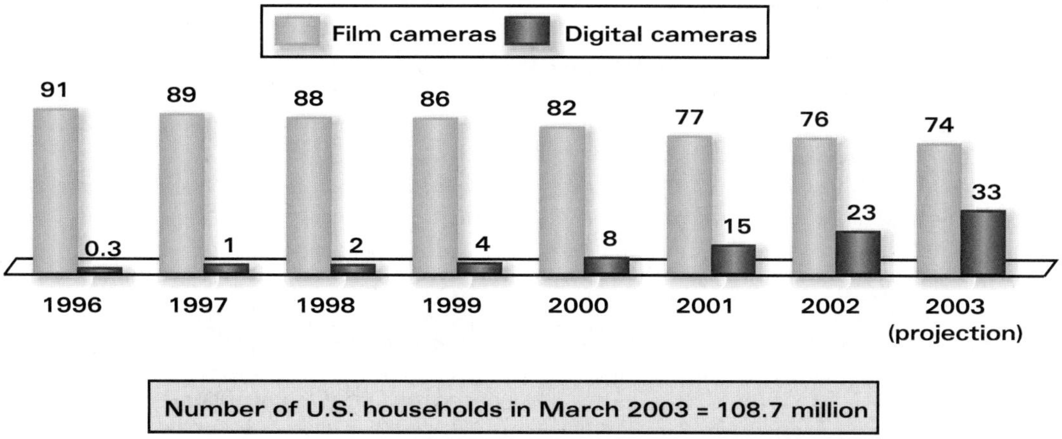

Number of U.S. households in March 2003 = 108.7 million

Source: PMA Marketing Research.

Demand for Digital Cameras

Digital photography was catching on fast in mainstream America as digital camera prices fell and image quality increased. The number of U.S. households owning a digital camera passed 1 million in 1997. By 2002, more than 23 million households owned digital cameras—this represented a 57 percent increase over 2001. Demand for digital cameras was expected to continue to increase, with more than 33 million households expected to own a digital camera in 2003. Exhibit 3 shows the growth in digital cameras and the decline in the number of households owning traditional film cameras. The 2.6 percent decline in traditional film cameras in 2002 was attributed in part to the growing demand for digital cameras and the rising popularity of one-time-use cameras. Market research projected continued further declines in traditional camera ownership.[15] Declines were also projected for sales of traditional film (down by 4 percent) and film processing (down by 3 percent) in 2003.

Although digital photography was making significant inroads with the mass market, technically sophisticated users were adopting digital technology at a higher rate. Among Internet-connected U.S. households, the estimate was that 60 percent had converted to digital cameras by the end of 2002.

Digital cameras generated a significant portion of industry revenues, accounting for $2.96 billion in revenues for 2002. This figure represented an increase of 22 percent over 2001 revenues. Revenues for traditional film, film processing, and traditional cameras had declined during this same period, as shown in Exhibit 4.

Industry experts predicted that the consumer shift to digital photography would be nearly complete by 2008, with sales of digital cameras nearly replacing sales of traditional film cameras such as 35-millimeter film cameras.[16] One-time-use cameras would continue to be popular, thus providing continued, although reduced, demand for film processing services.

What made digital cameras so attractive for consumers? Digital cameras gave users capabilities that were not possible with traditional cameras. Experts attributed the growth in digital photography to four factors—instant preview, sleek design, features, and price.[17] The technology of digital cameras allowed users to instantly view the shots they had taken and reshoot until they were satisfied with the results. The sleek design of many digital cameras made carrying one a fashion statement or a must-have item for teenagers and young professionals. Camera features also allowed digital users to capture short movies and to manipulate the images using photo-editing software that often came bundled with the camera. Price declines had made digital cameras much more affordable.

Michelle Slaughter, director of digital photography trends at InfoTrends Research Group, described digital cameras as an "essential communications device" for consumers.[18] "Consumers are becoming accustomed to the immediacy of digital photography

Exhibit 4   **Consumer Photographic Market Revenue, 2000–2002 (in billions of $)**

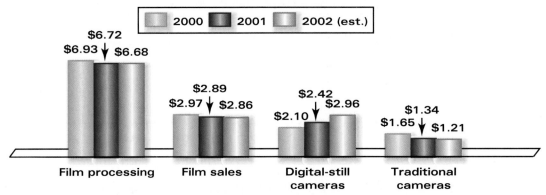

Source: PMA Marketing Research; www.pmai.org/pdf/0403_pixels_to_prints.pdf.

and are integrating digital photos into their daily communications with friends and family and for work. As a result, digital cameras have a higher intrinsic value to consumers than film cameras. This, in turn, paves the way for digital camera sales to exceed film camera sales," predicted Slaughter.

Although the price of digital cameras had declined sharply, the average price of a digital camera was still significantly more expensive than for 35-millimeter cameras. In 2002, the average price for a digital camera was $328.[19] When compared with an average price of $137 for a 35-millimeter camera, it was no surprise that more than half of digital camera buyers were in households where the annual income was $75,000 or more. Half of the digital camera buyers in 2002 were between the ages of 35 and 54. Buyers in this age group and income bracket were in the prime segment for capturing family photos and often traveled more frequently than those in other age groups and income brackets. Age and income statistics for digital camera buyers in 2002 are shown in Exhibit 5.

Although market research showed that men tended to purchase digital cameras more frequently than women (58 percent versus 42 percent), women tended to be the primary users of the equipment.[20] Women were described as the preservers of family memories and were increasingly using digital cameras to capture birthday parties, holiday celebrations, or family vacations. Women were becoming more likely to spur the decision to buy a digital camera for the household.[21] Women with children were described as the "most photo active consumers"[22]

and were expected to lead the demand for services such as digital printing.

Digital Printing Trends

Early adopters of digital photography consistently cited sending photos by e-mail as the number one reason for taking pictures with digital cameras.[23] Although mothers might e-mail friends and family the latest batch of baby photos, showing them off to a crowd gathered around a computer screen did not

Exhibit 5   **Percentage of Consumers Who Bought Digital Cameras in 2002**

By Age	
Age Group	**Percent**
18–24	9%
25–34	25
35–54	50
55 or older	17

By Income	
Household Income	**Percent**
Less than $25,000	6%
$25,000–$49,999	19
$50,000–$74,999	23
$75,000 or more	52

Source: *American Demographics*, July 1, 2003, p. 6.

Exhibit 6   **Destination of Digital Pictures after Capture**

Picture Destination	Year		
	2000	2001	2002
Save, store, or keep	63%	68%	71%
E-mail	16	13	13
Print	12	14	20

Source: Photomarketing Association International, April 2003.

provide the same gratification and ease of use as looking at photos in an album. Consumers saw the ability to preview digital photos and to print only those they wanted as one of the strengths of the medium.

Few digital images were ever actually printed on paper. In 2000, only 12 percent of all digital images taken were printed. By 2002, this had increased to 20 percent of images taken.[24] Trends in the destination for digital images are shown in Exhibit 6.

The low ratio of printed photos to digital images was a big problem for companies wanting to profit from the printing process. According to analysts' estimations, companies such as Hewlett-Packard (HP), Lexmark, Canon, Seiko Epson, Olympus, and Eastman Kodak made almost nothing on the printers they sold. The money and profits were in the materials used to make prints. For instance, in summer 2003, HP saw profit margins of about 65 percent on ink-jet paper and ink, and roughly 30 percent margins on laser printing supplies.[25]

Consumers had a wide variety of options to choose from in obtaining prints from digital images. Digital photographers printed 2.1 billion images from digital cameras in 2003. Of these, 77 percent were printed with home printers, 6.4 percent were ordered from online photo services, 8.7 percent were made at a local retailer, and 3.6 percent were made using digital self-service kiosks. Consumers reported using "some other means" to produce 4.2 percent of all digital prints in 2003.[26]

Most consumers used their personal computers and home printers for printing their digital pictures; however, these were often perceived as lower-quality, more time-consuming, and more expensive than traditional film prints. More than half of digital camera users indicated they would print more digital images if they could make high-quality prints on their home printers.[27] Almost as many also indicated the printing

of digital images at home would need to be easier and less time-consuming. Consumers often got confused while transferring pictures from their digital cameras to their computers. "There are so many ways for people to get into trouble when they try to print photos at home," said Kristy Holch, a principal at InfoTrends Research Group.

Online photo services provided another option. Services such as Snapfish, Shutterfly, and Ofoto allowed consumers to upload their photos; preview, crop, and manipulate them; and obtain high-quality snapshots by mail. Pictures could further be shared online with friends and relatives via online albums. Custom calendars, cards, books, and mouse pads could be ordered with the customer's photos. Prints were priced significantly less than those printed at home at 19–29 cents per print versus the 62-cent cost of a print made on a Kodak Easyshare printer.[28] Disadvantages to online photo services included slow photo uploads (especially for consumers with dial-up Internet connections) and the four to six days it took to receive the prints by mail.

In September 2003, 18.4 million people visited online photography sites that could be used for sharing and printing, according to Nielsen//Net Ratings. Yahoo! Photos had 4.7 million unique visitors, followed by the Time Warner AOL unit, You've Got Pictures, with 2.7 million. Ofoto and Snapfish each had 1.67 million users, and Kodak's online site drew 1.5 million.

Local retailers such as Costco, Wal-Mart, and Walgreens provided another option for obtaining prints of digital images; however, these services failed to catch on with consumers. Many consumers did not realize that they could drop off their digital camera's memory card at the photo counter for printing. Others were reluctant to entrust the expensive memory cards to film processors. Retailers attempted to resolve these problems by adding self-service photo printing kiosks in their stores. Consumers could use the kiosks to edit photos and make their own prints from digital memory cards. Retailers launched advertising emphasizing ease of use and the immediacy of prints from the kiosks to overcome consumer's lack of awareness of this option. Expectations for growth in print volume at self-service kiosks were strong. "As digital camera users begin to use photo kiosks, print volumes on photo kiosks will increase dramatically," reported Kerry Flatley, a research analyst.[29] "Digital camera customers . . . will use photo kiosks as a high-volume source for their original photo prints," Flatley stated.

Impact on Demand for Traditional Film

The widespread adoption of digital photography had taken a toll on demand for traditional film and film processing. The volume of prints made from traditional films in 2002 declined by 700,000 over 2001 volumes. During the same time, digital prints grew by 1.3 million units. Digital images accounted for 6.1 percent of the total volume of prints made in 2002, up from only 2.4 percent in 2001.[30] Film sales were expected to decline by 4 percent in 2003, as shown in Exhibit 7.

One-time-use cameras were popular with consumers due to their convenience and low price, although the growth had slowed from 25 percent in 1999 to 8 percent in 2003. Film processing, which included both film rolls and one-time-use cameras, had declined significantly over the period from 1999 to 2003 due to the decrease in the use of traditional film among digital camera owners and the economic slowdown.

Other Digital Imaging Options

Another interesting market situation was developing—photo-capable cell phones. According to a survey done by experts in September 2003, more cell phones with integrated digital cameras than other types of digital cameras were sold in the first half of the year.[31] The research group Strategy Analytics stated that 25 million camera phones were purchased by consumers worldwide in the first half of 2003, compared with only 20 million digital still cameras.

"This is a milestone event, but it is just the first step towards the industry goal of getting a camera phone in every pocket," said Neil Mawston, senior analyst at Strategy Analytics' Global Wireless Practice. Mobile operators wanted to get customers to send picture messages regularly over their recently enhanced networks, in hopes of replicating the surprise success of text messaging. As the market for voice calls was becoming more competitive, non-voice data revenues could prove vital for operators' profitability.

However, security and privacy concerns among companies represented one potential problem for the camera phone market. Besides, Strategy Analytics said, camera phones represented no major threat to the digital still camera market because the difference in picture quality between the two technologies was too great. A Canon marketing director expressed the view of most camera manufacturers when it called even the two-megapixel camera phone just a "distraction." "It's good to have mobile phone cameras," the marketing director said, "but their functionalities are limited in terms of storage, picture quality, zooming

Exhibit 7   **Annual Change in Unit Sales of Film Rolls, One-Time-Use Cameras, and Film Processing, 1999–2003**

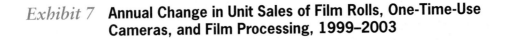

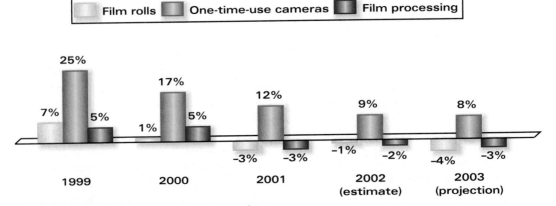

Note: Film processing includes both film rolls and one-time-use cameras.
Source: PMA Monthly Processing Surveys.

functionality, and power supply. Consumers will still go for the 'real camera' even though they have camera phones. Cameras on phones are just add-ons to give phones more functionalities."[32]

The Economist reported that camera phones might create a "nightmare scenario" for the traditional photography industry by hastening the decline of printed photos.[33] As camera phones improved, consumers might view on-screen images on phones, PCs, televisions, or even by beaming photos to a wireless-enabled picture frame. If this came to pass, "printing could become a niche, like film is expected to," said Chris Chute of the telecommunications consulting firm IDC.[34] Increased popularity of on-screen photo viewing would prove damaging for the photography industry, which depended on revenues from film processing and printing. Digital photography was threatening the first source of revenue. If camera phones caught on, cell phone operators could capture the second source, earning revenues by charging users for transmitting images.

GLOBAL TRENDS IN PHOTOGRAPHY

Income distribution among countries influenced the sales of the cameras around the world. While sales of digital cameras were booming in developed countries like the United States and Japan, consumers from emerging economies such as China bought more traditional cameras.

China was developing into a center of photography—and was doing so more rapidly than anyone would have expected only a few years ago. More than 5 million cameras were sold in China in 2002, and 400,000 of those were digital models (see Exhibit 8). This figure was set to increase, and Chinese consumers were expected to buy more than 3 million digital cameras by 2005. However, there were also other reasons why China was so important for the photographic and imaging sector, since every market segment was still growing in this country, not just the one for digital devices.

A large amount of additional sales potential remained unexploited in China. China's per capita consumption of film in 2003 was a mere 0.1 a year, compared to an average of 3.1 in Europe and 3.6 in the United States. China was still a long way from reaching market saturation even though film sales were rapidly increasing. Revenues from digital camcorders, photographic paper, data projectors, scanners, and printers were growing rapidly as well.

COMPETITIVE STANDINGS AND DIGITAL STRATEGIES

In the segment of traditional photography, Kodak's main brand competitors were Canon, Sony, and Fuji,

Exhibit 8   **Camera Sales in China, 2000–2002, with Projections for 2003–2005**

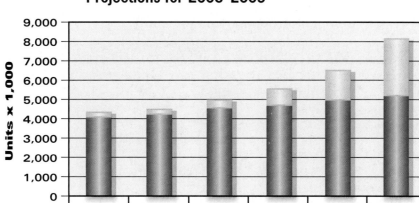

Source: www.prophoto-online.de/photokina/photokinanewsEnglish.pdf.

Exhibit 9   **Market Shares in Digital Imaging**

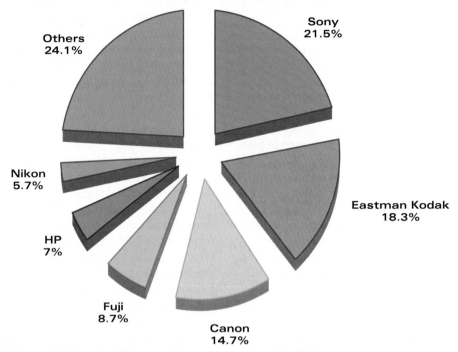

Source: "Digital Imaging's Winners and Losers," *Forbes,* August 9, 2004.

with Fuji being the biggest competitor. According to analysts' estimations, Kodak's competitors in the digital photography industry were Sony, HP, and Fuji.

Eastman Kodak captured 18.3 percent of the digital market, compared with the 15.3 percent share it had captured in the first six months of 2003. Sony led the market with a 21.5 percent share, with Canon, Fuji, HP, and Nikon following, with 14.7 percent,

8.7 percent, 7 percent, and 5.7 percent, respectively.[35] The market shares are shown in Exhibit 9.

Although Kodak was a major player in the photography market (both digital and traditional), it was far from being the biggest (see Exhibit 10). Eastman Kodak's earnings before interest, taxes, depreciation, and amortization (EBITDA) of $1.2 billion were just a fraction of its closest competitor

Exhibit 10   **Competitor Comparison for 2003**

	Kodak	Canon	Fuji	Sony
Market capitalization	$8.32 billion	$43.19 billion	$15.80 billion	$36.56 billion
Employees	70,000	98,873	72,569	161,100
Revenue growth	−3.00%	11.80%	0.4%	9.10%
Gross margin	32.17%	50.31%	41.64%	25.28%
EBITDA	$1.20 billion	$6.05 billion	$3.11 billion	$7.06 billion
Operating margins	2.79%	14.21%	6.20%	1.25%
Net income	$238 million	$2.62 billion	$532 million	$170 million
Earnings per share	$0.83	$2.948	$1.036	$0.09
Price/earnings ratio	35x	17x	30x	440x

Source: Company annual reports and Web sites.

Fuji's of $3.11 billion. Competitors Sony and Canon had EBITDA figures of $7.06 and $6.05 billion, respectively.

Sony

Sony had been on the digital wave since the mid-1990s, when it introduced its first PlayStation.[36] Nobuyuki Idei, chairman and CEO, played a key role in moving Sony into the digital network era by emphasizing the integration of audiovisual and information technology products. He was responsible for Sony's image campaign "Do you dream in Sony?" and helped coin the term "digital dream kids."[37]

Sony was a Japanese consumer electronics and multimedia giant. The firm produced music, movies, and television shows as well as the devices to bring them to the consumer. The electronics division produced video game consoles, personal digital assistants, DVD and MP3 players, digital camcorders, digital cameras, computers, and car audio products.

A team of developers gathered at a Sony laboratory in 1995 to "develop a digital still camera filled with enjoyment."[38] Sony's Cyber-Shot cameras were developed as the first "self-shooting" digital still cameras. Unburdened by a legacy in traditional film, developers relied on Sony's experience as a leading consumer technology company to develop a full line of digital cameras targeted to men and women between the ages of 25 and 55. Sony positioned its cameras at a premium or fair price based on cutting-edge technology and design. "You'll never see Sony offer a $99 camera," predicted one senior digital imaging analyst.[39] Sony's digital cameras ranged from about $180 for a point-and-shoot model to just under $1,000 for an advanced-featured Pro model.

Canon

Japan's Canon Inc. had come a long way since its days as a producer of cheap cameras. Much of Canon's success against its archrival had come on the watch of the company's president, Fujio Mitarai. A nephew of a Canon founder, Mitarai spent 23 years working in New York before returning to Japan in 1995 to head the company. Canon operated in the document reproduction markets producing copiers, fax machines, and scanners. Canon's optical segment produced diverse products such as television broadcast lenses and semiconductor manufacturing equipment. The camera division produced camcorders, binoculars, lenses, and digital cameras. Canon was relatively late to the market with its digital products, but the products it had introduced were hits.[40]

On November 21, 2001, Canon U.S.A. Inc., a subsidiary of Canon Inc., launched a marketing campaign featuring its PowerShot digital cameras and Bubble Jet printers working in concert to showcase Canon's leadership in digital photo solutions for the 2001 holiday season.[41] "The camera and printer are the stars of this 'production' number from beginning to end. Canon has a 60-year history in optics/lens technology for cameras, as well as creating its own printing technology—a combination our competitors cannot claim. By showcasing the 'digital duet' of our digital cameras and printers, we show the viewer that Canon products create picture perfect results that are unmatched by our competition," said Rick Booth, assistant director of advertising for the Canon Photographic Products Group.

Canon offered digital cameras for a wide variety of users at different price points. A simple point-and-shoot model was priced at slightly less than $200, while a professional-level digital single-lens reflex (SLR) camera sold for almost $8,000.

Fuji

Fuji, a longtime rival of Kodak, offered a complete portfolio of imaging, information, and document products, services, and e-solutions to retailers, consumers, professionals, and business customers. Fuji had been digital since 1998, when it introduced the first digital camera. "Fuji's solution was to start a suite of online options to share, order, pay for and collect digital photos," Dane Anderson of IDC, pointed out. By the summer of 2003, Fuji had developed a program for digital photography called Image Intelligence. This integrated system of digital image-processing software technologies came from the culmination of nearly 70 years of imaging expertise.

Fuji's traditional film, photo paper, developing chemicals, and nondigital printers accounted for 42 percent of the firm's 2003 sales. Experts expected the percentage of sales due to traditional photography to shrink to 31 percent by 2006.[42]

Fuji had introduced digital minilabs in the market. A minilab offered a service similar to that of traditional picture printing—consumers could print their digital photos by dropping off their digital memory cards and returning later to pick up finished prints. With more than 5,000 labs in the marketplace, Fuji had about 60 percent of the U.S. digital mini-lab market, including deals to put machines in 2,500 Wal-Mart and about 800 Walgreens outlets. Those two chains handled about 40 percent of the U.S. photo-processing market.

Hewlett-Packard (HP)

HP provided consumer and business customers with a full range of technology-based products, including personal computers, servers, storage devices, networking equipment, and software. The company also included an information technology service organization that was among the world's largest. Known primarily by consumers for its dominance in computer printers, HP expanded into the digital imaging segment as a way to continue to fuel demand for HP printers and ink cartridges.

HP's breadth also provided an important advantage to consumers, according to HP vice president Chris Morgan. "We think consumers are going to want their products to be interoperable. Digital photography is a natural extension given our strength in computing and image processing," said Morgan. Consumers will "want to move content from camera to computer to email or DVD, from camcorder to computer to TV, or just skip the computer and go directly from device to playback system. That plays to our advantage. Not only are we the No. 1 consumer computer company in the world, we think that our understanding of big-business ecosystems will be a powerful advantage in helping us develop these solutions," he continued.[43]

Prices for HP's digital cameras ranged from about $100 to $400. As part of the firm's strategy to provide interoperable solutions that allowed consumers to connect various devices, HP offered several different camera and photo printer bundles and camera and docking station bundles.[44]

HP had a personal computer dubbed Photo Smart, which had a built-in docking slot for uploading photos only from HP's latest digital cameras and unified photo software that handled downloading, storing, exchanging, and printing photos.

HP was also trying to get more people to share digital pictures electronically because that got more people making prints. HP's Instant Share software allowed consumers to preprogram e-mail addresses and photo-sharing Web sites into their cameras. After making pictures, users specified where they wanted the images sent, and the pictures were mailed the next time the camera was connected to the PC.

Nikon

Nikon was well known for its traditional photography products—35-millimeter cameras, lenses, and other consumer optical products. Nikon also produced equipment used in the manufacturing of semiconductors and a broad range of other optical products such as binoculars, microscopes, eyewear, and surveying equipment. Imaging products such as camera equipment comprised 57.6 percent of Nikon's net sales in 2003.[45]

Nikon targeted amateur photographers with its line of Coolpix cameras. These cameras ranged in price from about $140 to $850. The Coolpix line offered a full range of stylish and simple-to-use cameras designed to appeal to the first-time user and the more advanced photography hobbyist. Nikon also offered a line of digital single lens reflex (SLR) cameras that targeted advanced and professional photographers who wanted multifeatured, easy-to-use digital cameras. Digital SLR cameras permitted the use of interchangeable lenses and were designed to provide sharper, clearer images at faster shutter speeds than other digital cameras. Nikon digital SLR cameras ranged in price from $900 (camera body only) to well over $1,200. Nikon used the trademarked phrase "Nikon . . . If the picture matters, the camera matters" in the marketing of its cameras.[46]

KODAK'S PHOTOGRAPHY UNIT

Eastman Kodak was primarily engaged in developing, manufacturing and marketing traditional and digital imaging products, services, and solutions for consumers, professionals, health care providers, and other commercial customers. The company operated in four segments: components, health imaging (18 percent of company's total revenue), commercial imaging (11 percent of total sales), and photography (70 percent of revenue).

The photography segment included traditional and digital product offerings for consumers, professional photographers, and the entertainment industry. This segment combined traditional and digital photography and photographic services in all its forms—consumer, advanced amateur, and professional. Kodak manufactured and marketed various components of these systems, including films (consumer, professional, and motion picture); photographic papers; processing services; photofinishing equipment; photographic chemicals; and cameras (including one-time-use and digital).

Product and service offerings included kiosks and scanning systems to digitize and enhance images, digital media for storing images, and a network for transmitting images. In addition, other digitization options were available to stimulate more pictures in use, adding to the consumption of film and paper. These products served different groups of customers, including amateur photographers as well as professional, motion picture, and television customers. Technically, Eastman Kodak provided the services of picture creation to everyone who requested it, adjusting these services for specific groups of consumers.

Since Kodak's bread-and-butter unit was its photography unit, the company's stock price heavily depended on this unit's performance. The firm's stock price declined from more than $80 to $20 per share (see Exhibit 11) as revenues from traditional photography declined. In June 2003, Standard & Poor's (S&P) Rating Service placed Kodak on a CreditWatch, with negative implications, expressing concerns that economic, competitive, and leisure travel pressures would continue to impair Kodak's sales and earnings.[47] S&P analysts expressed concern that Kodak's transition to digital imaging would hurt future profitability for the firm by reducing high-margin film sales. Kodak's migration to digital technologies might also require additional restructuring as the firm adapted to evolving market conditions.

Kodak's restructuring actions prior to 2003 were primarily of a tactical nature. Three modifications between 1999 and 2003 indicated that the company's traditional film and photography businesses, while still hugely important as a source of cash, were becoming less of a central focus in a world where images were increasingly captured as bytes and bits. These modifications signaled management's attempt to keep up with the market, meaning that Eastman Kodak was losing the role of market maker.

Exhibit 11   **Eastman Kodak's Stock Price, January 1999–September 2003**

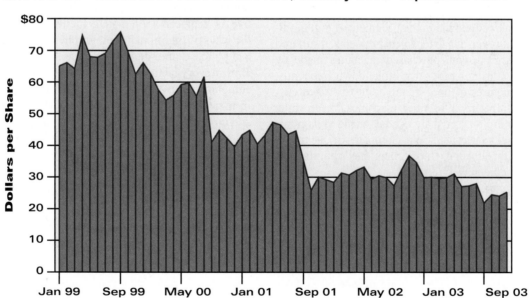

TOUGH CHOICES FOR A TRADITIONAL PHOTOGRAPHY COMPANY

Although it did not announce a change to a digital strategy until 2003, Eastman Kodak was moving toward this objective through acquisitions of smaller companies successful in the digital area. "Digital imaging is going to be like the cellular telephone business," George Fisher, Kodak's then CEO, predicted in 1997. "Highly competitive, very high growth, good profits for the leader, but not for the followers."[48]

In general, Kodak's performance in the new market conditions was varied. In some areas it was successful; in others it was not. Kodak's president and chief operating officer, Antonio Perez, had conceded that the company was behind the curve in printers, an area it regarded as key to its future digital profits. This was not for lack of effort. A joint attempt in 2000 to introduce a desktop photo ink-jet printer with Lexmark flopped, partly because the product's direct-to-camera interface never caught on. Most consumers made their digital prints via PC-to-printer links. Kodak said its newly introduced system for docking a thermal printer with a PC, designed for greater ease of use, was faring much better, and would generate a respectable $100 million in sales in 2003, its first year.

Kodak entered the market segment of digital minilabs. However, due to technical problems, it suffered some losses. Kodak purchased machines made by a manufacturing partner that broke down frequently, printed pictures of poor quality, and frustrated customers. Fuji's rival Frontier machines, meanwhile, were gaining market share. Kodak changed its minilab partner to Noritsu Koki Company of Japan. As result of this change, Kodak mentioned that the machines had been well received.

Phogenix, a joint venture between HP and Kodak to develop smaller digital photo printers for retail outlets, crumbled in May 2003 because the technology had already become obsolete by the time the machines were brought to market. In a joint statement, Matthias Freund, chairman of the Phogenix board of directors and chief operating officer of Kodak's Consumer Imaging Products and Services business, and Mary Peery, member of the Phogenix board of directors and senior vice president of HP's Digital Imaging & Publishing business, said, "Both HP and Kodak believe the technology being developed by Phogenix continues to offer a viable solution for on-site digital photo processing. However, based on the anticipated return on invested capital for the parent companies, each company has separately decided to focus its own investments on other opportunities."[49]

The Phogenix labs, small enough to fit in stores typically unequipped to house typical automated film-developing machines, would have cost retailers about $40,000 but could produce only about 250 prints an hour, compared with more than 1,000 for Fuji's Noritsu minilab. Fuji's system cost $139,000 to $245,000, analysts estimated.

Kodak had had some notable digital successes. Kodak's popular EasyShare cameras were the second best-selling digital cameras in the United States in the first half of 2003, behind only those of Sony. After successfully focusing on the lower end of the camera market, Kodak was planning to begin selling more-expensive digital cameras aimed at tech-savvy shutterbugs. The company was diversifying its product line's depth and width, aiming at new segments of the market.

Finally, Kodak believed it had a strong management team. CEO Daniel Carp was considered to have good leadership skills. He was helped by other specialists, known for their extensive experience in the digital photography industry. Executive by executive, he replaced a top management cadre steeped in the ways of traditional photography with a team that had almost a pure digital pedigree. Except for Carp, almost every senior executive was from outside the company. Carp's management team was composed from new hires from Lexmark, HP, General Electric, and Olympus Optical.

SHIFT FROM TRADITIONAL PHOTOGRAPHY TO DIGITAL PHOTOGRAPHY

On September 25, 2003, Kodak unveiled its digitally oriented strategy. "We are acting with the knowledge that demand for traditional products is declining, especially in developed markets," Carp said. "Given this reality, we are moving fast—as digital markets demand—to transform our business portfolio, with an emphasis on digital commercial markets. The digital world is full of opportunity for Kodak, and we intend to lead it, as we have led innovation in the imaging industry for more than a century."[50]

Kodak was among the last photographic giants to announce its digital plans. The truly global scale of Kodak's operations represented an additional complexity for Kodak. While some parts of the world were outgrowing the shoes of traditional photography (e.g., developed countries like the United States, western European countries, and Japan), other parts of the world still exhibited growth opportunities for old film production.

Kodak recognized that, on the one hand, there were growth opportunities in areas that provided 30 percent profit margins (traditional film). These opportunities were in unstable emerging economies of countries like China, India, and the Russian Federation. On the other hand, opportunities in new digital photography looked better than those in traditional photography. The expected growth rate of the digital photography industry was about 26 percent until 2012. However, pursuing these opportunities would require substantial capital investment of up to $3 billion (according to stock analysts).

Daniel Carp's PowerPoint presentation for the September announcement showed that Kodak's new strategy would be based on three pillars—commercial imaging, health imaging, and consumer imaging.[51] Additional pillars under construction were ink-jet printers, commercial workflow management, and flat-panel displays.

The digital and film imaging strategy focused on four components:[52]

1. Manage the traditional film business for cash and manufacturing share leadership.
2. Lead in distributed output.
3. Grow the digital capture business.
4. Expand digital imaging services.

Under the first of these components, Kodak planned to reduce costs in its traditional film businesses and cut back on marketing expenditures for film (shifting instead to processing). The firm would continue to offer premium, high-margin products such

as Perfect Touch processing and High Definition film in developing markets, while establishing leadership in emerging markets such as China and Russia.

Leading in distributed output referred to Kodak's plan to capture more of the demand for digital prints, whether produced in retail locations or at home. Kodak's plan called for the development of improved minilabs and kiosks that could print images faster, and for an increase of 50,000 kiosks by 2004. Kodak's home output strategy centered on the printer dock that allowed Kodak EasyShare users to transfer images directly from their cameras to a printer through a docking station. Users could then select and print images without a PC. Increasing use of Kodak's online photo service, Ofoto, was also a part of this strategy.

The digital capture business component referred to the further development of Kodak's digital cameras. Kodak intended to obtain a top-three worldwide market position for digital cameras by 2006. This goal would be reached by becoming the industry standard for ease of use and by moving to more sophisticated cameras.

Kodak planned to expand its digital imaging services by expanding the products and services offered through Ofoto to include items such as picture frames, calendars, and photo albums. Kodak also planned to develop kiosks that could print images from mobile phones. Rollout of this product had already begun in Asia and Europe and was expected to be ready for the U.S. market by the end of the fourth quarter of 2003.

On October 22, 2003, about 60 institutional shareholders met in New York City to examine other strategy alternatives, objecting to Carp's "risky" strategy of investing $3 billion into emerging digital markets.[53] Investors attending the meeting controlled about 25 percent of Kodak's stock. They felt that Kodak had been struggling with the transition to digital photography for almost 10 years and that, while it had enjoyed some success, the progress had not been enough, especially given the billions of dollars that had already been spent. Investors pushed for radical cost cuts to quickly boost earnings but had not yet come to an agreement about any long-term strategies for Kodak.

Carp argued that the cost-cutting plans touted by the investors "really aren't viable, practical options" and that Kodak had few alternatives other than slashing its dividends and pouring its resources into digital technologies.[54] Herbert A. Denton, president of Providence Capital, the host for the meeting, said, "We want them [Kodak] to let us under the tent and really show us why this strategy is best."[55] Was Carp's strategy best? Would Kodak's transition to a digital strategy be enough to help it reach its goal of becoming a $20 billion company by 2010?[56]

Endnotes

[1]C. Wolf, "Kodak Stock Plummets as Dividend Cut: Slashed by 72%," *Bloomberg News,* September 26, 2003, p. FP03.

[2]Ibid.

[3]C. H. Deutsch, "Some Positive News Aside, Kodak's Quarterly Profit Falls 63%," *New York Times,* October 23, 2003, p. C9.

[4]Wolf, "Kodak Stock Plummets."

[5]B. Dobbin, "Kodak Works Through Profit Drop," *Times Union,* October 23, 2003, p. E4.

[6]Wolf, "Kodak Stock Plummets."

[7]Ibid.

[8]Ibid.

[9]Dobbin, "Kodak Works Through Profit Drop."

[10]"What It 'Boils Down To' for Kodak," *BusinessWeek,* November 23, 2003.

[11]www.kodak.com.

[12]"Kodak Struggles to Find Its Focus," *Leader-Post,* July 28, 2003, p. B5.

[13]"Milestones—The Chronology," http://kodak.com/US/en/corp/kodakHistory/1930_1959.shtml (accessed December 6, 2004).

[14]A. Mutz, "Digital Photography Fundamentals and Trends," www.codesta.com/knowledge/technical/digital_photography/printable_version.aspx, March 26, 1993 (accessed December 6, 2004).

[15]Photo Marketing Association International, "The Path From Pixels to Print: The Challenge of Bringing Digital Imaging to the Mass Market," from www.pmai.org/pdf/0403_pixels_to_prints.pdf, April 2003 (accessed November 22, 2004).

[16]InfoTrends Research Group, "Digital Cameras Will Nearly Replace Film Cameras by 2008," press release, www.infotrends-rgi.com/home/Press/itPress/2003/6.25.03.html, June 25, 2003 (accessed November 29, 2004).

[17]I. Ismail, "Digital Photography Is Hot," *New Straits Times Press* (Malaysia), June 7, 2004, p. 9.

[18]InfoTrends Research Group, "Worldwide Consumer Digital Camera Sales to Reach Nearly 53 Million in 2004," press release, www.infotrends-rgi.com/home/press/itPress/2003/11.19.03.html, November 19, 2003 (accessed November 29, 2004).

[19]S. Yin, "Picture This," *American Demographics,* July 1, 2003, p. 6.

[20]Photo Marketing Association International, "The Path From Pixels to Print."

[21]"Digital Camera Ownership Moving Deeper into Mainstream Market, According to New InfoTrends/CAP Ventures Study," *Business Wire,* October 12, 2004.

[22]Photo Marketing Association International, "The Path From Pixels to Print."

[23]Ibid.

[24]Ibid.

[25]A. Ferrari, "The Push for More Digital Photo Prints," www.forbes.com/2003/10/30/cx_af_1030printing.html, October 30, 2003 (accessed December 6, 2004).

[26]R. A. Dalton Jr., "In a Tech World, It's a Snap," *Newsday,* September 26, 2004, p. E6.

[27]Photo Marketing Association International, "The Path From Pixels to Print."

[28]Dalton, "In a Tech World, It's a Snap."

[29]InfoTrends Research Group, "New Wave of Photo Kiosk and Digital Print Solutions Driven by Digital Photography," press release, www.infotrends-rgi.com/home/Press/itPress/2002/5.20.02.html, May 20, 2002 (accessed November 30, 2004).

[30]Photo Marketing Association International, "The Path From Pixels to Print."

[31]"Camera Phones Outselling Digital Cameras—Report," www.forbes.com/newswire/2003/09/26/rtr1092489.html, September 26, 2003 (accessed December 6, 2004).

[32]Ismail, "Digital Photography Is Hot."

[33]"Mobile Snaps," *The Economist,* July 3, 2003.

[34]Ibid.

[35]A. Ferrari, "Digital Imaging's Winners and Losers," www.forbes.com/infoimaging/2004/08/09/cx_af_0809imagingupdate_ii.html, August 9, 2004 (accessed December 3, 2004).

[36]"Sony History," www.sony.ca/sonyca/view/english/corporate/corporate_sonyhistory1.shtml (accessed December 6, 2004).

[37]"Executive Biographies," www.sony.com/SCA/bios/idei.shtml (accessed December 6, 2004).

[38]"Cybershot: The Roots," www.sony.net/Products/cybershot/the_roots_01.html (accessed December 6, 2004).

[39]B. S. Bulik, "Sony, Kodak Lead U.S. Battle for Share in Digital Cameras," *Advertising Age* 75, no. 22 (May 31, 2004).

[40]P. Klebinkov and B. Fulford, "Canon on the Loose," www.forbes.com/global/2001/0723/036_3.html, July 23, 2001 (accessed December 6, 2004).

[41]"New Canon Marketing Campaign Highlights 'Digital Duet' of Digital Cameras and Printers," *Business Wire,* November 21, 2001 (accessed via Lexis/Nexis November 30, 2004).

[42]"Fuji's Digital Picture Is Developing Fast," www.businessweek.com/print/magazine/content/04_08/b3871064.htm, February 23, 2004 (accessed November 29, 2004).

[43]"HP's Strategy: Connect 'Device Islands,'"www.businessweek.com/technology/content/dec2003/tc2003129_2679_tc137.htm, December 9, 2003 (accessed November 29, 2004).

[44]"Digital Cameras," www.shopping.hp.com (accessed November 29, 2004).

[45]"Nikon Portfolio," www.nikon.co.jp/main/eng/portfolio/index.htm (accessed November 29, 2004).

[46]Nikon Web site, www.nikonusa.com/home.php (accessed November 29, 2004).

[47]"Kodak Debt Placed on CreditWatch Negative," www.businessweek.com/print/investor/content/jun2003/pi20030619_9134_pi036.htm?chan=pi&, June 19, 2003 (accessed November 29, 2004).

[48]S. N. Chakravarty, "How an Outsider's Vision Saved Kodak," www.forbes.com/forbes/1997/0113/5901045a_3.html, January 13, 1997 (accessed December 6, 2004).

[49]"HP, Kodak to Dissolve Phoenix Venture," www.printondemand.com/MT/archives/000142.html, May 23, 2003 (accessed December 6, 2004).

[50]Kodak press release, www.kodak.com/eknec/PageQuerier.jhtml?pq-path=2709&pq-locale=en_US&gpcid=0900688a8022df48, September 25, 2003 (accessed November 29, 2004).

[51]"Kodak Strategy Review," http://media.corporate-ir.net/media_files/IROL/11/115911/Reports/Carp_Sept25.pdf, September 25, 2003 (accessed December 6, 2004).

[52]"Kodak Strategy Review: Digital and Film Imaging," http://media.corporate-ir.net/media_files/IROL/11/115911/Reports/Masson_sept25.pdf, September 25, 2003 (accessed December 6, 2004).

[53]W. Symonds, "Not Exactly a Kodak Moment," *BusinessWeek,* November 24, 2003, p. 44.

[54]Ibid.

[55]C. H. Deutsch, "Some Positive News Aside, Kodak's Quarterly Profit Falls 63%," *The New York Times,* October 23, 2003, p. C9.

[56]Kodak press release, www.kodak.com/eknec/PageQuerier.jhtml?pq-path=2709&pq-locale=en_US&gpcid=0900688a8022df48, September 25, 2003 (accessed November 29, 2004).

Adam Aircraft

Carl Hedberg
Babson College

William Bygrave
Babson College

John Hamilton
Babson College

As the sleek, six-seat Adam A500 performed a graceful arc overhead, Babson College MBA John Hamilton, vice president of marketing for Adam Aircraft Industries (AAI), had to smile. Earlier that morning, he had read an article describing the difficulties and pitfalls associated with designing, building, and certifying new aircraft. In the last 30 years, there were countless examples of start-up aircraft manufacturers that had tried and failed to deliver new products to the small and midsized aircraft markets. In fact, the only two start-up companies that had recently succeeded had been builders of very basic, single-engine aircraft.

Like most MBAs, John had been taught to analyze companies based on all the standard metrics: the management team, product viability and appeal, market demand, capitalization, and financing potential. While Adam Aircraft appeared to be a winner on all counts—including the progress it was making in the lengthy and complex certification process—the

Carl Hedberg and John Hamilton prepared this case under the supervision of Professor William Bygrave, Babson College, as a basis for class discussion rather than to illustrate either effective or ineffective handling of an administrative situation. Funding provided by the F. W. Olin Graduate School and the gift of the class of 2003, and the Frederic C. Hamilton Chair for Free Enterprise.

company did not have the many millions of dollars it would need to bring its products to market and reach positive cash flow.

Talking with some of his peers in venture capital, John had come to understand that private equity investors were a fickle bunch. The vast majority preferred to invest in biotechnology, telecommunications, and other industries with historically well-defined harvest potential. Following the market correction in 2000, the flow of venture capital had significantly diminished, and investments outside of these core industries had all but ceased.

John had grown up in a family of aviators. He had been a licensed pilot for over 18 years. Since flying machines were not only his vocation but also his passion, he had to wonder whether this love was clouding his analysis. The market was clearly desperate for products like the plane performing flawlessly overhead, but did Adam Aircraft have what it took to succeed where so many had failed? Could it continue to advance toward certification and full-production capability, or would the challenges that lay ahead slow it down enough to increase its burn rate to a level that would discourage even the most ardent investor?

John did know that in less than five years company founder Rick Adam had orchestrated the fabrication of two flying prototypes—the A500 twin piston and the A700 jet—at a speed of design and production that had turned heads in all sectors of the aviation industry. Certification on both models was expected in the coming year—two years ahead of a number of well-funded competitors. With their third product—the A600 twin turboprop—nearly ready to fly, Adam Aircraft had become the one to watch in 2004.

John zipped up against the cold December wind and tracked the A500 as it snapped a sharp wing-turn on its approach to their home field at Centennial Airport in Englewood, Colorado. Another successful flight test. He smiled; definitely the one to watch . . .

THE ENTREPRENEUR

George Adam Sr. had been a career Air Force officer who had flown B-17 and B-29 bombers during World War II. His son Rick, born in 1946, grew up on Air Force bases and had always expected to follow his father into the military cockpit. When a color-vision deficiency kept him out of the Air Force Academy flight program, he joined the Army, attended West Point Academy, and then switched his commission to the Air Force.

Rick specialized in computer science, and as an Air Force captain he ran the Real Time Computer Centers at the Kennedy Space Center and at Vandenberg Air Force Base. During that time he earned his MBA at Golden Gate University, and later, as a civilian, he found his way to Wall Street. At Goldman Sachs he ran the IT department as a general partner. In 1993, Rick left Goldman to start his own business: New Era of Networks, an enterprise application integration software developer. The wildly successful company went public and grew to a market capitalization of over $1 billion. It was later acquired by the Sybase Corporation.

All the while, Rick had never lost sight of his first love, and in the early 1990s he learned to fly. Since his business required lots of travel, he was able to log over a thousand pilot-hours in just a few years by flying himself to meetings. He started in an old Skymaster, moved into a 1978 Mitsubishi MU2, and ultimately got type-rated in a 1993 Citation jet. While Rick had the opportunity and the personal wealth to progress quickly as a pilot, he recognized that the majority of owner-operators weren't as fortunate:

> As a pilot you have to go in steps; you can't get ahead of yourself. So, as you log more and more hours in the air, you can begin to fly increasingly more complex airplanes. The problem is that when you are ready to make the move from a single to a twin-engine aircraft, there are very few products to choose from. Most of the aircraft are based on old designs, which makes them tough to fly and expensive to own and operate.

One of the most popular production twin-engine planes on the market is the Beechcraft Baron—introduced in 1961! Because they quit building their more capable pressurized twins in the mid-80s, and stopped innovating at the same time, the old Baron is still their frontline light twin—and a new one costs over a million dollars. See, as the volume of orders has gone down, the prices have continued to climb (see Exhibit 1).

Rick added that the alternative to buying a new version of an old design was far worse:

> Demand for used planes is huge, because they are cheaper than new ones, and, since nothing has changed in the industry, pilots can buy something that may have been manufactured in the 70s or 80s, but it looks like a new plane. Right now the average age of a general aviation[1] aircraft is over 30 years (see Exhibit 2), and it's getting one year older every year.
>
> And frankly, these airplanes become unsafe. If you look at the accident rate in aircraft, it climbs dramatically with age. So even though there are strict regulations on maintaining these aircraft, it's hard to keep an old plane in good shape. Systems like the wiring just get to a point where they are too old to be reliable.

The more Rick thought about this aging factor, the more certain he became that the only solution would be an entirely new generation of general aviation products. It wasn't long before he had begun to evaluate the commercial viability of such a venture.

SPOTTING THE OPPORTUNITY

Almost immediately upon joining the ranks of experienced aviators, Rick began to contemplate the type of effort that would be required to deliver a new plane to the marketplace:

> Every time I went to a cocktail party or barbeque, all the pilots would go off into a corner and start talking pilot stuff. And since everybody was moaning about the lack of new products, I became convinced that there was a huge demand. So in the early 90s I started developing strategies for launching a new aircraft company.
>
> Now, I have launched a few entrepreneurial ventures, and when you think there is a big opportunity, you make sure to stop and evaluate why it hasn't been

Exhibit 1   **Annual New U.S. Manufactured General Aviation Unit Shipments/Billings, 1974–2002**

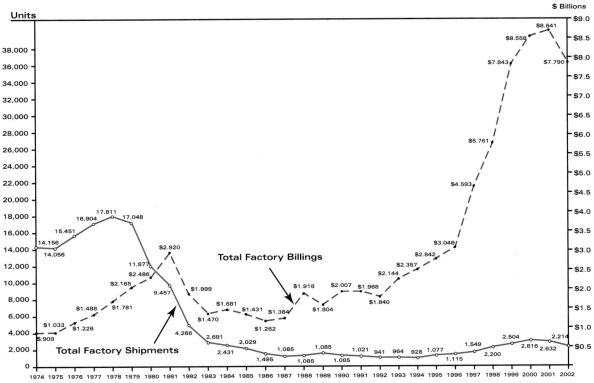

Source: General Aviation Manufacturers Association (GAMA) Statistical Databook 2002.

Exhibit 2   **Average Age of U.S. General Aviation Fleet in 2002**

Aircraft Type	Engine Type	Seats	Average Age in Years
Single-engine	Piston	1–3	36
		4	33
		5–7	28
		8+	43
	Turboprop	All	12
	Jet	All	31
Multi-engine	Piston	1–3	36
		4	33
		5–7	33
		8+	37
	Turboprop	All	26
	Jet	All	28
All aircraft			31

Source: General Aviation Manufacturers Association (GAMA) Statistical Databook 2002.

done before. Why isn't anyone pursuing this opportunity? What do I know, or what do I see that nobody else is seeing? Very often, entrepreneurial opportunities occur when a series of prior developments makes it possible to accomplish the once unachievable. You reach a point where you finally have all the ingredients to make it happen.

To illustrate, Rick referred to the electronic organizer on the table:

> There were at least a dozen attempts to bring out handheld devices ahead of the PalmPilot. The most notable was Jerry Kaplan's GO Corporation. Kaplan saw the opportunity, had the right idea, and raised $50 million in funding back in the early 90s. But since the chips weren't small enough, the displays weren't big enough, and the batteries weren't powerful enough, his product looked like a brick. He spent 50 million bucks and failed, simply because his great idea was ahead of the prevailing technology.

In a similar way, the Beechcraft Corporation was ahead of its time when, in the late 1970s, it set out to develop a new class of business aircraft. The five-and-a-half-year, $300-million development program resulted in the federally certified Starship (see Exhibit 3). The futuristic craft was the world's first pressurized, all-composite business turboprop.[2] Many in the industry had high hopes that the Starship would usher in a new age of modern propeller-driven aircraft, but that was not to be.

Developed by Scaled Composites, a cutting-edge aircraft design enterprise founded by visionary Burt Rutan,[3] the Starship project brought about the development of Federal Aviation Authority (FAA) standards for the construction of composite aircraft. Unfortunately for Beechcraft, this was a very long and difficult process resulting in an aircraft that was heavier and more expensive than predicted. As a result, the Starship's performance was only marginally better than the existing fleet—and yet its price was far higher. Despite its commercial failure, this project was the first in a series of events that would begin to spark new life into the long-ailing general aviation aircraft industry in America.

Exhibit 3   **The Beechcraft Starship**

The Beechcraft Starship, a twin-turboprop pusher design, was the first all-composite pressurized airframe ever certified by the FAA. The task was larger than simply developing an all-new aircraft. Beech had to master an innovative technology, work hand-in-hand with FAA regulators, build a new manufacturing facility, and train a specialized workforce. Much of this effort was concentrated on areas the industry had not addressed before. The company built 53 Starships in all before ceasing production in the early 1990s.

A CONVERGENCE OF FACTORS

Between 1978 and 1992, the general aviation industry had suffered a 95 percent unit sales decline and the loss of over 100,000 jobs. Over that same period, general aviation (GA) manufacturers had spent as much to defend product liability suits as they had spent to develop new aircraft in the 30 years following the Second World War.

When Congress enacted the General Aviation Revitalization Act (GARA) in 1994 to protect aircraft builders from lawsuits on planes that were older than 18 years, it revitalized an industry nearly wiped out by two decades of what lawmakers were calling lawsuit abuse and trial lawyer profiteering.

The 1990s also brought about enormous advances in computing power and computer-aided design and modeling (CAD/CAM) software. Airframe geometry could now reside in the computer, with all of its internal structures defined electronically as three-dimensional models. By the end of that decade, expensive wind tunnels and physical scale models were being replaced by computational fluid dynamics software. Manufacturing and tooling capabilities had made great strides as well.

Rick said that after a couple of kit manufacturers[4] managed to achieve commercial certification for their composite designs, he figured that the time was right:

> In the early 90s, all the innovation was being done in composites and kits. Then Lancair and Cirrus announced that they were going to take what they had learned and build production airplanes. Everybody who loves flying was rooting for them, hoping they would make it, and sure enough, they both got certified.
>
> I'm watching this process and realizing that while there were quite a few single-engine, nonpressurized, fixed-gear start-ups out there, nobody had yet brought an innovative product into the middle market. It was real clear to me that pilots wanted a new twin, and once I had seen the success that the composite guys had down in single engines, I came to the conclusion it could be done in the twin-engine area.

By the latter half of the 1990s, a number of well-financed firms were competing to introduce a personal jet into this middle-market space by 2006.

Rick looked at these projects and wondered: Would it be possible to design a single airframe that could accommodate jet engines as well as twin pistons? He didn't have the answer, but he knew who would.

THE PROJECT BEGINS

Although he was still running his software venture, in 1998 Rick decided to put up a million dollars to get into the aviation business. At the same time, he brought in a talented partner: former FAA trial attorney John Knudsen, an experienced aviator with a career in the U.S. Navy as a carrier-based attack pilot. Understanding that a commercially viable new design—whether it was a jet or a twin piston—would have to blend superior performance capabilities with curb appeal, Rick said that they contacted the best in the business:

> We met with Burt Rutan and showed him some requirements, definitions, and preliminary designs for a twin piston. Since carbon fiber lends itself to much more aerodynamic shapes than you can get with aluminum construction—I told him to make it look as much like a jet as possible.
>
> As always, he had some wild stuff and he had some stuff that was more middle of the road. We narrowed four or five design concepts down to an inline, front and back engine configuration, with twin booms to get to the tail.

If this plane was going to be the step up for single-engine pilots that Rick was envisioning, they understood that ease of operation would be critical. With this in mind, they chose a centerline thrust arrangement, since, compared to twins with the power plants mounted on the wings, the push-pull design significantly reduced the difficulty of flying with one engine not functioning. Having settled on what he felt was an exciting airframe, Rick noted that they had no desire to conquer more than one frontier at a time:

> The Eclipse 500 project has raised $400 million so far in its effort to build a light business jet. They tried to develop a new airframe and a new engine at the same time. The engine didn't work, and now they are two years off schedule.
>
> I'm a raging incrementalist; the way to innovate is to take one step at a time. We chose power plants, avionics, and construction methods that had

previously been certified by the FAA for other planes; our only major innovation initially will be with the shape of the airframe. I figured that once we had that done, we could innovate on something else later on. It's just so tough to bring a certified new airplane to market; we had to be very careful to avoid adding layers of complexity—and lots of time and money.

The team at Scaled Composites began work on the conceptual designs for Adam Aircraft in May of 1999, and cut the first tool in late August.[5] When the M-309 (see Exhibit 4) lifted off on its maiden flight in March 2000, it marked the most rapid manned-aircraft development program in the company's history.

Despite the price tag, Rick understood that this "experimental" was a one-of-a-kind, hand-built model that would serve only as a research vehicle. Conventional evidence suggested that the development of

an FAA-certified version of the M-309 would take a few years, at least a couple more flying test planes, millions of engineering man-hours, and hundreds of millions of dollars. Rick was determined, however, to make sure that his aircraft company was anything but conventional.

RESEARCH AND INNOVATION

With the M-309 outfitted with an array of data collection equipment, the AAI team proceeded to log over 300 flight hours in 2000 as they scrutinized the full range of the craft's aerodynamic characteristics and performance capabilities. Rick explained that with regard to understanding the commercial viability of

Exhibit 4   **The M-309**

Named for Burt Rutan's 309th completed design, the Model 309 was built with the aim of delivering a very safe twin-engine aircraft that would give good performance and benign single engine handling qualities. The pressurized cabin was designed to carry a pilot and five passengers.

The central goal of this program was to develop an aerodynamically refined aircraft. However, there were several features that were more representative of a full-production airplane. For example, there were several major structural components that had been produced as single-cure parts. The outboard wings, horizontal tail, elevator, rudders, and flaperons had no secondary bonds in their primary structure. This allowed for a lighter, stronger, and safer structure due to the significant elimination of fasteners and secondary bonds.

Source: www.scaled.com.

the plane, their destinations were often just as important as their in-flight calculations:

> We collected aerodynamic data as we flew the M-309 to air shows around the country, and that gave us the opportunity to survey the market and listen to what potential customers had to say. We completely reengineered the original design. For example, we increased the size of the empennage,[6] and also moved the door for easier access to the cabin. By the fall of 2000, I had come to the conclusion that there was a significant market for this kind of aircraft.

Rick, who was self-funding most of the start-up costs, had been busy recruiting a top-tier management group. Nearly everyone on his 10-member executive staff was an accomplished pilot, and collectively they had many years of experience from all corners of the aviation industry, including Boeing, Beechcraft, Martin Marietta, Cirrus, Lancair, Scaled Composites, Eclipse, the U.S. military, and the FAA.

In December, Adam Aircraft established its home base at Centennial Field, just south of Denver. As they got down to the business of fitting the factory in advance of tooling design for the first production model, now called the Adam A500, Rick said that because of the direct relationship between time to market and project cost, they had no choice but to innovate:

> I had recently heard from an industry expert that the standard budget for a new airplane project is about $250 million. Since there has been so little success in this industry to date, it would be nearly impossible to raise that kind of money for a start-up airplane company like ours. That's a long way from $250 million, but still, we knew that the only way we could make financing achievable was by cutting development costs by at least 75 percent.

He added that to accomplish such a feat would require not only brilliant engineering but also the development of a culture unheard of in aviation manufacturing:

> Being a lifetime computer guy, speed and innovation seem very natural to me. We knew right off that time was not our friend; either we get this plane up and certified quickly, or we'd attract competitors and run out of money. One of the first things we did was to institute the kind of 24-hour scheduling that we had used to run our data centers and networks.
>
> Our people now work 12-hour, overlapping shifts; three-day weeks, with voluntary overtime on Sundays. So while our competitors are putting in five

shifts in a calendar week, we are getting up to 21—in addition to high morale and very low attrition.

Over the past few decades, powerful aircraft builders like McDonnell Douglas, Lockheed, and Boeing had developed highly sophisticated modeling design tools that were powered by multimillion-dollar mainframe computers. The PC age had put those capabilities into the hands of small shops like Adam Aircraft. For an off-the-shelf cost of about $3,000 per system, the company was able to set up a 40-station CAD/CAM engineering center with all the capabilities of the big guys. Rick said that by tying this powerful design architecture into the tooling mill downstairs (see Exhibit 5), the company was able to add efficiencies by keeping the entire design process in-house:

> With aluminum technology, you design the part, and then you bid it out for tooling. You award the tooling—which typically costs over a million dollars—and

Exhibit 5   **Five Axis Tooling Mill**

Fabricating the Air-Stair door tool out of dense foam material

six to nine months later, the tool comes back. If it's wrong or you want to make a design change, you have to start all over, Because we have our own tooling mill, we can do it fast the first time, and more importantly, continue to modify the tool quickly until we get it right.

The management team understood that merely coupling rapid application development with a 24/7 working environment would not provide enough of an edge to develop the full line of airplanes they were envisioning. Rick explained that for that to happen, they would need to adopt a computer industry concept that, if successful, would change the face of general aviation manufacturing forever:

> PCs are developed around a common set of rules as to how the parts interact with each other. That way, you can change the keyboard, the disc drive, the screen, whatever you want, and it won't tear up your memory or your software; that's called modular architecture.
>
> There has been little progress in modular architecture in airplanes—until now. We are building enormous modularity into our design so we can do things like move the wing location, modify the cabin size, change the power plants; all kinds of things. What that means is that we will bring this first plane to certification status for about 50 million bucks. For another 10 million, we'll adjust the modules slightly and get a jet. For another 5 million, we'll get a turboprop.[7]

Detractors felt that this was wishful thinking, and pointed out that the modular architecture approach could potentially compromise performance. Some noted that since each power plant system would have different weight and structural characteristics, installing all three on essentially the same airframe could cause center-of-gravity problems. In addition, critics felt that using a single-wing and empennage design would mean that two of the planes, or maybe even the whole line of products, would fly at less than optimum performance.

The AAI team felt that they were on top of those challenges with innovations like their "smart tunnel," a device that enabled engineers to shift the wing location on the fuselage in order to control the range of the aircraft's center of gravity. The team felt that this technology and other specialized systems they were devising would give AAI engineers the means to modify the underlying airframe to accommodate a wide range of engine choices and configurations.

In addition, they felt that this engineering strategy would enable them to leverage their research and development spending over at least three commercially viable aircraft designs. Time would tell.

WORKING WITH THE FAA

Throughout 2001, all manner of government and industry groups had visited the plant to witness the A500 project as it came together very nearly on schedule, and on budget. Predictably, the one group that would not be offering praise or extra points for speed of design and assembly was the Federal Aviation Authority (FAA).

The task of the FAA was to see to it that the Type Certification (TC) approval process (see Exhibit 6) proceeded in a careful and thorough manner. The complex system of inspections and testing was similar to what health care companies faced with the Federal Drug Administration (FDA). Like the FDA, the FAA required exhaustive proof that products were safe before they could be marketed to consumers. In the aviation industry, that regulatory oversight translated into lots of time and money. While it was true that successful new entrants like Lancair and Cirrus had helped pave the way for subsequent efforts, Rick said that getting through the regulatory process would still be one of AAI's greatest challenges:

> Although the FAA is constantly working to improve the aircraft certification process, for good reason it is designed to be extremely arduous. Nevertheless, we do have a number of advantages over our predecessors. For example, as opposed to submitting aircraft designs on paper, we can now send designs to the FAA electronically. By doing this, we save a ton of time and, most importantly, are assured of the highest degree of accuracy in our documentation process.

By the time the A500 had been cleared for its inaugural flight in July of 2002, a second test aircraft was already under construction (see Exhibit 7), and fabrication of parts for a third had begun as well. Comprising the entire testing fleet, these three aircraft would each undergo a series of exhaustive flight and static tests—many requiring the construction of customized systems and fixtures (see Exhibit 8). If all proceeded as planned, AAI expected to achieve certification for the A500 by the first half of 2004.

THE CUSTOMERS

When AAI flew its A500 to the Experimental Aircraft Association's (EAA) AirVenture Convention in Oshkosh, Wisconsin, that summer, the company brought along a full-size mockup of the plane's cockpit and fully appointed interior. Vice President of Marketing John Hamilton noted that Oshkosh was an excellent show since it attracted buyers from all the major markets for its $895,000 twin piston:

There are two basic markets for aircraft like the A500; owner-flown, and professionally flown. The owner-flown market is just that. The owner of the aircraft is also the pilot in command. In the professionally flown market, non-owners fly the aircraft. It sounds like a silly distinction but it makes a difference in how you market the aircraft.

I would say between 70 and 80 percent of our A500 customers will be owner-operators. These folks are evaluating our aircraft from the pilot's seat. They will be very tuned in to things like the performance of the aircraft, its handling characteristics, and the

Exhibit 6   **FAA Type Certification Process**

Familiarization Meeting

Meeting to establish a partnership with the applicant. It is an opportunity to develop mutual understanding of the type certification process as it applies to the applicant's design. It's highly recommended as a beginning point in the process.

Formal Application

Applicant's formal application for a Type Certification (TC) includes a cover letter, Form 8110-2, and a three-view drawing.

Preliminary Type Certification Board

At this initial formal meeting, the project team collects data about the technical aspects of the project and the applicant's proposed certification basis and identifies other information needed to start developing the Certification Program Plan. Special-attention items are also identified at this time.

Certification Program Plan (CPP)

A key document, the Certification Plan addresses:

- The proposed FAA certification basis.
- Noise and emission requirements.
- Issue papers.
- Special conditions, exemptions, and equivalent level of safety findings.
- Means of compliance.
- Compliance checklists and schedules.
- Use of delegations/designees.

Technical Meetings

Held throughout the project, technical meetings (e.g., specialist and interim TC meetings) cover a variety of subjects. Team members may:

- Approve test plans and reports.
- Review engineering compliance findings.
- Close out issue papers.
- Review conformity inspections.
- Review minutes of board meetings.
- Revise the Certification Program Plan.
- Issue new FAA policy guidance.
- Review airworthiness limitations.
- Review instructions for continued airworthiness.

(Continued)

Exhibit 6   **Continued**

Preflight Type Certification Board

Discussions at the preflight TC board center on the applicant's flight test program, including conformity inspections and engineering compliance determinations.

Type Inspection Authorization (TIA)

Prepared on FAA Form 8110-1, the TIA authorizes conformity and airworthiness inspections and flight tests to meet certification requirements. The TIA is issued when examination of technical data required to TC is completed or has reached a point where it appears that the product will meet pertinent regulations.

Conformity Inspections and Certification Flight Tests

Conformity inspections ensure that the product conforms with the design proposed for type certification. Flight tests are conducted in accordance with the requirements of the TIA.

Aircraft Evaluation Group (AEG) Determinations

The AEG works with certification engineers and FAA flight test pilots to evaluate the operational and maintenance aspects of certified products through such activities as:

Flight Standardization Board (FSB)
- Pilot type rating.
- Pilot training checking, currency requirements.
- Operational acceptability.

Flight Operations Evaluation Board (FOEB)
- Master minimum equipment list (MMEL).

Maintenance Review Board (MRB)
- Maintenance instructions for continued airworthiness.

Final Type Certification Board

When the applicant has met all certification requirements, the ACO schedules the final formal TC board. The board wraps up any outstanding items and decides on the issuance of the TC.

Type Certificate

The certifying ACO issues the TC when the applicant completes demonstration of compliance with the certification basis. The TC data sheet is part of the TC and documents conditions and limitations to meet FAR requirements.

Postcertification Activities

This includes the Type Inspection Report (TIR)—to be completed within 90 days of issuance of the unique technical requirements and lessons learned—the Certification Summary Report (CSR), and the Postcertification Evaluation, which closes out the TC project and provides the foundation for continued FAA airworthiness monitoring activities such as service bulletins, revisions to type design, malfunction/defect reports, and Certificate Management for the remainder of the aircraft's life cycle.

electronic systems in the instrument panel. In addition, because they also manage the scheduled maintenance requirements, they will be very sensitive to serviceability.

Marketing to the professionally flown segment is a bit different since they are more focused on the needs of their client-passengers. They'll be interested in things like how comfortable the seating is, how much baggage area is available, whether the plane has a toilet or an entertainment system. They'll also want a pressurized cabin so they can fly over weather, a plane that looks and feels safe and substantial—and a plane that is appealing to the eye.

In addition, John emphasized that aviation consumers of all types demanded top service and easily maintainable aircraft:

You've got to have absolute first-rate service. Customers can't have difficulty getting parts or finding somebody to work on their airplane.

Pilots are also hesitant to adopt something that is new. We're not Cessna, we're not Beechcraft, and we're not Piper. Those guys have been around forever, and they've built a ton of airplanes.

That's why with everything we do—from delivery, to flight training, to service and parts—we

Exhibit 7   **Fuselage Construction of the A-500 SN002**

Vacuum bag on fuselage tool

Laying up the carbon material into the tail boom tool

Exhibit 8   **Custom-Built Static Test Rig**

have to prove to our customers that there is a very compelling reason why they should adopt this new aircraft.

John added that the company's unique design modularity would play an important role in serviceability:

One feature of the A500 that customers will love is how easy it is to access the systems on the aircraft that need to be inspected and/or replaced. A great deal of engineering work has been performed to dramatically reduce the amount of time it takes maintenance personnel to complete the necessary service tasks. This will result in reduced downtime and lower costs of operation. Going the extra mile for owners in this area will pay substantial dividends in customer satisfaction.

EYEING THE FUTURE

In October 2002, the company announced its plan to introduce the next aircraft. The company also indicated that due to the modular systems, the A700, a six- to eight-seat stretched-fuselage twin-jet, would share 80 percent part commonality with the A500. Some critics doubted Rick's assertion that since the A700 would present only an incremental development challenge for his talented engineers, AAI would be able to build a flying model within a year.

Ten months after completing preliminary design work, the A700 jet shocked and amazed the general aviation world by making a surprise appearance at the 2003 EAA AirVenture event. Industry dignitaries such as Secretary of Transportation Norman Minetta and FAA administrator Marion Blakey welcomed the aircraft with words of support and congratulations. The aviation press was buzzing; if the company was able to hold to its schedule and achieve FAA certification for the A700 in the fourth quarter of 2004, the $1.995 million craft would be the first to market in this emerging, closely watched segment (see Exhibit 9).

John explained that this keen interest in light jets was directly related to the need for more efficient transportation solutions:

> The average mission is less than a two-hour flight, with three and a half people on board—meaning nearly every business jet in America is oversized for what it does.
>
> This emerging personal jet segment is based on the same concept that Japanese automakers used to take on Detroit 30 years ago. With gas prices going up, why not build a car which was more suitably sized to the average driver's need? Reducing the size and weight of the machine dramatically improved its operating efficiency. We're building a smaller and lighter aircraft designed for the most common trip length and passenger load to deliver optimal efficiency in the twin-jet category.

In addition to the benefits of an incremental improvement in the efficiency of twin-engine jets, personal jet aircraft were being viewed by some as the solution to the gridlock in the hub-and-spoke airline system. Rick Adam described one official's views on the subject:

> Dr. Bruce Holmes at NASA[8] has performed extensive studies of the transportation system and has concluded that the best way to increase capacity in the air is by directing more traffic to the 5,000 underutilized regional airports in this country. Regional travelers would fly point-to-point out of small airports and never enter the hub and spoke system unless they plan to fly across the country or abroad.
>
> Because this air taxi system would require a massive fleet of aircraft to achieve network coverage, the price of the aircraft and its operating cost are critical components to the success of the system. Aircraft like the A700 could get the cost per seat mile down to a level where the average business traveler could afford the service.
>
> We don't need the air taxi model to take off for the A700 to be a successful project, but it would certainly provide a fantastic upside to our company.

With two distinct models flying, Rick and his company now had a real story to tell. CFO Mike Smith observed that for outside investors and municipal development groups, one of the most attractive aspects of the AAI plan was that the economics seemed entirely within the range of possibility:

> We could break even right out of this facility [at Centennial Field] by adding roughly 100 production people to our current staff of 150. With the A500, the current overhead breaks even at somewhere between 35 and 40 planes a year, and the jet would be roughly a third of that. We have a component capacity for about 100 planes a year, and an assembly capacity for about 40 or 50. The great thing about this company is at just 50 airplanes a year, we're making money. So far we have taken deposits for over 50 twin pistons.[9] Once we are certified, we anticipate a surge in orders.

By late 2003 the planes had appeared on a host of aviation magazine covers (see Exhibit 10) and in a wide range of business publications including the *New York Times, The Wall Street Journal,* and *Forbes* magazine. Nearly all seemed to be anticipating a significant American success story.

THE CRITICAL JUNCTURE

Heading out for a meeting over in Boulder, John fired up his twin-engine Beechcraft as the A500 crossed his path on its way back to the hanger for further testing. As he taxied out in preparation for take-off, John recalled an earlier meeting with a reporter from an aviation magazine. When she had asked him whether he thought much about the possibility of failure, he prefaced his response with a story:

> You know, we were speaking with some guys in the airborne fire-fighting business. They currently use airplanes that are roughly in the A500 class to fly lead-in for fire-fighting tankers. These spotter planes fly low and left of the tankers, and tell those pilots where to make the drop.
>
> They asked if we could put a window overhead on the A500 so their lead pilots could have good visibility of the tanker high and right. They told us that none of the established competitors they had spoken with would even consider that kind of modification. Our engineers told him that it would take us about a week to figure that out.
>
> The point is, that's why I don't spend much time thinking about the business risk of this venture. Adam Aircraft has been surprising the experts and our potential customers from the very beginning; there is no reason to assume we won't continue to do so.

Exhibit 9 **Very Light Jet Segment: Competitor Profiles**

Manufacturer	Product	List Price ($000)	Seats	Cruise Speed	First Delivery	Orders to Date (11/03)	Home Base
Avocet	Pro-Jet	$2,000	6–8	420	Late 2006	200	Westport, Connecticut
Cessna	Citation Mustang	$2,295	6	391	Late 2006	300+	Wichita, Kansas
Safire	Safire Jet	$1,395	6	437	2006	300+	Miami, Florida
Eclipse	Eclipse 500	$ 950	3–6	432	2006	2,060	Albuquerque, New Mexico

Exhibit 10 **Magazine Cover: AAI's A700 and A500**

As John lifted off and banked north toward Boulder, he realized that his thrill of flying had never waned since he was a kid. Although he loved his 30-year-old Beech, he knew it wouldn't last forever—and there were a bunch of pilots just like him out there waiting for something new. He felt certain that Adam Aircraft would be the one to answer that call.

Endnotes

[1]General aviation (GA) is a term comprising all of aviation other than government and scheduled air transport (commercial airlines), and includes privately owned aircraft, charter services, business-owned aircraft, and many more types of working aircraft that are not, strictly speaking, for transportation. Although a large part of GA consists of recreational flying, an equally large part involves important commercial activities such as flight training, shipping, surveying, agricultural application, air taxi, charter passenger service, corporate flying, emergency transport, and firefighting.

[2]An easy-to-understand composite material would be an adobe brick; wet mud and straw—mixed together and dried. The result is a material stronger than either mud or straw. Composite airframes typically consisted of a carbon, graphite, or glass fiber reinforcing material, and an epoxy resin binder. Alone, these substances had very little strength, but when combined and properly cured, they became a composite structure that was very strong. Since this construction process lent itself to fluid design, composite airframes were often sleeker and more pleasing to the eye than their aluminum counterparts.

[3]As a schoolboy, Burt Rutan had designed award-winning model aircraft, and by age 16 had learned to fly. After receiving a bachelor's degree in aeronautical engineering from Cal Poly, he worked for the U.S. Air Force as a Flight Test Project Engineer at Edwards Air Force Base in California. In 1972, at age 29, he founded Rutan Aircraft Factory, which sold plans and kits for Rutan-designed aircraft. His science-fiction-like aircraft designs were considered risky by established aircraft manufacturers, who made sure that the regulators of the Federal Aviation Administration were aware of their concerns. While he successfully sold a number of different unique designs, he became frustrated by the litigious regulatory environment and substantial liability claims that had put many private aircraft manufacturers out of business. In 1982, Rutan chose to leave the homebuilt industry in favor of larger-scale designs for companies. His new firm was Scaled Composites.

[4]Kit planes were considered experimental by the Federal Aviation Administration. This designation was originally intended for aircraft designers who wanted to do research, or for amateur pilots who wanted to learn about aerodynamics as they built their own planes. Because these aircraft were barred from commercial use, the FAA felt that there was no need to impose its exhaustive and very expensive certification process on this class of aircraft.

[5]In composite engineering, a tool was the master mold that the composite material was layered into before being vacuum-compressed, and then oven-cured—a process known as thermosetting—at 240 degrees.

[6]The empennage, commonly called the tail assembly, was the rear section of the body of the airplane. Its main purpose was to provide stability to the aircraft.

[7]Turboprops were designed to carry high passenger (or cargo) loads over relatively short distances (under 300 miles or so). Short-field take-off and landing capabilities, and the ability to use kerosene instead of aviation fuel, had contributed to the popularity of turboprops, particularly in developing countries.

[8]Dr. Bruce Holmes led the Small Aircraft Transportation System Program (SATS) unit at NASA. SATS was a driving force in the incubation of innovative technologies necessary to bring affordable, on-demand flight service by small aircraft in near-all-weather conditions to small community airports.

[9]Initial deposits to secure a delivery position for an A-500 were between $50,000 (non-escrowed) and $100,000 (escrowed). An additional $50,000 progress payment would be due at aircraft type certification, with an additional $100,000 progress payment due six months prior to the scheduled delivery date of the aircraft. The balance would be due upon delivery.

KRCB Television and Radio: The Canary in the Coal Mine?

Armand Gilinsky Jr.
Sonoma State University

Robert H. Girling
Sonoma State University

Teresa M. Shern
Sonoma State University

The October 2003 board meeting had been difficult for Nancy Dobbs, president and CEO of KRCB Television and Radio in California's Sonoma County, and for her board of directors. KRCB had always run on an extremely thin financial margin, and things were not improving. The national Public Broadcasting System (PBS) funding model, based on pledge drives, appeared to be floundering at stations across the country. PBS and the Corporation for Public Broadcasting (CPB) were working against the clock to make necessary, and as yet unknown, course corrections. All PBS stations, particularly those small stations competing with larger public broadcast stations in major markets, were scrambling to find answers. The KRCB-FM pledge drive had significantly missed its goal, as had pledge drives at other National Public Radio (NPR) stations across the San Francisco Bay Area. On the television side, KRCB faced increased fixed operating costs to support its new digital transmitter. Meanwhile, noncommercial and commercial television stations alike were in danger of losing their audiences because the fundamental television broadcast model of distribution was changing. TiVo and other devices with the ability to cut out commercials and pledge drives had already come into widespread use.

This case was presented at the annual meeting of the North American Case Research Association, October 7–9, 2004, Sedona, Arizona, and also was published in the Winter 2005 issue of the *Case Research Journal*. Copyright © 2005 by the case authors. All rights reserved by the case authors and NACRA.

Walking from the portable building that housed the station to her car, Dobbs turned to her business manager, Jane Kirchman, and said:

> KRCB is my "second family," but how long can we continue to stay together? Support from the business community, especially in the form of program underwriting by local businesses, has taken a serious hit across the system in the past year. TiVo is a major threat to our fund-raising model. And now we are facing competition from other Bay Area public broadcasters who really should be working together with us, instead of vying for our members and underwriting support. It's becoming increasingly likely that our station will need to undertake an expensive purchase of our leased land or move the broadcasting studios and offices within the next three to four years. We are like the canary in the coal mine. If smaller stations like ours cannot survive, then what will happen to the entire public broadcasting system?

Contributing to Dobbs's stress at the board meeting had been the irrefutable fact that the operating budget was precariously lean. The station did not have any cash reserves; it was operating hand to mouth, according to the preliminary year-end financial reports that Kirchman had prepared. Dobbs felt strongly that these budget weaknesses needed to be addressed and reconciled if the station was to survive. The precarious financial situation, in particular with respect to support for the radio station, also prompted Dobbs to reassess KRCB's current strategy. As Dobbs opened the door of her 1987 Volvo and wearily sank into the driver's seat, she wondered which challenge she needed to tackle first.

PUBLIC BROADCASTING: MARKETS AND COMPETITION

KRCB was an affiliate of PBS, which consisted of 170 noncommercial television stations in the United States, and NPR, which comprised 730 noncommercial radio stations nationwide. The station transmitted both television and FM radio programming. Its television signal was available to cable and satellite TV subscribers throughout the North Bay and the greater San Francisco Bay Area. Due to "must-carry" laws that required KRCB-TV to be carried over cable, EchoStar's Dish Network, and DIRECTV, station management believed it had an opportunity to widen both its audience and its potential membership and underwriting base. On June 1, 2003, Comcast, the local cable provider, began carrying KRCB-TV in San Francisco; as a result, KRCB did indeed witness an increase in its membership base.

The station competed directly with four educational TV broadcast stations and 15 public radio stations. Indirect competitors in the Bay Area, the nation's fifth-largest commercial media market, consisted of 15 commercial television stations and 21 commercial radio stations, according to Nielsen Media Research. KRCB-TV (cable, satellite, and broadcast Channel 22) aired a mix of local programs and those produced by other public and international television stations (see www.krcb.org/television/index.html for TV programming information). Prominent local public television competitors included KCSM-TV in San Mateo, KTEH-TV in San Jose, and KQED-TV in San Francisco (see Exhibit 1). Although each public television station felt it had a distinct programming niche, all were affiliated with PBS, airing at least the "marquee" PBS-produced programs, such as *Sesame Street* and *The NewsHour with Jim Lehrer,* as well as independently made programs. These stations competed for similar viewing audiences, and an increasing portion of their viewing audience markets overlapped.

On the radio side, KRCB-FM broadcast on 91.1 and 90.9. Its blend of locally produced and national programming reflected an eclectic format, ranging from news to classical to jazz to bluegrass to rock

music (see www.krcb.org/radio/index.htm for radio programming information). The station competed for listeners and members with KCSM-FM (91.1, primarily jazz); KQED-FM (88.5 and 88.3, exclusively news and talk); and nonprofit Pacifica Radio's Berkeley station, KPFA-FM (94.1, wide range of music and news). The latter two stations had broadcast signals strong enough to reach most of Northern California. KRCB's radio station also competed with 16 other local FM radio stations in Sonoma County, five of which were locally owned and one of which was a college station.

KRCB-FM had filed applications with the Federal Communications Commission (FCC) in 1997 and 1998 for a new broadcast license that would enable it to transmit at a higher level of power. The intent was to move broadcasts from 91.1 to 88.3 FM, the latter a "clear" frequency in Santa Rosa, the largest city in Sonoma County. Stockton Christian College won the license and then sold it in 2001 to KQED-FM, which received permission from the FCC to erect a new transmitter in Santa Rosa, thus enabling its San Francisco–based broadcasts to reach the entire North Bay.

In February 2003, KQED-FM announced that it had acquired a Sacramento public FM station, KQEI (89.3), for $3 million, boosting its coverage area to the rapidly growing counties in California's Central Valley (see Exhibit 2).[1] Subsequently, in July 2003, KQED announced a budget reduction of $4 million, layoffs of 10 percent of its staff, and a reduction of workweeks from 40 to 36 hours for its remaining 234 employees. According to a report in the *San Francisco Chronicle,* these layoffs, hour reductions, and other changes were expected to trim KQED's operating budget from $44.7 million in 2002 to $40.5 million in 2003.

KRCB-FM's radio broadcast signal did not reach beyond Sonoma and Marin counties (the latter via cable). Dobbs still hoped to boost the signal via a translator on Sonoma Mountain, the highest peak in Sonoma County. "Our application to the FCC for the translator has been pending for a number of years, but the slowness with which the FCC moves has been a big roadblock to improving our signal." Meanwhile, plans were under way to begin offering radio broadcasts to a potentially vast audience via streaming audio online in November 2003. On the air, however, the station's broadcasts often overlapped with those of San Mateo Community College's radio station, KCSM-FM. Both radio stations broadcast on 91.1 FM.

As a stopgap, KRCB-FM tried to improve its signal to reach a greater number of Sonoma County

Exhibit 1   **Profiles of Public TV and Radio Broadcasters in the San Francisco Bay Area**

	KRCB	KCSM	KTEH	KQED
Nonprofit organization	Yes	Yes	Yes	Yes
TV station	Yes	Yes	Yes	Yes
Broadcasting debut	1984	1964	n/a	1954
Areas served (counties)	• Alameda • Contra Costa • Marin • Mendocino • Napa • San Francisco • San Mateo • Solano • Sonoma	• Alameda • Contra Costa • Marin • Napa • San Francisco • San Mateo • Santa Clara • Santa Cruz • Solano • Sonoma	• San Francisco • San Jose	• North to Mendocino • South to Monterey • East to Lake Tahoe • Portions of Nevada
PBS programming	Yes	Yes	Yes	Yes
Programming focus	• Child and adult viewers • GED courses • PBS, BBC, APT programs • Local programs	• Adult viewers • College-level telecourses • PBS programs • Local programs	• Child and adult viewers • Community outreach • PBS, nationwide distributors • Local programs	• Child and adult viewers • PBS, nationwide distributors • Local programs
Number of viewers	n/a	500,000	n/a	5,000,000
Digital broadcasting?	November 2003	November 2003	November 2003	May 2000
Radio station	Yes	Yes	No	Yes
Broadcasting debut	1990	1964		1969
Areas served (counties)	• Sonoma • Marin	• San Francisco • Peninsula • South Bay Area		• North coast of CA • South to Monterey • East to the Sierra Nevada mountains
NPR programming	Yes	Yes		Yes
Programming focus	• Classical music • NPR news • Local music • Local information shows	• Jazz music • Jazz education • NPR news		• News and information • NPR, PRI, BBC
Number of listeners	n/a	200,000		745,000
Web streaming	November 2003	Yes (1999)		Yes (2000)
Operations				
Headquarters	Rohnert Park	San Mateo	San Jose	San Francisco
Web site	www.krcb.org	www.kcsm.org	www.kteh.org	www.kqed.org
Membership program	Yes	Yes	Yes	Yes
Volunteer program	Yes	Yes	Yes	Yes
For-profit ventures	No	n/a	Yes (partnership with barnesandnoble.com)	n/a

n/a = Not available or not applicable.

Sources: Information posted at www.krcb.org, www.kcsm.org, www.kteh.org, and www.kqed.org.

Exhibit 2   **Forecast Population Growth in Northern California, 2000–2040**

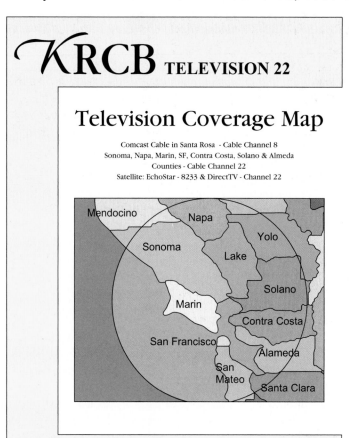

County	Forecast Population Change 2000–2040	County	Forecast Population Change 2000–2040
Alameda	41%	San Francisco	(−14)%
Contra Costa	36	San Joaquin	116
Lake	113	San Mateo	26
Marin	20	Santa Clara	47
Mendocino	66	Santa Cruz	91
Merced	114	Solano	75
Monterey	113	Sonoma	64
Napa	51	Stanislaus	118
Sacramento	75	Yolo	82
San Benito	122		

Source: Association of Bay Area Governments, www.abag.ca.gov/abag/overview/pub/p2000/intro.html.

listeners by installing a second signal (with its own transmitting antenna) on 90.9 FM. Even then, the radio station was only licensed to broadcast at 125 watts (effective radiated power) on either 90.9 or 91.1. At 125 watts, KRCB's signal was roughly the amount of power one might get from a common lightbulb. The station's low power had been mandated by the FCC's licensing rules and regulations, which remained in place to protect KCSM-FM's much stronger signal. Other regional, low-power noncommercial FM radio stations included KWMR, broadcasting from Point Reyes Station and Bolinas (Marin County); KMUD (broadcasting in Humboldt, Northern Mendocino, and Western Trinity counties); and KZYX (serving Mendocino County and beyond).

Emerging Technologies

In addition to rival broadcasters, print media, and other formats for news, education, arts, and culture, KRCB faced competition from the Internet and digital transmission via satellite. By July 2003, 80 percent of Americans had access to the Internet from at least one location. Edison Media Research estimated that the weekly Internet broadcast TV and radio audience had reached 30 million, or 30 percent of all Americans.[2] According to Edison Media Research, approximately 50 million Americans, or 21 percent of the adult population, watched video online or listened to audio online in 2003. Listeners tuned in most frequently to the Internet to hear radio formats such as alternative rock, urban, contemporary hit radio, and public radio (see Exhibit 3).

On the television side, the Internet video audience experienced significant gains in 2003, growing to 12 percent of the total video audience, according to the Nielsen Television Index (NTI). Movie trailers and music videos were the most-watched online video programming in 2003. In addition to Internet video, the penetration of subscriber satellite television had grown steadily from 18 percent in July 2001 to 22 percent in July 2003.[3]

Satellite radio represented a more distant threat to traditional "terrestrial" radio broadcasters.[4] The two leading satellite radio companies were XM Satellite Radio Holdings Inc. (partly owned by General Motors and Honda Motor) and Sirius Satellite Radio Inc. Each satellite station provided about 100 channels of music and other uninterrupted, static-free programming with limited commercials. Unlike terrestrial radio, however, satellite radio services depended on a subscription model. As of June 2003, XM (70 music channels) and Sirius (61 music channels) had approximately 692,000 and 105,000 subscribers, respectively, charging monthly rates of $9.99 and $12.95. Both companies believed that building strong ties with automobile manufacturers would be critical to establishing satellite radio as a potential alternative to terrestrial broadcasting. Both GM and Honda had plans to add factory-installed XM satellite radios in select 2003–2004 models; Sirius already had deals with DaimlerChrysler, Ford, and BMW.

Government Regulation and Digital Conversion

Upon congressional passage of the Telecommunications Act of 1996, the FCC required all commercial broadcasters to convert from "legacy" analog systems to all-digital programming known as high-definition television (HDTV). Digitalization enabled the transmission of either HDTV signals or multiple program streams. With up to 10 times the resolution of standard analog television signals, digital formats generated much sharper picture quality. However, optimal HDTV picture clarity required that digitalization be used throughout the system. HDTV also required using the entire digital broadcast bandwidth as a single program stream, which precluded broadcasters from transmitting multiple digital program streams. TV stations must broadcast in digital format, programs must be transmitted digitally via cable or satellite, and reception must be digital (see Exhibit 4 for a schematic diagram).

The deadline for commercial broadcasters to convert to HDTV was May 2002, and for noncommercial broadcasters, May 2003. Since not all of the estimated 1,300 commercial TV stations could meet the original deadline set by the FCC, the build-out deadline was extended to May 1, 2003. Of the estimated 900 noncommercial stations, 215 applied for extensions to convert from analog to digital beyond the May 1, 2003, deadline; 212 extensions were granted, and KRCB-TV's was among them. A new deadline for noncommercial stations was set

Exhibit 3   **Media Usage by U.S. Internet Users, July 2000–July 2003**

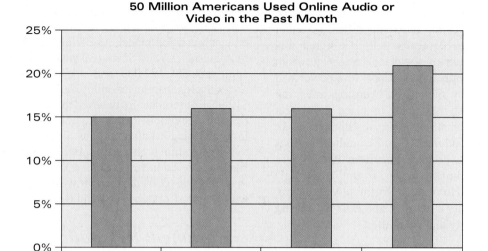

...and they listened to:		...and they listened to:	
Contemporary hit radio	26%	Other	13%
Public radio	22	Country	13
Alternative rock	20	Oldies	11
Urban	18	Big band	8
Religious	18	Jazz	7
News/talk	18	Classical	7
AOR	17	Spanish programming	6
AC	15		

Source: Internet and Multimedia II: New Media Enters the Mainstream (Arbitron/Edison Media Research).

for November 7, 2003. After that date, noncompliant stations faced fines or revocation of licenses.

Aside from picture quality, one of the most important benefits of HDTV was that it freed up parts of the broadcast spectrum and allowed its return to the government for other important uses such as public safety, police, and fire. Congress hoped to auction off the returned analog channels to help balance the federal budget, and subsequently introduced legislation to force a return of the analog spectrum to the government by December 31, 2006. However, to get the full benefits of HDTV after 2006, consumers would have to buy HDTV-ready receivers and monitors. Retail prices in 2003 for HDTV-ready receiving equipment ranged from $1,500 to $2,000. As a consequence,

penetration of this technology was projected to reach about 5 million HDTV units, or only 5 percent of all U.S. TV households in that year, according to data reported by Standard & Poor's in November 2003.

Radio was also going digital. In October 2002, the FCC endorsed a technology for radio stations to begin the conversion from analog to digital broadcasting. The commission's decision opened a transition path for public radio stations to expand and enhance their service to listeners, using digital broadcast technology to carry two or more streams of programming on the same channel, or frequency. Dobbs commented, "One of the promises of digital conversion [in radio] is that you can broadcast several streams, that is, separate channels. KCSM-FM has

Exhibit 4   **Schematic of Sample HDTV Receiving Apparatus**

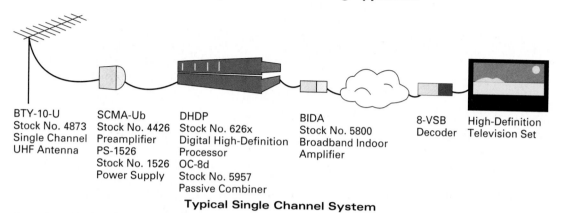

BTY-10-U
Stock No. 4873
Single Channel
UHF Antenna

SCMA-Ub
Stock No. 4426
Preamplifier
PS-1526
Stock No. 1526
Power Supply

DHDP
Stock No. 626x
Digital High-Definition
Processor
OC-8d
Stock No. 5957
Passive Combiner

BIDA
Stock No. 5800
Broadband Indoor
Amplifier

8-VSB
Decoder

High-Definition
Television Set

Typical Single Channel System

Source: www.blondertongue.com/pages/products/HDTV-processor_DHDP.php.php.

called us to ask if we want them to carry our signal on their second channel but the problem is that no one has digital radios, yet."

Kevin Klose, president and CEO of National Public Radio, estimated that the average cost of converting public radio stations to digital programming would be about $150,000. By comparison, the cost of providing the 90 public radio FM stations serving 25 top U.S. markets with another signal in the traditional but more burdensome fashion of acquiring a new channel was estimated by Klose to be between $250 and $300 million. The high cost of new station purchases enhanced the appeal of digital radio to public radio broadcasters, as that technology promised to be more affordable and cost-efficient.[5]

Viewer and Listener Demographics

Reliable and current demographic data regarding KRCB's members and audiences were not available to KRCB's management team. The station could not afford to buy ratings reports—at a cost of approximately $45,000 per year—from either of the two major media ratings services, Nielsen (a New York–based television ratings service) or Arbitron/Scarborough Research (a New York–based radio tracking and market data service). On an interim basis, KRCB hired a local survey research firm to gather data on demographics and viewing habits. The results

of this survey indicated that KRCB's audience tended to closely mirror the audiences of PBS and NPR, which reflected the social and economic makeup of the nation.

Exhibit 5 provides a breakdown of the full-day public TV audience for an average week from October to December 2002.[6] On the radio side, National Public Radio (NPR) attracted an audience that it perceived as thoughtful and discerning consumers, savvy business leaders, and influential and active community members.[7] The most recent national NPR audience profile is shown in Exhibit 6.

To reach and serve an estimated 250,000 people in the community who could not receive PBS programs from other stations, KRCB staff and volunteers worked hard to dispel the notion that the station targeted only the elite and highly educated segments of the population. KRCB sought to make culture and education more accessible to everyone in its signal range, and to broadcast local programs that met the unique needs of its North Bay community, including Spanish-language programming, quality children's programming, college courses, and adult literacy programming.[8]

KRCB'S HISTORY

Early in 1981, the North Bay counties of Sonoma, Marin, and Napa enjoyed the largest population growth spurt in their collective histories. At that time, a small group of citizens banded together to create a

Exhibit 5 **The Public Television Audience in the United States (average week, October–December 2002)**

Characteristic	Percentage of U.S. TV Households Watching Public TV	Percentage of Total TV Audience Watching Public TV
Race*		
Black	12.0%	10.7%
Spanish origin	9.1	8.5
Education*		
Less than 4 years of high school	14.9%	14.6%
4 years of high school	30.5	29.1
1–3 years of college	27.6	27.4
4+ years of college	27.0	28.9
Occupation*		
Professional/owner/manager	25.8%	25.1%
Clerical and sales	16.3	15.9
Skilled and semiskilled	26.7	23.9
Not in labor force	31.2	35.2
Household Income*		
Less than $20,000	20.0%	19.7%
$20,000–$39,999	23.9	23.3
$40,000–$59,999	18.2	18.0
$60,000+	37.9	39.0
Age—Children		
2–5	5.7%	9.0%
6–11	9.0	8.3
12–17 (teenagers)	9.1	4.7
Age—Women		
18–34	12.0%	8.3%
35–49	12.0	11.8
50–64	8.7	10.1
65+	7.1	11.3
Age—Men		
18–34	11.8%	7.4%
35–49	11.5	11.3
50–64	8.0	9.7
65+	5.1	8.2

*Head of household.
Source: Nielsen Television Index, March 2003.

Public Broadcasting station as a means to preserve, shelter, and protect their sense of community and local identity. In January 1981, the Rural California Broadcasting Corporation (KRCB) was incorporated in Rohnert Park, California, as a 501(c)(3) nonprofit organization.[9]

According to Dobbs, "The City of Rohnert Park was bemused by us. A non-profit organization didn't make sense in a city that had been developed and run primarily by leaders from the business sector." Once the land was secured, the next issue became how to get buildings on the

Exhibit 6   **National Public Radio (NPR), Nationwide Audience Profile, 2002**

	Demographics*		Lifestyles†
54%	**Men**	76%	**Public involvement**
	46% women		62% vote
67%	**Aged 25 to 54**		15% fund-raising
	24% aged 18 to 34	51%	**Theater/concert/dance**
	50% aged 35 to 54		31% attend live music performances
58%	**College degree or beyond**		65% dine out
	28% graduate school attended/degree		55% read books
73%	**Household income $50,000+**	55%	**Regular fitness program**
	49% HHI $75,000+		26% swim
	(mean HHI $85,675)		45% walk for exercise
64%	**Married**	41%	**Own financial securities**
	22% single		30% own stock/bond mutual funds
76%	**Employed**		20% own common/preferred stocks
	28% professional	86%	**Household owns computer**
	16% managerial		92% use online service
	35% business purchases	74%	**Domestic travel**
	57% view job as "career"		40% foreign travel over past 3 years

Base: Adults 18+ who listen to an NPR station.
*Reads: Over half (54%) of NPR listeners are men, etc.
†Past-year activities.
Source: MRI, Fall 2002.

property. Station funding was non-existent, and this meant that a creative solution was in order. Through legwork and strong community ties, a staff member identified a former drug rehabilitation center located just to the south in Marin County that had gone bankrupt. This company had several portable buildings and since their need for them had run out, they donated them to the station. These portables formed the core of the station's infrastructure. In 1983, the station obtained a 40-year lease from the City of Rohnert Park, with an option to purchase the land should the city eventually decide to sell.

President and CEO of the station since its founding, Dobbs had moved to Sonoma County in 1972 and worked in health care and as a legislative staffer during her previous careers. A former field representative for California legislator Barry Keane, Dobbs had left her position as house committee analyst and come to KRCB at age 35, bringing with her extensive experience in legislature, government, the media, and fund-raising. Paula Wrenn, writing in *North Bay Biz,* noted: "As the station had yet to grow grassroots or construct even a ground floor, her

[Dobbs's] skills were far more important than broadcast experience during the planning stages."[10]

Dobbs and her founding team considered the launch of the television station opportunistic. Because a frequency was immediately available for television in Sonoma County, KRCB-TV had gone on the air before the FM radio station. Dobbs recalled, "Shortly after KRCB-TV signed on the air in December 1984, we received our first donation. It was 35 cents taped on a piece of cardboard from a little boy in Glen Ellen, California. 'Finally,' he wrote, 'I can see *Sesame Street.*' We should have saved it but we needed the money."

KRCB-TV had been created to serve three specific purposes. Its primary purpose was to extend public television to 250,000 people in the region who had previously been unable to receive a signal from distant Public Broadcasting System (PBS) stations. Its secondary purpose was to extend an educational television signal to the many schools then outside the existing signal range of the other public stations. Finally, KRCB intended to provide as much local programming as possible. Volunteer producers, directors, and camera people stepped forward to run the television station and produce the local programming that would be the hallmark of the station's early years.

During the next decade, as the television station grew and achieved financial stability, the station's board of directors started to plan for a sister radio station. "It was quite remarkable that a county the size of Sonoma County did not have its own public radio station," Dobbs recalled. When a noncommercial frequency became available in 1991, the board set to work putting together a radio station to fill this void. Almost on the very day KRCB-FM signed on the air, a popular Bay Area classical station signed off the air, leaving the greater Bay Area without a source for classical music. Seizing the opportunity, the station began to offer classical music as its core program schedule, bracketed by NPR news feeds and local music and information shows. Once again, as with its television launch, volunteers helped build and staff the radio station.

KRCB-FM positioned itself as the North Bay's classical music station; Dobbs assumed that the station's listeners were expected to be similar to the NPR classical audience profile shown in Exhibit 7. Just 50 miles north of San Francisco, Sonoma County was best known for its agriculture (dairy and grapes), tourism, and technology in Telecom Valley, a spin-off of the famed Silicon Valley. Rohnert Park, where KRCB was based, was a town with a population of 42,000, in the growing and increasingly affluent Sonoma County region. Exhibit 8 shows recent population data for Sonoma County in comparison to other counties in the KRCB's viewing audience area.

Operations and Staffing

KRCB's portable buildings housing its studios and offices in Rohnert Park were old and modest, surrounded by vacant fields. Originally, the station shared a parcel of land that was also used by the minor league baseball team, the Sonoma County Crushers. The Crushers dissolved after the 2002 season, and the fate of the stadium and surrounding land was in the hands of the City of Rohnert Park. The city signed an exclusive option that would permit the development of additional big-box retailers on the site. Costco had in 2002 completed

Exhibit 7   National Public Radio (NPR), Classical Music Audience Profile, 2002

	Demographics*		Lifestyles†
51%	**Men** 49% women	83%	**Public involvement** 69% vote 14% fund-raising
61%	**Aged 25 to 54** 16% aged 18 to 34 51% aged 35 to 54	56%	**Theater/concert/dance** 37% attend live music performances 70% dine out
63%	**College degree or beyond** 32% graduate school attended/degree		64% read books
80%	**Household income $50,000+** 54% HHI $75,000+ (mean HHI $91,933)	56%	**Regular fitness program** 29% swim 49% walk for exercise
71%	**Married** 16% single	53%	**Own financial securities** 37% own stock/bond mutual funds 23% own common/preferred stocks
74%	**Employed** 30% professional 17% managerial 33% business purchases 58% view job as "career"	87%	**Household owns computer** 94% use online service
		81%	**Domestic travel** 44% foreign travel over past 3 years

Base: Adults 18+ who listen to an NPR classical station.

**Reads:* Over half (51%) of NPR classical music listeners are men, etc.

† Past-year activities.

Source: MRI, Fall 2002.

Exhibit 8   **Bay Area Population Estimates as of January 1, 2003**

Bay Area County	Population
Alameda (Oakland/Berkeley)	1,496,200
Contra Costa	994,900
Marin	250,400
Napa	129,800
San Francisco	791,600
San Mateo	717,000
Sonoma*	472,700

*Since 1980, Sonoma County had enjoyed an average annual increase in population of 7,923 (2.1%). From 1993 to 2002, the county witnessed a population growth of 14.7%; from 2001 to 2002, its population increased by 6,700 (1.4%). The population of Sonoma County was expected to increase to 498,600 (1.7%) in 2005, and to 541,100 (1.6%) in 2010.

In 2000, those who attended some college but did not graduate were the majority in both Sonoma County and California, at 27.9% and 24.3%, respectively.

In 2002, 40–49-year-olds accounted for 17.0% of the county's population, more than any other age group. The 40–49 age group was expected to account for 12.7% of the county's population in 2005, and 16.9% in 2010.

In 2002, Sonoma County's population by race/ethnicity could be described as largely white (80.7%) followed by Hispanic (13.3%), Asian (3.6%), African American (1.5%), and American Indian (0.92%). Hispanics were forecast to represent 28.3% of Sonoma County's population by 2005, and 41.7% by 2010.

The median household income in Sonoma County in 1999 was $53,076, compared to $47,493 in California statewide.

Source: California Department of Finance, Demographic Research Unit.

a new store opening just to the east of the stadium and the station's facilities. Due to Costco's success and in light of a budgetary crisis in 2003, the City of Rohnert Park was publicly reviewing the option to sell the land to developers known to be planning more big-box stores, which would, in turn, lead to increased retail tax revenues. Once the property was appraised, KRCB had a contractual right of first refusal to purchase the land if sufficient financing could be found.

The station's main building conveyed a sense of community, family, and pride. Paintings of Sonoma Mountain by local artist Jack Stuppin decorated the walls. The waiting area was modest, the ceilings were low, and the hallways were maze-like, lending a sense of mystery and curiosity. It was apparent that this organization was running lean financially. A station volunteer commented, "I couldn't help but notice the telephone lines hanging down from the

ceiling and the old equipment people were expected to use every day to complete their work. I wonder how KRCB entices people to work there." The station's transmission facility was located in nearby Santa Rosa, on the northernmost fringe of the San Francisco Bay Area.

Station staff consisted of 20.5 full-time equivalent (FTE) employees for television and 9 FTE employees for radio. While several staff members had been with the station since its inception, Dobbs considered volunteers to be a key component of daily operations. The volunteer staff size varied between 3 and 10, depending on the activities occurring at the station at any given time. Volunteers assisted with programming, filing, writing public service announcements, and acting as program hosts ("DJs"). The station also had four to five volunteers who helped with various functions such as landscaping, facilities work, mailing, filing, fielding phone calls, and general office duties. The production department also had a group of volunteers who worked exclusively on special events such as election nights and pledge drives. These volunteers operated cameras, directed programming, and switched programming between live studio action and taped footage.

Coordinating volunteers was vital to the station's operations. Volunteers performed myriad duties at the station; they staffed its television and radio pledge drives, the annual televised auction in April, the wine auction in September, and the travel auction in November. Vanessa Bergamo, KRCB's volunteer and outreach manager explained, "Television has three auctions and four pledge drives per year. They each require phone and support teams as well as production volunteers. Last year we logged 10,000 volunteer hours, the year before 25,000, and this year we are tracking to about 12,000." For each auction, the station needed 21 phone volunteers, 15 support volunteers, and 13 production volunteers over six nights. This was a total of 294 volunteers for one auction. TV station pledge drives required eight phone volunteers, two support volunteers, and six production volunteers over four nights, for a total of 64 volunteers. In addition, two FM radio pledges per year also required volunteer support. Yet recruiting volunteers had become more difficult following the onset of the war in Iraq and the weakened U.S. economy. According to Bergamo, "People were less interested in volunteering due to the war. What I was hearing were people who wanted to 'take care of their own' in a time of uncertainty."

The station was also plagued by turnover of its paid staff. The development director had left one year earlier to pursue other interests, and that position had remained unfilled. In the interim and as part of a cost-savings initiative, Dobbs had assumed those duties on a part-time basis. In early October 2003, just as KRCB was about to enter its fall season for fund-raising, Bergamo, the volunteer coordinator, had given her two weeks' notice.

The station's organization chart, as of November 2003, is shown in Exhibit 9. Dobbs was curious to see the organization charts of other small public broadcast stations to compare staff turnover rates and also how full- and part-time employees were split between television and radio. Dobbs was also interested in other stations' staff sizes versus dollars raised, or versus numbers of members. "I think we're lean and mean because we work like crazy, but are we organized in the best possible way? I just don't know," she lamented.

Leadership and Governance

The station's mission had remained unchanged since its inception: "In order to encourage full participation in society and community, KRCB provides educational, informational, and cultural telecommunication services in partnership with our community." Three key goals associated with the mission statement focused on programming, education, and finances. The station's board of directors sought to promote community awareness of cultural richness and human diversity through the production and broadcast of local, national, and regional programs. The station hoped that its broadcast and nonbroadcast resources would serve students in various and diverse settings. The station's financial objective was to remain a stable and enduring institution by exercising sound financial management.

The station's board of directors functioned as part of the top management team. The board was responsible for setting station policy through strategic planning and tackling tough issues such as radio signal quality, differentiation among stations, and underwriting as a means to raise money (see Exhibit 10). As in most nonprofit organizations, the board was comprised of professionals who were active in the local community (see Exhibit 11). Board members were not required to have any specific qualifications. A passion for public broadcasting and the ability to

attend the board meetings were the only two requirements. Dobbs reflected, "This is a good board. We've had very few times when the situation has been difficult enough that we've actually needed to vote on something. Each member has his or her own style."

Board members served two-year terms with no limit to the number of terms that could be served. When board members joined, Dobbs spoke to them about "the need to be supportive to the station in a level that was clearly meaningful for them." Dobbs expected the board members to act as ambassadors between the station and their respective business and social networks. She appreciated introductions by the board to members of the business community and was comfortable putting herself in the position of asking for donations. Since staffing resources to properly train the board were not available, few board members were actively involved in fund-raising. Unlike many nonprofit boards, KRCB's required no fixed level of personal contribution from board members, and no individual fund-raising quotas had been set. Still, the station's board members had contributed $45,000 from their own pockets over a period of three years for the Capital Campaign, which raised money for the digital conversion.

Dobbs herself was one of only two women on the station's board of directors, which consisted solely of white, upper-income professionals. Dobbs felt that finding a board that was passionate about public broadcasting was the most important factor and that everything else would fall into place. However, when the station applied for certain types of grants, the ethnic makeup of its board was occasionally a hindrance. Dobbs had looked for people from the minority community who were passionate about public broadcasting and could join the team, but had had only limited success. At one point there had been two Hispanic board members, but they had departed by 2003.

Fund-raising

With an annual operating budget of $2.1 million for television and radio, KRCB was considered a small station in the realm of public broadcasting. Statements of activities for fiscal years ended September 30, 2000–2002, are shown in Exhibit 12. Preliminary estimates of revenue and expenses for fiscal year 2003 are shown in Exhibit 13. Approximately 30 percent of KRCB's budget came from membership dollars (about $750,000 per year), 30 percent

Exhibit 9 **KRCB's Organization Chart**

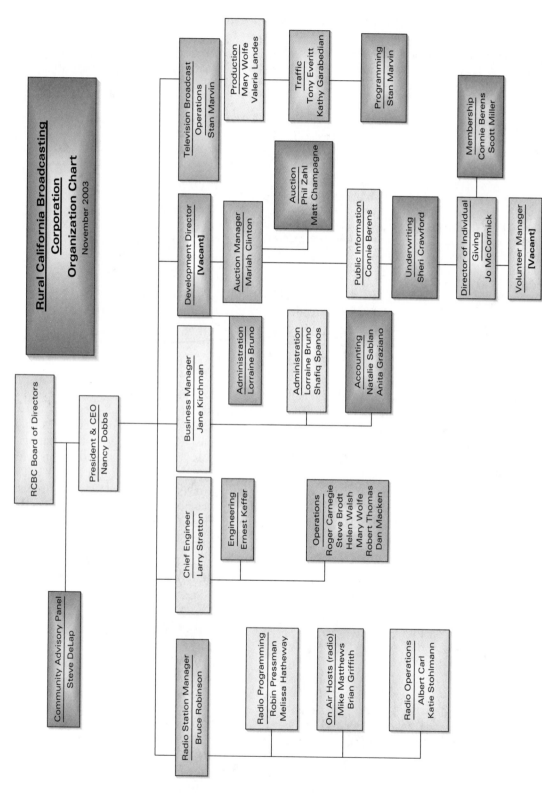

Rural California Broadcasting Corporation
Organization Chart
November 2003

RCBC Board of Directors

Community Advisory Panel
Steve DeLap

President & CEO
Nancy Dobbs

Television Broadcast
Operations
Stan Marvin

Production
Mary Wolfe
Valerie Landes

Traffic
Tony Everitt
Kathy Garabedian

Programming
Stan Marvin

Development Director
[Vacant]

Auction Manager
Mariah Clinton

Auction
Phil Zahl
Matt Champagne

Public Information
Connie Berens

Membership
Connie Berens
Scott Miller

Underwriting
Sheri Crawford

Director of Individual
Giving
Jo McCormick

Volunteer Manager
[Vacant]

Business Manager
Jane Kirchman

Administration
Lorraine Bruno

Administration
Lorraine Bruno
Shafiq Spanos

Accounting
Natalie Sablan
Anita Graziano

Chief Engineer
Larry Stratton

Engineering
Ernest Keffer

Operations
Roger Carnegie
Steve Brodt
Helen Walsh
Mary Wolfe
Robert Thomas
Dan Macken

Radio Station Manager
Bruce Robinson

Radio Programming
Robin Pressman
Melissa Hathaway

On Air Hosts (radio)
Mike Matthews
Brian Griffith

Radio Operations
Albert Carl
Katie Stohlmann

Source: KRCB, November 2003.

Exhibit 10   **Statement of Board of Directors of KRCB**

Service on the Board of Directors of Rural California Broadcasting Corporation allows individuals to make a significant contribution to the community of Northern California through development and shaping of telecommunications resources available to and owned by the public (more commonly known as "public broadcasting"). The Board, through stations and resources of which it is the steward, is truly creating the voice and vision of our community.

While the responsibility and satisfaction are notable, Board membership carries no financial remuneration. It is important for all members to understand the particulars of those responsibilities as well as the general mutual expectations that accompany membership with RCBC. In addition to the following points, Board Members should familiarize themselves with the corporate by-laws.

- As with any non-profit Board of Directors, Members are fiscally and legally responsible and liable for the conduct of the corporation. Adequate and timely information will be provided by management as to allow the BOD to make informed decisions. The station carries Officers and Directors Liability Insurance.
- Board Members are expected to attend all Board meetings, serve on Board committees and participate annually in KRCB fundraising and other activities. Board activities normally require four to five hours per month.
- Board Members are expected to support the fundraising efforts of RCBC. Each Member will contribute what is, for them, a substantial donation annually. Each will also actively support the fundraising of the organization in whatever way is best suited to each one.
- Underlying all aspects of participation is of course a strong belief in the purpose and mission of RCBC, and the good-faith assumption that all Members of the Board are operating with the same commitment, concern and level of involvement.

Source: KRCB.

from underwriting, and 30 percent from federal and CPB grants (the State of California did not provide ongoing government funding to public television or radio stations). Revenues from the televised live auctions rounded out the last 10 percent of the budget.

Membership contributions accounted for nearly one-third of station operating revenues. These covered membership expenses such as direct mail pieces (developing, printing, and mailing), telemarketing, thank-you gifts, software, and salaries (administration, volunteer manager, and graphic artist). The station's nonprofit status meant that all membership fees and donations qualified for tax deductions as charitable contributions. KRCB-FM estimated that its radio audience was 20 percent of the size of its television audience. Moreover, the fact that KRCB-FM's radio signal did not reach beyond Sonoma County and often overlapped with KCSM-FM's signal within the populous southern section of Sonoma County posed a huge challenge in growing the membership

Exhibit 11   **KRCB Board Members and Their Affiliations (as of October 2003)**

Steve De Lap	Santa Rosa Community Access Center, staff
Nancy Dobbs	President and CEO, KRCB
Mark Epstein	California Financial Services, owner
Paul Ginsberg	Attorney
John Kramer	Professor, Sonoma State University, station cofounder
Dan Lanahan	Attorney at law
Carol Libarle	Community volunteer
Michael Musson	Linkenheimer LLP, CPA
Howard Nurse	Engineer (retired)
Marshall Taxer	Flex Products Inc., manager of information systems
David Wolf	The Accrediting Commission for Community & Junior Colleges, retired executive director

Source: KRCB.

Exhibit 12 **KRCB Television & Radio's Statement of Activities, Fiscal Year Ending September 30, 2003, with Comparisons for Fiscal Years 2000-2002**

	Unrestricted		Temporarily Restricted	2003	2002	2001	2000
	Television	Radio					
Changes in net assets:							
Support and revenue:							
Grants:							
Corporation for Public Broadcasting	$ 322,382	$ 118,013	—	$ 440,395	$ 432,356	$ 423,300	$ 351,319
Corporation, foundation, government, and other	51,820	4,430	—	56,250	544,113	364,152	23,340
Underwriting contributions	400,787	139,755	—	540,542	412,749	359,050	393,978
Membership contributions	538,968	163,902	—	702,870	653,064	677,705	618,611
Capital campaign	—	—	$ 9,722	9,722	40,521	644,592	—
Annual auction and other fundraising activities	218,642	—	—	218,642	228,916	180,231	261,252
Services and other revenues	136,664	24,865	—	161,529	151,161	147,976	156,516
Interest and dividends	6,877	16	7,677	14,570	10,401	8,880	8,967
Net unrealized and realized gains (losses) on endowment	—	—	—	—	—	(5,125)	17,052
Donated goods and services	139,437	31,739	—	171,176	103,159	138,244	169,875
Total support and revenue	1,815,577	482,720	17,399	2,315,696	2,576,440	2,939,005	2,000,910
Net assets released from restrictions	890,826	—	(890,826)	—	—	—	—
Total support, revenue, and net assets released from restrictions	$2,706,403	$ 482,720	$(873,427)	$2,315,696	$2,576,440	$2,939,005	$2,000,910
Expenses:							
Program services:							
Programming and production	$ 315,854	135,082	—	450,936	404,856	463,676	434,786
Broadcasting	404,016	136,818	—	540,834	575,566	471,819	485,508
Program information and promotion	209,921	70,637	—	280,558	168,940	120,806	140,887
Supporting services:							
Management and general	509,037	139,865	—	648,902	587,238	557,530	570,214
Fundraising	462,856	70,302	—	533,258	488,157	464,983	401,294
Total expenses	$1,901,684	$ 552,704	$ —	$2,454,388	$2,224,757	$2,078,814	$2,032,689
Increase (decrease) in net assets	804,719	(69,984)	(873,427)	(138,692)	351,683	860,191	(31,779)
Net assets, beginning of year	639,970	(446,153)	1,386,611	1,580,428	1,228,745	368,554	400,333
Net assets, end of year	$1,444,689	$ (516,137)	$ 513,184	$1,441,736	$1,580,428	$1,228,745	$ 368,554

Source: KRCB.

Exhibit 13   KRCB TV & Radio's Preliminary Statement of Revenues and Expenses, Fiscal Year Ending September 30, 2003

	Actual			Annual Budget	Budget Variance	Capital Campaign
	TV	Radio	Total			
Revenue						
Grants—CPB	$ 322,382	$118,013	$ 440,395	$ 413,780	$ 26,615	$116,666
Grants—Other	59,510	4,430	63,940	77,200	(13,260)	0
Underwriting—cash	116,565	67,363	183,928	313,410	(129,482)	0
Underwriting—trade	276,046	71,527	347,573	249,559	98,014	0
Open air—advertising	6,400	1,600	8,000	42,000	(34,000)	0
Membership	511,156	155,182	666,338	714,297	(47,959)	0
Major donors	27,813	8,720	36,533	40,520	(3,987)	450,117
Auction	260,603	0	260,603	301,400	(40,797)	0
Special events	0	4,618	4,618	6,500	(1,882)	0
Creative services	124,072	16,701	140,773	134,600	6,173	0
Miscellaneous	10,782	3,012	13,794	5,220	8,574	7,677
In-kind services	37,294	11,289	48,583	18,282	30,301	0
In-kind goods	5,039	14,595	19,634	700	18,934	0
Total revenue	$1,757,662	$477,050	$2,234,712	$2,317,468	$(82,756)	$574,460
Expense						
Employee expense	$ 723,667	$283,886	$1,007,553	$1,075,500	$(67,947)	$ 35,127
Advertising	176,454	59,784	236,238	192,660	43,578	0
Commissions	5,980	495	6,475	0	6,475	0
Fundraising/events	108,931	11,424	120,355	151,924	(31,569)	0
Insurance	25,122	5,743	30,865	34,416	(3,551)	0
Interest expense	46,389	5,738	52,127	43,400	8,727	0
Land lease	20,033	8,109	28,142	29,136	(994)	0
Maintenance—facility	17,997	4,493	22,490	19,992	2,498	0
Maintenance—equipment	15,503	5,335	20,838	57,108	(36,270)	0
Meetings, travel, mileage	8,969	3,299	12,268	11,250	1,018	0
Miscellaneous	5,814	2,384	8,198	2,400	5,798	0
Office supplies	10,898	2,428	13,326	11,880	1,446	0
Postage & shipping	38,548	7,179	45,727	45,821	(94)	0
Printing	39,634	4,744	44,378	41,075	3,303	0
Production	19,685	0	19,685	4,300	15,385	0
Professional services—L&A	58,636	11,034	69,670	48,399	21,271	0
Professional services—Other	80,360	12,064	92,424	73,744	18,680	0
Program acquisition	148,031	50,780	198,811	205,116	(6,305)	0
Program guide	30,550	7,638	38,188	42,000	(3,812)	0
Pub/sub/dues/fees	21,573	5,737	27,310	24,546	2,764	0
Rental equipment	1,730	319	2,049	3,776	(1,727)	0
Recording materials	7,755	1,243	8,998	27,201	(18,203)	0
Telephone	49,103	19,929	69,032	63,205	5,827	0
Utilities	49,704	6,278	55,982	44,304	11,678	0
Total expense	$1,711,066	$520,063	$2,231,129	$2,253,153	$(22,024)	$ 35,127
Excess of revenue over expense	$ 46,596	$ (43,013)	$ 3,583	$ 64,315	$(60,732)	$539,333

(Continued)

Exhibit 13   **Continued**

| | Actual | | | | | |
	TV	Radio	Total	Annual Budget	Budget Variance	Capital Campaign
Capital expenditures:						
Principal payments			$ 66,482	$63,587	$2,895	
Equipment acquisition			10,219	0	10,219	
Software			0	3,200	(3,200)	
Building/construction			0	0	0	
Total capital expenditures			$ 76,701	$66,787	$9,914	
Cash needed (cumulative)			$ (73,118)	$ (2,472)	$ (70,646)	
Digital capital expenses			$458,464	$ 0	$458,464	$458,464

at KRCB-FM. A related membership challenge was how to retain current members.

New members joined for two reasons: first, because they were excited about a current offer and wanted to take advantage of it while it lasted, and, second, because they were committed to being part of their community and supporting a public institution. This second group of members was much easier to retain. Jo McCormick, KRCB's director of individual giving, believed that most members felt that "civic duty [was] the right thing to do." McCormick had been pleased with the results of the summer and fall pledge drives, but was concerned about retaining these new members. Pledge drives involved special programming on radio and TV as well as teams of volunteers working the phones, in order to take information from callers who wished to join as members or renew their memberships. Local chains such as Deaf Dog Coffee and High Tech Burrito provided coupons for free mochas or burritos as incentives for members to join. Other local firms or anonymous donors provided dollar-for-dollar matches to encourage new members to join.

Annual live fund-raising auctions on KRCB-TV were scheduled three times per year. Fall auctions featured a harvest theme, showcasing locally produced wine and dining. Companies were solicited to donate goods and services for the auctions. Winter auctions featured travel packages to resorts and other destinations near and far. Spring auctions featured leisure and personal pampering products and services, such as spas, massage, and personal care products. Auctions were televised Friday through Sunday nights; as goods and services were introduced, viewers were encouraged to place bids on auction items via telephone. During the live auctions, volunteers from local

businesses and other community organizations worked the phone banks, receiving bids and handing those to "runners," who would post the bids on various whiteboards visible to viewers. As the evening progressed and once individual bid boards had closed, another volunteer team called winning bidders to obtain payment information. McCormick explained further, "We're hoping our annual wine and holiday auctions will bring additional bidders from our new broadcasting area. We just don't have the PR budget to get our name out in new markets. At this time, the best we can do is trade air time to make up for the current lack of advertising dollars." Despite this, McCormick stressed that the growing donor base would be a major benefit, in particular to the station's public television audience, as it would eventually provide funds to produce local television programming.

Corporate giving or underwriting provided another third of the station's revenues. In addition to tax incentives, underwriting provided several nonmonetary benefits for its donors. First, public broadcasting members and loyal viewers and listeners who appreciated the broadcasting alternative provided by the station tended to support the businesses and organizations that supported Public Broadcasting. Second, unlike commercial stations, KRCB's non–program content constituted less than five minutes per hour, thereby retaining viewer/listener attention. Third, an organization's presence in local public broadcasting distinguished that organization as one that cared about and supported its community. Finally, for an underwriter, its continued on-air presence helped build name recognition and a positive association in the minds of existing and potential new customers, associates, and employees. The key challenge with underwriting was making organizations recognize these benefits so that they were willing to make sustained contributions.

The remaining third of revenues came from federal grants, separate for television and radio. The largest annual source of grant money was the Corporation for Public Broadcasting (CPB), created by Congress in 1967. The CPB was a private, nonprofit organization that funded over 1,000 public television and radio stations nationwide using an annual appropriation of funds from Congress, which in turn represented 12 percent of public broadcasting's revenues. The CPB provided the largest source of funds for radio programming and television programming for broadcast on NPR and PBS. CPB also led the way for public broadcasting's transition to digital service and digital programming and funded production of innovative educational programming.

According to Dobbs, "KRCB-TV would not have converted if it had not been required." KRCB's cost to get its digital TV transmitter operational was approximately $800,000. Most of this money had been raised from a Capital Campaign that had been launched in 2001, specifically to pay for the digital conversion. The remainder of funding for the project had come from grants provided by the CPB, PBS, and the State of California. In 2001, the State of California had distributed $7 million among 14 public television stations statewide to help fund the digital conversion. In return for state funds, KRCB had promised the state's Office of Emergency Services to make any unused new digital capacity available to the state in the event of emergency.

Larry Stratton, KRCB's chief engineer, said he was unsure "whether [or not] there would be a significant long-term future [for KRCB] in the digital arena." Still, Stratton had been concerned about the state of the station's aging transmission technology for some time. With the exception of an air-conditioning unit, KRCB-TV had already purchased all of the equipment required to broadcast a digital signal, but sufficient funds had not been available to upgrade the entire studio to digital all at once. As old analog equipment broke down, it was being replaced with new digital equipment. So far, the studio equipment had been installed, configured, and operational as the link to the transmitter. By mid-October 2003, the major installation of equipment at the transmitter site was expected to be complete. KRCB-TV scheduled signing on to its new digital signal for November 3, 2003.

In addition to completing the retrofits of new equipment, KRCB's technical staff had to cope with the challenge of learning how to use new technology and master the potential marketing opportunities that accompanied its use. Digital transmission technology not only could offer KRCB potential new revenue streams from licensing unused broadband capacity to other broadcasters but also could incur higher fixed operating costs and unknown variable costs associated with managing those licensed channels.

The station was also exploring the prospects of banding together with other local public broadcasters to help California with some of the projects on the statewide agenda in return for funds. One such mandate was Proposition 10, which provided funds for the education of young people about the dangers of smoking. Dobbs commented, "We're looking to partner to use our air time in a way we have never done before, realizing that we don't want to all look the same. Still, we ought to be speaking with the same voice about the value of public broadcasting in Sacramento [the state capital], San Francisco, and Los Angeles—if we want to get some of these monies."

Underwriting

An underwriter was a third party, typically a local company or foundation, that voluntarily contributed cash or trade (such as printing, mailing, or food for volunteer staff at auctions and pledge drives). Underwriting financed the production and transmission of programming. Underwriters received on-air recognition for their support. Yet tax-deductible donation patterns from underwriters with respect to nonprofit organizations were changing, and not necessarily to the station's advantage. Dobbs had read that one radio station in Los Angeles experienced a 30 percent decline in underwriting during the first nine months of 2003. She believed that the decline in revenues from underwriting was a direct result of the poor state and regional economy; as a result, local businesses did not have excess cash to spend on charitable causes. Dobbs noted that several companies who had funded KRCB-TV for nearly 20 years had decided not to renew their underwriting, instead contributing to other vital community services that had suffered from draconian State of California budget cuts.

Nationwide trends compiled by the Corporation for Public Broadcasting (CPB) showed that the public radio system's "net" revenue had declined since 1999 (see Exhibit 14). Reflecting these trends, on the radio side, KRCB-FM was operating at a loss greater than projected in the budget for 2003. The station's fund balances to fiscal year end September 30, 2003, are shown in Exhibit 15.

Exhibit 14 **Corporation for Public Broadcasting, Systemwide Financial Data, Fiscal Years 1999–2002 ($ in millions)**

	FY 1999	FY 2000	FY 2001	FY 2002
System operating revenue*†	$523	$581	$626	$654
System operating expenses*	509	567	619	655
System net revenue‡	$ 14	$ 14	$ 7	$ (1)
Number of licensees "in the red"	133			142
Number of licensees "in the black"	181			172
Average loss ($000)	$168			$257
Median loss ($000)	$ 67			$ 78
Number of licensees with losses >$1 million	4			7
Number of licensees with profits >$1 million	5			7
Four-year growth (%)				
Operating Revenue				25%
Operating Expense				29%
Programming (two-thirds of expense)				28%
Fund-raising (one-fifth of expense)				37%
Expense growth by function ($ millions)				
Programming				$ 86
Production				58
Broadcasting				21
Promotion				7
Fund-raising and underwriting				34
Management and general				20
Other				5

*Data compiled from 314 CPB radio licensees receiving annual grants of $65,000 or greater.

†Total operating revenue includes reported "in-kind" and "indirect" support.

‡Net operating revenue equals total operating revenue minus total operating expenses, but excludes capital, securities income and endowments.

Source: Corporation for Public Broadcasting, Public Radio Futures Project, www.cpb.org, July 31, 2004.

Still, noncash or trade underwriting (trading on-air acknowledgements for donated goods and services) was running well above what had been budgeted for 2003. Dobbs made a mental note that she would need to work with the KRCB underwriting staff to promote the station in such a way that when the economy turned around, they would be in front of all potential underwriters.

STRATEGIC PLANNING CHALLENGES

As KRCB-TV approached its 20th anniversary and KRCB-FM its 10th anniversary on the air, Dobbs reflected back on the events that had taken place over the years and contemplated the future of KRCB and her role in shaping and guiding that future:

> It's so easy given my upbringing to say, "Aw, shucks, I can't do that." I guess I'm not using the connections in the community as effectively as I could be. The investment the community has made in me the past 20 years needs to be utilized and built upon for expanding the station. This organization has invested in me and has a right to have a payoff, too. False modesty has not got much place here at KRCB. When all is said and done, you have to be able to live with yourself and come to terms with your own strengths and weaknesses.

As Dobbs pulled her car out of the parking lot, she pondered the challenges the station was facing. While locally KRCB had been known as "the little station that could," it was in need of a new strategy and direction.

Exhibit 15 **KRCB Television & Radio's Statements of Financial Position, Fiscal Years 2003 Versus 2002**

	Unrestricted		Temporarily Restricted	2003 Total	2002 Total
	Television	Radio			
Assets					
Current assets:					
Cash	$ 53,214	$ —	$ —	$ 53,214	$ 86,457
Accounts receivable	9,358	—	—	9,358	16,393
Grants receivable	—	—	50,000	50,000	501,000
Contributions receivable (net of allowance for uncollectibles of $2,000)	37,159	15,818	—	52,977	55,598
Unconditional promises to give, current portion	—	—	108,100	108,100	118,849
Program license agreements	87,792	23,348	—	111,140	83,314
Prepaid expenses	162,699	23,027	—	185,726	105,184
Inventory	33,565	—	—	33,565	17,346
Total current assets	383,787	62,193	158,100	604,080	984,141
Capital campaign fund	—	—	482,277	482,277	671,450
Unconditional promises to give, net of current portion	—	—	—	—	96,312
Structures and equipment	1,151,459	100,072	—	1,251,531	733,415
Broadcast licenses	908	6,490	—	7,398	10,931
Total assets	$1,536,154	$168,755	$640,377	$2,345,286	$2,496,249
Liabilities and net assets					
Current liabilities:					
Accounts payable	$ 268,499	$ 62,754	$127,193	$ 458,446	$ 370,174
Accrued expenses	51,785	17,629	—	69,414	61,478
Deferred revenue	9,029	—	—	9,029	—
Inter-company payable	(604,509)	604,509	—	—	—
Line of credit	—	—	—	—	50,000
Current portion of long-term debt	28,062	—	—	28,062	57,603
Current portion of obligation under capital lease	1,751	—	—	1,751	9,523
Total current liabilities	(245,383)	684,892	127,193	566,702	548,778
Long-term debt, less current	336,848	—	—	336,848	365,292
Obligation under capital lease, less current	—	—	—	—	1,751
Total liabilities	91,465	684,892	127,193	903,550	915,821
Net assets	1,444,689	(516,137)	513,184	1,441,736	1,580,428
Total liabilities and net assets	$1,536,154	$168,755	$640,377	$2,345,286	$2,496,249

Back in 1997, station management and the board developed the "KRCB Television and Radio 20 Point Strategic Plan," summarized in Exhibit 16. That plan was later revised in March 1998, but had not been revisited since then. Dobbs hoped that a meeting with station staff in early 2004 to update the strategic plan, facilitated by an independent consultant, would be sufficient to satisfy the needs of KRCB and its board. The external facilitator had come highly recommended by one of the board members.

Exhibit 16   **Summary of the "KRCB-TV and KRCB-FM 16 Point Strategic Plan"**

In June 1996, the Board of Directors of KRCB began the process of strategic planning for the next three to five years. The original version of the strategic plan was published on June 7, 1997 and a revision was published on March 4, 1998.

The strategic planning committee arrived at two goals and 16 points or objectives as listed below.

Goal 1: Strengthen the quality, quantity, visibility and support of KRCB's local programs and services.

1. Establish KRCB-TV and KRCB-FM as the cultural voice and educational resource of the North Bay.
2. Establish a highly visible on-air local presence for both TV and radio which differentiates KRCB from other public television and public radio services in our area.
3. Develop KRCB-FM into a full service county-wide station.
4. Serve the programming needs/interests of diverse audiences in our coverage area.
5. Promote KRCB to build audiences, and to secure audience loyalty and support.
6. Expand KRCB's sphere of influence, community connections, and alliances, including possible collaborations.
7. Strengthen KRCB's image.
8. Develop the Board of Directors.
9. Enhance workplace professionalism.
10. Develop volunteer support.
11. Develop membership and increase fundraising capabilities to achieve financial stability.
12. Intensify ties between KRCB-TV and KRCB-FM.

Goal 2: Enhance KRCB's options in providing and responding to new technologies.

13. Prepare KRCB to change from analog to digital (DTV) transmission.
14. Position KRCB to take advantage of its technological assets by means including collaborations and partnerships.
15. Enhance technical facilities and equipment.
16. Establish profit-making services.

Source: KRCB.

On the other hand, perhaps the process would be better served by developing an entirely new plan, as if the station were starting from scratch. Either way, Dobbs needed to set a strategic plan in motion in order to ensure KRCB's future as a resource to the community.

Bibliography

Arbitron.com, "Radio Today: How America Listens to Radio." Available at www.arbitron.com/home/content.stm.

Arbitron Radio Research Consortium, Inc., "Top 30 Public Radio Subscribers—Spring 2003." Available at www.RRConline.org.

California Department of Finance, Demographic Research Unit, "California City/County Estimates with Annual Percentage Change, January 1, 2002 and 2003." Available at www.dof.ca.gov/HTML/FS_DATA/profiles/pf_home.htm.

Competitor profiles, 2003, available at www.krcb.org, www.kcsm.org, www.kteh.org, www.kqed.org.

Corporation for Public Broadcasting, "Public Radio Futures Project," July 31, 2004. Available at www.cpb.org.

Digital Television FAQ, DTV Tower Siting Fact Sheet, and RF Guide. Available at www.fcc.gov/mb/policy/dtv.

Dobbs, Nancy. "KRCB: Expanding the Voice and Vision of the North Bay." KRCB handout, 2003.

———, and KRCB staff. Author interviews, August 2003–March 2004, Rohnert Park, CA.

Hand, M., and S. Harmon. "A Most Deliberate Rush for Frequencies." *Current: The Newspaper about Public TV & Radio,* July 26, 2004.

Klose, Kevin. Testimony to House Appropriations Subcommittee on Labor, Health and Human Services, Education and Related Agencies, February 25, 2004. Available at http://appropriations.house.gov/files/KevinKloseTestimony.pdf

"KRCB Board Members and Their Affiliations." KRCB company information, 2003.

"KRCB/Channel 22 Program Schedule." Available at www.pbs.org/tvschedules/?station=KRCB.

"KRCB Mission Statement." Available at www.krcb.org/inside/mission/htm.

"KRCB Organization Chart." KRCB company information, November 2003.

"KRCB Statement of Board of Directors." KRCB company information, 2003.

"KRCB TV and FM 20 Point Strategic Plan." KRCB company information, 1998.

MRI, "NPR Audience Profile," Fall 2002.

Nielsen Television Index. "Public Television Audience in the United States," March 2003.

"Open Air." KRCB monthly program guide for members, October 2003. Available at www.krcb.org/radio/new schedule.htm.

"The Public Broadcasting Service: An Overview." Available at www.pbs.org/insidepbs/facts/faq1.html.

Rose, B., and L. Rosin. *Internet and Multimedia II: New Media Enters the Mainstream* (Arbitron Internet Broadcast Services and Edison Media Research, 2003).

Sonoma County Economic Development Board, "2003 Sonoma County Economic and Demographic Profile," available at www.sonoma-county.org/edb/Reports.htm.

Standard & Poor's. "Broadcasting and Cable Industry Survey," November 20, 2003, pp. 13–14.

"Who Owns What in the Bay Area." *San Francisco Chronicle,* June 3, 2003, p. A1.

Wrenn, P. "KRCB Turns 20!" *North Bay Biz* 28, no. 8 (July 2003), pp. 62–64.

Endnotes

[1]Opportunities to buy radio stations could be scarce and expensive. There were few or no vacant frequencies left in major radio markets. One reason was that, since the early 1990s, noncommercial religious broadcasters had outpaced public radio's growth and outbid public radio for vacant frequencies. Another reason was cost. In the top 50 markets, single commercial FM stations had sold for an average of about $22.5 million in the three years prior to 2003. In contrast, single AM stations in those same markets sold for an average of about $5.5 million. Noncommercial FM stations were selling in the range of $500,000 to $5,500,000, according to M. Hand, and S. Harmon, "A Most Deliberate Rush for Frequencies," *Current: The Newspaper about Public TV & Radio,* July 26, 2004.

[2]Edison Media Research, based in Somerville, New Jersey, conducted survey research and provided strategic information to radio stations, television stations, Internet companies, newspapers, cable networks, record labels and other media organizations. See www.edisonresearch.com/aboutus.htm.

[3]Nielsen Television Index, *Public Television Audience in the United States, 2003* (March 2003).

[4]Standard & Poor's, *Broadcasting and Cable Industry Survey,* November 20, 2003, p. 13.

[5]Testimony of Kevin Klose, president and CEO, National Public Radio, to House Appropriations Subcommittee on Labor, Health and Human Services, Education and Related Agencies, February 25, 2004, available at http://appropriations.house.gov/_files/KevinKloseTestimony.pdf.

[6]Most recent estimates from Nielsen showed that 70.9 percent of all American television-owning families watched public television in October 2002, with the average home tuning in for approximately eight hours a month. From October to December 2002, 88 million viewers in 50.6 million households watched public TV each week. This represented 47.4 percent of America's 106.7 million TV households. During the October–December 2002 period, public TV's average prime-time rating was 1.7. This rating compared with 1.4 for Lifetime, 1.3 for USA, 1.3 for Nick at Nite, 1.2 for TBS, 1.0 for Fox News, 0.8 for Discovery Channel, 0.7 for CNN, 0.7 for A&E, and 0.6 for the History Channel. Cable TV, available only to subscribers who paid about $600 per year, could be seen by only 82 percent of television owners. Public TV was freely available to 99 percent of all U.S. homes.

[7]According to Arbitron/Scarborough Research, Americans spent about 20 hours per week on average listening to their favorite radio stations in 2002. Radio listening peaked most noticeably during wake-up and commute times at 7:00 a.m. on weekdays and listening remained strong through 6:00 p.m., after which it began to taper off. On weekends, listening was at its highest between the hours of 9:00 a.m. and 3:00 p.m. In general, radio was an out-of-home medium for adults ages 18–64, while those over 65 tended to spend more time listening at home. Adults over 55 accounted for 57 percent of all commercial and noncommercial classical station listeners in the United States. By contrast, about one-third of all news/talk/information listeners nationwide were adults over 65 and over 59 percent were men. The news/talk/information format performed best in the Pacific and New England regions, where 40 percent of listeners had college degrees and 34.6 percent earned more than $75,000 per year.

[8]P. Wrenn, "KRCB Turns 20!" *North Bay Biz* 28, no. 8 (July 2003), p. 63.

[9]501(c)(3) organizations: This section of the IRS Code exempted corporations and certain trusts from federal income tax. Organizations with 501(c)(3) status were also called *public charities.* Those who contributed money, services, or materials to a recognized 501(c)(3) organization could usually deduct the value of that contribution from their taxable income. The restrictions on deductibility of contributions were less restrictive with 501(c)(3) organizations, than they were with private foundations. The code prohibited the private inurnment from net earnings of any shareholder or private individual. The code also severely limited the activities of 501(c)(3) organizations that were directed at influencing legislation or political campaigns.

[10]Wrenn, "KRCB Turns 20!"

Western States Insurance Agency

Jeffrey Shay
University of Montana

Keith Jakob
University of Montana

Tony Crawford
University of Montana

Sally Baack
San Francisco State University

Ed Kirby, a 38-year-old professor of entrepreneurship and a management consultant, did not know what to expect as he drove into the country club in Missoula, Montana, on March 5, 2003. Larry Gianchetta, dean of the business school where Kirby worked, had asked Kirby to meet with Dennis Toussaint to discuss a potential consulting project. Toussaint was the president and chief executive officer (CEO) of Combined Benefits Management Inc. (CBMI), a wholly owned subsidiary of Blue Cross and Blue Shield of Montana (BCBS-MT) with managing responsibilities for a group of subsidiary companies that included Western States Insurance Agency (WSI). Toussaint had previously been the president and CEO of WSI.

As Kirby approached the table, Gianchetta and Toussaint rose to their feet. Gianchetta shook Kirby's hand and proceeded to make the introductions. The three ordered their lunch, discussed the approaching golf season, and became acquainted. Shortly after finishing their lunch, Gianchetta stood up and said, "Well, I'm going to leave you guys to discuss business here. I have a few appointments that I need to get back for, so I'll see you both later." After Gianchetta left the table, the conversation quickly turned to the impending consulting project. Toussaint described the parameters of the project to Kirby:

> Larry [Gianchetta] suggested that I approach you to do some consulting for us. With the rapidly changing health care environment, Blue Cross and Blue Shield

This case was presented at the Fall 2005 meeting of the North American Case Research Association, October 27–29, 2005, North Falmouth, Massachusetts. Copyright © 2005 by the case authors. All rights reserved.

is concerned about our overreliance on this segment. Therefore, we are exploring other opportunities for diversifying our risk while continuing to grow the company as a whole. Western States Insurance, the agency that I ran a few years ago before selling it to Blue, is seen by our president, Peter Babbin, as the vehicle for that growth. Peter has asked me to examine the possibility of growing Western States Insurance to the revenue level needed to raise additional capital through an initial public offering. This target revenue level not only would allow Western States to go public but also would bring in the capital necessary to continue its growth through acquisition strategy, and in turn allow Blue to underwrite its own insurance policies. That's where you come in. I'd like you to conduct an analysis of our ability to grow from our $21 million revenue level in 2002 to our target revenue level. Here are a few of the parameters for the project. First, in our recent discussions with investment bankers, we were told Western States would need annual revenues of at least $100 million in order to be considered a viable candidate for an IPO. Second, given the rapid changes in the health care industry and Peter's desire to leave the company in good shape when he retires in five years, we'd like to explore completing the IPO in five years. So . . . is this something that you'd be able to do for us? We have board meetings in June and will be discussing our options at that time.

Kirby and Toussaint continued to discuss the project's parameters, access to the appropriate managers to conduct the research, and the fee schedule for the consulting project. Kirby agreed to take on the project, and Toussaint took notes about the materials that Kirby requested to get started. The two agreed to meet again in a few weeks.

BLUE CROSS/BLUE SHIELD MONTANA

Through the subsidiaries of Blue Cross and Blue Shield of Montana (BCBS-MT), customers had the convenience of one-stop shopping for a broad range of insurance, employee benefits, and related services that complemented the company's health care benefit plans. BCBS-MT subsidiaries included Combined Benefits Management Inc. (CBMI), Western States Insurance Agency (WSI), Combined Benefits Insurance Company (CBIC), Health-e-Web, and Insurance Coordinators of Montana Inc. (ICMI). CBMI was set up as a BCBS-MT holding company for several of its Montana businesses, including all those listed above. WSI was a full-service insurance agency with offices located in 17 communities throughout Montana and Oregon (see Exhibit 1). It employed over 145 professionals and served over 60,000 customers. CBIC specialized in providing policyholder services to other insurance carriers and reinsurers. Health-e-Web was an electronic claims clearinghouse for physicians, clinics, hospitals, other health care providers, and third-party administrators. ICMI offered employee benefits including life insurance, long-term and short-term disability, and nursing home/long-term care plans.

WESTERN STATES INSURANCE AGENCY

At the end of 1995, WSI was an insurance agency with nine locations throughout the state of Montana. That would change over the next eight years, with the company acquiring eight agencies. Four of the newly acquired agencies were located in Montana (Kalispell, Stevensville, Great Falls, and Helena). The additional four agencies were located in Oregon and represented the first time that WSI had competed in another state

Exhibit 1   **Western States Insurance Agency Locations in Oregon and Montana, Spring 2003**

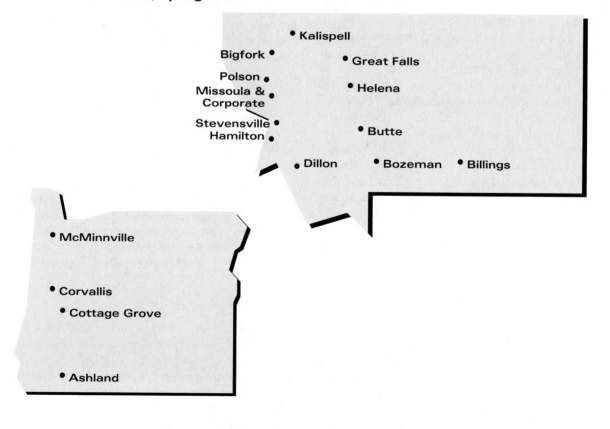

Exhibit 2 **Western States Insurance Agency's Acquisitions, 1996–2003**

Year	Number of Acquisitions	Acquisitions
1996	2	Kalispell and Helena, Montana
1997	0	
1998	1	Great Falls, Montana
1999	0	
2000	0	
2001	2	McMinnville, Oregon, and Stevensville, Montana
2002	2	Cottage Grove and Ashland, Oregon
2003*	1	Corvallis, Oregon

*WSI had already completed the Corvallis transaction, and executives felt they would close the deal on two additional acquisitions by the end of 2003.

executives emphasized the following characteristics to describe what the company was known for:

- Providing exceptional products and services.
- Offering linked solutions to protect and grow clients' assets with insurance, risk management, financial management, and employee benefits.
- Maximizing the value of the total client relationship.
- Using its status as a regional insurance agency with over $100 million in annual premium volume to form strategic alliances with insurance carriers.
- Recruiting top-caliber producers and managers.

The company Web site claimed that WSI's branches were characterized by "strong management, strong market relationships, strong local presence and community involvement, specialized areas of expertise, a history of growth, and broad financial services capabilities." WSI's management structure blended a centralized financial, administrative, and technical structure with a decentralized operating structure that was designed to allow the local branches to respond to the day-to-day needs of their clients. These centralized controls encompassed broad initiatives, such as regional sales strategy and financial reporting that were balanced by the preservation of hometown ethics and entrepreneurial drive.

Over the years, WSI had configured mix of commercial insurance, personal insurance, and financial services that was designed to fully meet its clients' needs. Exhibit 3 illustrates the mix of WSI's products and services. This range of products and services allowed WSI to offer single-source professional services for client insurance, risk management, financial management, and employee benefits programs, including property and casualty insurance; employee benefits; retirement plans; and life, health, and disability plans.

(see Exhibit 2 for acquisitions). Though still only a regionally based agency, by 2003 the company had over 200 employees, was in the top 100 largest insurance agencies in the United States, and was the top employees benefits broker in Montana.

The company's Web site stated that WSI was "a growing and diversified insurance agency, focused on a technology enabled, fully integrated delivery of commercial & personal property/casualty insurance, group & individual life & health insurance, employee benefits and retirement planning." The regionally focused agency was capable of delivering high-quality insurance and financial products and services throughout the United States. WSI

Exhibit 3 **WSI Service and Product Mix**

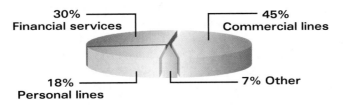

WSI'S COMPETITIVE ENVIRONMENT

WSI executives considered the insurance agency industry to be very competitive due to the diversity of competitors and high degree of product and service differentiation. This left the end consumer with a variety of agencies and products (health, property, home, business, life, automobile, etc.) to choose from. Insurance customers also came in a wide variety. For example, large corporations that purchased health care plans for employees and had the ability to negotiate lower rates per individual than the rates available to individual customers. Individual customers had recently gained some advantages as a result of the information available on the Internet. However, customers were still left with few alternatives to the products offered by insurance agencies (e.g., depositing money into a bank account to cover unforeseeable future losses).

Although the industry had recently undergone some consolidation as a result of agencies pursuing acquisition strategies similar to WSI's, there were very few that possessed dominant positions in regional markets. This left many agencies scanning the competitive landscape to see if smaller companies were gaining market presence or if larger companies were expressing an interest in entering their market. After all, getting started required gaining the necessary professional qualifications, establishing a network with larger insurance underwriters, and making capital investments (e.g., renting office space, furnishing it, purchasing computers, and hiring a few employees).

For agencies that were unable to reach the critical mass necessary to underwrite their own insurance policies, securing a larger underwriter was an important first step to starting the agency. The amount of negotiating leverage that an individual agency possessed with these larger underwriters was highly dependent on the size of the agency. As the size of the agency increased, so did its ability to negotiate more favorable terms with underwriters. Smaller agencies often relied on several different underwriters for their policies in order to maintain competitive pricing.

Expansion beyond an agency's established market presented many challenges. The agency's name recognition, for example, was usually limited to its established markets. In addition, agencies were limited by access to underwriters that traditionally focused on specific regions. For example, an agency such as WSI had established relationships with carriers in its region, but many of these carriers did not provide their products and services in other markets. This was primarily because underwriters focused on specific products and services that they knew best. For example, underwriters focusing on the Midwest had expertise in providing insurance for homeowners who faced the threat of tornadoes while underwriters in the Southeast focused on providing homeowner coverage for hurricanes. The focus of these underwriters therefore made it difficult for agencies to penetrate markets in which their underwriters had no market presence because such expansion required establishing a new network with regional underwriters.

WSI'S GROWTH THROUGH ACQUISITIONS

Although the company had undergone rapid growth (from nearly $5 million in revenues in 1995 to just over $21 million in 2003), WSI executives felt that they had maintained the organizational culture. These executives believed they had worked hard and had a vested interest in maintaining the organizational culture they helped create. Accomplishing this while pursuing an aggressive growth through acquisition strategy was considered risky by executives, but they were proud of their success thus far. Bruce Mahelish, president of WSI, explained his philosophy on maintaining the culture as follows: "We try to recruit strong agencies to bring into the WSI family. These agencies usually have highly qualified, experienced employees . . . the type that fit well in our culture and will also help us continue with our growth plans."

WSI's acquisition team included Mahelish; the chief financial officer, Craig Stahlberg; and usually one or two additional senior-level executives. Mahelish estimated that in total approximately two full-time equivalent (FTE) executives were currently being allocated to the acquisition process, but he commented, "We know that we'll need to increase the number of FTEs in the future because we're really stretched right now. I can't imagine increasing our growth rate much more without adding qualified members to our [acquisition] team."

Prospective new branch managers came under close scrutiny by the acquisition team and vice versa. Smaller agency managers typically sought long-term security for themselves and wanted to see their agency survive and thrive beyond their own work lives. WSI offered these managers economies of scale in purchasing and back-office functions, as well as advanced technologies and automation of many labor-intensive procedures. Existing WSI branch managers, in contrast, primarily needed to be assured that the high level of service and support to which they became accustomed would not degenerate as new branches were brought into the fold.

WSI's parent company, BCBS-MT, had its own unique needs with respect to the company's growth plans. BCBS-MT needed WSI to act as the point of its comprehensive strategy. The strategic plan was based on increasing WSI's customer base to the point where BCBS-MT could launch its own underwriting and reinsurance services. BCBS-MT executives believed that this would increase the company's stability and make it better prepared to face any further changes to the industry.

BCBS-MT also had to be concerned with the motives behind the investment bankers that were interested in facilitating the initial public offering (IPO) and accompanying process. Although WSI had a history of growth and a time-proven model of acquisition-fueled growth, the investment bankers needed WSI to be a significantly larger company before entering the IPO process in order for the offering to be attractive on the financial markets. One crucial aspect that investment bankers considered highly important was that WSI needed to establish a presence beyond its current geographic scope (i.e., Montana and Oregon).

WSI'S TARGET MARKET FOR ACQUISITIONS

The market that WSI targeted for acquisitions was small insurance agencies ($500,000 to $2 million) in the northwestern United States. These agencies were small relative to those found in other regional markets and were basing their decisions of whether to be acquired on what was best for them and their company. These agency owners were usually looking for a good exit strategy for their business. "Agency owners have often spent their whole life building up their business,

and it is very difficult to let go. To them, the most important thing is knowing that they are selling the business to a company that will take care of their employees. They need to know that they are leaving the agency in good hands. Of course they are also looking for a fair price for their business because they are often looking at using the money for their own retirement."

Some agency owners were not ready to exit the business right away, so it was very important to them that WSI could offer a smooth transition and still maintain the steady flow of business. Aside from the money, agency owners were looking for extra benefits that they could not get on their own, such as high-tech information systems and economies of scale.

The insurance industry in the United States, and more specifically the Northwest, was fairly fragmented but becoming increasingly consolidated. Medium-sized companies, like WSI, that were acquiring smaller companies, were now being acquired themselves by larger companies like Brown & Brown. In turn, companies the size of Brown & Brown were being acquired by industry leaders such as Aon.

There was an increasing number of large competitors in the Northwest. For example, in 2001, Brown & Brown, based in Tampa, Florida, acquired Raleigh Schwarz & Powell of Seattle, Washington. Raleigh Schwarz & Powell had about $170 million in premiums.[1] Most of the largest competitors that were acquiring agencies in the Northwest were not based in the region.

WHAT WSI OFFERED PROSPECTIVE AGENCY OWNERS

WSI executives felt that they offered value to prospective agency owners in two principal ways. First, WSI offered back-office support activities that it performed for the agency. These support activities involved functional support in areas such as human resources and information technology that smaller agencies often did not have the resources to perform on their own. Second, WSI offered formalized activities designed to support the individual agency's primary, front-office operations such as operations, marketing, and sales.

WSI was able to perform back-office functions on behalf of its agencies because of the economies of scale inherent in an organization of its size. The human resources support helped agencies attract and retain qualified producers and helped facilitate active employee participation in the WSI benefit programs. The types of programs included a generous employee referral program, producer scholarships, various employee education programs and e-access to human resources information by employees.

In the area of technology, WSI often brought a level of automation that a smaller independent agency could not easily achieve or afford on its own. This level of automation enhanced the productivity of an agency's employees and decreased the amount of time it took for a newly acquired agency to be integrated into the WSI family. In addition to a Web-based enrollment system for L&B producers and clients and innovative online training via WebEx, WSI was developing telecommunications solutions that were on the cutting edge of the telecom world. These included building the infrastructure for a Voice over Internet Protocol (VoIP) telecom system for use by distributed customer service centers and developing an e-accounting system for future use in regionalized accounting centers.

WSI was also able to offer its agencies support in their primary activities such as operations, marketing, and sales. Some of these activities existed behind the scenes in the work that the company did to instill the WSI culture into its agencies, the management of its computer network security, and the database-mining support functions that it performed. Other activities such as the formalized sales training program (called CRISP) and the cross-selling program (called Treble-Hook) served to enhance the profitability of the agency and the firm as a whole.

One last set of support functions that WSI performed on behalf of its agencies was its management of its carrier relationships. WSI was able to ensure that an agency could offer a wider range of carriers at more favorable rates than a smaller independent agency. Similarly, a WSI agency could offer its customers a greater variety of ancillary products, which enabled the agency to differentiate itself from its smaller competitors.

Executives noted that the value of these propositions to a given agency is inversely proportionate to the size of agency being considered. Smaller agencies possessed fewer of links in the value chain that WSI offered to them. They likely had no formalized sales or human resource programs and none of the technological automation features that made a WSI agency so efficient. WSI sold prospective agencies on the idea that they could derive competitive advantage by joining the WSI family. Mahelish noted, "The owners of these smaller agencies are typically less likely to 'shop' their agency to other potential buyers because of the time required for and costs associated with engaging in these activities." These agencies were thus easier to acquire relative to the acquisition of a larger agency that might possess the resources to shop their agency around.

Larger agencies, in contrast, already possessed many of the advantages that WSI had to offer. As such, they generally possessed the resources necessary to use information technology and human resource staff members to enhance the productivity of their employees. For these agencies, the prime motivating factor in an acquisition was cash. As such, these agencies were much more likely to "shop" their agency to several potential buyers, looking for the best overall monetary settlement. This dynamic made an acquisition of larger agencies more difficult, time-consuming, and expensive relative to the acquisition of a smaller agency. "The larger the agency," Mahelish commented, "the more difficult it is for us to get them interested in being acquired by us. The main reason is that we just don't have as much to offer them as we can offer to smaller agencies."

WSI'S COMPETITORS FOR ACQUISITIONS

WSI broke its competitors for acquisitions into two different groups: primary and secondary competitors. Primary competitors consisted of banks and other insurance agencies that competed in the western region of the United States. Banks presented serious concerns for WSI, as they were known to offer 3 to 3.5 times agency revenues for acquisitions, while WSI usually offered between 1.4 and 2 times agency revenues. According to Bruce Mahelish, "Banks have recently realized that they may be overpaying, and we expect them to lower their offering prices soon." When competing with banks for acquisitions, WSI tried to emphasize that it offered significant opportunities for improving the acquired agency, paid producers a much higher commission, and spent a great deal of time and effort courting potential acquisitions to make sure that it represented a strong fit with the organization that they were growing. Mahelish argued that "banks generally have little to offer because they do not understand the agency business. As a result, we think we are in a better position to offer the acquired agency much more than banks can."

A second source of primary competition for acquiring agencies was from other agencies that competedin the potential acquisition's market. WSI's acquisition team believed that this was due to the potential acquisition's desire to sell its business to someone it knew locally. "When we try to make acquisitions outside of our region," Mahelish commented, "we're really at a disadvantage and often end up very frustrated. We'll spend a significant amount of time courting an agency and even reach the stage where we place a deal in front of the owner. Then, the owner will often shop the offer with agencies in their market. If the local agency can come close to matching the bid that we've made, then they'll sign with the local [owner]. This is because we're seen as an unknown . . . as an outsider." As a result, members of WSI's acquisition team believed that they had to stress the technological and economies of scale advantages that WSI had to offer the potential acquisition—something that most local agencies could not offer.

Regardless of whether WSI faced competition from banks or local agencies, the company realized that this type of competition increased significantly as it went into markets outside of its current geographic area. Without brand recognition in a specific market and established trust-based relationships, many agency owners would consider WSI to be an outsider and might choose to sell to local banks or agencies.

In the search for possible acquisitions, WSI also recognized that it was increasingly facing competition from larger companies such as Aon, Marsh & McLennan, Brown & Brown, and Arthur Gallagher (competitors identified by WSI executive team). These competitors were billion-dollar companies that had a great deal of power in the insurance industry. For example, Aon and Marsh & McLennan reported $8.8 billion and $10.4 billion in sales for 2002, respectively. These companies completed acquisitions in the past that ranged from $1 million to billions of dollars. In 1997, Marsh & McLennan acquired Johnson & Higgins for $1.8 billion; and a year later became the largest insurance brokerage company when it acquired Sedgwick Group for $2.2 billion (see Exhibit 4).

Aon was an international company that made acquisitions worldwide. Competitors like Aon also had an advantage over smaller companies like WSI because they had their own in-house consulting divisions. Aon's consulting segment evaluated mergers and acquisitions for its customers.

The amount of competition WSI faced in acquiring agencies differed depending on the agency's size. If WSI wanted to acquire a $3 million (or larger) agency, it faced competition with larger, more powerful companies such Aon and Brown & Brown. In addition, the larger the agency was, the more complicated the acquisition became. Some larger prospective agencies already had many of the benefits WSI offered so they would be drawn to the extra benefits that companies like Aon possessed.

Larger prospective acquisition agencies were also more likely to hire lawyers and consultants that could impede or stop the acquisition process. Competitors such as Brown & Brown, with a large staff and acquisition team, were much better equipped to deal with these lawyers and consultants. Smaller agencies, worth $1 million or less, were not courted by the bigger competitors, especially if they were not the largest player in their market.

WSI'S ACQUISITION PROCESS

The acquisition process for WSI required a continuous effort throughout the year. More than 100 possible agencies were considered in a given year, with new agencies being added to the list as others were dropped. WSI narrowed the pool of 100 to approximately 10 agencies that seemed to have a good fit (see Exhibit 5). Of the 10, about 4 agencies prequalified and signed confidentiality agreements. Once WSI selected its first choice, it assessed the fit of the company and started preliminary discussions.

Conducting due diligence, the next step in the the process, usually took six months. It often took longer because some agencies did not share financials until later in the process. If the evaluation went well, WSI started financial negotiations with the agency. After the initial deal was made, it went to the WSI and CBIC boards for approval. This process could take three to four months, depending on whether the deal needed to be renegotiated. After an announcement was made, the companies closed the deal and moved on to the orientation and integration processes. The entire process to this point took approximately two years.

The orientation/integration process took anywhere from two to eight years, depending on the agency involved. After the deal was closed, operational integration began with an immediate office visitation, welcoming employees to the fold. Automation

Exhibit 4   **WSI's Secondary Competitors for Acquisitions**

Aon	Marsh & McLennan	Brown & Brown Inc.	Arthur Gallagher
Second largest insurance brokerage company in the industry	Largest insurance brokerage company in the industry		
Business Segments • Commercial brokerage • Consulting service • Consumer insurance • Underwriting	**Business Segments** • Reinsurance (Guy Carpenter) • Insurance • Program/management services (Seabury & Smith) • Insurance industry investment and advisory services (Seabury & Smith) • Human resources and management consulting (Mercer Consulting)	**Business Segments** • Insurance agency • Brokerage firm	**Business Segments** • Insurance brokerage and risk management
2002 sales: $8,822 million	2002 sales: $10,440 million	2002 sales: $455.7 million	2002 sales: $1,052 million
2002 net income: $466 million	2002 net income: $1,365 million	2002 net income: $83.1 million	2002 net income: $1,052 million
2002 employees: 55,000	2002 employees: 59,500	2002 employees: 3,384	2002 employees: 7,100
Acquisitions • Acquires companies worldwide • Consults for other companies doing acquisitions	**Acquisitions** • In 1997 acquired Johnson & Higgins for $1.8 billion in cash and stocks • In 1998 acquired UK broker Sedwick Group for $2.2 billion	**Acquisition** • The purchase of Schwarz & Powell, a company with a premium volume of $170 million	

was usually the step that took the longest because of producer/employee resistance to the new learning curve. One of the final steps was the orientation of branch managers. These training sessions spanned from 6 to 12 months. Finally, trainers were sent to the new branch to teach employees proper work flows and establish a sales culture and focus that was in line with WSI's sales.

PARAMETERS FOR WSI'S STRATEGIC ALTERNATIVES

Between March and April, Ed Kirby gathered a vast amount of data regarding the parameters for the alternatives WSI was exploring. Most of the

parameters were consistent with Kirby's experience and research, but others required much more thought. The first parameter was in regard to the revenue benchmark that WSI needed to reach before going public through the initial public offering (IPO) process. In Kirby's initial meeting with Dennis Toussaint, the revenue benchmark for WSI was set at $100 million. However, a second benchmark of $50 million for WSI plus the acquisition of a similar-sized agency that could reach $50 million was added to Kirby's project a few weeks later, after senior executives discussed alternative methods to reach the $100 million target. WSI executives had already developed a plan to reach $50 million in revenue by penetrating a number of new markets.

Exhibit 5   **WSI's Acquisition Process**

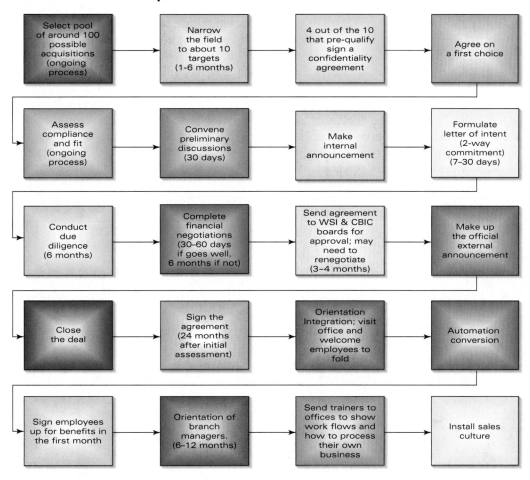

In mid-April, a third revenue target was added. The latest revenue target was reached after Terry Cosgrove, Sherry Cladouhos, Wayne Knutson, Dennis Toussaint, and Peter Babin (all senior executives with BCBS-MT)visited with investment bankers in New York City. In their discussions the investment bankers suggested that the benchmark be raised to $250 million. As a result, Kirby now had three alternatives to consider in his study:

1. Expand WSI to $50 million in revenues while simultaneously acquiring a similar-sized agency and expanding it to $50 million.

2. Expand WSI to $100 million in revenues.

3. Expand WSI to $250 million in revenues.

The second parameter that required more thought was that BCBS-MT indicated that it wanted WSI to complete the IPO in five years. That meant that the

IPO would have to be completed by 2007. WSI had completed 11 acquisitions in the past eight years and would have to increase the number of acquisitions per year considerably if the company was to reach the target revenue level by 2007. Kirby was told to use $1 million as the average for each acquired agency in his forecasting to determine the number of acquisitions per year to reach the target. Based on the time frame and the average sales of acquired firms, Kirby wondered whether it was reasonable for the company to complete the number of acquisitions needed.

Kirby's initial research concluded that the time frame that the company had to reach the target revenue level needed to be considered. The IPO process takes a minimum of six months, and can take up to two years or more. Therefore, the time horizon for reaching the revenue target was actually between

3 and 4.5 years. Since it was already nearing the midyear mark of 2003, Kirby needed to take an additional six months off the time frame. This left WSI with 2.5 to 4 years as the window in which the firm had to reach the revenue target. Thus, Kirby felt that WSI would need to be at or above its revenue target by the end of 2005.

During the time frame specified, WSI also had to realize constraints regarding the time it takes to complete each individual acquisition. As discussed earlier, it takes WSI approximately two years from the time an agency is identified as a potential match to the time that the acquisition actually closes. Thus, in order for WSI to complete the acquisitions necessary for 2004, it would have needed to begin the acquisition process in 2002 for those specific agencies. Kirby wondered whether the company was far enough along in the process to make the acquisitions necessary in 2004.

A third parameter that had not been discussed by the executives at BCBS-MT or WSI concerned

the population of agencies that were attractive acquisition targets. In order to increase the chance that integration of acquired agencies was successful, WSI needed to consider the product mix, market position, market size and potential, and possible cultural match of its pool of acquisition targets. These characteristics limited the number of agencies that could be seriously considered. Currently WSI develops a pool of approximately 100 potential acquisition targets and narrows it down to a field of four for closer evaluation. From the group of four, one is selected. Kirby felt that WSI needed to recognize the fact that there were a discrete number of attractive acquisition targets in the region in which it operated.

WSI'S FINANCIALS

Craig Stahlberg, WSI's chief financial officer, provided Kirby with the company's audited financial statements from 1998 to 2002 (Exhibits 6 and 7).

Exhibit 6   **WSI's Historical Consolidated Income Statements, 1998–2002 and Pro Forma for 2003**

	1998	1999	2000	2001	2002	2003 (est.)
Number of agencies	13	13	13	15	17	20
Net revenues	$ 9,509,906	$11,347,194	$12,369,457	$16,491,614	$21,279,562	$26,103,744
Total compensation	6,127,002	6,959,641	7,827,001	10,185,876	12,975,053	16,281,794
Selling & administrative expenses	443,060	477,298	461,534	539,551	804,340	940,834
Total operating expenses	1,546,879	1,656,656	1,771,101	2,055,184	2,525,016	3,583,618
EBITDA	$ 1,392,965	$ 2,253,599	$ 2,309,821	$ 3,711,002	$ 4,975,153	$ 5,297,498
Depreciation and amortization	629,544	633,000	644,123	649,852	653,165	717,876
EBIT (operating profits)	$ 763,421	$ 1,620,599	$ 1,665,698	$ 3,061,150	$ 4,321,988	$ 4,579,622
Other expenses	1,634,951	1,986,126	1,113,997	1,326,703	1,763,023	1,897,925
EBT	$ (871,530)	$ (365,527)	$ 551,700	$ 1,734,447	$ 3,212,130	$ 3,399,573
Income tax expense	283,962	213,000	(387,000)	(755,106)	(1,279,531)	(1,353,886)
Net profit	$ (587,568)	$ (152,527)	$ 164,700	$ 979,341	$ 1,932,599	$ 2,045,686

*As of March 2003 WSI had acquired one new agency (Corvallis, Oregon) but predicted that it would complete two additional acquisitions by year-end. The 2003 figures represent management's projections and reflect the completion of three acquisitions in the year.

Exhibit 7 **WSI's Historical Consolidated Balance Sheets 1998–2002 and Pro Forma for 2003**

Assets	1998	1999	2000	2001	2002	2003 (est.)
Current assets						
Cash and cash equivalents	$ 658,748	$ 416,507	$ 405,884	$ 956,081	$ 2,692,121	$ 6,144,638
Accounts receivable	2,242,934	2,382,911	2,535,739	3,298,323	3,773,361	5,054,617
Other current assets	235,867	226,944	247,389	329,832	390,947	408,003
Total current assets	$3,137,549	$ 3,026,362	$ 3,189,012	$ 4,584,236	$ 6,856,429	$11,607,258
Property plant and equipment, net	2,182,383	2,496,383	2,721,281	3,628,155	4,834,458	5,813,209
Other assets	4,190,425	4,879,293	5,318,867	7,091,394	9,281,567	10,926,783
Total assets	$9,510,357	$10,402,038	$11,229,159	$15,303,785	$20,972,454	$28,347,250
Liabilities and stockholders' equity						
Current liabilities						
Accounts payable	$1,886,383	$2,609,855	$2,844,975	$3,628,155	$ 4,963,052	$ 6,053,563
Current maturities long-term debt	712,647	737,568	804,015	659,665	933,562	967,270
Operating line of credit	150,000	—	—	—	—	—
Deferred compensation	189,902	113,472	123,695	82,458	34,545	25,045
Taxes payable	272,749	567,360	680,320	907,039	1,291,083	1,542,029
Total current liabilities	$3,211,681	$4,028,254	$4,453,005	$5,277,316	$ 7,222,242	$ 8,587,907
Long-term debt	2,994,680	2,450,000	2,253,720	2,628,516	2,974,360	3,752,902
Other	1,386,891	1,531,871	1,608,029	2,061,452	2,570,470	3,906,919
Total liabilities	$7,593,252	$8,010,125	$8,314,754	$9,967,284	$12,767,072	$16,247,728
Stockholders' equity						
Common stock	566,269	566,269	566,269	566,269	566,269	566,269
Additional paid-in capital	3,344,183	3,971,518	4,329,310	5,772,065	7,169,183	8,339,183
Treasury stock	(1,431,105)	(1,431,105)	(1,431,105)	(1,431,105)	(1,431,105)	(1,431,105)
Retained earnings	(562,242)	(714,769)	(550,068)	429,273	2,361,872	4,407,558
Accumulated other comprehensive income (loss)	—	—	—	—	(460,837)	217,617
Total shareholders' equity	$1,917,105	$ 2,391,913	$ 2,914,406	$ 5,336,501	$ 8,205,382	$ 12,099,522
Total liabilities and equity	$9,510,357	$10,402,038	$11,229,159	$15,303,785	$20,972,454	$ 28,347,250

Over the four-year period WSI acquired four additional agencies and revenues grew from $9.5 million in 1995 to more than $21 million in 2002. The company's profits had also grown from a net loss of $587,568 in 1998 to profits of more than $1.9 million in 2002. Stahlberg also provided Kirby with pro forma statements for 2003 reflecting management's estimates for the remainder of the year. The projections for 2003 included the acquisition of three additional agencies, one of which was completed and two of which were in process. The pro forma statements estimated revenues of more than $27 million and profits of more than $2 million in 2003. Stahlberg estimated that *organic* growth for existing agencies ranged between 7 and 10 percent. Additional growth during the period from 1998 to 2002 was attributed to its recent acquisitions, increasing the number of locations from 13 to 17, and sales, including organic growth, from $9.5 million to $21 million.

Kirby collected some current performance ratios for WSI's primary competitors and the industry as a whole (see Exhibit 8). He planned to evaluate WSI's performance relative to the performance of its

peers, especially those it was competing against in the acquisition market.

As he prepared to perform his analysis, Kirby remembered that Toussaint had indicated that Kirby's financial analysis should assume that the average revenue for acquired agencies would be $1 million and that WSI would pay 1.4 times revenue for each acquisition. Thirty-three percent of the price would be paid in cash, with the remaining 67 percent coming from a seven-year loan with a 7 percent interest rate. WSI provided Kirby with forecasted revenues for existing locations that included organic growth (see Exhibit 9) and suggested that organic growth for new acquisitions would be 15 percent for the first year after acquisition, 10 percent for the second and third years, and 8 percent for the fourth year and beyond. WSI expected to complete one more acquisition in the remainder of 2003, and all other components of the income statement were expected to remain constant as a percentage of revenues. WSI executives believed that they could generate $10 million in cash internally, and BCBS-MT had already committed a minimum of $5 million to foster acquisitions during the next five years.

Exhibit 8 **Western States Insurance Peer Performance Ratios, 2002**

	Marsh & McLennan	Aon	Brown & Brown	Arthur Gallagher	Peer Average	Industry Average
Profit margin	−0.97%	5.79%	19.82%	5.10%	7.44%	4.27%
Asset turnover	0.72	0.36	0.58	0.47	0.52	0.48
Return on assets (ROA)	−0.70%	2.11%	11.58%	2.42%	3.85%	2.05%
Equity multiplier	3.64	5.64	1.95	4.43	3.92	2.92
Return on equity (ROE)	−2.55%	11.91%	22.59%	10.73%	10.67%	5.99%
Dividend payout ratio	0.00%	32.99%	15.28%	124.10%	43.09%	27.36%
Internal growth rate	−0.70%	1.43%	10.88%	−0.58%	2.24%	1.51%
Sustainable growth rate	−2.49%	8.67%	23.67%	−2.52%	6.46%	4.55%
P/E ratio (TTM)	NM	14.16	23.71	34.73	24.20	20.60
Price to sales (TTM)	1.26	0.82	4.7	1.72	2.41	1.56
Price to book (MRQ)	3.01	1.62	4.82	3.71	3.38	2.85

KIRBY PREPARES THE REPORT

By the middle of May 2003, Kirby had gone through the volumes of information provided by WSI and BCBS-MT and additional information gathered from a variety of resources. Now Kirby had to organize the information into a cohesive report that analyzed the three strategic alternatives presented to him. He realized that he faced a challenging situation. On the one hand, his report might show that the company was poised for reaching the revenue targets; on the other hand, his report might have to tell the executives something they didn't want to hear.

Exhibit 9 **WSI Forecasted Revenues by Existing Agency Location**

	2003	2004	2005	2006	2007
Kalispell	$ 2,721,600	$ 2,939,328	$ 3,174,474	$ 3,428,432	$ 3,702,707
Helena	3,043,691	3,287,186	3,550,161	3,834,174	4,140,908
Great Falls	1,764,000	1,905,120	2,057,530	2,222,132	2,399,903
McMinnville	1,254,400	1,354,752	1,463,132	1,580,183	1,706,597
Stevensville	892,600	981,860	1,060,409	1,145,242	1,236,861
Cottage Grove	931,000	1,024,100	1,126,510	1,216,631	1,313,961
Ashland	579,000	636,900	700,590	756,637	817,168
Corvallis	1,488,218	1,711,451	1,882,596	2,070,855	2,236,524
Hamilton	703,000	759,240	819,979	885,578	956,424
Polson	747,600	807,408	872,001	941,761	1,017,102
Bozeman	1,451,000	1,567,080	1,692,446	1,827,842	1,974,069
Big Fork	962,190	1,039,165	1,122,298	1,212,082	1,309,049
Butte	502,445	542,641	586,052	632,936	683,571
Billings	2,801,000	3,025,080	3,267,086	3,528,453	3,810,730
Missoula	3,789,000	4,092,120	4,419,490	4,773,049	5,154,893
Dillon	453,500	489,780	528,962	571,279	616,982
Corporate	2,019,500	2,181,060	2,355,545	2,543,988	2,747,507
Total from existing locations	$26,103,744	$28,344,271	$30,679,261	$33,171,254	$35,824,954

Endnotes

[1] http://seattle.bizjournals.com/seattle/stories/2001/07/02/daily8.html.

eBay: Facing the Challenge of Global Growth

Louis Marino
The University of Alabama

Patrick Kreiser
Ohio University

At the beginning of 2006, the eBay name was synonymous with the online auction industry. The company had been the dominant player in the online auction industry since its inception in 1995. On September 20, 2000, eBay surprised the financial community and announced ambitious growth objectives including yearly revenue of $3 billion by year-end 2005. Given that the company's annual sales at the time were only $400 million, the $3 billion goal would require annualized growth of 50 percent from the end of 2000 to 2005, an objective that some analysts criticized as being too aggressive. However, the company was able to meet those ambitious goals—a year early! The company's 2004 revenues were over $3.2 billion, and its expected revenues for 2005 were well over $4 billion. By most any account, eBay's record of financial and competitive success had been rather impressive (see Exhibit 1).

Building on the vision of its founder, Pierre Omidyar (pronounced oh-*mid*-ee-ar), eBay was initially conceived as a marketplace that would facilitate a person-to-person trading community based on a democratized, efficient market in which everyone could have equal access through the same medium, the Internet. Leveraging a unique business model and the growing popularity of the Internet, eBay has dominated the market since its beginning, growing to include over 168 million registered users heading into 2006. This diverse base of registered users ranged from high school and college students looking to make a few extra dollars, to Fortune 500 companies such as IBM selling excess inventory, to large

government agencies like the U.S. Postal Service selling undeliverable parcels. This differed greatly from the individuals and small companies from the United States that comprised eBay's original user base.

However, eBay's continued growth was unable to completely mask several emerging threats the company needed to address. In recognition of these challenges, Standard & Poor's had classified eBay as a "hold" stock throughout all of 2005, citing potential domestic market saturation and concern over the pace and size of the company's recent acquisitions. Why was a company that had been so financially successful, and that had been number one in terms of market share in its industry for the past decade, drawing the concern of investors? Two main issues were primarily responsible: (1) increased competition and market saturation facing eBay's domestic business, and (2) concerns over eBay's ability to compete successfully over the long term in global markets. The company readily acknowledged that it saw both of these issues as significant threats. In regard to domestic competition, eBay noted the relative lack of entry barriers into the industry and expected "competition to intensify in the future."[1] The company also acknowledged its potential difficulties in competing globally, citing its lack of experience in adapting its service to local customs, the large amount of resources required to compete globally, and the existence of established competitors in many foreign markets.[2] The company claimed that "even if we are successful, we expect the costs of operating new sites to exceed our net revenues for at least 12 months in most countries."[3] In fact, eBay had to discontinue its operations in the Japanese market in

Exhibit 1   **Selected Indicators of eBay's Growth, 1996–2005 (in millions)**

	1996	1997	1998	1999	2000	2001	2002	2003	2004	2005
Number of registered users	.041	.341	2.2	10.0	22.0	42.4	61.7	94.9	135.5	168.1
Active users	NA	NA	NA	NA	NA	18.0	27.7	41.2	56.1	68.0
Gross merchandise sales	$7	$95	$745	$2,800	$5,400	$9,300	$14,900	$24,000	$34,200	$43,067*
Number of auctions listed	0.29	4.4	33.7	129	264	423	638	971	1,412.6	1,774*

*The gross merchandise sales and number of auctions listed for 2005 are projections based on eBay estimates and on third-quarter actual results.

2002 due to rising costs and a lack of profits. Yet if the company was going to continue to experience the same levels of financial success it had enjoyed during its first 10 years of operation, it needed to develop strategies that would allow it to negate both of these potential threats.

THE GROWTH OF E-COMMERCE AND ONLINE AUCTIONS

The concepts underlying the Internet were first conceived in the 1960s, but it wasn't until the 1990s that the Internet garnered widespread use and became a part of everyday life. International Data Corporation (IDC) estimated that in 2004 there were approximately 700 million Internet users worldwide in over 150 countries, and it estimated that number would grow to 1.1 billion users worldwide by 2007, with a compound annual growth rate of 12 percent. While the top 15 countries accounted for more than 70 percent of the computers in use, slightly less than one-fourth of these Internet users (160 million) resided in the United States, whose share as a percentage of total Internet users worldwide was falling. In the United States, 87 percent of households were expected to have Internet access in 2009, and the number of households with a broadband connection was expected to be 60 percent at that time. However, the highest areas of Internet usage growth were expected to be in developing countries, where Internet penetration was currently low, such as Asia, Latin America, and Eastern Europe due to increasing access through new technologies such as Web-enabled cell phones.

IDC predicted that the worldwide market for business-to-consumer Internet spending would increase from $216.2 billion in 2003 to $759.4 billion in 2007. Forrester Research forecasted a similar increase in the online auction market, from $13 billion in revenues in 2002 to $54 billion in revenues in 2007. North America accounted for approximately 50 percent of total e-commerce sales in 2004, with the Asia-Pacific region accounting for approximately 25 percent, Western Europe accounting for approximately 20 percent, and Latin America accounting for over 10 percent of total sales. Within the business-to-consumer segment, where eBay primarily operated, U.S. e-commerce accounted for over 65 percent of all Internet transactions in 1999 but accounted for less than 40 percent in 2003 and potentially less in the future, due to rapid expansion in other parts of the world. Asia was expected to grow especially rapidly with the 2001 decision to include China in the World Trade Organization. According to IDC in 2005, the Asia-Pacific region (excluding Japan) was expected to experience a strong annual growth rate of 25 percent for Internet devices, 19 percent for online users, and 46 percent for Internet buyers. European markets were also expected to experience rapid growth in 2006 and beyond. In 2002, Germany, the United Kingdom, France, and Italy accounted for 70 percent of the e-commerce revenues in Western Europe, but this share was expected to decline as business-to-business e-commerce in Europe was expected to triple from 2003 to 2006.

KEY SUCCESS FACTORS IN ONLINE RETAILING

While it was relatively easy to create a Web site that functioned like a retail store, the more significant challenge was for an online retailer to generate traffic to the site in the form of both new and returning customers. To reach new customers, some online retailers partnered with shopping search engines (such as Google, MySimon, or StreetPrices) that allowed customers to compare prices for a given product from many retailers. Other tactics employed to build traffic included direct e-mail, online advertising at portals and content-related sites, and some traditional advertising such as print and television advertising. Once customers found their way to a site, most online retailers endeavored to provide extensive product information, include pictures of the merchandise, make the site easily navigable, and have enough new things happening at the site to keep them coming back. (A site's ability to generate repeat visitors was known as "stickiness.") Retailers also had to overcome new users' nervousness about using the Internet itself to shop for items they generally bought in stores. Web sites had to appease concerns about sending credit card numbers over the Internet and the possible sale of personal information to marketing firms. Online retailing had severe limitations in the case of those goods and services people wanted to see in person to verify their quality. From the retailer's perspective, there was the issue of collecting payment from buyers who wanted to use checks or money orders instead of credit cards.

ONLINE AUCTIONS

The first known auctions were held in Babylon around 500 BC. In AD 193, the entire Roman Empire was put up for auction after the emperor Pertinax was executed. Didius Julianus bid 6,250 drachmas per royal guard and was immediately named emperor of Rome. However, Julianus was executed only two months later, suggesting that he may have been the first-ever victim of the winner's curse (bidding more than the good would cost in a nonauction setting).

Auctions have endured throughout history for several reasons. First, they give sellers a convenient way to find a buyer for something they would like to dispose of. Second, auctions are an excellent way for people to collect difficult-to-find items, such as Beanie Babies or historical memorabilia that have a high value to them personally. Finally, auctions are one of the "purest" markets that exist for goods, in that they bring buyers and sellers into contact to arrive at a mutually agreeable price. As technological advances led to the advent and widespread adoption of the Internet, this ancient form of trade found a new medium.

Online auctions worked in essentially the same way as traditional auctions, the difference being that the auction process occurred over the Internet rather than at a specific geographic location with buyers and sellers physically present. There were three basic categories of online auctions:

1. Business-to-business auctions, typically involving equipment and surplus merchandise.
2. Business-to-consumer auctions, in which businesses sold goods and services to consumers via the Internet. Many such auctions involved companies interested in selling used or discontinued goods, or liquidating unwanted inventory.
3. Person-to-person auctions, which gave interested sellers and buyers the opportunity to engage in competitive bidding.

Online auction operators could generate revenue in four principal ways:

1. Charging sellers for listing their good or service.
2. Charging a commission on all sales.
3. Selling advertising on their Web sites.
4. Selling their own new or used merchandise via the online auction format.

More recently, however, online auction sites had also added a new revenue-generation option:

5. Selling their own goods or allowing other sellers to offer their goods in a fixed-price format.

Most sites charged sellers either a fee or a commission and sold advertising to companies interested in promoting their goods or services to users of the auction site.

Online Auction Users

Participants in online auctions could be grouped into six categories: (1) bargain hunters, (2) hobbyists and collectors, (3) professional buyers, (4) casual sellers, (5) hobbyist and collector sellers and (6) corporate and power sellers.

Bargain Hunters   Bargain hunters viewed on-line auctions primarily as a form of entertainment; their objective usually was to find a great deal. Bargain hunters were thought to make up only 8 percent of active online users but 52 percent of eBay visitors. To attract repeat visits from bargain hunters, industry observers said, sites must appeal to them on both rational and emotional levels, satisfying their need for competitive pricing, the excitement of the search, and the desire for community.

Hobbyists and Collectors   Hobbyists and collectors used auctions to search for specific goods that had a high value to them personally. They were very concerned with both price and quality. Collectors prized eBay for its wide variety of product offerings.

Professional Buyers   As the legitimacy of on-line auctions grew, a new type of buyer began to emerge: the professional buyer. Professional buyers covered a broad range of purchasers ranging from purchasing managers acquiring office supplies to antique and gun dealers purchasing inventory. Like bargain hunters, professional buyers were looking for a way to help contain costs; and, like hobbyists and collectors, some professional buyers were seeking unique items to supplement their inventory. The primary difference between professional buyers and other types, however, was their affiliation with commercial enterprises. With the growth of online auction sites dedicated to business-to-business auctions, professional buyers were becoming an increasingly important element of the online auction landscape.

Casual Sellers   Casual sellers included individuals who used eBay as a substitute for a classified ad listing or a garage sale to dispose of items they no longer wanted. While many casual sellers listed only a few items, some used eBay to raise money for a specific project or other undertaking.

Hobbyist and Collector Sellers   Sellers who were hobbyists or collectors typically dealt in a limited category of goods and looked to eBay as a way to sell selected items in their collections to others who might want them. Items ranged from classic television collectibles, to hand-sewn dolls, to coins and stamps. The hobbyists and collectors used a range of traditional and online outlets to reach their target markets. A number of the sellers used auctions to supplement their retail operations, while others sold exclusively through online auctions and in fixed-price formats such as Half.com.

Power and Corporate Sellers   Power sellers were typically small to medium-sized businesses that favored eBay as a primary distribution channel and often sold tens of thousands of dollars' worth of goods every month on the site. One estimate suggested that while these power sellers accounted for only 4 percent of eBay's population, they were responsible for 80 percent of eBay's total business.[4] Individuals who were power sellers could often make a full-time job of the endeavor.

As with the evolution of buyers, commercial enterprises were becoming an increasingly important part of the online auction industry. These commercial enterprises generally achieved power-seller status relatively rapidly. On eBay, for example, some of the new power sellers were familiar names such as IBM, Compaq, and the U.S. Postal Service (which sells undeliverable items on eBay under the user name usps-mrc).

PIERRE OMIDYAR AND THE FOUNDING OF eBAY

Pierre Omidyar was born in Paris, France, to parents who had left Iran decades earlier. The family emigrated to the United States when Pierre's father began a residency at Johns Hopkins University Medical Center. Pierre attended Tufts University, where he met his future wife, Pamela Wesley, who came to Tufts from Hawaii to get a degree in biology. Upon graduating in 1988, the couple moved to California, where Pierre, who had earned a bachelor's degree in computer science, joined Claris, an Apple Computer subsidiary in Silicon Valley, and wrote a widely used graphics application, MacDraw. In 1991, Omidyar left Claris and cofounded Ink Development (later renamed eShop), which became a pioneer in online shopping and was eventually sold to Microsoft in 1996. In 1994,

Omidyar joined General Magic as a developer services engineer and remained there until mid-1996, when he left to pursue full-time development of eBay.

Internet folklore has it that eBay was founded solely to allow Pamela to trade Pez dispensers with other collectors. While Pamela was certainly a driving force in launching the initial Web site, Pierre had long been interested in how one could establish a marketplace to bring together a fragmented market. Pierre saw eBay as a way to create a person-to-person trading community based on a democratized, efficient market where everyone could have equal access through the same medium, the Internet. Pierre set out to develop his marketplace and to meet both his and Pamela's goals. In 1995 he launched the first online auction under the name of Auctionwatch at the domain name of www.eBay.com. The name eBay stood for "electronic Bay area," coined because Pierre's initial concept was to attract neighbors and other interested San Francisco Bay area residents to the site to buy and sell items of mutual interest. The first auctions charged no fees to either buyers or sellers and contained mostly computer equipment (and no Pez dispensers). Pierre's fledgling venture generated $1,000 in revenue the first month and an additional $2,000 the second. Traffic grew rapidly, however, as word about the site spread in the Bay area, and a community of collectors emerged, using the site to trade and chat—there were even some marriages that resulted from exchanges in eBay chat rooms.[5]

By February 1996, the traffic at Pierre Omidyar's site had grown so much that his Internet service provider informed him that he would have to upgrade his service. When Omidyar compensated for this by charging a listing fee for the auction, and saw no decrease in the number of items listed, he knew he was on to something. Although he was still working out of his home, Omidyar began looking for a partner and in May asked his friend Jeffrey Skoll to join him in the venture. While Skoll had never cared much about money, his Stanford MBA degree provided the firm with the business background that Omidyar lacked. With Omidyar as the visionary and Skoll as the strategist, the company embarked on a mission to "help people trade practically anything on earth."

Their concept for eBay was to "create a place where people could do business just like in the old days—when everyone got to know each other personally, and we all felt we were dealing on a one-to-one basis with individuals we could trust."

In eBay's early days, Omidyar and Skoll ran the operation alone, using a single computer to serve all of the pages. Omidyar served as CEO, chief financial officer, and president, while Skoll functioned as co-president and director. It was not long until Omidyar and Skoll grew the company to a size that forced them to move out of the Omidyars' living room, due to the objections of Pamela, and into Skoll's living room. Shortly thereafter, the operations moved into the facilities of a Silicon Valley business incubator for a time until the company settled in its current facilities in San Jose, California. Exhibits 2 and 3 present eBay's recent financial statements.

eBAY'S TRANSITION TO PROFESSIONAL MANAGEMENT

From the beginning, Pierre Omidyar intended to hire a professional manager to serve as the president of eBay: "[I would] let him or her run the company so . . . [I could] go play."[6] In 1997, both Omidyar and Skoll agreed that it was time to locate an experienced professional to function as CEO and president. In late 1997, eBay's headhunters came up with a candidate for the job: Margaret Whitman, then general manager for Hasbro Inc.'s preschool division. Whitman had received her bachelor of arts degree in economics from Princeton and her master of business administration from the Harvard Business School; her first job was in brand management at Procter & Gamble. Her experience also included serving as the president and CEO of FTD, the president of Stride Rite Corporation's Stride Rite Division, and as the senior vice president of marketing for the Walt Disney Company's consumer products division.

When first approached by eBay, Whitman was not especially interested in joining a company that had fewer than 40 employees and less than $6 million in revenues the previous year. It was only after repeated pleas that Whitman agreed to meet with Omidyar in Silicon Valley. After a second meeting, Whitman realized the company's enormous growth potential and agreed to give eBay a try. According to Omidyar, Meg Whitman's experience in global marketing with Hasbro's Teletubbies, Playskool, and Mr. Potato Head brands made her "the ideal choice to build upon eBay's leadership position in the

Exhibit 2   **eBay's Income Statements, 2000–2005 (in thousands of $, except per share figures)**

	2000	2001	2002	2003	2004	First Nine Months of 2005
Net revenues	$431,424	$748,821	$1,214,100	$2,165,096	$3,271,309	$3,223,542
Cost of net revenues	95,453	134,816	213,876	416,058	614,415	578,584
Gross profit	$335,971	$614,005	$1,000,224	$1,749,038	$2,656,894	$2,644,958
Operating expenses:						
Sales and marketing	166,767	253,474	349,650	567,565	857,874	852,239
Product development	55,863	75,288	104,636	159,315	240,647	224,309
General and administrative	73,027	105,784	171,785	304,703	415,725	410,016
Patent litigation expense				29,965		
Payroll taxes on stock options	2,337	2,442	4,015	9,590	17,479	9,582
Amortization of acquired intangibles	1,443	36,591	15,941	50,659	65,927	77,516
Merger-related costs	1,550	0	0	0	0	0
Total operating expenses	$300,977	$473,579	$ 646,027	$1,119,797	$1,597,652	$1,573,662
Income (loss) from operations	$ 34,994	$140,426	$ 354,197	$ 629,241	$1,059,242	$1,071,296
Interest and other income (expense), net	46,337	41,613	49,209	37,803	77,867	85,585
Interest expense	−3,374	−2,851	−1,492	−4,314	−8,879	−2,556
Impairment of certain equity investments	0	−16,245	−3,781	−1,230	0	0
Income before income taxes and minority interest	$ 77,957	$162,943	$ 398,133	$ 661,500	$1,128,230	$1,154,325
Provision for income taxes	−32,725	−80,009	−145,946	−206,738	−343,885	−351,455
Minority interests in consolidated companies	3,062	7,514	−2,296	−7,578	−6,122	−48
Net income	$ 48,294	$ 90,448	$ 249,891	$ 447,184	$ 778,223	$ 802,822
Net income per share:						
Basic	$0.19	$0.34	$0.43	$0.69	$0.59	$0.59
Diluted	0.17	0.32	0.43	0.67	0.57	0.58
Weighted average shares:						
Basic	251,776	268,971	574,992	638,288	1,319,458	1,350,836
Diluted	280,346	280,595	585,640	656,657	1,367,720	1,383,024

Source: Company financial documents.

one-to-one online trading market without sacrificing the quality and personal touch our users have grown to expect."[7] In addition to convincing Whitman to head eBay's operations, Omidyar had been instrumental in helping bring in other talented senior executives and in assembling a capable board of directors. Notable members of eBay's board of directors included Scott Cook, the founder of Intuit, a highly successful financial software company, and

Fred D. Anderson, executive vice president and chief financial officer of Apple.

HOW AN eBAY AUCTION WORKED

eBay endeavored to make it very simple to buy and sell goods. In order to sell or bid on goods, users first

Exhibit 3   **eBay's Consolidated Balance Sheets, 2000–2005 (in thousands of $)**

	Period Ending					
	12/31/00	12/31/01	12/31/02	12/31/03	12/31/04	9/30/05
Assets						
Current assets:						
Cash and cash equivalents	$ 201,873	$ 523,969	$1,109,313	$1,381,513	$1,330,045	$2,180,598
Short-term investments	354,166	199,450	89,690	340,576	682,004	888,783
Accounts receivable, net	67,163	101,703	131,453	225,871	240,856	274,238
Funds receivable	—	—	41,014	79,893	123,424	210,593
Other current assets	52,262	58,683	96,988	118,029	534,820	436,781
Total current assets	$ 675,464	$ 883,805	$1,468,458	$2,145,882	$2,911,149	$3,990,993
Long-term investments		286,998	470,227	934,171	1,266,289	827,191
Restricted cash and investments		129,614	134,644	127,432	1,418	—
Property and equipment, net	125,161	142,349	218,028	601,785	709,773	762,413
Goodwill		187,829	1,456,024	1,719,311	2,709,794	3,529,895
Investments	—	—	—	—	—	—
Deferred tax assets	—	21,540	84,218	—	—	—
Intangible and other assets, net	23,299	26,394	292,845	291553	392,628	515,551
Total assets	$1,182,403	$1,678,529	$4,040,226	$5,820,134	$7,991,051	$9,626,043
Liabilities and Stockholders' equity						
Current liabilities:						
Accounts payable	$ 31,725	$ 33,235	$ 47,424	$ 64,633	$ 37,958	$ 42,726
Funds payable and amounts due to customers	—	—	50,396	106,568	331,805	517,309
Accrued expenses and other current liabilities	60,882	94,593	199,323	356,491	421,969	523,584
Deferred revenue and customer advances	12,656	15,583	18,846	28,874	50,439	44,222
Debt and leases, current portion	15,272	16,111	2,970	2,840	124,272	—
Income taxes payable	11,092	20,617	67,265	87,870	118,427	138,951
Deferred tax liabilities, current	—	—	—	—	—	—
Other current liabilities	5,815	—	—	—	—	—
Total current liabilities	$ 137,442	$ 180,139	$ 386,224	$ 647,276	$1,084,870	$1,266,792
Debt and leases, long-term portion	11,404	12,008	13,798	124,476	75	—
Deferred tax liabilities, long-term	—	3,629	27,625	79,238	135,971	298,197
Other liabilities	6,549	15,864	22,874	33,494	37,698	33,690
Minority interests	—	37,751	33,232	39,408	4,096	—
Total liabilities	$ 168,643	$ 249,391	$ 483,753	$ 923,892	$1,262,710	$1,598,679
Series B redeemable convertible preferred stock and Series B warrants	—	—	—	—	—	—
	1,013,760	1,429,138	3,556,473	4,896,242	6,728,341	8,027,364
Total stockholders' equity	$1,182,403	$1,678,529	$4,124,444	$5,820,134	$7,991,051	$9,626,043

Source: Company financial documents.

had to register at the site. Once they registered, users selected both a user name and a password. Unregistered users were able to browse the Web site but were not permitted to bid on any goods or list any items for auction.

On the Web site, search engines helped customers determine what goods were currently available. When registered users found an item they desired, they could choose to enter a single bid or to use automatic bidding (called proxy bidding). In automatic bidding, the customer entered an initial bid sufficient to make him or her the high bidder; the bid would be automatically increased as others bid for the same object until the auction ended and either the bidder won or another bidder surpassed the original customer's maximum specified bid. Regardless of which bidding method they chose, users could check bids at any time and either bid again, if they had been outbid, or increase their maximum amount in the automatic bid. Users could choose to receive e-mail notification if they were outbid.

Once the auction had ended, the buyer and seller were both notified of the winning bid and were given each other's e-mail address. The parties to the auction would then privately arrange for payment and delivery of the good.

Fees and Procedures for Sellers

Buyers on eBay were not charged a fee for bidding on items on the site, but sellers were charged an insertion fee and a "final value" fee; they could also elect to pay additional fees to promote their listing. Listing, or insertion, fees ranged from 30 cents for auctions with opening bids, minimum values, or reserve prices of between $0.01 and $0.99, to $4.80 for auctions with opening bids, minimum values, or reserve prices of $500 and up. Final value fees ranged from 1.25 to 5 percent of the final sale price and were computed according to a graduated fee schedule in which the percentage fell as the final sales price rose. As an example, in a basic auction with no promotion, if the item had brought an opening bid of $200 and eventually sold for $1,500, the total fee paid by the seller would be $35.48—the $3.60 insertion fee plus $31.88. The $31.88 was based on a fee structure of 5 percent of the first $25 (or $1.25), 2.5 percent of the additional amount between $25.01 and $1,000 (or

$24.38), and 1.25 percent of the additional amount between $1,000.01 and $1,500 (or $6.25). Auction fees varied for special categories of goods such as passenger vehicles in eBay Motors, which were charged a $40 transaction fee when the first successful bid was placed, and residential, commercial, and other real estate, which carried a $100 insertion fee.

Sellers could also customize items by adding photographs and featuring their item in eBay's Gallery section. Sellers could indicate a photograph in the item's description if the seller posted the photograph on a Web site and provided eBay with the appropriate Web address. Items could be showcased in the Gallery section with a catalog of pictures rather than text. A seller who used a photograph in his or her listing could have this photograph included in the Gallery section for 25 cents or featured there for $19.95. A Gallery option was available in all categories of eBay, but fees varied among categories and according to the prominence of the Gallery. For example, a simple Gallery listing cost 25 cents, whereas a featured Gallery listing, which included a periodic listing in the featured section above the general Gallery, cost $19.95. In the eBay Motors Gallery, options could cost as much as $99.95.

To make doing business on eBay more attractive to potential sellers, eBay introduced several features. To ensure receiving a minimum price for an auction, the seller could either specify an opening bid or set a reserve price on the auction. If the bidding did not top the reserve price, the seller was under no obligation to sell the item to the highest bidder and could relist the item at no extra cost. For items with a reserve price between $0.01 and $49.99, the fee was $1.00; for prices between $50.00 and $199.99, the fee was $2.00; and for prices over $200, the fee was 1 percent of the reserve price. If the seller wished, he or she could also set a "buy-it-now" price that allowed bidders to pay a set amount for a listed item. The fee for this service was $1.00. If the buy-it-now price was met, the auction would end immediately.

As of June 11, 2001, new sellers at eBay were required to provide both a credit card number and bank account information. While eBay admits that these requirements are extreme, it argues that they help protect everyone in the community against fraudulent sellers and ensure that sellers are of legal age and are serious about listing an item on eBay.

How Transactions Were Completed

Under the terms of eBay's user agreement, if a seller received one or more bids above the stated minimum, or reserve, price, the seller was obligated to complete the transaction, although eBay had no enforcement power beyond suspending a noncompliant buyer or seller from using eBay's service. In the event the buyer and seller were unable to complete the transaction, the seller notified eBay, which then credited the seller the amount of the final value fee.

When an auction ended, the eBay system validated that the bid fell within the acceptable price range. If the sale was successful, eBay automatically notified the buyer and seller via e-mail; the buyer and seller could then work out the transaction details independent of eBay, or they could use eBay's checkout service and eBay's payment service to complete the transaction. In its original business model, eBay did not take possession of either the item being sold or the buyer's payment at any point in the process. In an effort to increase revenues, eBay expanded its offerings to facilitate buyers paying for auctions by first offering services that accepted credit card payments and electronic funds transfers on behalf of the seller and then, in 2003, purchasing PayPal, the leading third-party online payment facilitator. To make selling easier, eBay also had alliances with two leading shippers, the U.S. Postal Service (USPS) and UPS. Both of these shippers had centers on eBay that would allow sellers to calculate postage and to print postage-paid labels. However, the buyer and seller still had to independently arrange shipping terms, with buyers typically paying for shipping. Items were sent directly from the seller to the buyer unless an independent escrow service was arranged to help ensure security.

To encourage sellers to use eBay's ancillary services, the company offered an automated checkout service to help expedite communication, payment, and delivery between buyers and sellers.

FOSTERING COMMUNITY AFFINITY

From its founding, eBay considered developing a loyal, vivacious trading community to be a cornerstone of its business model. This community was nurtured through open and honest communication and was built on five basic values that eBay expected its members to honor:

> We believe people are basically good.
>
> We believe everyone has something to contribute.
>
> We believe that an honest, open environment can bring out the best in people.
>
> We recognize and respect everyone as a unique individual.
>
> We encourage you to treat others the way that you want to be treated.[8]

The company recognized that these values could not be imposed by fiat. According to Omidyar, "As much as we at eBay talk about the values and encourage people to live by those values, that's not going to work unless people actually adopt those values. The values are communicated not because somebody reads the Web site and says, 'Hey, this is how we want to treat each other, so I'll just start treating people that way.' The values are communicated because that's how they're treated when they first arrive. Each member is passing those values on to the next member. It's little things, like you receive a note that says, 'Thanks for your business.'"[9] Consistent with eBay's desire to stay in touch with its customers and be responsive to their needs, the company flies in 10 new sellers every few months to hold group meetings known as Voice of the Customer; 75–80 percent of new features are originally suggested by community members.

An example of eBay values in action took place when eBay introduced a feature that referred losing bidders to similar auctions from other eBay sellers, eliciting a strong outcry from the community. Sellers demanded to know why eBay was stealing their sales, and one longtime seller even went so far as to auction a rare eBay jacket so that he could use the auction as a forum to complain about "eBay's new policy of screwing the folks who built them."[10] This caught the attention of Omidyar and Whitman, who met with the seller in his home for 45 minutes. After the meeting, eBay changed its policy.

Recognizing that many new users may not get the most out of their eBay experience, and hoping to introduce new entrepreneurs to the community, the company created eBay University in August 2000. The university travels across the country and holds two-day seminars in various cities. These seminars attract between 400 and 500 people who each pay $25 for the experience. Courses range from freshmen-level classes that offer an introduction to buying and selling to graduate classes that teach the intricacies of bulk listing and competitive tactics. The eBay University has been so successful that the company has partnered with Evoke Communications to offer an online version of the classes. While community members gain knowledge from these classes, so does eBay. The company keeps careful track of questions and concerns and uses them to uncover areas that need improvement.

A second important initiative to make the eBay community more inclusive was aimed at the fastest-growing segment of the U.S. population, adults ages 50 and over. In an effort to bridge the digital divide for seniors, eBay launched its Digital Opportunity Program for Seniors and set a goal of training and bringing online 1 million seniors by 2005. Specific elements of this plan included partnering with SeniorNet, the leading nonprofit computer technology trainer of seniors, and donating $1 million to this organization for training and establishing 10 new training facilities by 2005, developing a volunteer program for training seniors, and creating a specific area on eBay for senior citizens (www.ebay.com/seniors).

To foster a sense of community among eBay users, the company employed tools and tactics designed to promote both business and personal interactions between consumers, to foster trust between bidders and sellers, and to instill a sense of security among traders. Interactions between community members were facilitated through the creation of chat rooms based on personal interests. These chat rooms allowed individuals to learn about their chosen collectibles and to exchange information about items they collected.

To manage the flow of information in the chat rooms, eBay employees went to trade shows and conventions to seek out individuals who had knowledge about and a passion for either a specific collectible or a category of goods. These enthusiasts would act as community leaders or ambassadors; they were never referred to as employees but were compensated $1,000 a month to host online discussions with experts.

Feedback Forum

Although personal communication between members fostered a sense of community, as eBay's community grew from "the size of a small village to a large city" additional measures were necessary to ensure a continued sense of trust and honesty among users.[11] One of eBay's earliest trust-building efforts

was the 1996 creation of the Feedback Forum, which encouraged individuals to record comments about their trading partners. At the completion of each auction, both the buyer and seller were allowed to leave positive, negative, or neutral comments about each other. Individuals could dispute feedback left about them by annotating any comments in question.

As users assigned values of +1 for a positive comment, 0 for a neutral comment, and −1 for a negative comment, each trader earned a ranking that was attached to his or her user name. A trader who had developed a positive reputation over time had a color-coded star symbol displayed next to his or her user name to indicate the amount of positive feedback. The highest ranking a trader could receive was "over 100,000," indicated by a red shooting star. Well-respected, high-volume traders could have rankings well into the thousands.

Traders who received a sufficiently negative net feedback rating (typically a −4) had their registrations suspended and were thus unable to bid on or list items for sale. Users could review a person's feedback profile before deciding to bid on an item listed by that person or before choosing payment and delivery methods. A sample user profile is shown in Exhibit 4.

The terms of eBay's user agreement prohibited actions that would undermine the integrity of the Feedback Forum, such as leaving positive feedback about oneself through other accounts or leaving multiple negative comments about someone else through other accounts. The Feedback Forum system had several automated features designed to detect and prevent some forms of abuse. For example, feedback posted from the same account, positive or negative, could not affect a user's net feedback rating by more than one point, no matter how many comments an individual made. Furthermore, a user could only make comments about his or her trading partners in completed transactions. Prior to 2004, a feedback comment could not be altered once it was made. However, as of February 9, 2004, the system was changed in response to suggestions by community members for all users to be able to mutually withdraw feedback. Withdrawn feedback would no longer impact a user's feedback rating.

The company believed its Feedback Forum was extremely useful in overcoming users' initial hesitancy about trading over the Internet, since it reduced the uncertainty of dealing with an unknown trading partner. However, there was growing concern among sellers and bidders that feedback could be positively

Exhibit 4   **A Sample Feedback Forum Profile**

Member Profile: nuggett12 (109 ⭐)

| Feedback Score: | 109 |
| Positive Feedback: | 100% |

Members who left a positive:	109
Members who left a negative:	0
All positive feedback received:	118

Learn about what these numbers mean.

Recent Ratings:		Past Month	Past 6 Months	Past 12 Months
⊕	positive	4	18	34
⊙	neutral	0	0	0
⊖	negative	0	0	0

Bid Retractions (Past 6 months): 0

Member since: May-17-99
Location: United States
- ID History
- Items for Sale
- Add to Favorite Sellers
- View my Reviews & Guides

Contact Member

Feedback Received | **From Buyers** | **From Sellers** | **Left for Others**

118 feedback received by nuggett12 (0 ratings mutually withdrawn)   Page 1 of 5

Comment	From	Date / Time	Item #
⊕ BUY IT NOW-PAID IT NOW-w/PAY-PAL WAY TO GO !!!!!! Thank You Much !	Seller krystalriver (2930 ⭐)	Dec-07-05 12:19	6233794219
⊕ Verrrrrrrrrrrrry quick payment. A credit to ebay. AAAAAAAAAAAA+++++++++++++	Seller thegoodpackage (3859 ⭐)	Dec-07-05 04:23	6586487441
⊕ Great ebayer! Lightning quick shipping and kept his word about everthing!	Buyer ngun0003 (34 ☆)	Nov-27-05 07:12	8236266960
⊕ Prompt payment, ****** WWW.STORES.EBAY.COM/COMPUTERMEMORYSTORE *******	Seller mwdusa (13146 ☆)	Nov-26-05 15:13	6823044281
⊕ GoGamers.Com - A+++ Great eBayer. Transaction was a breeze!	Seller gogamerscom (57249 ⭐)	Oct-28-05 08:00	8228611496
⊕ A pleasure dealing with. Smooth transaction.	Seller bkhtrains (532 ⭐)	Aug-03-05 05:23	5790615702
⊕ Perfectly Smooth transaction. A Credit to eBay ! A++++	Seller nup (1500 ⭐)	Aug-03-05 04:29	6788040863
⊕ Customers like you are *priceless* Excellent eBay member! A+ Thanks	Seller dans_cellular_accessories (55137 ☆) no longer a registered user	Aug-03-05 00:21	5789528933
⊕ Successful completion. Great customer. Thank you from THE SHARPER IMAGE!	Seller the_sharper_image (138164 ☆)	Jul-25-05 05:33	5791564203
⊕ Good buyer, prompt payment, valued customer, highly recommended.	Seller vcom (9318 ⭐)	Jul-21-05 16:17	5789130422
⊕ FAST PAYMENT! GREAT BIDDER. THANKS!!! AAAAA +++++++	Seller allbest4u (17890 ☆)	Jul-16-05 14:53	5788315854
⊕ Great buyer, awesome ebayer, and thank you from ECBURBANK	Seller ecburbank (14787 ☆)	Jul-16-05 14:52	5788869114
⊕ Great buyer, awesome ebayer, and thank you from ECBURBANK	Seller ecburbank (14787 ☆)	Jul-16-05 14:52	5777441953
⊕ Great buyer, awesome ebayer, and thank you from ECBURBANK	Seller ecburbank (14787 ☆)	Jul-16-05 14:52	5777441968
⊕ excellent customer, fast payment, A++	Seller ericapaul (14274 ☆)	Jul-05-05 22:42	8201576635
⊕ Great communication. A pleasure to do business with.	Seller p_accessory (187 ⭐) no longer a registered user	Jul-01-05 19:21	5785729365
⊕ great seller--excellent communication--very helpful. would recommend! A+A+A+A+A+	Buyer faye608 (20 ☆)	Jun-23-05 18:59	3981329520
⊕ GREAT BUYER AND VERY QUICK PAYMENT ! A REAL PLEASURE !	Seller bug_n_y2k (private)	Jun-23-05 18:50	8197028457
⊕ Top Notch Buyer - It doesn't get any better than this!!	Seller swdiscounters (12886 ☆)	Jun-17-05 19:10	8195154724
⊕ THANKS FOR YOUR ORDER	Seller jagktbs (397 ⭐)	Jun-17-05 14:59	243802489476
⊕ Nice ebayer. Easy smooth transaction. Thanks!	Seller 1blue1browncody (131 ⭐)	Jun-07-05 12:49	4385815724
⊕ Great communication. A pleasure to do business with.	Seller amazon-books (15683 ☆)	May-22-05 06:53	4544184186
⊕ Fast shipping, great comunication...	Buyer ctrfreak (35 ☆)	May-16-05 08:18	5770942373
⊕ Excellent Buyer! A Pleasure To Do Business With. A++++	Seller businessbagsonline (1671 ⭐)	May-09-05 11:19	8184800507
⊕ Great Ebay buyer!! A++++++++++++++	Seller cleanpureice (827 ⭐)	May-08-05 19:44	4373083958

Source: www.ebay.com, December 19, 2005.

skewed, as many eBayers were afraid to leave negative feedback for fear of unfounded retribution that could damage their carefully built reputations. This concern was heightened by the fact that buyers and sellers could agree to mutually withdraw negative feedback and thus expunge evidence of a failed transaction as if it never occurred.

Unfortunately, eBay's Feedback Forum was not always sufficient to ensure honesty and integrity among traders. The company estimated that far less than 1 percent of the millions of auctions completed on the site involved some sort of fraud or illegal activity, but some users, like Clay Monroe, disagreed. Monroe, a Seattle-area trader of computer equipment, estimated that "ninety percent of the time everybody is on the up and up . . . [but] . . . ten percent of the time you get some jerk who wants to cheat you." Fraudulent or illegal acts perpetrated by sellers included misrepresentation of goods; trading in counterfeit goods or pirated goods that infringed on others' intellectual property rights; failure to deliver goods paid for by buyers; and shill bidding, whereby sellers would use a false bidder to artificially drive up the price of a good. Buyers could manipulate bids by placing an unrealistically high bid on a good to discourage other bidders and then withdraw their bid at the last moment to allow an ally to win the auction at a bargain price. Buyers could also fail to deliver payment on a completed auction.

SafeHarbor

Recognizing that fraudulent activities represented a significant danger to eBay's future, management took the Feedback Forum a step further in 1998 by launching the SafeHarbor program to provide guidelines for trade, provide information to help resolve user disputes, and respond to reports of misuse of the eBay service. The SafeHarbor initiative was expanded in 1999 to provide additional safeguards and to actively work with law enforcement agencies and members of the trading community to make eBay more secure. New elements of SafeHarbor included:

- Free insurance, with a $25 deductible for transactions under $200 and further protection for buyers and sellers who used PayPal.
- Cooperation with local, national, and international law enforcement agencies to identify and prosecute fraudulent buyers and sellers.
- Enhancements to the Feedback Forum such as listing whether the user was a buyer or a seller in a transaction.

- A partnership with SquareTrade, an online dispute resolution service.
- A partnership with Escrow.com to promote the use of escrow services on purchases over $500.
- A new class of verified eBay users with an accompanying icon.
- Easy access to escrow services.
- Tougher policies relating to nonpaying bidders and shill bidders.
- Clarification of which items were not permissible to list for sale (such as items associated with Nazi Germany or organizations such as the Ku Klux Klan that glorify hate, racial, intolerance, or racial violence).
- A strengthened antipiracy and anti-infringement program known as the Verified Rights Owner (VeRO) program, and the introduction of dispute resolution services.

The use of verified buyer and seller accounts was viewed as especially significant because it allowed eBay to ensure that suspended users did not open new eBay accounts under different names. User information was verified through Atlanta-based Equifax Inc. To further ensure that suspended users didn't register new accounts with different identities, eBay partnered with Infoglide to use a similarity search technology to examine new registrant information.

To implement these new initiatives, eBay increased the number of positions in its SafeHarbor department from 24 to 182, including full-time employees and independent contractors. It also organized the department around the functions of investigations, community watch, and fraud prevention. The investigations group was responsible for examining reported trading violations and possible misuses of eBay. The fraud prevention group mediated customer disputes over such things as the quality of the goods sold. If a written complaint of fraud was filed against a user, eBay generally suspended the alleged offender's account, pending an investigation. Despite all of these initiatives, innovative thieves were developing new ways to cheat honest bidders and sellers as quickly as eBay could identify and ban them from the system, and many eBayers still viewed this as one of the most significant threats to the eBay community.

The community watch group worked with over 100 industry-leading companies, ranging from software publishers to toy manufacturers to apparel makers, to protect intellectual property rights. To ensure that illegal items were not being sold and sale items listed did not violate intellectual property rights, this SafeHarbor group automated daily keyword searches on auction content. Offending auctions were closed and the seller was notified of the violation. Repeated violations resulted in suspension of the seller's account.

As eBay expanded its categories to include Great Collections and the new automobile categories, safeguards were introduced to meet the unique needs of these areas. In the eBay Great Collections category, the company partnered with Collector's Universe to offer authentication and grading services for specific products such as trading cards, coins, and autographs. In the automobile area, one of eBay's fastest-growing segments, eBay partnered with Saturn to provide users with access to a nationwide automobile brand and offered a free limited one-month or 1,000-mile warranty, free purchase insurance up to $20,000 with a $500 deductible, and a special escrow service (Secure Pay) designed for the needs of automotive buyers and sellers.

eBAY'S STRATEGY TO SUSTAIN ITS MARKET DOMINANCE

Meg Whitman assumed the helm of eBay in February 1998 and began acting as the public face of the company. In an effort to stay in touch with her customers, Whitman hosted an auction on eBay herself. She found the experience so enlightening that she then required all of eBay's managers to sell on eBay. Pierre Omidyar stepped back to become chairman of eBay's board of directors and focused his time and energy on overseeing eBay's strategic direction and growth, business model and site development, and community advocacy. Jeff Skoll, who became the vice president of strategic planning and analysis, concentrated on competitive analysis, new business planning and incubation, the development of the organization's overall strategic direction, and supervision of customer support operations.

The Move to Go Public

On September 24, 1998, eBay's initial public offering (IPO) began at a price of $18 per share. The IPO closed the day up 160 percent at $47, generated $66 million in new capital for the company, and was recognized by several investing publications. The success of the offering led eBay to issue a follow-up offering in April 1999 that raised an additional $600 million. As a qualification to the IPOs, eBay's board of directors retained the right to issue as many as 5 million additional shares of preferred stock with no further input from the current shareholders in case of a hostile takeover attempt.

eBay's Business Model

According to eBay's Meg Whitman, the company could best be described as a dynamic, self-regulating economy. Its business model was based on creating and maintaining a person-to-person trading community in which buyers and sellers could readily and conveniently exchange information and goods. The company's role was to function as a value-added facilitator of online buyer–seller transactions by providing a supportive infrastructure that enabled buyers and sellers to come together in an efficient and effective manner. Success depended not only on the quality of eBay's infrastructure but also on the quality and quantity of buyers and sellers attracted to the site; in management's view, this entailed maintaining a compelling trading environment, a number of trust and safety programs, a cost-effective and convenient trading experience, and strong community affinity. By developing the eBay brand name and increasing the customer base, eBay endeavored to attract a sufficient number of high-quality buyers and sellers necessary to meet the organization's goals. The online auction format meant that eBay carried zero inventory and could operate a marketplace without the need for a traditional sales force.

The eBay business model was built around three profit centers: the domestic business (auction operations within the United States), international business (auction operations outside of the United States) and payments (e.g., PayPal). For the first nine months of 2005, the company's U.S. operations accounted for 40.7 percent of revenue growth, the international share was 37.0 percent, and the remaining 22.3 percent was from payments (see Exhibit 5).

Specific elements of eBay's business model that the company particularly recognized as key to the company's success included:[12]

1. The fact that eBay was the world's largest online trading forum, with a critical mass of buyers, sellers, and items listed for sale.

Exhibit 5   **Sources of eBay's Revenue Growth, 2001–2005**

	2001	2002	2003	2004	2005 (3 quarters)
U.S. auctions	62.8%	48.0%	49.1%	42.8%	40.7%
International auctions	32.6	36.9	30.7	35.9	37.0
Payment fees (Pay Pal)	4.7	15.1	20.2	21.3	22.3

2. The compelling and entertaining trading environment, which had strong values, established rules, and procedures that facilitated communication and trade between buyers and sellers.
3. Established trust and safety programs such as SafeHarbor.
4. Cost-effective convenient trading.
5. Strong community affinity.
6. An intuitive user experience that was easy to use, arranged by topics, and fully automated.

In implementing its business model, eBay employed three main competitive tactics. First, it sought to build strategic partnerships in all stages of its value chain, creating an impressive portfolio of over 250 strategic alliances with companies such as America Online (AOL), Yahoo, IBM, Compaq, and Walt Disney. Second, it actively sought customer feedback and made improvements on the basis of this information. Third, it actively monitored the environment, both externally and internally, for developing opportunities. Two ways eBay executives keep in touch with internal trends were by hosting online town hall meetings and by visiting cities with large local markets. The feedback gained from these meetings and visits was used to adopt and adjust practices to keep customers satisfied.

eBay's Strategy

eBay's strategy to sustain growth rested on three key elements:[13]

1. *Categories:* Broaden the existing trading platform within existing product categories, across new product categories, and through geographic expansion, both local and international.
2. *Formats:* Continue to introduce additional pricing formats such as fixed-price sales, Dutch auctions (which allow a seller to sell multiple identical items to the highest bidders), eBay stores, and classified listings. Also, expand value-added services in order to offer end-to-end personal trading service by offering a variety of pretrade and posttrade services to enhance the user experience and make trading easier.
3. *Geographies:* Continue to develop U.S. and international markets that employ the Internet to create an efficient trading platform in local, national, and international markets that can be transformed into a seamless, truly global trading platform.

Categories

Efforts intended to broaden the eBay trading platform concentrated on growing the content within current categories, broadening the range of products offered according to user preferences, and developing regionally targeted offerings. Growth in existing product categories was facilitated by deepening the content within the categories through the use of content-specific chat rooms and bulletin boards as well as targeted advertising at trade shows and in industry-specific publications.

To broaden the range of products offered, eBay developed new product categories, introduced specialty sites, and developed eBay stores. Over 2,000 new categories were added between 1998 and 2000; by 2005, eBay offered over 50,000 categories of items (greatly expanded from the original 10 categories in 1995). Projected over all of 2005, 12 of these categories had gross merchandise sales of over $1 billion, including eBay Motors ($14.3 billion), Clothing and Accessories ($3.3 billion), Consumer Electronics ($3.2 billion), Computers ($2.9 billion), Home and Garden ($2.5 billion), Books/Movies/Music ($2.4 billion), Sports ($2.1 billion), Collectibles ($2.0 billion), Toys ($1.6 billion), Jewelry and Watches ($1.5 billion), Business and Industrial ($1.5 billion), and Cameras and Photo ($1.3 billion). As of June 2005, over 55 million items were available on eBay worldwide and approximately 5 million items were being added per day.[14]

Significant new product categories and specialty sites developed since eBay's early days included:

- The eBay Motors category, which was developed when eBay noticed that an increasing number of automobile transactions were taking place on its site. In 2002, eBay Motors sold more than $3 billion worth of vehicles and parts and was currently the largest online marketplace for buying and selling autos, with over $14 billion in sales expected in 2005. According to Whitman, "One month, we saw the miscellaneous category had a very rapid growth rate, and someone said we have to find out what's going on. It was the buying and selling of used cars. So we said, maybe what we should do is give these guys a separate category and see what happens. It worked so well that we created eBay Motors."[15] In partnership with AutoTrader.com, this category was later expanded to a specialty site.

- The LiveAuctions specialty site, which allows live bidding via the Internet for auctions occurring in brick-and-mortar auction houses around the world. Through an alliance with Icollector.com, eBay users had access to more than 300 auction houses worldwide. Auction houses that participated in this agreement were well rewarded as more than 20 percent of their sales went to online bidders. One auction broadcast on the LiveAuctions site was held in February 2001 and featured items from a rare Marilyn Monroe collection, including a handwritten note from Monroe that listed her reasons for divorcing her first husband.

- The eBay Business marketplace, launched in 2002, which allowed business-related items to be sold in one location. Items such as office technology, wholesale lots, and marketplace services were offered at this destination. By the end of 2002, over 500,000 items were listed in eBay Business per week and more than $1 billion in annualized gross merchandise sales occurred across these categories. The Business and Industrial category of eBay's Web site was expected to generate $1.5 billion in revenues in 2005.

- The eBay Real Estate category was launched to foster eBay's emerging real estate marketplace. The offerings within this category were significantly enhanced by eBay's August 2001 acquisition of Homesdirect, which specialized in the sale of foreclosed properties owned by government agencies such as Housing and Urban Development and the Department of Veterans Affairs (formerly known as the Veterans Administration). The company estimated that a parcel of land was sold through the Real Estate category every 45 minutes. In February 2005, eBay also completed the acquisition of Rent.com, a leading online listing service in the apartment and rental housing industry.

Other notable moves to broaden the platform included:

- Launching the Application Program Interface (API) and Developers Program, which allowed other companies to use eBay's commerce engine and technology to build new sites.

- Launching, as of 1999, over 60 regional sites to give a more local flavor to eBay's offerings. These regional sites focused on the 50 largest metropolitan areas in the United States. Regional auction sites were intended to encourage the sale of items that were prohibitively expensive to ship, items that tended to have only a local appeal, and items that people preferred to view before purchasing. To supplement the regional sites, in mid-2001 eBay began offering eBay sellers the option of having their items listed in a special eBay seller's area in the classified sections of local newspapers. Sellers could highlight specific items, their eBay store, or their user ID in these classifieds.

- Reaching an agreement with Accenture, in May 2002, to develop a service intended to allow large sellers to more efficiently sell their products. These sellers were able to use a wide range of tools, such as high-volume listing capabilities, expanded customer service and support, and payment and fulfillment processes.

Formats

eBay also concentrated on expanding the number of formats in which its auctions were available. The company claimed that "in addition to our more established eBay Marketplace formats, we are continually looking for ways to better enable members of our community to interact and transact with one another online."[16] The company continued to develop additional pricing formats such as fixed-price sales, Dutch auctions, eBay stores, and classified listings. While eBay was primarily known for its traditional auction format, the company generated 29 percent of its gross merchandise volume through fixed-price auctions during the second quarter of 2005.[17]

Initiatives to create and develop new auction formats included:

- The establishment of a fixed-price format through the acquisition of Half.com that allowed eBay to compete more directly with competitors such as Amazon.com. Half.com was a fixed-price, person-to-person format that enabled buyers and sellers to trade books, CDs, movies and video games at prices starting at generally half of the retail price. Like eBay, Half.com offered a feedback system that helped buyers and sellers to build a solid reputation. eBay intended to eventually fully integrate both Half.com's listings and the feedback system into eBay's current site.

- The June 2001 eBay introduction of eBay stores to complement new offerings, to make it easier for sellers to build loyalty and for buyers to locate goods from specific sellers, and to prevent sellers from driving bidders to the seller's own Web site. In an eBay store, the entirety of a seller's auctions would be listed in one convenient location. These stores could also offer a fixed-price option from a seller and the integration of a seller's Half.com listings with his or her auction listings. While numerous sellers of all sizes moved to take advantage of eBay stores, the concept was especially appealing to the larger retailers such as IBM, Hard Rock Café, Sears, and Handspring, which were moving to take advantage of eBay's reach and distribution power. As of June 2005, the company had approximately 299,000 stores worldwide, with approximately 173,000 of these stores in the United States and the other 126,000 stores hosted on international sites.

- The August 2004 acquisition of a minority share in Craigslist, a company that offered online classifieds and forums. Of particular concern to eBay was penetrating international markets with classified listings. In February 2005, eBay launched online classifieds Web sites in select international markets. The international Web site was launched under the brand name Kijiji, which means "village" in Swahili. As of March 2005, Kijiji was available in over 50 cities in Canada, China, France, Germany, Italy, and Japan. Alex Kazim, eBay's senior vice president of new ventures, claimed that "Kijiji builds local communities online, giving neighbors a way to come together around local needs and interests. We're excited about making Kajiji the online neighborhood meeting place for local residents in cities across the world."[18]

- In August 2005, eBay completed the acquisition of shopping.com. Shopping.com, which had over 50 million unique visitors per month in the United States, the United Kingdom, and France, was the world's third-largest Internet shopping destination. eBay saw this as an opportunity to acquire a leading company in online comparison shopping and consumer reviews.[19]

Since its earliest days, eBay had realized that in order to be successful, its service had to be both easy to use and convenient to access. In September 2005, the company introduced member-generated product reviews and buying guides, in order to facilitate the dissemination of buying information to users. The company also sought to add services to fill these needs by offering a variety of pretrade and posttrade services to enhance the user experience and provide an end-to-end trading experience.

Early efforts in this direction included alliances with:

- Leading shipping services (USPS and UPS).
- Two companies that helped guarantee that buyers would get what they paid for (Tradesafe and I-Escrow).
- The world's largest franchiser of retail business, communications, and postal service centers (Mailboxes, Etc.).
- The leader in multicarrier Web-based shipping services for e-commerce (iShip.com).

To facilitate person-to-person credit card payments, eBay acquired PayPal, a company that specialized in transferring money from one cardholder to another, in October 2002. Using the newly acquired capabilities of PayPal, eBay was able to offer sellers the option of accepting credit card payments from other eBay users. As of the second quarter 2005, PayPal had over 78 million user accounts in 56 countries.

eBay's objective was to make credit card payment a "seamless and integrated part of the trading experience."[20] The total value of transactions on PayPal was $18.9 million in 2004. During the second quarter of 2005, over 35 percent of PayPal's revenues were from international business.

Developing International Markets

As competition increased in the online auction industry, eBay began to seek growth opportunities in international markets in an effort to create a global trading community. As of June 2005, eBay had a presence in 33 countries including Australia, Austria, Belgium, Canada, China (through an investment in the Chinese company Eachnet), France, Germany, Hong Kong, India, Ireland, Italy, Malaysia, the Netherlands, New Zealand, the Philippines, Singapore, South Korea, Spain, Sweden, Switzerland, Taiwan, Great Britain, and Latin America (through an investment in MercadoLibre.com). Through the first three quarters of 2005, 37 percent of eBay's revenues came from its international sources and over half of eBay's registered users were from countries outside the United States (82 million out of 157 million total registered users). Growth opportunities were especially appealing in Asia (due to rapid increases in Internet access) and Europe. In entering international markets, eBay considered three options: building a new user community from the ground up, acquiring a local organization, or forming a partnership with a strong local company. In realizing its goals of international growth, eBay employed all three strategies.

In late 1998, eBay's initial efforts at international expansion into Canada and the United Kingdom relied on building new user communities. The first step in establishing these communities was to create customized home pages for users in those countries. These home pages were designed to provide content and categories locally customized to the needs of users in specific countries, while providing them with access to a global trading community. Local customization in the United Kingdom was facilitated through the use of local management, grassroots and online marketing, and participation in local events.[21] In February 1999, eBay partnered with PBL Online, a leading Internet company in Australia, to offer a customized Australian and New Zealand eBay home page. When the site went live in October 1999,

transactions were denominated in Australian dollars, and, while buyers could bid on auctions anywhere in the world, they could also search for items located exclusively in Australia. Further, local chat boards were designed to facilitate interaction between Australian users, and country-specific categories, such as Australian coins and stamps as well as cricket and rugby memorabilia, were offered.

To further expand its global reach, eBay acquired Germany's largest online person-to-person trading site, Alando.de AG, in June 1999. Management handled the transition of service in a manner calculated to be smooth and painless for Alando.de's users. While users would have to comply with eBay rules and regulations, the only significant change for Alando.de's 50,000 registered users was that they would have to go to a new Web address to transact their business.

To establish an Asian presence, in February 2000 eBay formed a joint venture with NEC to launch eBay Japan. According to the new CEO of eBay Japan, Merle Okawara, an internationally renowned executive, NEC was pleased to help eBay in leveraging the tried-and-trusted eBay business model to provide Japanese consumers with access to a global community of active online buyers and sellers. In customizing the site to the needs of Japanese users, eBay wrote the content exclusively in Japanese and allowed users to bid in yen. The site had over 800 categories ranging from internationally popular categories (such as computers, electronics, and Asian antiques) to categories with a local flavor (such as Hello Kitty, Pokémon, and pottery). The eBay Japan site also debuted a new merchant-to-person concept known as Supershops, which allowed consumers to bid on items listed by companies. However, eBay discontinued its operations in the Japanese market in 2002 due to rising costs.

In 2001, eBay expanded into South Korea through an acquisition of a majority ownership position in the country's largest online trading service Internet Auction Company Ltd., and into Belgium, Brazil, Italy, France, the Netherlands, Portugal, Spain, and Sweden through the acquisition of Europe's largest online trading platform, iBazar. Further expansion in 2001 included the development of a local site in Singapore, and an equity-based alliance with the leading online auction site for the Spanish- and Portuguese-speaking communities in Latin America, MercadoLibre.com. By the end of 2004, eBay was using MercadoLibre.com to reach nine markets: Argentina, Brazil, Chile, Colombia, Ecuador, Mexico, Peru, Uruguay, and Venezuela.

Due to increasing saturation in their domestic market during 2004 and 2005, eBay implemented aggressive international expansion plans in an effort to increase the company's global presence. Among the strategic moves that the company implemented during this time were:

- The acquisition in September 2005 of Skype Technologies, a global Internet communications company. At the time of the acquisition, Skype had 54 million members in over 225 countries. eBay believed that this move would allow it to develop an enhanced global marketplace and payments platform.[22]

- The 2004 launch of a European Business Center in Dublin, Ireland, to serve as PayPal's European headquarters. This was PayPal's first facility outside the United States and hosted its European customer service and fraud prevention operations. This facility was expected to have over 400 employees by the end of 2005.

- The November 2004 launch of eBay Philippines. IDC expected business-to-consumer e-commerce in the Philippines to increase from $828 million in 2004 to $2.9 billion in 2007.[23]

- The December 2004 launch of eBay Malaysia. IDC reported that business-to-consumer e-commerce in Malaysia would increase from $1.1 billion to $3.0 billion between 2005 and 2008.[24]

- The launch of eBay Poland in April 2005. IDC predicted that business-to-consumer e-commerce would grow by over 400 percent in Poland between 2005 and 2008.[25]

- The August 2004 acquisition of Baazee.com, the largest online marketplace in India with over 1 million confirmed registered users. At that time, there were 17 million Internet users in India, and that number was expected to increase to more than 30 million by 2006.[26]

- The September 2004 acquisition of Internet Auction Company, an online trading company based in Korea.

- The November 2004 acquisition of Marktplaats. nl, the leading classifieds site in the Netherlands.

- The acquisitions in May 2005 of Gumtree.com and LoQUo.com. These two companies had

classified sites in international cities. Gumtree. com offered multiple sites in countries including the United Kingdom, Australia, New Zealand, and South Africa. LoQUo.com offered a classifieds site to the Spanish market.

- The acquisition in June 2005 of Opusforum, a leading German classifieds site. Opusforum had over 1 million visitors in May 2005 and advertised jobs, housing, and services to the German market. This followed the April 2004 acquisition of Mobile.de, the leading classifieds Web site for vehicles in Germany.

HOW eBAY'S AUCTION SITE COMPARED WITH THAT OF RIVALS

Auction sites varied in a number of respects: their inventory, the bidding process, extra services and fees, technical support, functionality, and sense of community. Since its inception, eBay had gone to great lengths to make its Web site intuitive, easy to use by both buyers and sellers, and reliable. Efforts to ensure ease of use ranged from narrowly defining categories (to allow users to quickly locate desired products) to introducing services designed to personalize a user's eBay experience. Two specific services developed by eBay and launched in 1998 to increase personalization were My eBay and About Me. My eBay gave users centralized access to confidential, current information regarding their trading activities. From his or her My eBay page, a user could view information pertaining to his or her current account balances with eBay; feedback rating; the status of any auctions in which he or she was participating, as either a buyer or a seller; and auctions in favorite categories. In October, eBay introduced the About Me service, which allowed users to create customized home pages that could be viewed by all other eBay members and could include elements from the My eBay page such as user ratings or items the user had listed for auction, as well as personal information and pictures. This service not only increased customer ease of use but also contributed to the sense of community among the traders; one seller stated that the About Me service "made it easier and more rewarding for me to do business with others."[27] New features and services added in 2000 included new listing functions that could make an auction standout including Highlight and Feature Plus as well as the ability for sellers to cross-list their products in two categories, a tool to set prequalification guidelines for bidders, a new imaging and photo hosting service that made it easier for sellers to include pictures of their goods, and the introduction of the Buy It Now tool.

Throughout its history, eBay had struggled to balance its explosive growth with its technological infrastructure. To counter several significant service outages the company had faced in its early days, eBay hired Maynard Webb, a premier software engineer and troubleshooter who was working at Gateway Computer. Webb took swift action, forming alliances with key vendors such as Sun, IBM, and Microsoft, and outsourcing its technology and Web site operations to Exodus Communications and Abovenet. These outsourcing agreements were intended to allow Exodus and Abovenet to "manage network capacity and provide a more robust backbone" while eBay focused on its core business.[28] While eBay still experienced minor outages when it changed or expanded services (for example, a system crash coincided with the introduction of the original 22 regional Web sites), system downtime decreased. However, the stability of the system under eBay's explosive growth and continuous introduction of new features was a continuing management concern, especially as competitors continued to strengthen their competencies.

eBay's Main Competitors

The ability to attract buyers, the volume of transactions and selection of goods, customer service, and brand recognition were among the competitive factors eBay considered most important in the online auction industry. In October 2005, eBay introduced the "It" broadcasting campaign, in an effort to draw attention to the expansive amount of product variety offered by the company. The campaign used the slogan "Whatever It is that you are looking for, you can find It on eBay." In addition to factors such as variety and brand image, eBay was also attempting to compete along several other dimensions: sense of community, system reliability, reliability of delivery and payment, Web site convenience and accessibility, low levels of service fees, and efficient information exchange.[29]

Early in eBay's history, the company's main rivals could be considered classified advertisements in newspapers, garage sales, flea markets, collectibles shows, and other venues such as local auction houses and liquidators. As eBay's product mix and selling techniques evolved, the company's range of competitors did as well. The broadening of eBay's product mix beyond collectibles to include practical household items, office equipment, toys, and so on brought the company into more direct competition with brick-and-mortar retailers, import/export companies, and catalog and mail order companies. Further, with the acquisition of Half.com, the introduction of eBay stores, and the growing percentage of fixed-price and Buy It Now sales as a percentage of eBay's revenue, eBay considered itself to be competing in a broad sense with a number of other online retailers, such as Wal-Mart, Kmart, Target, Sears, JCPenney, and Office Depot. In competing with these larger sellers, eBay began to adopt some of their tools, such as the use of gift certificates. The company also felt that it was competing with a number of specialty retailers, such as Christie's (antiques), KB Toys (toys), Blockbuster (movies), Dell (computers), Foot Locker (sporting goods), Ticketmaster (tickets), and Home Depot (tools).[30] Exhibit 6 displays eBay's customer service rankings as compared to a variety of rivals.

Management saw traditional competitors as inefficient because their fragmented local and regional nature made it expensive and time-consuming for buyers and sellers to meet, exchange information, and complete transactions. Moreover, they suffered from three other deficiencies: (1) They tended to offer limited variety and breadth of selection as compared to the millions of items available on eBay, (2) they often had high transactions costs, and (3) they were information-inefficient in the sense that buyers and sellers lacked a reliable and convenient means of setting prices for sales or purchases. Management saw eBay's online auction format as competitively superior to these rivals because (1) it facilitated buyers and sellers meeting, exchanging information, and conducting transactions; (2) it allowed buyers and sellers to bypass traditional intermediaries and trade directly, thus lowering costs; (3) it provided global reach to greater selection and a broader base of participants; (4) it permitted trading at all hours and provided continuously updated information; and (5) it fostered a sense of community among individuals with mutual interests.

Exhibit 6   **Customer Service Rankings for Selected Companies, 2000–2004 (scores out of 100)**

Company/Sector	2000	2001	2002	2003	2004
Online Auctions					
Online auctions overall	72	74	77	78	77
eBay	80	82	82	84	80
uBid	67	69	70	73	73
Priceline.com	66	69	71	71	73
All others	73	75	78	79	76
Internet Retail					
Internet retail overall	75.2	74.3	77.6	80.8	78.6
Barnesandnoble.com	77	82	87	86	87
Amazon.com	84	84	88	88	84
Buy.com	78	78	80	80	80
1-800-Flowers.com	69	76	78	76	79
General Retail					
General retail overall	78	77	83	84	80
Target	73	77	78	77	75
Wal-Mart	73	75	74	75	73
Sears	73	76	75	73	74
Kmart	67	74	70	70	67

Source: American Customer Satisfaction Index, www.theacsi.org.

The most significant competitors to eBay's auction business included Amazon Auctions, Yahoo Auctions, uBid, and Overstock.com. Two of the smaller competitors in the online auction industry included Bidville (an auction site with no listing fees and no final value fees) and ePier (over 60,000 members as of 2004). Both of these had closely copied eBay's look and feel and touted themselves as "alternatives to eBay."

Amazon.com Auctions

Amazon.com's business strategy was to be "Earth's most customer-centric company, where customers can find and discover anything they may want to buy online, and [we] endeavor to offer customers the lowest possible prices."[31] With its customer base of 35 million users in over 220 countries and a well-known brand name, Amazon.com was considered the closest overall competitive threat to eBay, especially as eBay expanded its business model beyond is traditional auction services. Created in July 1995 as an online bookseller, Amazon had rapidly transitioned into a full-line, one-stop-shopping retailer with a

product offering that included books, music, toys, electronics, tools and hardware, lawn and patio products, video games, software, and a mall of boutiques (called zShops). Amazon.com was the Internet's number one music, video, and book retailer. One of the distinctive features customers appreciated about Amazon.com was the extensive reviews available for each item. These product reviews were written both by professionals and by regular users who had purchased a specific product. The company's 2004 net income was over $440 million, which was an increase of over 600 percent from 2002 (see Exhibit 7). One significant weakness analysts noted in Amazon's financials was that the company's free shipping policies, put in place to draw more customers, had a significant negative impact on net income.

By 2003 Amazon's management felt that it was in a position that would allow it to balance demands of both cost control and growth in executing a strategy intended to enhance Amazon's position as leader in retail e-commerce. As an indication of the company's success in executing its strategy, its customer base rose from 14 million to 20 million during 2000 and to 35 million by 2004. The company invested

Exhibit 7   **Operating Income (Loss) for Amazon.com, 1996–2004**

Year	Income or (Loss) from Operations (in millions)
1996	$(6.2)
1997	(31.0)
1998	(124.5)
1999	(720.0)
2000	(863.9)
2001	(412.3)
2002	64.1
2003	270.5
2004	440.4

more than $300 million in infrastructure in 1999 and opened two international sites, Amazon.co.uk (the United Kingdom) and Amazon.de (Germany), and later added Amazon.ca (Canada), Amazon.co.jp (Japan), and Amazon.fr (France). These sites, along with Amazon.com, were among the most popular online retail domains in Europe. By 2004 international sales had grown to over $2 billion from just $168 million in 1999 and accounted for 38 percent of all Internet sales.

Some analysts felt that, in expanding its position both internationally and abroad, Amazon had conceded the top spot in online auctions to eBay and was looking for other avenues to expand its business. Amazon was continually looking for innovative ways to expand its product offering and often used strategic alliances to support these initiatives. For example, the company had agreements with Borders Books to allow customers to pick up Amazon.com book orders in-store, as well as e-commerce partnerships with Ashford.com, Drugstore.com, CarsDirect.com, and Sotheby's (a leading auction house for art, antiques, and collectibles), and opened a co-branded toy and video game store online with Toysrus.com. During 2003, the company announced an agreement with the band Pearl Jam to sell the group's music directly to fans through Amazon's Advantage program. By 2003, Amazon.com had over 550,000 active third-party sellers on its site and 350 branded sellers, most of them selling through shops rather than auctions. These third-party sellers accounted for over 22percent of U.S. sales. To further expand its reach, in September 2003 Amazon established an independent

unit called A9 that was charged with creating the best shopping search tool for Amazon's use and for use by other companies and third-party Web sites. To compete with eBay's fixed-price formats, Amazon began including links on product pages that allowed customers to view identical new and used items from third-party sellers.

Yahoo Auctions

Yahoo.com, the first online navigational guide to the Web, launched Yahoo Auctions in 1998. Yahoo.com offered services to nearly 200 million users every month in North America, Europe, Asia, and Latin America. The Web site was available in 24 countries and 12 languages. Yahoo had entered into numerous alliances and marketing agreements to generate additional traffic at its site and was investing in new technology to improve the performance and attractiveness of its site. Its auction services were provided to users free of charge in the early days, and the number of auctions listed on Yahoo increased from 670,000 to 1.3 million during the second half of 1999. However, when Yahoo decided to start charging users a listing fee in January 2001, listings fell from over 2 million to about 200,000.[32] In recognition of the fall in listings due to the listing fee instituted in January, Yahoo! Auctions announced a revamped performance-based pricing model for its U.S. auctions in November, 2001. In this system, which was relatively similar to eBay's, listing fees were reduced and sellers were charged according to the value of an item sold. In response to this change, the number of listings rose to more than 500,000 by December 7, 2001. In an effort to gain even greater market share in the online auction industry, Yahoo Auctions stopped charging fees for any of its auction services on June 6, 2005. Yahoo Auctions also offered many extra services to its users. For example, the Premium Sellers Program was designed to reward the sellers that were consistently at the top of their category. These Premium Sellers were allowed enhanced promotions, premium placement, and direct access to customer support.

While Yahoo had significant reach throughout the world, including over 25 local auction sites internationally, Yahoo Auctions had, by 2004, reduced its international operations from 16 countries to 7 (Brazil, Canada, Hong Kong, Japan, Mexico, Singapore, and Taiwan). In 2002 alone, Yahoo conceded its auction sites in France, Germany, Italy, Spain, the United Kingdom, and Ireland and promoted eBay's sites in each of those countries via banner ads and text links. In 2003, Yahoo sold its Australian site as well. In 2004, however, Yahoo began offering auctions in China through a joint venture with the dominant Chinese Web portal Sina, indicating that it had not completely abandoned the international auction market. Further reinforcing its commitment to online retail, in July 2003 Yahoo acquired Overture, which was the leading provider of commercial search as of the end of the first quarter of 2003 with more than 88,000 advertisers globally as well as an extensive affiliate distribution network. Many of the sellers who advertised on Overture also advertised on eBay, and some analysts estimated that the amount of sales by merchants through the combination of Yahoo's and Overture's offerings would total between one-half to two-thirds of that available on eBay. In August 2005, Yahoo further strengthened its position in China by paying $1 billion in cash for a 40 percent stake in Alibaba.com, an e-commerce company that was one of the largest Internet companies in China, and turned its Chinese operations over to Alibaba.com. Alibaba's Chinese online auction company, TaoBao (which means "searching for treasure"), claimed to be the largest in the country, with 41 percent of the market.[33] The deal was brokered by Softbank, a Japanese broadband Internet provider that aggressively invested in new technologies and successfully paired with Yahoo in 2002 to drive eBay out of Japan. Yahoo believed that this partnership clearly showed Yahoo's long-term commitment to the region, and that the agreement represented the "best approach for Yahoo! to win in this region."[34]

uBid.com

The auction site uBid was founded in April 1997 and offered an initial public offering on the Nasdaq in December 1998. According to its mission statement, uBid was to "be the most recognized and trusted business-to-consumer marketplace, consistently delivering exceptional value and service to its customers and supplier partners."[35] As of 2005, uBid believed that its core values of integrity, agility, execution, caring, and innovation would allow the company to deliver competitive success in the online auction industry and to build valuable relationships with its customers, employees, and suppliers.[36] As

such, uBid considered itself to be in direct competition with eBay, although the company had difficulty denting the portion of eBay's business that was derived from large corporations and smaller companies wanting to sell their products through an auction format. As a company, uBid had experienced increased revenues almost every year since its inception; however, it had never captured the share of the auction market that its founders hoped was possible, although it at one time had a 14.7 percent share of revenues in the online auction market. The company was sold to CGMI Networks in mid-2000, and then it was sold again to Petters Group Worldwide in 2003. With each sale, the number of workers employed by uBid fell and the product mix was changed in an attempt to find a niche market that would insulate the company from the competitive power of eBay.

The business model uBid chose centered on offering brand-name (often refurbished and closeout) merchandise at a deep discount in a relatively broad range of categories from over 1,000 leading manufacturers such as Sony, Hewlett-Packard, IBM, Compaq, AMD, and Minolta. Categories included Computer and Office, Consumer Electronics, Music Movies & Games, Jewelry & Gifts, Travel & Events, Home & Garden, Sports, Toys & Hobbies, Apparel, Collectibles, and Everything Else. The merchandise was offered in both an online auction format in which prices started at $1.00 and through uBid's fixed-price superstore. The merchandise was sourced from corporate partners and from uBid's own operations, which included a 400,000-square-foot warehouse and refurbishment center, and its current parent company Petters Group Worldwide, and from small and medium-sized companies that were members of uBid's Certified Merchant Program. Although uBid had offered consumer-to-consumer auctions at one time, the company had discontinued this option as of 2002 due to the costs associated with policing fraud and concerns over product quality.

Overstock.com

Overstock.com was another online auction company that was beginning to compete more directly with eBay. Founded in 1999, the company was emerging as a growing competitive threat in the online auction industry. Overstock.com specialized in selling excess inventory via the Internet. However, it also enacted an auction feature on its Web site. Sellers listed the opening bid price, the duration of the auction, and the Make It Mine price (which was optional). As evidence of its growing importance in the industry, Overstock's revenues had increased from $1.8 million in 1999 to over $540 million in 2004. The company also claimed to have over 650,000 products listed on its Web sites as of June 2005.

eBAY'S NEW CHALLENGES

Throughout its history, eBay faced each new challenge with an eye on its founding values and an ear for community members. Omidyar stated,

> What we do have to be cautious of, as we grow, is that our core is the personal trade, because the values are communicated person-to-person. It can be easy for a big company to start to believe that it's responsible for its success. Our success is really based on our members' success. They're the ones who have created this, and they're the ones who will create it in the future. If we lose sight of that, then we're in big trouble.[37]

The company applied this perspective in response to significant customer concerns regarding the growing presence of corporate sellers on eBay.

Omidyar and Whitman recognized the importance of eBay's culture and were aware of the potential impact rapid growth and the evolution of the product line could have on this valued asset. When asked about the importance of the culture, Omidyar said, "If we lose that, we've pretty much lost everything."[38] Whitman agreed with Omidyar about the importance of eBay's culture, but she did not see the influx of larger retailers and liquidators as a significant problem. Even as these sellers grew to account for 5 percent of eBay's total business in 2004 (from 1 percent in 2001), these large sellers received no favorable treatment. Whitman stated, "There are no special deals. I am passionate about creating this level playing field."[39] While this view was applauded by the smaller sellers, some larger sellers viewed these policies as overly restrictive and were searching for additional sales outlets.

Heading into 2006, eBay faced two fundamental challenges:

1. How could eBay continue to maintain strong international growth, which was necessary given the maturing of its domestic market?

2. As eBay's business model evolved to include more fixed-price sales in an effort to combat the saturation of its domestic market, could the company transfer its competitive advantage in the online auction industry into the more general area of online retail?

Continued International Growth

While eBay had been able to secure a significant market share in many of the countries in which it was operating, the company was still well aware of its failed venture into the Japanese market. The company had decided to pull out of Japan in 2002 as a result of stiff competition from Yahoo and eBay's unwillingness to cede decision-making authority to local Japanese managers. The Japanese experience was especially salient as it appeared that the primary battleground in the online auction industry for the foreseeable future would be another Asian market—China—and that its main competition would be the Yahoo-backed competitor TaoBao. As early as 2000, eBay had begun to cautiously build its presence in the Chinese online auction industry. However, there were a number of significant challenges in penetrating the Chinese market, including the fact that many Chinese consumers were suspicious of online transactions, many of these consumers did not have credit cards, and the Chinese transportation system was not sufficient to guarantee timely delivery of items won in online auctions.[40] In 2002, eBay bought a 33 percent stake in Eachnet, a Chinese online auction company patterned after eBay, and then purchased the remaining 67 percent of the company in 2003. By the end of 2005, eBay was still losing money in its Chinese operations despite having 13.2 million registered Chinese users.

The company's position in China was especially troubling, given Amazon.com's recent announcement that it had made the Chinese market a top priority and the new partnership between Yahoo and Alibaba. Alibaba's online auction subsidiary (Tao Bao) was overseen by Alibaba's CEO, Jack Ma, who had a reputation as a scrappy competitor. Since its founding in 2003, TaoBao had been an aggressive challenger to eBay's Eachnet. In an attempt to build a large user base, TaoBao did not charge any fees for its services and did not plan to do so until 2006 at the earliest. Additionally, the company claimed to have tailored its offerings particularly well to the Chinese market by offering services such as instant messaging between users and having online forum managers take the names of heroes from Chinese literature. In order to complete the business model, the company established AliPay, an online payment service, in 2003. In an effort to attract customers, it had shunned TV advertising such as that used by eBay in China and instead relied on word of mouth, which many analysts believed was the key to Chinese marketing, and it had also directly targeted eBay's users through a variety of unconventional means.[41] In one guerrilla marketing campaign, a contingent from TaoBao disrupted an eBay user seminar by hanging a TaoBao sign in the conference room, having the waitstaff hand out TaoBao flyers to seminar attendees, and then offering to reimburse the attendees for their registration fees and inviting them to dinner.[42]

By the end of 2005, TaoBao had established itself as a legitimate contender for the Chinese online auction industry and had developed strong customer loyalty among its user base. In fact, TaoBao claimed to be the largest Chinese online auction company, with 7.2 million registered users and $200 million in sales during the second quarter of 2005, as compared to eBay's 13.2 million registered users and $100 million in sales in China. However, the Chinese online auction industry was still in its early stages, with less than 8 percent of China's population of 1.3 billion people using the Internet. As such, experts believed there was still significant room for growth in the Chinese market. While Whitman and eBay had learned a lesson from eBay's failure in the Japanese market and had given more authority to local Chinese managers, Ma felt that TaoBao would prevail due to his personal knowledge of the Chinese market and that the company would be profitable 18 months after it started charging fees.[43] Not willing to surrender in the Chinese market as it had in Japan, eBay had consistently reaffirmed its commitment to the market and had even used phone calls and special promotions to pursue individual power sellers who had moved to TaoBao.

Evolution of the Business Model

By virtually any measure, eBay's growth had been outstanding. However, this impressive track record, coupled with the progress the company had made

in reaching its stated goals, had created high expectations among investors. These lofty expectations began to cause some concern among analysts as eBay's domestic core market of online auction sales began to show some warning signals. In many categories, as the number of sellers grew supply was beginning to outstrip demand. Almost half of eBay's registered users were from the United States and represented almost one-third of all U.S. Internet users. With the U.S. online auction market maturing and eBay's dominant market share, analysts were concerned with how much more penetration eBay could achieve.

In response to these concerns, eBay cited new trends indicating that even in the United States the company was reaching new customers and had room to grow. One of the trends eBay saw as particularly promising was the increasing use of eBay's more than 50,000 registered Trading Assistants and the emergence of drop-off eBay consignment services. Trading Assistants were experienced eBay sellers who, for a fee, would help users sell their items on eBay. Extending this service, drop-off consignment services begin to spring up as early as 2000. These consignment services, such as AuctionDrop, Quick-Drop, and Picture-It-Sold, would take physical possession of a customer's items, typically those with an eBay value of over $50, and sell them on eBay for a fee equal to between 30 and 40 percent of the item's final sale price. The company was encouraged by these activities, which allowed it reach sellers who would not normally use the Internet.

There was little concern that anyone would seriously threaten eBay in its core auction business in the near future. However, the increasing use of tools such as gift certificates, the growing importance of fixed-price sales, the purchase of Half.com, and the growing popularity of Buy It Now put eBay into more direct competition with retailers such as Amazon.com, with e-commerce solutions, and with the likes of Microsoft. When asked about how the evolution of its business model influenced eBay's sphere of competition, Whitman said,

> If we were a retailer, we'd be the 27th-largest in the world. So our sellers are competing [with retailers] for consumer dollars. If you're thinking about buying a set of golf clubs or a tennis racket or a jacket or a pair of skis, you decide whether you're going to do that at eBay, at Wal-Mart, a sporting-goods store, or Macy's. I would define our competition more broadly than ever before.[44]

The threat of these competitors increased as fixed-price sales comprised an ever-increasing percentage of eBay's total sales and growth. In mid-2005, fixed-price trading accounted for 29 percent of eBay's gross merchandise sales (the dollar value of merchandise sold) and was expected to experience continued growth throughout the foreseeable future.

THE FUTURE

Ten years since its inception, eBay had continued to enjoy heightened levels of financial success and was the dominant player in the online auction industry. However, there were several emerging issues that clouded the company's future, and this was reflected in the volatility of its stock price (see Exhibit 8). The recent downgrades of eBay's stock seemed to indicate

that Wall Street analysts were not as optimistic about eBay's ability to sustain its phenomenal growth rate and to extend its dominance to the global online auction industry. The company's executives needed to address several questions: Should additional expansion in the international markets be the highest priority? If so, in what countries should expansion efforts be focused? Alternatively, should eBay strive to broaden its offerings to include more categories, more specialty sites, and more sellers? And how much emphasis should be put on fixed-price options? If management opted to continue expanding eBay's fixed-price offerings and put the company into greater head-to-head competition with established online retailers, what competitive advantage could it hope to achieve? Would it be able to compete successfully against new, more diverse competitors such as paid search engines?

Exhibit 8   **eBay's Stock Price Performance, December 2004–December 2005**

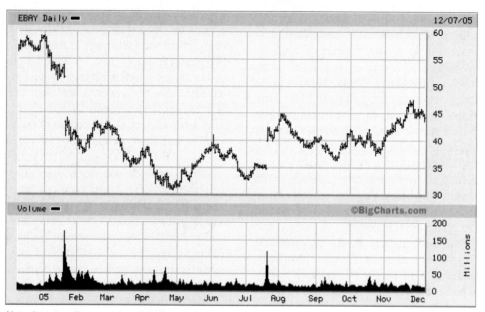

Note: A stock split occurred on February 17, 2005.
Source: www.bigcharts.com, December 8, 2005.

Endnotes

1 2004 eBay annual report.
2 Ibid.
3 Ibid.
4 Claire Tristram, " 'Amazing'Amazon," www.contextmag.com, November 1999.
5 Quentin Hardy, "The Radical Philanthropist," *Forbes,* May 1, 2000, p. 118.
6 "Billionaires of the Web," *Business 2.0,* June 1999.
7 eBay press release, May 7, 1998.
8 http://pages.ebay.com/help/community/values.html, December 18, 2005.
9 "Q&A with eBay's Meg Whitman," *BusinessWeek E. Biz,* December 3, 2001.
10 Ibid.
11 Claire Tristram, "'Amazoning' Amazon," www.contextmag.com, November 1999.
12 2000 eBay annual report.
13 2004 eBay annual report.
14 Company press release, September 12, 2005.
15 "Q&A with eBay's Meg Whitman."
16 2004 eBay annual report.
17 Company press release, September 12, 2005.
18 Company press release, March 8, 2005.
19 Company press release, August 30, 2005.
20 Company press release, May 18, 1999.
21 1999 eBay annual report.
22 Company press release, September 12, 2005.
23 Company press release, November 16, 2004.
24 Company press release, December 1, 2004.

25 Company press release, April 22, 2005.
26 Company press release, June 22, 2004.
27 Ann Pearson, in an eBay press release dated October 15, 1998.
28 eBay press release, October 8, 1999.
29 2004 eBay annual report.
30 eBay 10Q Annual Report, November 14, 2001.
31 2004 Amazon annual report.
32 Troy Wolverton, "eBay Seeks to Sail into New Territory," CNET News.com, July 19, 2001.
33 "Hot Bidding: In a Challenging China Market, eBay Confronts a Big New Rival; Yahoo Backs a Local Firm; An Online-Auction Duel Stirs Memories of Japan; Mr. Ma's Plans for Alibaba," *The Wall Street Journal,* August 12, 2005, p. A1.
34 Yahoo company press release, August 10, 2005.
35 www.ubid.com/about/companyinfo.asp, December 18, 2005.
36 Ibid.
37 "Q&A with eBay's Pierre Omidyar," *BusinessWeek E. Biz,* December 3, 2001.
38 "The People's Company," *BusinessWeek E. Biz,* December 3, 2001.
39 "Queen of the Online Flea Market," Economist.com, December 30, 2003.
40 "Can Eachnet Become an eBay in China's Image?" *BusinessWeek Online,* March 27, 2000.
41 "Hot Bidding."
42 Ibid.
43 Ibid.
44 "Meg Whitman on eBay's Self-Regulation," *BusinessWeek Online,* August 18, 2003.

Google Inc. in 2006: Can the Strategy Support the Lofty Stock Price?

John E. Gamble
University of South Alabama

In 2005, Internet searches were the second most common online activity after e-mail. Advertisers spent an estimated $12 billion on paid search Internet ads in 2005—375 percent more than spending for such ads in 2004. Advertisers believed that search-based ads were particularly effective because they were highly targeted to what Internet users were immediately searching for. In 2005, Google was the leading search engine on the Web and the leading provider of search-based ads because of Internet users' faith in the search engine. The company did not collect information on search users, placed ads discreetly on its page listing search results, and did not intersperse paid search results with nonpaid search results. Perhaps Google's most important feature was its capability to retrieve highly relevant results to search queries that was made possible by its innovative PageRank technology.

When an Internet user entered a search query at Google.com, from a Google toolbar or deskbar, or from a Web site that licensed Google's search appliance, the search engine performed a computation of an equation involving 500 million variables and 2 billion terms to generate a list of best-matching search results. The results were generated in a fraction of a second and pulled from billions of Web sites that were constantly downloaded onto Google's farm of an estimated 250,000 PCs. The reason many Internet users found Google's search results more relevant than results generated by competing search engines was based on this equation, which assessed

how well the search terms matched and, most important, how many other Web sites pointed to a site. Google cofounder Larry Page suggested that Google's technology, which counted the number of "votes" for various Web sites that might match search requests, was superior to other search technologies, saying, "You're asking the whole Web who's the greatest site to ask about this subject."[1]

Internet users' preference for Google's search results allowed the company to establish hundreds of thousands of accounts with advertisers, which had produced 2004 revenues of nearly $3.2 billion and profits of more than $399 million. The company executed a successful initial public offering (IPO) in August 2004 that brought in an investment of $1.7 billion and made a subsequent offering of shares in September 2005 that added nearly $4.3 billion to its coffers. The company's cash and cash equivalents stood at $5.5 billion at the end of its third quarter of fiscal 2005. At year-end 2005, Google seemed poised to repeat its stellar 217 percent growth rate in revenues and 377 percent growth rate in net income between 2003 and 2004, since its revenues and net income for the first nine months of the fiscal year stood at $4.2 billion and $1.1 million, respectively. Google's highly scalable business model delivered profits for the first nine months of 2005 of more than $500,000 per employee.

Google's stock price had risen from its $85 IPO price in August 2004 to over $443 at year-end 2005. In late December 2005, the shares traded at a price/earnings multiple of 95—pushing its market capitalization over $131 billion. In comparison, the market capitalization for General Motors was $12 billion, the market value of Chevron's shares was $129 billion, and Intel's market cap was $159 billion. Some analysts still saw Google as a "strong buy" since as much as 30 percent of consumers' exposure to media was through the Internet and, as of 2005, only a small fraction of the $300–$400 billion spent on advertising in the United States was allocated to Internet ads.

Others considered Google's stock to be highly overvalued—pointing to a business model that relied almost exclusively on revenue from search-based ads. Over time, such ads might prove to be less effective than other forms of advertising or might reach more Internet users if provided by a rival search engine. Clearly, Web portals such as Yahoo and MSN were working furiously to improve search functionality to lure Google's loyal users to their sites. Yahoo had developed its own search capabilities in 2003 and severed its three-year agreement with Google to provide search results and ads for its own Web portal in July 2004. Microsoft had spent more than $150 million and taken 18 months to build a search engine in an effort to match Google feature for feature. MSN Search was launched in the winter of 2005 and provided direct links to MSN Encarta and other sites for searches written in plain language. In addition, MSN search users could search image files, music files, news stories, e-mails, and files residing on their PCs; they could also narrow search results locally and pull up satellite-based street maps for almost any part of the world.

Perhaps the biggest threat Microsoft posed to Google's dominance in search was its ability to embed MSN Search into Outlook, Internet Explorer, and Office applications. In fact, Microsoft had a long track record of exploiting Windows integration to upset incumbents as the market leader. During the late 1980s and early 1990s, Excel surpassed Lotus 1-2-3 as the market leader in spreadsheets within four years of its launch. Lotus held a 70 percent market share prior to Excel's development. Similarly, Word beat out WordPerfect as the dominant word processing program, and Netscape proved to be no match for Microsoft in the war for market share in the browser category.

Also of concern to some analysts was the mysterious nature of Google's cash reserves. International expansion and the development of new features such as Voice over Internet Protocol (VoIP) telephone service were obvious strategic initiatives Google should pursue, but the company had made no comments regarding the specific use of its $5.5 billion cash balance. The company also held $2.1 billion in marketable securities at the end of its third quarter of 2005. Google's management itself seemed uncertain what might drive future growth. The company's two founders, Sergey Brin and Larry Page, wrote in the company's IPO prospectus, "We would fund products that have a 10% chance of earning a billion dollars over the long term. Don't be surprised if we place smaller bets in areas that seem very speculative or even strange." The company's cash reserves had spawned hordes of Mountain View, California, entrepreneurs with the end goal of being acquired by Google. However, as of late 2005, Google had been a tough sell for those making pitches, having completed only five modestly sized acquisitions. The company's expanded advertising partnership with America Online (AOL) announced in December 2005 that involved Google acquiring a 5 percent stake in AOL for $1 billion was by far its most ambitious financial investment.

COMPANY HISTORY

The development of Google's search technology began in January 1996 when Stanford University computer science graduate students Larry Page and Sergey Brin collaborated to develop a new search engine they named BackRub. The name BackRub was chosen because of the engine's ability to rate Web sites for relevancy by examining the number of back links pointing to them. The approach for assessing the relevancy of Web sites to a particular search query used by other Web sites at the time was based on examining and counting metatags and keywords included on various Web sites. By 1997, the search accuracy of BackRub had allowed it to gain a loyal following among Silicon Valley Internet users. Yahoo cofounder David Filo was among the converted, and in 1998 he convinced Sergey Brin and Larry Page to leave Stanford to focus on making their search technology the backbone of a new Internet company.

BackRub would be renamed Google, which was a play on the word *googol*—a mathematical term for a number represented by the numeral 1 followed by 100 zeros. Brin and Page's adoption of the new name reflected their mission to organize a seemingly infinite amount of information on the Internet. In August 1998, a Stanford professor arranged for Brin and Page to meet at his home with a potential angel investor to demonstrate the Google search engine. The investor, who had been a founder of Sun Microsystems, was immediately impressed with Google's search capabilities but was too pressed for time to hear much of the informal presentation. The investor stopped the two during the presentation and suggested, "Instead of us discussing all the details, why don't I just write you a check?"[2] The two partners held the investor's $100,000 check made payable to Google Inc. for two weeks while they scrambled to set up a corporation named Google Inc. and open a corporate bank account. The two officers of the freshly incorporated company went on to raise a total of $1 million in venture capital from family, friends, and other angel investors by the end of September 1998.

Even with a cash reserve of $1 million, the two partners ran Google on a shoestring budget, with its main servers built by Brin and Page from discounted computer components and its four employees operating out of a garage owned by a friend of the founders. By year-end 1998 Google's beta version was handling 10,000 search queries per day and *PC Magazine* had named the company to its list of "Top 100 Web Sites and Search Engines for 1998."

The new company recorded successes at a lightning-fast pace, with the search kernel answering more than 500,000 queries per day and Red Hat agreeing to become the company's first search customer in early 1999. Google attracted an additional $25 million in funding from two leading Silicon Valley venture capital firms by midyear 1999 to support further growth and enhancements to Google's search technology. Google began to add employees, bringing the total number up to 39 by the end of 1999, and to add key customers for its search functionality—including AOL and Virgilio, the leading online portal in Italy—which helped push search requests to more than 3 million per day.

In 2000, Google Inc. grew to 60 employees, introduced wireless search technology, provided search services for new Web portal customers in the United States, Europe, and Asia, launched search capabilities in 10 non-English languages, expanded its index of ranked Web sites to 1.3 billion, was called the "Best Bet Search Engine" by *PC World*, and was named by *Yahoo Internet Life* magazine as the "Best Search Engine on the Internet." Yahoo also signed an agreement to make Google its default search provider, which helped make Google the largest search engine on the Web, with more than 100 million daily searches. During 2000, the company also introduced the Google Toolbar browser plug-in, which allowed computer users to search the Internet without first visiting a Google-affiliated Web portal or Google's homepage. Among its most important innovations in 2000 was the development of keyword-targeted advertising, which provided the company with an additional revenue source beyond fees for licensing its search appliance to other Web sites.

In 2001, Google signed agreements with such wireless providers as Sprint PCS, Cingular, and AT&T that gave mobile phone users access to Google's index of Web pages. Also that year, the company acquired Deja.com, which provided Google with the Internet's largest archive of searchable messages posted on Usenet discussion boards. In other developments, Google expanded its search capabilities to 28 languages—allowing it to establish licensing agreements with 130 Web portals and destination sites in Latin American, Asian, Middle Eastern, and European countries; introduced new capabilities that enabled Google users to search an index of 250 million images, review and search daily news, search more than 1,100 mail order catalogs, and search for any published phone number in the United States; and expanded its search-based advertising program to include small businesses and individuals with a self-service advertising system that gave small advertisers the capability to set up ads online and pay Google by credit card on a per click basis. The expansion of advertising-based revenue allowed Google to increase annual revenues from $220,000 in 1999 to more than $86 million in 2001 and end the year with a profit of nearly $7 million.

Google's rapid growth in services and revenues made it obvious to Sergey Brin and Larry Page that the company needed executive-level management with experience in managing a large, rapidly growing company. In March 2001, the two asked Novell CEO and chairman Eric Schmidt to chair Google's board of directors. Four months later, Google's founders and board asked Schmidt to become CEO of the company, which moved Page to president of products and Brin to president of technology. Schmidt was brought in to introduce formal processes, procedures, and financial systems to the almost anarchic business environment that resulted from the company's unorthodox corporate culture. Employees at the company's Googleplex headquarters in Mountain View, California, were encouraged to work on pet projects that might be unrelated to work assignments, bring dogs to work, and engage in twice-a-week hockey games where checking higher-ups was fair game. Also, prior to Schmidt's arrival, important strategy and operating issues were settled by upper-level management during weekly two-hour meetings that rarely had an agenda and wandered from topic to topic. Google's board wanted Schmidt to bring a sufficient level of structure to the company to prepare it for an IPO, but avoid a cumbersome bureaucracy that would limit Google's ability to sustain its technological advantage. Schmidt commented just prior to Google's registration for a public offering that his instruction from the board was "Don't screw this up now, Eric. This is a really, really good starting point . . . So it doesn't require some gross change."[3]

In a March 2004 interview with *The Wall Street Journal,* Eric Schmidt stated, "You do not want to take big-company structures and apply them to small companies. You want to evolve small-company structures on a need-appropriate basis."[4] Even though Schmidt was made Google's CEO, both Page and Brin were deeply involved in strategy making, forming what was described by the three as a "triumvirate."[5] When asked about the roles of the two founders in decision making, Schmidt, who many business journalists suggested should have been given the title of chief operating officer instead of CEO, commented, "Whenever we have something important, two people have to agree . . . Now, often the two are the founders. When it's managerial things, things Larry and Sergey aren't as focused on, we try to get two of the vice presidents to agree."[6] Under Eric Schmidt's leadership as CEO, Google continued to add new features such as Google Compute, parcel tracking, flight information, vehicle identification number searches, Google News, Froogle, Google Deskbar, Local Search, and Gmail. A complete list of Google services and tools at year-end 2005 is presented in Exhibit 1. Exhibit 2 provides an overview of free software downloads from Google at year-end 2005.

THE INITIAL PUBLIC OFFERING

Two and a half years after Eric Schmidt arrived at Google to institute formal policies, procedures, and controls to ensure that Google did not collapse under the pressures of its accelerated growth rate, the company filed its Form S-1 Registration Statement for an initial public offering (IPO) of common stock. Google's April 29, 2004, IPO registration became the most-talked-about planned offering involving an Internet company since the dot-com bust of 2000. The registration announced Google's intention to raise as much as $3.6 billion from the issue of 25.7 million shares through an unusual Dutch auction.

One of the 10 key beliefs that comprised Google's philosophy (presented in Exhibit 3) was "You can make money without doing evil."[7] The choice of a Dutch auction stemmed from this belief since Dutch auctions allowed potential investors, regardless of size, to place bids for shares. Small investors were typically locked out of participating in IPOs since brokers handling such trades favored institutional investors or individual investors with large portfolio balances or frequent trades. After a period when investors could bid for Google shares over the Internet, the Dutch auction set the clearing price for Google shares at the lowest bid that allowed all shares to be sold. On the day the IPO was finalized, any potential investor bidding the clearing price or higher was granted shares at the clearing price. A Dutch auction would also be favorable to Google since it involved considerably lower investment banking and underwriting fees and little or no commissions for brokers.

Google's financial advisers initially believed the company's shares would fetch between $108 and $135 per share, but the clearing price was ultimately set at $85 after it became apparent that the Dutch auction process would not generate sufficient demand for the company's shares. The poor demand was caused by a number of factors, which included institutional investors' uneasiness with placing a bid absent satisfactory pricing guidance; individual investors' unfamiliarity with the auction process; and even though 28 brokerage firms were involved in the underwriting syndicate, brokers' unwillingness to help clients purchase shares when few or no commissions were involved.

Regardless of the shortcomings of the Dutch auction process, Google's initial offering was the 25th-largest U.S. IPO of all time. Google's shares appreciated by 18 percent during first day trading, making both Brin and Page about $600 million richer by the end of the day and each worth approximately $3.8 billion. Also, an estimated 900 to 1,000 Google employees were worth at least $1 million, with 600 to 700 holding at least $2 million in Google stock. On average, each of Google's 2,292 staff members held approximately $1.7 million in company stock, excluding the holdings of the top five executives.

Exhibit 1   **List of Google Services and Tools at Year-End 2005**

 Alerts
Receive news and search results via email

 Answers
Ask a question, set a price, get an answer

 Blog Search
Find blogs on your favorite topics

 Book Search
Search the full text of books

 Catalogs
Search and browse mail-order catalogs

 Directory
Browse the web by topic

 Froogle
Shop smarter with Google

 Groups
Create mailing lists and discussion groups

 Images
Search for images on the web

 Labs
Try out new Google products

 Blogger
Express yourself online

 Code
Download APIs and open source code

 Desktop
Info when you want it, right on your desktop

 Earth
Explore the world from your PC

 Gmail
A Google approach to email

 Local
Find local businesses and services

 Maps
View maps and get directions

 Mobile
Use Google on your mobile phone

 News
Search thousands of news stories

 Scholar
Search scholarly papers

 SMS
Use text messaging for quick info

 Special Searches
Search within specific topics

 University Search
Search a specific school's website

 Web Search
Search over billions of web pages

 Web Search Features
Do more with search

 Local for mobile
View maps and get directions on your phone

 Picasa
Find, edit and share your photos

 Talk
IM and call your friends through your computer

 Toolbar
Add a search box to your browser

 Translate
View web pages in other languages

Source: Google.com.

Exhibit 2   **Free Software Downloads from Google at Year-End 2005**

 Software Downloads

Upgrade your computer with free Google downloads
Google can improve more than just your search experience. The free software on this page makes it easier to get the most out of your computer. Currently available for Windows® computers only (Gmail Notifier also available for Mac OS X).

Google Talk
- Make free calls and send IMs through your computer
- Talk anytime, anywhere and for as long as you want
- More info...

By downloading and installing, you agree to the Terms of Service and Privacy Policy

[Download Now]

Google Toolbar
- Add a search box to your browser
- Block annoying pop-ups
- Automatically fill in online forms
- *For Internet Explorer 5.5+* (*Firefox version* **also available**)
- More info...

[Download Now]

Google Desktop 2
- Find all your email, files, photos, web history, and more
- Get all your personalized info in one place with Sidebar
- More info...

By downloading and installing, you agree to the Terms & Conditions and Privacy Policy

[Download Now]

Picasa Photo Organizer
- Find photos on your computer
- Edit photos and remove red-eye
- Create and share albums
- Print your photos at home
- More info...

Google Earth (BETA)
- Fly over a 3D model of the globe
- Search for hotels, dining, and more
- Get directions and fly the route
- Tilt, rotate for 3D terrain and buildings
- More info...

Gmail Notifier (BETA)
- Get alerts of new messages
- Preview email in the alerts window
- Works with any Gmail account
- *Get a free account (US only)*
- Now available for Mac OS X
- More info...

Blogger for Word   Post from Microsoft Word 2000+ to your blog   More info...

Source: Google.com.

Stanford University realized a $179.5 million windfall from its stock holdings granted for its early investment in Brin and Page's search engine. Some of Google's early contractors and consultants also profited handsomely from forgoing fees in return for stock options in the company. One such contractor was Abbe Patterson, who took options for 4,000 shares rather than a $5,000 fee for preparing a PowerPoint presentation and speaking notes for one of Brin and Page's first presentations to venture capitalists. After two splits and four days of trading, her 16,000 shares were worth $1.7 million.[8]

The company executed a second public offering of 14,159,265 shares of common stock in September 2005. The number of shares issued represented the first eight digits to the right of the decimal point for the value pi (π). The issue added more than $4 billion to Google's liquid assets and, as with the proceeds from the company's IPO, its management offered no specific use for the cash infusion. In its filing with the U.S. Securities and Exchange Commission, the company's management triumvirate stated that the proceeds would be for "general corporate purposes, including working capital and capital expenditures,

Exhibit 3   **The Google Philosophy: "Ten things Google has found to be true"**

1. Focus on the user and all else will follow.

From its inception, Google has focused on providing the best user experience possible. While many companies claim to put their customers first, few are able to resist the temptation to make small sacrifices to increase shareholder value. Google has steadfastly refused to make any change that does not offer a benefit to the users who come to the site:

• The interface is clear and simple.

• Pages load instantly.

• Placement in search results is never sold to anyone.

• Advertising on the site must offer relevant content and not be a distraction.

By always placing the interests of the user first, Google has built the most loyal audience on the web. And that growth has come not through TV ad campaigns, but through word of mouth from one satisfied user to another.

2. It's best to do one thing really, really well.

Google does search. With one of the world's largest research groups focused exclusively on solving search problems, we know what we do well, and how we could do it better. Through continued iteration on difficult problems, we've been able to solve complex issues and provide continuous improvements to a service already considered the best on the web at making finding information a fast and seamless experience for millions of users. Our dedication to improving search has also allowed us to apply what we've learned to new products, including Gmail, Google Desktop, and Google Maps.

3. Fast is better than slow.

Google believes in instant gratification. You want answers and you want them right now. Who are we to argue? Google may be the only company in the world whose stated goal is to have users leave its website as quickly as possible. By fanatically obsessing on shaving every excess bit and byte from our pages and increasing the efficiency of our serving environment, Google has broken its own speed records time and again.

4. Democracy on the web works.

Google works because it relies on the millions of individuals posting websites to determine which other sites offer content of value. Instead of relying on a group of editors or solely on the frequency with which certain terms appear, Google ranks every web page using a breakthrough technique called PageRank™. PageRank evaluates all of the sites linking to a web page and assigns them a value, based in part on the sites linking to them. By analyzing the full structure of the web, Google is able to determine which sites have been "voted" the best sources of information by those most interested in the information they offer.

5. You don't need to be at your desk to need an answer.

The world is increasingly mobile and unwilling to be constrained to a fixed location. Whether it's through their PDAs, their wireless phones or even their automobiles, people want information to come to them.

6. You can make money without doing evil.

Google is a business. The revenue the company generates is derived from offering its search technology to companies and from the sale of advertising displayed on Google and on other sites across the web. However, you may have never seen an ad on Google. That's because Google does not allow ads to be displayed on our results pages unless they're relevant to the results page on which they're shown. So, only certain searches produce sponsored links above or to the right of the results. Google firmly believes that ads can provide useful information if, and only if, they are relevant to what you wish to find. Advertising on Google is always clearly identified as a "Sponsored Link." It is a core value for Google that there be no compromising of the integrity of our results. We never manipulate rankings to put our partners higher in our search results. No one can buy better PageRank. Our users trust Google's objectivity and no short-term gain could ever justify breaching that trust.

7. There's always more information out there.

Once Google had indexed more of the HTML pages on the Internet than any other search service, our engineers turned their attention to information that was not as readily accessible. Sometimes it was just a matter of integrating new databases, such as adding a phone number and address lookup and a business directory. Other efforts required a bit more creativity, like adding the ability to search billions of images and a way to view pages that were originally created as PDF files. The popularity of PDF results led us to expand the list of file types searched to include documents produced in a dozen formats such as Microsoft Word, Excel and PowerPoint. For wireless users, Google developed a unique way to translate HTML formatted files into a format that could be read by mobile devices. The list is not likely to end there as Google's researchers continue looking into ways to bring all the world's information to users seeking answers.

(Continued)

Exhibit 3 **Continued**

---

8. The need for information crosses all borders.

Though Google is headquartered in California, our mission is to facilitate access to information for the entire world, so we have offices around the globe. To that end we maintain dozens of Internet domains and serve more than half of our results to users living outside the United States. Google search results can be restricted to pages written in more than 35 languages according to a user's preference. We also offer a translation feature to make content available to users regardless of their native tongue and for those who prefer not to search in English, Google's interface can be customized into more than 100 languages.

9. You can be serious without a suit.

Google's founders have often stated that the company is not serious about anything but search. They built a company around the idea that work should be challenging and the challenge should be fun. To that end, Google's culture is unlike any in corporate America, and it's not because of the ubiquitous lava lamps and large rubber balls, or the fact that the company's chef used to cook for the Grateful Dead. In the same way Google puts users first when it comes to our online service, Google Inc. puts employees first when it comes to daily life in our Googleplex headquarters. There is an emphasis on team achievements and pride in individual accomplishments that contribute to the company's overall success. Ideas are traded, tested and put into practice with an alacrity that can be dizzying. Meetings that would take hours elsewhere are frequently little more than a conversation in line for lunch and few walls separate those who write the code from those who write the checks. This highly communicative environment fosters a productivity and camaraderie fueled by the realization that millions of people rely on Google results. Give the proper tools to a group of people who like to make a difference, and they will.

10. Great just isn't good enough.

Always deliver more than expected. Google does not accept being the best as an endpoint, but a starting point. Through innovation and iteration, Google takes something that works well and improves upon it in unexpected ways. Google's point of distinction however, is anticipating needs not yet articulated by our global audience, then meeting them with products and services that set new standards. This constant dissatisfaction with the way things are is ultimately the driving force behind the world's best search engine.

Source: Google.com.

---

and possible acquisitions of complementary businesses, technologies or other assets." The team added that the company had "no current agreements or commitments with respect to any material acquisitions."[9] Exhibit 4 tracks the performance of Google's common shares between August 19, 2004, and December 16, 2005.

GOOGLE'S BUSINESS MODEL

Google's business model generated revenue from only two sources: (1) the licensing fees it charged to supply search capabilities to corporations, other Internet sites, and wireless telephone companies, and (2) the advertising fees it charged for providing highly targeted text-only sponsor links adjacent to its search results. Page and Brin insisted that the company would only sell discreet text ads placed near search results and never mix paid keyword-based ads with legitimate search results even though the practice was standard among search engine companies. Also, Google would not place banner ads on its Web site, nor would it sell pop-up ads.

Google's founders also had no interest in the search engine evolving into a Web portal such as Yahoo, MSN, or AOL.com.

Google Search Appliance

Google's search technology could be integrated into a third party's Web site or intranet if search functionality was important to the customer. The Google search appliance could be installed in one day and could search both public Web pages and local intranets to return relevant results for search users. The search appliance was available in four models tailored to the size of the organization and its search requirements. The Google Mini allowed small businesses to search up to 100,000 documents stored on local PCs and servers. The Google Mini hardware and software package could be licensed online for $2,995. The model GB-1001 was designed for departments or midsized companies and could be licensed at prices beginning at $30,000. The GB-5005 was developed for companies needing searches for companywide intranets or customer-facing Web sites, with pricing beginning at $230,000. The GB-8008 was best suited for global business units and could be implemented at licensing fees beginning at $600,000.

Exhibit 4 **Performance of Google Inc.'s Stock Price, August 19, 2004, to December 19, 2005**

(a) Trend in Google Inc.'s Common Stock Price

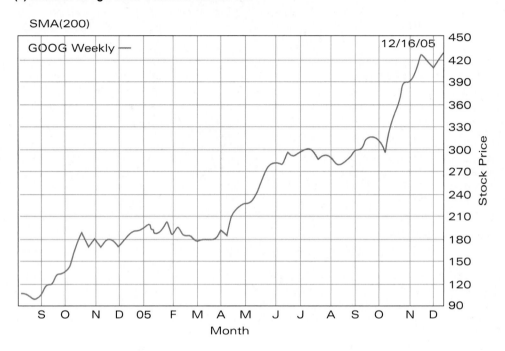

(b) Performance of Google Inc.'s Stock Price versus the S&P 500 Index

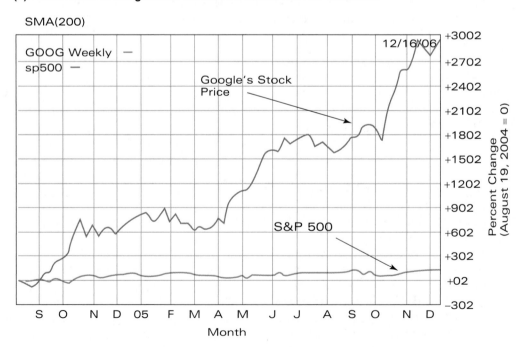

AdWords

Google AdWords allowed advertisers to, either independently through Google's automated tools or with the assistance of Google's marketing teams, create text-based ads that would appear alongside Google search results. AdWords users could evaluate the effectiveness of their advertising expenditures with Google through the use of performance reports that tracked the effectiveness of each ad. Google also offered a keyword targeting program that suggested synonyms for keywords entered by advertisers, a traffic estimator that helped potential advertiser anticipate cost-per-click (CPC) charges, and multiple payment options that included charges to credit cards, debit cards, and monthly invoicing. Google accepted payment for ads in 48 currencies.

Larger advertisers were offered additional services to help run large, dynamic advertising campaigns. Such assistance included the availability of specialists with expertise in various industries to offer suggestions for targeting potential customers, offer suggestions in identifying relevant keywords, and help develop ads that would increase click-through rates and purchase rates. Google also offered its large advertising customers bulk posting services that helped launch and manage campaigns including ads using hundreds or thousands of keywords.

Even though all advertisers were allowed to bid on keywords to achieve a more prominent placement, ads that were infrequently selected by Internet users moved to a less visible placement—regardless of the amount of the advertiser's bid for a keyword. Ads that were frequently clicked on by Internet users moved up the list, ensuring that the most relevant ads always had a good placement on Google's site.

Google also allowed users to pay a CPC rate lower than their bid price if their bid was considerably more than the next highest bid. For example, an advertiser who bid $0.75 per click for a particular keyword would only be charged $0.51 per click if the next highest bid was only $0.50. The AdWords discounter ensured that advertisers paid only 1 cent more than the next highest bid, regardless of the actual amount of their bid.

AdSense

Google's AdSense program allowed Web publishers to share in the advertising revenues generated by Google's CPC text ads. The AdSense program served content-relevant Google text ads to pages of Google Network Web sites. For example, an Internet user reading an article about the shortage of Splenda, an artificial sweetener popularized by the Atkins diet, at Foxnews.com would see two Google text ads from mail order sellers of Splenda embedded in the article. Google Network members did not pay a fee to participate in the program and received the majority of advertising dollars generated from the ads. Owners of dormant domain names could also participate in the AdSense program. During the first nine months of fiscal 2005, 79 percent of advertising revenue generated from such ads was paid to Google Network Web publishers.

The breakdown of Google's revenues by source is presented in the table below:

	Nine Months Ending September 30, 2005	2004	2003	2002	2001
Advertising revenues:					
Google Web sites	$2,278,848	$1,589,032	$772,192	$306,977	$66,932
Google Network Web sites	1,889,369	1,554,256	144,411	12,278	—
Total advertising revenues	4,168,217	3,143,288	916,603	319,255	66,932
Licensing and other revenues	51,251	45,935	45,271	28,593	19,494
Net revenues	$4,419,468	$3,189,223	$961,874	$347,848	$86,426

Source: Google Inc., Form S-1, filed April 29, 2004; 2004 Form 10-K; Form 10-Q, November 10, 2005.

GOOGLE'S COMPETITIVE POSITION AND STRATEGY GOING INTO 2006

Google's ability to sustain its competitive advantage among Internet search companies was a function of its ability to maintain strong relationships with Internet users, advertisers, and Web sites. In 2005, Internet users searching for information went to Google more often than to any other site with search capabilities. The breakdown of U.S. Internet searches among Web sites offering search capabilities in April 2005 is shown in the following table:

Search Company	% of Searches
Google	47%
Yahoo	21
MSN	14
AOL	—
Others	18
Total	100%

Source: Nielsen/NetRatings as reported by *Fortune Online,* April 18, 2005.

There was nothing that would prevent Internet users from abandoning Google to use a better search technology. Google's status in 2005 as the search engine of choice for most Internet users allowed its AdWords program to attract advertisers and its AdSense program attract Network members that would display Google ads. The development of a better search engine by a rival could lead to rapid erosion of advertising revenues for Google. Google management believed its primary competitors were Yahoo and Microsoft.

Google's Internet Rivals

Yahoo   Yahoo, founded in 1994, was the leading Internet destination worldwide in 2005, with 123 million unique visitors each month. Almost any information available on the Internet could be accessed through Yahoo's Web portal. Visitors could anonymously access content categorized by Yahoo or set up an account with Yahoo to maintain a personal calendar and e-mail account, check the latest news, check local weather, obtain maps, check TV listings, track a stock portfolio, maintain a golf handicap, keep an online photo album, or search personal ads or job listings. Yahoo's 2005 agreements with popular authors to write financial columns for its Web site was the company's first move into original content. Prior to the agreement, all Yahoo content was provided by public domain Internet sources. Also in 2005, the company also had launched a plan with the Open Content Alliance to scan out-of-copyright books that would be available on Yahoo.

Yahoo hosted Web sites for small businesses and Internet retailers and had established an alliance with SBC Communications to offer dial-up and broadband access to Internet users. SBC and Yahoo were developing a wireless telephone service that would allow users to access all Yahoo content from their wireless telephones. The company's broad range of services made it a key rival to just about any company with an Internet presence. Internet service providers, business-to-consumer e-commerce sites, business-to-business e-commerce companies, content providers, Web portals, and those who provided paid search advertising were all directly affected by the competitive moves of Yahoo.

Yahoo was among Google's earliest customers for its search appliance, but it initiated moves to distance itself from Google when it acquired Inktomi for $235 million in December 2002 and Overture Services for $1.6 billion in July 2003. Both Inktomi and Overture were developers of search technologies that would allow Yahoo to internally control its search capabilities. Yahoo began to replace Google with its own search capabilities in February 2004, and the two partners officially became rivals in July 2004 when they formally ended their relationship. After its acquisition of Overture, Yahoo filed a lawsuit against Google claiming the rival had infringed on certain Overture patents. The two parties settled the patent infringement case in August 2004, with Google acquiring the disputed technology rights in return for 2.7 million shares of Google stock.

Yahoo recorded revenues and earnings of $3.6 billion and $839.6 million, respectively, during 2004. The company's revenues and net earnings for the first nine months of 2005 were $3.8 billion and $1.2 billion, respectively. The revenue growth represented a 150 percent increase over the same period in 2004, while Yahoo's net income grew by 260 percent between the two nine-month periods.

MSN Search   After 18 months in development, Microsoft launched a preview version of its search engine in November 2004. Microsoft had spent more than $150 million developing Microsoft's MSN Search (www.search.msn.com) to enter the market for search-based advertising. MSN Search was closely modeled after Google with the appearance of its home page similar to the uncluttered, clean look of Google. Also, Microsoft's search engine returned results and text-only ads in 11 languages that looked like those offered by Google. MSN Search could perform some tasks Google was unable to carry out, such as answering plain-language questions like "When did Virginia become a state?," linking to Microsoft's online Encarta encyclopedia to answer questions, and linking to MSN Music for those wishing to purchase MP3s of specific songs. MSN Search matched Google features such as local searching, had a calculator built into its search box, and performed measurement conversions.

Microsoft's quest to overcome Google was led by its chairman and chief software architect, Bill Gates. Gates's concern over Google became heightened in 2003 when, while perusing Google's Web site, he noticed that many of the Google job postings on its site were nearly identical to Microsoft job specifications. Recognizing that the position announcements had more to do with operating-system design than search, Gates e-mailed key Microsoft executives, warning, "We have to watch these guys. It looks like they are building something to compete with us."[10] Gates later commented that Google was "more like us than anyone else we have ever competed with," and by mid-2005 Microsoft had lost more than 100 employees to Google, including the chief architect of Windows.[11]

Gates believed that Google's long-term strategy involved the development of software applications comparable to Word, Excel, PowerPoint, and other Microsoft products that could be accessed free of charge by Internet users. Under Gates's envisioned scenario, Google would record revenue from ads placed on the screens of Google application users. Microsoft's strategy to compete with Google was keyed to making MSN Search more effective than Google and integrating MSN Search into all Microsoft applications. In December 2005, the company matched Google's satellite-based mapping capabilities and began an alliance with MCI to add Voice over Internet Protocol (VoIP) capabilities to MSN Search. The VoIP service would allow MSN Search users to make local and long-distance telephone calls using a PC for as little as two cents per minute. Microsoft's ability to integrate search functionality into Outlook, Internet Explorer, and other Microsoft applications posed the greatest competitive hazard to Google. Gates believed that Microsoft could move computer users away from "Googling" topics to having search results "naturally available, based on the task they want to do."[12]

AOL   AOL, owned by Time Warner Inc., generated 2004 revenues of $8.8 billion from its Internet service provider (ISP), business, advertising sales, and sales of services to its ISP customers. More than 20 million households in the United States and 6 million European households subscribed to AOL, Netscape, or CompuServe in 2005 to gain dial-up access to the Internet. AOL also offered a service for broadband users with third-party broadband access. The company also owned destination sites such as Moviefone.com, ICQ.com, Mapquest.com, AOL Instant Messenger, and Love.com, which together attracted over 110 million unique visitors each month. In addition, AOL's sites were among the Internet's "stickiest" sites, with users averaging five hours per month on them. Yahoo users averaged just over four hours per month on the Yahoo site, while MSN users averaged slightly more than three hours per month on Microsoft's portal. AOL's exposure to vast numbers of Internet users allowed it to market banner ads and other forms of advertising to large companies that might also advertise on Time Warner cable channels or magazines. AOL accounted for 21 percent of Time Warner's 2004 revenues of $42 billion. The operating profit contributed by the AOL business unit in 2004 was $934 million. AOL's agreement with Google for search services on AOL's vast network of Web destinations generated more than $300 million in revenues during 2004.

Google's Strategy to Sustain Growth

Google's Cash Reserves   With Google's influx of cash generated from the proceeds of its 2004 IPO and successive 2005 offering, Internet companies beyond its key search rivals became concerned with the company's growth. It was believed that Google's Froogle feature would decrease traffic to Internet retailers like Amazon.com and eBay since users could perform price comparisons from Google. Amazon.com replaced Google with a search engine called A9 for searches on its site just prior to Google's IPO. Exhibit 5 presents a financial summary for Google that includes income statements and selected balance sheet and cash

Exhibit 5 **Financial Summary for Google, Inc., 2001 through First Nine Months of 2005 (in thousands, except per share amounts)**

	First Nine Months of 2005	Fiscal Year-End			
		2004	2003	2002	2001
Income statement data:					
Revenues	$4,219,468	$3,189,223	$1,465,934	$439,508	$86,426
Costs and expenses:					
Cost of revenues	1,796,128	1,457,653	625,854	131,510	14,228
Research and development	326,906	225,632	91,228	31,748	16,500
Sales and marketing	284,972	246,300	120,328	43,849	20,076
General and administrative	221,268	139,700	56,699	24,300	12,275
Stock-based compensation*	142,555	278,746	229,361	21,635	12,383
Nonrecurring portion of settlement of disputes with Yahoo	—	201,000	—	—	—
Total costs and expenses	2,771,829	2,549,031	1,123,470	253,042	75,462
Income (loss) from operations	1,447,639	640,192	342,464	186,466	10,964
Interest income (expense) and other, net	54,205	10,042	4,190	−1,551	−896
Income (loss) before income taxes	1,501,844	650,234	346,654	184,915	10,068
Provision for income taxes	408,655	251,115	241,006	85,259	3,083
Net income (loss)	$1,093,189	$ 399,119	$ 105,648	$ 99,656	$ 6,985
Net income (loss) per share:					
Basic	$4.04	$2.07	$0.77	$0.86	$0.07
Diluted	$3.80	$1.46	$0.41	$0.45	$0.04
Number of shares used in per share calculations:					
Basic	270,665	193,176	137,697	115,242	94,523
Diluted	287,841	272,781	256,638	220,633	186,776

(*Continued*)

Cash flow and balance sheet data:

Net cash provided by operating activities	$1,800,988	$ 977,044	$ 395,445	N/A
Net proceeds from public offerings	4,287,621	1,161,466	—	—
Cash and cash equivalents	5,518,569	426,995	148,995	57,752	N/A
Marketable securities	2,111,578	1,705,424	185,723	88,579	N/A
Total current assets	8,382,685	2,693,465	560,234	231,796	N/A
Total assets	$9,451,001	$3,313,351	$ 871,458	$286,892	N/A
Total current liabilities	559,848	340,368	235,452	89,508	N/A
Total stockholders' equity	8,793,068	2,929,056	588,770	173,953	N/A
Total liabilities and stockholders' equity	$9,451,001	$3,313,351	$ 871,458	$286,892	N/A

*Stock-based compensation, consisting of amortization of deferred stock-based compensation and the fair value of options issued to non-employees for services rendered, is allocated as follows:

Cost of revenues	$ 3,925	$ 11,314	$ 8,557	$ 1,065	$ 876
Research and development	82,733	169,532	138,377	8,746	4,440
Sales and marketing	20,549	49,449	44,607	4,934	1,667
General and administrative	35,348	48,451	37,820	6,890	5,400
	$142,555	$278,746	$229,361	$21,635	$12,383

Source: Google Inc. From S-1 filed April 29, 2004; Google Financial Release, October 21, 2004; Google Inc. 2004 10-k; Google Inc. 10-Q, November 10, 2005.

flow items for 2001 through the first nine months of fiscal 2005.

Continuing International Expansion By 2005, Google's 112 international domains allowed 380 million unique users worldwide search billions of Web pages each month. More than 50 percent of Google searches originated outside the United States. However, at the end of Google's third quarter of 2005, only 39 percent of Google's advertising revenues originated from accounts located outside the United States. Google management opened an operation center in Brazil and Mexico in late 2005 to improve sales and services to Latin American advertisers. The company also hired one of Microsoft's most valuable employees in China in late 2005 to aid the company in its expansion efforts in China. Google had been slow to enter the world's second largest market of Internet users because the founders believed China's restrictions on speech and information conflicted with key principals of its corporate philosophy. A 2005 event seemed to confirm the founders' worst fears when the Chinese government forced Yahoo to turn over e-mail records of a journalist suspected of writing unflattering remarks about the government. The e-mail records from the journalist's Yahoo account were used to convict him and sentence him to 10 years in prison. Yahoo began conducting business in China in 1999.

Google had offered Chinese-language search results since 2000, but its site was blocked from Chinese Internet users in 2002. Google's site was reinstated in China after two weeks, but users could no longer access sites listed among Google search results that the Chinese government had found politically sensitive. In June 2004, Google became more involved in the Chinese market when it acquired a 2.6 percent stake in Baidu—the number one search engine in China. Google believed it was essential to develop a local presence in China if it were to aggressively pursue search-based advertising customers in that market since the Chinese language was so complex (for example, there were 38 different ways to say the pronoun "I" in Chinese) and since only 50 percent of Chinese Internet users who were familiar with Google could spell "Google."[13] In late 2005, Google was moving forward with its strategy in China by recruiting employees for an office located in China, developing a separate brand name for the Chinese market, and launching a Chinese ".cn" site. Adding a .cn suffix would establish Google as a Chinese site and make it subject to censorship by Chinese authorities. Google intended to give Chinese search users the "greatest amount of information possible."[14]

Google Feature Additions Among Google's most controversial new features was its Book Search addition. The plan to digitally scan millions of books from the libraries of Harvard, Stanford, the University of Michigan, and the University of Oxford as well as from the collections of the New York Public Library brought copyright infringement lawsuits soon after the company announced the new feature. A suit filed by McGraw-Hill, Pearson, Viacom, Simon & Schuster, and John Wiley & Sons, along with a suit filed by a group of 8,000 authors, attempted to require Google to obtain permission to scan books before instructing libraries to do so. Even though the suits were still pending, Google scaled back its initiative to include only public domain works—such as classic novels, government documents, and historical books—when the feature went live in November 2005.

Google Earth allowed Internet users to view satellite images of any location in the world and create maps using satellite images. The feature could give users close-up aerial views of the Eiffel Tower, the Taj Mahal, the Grand Canyon, or their own residence. The images were not real-time images but rather were taken by commercial satellites within the past few years. However, many governments were concerned with the availability of such information to anyone with access to Google. India's secretary of science and technology stated that the feature "could severely compromise a country's security," while a Russian security agency analyst suggested, "Terrorists don't need to reconnoiter their target. Now an American company is working for them."[15] However, image resolution varied greatly across locations and the dated nature of the images made them less useful for reconnaissance. A private security analyst in the United States discounted the strategic importance of the images with the comment, "You can get imagery to determine whether there is a military base or airfield, but if you want to count aircraft, or determine there are troops there at a particular time, it is very difficult to do. It's not video."[16]

Google Talk was a new Google feature that caused great concern among those in the telecom and cable industries. Google Talk provided instant messaging services to Google users, along with free local and long-distance telephone service in some areas. For example, users might run a Google search for the phone number of a merchant locally or in another state. If a telephone icon was displayed by the merchant's phone number, the Google user could click on the icon to make a toll-free call to the merchant. Users were asked to enter their phone number once they clicked on the icon so that their phone could be called as soon as the merchant's number was dialed. Neither party incurred any phone charges using Google's VoIP technology. Google also made Google Wi-Fi service available to the entire city of San Francisco in September 2005. Google Wi-Fi not only allowed users to make free VoIP local or long-distance telephone calls but also allowed Wi-Fi-enabled users to do so without an ISP or broadband provider. Both telephone companies and cable companies alike were worried that Google Wi-Fi could dramatically affect their revenue streams. Google management said that it did not have intentions to make the service available outside San Francisco, but many analysts believed that Google would roll out the program to all major U.S. cities that could be serviced with wireless networks. Commenting on emerging technologies such as VoIP, News Corporation's Rubert Murdoch stated in September 2005,

"I believe that free voice is going to be ubiquitous not in 10 years [but] within two or three years."[17]

Google's Investment in AOL   Google's largest investment since its IPO was its proposed strategic alliance with AOL that would give Google a 5 percent stake in AOL in return for a $1 billion cash payment. The terms of the partnership would allow AOL not only to host Google ads and share in advertising revenues but also to sell search-based ads directly to advertisers and share in revenues generated from those ads when they appeared on Google Network partner Web sites. In addition, the agreement called for Google to promote content featured on AOL in its search results. The move was in large part defensive since Microsoft was very close to signing an agreement with AOL that would make MSN Search its search provider. Microsoft sought the alliance to expand the availability of MSN Search beyond MSN.com, which had approximately 100 million unique users each month. Microsoft believed it would be much easier to sell text-based advertising if its search results were available to AOL's 100 million monthly unique visitors as well as those visiting MSN.com each month.

Endnotes

[1]As quoted in "High-Tech Search Engine Google Won't Talk about Business Plan," *The Wall Street Journal Online,* June 14, 1999.
[2]As quoted in Google's Corporate Information, www.google.com/corporate/history.html.
[3]As quoted in "The Grownup at Google," *The Wall Street Journal Online,* March 29, 2004, p. B1.
[4]Ibid.
[5]Google Inc. Form S-1, ii.
[6]Ibid.
[7]As listed under "Our Philosophy," Google Corporate Information, www.google.com/corporate/tenthings.html.
[8]As reported in "For Some Who Passed on Google Long Ago, Wistful Thinking," *The Wall Street Journal Online,* August 23, 2004.

[9]As quoted in "Slice of Pi: New Google Mystery Centers on $4 Billion Share Sale," *The Wall Street Journal Online,* August 19, 2005.
[10]As quoted in "Gates vs. Google," *Fortune,* April 18, 2005.
[11]Ibid.
[12]Ibid.
[13]As reported in "As Google Pushes into China, It Faces Clashes with Censors," *The Wall Street Journal Online,* December 16, 2005, p. 1.
[14]Ibid.
[15]As quoted in "Governments Tremble at Google's Bird's-Eye View," *New York Times,* December 20, 2005.
[16]Ibid.
[17]As quoted in "Google's Wireless Plan Underscores Threat to Telecom," *The Wall Street Journal Online*, October 3, 2005, p. 1.

Copperfield's Books Inc.

Armand Gilinsky
Sonoma State University

Tom Scott
Sonoma State University

When I started in this business, it was the heyday of independent booksellers. The national corporations had not yet discovered the mass market. We could make some serious mistakes and still make money. We were a very loose company, certainly founded on business principles, but it was more like a community than a corporation. We had a lot of fun doing our jobs then. We didn't get as stressed out. —Tom Montan, CEO of Copperfield's Books

In late October 2004, Tom Montan, CEO of Copperfield's Books, stood in the middle of a vacant 9,700-square-foot space in Napa, California's Bel Aire Plaza shopping center. Copperfield's employed 120 people and operated six stores in Sonoma and Napa counties, located about 50 miles north of San Francisco. (See Exhibit 1 for a map of Copperfield's retail store locations.) Montan's dilemma was how to achieve his primary goals: to grow Copperfield's revenues from approximately $8 million in 2003 to $15 million by 2007, and to improve the chain's profitability. He considered the possibility of opening two or more new stores in local markets that lacked national chain penetration. While imagining how a new Bel Aire Plaza store would look full of holiday book shoppers, Montan agonized over the quarter-million-dollar annual cost of leasing the new space, located about two miles from the existing downtown Napa Copperfield's bookstore. Just then, his cell phone rang. It was Joel Jaman from Keegan & Coppin, a leading local commercial realtor.

"Tom, it's true! Borders Books is going into that new shopping center just off Highway 101. It's only a mile away from your Petaluma store," Jaman said.

"Thanks for the heads-up, Joel," Montan replied. At the moment, I'm in Napa looking at the Bel Aire Plaza site you suggested. I'll get back to you with a definite 'yes' or 'no' on this new store location by the end of next week. I'd better call Matt Brown, our Petaluma store manager, right away and give him the news about Borders."

Montan then called Brown to bring him up to date. "Matt, what are we going to do about Borders?"

"Maybe we should just work with the stores we already have, Tom," Brown said crisply. "If we could reduce our administrative overhead further, we could be much more cost-competitive with Borders."

Montan reminisced with Brown about a location they had once considered in Novato, about 10 miles south of the Petaluma store but in neighboring Marin County. A Novato outlet would have provided Copperfield's with its first entry into the affluent Marin County market. "The rent [there] was so high, Matt, but the demographics were spot-on and there was no other bookstore within 10 miles." Then he told Brown, "Maybe we'd be better off betting the farm on a 25,000-square-foot superstore format, and go after the chains where they live. After all, Matt, if we prove this Napa market with a nearly 10,000-square-foot store, what's to stop Barnes & Noble or Borders from swooping in and trying to steal what we've built? We could lose everything!"

The idea of competing head-to-head with the superstores spurred Montan's thinking about Copperfield's competitive advantage in used and rare books. "The chains can't compete with us in that market," he told Brown. "Perhaps we should work harder on a used and antiquarian megastore concept. If we did it right, we could draw bibliophiles from 50 miles in all directions. We could use it as a *monster* Internet fulfillment center for used and rare books as well. Isn't

Exhibit 1   **Copperfields' Books Inc.—Store Locations as of October 2004**

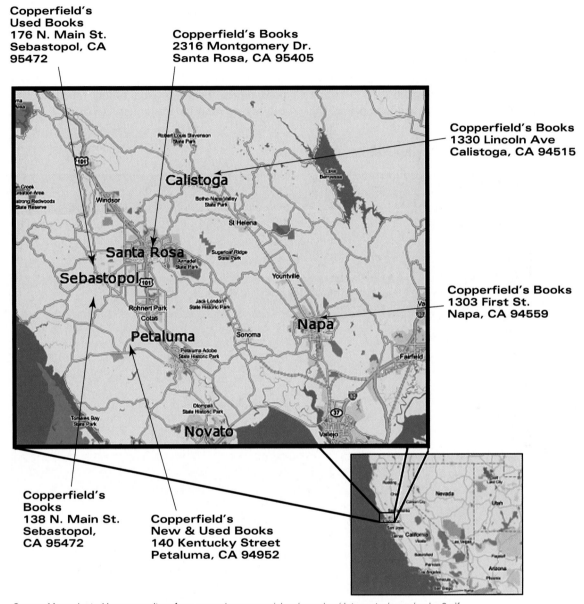

**Copperfield's
Used Books
176 N. Main St.
Sebastopol, CA
95472**

**Copperfield's Books
2316 Montgomery Dr.
Santa Rosa, CA 95405**

**Copperfield's Books
1330 Lincoln Ave
Calistoga, CA 94515**

**Copperfield's Books
1303 First St.
Napa, CA 94559**

**Copperfield's
Books
138 N. Main St.
Sebastopol,
CA 95472**

**Copperfield's
New & Used Books
140 Kentucky Street
Petaluma, CA 94952**

Source: Map adapted by case writers from www.abag.ca.gov/abag/overview/datacenter/maps/region2.gif.

the Internet, after all, where the action is in bookselling these days? See you at the store managers' team meeting tomorrow morning."

Turning off his cell phone, Montan walked around the vacant building, internally debating whether an independent bookstore chain like Copperfield's even *had* a future in a market that was now dominated by national chain superstores and Internet retailers. In his

two years as CEO, Montan had downsized Copperfield's warehouse operations and made some progress in reducing the company's administrative overhead. Still, the addition of two high-performing stores like the Montgomery Village store, he felt, could provide the scale necessary to be competitive with the national chains, or the answer might be found in a new, as yet undetermined format.

THE U.S. BOOKSELLING INDUSTRY

According to *Book Industry Trends 2004,* U.S. consumer expenditures on books exceeded $37.9 billion in 2003.[1] Analysts forecasted that expenditures would increase by 2.9 percent in 2004 to $39 billion and grow to $44 billion by 2008. In addition, analysts predicted that consumer expenditures on general trade books, commonly considered the bread-and-butter of the retail bookstores, would increase from about $11.8 billion in 2003 to $12.2 billion in 2004.[2] Annually, each U.S. household spent an average of $185 on books.[3] Income and education levels were, according to industry analysts, strong predictors of book-buying behavior. Booksellers relied on affluent, highly educated customers.[4] (Exhibit 2 presents

Exhibit 2   **U.S. Book-Buying Habits and Trends**

Compound Annual Growth Rates, 1992–2002			
Years	1992–2002	1992–1996	1997–2002
Unit growth	2.4%	3.6%	1.3%
Dollar growth	4.0	6.6	1.3
Population growth	1.1	0.9	1.2

Household Book Buying Trends, 1998–2002					
	1998	1999	2000	2001	2002
Total U.S. households (millions)	102.5	103.9	104.7	111.3	111.3
Buying households (millions)	59.7	59.5	57.4	58.6	58.2
% of total U.S. households	59.3%	58.7%	56.0%	56.1%	55.1%
Units/buying household	17.4	18.0	18.8	18.7	19.3
Dollars/buying household	$168	$174	$182	$180	$185

Book Buyer Purchasing Trends by Channel, 1992, 1995, and 1999–2002 (% units sold, by retail format)						
	1992	1995	1999	2000	2001	2002
Independent/small chain bookstores	24.9%	19.5%	15.1%	14.8%	14.8%	15.5%
Large chain superstores	5.0	9.5	12.4	14.7	14.2	13.9
Large chain other	19.1	16.0	12.2	9.0	9.2	8.6
Book clubs	16.8	18.1	17.7	18.6	19.9	19.2
Internet	—	—	5.5	7.1	7.5	8.1
Warehouse clubs	4.7	6.1	6.5	6.6	6.6	6.8
Mass merchandisers	4.4	5.6	6.2	5.9	5.6	5.8
Mail order catalogs	3.9	4.9	4.4	3.4	3.1	2.5
Variety stores	2.7	1.9	3.0	3.2	2.6	2.3
Food/drugstores	5.2	4.6	3.5	3.1	3.3	3.1
Used bookstores	4.9	4.0	3.0	2.9	3.3	4.8
Other	8.4	9.8	10.5	10.7	9.9	9.4
Total	100.0%	100.0%	100.0%	100.0%	100.0%	100.0%

(Continued)

Exhibit 2   **Continued**

Household Book-Buying Habits by Household Income, 2002		
	Units Sold (%)	Buying HH (%)	$ Purchases per Buying HH
Less than $30,000	25.7%	32.5%	$160
$30,000 to $49,999	21.9	24.8	159
$50,000 to $74,999	19.3	18.7	154
Over $75,000	33.1	24.0	236
Total	100.0%	100.0%	$185

Household Book-Buying Habits by Level of Educational Attainment, 2002		
	Units Sold (%)	Buying HH (%)	$ Purchases per Buying HH
Less than high school	6.9%	9.9%	$149
High school grad/some college	54.7	61.9	164
College grad	21.4	17.7	209
Post college	16.9	10.6	256
Total	100.0%	100.0%	$185

Note: Numbers in percentages may not add up to 100% due to rounding. The base for all of the data is general trade print books, which excludes children's books and audio and digital purchases.

Sources: IPSOS-Insight, *BookTrends, 2002* (most recent year available), www.ipsosinsight.com/knowledgecenter/syndicatedreports/bookstocadult.aspx, and the *Statistical Abstract of the United States,* www.census.gov/statab/www.

demographic and channel share data regarding U.S. customers' book-buying habits.) Meanwhile, adult readership in the United States had been on the decline for over 20 years (see Exhibit 3). Some book lovers expressed concerns regarding the power held by mass-market chains to act as "content gatekeepers" for book buyers. In 2003, the mass-market portion of the retail supply chain "often accounted for more than 40 percent of a best selling book."[5] Book publishers began issuing books with content targeted

Exhibit 3   **Trends in Domestic Literary Reading**

	1982	1992	2002
% of U.S. adult population reading literature	56.9	54.0	46.7
Number of literary readers (in millions)	96	100	96

Source: National Endowment for the Arts, *Reading at Risk: A Survey of Literary Reading in America,* 2004.

to sell in these stores. Book publishers also often self-censored books and started Christian imprints and other lines that would appeal to the religious, small-town, family values of the patrons of those stores.[6]

Nationwide, there were 10,900 bookstores in 2002; however, the industry was consolidating, as the number of retail establishments decreased by 11.9 percent between 1997 and 2002.[7] Consolidation was more acute among independent booksellers. Between 1993 and 2004, the number of independent retailers belonging to the American Booksellers Association (ABA), a trade group representing independent bookstores, decreased from 4,700 to 1,885.[8] These trends were, in part, attributed to the proliferation of national chain superstores, which offered vastly broader selections than did independent booksellers or mall chain outlets. Independent booksellers and mall chain stores had dominated the bookselling industry between 1970 and 1990, whereas superstores began to dominate in the 1990s.

Superstores ranged from 20,000 to 25,000 square feet of retail space and offered as many as 200,000 titles. Larger stores generated stronger foot traffic, which typically translated into higher sales, because 50 percent of adult trade book purchases were impulse purchases.[9] Superstore formats varied by operator but typically offered value pricing as well as a large assortment of music, magazines, newspapers, cards, and stationery in addition to books. Superstores provided inviting and comfortable environments designed to encourage browsing, and many included cafés. The trend toward superstores appeared to be driving industry growth: Barnes & Noble had opened 31 superstores in 2003, increasing its total to 647, and Borders had opened 41 new superstores in the same year, increasing its total to 445.[10] Favorable local government regulations promoted the expansion of retail tax bases by encouraging big-box development alongside freeways at the outskirts of major towns. Barnes & Noble reported that each new store opening, on average, cost about $1.9 million; this figure included $900,000 for fixtures and leasehold improvements, $700,000 for inventory, and $300,000 in pre-opening expenses.[11]

Supply Chain

Retail booksellers purchased books directly from publishing houses, which owned the distribution rights to a current, or front list, of titles. Demand for front-list titles offered by different houses was determined by consumer demand and merchandising placement at the retail level. While federal law precluded exclusive supply agreements in the publishing industry, publishing houses offered volume discounts that favored larger chains. Publishers shipped books in minimum quantities, enabling major chains to negotiate large discounts based on volume and merchandising commitments. As supplies of new titles on bestseller lists could be in short supply, publishing houses tended to supply their highest-volume retail customers first. Smaller independent retail booksellers like Copperfield's acquired merchandise from wholesale distributors that charged premium prices for acting as the intermediary but sold in smaller quantities than publishing houses. Wholesaler distributors, in turn, had developed proprietary technology interfaces that could reduce their throughput costs for smaller transaction volumes but could, in time, become a barrier to independent booksellers that wished to purchase from other wholesalers.

"Either you have to be very 'niche' or you need a physical presence that says you're significant," said Michael Powell, owner of Powell's Books in Portland, Oregon, which operated a 70,000-square-foot downtown store as well as three smaller stores that specialized in technical books, travel books, and gardening books.[12] Exhibit 4 presents comparative financial and operating data for Amazon, Barnes & Noble, and Borders Books covering the years 2001–2003.

Changing Dynamics

Accompanying the rise of national chain superstores, the emergence of Internet-based retailers like Amazon.com and the growth of book sales at mass-market retailers like Wal-Mart and Costco had dramatically changed the dynamics of the bookselling industry. Between 1992 and 2000, the independent and small chain bookstores' share of the domestic book market decreased from 24.9 to 14.8 percent.[13] During that same period, mass-market retailers' shares increased from 9.1 to 12.6 percent, and Internet retailers captured 8.1 percent of the market. However, large chain bookstores' market share decreased slightly from 24.1 to 22.5 percent between 1992 and 2000. Industry observers attributed this decline to the fact that the market-share increases produced by chains' superstores had been offset by losses at their legacy, mall-based outlets. For example, since 1989, Barnes & Noble had closed 772 of its B. Dalton subsidiary locations in shopping malls.[14] Moreover, erosion of independent booksellers' market share began to plateau after 2000. By 2003, independent and small chain sellers claimed 16 percent of the domestic market.[15]

The Book Industry Study Group reported that overall consumer spending for general trade books, which was $11.3 billion in 2002, declined by 2.7 percent to $11 billion in 2003, despite the fact that Americans purchased an approximately equivalent number of books (1.18 billion) during the same period. Between April and December 2003, consumers purchased 5 percent more books than in the same period in 2002.[16]

Emerging retail channels increased the depth of selection available to consumers: For example, Barnes & Noble's largest superstore carried 200,000 titles and Amazon.com carried an inventory of over 2 million titles, whereas Copperfield's largest store offered 72,000 titles.[17] Industry analysts credited an increased availability of obscure titles as a major driver of demand: by 2003, Amazon's sold 59 percent of all books from *outside* its list of 130,000 top titles.[18]

Used Books

In addition to discounting on new hardcover books, the growing popularity of used books contributed to the decline in dollar expenditures per book. Typically, used books were purchased through four main channels: used bookstores, independent bookstores, online retailers, and others (libraries, churches, garage sales, thrift shops, etc.). Price was a key motivator for used-book purchases. A 2003 survey of the used-book market stated that, of the purchase motivators across the four main channels, price prompted at least one out of every five used-book purchases by consumers; however, cover art, reviews, and readers' endorsements also prompted used-book buying. The survey also noted that the Internet was rapidly becoming a convenient resource for collectors of antiquarian (rare and first edition) books, which tended to fetch higher resale prices in comparison to other used books and even to some new titles.[19] Exhibit 5 presents profiles of selected Internet and storefront used booksellers. Exhibit 6 highlights recent trends in the used book segment of the bookselling industry, excerpted from a PowerPoint presentation prepared by two analysts for the Book Industry Study Group.

Digital Books

The emergence of digital content books (e-books) at the beginning of the new millennium posed a more distant threat to retail booksellers. Consumers could now download e-books directly to their computers or to a portable e-book device. Digital content downloading had already significantly changed the business model for the retail music industry, costing music retailers $700 million in sales in 2002.[20] By 2004, the bookselling industry still lacked a commercially viable platform, similar to Apple's iPod in the music industry, which could make using e-books user-friendly, for example, replicating the ease of page turning. Digital-content literature thus remained relatively user-unfriendly, lacking the tactile pleasures that many readers associated with book enjoyment. Susan Kevorkian, of IDC, an independent research firm, reported that "e-book devices remain[ed]

expensive and e-book titles [had] yet to provide readers with a broad selection of current reading material."[21] Analysts estimated the industry would sell 1.7 million e-book devices worldwide in 2004.[22]

Another potential threat posed by digital content to booksellers was emerging at Web sites like Gutenberg.org, which offered free electronic book downloads of public-domain literature. Gutenberg offered 13,000 e-books consisting primarily of books originally published prior to 1923 and including classics. In 2004, Google announced that it had begun working with university libraries to digitize books in their collections and make them accessible via Google Print.[23]

Key Industry Metrics

Profit margins in the bookselling industry reached historical lows in 2003, as large chains achieved net before-tax profit margins of approximately 5 percent.[24] Profitability among independent booksellers varied widely. A 2003 survey of 179 American Booksellers Association members revealed net before-tax profit margins ranging from 5.3 percent to −11.1 percent, with an average of 0.2 percent.[25] Exhibit 7 shows U.S. independent booksellers' average 2003 operating expenses grouped by store size in total dollar sales. Exhibit 8 shows U.S. independent booksellers' average 2003 operating expenses grouped by store size in sales per square foot.

The bookselling business was highly seasonal. With the possible exception of summer releases of blockbuster titles such as J. K. Rowling's HarryPotter series, the majority of book sales generally took place in the fourth quarter, due to the confluence of fall releases of major new titles and the holiday buying season. Borders Group Inc. reported that it realized 35.5 percent of its sales for 2003 in the fourth quarter.[26] By comparison, approximately 50 percent of Copperfield's 2003 annual sales occurred during the fourth quarter of that year. Also, sales of books were historically dependent on discretionary consumer spending, which was often affected by fluctuations in the business cycle. An equally important dynamic underlying book-buyer behavior was the hit-driven nature of the industry's merchandising strategy. Bookstore revenue and financial performance could fluctuate dramatically, depending on the number of blockbuster titles available for sale during a given time.

Exhibit 4 **Comparative Financial and Operating Highlights for Amazon.com, Barnes & Noble, and Borders Books, 2001–2003**

	Amazon.com			Barnes & Noble			Borders Books		
	12/31/03	12/31/02	12/31/01	1/31/04	2/1/03	2/2/02	1/25/04	1/26/03	1/27/02
Income statements ($ millions)									
Net sales	$5,263.7	$3,932.9	$3,122.4	$5,951.0	$5,269.3	$4,870.4	$3,731.0	$3,513.0	$3,387.9
Cost of sales*	4,006.5	2,940.3	2,323.9	4,323.8	3,855.8	3,560.0	2,682.6	2,439.2	2,439.2
Gross profit	1,257.2	992.6	798.6	1,627.2	1,413.5	1,310.4	1,048.4	1,073.8	948.7
Operating expenses									
Marketing and fulfillment	599.8	517.9	512.5	1,124.6	965.1	904.3	820.0	745.2	744.8
Selling, general, and administrative	88.3	79.0	89.9	163.6	148.7	147.8	11.5	14.9	25.4
Depreciation and amortization	2.8	5.5	181.0	8.8	35.6	12.5	11.3	119.8	21.5
Other	295.7	326.1	427.4						
Total Operating Expenses	986.6	928.5	1,210.8	1,297.0	1,149.4	1,064.6	842.8	879.9	791.7
Operating profit (loss)	270.6	64.1	(412.3)	330.3	264.1	245.8	205.6	193.9	157.0
Interest expense	130.0	142.9	139.2	20.1	21.5	36.3	8.7	12.6	14.4
Other non-operating expenses (income)	104.9	67.0	(25.1)	14.3	43.3	100.1	0.0	0.0	0.0
Income (loss) before tax	35.7	(145.8)	(526.4)	295.8	199.3	109.3	196.9	181.3	142.6
Taxes	—	—	—	(120.6)	(80.2)	(45.4)	(74.8)	(69.6)	(55.2)
Net income (loss)	35.7	(145.8)	(526.4)	175.3	119.1	64.0	122.1	111.7	87.4
Net income (loss), as reported†	$ 35.3	($149.1)	($567.3)	$ 151.9	$ 99.9	$ 64.0	$ 120.0	$ 111.7	$ 87.4
Total number of employees, year-end	7,800	7,500	7,800	43,000	50,000	45,000	32,300	32,700	32,000
Selected balance sheet data ($ millions)									
Current assets									
Cash and marketable securities	$1,394.8	$1,301.0	$ 996.6	$ 487.2	$ 267.6	$ 108.2	$ 378.8	$ 269.1	$ 190.2
Accounts receivable—trade	132.1			60.5	66.9	98.6	98.3	88.9	73.1
Accounts receivable—other					55.2		74.5		
Inventories	293.9	202.4	202.4	1,526.2	1,395.9	1,285.0	1,235.6	1,183.3	1,178.8
Other				119.6	101.2	99.2			
Total current assets	1,820.8	1,503.4	1,199.0	2,193.5	1,886.9	1,591.0	1,712.7	1,541.3	1,442.1
Fixed assets, net of depreciation	224.3	239.4	271.8	686.6	622.3	595.8	577.7	553.8	529.4
Other assets	116.9	247.7	166.8	627.2	486.3	436.5	175.8	173.1	207.8
Total assets	$2,162.0	$1,990.4	$1,637.5	$3,507.3	$2,995.4	$2,623.2	$2,466.2	$2,268.2	$2,179.3

(Continued)

Current liabilities	$1,252.7	$1,066.0	$921.4	$1,441.8	$1,231.4	$1,140.2	$1,164.1	$1,087.6	$1,106.7
Long-term debt	1,945.4	2,277.3	2,156.1	300.0	300.0	449.0	57.2	50.0	122.7
Deferred taxes and other				278.5	235.2	145.9	90.2	100.0	
Total liabilities	3,198.1	3,343.3	3,077.5	2,020.3	1,766.7	1,735.1	1,311.5	1,237.6	1,229.4
Minority Interest				227.3	201.0		1.7		
Shareholders' equity									
Common stock & paid-in capital	1,938.3	1,656.9	1,420.6	716.2	636.1	596.4	669.8	661.2	692.2
Retained earnings (accum. deficit)	(2,974.4)	(3,009.7)	(2,860.6)	543.5	391.7	291.7	483.2	369.4	257.7
Total shareholders' equity (deficit)	(1,036.1)	(1,352.8)	(1,440.0)	1,259.7	1,027.8	888.1	1,153.0	1,030.6	949.9
Total liabilities and shareholders' equity	$2,162.0	$1,990.4	$1,637.5	$3,507.3	$2,995.4	$2,623.2	$2,466.2	$2,268.2	$2,179.3
Selected financial ratios									
Profitability									
Gross profit margin	23.9%	25.2%	25.6%	27.3%	26.8%	26.9%	28.1%	30.6%	28.0%
Operating profit margin	5.1	1.6	-13.2	5.6	5.0	5.0	5.5	5.5	4.6
Net profit margin	0.7	-3.8	-18.2	2.6	1.9	1.3	3.2	3.2	2.6
Operating profit as % of total assets (ROA)	12.5	3.2	-25.2	9.4	8.8	9.4	8.3	8.5	7.2
Net income as a % of year-ending shareholders' equity (ROE)	nmf	nmf	nmf	12.1%	9.7%	7.2%	10.4%	10.8%	9.2%
Sales per employee	$455,732	$344,994	n/a	$87,515	$72,680	$70,585	$76,025	$71,583	$72,083
Activity									
Total asset turnover (sales/total assets)	2.4	2.0	1.9	1.7	1.8	1.9	1.5	1.5	1.6
Inventory turnover (cost of goods sold/inventory)	13.6	14.5	11.5	2.8	2.8	2.8	2.2	2.1	2.1
Fixed asset turnover (net sales/fixed assets)	23.5	16.4	11.5	8.7	8.5	8.2	6.5	6.3	6.4
A/R collection period, days	9.2	nmf	nmf	3.7	4.6	7.4	9.6	9.2	7.9
Leverage									
Total liabilities as a % of total assets	147.9%	168.0%	187.9%	57.6%	59.0%	66.1%	53.2%	54.6%	56.4%
Total liabilities as a % of shareholders' equity	nmf	nmf	nmf	160.4%	171.9%	195.4%	113.7%	120.1%	129.4%
Long-term debt as a % of shareholders' equity	nmf	nmf	nmf	45.9%	52.1%	67.0%	12.8%	14.6%	12.9%
Times interest earned ratio	2.1	0.4	(3.0)	16.4	12.3	6.8	23.6	15.4	10.9
Liquidity									
Net working capital ($ millions)	$568.1	$437.4	$277.6	$751.6	$655.4	$450.8	$548.6	$453.7	$335.4
Current ratio	1.5	1.4	1.3	1.5	1.5	1.4	1.5	1.4	1.3
Quick ratio	1.2	1.2	1.1	0.5	0.4	0.3	0.4	0.3	0.2

*Includes occupancy costs for Barnes & Noble and Borders.

†Includes adjustments for changes in accounting principles (Amazon, Borders) and minority interests (Barnes & Noble).

nmf = Not meaningful figure; n/a = Not available or not applicable.

Sources: Calculated by case writers from data provided by Mergent On-Line, company annual reports, and SEC filings; all ratios calculated based on year-end figures except where noted.

Exhibit 5 **Profiles of Selected Internet and Used Booksellers**

Company Name	Web Site	Year Founded	HQ	Ownership	Latest Sales ($ millions)	Latest Net Inc. ($ millions)	Number of Employees	Key Characteristics
Advanced Book Exchange	www.abebooks.com	1995	Victoria, BC (Canada)	Private	WND	WND	WND	>70 million new, used, rare, and out-of-print titles listed at over 13,000 independent booksellers; 5 global Web sites. Acquired BookFinder.com (Berkeley, CA) in 11/05. Partners include Alibris, Amazon.com, Barnes & Noble.com, Biblio.com, Buy.com, ILAB (International League of Antiquarian Booksellers), Overstock.com, and Powell's Books.
Alibris*	www.alibris.com	1998	Emeryville, CA	Private	$45.5	($4.8)	49	Offers >50 million used, new, & out-of-print titles from >10,000 sellers. Backed by venture capital firms. Recently postponed initial public offering.
Bookcrossing	www.bookcrossing.com	2001	Sandpoint, ID	Private	WND	WND	WND	Free paperback book swapping service. "Read, register on the Web, and release into the wild" business model. 2.6 million books "released" to 12/05.
Books-A-Million†	www.bamm.com	1917	Birmingham, AL	Public (Nasdaq: BAMM)	$475.2	$10.2	4,900	#3 U.S. book chain with 170 Books-A-Million and Books & Co. stores in 18 southeastern states. Runs 35 smaller Bookland & Books-A-Million stores. Web site inaugurated in 1998. Owns Joe Muggs' Newsstands & American Wholesales Books.

(Continued)

Company	Website	Year	Location						Notes
Half Price Books	www.halfpricebooks.com	1972	Dallas, TX	Private	WND	WND	WND	WND	85 Stores in 13 states, primarily in Texas. About 50% of merchandise is new.
Paperbackswap.com	www.paperbackswap.com	2004	Clermont, FL	Private	WND	WND	WND	WND	One-for-one used book exchange. Fee free. 6,000–10,000 books per day.
Powells Books	www.powells.com	1971	Portland, OR	Private	WND	WND	WND	WND	Web site started 1994 now accounts for >40% of total sales. Offers more than 1.5 million books. Supplies used books to Amazon.com.
Tattered Cover Book Store	www.tatteredcover.com	1974	Denver, CO	Private	WND	WND	WND	WND	Stocks over 500,000 titles at 3 locations Runs Fourth Story restaurant at Cherry Creek location.

WND = Would not disclose.

* 2003 fiscal year data from *Hoovers Company Reports*; 1-year sales growth was 46.4% and employee growth was 8.9%.

† 2004 fiscal year data from *Hoovers Company Reports*; 1-year sales growth was 3.3%; net income growth was 41.7%; employee growth was 2.1%.

Sources: *Hoover's Company Reports*; company Web sites (accessed 12/20/05), and N. Lewin, "The Book Trade," Public Radio International's *Marketplace*, December 19, 2005, http://marketplace.publicradio.org/shows/2005/12/19/pm.html.

Exhibit 6   **The U.S. Used-Book Market in 2004**

- $2.2 billion in used-book sales; 11.1% growth over 2003
  —$1.6 billion in education and $600 million in other genres
- 111.2 million used-book units
  —38.6 million units in education and 72.6 million units in other genres
- Online used-book sales = $609 million; 33.3% growth over 2003
  —Bookstores (point-of-sale) = $1.57 billion; 4.6% growth over 2003
  —Other locations = $46 million and 19 million units; 1% growth over 2003
- Bookstores
  —Independents (used, new), national, college, religious, other
  —11,036 establishments per Census Bureau
  —22,321 per *Information Today* (7,131 are various retail stores)
  —Industry consensus of around 15,000 to 17,000 total bookstores
  —We estimate around 11,600 sell used books
- Online
  —*Retailers:* Barnes & Noble, Books-A-Million, Powells—emphasize new & used; tied into online specialists and marketplaces
  —*Marketplaces:* Abebooks, Alibris, Amazon, Biblio, eBay—portal for the industry inventory, transaction systems for e-commerce
  —*Online specialists* (1,000+): Individuals working out of home and selling through marketplaces, ex-used-book dealers, part-time businesses ($10K, <10,000 books/year)
  —Rapid growth in segment (30% + year over year)
  —Transforming the adult trade and professional used-book segments
  —Expanding into textbooks
  —Achieving significantly higher prices and margins than other channels
- College bookstores
  —4,650 stores serving 4,168 institutions in the United States, 200 in Canada
  —2,500 university-owned, 2,150 managed or privately owned
  —$10.9 billion revenue (North America)
  —$5.0 billion new textbooks, $220 million course packs, $440 million trade books
  —$1.75 billion used books
  —Sales via Web around $275 million
  —Facing increased competition from third parties
- Other locations: book fairs, Friends of the Library, Goodwill and thrift stores, yard sales

Source: J. Abraham and J. Hayes, "Used Book Market Analysis: Initial Preview," *Book Industry Study Group,* 2005, www.bisg.org.

Trade Area Characteristics

Copperfield's operated four store locations in Sonoma County, California, and two in neighboring Napa County. Sonoma and Napa counties were world-renowned wine-producing regions and boasted personal income levels and property values that exceeded state and national averages. According to the 2000 census, the median family household income in these counties was $61,812, about 14 percent higher than California at large.[27] (Exhibit 9 provides 2003 demographic information.) Higher *per capita* income levels were a result of a diverse local economy, itself driven by the growing wine, tourism, telecommunications, and medical equipment industries. The local economy weakened in the early 2000s due to post-9/11 fears, declining wine prices, and a major downturn for high-technology companies.

Despite the economic uncertainty, the retail segment of the local economy continued to expand

Exhibit 7   **Average Operating Expenses for U.S. Independent Booksellers by Store Size (in Sales), 2003**

				Store Sales Volume[1]			
	<$250K	$250K–$500K	$500K–$1 MM	$1 MM–$2.5 MM	$2.5 MM–$5 MM	>$5 MM	Averages[2]
Sales per square feet	$122.00	$209.00	$337.00	$370.00	$456.00	$436.00	$321.67
Gross profit margin	39.5%	21.7%	39.2%	39.7%	41.6%	37.7%	39.9%
Payroll expense as a % of sales	20.9%	41.5%	20.8%	21.6%	23.4%	20.4%	21.5%
Occupancy expense as a % of sales	12.0%	10.0%	7.2%	7.0%	7.4%	8.0%	8.6%
Advertising as a % of sales	4.1%	1.9%	1.8%	1.5%	1.3%	1.0%	1.9%
Other expenses as a % of sales	12.8%	11.8%	10.0%	7.5%	9.2%	6.5%	9.6%
Net income as a % of sales	−10.3%	−2.9%	0.4%	2.1%	0.2%	1.7%	−1.5%

[1]N = 197 respondents, or 11% of ABA member booksellers.
[2]Unweighted means.
Source: Adapted and compiled by case writers from American Booksellers Association, *ABACUS Survey, 2003,* available from http://news.bookweb.org/news/2858.html.

between 2000 and 2004.[28] This expansion resulted in a shortage of supply of retail space in local trade area. In June 2004, the supply of available retail space in Sonoma County was less than 5 percent.[29] As a result of the shortage of supply and high area income levels, trade area commercial rents were among the highest in the state. In late 2004, commercial rents for Sonoma County averaged between $2.00 and $3.50 per square foot (on a monthly basis) depending on a number of variables, including location, tenant mix, and footprint of the leased premise. See Exhibit 10 for more detail and selected comparisons to market data for neighboring Marin and Napa Counties.

In addition to six Copperfield's stores, Sonoma and Napa Counties were home to over 30 independent

Exhibit 8   **Comparative Expenses for U.S. Independent Booksellers Based on Sales per sq. ft., 2003**

	Store Sales per Square Foot				
	≤$100	$100–$200	$200–$300	$300–$400	>$400
Sales	100.0%	100.0%	100.0%	100.0%	100.0%
Gross profit margin	46.7	39.4	39.8	38.8	39.2
Salaries, wages, and benefits	24.4	20.6	21.2	21.4	21.4
Occupancy costs (including utilities and maintenance)	14.8	9.3	7.2	6.1	6.8
Advertising	3.2	2.1	2.0	1.6	1.1
Depreciation	0.6	1.4	0.8	0.4	0.8
Other expenses	53.5	36.2	30.8	27.2	27.8
Net income before tax	−10.4%	−2.6%	0.6%	2.4%	2.4%

Note: Numbers may not add to 100% due to rounding.
Source: American Booksellers Association, *ABACUS Survey, 2003,* available from http://news.bookweb.org/news/2858.html.

Exhibit 9   **Copperfield's Books Inc., Population Demographics Analysis, 2003**

	5-Mile Trade Area*				State of California[†]	United States[‡]
	Napa	Santa Rosa	Petaluma	Sebastopol		
Household income						
Less than $15,000	8.46%	6.60%	8.50%	14.20%	14.29%	8.87%
$15,000–$24,999	8.79	8.00	7.40	12.40	11.77	10.82
$25,000–$34,999	11.11	9.30	8.30	10.90	10.25	11.20
$35,000–49,999	15.57	17.40	13.70	15.40	14.14	15.21
$50,000–74,999	19.44	22.80	22.70	25.40	17.42	20.59
$75,000–$99,999	13.82	16.00	16.10	9.00	11.83	10.21
Over $100,000	22.81	19.90	23.30	12.70	20.31	23.11
Estimated mean household income	$77,169	$74,640	$73,615	$54,608	$66,915	n/a
Estimated median household income	$57,791	$56,945	$61,679	$46,436	$49,320	$53,991
Educational attainment for population 25 and older						
Less than high school grad	20.72%	8.30%	14.10%	11.60%	18.73%	16.38%
High school grad (income equivalent)	20.69	18.50	19.30	16.50	21.29	29.80
Some college, no degree	25.56	26.80	27.30	28.70	27.68	20.29
Associate degree	8.66	11.10	9.20	7.70	n/a	6.99
Bachelor's degree	15.47	23.30	20.80	22.80	21.21	16.89
Graduate degree	8.90	12.00	9.30	12.70	10.47	9.65
High school grad or higher	79.28%	91.70%	85.90%	88.40%	81.27%	83.62%
Bachelor's degree or higher	24.37%	35.30%	30.10%	35.50%	31.68%	26.54%
Hispanic or Latino						
Not Hispanic or Latino	70.54%	91.20%	85.40%	90.70%	67.60%	87.45%
Hispanic or Latino	29.46	8.80	14.60	9.30	32.40	12.55

n/a = Not available.

*Napa and Sonoma data for a 5-mile radius Copperfield's store locations, obtained from www.clusterbigip1.claritas.com/claritas/Default. jsp?ti=3&ci=1&pn=freeinfo (accessed October 20, 2004).

[†]Demographic data for State of California obtained from State of California, Department of Finance Demographic Research Unit, *California Population Survey Basic Report,* March 2004 Data, Tables 14 and 15, www.dof.ca.gov/HTML/DEMOGRAP/DRU_datafiles/ DRU_DataFiles.asp (accessed December 27, 2005).

[‡]Demographic data for United States obtained from U.S. Census Bureau, *Statistical Abstract of the United States, 2006 edition,* Tables 37 and 45, www.census.gov/prod/www/statistical-abstract.html (accessed December 27, 2005).

bookstores and two chain superstores. Copperfield's stores were the largest independent bookstores in its trade area; its Montgomery Village and Petaluma stores each comprised more than twice the square footage as the next largest independent local competitor, thus Montan perceived chain superstores as his primary direct competitors. Exhibit 11 lists rival retail book-sellers in Napa and Sonoma.

COPPERFIELD'S HISTORY

In 1981, Barney Browne and Paul Jaffe founded Copperfield's Books in Sebastopol, California. Their first store was located in a century-old brick storefront on Sebastopol's Main Street. The store's business grew steadily by focusing on customers' needs and community service. In 1985, Copperfield's

Exhibit 10   **Late 2004 Market Data for San Francisco North Bay Area Commercial Retailers: Inventories, Vacancy Rates, and Rents**

County/Submarket	Inventory (sq. ft.)	Available Space (sq. ft.)	Vacancy Rate	Rent Range ($/sq. ft.)
Sonoma County*				
Petaluma	1,644,432	22,773	1.4%	$1.65–2.50
Rohnert Park	1,946,365	29,131	1.5	1.25–2.25
Santa Rosa	5,665,973	101,664	1.8	1.70–3.30
Windsor	632,000	13,720	2.2	1.85–2.95
Total	9,888,770	167,288	1.7	1.25–3.30
Marin County*				
Southern/Central Marin	1,832,986	52,867	2.9	1.85–4.00
San Rafael	1,517,961	25,627	1.9	1.75–3.25
Novato	1,218,459	64,390	5.3	1.45–2.25
Total	4,569,406	142,884	3.1	1.45–4.00
Napa County†				
Napa	8,800,000	290,000	3.3	1.25–2.25
Total	8,800,000	290,000	3.3	1.25–2.25

*Orion Commercial Real Estate Services, www.orionre.com.
†Napa Valley Economic Development Corporation, www.nvedc.org/nvedc/default.asp?idPage = 1031.

opened a second store in Santa Rosa, and in a 50 percent partnership with Paul's brother, Dan Jaffe, a third store in Petaluma. The Santa Rosa store was located in Montgomery Village, an older but prestigious regional shopping center. The Petaluma store was located in the heart of downtown Petaluma, in a century-old brick storefront, linking it aesthetically to the Sebastopol store. The first three stores thrived during the mid-1980s, benefiting from strong population growth in Sonoma County, the affluent educated demographics surrounding their locations, and a general lack of direct competition in the trade area.

By the mid-1990s, Copperfield's decided to establish a more traditional corporate hierarchy. Dan Jaffe became the director of operations, Paul the chief executive officer, and the two brothers embarked on a bold growth plan. They moved two stores into bigger spaces: Montgomery Village and Petaluma. Dozens of volunteers did most of the work of moving the stores. A year later, Copperfield's purchased the assets of Books Inc., a regional chain that had recently filed for bankruptcy protection, and took over its lease in the Coddingtown Center, a regional shopping mall in Santa Rosa. Copperfield's transferred inventory and personnel

from Rohnert Park to the new location and opened a second used and rare bookstore in Sebastopol, down the street from its original location. See Exhibit 12 for a list of Copperfield's store openings and closings.

In 2004, Copperfield's closed its downtown Santa Rosa location, finally succumbing to the competitive forces set in play a decade earlier when Barnes & Noble had first come to town and set up shop across the street. "We had grown out of that business model in that location," Montan told the *Santa Rosa Press Democrat.*[30] The Santa Rosa downtown store property was sold to an investment group in spring 2004 for about $826,000 after taxes, a substantial profit. Copperfield's board distributed the after-tax proceeds from the sale to shareholders, foregoing the opportunity to reinvest the proceeds in the chain. In an attempt to capture emerging Internet channel as well as the recent growth in demand for used books, Copperfield's transferred its Santa Rosa store's inventory to an unused portion of the Petaluma store's basement, which formed the foundation for a nascent Internet fulfillment center. Consolidated 1998–2003 financial statements for Copperfield's are shown in Exhibits 13 and 14. Exhibits 15 and 16

Exhibit 11   **Competing Retail Booksellers in Sonoma and Napa Counties**

Company	Location	Estimated Size	Type
Barnes & Noble	Santa Rosa	Estimated sales $2.5 mm–$ 5.0 mm	New
Bookends Napa	Napa	Estimated sales $500K–$1 mm	New
Bookends Sonoma	Sonoma	Estimated sales $500K–$1 mm	New
Book Market Inc.	Santa Rosa	Estimated sales $250K–$500K	New
Book Outlet Store	Napa	Estimated sales $250K–$500K	New
Book Warehouse	Petaluma	Estimated sales $250K–$500K	New
Borders	Santa Rosa	Estimated sales >$5 mm	New
Calistoga Books	Calistoga	Estimated sales $250K–$500K	New
Campus Textbooks	Santa Rosa	Estimated sales $250K–$500K	College
Cover to Cover	Cloverdale	Estimated sales $250K–$500K	New
Full Circle Books	Cotati	Estimated sales <$250K	Used
Gramma Queenies	Penngrove	Estimated sales <$250K	Used
Knight's Books	Santa Rosa	Estimated sales <$250K	Used
Lakeside Village Bookstore	Santa Rosa	Estimated sales <$250K	Used
Liberia Christiana	Rohnert Park	Estimated sales $250K–$500K	Religious
Liberia Christiana	Santa Rosa	Estimated sales $250K–$500K	Religious
Many Rivers Books and Tea	Sebastopol	Estimated sales $250K–$500K	New
Napa Booktree	Napa	Estimated sales $250K–$500K	New
North Light Books	Cotati	Estimated sales <$250K	New/College
Occidental Books	Occidental	Estimated sales <$250K	Used
Pages Books	Windsor	Estimated sales $250K–$500K	New
Paperbacks Unlimited	Santa Rosa	Estimated sales <$250K	Used
Parsons Books	Napa	Estimated sales <$250K	Used
Petaluma Paperbacks	Petaluma	Estimated sales <$250K	Used
Readers Books	Sonoma	Estimated sales $500K–$1 mm	New
River Reader	Guerneville	Estimated sales $250K–$500K	New
Sonoma State Bookstore	Rohnert Park	Estimated sales $500K–$1 mm	College
Stepping Stones	Occidental	Estimated sales <$250K	New
Treehorn Books	Santa Rosa	Estimated sales $250K–$500K	Used
Twice Told Books	Guerneville	Estimated sales <$250K	Used
Vicarious Experience	Cotati	Estimated sales <$250K	Used
Waldenbooks	Santa Rosa	Estimated sales $250K–$500K	New
Waldenbooks	Napa	Estimated sales $250K–$500K	New
Western Christian Bookstore	Cotati	Estimated sales <$250K	Religious

Source: Copperfield's Books Inc. and casewriters' estimates.

Exhibit 12   **Copperfield's Books: Store Openings and Closings, 1981–2004**

New Book Stores	County	Type of Location	Date Opened	Date Closed
138 N. Main Street, Sebastopol	Sonoma	Downtown	1981	
140 Kentucky Avenue, Petaluma*	Sonoma	Downtown	1985	
Montgomery Village, 2316 Montgomery Drive, Santa Rosa	Sonoma	Upscale mall	1985	
1303 First Street, Napa	Napa	Downtown	1996	
540 Raley's Town Center, Rohnert Park	Sonoma	Shopping center	1996	2001
Coddingtown Center, 2402 Magowan Drive, Santa Rosa	Sonoma	Mall	1996	2001
650 Fourth Street, Santa Rosa	Sonoma	Downtown	1996	2001
1330 Lincoln Ave., Calistoga	Napa	Downtown	2001	
Used and Rare Book Stores				
140 Kentucky Avenue, Petaluma†	Sonoma	Downtown	1995	
176 N. Main Street, Sebastopol	Sonoma	Downtown	1996	

*Petaluma store was moved in 1995 to a new, larger location on the same street.

†Used bookstore located in basement of Petaluma store.

Source: Copperfield's Books Inc.

present comparative store revenue and expense data by location for 2003 and 2002, respectively.

Marketing

Copperfield's had earned a reputation for being Sonoma County's hometown bookseller. Active in the local community, Copperfield's was instrumental in promoting local authors, hosting cultural events, and providing a venue for writers across the country to meet Northern California literati. Special events were the cornerstone of Copperfield's marketing efforts, and these were advertised in the local press, including the daily *Press Democrat* newspaper and weekly free *Bohemian* magazine. Fall 2004 literary readings and book-signing events featured Leonard Nimoy, Newt Gingrich, George Carlin, Mo Willems (Emmy Award–winning writer for *Sesame Street*), former U.S. secretary of labor Robert Reich, and Pulitzer Prize–winning poet Gary Snyder. In addition, the chain's online newsletter promoted upcoming book signings with local authors including historian Simone Wilson and photographer Richard Blair. Copperfield's also published *The Dickens,* a free journal dedicated to literature of quality: poems, stories, and creative nonfiction that gave voice to the talents of writers from Northern California.

Newly released, or front-list, book titles were sold at list prices, though individual store managers had some discretion to match the 10–20 percent discounts off cover prices offered by the larger chains. Store layouts contained a simple, casual, down-to-earth quality that differentiated them from other chain booksellers. Shelving units were made of simple unfinished fir boards. Seating was limited or nonexistent in most stores. Store signage consisted primarily of poster-board placards with hand-drawn calligraphic lettering that described major sections of the store. Lighting in the stores was simple, primarily derived from ambient ceiling sources. Music in the stores consisted of new age, classical, and jazz selections. Front-list titles and sideline merchandise targeted upscale, liberal-minded customers.

Operations

Each Copperfield's store manager controlled the merchandising, staffing, and back-list (older new-book titles) inventory for his or her store. Store layouts and product offerings varied significantly throughout the chain; the Petaluma and Sebastopol new-book stores contained special children's sections, replete with colorful fixtures and huge butterflies, while other stores did not. Some managers placed magazines in the front, while others placed them in the rear of the store. Consequently, each store had its own flavor, but common fixtures, signage, and front-list selections gave the chain continuity and branding among store locations. Front-list inventories were controlled centrally, but Montan delegated the

Exhibit 13 **Copperfield's Books Inc. Comparative Statements of Income and Expenses, 1998–2003**

	Fiscal Year Ended December 31					
	2003	2002	2001	2000	1999	1998
Revenue*	$ 8,124,422	$ 5,865,625	$ 6,002,434	$ 6,632,445	$ 6,495,758	$ 6,499,505
Cost of goods sold	4,643,866	3,489,448	3,531,834	3,972,392	3,958,974	3,918,764
Gross profit	$ 3,480,556	$ 2,376,177	$ 2,470,600	$ 2,660,053	$ 2,536,784	$ 2,580,741
Operating Expenses						
Salaries and wages	$ 1,651,299	$ 1,203,163	$ 1,252,290	$ 1,353,143	$ 1,298,109	$ 1,267,844
Benefits	248,448	171,357	183,328	192,096	182,389	176,750
Occupancy	542,519	382,073	331,438	382,571	378,692	337,008
Advertising	88,953	67,069	51,621	71,659	(5,336)	54,333
Utilities	177,812	139,789	125,277	160,237	139,981	154,562
Depreciation and amortization	123,797	115,142	123,763	112,807	111,649	86,411
Repairs and maintenance	72,389	62,070	52,361	72,498	62,956	48,723
Other costs	448,540	253,660	259,631	276,173	237,837	239,361
Total expenses	$ 3,353,757	$ 2,394,323	$ 2,379,709	$ 2,621,184	$ 2,406,277	$ 2,364,992
Income from operations	126,799	(18,146)	90,891	38,869	130,507	215,749
Income from Petaluma	(77,670)	72,630	128,957	77,796	85,936	73,704
Other income†	915,876	41,345	(180,287)	64,526	(71,164)	(51,813)
Income before taxes	$ 965,005	$ 23,199	$ (89,396)	$ 103,395	$ 59,343	$ 163,936
Provision for income taxes	14,500	1,700	2,318	4,829	4,829	3,236
Net income	$ 950,505	$ 21,499	$ (91,714)	$ 98,566	$ 54,514	$ 160,700

*In 2003, Copperfield's changed the way it accounted for its 50% interest in the Petaluma store due to the death of one of the founders, Dan Jaffe. Prior to 2003, revenues excluded sales from Petaluma, and the firm's share of the Petaluma store's net income was shown as other income to reflect the fact that Jaffe had held 50% interest in that store location. In 2003, revenue from the Petaluma store was included as company revenue, and Jaffee's heirs' shares of earnings from the Petaluma store were charged against revenues. Revenues from the Petaluma store were $2,296,561 in 2003.

†2003 income reflects a one-time $826,414 gain net of income taxes on disposal of the downtown Santa Rosa store, which was closed in June 2004. Proceeds from the sale were distributed to Copperfield's shareholders.

Source: Copperfield's Books Inc.

Exhibit 14 **Copperfield's Books Inc., Comparative Balance Sheets, 1998–2003**

			Fiscal Year Ended December 31			
	2003	2002	2001	2000	1999	1998
Assets						
Current assets						
Cash	$ 38,720	$ 296,582	$ 53,776	$ 147,539	$ 204,998	$ 220,509
Accounts receivable	66,204	79,133	78,695	99,806	88,211	71,158
Accounts receivable—related party	6,988	264,750	234,566	60,956	41,442	156,047
Inventory	2,030,342	1,305,012	1,525,310	1,695,389	1,643,615	1,509,409
Note receivable	6,000	6,000	7,653	8,330	15,921	16,179
Other current assets	—	6,612	5,584	25,517	30,688	25,915
Total current assets	2,148,254	1,958,089	1,905,584	2,037,537	2,024,875	1,999,217
Property and equipment	654,503	1,371,765	1,461,084	1,470,262	1,428,181	1,372,840
Other assets	35,996	23,192	27,130	28,645	36,788	41,998
Investment in Petaluma store	—	118,903	147,816	181,098	158,756	106,734
Total assets	$ 2,838,753	$ 3,471,949	$ 3,541,614	$ 3,717,542	$ 3,648,600	$ 3,520,789
Liabilities and equity						
Current liabilities						
Accounts payable	$ 976,527	$ 1,043,131	$ 1,107,049	$ 1,257,228	$ 1,181,073	$ 1,077,431
Current maturities of long-term debt	162,142	105,029	106,186	114,595	178,054	196,631
Total current liabilities	1,138,669	1,148,160	1,213,235	1,371,823	1,359,127	1,274,062
Long-term debt*	180,077	901,212	978,338	961,907	999,494	992,409
Other commitments	4,800	5,700	7,400	4,100	8,791	15,130
Stockholders' equity						
Capital stock	204,002	204,002	204,002	204,002	204,002	204,002
Retained earnings	1,157,988	1,212,875	1,138,639	1,175,710	1,077,186	1,035,186
Related party interest in affiliate†	153,217	—	—	—	—	—
Total stockholders' equity	1,515,207	1,416,877	1,342,641	1,379,712	1,281,188	1,239,188
Total liabilities and equity	$ 2,838,753	$ 3,471,949	$ 3,541,614	$ 3,717,542	$ 3,648,600	$ 3,520,789

*Decrease in Long-Term Debt from 2002 to 2003 reflects debt retirement from the sale of the Santa Rosa store, net of taxes, for $826,414.

†Jaffe family's 50% ownership stake in Petaluma store.

Source: Copperfield's Books Inc.

Exhibit 15 **Copperfield's Books Inc., Comparative Store Data, 2003**

				Fiscal Year Ended December 31			
	Petaluma New & Used*	Santa Rosa Montgomery Village	Downtown Santa Rosa	Napa	Calistoga	Sebastopol	Sebastopol Used & Rare
Revenue	$ 2,296,561	$ 2,762,670	$ 514,271	$ 418,548	$ 646,056	$ 1,265,567	$ 199,470
Cost of goods sold	1,268,712	1,679,629	255,021	240,364	371,599	744,831	67,512
Gross margin	1,027,849	1,083,040	259,250	178,183	270,417	520,736	131,958
Salaries and wages	458,040	252,953	126,119	87,608	93,031	149,727	73,291
Benefits	37,049	27,799	12,837	1,439	6,664	9,938	4,819
Occupancy	115,005	181,699	39,080	34,019	60,000	66,321	14,526
Advertising	17,430	37,273	6,506	3,317	4,434	19,152	758
Utilities	32,425	67,280	23,122	10,495	14,107	9,945	5,230
Depreciation and amortization	21,035	20,503	15,058	4,923	29,065	10,091	2,702
Repairs and maintenance	17,151	10,175	6,121	4,669	6,796	11,049	2,300
Other costs	131,825	107,420	36,900	28,288	38,431	51,378	19,277
Total expenses	829,960	705,101	265,743	174,757	252,528	327,600	122,901
Income from operations	197,889	377,939	(6,493)	3,426	17,888	193,136	9,057
Other income	19,069	126	305	—	54	—	1,930
Other expense	61,618	150	8,446	—	3,258	—	300
Overhead allocation	—	276,020	38,326	39,033	64,129	124,789	9,325
Income before taxes	$155,340	$101,894	$ (52,961)	$ (35,606)	$ (49,445)	$ 68,347	$ 1,361
Employees	19	21	N/A	8	12	15	8
% of sales nonbooks	3.7%	8.4%	N/A	1.2%	10.3%	5.5%	N/A
Total selling square feet	6,900	9,750	N/A	3,400	5,000	3,850	2,800
Leasehold cost per square foot	$1.19	$1.55	N/A	$0.83	$1.00	$1.44	$0.43

N/A = Not available.

* Petaluma store 50% owned by Copperfield's Books Inc. and by heirs of Dan Jaffee. Petaluma statements include both new and used operations. Petaluma statements also reflect administration overhead allocation of $10,245 in 2003.

Source: Copperfield's Books Inc.

Exhibit 16 **Copperfield's Books Inc., Comparative Store Data, 2002**

	Petaluma (Both New & Used)	Santa Rosa Montgomery Village	Downtown Santa Rosa	Napa	Calistoga	Sebastopol	Sebastopol Used & Rare
			Fiscal Year Ended December 31				
Revenue	$2,190,608	$2,677,781	$631,382	$403,880	$581,382	$1,271,123	$224,659
Cost of goods sold	1,277,229	1,675,832	319,195	227,524	334,940	801,045	82,970
Gross margin	913,379	1,001,950	312,187	176,355	246,442	470,078	141,689
Salaries and wages	453,572	303,091	143,794	85,463	80,538	170,508	66,950
Benefits	72,160	45,851	24,684	10,437	12,303	23,489	10,680
Occupancy	95,919	174,080	12,298	32,871	60,000	62,906	21,343
Advertising	21,503	31,367	8,180	3,008	5,232	18,440	673
Utilities	28,158	17,755	23,097	10,600	11,355	10,837	5,230
Depreciation and amortization	14,649	18,039	30,084	5,169	26,125	11,367	4,926
Repairs and maintenance	14,584	9,030	7,954	5,858	4,173	12,757	2,732
Other costs	73,015	60,812	21,603	13,464	22,284	34,239	7,045
Total expenses	773,560	660,024	271,693	166,868	222,011	344,542	119,578
Income from operations	139,819	341,925	40,494	9,487	24,432	125,536	22,111
Other income	20,758	223	260	176	30	1,027	21,876
Other expense	42,855	808	33,627	—	5,179	—	21,080
Overhead allocation	—	269,246	50,820	37,824	59,651	127,148	10,329
Income before taxes	$ 117,722	$ 72,094	$ (43,693)	$ (28,162)	$ (40,369)	$ (585)	$ 12,578

Note: Petaluma store 50% owned by Copperfield's Books, Inc. and by heirs of Dan Jaffee. Petaluma statements include both new and used operations. Petaluma statements also reflect administration overhead allocation of $35,969 in 2002.

Source: Copperfield's Books Inc.

placement and arrangement of front-list titles to the respective store managers. "We are working to get a handle on how product should be merchandised in our stores," stated Montan. "I have been studying the use of 'plan-o-grams' in other industries and trying to develop metrics for how to position our inventory to produce optimal sales."

Montan attributed decentralized control to helping attract and retain good employees. "We do have much more loyal employees than the chains do because we give more autonomy and creativity to our staff," Montan opined. "This creates an undefined yet very noticeable level of ownership toward the individual's store, and this attitude gets filtered down." Most of Copperfield's employees had been with the company since the 1980s, and their longevity was considered by Montan to be a key component in connecting Copperfield's to customers.

In conjunction with decentralized operations at the store level, the company invested heavily in front-office infrastructure. The corporate office provided general administrative support for the stores, which included centralized purchasing, accounting, marketing, information technology management, and special event coordination. Many of the firm's administrative employees were long tenured and had developed personal relationships with the company's founders. In 2003, approximately 22 percent of Copperfield's payroll was attributable to the corporate office, and overall corporate administration expenses cost approximately 7 percent of net sales. Corporate book buyers' salaries alone amounted to approximately 2 percent of new book sales. Exhibit 17 shows Copperfield's administrative cost structure.

Information Technology

In part, the need for front-office personnel had arisen from inefficiencies related to the company's antiquated information system based on MS-DOS, an operating system that had been in use since the

Exhibit 17 **Copperfield's Books Inc., Comparative Statements of Administrative Expenses, 2001–2003**

	2003		2002		2001	
Salaries and wages—executive/general administration	$ 93,668	16.7%	$ 104,835	17.7%	$ 134,739	22.6%
Salaries and wages—accounting	72,574	12.9	65,445	11.1	70,631	11.8
Salaries and wages—advertising/promotion	40,370	7.2	45,762	7.7	49,804	8.4
Salaries and wages—information technology	13,085	2.3	—	0.0	—	0.0
Salaries and wages—purchasing	104,917	18.7	103,465	17.5	100,623	16.9
Salaries and wages—warehouse	52,040	9.3	65,203	11.0	56,435	9.5
Salaries and wages—maintenance/special events	2,109	0.4	6,768	1.1	9,943	1.7
Benefits	42,656	7.6	43,756	7.4	47,193	7.9
Occupancy	31,868	5.7	30,874	5.2	27,192	4.6
Utilities	16,611	3.0	18,596	3.1	18,460	3.1
Depreciation and amortization	13,623	2.4	19,020	3.2	17,684	3.0
Repairs and maintenance	10,881	1.9	28,441	4.8	7,333	1.2
Travel and business entertainment	16,722	3.0	16,634	2.8	11,008	1.8
Professional services	29,788	5.3	28,441	4.8	17,333	2.9
Other costs	20,956	3.7	13,747	2.3	28,026	4.7
Total administrative expenses	$ 561,868	100.0%	$ 590,987	100.0%	$ 596,404	100.0%

Note: Percentages may not add up to 100% due to rounding.
Source: Copperfield's Books Inc.

mid-1980s. The system issued purchase orders, created receiving documents, and maintained a perpetual inventory for the stores. It also suggested which books should be returned to the publisher or wholesaler and generated figures necessary to calculate "open-to-buy" budgets. However, the system's drawbacks were significant, according to Montan. Other chains had developed software that allowed for more connectivity with wholesalers. Different levels in the supply chain could share information to reduce costs. For example, the chains were able to receive shipments by box (instead of by individual book title, as was Copperfield's practice). Box book orders allowed other chains added efficiencies when fulfilling orders as well as receiving them. Montan believed that wholesalers would soon require this technology, or would charge a premium to ship merchandise on a per book basis, as currently required by existing software.

"There's just no new software available for us independent bookstores," Montan commented. "Because of the [consolidating] trends in the business, no one is writing software for independent bookstores." Montan related that a leading wholesaler, Ingram, was developing a proprietary software package that a bookseller could use to manage product purchased through its supply channel, but this product would not likely be comprehensive enough to meet all of Copperfield's needs for tracking inventory. Sales of new books accounted for 60 percent of chainwide revenues in 2003.

Copperfield's buyers procured new book inventory from a variety of sources. A large percentage of the backlist titles came from Ingram, which required smaller minimum purchases and shorter lead times. Copperfield's staff placed customers' special orders through Ingram. Corporate buyers also ordered directly from publishers like Random House, Penguin, and Houghton-Mifflin. Gross margins on books bought directly from publishers ranged from 41 to 43 percent, while margins on books from wholesalers averaged between 37 and 39 percent.

Copperfield's had explored outsourcing its buying functions to Ingram, which, in turn, could fill the role of a wholesaler/jobber for Copperfield's stores. Ingram purchased books from all major publishing houses and provided services to many independent booksellers that were not large enough to deal directly with publishers. Ingram offered to write all of Copperfield's orders and manage all returns, in exchange for an exclusive contract for all of the company's purchases. Montan and his team decided to turn down Ingram's offer, due to the risks of being associated with a one-source jobber, not to mention what might happen if Ingram itself should fail. Some team members were concerned that an exclusive contract would shift the retailer/supplier power balance to Copperfield's detriment. Others were worried about protecting the jobs of Copperfield's book buyers.

Copperfield's also purchased remainder books directly from publishers. Remainder books were overstocked older titles of new books that publishers sold to bookstores for "pennies on the dollar," according to Montan. The larger gross margins helped offset additional handling costs associated with remainder books. Montan said, "We have had to be careful. Remainder books have been addictive [to us] because of their higher margins and [to customers] because of their low prices."

As early as 2000, Montan had begun to worry about the decline of the downtown business districts where five of Copperfield's stores were located. The primary reason for Montan's concern arose from the flight from downtown areas of dynamic businesses that had previously helped to create a critical mass for attracting customers. This flight was a response to the development of malls in Copperfield's communities that offered free parking, security, and attractive store layouts. Montan believed that high parking fees, the rise in vacant storefronts, and a lack of after-dark foot traffic had restricted the downtown stores' performance. Meanwhile, retail development accelerated along major arterial highways, in all cases far removed from the downtown business districts. These developments were buoyed by declining state government budget allocations to local communities as well as regulations rewarding municipalities that fostered big-box retail development as a means of generating local tax revenue.

Leadership Style

Montan started working for Copperfield's in 1986, after earning a bachelor's degree in sociology. His first job was as a bookseller in the firm's Petaluma store, advancing to director of marketing in 1988. Copperfield's promoted him to be director of operations in 2002, shortly after the unexpected death of

Dan Jaffe, the preceding director of operations. He ascended to the position of CEO when founder and preceding CEO, Paul Jaffe, decided to step down from day-to-day operations.

Copperfield's mission statement emphasized customer service, respect for employees' contributions, community, independence, and free expression (see Exhibit 18). Montan stated:

> We were founded on ideals of being independent and creating a forum for ideas to be exchanged, but this path becomes more and more restricted as time goes on. So, we try to bend and adapt. The core values of the company are changing, too. I am continually frustrated with many within our industry who are very high on ideals but lack business models to support these ideals.

Montan believed that Copperfield's would have to upgrade its technology and improve organizational efficiencies. "Our goal is to make the bookstore experience increasingly exciting and locally focused with a supercharged back end that makes it easier for our stores to connect to their unique communities," he said. He created a slogan encompassing these beliefs: "Creating community, connecting with you."

Copperfield's board of directors gave Montan broad discretionary powers. His first order of business was to develop a vision for the company's growth and to make that vision a reality. During his first two years, he decentralized many of the buying functions, downsized the firm's warehouse operation, and cut staff. He standardized many human resource functions such as job descriptions and staff training

programs, and implemented time and attendance controls. Montan also increased corporate communication through regular meetings with store management and weekly memos to all store employees.

Montan's management style inspired loyalty among his staff. "He really stepped up, and made it happen," exclaimed Aaron Smith, manager of the Montgomery Village store. "I had reservations when he was promoted, but now we all have a high level of trust in his intentions as well as his vision for the company. He impressed all of us in the way he dealt with the warehouse issue."

'[Standardizing human resource procedures] was something that had needed to happen for a long time," recalled Noreen Roberts, Copperfield's human resource manager. "He saw the opportunity and took it. I think he earned a lot of respect for that."

Governance and Corporate Structure

Copperfield's Inc. was organized as a subchapter S corporation at its inception with two founding stockholders: Barney Brown and Paul Jaffe. As the company grew, the board issued additional shares and sold them to members of the founders' families. As of October 2004, Copperfield's Inc. remained closely held by the Brown and Jaffe families, with the Brown family controlling a majority interest. The board of directors consisted of three members of the Brown family, one member of the Jaffe family, and one nonequity holding adviser.

Exhibit 18   **Copperfield's Books Inc. Mission Statement**

Our Intention
To create an extraordinary bookstore that is the pride of our community and staff.

Our Commitment
Service: *We strive to provide great customer service and recognize that it is only in our ability to uniquely serve our customers that we will succeed as a business.*

Responsibility: *We are committed to providing a forum for readers and writers that encourages the free expression of ideas. We are committed to remaining an independently owned and operated bookstore. We take personal responsibility for respecting one another and valuing the contributions we all make. We are committed to running a profitable business.*

Environment: *To carry a selection of books and gifts that nurtures the spirit and feeds the mind. To be a fun place to work.*

Source: Copperfield's Books Inc.

Internet

Capitalizing on the opportunities promised by the Internet posed a great challenge. Depth of selection, customized recommendations fueled by algorithms tracking previous purchasing behavior, discount pricing, and other value-added services provided by on-line retailers were all difficult—if not impossible—to duplicate in a storefront retail environment. While the setup costs for developing a presence on the Web were minimal and hundreds of people were selling used and rare books over the Internet, some via Web sites such as eBay, Bookfinder.com, the used-books division of Amazon.com, or Half.com, to name just a few sites, incumbent Internet booksellers erected barriers to fledgling online rivals through intensive capital investment and technical expertise. According to Montan:

> The independent book industry as a whole missed the Internet market per se [for new books]. Amazon just came and chose books as its ideal marketplace for Internet retailing. They were quite wise to do so; books are easily definable, you can have a lot of customer interactivity in terms of ratings and reviews, and it's a one-size-fits-all product that's not perishable. There are a lot of things going for books that makes a lot of sense to sell online.

As a way of providing value-added services for its existing customer base, Copperfield's used a Web site template developed by the American Booksellers Association (ABA). Through the site, customers could order books 24 hours a day. In addition, Copperfield's offered the value-added service of allowing in-store returns for online purchases, a service also offered by other retail stores that had Internet operations. Staff at the Montgomery Village store transmitted orders to a third-party wholesaler who fulfilled the orders, shipping directly to customers. Access to the ABA template cost $250 annually. Copperfield's earned a 5 percent finder's fee on sales through the site. "It's sort of a minimal cost, minimal work solution, that is certainly not the best," said Montan. In the 12 months ending in June 2004, Copperfield's posted revenues of $4,655 via this distribution channel.

Opportunities for selling used books online nevertheless appeared to be promising. Montan's belief that the Internet would be important to Copperfield's future competitiveness in the used-book market spurred his decision in 2004 to move staff and inventory of the abandoned downtown Santa Rosa location to the Petaluma store. Montan hoped to complete the first phase of operations in the new location by the end of 2004. He estimated that Copperfield's would receive one dollar in revenue per month for each title listed online. He hoped to list 10,000 titles by the end of 2004, estimating that should it achieve approximately $120,000 per year in Internet book sales, Copperfield's could then cover the online operation's overhead, realize a small profit, and begin to develop metrics for operating an online fulfillment operation. "We're learning how to do this business, but we are a long way from breakeven," Montan noted.

One problem with the fulfillment center was that there was no coordination between the other business units within the firm. Both of Copperfield's used bookstores sold online independently of the fulfillment center. There was no plan to integrate online sales of new books. Moreover, books inventoried in the fulfillment center were not available for sale in the stores. There were no mechanisms to coordinate the inventories between the used bookstores and the fulfillment center. It was possible that a customer looking for a particular book at one of the stores could be turned away, despite the fact that the book was inventoried in the fulfillment center. Conversely, shoppers looking for a particular book online did not have access to the inventories in the stores. Montan's long-range vision for the fulfillment center included "creating a 'mega-warehouse' used bookstore that could act as a warehouse for Internet sales, while developing large enough girth to attract customers from around the San Francisco Bay Area."

Used and Rare Books

Copperfield's primarily targeted the upper strata of the used-book market, that is, books valued at $20 or higher. Montan reflected:

> Used-book customers represent a different breed from new book people. They don't care about best sellers. They want what they want. They want the best copy. They are bibliophiles to the nth degree. They curmudgeonly want to get into the stacks so they can climb up the ladder and find that rare dusty "whatever" on the back shelf.

Copperfield's inventory of used and rare books was considered to be the largest in Sonoma County. The collection included a large percentage of antiquarian books and first editions, which were merchandised conspicuously throughout the stores to provide a sense of weight and refinement.

Copperfield's acquired its used books primarily from existing customers, junk dealers, and book scouts, but occasionally buyers went beyond these supply channels. In 2003, for example, the firm purchased an entire library in the Midwest. Determining the value of used books required specialized knowledge and experience. Art Kusnetz, manager of Copperfield's Petaluma Used and Rare Bookstore, had over 20 years' experience as a book scout and working with antiquarian book dealers. The need for expert employees was a significant barrier to expansion, as qualified, expert book buyers were scarce. Because key personnel were vital to success in the used-book business, Montan had considered equity sharing with managers of Copperfield's two used bookstores. Montan felt that owning a stake in the operation might increase their drive to grow the used-book business while protecting Copperfield's from the cost of replacing employees with rare skill sets.

THE NAPA OPPORTUNITY

After 10 years of disappointing operations in Copperfield's Napa store, Montan had begun looking for another way to access what he believed was an underserved market for books in Napa. "The fact that we secured what we felt was a sweetheart lease, [at] 80 cents per square foot, afforded us the ability to be patient," he said. "I think we had a distant hope that this area would explode, and we would be left holding the bag o' gold. But the trend currently is that this downtown space is flatter than flat." Early in 2004, Montan decided to give up on the Napa store and scheduled it for closure when the lease expired at the end of the year.

"We need to develop a store that will create a compelling gravity to attract customers," Montan said. He hoped to replicate his previous experience in Montgomery Village, consistently the most profitable store in the chain, which unlike its downtown locations, did not suffer from the lack of adequate parking, the impact of loitering transients that deterred customers from browsing, or a lack of evening foot traffic. Montan believed that new stores in regional lifestyle shopping centers with ample free parking could generate sales between $2.5 and $3 million annually, assuming that chain superstores refrained from entering into the same trade area.

Montan had located a space in a regional lifestyle center located at the intersection of two major arterial highways in Napa. The center had attracted other strong tenants like Trader Joe's, Cost Plus, and Orchard Hardware, retailers that could complement Copperfield's and help attract impulse purchasers and book browsers. To assess the market opportunity for a new Napa location, Montan pored over the demographic information for the Napa trade area, which, compared to Copperfield's current locations, had significantly larger Hispanic/Latino populations. His analysis suggested that the trade area was underserved, with over half of the area's potential book sales revenue "leaking" out of the trade area (see Exhibit 19). Yet his analysis also suggested that the surrounding area's demand could, at best, marginally support the additional retail space, because the levels of educational attainment in the Napa trade area appeared to be significantly lower than in the areas surrounding Copperfield's more successful stores (see Exhibit 20).

Copperfield's planned to recycle fixtures salvaged from the recent closure of the downtown Santa Rosa store along with those that would be transferred from the existing Napa store. By reusing fixtures, Montan felt that he could dramatically decrease the cost of opening a new store, which would still include $150,000 in tenant improvements (including $60,000 provided by the landlord), $450,000 in inventory ($150,000 of which would be transferred from the existing Napa location), and $30,000 in pre-opening expenses. An estimated total capital investment of nearly $500,000 would represent a level far exceeding any new store development Copperfield's had undertaken. The company would finance the project through bank loans collateralized by a company-owned building in Sebastopol.

The Future

When asked about the realism of his goal to grow Copperfield's Books from $8 million to $15 million in four years, Montan replied, "The biggest issue facing our company is growing to a size where we can develop a level of efficiency. We will need to develop this level of scale quickly to cover prospective increases in [administration] costs."

Exhibit 19   **Copperfield's Books Inc., Potential New Sales Analysis for Proposed Napa Store**

(1) Total trade area households*		31,885
(2) Annual average household spending at bookstores†		$162
(3) Total annual trade area potential [= (1) × (2)]		$5,165,370
(4) Existing supply‡		
Readers' Books	$600,000	
Copperfield's	420,000	
Napa Booktree	250,000	
Bookends Bookstore	550,000	
Waldenbooks	372,000	
Book Outlet Store	372,000	
(5) Total existing annual trade area sales		$2,564,000
(6) Current annual trade area "leakage" (potential sales) [= (3) − (5)]		$2,601,370
(7) Expressed as percentage of total annual trade area potential [= (6)/(3)]		50.36%

*Claritas, a marketing information resources company www.clusterbigip1.claritas.com/claritas/Default.jsp?ti=3&ci=1&pn=freeinfo (accessed October 2004).

†Represents average spending for *all* households on books, excluding children's, audio, and digital books. Household bookstore expenditures provided by *Press Democrat* and U.S. Census data from *Statistical Abstract of the United States, 2006.*

‡Supply data provided by Copperfield's; Waldenbooks and Book Outlet volumes reflect industry average per square foot; Copperfield's volume based on estimate using 2003 sales data.

Exhibit 20   **Copperfield's Books Inc., Demographic Analysis for Proposed Napa Store**

(1) Total trade area households*		31,885
(2) Annual average household spending at bookstores†		$162
(3) Total annual trade area potential [= (1) × (2)]		$5,165,370
(4) Average annual independent bookstore sales/sq. ft.‡		$248
(5) Supportable trade area bookstore space, sq. ft. [= (3)/(4)]		20,828
(6) Existing supply, sq. ft.§		
Readers' Books	3,000	
Copperfield's	3,400	
Napa Booktree	1,500	
Bookends Bookstore	4,000	
Waldenbooks	1,500	
Book Outlet Store	1,500	
(7) Total existing trade area supply, sq. ft.		14,900
(8) Additional supply trade area will support, sq. ft. [= (5) − (6)]		5,928
(9) Proposed Copperfield's store in Bel Aire Plaza, sq. ft.	9,700	
Existing Copperfield's store in downtown Napa, sq. ft.	(3,400)	
Net expansion, sq. ft.		6,300
(10) Trade area deficit after expansion, sq. ft. [= (8) − (9)]		(372)

*Claritas, a marketing information resources company, www.clusterbigip1.claritas.com/claritas/Default.jsp?ti=3&ci=1&pn=freeinfo (accessed October 2004).

†Represents average spending for *all* households on books, excluding children's, audio, and digital books. Household bookstore expenditures provided by *Press Democrat* and U.S. Census data from *Statistical Abstract of the United States, 2006.*

‡American Booksellers Association, *ABACUS Survey,* 2003.

§Supply data provided by Copperfield's; Waldenbooks and Book Outlet square footage estimated by using industry average per square foot.

The offer on the retail space in Napa expired in a week. Montan decided to take a few days with his management team and review several alternative strategies he had considered. These alternatives included opening as many as two 10,000-square-foot stores in North Bay markets, such as the proposed Napa location and perhaps also Novato (in neighboring Marin County to the south) within the next four years. Other options included increasing Copperfield's focus on the growing used- and rare-books segments, or accelerating its investment in Internet sales to complement its retail stores' sales.

Bibliography

Abraham, J., and J. Hayes. (2005). "Used Book Market Analysis: Initial Preview," Book Industry Study Group, www.bisg.org, preliminary report released September 2005.

Amazon.com, 2003 annual report.

American Booksellers Association. *ABACUS Survey 2003.*

Anderson, C. (2004, October). "The Long Tail." *Wired.*

Anonymous. (2003, September 10). "Adult Book Purchases Up Two Percent in 2002." *Bookselling This Week,* http://news.bookweb.org/news/1782.html.

Anonymous. (2004, May 6). "BookTrends Study Shows Independents Buck Trend and Gain Market Share." *Bookselling This Week,* http://news.bookweb.org/news/2514.html.

Anonymous. (2004, May 19). "BISG's Trends Predicts $44 Billion Book Market in 2008." *Bookselling This Week,* http://news.bookweb.org/news/2548.html.

Anonymous. (2004, August 24). "Independent Sellers Gain with Size, Service." *The Wall Street Journal (Eastern Edition),* Section A1.

Barnes & Noble. 2003 annual report.

Bernoff, J., C. Charron, A. Lonian, C. Stohm, and G. Fleming. (2004). "From Discs to Downloads." Forrester Research, www.forrester.com/ER/Research/Report/Summary/0,1338,16076,00.html.

Borders Group Inc., 10-K report filed with the Securities and Exchange Commission, FYE January 25, 2004.

Claritas, a Market Research Company. www.claritas.com/claritas/Default.jsp?ti = 3&ci = 1&pn = freeinfo (accessed October 20, 2004).

Howell, K. (2004, September 20). "Tattered Cover Expands to the Burbs," *Publishers Weekly.*

IPSOS-Insight. "BookTrends." www.ipsos-insight.com (accessed October 19, 2004).

Kirch, C. (2004, July 26) ."Creating an Experience." *Publisher's Weekly.*

Lewin, N. (2005, December 19). "The Book Trade," Public Radio International's *Marketplace,* http://marketplace.publicradio.org/shows/2005/12/19/pm.html.

Mariano, G. (2001, May 2). "E-book Devices Yet to Hit Bestseller's List." *CNET,* http://news.com.com/2100-1023-256938.html.

National Endowment for the Arts. (2004, June). "Reading at Risk: A Survey of Literary Reading in America." *National Endowment for the Arts,* www.arts.gov.

Patterson, W. (2004, June 6). "Retail Grows, with Vacancies under 5%," *Santa Rosa Press Democrat,* Outlook Section.

Patterson, W. (2004, June 24). "Copperfield's Moves On." *Santa Rosa Press Democrat,* p. E1.

Price, G. (2004). "Google Partners with Oxford, Harvard & Others to Digitize Libraries." *SearchEngineWatch,* http://searchenginewatch.com/searchday/article.php/3447411.

Rappaport, B. (2003, Fall). "The Used Book Marketplace: Fact or Fiction?" *Publishing Research Quarterly,* pp. 3–12.

Small Business Administration. www.onlinewbc.gov/docs/finance/fs_ratio1.html.

Trachtenberg J. (2004, August 24). "Plot Twist: To Compete with Book Chains, Some Think Big; Independent Sellers Gain with Size, Service." *The Wall Street Journal (Eastern Edition),* p. A1.

U.S. Census Bureau. (2000). *Income Distribution in 1999 of Households and Families: 2000,* QT-P32, http://factfinder.census.gov/servlet/QTTable?_bm=y&-geo_id=D&-qr_name=DEC_2000_SFAIAN_QTP32&-ds_name=D&-_lang=en.

U.S. Department of Commerce. (2004). "Sector 44: Retail Trade: Industry Series: Comparative Statistics for the United States (1997 NAICA Basics): 2002 and 1997." *2002 U.S. Economic Census* (Release Date: July 29, 2004), www.census.gov/econ/census02/guide/INDRPT44.HTM.

Endnotes

[1]Anonymous. (2004, May 19). "BISG's Trends Predicts $44 Billion Book Market in 2008." *Bookselling This Week,* http://news.bookweb.org/news/2548.html.

[2]Ibid.

[3]IPSOS. (2003). "Book Industry Struggles with Slow Growth." www.ipsos-ideas.com/article.cfm?id=2148.

[4]According to one industry observer, "The trade book industry is faced with the need to develop a strategic marketing plan that will excite customers and bring them back into the stores. Programs designed to attract the affluent, educated customer without alienating the remaining customer base are key." Rappaport, B. (2003, Fall). "The Used Book Marketplace: Fact or Fiction?" *Publishing Research Quarterly,* p. 5.

[5]Anonymous. (2003, June 22). "Wal-Mart and Other Discounters: Cultural Oligopsony?" *Oligopoly Watch,* www.oligopolywatch.com/2003/06/22.html.

[6]Ibid.

[7]"Sector 44: Retail Trade: Industry Series: Book Stores," *2002 U.S. Economic Census* (release date: July 29, 2004), www.census.gov/econ/census02/guide/INDRPT44.HTM.

[8]Trachtenberg J. (2004, August 24). "Plot Twist: To Compete with Book Chains, Some Think Big; Independent Sellers Gain with Size, Service." *The Wall Street Journal (Eastern Edition),* p. A1.

[9]Anonymous. (2003, September 10). "Adult Book Purchases Up Two Percent in 2002." *Bookselling This Week,* http://news.bookweb.org/news/1782.html.

[10]Borders Group Inc., form 10-K for the fiscal year ended January 25, 2004, p. 9.

[11]Milevoj, A., Manager of Investor Relations, Barnes & Noble, e-mail message to authors, October 18, 2004.

[12]Trachtenberg, J. op. cit.

[13]Anonymous. (2004, May 6). "BookTrends Study Shows Independents Buck Trend and Gain Market Share." *Bookselling This Week,* http://news.bookweb.org/news/2514.html.

[14]Barnes & Noble, 2003 annual report, p. 10.

[15]Anonymous. (2004, May 6), op. cit.

[16]Ibid.

[17]Anderson, C. (2004, October). "The Long Tail." *Wired,* pp. 171–77.

[18]Ibid.

[19]Rappaport, B. (2003). op. cit., pp. 9–10.

[20]Bernoff, J. et. al. (2004). "From Discs to Downloads." Forrester Research, www.forrester.com/ER/Research/Report/Summary/0,1338,16076,00.html.

[21] Mariano, G. (2004). "E-book Devices Yet to Hit Bestseller's List," *CNET,* http://news.com.com/2100-1023-256938.html.

[22]Ibid.

[23]Price, G. (2004). "Google Partners with Oxford, Harvard & Others to Digitize libraries." SearchEngineWatch.com, http://searchenginewatch.com/searchday/article.php/3447411.

[24]Borders Group Inc., form 10-K for the fiscal year ended January 25, 2004, p. 17; Barnes & Noble, 2003 annual report, p. 13.

[25]American Booksellers Association, *ABACUS Survey 2004.*

[26]Borders Group Inc., form 10-K for the fiscal year ended January 25, 2004, p. 9.

[27]U.S. Census Bureau. (2000). *QT-P32. Income distribution in 1999 of households and families: 2000,* http://factfinder.census.gov/servlet/QTTable?_bm=y&-geo_id=D&-qr_name=DEC_2000_SFA-IAN_QTP32&-ds_name=D&-_lang=en.

[28]Patterson, W. (2004, June 6). "Retail Grows, with Vacancies Under 5%." *Santa Rosa Press Democrat,* Outlook Section.

[29]Ibid.

[30]Patterson, W. (2004, June 24). "Copperfield's Moves On." *Santa Rosa Press Democrat,* p. E1.

Harley-Davidson in 2004

John E. Gamble
University of South Alabama

Roger Schäfer
University of South Alabama

Harley-Davidson's management had much to be proud of as the company wrapped up its Open Road Tour centennial celebration, which began in July 2002 in Atlanta, Georgia, and ended on the 2003 Memorial Day Weekend in Harley's hometown of Milwaukee, Wisconsin. The 14-month Open Road Tour was a tremendous success, drawing large crowds of Harley owners in each of its five stops in North America and additional stops in Australia, Japan, Spain, and Germany. Each stop along the tour included exhibits of historic motorcycles, performances by dozens of bands as diverse as Lynyrd Skynyrd, Earl Scruggs, and Nickelback, and brought hundreds of thousands of Harley enthusiasts together to celebrate the company's products. The Ride Home finale brought 700,000 biker-guests from four points in the United States to Milwaukee for a four-day party that included concerts, factory tours, and a parade of 10,000 motorcycles through downtown Milwaukee. The company also used the Open Road Tour as a platform for its support of the Muscular Dystrophy Association (MDA), raising $7 million for the MDA during the 14-month tour. Photos from the Open Road Tour and Harley's new V-Rod model are presented in Exhibit 1.

Harley-Davidson's centennial year was also a year to remember for the company's being named to *Fortune*'s annual list "The 100 Best Companies to Work For" and judged third in automotive quality behind Rolls-Royce and Mercedes-Benz by Harris Interactive, a worldwide market research and consulting firm best known for the Harris Poll. Consumer loyalty to Harley-Davidson motorcycles was unmatched by almost any other company. As

a Canadian Harley dealer explained, "You know you've got strong brand loyalty when your customers tattoo your logo on their arm."[1] The company's revenues had grown at a compound annual rate of 16.6 percent since 1994 to reach $4.6 billion in 2003—marking its 18th consecutive year of record revenues and earnings. In 2003, the company sold more than 290,000 motorcycles, giving it a commanding share of the market for motorcycles in the 651+ cubic centimeters (cc) category in the United States and the leading share of the market in the Asia/Pacific region. The consistent growth had allowed Harley-Davidson's share price to appreciate by more than 15,000 percent since the company's initial public offering in 1986. In January 2004, the company's CEO, Jeffrey Bleustein, commented on the centennial year and the company's prospects for growth as it entered its second century:

> We had a phenomenal year full of memorable once-in-a-lifetime experiences surrounding our 100th Anniversary. As we begin our 101st year, we expect to grow the business further with our proven ability to deliver a continuous stream of exciting new motorcycles, related products, and services. We have set a new goal for the company to be able to satisfy a yearly demand of 400,000 Harley-Davidson motorcycles in 2007. By offering innovative products and services, and by driving productivity gains in all facets of our business, we are confident that we can deliver an earnings growth rate in the mid-teens for the foreseeable future.[2]

However, not everyone was as bullish on Harley-Davidson's future, with analysts pointing out that the company's plans for growth were too dependent on aging baby boomers. The company had achieved its record growth during the 1990s and

Exhibit 1   **Photos from Harley-Davidson's Open Road Tour and Its VRSC V-Rod**

Source: Harley-Davidson Web site.

early 2000s primarily through the appeal its image held for baby boomers in the United States. Some observers wondered how much longer boomers would choose to spend recreational time touring the country by motorcycle and attending motorcycle rallies. The company had yet to develop a motorcycle that appealed in large numbers to motorcycle riders in their 20s or cyclists in Europe, both of whom preferred performance-oriented bikes over cruisers or touring motorcycles. Another concern of analysts watching the company was Harley-Davidson's short-term oversupply of certain models

Exhibit 2   **Summary of Harley-Davidson's Financial Performance, 1994–2003 (in thousands, except per share amounts)**

	2003	2002	2001
Income statement data			
Net sales	$4,624,274	$4,090,970	$3,406,786
Cost of goods sold	2,958,708	2,673,129	2,253,815
Gross profit	1,665,566	1,417,841	1,152,971
Operating income from financial services	167,873	104,227	61,273
Selling, administrative and engineering	(684,175)	(639,366)	(551,743)
Income from operations	1,149,264	882,702	662,501
Gain on sale of credit card business	—	—	—
Interest income, net	23,088	16,541	17,478
Other income (expense), net	(6,317)	(13,416)	(6,524)
Income from continuing operations before provision for income taxes and accounting changes	1,166,035	885,827	673,445
Provision for income taxes	405,107	305,610	235,709
Income from continuing operations before accounting changes	760,928	580,217	437,746
Income (loss) from discontinued operations, net of tax	—	—	—
Income before accounting changes	760,928	580,217	437,746
Cumulative effect of accounting changes, net of tax	—	—	—
Net income (loss)	$ 760,928	$ 580,217	$ 437,746
Weighted average common shares:			
Basic	302,271	302,297	302,506
Diluted	304,470	305,158	306,248
Earnings per common share from continuing operations:			
Basic	$ 2.52	$ 1.92	$ 1.45
Diluted	2.50	1.90	1.43
Dividends paid	0.195	0.135	0.115
Balance sheet data			
Working capital	$1,773,354	$1,076,534	$ 949,154
Current finance receivables, net	1,001,990	855,771	656,421
Long-term finance receivables, net	735,859	589,809	379,335
Total assets	4,923,088	3,861,217	3,118,495
Short-term finance debt	324,305	382,579	217,051
Long-term finance debt	670,000	380,000	380,000
Total debt	$ 994,305	$ 762,579	$ 597,051
Shareholders' equity	$2,957,692	$2,232,915	$1,756,283

Source: Harley-Davidson Inc. 2003, 2002, and 1998 10-K reports.

brought about by the 14-month production run for its 100th anniversary models. The effect of the extended production period shortened the waiting list for most models from over a year to a few months and left some models on showroom floors for immediate purchase. The combined effects of a market focus on a narrow demographic group, the difficulty experienced in gaining market share in Europe, and short-term forecasting problems led to a sell-off of Harley-Davidson shares going into 2004. Exhibit 2 presents a summary of Harley-Davidson's financial and operating performance for 1994–2003. Its market performance for 1994 through January 2004 is presented in Exhibit 3.

2000	1999	1998	1997	1996	1995	1994
$2,943,346	$2,482,738	$2,087,670	$1,762,569	$1,531,227	$1,350,466	$1,158,887
1,979,572	1,666,863	1,414,034	1,176,352	1,041,133	939,067	800,548
963,774	815,875	673,636	586,217	490,094	411,399	358,339
37,178	27,685	20,211	12,355	7,801	3,620	—
(485,980)	(427,701)	(360,231)	(328,569)	(269,449)	(234,223)	(204,777)
514,972	415,859	333,616	270,003	228,446	180,796	153,562
18,915	—	—	—	—	—	—
17,583	8,014	3,828	7,871	3,309	96	1,682
(2,914)	(3,080)	(1,215)	(1,572)	(4,133)	(4,903)	1,196
548,556	420,793	336,229	276,302	227,622	175,989	156,440
200,843	153,592	122,729	102,232	84,213	64,939	60,219
347,713	267,201	213,500	174,070	143,409	111,050	96,221
—	—	—	—	22,619	1,430	8,051
347,713	267,201	213,500	174,070	166,028	112,480	104,272
$ 347,713	$ 267,201	$ 213,500	$ 174,070	$ 166,028	$ 112,480	$ 104,272
302,691	304,748	304,454	151,650	150,683	149,972	150,440
307,470	309,714	309,406	153,948	152,925	151,900	153,365
$ 1.15	$ 0.88	$ 0.70	$ 1.15	$ 0.95	$ 0.74	$ 0.64
1.13	0.86	0.69	1.13	0.94	0.73	0.63
0.098	0.088	0.078	0.135	0.110	0.090	0.070
$ 799,521	$ 430,840	$ 376,448	$ 342,333	$ 362,031	$288,783	$189,358
530,859	440,951	360,341	293,329	183,808	169,615	—
234,091	354,888	319,427	249,346	154,264	43,829	—
2,436,404	2,112,077	1,920,209	1,598,901	1,299,985	980,670	676,663
89,509	181,163	146,742	90,638	8,065	—	—
355,000	280,000	280,000	280,000	250,000	164,330	—
$ 444,509	$ 461,163	$ 426,742	$ 391,572	$ 285,767	$185,228	$ 10,452
$1,405,655	$1,161,080	$1,029,911	$ 826,668	$ 662,720	$494,569	$433,232

COMPANY HISTORY

Harley-Davidson's history began in Milwaukee, Wisconsin, in 1903 when 20-year-old Arthur Davidson convinced his father to build a small shed in their backyard where Arthur and 21-year-old William Harley could try their hand at building a motorcycle. Various types of motorized bicycles had been built since 1885, but the 1901 development of a motorcycle with an integrated engine by a French company inspired Davidson and Harley to develop their own motorcycle. The two next-door neighbors built a two-horsepower engine that they fit onto a

Exhibit 3   **Yearly Performance of Harley-Davidson Inc.'s Stock Price, 1994 to January 2004**

(a) Trend in Harley-Davidson Inc.'s Common Stock Price

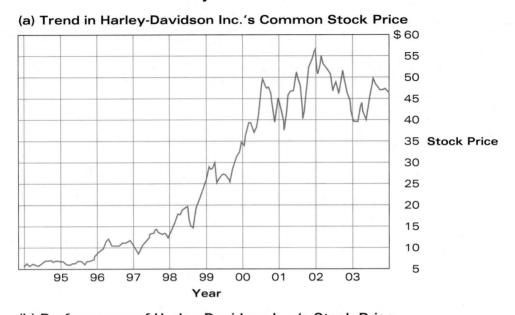

(b) Performance of Harley-Davidson Inc.'s Stock Price versus the S&P 500 Index

modified bicycle frame. At first the motorcycle could not pull itself and a rider up a steep hill, but after some additional tinkering, the first Harley-Davidson motorcycle could run as fast as 25 miles per hour. Milwaukee residents were amazed as Harley and Davidson rode the motorcycle down local streets, and by the end of the year the partners were able to produce and sell three of their motorcycles. Walter Davidson

joined his brother and William Harley during the year to help assemble and race the company's motorcycles. In 1905, a Harley-Davidson motorcycle won a 15-mile race in Chicago with a time of 19:02, and by 1907 the company had developed quite a reputation in motorcycle racing with numerous wins in Milwaukee-area races. In 1907, another Davidson brother, William, joined the company and the company began adding dealers. Harley-Davidson's dealers helped the company sell 150 motorcycles in 1907.

In 1909, Harley-Davidson developed a more powerful seven-horsepower motorcycle engine to keep its edge in racing, an innovation that turned out to define the look of the company's motorcycles for the next century. Twin cylinders joined at a 45-degree angle became a trademark Harley-Davidson engine design characteristic and created a distinctive "potato-potato-potato" sound. Harley designed his V-twin engine with two pistons connected to a single crankpin, whereas later designs used crankpins for each piston. The single-crankpin design had been called an inferior design because it caused the pistons to come into firing positions at uneven intervals, which produced an uneven cadence in sound and excessive vibrations. Nevertheless, the vibrations and distinctive rumble of a Harley engine were accepted by the market in the early 1900s and continued to appeal to motorcyclists in the early 2000s.

The stronger engine allowed the company to produce 17,000 motorcycles for the U.S. military during World War I and become the largest motorcycle producer in the world in 1920, with 2,000 dealers in 67 countries. A number of features that make up Harley-Davidson's image originated during the 1920s, including the teardrop gas tank, the "Hog" nickname, and the "Flathead" engine design. Harley-Davidson was one of two U.S. motorcycle companies to survive the Great Depression—the other being Indian—by relying on exports and sales to police departments and the U.S. military. The 1930s saw Harley-Davidson win more races and develop additional elements of its differentiated image, including the art deco eagle design painted on its gas tanks, three-tone paint, and the "Knucklehead" engine rocker boxes. Harley-Davidson's 1936 EL model, or "Knucklehead," became its first highly styled motorcycle and formed the foundation of style elements that remained present in the highly demanded 2004 Softail Fat Boy. The company suspended production of civilian motorcycles in 1941 to produce almost 90,000 motorcycles for the U.S. military during World War II.

The recreational motorcycle market grew dramatically after World War II, as ex-GIs purchased motorcycles and led enthusiasm for riding. Harley-Davidson introduced new models for enthusiasts, including the Hydra-Glide in 1949, the K-model in 1952, the Sportster in 1957, and the Duo-Glide in 1958. The combination of racing success

(Harley-Davidson riders won 18 of 24 races and set six new racing records in 1950 alone) and innovative new Harley-Davidson models led to rival company Indian's demise in 1953. Harley-Davidson would remain the sole U.S. manufacturer of motorcycles until 1998, when the Indian brand was revived.

Harley-Davidson continued to win races throughout the 1960s, but its reputation began to erode soon after its acquisition by American Machine and Foundry Company (AMF) in 1969. Harley-Davidson under AMF was known for its leaking engines, unreliable performance, and poor customer service. At one point during AMF's ownership of the company, more than one-half of its bikes had to be repaired before leaving the factory. The company attempted to offset its declining sales of road bikes with the introduction of dirt bikes and snowmobiles in the early 1970s, but by the late 1970s AMF lost faith in the acquisition and slated it for divestiture. When no buyers for the company emerged, 13 executives engineered a leveraged buyout of Harley-Davidson in 1981. Harley-Davidson struggled under the heavy debt load and came within four hours of bankruptcy in 1985, before then-CEO Richard Teerlink was able to convince new creditors to step in and restructure Harley with less costly financing terms. Teerlink also launched a restructuring program that updated manufacturing methods, improved quality, and expanded the model line.

U.S. tariffs imposed on 651+cc Japanese motorcycles also aided Harley-Davidson in gaining financial strength and competitiveness in the heavyweight segment of the U.S. motorcycle industry. Harley-Davidson completed an initial public offering in 1985 and petitioned the International Trade Commission to terminate tariffs on Japanese heavyweight motorcycles in 1987 when its market share in the U.S. heavyweight category had improved to 25 percent from 16 percent in 1985. In 1998, the company purchased Wisconsin-based Buell Motorcycle, a performance brand using Harley-Davidson engines that began as a venture between Erik Buell and Harley-Davidson in 1992. Harley-Davidson opened its 358,000-square-foot Kansas City, Missouri, plant in 1998 to produce Sportster, Dyna Glide, and V-Rod models and built an assembly plant in Brazil in 1999 to aid in its Latin American expansion. The new capacity allowed Harley-Davidson to set production records each year during the early 2000s to reach 290,000 units by year-end 2003.

OVERVIEW OF THE MOTORCYCLE INDUSTRY

Demand for motorcycles in developed countries such as the United States, Germany, France, Spain, and Great Britain, grew dramatically at the end of World War II as veterans who enjoyed riding motorcycles during the war purchased their own bikes upon return to civilian life. Groups of enthusiasts began to form motorcycle clubs that allowed them to socialize and participate in rallies and races. Two of the earliest motorcycle rallies in the United States were the Daytona Bike Week and the Sturgis Rally. The first Daytona 200, which occurs during Bike Week, was run in 1937 on a 3.2-mile beach and road course. The first Sturgis, South Dakota, race took place in 1938 when nine participants raced a half-mile track and performed such stunts as jumping ramps and crashing through plywood walls. These and other such events grew dramatically in popularity beginning in the 1970s, with both Daytona Bike Week and the Sturgis Rally each drawing over 200,000 bikers in 2003. The Sturgis Rally was said to be among the most raucous motorcycle rallies in the United States, with plenty of public drunkenness and lewd behavior accompanying the seven days of races. Such behavior was common enough that the Rally Web site (www. sturgis.com) provided the fines and bonds associated with such offenses as indecent exposure, disorderly conduct, open container in public, and possession of controlled substances.

The rowdy and rebellious image of bikers is traced to some of the motorcycle clubs that began after World War II. The outlaw image of cyclists first developed in 1947 when *Life* magazine photographers captured images of an impromptu rally at Hollister, California, by a motorcycle group calling themselves the Boozefighters. The group became quite rowdy during their motorcycling exhibition, but *Life* reporters embellished the story significantly, claiming the Boozefighters descended on the town and proceeded to terrorize its residents by drag-racing down the main street, tossing beer bottles, and riding motorcycles through the front doors of the town's saloon. The imagery of the drunken Fourth of July attack on the town became etched deeper into the minds of the world when the story became the subject of *The Wild One,* a 1954 movie starring Marlon Brando. When asked by a local resident what he was rebelling against, Brando's character, Johnny, replied, "Whaddya got?"[3] The general public came to dislike bikers because of incidents like the one in Hollister and because of the Hollywood treatment of the event, but the Hells Angels made many people fearful of bikers and put motorcycle gangs under the close scrutiny of law enforcement at local, state, and federal levels.

The Hells Angels were established in 1948 in Fontana, California, by a group of young cyclists who had read of the Hollister rampage and wished to start their own outlaw biker group. The Hells Angels, who took their name and symbols from various World War II flying units, became notorious during the 1960s when they became linked to drug trafficking and other organized crime activities. Sonny Barger, a founder of the Oakland, California, chapter in the late 1950s, became the United States' most infamous biker after organizing a disastrous security effort for the 1969 Rolling Stones concert in Altamont at which one concertgoer was stabbed and killed by Hells Angels members. Barger, who had been convicted of attempted murder, possession of narcotics with intent to sell, and assault with a deadly weapon, commented in an interview with the British Broadcasting Corporation (BBC) that he pressed a pistol into Keith Richards' ribs and ordered him to continue to play after the Rolling Stones' guitarist threatened to end the show because of Hells Angels' rough tactics with fans.[4]

The Hells Angels and rival motorcycle clubs like the Pagans, the Banditos, and the Outlaws, rode only Harleys, which hurt Harley-Davidson's image with the public in the 1960s. Honda successfully exploited Harley's outlaw image with the slogan "You meet the nicest people on a Honda" to become the largest seller of motorcycles in the United States during the late 1960s and early 1970s.[5] The image of the Hells Angels had spilled over to the entire industry and contributed to declines in motorcycle demand in the United States and Europe during the 1960s before a new Hollywood film resurrected interest in motorcycles. *Easy Rider* (1969) portrayed bikers as less villainous rebels and appealed greatly to young people in the United States and Europe. The movie eventually gained cult status and helped charge a demand for motorcycles that began in the 1970s and continued through 2003. The red-white-and-blue 1951 Harley "Captain America" chopper ridden by Peter Fonda's Wyatt character helped

Harley-Davidson break the outlaw image and come to represent less malevolent rebellion.

Industry Conditions in 2003

In 2003, more than 950,000 motorcycles were sold in the United States and 28 million motorcycles were in operation worldwide. The industry was expected to grow by approximately 5 percent annually through 2007 with light motorcycles, Mopeds, and scooters accounting for most of the expected growth. A general increase in incomes in such emerging markets as China, India, and Southeast Asia was the primary force expected to drive industry growth. Demand growth for the heavyweight motorcycle category had outpaced smaller motorcycles in the United States during the 1990s and into 2003, but analysts projected that demand for larger motorcycles would decline as the population aged and became less able to travel on two-wheelers. In 2002, demand for heavyweight motorcycles in the United States grew by 17 percent compared to an industrywide growth rate of 10 percent.

The industry was segmented into various groups on the basis of engine size and vehicle style. Mopeds, scooters, and some small motorcycles were equipped with engines having displacements of 50 cubic centimeters (cc) or less. These motorbikes were best suited for urban areas where streets were narrow and parking was limited or for developing countries where personal incomes were limited and consumers could make only small investments in transportation. Motorcycles used for basic transportation or for motocross events were typically equipped with engines ranging from 125cc to 650cc. Larger street bikes required more power and usually had engines over 650cc. Large motorcycles with engine displacements greater than 651cc accounted for the largest portion of demand in North America and Europe as riders increasingly chose motorcycles with more horsepower and better performance. Exhibit 4 presents registrations of 651+cc motorcycles in the United States, Europe, and Asia-Pacific for 1998–2003. Even though Europe had fewer registrations of 651+cc motorcycles than the United States, it was the world's largest market for motorcycles, with 1.1 million registrations of 125+cc motorcycles in 2002. Registrations of motorcycles with engine displacements greater than 125cc in the largest European markets are presented in Exhibit 5.

Segmentation within the 651+cc Category

Motorcycles in the 651+cc segment were referred to as heavyweights and were grouped into four categories. Standard heavyweight motorcycles were designed for low-cost transportation and lacked many of the features and accessories of more expensive classes of heavyweights. Performance bikes had streamlined styling, low-profile fairings, and seat and handlebar configurations that required the rider to lean forward; they were characterized by responsive handling, rapid acceleration, and high top-end speeds. Custom motorcycles ranged from motorcycles with a custom paint scheme to highly personalized bikes painted with murals or other designs, chromed frames and other components, and accessories not found on stock motorcycles. The chopper, among the more unusual custom styles, was limited only by designers' imaginations but typically had extended forks, high handlebars, a narrow front tire, and a rigid "hardtail" frame design that lacked rear shocks and was stretched longer than normal motorcycles. Another notable feature of custom choppers was that they were almost always built from stock Harley-Davidson motorcycles, sometimes retaining only the engine.

Custom bikes were the largest segment of the U.S. heavyweight market for motorcycles and had become a curiosity for noncyclists. The Discovery Channel regularly aired two programs dedicated to the topic of choppers and other custom vehicles. The names of two custom motorcycle shops, West Coast Choppers (WCC) and Orange County Choppers, frequently made the Internet search engine Lycos's list of 50 most-searched terms. Jesse James, a descendent of the famous American Old West outlaw and owner of West Coast Choppers, also made Lycos's list of most-searched terms. WCC charged between $60,000 and $150,000 for its custom motorcycles, which were usually sold to celebrities such as movie stars, professional athletes, and rock musicians.

Touring bikes were set apart from other categories by creature comforts and accessories that included large fairings, storage compartments, CD players, cruise control, and other features typically found on cars rather than on motorcycles. Touring bikes were popular in the United States since many baby boomers wished to enjoy biking, but with some

Exhibit 4   **Market Shares of the Leading Producers of Motorcycles by Geographic Region for the Heavyweight Segment, 1998–2003 (engine displacement of 651+cc)**

	2003	2002	2001	2000	1999	1998
New U.S. registrations (thousands of units)						
Total market new registrations	461.2	442.3	394.3	340	275.6	227.1
Harley-Davidson new registrations	228.4	209.3	177.4	155.1	134.5	109.1
Buell new registrations	3.5	2.9	2.6	4.2	3.9	3.2
Total company new registrations	231.9	212.2	180.0	159.3	138.4	112.3
Percentage market share						
Harley-Davidson motorcycles	49.5%	47.5%	45.0%	45.6%	48.8%	48.1%
Buell motorcycles	0.8	0.7	0.7	1.2	1.4	1.4
Total Harley-Davidson	50.3%	48.2%	45.7%	46.8%	50.2%	49.5%
Honda	18.4%	19.8%	20.5%	18.5%	16.4%	20.3%
Suzuki	9.8	9.6	10.8	9.3	9.4	10.0
Kawasaki	6.7	6.9	8.0	9.0	10.3	10.1
Yamaha	8.5	8.9	7.9	8.4	7.0	4.2
Other	6.3	6.6	7.1	8.0	6.7	5.9
Total	100.0%	100.0%	100.0%	100.0%	100.0%	100.0%
New European registrations (thousands of units)						
Total market new registrations	323.1	303.5	292.1	293.4	306.7	270.2
Total Harley-Davidson new registrations	26.3	20.1	19.6	19.9	17.8	15.7
Percentage market share						
Total Harley-Davidson	8.1%	6.6%	6.7%	6.8%	5.8%	5.8%
Honda	16.7	21.0	17.4	21.8	22.2	24.1
Yamaha	16.0	17.7	16.4	17.3	18.0	16.3
BMW	15.3	15.1	15.1	13.0	13.0	13.4
Suzuki	15.5	14.8	16.5	14.3	15.4	17.2
Other	28.4	24.8	27.9	26.8	25.6	23.2
Total	100.0%	100.0%	100.0%	100.0%	100.0%	100.0%
New Asia-Pacific registrations (thousands of units)						
Total market new registrations	58.9	63.9	62.1	62.7	63.1	69.2
Total Harley-Davidson new registrations	15.2	13.0	12.7	12.2	11.6	10.3
Percentage market share						
Total Harley-Davidson	25.8%	21.3%	20.4%	19.5%	18.5%	14.8%
Honda	17.8	19.1	17.3	20.4	22.4	28.0
Kawasaki	13.8	15.8	15.6	18.9	19.0	22.1
Yamaha	11.4	13.6	15.8	17.0	19.0	16.0
Suzuki	10.7	10.1	12.8	10.4	9.3	7.9
Other	20.5	20.1	18.1	13.8	11.8	11.2
Total	100.0%	100.0%	100.0%	100.0%	100.0%	100.0%

Source: Harley-Davidson Inc. 10-K reports and annual reports.

Exhibit 5   **Registrations of New Motorcycles in Major European Markets, 1998–2003 (engine displacement of 125+cc)**

Country	1998	1999	2000	2001	2002	2003
Germany	175,937	187,192	170,636	158,270	145,369	138,712
Italy	79,400	103,800	122,085	126,400	129,261	130,224
France	88,500	109,105	103,900	106,802	113,852	N/A
Great Britain	84,500	98,186	93,634	91,543	93,557	N/A
Spain	35,600	39,200	38,052	31,829	35,252	N/A

N/A = Not available.

Sources: Association des Constructeurs Europeens de Motocycles, Brussels; Industrieverband Motorrad Deutschland e.V.

comfort. Comfortable saddles, upright riding positions, and other features found on touring bikes were especially welcomed by those who took cross-country or other long-distance journeys on their motorcycles. Custom and touring motorcycles were less popular outside of the United States since cyclists in other countries were more likely to travel only short distances and did not necessarily identify with the individualist or outlaw image associated with heavyweights in the United States. The largest segment of the heavyweight motorcycle category outside the United States was the performance bike category since most riders in other countries preferred sleek styling and were more interested in speed and handling rather than in comfort and tradition. In addition, motorcyclists in Europe and Asia tended to choose performance bikes over motorcycles in the custom and touring categories because of the high relative prices of such motorcycles. Exhibit 6 presents a regional comparison of motorcycle registrations by heavyweight category for 1998 through 2002.

Competition in the Global Motorcycle Industry

Rivalry in the motorcycle industry centered on performance, styling, breadth of product line, image and reputation, quality of after-the-sale service, and price. Most motorcycle manufacturers had good reputations for performance and styling with the greatest variance between brands occurring in pricing, variety of models, and quality of dealer service. Most cyclists preferred not to purchase specific brands, even if they were attracted to specific models, if the company's dealers did not have trained mechanics or had a reputation for shoddy workmanship or poor parts availability. There was also a great degree of price variability in the industry with comparable models of Japanese motorcycles typically carrying retail prices far below that of U.S.- or European-made motorcycles.

Exhibits 7 and 8 illustrate the difficulty U.S. and European manufacturers had experienced in attracting price-sensitive buyers in Europe. The Japanese producers were able to offer high-performance motorcycles at prices below those of Harley-Davidson, Ducati, Triumph, or Moto Guzzi. BMW had achieved considerable success in Europe, especially in Germany, because of exceptional performance and reputation, a strong dealer network, and regional loyalty to the brand.

Motorcycle manufacturers, like automobile manufacturers, maintained relationships with suppliers to produce or assemble components such as upholstery, tires, engine parts, brake parts, wiring harnesses, shocks, and rims. Almost without exception, the manufacturer designed and manufactured its engines and frames. Design and assembly of motorcycles took place in the manufacturers' home country, and completed motorcycles were exported to country markets where dealer networks had been established.

Consumers typically evaluated brands by talking to other cyclists, reading product reviews, perusing company Web sites, noting ads in print and other media, and noting a manufacturer's performance in competitive events. Typically, consumers had some

Exhibit 6   **Regional Comparison of the 651+cc Motorcycle Market by Segment,* 1998–2002 (percent of units registered)**

	1998	1999	2000	2001	2002
United States					
Custom	58.4%	57.7%	56.6%	58.9%	60.3%
Touring	20.4	21.7	21.1	20.3	20.2
Performance	19.4	18.9	20.4	19.1	17.3
Standard	1.8	1.8	2.0	1.7	2.2
	100.0%	100.0%	100.0%	100.0%	100.0%
Europe					
Custom	22.8%	20.2%	17.6%	17.8%	13.8%
Touring	5.3	5.5	5.2	5.2	4.8
Performance	59.8	58	61.7	59.8	61.2
Standard	12.1	16.3	15.5	17.2	20.2
	100.0%	100.0%	100.0%	100.0%	100.0%
Asia-Pacific					
Custom	18.3%	28.6%	26.7%	23.9%	n/a
Touring	3.9	4.7	3.7	7.2	n/a
Performance	76.1	64.5	66.2	65.5	n/a
Standard	1.7	2.2	3.5	3.4	n/a
	100.0%	100.0%	100.0%	100.0%	n/a

*Category definitions:

Custom: Characterized by "American styling." Often personalized by accessorizing.

Touring: Designed primarily for long trips, with an emphasis on comfort, cargo capacity, and reliability. Often have features such as two-way radios (for communication with passenger), stereo, and cruise control.

Performance: Characterized by quick acceleration, top speed, and handling. Commonly referred to as "sport bikes."

Standard: A basic, no-frills motorcycle with an emphasis on low price.

Source: Harley-Davidson Inc. 2003 and 2002 10-K reports.

ability to negotiate prices with dealers, but most preferred to buy from dealers with good service departments, large parts inventories, and attractive financing programs. Similarly, strong motorcycle dealers preferred to represent manufacturers with good reputations and strong consumer demand, responsive customer service and parts delivery, formal training programs for service technicians, and financing divisions that offered competitive rates and programs.

Consumers purchased motorcycles for various reasons. Some individuals, especially in developing countries, were looking for low-cost transportation. Lightweight motorcycles, mopeds, and scooters were priced inexpensively compared to cars and used far less gasoline. However, motorcycles provided no protection from the elements and were used only for fair-weather transportation by most riders who also owned a car. In the United States and Europe, most consumers who purchased a motorcycle also owned a car and preferred to travel by motorcycle on weekends or other times they were not working. Some in Europe did choose to commute to and from work on motorcycles when weather permitted because of limited parking available in large European cities and the high cost of fuel. Many motorcycle owners, particularly so in the United States, looked at riding as a form of recreation and had given up other sports or hobbies to spend time touring on motorcycles. Many middle-aged bikers in the United States had

Exhibit 7   **Market Shares of the Leading Sellers of Motorcycles in Germany, 2001–2003 (engine displacement of 125+cc)**

Brand	2001 Market Share	2002 Market Share	2003 Market Share
BMW	16.0%	18.1%	19.5%
Suzuki	21.7	20.3	19.2
Yamaha	16.3	16.0	15.9
Honda	16.8	17.3	15.5
Kawasaki	11.1	10.7	10.6
KTM	3.1	3.8	4.4
Harley-Davidson	3.6	3.7	4.2
Ducati	2.8	2.8	2.9
Triumph	2.5	1.8	2.0
Aprilia	1.7	1.5	1.4
Moto Guzzi	0.6	0.7	0.9
Buell	0.4	0.3	0.6
MV/Cagiva	1.2	0.8	0.6
MZ	0.5	0.4	0.3
Sachs	0.3	0.2	0.2
Other	1.4	1.6	1.9
Total	100.0%	100.0%	100.0%

Sources: Kraftfahrtbundesamt; Industrieverband Motorrad Deutschland e.V.

Exhibit 8   **Best-Selling Motorcycle Models in Germany, November 2003**

Rank	Brand	Model	Manufacturers' Recommended Price ($ US)	Year-to-Date 2003 Registrations	Heavyweight Classification
1	BMW	R 1150 GS	$14,500	6,242	Enduro/Touring
2	Suzuki	GSF 1200 (KL)	7,399	4,023	Performance
3	BMW	F 650 GS	8,190	3,524	Enduro/Touring
4	Suzuki	SV 650	6,299	3,444	Standard
5	Yamaha	FZS 600	6,499	3,294	Standard
6	Suzuki	GSF 600	6,299	3,182	Standard
7	Suzuki	GSX-R 1000	10,599	2,836	Performance
8	Kawasaki	Z1000	8,499	2,825	Performance
9	BMW	R 1150 RT	16,290	2,607	Touring
10	BMW	R 1150 R	9,990	2,539	Performance

Sources: Kraftfahrtbundesamt; Industrieverband Motorrad Deutschland e.V.

purchased motorcycles after giving up sports and activities requiring more athleticism or endurance.

REGULATION AND LEGAL CHALLENGES

The motorcycle industry was subject to laws and regulations in all countries where motorcycles were operated. The European Parliament and the European Council included motorcycles in their agreement to reduce exhaust gas values during their March 2002 meeting. The agreement required producers of motorcycles and scooters to reduce pollutants by 60 percent for all new cycles produced after April 2003. A further 60 percent reduction would be required for motorcycles produced after January 2006. Demand for motorcycles in Europe was impacted to a great degree by the implementation of the euro in 2002; prices of motorcycles increased substantially in some countries when the currency exchange took effect. For instance, because Germany's currency was much stronger than that of many other European Union countries, prices of most products and services increased in Germany after the change to the euro since the euro attempted to equalize the differences between currencies. The difficulty in obtaining a driver's license for motorcycles in some European countries also affected demand for motorcycles. German laws required separate automobile and motorcycle licenses for riders of motorcycles larger than 125cc, and France required those applying for motorcycle licenses to have first held an automobile license for two years. Austria's licensing laws were the most restrictive, requiring applicants to first hold an automobile license for five years and to complete six training sessions prior to obtaining a motorcycle license. Motorcycles that produced excessive noise were also under attack in most European countries.

In the United States, motorcycle producers were subject to certification by the Environmental Protection Agency (EPA) for compliance with emission and noise standards, as well as agencies in some states imposing more stringent noise and emission standards. The California Air Resources Board (CARB) had outlined new tailpipe emission standards that would go into effect in 2004 and 2008. The EPA developed new emission standards that would go into effect in 2006 and 2010 to match national standards with those in California. Motorcycle producers in the United States were also required to meet the product safety standards imposed by the National Highway Traffic Safety Administration (NHTSA).

Also in the United States, many motorcyclists found that their health insurance providers excluded coverage for any injuries sustained while on a motorcycle. The American Motorcyclists Association (AMA) had successfully petitioned the U.S. Senate to pass a bill in October 2003 that would prohibit insurance companies from denying coverage to someone hurt while riding a motorcycle, a snowmobile, or an all-terrain vehicle. Insurance companies had based their policies on NHTSA statistics that found motorcycling to be much more dangerous than traveling by car. While traffic fatalities per 100 million vehicle miles traveled hit a historic low in 2002, motorcycle fatalities had increased for a fifth consecutive year, to reach 3,244 deaths. There were 42,815 traffic fatalities in 2002 involving occupants of automobiles. Fatalities involving motorcyclists ages 50 and older increased by 26 percent during 2002—a higher rate of increase than any other age demographic. State legislatures in some states where helmets were optional had attempted to force motorcyclists who chose not to wear helmets to become mandatory organ donors. However, the AMA and its membership had successfully stopped all such attempts to pass mandatory organ donor laws.

HARLEY-DAVIDSON'S STRATEGY FOR COMPETING IN THE MOTORCYCLE INDUSTRY

Harley-Davidson was reincorporated in 1981 after it was purchased from AMF by 13 of its managers through a leveraged buyout (LBO). The management team's main focus at the time was to preserve jobs, but its members soon realized the company would need to be rebuilt from the ground up to survive. The company's market share in the United States had fallen to 3 percent, primarily because its products were unreliable and had poorer performance relative to less-expensive Japanese motorcycles. In addition, its network of dealers ran greasy, run-down shops that many people didn't feel comfortable visiting. Upon assessing the company's situation, the management team concluded that a strong allegiance to the Harley brand by many bikers was the company's only resource strength. However, when managers began to meet with customers, they found that long-time Harley riders felt cheated by the company and were angry about the lack of attention to product quality and customer service under AMF ownership. Some of the most loyal Harley riders refused to call models produced in the 1970s Harleys, preferring to label them as AMFs. After the LBO, Harley management tried to win over previous customers by attending any function at which motorcyclists congregated. The company's director of communications at the time commented in a 2003 interview with a trade publication, "At first we found that our customers didn't like us, and they didn't trust us."[6] However, the distrust subsided when Harley owners saw their suggestions being implemented by the company.

Harley-Davidson's turnaround strategy including improving product quality by adopting Japanese management practices, abandoning a reliance on advertising in favor of promotions at motorcycle rallies, and improving its dealer network to broaden its appeal to new customers. After hearing complaints about dealers from Harley riders at rallies and other bike events, Harley-Davidson conducted a pilot program with two dealers in Milwaukee that called for the dealers to build clean, attractive stores to showcase the company's improved motorcycles and display apparel and other merchandise that cyclists might wish to purchase. The two dealerships recaptured their investments within 18 months, while other dealers struggled. The pilot program led to new or remodeled dealerships across the Harley-Davidson network and helped the company enter into a new product category. Harley showrooms offered a large assortment of clothing items and accessories—for example, leather jackets, T-shirts, helmets, and boots—in addition to new motorcycles. In 2003 Harley-Davidson introduced 1,200 new clothing items and licensed its name to more than 100 manufacturers making everything from Harley-Davidson Edition Ford F-150 pickups to Harley Barbie dolls. Apparel and accessories were so important

to the company and its dealers that in 2003 every dealer had a fitting room.

Cultivating Loyalty Through HOG Membership

After Harley-Davidson's product quality issues had been resolved, the company focused on cultivating the mystique of Harley ownership. The company formed Harley Owners Groups (HOGs) in 1983 to provide Harley owners with local chapters through which they could socialize and ride with other owners. Harley-Davidson established HOGs in cities where dealers were located, but did not interfere with HOG operations or try to use the organization in a self-serving way. The company's primary interest in setting up the chapters was to give motorcycle buyers a sense of community. Management understood that once new owners came to feel they belonged to the Harley community, they would bring new buyers to the company without any encouragement from Harley-Davidson.

The company provided each new Harley buyer with a free membership to a HOG where they could not only meet other area bikers but also learn the ins and outs of the biker world. HOGs also organized rides, raised money for charities, and participated in nationwide HOG events. Owners were required to renew their free memberships each year to ensure that only active participants would be on chapter roles. The HOG organization started with 33,000 members in 1983 and had grown to 793,000 members in 1,200 chapters in 2003. The company sponsored about 100 HOG rallies in 2003, with thousands of additional events organized by local chapters.

Harley's Image and Appeal with Baby Boomers

Even though Harley sold many motorcycles to construction workers, mechanics, and other blue-collar workers, Harley riders included a great many accountants, lawyers, bankers, and corporate executives. In 2003, Harley-Davidson's typical customer was a 46-year-old male earning $78,000 per year. The company had successfully added upscale consumers to its list of customers without alienating traditional bikers. Some of the more traditional bikers did complain about the new breed of "bean counter Harley owners," sometimes calling them "rubbers"—rich urban bikers. Such concern had been calmed to some degree by William G. Davidson's continuing involvement with the company. "Willie G." was the grandson of the company's cofounder and, as chief designer, had designed every motorcycle for the company since the 1960s. Willie G. was an "old-school" biker himself and rationalized the company's alliance with upscale baby boomers with comments such as "There's a lot of beaners, but they're out on the motorcycles, which is a beautiful thing."[7]

Part of the appeal of HOG membership was that new motorcyclists could experience freedom of the open road, much like a Hells Angel might, if only during occasional weekends when the weather was nice. Some middle-aged professionals purchased Harleys because riding was an opportunity to recreate and relax without being reminded of their daily responsibilities. Belonging to a HOG or other riding group was different from joining a country club or other club dominated by upper-income families; as the CEO of a Fortune 500 company explained, "Nobody cares what anybody else does. We share a common bond of freedom on a bike." This same Harley owner claimed that after a few hours of riding, he forgets he's a CEO.[8] Another affluent Harley owner suggested that Harley owners from all walks of life shared the brotherhood of the open road: "It doesn't matter if you make $10,000 a year or $300,000."[9] Others suggested that Harley ownership gave you an identity and provided you with a close group of friends in an increasingly anonymous culture.

However, other Harley owners were lured by the appeal of Harley-Davidson's outlaw image. The editor of *AARP Magazine* believed that baby boomers purchased Harleys because of a desire to feel "forever young."[10] The *AARP Magazine* editor said that riding a Harley helped take boomers back to a time when they had less responsibility. "You saw 'Easy Rider.' As a kid, you had a bit of a wild period in the '70s and you associate the motorcycle with that. But you got married. You had kids and a career. Now you can afford this. It's a safe way to live out a midlife crisis. It's a lot safer than running off with a stewardess."[11] In fact, many of Harley-Davidson's competitors have claimed that Harley sells lifestyles, not motorcycles. Harley-Davidson CEO Jeffrey Bleustein commented on the appeal of the company's motorcycles by stating, "Harley-Davidson stands for freedom, adventure, individual expression and being a little on the edge, a little bit naughty. People are drawn to the brand for those reasons."[12]

The desire to pose as a Hells Angel, Peter Fonda's Wyatt character, or Brando's Johnny helped Harley-Davidson sell more than 290,000 motorcycles and over $200 million in general merchandise in 2003. Many of Harley-Davidson's 1,400 dealers dedicated as much as 75 percent of their floor space to apparel and accessories, with most suggesting that between 25 and 40 percent of their annual earnings came from the sale of leather jackets, chaps, boots, caps, helmets, and other accessories. One dealer offered her opinion of what drove merchandise sales by commenting, "Today's consumer tends to be a little more affluent, and they want the total look."[13] The dealer also said that approximately 5 percent of the dealership's apparel sales were to non–bike owners who wanted the biker image. Even though some high-income baby boomers wanted to be mistaken from a distance for Hells Angels' "1 percenters"—the most rebellious 1 percent of the population—for most it was all show. When looking out at the thousands of leather-clad bikers attending Harley-Davidson's 2003 Memorial Day centennial celebration in Milwaukee, a Harley owner said, "The truth is, this is mostly professional people . . . People want to create an image. Everybody has an alter side, an alter ego. And this is a chance to have that."[14]

Another Harley owner who had ridden his Heritage Softail from his home in Sioux Falls, South Dakota, to attend the centennial event commented on his expectations for revelry during the four-day celebration by pointing out, "Bikers like to party pretty big. It's still a long way to go before you forget the image of the Hells Angels."[15] However, weekend bikers were quite different from the image they emulated. The Hells Angels continued to be linked to organized crime into 2003, with nine Hells Angels members being convicted in September 2003 of drug trafficking and murdering at least 160 people, most of whom were from rival gangs.[16] Similarly, Hells Angels organizations in Europe had been linked to drug trafficking and dozens of murders.[17] Fifty-seven Angels in the United States were arrested in December 2003 for crimes such as theft of motorcycles, narcotics trafficking, and firearms and explosives trafficking following a two-year investigation of the motorcycle club by the Bureau of Alcohol, Tobacco, Firearms and Explosives.[18]

Harley-Davidson balanced its need to promote freedom and rebellion against its need to distance the company from criminal behavior. Its Web site pointed out that "the vast majority of riders throughout the history of Harley-Davidson were law-abiding citizens," and the company archivist proposed, "Even those who felt a certain alienation from society were not lawless anarchists, but people who saw the motorcycle as a way to express both their freedom and their identity."[19] When looking at the rows of Harleys glistening in the sun in front of his Southern California roadside café, the longtime proprietor of one of the biggest biker shrines in the United States commented, "There used to be some mean bastards on those bikes. I guess the world has changed."[20] A Harley-Davidson dealer commented that dealers considered hardcore bikers "1 percenters" because they made up less than 1 percent of a dealer's annual sales. The dealer found that very affluent buyers made up about 10 percent of sales, with the remainder of customers making between $40,000 and $100,000 per year.[21]

Harley-Davidson's Product Line

Unlike Honda and Yamaha, Harley-Davidson did not produce scooters and mopeds, nor did it manufacture motorcycles with engine displacements less than 651cc. In addition, Harley-Davidson did not produce dirt bikes or performance bikes like those offered by Kawasaki and Suzuki. Of the world's major motorcycle producers, BMW produced bikes that most closely resembled Harley-Davidson's traditional line, although BMW also offered a large number of performance bikes. In 2004, Harley-Davidson's touring and custom motorcycles were grouped into five families: Sportster, Dyna Glide, Softail, Touring, and the VRSC V-Rod. The Sportster, Dyna Glide, and VRSC models were manufactured in the company's Kansas City, Missouri, plant, while Softail and Touring models were manufactured in York, Pennsylvania. Harley-Davidson considered the Sportster, Dyna Glide, and VRSC models custom bikes, while Softails and Touring models fell into the Touring industry classification. Sportsters and Dyna Glides each came in four model variations, while Softails came in six variations and Touring bikes came in seven basic configurations. The VRSC V-Rod came in two basic styles. Harley-Davidson produced three models of its Buell performance bikes in its East Troy, Wisconsin, plant. In 2004, Harley Sportsters carried retail prices ranging from $6,495 to $8,675; Dyna Glide models sold at price points between $11,995 and $16,580; VRSC V-Rods

sold between $16,895 and $17,995; Softails were offered between $13,675 and $17,580; and the Road King and Electra Glide touring models sold at prices between $16,995 and $20,405. Consumers could also order custom Harleys through the company's Custom Vehicle Operations (CVO) unit, started in 1999. Customization and accessories on CVO models could add as much as $10,000 to the retail price of Harley-Davidson motorcycles. Images of Harley-Davidson's five product families and CVO models can be viewed at www.harley-davidson.com.

Honda, Kawasaki, Suzuki, and Yamaha had all introduced touring models that were very close replicas of Harley Sportsters, Dyna Glides, Road Kings, and Electra Glides. The Japanese producers had even copied Harley's signature V-twin engine and had tuned their dual-crankpin designs in an attempt to copy the distinctive sound of a Harley-Davidson engine. However, even with prices up to 50 percent less on comparable models, none of the Japanese producers had been able to capture substantial market share from Harley-Davidson in the United States or in their home markets. (Refer back to Exhibit 4 for a breakdown of market shares in the heavyweight segment in the U.S., European, and Asia-Pacific regions.) Indian Motorcycle Corporation had experienced similar difficulties gaining adequate market share in the U.S. heavyweight segment and ceased its operations for a second time in September 2003.

Harley-Davidson's difficulties in luring buyers in the performance segment of the industry were similar to challenges that Japanese motorcycle producers had encountered in their attempts to gain market share in the custom and touring categories of the U.S. heavyweight motorcycle segment. Harley-Davidson had co-developed and later purchased Buell to have a product that might appeal to motorcyclists in the United States who were in their 20s and did not identify with the *Easy Rider* or Hells Angels images or who did not find Harley-Davidson's traditional styling appealing. Harley management also believed that Buell's performance street-racer-style bikes could help it gain market share in Europe, where performance bikes were highly popular. The Buell brand competed exclusively in the performance category against models offered by Honda, Yamaha, Kawasaki, Suzuki, and lesser-known European brands such as Moto Guzzi, Ducati, and Triumph. Buell prices began at $4,595 for its Blast model to better compete with Japanese motorcycles on price as well as on performance and styling. Buell's Lighting and Firebolt models were larger, faster motorcycles and retailed for between $9,000 and $11,000. The VSRC V-Rod, with its liquid-cooled, Porsche-designed engine, was also designed to appeal to buyers in the performance segment of the industry, both in the United States and Europe.

As of 2004, Harley-Davidson had not gained a significant share of the performance motorcycle segment in the United States or Europe. Some industry analysts criticized Harley-Davidson's dealers for the lackluster sales of V-Rod and Buell models since most dealers did little to develop employees' sales techniques. Demand for Harleys had exceeded supply since the early 1990s, and most dealers' sales activities were limited to taking orders and maintaining a waiting list. In addition, most Harley-Davidson dealers had been able to charge $2,000 to $4,000 over the suggested retail price for new Harley-Davidson motorcycles, although most dealers had begun to sell Harleys at sticker price in 2003. Harley-Davidson's revenues by product group are shown below:

Harley-Davidson Revenues by Product Group (in millions)

	2003	2002	2001
Harley-Davidson motorcycles	$3,621.5	$3,161.0	$2,671.3
Buell motorcycles	76.1	66.9	61.7
Total motorcycles	$3,697.6	$3,227.9	$2,733.0
Motorcycle Parts and Accessories	712.8	629.2	509.6
General Merchandise	211.4	231.5	163.9
Other	2.5	2.4	0.3
Net revenue	$4,624.3	$4,091.0	$3,406.8

Source: Harley-Davidson Inc. 2002 and 2003 annual reports.

The number of Harley-Davidson and Buell motorcycles shipped annually between 1998 and 2003 is presented in Exhibit 9.

Distribution and Sales in North America, Europe, and Asia-Pacific

Harley-Davidson's dealers were responsible for operating showrooms where motorcycles could be examined and test-ridden, stocking parts and accessories that existing owners might need, operating service departments, and selling biking merchandise such as apparel, boots, helmets, and various Harley-Davidson-branded gift items. Some Harley owners felt such strong connections to the brand that they either gave or asked for Harley gifts for birthdays, weddings, and anniversaries. Some Harley owners had even been married at Harley-Davidson dealerships or at HOG rallies. Harley-Davidson dealers were also responsible for distributing newsletters and promoting rallies for local HOG chapters. The 10,000-member Buell Riders Adventure Group (BRAG) was also supported by Harley-Davidson dealers.

Harley mechanics and other dealership personnel were trained at the Harley-Davidson University (HDU) in Milwaukee, where they took courses in such subjects as retail management, inventory control, merchandising, customer service, diagnostics, maintenance, and engine service techniques. More than 17,000 dealership employees took courses at the company's university in 2002. Harley-Davidson also provided in-dealership courses through its Web-based distance learning program. In 2002, HDU held 665 instructor-led classes, 115 online classes, and had participation in their courses by 96 percent of the company's dealers.

The company also held demo rides in various locations throughout the United States, and many Harley dealers offered daily rentals designed to help novices decide whether they really wanted a motorcycle. Some dealers also rented motorcycles for longer periods to individuals who wished to take long-distance trips. Harley-Davidson motorcycles could

Exhibit 9   **Annual Shipments of Harley-Davidson and Buell Motorcycles, 1998–2003**

	2003	2002	2001	2000	1999	1998
Harley-Davidson						
Sportster	57,165	51,171	50,814	46,213	41,870	33,892
Custom*	151,405	141,769	118,303	100,875	87,806	77,434
Touring	82,577	70,713	65,344	57,504	47,511	39,492
	291,147	263,653	234,461	204,592	177,187	150,818
Domestic	237,656	212,833	186,915	158,817	135,614	110,902
International	53,491	50,820	47,546	45,775	41,573	39,916
	291,147	263,653	234,461	204,592	177,187	150,818
Buell						
Buell (exc. Blast)	8,784	6,887	6,436	5,043	7,767	6,334
Buell Blast	1,190	4,056	3,489	5,416	—	—
	9,974	10,943	9,925	10,189	7,767	6,334

*Custom includes Softail, Dyna Glide, and VRSC.
Source: Harley-Davidson Inc. 2002 and 2003 annual reports.

also be rented from third parties like EagleRider—the world's largest renter of Harleys, with 29 locations in the United States and Europe. Harley-Davidson's Riders Edge motorcycle training courses were also offered by quite a few dealers in North America, Europe, and Asia-Pacific. The company had found that inexperienced riders and women were much more likely to purchase motorcycles after taking a training course. Harley-Davidson management believed the 25-hour Riders Edge program had contributed to the company's increased sales to women, which had increased from 2 percent of total sales prior to the adoption of the program to 9 percent in 2003.

In 2003, Harley-Davidson motorcycles were sold by 644 independently owned and operated dealerships across the United States. Buell motorcycles were also sold by 436 of these dealers. There were no Buell-only dealerships, and 81 percent of Harley dealers in the United States sold Harley-Davidson motorcycles exclusively. The company also sold apparel and merchandise in about 50 nontraditional retail locations such as malls, airports, and tourist locations. The company's apparel was also available seasonally in about 20 temporary locations in the United States where there was significant tourist traffic. The company also had three nontraditional merchandise outlets in Canada, where it had 76 independent dealers and one Buell

dealership. Thirty-two of its Canadian Harley dealers also sold Buell motorcycles.

Harley-Davidson had 161 independent dealers in Japan, 50 dealers and three distributors in the Australia/New Zealand market and seven other dealers scattered in smaller East and Southeast Asian markets. Only 73 of Harley-Davidson's Asia-Pacific also sold Buell motorcycles. The company also had two dealers that sold Buell but not Harley-Davidson motorcycles. Harley-Davidson motorcycles were sold in 17 Latin American countries by 32 dealerships. The company did not have a dealer for its Buell motorcycles in Latin America, but had 13 retail stores carrying only apparel and merchandise in the region.

The company's European distribution division based in the United Kingdom served 32 countries in Europe, the Middle East, and Africa. The European region had 436 independent dealers, with 313 choosing to also carry Buell motorcycles. Buell motorcycles were also sold in Europe by 10 dealers that were not Harley dealers. Harley-Davidson also had 26 nontraditional merchandise retail locations in Europe.

Exhibit 10 presents the company's revenues by geographic region, along with the division of assets in the United States and abroad and a breakdown of financial services revenues by region. The company's financial services unit provided retail financing

Exhibit 10   **Harley-Davidson's Net Revenues and Long-Lived Assets by Business Group and Geographic Region, 2000–2003**

	2003	2002	2001	2000
Motorcycles net revenue				
United States	$3,807,707	$3,416,432	$2,809,763	$2,357,972
Europe	419,052	337,463	301,729	285,372
Japan	173,547	143,298	141,181	148,684
Canada	134,319	121,257	96,928	93,352
Other foreign countries	89,649	72,520	57,185	57,966
	$4,624,274	$4,090,970	$3,406,786	$2,943,346
Financial services income				
United States	$ 260,551	$ 199,380	$ 172,593	$ 132,684
Europe	8,834	4,524	1,214	655
Canada	10,074	7,596	7,738	6,796
	$ 279,459	$ 211,500	$ 181,545	$ 140,135
Long-lived assets				
United States	$1,400,772	$1,151,702	$1,021,946	$ 856,746
Other foreign countries	41,804	36,138	33,234	27,844
	$1,442,576	$1,187,840	$1,055,180	$ 884,590

Source: Harley-Davidson Inc. 2002 and 2003 10-K reports.

to consumers and wholesale financial services to dealers, including inventory floor plans, real estate loans, computer loans, and showroom remodeling loans.

CHALLENGES CONFRONTING HARLEY-DAVIDSON AS IT ENTERED ITS SECOND CENTURY

As Harley-Davidson entered its second century in 2004, the company not only celebrated a successful centennial celebration that brought more than 700,000 of Harley's most loyal customers to Milwaukee but also a successful year with record shipments, revenues, and earnings. New capacity had allowed the company's shipments to increase to more than 290,000 units, which drove annual revenues to $4.6 billion and net earnings to nearly $761 million. The company's planned 350,000-square-foot expansion of its York, Pennsylvania, plant would allow the

company to increase production to 400,000 units by 2007. However, there was some concern that the company might not need the additional capacity.

Some market analysts had begun to believe Harley-Davidson's stock was approaching its apex because of the aging of its primary baby boomer customer group. Between 1993 and 2003, the average age of the company's customers had increased from 38 to 46. The average age of purchasers of other brands of motorcycles in 2003 was 38. Some analysts suspected, that within the next 5 to 10 years, fewer baby boomers would be interested in riding motorcycles and Harley's sales might begin to decline. Generation X buyers were not a large enough group to keep Harley's sales at the 2003 level, which would cause the company to rely on Generation Y (or echo boomer) consumers. However, most Generation Y motorcyclists had little interest in the company's motorcycles and did not identify with the *Easy Rider* or outlaw biker images that were said to appeal to baby boomers. The company's V-Rod motorcycle had won numerous awards for its styling and performance, but its $17,000-plus price tag kept most 20-year-olds away from Harley showrooms. Similarly, Buell motorcycles were critically acclaimed in terms of performance and styling but had been unable to draw performance-minded consumers in the United States or Europe away from Japanese street-racing-style bikes to any significant degree.

Europe was the largest market for motorcycles overall, and the second largest market for heavy-weight motorcycles, but Harley-Davidson had struggled in building share in the region. In some ways the company's 6+ percent market share in Europe was impressive since only 4.8 percent of motorcycles purchased in 2002 were touring cycles and custom cycles accounted for only 13.8 percent of motorcycles sold in Europe during 2002. The V-Rod's greatest success was in Europe, but neither the V-Rod nor any other HD model had become one of the top-10 best-selling models in any major European market.

There was also some concern that Harley-Davidson's 14-month production run had caused an unfavorable short-term production problem since the company's waiting list, which required a two-year wait in the late 1990s, had fallen to about 90 days beginning in mid-2003. The overavailability of 2003 models had caused Harley-Davidson's management to adopt a 0 percent down payment financing program that began at midyear 2003 and would run through February 2004. When asked about the program during a television interview, Harley-Davidson CEO Jeffery Bleustein justified it by noting, "It's not zero percent financing, as many people understood it to be, its zero dollars down, and normal financing. The idea there was to get the attention of some of the people who aren't riding Harleys and are used to a world of other motorcycles where there's always a financing program of some sort going on. We just wanted to get their attention."[22] By year-end 2003, dealer inventories had declined to about 2,000 units and many dealers again began charging premiums over list price, but not the $2,000–$4,000 premiums charged in prior years.

Endnotes

[1]As quoted in "Analyst Says Harley's Success Had Been to Drive into Buyers' Hearts," *Canadian Press Newswire,* July 14, 2003.

[2]As quoted in January 21, 2004, press release.

[3]As quoted in "Wings of Desire," *The Independent,* August 27, 2003.

[4]As quoted in "Born to Raise Hell," *BBC News Online,* August 14, 2000.

[5]"Wheel Life Experiences," *Whole Pop Magazine Online.*

[6]As quoted in "Will Your Customers Tattoo Your Logo?" *Trailer/Body Builders,* March 1, 2003, p. 5.

[7]As quoted in "Will Harley-Davidson Hit the Wall?" *Fortune,* July 22, 2002.

[8]As quoted in "Even Corporate CEOs Buy Into the Harley-Davidson Mystique, *Milwaukee Journal-Sentinel,* August 24, 2003.

[9]As quoted in "Harley-Davidson Goes Highbrow at Annual Columbia, S.C., H.O.G. Rally," *The State,* September 26, 2003.

[10]As quoted in "Even Corporate CEOs."

[11]Ibid.

[12]As quoted in "Milwaukee-Based Harley-Davidson Rides into Future with Baby Boomers Aboard," *The News-Sentinel,* August 5, 2003.

[13]As quoted in "Harley-Davidson Fans Sport Motorcycle Style," *Detroit Free Press,* August 28, 2003.

[14]As quoted in "Bikers Go Mainstream 100 Years On," *Global News Wire,* September 11, 2003.

[15]Ibid.

[16]"Nine Montreal Hells Angels Sentenced to 10 to 15 Years in Prison," *CNEWS,* September 23, 2003.

[17]"Hells Angels: Easy Riders or Criminal Gang?," *BBC News,* January 2, 2004.

[18]"Feds Raid Hells Angels' Clubhouses," *CBSNews.com,* December 4, 2003.

[19]As quoted in "Wings of Desire," *Global News Wire,* August 27, 2003.

[20]Ibid.

[21]Interview with Mobile, Alabama, Harley-Davidson dealership personnel.

[22]As quoted in a CNNfn interview conducted on *The Money Gang,* June 11, 2003.

adidas: Will Restructuring Its Business Lineup Allow It to Catch Nike?

John E. Gamble
University of South Alabama

Adidas's 1998 acquisition of diversified sporting goods producer Salomon was expected to allow the athletic footwear company to vault over Nike to become the leader of the global sporting goods industry. Salomon had several businesses that adidas's management viewed as attractive—its Salomon ski division was the leading producer of ski equipment; TaylorMade Golf was the second-largest seller of golf equipment; and Mavic was the leading producer of high-performance bicycle wheels and rims. Other Salomon businesses included Bonfire snowboard apparel and Cliché skateboard equipment. Adidas had been the best-selling brand of sporting goods throughout the 1960s and 1970s, but Nike had overtaken adidas as leader of the athletic footwear industry in the late 1980s and had grown to three times the size of adidas by 1997.

Almost as soon as the deal was consummated, it looked doubtful that the €1.5 billion acquisition of Salomon would boost the corporation's performance. Chief concerns with the acquisition were the declining attractiveness of the winter sports industry and integration problems between the adidas footwear and apparel business and Salomon's business units. Not until 2003, five years after the acquisition, had adidas's earnings per share returned to the level that shareholders enjoyed in 1997. In addition, the company's stock price failed to return to its 1998 trading range until 2004. The Salomon winter sports business had contributed very little operating profit to the company's overall financial performance since its acquisition and the TaylorMade-adidas Golf division had struggled at various times to deliver good earnings. However, TaylorMade seemed to have turned the corner in 2005, with sales and operating earnings improving by 12 percent and 185 percent, respectively, during the first six months of 2005. Salomon's operating loss of €54 million during the first six months of 2005 was 7 percent greater than its €50 million loss during the same period in 2004.

The company announced near the end of its second quarter 2005 that it would divest its winter sports brands and Mavic bicycle components business before the end of the year. In May 2005, Amer Sports Corporation, the maker of Atomic skis and Wilson sporting goods, agreed to acquire the winter sports and bicycle wheel businesses for €485 million. Adidas's October 2005 announcement that it would acquire Reebok International Ltd. for €3.1 billion ($3.8 billion) was the final component of a restructuring initiative that would focus the company's business lineup primarily on athletic footwear and apparel and golf equipment by 2006. Reebok also designed, marketed, and sold Rockport footwear, Ralph Lauren footwear, Greg Norman apparel, and CCM, Koho, and Jofa hockey equipment. In 2004, Rockport and Reebok's hockey brands contributed $377.6 million and $146.0 million, respectively, to the company's total sales of $3.8 billion. Reebok did not disclose the sales contributions of its Ralph Lauren or Greg Norman product lines. The acquisition would increase adidas's annual revenues to nearly €9 billion ($11 billion) and give the company a much stronger presence in North America, which accounted for 50 percent of the global

Exhibit 1   **Net Sales by Product Type and Geographic Region for Reebok International, 2002–2004**

	2004	2003	2002
Reebok International's net sales by product type			
Footwear	$2,430,311	$2,226,712	$2,060,725
Apparel	1,354,973	1,258,604	1,067,147
	$3,785,284	$3,485,316	$3,127,872
Reebok International's net sales by geographic region			
United States	$2,069,055	$2,021,396	$1,807,657
United Kingdom	474,704	444,693	416,775
Europe	810,418	692,400	607,381
Other countries	431,107	326,827	296,059
	$3,785,284	$3,485,316	$3,127,872

Source: Reebok International Ltd. 2004 10-K report.

sporting goods market. In addition, the new mix of businesses would draw adidas closer to overtaking Nike, which had 2004 revenues of $13.7 billion. Reebok's sales by product line and geographic region for 2002 through 2004 are presented in Exhibit 1.

COMPANY HISTORY

In 1920, a 20-year-old German baker-by-trade named Adolph Dassler began making simple canvas shoes in the rear of his family's small bakery in the North Bavarian town of Herzogenaurach. Dassler, a sports enthusiast, had little interest in working as a baker and wanted to make shoes for athletes competing in soccer, tennis, and track-and-field events. Adolph (nicknamed Adi) Dassler thought that proper footwear might improve an athlete's performance and began to study ways to improve athletic shoe design to give athletes wearing his shoes an edge in competitive events.

In 1924, Adi Dassler's brother, Rudolph, joined him in shoemaking to establish Gebrüder Dassler Schuhfabrik (Dassler Brothers Shoe Factory)—a new company specializing in innovative sports shoes. The two brothers realized that athletes should have shoes designed specifically for their respective sport and developed a variety of styles. In 1925, the Dasslers made their first major innovation in athletic shoe design when they integrated studs and spikes into the soles of track-and-field shoes. The Dassler brothers also developed other key innovations in footwear such as the arch support. Many of the standard features of today's athletic footwear were developed by Dassler brothers, with Adi Dassler alone accumulating 700 patents and property rights worldwide by the time of his death in 1978.

The Dasslers were also innovators in the field of marketing—giving away their shoes to German athletes competing in the 1928 Olympic Games in Amsterdam. By the 1936 Olympic Games in Berlin, most athletes would compete only in Gebrüder Dassler shoes, including Jesse Owens, who won four gold medals in the Berlin games. By 1937, Dassler was making 30 different styles of shoes for athletes in 11 sports. All of the company's styles were distinguished from other brands by two stripes applied to each side of the shoe.

The Dasslers' sports shoe production ceased during World War II when Gebrüder Dassler Schuhfabrik was directed to produce boots for the armed forces of Nazi Germany. Adi Dassler was allowed to remain in Herzogenaurach to run the factory, but Rudolph (or Rudi) Dassler was drafted into the army and spent a year in an Allied prisoner-of-war camp after being captured. Upon the conclusion of the war, Rudi Dassler was released by the Allies and returned to Herzogenaurach to rejoin his family. The Dasslers returned to production of athletic shoes in 1947, but the company was dissolved in 1948 after the two brothers entered into a bitter feud. Rudi Dassler moved to the other side of the small village to establish his own shoe company, Puma Schuhfabrik Rudolph Dassler. With the departure of Rudi Dassler, Adi renamed the company adidas—a combination of the first three letters of his nickname and the first three letters of his last name. Adi Dassler also applied an additional stripe to the sides of adidas shoes and registered the three-stripe trademark in 1949.

The nature of the disagreement between the Dassler brothers was not known for certain, but the two never spoke again after their split and the feud became the foundation of both organizations' cultures while the two brothers were alive. The two rival companies were highly competitive, and both discouraged employees from fraternizing with cross-town rivals. An adidas spokesperson described the seriousness of the feud by stating, "Puma employees wouldn't be caught dead with adidas employees," and continuing, "It wouldn't be allowed that an adidas employee would fall in love with a Puma employee."[1]

Adi Dassler kept up his string of innovations with molded rubber cleats in 1949 and track shoes with screw-in spikes in 1952. He expanded the concept to soccer shoes in 1954 with screw-in studs, an innovation that has been partially credited for Germany's World Cup Championship that year. By 1960, adidas was the clear favorite among athletic footwear brands, with 75 percent of all track-and-field athletes competing in the Olympic Games in Rome wearing adidas shoes. The company began producing soccer balls in 1963 and athletic apparel in 1967. The company's dominance in the athletic footwear industry continued through the early 1970s with 1,164 of the 1,490 athletes competing in the 1972 Olympic Games in Munich wearing adidas shoes. In addition, as jogging became popular in the United States during in the early 1970s, adidas was the leading brand of consumer jogging shoe in the United States. Also, T-shirts and other apparel bearing adidas's three-lobed trefoil logo were popular wardrobe items for U.S. teenagers during the 1970s.

At the time of Adi Dassler's death in 1978, adidas remained the worldwide leader in athletic footwear, but the company was rapidly losing market share in the United States to industry newcomer Nike. The first Nike shoes appeared in the 1972 U.S. Olympic Trials in Eugene, Oregon, and had become the best-selling training shoe in the United States by 1974. Both Adi Dassler and his son, Horst, who took over as adidas's chief manager after Adi Dassler's death, severely underestimated the threat of Nike. With adidas perhaps more concerned with cross-town adversary Puma, Nike pulled ahead of its European rivals in the U.S. athletic footwear market by launching new styles in a variety of colors and by signing recognizable sports figures to endorsement contracts. Even though Nike was becoming the market leader in U.S. athletic footwear market, adidas was able to retain its number one ranking among competitive athletes, with 259 gold medal winners in the 1984 Olympic Summer Games in Los Angeles wearing adidas products. Only 65 Olympic athletes wore Nike shoes during the 1984 Summer Games, but the company signed up-and-coming NBA star Michael Jordan to a $2.5 million endorsement contract after adidas passed on the opportunity earlier in the year. At the time of Horst Dassler's unexpected death in 1987, Nike was the undisputed leader in the U.S. athletic footwear market, with more than $1 billion in annual sales.

Adidas's performance spiraled downward after the death of Horst Dassler, with no clear direction from the top and quality and innovation rapidly deteriorating. By 1990, adidas had fallen to a number eight ranking in the U.S. athletic footwear market and held only a 2 percent share of the market. A number of management and ownership changes occurred between Horst Dassler's death in 1987 and 1993, when a controlling interest in the company was acquired by a group of investors led by French advertising executive Robert Louis-Dreyfus. Louis-Dreyfus launched a dramatic turnaround of the company—cutting costs, improving styling, launching new models such as the Predator soccer shoe, and creating new promotional events like the adidas Predator Cup tournament for young soccer players in Germany. The turnaround was also aided by a trend among teenagers that repopularized 1970s styles and teens' preference for niche brands that weren't likely to be purchased by adults. At year-end 1994, adidas had increased its annual sales in the United States by 75 percent from the prior year and improved its market share enough to become the third largest seller of athletic footwear in the United States, trailing only Nike and Reebok.

The company's turnaround continued in 1995 with it going public and recording annual sales of nearly €1.8 billion. In 1996, adidas outfitted more than 6,000 athletes in the Olympic Games held in

Atlanta and supplied the Official Match Ball for the European Soccer Championship. Louis-Dreyfus's turnaround also included a push in 1997 to sign athletes such as Kobe Bryant, Anna Kournikova, and David Beckham to offset the appeal of Nike's Michael Jordan with athletic footwear and apparel consumers in the United States. The company's mid-1990s image revival was also aided when celebrities such as Madonna and Elle MacPherson appeared in magazines or on television wearing adidas shoes without any prompting from the company.

Even though the company's turnaround had produced outstanding results, with sales and earnings growing at annual rates of 38.3 percent and 37.5 percent, respectively, between 1995 and 1997, the company was a distant number three in the worldwide athletic footwear and apparel industry. Nike's 1997 revenues of $9.2 billion were nearly three times greater than those of adidas, and Nike continued to grow at a fast pace as it expanded into more international markets. In addition, Nike had begun to diversify outside of athletic footwear and apparel with the 1988 acquisition of Cole-Haan and the 1995 acquisition of Bauer hockey equipment. In 1997, it was rumored that Nike was eyeing French ski maker Skis Rossignol SA. (Nike did not acquire Rossignol, but it did acquire Converse basketball shoes and Hurley skateboard equipment in 2003 and Starter athletic apparel in 2004.) In late 1997, Louis-Dreyfus and the family owners of Salomon SA, a French sports equipment manufacturer, agreed to a €1.5 billion buyout that would diversify adidas beyond footwear and apparel and into ski equipment, golf clubs, bicycle components, and winter sports apparel. The acquisition would also give adidas a stronger sales platform in North America and Asia—two markets where adidas was still struggling.

THE SALOMON SA ACQUISITION

Adidas's €1.5 billion acquisition of Salomon allowed it to surpass Reebok to become the world's second-largest sporting goods company, with projected 1998 sales of nearly €5.1 billion. Nike remained the leader of the $90 billion global sporting goods industry, but the acquisition added the

number one winter sports equipment producer, the second-largest golf equipment company, and the leading producer of performance bicycle wheels and rims to adidas's lineup of businesses. The acquisition was a move toward achieving CEO Robert Louis-Dreyfus's vision of building "the best portfolio of sports brands in the world."[2]

The price of adidas's shares fell upon the announcement of the acquisition over concerns about the price adidas agreed to pay for Salomon and how the company might finance the acquisition. There was also some concern among investors that adidas did not have expertise in manufacturing sports equipment since its apparel and footwear were produced by contract manufacturers. A Merrill Lynch analyst suggested that the Salomon acquisition might prove troublesome for adidas since other athletic shoe companies had "dabbled in the hard goods segment, but they have been unsuccessful to date in making inroads."[3]

Louis-Dreyfus used 100 percent debt financing to create adidas-Salomon but was not concerned with the merged company's ability to service the debt since adidas's annual free cash flow in 1997 was projected to be more than €200 million. Adidas's 1997 results (prior to the integration of Salomon) reached record levels, with the company's annual revenues increasing 42 percent from the prior year as a result of footwear sales growing by 32 percent and apparel sales increasing by 55 percent. Gains were recorded for all geographic regions, with North American sales increasing by 66 percent during 1997, sales in Europe increasing by 31 percent, and Asia-Pacific revenues growing by 38 percent between 1996 and 1997.

Louis-Dreyfus expected the new business units to boost adidas's pretax profits by 20–25 percent in 1998 and by an additional 20 percent in 1999. He believed 2000 would be the first year shareholders would see the full potential of the acquisition. However, Louis-Dreyfus's projections never materialized, with adidas taking control of Salomon just as the winter sports equipment and golf equipment industries were becoming less attractive. The poor performance of Salomon and TaylorMade in 1998 led to a net loss of $164 million for adidas-Salomon during the first nine months of its fiscal year. To make matters worse, the integration of Mavic, Salomon, Bonfire, Cliché, and TaylorMade were not going as smoothly as Louis-Dreyfus and adidas's shareholders had expected.

Adidas's core footwear and apparel business performed commendably during 1998 to contribute to a net profit of €205 million for the fiscal year. In early 1999, adidas-Salomon's management announced that synergies from the merger would amount to less than one-half of what was initially projected. By the summer of 1999, adidas-Salomon's share price had declined by more than a third from its early 1998 high, and most large investors believed that adidas had bitten off more than it could chew with the acquisition.[4] Robert Louis-Dreyfus announced in early 2000 that he would step down from adidas-Salomon and rejoin his family's business France in early 2001. Herbert Hainer, the company's head of marketing in Europe and Asia, was tapped as his replacement to run the diversified sporting goods company.

Under Hainer's leadership, the company cut costs, introduced new apparel and footwear products, increased the company's advertising, signed additional athletes to endorsement contracts, and supplied apparel, equipment, and footwear to more than 3,000 athletes competing in 26 sports during the 2000 Olympic Games in Sydney. Also, the company expanded into company-owned retail stores in 2001 with its first adidas Originals store opening in Berlin in September, followed by stores in Tokyo, Amsterdam, and Paris by year-end. In December 2001, Hainer added to the company's lineup of sports businesses with the acquisition of Arc'Teryx, the producer of technical winter sports apparel. Adidas-Salomon recorded sales of €6.1 billion in 2001 and ended the year as the top performer in the DAX 30. The performance of adidas-Salomon's common shares is presented in Exhibit 2.

ADIDAS-SALOMON'S CORPORATE STRATEGY IN EARLY 2005

In early 2005, adidas-Salomon's businesses were organized under three units based around the company's core brands—adidas, Salomon, and TaylorMade-adidas Golf. Innovation and excellence in strategy execution were common themes in all of adidas-Salomon's three business segments. The company expected its product design teams to develop at least one major product innovation per year in each product category. In 2004, TaylorMade Golf introduced its r7 Quad driver, which was a first-of-its-kind product that incorporated four movable weights. The movable weights allowed golfers to make adjustments to the club that could produce six different ball flight trajectories. TaylorMade extended the movable weight concept to irons and hybrid clubs in 2005. The adidas Sport Performance group introduced its Roteiro soccer ball, which was the industry's first thermal-bonded soccer ball. Also, the adidas Sport Performance group and the Salomon group collaborated to develop footwear featuring a Ground Control System that adjusted for uneven ground. Adidas T-MAC HUG laceless shoes and the adidas 1 were shoe innovations developed in 2004 and 2005. The $250-per-pair adidas 1 was the first running shoe with an embedded microprocessor. The microprocessor evaluated the runner's weight, the terrain, and speed to vary the compression in the heel of the shoe with the use of mechanical shock-absorbing components.

Adidas-Salomon also relied heavily on ongoing brand-building activities to further differentiate adidas, TaylorMade, and Salomon from competing brands of sporting goods. Partnerships with major sporting events around the world and with notable athletes competing in winter sports, track and field, soccer, basketball, tennis, and golf were critical to creating a distinctive image with consumers. The company also attempted to provide its retailers with superior customer service, including on-time deliveries, since the retailer was a crucial element of the sporting goods industry value chain. Efficient supply chain management and manufacturing efficiencies were also vital to the success of the company since poor product quality might discourage repeat sales to consumers. Even though the majority of adidas-Salomon products were produced by contract manufacturers, the company employed more than 100 quality control officers to monitor supplier standards.

Adidas-Salomon management expected visible improvements in operating margins each year and anticipated that the company would achieve an overall 10 percent operating profit margin in 2006. Increased profitability in Europe, strong top-line and bottom-line growth in Asia, and steady growth in North America were expected to deliver sought-after gains in operating profit margins. The company's chief managers believed that operational efficiency coupled with product innovation would allow it to

Exhibit 2   **Performance of adidas-Salomon's Stock Price, 1999–2005**

(a) Trend in adidas-Salomon's Common Stock Price

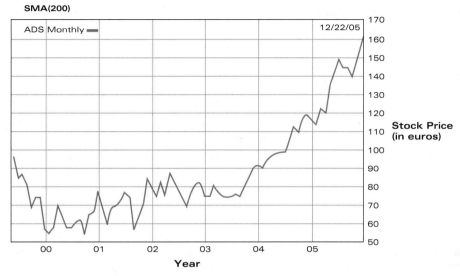

(b) Performance of adidas-Salomon's Stock Price versus the DAX 30 Index

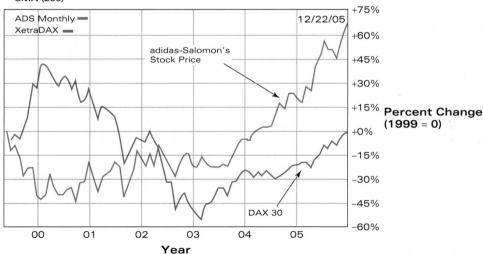

attain number one or number two positions in each sporting goods segment in which it competed.

Adidas Footwear and Apparel

Adidas footwear and apparel was organized under three categories based on the clothing needs of the consumer. The adidas Sport Performance group developed sports shoes and attire suitable for use by athletes in running, football and soccer, basketball, tennis, and general training. Adidas held number one or number two positions globally in these athletic

categories and maintained its advantage primarily through innovations like its ClimaCool 360-degree footwear ventilation system, its a^3 energy management system, and endorsements by individual athletes or league sponsorships. Tim Duncan, Kevin Garnett, and Tracy McGrady were among the latest NBA athletes to endorse adidas footwear and apparel. In soccer, players such as David Beckham and Zinedine Zidane, and even entire clubs, endorsed adidas soccer shoes and clothing. Adidas was the official sponsor for the German national women's team and the UEFA European soccer league teams in Munich,

Amsterdam, Milan, and Madrid. Also, the adidas Roteiro was the Official Match Ball for all UEFA games. Adidas was also the official supplier to 18 National Olympic Committees competing in the 2004 Olympic Games in Athens and fully equipped athletes from 45 nations competing in 26 of the 28 disciplines included in the Olympics.

The company's Sport Heritage group was established in 2000 and designed new styles of shoes and apparel that were similar to the performance-oriented styles of the 1970s. Although athletes in the early 2000s would not compete in products based on 1970s technology, many teenagers and urban trend-followers liked the look of adidas's older products. Adidas limited distribution of its Sport Heritage products to avoid dilution of the brand.

As with Sport Heritage products, few purchasers of adidas Sport Style products were likely to wear such products while engaged in athletic endeavors. The Y-3 collection of sportswear, which was designed by Yohji Yamamoto, was based on athletic styles but would be only marginally suitable for sports. Most of the Y-3 line was best suited for consumers looking for trendy and comfortable casual wear with a mild sports influence. The line was launched in 2003, and adidas-Salomon management believed the division could eventually account for €100 million in sales. The company also believed that its Stella McCartney performance apparel line, David Beckham Sport Style line, and Mohammad Ali and Missy Elliott Heritage lines would prove successful.

North America   The North American market for sporting goods showed virtually no growth between 2000 and 2004 and was characterized by fierce competition among manufacturers and deep promotional discounting by retailers. All of adidas's brand-building efforts and product innovations were directed toward building on its number four ranking in North America, which was the company's weakest region in the $33 billion global athletic footwear market. In 2004, adidas held an 8.9 percent market share—behind Nike, with 36 percent market share; Reebok, with a 12.2 percent market share; and New Balance, with an approximate 11 percent market share.

In late 2004, adidas held a 55 percent market share in soccer shoes in the United States compared to Nike's 33 percent market share. However, in the overall U.S. cleated shoe segment, Nike led adidas by a 48 to 23 percent margin. Adidas was not a contender in the $3 billion basketball category, where Nike held a 70 percent market share. Adidas, Nike, and New Balance were all tied, with about 20 percent market share each in the tennis category. Nike, asics, New Balance, and Reebok all recorded gains in the running category during the first nine months of 2004, but analysts suggested that adidas missed out on growth in the category because its new technologies had not been a hit with consumers. Sales of casual sports shoes similar to those included in the adidas Heritage and adidas Sport Style lines were up 30 percent during the first nine months of 2004, but adidas did not make the list of top four brands in the category. The category was expected to grow by 40 percent in 2005 to displace running as the second-largest category of athletic shoes in the United States.

To achieve its revenue growth objectives of 10 percent annually in 2005 and 2006, adidas developed new styles and models offered in all three adidas segments, placed a strong emphasis on basketball, established marketing partnerships with college sports teams, major league soccer, and major league baseball teams, and improved retailer relations. Also, adidas expanded distribution to additional sporting goods stores, mall-based stores, department stores, urban distribution locations, and company-owned stores. Adidas also hoped to encourage retailers to create shop-within-a-shop merchandising sections and provide permanent wall space for adidas shoes. In 2004, Foot Locker agreed to give adidas's Kevin Garnett shoes permanent wall space in its best locations and feature the sub-brand in its television and print ads. Adidas also planned to expand distribution into additional urban retail stores that might not be a part of a large chain but were close to urban consumers. Adidas estimated the U.S. urban retail market for athletic footwear and apparel to be over $6 billion. Adidas also opened company-owned retail stores in Las Vegas, New York, Chicago, and San Francisco in 2005. Store openings in Portland, Boston, Washington, Philadelphia, Los Angeles, and Atlanta were planned for 2006.

Europe   Growth plans in Europe were focused on building on adidas's number one ranking in the region through its sponsorship of youth and professional soccer and continued support for running. The European athletic footwear and apparel market was growing at a modest rate, but retailers in Europe had relied even more on promotional pricing than retailers in North America. Prices for children's apparel had declined by 10 percent during 2004, and prices of adult apparel had decreased by 8.5 percent between 2003 and 2004. Adidas believed that its emphasis on product innovation and its strong brand loyalty would help protect the company from margin erosion due to price competition. Adidas also planned to increase its number of retailers in Europe by 25 percent between 2004 and 2006, with most new locations coming in emerging country markets. Adidas also intended to open additional company-owned stores in Europe during 2005 and 2006.

Asia   In 1999, adidas held a 6 percent market share in Japan, but its market share had grown to 18 percent in 2004 and its management expected a 20–24 percent market share in Japan by 2006. Adidas's increase in market share had come mainly at the expense of local brands such as asics and Mizuno. In 2004, Japan accounted for 50 percent of athletic apparel sales in Asia, but adidas and other consumer goods companies were directing considerable efforts to building brand awareness in China and other emerging Asian markets. The region's growth in gross domestic product was projected to be the highest in the world between 2005 and 2010, with much of the growth resulting from domestic-driven demand rather than exports. The size of the middle class in the region was also expected to grow dramatically in the region by 2010, with China's middle class growing from 60 million in 2002 to 160 million by 2010. Adidas's management estimated that every 1 percent increase in consumption by China's population translated into a $70 billion increase in sales of consumer goods. Adidas expected the 2008 Olympic Games in Beijing to generate interest in athletic footwear and apparel in China.

The company was rapidly adding retail stores to ensure that its products were available for purchase by China's growing consumer base. The company was adding more than 40 stores per month in urban locations in China since 55 percent of the country's population was expected to migrate from the countryside to cities by 2012. In 2004, adidas had more than 150 retail locations in only 1 province of China but expected to have more than 150 retail locations in 10 provinces by the 2008 Olympics. In 2004, adidas's revenues of more than €100 million made it the number two brand of athletic footwear and apparel in China. Nike was the leading seller of athletic goods in China. Adidas's management expected the company to double its sales in China by 2008.

Salomon

Like athletic footwear and apparel, the winter sports industry was mature, with the market declining by 3.1 percent during the 2003–2004 ski season. The 2003–2004 decline followed a 3.6 percent decline during the 2002–2003 season and a 1.8 percent decline in the 2001–2002 season. Some categories within the winter sports industry were declining at a more rapid pace, with the snowboard industry falling from €428.9 million in 2000–2001 to €344.5 million in 2003–2004. Nordic (cross-country) skiing was the only bright spot in the industry, with a 3.1 percent growth rate during the 2003–2004 ski season. The total value of worldwide winter sports equipment market in 2004 was €1.5 billion.

Revenue increases for most winter sporting goods producers had come from adding summer outdoor-inspired apparel and footwear to their product lines. Salomon was the number one producer of winter sports equipment, with a number one position in alpine (downhill) ski boots and high-end skis, a number two position in alpine skis overall and snowboard boots, and a number three position in snowboards. The company held an 80 percent market share in nordic (cross-country) ski systems. The Salomon business group also included Mavic, which was the number one brand of performance bicycle wheels and rims. The performance bicycle category was also mature, but growing a modest rate because of the popularity of road racing in the United States and Europe. Other businesses in the portfolio included Bonfire, a producer of snowboard apparel; Arc'Teryx, which produced technical winter sports apparel; and Cliché, a maker of skateboard equipment and apparel.

The businesses included in the Salomon division utilized competitive approaches similar to those of adidas-branded products. The division was committed to innovation in products in its snow, outdoor, and asphalt categories and attempted to benefit from synergies with the core adidas business when feasible. An example of such cross-division strategic fit was Salomon and adidas's collaboration on the development of the Ground Control System running shoe. Shoes using the design were marketed under both the adidas and Salomon brand names and were sold in different retail channels. The division also exploited adidas's apparel design expertise in its development of winter sports, cycling, and skateboard apparel. The collaboration between adidas and Salomon brands in apparel design had contributed to a 400 percent increase in soft goods sales for the division since 1995.

In 2004, sales for the Salomon group were nearly evenly split between winter sports hard goods and other products. The Salomon group was undertaking efforts to increase soft goods sales to 50 percent of the group's sales by expanding apparel lines, developing dedicated soft goods sales forces for each brand, and developing advertising targeting women since studies had shown that a large percentage of winter sports apparel purchases were made by women.

Improvement in operating margins was also a strategic priority at Salomon since top-line growth was limited. Since 2001, the division had shifted hardware production from France to Eastern Europe and Asia, developed a new production process in skis that lowered materials costs, reduced production time, and lowered labor costs per unit. In addition, Salomon had reduced total employment between 2002 and 2004 through early retirements and an increased number of temporary employees.

Even with Salomon management's efforts to improve operating margins for the division, there were some characteristics of the winter sports industry that precluded options that might be pursued in other industries. When asked by an investment banker why Salomon didn't shift all production to Asia, the head of Salomon, Christian Finell, responded, "The reason for this is that the main part of our business in winter sports is done in Europe. We believe it makes much more sense to have our production close to our customers. Also most of the relevant raw materials are found in Europe and not in Asia. And lead times are relatively long in this business. So by adding both the lead time and additional transportation costs it doesn't make sense to shift the production to Asia."[5]

TaylorMade-adidas Golf

TaylorMade Golf was the second largest producer of golf equipment in the $5.5 billion industry. The golf equipment industry had experience little growth since 1999 when golf's chief governing body in the United States began to ban golf clubs that it deemed performed too well. Golf equipment sales had grown dramatically during the mid- to late-1990s as golf equipment manufacturers like Callaway Golf Company, Titleist, Ping, and TaylorMade Golf introduced better-performing clubs that were more forgiving of recreational golfers' poor swing characteristics. Professional golfers using the technologically advanced equipment saw improvements in their games as well—particularly in driving distance. The United States Golf Association (USGA) began to believe that these new high-tech clubs provided a springlike effect and developed a coefficient of restitution (COR) limitation that would prevent any such effect

for golf equipment sold in the United States. Golf equipment manufacturers scoffed at the idea that clubs could produce a timed springlike or trampoline effect that could help propel the ball forward but were nevertheless obliged to discontinue research and development projects that would produce clubs exceeding a COR of 0.83.

By 2000, most golf club manufacturers had reached the 0.83 COR limitation and were compelled to find new approaches to innovation. In 2004, there was little differentiation among golf clubs until TaylorMade developed its r7 Quad driver. The driver was unique in that it allowed golfers to reposition movable weights screwed into the clubhead. The golfer could move the weights to provide a higher or lower launch angle and cause the flight path to pull to the left or fade to the right. The new innovation created 8 percent growth in driver sales for the year and made TaylorMade the number one producer of drivers and metalwoods. Prior to TaylorMade's introduction of the r7 Quad driver, Callaway Golf had held the number one position in the industry since 1991. The r7 lost its number one ranking in 2005 to Ping's G5 driver.

In 2005, the golf equipment industry had seemingly reached maturity as a sport, with the number of new participants each year barely exceeding the number who were giving up the sport. Asia's 2–3 percent annual growth in the number of new golfers made it the only geographic region to experience growth between 1999 and 2003. Poor economic conditions in the United States during 2000 caused many frequent golfers to scale back their participation levels that year, but the number of core golfers had rebounded in 2001 through 2004. However, the overall number of rounds played by golfers had declined until 2004, when the number of rounds played increased by nearly 7 percent. Exhibit 3 provides the retail value, number of units sold, and average selling price for various golf equipment categories for 1997 through 2004.

TaylorMade-adidas Golf management expected to increase sales primarily through market share gains since they had concluded that it would be unwise to count on growth of the game. TaylorMade believed it could increase market share through endorsement contracts with touring professionals on the Professional Golf Association (PGA) Tour and other professional tours and through new product innovations like the movable weight system used in its r7 driver. TaylorMade management also wished to

Exhibit 3   **Retail Value, Units Sold, and Average Selling Price of Golf Equipment in the United States, 1997–2004**

	Year	Retail Value	Units Sold	Average Selling Price
Metalwoods	1997	$676.8 million	2.93 million	$231.00
	1998	601.1	2.81	214.00
	1999	583.8	2.91	201.00
	2000	599.1	2.94	204.00
	2001	626.6	2.99	210.00
	2002	608.7	3.09	197.00
	2003	660.4	3.28	201.00
	2004	654.1	3.56	184.00
Irons	1997	$533.4 million	7.12 million	$ 74.90*
	1998	485.4	6.87	70.71
	1999	447.9	6.97	64.28
	2000	475.3	7.14	66.57
	2001	459.3	7.17	64.06
	2002	456.4	7.42	61.50
	2003	461.4	7.66	60.23
	2004	482.6	8.06	59.88
Golf balls	1997	$458.7 million	19.97 million	$ 22.97†
	1998	487.4	20.06	24.30
	1999	518.1	20.46	25.32
	2000	530.8	20.80	25.52
	2001	555.6	21.32	26.06
	2002	529.9	20.81	25.46
	2003	496.4	19.85	25.01
	2004	506.3	19.98	25.34
Footwear (pairs)	1997	$214.3 million	2.48 million	$ 86.49
	1998	204.3	2.43	84.13
	1999	206.9	2.47	83.77
	2000	220.8	2.52	87.68
	2001	217.8	2.57	84.62
	2002	211.7	2.68	78.95
	2003	217.1	2.82	76.97
	2004	234.4	3.00	78.22

*Per club.
†Per dozen.
Source: Golf Datatech.

achieve revenue growth by increasing sales in Asia. The company had successfully increased its sales in Asia from 13 percent of sales in 1999 to 31 percent of sales in 2004, and the United States accounted for only 52 percent of sales in 2004 versus 69 percent of sales in 1999. TaylorMade CEO Mark King

designated Asia as a high-priority market: "Asia is very, very profitable as a region. The main reason is because the selling prices in Asia for golf equipment are higher than in any other place in the world. So the margins there are very, very strong. Profitability in North America is also very strong. The only area that we are struggling in right now a little bit is in Europe."[6] In addition, USGA rules did not apply to play in Asia and most golf club manufacturers produced models with high COR ratings for sale in Asia.

Even though TaylorMade had achieved the number one ranking in metalwoods during 2004, its market share in irons was about one-half that of industry leader, Callaway Golf Company, and its market share in putters was negligible. The division's sales of Maxfli golf balls, which was acquired by adidas-Salomon in 2002, had yet to earn profits and accounted for less than 5 percent of industry sales in 2005. Segment leader Titleist had held a 70 percent or greater market share in golf balls for decades. TaylorMade-adidas Golf's share of the metalwoods, irons, and golf footwear for January 2002–July 2004 is presented in Exhibit 4.

Like Salomon, TaylorMade-adidas Golf division attempted to benefit from adidas's core competencies in footwear and apparel design. The company offered a full line of golf apparel and footwear that was sold

in golf shops in North America, Europe, and Asia. The division expected double-digit annual growth rates in apparel and footwear revenues. Exhibit 5 presents key financial data for each of adidas-Salomon's operating divisions between 1998 and 2004. The company's financial information by geographic region for 1998–2004 is presented in Exhibit 6. Income statements for and balance sheets for 2003–2004 are provided in Exhibits 7 and 8, respectively.

ADIDAS'S DIVESTITURE OF SALOMON BUSINESS UNITS AND ITS PLANNED ACQUISITION OF REEBOK

With the Amer's acquisition of Salomon's business units completed in October 2005, adidas was able to report that its revenues and earnings for the first nine months of 2005 were quite improved when compared

Exhibit 4   **Market Shares of Leading Sellers of Golf Equipment for Metalwoods, Irons, and Footwear, January 2002–July 2004**

Metalwoods

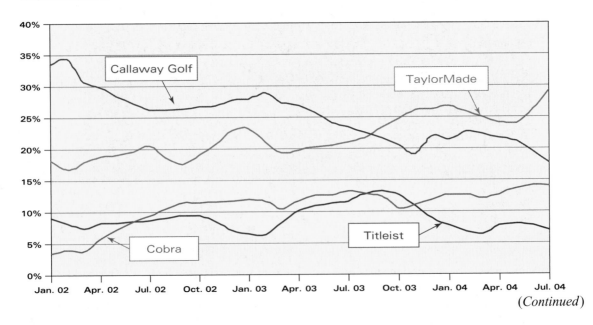

(*Continued*)

Exhibit 4   **Continued**

Irons

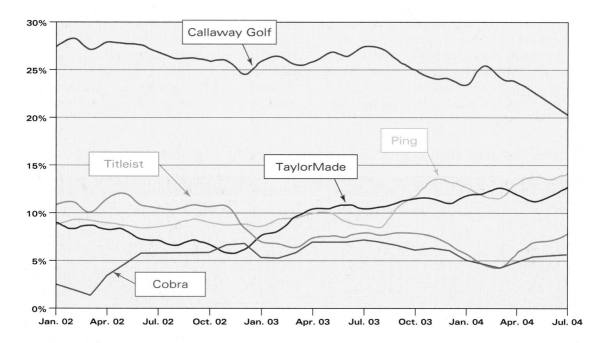

Footwear

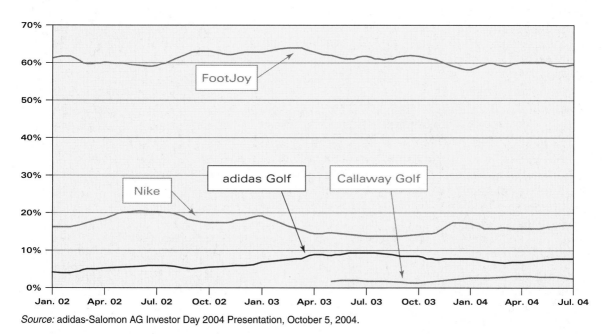

Source: adidas-Salomon AG Investor Day 2004 Presentation, October 5, 2004.

to the first nine months of 2004. The company's revenues had increased by 10 percent on a currency-neutral basis, its operating profits had increased by 12 percent, and its net income from continuing operations during the third quarter of 2005 was 28 percent better than the same period in 2004. Much of the company's sales growth was attributable to new models such as the T-Mac, which was expected to sell more than 1 million pairs in 2005 and 2006, and adidas 1, which was expected to become a €20 million product line addition by 2006. Also, adidas's Sport Heritage line was expected to account for €1 billion in sales during 2005 and the company's 680 company-owned retail stores were expected to record sales of €750 million by year-end 2005. Sales grew at double digits in all geographic regions except Europe, were sales were stable on a currency-neutral basis. Adidas-Salomon was scheduled to change its name to adidas AG during its 2006 annual stockholders' meeting.

Exhibit 5   **adidas-Salomon Financial Data by Operating Segment, 1998–2004**

	2004	2003	2002	2001	2000	1999	1998
Adidas							
Net sales	€5,174	€4,950	€5,105	€4,825	€4,672	€4,427	€4,316
Gross profit	2,284	2,008	2,004	1,845	1,907	1,827	1,818
Operating profit	523	365	343	352	391	431	412
Operating assets	1,393	2,172	2,294	1,954	2,286	1,987	1,730
Capital expenditures	85	63	84	113	93	105	102
Amortization and depreciation, excluding goodwill amortization	56	63	57	52	45	48	38
Salomon							
Net sales	€653	€658	€684	€714	€703	€587	€487
Gross profit	259	264	279	313	296	233	188
Operating profit	9	35	39	63	61	32	6
Operating assets	505	521	581	679	566	533	598
Capital expenditures	19	18	18	38	24	17	20
Amortization and depreciation, excluding goodwill amortization	7	7	7	7	7	5	7
TaylorMade-adidas Golf							
Net sales	€633	€637	€707	€545	€441	€327	€263
Gross profit	298	290	345	281	221	160	118
Operating profit	60	67	74	63	44	30	20
Operating assets	335	391	433	316	219	156	99
Capital expenditures	9	12	49	16	12	10	16
Amortization and depreciation, excluding goodwill amortization	11	9	7	6	4	4	2
Headquarters/consolidation							
Net sales	€ 18	€ 22	€ 27	€ 28	€ 19	€ 10	—
Gross profit	218	252	191	162	104	—	—
Operating profit	(12)	23	21	(3)	(59)	(14)	(22)
Operating assets	1,648	1,104	953	1,234	947	903	782
Capital expenditures	27	29	22	20	16	—	—
Amortization and depreciation, excluding goodwill amortization	28	17	26	25	23	6	6

Source: adidas-Salomon annual reports.

Exhibit 6   **adidas-Salomon Financial Data by Geographic Region, 1998–2004**

	2004	2003	2002	2001	2000	1999	1998
Europe							
Net sales	€3,470	€3,365	€3,200	€3,066	€2,860	€2,723	€2,774
Gross profit	1,573	1,383	1,268	1,153	1,171	1,133	1,127
Operating profit	644	534	471	444	454	382	357
Operating assets	1,461	1,428	1,396	1,419	1,107	1,167	1,114
Capital expenditures	46	44	56	74	55	40	35
Amortization and depreciation, excluding goodwill amortization	30	30	27	24	22	20	19
North America							
Net sales	€1,486	€1,562	€1,960	€1,818	€1,907	€1,826	€1,784
Gross profit	534	552	742	697	729	731	713
Operating profit	79	92	162	161	177	234	276
Operating assets	768	778	969	945	862	848	666
Capital expenditures	27	22	82	68	54	26	29
Amortization and depreciation, excluding goodwill amortization	21	21	20	17	16	12	11
Asia							
Net sales	€1,251	€1,116	€1,166	€1,010	€875	€663	€383
Gross profit	615	525	562	481	416	301	156
Operating profit	244	191	189	170	129	96	26
Operating assets	480	447	505	743	455	390	201
Capital expenditures	23	12	16	15	17	18	9
Amortization and depreciation, excluding goodwill amortization	16	14	15	12	10	5	3
Latin America							
Net sales	€224	€179	€163	€178	€171	€126	€112
Gross profit	87	70	65	73	72	50	43
Operating profit	38	25	24	16	23	15	11
Operating assets	56	93	79	98	109	75	66
Capital expenditures	1	1	1	2	3	3	2
Amortization and depreciation, excluding goodwill amortization	1	1	1	2	2	1	1
Headquarters/ consolidation							
Net sales	€ 47	€ 45	€ 34	€ 40	€ 23	€ 34	€ 12
Gross profit	248	284	182	197	140	—	—
Operating profit	(426)	(352)	(369)	(316)	(346)	(239)	(254)
Operating assets	1,601	1,442	1,312	978	1,485	1,108	1,162
Capital expenditures	43	43	15	28	16	45	63
Amortization and depreciation, excluding goodwill amortization	34	30	34	35	29	25	19

Source: adidas-Salomon annual reports.

Exhibit 7   **adidas-Salomon Income Statements, 2003–2004
(in thousands except per share data)**

	2004	2003
Net sales	€6,478,072	€6,266,800
Cost of sales	3,419,864	3,453,132
Gross profit	3,058,208	2,813,668
Selling, general and administrative expenses	2,376,266	2,228,135
Depreciation and amortization (excluding goodwill)	101,764	95,519
Operating profit	580,178	490,014
Goodwill amortization	46,352	44,809
Royalty and commission income	43,166	42,153
Financial expenses, net	56,832	49,170
Income before taxes	520,160	438,188
Income taxes	196,691	166,712
Net income before minority interests	323,469	271,476
Minority interests	(9,221)	(11,391)
Net income	€ 314,248	€ 260,085
Basic earnings per share (in euros)	€6.88	€5.72
Diluted earnings per share (in euros)	€6.54	€5.72
Dividends per share (in euros)	€1.30	€1.00
Number of shares outstanding (Basic)	46,649,560	45,452,361
Number of shares outstanding (Diluted)	49,669,346	45,469,366

Source: 2004 adidas-Salomon annual report.

The Reebok acquisition, which was announced in August 2005 and was expected to be finalized sometime during the first half of 2006, would give the company pro forma aggregate 2004 revenues of €8.9 billion ($11.1 billion) and allow it to more than double its sales in North America to €3.1 billion ($3.9 billion). In addition, adidas expected to capture annual cost-sharing benefits of approximately €125 million ($150 million) within three years of the closing date. The company placed 4,531,250 shares with institutional investors in November 2005 to raise approximately €648 million to contribute to the financing of the Reebok acquisition.

Perhaps the greatest opportunity presented by the planned Reebok acquisition was the company's ability to position adidas as a technologically superior shoe designed for serious athletes, while Reebok could be positioned as leisure shoe that would sell at middle price points. In addition, the company could maintain its strategy of signing respected athletes to adidas endorsement contracts, while gaining endorsements from more edgy Reebok celebrities such as Allen Iverson, Jay-Z,

and Fifty Cent. In addition, Reebok would retain its founder and CEO Paul Fireman to lead Reebok after the acquisition.

Even though the restructured lineup of businesses offered adidas an improved chance of catching Nike in its race to be the world's largest sporting goods company, some observers were not convinced the move would prove to be any more successful than the company's 1998 acquisition of Salomon. The president of a sports marketing firm and former New Balance executive said he doubted that adidas's "German mentality of control, engineering, and production" would prove to be compatible with Reebok's "U.S. marketing-driven culture" and added, "In reality, I don't think [the merged company] is going to dent the market, because Nike is already too far ahead."[7] New Balance's CEO, Jim Davis, concurred with his former colleague's assessment by commenting, "You can try to take on Nike, but . . . Nike is Nike and will continue to be Nike.[8] A Goldman Sachs analyst added, "We fail to see how this combo will erode Nike's franchise as the global brand leader."[9]

Exhibit 8   **adidas-Salomon Balance Sheets, 2003–2004 (in thousands)**

Assets	December 31	
	2004	2003
Cash and cash equivalents	€ 195,997	€ 189,503
Short-term financial assets	258,950	89,411
Accounts receivable	1,046,322	1,075,092
Inventories	1,155,374	1,163,518
Other current assets	378,303	259,427
Total current assets	€3,034,946	€2,776,951
Property, plant and equipment, net	367,928	344,554
Goodwill, net	572,426	591,045
Other intangible assets, net	96,312	103,797
Long-term financial assets	93,134	88,408
Deferred tax assets	160,135	178,484
Other noncurrent assets	102,599	104,569
Total noncurrent assets	€1,392,534	€1,410,857
Total assets	€4,427,480	€4,187,808
Liabilities, minority interests and shareholders' equity		
Short-term borrowings	€ 185,837	€ —
Accounts payable	591,689	592,273
Income taxes	167,334	157,764
Accrued liabilities and provisions	558,121	454,573
Other current liabilities	184,332	139,095
Total current liabilities	€1,687,313	€1,343,705
Long-term borrowings	862,845	1,225,385
Pensions and similar obligations	111,321	105,264
Deferred tax liabilities	77,951	65,807
Other noncurrent liabilities	30,784	35,278
Total noncurrent liabilities	€1,082,865	€1,431,734
Minority interests	28,850	56,579
Shareholders' equity	€1,628,452	€1,355,790
Total liabilities, minority interests and shareholders' equity	€4,427,480	€4,187,808

Source: 2004 adidas-Salomon annual report.

Endnotes

[1] As quoted in "The Brothers Dassler Fight On," *Deutsche Welle,* dw-world.de.

[2] As quoted in "Adidas Foots $1.5B to Buy Sporting Firm," *USA Today,* September 17, 1997.

[3] As quoted in "Sporting Goods Consolidation Off to the Races," *Mergers & Acquisitions Report,* November 10, 1997.

[4] As quoted in "Sports Goods/Shareholders Criticize Salomon Takeover," *Handelsblatt,* May 21, 1999.

[5] Ibid.

[6] Ibid.

[7] As quoted in "Reebok and adidas: A Good Fit," *BusinessWeek Online,* August 4, 2005.

[8] Ibid.

[9] Ibid.

Procter & Gamble's Acquisition of Gillette

John E. Gamble
University of South Alabama

Between 2001 and 2005, Procter & Gamble's revenues increased by more than 40 percent to reach $56.7 billion; its profits more than doubled to approach $7.3 billion; and its number of billion-dollar brands such as Crest, Bounty, Charmin, Tide, Ivory, and Folgers increased from 10 to 16. The company's outstanding financial performance during the four-year period generated adequate free cash flows to fund dividend payments of $11 billion and allowed its market capitalization to increase by more than 100 percent. The company also utilized free cash flows to build its lineup of marquee brands through the acquisitions of Clairol in 2001 and Wella hair care products in 2003.

At the close of its fiscal year ending September 30, 2005, Procter & Gamble executed its largest acquisition ever with the $57 billion takeover of the Gillette Company. The acquisition delivered five additional billion-dollar brands to Procter & Gamble's business mix and made it the global leader in the market for razors and blades. In addition, Gillette's Duracell business unit was the world's number-one seller of alkaline batteries to consumers, its Oral B business was the worldwide leader in manual and electric toothbrushes, and the Braun unit produced and marketed the best-selling brand of foil electric shavers for men and the number-one hair epilator for women. The Gillette Company's sales of Gillette, Foamy, Satin Care, Right Guard, Soft & Dri, and Dry Idea also made it a leading producer of personal care products.

The $57 billion acquisition price represented a 20 percent premium over Gillette's market capitalization one week prior to the January 28, 2005, merger announcement and would allow Gillette shareholders to exchange each Gillette share held for 0.975 shares of Procter & Gamble (P&G) stock. P&G planned to buy back $18 billion to $22 billion of its outstanding common shares within 12 to 18 months of the completion of the October 1, 2005, merger. The share buyback plan would have the effect of financing the acquisition with 60 percent equity and 40 percent debt.

P&G management expected a $1 + 1 = 3$ effect from the merger since the acquisition of Gillette would give P&G a stronger business lineup and brand portfolio and provide significant cost-sharing opportunities between the two companies' businesses. Procter & Gamble's ability to introduce Gillette brands to new country markets served by its distribution system caused management to increase its near-term annual sales growth objective from 4–6 percent to 5–7 percent. In addition, P&G management had identified approximately $1 billion in annual cost savings resulting from value chain synergies between P&G businesses and Gillette business units. The company planned an immediate workforce reduction of 6,000 employees who would no longer be needed because of duplication of responsibilities and activities.

By all appearances, the Gillette acquisition seemed to offer P&G attractive new consumer products segments and ample strategic-fit opportunities that would benefit the overall performance of both business groups, but P&G shareholders had reason to question whether the company's bid for Gillette was too rich. According to an analysis by Goldman Sachs and UBS, the 20 percent purchase-price premium P&G offered to Gillette shareholders was within the range offered in other recent consumer goods mergers, but the acquisition price seemed high when comparing the merger price sales and earnings before interest and taxes (EBIT) multiples to those of other recent mergers. The $57 billion price offered for Gillette was 5.5 times greater than Gillette's most recent sales and 18.8 times greater than its most recent EBIT. The sales multiple for other acquisitions examined by Goldman Sachs/ UBS ranged from 1.1 to 4.1. EBIT multiples for previous consumer goods acquisitions included in the investment firms' analysis ranged from 8.4 to 17.6. Projections that the addition of Gillette's business units to P&G's lineup would dilute P&G's EPS for up to three years was also worrisome to investors who believed the 0.975 exchange ratio was overly generous. However, as Procter & Gamble closed its first quarter as a merged company on December 31, 2005, the company was performing at the high end of analysts' expectations. In addition, the merged company's ample free cash flows had allowed it to acquire four leading detergent brands sold in Southeast Asia from Colgate-Palmolive. The new brands would dramatically improve P&G's market share in its weakest region in Asia.

COMPANY HISTORIES AND OVERVIEW OF THE MERGER

Procter & Gamble

The Procter & Gamble Company (P&G) was begun when immigrants William Procter and James Gamble settled in Cincinnati, Ohio, in 1837 and soon thereafter married sisters. At the urging of their father-in-law, the two men, one a candle maker and other a soap maker, created a partnership to manufacture and market their products in the Cincinnati area. The company's sales reached $1 million in 1859, but the company had yet to produce and market a national brand until 1879, when James Norris Gamble, son of the founder and a trained chemist, developed Ivory soap. Ivory quickly transformed Procter & Gamble into a national consumer products company with 30 brands and production facilities across the United States and Canada by 1890. The company added a food products division in 1911 when it introduced

Crisco and began a chemicals division to formalize research procedures and develop new products in 1917. P&G entered the hair care business in 1934 when it developed the first detergent-based shampoo. The company introduced popular-selling brands like Tide, Crest, Pampers, and Downy throughout the 1940s, 1950s, and 1960s.

The company expanded its presence in the cosmetics, fragrances, and toiletries industry in the 1980s with the acquisitions of Richardson-Vicks and Noxell. Richardson-Vicks was the producer of Oil of Olay and Pantene products, and Noxell manufactured and marketed Cover Girl, Noxema, and Clarion products. The company acquired Old Spice in 1990, Max Factor in 1991, Giorgio Beverly Hills in 1994, and Tambrands in 1997. Acquisitions during the 2000s included Clairol in 2001 and Wella shampoos and hair care products in 2003. In 2005, the company sold more than 300 brands in 160 countries. The company's business lineup included 16 billion-dollar brands, and P&G was the global market share leader in 7 of the 12 product categories in which it competed. Its closest rival was the market share leader in only two global markets.

P&G's businesses were organized into three product-based segments: Household Care; Health, Baby, and Family Care; and Beauty Care. The company's Household Care segment included fabric care, home care, snacks, coffee, and commercial services businesses. The Health, Baby, and Family Care division businesses included oral care, personal health care, pharmaceuticals, and pet health and nutrition. Beauty Care businesses manufactured and marketed retail and professional hair care products, feminine care products, cosmetics, fine fragrances, and personal cleansing products. The company's best-known brands in each of its business units are presented in Exhibit 1.

The Gillette Company

The history of shaving dates back to at least 3000 BC, when the first copper-bladed razors were fashioned. Razors through the 1800s were knifelike in their appearance and were prone to leaving gashes or nicks in the skin. The razor of the 21st century can be traced to the efforts of King C. Gillette and William Nickerson, who collaborated to invent the first razor with a safe, inexpensive, disposable blade. The invention

Exhibit 1   **P&G's Best-Known Brands Prior to Gillette Acquisition**

Household Care		
Brand Name	**Product Categories**	**Markets**
Ariel	Laundry detergent	Latin America, Europe, Middle East, Africa
Bounce	Dryer sheets	North America, Latin America, Asia
Dawn	Dishwashing liquid	North America, Latin America
Downy	Fabric softener	North America, Latin America, Europe, Middle East, Africa
Folgers	Whole bean, ground, and instant coffees	North America, Latin America
Gain	Laundry detergent	North America
Millstone	100% premium arabica bean coffees with over 65 varieties	North America
Mr. Clean	Multipurpose cleaner	North America, Asia
Pringles	Snack foods	North America, Latin America, Europe, Middle East, Africa, Asia
Swiffer	Sweeper system	North America, Latin America, Europe, Middle East, Africa
Tide	Laundry detergent	North America, Latin America, Europe, Middle East, Africa, Asia

Beauty Care		
Brand Name	**Product Categories**	**Markets**
Always	Sanitary pads	North America, Latin America, Europe, Middle East, Africa
Aussie	Shampoo and styling products	North America, Europe, Middle East, Africa
CoverGirl	Full line of beauty products for face, lips, eyes, and nails	North America, Latin America, Europe, Middle East, Africa, Asia
Giorgio	Fragrances	North America, Latin America, Europe, Middle East, Africa, Asia
Head & Shoulders	Shampoo	North America, Latin America, Europe, Middle East, Africa, Asia
Herbal Essences	Line of shampoos, conditioners, styling aids, and body washes	North America, Europe, Middle East, Africa, Latin America, Asia
Hugo Boss	Fragrances	North America, Latin America, Europe, Middle East, Africa, Asia
Infusium	Line of therapeutic, premium hair care products	North America, Latin America
Ivory	Line of detergent, dishwashing liquid, and body soap	North America, Latin America, Europe, Middle East, Africa, Asia
Max Factor	Full line of beauty products for face, lips, eyes, and nails	North America, Latin America, Europe, Middle East, Africa, Asia
Miss Clairol	Permanent hair color	North America, Europe, Middle East, Africa, Latin America, Asia
Nice 'n Easy	Permanent hair color	North America, Europe, Middle East, Africa, Latin America, Asia
Noxzema	Line of skin care products	North America, Latin America, Europe, Middle East, Africa
Olay	Line of skin care and cleansing products	North America, Latin America, Europe, Middle East, Africa, Asia

(Continued)

Exhibit 1   **Continued**

Beauty Care		
Brand Name	**Product Categories**	**Markets**
Old Spice	Line of shaving and fragrance products for men	North America, Latin America, Europe, Middle East, Africa, Asia
Pantene	Shampoos, conditioners, hairsprays, and styling aids	North America, Latin America, Europe, Middle East, Africa, Asia
Pert Plus	2-in-1 shampoo/conditioner, individual shampoos and conditioners	North America, Latin America, Europe, Middle East, Africa, Asia
Scope	Mouthwash	North America, Latin America
Secret	Antiperspirant	North America, Latin America, Europe, Middle East, Africa
Tampax	Tampons	North America, Latin America, Europe, Middle East, Africa, Asia
Vidal Sassoon	Hair washes, therapies, stylers, and specialty products	North America, Latin America, Europe, Middle East, Africa, Asia

Family Care		
Brand Name	**Product Categories**	**Markets**
Bounty	Paper towels	North America, Latin America
Charmin	Bathroom tissue	North America, Latin America, Europe, Middle East, Africa
Iams	Complete line of premium dog and cat foods	North America, Europe, Middle East, Africa, Latin America
Puffs	Facial tissues	North America, Latin America
PUR	Water filtration systems, including pitchers and faucet mounts	North America

Baby Care		
Brand Name	**Product Categories**	**Markets**
Luvs	Disposable diapers and wipes	North America, Latin America
Pampers	Disposable diapers, wet wipes, and bibs	North America, Latin America, Europe, Middle East, Africa, Asia

Health Care		
Brand Name	**Product Categories**	**Markets**
Crest	Toothpastes and toothbrushes	North America, Latin America, Europe, Middle East, Africa, Asia
NyQuil	Nighttime relief for temporary relief of cold/flu symptoms	North America, Latin America, Europe, Middle East, Africa
Pepto-Bismol	Antacidum that relieves most common stomach discomforts	North America, Latin America
Prilosec OTC	Over-the-counter medication used to treat frequent heartburn	North America
Vicks	Line of temporary cold symptom relief products and throat drops	North America, Latin America, Europe, Middle East, Africa, Asia

Source: www.pg.com.

led to the founding of the Gillette Company in 1901, which sold its first razors in 1903. The double-edged safety razor proved so popular with men that Gillette began to expand abroad in 1905, with the company opening a European headquarters in London. On the company's 25th anniversary in 1926, King C. Gillette heralded the success of the company's safety razor by stating, "There is no other article for individual use so universally known or widely distributed. In my travels, I have found it in the most northern town in Norway and in the heart of the Sahara Desert."[1]

In 2005, Gillette had expanded into five business segments: Blades and Razors, Duracell, Oral Care, Braun, and Personal Care. The company has maintained manufacturing operations in 14 countries and sold its products in over 200 countries. Five of Gillette's brands each accounted for more than $1 billion in annual sales. In addition to its blades and razors business unit holding the number-one position worldwide, Duracel was the global leader in alkaline battery sales to consumers, Oral B was the worldwide leader in manual and electric toothbrushes, and Braun was the best-selling brand of foil electric shavers for men and the number-one hair epilator for women. The company's Personal Care segment sold shaving creams, skin care products, and antiperspirants under the Gillette, Foamy, Satin Care, Right Guard, Soft & Dri, and Dry Idea brand names.

Rationale for Merger

Both P&G and Gillette management agreed that a merger between the two companies would offer four key benefits: (1) The companies had complementary strengths in product innovation and selling activities, (2) the merger would result in a stronger lineup of brands, (3) a merged company would generate additional opportunities for scale economies, and (4) a stronger lineup of brands would enhance relationships and bargaining power with retail buyers. Immediately upon consummation of the merger, management was to take Gillette products into developing markets such as China that were served by P&G, but not by Gillette. In addition, company managers planned to share R&D costs between P&G and Gillette products and to reduce more than $1 billion in non-value-adding costs in both business groups through synergies in purchasing and asset utilization. The companies' managers also agreed that both companies had similar cultures, visions, and values, which should facilitate their integration.

The acquisition would also better balance P&G's sales between Beauty Care, Health Care, Baby Care, Family Care, and Household Care, with approximately 50 percent of the combined company's revenues originating from the sales of Beauty and Health and 50 percent coming from the sales of Baby, Family, and Household. Also, the acquisition would give P&G 10 billion-dollar brands in Beauty and Health and 12 billion-dollar brands in Baby, Family, and Household. The merged company's nearly $2 billion R&D budget would be more than most of P&G's direct rivals combined, which should allow it to turn some if its 13 $500 million brands into billion-dollar brands. The combination of merger benefits led P&G management to increase its annual sales growth objectives through 2010 from 4–6 percent to 5–7 percent.

COMPETITIVE POSITION AND PERFORMANCE OF P&G AND GILLETTE BUSINESS UNITS

Procter & Gamble

In 2005, P&G's five business units held an average global market share of 30 percent and held 50–60 percent market shares in the Western Europe Baby Care and Feminine Care markets and the North American Fabric Care market. The company's management believed that P&G had a $15 billion opportunity for organic growth in its existing lineup of brands through continued international expansion. In 2005, emerging markets accounted for only 23 percent of P&G's sales, but accounted for 86 percent of the world's population. The combined GDPs of emerging markets represented 25 percent of the global GDP, but were expected to grow to 30 percent of global GDP by 2009.

P&G Beauty Care sales grew by 14 percent based on volume and 12 percent based on revenues in fiscal 2005, with its net earnings increasing by 22 percent for the year. The Beauty Care division held five billion-dollar brands. Pantene was the world's leading hair care brand in 2005, with sales of more than $2 billion and a 10 percent global share of the market. Head & Shoulders was the world's second best-selling brand of shampoo, with just under

10 percent of the market in 2005. P&G's fragrance lines had also experienced notable growth with the sales of Hugo Boss and Lacoste, each growing by more than 1,000 percent since 2001. Overall, the division's net sales had increased from $12.2 billion in fiscal 2003 to $19.5 billion in fiscal 2005, while net earnings for the division grew from $1.9 billion to $2.9 billion during the three-year period.

Net sales grew by 11 percent and net earning grew by 28 percent in fiscal 2005 for P&G's Family Care and Baby Care divisions. The Baby Care division held a 37 percent global market share in the category with products such as its Pampers line of disposable diapers and baby wipes. Billion-dollar brands in the Family Care division included Crest, Bounty, Charmin, and Iams. Health Care sales grew by 11 percent as well during fiscal 2005, but net income for the business segment increased by only 8 percent during the year. The company's best-known pharmaceutical products were Actonel and Prilosec OTC. Prilosec OTC held 35 percent of the U.S. heartburn treatment market, while Actonel had achieved a 33 percent global market share in the osteoporosis prevention market. The combined sales of all Baby, Family, and Health products increased from $15.7 billion in 2003 to $19.7 billion in 2005. Net income attributable to the divisions increased from $1.6 billion in fiscal 2003 to $2.3 billion in fiscal 2005.

The company's Household Care division recorded sales and earnings of $18.4 and $2.5 billion in fiscal 2005, respectively. The division's sales had grown from $15.2 billion in 2003, while net earnings contribution had increased from $2.3 billion. The company's top 10 household care products in 2005 were Folgers, Tide, Ariel, Downy, Pringles, and Dawn—all bringing in sales of more than $1 billion each. Gain, Ace, Mr. Clean, and Swifter were other best-selling P&G household products brands.

Approximately 52 percent of P&G's fiscal 2005 sales were from outside North America, with 24 percent originating in Western Europe, 5 percent coming from Northeast Asia, and 23 percent originating from developing geographies. The company's gross margins had improved from 49.0 percent in 2003 to 51.0 percent in 2005. Free cash flow and free cash flow productivity (the ratio of free cash flow to net income) had declined slightly between 2004 and 2005. Exhibit 2 presents a financial summary for Procter & Gamble.

The Gillette Company

The strong competitive position of Gillette's business units in their respective consumer segments was among the most enticing attributes of the company as an acquisition target for P&G. Gillette held the number-one position in each of its primary product categories in 2005, including a 70 percent market share in the global razor and razor blade market, a 40 percent global market share in alkaline

Exhibit 2   **Financial Summary for Procter & Gamble, Fiscal 2000–Fiscal 2005 (in millions, except per share amounts)**

	Year Ended June 30					
	2005	2004	2003	2002	2001	2000
Net sales	$56,741	$51,407	$43,377	$40,238	$39,244	$39,951
Operating income	10,927	9,827	7,853	6,678	4,736	5,954
Net earnings	7,257	6,481	5,186	4,352	2,922	3,542
Diluted net earnings per common share	$ 2.66	$ 2.32	$ 1.85	$ 1.54	$ 1.03	$ 1.23
Dividends per common share	1.03	0.93	0.82	0.76	0.70	0.64
Total assets	61,527	57,048	43,706	40,776	34,387	34,366
Long-term debt	12,887	12,554	11,475	11,201	9,792	9,012
Free cash flow*	6,541	7,338	7,218	6,063	3,318	1,657
Free cash flow productivity†	90.1%	113.2%	139.2%	139.3%	113.6%	46.8%

*Free cash flow represents operating cash flow less capital spending.
†Free cash flow productivity is the ratio of free cash flow to net earnings.
Source: Procter & Gamble 2002 and 2005 10-Ks and 2005 S-4.

batteries, a 36 percent market share of the world-wide market for manual and electric toothbrushes. Net sales for the entire company grew by 13 percent to $10.5 billion in 2004, while gross profit increased by 16 percent and net income grew by 22 percent in 2004. In 2004, 37.8 percent of Gillette's sales were in North America, 33.8 percent came from European markets, 11.2 percent originated in Africa and the Middle East, 9.6 percent came from Asia, and 7.4 percent were in Latin America.

The Gillette Company's management believed that its growth and margin opportunities were better than those available to other consumer staple producers because of consumers' preference for branded products. The overall private-label market share for consumer staple items in the United States was 15 percent, according to a 2003 ACNielsen survey. Some categories experienced even greater pricing pressure from private-label brands, with store brands capturing 18 percent of U.S. food and beverage sales in 2003. Sales of private-label razor blades represented only 5.3 percent of the market in 2003, private-label toothbrushes held only a 6.5 percent market share, and private-label alkaline batteries had captured only 12.7 percent of the U.S. market in 2003. P&G was similarly protected from private-label brands in many categories, with private-label antiperspirants accounting for just 0.4 percent of U.S. sales of such products in 2003.

Gillette had also been successful in urging consumers to trade up to higher-price-point personal care items. For example, the company sold low-cost Gillette double-edged blades for safety razors, entry-level shaving systems like the Gillette Sensor 3, and premium shaving systems such as the battery-powered M Power Mach 3. Consumers in developed markets such as the United States were increasingly trading up to higher-priced and higher-margin personal care products. In 2004, 56 percent of the U.S. blade market was held by brands charging more than $1.50 per blade, 37 percent of the market sold at price points between $0.45 and $1.50, and only 7 percent of the market was held by brands selling at less than $0.45 per blade. Gillette saw great opportunity for higher-end shaving systems in emerging markets since such shavers held only 8 percent of sales in regions such as Asia, Latin America, and Africa–Middle East. The company saw similar opportunities in the markets for power toothbrushes, alkaline batteries, and electric shavers. The transition

to higher-priced personal care products was already evident in growing economies such as Russia, where the sales of blades priced over $1.50 grew by 33 percent in 2004 to account for 41 percent of all blade sales. The sales of the lowest-priced blades declined by 19 percent in Russia during 2004.

Buyers of premium personal care products also tended to be highly loyal, with only 23 percent of Mach3 users indicating in a 2003 NCS-USA survey that they would try another brand if Mach3 shavers were out of stock during their trip to the supermarket. Seventy-two percent of men using less expensive disposable shavers indicated that they would purchase whatever brand was available. Women surveyed in the NCS-USA survey were equally loyal to Gillette shavers, with only 22 percent of Venus users suggesting they would purchase a different brand if no Venus blades were in stock.

The company had recorded its second consecutive year of record results in 2004, with its turnaround that began in 2000 fully completed. The company's net sales had grown at a 9 percent compounded annual growth rate between 2001 and 2004, while earnings per share had grown at a 19 percent compounded annual growth rate during the four-year period. The company's gross margins had also improved by 350 basis points between 2001 and 2004, and free cash flow had improved dramatically after the turnaround began in 2000. The company's total free cash flow between 1997 and 2000 was only $1.9 billion, while free cash flow generated between 2001 and 2004 exceeded $7 billion. Exhibit 3 presents a financial summary for the Gillette Company.

P&G'S SHARE PRICE OFFER

Most analysts understood the attractiveness of a Gillette acquisition for P&G. The two companies both enjoyed strong market positions and competed in relatively attractive consumer goods segments. Also, both companies had achieved outstanding recent financial performance—including the generation of free cash flows that would support further growth. In addition, the two companies management teams believed that P&G and Gillette had similar organizational cultures, which should prove to aid in the integration of the two companies and help P&G

Exhibit 3   **Financial Summary for the Gillette Company, 2000–2004 (in millions, except per share amounts)**

	2004	2003	2002	2001	2000
Net sales	$10,477	$ 9,252	$8,453	$8,084	$8,310
Operating income	2,465	2,003	1,809	1,498	1,512
Net earnings	1,691	1,385	1,216	910	392
Diluted net earnings per common share	1.68	1.35	1.15	0.86	0.37
Dividends per common share	0.65	0.65	0.65	0.65	0.65
Total assets	10,731	10,041	9,883	9,961	10,246
Long-term debt	2,142	2,453	2,457	1,654	1,650
Free cash flow*	1,630	2,232	1,672	1,468	811
Free cash flow productivity†	96.4%	161.2%	137.5%	161.3%	206.9%

*Free cash flow represents operating cash flow less capital spending.
†Free cash flow productivity is the ratio of free cash flow to net earnings.
Source: Gillette 2001 and 2004 10-Ks.

deliver its expected $1 billion–plus cost savings from cross-business strategic fits. There was also reason to believe that the combined company's key product categories would grow at high enough rates to support future increases in shareholder value. Gillette's calculation of compounded annual growth rates for consumer goods categories between 2000 and 2004 is presented in Exhibit 4. Exhibit 5 provides perpetuity growth rates for selected consumer product categories as prepared by Merrill Lynch for P&G shareholders evaluating the merger.

Merrill Lynch analysts expected the integration of the two companies and the elimination of duplicate value chain activities to take as long as three years, which might have a dilution effect on P&G's earnings per share (EPS). Specifically, Merrill Lynch's analysis indicated P&G's EPS might be higher between 2006 and 2008 if it were to continue to operate without the inclusion of Gillette's products. Merrill Lynch also suggested P&G's EPS might show positive effects from the merger if integration went quicker than expected and cost savings from synergies between

Exhibit 4   **Gillette's Compounded Annual Growth Rates for Consumer Products Categories, 2000–2004**

Consumer Product Category	Growth Rate for Global Market (CAGR for 2000–2004)
Blades and razors	8.2%
Oral care—toothbrushes	7.3
Skin care	6.8
Chocolate confectionery	6.5
Pet food/pet cares	6.5
Baked goods	4.9
Hair care	4.4
Alkaline batteries	3.7
Oral care—toothpaste	3.5
Laundry detergent	3.4
Carbonated soft drinks	3.4

Source: Gillette presentation to the CAGNY Conference, February 24, 2005.

Exhibit 5   Gillette's Perpetuity Growth Rates for Selected Consumer Product Categories

Consumer Product Category	Perpetuity Growth Rate Range
Blades and razors	2.8%–3.8%
Personal care	1.5%–2.5%
Duracell	(0.1%)–0.9%
Oral care	2.4%–3.4%
Braun	0.5%–1.5%

Source: P&G 2005 S-4.

brands were captured in fewer than three years. The projected impact of the Gillette acquisition on P&G's financial performance as calculated by Merrill Lynch is shown in Exhibit 6.

The $57 billion price P&G's board of directors agreed to pay for Gillette would give Gillette shareholders a 20.1 percent premium over Gillette's trading price one week prior to the January 28, 2005, merger announcement. P&G believed that the 20.1 percent share price premium would provide Gillette's board of directors with an adequate incentive to approve the merger and prevent outsiders from interfering with the outright purchase of the company. The $57 billion deal also represented a 5.5 multiple of Gillette's 2004 net sales and an 18.8 multiple of the company's 2004 earnings before interest, taxes, depreciation, and amortization (EBITDA). A comparison of purchase-price multiples and stock-price premiums for selected consumer goods acquisitions as prepared for Gillette shareholders by Goldman Sachs and UBS is presented in Exhibit 7. While the 20.1 percent per share purchase-price premium is within the range for other acquisitions examined by

Exhibit 6   Projected Range of Impact on P&G Performance by Gillette Acquisition

	Fiscal Year Ending June 30		
	2006E	2007E	2008E
Earnings per share	$(0.25)–$(0.30)	$(0.10)–$0.05	$(0.05)–$0.15
Earnings per share excluding one-time charges	$(0.21)–$(0.26)	$(0.09)–$0.06	$(0.05)–$0.15
Earnings per share excluding one-time charges and new amortization	$(0.16)–$(0.21)	$(0.03)–$0.12	$ 0.00–$0.20

Source: P&G 2005 S-4.

Exhibit 7   Gillette's Purchase-Price Multiples and Stock-Price Premiums for Selected Consumer Goods Acquisitions

	Purchase-Price Multiples for Selected Consumer Goods Acquisitions		Per Share Purchase-Price Premium based on Stock Price
	Sales	EBITDA	One Week Prior to Announcement
Median	2.2x	13.0x	19.30%
Mean	2.2x	13.2x	29.10%
Range	1.1x–4.1x	8.4x–17.6x	5.3%–92.6%
Gillette at $54.05	5.5x	18.8x	20.1%*

*Relative to closing price on Wednesday, January 19, 2005.
Source: P&G 2005 S-4.

Exhibit 8   **Transaction Value and Per Share Purchase-Price Premiums Paid in Selected Consumer Goods Acquisitions, 1994–2004**

Announcement Date	Acquirer	Target	Transaction Value (in billions)	Premium to Share Price One Week Prior to Announcement
6/2000	Phillip Morris	Nabisco	$19.2	103.2%
8/1994	Johnson & Johnson	Neutrogena	1.0	76.3
11/2004	Constellation Brands	Robert Mondavi	1.4	52.3
3/2003	Procter & Gamble	Wella	7.0	47.3
10/2003	Tchibo	Beiersdorf	13.0	45.7
6/2000	Unilever	Bestfoods	23.7	39.9
12/2000	PepsiCo	Quaker Oats	15.1	24.0
				Average 55.5%

Source: P&G 2005 S-4.

UBS and Goldman Sachs, the purchase-price multiple exceeds that of prior acquisitions.

Merrill Lynch's analysis of the per share purchase-price premiums paid to acquire selected consumer goods between 1994 and 2004 left room for debate as to whether P&G's 20.1 percent offer was fair to Gillette shareholders. Merrill Lynch's purchase-price evaluation based on Gillette's January 26, 2005, closing price indicates the price might be considered low, although calculations based on Gillette's 52-week low and three-year average stock price was near the average paid in other acquisitions (see Exhibits 8 and 9).

Exhibit 9   **Multiples and Premium for P&G's Share Price Offer for Gillette as Calculated by Merrill Lynch**

	Gillette at Offer Price
2004 sales	5.5x
2004 EBITDA	18.8
Premium to:	
1 day (based on Gillette closing price of ($45.00 on 1/26/05)	20.1%
52-week high	18.7%
52-week low	45.9
3-year average	52.4

Source: P&G 2005 S-4.

Since P&G's shares traded for a higher price at the time of the merger than Gillette shares, Gillette shareholders received a fraction of a P&G share in exchange for their Gillette holdings. The relationship between P&G's prevailing stock price and Gillette's price resulted in an exchange ratio of 0.975. For example, a Gillette stockholder owning 1,000 Gillette shares would receive 975 P&G shares upon the completion of the merger. Fractional shares were not awarded, so a Gillette shareholder owning 100 shares would receive only 97 P&G shares.

Merrill Lynch also calculated a range of appropriate exchange ratios based on Gillette's expected contribution to the combined company's net income and the amount of levered free cash flow provided by Gillette brands (see Exhibit 10). Levered free cash flow represents free cash flow less additional debt service taken on as a result of the acquisition of Gillette. Based on the analysts' estimates of net income contributed by Gillette brands, P&G would be required to capture at least two-thirds of the expected synergies between the company's brands to approach the 0.975 exchange ratio offered to Gillette shareholders. Using the estimates based on levered free cash flow, the 0.975 exchange ratio could be justified if at least some expected synergies were achieved.

Exhibit 11 shows the financial projections used in Merrill Lynch's exchange ratio calculations to estimate the importance of Gillette's brands to the combined company's performance through 2008.

Exhibit 10   **Merrill Lynch's Estimation of Appropriate Exchange Ratios**

	Assuming No Expected Synergies Are Achieved	
	Low Estimate	High Estimate
Exchange ratio based on net income contribution for Gillette brands	0.654	0.684
Exchange ratio based on levered free cash flow provided by Gillette brands	0.848	0.875
	Assuming 50% of Expected Synergies Are Achieved	
	Low Estimate	High Estimate
Exchange ratio based on net income contribution for Gillette brands	0.876	0.886
Exchange ratio based on levered free cash flow provided by Gillette brands	1.108	1.152
	Assuming 2/3 of Expected Synergies Are Achieved	
	Low Estimate	High Estimate
Exchange ratio based on net income contribution for Gillette brands	0.941	0.963
Exchange ratio based on levered free cash flow provided by Gillette brands	1.190	1.252

Source: P&G 2005 S-4.

Exhibit 11   **Financial Projections**

	Procter & Gamble's Contribution to Combined Company	Gillette's Contribution to Combined Company
Sales		
CY* 2004E	83.6%	16.4%
CY 2005E	83.8	16.2
EBITDA		
CY 2004E	80.0	20.0
CY 2005E	79.1	20.9
EBIT		
CY 2004E	80.9	19.1
CY 2005E	79.7	20.3
Net Income		
CY 2004E	80.3	19.7
CY 2005E	78.9	21.1
CY 2006E	78.4	21.6
CY 2007	78.3	21.7
CY 2008	78.3	21.7

*Contributions based on calendar year (CY), since P&G's fiscal year ends June 30 and Gillette's fiscal year ends December 31.

Source: P&G 2005 S-4.

P&G'S EARLY POSTMERGER PERFORMANCE

As the 2005 calendar year ended and P&G closed out its first quarter as a merged company, its managers were pleased that the company's performance seemed to be exceeding analysts' predictions. The company anticipated that its audited reports would show sales growth for the quarter ending December 31, 2005, to come in at 25–26 percent. Prior to the consummation of the merger, the company's managers and financial advisers had projected sales growth for the quarter to be in the 23–26 percent range. The company's managers attributed the increase in revenues to 6–7 percent organic sales growth in its Household Care and Beauty Care business units. Much of that increase was attributable to the performance of Gillette's blades and razors, Duracell, and Braun brands, which had grown by an estimated 17 percent during the quarter. Prior to the merger, Gillette's brands had been expected to grow at a low-single-digit rate.

Procter & Gamble managers also expected that final tabulations for the quarter would report a quarterly EPS of $0.68–$0.69, which was at the very top end of the $0.66–$0.69 projected for the quarter. The achievement of best-case quarterly EPS estimate led P&G managers to predict EPS dilution for the 2006 fiscal year to be no more than $0.20 to $0.26 per share. In assessing the impact of the merger on P&G performance for 2006, Merrill Lynch analysts had expected EPS dilution to fall between $0.25 and $0.30 per share.

P&G announced on January 4, 2006, that it would acquire the Fab, Trojan, Dynamo, and Paic laundry detergent brands marketed in Hong Kong, Singapore, Thailand, and Malaysia from Colgate-Palmolive. The new brands would boost P&G's market share in the category from 2.1 percent to 12.9 percent in Singapore, from 0.3 percent to 7.9 percent in Thailand, from 0.3 percent to 12.5 percent in Malaysia, and from 1.2 percent to 12.5 percent in Hong Kong. The company's market performance relative to the S&P 500 from January 1996 to December 2005 is presented in Exhibit 12. The exhibit also provides a comparison of P&G's stock performance relative to the S&P 500 for the January–December 2005 period.

Exhibit 12   **Performance of Procter & Gamble's Stock Price, January 1996–December 2005**

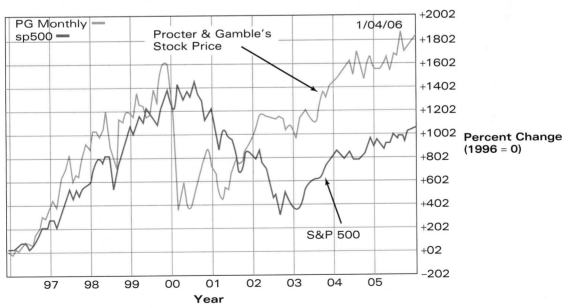

(a) Performance of Procter & Gamble's Stock Price versus the S&P 500.

(Continued)

Exhibit 12   **Continued**

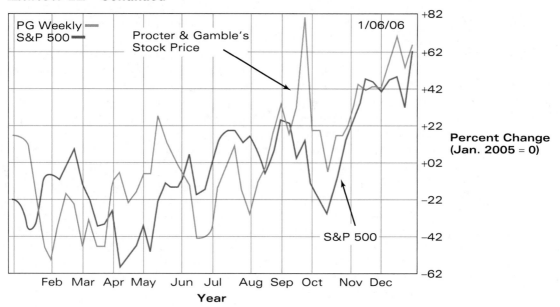

(b) Performance of Procter & Gamble's Stock Price versus the S&P 500 between January 2005 and December 2005.

Endnotes

[1]As quoted in "Gillette at a Glance," http://www.gillette.com/company/gilletteataglance.asp

Robin Hood

Joseph Lampel
New York University

It was in the spring of the second year of his insurrection against the High Sheriff of Nottingham that Robin Hood took a walk in Sherwood Forest. As he walked he pondered the progress of the campaign, the disposition of his forces, the Sheriff's recent moves, and the options that confronted him.

The revolt against the Sheriff had begun as a personal crusade. It erupted out of Robin's conflict with the Sheriff and his administration. However, alone Robin Hood could do little. He therefore sought allies, men with grievances and a deep sense of justice. Later he welcomed all who came, asking few questions and demanding only a willingness to serve. Strength, he believed, lay in numbers.

He spent the first year forging the group into a disciplined band, united in enmity against the Sheriff and willing to live outside the law. The band's organization was simple. Robin ruled supreme, making all important decisions. He delegated specific tasks to his lieutenants. Will Scarlett was in charge of intelligence and scouting. His main job was to shadow the Sheriff and his men, always alert to their next move. He also collected information on the travel plans of rich merchants and tax collectors. Little John kept discipline among the men and saw to it that their archery was at the high peak that their profession demanded. Scarlock took care of the finances, converting loot to cash, paying shares of the take, and finding suitable hiding places for the surplus. Finally, Much the Miller's son had the difficult task of provisioning the ever-increasing band of Merrymen.

The increasing size of the band was a source of satisfaction for Robin, but also a source of concern. The fame of his Merrymen was spreading, and new recruits were pouring in from every corner of England. As the band grew larger, their small bivouac became a major encampment. Between raids the men milled about, talking and playing games. Vigilance was in decline, and discipline was becoming harder to enforce. "Why," Robin reflected, "I don't know half the men I run into these days."

The growing band was also beginning to exceed the food capacity of the forest. Game was becoming scarce, and supplies had to be obtained from outlying villages. The cost of buying food was beginning to drain the band's financial reserves at the very moment when revenues were in decline. Travelers, especially those with the most to lose, were now giving the forest a wide berth. This was costly and inconvenient to them, but it was preferable to having all their goods confiscated.

Robin believed that the time had come for the Merrymen to change their policy of outright confiscation of goods to one of a fixed transit tax. His lieutenants strongly resisted this idea. They were proud of the Merrymen's famous motto: "Rob the rich and give to the poor." "The farmers and the townspeople," they argued, "are our most important allies. How can we tax them, and still hope for their help in our fight against the Sheriff?"

Robin wondered how long the Merrymen could keep to the ways and methods of their early days. The Sheriff was growing stronger and becoming better organized. He now had the money and the men and was beginning to harass the band, probing for its weaknesses. The tide of events was beginning to turn against the Merrymen. Robin felt that the campaign must be decisively concluded before the Sheriff had a chance to deliver a mortal blow. "But how," he wondered, "could this be done?"

Robin had often entertained the possibility of killing the Sheriff, but the chances for this seemed increasingly remote. Besides, killing the Sheriff might satisfy his personal thirst for revenge, but it would not improve the situation. Robin had hoped that the perpetual state of unrest, and the Sheriff's failure to collect taxes, would lead to his removal from office. Instead, the Sheriff used his political connections to obtain reinforcement. He had powerful friends at court and was well regarded by the regent, Prince John.

Prince John was vicious and volatile. He was consumed by his unpopularity among the people, who wanted the imprisoned King Richard back. He also lived in constant fear of the barons, who had first given him the regency but were now beginning to dispute his claim to the throne. Several of these barons had set out to collect the ransom that would release King Richard the Lionheart from his jail in Austria. Robin was invited to join the conspiracy in return for future amnesty. It was a dangerous proposition. Provincial banditry was one thing, court intrigue another. Prince John had spies everywhere, and he was known for his vindictiveness. If the conspirators' plan failed, the pursuit would be relentless, and retributions swift.

The sound of the supper horn startled Robin from his thoughts. There was the smell of roasting venison in the air. Nothing was resolved or settled. Robin headed for camp promising himself that he would give these problems his utmost attention after tomorrow's raid.

Dilemma at Devil's Den

Allen Cohen
Babson College

Kim Johnson
Babson College

My name is Susan, and I'm a business student at Mt. Eagle College. Let me tell you about one of my worst experiences. I had a part-time job in the campus snack bar, The Devil's Den. At the time, I was 21 years old and a junior with a concentration in finance. I originally started working at the Den in order to earn some extra spending money. I had been working there for one semester and became upset with some of the happenings. The Den was managed by contract with an external company, College Food Services (CFS). What bothered me was that many employees were allowing their friends to take free food, and the employees themselves were also taking food in large quantities when leaving their shifts. The policy was that employees could eat whatever they liked free of charge while they were working, but it had become common for employees to leave with food and not to be charged for their snacks while off duty as well.

I felt these problems were occurring for several reasons. For example, employee wages were low, there was easy access to the unlocked storage room door, and inventory was poorly controlled. Also, there was weak supervision by the student managers and no written rules or strict guidelines. It seemed that most of the employees were enjoying freebies, and it had been going on for so long that it was taken for granted. The problem got so far out of hand that customers who had seen others do it felt free to do it whether they knew the workers or not.

The employees who witnessed this never challenged anyone because, in my opinion, they did not care and they feared the loss of friendship or being frowned upon by others. Apparently, speaking up was more costly to the employees than the loss of money to CFS for the unpaid food items. It seemed obvious to me that the employees felt too secure in their jobs and did not feel that their jobs were in jeopardy.

The employees involved were those who worked the night shifts and on the weekends. They were students at the college and were under the supervision of another student, who held the position of manager. There were approximately 30 student employees and 6 student managers on the staff. During the day there were no student managers; instead, a full-time manager was employed by CFS to supervise the Den. The employees and student managers were mostly freshmen and sophomores, probably because of the low wages, inconvenient hours (late weeknights and weekends), and the duties of the job itself. Employees were hard to come by; the high rate of employee turnover indicated that the job qualifications and the selection process were minimal.

The student managers were previous employees chosen by other student managers and the full-time CFS day manager on the basis of their ability to work and on their length of employment. They received no further formal training or written rules beyond what they had already learned by working there. The student managers were briefed on how to close the snack bar at night but still did not get the job done properly. They received authority and responsibility over events occurring during their shifts as manager, although they were never actually taught how and when to enforce it! Their increase in pay was small, from a starting pay of just over minimum wage to an additional 15 percent for student managers. Regular employees received an additional nickel for each semester of employment.

Although I only worked seven hours per week, I was in the Den often as a customer and saw the problem frequently. I felt the problem was on a large enough scale that action should have been taken, not only to correct any financial loss that the Den might have experienced but also to help give the student employees a true sense of their responsibilities, the limits of their freedom, respect for rules, and pride in their jobs. The issues at hand bothered my conscience, although I was not directly involved. I felt that the employees and customers were taking advantage of the situation whereby they could "steal" food almost whenever they wanted. I believed that I had been brought up correctly and knew right from wrong, and I felt that the happenings in the Den were wrong. It wasn't fair that CFS paid for others' greediness or urges to show what they could get away with in front of their friends.

I was also bothered by the lack of responsibility of the managers to get the employees to do their work. I had seen the morning employees work very hard trying to do their jobs, in addition to the jobs the closing shift should have done. I assumed the night managers did not care or think about who worked the next day. It bothered me to think that the morning employees were suffering because of careless employees and student managers from the night before.

I had never heard of CFS mentioning any problems or taking any corrective action; therefore, I wasn't sure whether they knew what was going on, or if they were ignoring it. I was speaking to a close friend, Mack, a student manager at the Den, and I mentioned the fact that the frequently unlocked door to the storage room was an easy exit through which I had seen different quantities of unpaid goods taken out. I told him about some specific instances and said that I believed that it happened rather frequently. Nothing was ever said to other employees about this, and the only corrective action was that the door was locked more often, yet the key to the lock was still available upon request to all employees during their shifts.

Another lack of strong corrective action I remembered was when an employee was caught pocketing cash from the register. The student was neither suspended nor threatened with losing his job (nor was the event even mentioned). Instead, he was just told to stay away from the register. I felt that this weak punishment happened not because he was a good worker but because he worked so many hours and it would be difficult to find someone who would work all those hours and remain working for more than a few months. Although a customer reported the incident, I still felt that management should have taken more corrective action.

The attitudes of the student managers seemed to vary. I had noticed that one in particular, Bill, always got the job done. He made a list of each small duty that needed to be done, such as restocking, and he made sure the jobs were divided among the employees and finished before his shift was over. Bill also stared down employees who allowed thefts by their friends or who took freebies themselves; yet I had never heard of an employee being challenged verbally, nor had anyone ever been fired for these actions. My friend Mack was concerned about theft, or so I assumed, because he had taken some action about locking the doors, but he didn't really get after employees to work if they were slacking off.

I didn't think the rest of the student managers were good motivators. I noticed that they did little work themselves and did not show much control over the employees. The student managers allowed their friends to take food for free, thereby setting bad examples for the other workers, and allowed the employees to take what they wanted even when they were not working. I thought their attitudes were shared by most of the other employees: not caring about their jobs or working hard, as long as they got paid and their jobs were not threatened.

I had let the "thefts" continue without mention because I felt that no one else really cared and may even have frowned upon me for trying to take action. Management thus far had not reported significant losses to the employees so as to encourage them to watch for theft and prevent it. Management did not threaten employees with job loss, nor did they provide employees with supervision. I felt it was not my place to report the theft to management, because I was just an employee and I would be overstepping the student managers. Also, I was unsure whether management would do anything about it anyway—maybe they did not care. I felt that talking to the student managers or other employees would be useless, because they were either abusing the rules themselves or were clearly aware of what was going on and just ignored it. I felt that others may have frowned upon me and made it uncomfortable for me to continue working there. This would be very difficult for me, because I wanted to become a student manager the next semester and did not want to create any waves that might have prevented me from doing so. I recognized the student manager position as a chance to gain some managerial and leadership skills, while at the same time adding a great plus to my resume when I graduated. Besides, as a student manager, I would be in a better position to do something about all the problems at the Den that bothered me so much.

What could I do in the meantime to clear my conscience of the freebies, favors to friends, and employee snacks? What could I do without ruining my chances of becoming a student manager myself someday? I hated just keeping quiet, but I didn't want to make a fool of myself. I was really stuck.

Wal-Mart Stores Inc.: Combating Critics and Sustaining Growth

Arthur A. Thompson
The University of Alabama

Throughout 2005, Wal-Mart executives were engaged in a charm offensive to combat growing outcries from the company's critics. Numerous journalists, union leaders, community activists, and so-called cultural progressives were uniting in a campaign to bash Wal-Mart on a variety of fronts and turn public opinion against the company and its seemingly virtuous business model of relentlessly wringing cost efficiencies out of its supply chain and providing customers with everyday low prices. At the center of the crusade to cast Wal-Mart in a bad light were Wal-Mart Watch and Wake Up Wal-Mart.[1] Wal-Mart Watch was founded by Andrew Stern, president of the Service Employees International Union. Wake Up Wal-Mart was a project of the United Food and Commercial Workers International Union (UFCW). Wal-Mart Watch had an e-mail utility that visitors could use to direct the recipient to anti–Wal-Mart "facts"; the e-mail had the tag line, "I thought you might enjoy this story from Wal-Mart Watch, a group who is starting to expose Wal-Mart for their bad labor standards, political corruptness and overall bad citizenship. It's getting a lot of attention in the press. Take a look."[2]

The biggest complaint of critics was that Wal-Mart's zealous pursuit of low costs had resulted in substandard wages and insufficient medical benefits for Wal-Mart's 1.3 million U.S. employees. Others opposed Wal-Mart on the grounds that it sourced too much of its merchandise from Chinese suppliers (about $18 billion), thus costing jobs for American workers and hastening the decline of the U.S. manu-

facturing sector. Some said the "Beast of Bentonville" was too big and too powerful.

Community activists in California, New York, Vermont, Massachusetts, and several other areas were vigorously opposing the company's attempts to open big-box stores in their locales, claiming that they were unsightly and detracted from the small-merchant atmosphere they wanted to preserve. Wal-Mart's low prices tended to attract customers away from apparel shops, general stores, pharmacies, sporting goods stores, shoe stores, hardware stores, supermarkets, and convenience stores operated by local merchants. It was common for a number of local businesses that carried merchandise similar to Wal-Mart's lines to fail within a year or two of Wal-Mart's arrival—this phenomenon, known as the "Wal-Mart effect," was so potent that it had spawned sometimes fierce local resistance to the entry of a new Wal-Mart among both local merchants and area residents wanting to preserve the economic vitality of their downtown areas.

Union leaders at the UFCW, which represented workers at many supermarket chains, were adamant in their opposition to the opening of Wal-Mart Supercenters that had a full-sized supermarket in addition to the usual merchandise selection. The UFCW and its Wake Up Wal-Mart organization were exerting all the pressure they could to force Wal-Mart to raise its wages and benefits for associates to levels that would be comparable to union wages and benefits at unionized supermarket chains. A UFCW spokesperson said:

> Their productivity is becoming a model for taking advantage of workers, and our society is doomed

if we think the answer is to lower our standards to Wal-Mart's level. What we need to do is to raise Wal-Mart to the standard we have set using the supermarket industry as an example so that Wal-Mart does not destroy our society community by community.[3]

Wal-Mart's labor costs were said to be 20 percent less than those at unionized supermarkets.[4] In Dallas, 20 supermarkets had closed once Wal-Mart had saturated the area with its Supercenters. According to one source, for every Wal-Mart Supercenter opened in the next five years, two other supermarkets would be forced to close.[5] A trade publication had estimated that Wal-Mart's plans to open more than 1,000 Supercenters in the United States in the 2004–2008 period would boost Wal-Mart's grocery and related revenues from $82 billion to $162 billion, thus increasing its market share in groceries from 19 percent to 35 percent and its share of pharmacy and drugstore-related sales from 15 percent to 25 percent.[6]

Wal-Mart's public image had also taken a hit in late 2003 when federal agents had arrested nearly 250 illegal immigrants after cleaning shifts at 61 Wal-Mart stores in 21 states. Agents had searched a manager's office at Wal-Mart's Bentonville headquarters and taken 18 boxes of documents relating to cleaning contractors dating back to March 2000.[7] Federal officials reportedly had wiretaps showing that Wal-Mart officials knew its janitorial contractors were using illegal cleaning crews. Wal-Mart, however, was indignant about the charges, saying that Wal-Mart had cooperated with federal authorities in the investigations for almost three years, helped agents tape conversations between some of its store managers and employees of the cleaning contractors suspected of using illegal immigrants, and revised its cleaning contracts in 2002 to include language that janitorial contractors comply with all federal, state, and local employment laws (because of the information developed in 2001), and begun bringing all janitorial work in-house because outsourcing was more expensive— at the time of the arrests, fewer than 700 Wal-Mart stores used outside cleaning contractors, down from almost half in 2000. In March 2005, Wal-Mart settled the charges with the Justice Department.

Wal-Mart had been criticized for refusing to stock CDs or DVDs with parental warning stickers (mostly profanity-laced hip-hop music) and for either pulling certain racy magazines (*Maxim, Stuff,* and *FHM*) from its shelves or obscuring their covers. Critics contended that Wal-Mart made no effort to survey shoppers about how they felt about such products but rather that it responded in ad hoc fashion to complaints lodged by a relative handful of customers and by conservative outside groups.[8] Wal-Mart had also been the only one of the top 10 drugstore chains to refuse to stock Preven, a morning-after contraceptive introduced in 1999, because company executives did not want its pharmacists have to grapple with the moral dilemma of abortion.

Moreover, Wal-Mart's high profile had made it a lightning rod for lawsuits. It was confronting roughly 6,000 lawsuits on a variety of issues, including one that it discriminated against female employees and another that claimed Wal-Mart forced employees to work beyond their shifts.

Initially, H. Lee Scott, Wal-Mart's CEO, and other top Wal-Mart executives had shrugged off the criticism and concentrated their full attention on running the business and expanding the company's operations into more countries and more communities. But in 2004–2005, Scott started to see that all the Wal-Mart bashing was taking a toll on the company's sales growth and throwing up roadblocks to its expansion plans. He decided that Wal-Mart ought to reach out to its critics, see if their concerns had merit, and explore whether Wal-Mart ought to alter some of its practices. But, while it made good business sense for Wal-Mart to be responsive to societal expectations, he knew that the company could not simply abandon doing things that were the keys to its success.[9]

COMPANY BACKGROUND

Wal-Mart's journey from humble beginnings in the 1960s as a folksy discount retailer in the boondocks of Arkansas to a global retailing juggernaut in 2006 was unprecedented among the companies of the world:

	1962	1970	1980	1990	2000	2005
Sales	$1.4 million	$31 million	$1.2 billion	$26 billion	$191 billion	$285 billion
Profits	$112,000	$1.2 million	$41 million	$1 billion	$6.3 billion	$10.3 billion
Stores	9	32	276	1,528	4,188	5,289

Wal-Mart grew its sales by $29 billion in 2004 and by $30 billion in 2005; sales were expected to reach $315 billion in fiscal 2006. It was the largest retailer in Canada and Mexico, as well as in the United States and the world as a whole. According to a 2003 report by the prominent Boston Consulting Group, "The world has never known a company with such ambition, capability, and momentum."

Just as unprecedented was Wal-Mart's impact on general merchandise retailing and the attraction its stores had to shoppers in locations where it had stores. In 2005, about 140 million people in 16 countries shopped Wal-Mart's 5,300 stores every week. More than half of American shoppers visited a Wal-Mart at least once a month, and one-third went once a week—in 2002 an estimated 82 percent of American households made at least one purchase at Wal-Mart.[10] Since the early 1990s, the company had gone from dabbling in supermarket sales to number one in grocery retailing worldwide. In the United States, Wal-Mart was the biggest employer in 21 states. The company employed about 1.7 million people worldwide and was expanding its workforce by about 120,000 new jobs annually.[11]

Wal-Mart's performance and prominence in the retailing industry had resulted in numerous awards. It had been named "Retailer of the Century" by *Discount Store News,* made the *Fortune* magazine lists of "Most Admired Companies in America" (it was ranked first in 2003 and 2004 and fourth in 2005) and "100 Best Companies to Work for in America," and been included on *Financial Times'* "Most Respected in the World" list. In 2005, Wal-Mart was ranked second on *Fortune's* list of the "Global Most Admired Companies." In 2002, 2003, 2004, and 2005, Wal-Mart was number one on the Fortune 500 list of the largest companies in America and also on the Fortune Global 500 list. Wal-Mart received the 2002 Ron Brown Award, the highest presidential award recognizing outstanding achievement in employee relations and community initiatives. In 2003, American Veterans Awards gave Wal-Mart its Corporate Patriotism Award. Wal-Mart was the largest corporate contributor to charitable causes in the United States, with 2005 contributions of over $200 million.

Exhibit 1 provides a summary of Wal-Mart's financial and operating performance for the 1993–2005 fiscal years. Wal-Mart's success had made the Walton family (Sam Walton's heirs and living relatives) exceptionally wealthy—in 2005, five Walton family members controlled about 1.73 billion shares of Wal-Mart stock worth about $87 billion. Increases in the value of Wal-Mart's stock over the years had made hundreds of Wal-Mart employees, retirees, and shareholders millionaires or multimillionaires. Since 1970, when Wal-Mart shares were first issued to the public, the company's stock had split 11 times. A 100-share investment in Wal-Mart stock in 1970 at the initial offer price of $16.50 equated to 204,800 shares worth $10.2 million as of December 2005.

Sam Walton, Founder of Wal-Mart

Sam Walton graduated from the University of Missouri in 1940 with a degree in economics and took a job as a management trainee at J. C. Penney Company. His career with Penney's ended with a call to military duty in World War II. When the war was over, Walton decided to purchase a franchise and open a Ben Franklin retail variety store in Newport, Arkansas, rather than return to Penney's. When the lease on the Newport building was lost five years later, Walton decided to relocate his business to Bentonville, Arkansas, where he bought a building and opened Walton's 5 & 10 as a Ben Franklin–affiliated store. By 1960, Walton was the largest Ben Franklin franchisee, with nine stores. But Walton was becoming concerned about the long-term competitive threat to variety stores posed by the emerging popularity of giant supermarkets and discounters. An avid pilot, he took off in his plane on a cross-country tour studying the changes in stores and retailing trends, then put together a plan for a discount store of his own because he believed deeply in the retailing concept of offering significant price discounts to expand sales volumes and increase overall profits. Walton went to Chicago to try to interest Ben Franklin executives in expanding into discount retailing; when they turned him down, he decided to go forward on his own.

The first Wal-Mart Discount City opened July 2, 1962, in Rogers, Arkansas. The store was successful, and Walton quickly began to look for opportunities to open stores in other small towns and to attract talented people with retailing experience to help him grow the business. Although he started out as a seat-of-the-pants merchant, he had great instincts, was quick to learn from other retailers' successes and failures, and was adept at garnering ideas for

Exhibit 1   **Financial and Operating Summary, Wal-Mart Stores, Fiscal Years 1993–2005 (dollar amounts in billions, except earnings per share data)**

	Fiscal Year Ending January 31					
	2005	2004	2003	2002	2000	1993
Financial and operating data						
Net sales	$285.2	$256.3	$229.6	$204.0	$156.2	$55.5
Net sales increase	11.3%	11.6%	12.6%	12.8%	19.7%	26.0%
Domestic comparable store sales increase*	3%	4%	5%	6%	8%	11%
Cost of sales	219.8	198.7	178.3	159.1	121.8	44.2
Operating, selling, general and administrative expenses	51.1	44.9	40.0	35.1	26.0	8.3
Interest costs, net	1.0	0.8	0.9	1.2	0.8	0.3
Net income	$ 10.3	$ 8.9	$ 8.0	$ 6.4	$ 5.3	$ 2.0
Earnings per share of common stock (diluted)	$2.41	$2.07	$1.79	$1.47	$1.19	$0.44
Balance sheet data						
Current assets	$ 38.5	$ 34.2	$ 29.5	$ 26.6	$ 23.5	$10.2
Net property, plant, equipment, and capital leases	68.6	55.2	51.4	45.2	35.5	9.8
Total assets	120.2	104.9	92.9	81.5	69.0	20.6
Current liabilities	42.9	37.4	32.2	26.7	25.5	6.8
Long-term debt	20.1	17.5	16.6	15.7	13.7	3.1
Long-term obligations under capital leases	3.6	3.0	3.0	3.0	3.0	1.8
Shareholders' equity	49.4	43.6	39.5	35.2	25.9	8.6
Financial ratios						
Current ratio	0.9	0.9	0.9	1.0	0.9	1.5
Return on assets	9.3%	8.6%	9.2%	8.4%	9.8%	11.1%
Return on shareholders' equity	22.1%	20.6%	20.9%	19.4%	22.9%	25.3%
Other year-end data						
Number of domestic Wal-Mart discount stores	1,353	1,478	1,568	1,647	1,801	1,848
Number of domestic Wal-Mart Supercenters	1,713	1,471	1,258	1,066	721	34
Number of domestic Sam's Clubs	551	538	525	500	463	256
Number of domestic Neighborhood Markets	85	64	49	31	7	—
Number of international stores	1,587	1,355	1,272	1,154	991	10

*Based on sales at stores open a full-year that have not been expanded or relocated in the past 12 months.
Source: Wal-Mart annual reports for 2003 and 2005.

improvements from employees and promptly trying them out. Sam Walton incorporated his business as Wal-Mart Stores in 1969, with headquarters in obscure Bentonville, Arkansas—in 2005, the Wal-Mart-related traffic into and out of Bentonville was sufficient to support daily nonstop flights from New York City and Chicago. When the company went public in 1970, it had 38 stores and sales of $44.2 million. In 1979, with 276 stores, 21,000 employees, and operations in 11 states, Wal-Mart became the first company to reach $1 billion in sales in such a short period of time.

As the company grew, Sam Walton proved an effective and visionary leader. His folksy demeanor and his talent for motivating people, combined with a hands-on management style and an obvious talent for discount retailing, produced a culture and a set of values and beliefs that kept Wal-Mart on a path of continuous innovation and rapid expansion. Moreover, Wal-Mart's success and Walton's personable style of leadership generated numerous stories in the media that cast the company and its founder in a positive light. As Wal-Mart emerged as the premier discount retailer in the United States in the 1980s, an uncommonly large cross-section of the American public came to know who Sam Walton was and to associate his name with Wal-Mart. Regarded by many as "the entrepreneur of the century" and "a genuine American folk hero," he enjoyed a reputation of being concerned for employees, community-spirited, and a devoted family man who epitomized the American dream and demonstrated the virtues of hard work. People inside and outside the company held him in high esteem.

Just before Sam Walton's death in 1992, his vision was for Wal-Mart to become a $125 billion company by 2000. But his handpicked successor, David D. Glass, beat that target by almost two years. Under Glass's leadership (1988–2000), Wal-Mart's sales grew at an average annual compound rate of 19 percent, pushing revenues up from $20.6 billion to $156 billion. When David Glass retired in January 2000, Lee Scott was chosen as Wal-Mart's third president and CEO. In the five years that Lee Scott had been CEO, Wal-Mart's sales had grown over $145 billion, almost matching the company's growth in its first 30 years. Even though there were Wal-Mart stores in all 50 states and 15 foreign countries in 2005, Scott and other senior executives believed there were sufficient domestic and foreign growth opportunities to permit the company to grow at double-digit rates for the foreseeable future and propel Wal-Mart's revenues past $500 billion by 2010. Wal-Mart had only a 3 percent share of global retail sales in the merchandise lines it stocked.

WAL-MART'S STRATEGY

The hallmarks of Wal-Mart's strategy were multiple store formats, low everyday prices, wide selection, a big percentage of name-brand merchandise, a customer-friendly store environment, low operating costs, innovative merchandising, a strong emphasis on customer satisfaction, disciplined expansion into new geographic markets, and the use of acquisitions to enter foreign country markets. On the outside of every Wal-Mart store in big letters was the message "We Sell for Less." The company's advertising tag line reinforced the low-price theme: "Always low prices. Always." Major merchandise lines included housewares, consumer electronics, sporting goods, lawn and garden items, health and beauty aids, apparel, home fashions, paint, bed and bath goods, hardware, jewelry, automotive repair and maintenance, toys and games, and groceries.

Multiple Store Formats

In 2005, Wal-Mart was seeking to meet U.S. customers' needs with four different retail concepts: Wal-Mart discount stores, Supercenters, Neighborhood Markets, and Sam's Clubs:

- *Discount stores*—These stores ranged from 40,000 to 125,000 square feet, employed an average of 150 people, and offered as many as 80,000 different items, including family apparel, automotive products, health and beauty aids, home furnishings, electronics, hardware, toys, sporting goods, lawn and garden items, pet supplies, jewelry, housewares, prescription drugs, and packaged grocery items. Discount stores had sales in the $30 to $50 million range, depending on store size and location.
- *Supercenters*—Supercenters, which Wal-Mart started opening in 1988 to meet a demand for one-stop family shopping, joined the concept of a general merchandise discount store with that of a full-line supermarket. They ranged from 109,000 to 220,000 square feet, employed between 200 and 550 associates, had about 36 general merchandise departments, and offered up to 150,000 different items, at least 30,000 of which were grocery products. In addition to the value-priced merchandise offered at discount stores and a large supermarket section with more than 30,000 items, Supercenters contained such specialty shops as vision centers, tire and lube expresses, fast-food restaurants, portrait studios, one-hour photo centers, hair salons, banking, and employment agencies. Typical Supercenters had annual sales in the $80–$100 million range.
- *Sam's Clubs*—A store format that Wal-Mart launched in 1983, Sam's was a cash-and-carry,

members-only warehouse that carried about 4,000 frequently used, mostly brand-name items in bulk quantities along with some big-ticket merchandise. The product lineup included fresh, frozen, and canned food products, candy and snack items, office supplies, janitorial and household cleaning supplies and paper products, a selection of apparel, CDs and DVDs, and an assortment of big-ticket items (TVs, tires, large and small appliances, watches, jewelry, computers, camcorders, and other electronic equipment). Stores were approximately 110,000 to 130,000 square feet in size, with most goods displayed in the original cartons stacked in wooden racks or on wooden pallets. Many items stocked were sold in bulk quantity (five-gallon containers, bundles of a dozen or more, economy-size boxes). Prices tended to be 10–15 percent below the prices of the company's discount stores and Supercenters since merchandising costs and store operation costs were lower. Sam's was intended to serve small businesses, churches and religious organizations, beauty salons and barber shops, motels, restaurants, offices, local schools, families, and individuals looking for great prices on large-volume quantities or big-ticket items. Annual member fees were $30 for businesses and $35 for individuals—there were 46 million members in 2003. Sam's stores employed about 125 people and had annual sales averaging $67 million. A number of Sam's stores were located adjacent to a Supercenter or discount store.

- *Neighborhood Markets*—Neighborhood Markets, launched in 1998, were designed to appeal to customers who just needed groceries, pharmaceuticals, or general merchandise. They were always located in markets with Wal-Mart Supercenters so as to be readily accessible to Wal-Mart's food distribution network. Neighborhood Markets ranged from 42,000 to 55,000 square feet, employed 80–100 people, and featured fresh produce, deli foods, fresh meat and dairy items, health and beauty aids, one-hour photo and traditional photo developing services, drive-through pharmacies, stationery and paper goods, pet supplies, and household supplies—about 28,000 items in total.

During 2005 and 2006, Wal-Mart expected to open about 70 new discount stores, 525 new Supercenters, 45 new Neighborhood Markets, and 75 new Sam's Clubs in the United States. Approximately 300 of the planned new U.S. Supercenters were expansions or relocations of existing discount stores, and approximately 35 of the Sam's Clubs were relocations or expansions. Internationally, Wal-Mart planned to open 390 units in the 15 countries where it already had stores; of these, 50 were expected to be relocations or expansions. In February 2005, it had 660 million square feet of selling space in its almost 5,300 retail stores across the world; it expected to add 55 million square feet of retail space in 2005 and another 60 million square feet in 2006. Wal-Mart was expanding most aggressively in Mexico, Brazil, and China. Since 2003, Wal-Mart had opened 18 new stores in China, a country where French retailer Carrefour (the world's second-largest retailer behind Wal-Mart) and Germany's Metro AG had stores.

Exhibit 2 shows the number of Wal-Mart stores in each state and country as of January 2005. There were still many locations in the United States that were underserved by Wal-Mart stores. Inner-city sections of New York City had no Wal-Mart stores of any kind because ample space with plenty of parking was unavailable at a reasonable price. Wal-Mart's first Supercenter in all of California opened in March 2004, and the whole state only had three Supercenters in early 2005. There were no Supercenters in New Jersey, Rhode Island, Vermont, and Hawaii, and only 2 in Massachusetts and 2 in Connecticut (versus 219 in Texas, 116 in Florida, 88 in Georgia, 75 in Tennessee, 71 in Alabama, and 70 in Missouri). Lee Scott believed that opportunities existed to have at least 5,500 Supercenters in the United States alone. Wal-Mart's various domestic and international stores were served by about 120 regional general merchandise and food distribution centers.

Wal-Mart's Geographic Expansion Strategy

One of the most distinctive features of Wal-Mart's domestic strategy in its early years was the manner in which it expanded into new geographic areas. Whereas many chain retailers achieved regional and national coverage quickly by entering the largest metropolitan centers before trying to penetrate less-populated markets, Wal-Mart always expanded into adjoining geographic areas, saturating each area with

Exhibit 2   **Wal-Mart's Store Count, January 2005**

State	Discount Stores	Supercenters	Sam's Clubs	Neighborhood Markets
Alabama	18	71	11	2
Alaska	7	0	3	0
Arizona	18	33	11	5
Arkansas	26	54	5	6
California	149	3	33	0
Colorado	15	40	15	0
Connecticut	28	4	3	0
Delaware	3	4	1	0
Florida	53	116	38	6
Georgia	23	88	21	0
Hawaii	7	0	2	0
Idaho	3	14	1	0
Illinois	78	45	28	0
Indiana	31	56	15	4
Iowa	20	33	7	0
Kansas	19	34	6	3
Kentucky	26	52	5	2
Louisiana	26	56	12	1
Maine	11	11	3	0
Maryland	33	6	13	0
Massachusetts	42	2	3	0
Michigan	41	30	24	0
Minnesota	33	16	13	0
Mississippi	14	51	6	1
Missouri	46	70	14	0
Montana	4	7	1	0
Nebraska	8	16	3	0
Nevada	9	12	5	4
New Hampshire	19	7	4	0
New Jersey	38	0	9	0
New Mexico	3	24	5	0
New York	53	27	18	0
North Carolina	41	65	19	0
North Dakota	8	0	2	0
Ohio	69	45	27	0
Oklahoma	33	49	8	14
Oregon	20	7	0	0
Pennsylvania	49	60	21	0
Rhode Island	7	1	1	0
South Carolina	16	45	9	0
South Dakota	5	5	2	0
Tennessee	21	75	15	4
Texas	80	219	69	28
Utah	4	24	7	5
Vermont	4	0	0	0

(Continued)

Exhibit 2 **Continued**

State	Discount Stores	Supercenters	Sam's Clubs	Neighborhood Markets
Virginia	22	56	13	0
Washington	24	13	3	0
West Virginia	6	23	4	0
Wisconsin	38	37	11	0
Wyoming	2	7	2	0
U.S. totals	1,353	1,713	551	85
International/Worldwide				
Argentina	0	11	0	0
Brazil	118*	17	12	2*
Canada	256	0	6	0
China	0	38	3	2
Germany	0	91	0	0
South Korea	0	16	0	0
Mexico	529†	89	61	0
Puerto Rico	9	4	9	32**
United Kingdom	263‡	19	0	0
International totals:	942	285	91	37
Grand totals:	2,510	1,998	642	121

*Brazil includes 2 Todo Dias, 118 Bompreco.
†Mexico includes 162 Bodegas, 50 Suburbias, 48 Superamas, 269 Vips.
**Puerto Rico includes 32 Amigos.
‡United Kingdom includes 256 ASDA stores, 6 George stores, and 1 ASDA Living store.
Source: 2005 annual report.

stores before moving into new territory. New stores were usually clustered within 200 miles of an existing distribution center so that daily deliveries could be made cost-effectively; new distribution centers were added as needed to support store expansion into additional areas. In the United States, the really unique feature of Wal-Mart's geographic strategy had involved opening stores in small towns surrounding a targeted metropolitan area before moving into the metropolitan area itself—an approach Sam Walton had termed *backward expansion*. Wal-Mart management believed that any town with a shopping-area population of 15,000 or more was big enough to support a Wal-Mart discount store and that towns of 25,000 could support a Supercenter. Once stores were opened in towns around the most populous city, Wal-Mart would locate one or more stores in the metropolitan area and begin major market advertising. By clustering new stores in a relatively small geographic area, the company could share advertising expenses for breaking into a new market across all the area stores, a tactic Wal-Mart used to keep its advertising costs under 1 percent of sales (compared to 2 or 3 percent for other discount chains).

In recent years, Wal-Mart had been driving hard to expand its geographic base of stores outside the United States largely through acquisition and partly through new store construction. Wal-Mart's entry into Canada, Mexico, Brazil, Japan, Puerto Rico, China, Germany, South Korea, and Great Britain had all been accomplished by acquiring existing general merchandise or supermarket chains. In December 2005, Wal-Mart expanded its store base in Brazil by purchasing Portuguese retailer Sonae's 140-store Brazilian operations for $757 million; the acquisition boosted Wal-Mart's store portfolio in Brazil to 295 stores in 17 of Brazil's 26 states with sales totaling about $5 billion. In Mexico, Wal-Mart had sales of $12.5 billion in fiscal 2005 and had recently expanded its operations to a total of 756 stores with 112,000 employees. In late 2005, Wal-Mart had 47 stores and 27,000 employees in 20 China cities;

some of these stores had the highest traffic counts of any stores in the world. Wal-Mart China was ranked 8th among China's Top 50 Most Admired Companies by *Fortune China* in July 2004.

Wal-Mart also owned a 42 percent interest in Seiyu Ltd., Japan's fifth-largest supermarket chain, with 405 locations, and a 33⅓ percent interest in Central American Retail Holding Company (CARHCO), with 363 stores in Costa Rica, El Salvador, Guatemala, Honduras, and Nicaragua. Wal-Mart's entry into Japan via minority ownership of Seiyu had stirred a retailing revolution among Japanese retailers to improve their merchandising, cut their costs, lower their prices, and streamline their supply chains. Prior to buying the stake in Seiyu in 2002 (with an option to increase its ownership to 67 percent by 2007), Wal-Mart had studied the Japanese market for four years. Wal-Mart had a team of 15 people in Japan working with Seiyu to transition its operation to a low-cost, low-price retail structure. In late 2005, with Seiyu struggling to reduce its costs, Wal-Mart assumed control of Seiyu and stepped up efforts to bring down costs and integrate Seiyu into Wal-Mart's global procurement system and global data network.

Sales at Wal-Mart's international stores averaged over $35 million per store in fiscal 2005; the company's international division had fiscal 2005 sales of $56.3 billion (up 18.3 percent over fiscal 2004) and operating profits of $3.0 billion (up almost 26 percent). International sales accounted for nearly 20 percent of total sales in fiscal 2005, and the percentage was expected to rise in the coming years. Wal-Mart had more than 400,000 employees in its international operations.

Wal-Mart's international strategy was to "remain local" in terms of the goods it merchandised, its use of local suppliers where feasible, and in some of the ways it operated. Management strove to adapt the company's standard operating practices to be responsive to local communities and cultures, the needs and merchandise preferences of local customers, and local suppliers. Most store managers and senior managers in its foreign operations were natives of the countries where Wal-Mart operated; many had begun their careers as hourly employees. Wal-Mart did, however, have a program in which stores in different areas exchanged best practices.

Everyday Low Prices

While Wal-Mart had not invented the concept of everyday low pricing strategy, it had done a better job than any other discount retailer in executing the concept. Consumers widely saw the company as having the lowest everyday prices among general merchandise retailers. Studies showed that prices of its grocery items were 5 to 48 percent below such leading supermarket chain competitors as Kroger (which used the City Market brand in the states west of the Mississippi), Safeway, and Albertson's, after making allowances for specials and loyalty cards.[12] On average, Wal-Mart offered many identical food items at prices averaging 15 to 25 percent lower than traditional supermarkets. In-store services were also bargain-priced—customers could wire money for a flat $12.95 (versus a fee of $50 to wire $1,000 at Western Union) and could purchase money orders for 46 cents (versus the 90 cents charged by the U.S. Postal Service). Wal-Mart touted its low prices on its storefronts ("We Sell for Less"), in advertising, on signs inside its stores, and on the logos of its shopping bags.

Some economists believed that Wal-Mart's everyday low prices had reduced inflationary pressures economywide, allowing all U.S. consumers to benefit from the "Wal-Mart effect." Warren Buffet said, "You add it all up and they have contributed to the financial well-being of the American public more than any other institution I can think of."[13] A 2005 study showed that the competitive effect of Wal-Mart's low prices saved each American household an average of $2,329 in 2004.[14] The presence of Wal-Mart stores in a new geographic area created a direct price effect by offering a lower-price option to consumers and an indirect price effect stemming from lower prices on the part of nearby retailers to better compete with Wal-Mart.

Merchandising Innovations

Wal-Mart was unusually active in testing and experimenting with new merchandising techniques. From the beginning, Sam Walton had been quick to imitate good ideas and merchandising practices employed by other retailers. According to the founder of Kmart, Sam Walton "not only copied our concepts; he strengthened them. Sam just took the ball and ran with it."[15] Wal-Mart prided itself on its "low threshold for change," and much of management's time was spent talking to vendors, employees, and customers to get ideas for how Wal-Mart could improve. Suggestions were actively solicited from employees. Most any reasonable idea was tried; if it worked well in stores where it was first tested, then it was quickly implemented in other stores. Experiments in store layout, merchandise displays, store color schemes, merchandise selection (whether to add more upscale lines or shift to a different mix of items), and sales promotion techniques were always under way. Wal-Mart was regarded as an industry leader in testing, adapting, and applying a wide range of cutting-edge merchandising approaches. In 2005 Wal-Mart began upgrading the caliber of the merchandise it stocked in certain departments so as to be more competitive with Target, its major rival in discount retailing.

Advertising

Wal-Mart relied less on advertising than most other discount chains. The company distributed only one or two circulars per month and ran occasional TV ads, relying primarily on word of mouth to communicate its marketing message. Wal-Mart's advertising expenditures ran about 0.3 percent of sales revenues, versus 1.5 percent for Kmart and 2.3 percent for Target. Wal-Mart's spending for radio and TV advertising was said to be so low that it didn't register on national ratings scales. Most Wal-Mart broadcast ads appeared on local TV and local cable channels. Wal-Mart did no advertising for its Sam's Club stores. The company often allowed charities to use its parking lots for their fund-raising activities.

WAL-MART'S COMPETITORS

Discount retailing was an intensely competitive business. Competition among discount retailers centered around pricing, store location, variations in store format and merchandise mix, store size, shopping atmosphere, and image with shoppers. Wal-Mart's primary competitors were Kmart and Target. Like Wal-Mart, Kmart and Target had general merchandise stores and superstores (Super Target and Super Kmart) that also had a full-line supermarket on one side of the store. Wal-Mart also competed against category retailers like Best Buy and Circuit City in electronics; Toy "R" Us in toys; Goody's in apparel; Bed, Bath, and Beyond in household goods; and Kroger, Albertson's, and Safeway in groceries.

Wal-Mart's rapid climb to become the largest supermarket retailer via its Supercenters had triggered heated price competition in the aisles of most supermarkets. Wal-Mart's three major rivals—Kroger, Albertson's and Safeway—along with a host of smaller regional supermarket chains were scrambling to cut costs, narrow the price gap with Wal-Mart, and otherwise differentiate themselves so as to retain their customer base and grow revenues. Continuing increases in the number of Wal-Mart Supercenters meant that the majority of rival supermarkets would be within 10 miles of a Supercenter by 2010. Wal-Mart had recently concluded that it took fewer area residents to support a Supercenter than it had thought; management believed that Supercenters in urban areas could be as little as four miles apart and still attract sufficient store traffic.

The two largest competitors in the warehouse club segment were Costco and Sam's Clubs; BJ's Wholesale Club, a smaller East Coast chain, was the only other major U.S. player in this segment.[16] In 2005 Costco had sales of $51.9 billion at 464 stores versus $37.1 billion at 551 stores for Sam's. The average Costco store generated annual revenues of $112 million, over 65 percent more than the $67 million average at Sam's. Costco catered to affluent households with upscale tastes and located its stores in mostly urban areas. Costco's 45.3 million members averaged 11.4 store visits annually and spent an average of $94 per visit, which compared favorably with averages of 8.5 visits and expenditures of $78 at Sam's. Costco was the United States' biggest retailer of fine wines ($600 million annually) and roasted chickens (55,000 rotisserie chickens a day). While its product line included food and household items, sporting goods, vitamins, and various other merchandise, its major attraction was big-ticket luxury items (diamonds and plasma TVs) and the latest gadgets at bargain prices (Costco capped its markups at 14 percent). Costco had beaten Sam's in being the first to sell fresh meat and produce (1986 versus 1989), to introduce private-label items (1995 versus 1998), and to sell gasoline

(1995 versus 1997). Costco offered its workers good wages and fringe benefits (full-time hourly workers made about $40,000 after four years).

Internationally, Wal-Mart's biggest competitor was Carrefour, a France-based retailer with nearly 12,000 stores of varying formats and sizes across much of Europe and in such emerging markets as Argentina, Brazil, China, South Korea, and Taiwan. Both Wal-Mart and Carrefour were expanding aggressively in Brazil and China, going head-to-head in an increasing number of locations. In 2005, Carrefour had 1,330 stores in Asia and Latin America with sales approximating €12 million; there were 69 Carrefour hypermarkets in China. Overall, Carrefour had sales close to €95 billion in 2005.

WAL-MART'S APPROACHES TO STRATEGY EXECUTION

To profitably execute its everyday-low-price strategy, Wal-Mart put heavy emphasis on getting the lowest possible prices from its suppliers, forging close working relationships with key suppliers in order to capture win–win cost savings throughout its supply chain, keeping its internal operations lean and efficient, paying attention to even the tiniest details in store layouts and merchandising, making efficient use of state-of-the art technology, and nurturing a culture that thrived on customer service, hard work, constant improvement, and low prices.

Relationships with Suppliers

Wal-Mart was far and away the biggest customer of virtually all of its suppliers. Wal-Mart's scale of operation (see Exhibit 3) allowed it to bargain hard with suppliers and get their bottom prices. During part of 2005, Wal-Mart's requirements for PCs for the holiday sales season was so big that Hewlett-Packard devoted 3 of its 10 PC plants operated by contract manufacturers to turning out products solely for Wal-Mart. Wal-Mart looked for suppliers that were dominant in their category (thus providing strong brand-name recognition), could grow with the company, had full product lines (so that Wal-Mart buyers could both cherry-pick and get some sort of limited exclusivity on the products it chose to carry), had the long-term commitment to R&D to bring new and better products to retail shelves, and had

Exhibit 3 **The Scale of Wal-Mart's Purchases from Selected Suppliers and Its Market Shares in Selected Product Categories**

Supplier	Percent of Total Sales to Wal-Mart	Product Category	Wal-Mart's U.S. Market Share*
Tandy Brands Accessories	39%	Dog food	36%
Dial	28	Disposable diapers	32
Del Monte Foods	24	Photographic film	30
Clorox	23	Shampoo	30
Revlon	20–23	Paper towels	30
RJR Tobacco	20	Toothpaste	26
Procter & Gamble	17	Pain remedies	21
		CDs, DVDs, and videos	15–20
		Single-copy sales of magazines	15
Although sales percentages were not available, Wal-Mart was also the biggest customer of Disney, Campbell Soup, Kraft, and Gillette		Although market shares were not available, Wal-Mart was also the biggest seller of toys, guns, diamonds, detergent, video games, socks, and bedding.	

*Based on sales through food, drug, and mass merchandisers.

Sources: Jerry Useem, "One Nation Under Wal-Mart," *Fortune,* March 3, 2003, p. 66, and Anthony Bianco and Wendy Zellner, "Is Wal-Mart Too Powerful?" *BusinessWeek,* October 6, 2003, p. 102.

the ability to become more efficient in producing and delivering what they supplied. But it also dealt with thousands of small suppliers (mom-and-pop operations, small farmers, and minority businesses) that could furnish particular items for stores in a certain geographical area. Many Wal-Mart stores had a "Store of the Community" section that showcased local products from local producers; in addition, Wal-Mart had set up an export office in the United States to help small and medium-sized businesses export their American-made products (especially to Wal-Mart stores in foreign countries).

Wal-Mart buyers literally shopped the world for merchandise suitable for the company's stores—they purchased goods from 61,000 U.S. suppliers and 7,000 foreign suppliers in 2005; the purchases from U.S. suppliers totaled $150 billion. Procurement personnel spent a lot of time meeting with vendors and understanding their cost structure. By making the negotiation process transparent, Wal-Mart buyers soon learned whether a vendor was doing all it could to cut down its costs and quote Wal-Mart an attractively low price. Wal-Mart's purchasing agents were dedicated to getting the lowest prices they could, and they did not accept invitations to be wined or dined by suppliers. The marketing vice president of a major vendor told *Fortune* magazine:

> They are very, very focused people, and they use their buying power more forcefully than anybody else in America. All the normal mating rituals are verboten. Their highest priority is making sure everybody at all times in all cases knows who's in charge, and it's Wal-Mart. They talk softly, but they have piranha hearts, and if you aren't totally prepared when you go in there, you'll have your ass handed to you.[17]

All vendors were expected to offer their best price without exception; one consultant that helped manufacturers sell to retailers observed, "No one would dare come in with a half-ass price."[18]

Even though Wal-Mart was tough in negotiating for absolute rock-bottom prices, the price quotes it got were still typically high enough to allow suppliers to earn a profit. Being a Wal-Mart supplier generally meant having a stable, dependable sales base that allowed the supplier to operate production facilities in a cost effective manner. Moreover, once it decided to source from a vendor, then Wal-Mart worked closely with the vendor to find *mutually beneficial* ways to squeeze costs out of the supply chain. Every aspect of a supplier's operation got

scrutinized—how products got developed, what they were made of, how costs might be reduced, what data Wal-Mart could supply that would be useful, how sharing of data online could prove beneficial, and so on. Nearly always, as they went through the process with Wal-Mart personnel, suppliers saw ways to prune costs or otherwise streamline operations in ways that enhanced their profit margins. In 1989 Wal-Mart became the first major retailer to embark on a program urging vendors to develop products and packaging that would not harm the environment. In addition, Wal-Mart expected its vendors to contribute ideas about how to make its stores more fun insofar as their products were concerned. Those suppliers that were selected as "category managers" for such product groupings as lingerie or pet food or school supplies were expected to educate Wal-Mart on everything that was happening in their respective product category.

Some 200 vendors had established offices in Bentonville to work closely with Wal-Mart on a continuing basis—most were in an area referred to locally as "Vendorville." Vendors were encouraged to voice any problems in their relationship with Wal-Mart and to become involved in Wal-Mart's future plans. Top-priority projects ranged from using more recyclable packaging to working with Wal-Mart on merchandise displays and product mix to tweaking the just-in-time ordering and delivery system to instituting automatic reordering arrangements to coming up with new products with high customer appeal. Most recently, one of Wal-Mart's priorities was working with vendors to figure out how to localize the items carried in particular stores and thereby accommodate varying tastes and preferences of shoppers in different areas where Wal-Mart had stores. Most vendor personnel based in Bentonville spent considerable time focusing on which items in their product line were best for Wal-Mart, where they ought to be placed in the stores, how they could be better displayed, what new products ought to be introduced, and which ones ought to be rotated out.

A 2005 survey conducted by Cannondale Associates found that manufacturers believed Wal-Mart was the overall best retailer with which to do business—the seventh straight year in which Wal-Mart was ranked number one.[19] Target was ranked second and Costco was ranked sixth. The criteria for the ranking included such factors as clearest company strategy, store branding, best buying teams, most innovative consumer marketing/merchandising, best supply chain management practices, overall business fundamentals, and best practice management of individual product categories. One retailing consultant said, "I think most [suppliers] would say Wal-Mart is their most profitable account."[20] While this might seem surprising because of Wal-Mart's enormous bargaining clout, the potentially greater profitability of selling to Wal-Mart stemmed from the practices of most other retailers to demand that suppliers pay sometimes steep slotting fees to win shelf space and their frequent insistence on supplier payment of such extras as in-store displays, damage allowances, handling charges, penalties for late deliveries, rebates of one kind or another, allowances for advertising, and special allowances on slow-moving merchandise that had to be cleared out with deep price discounts. Further, most major retailers expected to be courted with Super Bowl tickets, trips to the Masters golf tournament, fancy dinners at conventions and trade shows, or other perks in return for their business. All of these extras represented costs that suppliers had to build into their prices. At Wal-Mart everything was boiled down to one price number, and no funny-money extras ever entered into the deal.[21]

Most suppliers viewed Wal-Mart's single bottom-line price and its expectation of close coordination as a win–win proposition, not only because of the benefits of cutting out all the funny-money costs and solidifying their relationship with a major customer but also because what they learned from the collaborative efforts and data sharing often had considerable benefit in the rest of their operations. Many suppliers, including Procter & Gamble, liked Wal-Mart's supply chain business model so well that they had pushed their other customers to adopt similar practices.[22]

Wal-Mart's Standards for Suppliers   In 1992 Wal-Mart began establishing standards for its suppliers, with particular emphasis on suppliers located in foreign countries that had a history of problematic wages and working conditions. Management believed that the manner in which suppliers conducted their business regarding long work hours, the use of child labor, discrimination based on race or religion or other factors, workplace safety, and lack of compliance with local laws and regulations could be attributed to Wal-Mart and affect its reputation with customers and shareholders. To mitigate the potential for

Wal-Mart to be adversely affected by the manner in which its suppliers conducted their business, Wal-Mart had established a set of supplier standards and formed an internal group to see that suppliers were conforming to the ethical standards and business practices stated in its published standards. The company's supplier standards had been through a number of changes as the concerns of Wal-Mart management evolved over time. In February 2003, Wal-Mart took direct control of foreign factory audits; factory certification teams based in offices in Bentonville, China, Singapore, India, United Arab Emirates, and Honduras were staffed with more than 200 Wal-Mart employees dedicated to monitoring foreign factory compliance with the company's supplier standards. All suppliers were asked to sign a document certifying their compliance with the standards and were required to post a version of the supplier standards in both English and the local language in each production facility servicing Wal-Mart. In 2004, Wal-Mart conducted 12,500 audits at 7,600 plants of suppliers; in 2005, about 20 percent of the audits conducted were to be unannounced.

Distribution Center Operations

Throughout the 1980s and 1990s, Wal-Mart had pursued a host of efficiency-increasing actions at its distribution centers. The company had been a global leader in automating its distribution centers and expediting the transfer of incoming shipments from manufacturers to its fleet of delivery trucks that made daily deliveries to surrounding stores. Prior to automation, bulk cases received from manufacturers had to be opened by distribution center employees and perhaps stored in bins, then picked and repacked in quantities needed for specific stores, and loaded onto trucks for delivery to Wal-Mart stores—a manual process that was error-prone and sometimes slow. Using state-of-the-art technology, Wal-Mart had automated many of the labor-intensive tasks, gradually creating an ever-more-sophisticated and cost-efficient system of conveyors, bar-coding machines, handheld computers, and other devices with the capability to quickly sort incoming shipments from manufacturers into smaller, store-specific quantities and route them to waiting trucks to be sent to stores to replenish sold merchandise. Often, incoming goods from manufacturers being unloaded at one section of the warehouse were immediately sorted into store-specific amounts and conveyed directly onto waiting Wal-Mart trucks headed for those particular stores—a large portion of the incoming inventory was in a Wal-Mart distribution center an average of only 12 hours. Distribution center employees had access to real-time information regarding the inventory levels of all items in the center and used the different bar codes for pallets, bins, shelves, and items to pick up for store orders. Handheld computers also enabled the packaging department to get accurate information about which items to pack for which store and what loading dock to have packages conveyed.

Wal-Mart's trendsetting use of cutting-edge retailing technologies and its best-practices leadership in supply chain activities had given it operating advantages and raised the bar not only for its competitors but for most other retailers as well. Distribution centers processed over 5 billion cases through the network to Wal-Mart's stores and Sam's Clubs.

Truck Fleet Operations

Wal-Mart used a fleet of more than 3,500 company-owned trucks and a force of more than 7,800 drivers to transport goods from its 120 distribution centers to its 5,300 stores. Wal-Mart hired only experienced drivers who had driven more than 300,000 accident-free miles with no major traffic violations. Distribution centers had facilities where drivers could shower, sleep, eat, or do personal business while waiting for their truck to be loaded. A truck dispatch coordinator scheduled the dispatch of all trucks based on the available time of drivers and estimated driving time between the distribution center and the designated store. Drivers were expected to pull their truck up to the store dock at the scheduled time (usually late afternoon or early evening) even if they arrived early; trucks were unloaded by store personnel during nighttime hours, with a two-hour gap between each new truck delivery (if more than one was scheduled for the same night.

In instances where it was economical, Wal-Mart trucks were dispatched directly to a manufacturer's facilities, picked up goods for one or more stores and delivered them directly, bypassing the distribution center entirely. Manufacturers that supplied certain high-volume items or even a number of different items sometimes delivered their products in truckload lots directly to some or many of Wal-Mart's stores.

Store Construction and Maintenance

Wal-Mart management worked at getting more mileage out of its capital expenditures for new stores, store renovations, and store fixtures. Ideas and suggestions were solicited from vendors regarding store layout, the design of fixtures, and space needed for effective displays. Wal-Mart's store designs had open-air offices for management personnel that could be furnished economically and featured a maximum of display space that could be rearranged and refurbished easily. Wal-Mart claimed that the design and aisle width at its new Supercenters would accommodate 100 million shoppers per week. Because Wal-Mart insisted on a high degree of uniformity in the new stores it built, the architectural firm Wal-Mart employed was able to use computer modeling techniques to turn out complete specifications for 12 or more new stores a week. Moreover, the stores were designed to permit quick, inexpensive construction as well as to allow for low-cost maintenance and renovation. All stores were renovated and redecorated at least once every seven years. If a given store location was rendered obsolete by the construction of new roads and highways and the opening of new shopping locations, then the old store was abandoned in favor of a new store at a more desirable site. In 2003–2005, stores were being expanded or relocated at the rate of 100–200 annually.

In keeping with the low-cost theme for facilities, Wal-Mart's distribution centers and corporate offices were also built economically and furnished simply. The offices of top executives were modest and unpretentious. The lighting, heating, and air-conditioning controls at all Wal-Mart stores were connected via computer to Bentonville headquarters, allowing cost-saving energy management practices to be implemented centrally and freeing store managers from the time and worry of trying to hold down utility costs. Wal-Mart mass-produced a lot of its displays in-house, not only saving money but also cutting the time to roll out a new display concept to as little as 30 days. It also had a group that disposed of used fixtures and equipment that could not be used at other store via auctions at the store sites where the surplus existed—a calendar of upcoming auctions was posted on the company's Web site.

Wal-Mart's Use of Cutting-Edge Technology

Wal-Mart's approach to technology was to be on the offense—probing, testing, and then deploying the newest equipment, retailing techniques, computer software programs, and related technological advances to increase productivity and drive costs down. Wal-Mart was typically a first-mover among retailers in upgrading and improving its capabilities as new technology was introduced. The company's technological goal was to provide employees with the tools to do their jobs more efficiently and to make better decisions.

Wal-Mart began using computers to maintain inventory control on an item basis in distribution centers and in its stores in 1974. In 1981, Wal-Mart began testing point-of-sale scanners and then committed to systemwide use of scanning bar codes in 1983—a move that resulted in 25–30 percent faster check-out of customers. In 1984, Wal-Mart developed a computer-assisted merchandising system that allowed the product mix in each store to be tailored to its own market circumstances and sales patterns. Between 1985 and 1987, Wal-Mart installed the nation's largest private satellite communication network; this network allowed two-way voice and data transmission between headquarters, the distribution centers, and the stores and one-way video transmission from Bentonville's corporate offices to distribution centers and to the stores; the system was less expensive than the previously used telephone network. The video system was used regularly by company officials to speak directly to all employees at once.

In 1989, Wal-Mart established a direct satellite link with about 1,700 vendors supplying close to 80 percent of the goods sold by Wal-Mart; this link allowed the use of electronic purchase orders and instant data exchanges. Wal-Mart had also used the satellite system's capabilities to develop a credit card authorization procedure that took five seconds, on average, to authorize a purchase, speeding up credit check-out by 25 percent compared to the prior manual system. In the early 1990s, through pioneering collaboration with Procter & Gamble, it instituted an automated reordering system that notified suppliers as their items moved though store check-out lanes; this allowed suppliers to track sales and inventories of their products (so they could plan production and schedule shipments accordingly).

By 2003 the company had developed and deployed sophisticated information technology systems and online capability that not only gave it real-time access to detailed figures on most any aspect of its operations but also made it a leader in cost-effective supply chain management. It could track the movement of goods through its entire value chain—from the sale of items at the cash register backward to stock on store shelves, in-store backup inventory, distribution center inventory, and shipments en route. Moreover, Wal-Mart had collaborated with its suppliers to develop data-sharing capabilities aimed at streamlining the supply of its stores, avoiding both stock-outs and excess inventories, identifying slow-selling items that might warrant replacement, and spotting ways to squeeze costs out of the supply chain. The company's Retail Link system allowed 30,000 suppliers to track their wares through Wal-Mart's value chain, get hourly sales figures for each item, and monitor gross margins on each of their products (Wal-Mart's actual selling price less what it paid the supplier).

In mid-2003 in another of its trendsetting moves, Wal-Mart informed its suppliers that they had to convert to electronic product code (EPC) technology based on radio frequency identification (RFID) systems. The EPC technology involved embedding every single item that rolled off a manufacturing line with an electronic tag containing a unique number. When brought into range, EPC tags could be read by RFID scanners, thus allowing the company to locate and track items throughout the supply chain in real time. With EPC and RFID capability, every single DVD or can of soup or screwdriver in Wal-Mart's supply chain network or on its store shelves could be traced back to when it was made, where and when it arrived in a case or pallet of goods, and where and when it was sold or turned up missing. Further, EPC tags linked to an online database provided a secure way of sharing product-specific information with supply chain partners. Wal-Mart management believed that EPC technology, in conjunction with the expanding production of RFID-capable printers/encoders, had the potential to revolutionize the supply chain by providing more accurate information about product movement, stock rotation, and inventory levels; it was also seen as a significant tool for preventing theft and dealing with product recalls. An IBM study indicated that EPC tagging would reduce stock-outs by 33 percent, while an Accenture study showed that EPC/RFID technology could boost worker productivity by 5 percent and shrink working capital and fixed capital requirements by 5 to 30 percent. In 2005, EPC/RFID technology implementation was under way for Wal-Mart's top 200 suppliers, with around 20,000 suppliers to be involved in some way by the end of 2006.

In 2005, Wal-Mart's data center was tracking over 680 million stock-keeping units (SKUs) weekly. The company had over 75,000 associates in logistics and in its information systems division. The attention Wal-Mart management placed on using cutting-edge technology and the astuteness with which it deployed this technology along its value chain to enhance store operations and continuously drive down costs had, over the years, resulted in Wal-Mart's being widely regarded as having the most cost-effective, data-rich information technology (IT) systems of any major retailer in the world. It spent less than 1 percent of revenues on IT, far less than other retailers, and had stronger capabilities. According to Linda Dillman, Wal-Mart's chief information officer, "The strength of this division is, we are doers and do things faster than lightning. We can implement things faster than anyone could with a third party. We run the entire world out of facilities in this area [Bentonville] at a cost that no one can touch. We'd be nuts to outsource."[23] Wal-Mart rarely used commercial software, preferring to develop its own IT systems. So powerful had Wal-Mart's influence been on retail supply chain efficiency that its competitors (and many other retailers as well) had found it essential to follow Wal-Mart's lead and pursue "Wal-Martification" of their retail supply chains.[24]

Wal-Mart's Approach to Customer Service

Wal-Mart tried to put some organization muscle behind its pledge of "Satisfaction Guaranteed" and do things that would make customers' shopping experience at Wal-Mart pleasant. Store managers challenged store associates to practice what Sam Walton called "aggressive hospitality." A "greeter" was stationed at store entrances to welcome customers with a smile, thank them for shopping at Wal-Mart, assist them in getting a shopping cart, and answer questions about where items were located. Clerks and check-out workers were trained to be courteous and helpful and to exhibit a "friendly, folksy attitude." All store associates were called upon to display the "10-foot attitude" and commit to a pledge of friendliness: "I solemnly promise and declare that every customer that comes within ten feet of me, I will smile, look them in the eye, and greet them." Wal-Mart's management stressed five themes in training and supervising store personnel:

1. Think like a customer.
2. Sell what customers want to buy.
3. Provide a genuine value to the customer.
4. Make sure the customer has a good time.
5. Exceed the customer's expectations.

In all stores, efforts were made to present merchandise in easy-to-shop shelving and displays. Floors in the apparel section were carpeted to make the department feel homier and to make shopping seem easier on customers' feet. Store layouts were constantly scrutinized to improve shopping convenience and make it easier for customers to find items. Store employees wore blue vests with the tag line "How May I Help You?" on the back to make it easier for customers to pick them out from a distance. Fluorescent lighting was recessed into the ceiling to create a softer impression than exposed fluorescent lighting strips. Yet nothing about the decor conflicted with Wal-Mart's low-price image; retailing consultants considered Wal-Mart as being very adept at sending out an effective mix of vibes and signals concerning customer service, low prices, quality merchandise, and friendly shopping environment. Wal-Mart's management believed that the attention paid to all the details of making the stores more user-friendly and inviting caused shoppers to view Wal-Mart in a more positive light.

The Culture at Wal-Mart in 2005

Wal-Mart's culture in 2005 continued to be deeply rooted in Sam Walton's business philosophy and leadership style. Mr. Sam, as he was fondly called and remembered, not only was Wal-Mart's founder and patriarch but had also been its spiritual leader—and still was in many respects. Four key core values and business principles underpinned Sam Walton's approach to managing:[25]

- Treat employees as partners, sharing both the good and bad about the company so they will strive to excel and participate in the rewards. (Wal-Mart fostered the concept of partnership by referring to all employees as "associates," a term Sam Walton had insisted on from the company's beginnings because it denoted a partnerlike relationship.)
- Build for the future, rather than just immediate gains, by continuing to study the changing concepts that are a mark of the retailing industry and be ready to test and experiment with new ideas.
- Recognize that the road to success includes failing, which is part of the learning process rather than a personal or corporate defect or failing. Always challenge the obvious.
- Involve associates at all levels in the total decision-making process.

He practiced these principles diligently in his own actions and insisted that other Wal-Mart managers do the same. Until his health failed badly in 1991, he spent several days a week visiting the stores, gauging the moods of shoppers, listening to employees discuss what was on their minds, learning what was or was not selling, gathering ideas about how things could be done better, complimenting workers on their efforts, and challenging them to come up with good ideas.

The values, beliefs, and practices that Sam Walton instilled in Wal-Mart's culture and that still carried over in 2005 were reflected in statements made in his autobiography:

> Everytime Wal-Mart spends one dollar foolishly, it comes right out of our customer's pockets. Everytime we save a dollar, that puts us one more step ahead of the competition—which is where we always plan to be.
>
> One person seeking glory doesn't accomplish much; at Wal-Mart, everything we've done has been the result of people pulling together to meet one common goal.
>
> I have always been driven to buck the system, to innovate, to take things beyond where they've been.
>
> We paid absolutely no attention whatsoever to the way things were supposed to be done, you know, the way the rules of retail said it had to be done.
>
> I'm more of a manager by walking and flying around, and in the process I stick my fingers into everything I can to see how it's coming along . . . My appreciation for numbers has kept me close to our operational

statements, and to all the other information we have pouring in from so many different places.

> The more you share profit with your associates—whether it's in salaries or incentives or bonuses or stock discounts—the more profit will accrue to your company. Why? Because the way management treats the associates is exactly how the associates will then treat the customers. And if the associates treat the customers well, the customers will return again and again.
>
> There's no better way to keep someone doing things the right way than by letting him or her know how much you appreciate their performance.
>
> The bigger we get as a company, the more important it becomes for us to shift responsibility and authority toward the front lines, toward that department manager who's stocking the shelves and talking to the customer.
>
> We give our department heads the opportunity to become real merchants at a very early stage of the game . . . we make our department heads the managers of their own businesses . . . We share everything with them: the costs of their goods, the freight costs, the profit margins. We let them see how their store ranks with every other store in the company on a constant, running basis, and we give them incentives to want to win.
>
> We're always looking for new ways to encourage our associates out in the stores to push their ideas up through the system . . . Great ideas come from everywhere if you just listen and look for them. You never know who's going to have a great idea.
>
> A lot of bureaucracy is really the product of some empire builder's ego . . . We don't need any of that at Wal-Mart. If you're not serving the customers, or supporting the folks who do, we don't need you.
>
> You can't just keep doing what works one time, because everything around you is always changing. To succeed, you have to stay out in front of that change.[26]

Walton's success flowed from his cheerleading management style, his ability to instill the principles and management philosophies he preached into Wal-Mart's culture, the close watch he kept on costs, his relentless insistence on continuous improvement, and his habit of staying in close touch with both consumer and associates. It was common practice for Walton to lead cheers at annual shareholder meetings, store visits, managers' meetings, and company events. His favorite was the Wal-Mart cheer:

Give me a W!
Give me an A!
Give me an L!
Give me a squiggly! (Here, everybody sort of does the twist.)
Give me an M!
Give me an A!
Give me an R!
Give me a T!
What's that spell?
Wal-Mart!
Whose Wal-Mart is it?
My Wal-Mart!
Who's number one?
The Customer! Always!

In 2005, the Wal-Mart cheer was still a core part of the Wal-Mart culture and was used throughout the company at meetings of store employees, managers, and corporate gatherings in Bentonville to create a "whistle while you work" atmosphere, loosen everyone up, inject fun and enthusiasm, and get sessions started on a stimulating note. While the cheer seemed corny to outsiders, once they saw the cheer in action at Wal-Mart, they came to realize its cultural power and significance. And much of Sam Walton's cultural legacy remained intact in 2005, most especially among the company's top decision makers and longtime managers. As a *Fortune* writer put it:

> Spend enough time inside the company—where nothing backs up a point better than a quotation from Walton scripture—and it's easy to get the impression that the founder is orchestrating his creation from the beyond.[27]

The Three Basic Beliefs Underlying the Wal-Mart Culture in 2005 Wal-Mart's top management stressed three basic beliefs that Sam Walton had preached since 1962:[28]

1. *Every individual deserves to be treated with respect and dignity.* Management consistently drummed the theme that dedicated, hardworking, ordinary people who teamed together and who treated each other with respect and dignity could accomplish extraordinary things. Throughout company literature, comments could be found referring to Wal-Mart's "concern for the individual." Such expressions as "Our people make the difference," "We care about people," and "People helping People" were used repeatedly by Wal-Mart executives and store managers to create and nurture a family-oriented atmosphere among store associates.

2. *Service to customers is the top priority.* Management stressed that the company was nothing without its customers. To satisfy customers and keeping them coming back again and again, management emphasized that customers had to trust in Wal-Mart's pricing philosophy and to always be able to find the lowest prices with the best possible service. One of the standard Wal-Mart mantras preached to all associates was that the customer was number one and that the customer was boss. Associates in stores were urged to observe the rule regarding the "10-foot attitude."

3. *We must strive for excellence.* The concept of striving for excellence stemmed from Sam Walton's conviction that prices were seldom as low as they needed to be and that product quality was seldom as high as customers deserved. The thesis at Wal-Mart was that new ideas and ambitious goals made the company reach further and try harder—the process of finding new and innovative ways to push boundaries and constantly improve made the company better at what it did and contributed to higher levels of customer satisfaction. Wal-Mart managers at all levels spent much time and effort motivating associates to offer ideas for improvement, and to function as partners. It was iterated over and over that every cost counted and that every worker had a responsibility to be involved.

These three beliefs were supplemented by several supporting cultural themes and practices:

- *Go all out to exceed customers' expectations, and make sure that customers have a good time shopping at Wal-Mart.* Every associate repeatedly heard, "The customer is boss and the future depends on you."

- *Practice Sam Walton's 10 rules for building a business.* Management had distilled much of Sam Walton's business philosophy into 10 rules (see Exhibit 4); these were reiterated to associates and used at meetings to guide decision making and the crafting and executing of Wal-Mart's strategy.

- *Observe the Sundown Rule.* Answer requests by sundown on the day they are received. Management believed this working principle had to be taken seriously in a busy world where people's job performance depended on cooperation from others.

Wal-Mart's culture had unusually deep roots at the headquarters complex in Bentonville. The numerous journalists and business executives who had been to Bentonville and spent much time at Wal-Mart's corporate offices uniformly reported being impressed with the breadth, depth, and pervasive power of the company's culture. Jack Welch, former CEO of General Electric and a potent culture builder in his own right, noted that "the place vibrated" with cultural energy. There was little evidence that the culture in Bentonville was any weaker in 2005 than it had been 15 years earlier when Sam Walton personally led the culture-building, culture-nurturing effort. An atmosphere of frugality continued to prevail—Wal-Mart associates, including executives, flew coach, shared hotel rooms, and emptied their own trash. The philosophy was, "If we can go without something to save money, we do. It's the cornerstone of our culture to pass on our savings. Every penny we save is a penny in our customers' pockets."[29]

But Wal-Mart executives nonetheless were currently facing a formidable challenge in sustaining the culture in the distribution centers and especially in the stores. Annual turnover rates at Wal-Mart stores ran about 40 percent in 2002–2005 and had run as high as 70 percent in 1999 when the economy was booming and the labor market was tight. Such high rates of turnover among the company's 1.6 million worldwide workforce, coupled with the fact that Wal-Mart was adding about 120,000 additional associates annually to staff its new stores and distribution centers, made keeping the culture intact outside Bentonville a Herculean task. No other company in all of business history had been confronted with cultural indoctrination of so many new employees in so many locations in such a relatively short time.

Soliciting Ideas from Associates

Associates at all levels were expected to be an integral part of the process of making the company better. Wal-Mart store managers usually spent a portion of each day walking around the store checking on how well things were going in each department, listening to associates' comments, soliciting suggestions and discussing how improvements could be made, and praising associates who were doing a good job. Store managers frequently asked associates what needed to be done better in their department and what could be changed to improve store operations. Associates who believed a certain policy or procedure detracted from operations were encouraged to challenge and change it. Task forces to evaluate ideas and plan out future actions to implement them were common, and it was not unusual for the person who developed the idea to be appointed the leader of the group.

Listening to employees was a very important part of each manager's job. All of Wal-Mart's top executives relied on management by walking around; they visited stores, distribution centers, and support facilities regularly, staying on top of what was happening and listening to what employees had to say about how things were going. Senior managers at Wal-Mart's Bentonville headquarters believed that visiting stores and listening to associates was time well spent because a number of the company's best ideas had come from Wal-Mart associates—Wal-Mart's use of people greeters at store entrances was one of those ideas.

Compensation and Benefits

In 2005, Wal-Mart's average hourly wage for regular full-time associates in the United States was $9.68 an hour (the federal minimum wage was $5.15, and the average hourly wage of retail workers was $12.28—Costco, one of Wal-Mart's rivals paid its hourly workers an average of $16.00 per hour).[30] The average was higher in certain urban areas, for example, Chicago ($10.69), Atlanta ($10.80), and Los Angeles ($9.99).[31] Store clerks generally earned the lowest wage; workers who unloaded trucks and stocked store shelves could earn anywhere from $25,000 to $50,000. New hourly associates in the United States were paid anywhere from $1 to $6 above the minimum wage, depending on the type of job, and could expect to receive a raise within the first year at one or both of the semiannual job evaluations. Typically, at least one raise was guaranteed in the first year if Wal-Mart planned to keep the individual on the staff. The other raise depended on how well the associate worked and improved during the year. At the store level, only the store manager was salaried; all other associates, including the department managers, were considered hourly employees. Store managers generally had six-figure incomes.

Exhibit 4   **Sam Walton's Rules for Building a Business**

Rule 1: Commit to your business. Believe in it more than anybody else. I think I overcame every single one of my personal shortcomings by the sheer passion I brought to my work. I don't know if you're born with this kind of passion, or if you can learn it. But I do know you need it. If you love your work, you'll be out there every day trying to do it the best you possibly can, and pretty soon everybody around will catch the passion from you—like a fever.

Rule 2: Share your profits with all your Associates, and treat them as partners. In turn, they will treat you as a partner, and together you will all perform beyond your wildest expectations. Remain a corporation and retain control if you like, but behave as a servant leader in a partnership. Encourage your Associates to hold a stake in the company. Offer discounted stock, and grant them stock for their retirement. It's the single best thing we ever did.

Rule 3: Motivate your partners. Money and ownership alone aren't enough. Constantly, day-by-day, think of new and more interesting ways to motivate and challenge your partners. Set high goals, encourage competition, and then keep score. Make bets with outrageous payoffs. If things get stale, cross-pollinate; have managers switch jobs with one another to stay challenged. Keep everybody guessing as to what your next trick is going to be. Don't become too predictable.

Rule 4: Communicate everything you possibly can to your partners. The more they know, the more they'll understand. The more they understand, the more they'll care. Once they care, there's no stopping them. If you don't trust your Associates to know what's going on, they'll know you don't really consider them partners. Information is power, and the gain you get from empowering your Associates more than offsets the risk of informing your competitors.

Rule 5: Appreciate everything your Associates do for the business. A paycheck and a stock option will buy one kind of loyalty. But all of us like to be told how much somebody appreciates what we do for them. We like to hear it often, and especially when we have done something we're really proud of. Nothing else can quite substitute for a few well-chosen, well-timed, sincere words of praise. They're absolutely free—and worth a fortune.

Rule 6: Celebrate your successes. Find some humor in your failures. Don't take yourself so seriously. Loosen up, and everybody around you will loosen up. Have fun. Show enthusiasm—always. When all else fails, put on a costume and sing a silly song. Then make everybody else sing with you. Don't do a hula on Wall Street. It's been done. Think up your own stunt. All of this is more important, and more fun, than you think, and it really fools the competition. "Why should we take those cornballs at Wal-Mart seriously?"

Rule 7: Listen to everyone in your company. And figure out ways to get them talking. The folks on the front lines—the ones who actually talk to the customer—are the only ones who really know what's going on out there. You'd better find out what they know. This really is what total quality is all about. To push responsibility down in your organization, and to force good ideas to bubble up within it, you must listen to what your Associates are trying to tell you.

Rule 8: Exceed your customers' expectations. If you do, they'll come back over and over. Give them what they want—and a little more. Let them know you appreciate them. Make good on all your mistakes, and don't make excuses—apologize. Stand behind everything you do. The two most important words I ever wrote were on that first Wal-Mart sign, "Satisfaction Guaranteed." They're still up there, and they have made all the difference.

Rule 9: Control your expenses better than your competition. This is where you can always find the competitive advantage. For 25 years running—long before Wal-Mart was known as the nation's largest retailer—we ranked No. 1 in our industry for the lowest ratio of expenses to sales. You can make a lot of different mistakes and still recover if you run an efficient operation. Or you can be brilliant and still go out of business if you're too inefficient.

Rule 10: Swim upstream. Go the other way. Ignore the conventional wisdom. If everybody else is doing it one way, there's a good chance you can find your niche by going in exactly the opposite direction. But be prepared for a lot of folks to wave you down and tell you you're headed the wrong way. I guess in all my years, what I heard more often than anything was: a town of less than 50,000 population cannot support a discount store for very long.

Source: www.walmartstores.com (accessed December 19, 2005).

In fiscal 2005, nearly 11,000 hourly associates in the United States were promoted to management positions; 76 percent of those in management positions in Wal-Mart's stores had been promoted from hourly jobs. The company's U.S. workforce included 220,000 seniors 55 and older, 775,000 women, 139,000 Hispanics, and 208,000 African Americans.

A majority of Wal-Mart's hourly store associates in the United States worked full-time—at most U.S. retailers, the percentage of full-time employees ranged between 20 and 40 percent. Part-time jobs at Wal-Mart were most common among sales clerks and check-out personnel in the stores where customer traffic varied appreciably during days of the week and months of the year. New full-time and part-time associates became eligible for health care benefits after a six-month wait and a one-year exclusion for preexisting conditions.

As of 2005, about 620,000 of Wal-Mart's 1.3 million associates in the United States (48 percent) had signed up for health insurance coverage in a Wal-Mart-sponsored plan (compared with an average of 72 percent for the whole retailing industry). Many Wal-Mart associates did not sign up for health coverage because another household member already had family coverage at his or her place of employment. Worker premiums for coverage were as little as $11 per month for individuals and 30 cents per day for children (no matter how many children an associate had). There were several plans that workers could choose from; usually, the lower the premium, the higher the annual deductible. The health benefit package covered 100 percent of most major medical expenses above $1,750 in employee out-of-pocket expenses and entailed no lifetime cap on medical cost coverage (a feature offered by fewer than 50 percent of employers).[32] The company's health benefits also included dental coverage, short- and long-term disability, an illness protection plan, and business travel accident insurance. But to help control its health costs for associates, Wal-Mart's health care plan did not pay for flu shots, eye exams, child vaccinations, chiropractic services, and certain other treatments allowed in the plans of many companies; further, Wal-Mart did not pay any health care costs for retirees. Due to Wal-Mart management's recent efforts to control costs for health benefits, the company's health care costs compared very favorably with those of other organizations:[33]

	Average Cost per Eligible Employee	
	2001	2002
U.S. employees of a cross-section of large, medium, and small companies	$4,924	$5,646
Employees of wholesale/retail stores	4,300	4,834
Wal-Mart employees (estimated)	3,000	3,500

However, critics assailed Wal-Mart's health care offering on grounds that the coverage was skimpier than that of many employers and that far too few Wal-Mart employees were eligible for coverage. According to 2005 data, 5 percent of Wal-Mart associates were on Medicaid, compared to an average for national employers of 4 percent, and 27 percent of associates' children were on such programs, compared to a national average of 22 percent. In total, 46 percent of associates' children were either on Medicaid or were uninsured.[34] Wal-Mart recognized that its critics had made valid points regarding the shortcomings of the company's health care offering. Starting in January 2006, Wal-Mart began providing health insurance to more than 1 million of its 1.7 million associates and offering up to 18 different plans.

Wal-Mart's package of fringe benefits for full-time employees (and some part-time employees) also included:

- Vacation and personal time.
- Holiday pay.
- Jury duty pay.
- Medical and bereavement leave.
- Military leave.
- Maternity/paternity leave.
- Confidential counseling services for associates and their families.
- Child care discounts for associates with children (through four national providers).
- GED reimbursement/scholarships for associates and their spouses.
- Discounts on selected merchandise (Sam's Club associates received a Sam's membership card at no cost).

In fiscal 2005, Wal-Mart spent $4.2 billion on benefits for its associates (equal to 1.9 percent of revenues), up from $2.8 billion in 2002 (1.5 percent of revenues). The company's benefit expenses were growing by 15 percent annually due to a combination of factors: growing workforce size, increased age and average tenure of associates, and rising cost trends for benefits, particularly health care. Top management and the board of directors were actively looking at strategies to contain the rising costs of the company's fringe benefit package, while at the same time preserving employee satisfaction with the benefit package and avoiding outcries from critics—in late 2005, a Wal-Mart executive provided the board of directors with a 12-page memo outlining "limited-risk" and "bold step" options for revising the company's benefits strategy.[35] Recent surveys of associates indicated overall satisfaction with the current benefit package (although this varied by benefit and associate demographics), but there was opposition to higher deductibles. Interestingly, the least healthy, least productive employees tended to be the most satisfied with their benefits and expressed interest in longer careers with Wal-Mart.

The Profit Sharing Plan   Wal-Mart maintained a profit-sharing plan for full and part-time associates; individuals were eligible after one year and 1,000 hours of service. Annual contributions to the plan were tied to the company's profitability and were made at the sole discretion of management and the board of directors. Employees could contribute up to 15 percent of their earnings to their 401(k) accounts. Wal-Mart's contribution to each associate's profit-sharing account became vested at the rate of 20 percent per year beginning the third year of participation in the plan. After the associate had been employed for seven continuous years, the company's contribution became fully vested; however, if the associate left the company prior to that time, the unvested portions were redistributed to all remaining employees. The plan was funded entirely by Wal-Mart, and most of the profit-sharing contributions were invested in Wal-Mart's common stock. In recent years, the company's contribution to profit sharing and the 401(k) plan had averaged 4 percent of an associate's eligible pay and amounted to $756 million in fiscal 2005 and $662 million in fiscal 2004; more than $4 billion had been contributed to associates' profit-sharing and 401(k) accounts since 1972. Associates could begin withdrawals from their account upon retirement or disability, with the balance paid to family members upon death.

Stock Purchase and Stock Option Plans   A stock purchase plan was adopted in 1972 to allow eligible employees a means of purchasing shares of common stock through regular payroll deduction or annual lump-sum contribution. Prior to 1990, the yearly maximum under this program was $1,500 per eligible employee; starting in 1990, the maximum was increased to $1,800 annually. The company contributed an amount equal to 15 percent of each participating associate's contribution. Longtime employees who had started participating in the early years of the program had accumulated stock worth over $100,000. About one-fourth of Wal-Mart's employees participated in the stock purchase plan in 1993, but this percentage had since declined, as many new employees opted not to participate.

In addition to regular stock purchases, certain employees qualified to participate in stock option plans; options expired 10 years from the date of the grant and could be exercised in nine annual installments. In 2005 over 80 million shares, with an estimated value of $3.8 billion, were reserved for issuance under the stock option plan.

Training

Top management was committed to providing all associates state-of-the-art training resources and development time to help achieve career objectives. The company had a number of training tools in place, including classroom courses, computer-based learning, distance learning, corporate intranet sites, mentor programs, satellite broadcasts, and skills assessments. In November 1985 the Walton Institute of Retailing was opened in affiliation with the University of Arkansas. Within a year of its inception, all Wal-Mart managers from the stores, the distribution facilities, and the general office were expected to take part in special programs at the Walton Institute to strengthen and develop the company's managerial capabilities.

Management Training   Wal-Mart store managers were hired in one of three ways. Hourly associates could move up through the ranks from sales to department manager to manager of the check lanes into store management training—more than 65 percent of Wal-Mart's managers had started out as hourly associates. Second, people with outstanding merchandising skills at other retail companies were recruited to join the ranks of Wal-Mart managers. And third, Wal-Mart recruited college graduates to enter the company's training program. Store management trainees went through an intensive on-the-job training program of almost 20 weeks and were then given responsibility for an area of the store. Trainees who progressed satisfactorily and showed leadership and job knowledge were promoted to an assistant manager, which included further training in various aspects of retailing and store operations. Given Wal-Mart's continued store growth, above-average trainees could progress to store manager within five years. Through bonuses for sales increases above projected amounts and company stock options, the highest-performing store managers earned well into six figures annually.

Associate Training   Wal-Mart did not provide a specialized training course for its hourly associates. Upon being hired, an associate was immediately placed in a position for on-the-job-training. From time to time, training films were shown in associates' meetings. Store managers and department managers were expected to train and supervise the associates under them in whatever ways were needed. As one associate put it, "Mostly you learn by doing. They tell you a lot; but you learn your job every day."

Special programs had been put in place to ensure that the company had an adequate talent pool of women and minorities who were well prepared for management positions. If company officers did not meet their individual diversity goals, their bonuses were cut 15 percent.

Meetings and Rapid Response

The company used meetings both as a communication device and as a culture-building exercise. In Bentonville, there were Friday merchandising meetings and Saturday morning meetings at 7:30 a.m. to review the week. The weekly merchandising meeting included buyers and merchandising staff headquartered in Bentonville and various regional managers who directed store operations. David Glass, Wal-Mart's former CEO explained the purpose of the Friday merchandise meeetings:

> In retailing, there has always been a traditional, head-to-head confrontation between operations and merchandising. You know, the operations guys say, "Why in the world would anybody buy this? It's a dog, and we'll never sell it." Then the merchandising folks say, "There's nothing wrong with that item. If you guys were smart enough to display it well and promote it properly, it would blow out the doors." So we sit all these folks down together every Friday at the same table and just have at it.

> We get into some of the doggonedest, knock-down drag-outs you have ever seen. But we have a rule. We never leave an item hanging. We will make a decision in that meeting even if it's wrong, and sometimes it

is. But when the people come out of that room, you would be hard-pressed to tell which ones oppose it and which ones are for it. And once we've made that decision on Friday, we expect it to be acted on in all the stores on Saturday. What we guard against around here is people saying, "Let's think about it." We make a decision. Then we act on it.[36]

At the Saturday-morning meetings—a Wal-Mart tradition since 1961—top officers and other key personnel gathered to exchange ideas on how well things were going and talk about any problems relating to the week's sales, store performance, special promotion items, store construction, distribution centers, transportation, supply chain activities, and so on. Management described the nature and purpose of the Saturday meetings as follows:

> Created with a sense of the unpredictable and intended to entertain as well as inform, the Saturday morning meeting lets everyone know what the rest of the company is up to.

> The agenda constantly changes, so each meeting has an element of spontaneity. Sometimes we'll bring associates from the field in to Bentonville to praise them in front of the whole meeting. Other mornings, an associate may get a standing ovation as he receives a 20-year service award.

> On any given Saturday, we may invite special guests to promote product launches or just to share insights. We've had CEOs of other Fortune 500 companies, musicians, actors, journalists, authors, athletes, politicians, and children's characters . . . That kind of unpredictability keeps things interesting.

> But beyond focusing on giving good news, entertaining special guests, and having a good time, we use that valuable time to critique our business. We review what we could do better and encourage suggestions about correcting those weaknesses. If the solution is obvious, we can order changes right then and carry them out over the weekend, while almost everyone else in retail business is off.

> The meeting is where we discuss and debate management philosophy and strategy. It's the focal point of our communication efforts, where we share ideas. We look at what our competition is doing well and look for ways to improve upon their successes in our own business. Often, it's the place where we decide to try things that seem unattainable, and instead of shooting those ideas down, we try to figure out how to make them work.

> The Saturday morning meeting remains the pulse of our culture.

As with the Friday merchandise meetings, decisions were made about what actions needed to be taken.

The store meetings and the Friday/Saturday meetings in Bentonville, along with the in-the-field visits by Wal-Mart management, created a strong bias for action. A *Fortune* reporter observed, "Managers suck in information from Monday to Thursday, exchange ideas on Friday and Saturday, and implement decisions in the stores on Monday."[37]

WAL-MART'S FUTURE

Sam Walton had engineered the development and rapid ascendancy of Wal-Mart to the forefront of the retailing industry—the discount stores and Sam's Clubs were strategic moves that he directed. His handpicked successor, David Glass, had directed the hugely successful move into Supercenters and grocery retailing, as well as presiding over the company's growth into the world's largest retailing enterprise; the Neighborhood Market store format also came into being during Glass's tenure as CEO. Lee Scott, Wal-Mart's third CEO, had the challenge of sustaining the company's growth, globalizing Wal-Mart's operations, continuing the long-term process of saturating the U.S. market with Supercenters, overseeing Wal-Mart's ever-larger business operations, and most recently, figuring out how to counteract the anti-Wal-Mart campaign being orchestrated by the company's critics and adversaries. Some of the issues that had come to his desk were embarrassing:

- In December 2005, Wal-Mart became the subject of a criminal investigation in Los Angeles over how it handled merchandise classified as hazardous waste. Wal-Mart apparently transported the materials from stores in California to a return center in Las Vegas before dumping them at a disposal site. But federal prosecutors said that process violated the U.S. Resource Conservation and Recovery Act. Instead of going to the return center in Vegas, the materials should have gone straight to the disposal site.

- Wal-Mart was ordered to compensate a number of former employees in Canada after it was ruled that the retail giant closed a store as a reprisal against unionization attempts. In Colorado, the United Food and Commercial Workers Union had accused Wal-Mart of harassing workers to keep them from joining its local in Denver and elsewhere; the number of such complaints had grown in recent years. A Wal-Mart board member, a high-level executive, and two Wal-Mart associates were dismissed following an internal investigation of improper expense account charges, improper payment of third-party invoices, and improper use of gift cards (some of which, according to critics, entailed efforts to finance anti-union activities and defeat unionization efforts at various Wal-Mart stores).

- An internal memo to Wal-Mart's board of directors, leaked to Wal-Mart Watch and the *New York Times,* proposed ways to control Wal-Mart's health care costs, including changing the benefits package in ways that would attract a healthier workforce and dissuade unhealthy people from coming to work at Wal-Mart. The memo stated that Wal-Mart associates spent an average of 8 percent of their incomes on heath care (premiums plus deductibles plus out-of-pocket expenses), an amount about twice the national average; the 8 percent number rose to as high as 13 percent on some of the plans that the company offered to employees. In 2004, 38 percent of Wal-Mart associates spent more than 16 percent of their Wal-Mart income on health care costs. Furthermore, the memo stated that Wal-Mart associates on the Family Plan for heath care sometimes had to spend 74 to 150 percent of annual income on health care costs before insurance took over the remaining costs of a serious health problem. All this was said to be a prime reason for Wal-Mart's expansion of health insurance coverage to more of its workforce as of January 2006.

- Wal-Mart had to temporarily stop selling guns at its 118 stores across California following what California's attorney general said were hundreds of violations of state laws. Investigations by California authorities revealed that six Wal-Mart stores had released guns before the required 10-day waiting period, failed to verify the identity of buyers properly, sold illegally to felons, and allowed other violations. Wal-Mart cooperated with governmental officials and agreed to immediately suspend firearm sales until correction action could be taken and store associates properly trained on state firearms laws.

- In New York state, Wal-Mart had run afoul of New York's 1988 toy weapons law. The toy guns Wal-Mart sold had an orange cap at the end of the barrel but otherwise looked real, thus violating New York laws banning toy guns with realistic colors such as black or aluminum and not complying with New York's requirement that toy guns have unremovable orange stripes along the barrel. Investigators from the state attorney general's office shopped 10 Wal-Marts in New York state from Buffalo to Long Island and purchased toy guns that violated the law at each of them. Wal-Mart had sold more than 42,000 toy guns in the state.

- In December 2005, federal agents executed search warrants on trailers belonging to five subcontracting companies working at the construction site of a new Wal-Mart distribution center in Pennsylvania. The warrants sought evidence of possible money laundering and using illegal immigrants to work on the project; 125 illegal aliens from Costa Rica, El Salvador, Guatemala, Honduras, and Mexico were detained shortly after they arrived to work at the construction site and placed into deportation proceedings.

- The discrimination lawsuit filed in 2003 by six female employees claimed that the company discriminated against women in pay, promotions, training, and job assignments—plaintiffs' attorneys asked for class action status for the lawsuit on behalf of all past and present female workers at Wal-Mart's U.S. stores. According to data from various sources, while two-thirds of Wal-Mart's hourly employees were women, less than 15 percent held store manager positions. There were also indications of pay gaps of 5–6 percent between male and female employees doing similar jobs and with similar experience levels; the pay gap allegedly widened higher up the management ladder. Male management trainees allegedly made an average of $23,175 a year, compared with $22,371 for women trainees.

- A 98-minute documentary entitled *Wal-Mart: The High Cost of Low Price* premiered in November 2005 and bashed the company for destroying once-thriving downtowns, running local merchants out of business, paying meager wages, selling goods produced in sweatshops in third world countries, and assorted other corporate sins. It showed testimony from ex-employees describing seedy practices and clips of individuals, families, and communities that had struggled to fight the company on various issues. Canadian unions had urged

their 340,000 members to take time to see the documentary and, where possible, to arrange screenings at local meetings and other union events. Anti-Wal-Mart journalists had praised the documentary. The *San Francisco Bay Guardian* said the movie "will make you fear and loathe [Wal-Mart] even more. The unscrupulous megaretailer is exposed from every angle: its devastating effect on small businesses and communities; its inadequate health care plans; its rabid antiunion stance; the racism and sexism sprinkled throughout its ranks; its blatant disregard for environmental issues; its practice of importing nearly all of its goods (churned from company sweatshops in countries like China, Bangladesh, and Honduras); and—perhaps most offensively— its faux-homespun television advertisements, which cast a golden glow on a corporation that clearly cares not for human beings, but for cold, hard cash."[38]

But Wal-Mart was beginning to fight back. It had hired a public relations firm that had put a staff of seven professionals in Bentonville to assist Wal-Mart's own PR staff to get the company's story out and respond within hours to any new blast of criticism.[39] Since mid-2004, Lee Scott had done nine interviews on TV, met with the editorial boards of *The Wall Street Journal* and the *Washington Post*, been interviewed by numerous newspaper journalists, and spoken to business and community leaders in Chicago, Los Angeles, Istanbul, and Paris. The company was striving to build relationships with congressional delegations, governors, mayors, community leaders, and activists in key locations. It had run ads in more than 100 newspapers. And it created a Web site (walmartfacts.com) to help set the record straight about what Wal-Mart did and did not do.

Wal-Mart had received favorable publicity in the media following hurricane Katrina, when its response with food, supplies, and cash assistance was faster than the U.S. government's effort; Wal-Mart had also donated $15 million to the Katrina relief effort. And there was growing interest on the part of academic researchers over whether Wal-Mart had a positive or negative effect on the economy. A New York University economist reported that a Wal-Mart store opening in Glendale, Arizona, received 8,000 applications for 525 jobs. A University of Missouri economist in an article published in the prestigious

Review of Economics and Statistics found that the entry of a Wal-Mart store increased a county's retail employment by 100 jobs in the first year and over time led to the elimination of 50 jobs at less-efficient retailers. Studies also showed that new businesses quickly sprang up near Wal-Mart stores; both new and existing stores along the routes leading to a Wal-Mart tended to flourish because of the heavy traffic flow to and from the company's stores.

But heading into 2006, stories in the media continued to be critical of Wal-Mart's operating practices and of the company in general. It was unclear whether the company's charm offensive was having the desired impact on public opinion and whether Wal-Mart's growth and profitability would be adversely affected by its critics and adversaries.

Endnotes

[1]Kevin Haslett, "Unions Wage Vicious, Misguided War on Wal-Mart," December 19, 2005, posted at www.bloomberg.com (accessed December 20, 2005).

[2] www.walmartwatch.com (accessed December 20, 2005).

[3]As quoted in Lorrie Grant, "Retail Giant Wal-Mart Faces Challenges on Many Fronts," *USA Today,* November 11, 2003, p. B2.

[4]Anthony Bianco and Wendy Zellner, "Is Wal-Mart Too Powerful?" *BusinessWeek,* October 6, 2003, p. 103.

[5]Ibid.

[6]Ibid., p. 108.

[7]Ann Zimmerman, "After Huge Raid on Illegals, Wal-Mart Fires Back at U.S.," *The Wall Street Journal,* December 19, 2003, pp. A1, A10.

[8]Bianco and Zellner, "Is Wal-Mart Too Powerful?" pp. 104, 106.

[9]As quoted in "Can Wal-Mart Fit into a White Hat?" *BusinessWeek,* October 3, 2005, p. 94.

[10]Anthony Bianco and Wendy Zellner, "Is Wal-Mart Too Powerful?" *BusinessWeek,* October 6, 2003, p. 102.

[11]Jerry Useem, "One Nation Under Wal-Mart," *Fortune,* March 3, 2003, p. 66.

[12]The most recent study was done by Jerry Hausman (Ph.D. from MIT) and Ephraim Leibtag (from U.S. Department of Agriculture) in a paper entitled "Consumer Benefits from Increased Competition in Shopping Outlets: Measuring the Effect of Wal-Mart." The paper was presented at the Economic Impact Research Conference: An In-Depth Look at Wal-Mart and Society, held in Washington, D.C., on November 4, 2005.

[13]As quoted in Jerry Useem, "One Nation Under Wal-Mart," *Fortune,* March 3, 2003, p. 68.

[14]Global Insight, *The Economic Impact of Wal-Mart,* November 2005.

[15]As quoted in Bill Saporito, "What Sam Walton Taught America," *Fortune,* May 4, 1992, p. 105.

[16]The information in this paragraph is drawn from John Helyar, "The Only Company Wal-Mart Fears," *Fortune,* November 24, 2003, pp. 158–66.

[17]As quoted in *Fortune,* January 30, 1989, p.53.

[18]As quoted in Useem, "One Nation Under Wal-Mart;" p. 68.

[19]Cannondale Associates, 2005 PoweRanking Results, November 2, 2005; press release at www.cannondaleassoc.com (accessed December 15, 2005).

[20]As quoted in Useem, "One Nation Under Wal-Mart," p. 74.

[21]Ibid.

[22]Ibid.

[23]As quoted in "Wal-Mart's Way," *Information Week,* September 27, 2004,

[24]Paul Lightfoot, "Wal-Martification," *Operations and Fulfillment,* June 1, 2003, posted at www.opsandfulfillment.com.

[25]Sam Walton with John Huey, *Sam Walton: Made in America* (New York: Doubleday, 1992), p. 12.

[26]Ibid., pp. 10, 12, 47, 63, 115, 128, 135, 140, 213, 226–29, 233, 246, 249–54, and 256.

[27]Useem, "One Nation Under Wal-Mart," p. 72.

[28]Information posted at www.walmartstores.com (accessed December 19, 2005).

[29]Quote taken from the section on Wal-Mart Culture, posted at www.walmartstores.com (accessed December 19, 2005).

[30]Data for Wal-Mart are from company sources; the wage data for retail workers and Costco workers were cited in a May 3, 2005, article appearing in the *New York Times* that was quoted in part at www.walmartwatch.com (accessed December 20, 2005).

[31]Information posted at www.walmartstores.com (accessed December 19, 2005).

[32]Bernard Wysocki and Ann Zimmerman, "Wal-Mart Cost-Cutting Finds Big Target in Health Benefits," *The Wall Street Journal,* September 30, 2003, pp. A1, A16.

[33]Ibid.

[34]Based on an internal memo by Susan Chambers to Wal-Mart's board of directors that was leaked to Wal-Mart Watch and posted at www.walmartwatch.com (accessed December 20, 2005).

[35]The contents of the memo were obtained by Wal-Mart Watch and posted at www.walmartwatch.com (accessed December 2005).

[36]Walton with Huey, *Sam Walton,* pp. 225–26.

[37]Saporito, "What Sam Walton Taught America," p. 105.

[38]*San Francisco Bay Guardian,* November 23–29, 2005, posted at www.sfbg.com (accessed December 20, 2005).

[39]Robert Berner, "Can Wal-Mart Fit into a White Hat?" *BusinessWeek,* October 3, 2005, p. 94.

Case 26

Outback Steakhouse

Sarah June Gauntlett
The University of Alabama

In the wake of changing executive leadership and rising energy and commodity costs, Outback Steakhouse Inc. was struggling to retain and increase market share in the casual-dining segment of the restaurant industry. Additionally, the 2005 hurricane season was devastating—15 percent of Outback restaurants were located in the areas hit by the hurricanes. From its inception, Outback had experienced tremendous growth, adding 30–65 new locations a year domestically and internationally, but the company had experienced soft revenue growth in 2004 as same-store sales did not increase. In response, Outback reinvented its menu by focusing on core specialties and introducing smaller portions for health-conscious consumers. Despite numerous obstacles and challenges, the company remained focused on its "Recipe for Success," which included preparing each meal from scratch and treating people as individuals. Outback's goal was to succeed one restaurant, one person at a time.

To help drive company growth, management had diversified into eight different restaurant formats and menus that spanned both casual and upscale dining:

- *Outback Steakhouse*—From the signature "Bloomin' Onion" to the full-flavored steaks, chops, ribs, chicken, and seafood, Outback Steakhouse offered quality food in a casual, Australian-themed atmosphere. Outback's service was defined by a promise of "No Rules. Just Right."

- *Carrabba's*—Carrabba's Italian Grill featured warm Italian hospitality; authentic aromas from a lively exhibition kitchen; and flavorful, hearty, handmade dishes prepared from original Carrabba family recipes.

- *Lee Roy Selmon's*—Lee Roy Selmon's was a family sports restaurant featuring heartwarming hospitality and generous portions of soul-satisfying comfort food. It was a favorite place to eat, drink, relax, and be with friends and family.

- *Cheeseburger in Paradise*—At Cheeseburger in Paradise, Jimmy Buffet's famous song came to life with the signature cheeseburger in a Key West–style setting. Great food, cool cocktails, and live music every night of the week combined for the ultimate experience in an escape to paradise.

- *Bonefish Grill*—Bonefish Grill specialized in market-fresh fish from all over the world, prepared over a wood-burning grill to ensure a tasty, even flavor. A tantalizing array of sauces and original toppings was offered to enhance the flavor of the fish, each in a fun and different way.

- *Fleming's Prime Steakhouse and Wine Bar*—Fleming's offered the best in steakhouse dining in a stylish, contemporary setting. Featuring the finest prime steaks, chops, fresh grilled fish, seafood and chicken, the menu was complemented by a unique and notable wine list featuring 100 fine wines by the glass.

- *Roy's*—Founded by James Beard Award winner Chef Roy Yamaguchi, Roy's exciting and innovative Hawaiian fusion cuisine incorporated the freshest local ingredients, European sauces, and bold Asian spices, with a focus on fresh seafood.

- *Paul Lee's Chinese Kitchen*—Friends and family delighted in traditional favorites and new specialties at Paul Lee's Chinese Kitchen, where only the freshest meats, fish, and vegetables are prepared in Chinese woks. For those too busy to dine in a warm, relaxed setting, there was a second kitchen dedicated solely to take-out.

AUSSIE BEGINNING

One evening in late 1987, Chris Sullivan, Bob Basham, and Tim Gannon gathered at a jazz club in Tampa, Florida, to brainstorm the name of their new restaurant venture. Their objective was to create a dining "experience" offering high-quality food and service, generous portions at moderate prices, and a casual atmosphere entrenched with an Australian theme. After the young men had downed several brews, the name Outback emerged as a suggestion and was unanimously agreed on. Shortly thereafter, Trudy Cooper joined the team and plans were made to open the very first Outback Steakhouse on Henderson Boulevard in Tampa, Florida. Tim Gannon, known as the "Food Guy," brought in world-renowned chef Warren Larue to design and create the menu for the new restaurant venture. Larue created bold, distinctive spices and a unique flavor for each dish. Originally, the Outback business plan consisted of four restaurants, one for each respective founder. The cofounders' intent was to have fun, earn a nice income, and enjoy a Florida lifestyle. The first restaurant, which opened in 1988, met with tremendous success. Word spread quickly among consumers and industry peers regarding the quality of food, with its bold flavors, and the "no rules" service style. The number of Outback Steakhouses grew rapidly: One restaurant soon became 4, then 10, then 20, and so on (see Exhibits 1 and 2).

Exhibit 2   International Locations of Outback Restaurants, 2004

Australia	Japan
Bahamas	Korea
Brazil	Malaysia
Canada	Mexico
China	Philippines
Costa Rica	Puerto Rico
Dominican Republic	Singapore
Guam	Thailand
Hong Kong	United Kingdom
Indonesia	Venezuela

Source: Outback Steakhouse Inc. 2004 annual report.

The Outback Steakhouse concept was clearly well accepted by customers, Outbackers (i.e., employees), and industry peers. Company-owned restaurants consisted of restaurants owned by partnerships (with the company as the general partner) and joint ventures (with the company as one of the two members). The company's ownership interests in partnerships and joint ventures generally ranged from 50 to 90 percent. Unique to the restaurant industry, Outback provided the opportunity for true ownership and self-responsibility, cutting the managing partner a 10 percent share of ownership in his or her restaurant. Company-owned restaurants also included restaurants owned by Roy's consolidated venture, in which the company had less than a majority ownership. The rationale for consolidating this venture was that Outback Steakhouse Inc. controlled the executive committee

Exhibit 1   Outback Steakhouse Inc. Locations, 2004

Outback Steakhouse Inc. and Affiliates	Outback Steakhouse (Domestic)	Outback Steakhouse (International)	Carrabba's Italian Grill	Bonefish Grill	Fleming's	Roy's	Other	Total
Company-owned	652	69	168	59	31	18	14	1,011
Development joint venture	1	12	—	—	—	—	—	13
Franchise	103	44	—	4	—	—	—	151
Total	756	125	168	63	31	18	14	1,175

Source: Outback Steakhouse Inc. 2004 annual report.

and had control through representation on the committee by related parties, enabling the company to direct management and daily operations. The company was responsible for 50 percent of the costs of new restaurants operated under this consolidated venture, and the joint venture partner was responsible for the other 50 percent. Restaurants with no direct investment from the company operated under franchise agreements with the company, receiving a specified percentage of net income. The results of company-owned restaurants were included in the consolidated statements of income, and the results of development-joint-venture restaurants were accounted for under the equity method of accounting.

FINANCIAL POSITION

Outback management periodically brainstormed options for funding capital to grow. On June 18, 1991, Outback Steakhouse Inc. held an initial public offering (IPO) for its common stock, selling 1.57 million shares at a price of $15 per share; the stock began trading on the Nasdaq. Between December 1991 and March 1999, Outback's stock split four times; in April 2000, the company moved trading from the Nasdaq to the New York Stock Exchange (NYSE). Chris Sullivan, Outback's chief executive officer, felt the move would benefit the shareholders by providing greater visibility and a broader investor base. The NYSE presented lower price volatility and smaller order execution costs that benefited investors. On October 23, 2002, the company declared its first quarterly dividend of $0.12 per share of common stock.

Beginning in December 2004, Outback started revising its accounting lease practices to include option renewals reasonably assumed to be exercised resulting in the restatement of the financial statements for the years ended December 31, 2004, 2003, and 2002. The restatement reflected estimated reductions of net income of approximately $3,346,000, $2,951,000, and $2,855,000 for the years ended December 31, 2004, 2003, and 2002, respectively. These restatement adjustments were noncash and had no impact on revenues or net operating cash flow. The company also changed its accounting method for partnership programs to the "stock compensation" model from the "minority interest" model that was previously used. As a result, partnership cash flow distributions to general managers and area operating partners were treated as compensation expense instead of minority interest profit. Moreover, company purchases of partnership interests from area operating partners were treated as compensation expense instead of being recorded as an intangible asset. On July 26, 2000, the company initiated a program to repurchase up to 4 million shares of the company's stock with the timing, price, quantity, and manner of the purchases to be made at management's discretion dependent on market conditions. On July 23, 2003, the company initiated a second program to repurchase 2.5 million additional shares on a regular basis to offset shares issued due to the exercise of stock options. The company funded these repurchase programs with available cash and bank credit facilities. As of year-end 2004, 11,819,000 shares of common stock had been repurchased for approximately $400,259,000. Exhibits 3–5 show the company's restated financial statements for 2002–2004. Exhibit 6 gives details about restaurant operations during the same period.

NEW EXECUTIVE SUITE

On March 8, 2005, Outback announced that long-time chairman and CEO Chris Sullivan was stepping down immediately, turning over the reins to Bill Allen. Concurrently, the company announced that Paul Avery, who had been president, was transitioning into a co-chair role. Allen had previously headed up Outback's West Coast Concepts division. Becoming co-chair was a huge step up, as the West Coast Concepts division had fewer than 100 restaurants under its domain, whereas Outback Steakhouse Inc. had over 1,000 company-owned restaurants. Chris Sullivan and Bob Basham remained as co-chairs of the board to ensure an effective transition to new leadership. As with any company that experienced executive management transitions, Outback Steakhouse faced some level of execution risk from its changes. Even skilled executives and high-achieving companies stumbled a bit during a management transition. Although all signs indicated that Allen was a talented and motivated executive, even exceptional managers encountered a learning curve when taking on greatly expanded responsibilities.

Six weeks after Sullivan resigned, Bob Merritt, chief financial officer, announced his retirement. Merritt had been with the company since 1990 and justified his retirement decision on frustration with

Exhibit 3 **Statement of Operations, Outback Steakhouse Inc. and Affiliates, 2002–2004 (in thousands)**

	2004	2003	2002
Revenues			
Restaurant sales	$3,183,297	$2,647,991	$2,276,599
Other revenue	18,453	17,786	17,915
Total revenue	$3,201,750	$2,665,777	$2,294,514
Cost of revenue	1,193,262	983,362	856,951
Gross profit	$2,008,488	$1,682,415	$1,437,563
Operating expenses			
Selling, general, and administrative	1,562,467	1,273,478	1,078,107
Depreciation and amortization	104,310	84,876	73,294
Other	89,680	65,143	58,819
Total operating expenses	$1,756,457	$1,423,497	$1,210,220
Operating income	252,031	258,918	227,343
Total other income/expenses	(4,384)	(1,431)	(2,110)
Elimination of minority partners' interest	9,415	2,532	(1,580)
Income before tax	$ 238,232	$ 254,955	$ 226,813
Provision for income tax	82,175	87,700	78,838
Cumulative effect of a change in accounting principle	—	—	(740)
Net income	$ 156,057	$ 167,255	$ 147,235

Source: Outback Steakhouse Inc. 2004 annual report.

overzealous regulators, accounting rules bordering on "lunacy," and "growing public perception that all businesspeople were dishonest." Merritt complained about the legal and regulatory burdens associated with the Sarbanes-Oxley Act of 2002. He said that those burdens left executives with little time for strategic planning or profit building and that he spent most of his time trying to comply with arcane rules and avoid making mistakes. What sent him over the edge were the accounting rules concerning the payment of rent and improvements to leased property. Although lease-accounting rules had changed little since 1976, public accountants made cautious after Sarbanes-Oxley began to question the way in which restaurants reported leases. Outback's accountants advised the company to restate prior earnings based on changing interpretations of existing lease-accounting rules. Merritt vowed to never work for a publicly traded company again but admitted he was willing to serve on public company boards if invited. Merritt was later invited to be an independent director on the board of directors for Cosi Inc., an operator and franchisor of bakery-café stores. In October 2005, Outback named Dirk Montgomery

as Merritt's successor. Montgomery had over 15 years' experience in the food and retail industry; he had previously served as retail senior financial officer for ConAgra Foods and chief financial officer of Express.

RESTAURANT PORTFOLIO

To capitalize on the growing popularity of casual dining, Outback decided in 1993 to begin expanding its restaurant portfolio, mainly through joint-venture partnerships. The company engaged in the ownership, development, and operation of casual-dining restaurants (primarily in the United States) that served lunch and dinner, featuring menus consisting of steaks, prime rib, pork chops, ribs, chicken, seafood, and pasta. The company's provision of capital and real estate expertise, procurement services, and unit-level engineering, as well as legal and financial support, allowed partners and management of each concept to focus on the basics of their business. Outback prided itself on having the most stable young brands, with the most growth

Exhibit 4 **Balance Sheet, Outback Steakhouse and Affiliates, 2003–2004 (in thousands)**

	2004	2003
Assets		
Current assets		
Cash and cash equivalents	$ 87,977	$ 102,892
Short-term investments	1,425	20,824
Inventories	63,448	59,608
Deferred income tax asset	12,969	11,757
Other current assets	53,068	37,529
Total current assets	$ 218,887	$ 232,610
Property, plant, and equipment, net	1,235,151	1,049,546
Investments in and advances to unconsolidated affiliates, net	16,254	31,209
Intangible assets	21,683	—
Goodwill	107,719	86,745
Other assets	78,098	74,008
Notes receivable collateral for franchisee guarantee	30,239	—
Total assets	$1,708,031	$1,474,118
Liabilities and stockholders' equity		
Current liabilities		
Accounts payable	$ 74,162	$ 58,533
Accrued expenses	97,124	80,248
Current portion of long-term debt	54,626	48,901
Unearned revenue	100,895	82,670
Other current liabilities	40,383	44,177
Total current liabilities	$ 367,190	$ 314,529
Deferred rent	44,075	37,454
Partner deposit and accrued buyout liability	63,102	42,628
Long-term debt	59,900	9,550
Other long-term liabilities	36,457	6,607
Total liabilities	$ 570,724	$ 410,768
Commitments and contingencies		
Interest of minority partners in consolidated partnerships	$ 48,905	$ 58,126
Stockholders' equity		
Common stock	788	788
Treasury stock	(206,824)	(161,808)
Additional paid-in capital	271,109	254,852
Retained earnings	1,025,447	913,470
Accumulated other comprehensive loss	(2,118)	(2,078)
Total stockholders' equity	$1,088,402	$1,005,224
Total liabilities and stockholders' equity	$1,708,031	$1,474,118

Source: Outback Steakhouse Inc. 2004 annual report.

potential, among the major multichain operators within the casual-dining segment. As of March 31, 2005, the company operated 888 Outback Steakhouses, 176 Carrabba's Italian Grills, 72 Bonefish Grills, 32 Fleming's Prime Steakhouse and Wine Bars, 19 Roy's, 2 Lee Roy Selmon's, 3 Paul Lee's Chinese Kitchens, and 14 Cheeseburger in Paradise restaurants in 50 states and 21 countries. In

Exhibit 5 **Statement of Cash Flows, Outback Steakhouse and Affiliates, 2002–2004 (in thousands)**

	2004	2003	2002
Cash flow from operating activities			
Net cash provided by operating activities	$ 322,265	$ 269,082	$ 294,000
Cash flow from investment activities			
Net cash used for investing activities	(290,860)	(230,061)	(168,066)
Cash flow from financing activities			
Net cash used in financing activities	(46,320)	(123,707)	(54,284)
Net change in cash and equivalents	(14,915)	(84,686)	71,650
Cash at beginning of period	102,892	187,578	115,928
Cash at end of period	$ 87,977	$ 102,892	$ 187,578

Source: Outback Steakhouse, Inc. 2004 Annual Report

August 2005, the company was approved by the U.S. Bankruptcy Court for the District of Delaware as the successful bidder for the rights to 76 properties of Chi-Chi's and its affiliates. Outback's objective for acquiring these rights was to have access to restaurant sites for conversion to one of its own concepts. The company's overall strategy focused on offering consumers an array of dining alternatives suited for differing needs or occasions.

Carrabba's Italian Grill

In April 1993, Outback purchased a 50 percent interest in the cash flows of two Carrabba's Italian Grill restaurants located in Houston, Texas, and entered into a 50–50 joint venture with the founders to develop more Carrabba's restaurants. Outback acquired sole ownership of this venture in early 1995. Johnny Carrabba and Damian Mandola, Carrabba's cofounders, both possessed immense passion for Carrabba's and kept their Italian roots and traditions at the forefront of the business. Carrabba's grasped diners' attention immediately with eye-catching rooftopgardens and a warm ambiance that featured handmade Italian dishes prepared in an exhibition-style kitchen. In addition to traditional Italian entrées, the menu featured fresh fish, seafood, wood-fired pizza, meats smothered in special seasonings, and an extensive wine list featuring wide selections of midrange to high-end wines. Each Carrabba's location offered a chef's daily special menu, in part to allow managing partners to accommodate local tastes and preferences.

In 2004, there was encouraging progress in the redesign of Carrabba's restaurants. The new stores were smaller and less expensive to operate. Average store sales volumes for the smaller units kept pace with the larger units, gaining the company's confidence that unit-level returns on invested capital justified widespread national expansion. In acknowledgment of emerging lifestyles, Carrabba's implemented a carside carry-out service and planned to continue enhancing this service. Advertising had also made a positive impact on revenues. Television commercials captured Johnny Carrabba and Damian Mandola's generous Italian spirit and passion for fresh, quality ingredients. Carrabba and Mandola snagged a spot on the PBS cooking show *Cucina Amore,* which aired in more than half of all TV markets. Carrabba's had a total of 168 restaurants domestically in 2004 and planned to open an additional 25 stores in 2005.

Bonefish Grill

To fill the niche between formal, upscale seafood restaurants and family-style seafood eateries, Outback formed a joint venture with Bonefish Grill. Bonefish was positioned as a casual-dining concept featuring fresh, high-quality seafood served in an upbeat environment with distinctive artwork inspired by Florida's natural coastal setting. The casual-dining seafood segment was ripe for a concept to go national. The menu featured a "cosmic" collection of finfish cooked over an oak-burning grill and hand-cut beef, pasta, and chicken dishes garnished with special sauces. Menu selections featured quality ingredients, including hearts of palm, pine nuts, artichokes, goat cheese, and sun-dried tomatoes. Bonefish showed its commitment to serving fresh food by receiving,

Exhibit 6   **Restaurant Operations, 2002–2004**

	2004	2003	2002
Average unit volumes for restaurants opened for one year or more (in thousands):			
Outback Steakhouse	$ 3,465	$ 3,375	$ 3,311
Carrabba's Italian Grill	3,108	3,103	3,050
Fleming's Prime Steakhouse and Wine Bar	4,783	3,893	4,197
Roy's	3,496	3,157	3,364
Bonefish Grill	3,220	3,124	N/A
Average unit volumes for restaurants opened for less than one year (in thousands):			
Outback Steakhouse	$ 3,179	$ 3,212	$ 3,058
Carrabba's Italian Grill	2,939	2,964	2,901
Fleming's Prime Steakhouse and Wine Bar	3,492	3,995	3,209
Roy's	3,414	3,195	2,764
Bonefish Grill	2,965	3,022	3,069
Operating weeks:*			
Outback Steakhouse	33,304	31,058	28,897
Carrabba's Italian Grill	8,228	5,327	4,221
Fleming's Prime Steakhouse and Wine Bar	1,302	1,010	711
Roy's	941	826	640
Bonefish Grill	2,234	1,070	309
Year-to-year percentage change:			
Menu price increases:†			
Outback Steakhouse	2.4%	0.8%	1.6%
Carrabba's Italian Grill	1.5	0.9	1.0
Bonefish Grill	3.0	0.3	N/A
Same-store sales (stores open 18 months or more):			
Outback Steakhouse	2.7	1.9	−0.1
Carrabba's Italian Grill	3.3	1.8	1.7
Fleming's Prime Steakhouse and Wine Bar	17.1	12.7	10.2
Roy's	11.5	10.0	11.0
Bonefish Grill	7.5	2.0	N/A

*Represents the combined number of weeks that all units in each restaurant chain were in operation and open for business; existing units were typically open all 52 weeks, but newly-opened units were open only a portion of the 52 weeks.

†Reflected nominal amounts of menu price changes, prior to any change in product mix because of price increases, and may not reflect amounts effectively paid by the customer. Menu price increases were not provided for Fleming's and Roy's as a significant portion of their sales come from specials, which fluctuate daily.

Source: Outback Steakhouse Inc. 2004 annual report.

inspecting, and hand-cutting its fish daily and preparing its dishes with modern culinary techniques. It cultivated relationships with suppliers to distribute seafood daily to the restaurant. Bonefish had 63 locations by the end of 2004 and planned to develop 35 to 40 more locations in 2005. It possessed great growth potential, evidenced by the success and acceptance of the original restaurants and new locations.

The Upscale-Dining Segment: Fleming's Prime Steakhouse and Roy's

In 1998, Outback identified upscale casual dining as a new target segment. This segment was attractive because of its revenue potential. Outback decided to break into this new segment through forming joint ventures with two proven winners: Fleming's Prime Steakhouse and Wine Bar and Roy's. Paul Fleming and Bill Allen, founders of Fleming's, had a long and successful track record in the restaurant industry, especially with restaurant chains such as P. F. Chang's China Bistro. Fleming's was embedded as a high-end prime steakhouse whose contemporary style featured light woods, high ceilings, and 100 quality wines by the glass.

The vast selection of high-end wines and the shape of its crystal glasses differentiated Fleming's from competitors. Fleming's offered an exceptional wine list featuring boutique vintages from California, Oregon, and Washington, augmented by selections from France, Italy, Australia, and South Africa. Fleming's served only the finest in USDA prime beef. USDA prime beef came from corn-fed cattle (to keep the meat tender, these cattle were given no grazing privileges). To achieve distinctive taste, Fleming's aged its steaks up to four weeks for flavor and texture, then hand-cut and broiled them at 1,600 degrees to seal in the juices. Fleming's menu featured flavorful dishes ranging from fresh seafood such as ahi tuna, swordfish, and lobster tails to chicken, pork, and lamb specialties in addition to its superior prime beef. *Nation's Restaurant News* gave Fleming's its "Hot New Concept" award in May 2000. Fleming's was the strongest earnings performer in Outback's restaurant portfolio, achieving a 10.7 percent growth of average sales volume in 2004. The company exercised its option in September 2004 to purchase an additional 39 percent interest in Fleming's from the concept's founders. As of March 31, 2005, Fleming's had 32 locations in areas such as Las Vegas, Newport Beach, Houston, El Segundo, Birmingham, and North Scottsdale, and was expected to open 9 more new locations later in the year.

In 1999, Outback established a joint venture with Roy Yamaguchi to develop and operate Roy's restaurants worldwide. Chef Roy Yamaguchi had won many prestigious awards, including the James Beard Award and admittance to the Fine Dining Hall of Fame, and Roy's had garnered acclaim as the "crown jewel of East-West eateries." Yamaguchi acted as a tireless ambassador for his cuisine and inspired and motivated chef partners while investing time visiting each restaurant location. Roy's Hawaiian fusion cuisine fit nicely in the high-end seafood segment, where attention was focused heavily on the

food: textures, colors, and bold flavors appealing to all the senses. Roy's dishes were complemented well by exclusive wines blended solely for Roy's by some of the finest winemakers in the world. The menu incorporated a variety of fish and seafood, beef, short ribs, pork, lamb, and chicken with blends of flavorful sauces and Asian spices. Roy's created an upscale casual-dining experience featuring spacious dining rooms, an expansive lounge area, and an exhibition-style kitchen finished in stainless steel and appointed with copper accents. Guests of Roy's were often well-traveled individuals seeking an upscale yet casual ambiance, and they wanted the convenience of reservations. Roy's experienced a sales momentum push beginning in 2003 and lasting through 2004. Average store sales volumes grew by 10.3 percent in 2004, making Roy's a sturdy revenue contributor in Outback's portfolio.

PRINCIPLES AND BELIEFS

While Outback was growing rapidly, the founders felt that the company's fun and caring culture was eroding as more managers and hourly Outbackers came in from other restaurants. A positive aspect of the influx was that the newcomers brought with them their previous experience, but they also brought ingrained habits. In 1990, the founders knew that they needed to take action quickly to uphold Outback's unique culture and business style. Thus, the four spent nine months in 1990 contemplating and verbalizing the values, beliefs, goals, keys to success, guiding principles, and direction of the company. They hoped to recapture the original flare of Outback's culture. During this process, they started over from the beginning to figure out what had been lost.

When the "visioneering" process was complete in 1999, the leadership team produced a document called the Principles and Beliefs (P&Bs). This five-and-a-half-page document quickly became Outback's operating manifesto and gained momentum over the years. The P&Bs outlined the founders' prescribed "recipe for success"; it defined Outback to its stakeholders and explained how the company's identity was to be created. Stakeholders included Outbackers, customers, purveyors, neighbors, and partners. The P&Bs incorporated Outback's core principles, commitments to Outbackers (see Exhibit 7) and other

Exhibit 7   **Outback Steakhouse Commitment to Outbackers**

We keep our nine commitments to Outbackers, guided by our five principles.
Our purpose is to prepare Outbackers to exercise good judgment and live our *Principles and Beliefs.*
There are no probationary Outbackers.
Because of our *Serious Food, Concentrated Service,* and *No Rules,*
Outbackers approach our Customers with confidence and a sense of ownership while demonstrating our principles
of Hospitality and Quality. They are proud to be Outbackers. Outback's environment requires people to be
tough on results, but kind with people.
It is an environment where managers are focused on serving Customers and supporting their Outbackers.
Outbackers know they are valued and that situations special to them will be handled with respect and concern.
How we take care of Outbackers is embodied in the details of our nine commitments to them.
*Clear Direction, Preparation, Involvement, Affecting One's Own Destiny, A Fair Hearing, Sharing in the Success,
Making a Commitment, Having a Good Time,* and *Compassion.*

stakeholders, and connections to exemplify that living the P&Bs was a source of happiness, remarkable success, and personal commitment to Outback. The leadership team recognized early that Outbackers were the faces, hearts, and hands of the company. The company considered its employees—approximately 80,000 Outbackers were employed by the company in 2004—to be its most valuable resource. They were the ones customers saw when visiting the restaurant, and the ones who established a connection with the customer. The first sentence of the P&Bs read, "We believe that if we take care of Our People, then the institution of Outback will take care of itself." Management believed that, if the P&Bs were followed, Outback would be in position to achieve the five following goals:

- *For Outbackers, A great place to work, have fun, and make money;*
- *For Customers, Favorite place to eat, drink, relax, and be with friends;*
- *For Purveyors, A great customer and source of comfort and pride;*
- *For Neighbors, A valued corporate citizen and neighbor; and*
- *For Partners, A superior financial and emotional investment opportunity.*

DAILY OPERATIONS AT OUTBACK

A typical day at an Outback Steakhouse began around nine in the morning with the arrival of the prep crew.

All signature ingredients, sauces, and soups were prepared from scratch daily. Food was delivered daily to the store and immediately placed in the preparation process. Management negotiated directly with food suppliers to ensure uniform quality and adequate supplies. The crew promptly began making salad dressings. Each dressing marinated for an extended time to ensure that the proper flavor was achieved, and croutons took three hours to season and toast. Outback used quality blends of freshly grated cheeses from Wisconsin, imported Parmesan cheese, and imported Swiss Gruyere. Outback prepared "Aussie chips," its version of French fries, in-house to guarantee quality by extensively rinsing the potatoes to remove excess starches and sugars. Desserts, including brownies and chocolate and caramel sauces—were prepared daily as well.

Outback used only top-grade USDA center-cut Choice steaks from Nebraska or Colorado and seasoned them with Outback seasoning, which consisted of a blend of various spices and 19 different peppers. To maintain quality, Outback required its beef suppliers to provide written documentation confirming that the cattle used for Outback steaks were raised and fed in compliance with U.S. government regulations designed to prevent bovine spongiform encephalopathy (mad cow disease). Additionally, the company prohibited suppliers from using mammal protein by-products in cattle feed. All chicken, beef, and fish were fresh, never frozen. About one hour before opening time, a line check took place, which consisted of tasting all the sauces, dressings, and soups to ensure quality for the customers. A heavy emphasis was placed on food quality, and extra cost was always absorbed to provide "serious food" to customers.

OUTBACK'S STRATEGY

In 2005, Outback was a well-established brand name among consumers worldwide. With 881 locations, customers knew they could dine in any Outback restaurant and receive a top-quality meal for a reasonable price. While continually growing, Outback reached consumers in new markets through creative television and radio advertising and sports affiliations. When Outback entered a new market, customers lined up to taste the beloved Bloomin' Onion. Although beef and steak items comprised a large portion of the menu, Outback restaurants also offered a variety of chicken, rib, seafood, and pasta dishes. The company's philosophy of "No Rules, Just Right" allowed customers to personalize their dining experience by choosing how menu selections were prepared. Outback chose to differentiate itself by offering generous portions of high-quality food and superior service in a casual Australian outback atmosphere.

Marketing and Advertising

In 2005, Outback's innovative, edgy advertisements drew the criticism that the company was trying too hard to be funny. The particular commercial that received the most criticism showed a man on one knee holding his beloved's hand, about to propose, when a boomerang thwacked him on the head. Instead of asking the woman to marry him, the man asked her to take him to Outback. When the boomerang returned and conked the woman on the head, she agreed. Widespread consumer disapproval caused Outback to stop using its "humor message" in core Outback brand marketing. The new advertising strategy, expected to launch around the beginning of 2006, would focus more on food and taste.

Outback engaged in a variety of promotional activities, such as contributing goods, time, and money to charitable, civic, and cultural programs. The Outback brand was attached to events ranging from NCAA college football, to Donald Trump's television show *Apprentice,* to NASCAR. Starting in 1994, the Outback Bowl attracted a national ESPN audience for the New Year's Day college football bowl game. The Outback Bowl was the sixth-highest-paying bowl game, with a matchup between the Big Ten and the Southeastern Conference. Outback's relationship with NASCAR consisted of an alliance with driver Dale Jarret and in-store driver appearances.

Broadcaster John Madden, who had an ongoing partnership with the company, traveled to his Monday-night football games in the Outback Steakhouse Madden Cruiser, providing exposure and promotional opportunities for the company. Also, the *Bloomin' Onion I,* the Outback blimp, traveled across the country providing coverage for ABC sports events, including Professional Golfers' Association tournaments, the Little League World Series, and National College Athletic Association football. The blimp aided in further enhancing awareness of Outback nationwide.

Focus on Customer and Customer Satisfaction

Outback went all out to guarantee that customers had a positive, fun dining experience. As customers walked up to the restaurant, they were greeted with a smiling face and a door that opened especially for them. Those who incurred a wait found many activities to engage in—magazines, children's toys, and free samples of Bloomin' Onion helped them pass the time. To help reduce wait times, Outback implemented call-ahead seating. This initiative increased the number of customer visits by regulating table turnover.

To address emerging consumer preferences and lifestyles, Outback began offering curbside take-away. Following this implementation, food-to-go sales represented a larger proportion of the company's total sales compared to prior years—nearly one out of three consumers used curbside take-away. Upon calling the neighborhood Outback, the customer was greeted by a warm, friendly voice and asked to place an order. The take-away server made sure to document the color and type of car the customer would be driving. As soon as the customer arrived and parked in a specially designated spot, the server brought the food directly to the car. This process provided Outback customers with a hassle-free way to obtain a quick, high-quality dinner.

Outback was convinced that its "Commitments to Customers" were the key to having a competitive advantage (see Exhibit 8). Outbackers worked hard to personalize each customer's experience, treating all customers as individuals and responding to their unique needs. Outbackers interacted with patrons in a friendly, energized, and extroverted manner and always gave an enthusiastic yes to special requests. For example, it was routine for Outback to make an

Exhibit 8   **Outback Steakhouse Commitment to Customers**

> We take care of our Customers.
> We totally indulge you with *Serious Food, Concentrated Service,* and *No Rules* in an environment that is welcoming, friendly, warm, energetic, and fun.
> During a wait, drinks are offered and food is shared.
> The menu is broad, the portions are generous, and the drinks poured full.
> Our serious food means freshness, flavors, attractive food, just-right temperatures.
> It is food prepared from scratch, using the finest ingredients, and to exacting standards.
> We are thick-cut steaks, fresh-cut fries, homemade croutons and salad dressings, fresh-baked brownies and meticulously prepared chocolate sauce.
> We have an intense desire to please you.
> You dictate the pace of service, from a quick meal to a relaxing evening with friends.
> We respect your privacy and tailor our service to your wants and needs.
> We delight customers one at a time ensuring everything is as you want it.
> We invite you to enjoy anything you want prepared any way you like it.
> We will please you, provide perfection your way, and enthusiastically say yes to your requests.
> We provide a hassle-free, personalized, and totally enjoyable experience.
> We do whatever it takes to deliver great food, drink, and services, are not distracted by the latest fads in the industry, and have the courage to put quality ahead of cost.

extraordinary effort to address special needs of customers who might not have otherwise been comfortable dining in public, kept special dietary items on hand for regular customers, pureed food for patrons who could not chew, sent an Outbacker to the nearest McDonald's in order to buy a Happy Meal for a customer's child, and sat customers ahead of the wait when it was obvious that waiting would have been a physical hardship. Overall, the philosophy was to treat people "Just Right."

Other Strategic Elements

- *Dinner-only hours at most locations.* Outback pioneered the strategy of having the vast majority of its restaurants open for dinner only during much of the week. In turn, this enhanced Outbackers' lifestyles by allowing them time to pursue personal interests in addition to work. Outback had the lowest labor turnover rate in the industry, which lessened its need to spend money on training replacement employees.

- *Limited seating.* The typical Outback restaurant was approximately 6,200 square feet with a seating capacity of around 220. The 220-person seating arrangement was chosen because it was considered the optimum seating capacity to guarantee a quality steak. Chris Sullivan and Bob Basham argued that an optimal facility was

more efficient and effective than a gigantic one and decided to build more Outbacks in new locations to keep up with demand.

- *Good pay for Outbackers.* Outbackers saw substantial monetary compensation as well as intangible rewards. One of the company's precepts was "Sharing in the Success of Outback." This was achieved through celebrations, recognizing individual Outbackers for their performance, and other bonus incentive programs. Overall, Outbackers earned a lot of money; a server typically left a shift with around $125 after working a three-table station.

- *Quality steaks and ingredients.* Outback's fine cuts of steak and bold, flavorful seasonings made customers crave and love their steaks. Emphasizing freshness and quality, Outback used specific methods for aging, cutting, seasoning, and searing its steaks. Outback knew that if it served a first-rate steak prepared with good seasoning, customers would be willing to wait two hours to get a seat.

- *Strong signature menu items.* The Bloomin' Onion was the menu item customers requested most often upon sitting down at a table. Many craved the zesty and bold seasonings. Approximately 35 percent of all customers ordered a Bloomin' Onion when dining in the restaurant. As for the drink menu, the Wallaby Darned proved to be a strong signature item unmatched by competitors. The bartenders mixed the drink daily from DeKuyper Peachtree schnapps, champagne, Smirnoff vodka, and secret mixers.

- *Fun and relaxed atmosphere.* Outback's lighting and ceiling reflected the unusual colors found at Ayers Rock, a formation that was a popular Australian tourist attraction. At sunset, the rock turned a burnt orange and the sky turned a deep purple. Outback replicated this scenery by painting the ceiling purple and the walls burnt orange and using pink lighting. Various Australian artifacts, such as boomerangs, surfboards, maps, and hats were hung on the walls. The floors and tables were made of a deep-colored wood with a glossy finish. Outback employed formula facilities so that a customer could walk into any Outback Steakhouse and feel at home. Customers came to recognize the green roof with red lettering as a place to dine casually and unwind.

- *Managing partner ownership.* To attract great, qualified, and motivated people—and to promote ownership and responsibility—Outback required each managing partner to purchase a 10 percent equity stake in his or her restaurant for $25,000. This interest gave the partner the right to receive a percentage of his or her restaurant's annual cash flows for the duration of the agreement. Additionally, managing partners signed a five-year employment agreement, which contributed to a stable environment and a low turnover of both managers and hourly Outbackers. During the employment term, managing partners were prohibited from selling or transferring the ownership interest; upon termination of employment, the partner was required to sell the ownership interest back to the company.

- *Large portions at reasonable prices.* Outback provided great value to its customers by serving generous portions of high-quality food at reasonable prices. The average ticket price for an adult at dinnertime was between $19 and $21. Outback customers never left the restaurant hungry.

OUTBACK'S CULTURE

Many companies' policy statements claimed that the customer came first. Outback, in contrast, realized that its employees were the company's most valuable asset and resource, so it fostered a culture that developed, recognized, and rewarded people. The founders discovered that the company had to show that it was as serious about taking care of Outbackers as it was about taking care of customers. In addition, the company recognized that Outbackers could not be asked to take care of customers if they were not being cared for themselves. The company's goal was to make work an enjoyable experience; the hope was that each Outbacker would look forward to coming in each day. Outback promised all Outbackers clear direction, extensive training, a fair hearing when a complaint arose, and a fun workplace environment (see again Exhibit 7).

A prominent feature of Outback's culture was caring. Outbackers showed compassion for one another and were always willing to help another in need. One story exemplified the nature of Outbackers: A dishwasher had his bicycle stolen during a shift. While thousands of bikes are stolen each year, this was the dishwasher's only means of transportation. Before the shift ended, the Outbackers at this particular location collected enough money among themselves to replace the bicycle. An Outbacker was sent to a nearby store to purchase a new bicycle and had it ready, including ribbons, by the end of the shift. Outback had a culture of respect and camaraderie that bred enthusiasm for helping others.

Recruitment, Screening, Promotion, and Hiring

Outback did not maintain internal or external recruiters and never created a human resource department but still boasted the lowest management and hourly turnover rate in the industry. Outback always accepted applications for employment because it believed another dedicated, fun-loving Outbacker would make a positive addition. It strove to hire people from different backgrounds to create synergy that came from great diversity. After completing an application, an individual was required to take a personality test to determine whether he or she would fit with Outback's culture and an analytical math test designed to measure quick thinking. An external third party scored the tests to prevent bias. Once hired, every new Outbacker was immediately welcomed as an integral member of the team; there were no probationary Outbackers.

Instead of requiring experience, Outback hired friendly people and provided training for work-related skills. Outback sought to hire people with enthusiasm, a positive outlook, and a winning attitude because it believed it was easier to add competence to friendliness than the reverse. The company defined a "Quality Hire" as an individual who performed the job, fit in with Outback's culture, and planned to stick around. It sought ambitious individuals who had a surplus of energy that drove them to achieve their goals and who understood that going the extra mile was the norm rather than exception.

Each Outbacker affected his or her own destiny through work ethic and commitment to the company's Principles and Beliefs. Outback initiated programs such as "Five for Our Future," in which management at all levels identified five or more Outbackers of underrepresented groups (i.e., minorities and women) with strong leadership potential and developed mentoring programs designed to help them earn more responsibility in the workplace. Outback sourced all managers internally from hourly Outbackers. These Outbackers knew what it took to be successful the Outback way. The internal promotion policy helped keep the fun-loving, generous culture alive on the management level.

Training

Outback believed that training was an essential component of providing opportunities for individuals and that exceptional training translated routine challenges in the restaurant into solutions because Outbackers felt empowered to perform their jobs. Every Outbacker underwent an intensive on-the-job training program in addition to classroom instruction. Each one-week training period on-the-job supervision by an experienced Outbacker. Classroom training programs were designed to teach Outbackers how to live the P&Bs and exercise good judgment. "Serious Food" seminars were conducted every month in each store to emphasize the importance of food quality to all Outbackers. The managing partner, front-of-house manager, and kitchen manager conducted mini-classes with groups of Outbackers to discuss how to achieve Outback's commitment to quality food. These mini-classes included kitchen tours, education regarding cuts of beef, tasting sessions, and discussions of the Outback way for food preparation. Quarterly, each restaurant held a "Concentrated Service" meeting to revisit the purpose and implementation of the P&Bs.

For managers, the Better Yourself Through Education (BYTE) program was established to enhance the skills of the management team. BYTE was a self-directed, 12-week, distance-learning program consisting of 16 classes focusing on business needs. The classes encompassed business skills, communication skills, human resources, and self-management skills. The classes were in workbook format and took roughly 10 to 32 hours to complete. In BYTE, each managing partner served as a "Working Mentor" for their managers taking the classes. The partner assisted the manager when he or she came across difficult material or sought advice on how to handle various situations. Outback's goal for the BYTE program was to prepare its managers by providing them with the resources they needed to achieve the next level of excellence.

The Outbacker Trust

Established in 1999, the Outbacker Trust was funded primarily through Outbackers. The purpose of the program was to financially support Outbackers experiencing significant hardships in life. Money was raised through voluntary contributions from Outbackers; a donor of $20 or more received a collector's pin designed for that particular year. Contributions were not solicited from suppliers, customers, or friends. Requests for disbursements from the Outbacker Trust funneled through the area joint-venture partner and were then presented to a trust committee in Tampa, Florida. The Outbacker Trust covered such cases as funeral and burial costs of loved ones; loss of housing and possessions by fire, flood, and other causes; costs of surgery; income loss during life-threatening operations; and other life-altering challenges. Outback's philosophy for this program was as follows:

> We all travel different journeys in life, all of which are filled with different hurdles along the way. It is comforting to know that even when we are faced with the most difficult times, we are surrounded by, at the very least, our incredible family of Outbackers.

The STARS Program

Outback instituted a bonus program called Sharing the Actions, Responsibilities and Success (STARS) to encourage Outbackers to live the P&Bs. The STARS program shared 25 percent of the restaurant's increase in quarterly profitability as compared to the same quarter of the prior year. Sales had to experience an increase, and cash flow had to be up a minimum of $4,000 for the quarter. Hourly Outbackers who worked a minimum average of 10 hours per week per quarter qualified for one share of the STARS bonus, and hourly Outbackers who worked a minimum average of 25 hours per week per quarter qualified for two shares. Outbackers had to be employed the entire quarter to qualify. A share of the bonus was calculated by taking the total bonus and dividing it by the total number of shares of all qualifying Outbackers. Overall, STARS encouraged Outbackers, with a sense of ownership, to support the team in building sales and profits in their respective restaurants while putting extra money in their pockets.

Community Involvement

Outback's culture strongly emphasized community involvement. Each year, Outback organized and contributed to more than 10,000 community events across the United States. The company strove to create a source of strength in times of crisis and could always be counted on to enhance the quality of life in the neighborhoods where its restaurants operated. This was achieved through continually identifying and acting on opportunities to give back to the community and to make it a better place to live, have fun, and conduct business. Outback took pride in supporting many meaningful organizations ranging from civic and charitable groups, to youth sports, to community restoration efforts, to parent teacher organizations.

Mission Outback was a program implemented to support the U.S. military and coalition troops while at war in Iraq. For the brave men and women overseas, an Outback meal was a taste of home and a reminder of how much they were appreciated. Outback sent 15 Outbackers in June 2002 to Kandahar, Afghanistan, to feed over 6,000 members of the military. An additional 15 were sent in January 2003 to Kandahar and Bagram to provide food for more than 13,000 troops, and an additional 21 Outbackers were sent in January 2004 to Al Asad, Baqubah, and Mosul (see Exhibit 9). Nearly 41,000 men and women of the military were served a dinner of Bloomin' Onions, Victoria's Filets, Rockhampton Rib-eyes, Grilled Shrimp on the Barbie, Aussie Chips, Jacket Potatoes, Mixed Veggies, and Cheesecake Olivia. The troops were overwhelmingly pleased and excited to see Outback Steakhouse in the middle of the desert. Outback received numerous letters and e-mails regarding Mission Outback. A retired veteran wrote,

Exhibit 9   **Mission Outback**

"The effort and sacrifice you and your supporters have made for our troops gladdened the hearts of numerous old vets who remember what it is like to be away from home for an extended tour and missing familiar foods." Mission Outback was a successful effort showing Outbackers' gratitude and appreciation for the men and women who risked their lives to protect freedom.

A nationwide coalition of restaurants, including Outback, designated October 5, 2005, as Dine Out for America Day. This industrywide fund-raising event raised money to aid the victims of Hurricanes Katrina and Rita. The initiative involved a record-setting 17,115 restaurants, which committed resources by designating up to 100 percent of daily sales for that day. The proceeds directly benefited the American Red Cross Disaster Relief Fund specifically earmarked for hurricane relief efforts. All Outback Steakhouse Inc. concepts contributed 100 percent of their sales on this day. Restaurants Unlimited generated the idea and was a leading force behind Dine Out for America Day in hopes the restaurant industry could cooperatively make a significant contribution to the hurricane survivors.

COMPETITORS

Lone Star Steakhouse & Saloon

Lone Star Steakhouse & Saloon positioned itself as a "destination restaurant" in the midpriced, full-service, casual-dining segment with a menu similar to that of Outback Steakhouse, but also lunchtime hours. Lone Star restaurants had a Texas-style ambiance with Texas artifacts and upbeat country-and-western music. Each restaurant was approximately 5,500 square feet with a seating capacity of 220 people featuring planked wooden floors, dim lighting, and flags and other Texas memorabilia to enhance the casual atmosphere. Moreover, Lone Star limited its menu to focus on high-quality USDA Choice-graded steaks, which were hand-cut daily, to create a competitive advantage. Generous "Texas-sized" portions were served for an average ticket price per customer of $12 for lunch and $18.50 for dinner in 2004.

Lone Star began operations in October 1989 in Winston-Salem, North Carolina. In March 1992, it became a public company traded on the Nasdaq. Through seasoned public offerings, the company satisfied all debt obligations through equity financing. In 2005, Lone Star had a total of 251 locations in the United States. In 2003, Lone Star divested its Australian operations to concentrate on domestic operations. Furthermore, the company suspended development of new stores in 2003 and 2004 to reduce the demand for additional managers, to focus on improving operations and guest relations in current stores, and to improve the quality of management. The company had plans to develop new stores in 2005. In January 2004, the company made a significant acquisition of the Texas Land & Cattle restaurants. The acquisition gave the company a stronger presence in Texas, where it also operated three Sullivan's and two Del Frisco's Double Eagle Steak Houses. Lone Star was met with intense competition from a variety of competitors, including locally owned, regional, and national restaurants. The company recognized that its ability to compete would depend on attraction and retention of loyal clientele, strong employees, experienced management, a continued offering of high-quality food, competitive prices, and an attractive dining atmosphere.

Texas Roadhouse

Founded in 1993, Texas Roadhouse was an up-and-coming competitor whose commitment to its customers was "Legendary Food, Legendary Service." Texas Roadhouse was a full-service, casual-dining restaurant chain offering an assortment of specially seasoned and aged steaks hand-cut daily on the premises and cooked to order over gas-fired grills. Guests were also offered a selection of rib, fish, chicken, and vegetable plates, and a variety of hamburgers, salads, and sandwiches, showcasing great menu diversity from hearty meals to leaner selections. Most entrées were accompanied by two made-from-scratch side items. The average dinner entrée prices ranged from $7.99 to $18.99.

Texas Roadhouse's operating strategy was designed to position each restaurant as the local hometown destination for a broad segment of customers seeking high-quality, affordable meals and friendly, attentive service. The key components to its operating strategy included high-quality, freshly prepared food; a focus on dinner only; moderate menu prices; performance-based management compensation; and a comfortable ambiance. The company successfully grew from 67 restaurants in 1999 to 193 by the end of 2004, representing a 23.6 percent compounded

Exhibit 10   **Lone Star's Statement of Income and Operating Ratios ($ thousands)**

	2004	2003	2002
Total revenue	$669,527	$591,617	$593,617
Cost of revenue	579,293	509,946	491,963
Gross profit	$ 90,234	$ 81,671	$101,654
Selling, general, and administrative expenses	45,269	43,346	45,085
Operating income	44,965	38,109	56,569
Net income from continuing operations	31,282	26,902	39,840
Net income	$ 31,213	$ 18,245	$ 38,667
Ratios			
Return on equity	7.73%	4.40%	8.75%
Return on assets	6.25	3.73	7.61
Gross profit margin	13.48	13.80	17.12
Net profit margin	4.66	3.08	6.51
Working capital	39,332	68,369	41,000
Current ratio	1.53	2.16	0.96
Debt to equity ratio	0	0	0

Source: Lone Star Steakhouse & Saloon 2004 annual report.

annual growth rate. The plan was to open 26 new restaurants in 2005. The focus remained primarily on midsize markets, where population size, income levels, and nearby shopping had proved to be fertile ground for expanding growth.

By any measure, 2004 was an exciting year for Texas Roadhouse due to achievement of significant milestones and goals. The company's initial public offering (IPO) in October 2004 was considered another way to prove itself to new partners who entrusted it with financial support. By the end of the closing bell on the day of Texas Roadhouse's IPO, the stock price had increased by 28 percent. As a result of the IPO, the company's balance sheet was stronger and more flexible. As for financial performance, total revenue increased by 27 percent in 2004 over the prior year, while comparable sales increased by 7.6 percent.

Exhibit 11   **Texas Roadhouse Financial Data ($ thousands)**

	2004	2003	% Change
Revenue:			
Restaurant sales	$354,190	$279,519	27%
Franchise royalties and fees	8,821	6,934	27
Total revenue	$363,011	$286,453	27
Income from operations	38,682	34,258	13
Total assets	276,663	148,193	87
Long-term debt including current portion	13,285	64,313	−79
Total stockholders' equity	$173,211	$ 37,902	357
Company restaurants			
Number open at end of period	107	87	23
Average unit volumes	$ 3,679	$ 3,401	8
Comparable restaurant sales growth	7.6%	3.4%	N/A

Source: Taxes Roadhouse 2004 annual report.

INDUSTRY ENVIRONMENT

Revenue for the U.S. restaurant industry was $1 trillion in 2004 and was expected to reach $1.2 trillion in 2005. This included revenues from related industries such as agriculture, transportation, wholesale trade, and food manufacturing. Food-and-drink revenues were projected to be $476 billion, with operations in 900,000 locations. This industry was complex and fragmented, with different types of establishments ranging from full-service restaurants to snack bars. On a typical day in 2005, the restaurant industry posted average sales of nearly $1.3 billion. Sales were forecasted to advance 4.9 percent in 2005 and to equal 4 percent of the U.S. gross domestic product. The major growth drivers for the industry included unit expansion, same-store sales, and efforts to increase margins.

Excluding the government, the restaurant industry, a labor-intensive environment, was the nation's largest employer, with an estimated 12.2 million employees. The industry provided work for more than 9 percent of the workforce in the United States. More than 4 out of 10 adults worked in the restaurant industry at some point in their lives, and 27 percent of adults got their first job experience in a restaurant. A typical employee in food service in 2005 was a single female under 30 years of age working an average of 25 hours a week and living in a household with two or more wage earners. Restaurant industry employment was expected to reach 13.3 million by 2012. The number of food-service managers was projected to increase by 11 percent from 2005 to 2015. The industry employed more minority managers than any other; more than two-thirds of supervisors were women, 16 percent were African Americans, and 13 percent were Hispanic.

In 2002, the typical American household spent an average of $2,276 (or $910 per person) on food away from home, according to the National Restaurant Association's *Restaurant Spending* report. Every dollar spent by consumers in restaurants generated an additional $1.98 spent in other industries allied with the restaurant industry. In 2004, the U.S. Department of Agriculture estimated the average annual per capita consumption of beef was 66.3 pounds, up 2.1 pounds from 2003. More than 50 percent of all consumers visited a restaurant on their birthday, therefore making it the most popular occasion to dine out, followed by Mother's Day and Valentine's Day. Researchers had determined that more customers dined out during the month of August than any other month, while Saturday was the most popular day to dine out. Demographic characteristics dictating restaurant spending included household income, head of household's age, and household composition. Restaurant patronage was strongly correlated with increases in household income. Consumers were driven to frequent restaurants for entertainment, convenience, socialization, and nutrition. The largest spenders in the industry had a household income of over $70,000, with the household head between the ages of 45 and 54 and children older than 18.

Issues and Conditions

Characterized by tight margins and a high failure rate, the restaurant industry witnessed incredibly intense competition. The measures on which restaurants competed included price, location, and food quality, and there was a large number of well-established competitors. The industry was highly fragmented and subject to risks from food cost and wage inflation, lifestyle trends, seasonality, and shifts in investor sentiment. These external forces—including the price and availability of commodities and consumer preferences—dictated how each restaurant conducted operations. Furthermore, the fast pace of society required companies to develop efficient take-out services to accommodate working families. With fitness and health issues on the forefront of consumers' minds, restaurants had to develop new menu additions to retain health-conscious customers. In 2004, nearly two out of three restaurants added low-carbohydrate menu items as a result of the low-carb diet trend. In the steakhouse restaurant industry, emerging concerns over the ever-present rising costs of meat and decrease in U.S. cattle supply was drastically decreasing profit margins. Since the mid-1970s, the U.S. cattle headcount had declined from 130 million to 95 million, representing a 28 percent decrease despite the rising average annual per capita consumption of beef. Macroeconomic challenges became an evolving problem for the industry as gas and energy prices were rapidly increasing, with no indication of slowing down; in response, consumers frequented restaurants less often. Annually, many companies entered the industry, creating an atmosphere in which each restaurant competed on the basis of food and service quality, ambiance, location, and price–value relationship.

With demand for the best beef up and supply down, some restaurants began cutting corners. As the steakhouse industry rapidly expanded at a time of record shortages of top-quality beef, many steakhouses changed the way they did business. Some used lower-quality meats; others raised prices, shrunk steaks, and designed menus steering diners to higher-margin cuts. Finding top-quality meat became a tough challenge due to the rapid growth of the steakhouse industry beyond its traditional base of business meals and corporate accounts. The industry began trying to attract a new clientele—women—by rolling out fruity cocktails and adding more fish to the menu. In 2004, sales were up 10.7 percent from the previous year. The menus in many steakhouses were misleading to consumers. They declared at the top of the menu that their meat was either "USDA prime" or "dry-aged" or both, even if those terms did not apply to all steaks on the list. This meant that steakhouses were charging prime meat prices while quietly serving lesser grades.

In 2005, amid the worst hurricane season to date in the United States, Hurricanes Katrina and Rita devastated the restaurant industry along the Gulf Coast. Although this region was braced for the storms, these hurricanes delivered a massive punch, closing some restaurants permanently. Hurricane Katrina resulted in the temporary closure of 26 and indefinite closure of 2 Outback Steakhouse locations in Florida, Alabama, Louisiana, and Mississippi. The company reported hurricane-related losses of approximately $2.2 million in revenues. Outback also incurred costs for financial and housing assistance to Outbackers displaced by the catastrophe. The 2004 hurricane season resulted in the permanent closure of Outback's operations in the Cayman Islands. Hurricane Katrina forced Ruth's Chris Steakhouse to relocate its headquarters to Orlando from its home in Metairie, Louisiana, near the historical heart of the wind-and-flood-ravaged New Orleans. The decision was a tough one but was necessary, company executives said, amid the uncertainty that surrounded the entire Gulf Coast area.

The restaurant industry was subject to various federal, state, and local laws. Each restaurant was subject to licensing and regulation by a number of government authorities such as the alcoholic beverage control and health and safety agencies. If a restaurant wanted to sell alcoholic beverages, it was required to apply to a state authority for a license or permit to sell alcoholic beverages on the premises and to open for extended hours. In addition, control regulations were in place for daily operations including minimum age of patrons and employees, hours of operations, advertising, wholesale purchasing, and inventory control. To protect patrons, "dram-shop" statutes were in place to provide a person injured by an intoxicated person to recover damages from the established that wrongfully served alcoholic beverages to the intoxicated person.

Despite operating in a challenging cost environment (the commodities market was the worst in history, particularly the prices of beef and dairy products), Outback was able to maintain its market share. Furthermore, higher gasoline prices, labor costs, and interest rates dampened industry sales and raised the operating costs of food supplies, which were often passed on to Outback. In addition, changing lifestyles and health concerns dictated change. Outback had to adapt to changing market conditions to sustain the growth experienced throughout the years by continuing to indulge customers with top-quality ingredients that were perfectly prepared; having well-trained Outbackers to provide customers with "Concentrated Service" and "No Rules" in a welcoming, friendly, warm, energetic, and fun environment; keeping the physical plant updated; and living the Principles and Beliefs every day to remain focused on the company's commitments to its stakeholders.

Moses at the Red Sea

Mark Meckler
University of Portland

Howard Feldman
University of Portland

Michele Snead
University of Portland

Moses sat on a rock that overlooked the shores of the Red Sea. The three-day journey by pack mule, east from his home in the Nile River valley, had brought him a full week of solitary contemplation on this windswept coast. He was considering his options, knowing he must make some decisions and act on them soon.

The situation had become untenable. It had been over a year since he assumed leadership of the Israelites. The initial nine miracles he performed had long since lost their luster—after all, the Israelites were all still slaves, still living in abject poverty. Their masters, as a result of the "plagues" strategy, had become angry and brutal. Since the first of the plagues occurred, the beatings by the guards had been applied more harshly and more randomly. Moses believed that if he unleashed his 10th and final plague, the Egyptian pharaoh would finally let his people go. But how could he kill the firstborn of anyone, let alone the firstborn of the whole kingdom? And what would his people do when they arrived here at the shores of the Red Sea?

The whole tribe seemed to be bickering. The expectations of imminent freedom since the arrival of Moses over a year ago had everyone impatient, wondering what was taking so long. The heads of some of the more powerful families, who had been so supportive just a year ago, were now talking about the lack of results they had experienced, about how they were worse off than ever before, and about the possible need for a change in leadership.

Aaron[1] had come to Moses some days earlier with news that after four years of work, enough boats had been built to carry about half of his people across the sea. "Half?" Moses questioned aloud to the sea. "How can I live with myself if I only lead half of us to freedom?" It would take another three years to build enough boats to save everyone. Cash flow was too low to purchase boats from the Africans to the south. Perhaps the women could secretly work in the papyrus scroll works after their Egyptian masters had left for the night. Papyrus scrolls, a product invented by the Egyptians, were highly prized outside of the empire and could easily be sold on the black market. Such a tactic would allow the Israelites to leave in perhaps a year and a half. However, the men couldn't do it; they were exhausted from their daily working in the mud pits and from the other hard duties forced on them by their Egyptian masters. The women might be able to do it, but the great majority had never worked anywhere but in the home or in the fields, and the conservative elders would fight this idea adamantly. Furthermore, if anyone was caught, there was no doubt the punishment would be severe.

Joshua's idea of a "ferry barge" that could carry 10 times the number of people that even the largest boat could carry was another option, but many criticized it as outlandish. Joshua had proposed to sail across the Red Sea with 15,000 paces of woven oiled rope that he would anchor at both this side and the other side so that barges could be pulled across. It was physically possible—Joshua had demonstrated

This case was presented at the fall 2005 meeting of the North American Case Research Association, October 27–29, 2005, North Falmouth, Massachusetts. All rights are reserved to the authors and NACRA. Copyright © 2005 by Mark Meckler and Howard Feldman.

the technology by pulling a boat across the Nile and back again—so perhaps men on these huge barges could pull themselves hand over hand across the Red Sea. Joshua had calculated that if they dedicated all of their extra resources to manufacturing rope, they could leave on barges within six months. However, should the rope break or a storm hit, the barges would be incapable of navigating themselves safely. They would have to leave before the beginning of the rainy season.

During secret meetings with a captain of a Hittite trade mission to the pharaoh, Moses had been offered passage for his people in exchange for helping the Hittites annex the promised land of Canaan into the Hittite empire. The Hittites had been harsh lords in the past, taxing their subjects to near poverty, but at least they promised that none of the tribes of Israel would be slaves. However, the Hittite captain made no such promises of freedom to their long-lost siblings, the Hebrews, who had remained behind in Canaan hundreds of years ago. Moses dreamed of returning and joining together with his Hebrew brethren to form one empire. He hoped for the Hebrews' welcome and help, not their enmity. Moses was also very reluctant to turn over their birthright, their promised land of Canaan waiting for them by the sea, to Hittite governance in exchange for their freedom.

Then Moses once again pondered the waking dream he had had in which the Almighty, Great Creator of All, ensured the Israelites safe passage through the Red Sea to the far shores *if they could come up with no better solution of their own.* Moses also knew from his dream that if they used this miracle to obtain freedom, it would come at a guaranteed cost of wandering the desert for 40 years before finding their way home, a home that Moses would never live long enough to see.

The food supply was even more miserable than usual; and with more and more mouths to feed, it would be only a matter of time before people began to starve. The growing chaos made Moses feel nervous and uncomfortable. "Can I do this?" he asked aloud in desperation to the sky, his feelings of inadequacy surfacing again. He knew that he needed a way to get everyone to pull together, to cooperate. We have indeed grown into a great nation, thought Moses, but how do I manage to bring my people to freedom?

Appendix: The Exodus Story from the Old Testament

The Wheel of Time turns, and Ages come and pass, leaving memories that become legend. Legend fades to myth. —Robert Jordan, *The Eye of the World*

The story of the Exodus takes place about 1445 BC. Originally, the Israelites had prospered in Egypt. Joseph, of the coat of many colors, had even become the prime minister of the country. Those days, however, were long forgotten. Over many generations, the Israelites had become slaves to the pharaohs of Egypt. The current pharaoh feared the strength of their numbers (estimated at 2 million). Moses was the firstborn of an Israelite slave family, who saved his life from a "slaying of the firstborn" edict by the pharaoh when they put him in a basket and floated him in the Nile River. Moses, found as an infant by a royal family member, was raised in the pharaoh's court. He later fell out of favor with the pharaoh, exiled from Egypt, and ended up living as a shepherd in the desert.

As he was tending his flocks in the desert, Moses saw a burning bush that was not consumed by the flames. He went to the bush, and God spoke to him from it: "Come now therefore, and I will send thee unto Pharaoh, that thou mayest bring forth my people the children of Israel out of Egypt" (Exodus 3:10). God instructed Moses on what to do when he arrived in Egypt, and Moses agreed to speak to the pharaoh and demand that he release the Israelites.

Moses was initially reluctant to take on this task. He was not a good speaker and feared that he would not be able to present God's case to the pharaoh. God told Moses' brother Aaron to meet Moses in the desert and travel into Egypt with him. God sent Aaron with Moses to act as Moses' voice: "And Aaron spake all the words which the LORD had spoken unto Moses, and did the signs in the sight of the people" (Exodus 4:30).

In Egypt, Moses, through Aaron, told the pharaoh to free the Israelites by command of the Lord. The pharaoh refused, saying he didn't know the Lord that Moses spoke of, and told the taskmasters to increase the labor burden on the Israelites. The Israelites blamed Moses and Aaron for their worsened conditions. Moses despaired and complained to God. God answered Moses and the Israelites: "Wherefore say unto the children of Israel, I am the LORD, and I will bring you out from under the burdens of the Egyptians, and I will rid you out of their bondage, and I will redeem you with a stretched out arm, and with great judgments" (Exodus 6:6).

Moses went before the pharaoh again and demanded the release of his people. The pharaoh laughed, and God, through Moses, turned all of the waters to blood. Another demand was made, another refusal, and another disaster followed. Plagues of frogs, gnats and flies, disease that killed their livestock, disease that caused the Egyptians boils, hailstones, locusts, and days of pitch darkness befell Egypt. The pharaoh promised to let the Israelites go if only Moses would bring an end to the plagues, but he didn't make good on the promise when the plagues were stopped.

Again, Moses and Aaron begged the pharaoh to capitulate and free the Israelites. Again he refused. Then the Lord told Moses that the next plague would take the firstborn of every Egyptian and the firstborn of all the Egyptians' animals. So that the Israelites would avoid the same fate, God instructed them through Moses to each sacrifice a lamb, prepare a special meal, and mark their doorposts with the blood of the lamb. Seeing the blood on the door, the angel of death would pass over their houses.

When the angel of death killed all the firstborn of Egypt, the pharaoh and the Egyptians begged the Israelites to leave. The Egyptians gave them all of their remaining wealth to speed them on their way. Moses led them into the wilderness and God showed them the way to go: "And the LORD went before them by day in a pillar of a cloud, to lead them the way; and by night in a pillar of fire, to give them

light; to go by day and night" (Exodus 13:21).

By the time the Israelites reached the Red Sea, the pharaoh had changed his mind about setting them free. He sent his armies after them and trapped them against the sea. The Israelites railed against Moses, thinking their death was certain. Despite all the disasters the Lord had brought against Egypt on the behalf of His people, they still doubted His ability and willingness to save them. Yet God was faithful to the Israelites: "And Moses stretched out his hand over the sea; and the LORD caused the sea to go back by a strong east wind all that night, and made the sea dry land, and the waters were divided." And the children of Israel went into the midst of the sea upon the dry ground: and the waters were a wall unto them on their right hand, and on their left." (Exodus 14:21-22) The Israelites passed safely through the Red Sea with the Egyptians on their trail. When all the Israelites passed through, the walls of water collapsed in and the Egyptians were drowned. God's people were free from Egypt. Ultimately, it took the Israelites 40 years of wandering until they found their way back to their historical home, and were reunited with the Hebrews living in the promised land of Canaan.

THE HITTITES

The Hittites ruled a great empire that stretched from Mesopotamia to Syria and Palestine. Their empire was at its greatest from 1600 to 1200 BC, and even after the Assyrians gained control of Mesopotamia after 1300 BC, the Hittite cities and territories thrived independently until 717 BC, when the territories were finally conquered by other peoples.

The Hebrew scriptures have little to say about the Hittites, and the Egyptians regarded them as barbarians. In fact, from 1300 to 1200 BC, the Hittites waged a war against Egypt that drained both empires tragically. The Hittites were perhaps one of the most significant peoples in Mesopotamian history. Because their empire was so large and because their primary activity was commerce—trading with all the civilizations and peoples of the Mediterranean—the Hittites were the people primarily responsible for transmitting Mesopotamian thought, law, political structure, economic structure, and ideas around the Mediterranean, from Egypt to Greece.

PAPYRUS

The writing surface papyrus, named after the plant from which it is made, was manufactured as early as the first Egyptian dynasty, circa 3100 BC. The emergence of writing and the concomitant use of papyrus appear to have been a necessary outcome of the imperial bureaucracy. Papyrus was invariably used by the Egyptians until the AD 800–1000, that is, for 4,000 years. The papyrus product was made by tearing off the "skin" of the papyrus reed. The strips thus formed were first beaten and dried in the sun and then were laid lengthwise and crosswise to attain strength, perhaps with the aid of some glue (made of plants). Finally, the papyrus was stretched and smoothed to be fit for use.

ROPE

There is evidence of rope being made as far back as 17,000 BC. These early ropes were twisted by hand or braided. The earliest indication of any type of mechanical advantage in making rope comes from early Egyptian evidence relating to the craft. The Egyptians tied rope-making material to a piece of finished rope that was weighted and tied to a stick; the material was then spun around the stick. The spinning imparted a twist to the strand. Three twisted strands would then be twisted together in the opposite direction. Finished rope was oiled for use in water.

Endnotes

[1] Aaron helped his brother Moses speak to the Israelites and the Pharaoh. Moses had a lifelong speech impediment. As a child, Moses had been put to a test by the court magicians. Two braziers—one full of gold and the other hot coals—were put before him to see which he would take. If Moses took the gold, he would have to be killed. An angel guided his hand to the coals, and he put one in his mouth, saving his life but ruining his ability to speak clearly.

Implementing Strategic Change: Monica Ashley's Experience

Allen R. Cohen
Babson College

David L. Bradford
Stanford University

Monica Ashley was stunned. Just as she was successfully completing a complex two-year project that could be a major contributor to the future growth of Health Equipment and Laboratories Inc. (HEAL-INC), her boss, Dan Stella, removed her as program manager.

Although Dan, vice president for design and manufacture of one of the top lines of HEAL-INC machines, asked her to stay on in his division, Monica felt that personal defeat had been snatched from the jaws of victory. The glory from her massive effort to enable HEAL-INC to adapt its hospital-oriented, technically driven products and strategies to much wider usage would go elsewhere. It wasn't that she was hung up on glory, but it didn't seem fair to be pulled out of this incredible accomplishment just as it was finally about to overcome the ferocious opposition that had made it even more difficult than it naturally was. And she feared—correctly as it turned out—that over a year would be lost in replacing her and getting a replacement up to speed.

HEAL-INC was a rapidly growing company making a wide range of advanced diagnostic and treatment equipment. Utilizing many complex technologies, from lasers to powerful magnets to semiconductors and signal processors, the company had thrived on the enormous latitude given its very bright employees to take initiatives and pursue opportunities.

Since its inception, HEAL-INC had found great success by creating equipment that appealed to the same kinds of technically sophisticated hospital researchers and technicians it employed. Early on, top management decided that creating an atmosphere of maximum freedom would be worth the waste and duplicated effort, since it would tap the creativity and energy of smart employees. The strategy had worked, and HEAL-INC's meteoric growth had been a source of pride to management and employees—and sometimes a source of puzzlement to those who had been taught to revere order and efficiency above all else. (See Exhibit 1 for a partial organization chart.)

MORE TECH, MORE TOUCH: NEW USERS AND THEIR NEEDS

In recent years, however, the market had begun to shift, along with the technology in the industry. The equipment was increasingly going to be used in doctors' offices, small clinics, and storefront test labs, rather than exclusively in teaching hospitals. New users of the equipment were less technical and more patient-oriented than the hospital staffers who had been the company's original customers.

Furthermore, in order to make the equipment easier for less sophisticated personnel to use, the technology had grown more complicated; thus, far

Exhibit 1 **Partial Organization Chart**

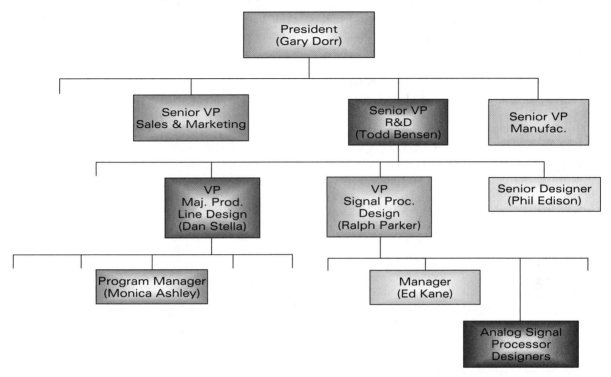

greater coordination and teamwork in design and manufacture became necessary. Many different, but interrelated, components had to be designed by teams of contributors, rather than be developed for special purposes by solo "geniuses." There were pressures for some key components to shift from analog to digital electronics. And purchasers were becoming more selective, so their interests had to be taken into account at an earlier stage of product design. Finally, it was increasingly difficult for any one company, no matter how big, to custom design all the components of the equipment. The industry leaders were beginning to form strategic alliances and purchase components from outside sources.

All of this caused considerable tension at HEAL-INC and entrepreneurial companies like it. The original ways of doing things had brought huge success, and the company was young enough so that many of those who had grown with it were still entrenched. They had a big stake in their hard-won lessons about growth, decentralization, encouragement of initiative, technical orientation, and the virtues of inventing everything within the company. The voices of those arguing the urgent strategic need for greater ease of operation, more coordination of previously autonomous units, and purchasing components and subsystems elsewhere were not readily heard.

THE PRESIDENT OF HEAL-INC RECRUITS MONICA FOR PROJECT HIPPOCRATES

Monica had been squarely in the middle of just such issues. She had taken on Project Hippocrates reluctantly, because, even though she was ready for a line job after many successful years in important staff positions, she knew there would be major opposition. Over her years at HEAL-INC, she had developed a special relationship with Gary Dorr, the president and founder, which began at a meeting early in her career when she caught his attention by challenging his conclusions. He liked her spirit and the hard work that had enabled her to back up her views with data when he asked why she disagreed. After that, Dorr had periodic long talks with Monica and once told her that he thought of her as his HEAL-INC daughter. So, before taking the assignment as program manager of Project Hippocrates, Monica went to see Dorr.

She explained to him her concerns, especially in relation to a key manager, Ralph Parker, the vice president in charge of designing the key signal processor used in several lines of HEAL-INC equipment. Monica had heard through the grapevine that Parker, who was in a different division from hers, was politically aggressive and had not been helpful on another project that her boss, Dan Stella, had pioneered. A different approach to signal processing—from analog to digital—would likely be needed for Project Hippocrates; and, as the main designer of HEAL-INC's original analog signal processors, Parker could be a major roadblock.

So many people in her division had talked about Parker's legendary resistance to new approaches and to customer input that Monica took their views as fact and didn't bother to talk with Parker directly. She just decided that she wouldn't be another in the long line of people she knew complaining about their inability to move him; she would set out to demonstrate overwhelmingly the correctness of the need for a new signal processor design. Dorr told Monica that he knew about the problem with Parker, and that he was working on it. He told her not to take Parker on directly, but to accept the program manager role, since she would "be protected." Before Monica could reply with her continuing concerns, Dorr ended the meeting by saying, "Monica, congratulations to the new program manager."

A WHIRLWIND OF ACTIVITIES

Monica plunged in, tackling the project with the same focused intensity that she brought to everything she did. She first interviewed the new kinds of purchasers to understand their very different needs; created a task force; recruited members from other parts of HEAL-INC; introduced to HEAL-INC for the first time to the Taguchi method, a highly disciplined product design process she had learned in Japan; and initiated a series of studies on just what would be

needed to alter HEAL-INC's equipment to make it more viable for new applications. All of this activity made people uncomfortable, because the structured Taguchi process was far more rigorous than anyone was used to; and it led to something that had never been done before at HEAL-INC: a total system outline for the product revisions, including all the elements and how they would have to fit together. She created a cross-department signal-processor study group to investigate whether the existing component could handle the redesigned equipment. As Monica had intuited, the study group determined that no in-house analog product could do the job and recommended the purchase from an outside vendor of the necessary digital signal processor.

JUST ONE MORE STUDY: DIFFICULTIES WITH OUTSIDE PURCHASE OF SIGNAL PROCESSORS

This recommendation set off many months of problems. The decision was made, restudied, made again, restudied, and remade four times. Twice Monica gave presentations before the senior management staff, with competing presentations given by the signal-processor design group under Parker. Parker was nasty to her and made numerous accusations, including one that the technical people she had used in her study group were not competent (even though some had come from lower levels of Parker's organization and two had been loaned by Phil Edison, the most respected technical person in the company). Parker had publicly declared that any kind of signal processor would be purchased outside only "over my dead body." And even after the senior management staff gave the go-ahead, Parker accused Monica of proceeding without permission. So still another independent task force was created to evaluate the decision; once again, the outcome was in Monica's favor.

At the first senior management staff meeting, Gary Dorr surprised Monica by being more critical and less friendly than Monica had ever experienced. He had often complained in the past about the need at HEAL-INC to define measures that would spell out the performance of an entire diagnostic and treatment system, not just its components. Worried about the common HEAL-INC problem of components being optimized but the complete system ending up suboptimized (the whole being less than the sum of its parts), Monica had developed detailed, integrated plans, but Dorr seemed annoyed rather than pleased. At the meeting, he criticized Monica for the comprehensive approach.

Monica was confused, then flabbergasted at Dorr's continued critical tone. At first she couldn't say anything, she was so taken aback. Then as the meeting went on, she realized that Dan Stella, her boss, wasn't speaking up and defending the massive amount of work she had done to ensure that components would not be suboptimized at the expense of the total equipment systems. Assuming that her past relationship with Dorr legitimized disagreement with him, she defended the decisions. She knew that customers used different criteria for measuring overall equipment performance than the designers of each component, and she wanted that recognized.

Parker had attended the meetings of the Project Hippocrates group, during which he challenged Monica constantly and, in her view, tried to provoke her. Because Dan Stella had advised Monica to keep cool, she avoided taking Parker's bait. Then, during one meeting at which Monica asked Parker a question, he accused her of being angry. She coolly replied, "It seems to me that you're the one who is angry." Parker exploded. Monica just let him yell, and then proceeded with the meeting.

After the meeting, all who attended, including Dan, congratulated Monica for "humiliating Parker," which had not been her intent at all. She was just trying to head off a fight, as she had been advised. But the battle lines hardened further. From then on, Parker assigned one of his managers, Ed Kane, to attend Project Hippocrates task force meetings on his behalf.

At one of the subsequent meetings, Kane heatedly accused Monica of not listening and of excluding signal processor people. She was embarrassed by the attack and unhappy about being falsely accused; but, as was her custom, she handled the unjust attacks by providing more accurate information. Thinking, "If he knows the truth, he'll cool off," she told Kane the history of how the original cross-functional design team, including people from his own organization, had agreed unanimously on the need for a switch to digital signal processing, and the requisite acquisition of an outside product.

There was so much conflict at that meeting that, as it broke up, Monica's boss, Dan Stella, called a spontaneous meeting of his own managers in a nearby conference room. Because Kane was standing outside the room and he was available to attend, Stella invited him "to c'mon in and help us plan."

Once inside, an obviously outraged Kane shouted, "Who the hell do you think you are, going to an outside vendor!" and called Stella a "traitor and a renegade." Stella retorted that if anyone was a traitor it was Kane, because the signal processor department of which Kane was a member had said to go ahead, and now he was trying to subvert their decision. In Monica's eyes, the confrontation was particularly brutal ("like dinosaurs slugging it out"), especially since she knew that Stella did not particularly like conflict.

Soon after, friends of Monica began to tell her that Kane was spreading nasty personal rumors about her, including innuendoes that she was having an affair with Stella. Stunned and hurt, she decided there was nothing she could do about it. Her friends would know how absurd the rumors were, and she believed that telling others she was innocent would only help dignify the rumors. She persevered in the project.

A month later, Parker once again challenged the outside purchase decision. Monica was called to an extended senior management staff meeting where she was given one day to make a presentation of the complete program; Parker was given the next day for his rebuttal.

TWISTING IN THE WIND: ABANDONED BY THE PRESIDENT

Monica was shocked by what happened at the meeting. She had barely started her presentation when Gary Dorr began to attack her. He said that no one person was going to be in control, that Monica in particular was trying to overcontrol things—"like an Imperial Chinese Emperor" was how he phrased it—and that central control was totally inappropriate for the company. Seeing Parker smirking in the background and feeling extraordinarily jittery after the attack by the president, Monica mustered her courage and told Dorr that she was only giving the complete system overview he had asked for. Every time she tried to give a detailed calculation, Dorr broke in again with criticism. Monica and her group were devastated; they were certain that Dorr had been totally prejudiced by Parker.

When Parker made his presentation the following day, Dorr was very receptive to him. In Monica's eyes, however, Parker had no solid data, and his presentation was devoid of content and filled with glib assertions and pronouncements. The main theme of his argument was "Haven't we always met hospital needs? Just look at our original analog signal processor: it's the best in the business, and it can be adapted to any need our customers have."

As she sat there in disbelief, Monica recalled a comment Dorr had once made to her privately. He had told her that there was no way the company could do without Parker because of his signal processor contributions. After Parker finished, the people in his group were slapping each other on the back; and Kane walked over to sneer, "Ha, ha, you lose!" at Monica. She was upset that Parker and his supporters had done so much behind-closed-doors political maneuvering and it absolutely infuriated her that "politics could beat out substance" in the company. Only Dorr's earlier warning about not confronting Parker kept her from retaliating.

Sticking the knife in was not enough for Parker. He had to twist it. At the end of the meeting, Parker again brought up Monica's negotiation for the digital processor with an outside company. Dorr exploded, and yelled at Monica, "How dare you negotiate on behalf of the company? You are a renegade and an empire-builder!"

Although by this point Monica was down for the count, she defended what had happened, explaining that she acted upon a decision that had been cleared by many groups. But then, when Dorr turned to Edison, the most respected technical expert, and asked him if it had gone through the review committee he headed, Edison claimed he did not remember. Monica was amazed and shocked, since the technical guru had always been friendly to her, and he certainly was present when his review committee had made the decision.

Dorr then said that he was going to go around the room and take a vote on going outside. He said that he personally would vote if there were a tie. As fate would have it, there was a tie. Dorr turned to Monica and asked her how she would interpret the tie.

Monica had been sitting near Dorr at the meeting. After his attack, he acted conciliatory, and they even exchanged whispered comments several times, so Monica was feeling a bit restored in relationship with him. Although she was scared of how it would be taken, she summoned up a sense of humor that she was rarely able to use when tense and deadpanned, "I would say that there was an overwhelming sentiment for going ahead with the outside negotiations." Dorr laughed and agreed. Monica was enormously relieved.

At the next senior management staff meeting, Dorr wanted one more vote on the issue of negotiating with an outside vendor. When the results were in, only one person had voted against the outside purchase: Parker. One of the executive vice presidents then turned to Parker and said, "You will have to speak now or forever hold your peace." Parker finally retorted that the move was against his better judgment and that, when it proved to be a giant mistake, it would be on the heads of Monica and her boss, Dan Stella.

HEAT IN THE KITCHEN: PUT OUT THE FIRE

Monica felt herself constantly being drawn into conflict even though she had wanted to accomplish the whole project by building consensus. In part, she had been driven by her assumptions about her relationship with Dorr. She had assumed that he still wanted her to stand up for what she believed in.

Upset, she went to talk to him about what had happened at various meetings. He told her that she was no longer behaving appropriately; because she was acting like a "hot competitor" when she came to the senior management staff, she was disturbing the company's once-peaceful and productive environment.

In her defense, she tried to explain that it was not she who was causing the problems but Kane and Parker. She reminded Dorr that he himself had said Parker was a problem, but Dorr replied, "That is none of your business." She knew that Dorr admired her for having the drive to complete her advanced studies and other complex company assignments, and that he counted on her as somebody who could carry things through, but she had overestimated the amount of support she would get from him in Project Hippocrates.

Throughout Monica's career at HEAL-INC, Dan Stella had phoned her on Sunday evenings to review the previous week and discuss what was coming up. As the infighting increased at the senior staff meetings, Stella told Monica in one of these Sunday-night phone conversations that she was going too fast and causing conflict. When things got very hot, he called her into his office and tried to slow her down. She said, "Don't these people understand we have all this work to do?"

Stella replied, "Don't you understand you have to build all these relationships and deal with the politics at the top?"

Nevertheless, caught up in the need to master enormous numbers of interrelated issues, Monica pressed on. She had set a date for bringing Project Hippocrates to market, and she was determined to meet it. She knew the external competition was getting increasingly tougher, and that it would be a severe strategic blow to HEAL-INC if the company missed the deadline.

Over the ensuing several months, a new team, which included many signal processor people, was formed to begin the technology transfer process and overcome all not-invented-here feelings in preparation for a contract with an outside vendor. Parker's people chose not to help specify the features of the digital signal processor. Technical experts from Stella's organization did the work, along with some people from sales and marketing. Exhaustive effort went into design and product specification documents to pave the way for a smoother-than-usual product introduction. During this period, there were vague promises from Parker's organization about modifying the existing analog signal processor to meet the new demands, but nothing tangible happened.

ONE MORE TIME: HARD DECISIONS ABOUT THE SIGNAL PROCESSOR

While plans to educate the sales force went forward, Parker stirred up a great deal of tension around the decision to purchase signal processors. He used every meeting he attended to say negative things about Project Hippocrates. Several important customers even told Monica that Parker and his people had visited them to say that their analog signal processor was being enhanced to adapt to new uses, and that the digital processor that HEAL-INC was thinking of purchasing outside was "a pile of crap."

This immobilized Monica at first, because she couldn't understand how top management could allow this malicious behavior to go on. She got Stella to talk to Dorr about it, but she saw nothing happen to stop it. Eventually, it just spurred her into redoubling efforts and pushing her project group to work harder. "I'd have gone crazy if I had paid attention to all that nasty political stuff, so I just poured more energy into the project," she reported later.

As a result of Parker's continued complaining, Dorr formed another committee chaired by a new engineering manager, who, because he had recently been hired away from a competitor, was assumed to be unbiased. Unbeknownst to Monica, the new manager began a series of secret meetings involving most of the same people who had been part of Monica's original task force to work on what the criteria should be for making the decision.

Within the next month, the company signed a contract with an outside vendor. Shortly thereafter, Monica learned of the secret study committee and found out it was still evaluating outside purchase. She warned that the company now had a legal obligation and could be sued if it did not go ahead with the new contract.

In spite of her troubles, Monica was proud of the negotiation and the amount of continuing vendor support that she had managed to get the vendor to include in the contract. In fact, her negotiation eventually became a model for the company to purchase components from outside.

Three months after the contract was signed, the "secret" committee announced that it was ready to hear a debate on the merits of the outside digital signal processor versus the existing HEAL-INC analog product. Kane and Monica made presentations.

Another three months went by before the committee announced its decision, which was to go ahead with the outside purchase. Meanwhile, people working on the project were completely confused;

they didn't know which side to support. Monica told them to forget politics because there was work to do, but she had to keep encouraging people to get them to do what was needed.

SUDDEN DEATH: MONICA LOSES HER POSITION

Two days before a major national meeting, which Monica had organized for HEAL-INC people from around the country to finalize the support strategy for implementing Project Hippocrates, she was called to a meeting with Dan Stella and a new personnel manager. There she was told that she would no longer be managing the program.

Crushed, Monica asked why. Stella told her that the secret committee had recommended that a more technical person replace her, but that he had removed her because he thought she might have a nervous breakdown as a result of all the intensity of her involvement. He believed that she had failed to read the signals he had sent her to slow down, build relationships more, hold back her angry opinions in meetings, and, in general, learn to act "more like a top executive." To him that meant fighting battles off-line rather than in public, and learning to sit quietly through public attacks, even when they were wrong. He told her that as long as she did not understand all of that, there was no place for her in Project Hippocrates. He told her, however, he wanted to keep her on and he gave her some time to think about what her new job might be. For almost a year after that, Monica worked on minor projects as part of Stella's group.

Subsequent events made Monica feel simultaneously vindicated and regretful. Following another eight months of study, the new program manager concluded that Monica's plans were correct; he proceeded with Project Hippocrates using the innovative strategy Monica had developed for HEAL-INC. Kane was removed from Parker's staff and was having trouble getting anyone in the company to take him on in a new position. The scope of Parker's job was eventually reduced considerably, and he lost control of the most important part of the signal processor design area. And, after a year in limbo, Monica began to acquire significant assignments again. Yet the way in which the project had lived but the leader of it had been killed off—or at least buried alive for a year—left wounds that still ached; and Monica was determined to learn from her experiences.

MONICA REFLECTS ON HER EXPERIENCES

In retrospect, and with a year to contemplate what had happened, Monica analyzed her own problems as follows:

I was very data-oriented in my approach to the project, which carried the day; but I didn't develop the interpersonal contacts to solidify my influence. Not being from the signal processor department, I was out of the design mainstream, yet there were many complex issues to deal with. I still haven't figured out why they allowed a female—especially one without an engineering background—to manage the project and whether they were setting me up for a big fall.

I know I could have had Parker's support if I hadn't challenged the sacred cow of their analog signal processor product, but I didn't see how to avoid that once we determined that the technology was too limited. When I invited the signal processor people in early in the process, they were surprised because, in their own organization, they couldn't get heard if they were not part of the original analog cult. Most of them had been trying to get the company to consider a move to digital technology for some time, but they were shot down from within their own organization.

I had heard that Parker was an authoritarian who could not be influenced and that no one dared challenge him, and I guess I was scared. There was so much work to be done and so much market opportunity that I focused on achieving the goals without trying to directly influence Parker. He had a much higher power position in the organization and was a formidable player, so I was afraid to challenge him.

I wanted Parker's people to recognize on their own that Project Hippocrates needed new signal processing capacity, but I see now that I should have dealt with Parker directly if I wanted to be treated as a senior executive.

Furthermore, I have to build my confidence; I still feel like a little kid from the sticks, despite all my success. Others see me as overconfident and aggressive, but I probably act that way to overcome my own fears of somehow being "found out." My peers tell me that they are afraid of me and don't argue with me because they know I would bowl them over with my arguments or my intensity. They see me as angry; but I feel that I am just intense. It surprises me when they act laid-back even when they have intense feelings about something; when I feel intensely, I show it.

I now see that the content of what I was doing—the plans, strategies, decisions—was the least important part. The most important is mobilizing support and resources. If the content is wrong, you can always change it; but if there is no support, you don't have a foundation. I was trying to work without a foundation under me.

Ironically, I'm getting *more* done now without having to push so hard. In the past, I thought I had to speak up and give lots of facts to prove I was credible and confident, but I no longer think that way. I don't want to be so personally exposed and vulnerable that I overreact to attacks or assume I'm being attacked when I'm not. When Dan pushed me to do some relationship building, I made excuses for why I couldn't take the time to do it. I see now that was wrong.

I did ask Phil Edison for his help on technical issues; and as evidence of his support and confidence, he gave me two key people early on. It is easier for me to ask for help when I feel that the person is supportive. Because Edison is calm and laid back, I was too. I felt I had to stay low-key or I would lose him. I didn't see how that same approach might have worked with others. Even when Edison and I disagreed, I would try to be calm and talk slowly, which is very hard for me. I would try not to fight too hard; instead I would go away and come back to him when I had the data.

Edison likes being "stroked," which was easy to do because his early support made me feel very positive toward him. It wasn't artificial at all. The two people he gave me were reputed to be very tough and ready to eat alive anyone who made a technical mistake. When they joined me, I went to them and told them I was not a technical expert and would need their help. They were great after that.

Even when Edison challenged my ideas, I would never feel personally attacked. I would just want to figure out what the right answer was. When Kane attacked me, however, he would intimidate me both verbally and physically. He would even stand much too close, and when I tried to back off, he would follow me around, trying to dominate, to win, both organizationally and technically. As an engineer, Kane had no sense of how to work through a problem

taking many views and business needs into account. With him it was all or nothing: if I didn't accept his position immediately, he would fight until I did. There was no sense of compromise or mutual learning. I got the impression that he would accept nothing short of complete acquiescence on my part, which I couldn't do, because the data I had simply didn't support his position. I also felt that I had to protect those people who had come to me from his organization. They appreciated my protecting them, of course; but he didn't.

He spent lots of time building interpersonal bridges. For example, he worked hard to influence Todd Benson, my division's senior vice president, who was a longtime supporter of mine. Although I knew what Kane was doing, I didn't bother to go talk to Todd. I figured that we had data on our side, so why spend time with somebody I already knew. And he had plenty else on his plate.

In the long run, Kane's position and strategy didn't help him any more than mine helped me. He lost his job, too. We were opposite sides of the coin— he had relationships and I had data, but we both lost. Both data and relationships, together, were necessary for success.

I never lobbied anyone, even when I knew the person that Kane had gone to. For example, an outside member of our board of directors went out of his way to congratulate me every time I made any kind of presentation on Project Hippocrates. Although, in retrospect, it is clear that he could have been a strong ally, I never followed up with him.

I had nothing to offer Kane to get him to back off, except to voluntarily disappear into the woodwork. Although people had told me he was a bad apple and I should leave him alone, Dan Stella had said that I shouldn't get down to Kane's level of behavior, so I didn't know how exactly to respond when he attacked me in meetings.

I suppose that I could have gone to Kane directly after his first nasty attack and warned him that if he didn't cut it out I would expose his behavior publicly. Then, when he acted up in a meeting, I could have said something like, "You're doing it again, Kane; you're being personal about the issues instead of using data. That's just what you do when you spread rumors about me instead of dealing with the issues. Let's deal with the issues here." If I had said it calmly, I probably wouldn't have been seen as descending to his level, and that might have stopped him.

I wish I could learn to use humor instead of just being a fighter. But if someone like Kane says (and he did), "You'll do this over my dead body," should

I say, "Lie down"? I suppose if I had said something like, "Anybody here know where I can find a gun to give Mr. Kane?" I might have broken the tension. When I am not feeling uptight and tense, I can inject humor. I see now that it works very well on senior executives here, but I haven't been able to joke when I am tense.

I could have stayed quiet when Dorr attacked me; maybe it was immature to take him on in front of witnesses. I could have done it later in private; but I don't like seeing my people attacked, and I think it is my role to publicly defend them.

I've seen Dorr get furious with his people, and they just seem to take it. I thought I could get away with challenging him not only because of the old relationship but also because he expected that of me.

Maybe when he attacked me, I could have replied quietly, "That's not how I see it," or, "We have to talk; I have a different view of the facts." That might have been a more mature way to do it.

I forget to take the long-term view because I feel I have to win every battle. I need to learn to roll with the punches. I haven't been savvy about when to speak and when to be quiet. It looks as if laying low is more effective.

I guess it never occurred to me that putting a senior executive in a bad light in front of others is not such a great idea. Dorr might have liked me for challenging him when I was junior, but I guess what I didn't realize was that, as you get nearer the top, you have to play by different rules.

Dan Stella didn't support me as much as I wanted him to. He claimed that he did, but I didn't see it. And sometimes he thinks he is helpful when he is not. For example, after I complained that my ideas weren't being listened to at his management committee meetings, he would make a special point of acknowledging my contribution after I said something. But, since he didn't do that for others, it was seen as an unfair advantage. So he thought he was helping when he wasn't. Similarly, he thought that removing me from Project Hippocrates was the best thing "for my health." I needed his support, not his protection. I'm not a delicate flower. He could have handled the whole conversation much better.

At the senior management staff meeting at which Dorr attacked me, Dan said nothing. He believes in working the tough issues in private. I know now that he was trying to work behind the scenes to back Parker and Kane off, but I would have appreciated something more visible. I got the program through for him and then got shit for it. He avoids conflict until there is a major explosion.

I believe Dan changed as he got to the vice-president level. He used to welcome and solicit direct feedback, but now he doesn't. He tells us, "Be senior managers; that is, be quiet and circumspect and don't engage in direct confrontation." In the old days, there was healthy disagreement, but now it is hard to get people stirred at his meetings.

I find Dan and I can no longer have the kind of conversations we used to have when he was more congenial and collegial. Now I have to agree wholeheartedly or disagree very gently and tentatively. When I perceived that Dan was threatened by my conversations with Dorr, I learned not to tell anybody about them. But now that Dan has his own conversations with the president, I don't think he is threatened by my closeness to Dorr.

I guess I must have given Dan fits because, in his eyes, I became unpredictable and seemingly uncontrollable, and therefore potentially embarrassing. I guess that doesn't help him look good when he wants to win the respect of the senior managers. I don't want to embarrass him; I want to learn how to function in a better way.

Dan has been pushing me to work more with other members of his management committee and not rely on him as my sole contact. I have been doing that, and I find that I now do feel more effective and comfortable with them.

One of HEAL-INC's senior executives kept telling me in regards to Project Hippocrates that I didn't have to own it all. He said that the more you give away, the more will be given to you; and I'm starting to understand that. Dan tells me the same thing. Before, I was volunteering for everything. Had I volunteered for less, I would have had time for more activities, including more relationship building.

It's a curse to see the big picture and have a strict, self-imposed deadline, because you know how much has to be done. Dan and Dorr would tell me that they knew I was right but they couldn't handle everything I was throwing at them in the moment. When they didn't know the overall strategic plan, how could they worry about one subsidiary issue that I was pushing at them? I made people feel overwhelmed early on, which wasn't useful, nor intended. I felt my team was being clever and comprehensive to think of all the angles; but Dan and Dorr—most of the senior staff, in fact—just felt that I was throwing too much at them. I needed to show them an overview rather than a step-by-step plan laid out in the minutest detail.

I guess what I really need to do is persuade myself that I am bright enough so that I can focus on what is important to others rather than on proving that I am really smart. I don't know what has to happen for me to finally accept that I am. Because I was taught to be self-critical and humble, it's been difficult for me to accept this positive view of myself, although deep down I know it's true.

STELLA LOOKS BACK

Dan Stella had his own views of what had happened, and the lessons for Monica:

Monica took Kane's attacks on her too personally. She should have stepped back and let him hang himself. Furthermore, when he was out doing countermarketing to the ideas of Project Hippocrates, Monica should have been selling the project; but she didn't. We're still repairing the damage.

I agree that there was no way to deal with Parker. He does not and will not understand the needs of customers other than hospital technicians. Because he had position power, the only battle strategy to use with him was to go underground. All you can do is neutralize him, using other people. You need to practice "octopus management": Get others to see that there's a problem, and get them to raise the issue with top management. If it comes from many sides, it can be effective eventually. But you have to be cautious how you word your concerns. The trick is to get marketing to do a full-court press, since they won't be able to sell machines that are not suited to other kinds of customers.

If Monica had been patient, others would have blocked Parker, but I couldn't back her off. She set a launch date and wouldn't budge. I kept trying to slow her down, but she wasn't having that. I was angry with Parker and Kane too, but I didn't want to add to Monica's boiling. Remember the old saying: In war, if there is no chance that you will lose your life waiting, patience wins.

I gave Monica a card that says "Listen; Remove the Urgency; Trust," but it didn't get through to her at the time. That's the hardest thing for a data-driven person to do! I know, because that's the way I am too; neither of us suffers fools gladly. We just want to pile more data on.

She became a bulldozer, which got her in trouble with Dorr. He wasn't comfortable with a woman being so aggressive and tenacious, refusing to grovel. Although I think he learned from that experience, he was not happy at the time. That hurt me a lot. I've had a 10-year relationship as Monica's boss and sponsor, and I wanted to help, but I couldn't. She's rarely wrong about data, so it was extremely frustrating. I keep telling her, "Give it away; it'll come back with interest."

Case 29

Starbucks' Global Quest in 2006: Is the Best Yet to Come?

Amit J. Shah
Frostburg State University

Thomas F. Hawk
Frostburg State University

Arthur A. Thompson
The University of Alabama

In early 2006, Howard Schultz, Starbucks' founder, chairman of the board, and global strategist, could look with satisfaction on the company's phenomenal growth and market success. Since 1987, Starbucks had transformed itself from a modest nine-store operation in the Pacific Northwest into a powerhouse multinational enterprise with 10,241 store locations, including some 2,900 stores in 30 foreign countries (see Exhibit 1). During Starbucks' early years when coffee was a 50-cent morning habit at local diners and fast-food establishments, skeptics had ridiculed the notion of $3 coffee as a yuppie fad. But the popularity of Starbucks' Italian-style coffees, espresso beverages, teas, pastries, and confections had made Starbucks one of the great retailing stories of recent history and the world's biggest specialty coffee chain. In 2003, Starbucks made the Fortune 500, prompting Schultz to remark, "It would be arrogant to sit here and say that 10 years ago we thought we would be on the Fortune 500. But we dreamed from day one and we dreamed big."[1]

Having positioned Starbucks as the dominant retailer, roaster, and brand of specialty coffees and coffee drinks in North America and spawned the creation of the specialty coffee industry, management's long-term objective was now to establish Starbucks as the most recognized and respected brand in the world. New stores were being opened at the rate of roughly 32 per week in 2005, and management

expected to have 15,000 Starbucks stores open worldwide going into 2006. Believing that the scope of Starbucks' long-term opportunity had been underestimated, Schultz had recently increased the targeted number of stores from 25,000 to 30,000 worldwide by 2013, at least half of which were to be outside the United States.[2] He noted that Starbucks had only an overall 7 percent share of the coffee-drinking market in the United States and perhaps a 1 percent share internationally. According to Schultz, "That still leaves lots of room for growth. Internationally, we are still in our infancy."[3] Although coffee consumption worldwide was stagnant, coffee was still the second-most-consumed beverage in the world, trailing only water.[4]

Starbucks reported revenues in fiscal 2005 of $6.4 billion, up 205 percent from $2.1 billion in fiscal 2000; after-tax profits in 2005 were $494.5 million, an increase of 423 percent from the company's fiscal 2000 net earnings of $94.6 million.

COMPANY BACKGROUND

Starbucks got its start in 1971 when three academics, English teacher Jerry Baldwin, history teacher Zev Siegel, and writer Gordon Bowker—all coffee aficionados—opened Starbucks Coffee, Tea, and Spice in touristy Pikes Place Market in Seattle. The three partners shared a love for fine coffees and exotic teas and believed they could build a clientele in Seattle that would appreciate the best coffees and

Exhibit 1   **Number of Starbucks Store Locations Worldwide, 1987–2005**

Fiscal Year	Number of Store Locations at End of Fiscal Year	Fiscal Year	Number of Store Locations at End of Fiscal Year
1987	17	1997	1,412
1988	33	1998	1,886
1989	55	1999	2,135
1990	84	2000	3,501
1991	116	2001	4,709
1992	165	2002	5,886
1993	272	2003	7,225
1994	425	2004	8,569
1995	676	2005	10,241
1996	1,015		

Licensed Locations of Starbucks Stores, 2005

Asia-Pacific		Europe–Middle East–Africa		Americas	
Japan	572	Spain	39	United States	2,435
China	185	Saudi Arabia	38	Canada	118
Taiwan	153	Greece	38	Mexico	60
South Korea	133	United Arab Emirates	37	Hawaii	51
Philippines	83	Kuwait	32	Puerto Rico	11
Malaysia	62	Turkey	24	Peru	6
New Zealand	41	Switzerland	21	The Bahamas	2
Indonesia	32	France	16		2,683
	1,261	Lebanon	10		
		Austria	9		
		Qatar	8		
		Bahrain	8		
		Cyprus	7		
		Oman	4		
		Jordan	4		
		United Kingdom	2		
			297		

Source: 2005 10-K report.

teas, much like what had already emerged in the San Francisco Bay area. They each invested $1,350 and borrowed another $5,000 from a bank to open the Pikes Place store. The inspiration and mentor for the Starbucks venture in Seattle was a Dutch immigrant named Alfred Peet, who had opened Peet's Coffee and Tea, in Berkeley, California, in 1966. Peet's store specialized in importing fine coffees and teas and dark-roasting its own beans the European way to bring out the full flavors. Customers were encouraged to learn how to grind the beans and make their own freshly brewed coffee at home. Baldwin, Siegel, and Bowker were well acquainted with Peet's expertise, having visited his store on numerous occasions and listened to him expound on quality coffees and the importance of proper bean-roasting techniques.

The Pikes Place store featured modest, hand-built, classic nautical fixtures. One wall was devoted to whole-bean coffees, while another had shelves of coffee products. The store did not offer fresh-brewed coffee by the cup, but tasting samples were sometimes available. Initially, Siegel was the only paid employee. He wore a grocer's apron, scooped out beans for customers, extolled the virtues of fine, dark-roasted coffees, and functioned as the partnership's retail expert. The other two partners kept their day jobs but came by at lunch or after work to help out. During the start-up period, Baldwin kept the books and developed a growing knowledge of coffee; Bowker served as the "magic, mystery, and romance man."[5] The store was an immediate success, with sales exceeding expectations, partly because of interest stirred by a favorable article in the *Seattle Times*. For most of the first year, Starbucks ordered its coffee-bean supplies from Peet's, but then the partners purchased a used roaster from Holland, set up roasting operations in a nearby ramshackle building, and developed their own blends and flavors.

By the early 1980s, the company had four Starbucks stores in the Seattle area and had been profitable every year since opening its doors. But then Zev Siegel experienced burnout and left the company to pursue other interests. Jerry Baldwin took over day-to-day management of the company and functioned as chief executive officer; Gordon Bowker remained involved as an owner but devoted most of his time to his advertising and design firm, a weekly newspaper he had founded, and a microbrewery that he was launching known as the Redhook Ale Brewery.

Howard Schultz Enters the Picture

In 1981, Howard Schultz, vice president and general manager of U.S. operations for a Swedish maker of stylish kitchen equipment and coffeemakers, decided to pay Starbucks a visit—he was curious about why Starbucks was selling so many of his company's products. The morning after his arrival in Seattle, he was escorted to the Pikes Place store by Linda Grossman, the retail merchandising manager for Starbucks. A solo violinist was playing Mozart at the door (his violin case open for donations). Schultz was immediately taken by the powerful and pleasing aroma of the coffees, the wall displaying coffee beans, and the rows of coffeemakers on the shelves. As he talked with the clerk behind the counter, the clerk scooped out some Sumatran coffee beans, ground them, put the grounds in a cone filter, poured hot water over the cone, and shortly handed Schultz a porcelain mug filled with freshly brewed coffee. After only taking three sips of the brew, Schultz was hooked. He began asking the clerk and Grossman questions about the company, about coffees from different parts of the world, and about the different ways of roasting coffee.

A bit later, he was introduced to Jerry Baldwin and Gordon Bowker, whose offices overlooked the com-pany's coffee-roasting operation. Schultz was struck by their knowledge about coffee, their commitment to providing customers with quality coffees, and their passion for educating customers about the merits of dark-roasted coffees. Baldwin told Schultz, "We don't manage the business to maximize anything other than the quality of the coffee."[6] The company purchased only the finest arabica coffees and put them through a meticulous dark-roasting process to bring out their full flavors. Baldwin explained that the cheap robusta coffees used in supermarket blends burned when subjected to dark roasting. He also noted that the makers of supermarket blends preferred lighter roasts, which allowed higher yields (the longer a coffee was roasted, the more weight it lost).

Schultz was also struck by the business philosophy of the two partners. It was clear that Starbucks stood not just for good coffee but also for the dark-roasted flavor profiles that the founders were passionate about. Top-quality, fresh-roasted, whole-bean coffee was the company's differentiating feature and a bedrock value. It was also clear to Schultz that Starbucks was strongly committed to educating its customers to appreciate the qualities of fine coffees. The company depended mainly on word of mouth to get more people into its stores, then built customer loyalty cup by cup as buyers gained a sense of discovery and excitement about the taste of fine coffee.

On his trip back to New York the next day, Howard Schultz could not stop thinking about Starbucks and what it would be like to be a part of the Starbucks enterprise. Schultz recalled, "There was something magic about it, a passion and authenticity I had never experienced in business."[7] The appeal of living in the Seattle area was another strong plus. By the time he landed at Kennedy Airport, he knew in his heart he wanted to go to work for Starbucks. At the first opportunity, Schultz asked Baldwin whether there was any way he could fit into Starbucks. While Schultz and Baldwin had established an easy, comfortable personal rapport, it still took a year, numerous meetings at which Schultz presented his ideas, and a lot of convincing to get Baldwin, Bowker, and their silent partner from San Francisco to agree to hire him. Schultz pursued a job at Starbucks far more vigorously than Starbucks pursued hiring Schultz. There was some nervousness about bringing in an outsider, especially a high-powered New Yorker who had not grown up with the values of the company. Nonetheless, Schultz continued to press his ideas about the tremendous potential of expanding the Starbucks enterprise outside Seattle and exposing people all over America to Starbucks coffee. He argued that there had to be more than just the few thousand coffee lovers in Seattle who would enjoy the company's products.

At a meeting with the three owners in San Francisco in the spring of 1982, Schultz once again presented his ideas and vision for opening Starbucks stores across the United States and Canada. He thought the meeting went well and flew back to New York, believing a job offer was in the bag. However, the next day Jerry Baldwin called Schultz and indicated that the owners had decided against hiring him because geographic expansion was too risky and they did not share Schultz's vision for Starbucks. Schultz was despondent, seeing his dreams of being a part of Starbucks' future go up in smoke. Still, he believed so deeply in Starbucks' potential that he decided to make a last-ditch appeal; he called Baldwin back the next day and made an impassioned, reasoned case for why the decision was a mistake. Baldwin agreed to reconsider. The next morning Baldwin called Schultz and told him the job of heading marketing and overseeing the retail stores was his. In September 1982, Howard Schultz took over his new responsibilities at Starbucks.

Starbucks and Howard Schultz: The 1982–1985 Period

In his first few months at Starbucks, Howard Schultz spent most of his waking hours in the four Seattle stores—working behind the counters, tasting different kinds of coffee, talking with customers, getting to know store personnel, and learning the retail aspects of the coffee business. By December, Jerry Baldwin concluded that Schultz was ready for the final part of his training, that of actually roasting the coffee. Schultz spent a week getting an education about the colors of different coffee beans, listening for the telltale second pop of the beans during the roasting process, learning to taste the subtle differences among Baldwin and Bowker's various roasts, and familiarizing himself with the roasting techniques for different beans.

Schultz made a point of acclimating himself to the informal dress code at Starbucks, gaining credibility and building trust with colleagues, and making the transition from the high-energy, coat-and-tie style of New York to the more casual, low-key ambience of the Pacific Northwest (see Exhibit 2 for a rundown on Howard Schultz's background). Schultz made real headway in gaining the acceptance and respect of company personnel while working at the Pikes Place store one day during the busy Christmas season that first year. The store was packed and Schultz was behind the counter ringing up sales of coffee when someone shouted that a shopper had just headed out the door with some stuff—two expensive coffeemakers it turned out, one in each hand. Without thinking, Schultz leaped over the counter and chased the thief up the cobblestone street outside the store, yelling, "Drop that stuff! Drop it!" The thief was startled enough to drop both pieces and run away. Howard picked up the merchandise and returned to the store, holding the coffeemakers up like trophies. Everyone applauded. When Schultz returned to his office later that afternoon, his staff had strung up a banner that read: "Make my day."[8]

Schultz was overflowing with ideas for the company. Early on, he noticed that first-time customers sometimes felt uneasy in the stores because of their lack of knowledge about fine coffees and because store employees sometimes came across as a little arrogant or superior to coffee novices. Schultz worked with store employees on customer-friendly sales skills and developed brochures that made it easy for customers to learn about fine coffees. However, Schultz's biggest inspiration and vision for Starbucks' future came during the spring of 1983 when the company sent him to Milan, Italy, to attend an international housewares show. While walking from his hotel to the convention center, he spotted an espresso bar and went inside to look around. The cashier beside the door nodded and smiled. The

Exhibit 2   **Biographical Sketch of Howard Schultz**

- His parents both came from working-class families residing in Brooklyn, New York, for two generations. Neither completed high school.
- He grew up in a government-subsidized housing project in Brooklyn, was the oldest of three children, played sports with the neighborhood kids and developed a passion for baseball, and became a die-hard Yankees fan.
- His father was a blue-collar factory worker and taxicab driver who held many low-wage, no-benefits jobs; his mother remained home to take care of the children during their preschool years, then worked as an office receptionist. The family was hard pressed to make ends meet.
- He had a number of jobs as a teenager—paper route, counter job at luncheonette, an after-school job in the garment district in Manhattan, a summer job steaming yarn at a knit factory. He always gave part of his earnings to his mother to help with family expenses.
- He saw success in sports as his way to escape life in the projects; he played quarterback on the high school football team.
- He was offered a scholarship to play football at Northern Michigan University (the only offer he got) and he took it. When his parents drove him to the campus to begin the fall term, it was his first trip outside New York. It turned out that he didn't have enough talent to play football, but he got loans and worked at several jobs to keep himself in school. He majored in communications, took a few business courses on the side, and graduated in 1975 with a B average—the first person in his family to graduate from college.
- He went to work for a ski lodge in Michigan after graduation, then left to go back to New York, landing a sales job at Xerox Corporation. He left Xerox to work for Swedish coffee-equipment maker Hammarplast, U.S.A., becoming vice president and general manager in charge of U.S. operations and managing 20 independent sales representatives.
- He married Sheri Kersch in July 1982 and later became the father of two children.
- His father contracted lung cancer in 1982 at age 60 and died in 1988, leaving his mother with no pension, no life insurance, and no savings.
- He became a principal owner of Seattle SuperSonics NBA team in 2001 and also a principal owner of Seattle Storm of WNBA.
- He owned about 32 million shares of Starbucks worth about $950 million in December 2005.

Source: Howard Schultz and Dori Jones Yang, *Pour Your Heart Into It* (New York: Hyperion, 1997).

barista behind the counter greeted Howard cheerfully and moved gracefully to pull a shot of espresso for one customer and handcraft a foamy cappuccino for another, all the while conversing merrily with those standing at the counter. Schultz thought the barista's performance was "great theater." Just down the way on a side street, he entered in an even more crowded espresso bar where the barista, whom he surmised to be the owner, was greeting customers by name; people were laughing and talking in an atmosphere that plainly was comfortable and familiar. In the next few blocks, he saw two more espresso bars. That afternoon, when the trade show concluded for the day, Schultz walked the streets of Milan to explore more espresso bars. Some were stylish and upscale; others attracted a blue-collar clientele. Most had few chairs, and it was common for Italian opera to be playing in the background. What struck Schultz was how popular and vibrant the Italian coffee bars were.

Energy levels were typically high, and they seemed to function as an integral community gathering place. Each one had its own unique character, but they all had a barista who performed with flair and maintained a camaraderie with the customers.

Schultz remained in Milan for a week, exploring coffee bars and learning as much as he could about the Italian passion for coffee drinks. Schultz was particularly struck by the fact that there were 1,500 coffee bars in Milan, a city about the size of Philadelphia, and a total of 200,000 in all of Italy. In one bar, he heard a customer order a caffe latte and decided to try one himself—the barista made a shot of espresso, steamed a frothy pitcher of milk, poured the two together in a cup, and put a dollop of foam on the top. Schultz liked it immediately, concluding that lattes should be a feature item on any coffee bar menu even though none of the coffee experts he had talked to had ever mentioned them.

Schultz's 1983 trip to Milan produced a revelation: The Starbucks stores in Seattle completely missed the point. There was much more to the coffee business than just selling beans and getting people to appreciate grinding their own beans and brewing fine coffee in their homes. What Starbucks needed to do was serve fresh-brewed coffee, espressos, and cappuccinos in its stores (in addition to beans and coffee equipment) and try to create an American version of the Italian coffee bar culture. Going to Starbucks should be an experience, a special treat, a place to meet friends and visit. Re-creating the authentic Italian coffee bar culture in the United States could be Starbucks' differentiating factor.

Schultz Becomes Frustrated

On Howard Schultz's return from Italy, he shared his revelation and ideas for modifying the format of Starbucks' stores with Jerry Baldwin and Gordon Bowker. But instead of winning their approval for trying out some of his ideas, Schultz encountered strong resistance. They argued that Starbucks was a retailer, not a restaurant or coffee bar. They feared that serving drinks would put them in the beverage business and diminish the integrity of Starbucks' mission as a purveyor of fine coffees. They pointed out that Starbucks had been profitable every year and there was no reason to rock the boat in a small, private company like Starbucks. But a more pressing reason not to pursue Schultz's coffee bar concept emerged shortly—Baldwin and Bowker were excited by an opportunity to purchase Peet's Coffee and Tea. The acquisition was finalized in early 1984, and to fund it Starbucks had to take on considerable debt, leaving little in the way of financial flexibility to support Schultz's ideas for entering the beverage part of the coffee business or expanding the number of Starbucks stores. For most of 1984, Starbucks managers were dividing their time between operations in Seattle and the Peet's enterprise in San Francisco. Schultz found himself in San Francisco every other week supervising the marketing and operations of the five Peet stores. Starbucks employees began to feel neglected and, in one quarter, did not receive their usual bonus due to tight financial conditions. Employee discontent escalated to the point where a union election was called. The union won by three votes. Baldwin was

shocked at the results, concluding that employees no longer trusted him. In the months that followed, he began to spend more of his energy on Peet's operation in San Francisco.

It took Howard Schultz nearly a year to convince Jerry Baldwin to let him test an espresso bar. Baldwin relented when Starbucks opened its sixth store in April 1984. It was the first store designed to sell beverages, and it was the first store located in downtown Seattle. Schultz asked for a 1,500-square-foot space to set up a full-scale Italian-style espresso bar, but Jerry agreed to allocating only 300 square feet in a corner of the new store. As a deliberate experiment to see what would happen, the store opened with no fanfare. By closing time on the first day, some 400 customers had been served, well above the 250-customer average of Starbucks' best-performing stores. Within two months the store was serving 800 customers per day. The two baristas could not keep up with orders during the early-morning hours, resulting in lines outside the door onto the sidewalk. Most of the business was at the espresso counter, while sales at the regular retail counter were only adequate.

Schultz was elated at the test results, expecting that Jerry's doubts about entering the beverage side of the business would be dispelled and that he would gain approval to pursue the opportunity to take Starbucks to a new level. Every day he went into Baldwin's office to show him the sales figures and customer counts at the new downtown store. But Baldwin was not comfortable with the success of the new store, believing that it felt wrong and that espresso drinks were a distraction from the core business of marketing fine arabica coffees at retail. Baldwin rebelled at the thought that people would see Starbucks as a place to get a quick cup of coffee to go. He adamantly told Schultz, "We're coffee roasters. I don't want to be in the restaurant business . . . Besides, we're too deeply in debt to consider pursuing this idea."[9] While he didn't deny that the experiment was succeeding, he didn't want to go forward with introducing beverages in other Starbucks stores. Schultz's efforts to persuade Baldwin to change his mind continued to meet strong resistance, although to avoid a total impasse Baldwin finally did agree to let Schultz put espresso machines in the back of possibly one or two other Starbucks stores.

Over the next several months, Schultz made up his mind to leave Starbucks and start his own company. His plan was to open espresso bars in high-traffic downtown locations, serve espresso drinks and coffee by the cup, and try to emulate the friendly, energetic atmosphere he had encountered in Italian espresso bars. Baldwin and Bowker, knowing how frustrated Schultz had become, supported his efforts to go out on his own and agreed to let him stay in his current job and office until definitive plans were in place. Schultz left Starbucks in late 1985.

Schultz's Il Giornale Venture

With the aid of a lawyer friend who helped companies raise venture capital and go public, Howard Schultz began seeking out investors for the kind of company he had in mind. Ironically, Jerry Baldwin committed to investing $150,000 of Starbucks' money in Schultz's coffee bar enterprise, thus becoming Schultz's first investor. Baldwin accepted Schultz's invitation to be a director of the new company, and Gordon Bowker agreed to be a part-time consultant for six months. Bowker, pumped up about the new venture, urged Schultz to take pains to make sure that everything about the new stores—the name, the presentation, the care taken in preparing the coffee—be calculated to elevate customer expectations and lead them to expect something better than competitors offered. Bowker proposed that the new company be named Il Giornale Coffee Company (pronounced *il jor NAHL ee*), a suggestion that Schultz accepted. In December 1985, Bowker and Schultz made a trip to Italy, where they visited some 500 espresso bars in Milan and Verona, observing local habits, taking notes about decor and menus, snapping photographs, and videotaping baristas in action.

About $400,000 in seed capital was raised by the end of January 1986, enough to rent an office, hire a couple of key employees, develop a store design, and open the first store. But it took until the end of 1986 to raise the remaining $1.25 million needed to launch at least eight espresso bars and prove that Schultz's strategy and business model were viable. Schultz made presentations to 242 potential investors, 217 of whom said no. Many who heard Schultz's hour-long presentation saw coffee as a commodity business and thought that Schultz's espresso bar concept lacked any basis for sustainable competitive advantage (no patent on dark roast, no

advantage in purchasing coffee beans, no ways to bar the entry of imitative competitors). Some noted that coffee couldn't be turned into a growth business—consumption of coffee had been declining since the mid-1960s. Others were skeptical that people would pay $1.50 or more for a cup of coffee, and the company's unpronounceable name turned some off. Being rejected by so many of the potential investors he approached was disheartening (some who listened to Schultz's presentation didn't even bother to call him back; others refused to take his calls). Nonetheless, Schultz maintained an upbeat attitude and displayed passion and enthusiasm in making his pitch. He ended up raising $1.65 million from about 30 investors; most of the money came from nine people, five of whom became directors.

The first Il Giornale store opened in April 1986. It had 700 square feet and was located near the entrance of Seattle's tallest building. The decor was Italian, and there were Italian words on the menu. Italian opera music played in the background. The baristas wore white shirts and bow ties. All service was stand-up—there were no chairs. National and international papers were hung on rods on the wall. By closing time on the first day, 300 customers had been served—mostly in the morning hours. But while the core idea worked well, it soon became apparent that several aspects of the format were not appropriate for Seattle. Some customers objected to the incessant opera music, others wanted a place to sit down, and many did not understand the Italian words on the menu. These "mistakes" were quickly fixed, but an effort was made not to compromise the style and elegance of the store. Within six months, the store was serving more than 1,000 customers a day. Regular customers had learned how to pronounce the company's name. Because most customers were in a hurry, it became apparent that speedy service was essential.

Six months after opening the first store, Schultz opened a second store in another downtown building. A third store was opened in Vancouver, British Columbia, in April 1987. Vancouver was chosen to test the transferability of the company's business concept outside Seattle. Schultz's goal was to open 50 stores in five years, and he needed to dispel his investors' doubts about geographic expansion early on to achieve his growth objective. By mid-1987, sales at the three stores were running at a rate equal to $1.5 million annually.

Il Giornale Acquires Starbucks

In March 1987 Jerry Baldwin and Gordon Bowker decided to sell the whole Starbucks operation in Seattle—the stores, the roasting plant, and the Starbucks name. Bowker wanted to cash out his coffee business investment to concentrate on his other enterprises; Baldwin, who was tired of commuting between Seattle and San Francisco and wrestling with the troubles created by the two parts of the company, elected to concentrate on the Peet's operation. As he recalls, "My wife and I had a 30-second conversation and decided to keep Peet's. It was the original and it was better."[10]

Schultz knew immediately that he had to buy Starbucks; his board of directors agreed. Schultz and his newly hired finance and accounting manager drew up a set of financial projections for the combined operations and a financing package that included a stock offering to Il Giornale's original investors and a line of credit with local banks. While a rival plan to acquire Starbucks was put together by another Il Giornale investor, Schultz's proposal prevailed—and within weeks Schultz had raised the $3.8 million needed to buy Starbucks. The acquisition was completed in August 1987. The new name of the combined companies was Starbucks Corporation. Howard Schultz, at the age of 34, became Starbucks' president and CEO.

STARBUCKS AS A PRIVATE COMPANY: 1987–1992

The following Monday morning, Howard Schultz returned to the Starbucks offices at the roasting plant, greeted all the familiar faces, and accepted their congratulations. Then he called the staff together for a meeting on the roasting plant floor:

> All my life I have wanted to be part of a company and a group of people who share a common vision . . . I'm here today because I love this company. I love what it represents . . . I know you're concerned . . . I promise you I will not let you down. I promise you I will not leave anyone behind . . . In five years, I want you to look back at this day and say "I was there when it started. I helped build this company into something great."[11]

Schultz told the group that his vision was for Starbucks to become a national company with values and guiding principles that employees could be proud of. He indicated that he wanted to include people in the decision-making process and that he would be open and honest with them.

Schultz believed that building a company that valued and respected its people, inspired them, and shared the fruits of success with those who contributed to the company's long-term value was essential, not just an intriguing option. His aspiration was for Starbucks to become the world's most respected brand name in coffee and for the company to be admired for its corporate responsibility. In the next few days and weeks, Schultz came to see that the unity and morale at Starbucks had deteriorated badly in the 20 months he had been at Il Giornale. Some employees were cynical and felt unappreciated. There was a feeling that prior management had abandoned them and a wariness about what the new regime would bring. Schultz decided to make building a new relationship of mutual respect between employees and management a priority.

The new Starbucks had a total of nine stores. The business plan Schultz had presented investors called for the new company to open 125 stores in the next five years—15 the first year, 20 the second, 25 the third, 30 the fourth, and 35 the fifth. Revenues were projected to reach $60 million in 1992. But the company lacked experienced management. Schultz had never led a growth effort of such magnitude and was just learning what the job of CEO was all about, having been the president of a small company for barely two years. Dave Olsen, a Seattle coffee bar owner Schultz had recruited to direct store operations at Il Giornale, was still learning the ropes in managing a multistore operation. Ron Lawrence, the company's controller, had worked as a controller for several organizations. Other Starbucks employees had only the experience of managing or being a part of a six-store organization. When Starbucks' key roaster and coffee buyer resigned, Schultz put Dave Olsen in charge of buying and roasting coffee. Lawrence Maltz, who had 20 years' experience in business and eight years' experience as president of a profitable public beverage company, was hired as executive vice president and charged with heading operations, finance, and human resources.

In the next several months, a number of changes were instituted. To symbolize the merging of the two companies and the two cultures, a new logo was created that melded the designs of the Starbucks logo and the Il Giornale logo. The Starbucks stores were equipped with espresso machines and remodeled to look more Italian than Old World nautical. Il Giornale green replaced the traditional Starbucks brown. The result was a new type of store—a cross between a retail coffee-bean store and an espresso bar/café that has now become Starbucks' signature.

By December 1987, the mood of the employees at Starbucks had turned upbeat. They were buying into the changes that Schultz was making and began to trust management. New stores were on the verge of opening in Vancouver and Chicago. One Starbucks store employee, Daryl Moore, who had started working at Starbucks in 1981 and who had voted against unionization in 1985, began to question the need for a union with his fellow employees. Over the next few weeks, Moore began a move to decertify the union. He carried a decertification letter around to Starbucks' stores securing the signatures of employees who no longer wished to be represented by the union. He got a majority of store employees to sign the letter and presented it to the National Labor Relations Board, which then decertified the union representing store employees. Later, in 1992, the union representing Starbucks' roasting plant and warehouse employees was also decertified.

Market Expansion Outside the Pacific Northwest

Starbucks' entry into Chicago proved far more troublesome than management anticipated. The first Chicago store opened in October 1987 and three more stores were opened over the next six months. Customer counts at the stores were substantially below expectations. Chicagoans did not take to dark-roasted coffee as fast as Schultz had anticipated. The first downtown store opened onto the street rather than into the lobby of the building where it was located; in the winter months, customers were hesitant to go out in the wind and cold to acquire a cup of coffee. It was more expensive to supply fresh coffee to the Chicago stores out of the Seattle warehouse (the company solved the problem of freshness and quality assurance by putting freshly roasted beans in special FlavorLock bags that used vacuum packaging techniques with a one-way valve to allow carbon dioxide to escape without allowing air and moisture in). Rents were higher in Chicago than in Seattle,

and so were wage rates. The result was a squeeze on store profit margins. Gradually, customer counts improved, but Starbucks lost money on its Chicago stores until, in 1990, prices were raised to reflect higher rents and labor costs, more experienced store managers were hired, and a critical mass of customers caught on to the taste of Starbucks products.

Portland, Oregon, was the next market Starbucks entered, and Portland coffee drinkers took to its products quickly. By 1991, the Chicago stores had become profitable and the company was ready for its next big market entry. Management decided on California because of its host of neighborhood centers and the receptiveness of Californians to high-quality, innovative food. Los Angeles was chosen as the first California market to enter. L.A. was selected principally because of its status as a trendsetter and its cultural ties to the rest of the country. L.A. consumers embraced Starbucks quickly, and the *Los Angeles Times* named Starbucks as the best coffee in America even before the first area store opened. The entry into San Francisco proved more troublesome because San Francisco had an ordinance against converting stores to restaurant-related uses in certain prime urban neighborhoods; Starbucks could sell beverages and pastries to customers at stand-up counters but could not offer seating in stores that had formerly been used for general retailing. However, the city council was soon convinced by café owners and real estate brokers to change the code. Still, Starbucks faced strong competition from Peet's and local espresso bars in the San Francisco market.

Starbucks' store expansion targets proved easier to meet than Schultz had originally anticipated, and he upped the numbers to keep challenging the organization. Starbucks opened 15 new stores in fiscal 1988, 20 in 1989, 30 in 1990, 32 in 1991, and 53 in 1992—producing a total of 161 stores, significantly above the 1987 objective of 125 stores.

From the outset, the strategy was to open only company-owned stores; franchising was avoided so as to keep the company in full control of the quality of its products and the character and location of its stores. But company ownership of all stores required Starbucks to raise new venture capital to cover the cost of new store expansion. In 1988, the company raised $3.9 million; in 1990, venture capitalists provided an additional $13.5 million; and in 1991, another round of venture capital financing generated $15 million. Starbucks was able to raise the needed funds despite posting losses of $330,000 in 1987,

$764,000 in 1988, and $1.2 million in 1989. While the losses were troubling to Starbucks' board of directors and investors, Schultz's business plan had forecast losses during the early years of expansion. At a particularly tense board meeting where directors sharply questioned Schultz about the lack of profitability, Schultz said:

> Look, we're going to keep losing money until we can do three things. We have to attract a management team well beyond our expansion needs. We have to build a world-class roasting facility. And we need a computer information system sophisticated enough to keep track of sales in hundreds and hundreds of stores.[12]

Schultz argued for patience as the company invested in the infrastructure to support continued growth well into the 1990s. He contended that hiring experienced executives ahead of the growth curve, building facilities far beyond current needs, and installing support systems laid a strong foundation for rapid, profitable growth on down the road. His arguments carried the day with the board and with investors, especially since revenues were growing by approximately 80 percent annually and customer traffic at the stores was meeting or exceeding expectations.

Starbucks became profitable in 1990; profits had increased every year since 1990 except for fiscal year 2000 (because of $58.8 million in investment write-offs in four dot-com enterprises). Exhibit 3 provides a financial and operating summary for 2000–2005. Exhibit 4 shows the performance of the company's stock price. The stock had split 2-for-1 five times. In September 2005, Starbucks' board of directors approved the repurchase of up to 5 million shares of common stock; a total of 35.7 million shares had been repurchased since the company went public.

HOWARD SCHULTZ'S STRATEGY TO MAKE STARBUCKS A GREAT PLACE TO WORK

Howard Schultz deeply believed that Starbucks' success was heavily dependent on customers having a very positive experience in its stores. This meant having store employees who were knowledgeable about the company's products, who paid attention to detail in preparing the company's espresso drinks, who eagerly communicated the company's passion for coffee, and who possessed the skills and personality to deliver consistent, pleasing customer service. Many of the baristas were in their 20s and worked part-time, going to college on the side or pursuing other career activities. The challenge to Starbucks, in Schultz's view, was how to attract, motivate, and reward store employees in a manner that would make Starbucks a company that people would want to work for and that would generate enthusiastic commitment and higher levels of customer service. Moreover, Schultz wanted to send all Starbucks employees a message that would cement the trust that had been building between management and the company's workforce.

One of the requests that employees had made to the prior owners of Starbucks was to extend health care benefits to part-time workers. Their request had been turned down, but Schultz believed that expanding health care coverage to include part-timers was the right thing to do. His father had recently passed away with cancer and he knew from his own experience of having grown up in a family that struggled to make ends meet how difficult it was to cope with rising medical costs. In 1988, Schultz went to the board of directors with his plan to expand the company's health care coverage to include part-timers who worked at least 20 hours per week. He saw the proposal not as a generous gesture but as a core strategy to win employee loyalty and commitment to the company's mission. Board members resisted because the company was unprofitable and the added costs of the extended coverage would only worsen the company's bottom line. But Schultz argued passionately that it was the right thing to do and wouldn't be as expensive as it seemed. He observed that if the new benefit reduced turnover, which he believed was likely, then it would reduce the costs of hiring and training—which equaled about $3,000 per new hire; he further pointed out that it cost $1,500 a year to provide an employee with full benefits. Part-timers, he argued, were vital to Starbucks, constituting two-thirds of the company's workforce. Many were baristas who knew the favorite drinks of regular customers; if the barista left, that connection with the customer was broken. Moreover, many part-time employees were called upon to open the stores early, sometimes at 5:30 or 6:00 a.m.; others had to work until closing, usually 9:00 p.m. or later. Providing these employees with health care benefits, he argued, would signal that the company honored their value and contribution.

The board approved Schultz's plan, and part-timers working 20 or more hours were offered the same health coverage as full-time employees starting in late 1988. Starbucks paid 75 percent of an employee's health care premium; the employee paid 25 percent. Over the years, Starbucks extended its health coverage to include preventive care, crisis counseling, dental care, eye care, mental health, and chemical dependency. Coverage was also offered for unmarried partners in a committed relationship. Since most Starbucks' employees were young and comparatively healthy, the company had been able to provide broader coverage while keeping monthly payments relatively low. The value of Starbucks' health care program struck home when one of the company's store managers and a former barista walked into Schultz's office and told him he had AIDS:

> I had known he was gay but had no idea he was sick. His disease had entered a new phase, he explained, and he wouldn't be able to work any longer. We sat

Exhibit 3 **Financial and Operating Summary for Starbucks Corporation, Fiscal Years 2000–2005 (dollars in 000s)**

	Fiscal Years Ending[1]					
	October 2, 2005	October 3, 2004	September 30, 2003	September 29, 2002	September 30, 2001	October 1, 2000
Results of operations data						
Net revenues:						
Retail	$5,391,927	$4,457,378	$3,449,624	$2,792,904	$2,229,594	$1,823,607
Specialty	977,373	836,869	625,898	496,004	419,386	354,007
Total net revenues	$6,369,300	$5,294,247	$4,075,522	$3,288,908	$2,648,980	$2,177,614
Cost of sales and related company costs	2,605,212	2,191,440	1,681,434	1,350,011	1,112,785	961,885
Store operating expenses	2,165,911	1,790,168	1,379,574	1,109,782	867,957	704,898
Other operating expenses	197,024	171,648	141,346	106,084	72,406	78,445
Depreciation and amortization expenses	340,169	289,182	244,671	205,557	163,501	130,232
General and administrative expenses	357,114	304,293	244,550	234,581	179,852	110,202
Income from equity ventures	76,745	59,071	36,903	33,445	27,740	20,300
Operating income	$ 780,615	$ 606,587	$ 420,850	$ 316,338	$ 280,219	$ 212,252
Internet-related investment losses[2]					2,940	58,792
Gain on sale of investment[3]				13,361		
Net earnings	$ 494,467	$ 388,973	$ 265,355	$ 210,463	$ 178,794	$ 94,564
Net earnings per common share—diluted[4]	$0.61	$0.49	$0.34	$0.54	$0.46	$0.24
Cash dividends per share	0	0	0	0	0	0
Balance sheet data						
Current assets	$1,209,334	$1,350,895	$ 924,029	$ 772,643	$ 593,925	$ 459,819
Current liabilities	1,226,996	746,259	608,703	462,595	445,264	313,251
Working capital[5]	(17,662)	604,636	335,767	328,777	165,045	146,568
Total assets	3,514,065	3,386,541	2,776,112	2,249,435	1,807,574	1,491,546
Long-term debt (including current portion)	3,618	4,353	5,076	5,786	6,483	7,168
Shareholders' equity	$2,090,634	$2,470,211	$2,068,689	$1,712,456	$1,366,355	$1,148,399

(Continued)

Exhibit 3   **Continued**

	Fiscal Years Ending[1]					
	October 2, 2005	October 3, 2004	September 30, 2003	September 29, 2002	September 30, 2001	October 1, 2000
Store operations data						
Percentage change in comparable store sales[6]						
United States	9%	11%	9%	7%	5%	9%
International	6	6	7	1	3	12
Consolidated	8	10	8	6	5	9
Systemwide stores opened during the year[7,8]						
United States						
Company-operated stores	574	514	506	503	498	388
Licensed stores	596	417	315	264	268	342
International						
Company-operated stores	161	141	124	117	151	96
Licensed stores	341	272	256	293	291	177
Total	1,672	1,344	1,201	1,177	1,208	1,003
Systemwide stores open at year-end[8]						
United States[9]						
Company-operated stores	4,867	293	3,779	3,209	2,706	2,208
Licensed stores	2,435	1,839	1,422	1,033	769	501
International						
Company-operated stores	1,133	972	831	707	590	411
Licensed stores	1,806	1,465	1,193	937	644	381
Total	10,241	8,569	7,225	5,886	4,709	3,501

[1]The company's fiscal year ends on the Sunday closest to September 30. All fiscal years presented include 52 weeks, except fiscal 2004, which includes 53 weeks.

[2]In fiscal 2000, the company wrote off most of its investment in four ill-fated dot-com businesses. In fiscal 2001, the company wrote off an additional $2.9 million in Internet-related investments.

[3]On October 10, 2001, the company sold 30,000 of its shares of Starbucks Coffee Japan Ltd. at approximately $495 per share, net of related costs, which resulted in a gain of $13.4 million.

[4]Earnings per share data for fiscal years presented above have been restated to reflect the 2-for-1 stock splits in fiscal 2006 and 2001.

[5]Working capital deficit as of October 2, 2005, was primarily due to lower investments from the sale of securities to fund common stock repurchases and increased current liabilities from short-term borrowings under the revolving credit facility.

[6]Includes only Starbucks company-operated retail stores open 13 months or longer. Comparable store sales percentage for fiscal 2004 excludes the extra sales week.

[7]Store openings are reported net of closures.

[8]International store information has been adjusted for the fiscal 2005 acquisitions of licensed operations in Germany, southern China, and Chile by reclassifying historical information from licensed store to company-operated stores.

[9]United States stores open at fiscal 2003 year end included 43 SBC and 21 Torrefazione Italia Company–operated stores and 74 SBC franchised stores.

Source: 10-K reports for 2005, 2004, 2003, 2002, and 2000. Notes reflect 2005 10-K report.

together and cried, for I could not find meaningful words to console him. I couldn't compose myself. I hugged him.

At that point, Starbucks had no provision for employees with AIDS. We had a policy decision.

Because of Jim, we decided to offer health-care coverage to all employees who have terminal illnesses, paying medical costs in full from the time they are not able to work until they are covered by government programs, usually twenty-nine months.

Exhibit 4   **The Performance of Starbucks' Stock, 1992–2005**

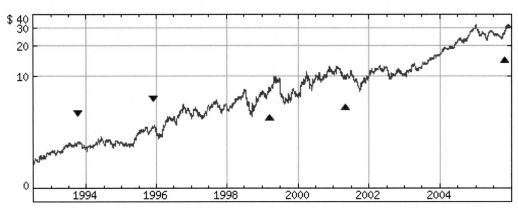

Source: http://finance.yahoo.com (accessed December 28, 2005).

After his visit to me, I spoke with Jim often and visited him at the hospice. Within a year he was gone. I received a letter from his family afterward, telling me how much they appreciated our benefit plan.[13]

In 1994 Howard Schultz was invited to the White House. He met one-on-one with President Bill Clinton to brief him on the Starbucks' health care program.

The Creation of an Employee Stock Option Plan

By 1991 the company's profitability had improved to the point where Schultz could pursue a stock option plan for all employees, a program he believed would have a positive, long-term effect on the success of Starbucks.[14] Schultz wanted to turn all Starbucks employees into partners, give them a chance to share in the success of the company, and make clear the connection between their contributions and the company's market value. Even though Starbucks was still a private company, the plan that emerged called for granting stock options to all full-time and part-time employees in proportion to their base pay. The plan, dubbed Bean Stock, was presented to the board in May 1991. Though board members were concerned that increasing the number of shares might unduly dilute the value of the shares of investors who had put up hard cash, the plan received unanimous approval. The first grant was

made in October 1991, just after the end of the company's fiscal year in September; each partner was granted stock options worth 12 percent of base pay. Each October since then, Starbucks has granted employees options equal to 14 percent of base pay, awarded at the stock price at the start of the fiscal year (October 1). When the Bean Stock program was presented to employees, Starbucks dropped the term *employee* and began referring to all of its people as *partners* because everyone, including part-timers working at least 20 hours per week, was eligible for stock options after six months. At the end of fiscal year 2004, Starbucks' employee stock option plan included 38.4 million shares in outstanding options; new options for about 9 million shares were being granted annually.[15]

Starbucks Stock Purchase Plan for Employees

In 1995, Starbucks implemented an employee stock purchase plan. Eligible employees could contribute up to 10 percent of their base earnings to quar-terly purchases of the company's common stock at 85 percent of the going stock price. As of fiscal 2005, about 14.8 million shares had been issued since inception of the plan, and new shares were being purchased at a rate close to 1 million shares annually by some 18,800 active employee participants (out of almost 55,100 employees who were eligible to participate).[16] During fiscal 2004, the U.K. Share Incentive Plan, a new employee stock purchase plan was introduced, discontinuing the original plan established in 2002. As of fiscal 2005, 10,732 shares had been issued.[17]

The Workplace Environment

Starbucks' management believed the company's pay scales (around $9–$12 per hour) and fringe benefit package allowed it to attract motivated people with above-average skills and good work habits. Store employees were paid several dollars above the hourly minimum wage. Whereas most national retailers and fast-food chains had turnover rates for store employees ranging from 150 to 400 percent a year, the turnover rates for Starbucks baristas ran about 65 percent. Starbucks' turnover for store managers was about 25 percent, compared to about 50 percent for other chain retailers. Starbucks executives believed that efforts to make the company an attractive, caring place to work were responsible for its relatively low turnover rates. One Starbucks store manager commented, "Morale is very high in my store among the staff. I've worked for a lot of companies, but I've never seen this level of respect. It's a company that's very true to its workers, and it shows. Our customers always comment that we're happy and having fun. In fact, a lot of people ask if they can work here."[18]

Starbucks' management used annual "Partner View" surveys to solicit feedback from the company's workforce of over 115,000 people worldwide, learn their concerns, and measure job satisfaction. In the latest sample survey of 1,400 employees, 79 percent rated Starbucks' workplace environment favorably relative to other companies they were familiar with, 72 percent reported being satisfied with their present job, 16 percent were neutral, and 12 percent were dissatisfied. But the 2002 survey revealed that many employees viewed the benefits package as only "average," prompting the company to increase its match of 401(k) contributions for those who had been with the company more than three years and to have these contributions vest immediately.

Exhibit 5 contains a summary of Starbucks' fringe benefit program. Starbucks was named by *Fortune* magazine as one of the "100 Best Companies to Work For" in 1998, 1999, 2000, 2002, 2003, 2004, and 2005. In 2005, Starbucks was ranked 11th, up from 34th in 2004. In October 2005, Starbucks had approximately 115,000 employees worldwide, of which 97,500 were in the United States. It had 91,200 employees in its U.S. company-owned stores. Employees at 10 stores in Canada were represented by a union.

Starbucks' Corporate Values and Business Principles

During the early building years, Howard Schultz and other Starbucks' senior executives worked to instill some key values and guiding principles into

---

Exhibit 5   **Elements of Starbucks' Fringe Benefit Program**

• Medical insurance	• Sick time
• Dental and vision care	• Paid vacations (first-year workers got one vacation week and two personal days)
• Mental health and chemical dependency coverage	• 401(k) retirement savings plan—the company matched from 25% to 150%, based on length of service, of each employee's contributions up to the first 4% of compensation.
• Short- and long-term disability	• Stock purchase plan—eligible employees could buy shares at a discounted price through regular payroll deductions
• Life insurance	• Free pound of coffee each week
• Benefits extended to committed domestic partners of Starbucks employees	• 30% product discounts
• Stock option plan (Bean Stock)	• Tuition reimbursement program

Source: Compiled by the case researchers from company documents and other sources.

the Starbucks culture. The cornerstone value in the effort "to build a company with soul" was that the company would never stop pursuing the perfect cup of coffee—it would continue buying the best beans and roasting them to perfection. Schultz remained steadfastly opposed to franchising; he wanted the company to be able to control the quality of its products and build a culture common to all stores. He was adamant about not selling artificially flavored coffee beans: "We will not pollute our high-quality beans with chemicals." If a customer wanted hazelnut-flavored coffee, Starbucks would add hazelnut syrup to the drink, rather than adding hazelnut flavoring to the beans during roasting. Running flavored beans through the grinders would result in chemical residues being left behind to alter the flavor of beans ground afterward; plus, the chemical smell given off by artificially flavored beans was absorbed by other beans in the store. Furthermore, Schultz didn't want the company to pursue supermarket sales because it would mean pouring Starbucks' beans into clear plastic bins where they could get stale, thus compro-mising the company's legacy of fresh, dark-roasted, full-flavored coffee.

Starbucks' management was also emphatic about the importance of employees paying attention to what pleased customers. Employees were trained to go out of their way—even to take heroic measures if necessary—to make sure customers were fully satisfied. The theme was "Just say yes" to customer requests. Further, employees were encouraged to speak their minds without fear of retribution from upper management—senior executives wanted employees to be straight with them, verbalizing what Starbucks was doing right, what it was doing wrong, and what changes were needed. Management wanted employees to be involved in and contribute to the process of making Starbucks a better company.

A values-and-principles crisis arose at Starbucks in 1989 when customers started requesting nonfat (skim) milk in making cappuccinos and lattes. Howard Schultz, who read all customer comments cards, and Dave Olsen, head of coffee quality, conducted taste tests of lattes and cappuccinos made with nonfat milk and concluded they were not as good as those made with whole milk. Howard Behar, recently hired as head of retail store operations, indicated that management's opinions didn't matter; what mattered was giving customers what they wanted.

Schultz said, "We will never offer nonfat milk. It's not who we are." Behar, however, stuck to his guns, maintaining that use of nonfat milk should at least be tested—otherwise, it appeared as if all the statements management had made about the importance of really and truly pleasing customers were a sham. A fierce internal debate ensued. One dogmatic defender of the quality and taste of Starbucks' coffee products buttonholed Behar outside his office and told him that using nonfat milk amounted to "bastardizing" the company's products. Numerous store managers maintained that offering two kinds of milk was operationally impractical. Schultz found himself in a quandary, torn between the company's commitment to quality and its goal of pleasing customers. Then, one day after visiting one of the stores in a residential neighborhood and watching a customer leave to go to a competitor's store because Starbucks did not make lattes with nonfat milk, Schultz authorized Behar to begin testing.[19] Within six months, all 30 stores were offering drinks made with nonfat milk. Currently, about half the lattes and cappuccinos Starbucks sells are made with nonfat milk.

Schultz's approach to offering employees good compensation and a comprehensive benefits package was driven by his belief that sharing the company's success with the people who made it happen helped everyone think and act like an owner, build positive long-term relationships with customers, and do things efficiently. He had vivid recollection of his father's employment experience—bouncing from one low-paying job to another, working for employers who offered few or no benefits and who conducted their business with no respect for the contributions of the workforce—and he had no intention of Starbucks being that type of company. He vowed that he would never let Starbucks employees suffer a similar fate, saying:

> My father worked hard all his life and he had little to show for it. He was a beaten man. This is not the American dream. The worker on our plant floor is contributing great value to the company; if he or she has low self-worth, that will have an effect on the company.[20]

The company's employee benefits program was predicated on the belief that better benefits attract good people and keep them longer. Schultz's rationale, based on his father's experience of going from one low-wage, no-benefits job to another, was that if you treat your employees well, they in turn will treat customers well.

STARBUCKS' MISSION STATEMENT

In early 1990, the senior executive team at Starbucks went to an off-site retreat to debate the company's values and beliefs and draft a mission statement. Schultz wanted the mission statement to convey a strong sense of organizational purpose and to articulate the company's fundamental beliefs and guiding principles. The draft was submitted to all employees for review and several changes were made based on employee comments. The resulting mission statement, which remained unchanged in 2005, is shown in Exhibit 6.

Following adoption of the mission statement, Starbucks' management implemented a "Mission Review" to solicit and gather employee opinions as to whether the company was living up to its stated mission. Employees were urged to report their concerns to the company's Mission Review team if they thought particular management decisions were not supportive of the company's mission statement. Comment cards were given to each newly hired employee and were kept available in common areas with other employee forms. Employees had the option of signing the comment cards or not. Hundreds of cards were submitted to the Mission Review team each year. The company promised that a relevant manager would respond to all signed cards within two weeks. Howard Schultz reviewed all the comments, signed and unsigned.

STARBUCKS' STORE EXPANSION STRATEGY

In 1992 and 1993 Starbucks developed a three-year geographic expansion strategy that targeted areas that not only had favorable demographic profiles but also could be serviced and supported by the company's operations infrastructure. For each targeted region, Starbucks selected a large city to serve as a hub; teams of professionals were located in hub cities to support the goal of opening 20 or more stores in the hub in the first two years. Once stores blanketed the hub, then additional stores were opened in smaller, surrounding spoke areas in the region. To oversee the expansion process, Starbucks created zone vice presidents to direct the development of each region and to implant the Starbucks culture in the newly opened stores. All of the new zone vice presidents Starbucks recruited came with extensive operating and marketing experience in chain store retailing.

Starbucks' strategy in major metropolitan cities was to blanket the area with stores, even if some stores cannibalized another store's business.[21] While a new store might draw 30 percent of the business of an existing store two or so blocks away, management believed its "Starbucks everywhere" approach cut down on delivery and management costs, shortened customer lines at individual stores, and increased foot traffic for all the stores in an area.

In 2002, new stores generated an average of $1.2 million in first-year revenues, compared to $700,000 in 1995 and only $427,000 in 1990. The steady increases in new-store revenues were due partly to growing popularity of premium coffee drinks and

Exhibit 6   **Starbucks' Mission Statement**

Establish Starbucks as the premier purveyor of the finest coffee in the world while maintaining our uncompromising principles while we grow.

The following six guiding principles will help us measure the appropriateness of our decisions:

- Provide a great work environment and treat each other with respect and dignity.
- Embrace diversity as an essential component in the way we do business.
- Apply the highest standards of excellence to the purchasing, roasting, and fresh delivery of our coffee.
- Develop enthusiastically satisfied customers all of the time.
- Contribute positively to our communities and our environment.
- Recognize that profitability is essential to our future success.

partly to Starbucks' growing reputation. In more and more instances, Starbucks' reputation reached new markets even before stores opened. Moreover, existing stores continued to post sales gains in the range of 2–10 percent annually. In 2005, Starbucks posted same-store sales increases averaging 8 percent (refer back to Exhibit 3), the 14th consecutive year the company had achieved sales growth of 5 percent or greater at existing stores. Starbucks' revenues had climbed an average of 20 percent annually since 1992.

One of Starbucks' core competencies was identifying good retailing sites for its new stores. The company was regarded as having the best real estate team in the coffee bar industry and a sophisticated system for identifying not only the most attractive individual city blocks but also the exact store location that was best; it also worked hard at building good relationships with local real estate representatives in areas where it was opening multiple store locations. The company's site location track record was so good that, as of 1997, it had closed only 2 of the 1,500 sites it had opened; its track record in finding successful store locations was still intact as of 2005 (although specific figures were not available).

International Expansion

In markets outside the continental United States (including Hawaii), Starbucks had a two-pronged store expansion plan: Either open company-owned and company-operated stores, or else license a reputable and capable local company with retailing know-how in the target host country to develop and operate new Starbucks stores. In most countries, Starbucks used a local partner/licensee to help it recruit talented individuals, set up supplier relationships, locate suitable store sites, and cater to local market conditions. Starbucks looked for partners/licensees that had strong retail/restaurant experience, had values and a corporate culture compatible with Starbucks', were committed to good customer service, possessed talented management and strong financial resources, and had demonstrated brand-building skills.

Starbucks had created a new subsidiary, Starbucks Coffee International, to orchestrate overseas expansion and begin to build the Starbucks brand name globally via licensees. (Refer back to Exhibit 1 for the number of licensed international stores in

each country.) Starbucks' management expected to have a total of 10,000 stores in 60 countries by the end of 2005. As of August 2005, Starbucks was located in 34 countries, with 1,049 company-operated stores and 1,734 licensed locations outside the United States. The company's first store in France opened in early 2004 in Paris. China was expected to be Starbucks' biggest market outside the United States in the years to come. Thus far, Starbucks' products were proving to be a much bigger hit with consumers in Asia than in Europe. In 2003, the Starbucks Coffee International division was only marginally profitable, with pretax earnings of only $3.8 million on sales of $603 million. However, the profitability picture improved in 2004, with pretax profits rising to $51.7 million on sales of $803 million. And it did even better in fiscal 2005, with pretax earnings of $86.4 million on sales of $1.03 billion.

So far, Starbucks had avoided franchising, preferring licensing because it permitted tighter controls over the operations of licensees. Often, Starbucks opened foreign stores as a minority partner with local companies. In 2005, Starbucks assumed 100 percent equity ownership of previously licensed operations in Germany and Chile (where it had been a 20 percent equity partner), and it boosted its ownership of stores in southern China from 20 percent to 51 percent.

In May 2005, Starbucks announced the first step into expanding its consumer products channel in the South Pacific region by launching the sales of its Frappuccino line in Japan and Taiwan. The combined ready-to-drink markets in these countries represented more than $10 billion in annual sales.[22] Marketing of Frappuccino products also began in South Korea through agreements with leading local distributors; the ready-to-drink coffee segment in South Korea represented $320 million in annual consumer sales.[23]

Employee Training and Recognition

To accommodate its strategy of rapid store expansion, Starbucks put in systems to recruit, hire, and train baristas and store managers. Starbucks' vice president for human resources used some simple guidelines in screening candidates for new positions, "We want passionate people who love coffee . . . We're looking for a diverse workforce, which reflects our community. We want people who enjoy what they're doing and for whom work is an extension of themselves."[24]

Every partner/barista hired for a retail job in a Starbucks store received at least 24 hours training in his or her first two to four weeks. The topics included classes on coffee history, drink preparation, coffee knowledge (four hours), customer service (four hours), and retail skills, plus a four-hour workshop titled "Brewing the Perfect Cup." Baristas spent considerable time learning about beverage preparation—grinding beans, steaming milk, learning to pull perfect (18- to 23-second) shots of espresso, memorizing the recipes of all the different drinks, practicing making the different drinks, and learning how to customize drinks to customer specifications. There were sessions on operating the cash register, cleaning the milk wand on the espresso machine, explaining the Italian drink names to unknowing customers, selling home espresso machines, making eye contact with customers, and taking personal responsibility for the cleanliness of the store. Everyone was drilled in the Star Skills, three guidelines for on-the-job interpersonal relations: (1) maintain and enhance self-esteem, (2) listen and acknowledge, and (3) ask for help. And there were rules to be memorized: Milk must be steamed to at least 150 degrees Fahrenheit but never more than 170 degrees; every espresso shot not pulled within 23 seconds must be tossed; never let coffee sit in the pot more than 20 minutes; always compensate dissatisfied customers with a Starbuck coupon that entitles them to a free drink.

In response to feedback through 2003 Partner View Survey, Starbucks expanded its training and career development offerings by adding the following:[25]

Coffee Masters Program: A set of courses in which partners deepen their coffee knowledge and expertise. More than 7,000 partners have taken advantage of this training either partially or fully.

Servant Leadership Workshop: A workshop that emphasizes trust, collaboration, people development, and ethics. Approximately 6,200 partners attended this workshop.

Career Power and Career Power for Coaches Workshop: A workshop designed to provide partners and their managers with an opportunity to reflect on their personal values,

career dreams, and development through coaching and feedback. More than 200 partners in Seattle attended the workshop.

Management trainees attended classes for 8 to 12 weeks. Their training covered not only the coffee knowledge and information imparted to baristas but also the details of store operations, practices and procedures as set forth in the company's operating manual, information systems, and the basics of managing people. Starbucks' trainers were all store managers and district managers with on-site experience. Among their major objectives were to ingrain the company's values, principles, and culture and to pass on their knowledge about coffee and their passion about Starbucks.

When Starbucks opened stores in a new market, it launched a major recruiting effort. Eight to 10 weeks before opening a store, the company placed ads to hire baristas and begin their training. It sent a Star team of experienced managers and baristas from existing stores to the area to lead the store-opening effort and to conduct one-on-one training following the company's formal classes and basic orientation sessions at the Starbucks Coffee School in San Francisco.

To recognize the partner contributions, Starbucks had created 19 different awards programs ranging from frequent awards to high-level cash awards. Some of the high-level awards included Manager of the Quarter for store manager leadership, Green Apron Awards for outstanding customer service, and Green Bean Awards for exceptional support for company's environmental mission.

Real Estate, Store Design, Store Planning, and Construction

Starting in 1991, Starbucks created its own in-house team of architects and designers to ensure that each store would convey the right image and character. Stores had to be custom-designed because the company didn't buy real estate and build its own freestanding structures like McDonald's or Wal-Mart; rather, each space was leased in an existing structure, making each store differ in size and shape. Most stores ranged in size from 1,000 to 1,500 square feet and were located in office buildings, downtown and suburban retail centers, airport terminals, university campus areas, and busy neighborhood shopping areas convenient for pedestrian foot traffic and/or drivers. Only a select few were in suburban malls.

Over the years, Starbucks had experimented with a broad range of store formats. Special seating areas were added to help make Starbucks a desirable gathering place where customers could meet and chat or simply enjoy a peaceful interlude in their day. Flagship stores in high-traffic, high-visibility locations had fireplaces, leather chairs, newspapers, couches, and lots of ambience. The company also experimented with drive-through windows in locations where speed and convenience were important to customers and with kiosks in supermarkets, building lobbies, and other public places.

A "stores of the future" project team was formed in 1995 to raise Starbucks' store design to a still higher level and come up with the next generation of Starbucks stores. The vision of what a Starbucks store should be like included such concepts as an authentic coffee experience that conveyed the artistry of espresso making, a place to think and imagine, a spot where people could gather and talk over a great cup of coffee, a comforting refuge that provided a sense of community, a third place for people to congregate beyond work or the home, a place that welcomes people and rewards them for coming, and a layout that could accommodate both fast service and quiet moments. The team researched the art and literature of coffee throughout the ages, studied coffee-growing and coffeemaking techniques, and looked at how Starbucks' stores had already evolved in terms of design, logos, colors, and mood. The team came up with four store designs—one for each of the four stages of coffeemaking: growing, roasting, brewing, and aroma—each with its own color combinations, lighting scheme, and component materials. Within each of the four basic store templates, Starbucks could vary the materials and details to adapt to different store sizes and settings (downtown buildings, college campuses, neighborhood shopping areas). In late 1996, Starbucks began opening new stores based on one of four formats and color schemes. But as the number of stores increased rapidly in 2000–2003, greater store diversity and layout quickly became necessary. Exhibit 7 shows the diverse nature of Starbucks stores.

To better control average store opening costs, the company centralized buying, developed standard contracts and fixed fees for certain items, and consolidated work under those contractors who displayed good cost control practices. The retail operations group outlined exactly the minimum amount of equipment each core store needed so that standard items could be ordered in volume from vendors at 20 to 30 percent discounts, then delivered just-in-time to the store site either from company warehouses or the vendor. Modular designs for display cases were developed. And the whole store layout was developed on a computer, with software that allowed the costs to be estimated as the design evolved. All this cut store opening costs significantly and reduced store development time from 24 to 18 weeks.

In August 2002, Starbucks teamed up with T-Mobile USA, the largest U.S. carrier-owned Wi-Fi service, to experiment with providing Internet access capability and enhanced digital entertainment to patrons at over 1,200 Starbucks locations. The objective was to heighten the "third-place" Starbucks experience, entice customers into perhaps buying a second latte or espresso while they caught up on e-mail, listened to digital music, put the finishing touches on a presentation, or accessed their corporate intranet. Since the August 2002 introduction of Wi-Fi at Starbucks, wireless Internet service had been added at over 1,700 more stores. Internal research showed that the average connection lasted approximately 45 minutes and that more than 90 percent of accesses were during the off-peak store hours.

During the early start-up years, Starbucks avoided debt and financed new stores entirely with equity capital. But as the company's profitability improved and its balance sheet strengthened, Schultz's opposition to debt as a legitimate financing vehicle softened. In 1996 the company completed its second debt offering, netting $161 million from the sale of convertible debentures for use in its capital construction program. This debt was successfully converted into common stock in 1997. Over the next eight years, strong internal cash flows allowed Starbucks to finance virtually all of its store expansion with internal funds; in 2005, the company had less than $3 million in long-term debt on its balance sheet despite having $1.8 billion in net investment in facilities and equipment, but it did have long-term liabilities of $193.6 million associated with lease obligations at its stores.

Store Ambience

Starbucks management viewed each store as a billboard for the company and as a contributor to

Exhibit 7   **Scenes from Starbucks Stores**

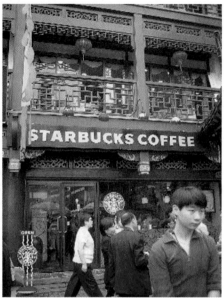

building the company's brand and image. Each detail was scrutinized to enhance the mood and ambience of the store, to make sure everything signaled "best-of-class" and reflected the personality of the community and the neighborhood. The thesis was "Everything matters." The company went to great lengths to make sure the store fixtures, the merchandise displays, the colors, the artwork, the banners, the music, and the aromas all blended to create a consistent, inviting, stimulating environment that evoked the romance of coffee, that signaled the company's passion for coffee, and that rewarded customers with ceremony, stories, and surprise. Starbucks was recognized for its sensitivity to neighborhood conservation with the Scenic America's award for excellent design and "sensitive reuse of spaces within cities."

To try to keep the coffee aromas in the stores pure, Starbucks banned smoking and asked employees to refrain from wearing perfumes or colognes. Prepared foods were kept covered so that customers would smell coffee only. Colorful banners and posters in tune with seasons and holidays kept the look of Starbucks stores fresh. Company designers came up with artwork for commuter mugs and T-shirts in different cities that were in keeping with each city's personality (peach-shaped coffee mugs for Atlanta, pictures of Paul Revere for Boston and the Statue of Liberty for New York). To make sure that Starbucks' stores measured up to standards, the company used "mystery shoppers" who posed as customers and rated each location on a number of criteria.

THE PRODUCT LINE AT STARBUCKS

Starbucks stores offered a choice of regular or decaffeinated coffee beverages, a special "coffee of the day," and an assortment of made-to-order Italian-style hot and cold espresso drinks. In addition, customers could choose from a wide selection of fresh-roasted whole-bean coffees (which could be ground or not on the premises for take-home in distinctive packages), fresh pastries, juices, hot and iced teas, coffeemaking equipment, coffee mugs and other accessories, and music CDs. From time to time, stores ran special promotions touting the company's special Christmas Blend coffee, shade-grown coffee from Mexico, organically grown coffees, and various

rare and exotic coffees from across the world. In 2003, Starbucks began offering customers a choice of using its exclusive Silk soymilk specifically designed to accentuate its handcrafted beverages using espresso roast coffee and Tazo chai teas; the organic, kosher soymilk appealed to some customers as a substitute for milk or skim milk in various coffee and tea beverages.

The company's retail sales mix in 2005 was 77 percent beverages, 15 percent food items, 4 percent whole-bean coffees, and 4 percent coffeemaking equipment and accessories.[26] The product mix in each store varied, depending on the size and location of each outlet. Larger stores carried a greater variety of whole coffee beans, gourmet food items, teas, coffee mugs, coffee grinders, coffeemaking equipment, filters, storage containers, and other accessories. Smaller stores and kiosks typically sold a full line of coffee beverages, a limited selection of whole-bean coffees, and a few hardware items.

The idea for selling music CDs (which, in some cases, were special compilations that had been put together for Starbucks to use as store background music) originated with a Starbucks store manager who had worked in the music industry and selected the new "tape of the month" Starbucks played as background in its stores. He had gotten compliments from customers wanting to buy the music they heard and suggested to senior executives that there was a market for the company's music tapes. Research through two years of comment cards turned up hundreds asking Starbucks to sell the music it played in its stores. The Starbucks CDs proved a significant seller and addition to the product line; some of the CDs were specifically collections designed to tie in with new blends of coffee that company was promoting. Starbucks had also co-produced a Ray Charles CD, *Genius Loves Company,* which became a multiplatinum album with significant sales from Starbucks stores.

In 2000, Starbucks acquired Hear Music, a San Francisco–based company, to give it added capability in enhancing its music CD offerings. In 2004, Starbucks introduced Hear Music media bars, a service that offered custom CD burning at select Starbucks stores, and it opened several Starbucks Hear Music Coffeehouses—a first-of-its-kind coffee and music establishment where customers could enjoy a freshly brewed cup of coffee while downloading music from the company's 200,000-plus song library and, if they wished, have the downloaded songs burned onto a CD for purchase.

In 2005, in an average week, an estimated 30 million-plus customers patronized Starbucks, up from about 5 million in 1998. U.S. stores did about half of their business by 11:00 a.m. Loyal customers patronized a Starbucks store 15 to 20 times a month, spending perhaps $50–$75 monthly. Some customers were Starbucks fanatics, coming in daily. Baristas became familiar with regular customers, learning their names and their favorite drinks. Christine Nagy, a field director for Oracle Corporation in Palo Alto, California, told a *Wall Street Journal* reporter, "For me, it's a daily necessity or I start getting withdrawals."[27] Her standard order was a custom drink: a decaf grande nonfat no-whip no-foam extra-cocoa mocha; when the barista saw her come through the door, she told the reporter, "They just say 'We need a Christine here.' " Since the inception of Starbucks Cards in 2001, 52 million Starbucks customers had purchased the reloadable cards that allowed them to pay for their purchases with a quick swipe at the cash register and also to earn and redeem rewards. The use of Starbucks Cards was a growing means of payment in Starbucks stores. In fiscal 2004, the company reached approximately $1 billion in total life-to-date activations and reloads on Starbucks cards. Due to its success in the United States the Starbucks Card was being launched internationally, with the initial rollouts starting in Japan and Greece.

In the fall of 2003, Starbucks, in partnership with Bank One, introduced the Duetto Visa card, which added Visa card functionality to the reloadable Starbucks Cards. By charging purchases to the Visa account of their Duetto card anywhere Visa credit cards were accepted, cardholders earned 1 percent back in Duetto Dollars, automatically loaded on their Starbucks card account after each billing cycle. Duetto Dollars could be used to purchase beverages, food, and store merchandise at any Starbucks location. The Duetto card was an example of the ongoing effort by Starbucks' management to introduce new products and experiences for customers that belonged exclusively to Starbucks; senior executives drummed the importance of always being open to reinventing the Starbucks experience.

So far, Starbucks had spent very little money on advertising, preferring instead to build the brand cup-by-cup with customers via word of mouth and the appeal of its storefronts. The company spent a total of $87.7 million on advertising in fiscal 2005, up from $49.6 million in fiscal 2003.

Joint Ventures and Acquisitions

In 1994, after months of meetings and experimentation, PepsiCo and Starbucks entered into a joint venture to create new coffee-related products for mass distribution through Pepsi channels, including cold coffee drinks in a bottle or can. Howard Schultz saw this as a major paradigm shift with the potential to cause Starbucks' business to evolve in heretofore unimaginable directions; he thought it was time to look for ways to move Starbucks out into more mainstream markets. Cold coffee products had historically met with poor market reception, except in Japan, where there was an $8 billion market for ready-to-drink coffee-based beverages. Nonetheless, Schultz was hoping the partners would hit upon a new product to exploit a good-tasting coffee extract that had been developed by Starbucks' recently appointed director of research and development. The joint venture's first new product, Mazagran, a lightly flavored carbonated coffee drink, was a failure; a market test in southern California showed that some people liked it and some hated it. While people were willing to try it the first time, partly because the Starbucks name was on the label, repeat sales proved disappointing. Despite the clash of cultures and the different motivations of PepsiCo and Starbucks, the partnership held together because of the good working relationship that evolved between Howard Schultz and Pepsi's senior executives. Then Schultz, at a meeting to discuss the future of Mazagran, suggested, "Why not develop a bottled version of Frappuccino?"[28] Starbucks had come up with Frappuccino in the summer of 1995, and the cold coffee drink had proved to be a big hot-weather seller; Pepsi executives were enthusiastic. After months of experimentation, the joint venture product research team came up with a shelf-stable version of Frappaccino that tasted quite good. It was tested in West Coast supermarkets in the summer of 1996; sales ran 10 times projections, with 70 percent being repeat business. Sales of Frappuccino reached $125 million in 1997 and achieved national supermarket penetration of 80 percent. Starbucks' management believed that the market for Frappuccino would ultimately exceed $1 billion.

In October 1995 Starbucks partnered with Dreyer's Grand Ice Cream to supply coffee extract for a new line of coffee ice cream made and distributed by Dreyer's under the Starbucks brand. The new line, featuring such flavors as Dark Roast Expresso Swirl, JavaChip, Vanilla MochaChip, Biscotti Bliss, and Caffe Almond Fudge, hit supermarket shelves in April 1996, and by July 1996 Starbucks' coffee-flavored ice cream was the top-selling superpremium brand in the coffee segment. In 1997, two new low-fat flavors were added to complement the original six flavors, along with two flavors of ice cream bars; all were well received in the marketplace.

The partnerships with Pepsi and Dreyer's produced about $20 million in revenues for Starbucks in fiscal 2005 (equal to about 2 percent of total specialty sales).

In 2004, Starbucks teamed with Jim Beam Brands to invent a Starbucks Coffee Liqueur that would be sold in bars, liquor stores, and restaurants; projections were for systemwide gross sales of over $8 million annually. Launched in February 2005, Starbucks Coffee Liqueur was the top-selling new spirit product through August 2005, according to Nielsen. In October 2005, again collaborating with Jim Beam Brands, Starbucks introduced Starbucks Cream Liqueur, a blend of cream, spirits, and a hint of Starbucks coffee. With 22 million cordial consumers in the U.S. market, the cream liqueur category was nearly three times the size of coffee liqueur category. Both Starbucks Coffee Liqueur and Starbucks Cream Liqueur were packaged in a 750-milliliter bottle priced at $22.99.

In April 2005, Starbucks purchased Ethos Water for $8 million in cash. The acquisition was made to expand the line of beverages in Starbucks' stores in the United States.

Licensed Stores and Specialty Sales

Starbucks had a licensing agreement with Kraft Foods to market and distribute Starbucks whole-bean and ground coffees in grocery and mass-merchandise channels across the United States. Kraft managed all distribution, marketing, advertising, and promotions and paid a royalty to Starbucks based on a percentage of net sales. The coffee that Starbucks sold in supermarkets featured distinctive, elegant packaging, prominent positions in grocery aisles, and the same premium quality as that it sold in its stores. Product freshness was guaranteed by Starbucks' FlavorLock packaging, and the price per pound paralleled the

prices in Starbucks' retail stores. Flavor selections in supermarkets were more limited than those at Starbucks stores. Going into 2006, Starbucks coffees were available in some 31,300 grocery and warehouse clubs (such as Sam's and Costco) with 30,000 in the United States and 1,300 in the international markets. Revenues from this category comprised 24 percent of specialty revenues in fiscal 2005.

Starbucks executives recognized that supermarket distribution entailed several risks, especially in exposing Starbucks to first-time customers. Starbucks had built its reputation around the unique retail experience in its stores where all beverages were properly prepared—it had no control over how customers would perceive Starbucks when they encountered it in grocery aisles. A second risk concerned coffee preparation at home. Rigorous quality control and skilled baristas ensured that store-purchased beverages would measure up, but consumers using poor equipment or inappropriate brewing methods could easily conclude that Starbucks packaged coffees did not live up to their reputation.

Starbucks had also entered into a limited number of licensing agreements for store locations in areas where it did not have ability to locate its own outlets. The company had an agreement with Marriott Host International that allowed Host to operate Starbucks retail stores in airport locations, and it had an agreement with Aramark Food and Services to put Starbucks stores on university campuses and other locations operated by Aramark. Starbucks received a license fee and a royalty on sales at these locations and supplied the coffee for resale in the licensed locations. All licensed stores had to follow Starbucks' detailed operating procedures, and all managers and employees who worked in these stores received the same training given to Starbucks managers and store employees. As of 2005, there were 2,435 licensed or franchised stores in the United States and 1,806 licensed stores in other countries. Licensing revenues increased from $241 million in fiscal 2001 to $673 million in fiscal 2005; domestic stores accounted for $515 million of the revenues from licensing in 2005.

Starbucks had a specialty sales group that provided its coffee products to restaurants, airlines, hotels, universities, hospitals, business offices, country clubs, and select retailers. One of the early users of Starbucks coffee was Horizon Airlines, a regional carrier based in Seattle. In 1995, Starbucks entered into negotiations with United Airlines to serve Starbucks coffee on all United flights. There was much internal debate at Starbucks about whether such a move made sense for Starbucks and the possible damage to the integrity of the Starbucks brand if the quality of the coffee served did not measure up (since there was different coffeemaking equipment on different planes). It took seven months of negotiations for Starbucks and United to arrive at a mutually agreeable way to handle quality control on United's various types of planes.

In recent years, the specialty sales group had won the coffee accounts at Hyatt, Hilton, Sheraton, Radisson, and Westin hotels, resulting in packets of Starbucks coffee being in each room with coffee-making equipment. Starbucks had entered into an agreement with Wells Fargo to provide coffee service at some of the bank's locations in California. A 1997 agreement with U.S. Office Products gave Starbucks an entrée to provide its coffee to workers in 1.5 million business offices. In addition, Starbucks supplied an exclusive coffee blend to Nordstrom's for sale only in Nordstrom stores, operated coffee bars in Barnes & Noble bookstores, and, most recently, had begun coffee bar operations in Chapters bookstores (Chapters was a Toronto book retailer that had sites throughout Canada) and Borders bookstores that had cafés. Starbucks also had an alliance with SYSCO Corporation to service the majority of its food-service and restaurant accounts. In fiscal 2005, Starbucks was supplying its coffees to 15,500 food-service accounts worldwide, producing fiscal 2005 revenues of $304 million, up from $179 million in 2001.

Other Starbucks initiatives included a 24-hour Starbucks Hear Music digital music channel available to all XM satellite radio subscribers and the availability of wireless broadband Internet service in company-owned stores in the United States and Canada. Collectively, these other initiatives accounted for 3 percent of specialty revenue in fiscal 2005.

Starbucks experimented with a mail order catalog and with online sales at its Web site, but it discontinued those operations in 2003 when sales fell off (chiefly because of the growing availability of Starbucks coffees in supermarkets and the company's expanding number of store locations).

STARBUCKS COFFEE PURCHASING STRATEGY

Starbucks personnel traveled regularly to coffee-producing countries—Colombia, Sumatra, Yemen, Antigua, Indonesia, Guatemala, New Guinea, Costa Rica, Sulawesi, Papua, Kenya, Ethiopia, Java, and Mexico—building relationships with growers and exporters, checking on agricultural conditions and crop yields, and searching out varieties and sources that would meet Starbucks' exacting standards of quality and flavor. The coffee-purchasing group, working with personnel in roasting operations, tested new varieties and blends of beans from different sources.

Coffee was grown in 70 tropical countries and was the second-most-traded commodity in the world after petroleum. The global value of the 2000–2001 coffee bean crop was about $5.6 billion. By World Bank estimates, some 25 million small farmers made their living growing coffee. Commodity-grade coffee, which consisted of robusta and commercial quality arabica beans, was traded in a highly competitive market as an undifferentiated product. Coffee prices were subject to considerable volatility due to weather, economic and political conditions in the growing countries, new agreements establishing export quotas, and periodic efforts to bolster prices by restricting coffee supplies. Starbucks used fixed-price purchase commitments to limit its exposure to fluctuating coffee prices in upcoming periods and, on occasion, purchased coffee futures contracts to provide price protection. In years past, there had been times when unexpected jumps in coffee prices had put a squeeze on Starbucks' margins, forcing an increase in the prices of the beverages and beans sold at retail.

Starbucks sourced approximately 50 percent of its beans from Latin America, 35 percent from the Pacific Rim, and 15 percent from East Africa. Sourcing from multiple geographic areas not only allowed Starbucks to offer a greater range of coffee varieties to customers but also spread the company's risks regarding weather, price volatility, and changing economic and political conditions in coffee-growing countries.

During 2002, a global oversupply of more than 2 billion pounds drove the prices of commodity coffees to historic lows of $0.40–$0.50 per pound. The specialty coffee market, which represented about 10 percent of worldwide production, consisted primarily of high-quality arabica beans. Prices for specialty coffees were determined by the quality and flavor of the beans and were almost always higher than prevailing prices for commodity-grade coffee beans. Starbucks purchased only high-quality arabica coffee beans, paying an average of $1.20 per pound in 2004. Its purchases represented about 1 percent of the world's coffee bean crop. The company's green coffee costs reached a historic low in 2002 and had gradually increased since then. Given the price volatility risk, the company entered into fixed-price purchase commitments in order to secure an adequate supply of quality green coffee. As of October 2005, the company had over $375 million in fixed-price purchase commitments, which along with existing inventory was expected to provide an adequate supply of green coffee through fiscal 2006.[29]

Believing that the continued growth and success of its business depended on gaining access to adequate supplies of high-quality coffees year-in and year-out, Starbucks had been a leader in promoting environmental and social stewardship in coffee-origin countries. Starbucks' coffee sourcing strategy was to contribute to the sustainability of coffee growers and help conserve the environment. In sourcing green coffee beans, Starbucks was increasingly dealing directly with farmers and cooperatives, and its policy was to pay prices high enough to ensure that small coffee growers, most of whom lived on the edge of poverty, were able to cover their production costs and provide for their families. About 40 percent of Starbucks purchases were made under three-to five-year contracts, which management believed enabled the company to purchase its future coffee bean requirements at predictable prices over multiple crop years. Coffee purchases negotiated through long-term contracts increased from 3 percent in 2001 to 36 percent in 2002. Farmers who met important quality, environmental, social, and economic criteria, which Starbucks had developed with the support of Conservation International's Center for Environmental Leadership in Business, were rewarded with financial incentives and preferred supplier status. In fiscal 2004, the company opened its Farmer Support Center in Costa Rica to support existing and potential Starbucks coffee suppliers and their communities.

Starbucks had $375 million in fixed-price purchase commitments in October 2005 but was not planning to increase this commitment in the near future due to a significant jump in the prices of green coffee beans (in some cases the going prices for green beans were above the fixed purchase prices). The high commodity prices for coffee beans made farmers less willing to enter into fixed-price arrangements.

Fair Trade Certified Coffee

A growing number of small coffee growers were members of democratically run cooperatives that were registered with the Fair Trade Labeling Organizations International; these growers could sell their beans directly to importers, roasters, and retailers at favorable guaranteed "Fair Trade" prices. The idea behind guaranteed prices for Fair Trade coffees was to boost earnings for small coffee growers enough to allow them to afford basic health care, education, and home improvements. Starbucks marketed Fair Trade Certified coffee at most of its retail stores and through other locations that sold Starbucks coffees. In October 2005, Starbucks introduced Café Estima Blend Fair Trade Certified Coffee as the coffee of the week to support Fair Trade Month 2005. Starbucks expected to purchase 10 million pounds of Fair Trade Certified coffee in 2005, and it planned to purchase 12 million pounds in 2006.

Environmental Best Practices

Since 1998, Starbucks had partnered with Conservation International to promote coffee cultivation methods that protected biodiversity and maintained a healthy environment. A growing percentage of the coffees that Starbucks purchased were grown "organically" without the use of pesticides, herbicides, or chemical fertilizers; organic cultivation methods resulted in clean groundwater and helped protect against degrading of local ecosystems, many of which were fragile or in areas where biodiversity was under severe threat. Another environmental conservation practice involved growing organic coffee under a natural canopy of shade trees interspersed with fruit trees and other crops; this not only allowed farmers to get higher crop yields from small acreages but also helped protect against soil erosion on mountainsides.

COFFEE ROASTING OPERATIONS

Starbucks considered the roasting of its coffee beans to be something of an art form, entailing trial-and-error testing of different combinations of time and temperature to get the most out of each type of bean and blend. Recipes were put together by the coffee department, once all the components had been tested. Computerized roasters guaranteed consistency. Each batch was roasted in a powerful gas oven for 12 to 15 minutes. Highly trained and experienced roasting personnel monitored the process, using both smell and hearing, to help check when the beans were perfectly done—coffee beans make a popping sound when ready. Starbucks' standards were so exacting that roasters tested the color of the beans in a blood-cell analyzer and discarded the entire batch if the reading wasn't on target. After roasting and cooling, the coffee was immediately vacuum-sealed in bags with one-way valves that let out gases naturally produced by fresh-roasted beans without letting oxygen in—one-way valve technology extended the shelf life of packaged Starbucks coffee to 26 weeks. As a matter of policy, however, Starbucks removed coffees on its shelves after three months, and, in the case of coffee used to prepare beverages in stores, the shelf life was limited to seven days after the bag was opened.

At the end of fiscal 2005, Starbucks had roasting plants in Kent, Washington; York, Pennsylvania; Minden, Nevada; and the Netherlands. In addition to roasting capability, the Kent, York, Minden, and Netherlands plants also had additional space for warehousing and shipping coffees. The roasting plants and distribution facilities in Kent supplied stores west of the Mississippi and in the Asia-Pacific region. The newly constructed Minden plant and distribution center was used to supply stores in the Mountain West and Midwest. The roasting and distribution facility in York, which could be expanded to 1 million square feet, supplied stores mainly east of the Mississippi. The 94,000-square-foot facility in the Netherlands supplied stores in Europe and the Middle East.

STARBUCKS' CORPORATE SOCIAL RESPONSIBILITY STRATEGY

Howard Schultz's effort to "build a company with soul" included broad-based initiatives to contribute positively to the communities in which Starbucks had stores and to the environment. The guiding theme of Starbucks' social responsibility strategy was "Giving back to our communities is the way we do business." The Starbucks Foundation was set up in 1997 to orchestrate the company's philanthropic activities. Since 1991 Starbucks had been a major contributor to CARE, a worldwide relief and development organization that sponsored health, education, and humanitarian aid programs in almost all of the third world countries where Starbucks purchased its coffee supplies. Stores featured CARE in promotions and had organized concerts to benefit

CARE. A second major philanthropic effort involved providing financial support to community literacy organizations. In 1995 Starbucks began a program to improve the conditions of workers in coffee-growing countries, establishing a code of conduct for its growers and providing financial assistance for agricultural improvement projects. In 1997, Star-bucks formed an alliance with Appropriate Technology International to help poor, small-scale coffee growers in Guatemala increase their income by improving the quality of their crops and their market access; the company's first-year grant of $75,000 went to fund a new processing facility and set up a loan program for a producer cooperative.

Starbucks had an Environmental Committee that looked for ways to reduce, reuse, and recycle waste, as well as contribute to local community environmental efforts. There was also a Green Store Task Force that looked at how Starbucks stores could conserve on water and energy usage and generate less solid waste. Customers who brought their own mugs to stores were given a 10-cent discount of beverage purchases (in 2002, customers used commuter mugs in making purchases about 12.7 million times). Coffee grounds, which were a big portion of the waste stream in stores, were packaged and given to customers, parks, schools and plant nurseries as a soil amendment. Company personnel purchased paper products with high levels of recycled content and unbleached fiber to help Starbucks minimize its environmental footprint. Stores participated in Earth Day activities each year with in-store promotions and volunteer efforts to educate employees and customers about the impacts their actions had on the environment. Suppliers were encouraged to provide the most energy-efficient products within their category and eliminate excessive packaging; Starbucks had recently instituted a Code of Conduct for suppliers of noncoffee products that addressed standards for social responsibility, including labor and human rights. No genetically modified ingredients were used in any food or beverage products that Starbucks served, with the exception of milk. (U.S. labeling requirements do not require milk producers to disclose the use of hormones aimed at increasing the milk production of dairy herds.)

Starbucks stores participated regularly in local charitable projects of one kind or another, donating drinks, books, and proceeds from store-opening benefits. Employees were encouraged to recommend and apply for grants from the Starbucks Foundation to benefit local community literacy organizations.

Exhibit 8   **Starbucks' Environmental Mission Statement**

Starbucks is committed to a role of environmental leadership in all facets of our business.

We fulfill this mission by a commitment to:

- Understanding of environmental issues and sharing information with our partners.
- Developing innovative and flexible solutions to bring about change.
- Striving to buy, sell, and use environmentally friendly products.
- Recognizing that fiscal responsibility is essential to our environmental future.
- Instilling environmental responsibility as a corporate value.
- Measuring and monitoring our progress for each project.

On the Fourth of July weekend in 1997, three Starbucks employees were murdered in the company's store in the Georgetown area of Washington, D.C.; Starbucks offered a $100,000 reward for information leading to the arrest of the murderer(s). The company announced it would reopen the store in early 1998 and donate all future net proceeds of the store to a Starbucks Memorial Fund that would make annual grants to local groups working to reduce violence and aid the victims of violent crimes. In 2005, Starbucks made a $5 million, five-year commitment to long-term relief and recovery efforts for victims of Hurricane Katrina and committed $5 million to support educational programs in China.

Starbucks felt so deeply about its responsibilities that it even developed an environmental mission statement to expand on its corporate mission statement (see Exhibit 8). In 2002, Starbucks also began issuing an annual Corporate Social Responsibility Report (the reports for recent years can be viewed in the Investors section at www.starbucks.com). Going into 2004, Starbucks had received 20 awards from a diverse group of organizations for its philanthropic, community service, and environmental activities.

THE SPECIALTY COFFEE INDUSTRY

While the market for traditional commercial grade coffees had stagnated since the 1970s, the specialty coffee segment had expanded, as interested, educated, upscale consumers became increasingly inclined to upgrade to premium coffees with more robust flavors. Whereas retail sales of specialty coffees amounted to only $45 million in 1969, by 1994 retail sales of specialty coffees had increased to $2 billion, much of which stemmed from sales in coffee bars or the shops of coffee bean retailers (like Peet's). The increase was attributed to wider consumer awareness of and appreciation for fine coffee, the emergence of coffee bars featuring a blossoming number of premium coffee beverages, and the adoption of a healthier lifestyle that prompted some consumers to replace alcohol with coffee. Coffee's image changed from one of just a breakfast or after-dinner beverage to a drink that could be enjoyed at any time in the company of others. Many coffee drinkers took to the idea of coffee bars where they could enjoy a high-caliber coffee beverage and sit back and relax with friends or business associates.

Some industry experts expected the gourmet coffee market in the United States would be saturated by 2005. But the international market was much more wide open as of early 2004. The United States, Germany, and Japan were the three biggest coffee-consuming countries.

COMPETITORS

Starbucks' primary competitors were restaurants, specialty coffee shops, doughnut shops, supermarkets, convenience stores, and others that sold hot coffee and specialty coffee drinks. In 2003, there were an estimated 14,000 specialty coffee outlets in the United States, with some observers predicting there would as many as 18,000 locations selling specialty coffee drinks by 2015.

Starbucks' success was prompting a number of ambitious rivals to scale up their expansion plans. Still, no other specialty coffee rival had as many as 400 stores, but there were at least 20 small local and regional chains that aspired to compete against Starbucks in their local market arenas, most notably Caribou Coffee (337 stores in 14 states and the District of Columbia), Tully's Coffee (98 stores in 4 states), Gloria Jean's (280 mall locations in 35 states and several foreign countries), New World Coffee (30 locations), Brew HaHa (13 locations in Delaware and Pennsylvania), Bad Ass Coffee (about 60 locations in 18 states, Japan, and South Korea),

Second Cup Coffee (the largest chain based in Canada), and Qwiky's (India). Caribou Coffee went public in late 2005, with a stock offering that raised about $68 million. McDonald's had begun opening McCafés. While it had been anticipated in the late 1990s that local and regional chains would merge in efforts to get bigger and better position themselves as an alternative to Starbucks, such consolidation had not occurred as of 2003. But numerous retail entrepreneurs had picked up on the growing popularity of specialty coffees and opened coffee bars in high-pedestrian-traffic locations to serve espresso, cappuccino, latte, and other coffee drinks. Growing numbers of restaurants were upgrading the quality of the coffee they served.

Starbucks also faced competition from nation wide coffee manufacturers—such as Kraft General Foods (the parent of Maxwell House), Procter & Gamble (the marketer of Folger's and Millstone brands), and Nestlé—that distributed their coffees through supermarkets. Both General Foods and Procter & Gamble had introduced premium blends of their Maxwell House and Folgers coffees on supermarket shelves, pricing them several dollars below Starbucks' offerings. But Starbucks' most important competitors in supermarkets were the increasing numbers of rival brands of specialty coffees—Green Mountain, Allegro, Peaberry, Brothers, and dozens of other brands. Because many consumers were accustomed to purchasing their coffee supplies at supermarkets, it was easy for them to choose whatever specialty coffee brand or brands were featured in their local supermarkets over Starbucks.

FUTURE CHALLENGES

In fiscal 2006, Starbucks planned to open 1,800 new stores globally. Top management believed that it could grow revenues by about 20 percent annually and net earnings by 20–25 percent annually for the next three to five years. Howard Schultz and CEO Jim Donald viewed China as a huge market opportunity, along with Brazil, India, and Russia. Howard Schultz believed that, to sustain its growth and make Starbucks one of the world's preeminent global brands, the company had to challenge the status quo, be innovative, take risks, and adapt its vision of who it was, what it did, and where it was headed. If the challenge was met successfully, in all likelihood the company's best years lay on the strategic road ahead.

Endnotes

[1] As quoted in Cora Daniels, "Mr. Coffee," *Fortune,* April 14, 2003, p. 139.
[2] 2004 annual report, letter to shareholders.
[3] 2002 annual report, letter to shareholders.
[4] Ibid.
[5] Howard Schultz and Dori Jones Yang, *Pour Your Heart Into It* (New York: Hyperion, 1997), p. 33.
[6] Ibid., p. 34.
[7] Ibid., p. 36.
[8] As told in ibid., p. 48.
[9] Ibid., pp. 61–62.
[10] As quoted in Jennifer Reese, "Starbucks: Inside the Coffee Cult," *Fortune,* December 9, 1996, p. 193.
[11] Schultz and Yang, *Pour Your Heart Into It,* pp. 101–2.
[12] Ibid., p. 142.
[13] Ibid., p. 129.
[14] As related in ibid., pp. 131–36.
[15] 2004 annual report, p. 36.

[16] Ibid.
[17] 2005 Starbucks 10-K report, p. 67.
[18] Ben van Houten, "Employee Perks: Starbucks Coffee's Employee Benefit Plan," *Restaurant Business,* May 15, 1997, p. 85.
[19] As related in Schultz and Yang, *Pour Your Heart Into It,* p. 168.
[20] As quoted in Ingrid Abramovitch, "Miracles of Marketing," *Success* 40, no. 3, p. 26.
[21] Daniels, "Mr. Coffee," p. 140.
[22] Company press releasse, May 31, 2005, and October 25, 2005.
[23] Company press release, October 25, 2005.
[24] Kate Rounds, "Starbucks Coffee," *Incentive* 167, no. 7, p. 22.
[25] CSR annual report, Starbucks, fiscal 2004.
[26] Fiscal 2005 annual report, p. 14.
[27] David Bank, "Starbucks Faces Growing Competition: Its Own Stores," *The Wall Street Journal,* January 21, 1997, p. B1.
[28] As related in Schultz and Yang, *Pour Your Heart Into It,* p. 224.
[29] Starbucks 2005 form 10-K report, p. 6.

Leadership at TDC sunrise: "Always a Smile" or "Communication Is Life"?

Preston Bottger
International Institute for Management Development

George Rädler
International Institute for Management Development

Early 2001: Although the Danish telecom company TDC increased its net income by 142% [y-on-y], the share price dropped by 17% following the announcement of the annual results. One reason for this is the concern about the newly acquired Swiss operation [sunrise]—*Neue Zürcher Zeitung (NZZ)*, **Swiss newspaper, February 23, 2001**

Early 2004: For the first time ever, sunrise [TDC's Swiss operation] recorded a net income in 2003. The numbers (. . .) show that sunrise has reached normal operating temperatures—*Neue Zürcher Zeitung (NZZ)*, **Swiss newspaper, March 2, 2004**

Leadership is about breaking rules—**Georg Baselitz, Artist**

Leadership is not about getting things done, but about getting the *right* things done!

December 2000: sunrise—initially a telecom operator for fixed line and Internet services—had just merged with an operator with a mobile/wireless license. The new company kept the sunrise name, but the ownership changed. TDC, the former Danish telephone monopoly who already held a minority share in the old sunrise, increased its stake from 19.5 percent to 78.5 percent of the new company.

In this merger, the typical harmonious "get to know each other phase" was very short. The desig-

nated CEO decided to leave less than one month after the merger. On December 15, TDC sent Kim Frimer, 41, to take over as CEO and president of sunrise. His job was "to fix" what was the biggest ever foreign takeover by a Danish company. Challenges came from many sides. While the whole telecom industry was suffering from massive overspending, sunrise in particular was also facing operational difficulties: The mobile division was losing 9% of its customers per month; operations had to be merged and a new company culture had to be established. The local press forecast an annual loss of up to 27 percent of sales for the year 2001.

So, how was sunrise able to reach very respectable profit levels by 2003—a year earlier than initially expected?

THE TELECOM INDUSTRY: FROM BOOM TO BUST

Since its invention in 1876, the telephone has seen many innovations on a sequential basis, some of which have been technical revolutions. Direct dialing (without an operator), touchtone instead of pulse, digital instead of analogue, caller ID, etc., have become integral parts of our daily life.

This was a high fixed-cost industry and asset utilization was key. Telecom companies were mostly operating as state monopolies and could easily cross-subsidize unprofitable operations with profits from other divisions, such as long-distance calls. However, starting in the early 1990s, several large shifts suddenly impacted the global telecom industry at once: (1) ownership changes due to privatization, (2) massive price drops due to deregulation, and (3) major changes in consumer behavior due to the arrival of mobile telephones.

The stock market hype catapulted the share prices of many newly listed, former state monopolies sky-high. For example, during their peak in 2000 France Telecom and Deutsche Telekom's shares reached €156 and €84, respectively, before beginning their decline into single digit figures.

The Swiss Market

Switzerland had always been a highly attractive market for telephone companies. High GDP levels, a considerable base of multinational companies and organizations, as well as a good private market accounted for telecom expenditure reaching 3.3 percent of GDP in 2000—the highest in Europe (refer to Exhibit 1 for key data on the Swiss telecommunications market).

In January 1998 Switzerland became the last telecommunication market in Europe to open its voice market to private enterprises (the data sector in Switzerland had been deregulated since 1992; the Internet market since 1995). State-run Swisscom, the incumbent player, traded its status of a government-owned monopoly for that of a

corporation. However, the government still owned/controlled 66 percent of Swisscom.

KIM FRIMER: EARLY DAYS

While studying economies with a focus on marketing and HR in Denmark, Kim Frimer set up and operated a trucking company which grew to 20 trucks before he sold it at the end of his studies. He recalled: "In my early days, I learned a lot about accounting, processes, how to earn money and above all, I learned to be disciplined."

After graduation, Frimer joined one of the regional telephone companies that later became part of TDC. Frimer: "I joined for practical reasons. The job was close to home." His job was to develop market strategies which "was easy, as it was still a monopoly." He became increasingly bored and decided to quit. However, the company wanted to keep him and offered him a job marketing new technologies. He rose through the ranks and became CEO of data networking. The division grew rapidly from 200 people in 1992 to 1,400 in 1995.

In 1997 he moved to Switzerland for the first time, where he oversaw the launch of sunrise as chief commercial officer. In this function, he had to lobby against heavy opposition from "all sides" for the sunrise name. Initially, it was seen as a good name for a travel agency, but for a telephone company? In the end, Frimer got his "sunrise" and

Exhibit 1   **Overview—The Swiss Market for Telecommunications (1998–2003)**

	1998	1999	2000	2001	2002	2003
Population (millions)	7.2	7.2	7.2	7.2	7.2	7.2
Telecommunications revenue ($ billion)	7.7	8.7	8.2	8.7	9.6	9.6
Main lines in service (thousands)	4,273.6	4,153.1	4,108.2	4,101.1	4,093.6	4,081.4
Main lines (% change y-o-y)	−8.8	−2.8	−1.1	−0.2	−0.2	−0.3
Main line penetration (%)	59.6	57.9	57.3	57.2	57.1	57
Mobile subscribers (thousands)	1,698.6	3,057.5	4,638.5	5,275.8	5,747	6,436.6
Mobile subscribers (% change y-o-y)	62.6	80	51.7	13.7	8.9	12
Mobile penetration (%)	23.7	42.6	64.7	73.6	80.2	89.9
Estimated Internet users (thousands)	939	1,473	2,096	2,224	2,556	2,878
Internet users (% change y-o-y)	71.4	56.9	42.3	6.1	14.9	14.9
Internet penetration (%)	13.1	20.5	29.2	31	35.7	40.2

Source: World Markets Research Center. "Country Report Switzerland (Telecoms)," May 21, 2004.

the company put great emphasis on being ready for the first day of liberalization—January 1, 1998—to challenge the incumbent. Competitor diAx later said, "sunrise favored speed over quality," but the marketing campaign on New Year's Day worked well. A company source explained:

> December 31, 1997, PM: With the countdown to liberalization only few hours away, Swisscom [state-owned telephone monopoly in Switzerland] decided to flaunt its market dominance in a way that no one could misunderstand. The people of Zurich were invited to a huge party at a central spot in downtown Zurich, where there were to be outstanding fireworks, music and drinks. The rockets were to have been set off on the dot of half past midnight, and literally all of Zurich was watching. Suddenly, however, something completely unexpected happened. The crowds spotted someone scaling the façade of Zurich's main church. And then a huge screen was unfurled and the band hired by Swisscom fell silent, as the power was needed for the "sunrise" laser show instead. The message [on the screen] was clear: "Today is the beginning of the end of telecommunism."[1]

Frimer later remembered:

> In order to use sunrise, people had to sign up by either sending or faxing us their application. Our campaign "end telecommunism" [on December 31] got us a lot of attention in the media. I had to send out my employees to buy fax machines. It seemed like wherever we hooked up the fax machines, they were spitting out applications. The success of the launch was huge. Within just three days, we exceeded the target we had set for the whole year.

The other newcomer, diAx, however, was not ready for service by early 1998 as it "was committed to the provision of top quality services, even at the cost of losing a certain amount of market share." Once it was operational—about five months after sunrise—it found that it was not attracting as many customers as initially planned.

Originally, sunrise only offered long-distance calls (on the fixed line), at around 25 percent less than the incumbent. In 1999, it started offering local calls and Internet service. Initially Frimer ran the marketing department before taking over as interim CEO for 10 months. After spending exactly two years in Switzerland, he left sunrise in April 1999 to run a telecom company owned by TDC in Germany. However, by the end of the following year, he was back in Switzerland.

FRIMER RETURNS TO ZURICH

When Frimer arrived at sunrise's headquarters in Zurich on December 15, 2000, it was his second time at sunrise but this time as president and CEO. However, the company was barely recognizable from the one he had left only two years earlier.

First Assessment

There was a considerable migration from wireline/fixed line calls to mobiles during that period. Mobile telephony was *the* major growth and profit driver[2] in this industry but sunrise had failed to secure an operating license for mobile telephony from the government. This was pretty much a death sentence since mobile communication was expected to dominate the future. However, sunrise merged with diAx, which had successfully secured a mobile license in addition to its fixed line business.

Frimer's employer, the former Danish incumbent TDC, decided to acquire the shares or parts thereof of the former partners and thereby raised its stake in the merged company from 19.5 percent to 78.5 percent, making it the biggest Danish foreign takeover ever. The plan was to float sunrise or parts thereof on the stock market within the next few years. At HQ in Denmark the thinking was that "a Swiss company should have a Swiss CEO." However, sunrise's Swiss CEO, who was also supposed to run the merged company, decided to step down a month after the merger was announced, and hence Frimer was sent back to Switzerland.

diAx's aim was "to make some money" from the deregulation. It was a consortium headed by the six biggest Swiss utilities, two insurance companies (Swiss Re and Winterthur) and SBC, from the United States as technical partner. However, diAx was facing serious problems:

- Mobile phone operations and fixed line services were operating as standalone businesses, resulting in very different marketing and advertising strategies, etc.
- After a difficult start in the fixed line business, the launch of mobile services needed to be a success. Within four months of mobile operations, the company already had 100,000 customers. This

was much faster than in neighboring countries, but was not without a price: it turned out that the handsets were heavily subsidized by diAx with contract lengths of only six months versus. the industry norm of either 12 or 24 months. Losses occurred with every mobile phone sold.

- While the company received positive press coverage for creating many jobs (900 in 1999), some of the initial marketing tools failed miserably. For example, a free concert tour around Switzerland was intended to create awareness and goodwill among the public. However, the band selection mostly covered the taste of punks,

while the Swiss public in general disapproved of the noise levels.

When diAx initially started its mobile operations, it only covered half of the country. By late 2000, 90 percent of the country was covered. The overall mobile market in Switzerland grew by 51.7 percent in 2000 (down from 80 percent in 1999). Orange, the other entrant into mobiles, added 473,000 new users in 2000, while diAx added less than 190,000 new mobile users over the same period (refer to Exhibit 2 for the sales data for mobile phones). Customer acquisition was deteriorating in the last quarter of 2000: diAx recorded net losses of around 30,000

Exhibit 2   **Swiss Market for Mobile Telephony, 1997–2003**

General Data on the Swiss Mobile Market

	1997	1998	1999	2000	2001	2002	2003
Coverage (as a % of the population)	14.7%	23.8%	42.7%	64.4%	72.7%	78.4%	84.4%
Number of customers (millions)	1.044	1.698	3.058	4.639	5.276	5.736	6.177
Growth rate	57.5%	62.6%	80.1%	51.7%	13.7%	8.7%	7.7%
Postpaid customers as a % of total	80	65.3	65.5	63.2	59.2	59.6	58.0
Prepaid customers as a % of total	20	34.7	34.5	36.8	40.8	40.4	42.0

Competition in the Swiss Mobile Market

	1997	1998	1999	2000	2001	2002	2003
Number of subscribers (thousands)	1,044	1,698	3,058	4,639	5,276	5,736	6,177
Swisscom	1,044	1,672	2,282	3,168	3,373	3,605	3,792
sunrise		26	463	653	944	1,134	1,260
Orange			313	786	925	963	1,085
Others				32	33	34	40
Subscriber growth (%)	57.5%	62.6%	80.1%	51.7%	13.7%	8.7%	7.7%
Swisscom	57.5	60.2	36.5	38.8	6.5	6.9	5.2
sunrise				41.0	44.7	20.0	11.1
Orange					17.7	4.1	12.7
Others					3.1	3.0	17.6
Market shares (%)							
Swisscom	100.0%	98.5%	74.6%	68.3%	63.9%	62.8%	61.4%
sunrise		1.5	15.1	14.1	17.9	19.8	20.4
Orange			10.2	16.9	17.5	16.8	17.6
Others				0.7	0.6	0.6	0.6

Source: Swiss Federal Office of Communications (Ofcom), "Sammlung aus diversen Quellen," May 2004: 11 & 12.

users in Q4, 2000 (equivalent to a monthly churn of 9 percent), while Orange added 60,000 users in the same quarter.

Incumbent Swisscom had a real first-mover advantage in mobile phones with about 1.6 million customers before competitors began to enter in 1998. Many of these were the very best customers (high usage, price insensitive business people). Before Frimer returned to Switzerland, the mobile market became a lot tougher. Swisscom sold a 25 percent stake of its mobile division to Vodafone and subsequently had access to Vodafone's technology as well as its 295 million customers.

Can Former Competitors Work Together?

In the past both sunrise and diAx were competitors in the fixed line business. Suddenly, former enemies had to work together. Frimer remembered the beginning:

> The following Monday, I was on the plane to Zurich to head right into a management meeting. What I saw was huge frustration and two companies desperately looking to move forward. I told the people in the room that I did not care where they came from, as long as they did a good job.

The diAx brand was well known since the company had spent much more on building the brand. Unfortunately, the brand perception was not always positive due to the weak network coverage.

Frimer was surprised by the general feeling among employees that the "whole thing was seen as a license to print money." Frimer and his team were not only facing an industry problem after the tech bubble, but also management problems. There was a lot of duplication between both companies, price plans had to be adjusted, managers had to be selected. And time was running out—newspapers reported

that sunrise was expected to record losses equivalent to around 27 percent of sales.

In the process of raising its stake to 78.5 percent, TDC paid SFr 3.53 billion[3] in cash and promissory notes, and fully consolidated sunrise's and diAx' debt of SFr 1.2 billion. In the new set-up, diAx holding, a holding company for Swiss Reinsurance, Winterthur Insurance and the six utilities, reduced its holdings to 16.7 percent, and UBS (Union Bank of Switzerland) reduced its stake to 2.6 percent while the Swiss Federal Railways kept 2.2 percent of the new company respectively (refer to Exhibit 3 for the initial set-up of both consortia).[4]

Some insiders have described sunrise in 2000 as being a "paralyzed company." Based on the scale of the issues, Frimer brought with him 25 colleagues from Denmark. Within TDC, there was a strong feeling that Frimer's skills combined with those of a strong CFO would be the right solution for sunrise. Klaus Pedersen, TDC's vice president, Group Accounting & Tax was a natural choice for this position. This was the first time he would be working with Frimer.

HISTORY OF TDC (FORMERLY TELE DANMARK)

TDC A/S (TDC) was the former state monopoly for telephones in Denmark. It resulted from a merger in 1990 between four regional Danish telephone companies and the international operations. TDC was formed with the clear aim to strengthen the telecommunications industry. The merger of the various companies was seen as a response to a recommendation from the European Union (EU). In a 1989 report the regulators saw no reason for the telecommunications market to be protected by

Exhibit 3 **Original Ownership Structure in 1998**

Sunrise	Ownership	diAx	Ownership
Swiss Federal Railways	11.8%	SBC	40%
UBS Bank	9.8	diAx Holding (Swiss Reinsurance,	60
TDC	44.0	Winterthur Insurance, utilities)	
British Telecom	34.4		

state monopolies. The EU suggested that telecom companies should become part of the private competition.

The integration of the various networks and the IT platforms took several years. But the efforts paid off in 1994. TDC had its initial public offering (IPO) on the stock market and thereby government ownership went down to 51 percent. It was also one of the European pioneers to list on the New York Stock Exchange. Some saw this as a first indicator of internationalization.

Growing by Leaving Denmark

The IPO started a rapid internationalization process drive with regard to international activities and ownership. TDC began to invest in consortia outside Denmark—initially with small investments in the Ukraine and Poland. The Danish market was fully deregulated and as early as 1993, two mobile operators were chasing customers in a country with 5.4 million inhabitants. Denmark was widely considered as one of the most deregulated markets in

Exhibit 4   **Overview of TDC's International Operations**

Country	Company	Businesses	TDC's Ownership Stake in 2003 (year-end)	TDC's Ownership Stake Initially and Year of Entry
Austria	Connect Austria-One	Mobile	15%	15.00% 1997
Belgium	Belgacom	Full service telecom provider	15.9	16.50% 1996
Czech Republic	Ceske Radiokommunikace	Fixed telephony & Internet	0	20.79% 1997
	Contactel	Fixed telephony & Internet	100	16.67% 1999
Finland	TDC Hakemistot	Directories	100	100.00% 2002
Germany	Talkline	Mobile	100	100.00% 1997
Hungary	HTCC	Fixed telephony & Internet	31.9	19.00% 1997
Norway	TDC Norway	Fixed telephony & Internet	100	51.00% 1999
Lithuania	Bite	Mobile	100	17.00% 1995
Poland	Polkomtel	Mobile	19.6	19.25% 1995
	TDC Internet Polska	Internet	0	51.00% 2001
Sweden	TDC Internordia AB	Fixed telephony & Internet	100	50.00% 1995
Switzerland	TDC Switzerland	Full service telecom provider	100	44.00%* 1997
Ukraine	UMC	Mobile	0	16.33% 1993

*The acquisition in 1997 relates to sunrise Communications AG. In January 2001 this company was merged with diAx to form a new company named TDC Switzerland.
Source: TDC.

Exhibit 5   **TDC's Net Revenues and Earnings Before Interest, Taxes, Depreciation and Amortization (EBITDA)**

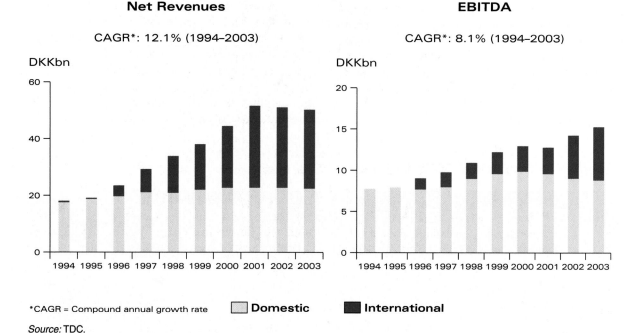

Net Revenues

CAGR*: 12.1% (1994–2003)

EBITDA

CAGR*: 8.1% (1994–2003)

*CAGR = Compound annual growth rate   ☐ **Domestic**   ■ **International**

Source: TDC.

Europe with very low price levels. Over the years, TDC made more investments in Europe (refer to Exhibit 4 for an overview of international operations). But by 1998, the strategy changed. Torben V. Holm, TDC's senior VP corporate business development, clarified:

> Until 1998, the strategy was to go abroad, plant flags and get some experience. This was followed by swapping assets. After 1998, the question was how to get control. [We] realized that with consortia it was impossible to realize synergies between the companies due to the limited sharing potential.

In fact, between 1998 and 2003 TDC kept investments in a total of 13 companies, but direct control

increased from 1 to 8. By 1999, international sales accounted for 40% of total (up from 2% in 1995) and two years later they surpassed domestic sales for the first time (refer to Exhibit 5 for net revenues from internationalization).

While TDC's sales grew rapidly in the ten years up to 2003 (refer to Exhibit 6), its ownership also became more international. In 1997 34 percent of the Danish government's 51 percent stake in TDC was sold to Ameritech of the United States, and the remaining 17 percent was bought back in a share buy-back program. Ameritech, which later raised its stake in TDC to 42 percent, was later sold to SBC, a company that held a share in diAx.[5]

Exhibit 6   **10-Year Performance of TDC ($ in millions)**

	1993	1994	1995	1996	1997	1998	1999	2000	2001	2002	2003
Sales	$2,693	$3,256	$3,400	$4,407	$4,474	$5,336	$5,173	$5,556	$6,457	$7,546	$8,770
Sales growth		20.9%	4.4%	29.6%	1.5%	19.3%	(3.1%)	7.4%	16.2%	16.9%	16.2%
Net income	$230	$423	$630	$523	$226	$630	$476	$1,133	$(88)	$641	$305
Employees	N/A	16,678	16,476	16,763	17,268	16,410	17,464	18,363	19,130	22,263	22,429

Note: Exchange rates fluctuated over the same period.
Source: Hoover's Profile.

In a move to improve TDC's competitive position and focus more clearly on high potential growth areas, TDC restructured its operations in 2000. Three core divisions emerged (refer to Exhibit 7 for further details on the organization). Within the group, TDC Switzerland was the largest foreign operation, accounting for around 19 percent of TDC's revenues. Part of the reorganization was the introduction of the "TDC" name to replace the Tele Danmark brand.

Managing at TDC

TDC's CEO, Henning Dyremose, a former Danish finance minister, joined the company in 1998. He remembered the early days:

> Our international expansion put us in the position of being a portfolio manager. Management was not ready for this [new environment] of competition and privatization.

As a result of this, TDC developed its vision model (refer to Exhibit 8 for the vision model). But with it, Dyremose believed in rotating his top managers. He explained:

> Over the years, only three out of the 100 top managers maintained the same position—including the legal counsel and CFO. I select people based on their intellectual capacity, honesty, capability to create results, loyalty and operational skills.

Dyremose continued:

> With this [selection] criteria, I'm out for trouble. This system attracts very skilled, but at the same time also somewhat difficult managers. In the case of Frimer, he is someone who delivers on time, is always well-prepared, sharp and precise, and employees are proud to work for him. He motivates them to go the extra mile.

TDC had a very small executive committee (three members) plus a senior management team which consisted of the six CEOs from the largest subsidiaries. They met monthly to exchange knowledge and business ideas.

The financial reporting system was clear. Karsten Hetland, executive vice president HR, clarified, "We lead by targets—both financial and operational. If we put more structure on there, this would not work." Managers in the various companies realized the importance of the financial controls and there was strong emphasis to adhere to these processes. Dyremose and his CFO, Hans Munk Nielsen, held monthly review updates with the CEOs and CFOs of the various subsidiaries. Nielsen, the CFO, explained his role:

> My role is to make sure that the figures are correct and evaluate forward-looking statements. In the case of sunrise, the critics said that TDC overpaid, the company was performing poorly and telecom was not necessarily a portable business. They were questioning TDC's business model. But time has shown that the sunrise business case was correct.

With rapid internationalization, leadership became a top priority. As part of the new vision, TDC reorganized its HR functions by combining various functions (compensation, performance, leadership development, succession management) into one

Exhibit 7   TDC's Structure, 2003 sales in millions of $

Division	Services Offered	Sales (% of total)	Customers (millions)	Employees
TDC Solutions	Full range of communications services for customers in Denmark and neighboring Nordic countries	$3,245 (37%)	4.4	11,675
TDC Mobile International	All mobile operations including the domestic operation	2,719 (31%)	6.1 (pro rata)	
TDC Switzerland	Fixed line, mobile, Internet services in Switzerland	1,666 (19%)	2.6	2,380
TDC Cable TV	TV network and broadband Internet access	263 (3%)	0.9	733
TDC Directories		248 (3%)		1,091
Other	TDC Service (billing and internal IT services)	629 (7%)		2,093
Total		$8,770 (100%)		22,429

Source: TDC.

Exhibit 8   **TDC Vision Model and TDC Values**

The TDC Vision

**TDC will strive to be the best provider
of communications solutions in Europe**

Stakeholder
Approach

| Customers | Employees | Shareholders | Society |

Strategies

Group

Business Lines

The TDC Values

We center our actions around the **customers**
We **demand the most of ourselves**
We are **trustworthy** in every context
We value **teamwork**
We **respect** the individual

We center our actions around the customers:

▸ We strive to understand our customers' requirements—and to meet these in the best possible way
▸ We encourage initiative and entrepreneurship
▸ We treat every customer as if they are our only customer

We demand the utmost of ourselves:

▸ We focus on execution and act with a sense of urgency
▸ We respect decisions taken
▸ We treat everyone like we wish to be treated
▸ We eliminate activities that are not creating value
▸ We live the values

We are trustworthy in every context:

▸ We are reliable
▸ We are good citizens

We value teamwork:

▸ We create good teams through cooperation
▸ We share knowledge across teams
▸ We secure orderly and fair decision making processes

We respect the individual:

▸ We evaluate on the basis of results
▸ We are fair to each other
▸ We seek a balance between work and private life
▸ We respect diversities and provide all with equal opportunity

Source: TDC.

department. In total, the department catered to the needs of over 100 expats.

The impact of the vision on daily jobs was measured by the climate survey. This survey consisted of 52 parameters, which measured how the focus areas of the vision model and the values were incorporated in the daily life of employees. Hetland explained, "This serves as a discussion and action tool and is the key tool for changing the company culture."

BACK TO SWITZERLAND—EARLY 2004: "SUNRISE REACHED OPERATING TEMPERATURE"[6]

Deregulation in Switzerland saw prices tumbling beyond expectations. According to Bakom, the local authorities, prices for domestic long-distance calls on fixed lines dropped by up to 83 percent between 1998 and 2003 while international calls dropped by

up to 77 percent over the same period.[7] The price decreases for mobile phones were less drastic, on average between 5 percent and 19 percent over the same period. Overall, the price index for telephony fell from a base of 100 in 1998 to 68.8 in 2003.

Complete Recovery Shows in the Results

While the company increased its revenues by 9.8 percent to SFr 1.937 billion in 2003, it increased its EBITDA[8] by 79.9 percent to SFr 451 million and net income reached SFr 171 million. Interestingly, sunrise was able to return to profitability one year earlier than expected (refer to Exhibits 9 and 10 for full financial details). Sunrise's profitability was impressive on different accounts. Net income came in at 8.8 percent of sales, even beating Swisscom (7.88 percent), France Telecom (6.94 percent), and Deutsche Telekom (2.33 percent).

More important, Swisscom's growth, still around 27 percent in 2000, almost came to a halt between 2001 and 2003 (refer to Exhibit 11 for further details). Orange, after a strong launch, had lost its 2nd

Exhibit 9   **Financial Overview of Sunrise, 2001–2003**

	2001	Change (in %)	2002	Change (in %)	2003	Change (in %)
Net sales (SFr million)	1,652		1,764	6.8%	1,937	9.8%
Mobile Communication	818		904	10.4	1,042	15.3
Fixed Line Communication	718		744	3.6	765	2.9
Internet & ADSL	117		117	0.5	130	11.4
Cost of Sales (SFr million)	(1,675)		(1,534)	(8.4)	(1,486)	(1.8)
Transmission Cost and Raw Materials (includes subsidized mobile phones)	(807)		(741)	(8.2)	(789)	6.5
Other External Expenses	(626)		(542)	(13.4)	(449)	(17.1)
Salaries, wages and pension payments	(242)		(251)	3.7	(248)	(1.2)
EBITDA	(23)		251	na	451	79.9
Net Income (SFr million)	na*		(93)		171	
Customer structure						
Mobile Communications	944,000	62%	1,100,000	20	1,260,000	11.1
Fixed Line Communications	786,000	15	852,000	8.4	824,000	(3.3)
Internet & ADSL	499,000	25	518,000	3.8	526,000	1.5
Employees	2,465		2,200	(12)	2,500	12

*Note: *Neue Zürcher Zeitung* (NZZ) estimated losses of SFr 400–450 million for 2001. See NZZ, "sunrise mit Verlust," June 7, 2002.
Source: sunrise, IMD Research.

Exhibit 10   **TDC Switzerland's Financial Performance (EBITDA)**

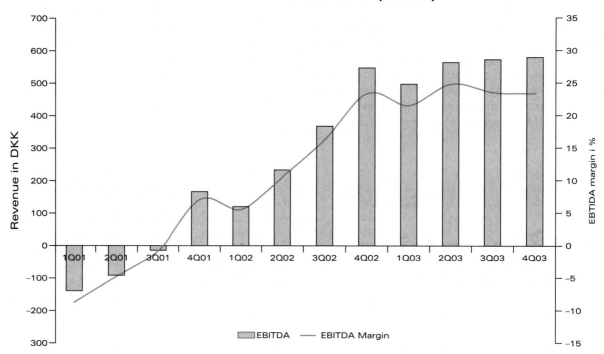

Source: TDC.

place position for mobile phones to sunrise, after Frimer and his team decided to drop the diAx brand altogether.

What did sunrise do to have such a successful turnaround?

STARTING THE TURNAROUND AT SUNRISE

Given the situation at sunrise when Frimer arrived in December 2000, he decided to call a management board[9] meeting without delay. For the board members, it sounded like a peculiar setup: The meeting was to be held in a chalet in the Swiss mountains over the weekend, and when they requested an agenda they were simply told "there is no agenda." At first they were reluctant since "there could not be a board meeting without an agenda." However, the meeting took place and Frimer began by raising two issues he wanted to discuss over the weekend: "Firstly, how to increase revenue and secondly how to reduce cost?" After the two days in the mountains, the management

board had a clear understanding of the turnaround strategy. Moreover, it set the basis for creating a "we" feeling among the top team.

The management team soon discovered that the merged company was "definitely not a license to print money" and personnel costs had to be cut. One round of layoffs was necessary and 240 employees (10 percent of the workforce) were asked to leave. However, the top management team made it clear that this was the last round of layoffs and that things would subsequently pick up.

From the beginning, Frimer and his team were worried that the wrong people were leaving. The newspapers reported an employee fluctuation rate of 32 percent.[10] Fast decisions had to be made. Frimer explained:

> I have seen it in the past, I don't care how we are organized, just get things done. I find people and then I design a structure around them. After one week, the management team was in place. This was an emergency and we did not have time to look for six months for an outsider to fill a position. We could take care of the wrong selections later on. When hiring people I look for commercial sense, people skills and operational focus. I have seen a lot of intelligent people with no people skills. It does not work.

Exhibit 11   **Competitive Data (General Data & Swiss Market)**

General Data (2003)	France Telecom	Deutsche Telekom	Swisscom	sunrise
Revenue	€46.1 billion	€55.8 billion	SFr 14.6 billion	SFr 1.937 billion
Net income	€ 3.2 billion	€ 1.3 billion	SFr 1.15 billion	SFr 0.171 billion
Net income as a % of revenue	6.94%	2.33%	7.88%	8.83%

Note: see also Appendix I.
Source: Annual reports, investor presentations.

Swiss Market: Revenues of Swisscom (SFr million)	1999	2000	2001	2002	2003
Net revenue	11,052	14,060	14,174	14,526	14,581
EBITDA	4,192	4,034	4,409	4,413	4,641
Net income	2,391	3,156	4,964	824	1,569
Number of mobile customers (in millions)	2.282	3.168	3.373	3.605	3.792

Note: 2001 net income includes a gain of SFr 3.8 billion from selling 25% of Swisscom's mobile division to Vodafone.

Swiss Market: Revenues of Orange (SFr million)	1999	2000	2001	2002	2003
Net revenue			886	1,018	1,169 (14.8%)
EBITDA		(523.7)	10.5	81	296
Number of mobile customers	313,000	786,000	925,000	962,733	1,085,000 (+12.7%)

Source: Press clippings.

In order to deal with the uncertainty among employees, HR decisions were communicated on a daily basis to all personnel via e-mail at 17:00. Communication between management and employees continued during the turnaround, and employees were closely involved both in the turnaround and the return to profitability. Early on, there was a decision that there "would be no consultants." The employees alone would be accountable for their actions. The new organizational structure was developed within just two weeks—in fact, fast decision making became a symbol of the turnaround—and it catered to the needs of Frimer's team (refer to Exhibit 12 for sunrise's structure). Legally the merger was completed on January 23, two months after the announcement.

There were some new faces on the board (refer to Exhibit 13 for the background of board members). Frimer was known for his open-door policy. He explained, "I hate [office] politics and I want to keep political infighting to a minimum by keeping discussions on a level of what helps customers." This customer orientation made the board members realize the shortcomings of their existing structure. The product groups had to join forces to serve business customers, since they often required several services at once. As a result, a key account management system was set up for business customers. These key accounters would handle all contact with sunrise. In addition, a business marketing board was set up to coordinate the various functions and this was later followed by a customer marketing board, too.

The targets for each division were ambitious. With the arrival of the Danish delegation at sunrise, it soon became clear that targets had to be met, "apologies were not accepted anymore." Board members also felt this desire to succeed. Klaus Pedersen, CFO, explained

Exhibit 12   **Organizational Chart—TDC Switzerland, May 2004**

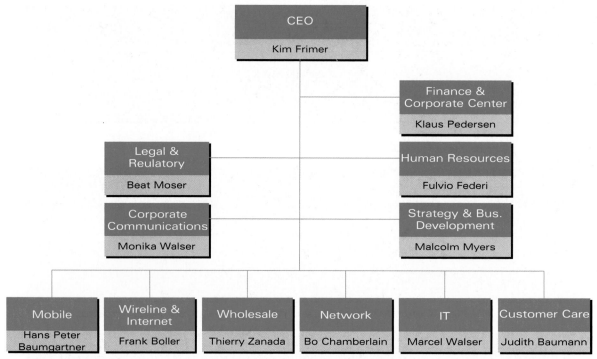

Source: Company information.

Mergers are difficult, but you can get people excited. The management board was extremely motivated, as everyone really felt part of sunrise. Failure was not an option for us.

sunrise: The Most Human Telecom Provider?

In line with "picking the low hanging fruit first," the management streamlined operations with the elimination of double functions, sunrise merged back-office functions including networks, call centers, IT, billing operations, corporate functions (HR, legal, strategy, communications), reduced office locations and fewer externals/contractors. This led to considerable cost savings, e.g., IT functions were reduced by SFr 12.5 million. Marketing budgets were cut by 25 percent. Expensive sponsoring engagements, such as the Swiss National Exhibition (Expo 2002), were stopped. Following the board meeting in the chalet, long lists were made up showing where costs could be cut. Growing the revenue was possible, too, since there was little overlap in the customer base. Only 15 percent of diAx's customers were also customers of sunrise and hence the potential was considerable.

Within two months, the management had decided on the new strategy. Sunrise was going to be the "most human telecom provider," easy, friendly, smart solutions for reasonable prices. This was quite different from the competition, which normally differentiated themselves based on hard facts such as network power and tradition (refer to Exhibit 14 for the product positioning). Some of the first advertising campaigns read: "we are here to stay," "you can hear the smile," "easy & understandable," "quality and reliability," "value for money." Although there were several entrants in the Swiss market for telecommunications, sunrise was the only alternative operator in Switzerland to offer mobile, fixed and Internet services.

The new positioning translated into the three pillars of strategy: excellent marketing and sales, cost consciousness, and customer loyalty (refer to Exhibit 15 for the strategy overview). The merged company was to fade out the diAx brand name.

Making Sure Employees Understand the Strategy

Sunrise's management put great effort into ensuring that employees understood the strategy: "We strive

Exhibit 13   **Background of Board Members**

Name	Age	Position	In This Position Since	Previous Professional Experience
Judith Baumann	39	Customer Care	2000	• Vice Director in the IT Customer Support/Private Banking division of UBS bank
Hans Peter Baumgartner	45	Mobile	2004	• Various management positions at Sony (1989–2004)
Frank Boller	46	Wireline & Internet	2003	• CEO of diAx
Bo Chamberlain	39	Network	2001	• Managing Director Technology and Network Operations at Talkline GmbH, Hamburg • Various positions within TDC incl. Manager at Switching Technology; Project Leader Central and Eastern Europe
Fulvio Federi	55	Human Resources	2004	• Various management positions in customer services/sales, HR Development
Klaus Pedersen	36	Finance	2000	• Vice President Group Accounting & Tax, TDC
Beat Moser	34	Legal & Regulatory	2000	• Attorney-at-law
Malcolm Myers	38	Strategy & Business Development	1999	• Product Manager at sunrise (1997–1999) • Senior Associate at Booz Allen & Hamilton • Marketing Manager Belgacom Mobile
Marcel Walser	44	IT	2000	• CIO Novartis Nutrition • Various senior IT positions at UBS bank
Monika Walser	38	Corporate Communications	2000	• Head of Marketing Communications at Computer 2000, a computer distributor (1998–2000) • Managing Director of a company producing traditional clothing for children (1994–1998)
Thierry Zanada	38	Wholesale	2000	• Manager at Interconnect

Source: Company information.

to be Switzerland's No. 1 or No. 2 communications provider for residential, business and wholesale customers in the product areas we are in." In practical terms, this was much easier. For mobile phones, the slogan was:

> We will beat Orange [main competitor] in mobiles.

By June 2001, the product offerings and price plans were harmonized, sunrise's new slogan was launched the same day—"Communication is life." In some cases, the slogan was used with the addition "sunrise: always a smile."

In order for the employees to get a better understanding of the strategy, Frimer and his team also set up special events. During 2001, the goal was to get a better utilization of its mobile network (after all, it was a high fixed-cost business). Frimer explained that this could be achieved with better marketing, but to some extent marketing is just "hot air." So, since the achievement of any strategic goal was generally

Exhibit 14   **Product Positioning**

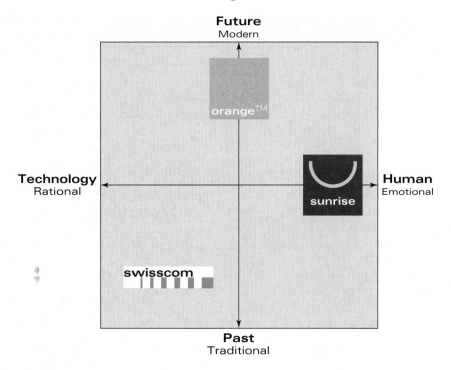

Exhibit 15   **Strategy Overview**

Excellent marketing & sales

- focus on being the most innovative in the market
- make sunrise the most appealing choice for each of our target customer segments

Cost consciousness

- take out cost by being smarter and more creative about how we do our work
- think "must have" rather than "nice to have" when spending the company's money

Customer loyalty

- put ourselves in our customers' shoes
- make sunrise number 1 in satisfaction

Source: Company information.

Exhibit 16   **sunrise's Year 2001 in Review (number of customers)**

	Q1 2001	Q2 2001	Q3 2001	Q4 2001
Postpaid mobile (in 000s)	376	391	407	421
Prepaid mobile (in 000s)	292	354	426	523
Fixed line (in 000s)	714	740	751	786
Internet (in 000s)	445	447	471	499

Source: sunrise Presentation to Investors, 2003, p. 10.

celebrated in style, they decided to install a hot-air balloon in the staircase of sunrise's HQ. Depending on the level of new acquisitions for mobile phone customers per week, they would lower or raise the balloon (refer to Exhibit 8 for the actual developments). sunrise was able to stop the high churn for mobiles, extend the contract length to a minimum of 12 months and grow by 62 percent in a market that was only growing at 14 percent (the slowest since 1993). Thanks to a boom in mobile phones, sunrise was adding customers fast. It was especially successful in pushing "prepaid" customers, i.e., mobile phones without a contract. These phones relied on "prepaid" cards, which were available in many different stores, and were particularly popular among teenagers. (refer to Exhibit 16).

By the end of 2001, sunrise had beaten Orange in numbers of subscribers—a cause for great celebration at the sunrise HQ! This was a celebration people would not forget in a long time and at a cost in excess of SFr 1 million for one day. But top management thought that this money was well invested. They gave short presentations on sunrise's strategy, the plan forward and organized games for employees to interact with each other.

Products, Products, Products

Over the years, sunrise remained innovative by adding new products or changing the rules of the game. For mobile phones, sunrise decided to sell packages of minutes (e.g., 75 minutes per month) at a fixed price, rather than mobile phone minutes. Other popular innovations included myzone, which was a mobile phone that would link to the local network at home. This implied that people could use their mobile phone (and pay local charges) while calling from their home zone. In 2002 sunrise was also the first in Switzerland to launch a multimedia service for mobile phones. This enabled customers to send pictures via their mobile phones.

For fixed-line customers, sunrise offered 60 minutes free of charge, but customers then had to sign up for 12 months. Also, sunrise was the first company to offer a flat rate for domestic telephone calls. This service was expected to start in mid-2004.

Streamlining Operations

Over the years, there was tremendous pressure to reduce cost. As sunrise was a smaller operator in comparison to some of the large players such as France Telecom (the owner of Orange), it could not reap similar economies of scale. Instead, it decided to start a new international alliance with smaller operators from Spain, Austria, Hungary, Norway and Italy. The goal was to reduce sourcing prices, with a combined purchasing volume of close to 40 million units.

While sunrise was reducing costs on the one hand, at the same time it was opening its own stores across Switzerland. The so-called sunrise centers were dedicated exclusively to selling sunrise products—a total of 20 shops were opened in 2003 with another 18 scheduled for 2004.

MANAGING INSIDE SUNRISE

Sunrise kept its promise of no further lay-offs. Since employees were actively engaged in the 2001 restructuring processes, they started to identify closely with sunrise. A member of the call center for business customers explained:

> Our internal processes and systems are designed to have maximum efficiency. For example, all customer contacts, such as e-mails, calls, voice messages and even letters are all available electronically, that makes it possible to deliver good value to customers.

As employees had a lot of contact with end customers, they needed not only technical skills, but also social competencies. For this, sunrise offered a considerable number of courses, including IT, sales, product infos, personality development, leadership and social competence, and project management. Overall, the company offered over 200 courses in 2002.

In fact, employees were even encouraged to air their opinions and regularly received an online employee survey aimed at measuring feelings among employees. Frimer explained:

> The frustration was huge initially, but now it has improved a lot. I use this survey widely and when it is very negative, you normally have a management problem.

"Communication Is Life" for Employees: Keeping in Touch with the Top

Sunrise's 2,500 employees had access to various methods of communication with top management. The most frequent, the "CEO News" e-mail, was sent out every four to five weeks. It was written by Frimer himself and outlined recent developments and major achievements by employees.

Employees were also able to have personal encounters with Frimer. Every six weeks his team organized a "power breakfast." Anyone could apply to attend these breakfast meetings which all followed the same format. The invited employees represented a wide pool of experiences and were first asked to introduce themselves before Frimer asked his question, "If you were CEO of sunrise for a week—what would you do?" This served as a platform for making improvements and it was not uncommon for employees to receive a personal letter from Frimer after highlighting important issues.

Since the number of places for the power breakfasts was limited, the top management team would actually visit the various locations, too. All the employees were invited to the "EMT [executive management team] on tour" event, which took place twice a year at each location. Normally, anywhere between 20 and 300 employees at each location attended the EMT on tour. There, the CEO would explain sunrise's overall strategy before two other board members clarified recent developments in their field. The board members accompanying Frimer rotated so that employees could get to know different board members. These meetings were set up in such a way that employees had enough time to ask questions. One board member commented: "A lot of good ideas come from down in the organization."

MANAGEMENT AT THE TOP: "I TRY TO DELEGATE"

Frimer was clear that "if you delegate, you have to make sure you control." Although sunrise transformed itself from a start-up to a "real" company, the delegation was key. In his approach, Frimer gave a lot of autonomy and trust, but he made it clear that his employees understood the rules: not to betray him. A member of the sunrise management board explained:

> This approach gives employees a real job: you feel you have a real job, your experience/knowledge is welcomed and you are a valued team member. This approach could only work with a level of discipline. There were very clear guidelines of what was needed/expected from the managers for "getting things done."

For board members, setting goals was a real dialogue, not a command. But once they committed, it was their job to achieve the goals! And goals become very visible. Frimer explained his style:

> There are so many systems, structures, PowerPoint presentations, and people forget what the value drivers are. My approach is to ask questions and then we will develop the conclusions together, rather than me saying you should do this . . . But sometimes you still have to say, this is not good enough.

Employees around Frimer said that they could feel the trust he placed in them. Another board member remarked: "As long as you deliver, you will not hear from him. If you are not delivering, you are told by him. If you are not delivering, it is not that much fun."

DECISION MAKING AND INFO GATHERING ON THE MANAGEMENT BOARD

Weekly Management Board Meeting on Monday   This was the major decision-making body within sunrise. Initially, the board members managing product lines also had their own commercial meeting, but this was soon stopped since there was too much overlap between the two. The meetings on Monday were seen as "holy" and board members were expected to be present. If they were unable to attend, there was a clear understanding that they had to respect the decisions taken by their colleagues.

1-on-1   These bi-weekly meetings were forums for exchange between Frimer and individual members of the board. There was no pre-arranged agenda except that the meeting would last for up to one hour. Board members would decide the issues to be discussed. Typical issues included brainstorming, operational issues or "things you do not need to discuss in a big group," e.g., at the Monday board meetings. One board member commented: "I have to tell him what I need, how it is running and where I expect help from him." If neither the board member nor the CEO had anything to discuss, then the meeting could be canceled.

Information Gathering in the Company

Business Unit Strategy Review Meetings ("Drill Down Meetings")   This was the informal meeting between Frimer and key managers (not only board members) of the various divisions. Although informal, the impact should not be underestimated as it was here that strategy discussions took place. Depending on the size of the division, these meetings would take place between once—for small units—and up to three times per year for large units. The meetings would start at 12 o'clock and be open ended. In the course of the afternoon, the responsible board members and their top managers would explain "what they were doing, what challenges and issues they were facing."

Project Board   When the new management team arrived in Switzerland they soon discovered that there was a lot of cash outflow leading to real "cash burn." Equipment was being purchased without any prior internal discussion. Now, every purchase valued at more than SFr 400,000 had to be discussed at this forum. Employees had to present their planned purchases together with a net present value (NPV) analysis. Although this board initially met with a lot of resistance, it soon became a forum for "selling ideas." The project board was jointly headed by the CEO and the following board members:

- Strategy & business development: Malcolm Myers
- Information technology (IT): Marcel Walser
- CFO: Klaus Pedersen
- COO Mobile: Geert Rieder (later replaced by Hans Peter Baumgartner)
- COO Wireline and Internet: Martin Staub (later replaced by Frank Boller)
- COO Wholesale: Thierry Zanada

Relations between CEO and Top Management

The IT system was quite detailed including a lot of data regarding performance measurement. Senior managers could have access to the performance data of sunrise from their PC at all times. This transparency also helped to highlight performance issues. In serious cases of non-performance, Frimer would, as a last resort, send in a task force. Once a problem was identified, board members were expected to fix it. If this did not happen, they would receive a warning. If the problem was not solved within the next three to four months, then Frimer would send in a task force. This team would then directly report to the CEO until the problem was fixed.

FRIMER'S DELEGATION: COMBINING THE OPPOSITES

Sunrise employees remembered well one of the first meetings with Frimer when he described the merger process. He explained that there were only two ways of pulling off a Band-Aid—slowly or fast. Frimer was very clear: "In any case it hurts, so let's pull it off fast."

For employees it soon became clear what it meant working for sunrise. Frimer's first bill to his private home read: "Frau Kim Frimer" [Mrs. Kim Frimer]. It was soon understood that there should be "no mistakes when dealing with customers." However, in other parts of the business, the management team was not averse to risk. If employees could provide the board with some hard data proving the potential of their initiatives (e.g., product launches), such as market research or surveys, then the board was willing to take the risk.

People within sunrise were constantly being challenged to take the customers' point of view, however, they were also strongly reminded of the profitability expectations from "up north"—a widely used term for referring to TDC's HQ. The reference to "up north" was a good indication that the EBITDA or net present values were too low.

Overall, employees enjoyed the trust and freedom they received from the board of management. A staff member working closely with Frimer explained his approach:

> You agree with him on what has to be done and then he leaves you all the freedom in the world. How you get it done is your responsibility.

However, a board member added:

> No one should misunderstand this freedom. Frimer did not like it if you did not think things through.

Sunrise was proud of its flexible and tolerant work environment. At the same time, it was clear to the managers that they "had to deliver" on whatever they agreed upon. While Frimer was perceived as a fun guy, everyone around him "definitely knew who the boss was." Going to his office with bad results was no fun.

While managers at various levels enjoyed the freedom, the possible threat of task forces put pressure on them to perform. After it became clear in various drill down meetings that there were operational problems in one division, this particular board member was asked to resign. In general, members of the management board were concerned not only about being overworked, but also about the general pressure to perform. Frimer commented: "Keep the pressure up and never be satisfied with the current situation!"

Also, Frimer was not afraid of taking positions. As internal communication became difficult in some instances when employees would communicate in German, although not all 56 Danes were able to read German, it was time for a message from the CEO: Starting immediately, the new official language was English, and only English.

Within sunrise, the structure remained mostly unchanged with only a few adjustments including the consumer and business marketing boards. The internal meeting structure did not change over time. However, a board member explained: "Frimer likes to disturb the balance."

While Frimer agreed with the statement about disturbing the balance, he also wondered how to maintain the balance. He was generally against organizational changes, which he believed should only be carried out if they were definitely adding value. Referring to the band aid example, it was clear that in the 2001 crisis situation, the band aid had to be removed quickly. Would Frimer take the same approach in 2003?

While sunrise reported a successful year for 2003, the pressure was going to continue. Dyremose explained:

> In Europe, our operations continue to thrive and contribute increasingly to our positive financial performance. TDC Switzerland has achieved a solid position as the second-largest telecom provider in the Swiss market. Its continued progress is illustrated by an increasing EBITDA margin and a positive net income development. We are very pleased to have been able to exploit the good growth opportunities outside Denmark.

But for Frimer, the question was how to maintain momentum. He believed in improving daily and for employees, this meant constantly moving forward.

Appendix: The Telecom Industry

HISTORIC OVERVIEW

In 1876 Graham Bell, a Scotsman in Boston, Massachusetts, succeeded in making the first "telephone" operational and started the Bell Telephone Company the following year. Bell's invention allowed sounds to be transmitted electrically via the telephone. "Tele"—the Greek word for afar—and "phone"—meaning voice or sound—soon started to replace the Morse code. For the first time, it was possible to send multiple messages over the same wireline, thereby reducing cost per call. By 1915, American telephone companies offered transcontinental service and by 1927, it was possible to make intercontinental calls to London.

Over the years, various innovations around the telephone became part of everybody's life. Direct dialing (without a switchboard operator) was followed by Touchtone in the 1960s. The 1980s saw the arrival of caller ID, the move from analogue to digital and the arrival of fiber optics. Demand from private households and corporations continued to increase, with corporations investing heavily in data networks linking various locations around the world. However, two massive shifts in the telephone industry changed the fundamentals of the industry starting in the early to mid-1990s:

1. *Privatization and deregulation*: Governments around the globe sold off their telephone companies. At the same time, they deregulated markets thereby prompting many companies and entrepreneurs to enter this "gold rush." Massive price reductions followed, especially on international calls, which often subsidized local calls. Within only a few years, the former state monopolies had to adapt to customer-driven markets.

2. *Arrival of mobile telephony*: Starting in the early 1990s, it was the arrival of mobile phone technology that truly revolutionized the industry. Annual sales of mobile handsets had reached 100 million units by 1997, before quadrupling to 400 million units in the following three years. Operators were required to invest heavily in infrastructure for mobile communications, but the price levels remained relatively high.

These shifts had far-reaching consequences: For decades this industry was seen as a commodity, utility type business with stable earnings and revenues. However, suddenly it was seen as a growth industry. Mobile telephony gave the industry a high-tech image, mobile penetration was skyrocketing and during the late 1990s, the growth phantasm of mobile operators could only be topped by Internet companies. This actual growth was for real—household expenditures on telecom have grown by more than 50 percent and revenues doubled.

However, this required massive investments in new infrastructure for mobile phones and other applications. A massive overestimation of the future demand led to overspending in capital-intensive infrastructure.

THE BUSINESS MODEL

Customers were mostly segmented across three groups: consumer, business accounts and multinational/global accounts. While consumer segments tended to be price sensitive, the corporate accounts were more interested in quality of the network, reliability, competence, innovation, partnership, one-stop-shopping and trustworthiness.

In terms of product offering, it remained difficult for telephone operators to differentiate the product offering due to "commoditization." The migration from fixed lines to mobile telephony was for real in developed countries, with revenues dropping due to the migration and decreasing price levels. Given these pressures, operators invested heavily in branding (e.g, Vodafone or T-Mobile), finer segmentation and scale.

EUROPEAN TELECOMS: FROM BOOM TO BUST

For many companies, the M& A boom was seen as a way to "create scale" and deregulation greatly facilitated such moves. In addition, European telecom companies were caught paying fictitious sums for acquiring future operating licenses for mobiles frequencies (UMTS) in 2000. They were estimated to have paid €109 billion for the next generation of mobile phone licenses.[11] Deutsche Telekom, invested €8.2 billion for acquiring such a UMTS license in its German home market—the equivalent of almost seven annual net incomes. In many cases, telecom operators overstretched their balance sheets and stock prices collapsed accordingly. Between March 2000 and September 2002, the share prices of former monopolies such as France Telecom, Deutsche Telekom and British Telecom collapsed from €156 to €6, from €84 to €8.7 and from €13.7 to €2.6, respectively. Given these adverse conditions, the strategies for telephone operators post-2001 were clear—tighten belts by reducing debt and cost, clean balance sheets (including writing off bad

investments) and removing management of non-performing units and becoming more customer-oriented. Many companies maintained heavy debt levels even in 2003 (refer to Exhibit 17 for a financial overview of European telecom operators).

After the bubble in the telecom industry, many industry executives identified mobile telephony, broadband Internet connections (ADSL) and business customers as growth markets. But the profitability dynamics in the various segments was very different:

- For mobile phones it was critical to keep a good balance of network coverage and utilization without spending too much on customer acquisition. In the European market, customers were used to receiving highly subsidized mobile phones in return for 12-month contracts. In some European markets, the subsidies would reach €250 per mobile phone.

- The profitability of high-speed Internet connections was based on the transfer pricing for the so-called "last mile." The term referred to the actual access to customers, which was in many countries still controlled by the incumbent.

Exhibit 17   **Key Financial Indicators for Former State Monopolies**

Company	Country	2003 Revenue (€ billion)	2003 Total Liabilities (€ billion)	Market Capitalization in Mid-2004 (€ billion)	Free Float (percentage of shares listed on the market)
Belgacom	Belgium	€ 5.377	€ 2.368	€ 8.6	€ 42.3%
BT Group	UK	27.696	35.112	24.0	100.0
Deutsche Telekom	Germany	55.838	82.268	59.5	57.2
France Telecom	France	46.121	73.914	50.2	45.5
KPN	Netherlands	11.870	14.917	14.7	80.7
Portugal Telecom	Portugal	5.217	8.564	11.0	90.3
TDC	Denmark	6.750	8.122	5.2	83.4
Telecom Italia	Italy	30.850	59.649	36.9	83.0
Telefonica	Spain	25.704	31.576	58.7	89.8

Note: BT publishes its numbers for year end March 31.

Source: Rossana Bird and Mike Jeremy, "TDC—To Be or Not to Be," ING Financial Markets Report, June 17, 2004: 6; Thomson Analytics.

- Business customers represented large markets, but "lack of reputation/credibility/experience of newcomers" was often the main reason for keeping the business with the incumbents.

- An executive summed up the key success factors in the industry: "What do customers want, how easily can they be contacted and what are they willing to pay for?"

Endnotes

1 "Thinking at the Speed of Light," sunrise Publication 2003: 37.

2 In telecommunications the earnings before interest, taxes, depreciation and amortization (EBITDA) is one of the key financial drivers. Mobile telephony generally records the highest EBITDA contributions. In 2002 Swisscom reported EBITDA margins of 48.1 percent for mobile and 29.9 percent for fixed line [*Neue Zürcher Zeitung* (NZZ), November 21, 2003].

3 Exchange rate: SFr 1 = US$0.83 on November 2, 2004.

4 In 2003 TDC eventually took over the minority shareowners of sunrise.

5 TDC bought back the SBC shares in 2004, thereby gaining full control.

6 *Neue ZürcherZeitung (NZZ)*, March 2, 2004.

7 Price declines were not a concern as long as usage was increasing faster.

8 EBITDA = earings before interest, taxes, depreciation and amortization (see also Footnote 2).

9 Companies in Switzerland operated on a two-tier board system: the management board took care of the operational issues; the supervisory board supervised the management board. In this case, we focus on the management board.

10 *Neue Zürcher Zeitung (NZZ)*, December 16, 2000.

11 See "Beyond the Bubble," supplement to *The Economist*, October 11, 2003: 109.

Merck and the Recall of Vioxx

Arthur A. Thompson
The University of Alabama

On September 30, 2004, officials at Merck & Company Inc., the sixth-largest pharmaceutical firm in the United States and a respected blue-chip company, announced that Merck was withdrawing its pain reliever Vioxx from the market because a new study indicated that the drug doubled the risks of heart attacks and strokes in patients taking it longer than 18 months. Merck's stock immediately plunged 27 percent and continued to fall further in upcoming weeks, in response to the $2.5 billion annual revenue loss from Merck's second best-selling drug and a rapidly mounting potential for costly lawsuits. An estimated 20 million Americans and another 60 million people in 80 foreign countries had taken Vioxx, primarily for relief of arthritis and acute pain, since it had been introduced in May 1999. Merck estimated that 105 million U.S. prescriptions were written for Vioxx from May 1999 through August 2004. An estimated 2 million people in the United States were taking Vioxx at the time of the recall.

As early as 2000, there had been warning signs of problems with Vioxx. Prior to the recall, roughly 30 lawsuits alleging that Vioxx was unsafe and had caused patients to suffer heart attacks and strokes, some resulting in death, had been filed in state and federal courts. In the weeks following the recall, the number of lawsuits multiplied quickly, reaching close to 700 by some counts. Some of these were class-action suits filed by high-profile trial lawyers on behalf of all potential claimants. Wall Street analysts estimated that Merck's legal costs associated with the Vioxx claims could range as high as $18 billion over the next decade.

As of 2004, the largest drug-product liability case on record involved Wyeth's recall of weight-loss remedies Redux and Pondimin in 1997, which contained a compound known as fen-phen and were estimated to cause heart-valve damage in as many as 30 percent of the people who took the pills. Some 6 million Americans had taken Redux or Pondimin; Wyeth's payouts to date had exceeded $13 billion of the $16.6 billion in reserves that the company had set aside to cover settlement costs.

Five weeks after the Vioxx recall, Standard & Poor's (S&P), which had placed a triple-A rating on Merck's debt since 1975, announced that it had put Merck's ratings on its watch list. Merck was one of only seven companies outside the financial services industry that had a triple-A S&P debt rating. The week following S&P's credit watch announcement, Moody's Investors Service lowered the rating of Merck's long-term debt two notches, to Aa2 from Aaa (its highest rating), and said it was keeping Merck's rating under review for a possible further downgrade. Moody's cited the loss in revenues and Merck's Vioxx litigation exposure as reasons for the downgrade. The Moody's downgrade and the threat of an S&P downgrade had little immediate impact on Merck—the company had $7 billion in cash and short-term investments and $10 billion in current assets to apply against its current liabilities of $2.2 billion and long-term debt of only $4.4 billion at the time of the recall, putting it in a position of strong liquidity. Nonetheless, the actions of the two credit rating agencies signaled concerns about the extent to which legal settlements would sap the company's financial resources down the road.

Moreover, the company's reputation as the gold standard of the pharmaceutical industry and one of the bluest of the blue-chip companies took a huge hit as the circumstances surrounding the recall came to light over the next several months. Internal e-mails, training aids sent to Merck salespeople, and pressures that Merck put on outside medical experts suggested that Merck personnel knew of or at least suspected Vioxx's dangers well before the recall. A front-page *Wall Street Journal* story on November 1, 2004, was headlined "E-Mails Suggest Merck Knew Vioxx's Dangers at Early Stage."

MERCK'S SITUATION IN 2004

In 2004, Merck & Company Inc., was a global research-driven company with annual sales of $22.5 billion; profits of $6.8 billion; 59,000 employees; 12 major drug research centers in the United States, Canada, Europe, and Japan; 32 manufacturing facilities; and a broad range of human and animal health care products marketed in 150 countries. Exhibit 1 shows the company's mission and core values.

MERCK'S STRATEGY

For the past 10 years or so, Merck's strategy had been to concentrate its considerable scientific and research expertise on developing blockbuster new drugs. The research-grounded strategy had three core elements:

- Develop a core competence in drug research by supporting the efforts of the best and brightest scientists and medical researchers Merck could assemble.
- Do very thorough clinical studies of promising drugs discovered in Merck's research labs to determine their effectiveness on patients and to explore the nature and extent of side effects.
- Seek to gain speedy regulatory approval of newly discovered medicines by using the results of the previously done research and clinical studies

Exhibit 1 **Merck's Mission and Core Values, 2004**

Our Mission

The mission of **Merck** is to provide society with superior products and services by developing innovations and solutions that improve the quality of life and satisfy customer needs, and to provide employees with meaningful work and advancement opportunities, and investors with a superior rate of return.

Our Values

1. **Our business is preserving and improving human life.** All of our actions must be measured by our success in achieving this goal. We value, above all, our ability to serve everyone who can benefit from the appropriate use of our products and services, thereby providing lasting consumer satisfaction.

2. **We are committed to the highest standards of ethics and integrity.** We are responsible to our customers, to Merck employees and their families, to the environments we inhabit, and to the societies we serve worldwide. In discharging our responsibilities, we do not take professional or ethical shortcuts. Our interactions with all segments of society must reflect the high standards we profess.

3. **We are dedicated to the highest level of scientific excellence and commit our research to improving human and animal health and the quality of life.** We strive to identify the most critical needs of consumers and customers, and we devote our resources to meeting those needs.

4. **We expect profits, but only from work that satisfies customer needs and benefits humanity.** Our ability to meet our responsibilities depends on maintaining a financial position that invites investment in leading-edge research and that makes possible effective delivery of research results.

5. **We recognize that the ability to excel—to most competitively meet society's and customers' needs—depends on the integrity, knowledge, imagination, skill, diversity and teamwork of our employees, and we value these qualities most highly.** To this end, we strive to create an environment of mutual respect, encouragement and teamwork—an environment that rewards commitment and performance and is responsive to the needs of our employees and their families.

Source: www.merck.com (accessed November 29, 2004).

to thoroughly document the benefits and safety of the drugs submitted for approval. Rapid approval to market new drugs could produce a significant competitive edge by not only allowing Merck to get its drug discoveries into the marketplace ahead of rivals but also giving it more time to sell the drug before patent expirations.

Merck's resource strengths in executing this strategy over the years had been a major factor in the company's success and in developing and fortifying what had come to be a storied reputation for first-rate scientific research and for having the best research personnel and research capabilities in the business. During the past two decades, Merck personnel had published more scientific papers than personnel at any other drug company, and Merck had patented more compounds than any of its competitors.[1] And the company's track record in getting new drugs approved expeditiously was excellent in comparison to other pharmaceutical manufacturers.

The central figure in executing Merck's research-based drug discovery strategy was Edward M. Scolnick, a graduate of Harvard Medical School who had published roughly 200 scientific papers and risen through the ranks at Merck to become its chief of research. Scolnick was reputed to have a superior intellect, and his persistent drive for research excellence permeated Merck's research activities. According to a former Merck cancer researcher, "You never went before him unprepared. He would begin probing very directly and very quickly. He would often identify some controlled experiment

that should have been done and wasn't."[2] For at least a decade before he retired in 2003, Scolnick was considered the de facto number two person at Merck (after CEO Raymond V. Gilmartin).[3] Scolnick was appointed to Merck's board of directors in 1997; he was the only inside executive on Merck's board besides the CEO. Merck's newest research lab, dedicated in October 2004—a multimillion-dollar building in Boston not far from Harvard Medical School—was named for Scolnick.

Under Scolnick's drug research leadership, Merck had racked up dazzling successes. Zocor, a cholesterol-reducing drug introduced in the early 1990s, soon became the market-leading prescription for lowering cholesterol and Merck's best-selling drug. Zocor had annual sales in 2003 of $5 billion. During the 1995–2001 period, Merck won approval from the U.S. Federal Drug Administration (FDA) for 15 new drugs, many of which became big market successes—Singulair (asthma), Fosamax (osteoporosis), Cozarr and Hyzarr (hypertension), Procepia (baldness), Vioxx (arthritis and pain relief), and Crixivan (HIV). These successful new drug introductions helped drive Merck's stock price to an all-time high of $95 per share in the fall of 2000. A breakdown of Merck's drug sales by category is shown in Exhibit 2.

But just as important to Merck's strategic success as a research-based drug-discovery organization was Scolnick's oversight of the process of gaining regulatory approval to introduce new drugs and the resulting competitive edge that accrued to Merck.

Exhibit 2   **Merck's Sales by Drug Category, 2001–2003 (in millions)**

Drug Category	2003	2002	2001
Atherosclerosis	$ 5,077.9	$ 5,552.1	$ 5,433.3
Hypertension/heart failure	3,421.6	3,477.8	3,584.3
Anti-inflammatory/analgesics (includes Vioxx)	2,677.3	2,587.2	2,391.1
Osteoporosis	2,676.6	2,243.1	1,629.7
Respiratory	2,009.4	1,489.8	1,260.3
Vaccines/biologicals	1,056.1	1,028.3	1,022.5
Antibacterial/antifungal	1,028.5	821.0	750.4
Ophthalmologicals	675.1	621.5	644.5
Urology	605.5	547.3	545.4
Human immunodeficiency virus (HIV)	290.6	294.3	380.8
Other	2,967.3	2,783.4	3,556.7
Total	$22,485.9	$21,445.8	$21,199.0

Source: Merck, 2003 10-K report.

The research-and-approval process for new drugs was known for being risky and tedious, both because of the need to conduct lengthy and convincing studies of drug effectiveness and safety (a high proportion of chemical compounds under investigation never survived this step) and because regulatory approval was rife with bureaucracy and sometimes contentious review procedures that could take several years. Scolnick's approach to dealing with the regulatory approval process was for Merck to submit fastidious supporting documentation for the new drugs it asked the FDA to approve, an approach that had worked well for Merck.

During the 1995–2001 period, Merck's vaunted scientific reputation, high-caliber clinical studies, and solid supporting documentation allowed the company to gain approval for all 13 new drugs it submitted to the FDA, with an average review time of 11 months. Vioxx won approval following a six-month review.[4] At Pfizer, the world's largest pharmaceutical firm in 2004, the new drug submissions during the same period had an average review time of two years. Analysts at Merrill Lynch estimated that Merck's drug research documentation capabilities and short approval times allowed the company to achieve extra sales of $3.3 billion during 1995–2001.[5]

MERCK'S RECORD OF CORPORATE SOCIAL RESPONSIBILITY AND GOOD CITIZENSHIP

Merck was strongly committed to being a solid corporate citizen and conducting its business in an ethical manner. This commitment had long been guided by the vision of the company's modern-day founder, George W. Merck, who said in 1950:

> We try never to forget that medicine is for the people. It is not for the profits. The profits follow, and if we have remembered that, they have never failed to appear.
>
> We cannot step aside and say that we have achieved our goal by inventing a new drug or a new way by which to treat presently incurable diseases, a new way to help those who suffer from malnutrition, or the creation of ideal balanced diets on a worldwide scale. We cannot rest till the way has been found, with our help, to bring our finest achievement to everyone.[6]

The two chief components of Merck's social responsibility strategy were charitable contributions and its actions to further the cause of public health by making its drugs more widely available. In 2003, Merck's philanthropic contributions totaled $843 million, consisting of cash contributions ($54 million), its patient assistance program ($393 million), and product donations ($396 million). Exhibit 3 shows Merck's recent record of charitable contributions.

Merck's efforts to live up to its commitment to make its drugs available to everyone are demonstrated in the following four examples of actions that the company had recently taken:[7]

1. Merck announced in February 2004 that the company would provide its medicines free for low-income Medicare beneficiaries who exhaust their $600 transitional assistance allowance in Medicare-endorsed drug discount cards. This action was consistent with Merck's long-standing Patient Assistance Program, which provided free medicine to patients who lacked drug coverage and could not afford Merck's drugs.

2. Since 1987, Merck had donated more than 300 million doses of its Mectizan drug to treat people in developing and third world countries who were suffering from onchocerciasis, a ravaging disease more commonly known as river blindness. Mectizan was a highly effective medicine that not only controlled and prevented river blindness but also helped limit the agonizing and disfiguring skin infections caused by the disease. The Mectizan Donation Program, a public/private partnership regarded as one of the world's most successful global health care collaborations, and funded in part by Merck, had long worked to improve the lives and prevent blindness for millions of people in Africa, Latin America, and Yemen. In 2004, doses of Mectizan reached more than 40 million people in 34 countries.

3. In poor African countries that had been hard hit by the AIDS epidemic, Merck had arranged to provide two of its HIV-fighting drugs, Stocrin and Crixivan, at prices at which it made no profit. Merck had also granted a royalty-free license to a South African pharmaceutical company to manufacture and sell a generic version of its HIV/AIDS drug Efavirenz.

4. In 2003, Merck launched the Merck Vaccine Network–Africa, an initiative designed to

Exhibit 3   **Merck's Corporate Philanthropy Contributions, 1998–2003**

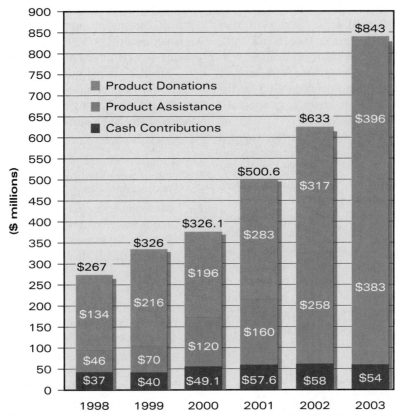

Total Merck Contributions/Donations

Legend:
- Product Donations
- Product Assistance
- Cash Contributions

Y-axis: ($ millions), scale 0 to 900

Year	Cash Contributions	Product Assistance	Product Donations	Total
1998	$37	$46	$134	$267
1999	$40	$70	$216	$326
2000	$49.1	$120	$196	$326.1
2001	$57.6	$160	$283	$500.6
2002	$58	$258	$317	$633
2003	$54	$383	$396	$843

*Total Merck cash contributions are the sum of contributions from The Merck Company Foundation, Merck & Co., Inc., and Merck Genome Research Institute.

Source: www.merck.com, accessed November 30, 2004.

contribute to improving the immunization infrastructure in Africa. Merck's initiative involved funding the establishment of a network of vaccination training centers at academic institutions in Kenya and Mali to provide a sustainable source of skilled health care workers in those countries and across the region. Africa had the highest per capita incidence of vaccine-preventable diseases in the world, with only half of all children in sub-Saharan Africa getting basic lifesaving vaccinations during their first year of life.

In 1999 Merck developed a lengthy code of conduct entitled "Our Values and Standards: The Basis of Our Success" and distributed it to Merck employees. The company's Web site postings, in elaborating on the company's core values (see Exhibit 1) and the conduct expected of Merck employees, said:

- Every Merck employee is responsible for adhering to business practices that are in accordance with the letter and spirit of the applicable laws and with ethical principles that reflect the highest standards of corporate and individual behavior.

- Improper behavior cannot be rationalized as being in the company's interest. No act of impropriety advances the interest of the Company.

In May 2004, *Business Ethics* magazine named Merck one of its "100 Best Corporate Citizens" for the fifth consecutive year. Merck, ranked 48, was the only pharmaceutical company to gain a spot on the list in each of the five years that *Business Ethics* had published it and was also one of only two pharmaceutical companies to make the list.

MERCK'S TROUBLES IN 2004 PRIOR TO THE VIOXX RECALL

Since 2001, Merck had been struggling to maintain its earlier momentum of growing sales via a stream of new product introductions. None of its recently introduced drugs had generated annual sales of $1 billion or more. During the 1999–2001 period, Merck had lost its patent protection on five of its best-selling drugs—Vasotec (hypertension), Pepcid (ulcers), Mevacor (cholesterol), Prilosec (ulcers), and Prinivil (hypertension). The company's market-leading treatment for high cholesterol, Zocor, which generated annual sales revenues of about $5 billion, was coming off patent in 2006 and, like most other drugs without patent protection, was expected to experience sharp sales erosion when lower-priced generic imitations came onto the market. In 2003, Merck had to cancel work on four major new drugs, which were in big, costly Phase III trials. All four were thought to have real promise and had been touted by management as having major revenue potential. One of the four drugs, for depression, failed a pivotal clinical trial, and a second, for diabetes, was found in animal studies to pose a risk of cancer.

As a consequence, Merck's sales had flattened (Exhibit 2) and its net profits had eroded from the all-time peak of $7.3 billion and earnings per share (EPS) of $3.14 in 2001 to $6.8 billion and an EPS of $3.03 in 2003. Investors were fully aware of Merck's struggling condition—the company's stock price, after having risen 475 percent from 1994 to its all-time high of $95 per share in the fall of 2000, had trended downward and was trading at around $45 per share in the weeks prior to the Vioxx recall. Shareholders were restless, having suffered a loss in market capitalization of over $130 billion during the past four years. While Merck still had a number of new products in the pipeline that it expected to be able to release in upcoming years—treatments for diabetes, shingles, and assorted viruses—most analysts did not believe

the new drugs had the sales potential to overcome the anticipated falloff of Zocor's sales in 2006–2007.

However, Merck was not alone in its struggle to discover and introduce new blockbuster drugs; virtually the whole pharmaceutical industry worldwide was finding the discovery of new drugs with big sales potential tough sledding. New drugs in the pipeline at a number of major pharmaceutical companies were disturbingly low from the standpoint of boosting future revenue growth and profitability—a condition that had already prompted several large mergers and acquisitions (to try to gain better scale economies in research), as well as strategy changes. New strategy elements already in place at Merck involved cost reduction, partnering with small innovative companies on new drug discovery, and licensing promising compounds.

EVENTS AT MERCK LEADING UP TO THE INTRODUCTION OF VIOXX

Vioxx was the last of Merck's multibillion-dollar drugs under Scolnick's leadership. Discovered in laboratory experiments by Merck researchers in 1994, the drug was one of a new class of painkillers, called Cox-2 inhibitors, that reduced pain and inflammation without such side effects as ulcers and gastrointestinal bleeding. Some people had experienced such side effects while taking daily doses of aspirin, ibuprofen (the painkiller in Advil and Motrin), and naproxen (the painkiller in Aleve) for chronic pain relief. Pain relievers containing aspirin, ibuprofen, and naproxen were designated nonsteroidal anti-inflammatory drugs (NSAIDs). By some estimates, intestinal bleeding associated with long-term use of NSAIDs was responsible for the deaths of 10,000 Americans annually.

Internal e-mails at Merck indicated that the company was well aware that Vioxx had limited market potential unless it could gain acceptance in the mass market for painkillers and be preferred to cheap over-the-counter NSAIDs. A November 1996 memo by a Merck official indicated that company personnel were wrestling with this marketing dilemma.[8] There was discussion of conducting a trial to demonstrate that Vioxx was gentler on the stomach than over-the-counter painkillers. To show the difference, takers of

Vioxx could not take any aspirin, which some arthritis patients took because of its blood-thinning and cardio-protective benefits. But the necessity of excluding aspirin raised concerns at Merck. The author of the memo noted that "there is a substantial chance that significantly higher rates" of cardiovascular problems would occur in the group taking only Vioxx. A February 1997 e-mail by another Merck official said that unless patients in the Vioxx group also took aspirin "you will get more thrombotic events and kill the drug."[9] In response, a Merck vice president for clinical research indicated the company was in a "no-win situation" because giving study subjects both Vioxx and aspirin could result in gastrointestinal problems and not giving them aspirin raised "the possibility of increased CV [cardiovascular] events."[10]

It is not clear what came out of the discussion Merck officials had about the study in 1996–1997.[11] But in early 1999, around the time that Merck won FDA approval to market Vioxx, Merck began an 8,000-person clinical trial that compared people taking a high dose of Vioxx against those taking naproxen. The patients taking Vioxx were not allowed to take aspirin.

In 1998 medical researchers at the University of Pennsylvania reported findings that Cox-2 inhibitors *might* interfere with enzymes thought to play key roles in warding off cardiovascular disease; the findings were communicated to the companies developing Cox-2 inhibitors and were also published.[12] In Merck's first round of clinical trials, patients taking Vioxx had about the same rate of heart attacks and strokes as did patients who took NSAIDs or a sugar placebo. An unpublished 1998 Merck clinical trial called "Study 090," which involved 978 patients, showed that serious cardiovascular events, including heart attack and stroke, occurred about six times more often in patients taking Vioxx than in patients taking another arthritis drug or a placebo.[13] Merck said that study was too small and the results were not statistically significant enough to allow the company to draw any conclusions.

Merck's application to the FDA for Vioxx approval in November 1998 included data on approximately 5,400 osteoarthritis patients who participated in eight studies. In these studies, there were similar rates of thrombotic cardiovascular adverse events with Vioxx, placebos, and three NSAIDs (ibuprofen, diclofenac, and nabumetone). After a six-month review, Vioxx gained FDA approval on May 21, 1999, despite apparent reservations on the part of some reviewers about its possible blood vessel effects.

But the studies of Vioxx reportedly did not establish that it was a more effective painkiller than NSAIDs. The real selling proposition for Vioxx—and the main basis for its approval by the FDA—was simply a lower incidence of stomach bleeding and gastrointestinal problems, as compared to conventional pain relievers like aspirin, Tylenol, Aleve, Advil, and other over-the-counter remedies (which cost about five cents a pill versus several dollars a pill for Vioxx).[14] Thus, the chief basis for Vioxx's approval by the FDA rested mainly on its relevance for the estimated 15 percent of arthritis sufferers who could not take over-the-counter pain relievers on a sustained basis because of the resulting gastrointestinal side effects.[15]

MERCK'S DIRECT-TO-CONSUMER MARKETING CAMPAIGN FOR VIOXX

When Vioxx won FDA approval in 1999, Merck's marketing strategy included sales pitches to doctors about the drug's benefits (along with the usual free samples they could try out on patients) and an aggressive direct-to-consumer advertising campaign. The cover of Merck's 1999 annual report headlined that Vioxx was the company's "biggest, fastest, and best launch ever." In the five or so years that arthritis pain reliever Vioxx was on the market, Merck spent roughly $100 million annually for television, newspaper, and magazine ads touting Vioxx's benefits and appealing to pain suffers to ask their doctor about Vioxx.[16] Sales of Vioxx climbed steadily from 1999 to 2004, and the drug became a $2.5 billion annual revenue source for Merck. It was the second best-selling Cox-2 inhibitor when it was pulled from the market, trailing only Celebrex, which had $3 billion in annual sales. Pfizer had become the marketer of Celebrex when it acquired rival drugmaker Pharmacia in 2003.

Vioxx was one among many blockbuster drugs that had benefited from direct-to-consumer advertising opportunities that opened up in 1997 when, during the Clinton administration, the FDA loosened regulations on how pharmaceutical companies could advertise to a general audience. Since then, drugs that were originally meant to treat specific medical problems had become used in far broader populations—partly because doctors had been willing to prescribe them when requested by patients (who presumably were intrigued by the newly allowed ads for prescription drugs) and partly because the costs of such prescriptions were paid for by patients' health insurance programs. A study by Bruce Stuart at the University of Maryland showed that the biggest determinant of whether a patient took a prescription Cox-2 inhibitor or a far cheaper over-the-counter pain reliever like Aleve, Motrin, or Advil was whether the patient had health insurance that would cover much of the prescription costs.[17]

WARNING SIGNS OF TROUBLE PRIOR TO THE RECALL

In March 2000, Merck found surprising results from an 8,000-person clinical trial it had initiated in early 1999 to see if Vioxx posed fewer gastrointestinal risks than NSAIDs. The trial showed that arthritis patients taking Vioxx had more than two times as many serious cardiovascular events as those on naproxen, an NSAID sold under the Aleve brand, among other brand names (see Exhibit 4). A total of 45 serious cardiovascular thrombotic events occurred among the 4,047 patients taking Vioxx, whereas only 19 had occurred among the 4,029 patients taking naproxen. According to Merck, the higher number was largely due to a difference in the incidence of *nonfatal* heart attacks: 18 for Vioxx and 4 for naproxen. The number of *fatal* cardiovascular thrombotic events was similar in patients treated with Vioxx ($n = 7$) compared to naproxen ($n = 6$). Deeper analysis, however, showed that the heart-attack rate in the Vioxx group appeared to be four times as high as the naproxen group. Something akin to these results had been seemingly anticipated in the 1996–1997 memos and e-mails.

In a March 9, 2000, e-mail with the subject line "Vigor"—the name Merck gave to the Vioxx–naproxen clinical trial—Merck's chief of research, Ed Scolnick, wrote that the results showed that the cardiovascular events "are clearly there. It is a shame but it is a low incidence and it is mechanism based as we worried it was." He compared Vioxx to other drugs with known side effects, writing, "There is always a hazard."[18] Scolnick went on to say that he wanted other data available before the Vioxx–naproxen results were made public, so that it would be "clear to the world" that hazard was a characteristic of all Cox-2 inhibitors, not just Vioxx.[19]

Medical experts outside Merck who were familiar with the Vioxx–naproxen study hypothesized that the results raised valid concerns that Vioxx could indeed be causing cardiac problems. Merck took the position that the differential risks could be attributable to the added side benefits of taking naproxen rather than to problems with Vioxx. Merck personnel reportedly believed that known properties of naproxen were responsible for the differential. Nonetheless, Merck immediately put out a press release describing the Vioxx–naproxen results and informed the FDA.

But, for unknown reasons, it was not until February 8, 2001, that the FDA Arthritis Advisory Committee met to discuss concerns about the potential cardiovascular risks associated with Vioxx. On May 22, 2001, a little over three months after the FDA advisory committee meeting, Merck issued a press release entitled "Merck Reconfirms Favorable Cardiovascular Safety of Vioxx"; this effort to address doubts about Vioxx was complemented by numerous papers in peer-reviewed medical literature by Merck employees and their consultants.[20] The company sponsored continuing medical "education" symposiums at national meetings in an effort to temper concerns about the adverse cardiovascular effects of Vioxx.[21] The essence of Merck's message was that Vioxx had no cardiovascular toxicity but, rather,

Exhibit 4   **Summary-Results of Vioxx–Naproxen Study in 2000**

	People Taking Vioxx	People Taking Naproxen
Total number of people in clinical trial	4,047	4,029
Number of adverse cardiovascular events	101	46
Number of digestive system adverse events	48	97

Source: FDA's analysis of the clinical trial results, as reported in Anna Wilde Mathews and Barbara Martinez, "E-Mails Suggest Merck Knew Vioxx's Dangers at Early Stage," *The Wall Street Journal,* November 1, 2004, p. A10.

naproxen was cardio-protective. (The FDA, how-ever, has said there is no conclusive evidence that naproxen protects the heart.)[22] In response to Merck's pro-Vioxx campaign, the FDA sent an eight-page warning letter to the company in September 2001 saying that sales representatives "have engaged in false or misleading promotional activities," and that the company's promotional campaign "minimizes the potentially serious cardiovascular findings" about Vioxx and "discounts the fact [that] patients on Vioxx were observed to have a four to five-fold increase" in heart attacks, compared with patients on naproxen.[23]

But it was not until two years later, in April 2002, that the FDA instructed Merck to include certain precautions about cardiovascular risks in its package insert. At about the same time, the FDA also decided to go a step further and do its own follow-up study of Vioxx safety, opting to sponsor a study of the medical records of 1.4 million patients insured by Kaiser Permanente, the nation's largest nonprofit health maintenance organization (HMO), serving 8.2 million members in nine states and the District of Columbia.

In November 2000, the results of the Vioxx–naproxen study were published in the *New England Journal of Medicine;* the article was co-authored by Merck employees and by academics who had re-ceived consulting contracts or research grants from Merck. But the Vioxx–naproxen trial also spurred Merck to do further clinical studies on the possible links between Vioxx and heart trouble. Shortly af-ter learning of the Vioxx–Naproxen cardiovascular differential, Merck embarked on a long-term study called APPROVe to see whether Vioxx would lead to a reduction of colon polyps (which if shown to be the case would give doctors another reason to prescribe Vioxx). APPROVe, which involved 2,600 patients, was a true controlled trial that compared Vioxx with a placebo instead of another drug, thereby provid-ing a more definitive test of whether Vioxx increased blood vessel risk.

MERCK'S "DODGE BALL VIOXX" TRAINING DOCUMENT

To help its sales personnel deal with questions doctors were asking about Vioxx's safety, Merck developed a sales aid entitled "Dodge Ball Vioxx." The 16-page document, addressed to "all field personnel" was intended as an "obstacle handling guide"; each of the first 12 pages listed one "obstacle" or concern that doctors might have about Vioxx, such as "I am concerned about the cardiovascular effects of Vioxx" and "The competition has been in my office telling me the incidence of heart attacks is greater with Vioxx than Celebrex."[24] Suggested responses for each obstacle were provided. The final four pages each contained a single word in capital letters: DODGE.[25] A former Merck sales representative told *60 Minutes* that when a doctor expressed concerns about the cardiovascular effects of Vioxx, "We were supposed to tell the physician that Vioxx did not cause cardiovascular events, that instead, in the studies, naproxen has aspirin-like characteristics which made naproxen a heart-protecting type of drug where Vioxx did not have that heart-protecting side."[26]

MERCK'S OFFENSIVE TO COMBAT THE CONCERNS OF ACADEMIC RESEARCHERS ABOUT VIOXX'S SAFETY

In 2000–2001, Merck took actions to combat the concerns of several academic researchers who were openly questioning the safety of Vioxx. A Stanford University professor who regularly gave prescription drug–related lectures sponsored by Merck and other drug companies pressed Merck for additional data about Vioxx.[27] When Merck failed to provide it, the professor added a slide to his lectures showing a man (representing the missing data) hiding under a blanket. Merck then canceled its sponsorship of several lectures by the professor, and a Merck official called Stanford Medical School, complaining that the professor's presentations were "irresponsibly anti-Merck and specifically anti-Vioxx." The Merck official suggested that if the lectures continued, the professor would "flame out" and there would be consequences for Stanford (presumably in the form of fewer Merck-sponsored research grants).

A professor at the University of Minnesota who had given Merck-sponsored lectures also got a call from Merck complaining about what was being said about Vioxx, as did a rheumatologist at Beth Israel Deaconess Medical Center in Boston who had worked on research with rival Celebrex but who had also worked with Merck on occasion. In the summer of 2002, a professor at the Catalan Institute of Pharmacology in Barcelona, Spain, edited a publication that repeated criticisms of Merck's handling of Vioxx that had been published in *The Lancet*, a respected British medical journal.[28] Merck approached the professor on three occasions to print a Merck-authored rebuttal. When the professor refused, Merck sued the professor and the Catalan Institute under a Spanish law that allowed plaintiffs to demand a public correction of inaccurate published information. In January 2004, the judge ruled in favor of the defendants and ordered Merck to pay the court costs. In March 2004, the professor was asked to give a featured presentation to a conference of 1,000 Spanish family physicians—a conference that Merck had helped sponsor for eight straight years. When Merck learned of the invitation, it called the conference organizer and indicated that it "preferred" that the professor not be on the program. When the organizer refused to delete the professor's presentation, Merck withdrew its $140,000 funding for the conference.[29]

OTHER EXTERNAL WARNING SIGNS OF TROUBLE WITH VIOXX

While Merck's multiyear APPROVe study was under way, several developments outside Merck further signaled there might be cardiovascular problems with Vioxx:

- An article by three medical researchers, published in the *Journal of the American Medical Association* on August 22, 2001, reviewed four studies with a total of about 18,000 patients and concluded that "the available data raise a cautionary flag about the risk of cardiovascular events with Cox-2 inhibitors."[30] One of the researchers communicated the results of the study to Merck's CEO, Ray Gilmartin, offering to visit Merck and present their findings. Neither Gilmartin nor anyone else at Merck responded to the researcher's phone calls. Merck reportedly asked the *New England Journal of Medicine* to

run a Merck-authored rebuttal, but the journal editors refused.[31]

- *The Wall Street Journal* ran a front-page story on the heart risks of Vioxx and other Cox-2 inhibitor drugs on August 22, 2001, citing the concerns of several medical researchers and the Vioxx–naproxen results.

- The National Trial Lawyers Guild formed a "Cox-2 litigation group" in early 2002 and at their national convention in 2003 devoted a session to Vioxx.

- Before the Vioxx recall, more than 400 lawsuits had been filed on behalf of Vioxx patients.[32]

- A Merck-sponsored analysis, conducted by researchers at Harvard and Merck, found that Vioxx was "associated with an elevated relative risk" of heart attacks compared to the use of Pfizer's painkiller Celebrex or no similar painkiller. When Merck asked the researchers to tone down the conclusion about the no-painkiller group and the Harvard researcher refused, Merck removed the name of the Merck researcher prior to the article's publication in *Circulation* in May 2004.[33]

- A book published in the summer of 2004 by John Abramson, a family doctor and clinical instructor at Harvard Medical School, concluded that even people who did not have a history of heart problems doubled their risk of developing a cardiovascular problem by taking Vioxx instead of naproxen.[34]

All of these developments served to switch the debate on Vioxx from whether it lacked some of the cardiac-related benefits of NSAIDs to whether it was inherently risky from a cardiac-stroke perspective.

Meanwhile, in the summer of 2004, the earlier study of the medical records of 1.4 million people insured by Kaiser Permanente was producing important findings. The study, financed by the FDA and conducted by David J. Graham, associate director for science and medicine in the FDA's Office of Drug Safety, compared the outcomes of 40,405 patients who took Celebrex and 26,748 patients who took Vioxx. The results, which were reported at a conference in France on August 25, 2004, showed two significant facts:

- Patients taking the typical starting dose of Vioxx had a 50 percent greater chance of heart attacks and sudden cardiac death than patients taking Celebrex.

- Patients taking the highest recommended daily dosage of Vioxx had nearly 2.7 times the risk of heart attack and sudden cardiac death as patients taking Celebrex.

Merck issued a press release saying it strongly disagreed with the FDA study's conclusions.[35]

THE RECALL DECISION

On Thursday afternoon, September 23, 2004, almost four and a half years after the APPROVe study began, Peter Kim, who had taken over as Merck's chief of research when Scolnick retired, met with Ray Gilmartin to inform him that the results of the APPROVe study were showing that patients on Vioxx longer than 18 months had begun experiencing heart attacks and strokes at about double the rate of the control group taking placebos. Results for the first 18 months of the study did not show an increased risk of cardiovascular problems with Vioxx; these results were similar to those of two prior placebo-controlled studies described in the current U.S. labeling for Vioxx. The decision to recall Vioxx came seven days later. Exhibit 5 presents a time line of Vioxx-related actions and events at Merck up to the recall.

THE FALLOUT FOLLOWING MERCK'S VOLUNTARY WITHDRAWAL OF VIOXX

A torrent of criticism was directed at Merck in the days and weeks following the withdrawal of Vioxx from the market. Some outsiders objected strongly to the company's hyped-up marketing tactics. With Merck's share price dropping from about $45 to the $27–$29 range, equal to a $42 billion loss in market capitalization, shareholders expressed concerns about management's handling of Vioxx, arguing that a better option to the recall was to (1) immediately inform doctors writing Vioxx prescriptions for patients of the above-average risks of heart attacks and strokes, and (2) seek FDA approval to amend the warning label on Vioxx to state that patients with heart-attack and stroke risk should not take Vioxx

for longer than 18 months. Indeed, the majority of the outside clinicians Merck consulted between September 23 and September 30, 2004, advised Merck to go to the FDA and other regulatory authorities and have the prescribing information for Vioxx updated with the new findings of increased cardiovascular risk, especially since millions of people were benefiting from use of Vioxx.

Medical experts opined that Merck should have done more studies when doubts about Vioxx first surfaced. William Castelli, former director of the Framingham Heart Study, which investigated cardiac risk factors, told *Fortune* that since Cox-2 inhibitors reduce inflammation (one of the risk factors for cardiac disease), a red flag should have immediately gone up when some studies suggested that Vioxx raised the risk of heart attacks instead of reducing them.[36]

Eric J. Topol, chairman of cardiology at the Cleveland Clinic and a vocal Merck critic, said in a commentary concerning Merck's withdrawal of Vioxx that was published in the October 21, 2004, issue of the *New England Journal of Medicine,* "Had the company not valued sales over safety, a suitable trial could have been initiated rapidly at a fraction of the cost of Merck's direct-to-consumer advertising campaign." Topol believed that the early estimates of 28,000 heart attacks that might be attributable to Vioxx were low and estimated that the number of people injured by Vioxx could be as high as 160,000 (a number Merck believed was far too high). But it was pretty clear that every person who took Vioxx during 1999–2004 and subsequently had a heart attack or stroke was a potential litigant.

A month after the Vioxx recall, on November 2, 2004, the FDA announced that David J. Graham's study of the Kaiser Permanente data indicated that Vioxx may have contributed to an additional 27,785 heart attacks, strokes, or deaths that might have been avoided if patients had taken Celebrex instead. Three days later, in a study published online by *The Lancet,* Swiss researchers at the University of Berne publicly reported their conclusions that Vioxx should have been "withdrawn several years earlier."[37] Their study, funded by the Swiss National Science Foundation, analyzed 18 randomized controlled Vioxx trials and 11 related observational studies; much of the information for the study was based on prior data and study results obtained primarily from the FDA. Merck posted a strongly worded rebuttal of the *Lancet* article on its Web site, citing a variety of problems with the analysis done by the Swiss researchers.

Exhibit 5   **Timeline of Information about Vioxx, as Compiled by Merck**

1998	April: Results of FitzGerald study first presented. Among the results of the study were indications that Cox-2 inhibitors may increase the risk of cardiovascular events.
	April: Trial of Vioxx versus placebo in the prevention of Alzheimer's in patients with mild cognitive impairment (MCI) begins.
1999	January: Vioxx–naproxen trial initiated; patients taking aspirin for cardiac protection were excluded from the study.
	February: First trial of Vioxx versus placebo for the treatment of Alzheimer's disease begins.
	April: Public meeting of FDA Arthritis Advisory Committee on Vioxx's approval.
	May: Vioxx approved by the FDA.
	October: Terms of APPROVe trial finalized, with enrollment of 2,600 patients, ages 40–96, beginning in February 2000. Purpose was to determine ability of Vioxx to reduce colon polyps over a period of three years, with cardiovascular events to be closely monitored. Patients were allowed to take aspirin.
2000	March: Preliminary results from Vioxx–naproxen study become available to Merck. News release on preliminary results of Vioxx–naproxen results issued by Merck; preliminary Vioxx–naproxen results submitted to the FDA. Two ongoing Alzheimer's studies—one for prevention and one for treatment—show no difference in cardiovascular event rates between Vioxx and placebo.
	April: Second trial of Vioxx versus placebo for the treatment of Alzheimer's begins.
	May: Article discussing preliminary Vioxx–naproxen data submitted to the *New England Journal of Medicine* for review and publication. Vioxx–naproxen preliminary results presented at Digestive Disease Week.
	June: Final Vioxx–naproxen study data submitted to FDA in a supplemental new drug application, which included a draft prescribing new disclosure information regarding uses and possible side effects.
	November: Vioxx–naproxen findings published in the *New England Journal of Medicine.* First Vioxx versus placebo trial in the treatment of Alzheimer's disease ends; second interim analysis of safety data from Alzheimer's prevention and treatment trials shows no difference in cardiovascular event rates between Vioxx and placebo.
2001	February: Public meeting of FDA Arthritis Advisory Committee on Vioxx–naproxen results.
	May: Second trial of Vioxx versus placebo for treatment of Alzheimer's disease stopped.
	September: Merck and Oxford University sign letter of intent to conduct a randomized, double-blind, placebo-controlled, international, multicenter study of Vioxx in 7,000 colorectal cancer patients following potentially curative therapy (designated as the VICTOR trial). The primary hypothesis to be tested in the study was that Vioxx administered for two years would result in greater overall survival compared with placebo. Cardiovascular events were to be monitored.
	October: Pooled analysis of cardiovascular data from Phase II/III studies published in *Circulation,* the journal of the American Heart Association. Analysis demonstrated that Vioxx was not associated with excess cardiovascular thrombotic events compared with either placebo or non-naproxen NSAIDs.
	November: APPROVe enrollment completed.
2002	April: U.S. prescribing information for Vioxx updated as a consequence of the Vioxx–naproxen study information and data from two placebo-controlled studies. First patient is enrolled in VICTOR trial.
	June: Pooled analysis of placebo-controlled studies in patients with Alzheimer's and MCI presented to European League Against Rheumatism. The incidence of serious cardiovascular adverse events in this population was similar for both Vioxx and placebo.
2003	March: Design of a study to test ability of Vioxx to reduce incidence of prostate cancer in 15,000 patients (named Vioxx in Prostate Cancer, or ViP, trial) finalized; adverse cardiovascular events were to be monitored.
	April: Trial of Vioxx versus placebo in MCI ends.
	June: ViP trial enrollment begins. Updated pooled analysis of Alzheimer's treatment and MCI data presented to European League Against Rheumatism. The cardiovascular event rate in patients taking 25-milligram doses of Vioxx continued to be similar to the rate in patients taking a placebo; mean duration of treatment was 1.2 years in Vioxx group and 1.3 years in placebo group.
	October: Updated pooled analysis published in the *American Heart Journal* demonstrated that Vioxx was not associated with excess cardiovascular thrombotic events compared with either placebo or non-naproxen NSAIDs.
2004	September: APPROVe External Data Safety Monitoring Board notifies Merck of its recommendation to end APPROVe trial due to high Vioxx incidence of cardiovascular problems. APPROVe, ViP, and VICTOR trials also terminated early. Merck voluntarily withdraws Vioxx from the market.

Source: Information posted at www.merck.com (accessed December 4, 2004).

REACTION AND RESPONSE IN REGULATORY CIRCLES

European prescription drug regulators launched investigations of other Cox-2 inhibitor drugs, such as Pfizer's Celebrex and Bextra. On November 30, 2004, Swiss pharmaceutical manufacturer Novartis announced that it was temporarily withdrawing its application for European Union approval of its new Cox-2 painkiller Prexige in order to gather more detailed data—Prexige had already been approved in Britain and 20 other countries. Novartis was also working with the FDA on what documentation was needed to win approval to market Prexige in the United States. It was unclear to what extent Merck's next big drug, Arcoxia, would be delayed at the FDA following the FDA's request for further safety and benefit data in October 2004.

Members of Congress, as well as prominent doctors, had recently called for an investigation of the FDA, its drug approval procedures, and whether the relationship between the pharmaceutical firms and FDA officials was too cozy to produce independent oversight and adequately protect the public interest. In a congressional hearing on November 18, 2004, the FDA's David J. Graham testified that the agency downplayed mounting negative data on Vioxx and that it "seriously undervalues, disregards and disrespects drug safety" in general. Graham listed five other potentially dangerous medications currently on the market—Accutane, Bextra, Crestor, Meridia, and Serevent. Exhibit 6 lists drugs that *Forbes* magazine identified as targets for litigation. In early 2005, concerns about the safety of Celebrex began to multiply.

In response to its critics, the FDA announced that it was moving to modify its system for evaluating the safety of drugs, particularly those already on the market and those applications where there was disagreement among FDA scientists reviewing new drug applications. Under the proposed new system, when FDA reviewers failed to reach consensus, an ad hoc panel would be convened, with the panel

Exhibit 6   **Other Drugs That Could Be the Target of Litigation**

Drug	Manufacturer	Global Sales	Possible Problems
Zyprexa	Eli Lilly	$4.3 billion	A group convened by the American Diabetes Association says that this drug, used to treat schizophrenia, raises diabetes risk relative to other drugs—75 lawsuits have been filed.
Paxil	GlaxoSmithKline	$3.1 billion	This antidepressant (and others) may be linked to suicidal thoughts in children.
Neurontin	Pfizer	$2.7 billion	In May 2004, a Pfizer subsidiary paid $430 million to promote this epilepsy drug for unapproved uses; a class-action lawsuit has been filed.
Prempro	Wyeth	$1.3 billion	Almost 2,000 lawsuits involving 3,136 women who took estrogen replacement drugs Premarin or Prempro have been filed following medical trials showing that both drugs raise the risk of heart attack and that Prempro raises the risk of breast cancer. Wyeth says the increased risk of breast cancer was disclosed.
Bextra	Pfizer	$990 million	Bextra, like Vioxx, was a Cox-2 inhibitor and was being scrutinized by trial lawyers because of two studies showing it raised risks in heart surgery patients. However, Bextra was not an approved drug for heart surgery patients.
Accutane	Roche	$410 million	This acne drug has been linked to causing birth defects and has alleged links to suicide. Roche says birth defect links were prominently disclosed.
Crestor	AstraZeneca	$130 million	Public Citizen, an advocacy group, is claiming possible liver and muscle side effects; one lawsuit is pending in Mississippi.

Source: "Merck's Mess," *Forbes,* November 1, 2004, p. 51.

consisting of scientists who were not involved in the original decision-making process, including some from outside the agency. The panel would have 30 days to make a recommendation to the director of FDA's Center for Drug Evaluation & Research. However, Senate Finance Committee chair Charles E. Grassley (R-Iowa) and other knowledgeable FDA observers believed that more far-reaching changes were needed to prevent another Vioxx debacle. At the close of the November 18 hearing, Grassley said he would be pushing for an autonomous board at the FDA to track the safety of drugs after they go on the market. The board would have the power to make label changes and to withdraw drugs from the market. Advocates of an independent board argued that it was unreasonable to expect that the same agency responsible for approval of drug licensing and labeling also be committed to the task of actively seeking evidence that might indicate its decisions to approve the drug or its warning label were wrong.[38]

Since adoption of the 1992 Prescription Drug User Fee Act, the FDA had received approximately $825 million in "user fees" from drug and biologic manufacturers from fiscal years 1993 through 2001 to augment its budget and help pay for the costs of streamlining its new drug-review-and-approval process.[39] During that time, median approval times for standard, or nonpriority, drugs decreased from 27 months in 1993 to 14 months in 2001. However, drug recalls following approval increased from 1.56 percent during 1993–1996 to 5.35 percent during 1997–2001. In addition, an investigation of 18 FDA expert advisory panels revealed that more than half of the members of these panels had direct financial interests in the drug or topic they were evaluating and for which they were making recommendations.[40]

THE SPECTER OF LITIGATION AND MERCK'S EXPOSURE

As of December 2004, trial lawyers in the United States and elsewhere were still taking calls from potential clients daily in regard to Vioxx. Several prominent law firms with expertise in product liability were in the process of (1) soliciting and interviewing potential clients who believed they

had been harmed by taking Vioxx, (2) preparing and/or filing lawsuits of one kind or another, and (3) identifying and working with medical experts who might be called to testify about Vioxx's causal connections to clients' health problems. While every person who took Vioxx and subsequently suffered a heart attack or stroke could be a potential litigant, the science seemed to indicate that the cardiovascular risks of Vioxx began after 18 months of usage (which could significantly limit the number of legitimate plaintiffs and Merck's litigation exposure). Moreover, a successful plaintiff would have to prove that it was Vioxx and not any of a myriad of other reasons— smoking, poor eating habits, excess weight, lack of exercise—that *caused* the health problem.

On the other hand, lawyers for the plaintiffs believed they could introduce documents and testimony showing that Merck swept adverse evidence about Vioxx's safety under the rug. In litigation in New Jersey and Alabama, where over 150 Vioxx cases were pending, plaintiffs' lawyers had successfully gotten discovery rights from the courts and obtained some 3 million Merck documents and e-mails relating to Vioxx.[41] In the New Jersey cases, plaintiffs' lawyers were also expected to claim that Merck's direct-to-consumer advertising campaign had induced patients to ask their doctors for Vioxx— in New Jersey (and other jurisdictions), a drugmaker that employed direct-to-consumer marketing lost the protection of a legal rule that says it need only provide safety warnings sufficient to alert doctors (not patients) to a drug's risks.

Some of the plaintiffs' lawyers were seeking to have their pending cases consolidated and transferred to jurisdictions where jury awards for damages were quite generous. Merck was trying to get many of the federal cases transferred to courts in Maryland, where it believed the judicial climate was more favorable to its position.[42]

MERCK'S POSITION ON ITS DECISION TO WITHDRAW VIOXX FROM THE MARKET

When Merck pulled Vioxx from the market on September 30, 2004, CEO Raymond Gilmartin said that the new study findings prompting Merck's decision were "unexpected" and that Merck's voluntary withdrawal was "really putting patient safety first"—needy patients could readily switch to other Cox-2 inhibitors such as Celebrex or NSAIDs.

Merck's position right up until it withdrew Vioxx was that the evidence about Vioxx's cardiovascular effects was inconclusive. For example, in the first round of clinical trials, patients who took Vioxx had about the same rate of heart attacks and strokes as patients who took NSAIDs or a sugar-pill placebo.[43] Merck said that it had conducted a number of studies before and after FDA approval that did not show the heart risk seen in the Vioxx–naproxen study.[44]

And management believed it had done the right things, pointing out that:[45]

- It had extensively studied Vioxx before seeking regulatory approval to market it.

- After it saw the results of the Vioxx–naproxen trial, it immediately put out a press release.

- It added warning language to its Vioxx label and prescription usage information.

- When questions arose, it took additional steps, including conducting further studies to gain more clinical information. For example, it voluntarily and ethically initiated the APPROVe study, which ultimately identified the increased cardiovascular risks of long-term use of Vioxx.

- When information from the additional clinical trials became available, Merck had put patient safety first and promptly recalled Vioxx rather than amend the prescription warnings.

According to Merck general counsel Kenneth Frazier:

We communicated appropriately about the product, we monitored it appropriately, we studied it appropriately, and in the end we took the actions that benefited patients.[46]

Endnotes

[1]John Simons and David Stipp, "Will Merck Survive Vioxx?" *Fortune,* November 1, 2004, p. 96.

[2]Ibid.

[3]Ibid., p. 94.

[4]Ibid., p. 96.

[5]As cited in ibid., pp. 96–97.

[6]Quotes posted at www.merck.com (accessed November 30, 2004).

[7]These examples are based on information in company press releases posted at www.merck.com (accessed November 30, 2004).

[8]Anna Wilde Mathews and Barbara Martinez, "E-Mails Suggest Merck Knew Vioxx's Dangers at Early Stage," *The Wall Street Journal,* November 1, 2004, p. A10.

[9]Ibid.

[10]Ibid.

[11]Ibid.

[12]Simons and Stipp, "Will Merck Survive Vioxx?" p. 102.

[13]"Prescription for Trouble," a *60 Minutes* documentary posted at www.cbsnews.com, November 14, 2004 (accessed December 4, 2004).

[14]Holman W. Jenkins Jr., "Was Withdrawing Vioxx the Right Thing to Do?" *Wall Street Journal,* November 10, 2004, p. A17.

[15]Ibid.

[16]Amy Isao, "Drug Ads—Without Harmful Side Effects," *Business Week Online,* posted November 8, 2004.

[17]Jenkins, "Was Withdrawing Vioxx the Right Thing to Do?" p. A17.

[18]Mathews and Martinez, "E-Mails Suggest Merck Knew," p. A10.

[19]Ibid.

[20]Eric J. Topol, "Failing the Public Health—Rofecoxib, Merck, and the FDA," *New England Journal of Medicine* 351, no. 17 (October 21, 2004), p. 1707.

[21]Ibid.

[22]"Prescription for Trouble."

[23]Ibid.

[24]Mathews and Martinez, "E-Mails Suggest Merck Knew," p. A10, and "Prescription for Trouble."

[25]Mathews and Martinez, "E-Mails Suggest Merck Knew," p. A10.

[26]"Prescription for Trouble."

[27]Mathews and Martinez, "E-Mails Suggest Merck Knew," p. A10.

[28]Ibid.

[29]Ibid., p. A11.

[30]Debabrata Mukherjee, Steven E. Nissen, and Eric J. Topol, "Risk of Cardiovascular Events Associated with Selected Cox-2 Inhibitors," *Journal of the American Medical Association* 286, no. 8 (August 22, 2001), pp. 954–59.

[31]Mathews and Martinez, "E-Mails Suggest Merck Knew," p. A10.

[32]According to LexisNexis "Mealey Reports," and cited in "Merck's Mess," *Forbes,* November 1, 2004, p. 51.

[33]Mathews and Martinez, "E-Mails Suggest Merck Knew," p. A11.

[34]John Abramson, *Overdosed America: The Broken Promise of American Medicine* (New York: HarperCollins, 2004); and Mathews and Martinez, "E-Mails Suggest Merck Knew," p. A10.

[35]Mathews and Martinez, "E-Mails Suggest Merck Knew," p. A11.

[36]Simon and Stipp, "Will Merck Survive Vioxx?" p. 104.

[37]Peter Jüni, Linda Nartey, Stephan Reichenbach, Rebekka Sterchi, Paul A Dieppe, and Matthias Egger, "Risk of Cardiovascular Events and Rofecoxib: Cumulative Meta-Analysis," *The Lancet* 364, no. 9450 (November 5, 2004), pp. 2021ff.

[38]Phil B. Fontanarosa, Drummond Rennie, and Catherine D. DeAngelis, "Postmarketing Surveillance—Lack of Vigilance, Lack of Trust," *Journal of the American Medical Association* 292, no. 21 (December 1, 2004), p. 2649.

[39]Ibid., p. 2647.

[40]Ibid., p. 2647.

[41]Roger Perloff, "How Bad Will the Lawsuits Get?" *Fortune,* November 1, 2004, p. 97.

[42]Barbara Martinez, "Preparing for Vioxx Suits, Both Sides Seek Friendly Venues," *The Wall Street Journal,* November 17, 2004, p. B1.

[43]Simon and Stipp, "Will Merck Survive Vioxx?" p. 102.

[44]"Prescription for Trouble."

[45]"An Open Letter from Merck," appearing in many newspapers, November 12, 2004.

[46]As quoted in Perloff, "How Bad Will the Lawsuits Get?" p. 96.

Kimpton Hotels: Balancing Strategy and Environmental Sustainability

Murray Silverman
San Francisco State University

Tom Thomas
San Francisco State University

Michael Pace faced a dilemma. He was Kimpton Hotels' West Coast director of operations and environmental programs, general manager of its Villa Florence Hotel in San Francisco, and the main catalyst for implementing its EarthCare program nationally. He was determined to help the boutique hotel chain walk the talk regarding its commitment to environmental responsibility, but he also had agreed not to introduce any new products or processes that would be more expensive than those they replaced. Now that the first phase of the program had been implemented nationwide, he and the company's team of "eco-champions" were facing some difficult challenges with the rollout of the second, more ambitious phase.

For example, the team had to decide whether to recommend the purchase of linens (towels, sheets, pillowcases, etc.) made of organic cotton, which vendors insisted would cost at least 50 percent more than standard linens. It would cost an average of $100,000 to $150,000 to switch out all the linens in each hotel. If Kimpton couldn't negotiate the price down, was there some way it could introduce organic cotton in a limited but meaningful way? All linens are commingled in the laundry, so they can't be introduced one floor at a time. Maybe the company could start with pillowcases—though the sheets wouldn't be organic, guests would be resting their heads on organic cotton. Would it even be worth spending so much on linens? From a public relations perspective,

would it make that much of a difference? Should the company wait and see, phase organic cotton in over time, or drop the idea altogether? Similar issues would arise when the company had to decide whether to recommend environmentally friendly carpeting or furniture.

And then there was recycling. The program had been field-tested at Kimpton hotels in San Francisco, a singular city in one of the most environmentally progressive states in the United States. Now the eco-champions team had to figure out how to make it work in cities like Chicago, which didn't even have a municipal recycling program in place. In Denver, recycling actually cost more than waste disposal to a landfill, due to the low cost of land in eastern Colorado. Pace knew that the environmental initiatives most likely to succeed would be those that could be seamlessly implemented by the general managers and employees of the 39 unique Kimpton hotels around the country. The last thing he wanted to do was to make their jobs more difficult by imposing cookie-cutter standards.

Kimpton had recently embarked on a national campaign to build brand awareness by associating its name with each unique property. Pace knew that the success of Kimpton's strategy would rest heavily on its ability to maintain the care, integrity, and uniqueness that customers had come to associate with its chain of boutique hotels. Other hotel companies had begun investing heavily in the niche that Kimpton had pioneered. To differentiate itself, the company had to continue to find innovative ways to offer services that addressed the needs and values of its customers, and EarthCare was a crucial part of its plans. But could Pace find a way to make it happen within Kimpton's budget, and without adversely affecting the customer experience? Would Kimpton be able to keep the promises made by its new corporate brand?

THE U.S. HOTEL INDUSTRY

By the summer of 2005, the absence of any major terror attacks since September 11, 2001, had encouraged Americans to begin traveling again. Buoyed by a rebound in business travel and continued growth in leisure related spending, the lodging industry had shown steady growth since mid-2003. In 2004, the industry posted impressive gains in room occupancy levels, revenue per available room (REVPAR), and average room rates (see Exhibit 1). In the previous year, demand had been dampened by the outbreak of the war with Iraq and the soft U.S. economy. Industry pretax profit increased in 2004 to $14.5 billion over $12.8 billion in 2003 but was still far below the recent peak of $22.5 billion in 2000.

The U.S. hotel industry was comprised of 55,000 properties and 4.5 million rooms. Its $112 billion in revenues in 2004 included room sales (75 percent), food and beverage sales (18 percent), and miscellaneous such as phone charges and movie rentals (7 percent). Revenues in 2003 were $105 billion. There were many large hotel chains (see Exhibit 2); however, no single lodging company accounted for more than 15 percent of all U.S. hotel rooms. Hotels were segmented into luxury (Four Seasons, Fairmont, Carlton); upscale (Embassy, Sheraton, Radisson, Courtyard); midmarket (Holiday Inn, Ramada, Comfort Inn); and economy (Motel 6, Days

Inn, Red Roof). Within the upscale segment there were two strategic niches: (1) boutique hotels in urban areas, which differentiated themselves through unique decor, amenities and service, and (2) bed and breakfasts (B&Bs), which were typically small, independent properties featuring unique settings and decor.

Kimpton Hotels had built a portfolio of unique properties in the upscale segment of the industry and had been credited with inventing the boutique hotel segment in 1981.[1] By 1999, boutique hotels accounted for about 15 percent of San Francisco's estimated 31,000 rooms, according to PKF Consulting. Boutique hotels constituted about 1 percent of the industry nationwide, and the segment was growing. The Starwood Hotel chain entered the segment with its W hotels, and Continental Hotels PLC entered with Hotel Indigo. In San Francisco, Kimpton was the recognized market leader, with 67 percent of the city's boutique hotels. Joie de Vivre Hotels had 20 percent of the local market, and Personality Hotels on Union Square had 12 percent. With 2004 sales of $400 million, up from $350 million in 2003, Kimpton planned to add at least three to five properties per year in major markets such as New York, Boston, Washington, D.C., and Miami.

Approximately 55 percent of hotel customers were individuals attending a business meeting, conference, or group meeting. Foreign travelers contributed significantly to room demand, especially in major cities. Competition for these customers was based on many factors, including price, location, brand loyalty, customer service, and value-added services. It appeared that the industry's earnings recovery had been limited by consumer price shopping on the Internet and by cost pressures driven by rising health care costs, energy costs, and property taxes. Companies were intensifying efforts to win customer loyalty. Efforts included establishing reward

Exhibit 1   **Hotel and Lodging Industry Trends**

	2000	2001	2002	2003	2004
Average room rates	$85.43	$85.35	$83.48	$83.41	$86.70
Occupancy rate	65.3%	61.9%	60.9%	60.8%	63.1%
Average revenue per available room per night*	$55.78	$52.83	$50.84	$50.71	$54.70
Estimated pretax income, industrywide (in billions)	$ 22.5	$ 16.2	$ 14.2	$ 12.8	$ 14.5

*Equal to the average room rate multiplied by the occupancy rate.
Source: Smith Travel Research.

Exhibit 2   **Large Hotel Companies (based on number of affiliated rooms worldwide)**

Company	Major Chains	Number of Properties	Number of Rooms
Cendant Corporation	Days Inn, Ramada (U.S.), Super 8, Howard Johnson, Travel Lodge	6,399	518,435
InterContinental Hotels Group	Holiday Inn, Inter-Continental	3,500	538,000
Marriott International	Marriott, Marriott Courtyard, Residence Inn, Fairfield Inn, Renaissance, Ramada (outside U.S.)	2,753	496,920
Arcor SA	Motel 6, Mercure, Ibis, Novotel, Red Roof Inns, Hotel Sofitel, Formule 1	3,950	455,000
Choice Hotels International	Comfort Inn, Quality Inn, Econo Lodge	4,678	375,859
Hilton Hotels	Hilton (U.S.), Hampton Inns, Doubletree, Embassy Suites, Homewood Suites	2,157	345,141
Best Western International	Best Western	4,105	312,329
Starwood Hotels & Resorts	Sheraton, Westin	736	227,815
Carlson Hospitality Group	Radisson, Country Inns & Suites by Carlson, Regent International Hotels	885	147,000
Hyatt Corporation	Hyatt Regency	121	59,000
Total		29,494	3,498,423

Source: Standard & Poors Industry Surveys, Lodging & Gaming (New York: McGraw-Hill, December 2004).

programs for frequent visitors and targeting a hotel's best customers for direct marketing programs.

The longer-term outlook for the industry seemed positive. U.S. demographic trends were highly favorable. Baby boomers, then in their peak earning years, would be seeking elaborate or expensive vacations. In addition, more and more Americans would be retiring and traveling in their leisure time.

THE GREENING OF THE U.S. HOTEL INDUSTRY

The U.S. hotel industry—with its 4.5 million rooms and its common areas, lobbies, convention rooms, restaurants, laundry facilities, and back offices—had a significant environmental impact. According to the American Hotel and Lodging Association, the average hotel toilet was flushed seven times per day

per guest, an average shower was 7.5 minutes long, and 40 percent of bathroom lights were left on as nightlights. A typical hotel used 218 gallons of water per day per occupied room. Energy use was pervasive, including lighting in guest rooms and common areas, heating and air-conditioning, and washing and drying towels and linens. The hotel industry spent $3.7 billion per year on electricity.[2]

Guestrooms generated surprisingly large amounts of waste, ranging from 0.5 pound to 28 pounds per day, and averaging 2 pounds per day per guest. In California, 2 percent of all food waste came from the hotel and lodging industry. A short list of other environmental impacts of the hotel industry included the following:

- Non refillable amenity bottles (shampoos, etc.) generated large amounts of plastic waste.
- Products used to clean bathrooms and furniture contained synthetic additives.

- Paints contained high levels of volatile organic compounds.
- Back-office and front-desk activities generated large amounts of wastepaper.
- Furniture, office equipment, and kitchen and laundry appliances were usually not selected for their environmental advantages.

Opportunities for reducing a hotel's environmental footprint were plentiful, and many could yield bottom-line savings. Reduced laundering of linens, at customer discretion, had already been adopted enthusiastically across the spectrum of budget to luxury hotels, to the point that 38 percent of hotels had linen reuse programs. Low-flow showerheads could deliver the same quality shower experience using half the water of a conventional showerhead. Faucet aerators also could cut the water requirements by 50 percent. A 13-watt compact fluorescent bulb gave the same light as a 60-watt incandescent, lasted about 10 times longer, and used about 70 percent less energy. Waste costs also could be significantly reduced. For many hotels, 50–80 percent of their solid waste stream was compostable, and a significant part of the remaining waste was recyclables such as paper, aluminum, and glass.

Fairmont Hotels & Resorts, a Canadian-based hotel chain, had generated considerable savings since implementing its environmental programs in the early 1990s. While concern for the environment drove Fairmont's program, many of its initiatives resulted in bottom-line benefits. Examples of the types of environmental initiatives and their associated savings at the Fairmont Hotels & Resorts are listed in Exhibit 3. Fairmont Hotels also pursued initiatives and made investments that did not produce readily apparent bottom-line benefits. For example, one of its hotels purchased 20 percent of their energy as renewable energy (solar, wind, and hydro) even though the cost was higher. The company supported the expense of a corporate office of environmental affairs and a manager of environmental affairs. It also financially supported efforts related to habitat restoration and preservation of endangered species.[3]

In addition to bottom-line savings, environmental programs held the potential to generate new business. Governmental bodies, nongovernmental organizations, corporations, and convention/meeting planners were showing increased interest in selecting hotels using environmental criteria. California had recently launched its Green Lodging Program (GLP). State employees were encouraged to select from the GLP's list of certified hotels. The state's $70 million annual travel budget was an incentive for hotels to be certified by the program. The criteria for certification included recycling, composting, energy- and water-efficient fixtures and lighting, and nontoxic or less toxic alternatives for cleaning supplies. State governments in Pennsylvania, Florida, Vermont, and Virginia also had developed green lodging programs.

Exhibit 3   **A Sampling of Fairmont Hotels & Resorts' Environmental Cost-Saving Initiatives**

- The Fairmont Royal York Hotel in Toronto recycled over 212,000 pounds of cardboard and paper annually, saving 2,025 trees and $79,000 in landfill fees.
- Prior to establishing a recycling program for kitchen grease, the Fairmont Winnipeg spent over $1 million to have its sewer system cleared of kitchen grease buildup. Kitchen grease was now picked up and recycled free of charge.
- The breakfast buffet at Fairmont Tremblant eliminated individual servings of jams in 22-milliliter glass jars. Instead, the kitchen prepared seven varieties of homemade jams and served them in large attractive jars with serving spoons. With over 49,500 breakfasts served annually, the restaurant saved over $19,000 per year.
- The Fairmont Royal York had over 34,000 light fixtures. The hotel switched 1,920 bulbs in the guest bathrooms and 5,500 bulbs in the guestrooms from incandescent to compact fluorescent bulbs, saving $57,135 annually. In public areas and staircases, over 773 bulbs had been switched, generating additional savings of $23,095 per year.
- The staff at the Fairmont Hotel Vancouver separated organic waste (from room service, meetings, and conference meals) from its regular waste stream. The organic waste was picked up from the hotel (free of charge) and used to make a rich organic fertilizer. This produced a 50 percent reduction in landfill wastes and an annual savings of $11,000.

Source: Fairmont Hotels & Resorts, *The Green Partnership Guide*, 2nd ed., 2001.

CERES, a well-respected environmental nonprofit organization, had developed the Green Hotel Initiative, designed to increase and demonstrate demand for environmentally responsible hotel services. Some major corporations endorsed the initiative, including Ford Motor Company, General Motors, Nike, American Airlines, and Coca-Cola. The Coalition for Environmentally Responsible Conventions (CERC) and the Green Meetings Industry Council were encouraging meeting planners to "green" their events by, among other things, choosing environmentally friendly hotels for lodging and meeting sites. This trend toward booking lodging and meeting sites based on green criteria was in its very early stages. Industry insiders believed that environmentally driven demand was extremely limited at this point, and the ultimate impact of this movement was uncertain.

Environmental progress in the U.S. hotel industry had been limited. With a few exceptions, most hotels were doing little beyond pursuing the low-hanging fruit, in the form of easy-to-implement cost-saving initiatives. Those hotels had been reducing their environmental footprint as a welcome consequence of their cost-cutting efforts, but they were not necessarily committed to a comprehensive environmental program. During a 1998 effort by Cornell University's School of Hotel Administration to identify hotels employing environmental best practices, researchers were "surprised by the dearth of nominations." The four U.S. hotels selected as champions—Colony Hotel, Hotel Bel Air, Hyatt Regency Chicago, and Hyatt Regency Scottsdale— were primarily focused on cost savings in energy and waste streams.[4] In contrast to those in the United States, hotels in Canada and Europe seemed to be embracing the hotel greening process, as exemplified by the Fairmont Hotel & Resorts' effort to institutionalize innovative approaches to reducing its environmental footprint throughout its operations.

KIMPTON'S BUSINESS PHILOSOPHY AND STRATEGY

Kimpton Hotels was founded in 1981 by Bill Kimpton, who once said, "No matter how much money people have to spend on big, fancy hotels, they're still intimidated and unsettled when they arrive. So the psychology of how you build hotels and restaurants is very important. You put a fireplace in the lobby and create a warm, friendly restaurant, and the guest will feel at home." By 2005, Kimpton had grown to include 39 hotels throughout North America and Canada, each one designed to create a unique and exceptional guest experience (see Exhibit 4). Every hotel lobby had a cozy fireplace and plush sitting area, where complimentary coffee was served every morning, and wine every evening. Guest rooms were stylishly decorated and comfortably furnished, offering amenities such as specialty suites that included Tall Rooms and Yoga Rooms. Every room offered high-speed wireless Internet access and desks with ample lighting. Rather than rewarding customer loyalty with a point program, Kimpton offered customization and personalization. "We record the preferences of our loyal guests," said Mike Depatie, Kimpton's CEO of real estate, "Someone may want a jogging magazine and a Diet Coke when they arrive. We can get that done."

Business travel (group and individual) accounted for approximately 65 percent of Kimpton's revenues, and leisure travel (tour group and individual) the other 35 percent. The selection of hotels for business meetings and conferences was through meeting and conference organizers. Around 35 percent of all rooms were booked through the company's call center, 25 percent through travel agents, and 25 percent through the company's Web site; the remainder of customers "came in off the street." The Internet portion of Kimpton's business continued to grow, but the company didn't cater to buyers looking for the steal of the century. Rather, Kimpton was increasingly being discovered by the 25 percent of the customer pool that market researchers called "unchained seekers," many of whom used the Internet to search for unique accommodations that matched their particular needs or values.

Steve Pinetti, senior vice president for sales and marketing, noted, "If I were to drive a customer to the airport after their stay and ask them what their experience was like, the right answer would be, 'It felt great.' They don't have to know why, it could be the bed, the room, the wine, or the friendly employees. The next time they want to book a room, though, they'll come to us." Kimpton's REVPAR tended to meet or exceed norms within its upscale segment, due primarily to its relatively high occupancy rates. Occupancy rates rose to 68 percent in the fourth quarter of 2004, up from 63 percent during the same

Exhibit 4   **List of Kimpton Hotels**

	Style/Theme	Rooms	Year
Aspen, Colorado			
• Sky Hotel	Play & Action	90	2001
Boston, Massachusetts			
• Onyx Hotel	Emerging Art	112	2004
Cambridge, Massachusetts			
• Hotel Marlowe	Discovery	236	2003
Chicago, Illinois			
• Hotel Allegro Chicago	Be a Star	483	1998
• Hotel Monaco Chicago	Indulge Your Senses via Body, Mind & Soul	192	1998
• Burnham Hotel	Architecture	122	1999
Cupertino, California			
• Cypress Hotel	Good Life: Body, Mind & Soul	224	2002
Denver, Colorado			
• Hotel Monaco Denver	Adventure	189	1998
Miami			
• Mayfair Hotel & Spa	Tranquility and Sensuality	179	2005
New Orleans, Louisiana			
• Hotel Monaco New Orleans	Indulge Your Senses via Exotic Pleasures	250	2001
New York, New York			
• 70 Park Avenue Hotel	Private Residence	205	2004
Portland, Oregon			
• Hotel Vintage Plaza	Italian Romance	107	1992
• Fifth Avenue Suites Hotel	Patron of the Arts	221	1996
Salt Lake City			
• Hotel Monaco Salt Lake City	Indulge Your Senses via Guilty Pleasures	225	1999
San Diego, California			
• Solamar	Art Lies Within	235	2005
San Francisco, California			
• Villa Florence Hotel	Celebration of Italy	183	1986
• Monticello Inn	Literary	91	1987
• Prescott Hotel	Private Residence	164	1989
• Tuscan Inn	Family	221	1990
• Harbor Court Hotel	Energy & Well-being	131	1991
• Hotel Triton	Art, Music and Eco	140	1991
• Sir Francis Drake Hotel	Classic San Francisco	417	1994
• Hotel Monaco San Francisco	Sophisticated World Travel	201	1995
• Serrano Hotel	Fun & Games	236	1999
• Palomar Hotel	Art in Motion	198	1999
• Argonaut Hotel	Adventure	252	2003

(Continued)

Exhibit 4 **Continued**

	Style/Theme	Rooms	Year
Seattle, Washington			
• Alexis Hotel	Art of Living	109	1992
• Hotel Vintage Park	Washington Wine	126	1992
• Hotel Monaco Seattle	Animals	189	1997
Tacoma, Washington			
• Sheraton Tacoma Hotel	Business, conference center	319	1984
Vancouver, British Columbia			
• Pacific Palisades	Fun, Fresh and in the Now	233	2000
Washington, D.C.			
• Hotel Rouge	Playful Interactions	137	2001
• Topaz Hotel	Wellness	99	2001
• Hotel Monaco DC	Indulge Your Senses	184	2002
• Hotel Madera	Home Away From Home	86	2002
• Hotel Helix	Your 15 Minutes	178	2002
• Hotel George	George Washington w/contemporary flair	139	2003
Whistler, British Columbia			
• Summit Lodge	Romance, premier ski resort	81	2000

quarter in 2003. REVPAR during the same period rose from $87 to $102.[5]

Historically, Kimpton prospered by purchasing and renovating buildings at a discount in strategic nationwide locations that were appropriate for its niche segment. The hotel industry in general had been slow to enter the boutique niche, and Kimpton enjoyed a substantial edge in experience in developing value-added services for guests. "All hotels are starting to look alike and act alike, and we are the counterpoint, the contrarians," said Tom LaTour, Kimpton president and CEO. "We don't look like the brands, we don't act like the brands, and as the baby boomers move through the age wave, they will seek differentiated, experience-oriented products."

Kimpton's top executives took pride in their ability to recognize and develop both undervalued properties and undervalued people. Kimpton's hotel general managers were often refugees from large branded companies who did not thrive under hierarchical, standardized corporate structures. At Kimpton, they were afforded a great deal of autonomy, subject only to the constraints of customer service standards and capital and operating budgets.

This sense of autonomy and personal responsibility was conveyed down through the ranks to all 5,000 Kimpton employees. Kimpton's flexible corporate structure avoided hierarchy, preferring a circular structure where executives and employees were in constant communication.[6] Steve Pinetti liked to tell the story of a new parking attendant who had to figure out how to deal with a guest who felt that he had not been adequately informed of extra charges for parking his car at the hotel. The attendant decided on the spot to reduce the charges and asked the front desk to make the necessary adjustments. He had heard his general manager tell employees that they should feel empowered to take responsibility for making guests happy, but he fully expected to be grilled by his general manager, at the very least, about his actions. A sense of dread took hold as he was called to the front of the room at a staff meeting the very next day, but it dissipated quickly when his general manager handed him a special award for his initiative.

ESTABLISHING THE KIMPTON BRAND

While Kimpton was known for designing hotels that reflected the energy and personality of its distinct locations, by 2004 the company's top executives realized that uniting its hotel portfolio under a single recognizable brand could add considerable value. Cross-selling of hotel rooms in different cities, for instance, would be easier for salespeople handling corporate accounts if the properties all shared the Kimpton name. So the company launched what it called the Lifestyle Hotel Collection, with the theme "Every Hotel Tells a Story." One aspect of the branding effort was to add the Kimpton name to each property, as in Hotel Monaco San Francisco, a Kimpton Hotel. According to CEO LaTour, "We think of our hotels as a family, all having their own first names and sharing the last name Kimpton. We are ready to tell the world the Kimpton story."[7]

The distinctive value proposition associated with the Kimpton brand guaranteed the customer a unique and satisfying experience along five different dimensions, what the company referred to as Care, Comfort, Style, Flavor, and Fun:

- *Care*—Just as Kimpton treated its guests with a strong dose of friendly personal attention and tender loving care, its culture also emphasized concern and responsibility for the communities in which it did business, and the people it employed. Each hotel's general manager and staff expressed this sense of care by engaging in their own forms of community outreach, employee diversity, and environmental quality initiatives.

- *Comfort*—Kimpton focused intently on making its guests feel comfortable, their plush rooms and intimate public spaces providing a home away from home. It kept overhead costs in check by limiting the range of services it provided, forgoing the gyms, spas, swimming pools, and other space-hungry amenities that larger chains regularly offered.

- *Style*—No two Kimpton hotels were alike. Each attempted to draw on the distinctive character of the city and neighborhood in which it was located. Interiors tended to be upscale and stylish rather than opulent or ornate.

- *Flavor*—The restaurants located in each hotel were designed to stand on their own, catering to local clientele rather than rely on hotel guests for the bulk of their business.

- *Fun*—Employees were encouraged to bring their personalities to work, and to make sure that guests enjoyed their stay. According to Mike Depatie, "We don't try to make people Kimpton people. We want them to express the best of what they are."

An important part of Kimpton's story was its long-standing commitment to social responsibility. Staff at each hotel had always been encouraged to engage with local community nonprofits that benefited the arts, education, the underprivileged, and other charitable causes. Kimpton maintained these local programs even in periods of falling occupancy rates and industry downturns. These local efforts evolved into the companywide Kimpton Cares program in 2004, as part of the company's corporate branding effort, expanding its social and environmental commitments to the national and global arenas. At the national level, Kimpton supported the National AIDS Fund's Red Ribbon Campaign and a program called Dress for Success (which assisted economically disadvantaged women struggling to enter the workforce) by allotting a share of a guest's room fee to the charity. At the global level, Kimpton embarked in a partnership with Trust for Public Land (TPL), a nonprofit dedicated to the preservation of land for public use. In July 2005, Kimpton committed to raising $15,000 from its total room revenues to introduce the TPL's Parks for People program, and created eco-related fund-raising events in each of its cities to further support the campaign. Kimpton's EarthCare program was designed to be instituted through a comprehensive environmental program rolled out to all of Kimpton's hotels. "As business leaders, we believe we have a responsibility to positively impact the communities we live in, to be conscious about our environment and to make a difference where we can," said Niki Leondakis, Kimpton's chief operating officer.

Kimpton's top executives considered the Kimpton Cares program, and its EarthCare component, essential parts of the company's branding effort. Steve Pinetti noted, "What drove it was our belief that our brand needs to stand for something. What do we want to stand for in the community? We want to draw a line in the sand. We also want our impact to be felt as far and wide as it can. Hopefully, through our good deeds, we'll be able to influence other companies."

The early evidence suggested that the branding effort also had financial payoffs. Kimpton was receiving significant public relations coverage of its EarthCare program in local newspapers and travel publications. According to Pinetti, "The number of people who visit our Kimpton Web site has tripled in the year since we began the branding effort. Membership in the company's 'InTouch' guest loyalty program, which markets to previous guests via e-mail, rose from 86,000 in the 1st quarter of 2004 to 112,000 in the 4th quarter."[8] Consumer surveys showed big gains in awareness that each hotel is part of a bigger organization, with properties in other cities." As for the firm's Kimpton Cares program and its new EarthCare initiative, anecdotal evidence pointed to top-line benefits. "We've booked almost half a million dollars in meetings from a couple of corporations in Chicago because of our ecological reputation," said Pinetti. "Their reps basically told us, 'Your values align with our values, and we want to spend money on hotels that think the way we do.' " Kimpton believed that companies that identified with being socially responsible would look for partners like Kimpton that shared those values, and that certifications like the California Green Lodging program would attract both individuals and corporate clientele.

However, Pinetti noted, "The cost-effectiveness wasn't clear when we started. I thought we might get some business out of this, but that's not why we did it. We think it's the right thing to do, and it generates a lot of enthusiasm among our employees." Kimpton's real estate CEO, Mike Depatie, believed that incorporating care for communities and the environment into the company's brand had been a boon to hiring: "We attract and keep employees because they feel that from a values standpoint, we have a corporate culture and value system that's consistent with theirs. They feel passionate about working here." While the hotel industry was plagued with high turnover, Kimpton's turnover rates were lower than the national averages.

THE HOTEL TRITON

Kimpton's environmental consciousness reached back to 1985, when the company introduced the Galleria Park Hotel in San Francisco as an urban retreat with an open-space "park" within the hotel. In 1995, Kimpton's commitment picked up steam as it converted an entire floor of the 140-room Triton Hotel in San Francisco into an "eco-floor." With assistance from Green Suites International, a supplier of environmental solutions for the lodging industry, the Triton introduced the following initiatives in the 24 rooms on its eco-floor:

- Energy-efficient lighting solutions, including compact fluorescent bulbs and sensor night-lights (cutting energy costs by 75 percent).
- Bathroom amenity dispensers using biodegradable hypoallergenic soaps, lotions, and shampoos.
- Programmable digital thermostats to control guestroom energy consumption.
- Low-flow/high-pressure showerheads and sink aerators, and toilets that reduced water use.
- A linen and towel reuse program.
- Nontoxic, nonallergenic, all-natural cleaning products.
- Facial and bathroom tissues made from 100 percent recycled materials with at least 30 percent postconsumer wastepaper.
- Recycling receptacles.
- Bedding and bath towels made from organically grown cotton. (On average, 1.5 pounds of agricultural chemicals were used to produce the conventionally grown cotton in a single set of queen-size sheets.)
- Water filters to improve water quality and air filters to improve air quality.
- Low-volatile-organic-compound (VOC) paints used to paint walls and ceilings.

For Michael Pace, the sustainability lightbulb came on when he was general manager of the Monticello Hotel, prior to taking over as general manager of the Triton. At first, his interest was piqued by recycling efforts at the Monticello. But one day, he said, "I had a personal epiphany, where I realized how lucky I am. I'm living the American Dream, and I pass by a dozen homeless people on my way to work every day. I just realized that I wanted to do more than focus on myself and my job. The more I got involved, the more I saw the positive impact these efforts could have."

When Pace became general manager of the Triton in 2003, he felt that the eco-floor concept should be expanded throughout the Triton hotel's rooms and common areas. He immediately began to institute most of the eco-floor initiatives in the hotel's other guestrooms. He worked closely with the hotel staff to sort the hotel's entire waste stream and was able to reduce waste-hauling expenses from $2,200 to $600 per month.

As a result of Pace's conservation efforts, in 1994, the Triton was recognized as one of four properties in Northern California to qualify at the

Leadership Level for the State's new Green Lodging program. More important, the Triton was ready to serve as the template for the EarthCare program and the rest of Kimpton's hotels.

PLANNING THE EARTHCARE PROGRAM ROLLOUT CAMPAIGN

Pinetti and Pace realized that they were too busy to handle all the planning and operational details of the national rollout, so they turned to Jeff Slye, of Business Evolution Consulting, for help. Slye was a process management consultant who wanted to help small and medium-sized business owners figure out how to "ecofy" their companies. He knew that entrepreneurs were typically far too busy to do much about the resources they didn't like to overuse, and the waste they didn't like to generate. He had heard that Kimpton was trying to figure out how to make its operations greener and integrate this effort into its branding. When they first met in October 2004, Pinetti and Pace handed Slye a 10-page document detailing their objectives and a plan for rolling out the initiative in phases. Kimpton's program was to have the following eco-mission statement:

> Lead the hospitality industry in supporting a sustainable world by continuing to deliver a premium guest experience through non-intrusive, high quality, eco-friendly products and services.
>
> Our mission is built upon a companywide commitment towards water conservation; reduction of energy usage; elimination of harmful toxins and pollutants; recycling of all reusable waste; building and furnishing hotels with sustainable materials; and purchasing goods and services that directly support these principles.

Slye worked with Pinetti and Pace to fill various gaps in their plan and develop an "ecostandards program," a concise report outlining a strategy for greening the products and operational processes that Kimpton used to deliver a superior experience to its guests. In December 2004, Pinetti asked Slye to present the report to Kimpton's chief operating officer, Niki Leondakis. Leondakis greeted the proposal enthusiastically, but noted that it needed an additional component: a strategy for communicating the program both internally (to management

and staff) and externally (to guests, investors, and the press). As important as these external audiences were, Slye knew that the internal communications strategy would be particularly crucial, given the autonomy afforded each Kimpton hotel, each with its own set of local initiatives. Getting everyone on board would require a strategy that respected that aspect of Kimpton's culture. Slye kept that in mind as he worked with Pace to draft a communications strategy.

They decided to create an ad hoc "eco-champions" network throughout the company. The national "lead" (Pace) and "co-lead" (Pinetti) would head up the communications effort and would be accountable for its success. Each of five geographic regions (Pacific Northwest; San Francisco Bay Area; Central United States; Washington, D.C.; and Northeast/Southeast), covering six or seven hotel properties, would also have a lead and co-lead who would help communicate the program to employees, and be the local point-person in the chain of command. One of their key roles would be to solicit employee suggestions regarding ways to make products and processes greener.

In addition, a team of national eco-product specialists (EPSs) would be key components of the network. These specialists would be responsible for soliciting staff input and identifying and evaluating greener products as potential substitutes for existing ones. Products would be tested for effectiveness and evaluated on the basis of their environmental benefits, effect on guest perceptions, potential marketing value, and cost. Pinetti and Pace determined that specialists would be needed initially for six product categories: beverages, cleaning agents, office supplies, engineering, information technology, and room supplies.

Pinetti and Pace knew that the various regional leads and national product specialists would have to be selected carefully. The program's success would depend largely on the enthusiasm and capability that team members would bring to the task. They faced a dilemma: Ask for volunteers, or handpick preferred candidates? They decided to identify likely candidates and invite them to participate, an approach made possible by Kimpton's tractable size and intimate culture. As they anticipated, everyone they approached responded enthusiastically and volunteered on the spot.

Meanwhile, Pace and Pinetti asked all general managers to report on their existing environmental initiatives, to get baseline feedback on what individual hotels were doing already. They turned the results into a matrix they could use to identify gaps and monitor progress for each hotel.

They also sent out to all Kimpton directors of operations (regional managers) a briefing that laid out the communications strategy, including the mission statement, a description of the new eco-champions network, an overview of the phased roll-out of products and processes (see Exhibit 5), and a "talking points" document that explained to employees the benefits of the new program (see Exhibit 6).

NATIONAL ROLLOUT OF THE EARTHCARE PROGRAM

By February 2005, Kimpton's new network of eco-champions was in place, and everyone had agreed on the two basic ground rules for the transition: New initiatives couldn't cost more than what was already budgeted for operations and capital improvements, and they couldn't adversely affect customer perceptions or satisfaction. The ground rules also mandated that any new product or service could not cost more than the product or service it replaced. All leads, co-leads, and product specialists began meeting via conference call every Friday morning to discuss the greening initiative and share accounts of employee suggestions, progress achieved, and barriers encountered. One revelation that emerged early in the process was that, due to the uniqueness of each hotel and autonomous nature of the organization, all plans and proposals would have to be presented in a clear, concise package in order to ensure effective implementation.

To help communicate the program's goals and achievements, and help motivate employees seeking recognition, the team began to post regular updates and success stories in Kimpton's internal weekly newsletter, *The Word,* which was distributed throughout the organization and read by all general

Exhibit 5   **Rollout of Kimpton's EarthCare Program**

Phase I:

Phase I initiatives are designed to make hotel staff comfortable with the concept of greener management by introducing non-disruptive and cost-reducing operational practices.

- Recycling program ("Back of house")—Bottles, cans, paper, cardboard.
- Cleaning chemicals—Tub & tile cleaners, glass cleaners, deoderizers, and disinfectants all have to be switched to non-toxic, natural products.
- Promotional materials printed on recycled paper, using soy-based inks.
- Complimentary coffee served in lobbies every morning must be organically grown.
- Towel/linen reuse—Sheets and towels are replaced only at guest's request.

Phase II:

Hotels that successfully complete their implementation of Phase I initiatives will then move to Phase II, which focuses on investments in water and energy conservation, organically-grown cottons, and extending Phase I initiatives.

- Water conservation—Install 2.0 GPM sink aerators, 2.5 GPM showerheads, and phase in 1.6 GPF toilets.
- Energy conservation—Install motion sensors in rooms, fluorescent bulbs in corridors and back-of-house.
- Use recycled content paper for copying and notepads back-of-house, toilet paper and tissues in-room.
- Serve organic coffee in rooms and meeting rooms, organic tea in lobby.
- Switch to organic linens and towels, if feasible.

Phase III:

The most fundamental changes are anticipated when hotels are renovated and new hotels are acquired and converted. In addition to implementing Phases I and II, this will require extensive investment in building materials, labor, and appliances. The good news is that rooms can be designed, rather than retrofitted, to be more energy efficient, and green building materials can be ordered in larger quantities, thus lowering costs.

- Install only Energy Star rated appliances, computers, and electronic.
- Use only low-VOC paints.
- Install energy efficient lighting, heating, and air conditioning.

Exhibit 6   **Internal Talking Points Document**

Quick Facts on the Difference You Will Make . . .

Printing on 35% post consumer recycled paper: Kimpton will save:
- 24,000 pounds (12 tons) of wood
- 3,720 pounds (1.75 tons) of solid waste
- 7,260 pounds (3.6 tons) of CO_2 emissions
- 58,230,000 BTUs of total energy
  (Assumes 30 hotels participate using 1 case/5,000 sheets per month)

Using Green/Eco friendly cleaning products: Kimpton will:
- Improve worker productivity by between 0.5 percent and 5 percent by reducing cleaning supply toxins (U.S. institutions spend more than $75 million a year on medical expenses and lost time wages due to chemical-related injuries).
- Reduce environmental pollution as traditional cleaning products are responsible for approximately 8% of total non-vehicular emissions of volatile organic compounds (VOCs).

Recycling waste: Recycling 50% of hotel waste Kimpton properties will:
- Save over $250,000 per year in waste disposal costs.
- Reduce unnecessary landfill waste by over 100,000 gallons per year.
  (Assumes 30 hotels participate)

Recycling glass: Recycling 100 glass bottles/month, Kimpton will:
- Save the equivalent of powering one hundred 100-watt light bulbs for 1,440 hours (60 days).

Recycling aluminum: Recycling 20 Aluminum cans/day, Kimpton will:
- Save the equivalent of nearly 1,500 gallons of gas—enough to run a car for nearly three years.

managers. They also ran an EarthCare contest to further galvanize interest, which generated over 70 entries for categories such as "Best Eco-Practice Suggestion," "Most EarthCare Best Practices Adopted," and "Best Art and Humor Depicting EarthCare."

Potential benefits of the program became clear when the team of eco-product specialists began researching the availability of nontoxic cleaning agents. Common cleaning products such as furniture polish, carpet cleaner, spot remover, air fresheners, disinfectants and bleach can contain hazardous compounds such as toluene, naphthalene, trichloroethylene, benzene and nitrobenzene, phenol, chlorine, and xylene. These and other hazardous ingredients found in many cleaning products are associated with human health concerns including cancer, reproductive disorders, respiratory ailments, and eye or skin irritation. An EPA-funded study by the Western Regional Pollution Prevention Network found that 41 percent of all standard cleaning products they tested were potentially hazardous to the health of individuals using them. Cleaning chemicals could also include ozone-depleting substances and toxic materials that can accumulate in the environment and harm plant and animal life. The health

and environmental consequences for Kimpton were substantial, as one of its suppliers (Sierra Environmental) estimated that every housekeeping worker handled 60 pounds of cleaning agents per year. With an average of 15 room cleaners, times 39 hotels, it added up.

The eco-specialists learned that one of Kimpton's incumbent vendors did have a Green Seal–certified nontoxic line, but the products were selling at a 10–15 percent premium over standard products. They discovered that virtually every product they were interested in was more expensive than those currently used. At the extreme, eco-friendly paper products were priced 50 percent above standard products.

The eco-specialists knew that this would not satisfy the imperative that the greening initiative should not increase operating costs. Determined, they just kept going back to the vendors and asking them to keep working on it until they could supply a greener product of the same quality at the same, or lower, price. Eventually, existing or new vendors were able to meet these criteria, and now the typical hotel used eco-friendly products such as organic coffee and tea, air fresheners, and cleaning agents at no extra cost, and saved thousands of dollars a month by recycling waste materials that were previously shipped to landfills.

By 2005, the Internet had become a popular supply channel, with BuyEfficent.com emerging as the major online catalog from which hotels purchased their products. Assisting the eco-product specialists, consultant Jeff Slye discovered that it could be a nightmare getting the Web site to add new eco-vendors; more than once he had to personally obtain and supply vendor and product codes in order to purchase greener products through the site. While efforts such as these were time-consuming, part of the long-term payoff for the company and its eco-champions was knowing that they'd made it easier for the entire industry to follow in their footsteps.

The team of eco-champions also quickly learned that the national roll-out effort would have its share of potential operational risks and challenges which would need to be addressed. Among them:

- *Resistance by general managers to centralized imperatives*—Kimpton's culture of uniqueness and autonomy might be threatened by a green management program mandated by corporate headquarters. General managers might chafe at what they saw as corporate intrusion on their autonomy. They might see it as just the first step in a trend that would ultimately lead to centralization of the firm as a result of its rebranding effort. Local vendors and distributors might not offer green products. Search and acquisition costs might increase if general managers had to work with a broader range of vendors.

- *Resistance by hotel staff to new products and procedures*—Kimpton's relatively low turnover meant that some employees had been working there for many years, and had become accustomed to familiar ways of doing things. (Informal queries by management, for example, revealed that many cleaning staff equated strong chemical odors with cleanliness.) Also, many of the service staff did not speak English fluently and potetentially had difficulty understanding and accepting management's rationales for switching to new procedures or greener cleaning products.

- *Few tangible benefits, a slow payback period, or a low rate of return*—Unless informed, guests would not be aware that their rooms had been painted with low-VOC paints. Likewise, organic cottons were not likely to feel or look

superior to traditional materials. The gains in operating costs achieved by installing longer-life and more energy-efficient fluorescent lighting could take years to pay off, while higher acquisition costs could inflate short-term expenses. The same logic applied to water conservation investments. Would general managers be around to enjoy the benefits? Would corporate executives and investors be patient? What if consumer tastes or Kimpton's branding strategies changed before investments had paid off?

- *Investments that exceeded existing budgets or failed to meet the cost parity criterion*—Linens and towels made from organic cotton could cost at least 50 percent more than conventional products, and the initial cost of converting an average Kimpton hotel to organic cotton linens would run between $100,000 and $150,000. Other environmentally friendly products, such as environmentally friendly carpeting and draperies and sustainable flooring, would also have a price premium. Would additional budget be provided? Would savings in other areas be allowed to pay for it?

- *Marketing challenges*—How should the Earth-Care program be promoted, given customer concerns regarding the impact of some environmental initiatives on the quality of their guest experience? Guests might be concerned, for example, about whether low-flow showerheads or fluorescent lighting would meet their expectations. Environmental awareness and concern varied considerably by geographic region, from very high on the West Coast and in the Northeast, to considerably lower in the South and Midwest. Would this affect customer perceptions and demand? Would the program affect the quality rating of Kimpton's hotels? According to the American Automobile Association's Diamond Rating Guidelines, some water-saving showerheads and energy-saving lightbulbs could lower a hotel's diamond rating.[9] Eventually, information about the EarthCare program was to be disseminated through Kimpton's Web site, guest directory, and sales brochures that would go to travel agents, corporate travel planners, and meeting planners. Should the program be marketed more aggressively?

- *Regional differences in recycling infrastructure and regulatory environment*—California had a mandated recycling program requiring

70 percent recycling of solid waste by 2007, so San Francisco's disposal service provided free recycling containers. Other localities might not be so generous.

Even in the face of these challenges, Kimpton executives believed that the EarthCare program was the smart, as well as the right, thing to do. According to Tom LaTour, chairman and CEO:

> It's good business. It's not just because we're altruistic, it's good for business. Otherwise the investors would say, what are you guys doing? A lot of people think it's going to cost more. It's actually advantageous to be eco-friendly than not.

Niki Leondakis, chief operating officer, saw the program's impact on marketing and employee retention:

> Many people say we're heading toward a tipping point: If you're not environmentally conscious, your company will be blackballed from people's choices. Also, employees today want to come to work every day not just for the paycheck but to feel good about what they're doing. . . . It's very important to them to be aligned with the values of the people they work for, so from the employee retention standpoint, this helps us retain and attract them so we can select from the best and the brightest.[10]

Investors appeared to be happy with Kimpton's efforts to manage their properties in a more sustainable manner, as the firm announced a new round of financing in June 2005. Private investors poured $157 million into the company for a new wave of expansion and renovation. Yale University put up most of the funds, making an investment valued at close to 1 percent of its $12.7 billion endowment.

By July 2005, Phase I of the EarthCare initiative had been successfully implemented at all Kimpton hotels. The percentage of waste materials recycled at its hotels in San Francisco had gone from 10–20 percent to over 50 percent (by volume) since the program's inception. Chemical cleaning agents were no longer used in any of Kimpton's hotel rooms. Every hotel served organic coffee in its lobby and printed promotional materials on recycled paper with soy-based ink. The challenges of Phase II lay ahead.

Endnotes

[1]Gene Sloan, "Let the Pillowfights Begin," *USA Today,* August 27, 2004.
[2]California Green Lodging Program, www. Ciwmb.ca.gov/epp.
[3]Fairmont Hotels & Resorts, *The Green Partnership Guide,* 2nd ed., 2001.
[4]Cathy A. Enz, and Judy A. Siguaw, "Best Hotel Environmental Practices," *Cornell Hotel and Restaurant Administartion Quarterly,* October 1999.
[5]Robyn Parets, National Real Estate Investor, www.nreionline.com, March 2005.

[6]Liz French, Americanexecutive.com, December 2004.
[7]"Boutique Meets Lifestyle as Kimpton Hotels Let the Secret Out with Launch of National Brand Campaign," Kimpton Hotels press release.
[8]Ryan Tate, "Kimpton Hotels Remakes Its Beds," *San Francisco Business Times,* January 28, 2005.
[9]*AAA Lodging Requirements & Diamond Rating Guidelines* (Heathrow, FL: AAA Publishing, June 2001).
[10]Carlo Wolff, "Environmental Evangelism: Kimpton Walks the Eco-Walk," *Lodging Hospitality,* March 1, 2005.

Case 33

Monsanto and the Genetic Engineering of Agricultural Seeds

Lisa Johnson
The University of Puget Sound

"This field's planted in mustard. That field's planted in oats," Percy Schmeiser explained on the windy summer 2005 day. "We can't plant canola anymore, on account of the volunteer plants. Our entire fields are contaminated with Monsanto's patent, so we just don't grow that anymore." As Schmeiser gazed over his fields in central Saskatchewan, he continued, "I remember in 1947 when a chemical representative came out here and met with my father. I was right there in that meeting. He told us if we would use his chemical herbicide, why, we'd never have to worry about weeds again. Those were in the days when chemical farming was just unheard of, and we all farmed using the traditional knowledge that had been accumulated over the years. No one needed chemicals. Today, our fields are so saturated with chemicals that a field requires a fair bit of preparatory work before it is even suitable for planting from year to year."

Schmiser continued: "With the introduction of genetically modified crops, Monsanto tells the young farmers when to spray, what to spray, what to plant, when to plant. The younger generation doesn't know anything of the farming methods of their fathers. There's a young farmer in this community who follows Monsanto's instructions and I said to him, 'Your father was one of the best farmers that this province had ever seen. Why don't you just follow

what you learned from him?' He doesn't know how to answer that. I asked him, 'Does Monsanto also tell you when it's going to rain?' He didn't like that comment too much." Percy chuckled.[1]

While Percy Schmeiser checked on his fields, Monsanto Company's legal department was wrestling with another suspected case of patent infringement. The company, which was a leading producer of genetically engineered agricultural products with 2005 revenues of approximately $6.3 billion, was highly committed to protecting its patents. The company's managers believed that farmers who had paid a technology fee for the use of patented products expected Monsanto to prevent other farmers from growing crops from Monsanto seeds without paying a fee. Even though there were cases of farmers deliberately acquiring and growing patented genetically modified organisms (GMOs) without paying a technology fee, there were unintentional natural causes of farmers improperly possessing patented Monsanto plants. Studies had shown that seeds from some types of patented plants could drift as far as 13 miles in heavy winds. In addition, some legal scholars had suggested that the existence of stray seeds constituted trespass or negligence on the part of the patent holder.

The decision to sue farmers was not taken lightly. "It is . . . [an] uncomfortable [position] for us," said Scott Baucum, Monsanto's chief intellectual property protector. "They are our customers, and they are important to us."[2] With 70 percent of all processed food in the United States being grown from genetically engineered plants and the percentage increasing each year, it seemed that Baucum and other chief managers at Monsanto would be forced to either pursue patent infringement cases on an increasingly regular basis or develop less aggressive patent protection measures.

PLANT HUSBANDRY: A BRIEF PRIMER

Civilizations historically relied on open-germination seeds to propagate the food supply in subsequent horticultural generations. Seeds could be saved from year to year, and since open-pollination plants had large gene pools, they were known for their stability and disease resistance. Hybridization, developed in the late 19th century, improved the reliability of food production by making plants stronger and more resistant and provided ownership interests in portions of the food supply. Genetically modified (GM) agricultural products were a relatively new technology, appearing in North American markets in the 1990s. GM agricultural technology provided resistance to herbicides, increased yield, and improved appearance of food. Developers of GM agricultural products were granted patents that provided a legal monopoly of the patented product and created incentives for further advancements in agricultural research and development. However, despite technological advances in agricultural production, one child died every five seconds from hunger and related causes.[3]

GENETICALLY MODIFIED ORGANISMS AND THE GLOBAL FOOD SUPPLY

In 2005, 85 percent of all soybeans in the United States were genetically engineered and subject to patent ownership.[4] Seventy percent of all processed food consumed by Americans and virtually all domestic animal feed in the United States came from genetically modified products.[5] At least 25 percent of all corn and 60 percent of all soybeans harvested in the United States, and more than 100 million acres of farmland worldwide were planted in genetically modified crops.[6] At least 200 million acres of biotech crops were planted in 2004, and the percentage of farmland in bioengineered crops had increased sharply every year.[7]

Much of the world's population relied on local farmers to save seeds from year to year. Annually, more than 1.4 billion people were fed from the food resulting from seed-saving farmers. Opponents of GM agricultural products feared that patent ownership may have threatened the rights of farmers worldwide to save seed. Many seed-saving farmers could not afford the technology fee or defend against lawsuits brought by patent-owning corporations.

Many countries that had resisted genetically modified crops had been pressured by the United States, and in some cases bribed by GM plant patent owners, to rethink their positions. Lifting the European Union (EU) ban on genetically modified plants had become a matter of U.S. national strategic priority, and, through pressure exerted by the United States, the EU reluctantly lifted the ban in 2004.[8] After the repeal of its ban on GMOs, the EU also unenthusiastically demanded that Austria, Luxembourg, France, Germany, and Greece all lift national bans.[9] The European commissioners felt they had "no alternative" but to "fulfill their legal obligations" and force through the decision to lift the ban, despite widespread opposition among its members' populations.[10] India, reluctantly, and Brazil had allowed this technology into their countries as well.[11] In 2005, Monsanto was fined $1.5 million by the U.S. Securities and Exchange Commission for bribing an Indonesian environmental official to permit genetically modified crops in Indonesia.[12]

MONSANTO AND ROUND-UP READY PATENTS

Monsanto was a global supplier of agricultural products whose revenues of $6.3 billion in 2005 were generated by two primary business units. Its Seeds and Genomics business unit developed, produced, and marketed DEKALB, Asgrow, Bollgard, and Roundup Ready brands of genetically engineered

Exhibit 1   **Financial Summary for Monsanto Company, Fiscal 2000–Fiscal 2005 (dollar amounts in millions, except per share and pro forma share amounts)**

	12 Months Ended Aug. 31,			Eight Months Ended Aug. 31,*		Year Ended Dec. 31,		
	2005	**2004**	**2003**	**2003**	**2002**	**2002**	**2001**	**2000**
Operating results								
Net sales	$ 6,294	$ 5,423	$ 4,924	$ 3,378	$ 3,129	$ 4,674	$ 5,450	$ 5,457
Income from operations	742	603	676	483	151	344	672	567
Income from continuing operations	157	266	98	—	48	146	318	196
Income (loss) on discontinued operations	98	1	(18)	(11)	(11)	(17)	(23)	(21)
Cumulative effect of a change in accounting principle	—	—	(12)	(12)	(1,822)	(1,822)	—	(26)
Net income (loss)	255	267	68	(23)	(1,785)	(1,693)	295	149
Basic earnings (loss) per share and per pro forma share								
Income from continuing operations	$ 0.59	$ 1.01	$ 0.37	$ —	$ 0.18	$ 0.56	$ 1.23	$ 0.76
Income (loss) on discontinued operations	0.37	—	(0.06)	(0.04)	(0.04)	(0.07)	(0.09)	(0.08)
Cumulative effect of accounting change	—	—	(0.05)	(0.05)	(7.00)	(6.99)	—	(0.10)
Net income (loss)	0.96	1.01	0.26	(0.09)	(6.86)	(6.50)	1.14	0.58
Diluted earnings (loss) per share and per pro forma share								
Income from continuing operations	$ 0.58	$ 0.99	$ 0.37	$ —	$ 0.18	$ 0.56	$ 1.21	$ 0.76
Income (loss) on discontinued operations	0.36	—	(0.06)	(0.04)	(0.04)	(0.07)	(0.09)	(0.08)
Cumulative effect of accounting change	—	—	(0.05)	(0.05)	(6.92)	(6.94)	—	(0.10)
Net income (loss)	0.94	0.99	0.26	(0.09)	(6.78)	(6.45)	1.12	0.58
Financial position at end of period								
Total assets	$10,579	$ 9,164	$ 9,536	$ 9,536	$ 9,175	$ 8,949	$11,454	$11,731
Working capital	2,485	3,037	2,920	2,920	2,804	2,537	2,373	2,213
Current ratio	2.15:1	2.60:1	2.45:1	2.45:1	2.62:1	2.36:1	1.99:1	1.80:1
Long-term debt	1,458	1,075	1,258	1,258	1,148	851	893	962
Debt-to-capital	24%	22%	23%	23%	27%	19%	19%	19%
Other data (applicable for periods subsequent to IPO)								
Dividends per share	$0.68	$0.68	$0.49	$0.25	$0.24	$0.48	$0.48	$0.09

(*Continued*)

Exhibit 1 Continued

	12 Months Ended Aug. 31,			Eight Months Ended Aug. 31,*		Year Ended Dec. 31,		
	2005	2004	2003	2003	2002	2002	2001	2000
Stock price per share:								
High	$69.23	$38.50	$26.35	$26.35	$33.29	$33.290	$38.800	$27.380
Low	34.15	23.08	13.55	13.55	13.01	13.010	26.875	19.750
End of period	63.84	36.60	25.71	25.71	18.37	19.130	33.800	27.060
Basic shares outstanding	266.8	264.4	261.6	261.7	260.3	260.7	258.1	258.0
Diluted shares outstanding	272.7	269.2	261.8	262.1	263.2	262.6	263.6	258.5

*Monsanto Company changed its fiscal year end from December 31 to August 31, effective August 31, 2003. Year-to-year comparisons between 2002 and 2003 should be done using the eight month ending data for those two years.

Source: Monsanto Company 2005 10-K report.

seeds. Monsanto's Agricultural Productivity business segment created and sold herbicides such as Roundup and genetically engineered products that, for instance, increased milk production in dairy cows. Exhibit 1 presents a summary of Monsanto's financial performance between 2000 and 2005. Exhibits 2 and 3 show the revenue and gross profit contributions of each business unit and key product categories.

Monsanto sold GM canola seeds in Canada and GM soybean seeds in the United States. Its patents in Canada covered genetically modified cells and genes contained in canola plants, and U.S. patents protected all GM soybeans produced from biolistics, which is a technique for inserting GM genes into cells. The Canadian canola patents specifically covered "the gene and the process for its insertion . . . and the cell

Exhibit 2 Sales and Gross Profit Contributions for Monsanto's Seeds and Genomics Business Segment, Fiscal 2001–Fiscal 2005 (in millions)

	12 Months Ended Aug. 31,			Eight Months Ended Aug. 31,		Year Ended Dec. 31,	
	2005	2004	2003	2003	2002	2002	2001
Net sales							
Corn seed and traits	$1,494	$1,145	$ 959	$ 592	$ 366	$ 734	$ 688
Soybean seed and traits	889	699	591	270	251	572	670
Vegetable and fruit seed	226	—	—	—	—	—	—
All other crops seeds and traits	643	476	371	322	247	295	375
Total net sales	$3,252	$2,320	$1,921	$1,184	$ 864	$1,601	$ 1,733
Gross profit							
Corn seed and traits	$ 825	$ 638	$ 505	$ 282	$ 117	$341	$ 298
Soybean seed and traits	613	429	334	127	103	310	384
Vegetable and fruit seed	113	—	—	—	—	—	—
All other crops seeds and traits	431	302	234	213	156	176	174
Total gross profit	$1,982	$1,369	$1,073	$ 622	$ 376	$ 827	$ 856
EBIT	$ 374	$ 196	$ 182	$ 17	$(2,254)	$(2,088)	$ (241)

Source: Monsanto Company 2005 10-K report.

Exhibit 3   **Sales and Gross Profit Contributions for Monsanto's Agricultural Productivity Business Segment, Fiscal 2001–Fiscal 2005 (in millions)**

	12 Months Ended August 31			Ended August 31		Year Ended December 31	
	2005	2004	2003	2003	2002	2002	2001
Net sales							
Roundup and other glyphosate-based herbicides	$2,049	$2,005	$1,844	$1,349	$1,393	$1,888	$ 2,488
All other agricultural productivity products	993	1,098	1,159	845	872	1,185	1,229
Total net sales	$3,042	$3,103	$3,003	$2,194	$2,265	$3,073	$ 3,717
Gross profit							
Roundup and other glyphosate-based herbicides	$ 637	$ 703	$ 695	$ 533	$ 661	$ 823	$ 1,234
All other agricultural productivity products	385	455	505	397	389	496	500
Total gross profit	$1,022	$1,158	$1,200	$ 930	$1,050	$1,319	$ 1,734
EBIT	$ (27)	$ 249	$ (24)	$ (33)	$ 353	$ 362	$ 760

Source: Monsanto Company 2005 10-K report.

derived from that process," which were glyphosate-resistant.[13] In Canada, Monsanto did not claim protection for the entire GM plant, but only for those genes and cells.[14] In the United States, Monsanto's patent covered the entire plant.

Roundup, an herbicide manufactured by Monsanto, contained glyphosate. Many generic herbicides also contained glyphosate. Unless they were genetically modified to be glyphosate-resistant, plants died when they were sprayed with Roundup. Monsanto Roundup Ready GM plants had increased resistance to glyphosate. Indeed, this was a stated object of the patented invention.[15] Genetically modified plants could not be distinguished from other plants on sight, but plants that did not die after being sprayed with Roundup were presumed to contain the patented GM cells or genes.[16] Monsanto marketed GM canola plants as Roundup Ready Canola and GM soybean plants as Roundup Ready Soybeans. Those names aptly implied that canola and soybean plants that emerged from seeds containing the patented gene or cell would survive a Roundup spraying, and that plants that did not contain the Roundup Ready patented gene or cell would die. Roundup Ready Canola and Roundup Ready Soybean plants were open-pollination plants. Their seeds could be saved from year to year and their progeny would display the same characteristics of the parent plants. In addition,

genetically modified plants such as Roundup Ready Canola or Roundup Ready Soybean plants could cross-pollinate with non-GM plants and the progeny would be genetically modified.

Farmers who wished to plant Roundup Ready Canola were required to sign a limited-use license agreement with Monsanto. This agreement allowed a one-time planting, prohibited seed saving, and allowed Monsanto to inspect farmers' fields to take samples for three years after the expiration of the agreement.[17] Similarly, Monsanto's Technology Use Guide expressly allowed Monsanto and its agents to enter on farmers' lands to take samples to verify compliance with the licensing agreement.[18] Monsanto contended that its licensing agreements protected its patents and ensured a return on its $400 million annual research expense.[19]

MONSANTO'S APPROACH TO PATENT PROTECTION

In 2005, Monsanto dominated large portions of the agricultural seed market with genetically modified seeds that gave rise to plants that were more resistant to disease and herbicides and provided higher yields than naturally occurring plants. The company had pressed its ownership claims successfully through the courts against both Canadian and U.S. farmers who had been found in possession of the GM agricultural products without a license. Courts in both countries had concluded that patented plants, and plants containing a patented gene or cell, were owned by the patent holder regardless of how those plants happened to arrive on private land, and regardless of whether the owner of that land consented or even had knowledge of their presence.

Given those court decisions, it appeared that intellectual property rights had trumped common law rights over agricultural products. Common law property rights supported the customary and age-old practice of seed saving for food security. Yet patent holders had effectively usurped this right with the introduction of patented plants, genes, and cells that contaminated the lands of farmers who did not wish for that technology to be present on those lands. Courts had upheld patent holders' claims against unsuspecting farmers for patent infringement, at great financial and emotional costs to the farmers. The courts had been reluctant to address those controversies through the lens of common law property rights or tort analysis, and favored as a threshold inquiry the intellectual property analysis. In other words, if there was a patent owner, then that was the end of the analysis, and the patent owner's legal monopoly over that product was protected.

Patent owners, like Monsanto, solicited information from members of farming communities about suspected patent infringement. In exchange for promotional items or free agricultural products, farmers who suspected that other farmers in their area were using agricultural products containing the patent were encouraged to call a hotline and report their suspicions.[20] This report would launch an inquiry by investigators hired by the patent owner—frequently retired police officers or retired Royal Canadian Mounted Police in Canada. Those investigations would include visiting the suspect farmers' homes, taking plants out of the farmers' fields—with or without permission of the farmer—and sending settlement letters to the farmer. Settlement terms demanded a payment for damages, frequently ranging from $25,000 to $50,000. These figures far exceeded the resources of most farmers, who often owed mortgages and other secured debts on their farm equipment.

Monsanto's patent protection policy had serious effects on farming communities. Built on generations of trust and long histories of family relationships, farming communities were suddenly divided by suspicion and fear. Sometimes farmers would report other farmers out of spite from some long-standing dispute unrelated to genetically modified crops, not out of factual evidence.

Farmers also were aware of the great financial and personal consequences suffered by the few farmers who had chosen to fight the legal charges leveled against them by Monsanto. Reports of serious health effects—such as stress-induced heart attacks and injuries resulting from lack of sleep—were not uncommon. Many defendant farmers who had equity in their property eventually mortgaged their homes, lands, and equipment simply to fight the lawsuit. The farmers' fears of losing their homes, health, and lands encouraged farmers accused of patent infringement to settle rather than to argue against Monsanto's contention.

PERCY SCHMEISER'S LEGAL TROUBLES WITH MONSANTO

Monsanto tested the validity of its Roundup Ready Canola patent under Canadian law in 1998 with a case against Percy Schmeiser. Schmeiser had farmed his land in Saskatchewan, Canada, for more than 50 years and was known as a seed saver and seed developer in his community.[21] He also used open-pollination seed on his land.[22, 23] Mr. Schmeiser primarily grew canola commercially, but he also kept some acreage in peas and wheat.[24] He farmed conventionally, not organically.[25] Schmeiser not only farmed but also had served as a member of the Canadian Parliament, as the mayor of his community, and on several federal and provincial agricultural committees.[26]

In 1996, five other farmers in Schmeiser's area planted Roundup Ready Canola.[27] Schmeiser did not plant Roundup Ready Canola but instead planted his own seed saved from prior harvests in his fields, which had been his practice for many decades. His own seed had been developed over his many years of farming, and was unique, hardy, and disease-resistant.[28] Schmeiser was proud of the superior performance of the seed he had developed.[29]

In the spring of 1997, he planted seeds saved from his 1996 harvest. As was customary, he sprayed approximately three acres in ditches and around power poles with Roundup and was puzzled by the number of "volunteer" plants, or plants that did not die. The power company paid Schmeiser approximately $120 to perform that service each year. He estimated that 60 percent of the canola plants were unaffected by the Roundup spraying.[30] Schmeiser did not spray to isolate any GM plants, but instead sprayed because it is a common practice among Saskatchewan canola farmers to chemically burn off, or "chem fallow," the field before spring planting or between growing seasons.[31]

In 1997, Monsanto agents heard a rumor that Schmeiser might have grown Roundup Ready Canola without a license.[32] An investigator hired by Monsanto took samples from the public road allowance bordering Schmeiser's land after that area had been sprayed with Roundup, and confirmed that those plants were Roundup Ready.[33] Monsanto put Schmeiser on notice of its belief that he had grown Roundup Ready Canola without a license. Schmeiser denied the allegation, stating that he had never purchased[34] and never intended to grow Roundup Ready Canola.

In 1998, Schmeiser planted his acreage with those seeds saved from his 1997 harvest.[35] He did not spray his crop with Roundup. Monsanto again took samples from the public road allowance bordering Schmeiser's land, and because Roundup Ready Canola was found, Monsanto filed a complaint against Schmeiser alleging patent infringement.[36] The lawsuit against Schmeiser eventually depleted all of his retirement funds of $200,000.[37] Exhibit 4 describes the lawsuit, including the Federal Court of Appeals and the Supreme Court of Canada's reasoning and the holding.

MONSANTO'S LEGAL PURSUIT OF PATENT INFRINGEMENT

After the Schmeiser case, many American farmers who saved genetically modified seeds settled with

or had judgments entered in favor of Monsanto. According to the Center for Food Safety's *Monsanto v. U.S. Farmer Report of 2005,*[38] several cases have resulted in judgments and settlements against farmers totaling in the millions of dollars. For example, a judgment in excess of $3 million was entered against Richard Anderson, a Texas farmer. A judgment against Ray Dawson, a Missouri farmer, was entered for more than $2.5 million. Not only was a judgment of more than $2 million entered against Kem Ralph, a Tennessee farmer, but Ralph was also sentenced to eight months in prison after he was caught lying about a hidden truckload of cottonseed. This was the first criminal prosecution associated with Monsanto's "seed wars." Interestingly, in *Monsanto Co. v. Mc-Farling,*[39] the liquidated damages clause requiring farmers to pay 120 times the technology fee was held to be unenforceable under Missouri law because it was a penalty rather than damages.[40] That farmer would likely end up paying Monsanto about $10,000 instead of $780,000 after the lower court computed the actual damages the farmer caused Monsanto.[41]

By 2005, Monsanto had filed multiple lawsuits in half of the U.S. states involving 147 farmers and 39 small farm businesses.[42] It maintained an annual budget of $10 million and 75 full-time employees "devoted solely to investigating and prosecuting farmers."[43] The company had won more than $15 million in judgments against farmers in the United States, ranging from $5,000 to more than $3 million and annually investigated about 500 tips that farmers were illegally using its seed.[44, 45] Exhibits 5 and 6 provide an overview of U.S. and Canadian Patent Law regarding genetically modified organisms.

THE NATURAL SPREAD OF GENETICALLY ENGINEERED PLANTS

In 2005, the Montana legislature considered the Farmer Limited Liability for Genetically Engineered Wheat Act, which ultimately failed. This bill would have shielded Montana wheat farmers from lawsuits and would have prevented patent holding companies from suing farmers for patent infringement if genetically engineered wheat drifted across property lines

Exhibit 4   **Background on the *Monsanto v. Schmeiser* Case**

Monsanto filed a complaint against Percy Schmeiser alleging patent infringement.[a] The trial court rejected Schmeiser's argument that the Roundup Ready Canola was the result of a natural occurrence, such as wind, because of the concentration of the Roundup Ready Canola discovered. It also noted that Schmeiser should have known that it was Roundup Ready Canola when he discovered that some plants on his land were Roundup tolerant.[b] The court also rejected Schmeiser's argument that the patent was invalid because the subject of its protection—i.e., entire plants—was not patentable. The trial court ruled in favor of Monsanto by concluding that the patent was valid, and that Schmeiser committed patent infringement because he knew, or should have known, that he saved and planted seed containing the patented genes and cells of Roundup Ready Canola.

After the Federal Court of Appeal upheld the trial court's ruling, Schmeiser appealed.[c] The Supreme Court of Canada held that the patent was valid, and that Schmeiser committed patent infringement when he saved and planted the seed, then harvested and sold the plants that contained the patented cells and genes.[d]

The Supreme Court found that it was irrelevant whether Schmeiser intended to infringe on the patent or whether Schmeiser knew about the patented product on his land, because "it is a settled issue in Canadian patent law that intention is irrelevant to infringement,"[e] though the presumption of use is rebuttable.[f] The court acknowledged that the plants containing the patented product could have been the result of pollen that blew onto Schmeiser's land but found that the manner in which the Roundup Ready Canola product got onto Mr. Schmeiser's land was irrelevant. The Court specifically declined to address the "innocent discovery by farmers of "blow-by" patented plants on their land or in their cultivated fields . . . [or] . . . the scope of the . . . patent or the wisdom and social utility of the genetic modification of genes and cells."[g]

Since Canada's Patent Act confers on the patent owner "the exclusive right, privilege and liberty of making, constructing and using the invention and selling it to others to be used,"[h] the only relevant inquiry was whether Schmeiser "used" the genetically modified plants and seeds and whether Schmeiser's acts interfered with the exclusive rights granted by the patent.[i] The Supreme Court found that Mr. Schmeiser "used" the patent and interfered with the exclusive rights granted by the patent to Monsanto, and affirmed the lower courts' rulings. The court held that "by cultivating a plant containing the patented gene and composed of the patented cells without license, [Schmeiser] deprived the respondents of the full enjoyment of the monopoly" created by the patent.[j] However, the damages awarded to Monsanto by the lower court were reversed, because Schmeiser did not earn profit from the use of the patented product, since he did not use Roundup herbicide on those plants.

According to the Court, despite the fact that Monsanto's patent only protects the genetically modified cell or gene, infringement does not require use of the cell or gene in isolation.[k] Indeed, if a plant containing a genetically modified cell or gene propagates, grows and is used by a nonlicensee farmer—even though the presence of the plant is unknown to the farmer—the farmer has committed patent infringement. Also, even though the object of the patent is to provide glyphosate-resistance, lack of use of Roundup herbicide is irrelevant. In other words, patent infringement can exist whether or not the unauthorized "user" of the patent utilizes the patent for its purpose.

When addressing whether a volunteer plant could appropriately fall under the patent's protection even though the Canadian patent was not intended to protect whole plants, the Court noted that "infringement is possible . . . [when] the patented invention is [only] part of . . . a broader unpatented structure or process." The Court was persuaded by the firm principle that "the main purpose of patent protection is to prevent others from depriving the inventor, even in part and even indirectly, of the monopoly that the law intends to be theirs: only the inventor is entitled, by virtue of the patent and as a matter of law, to the full enjoyment of the monopoly conferred."[l]

[a]*Monsanto Canada, Inc. v. Schmeiser* [2001] FTC 256.

[b]Ibid.

[c]*Schmeiser v. Monsanto Canada* [2004] SCC 34.

[d]Ibid.

[e]Ibid., The court also cites *Stead v. Anderson* (1847), 4 C.B. 806, 136 Eng. Rep. 724 (C.P.), at p. 736. The issue is "what the defendant does, not . . . what he intends," at para. 49.

[f]Ibid. at para. 56.

[g]Ibid. at para. 2.

[h]Ibid. at para. 25.

[i]Ibid.

[j]Ibid.

[k]Ibid.

[l]Ibid. at para. 43.

Exhibit 5   **Overview of Canadian Patent Law**

Canada stands virtually alone among developed countries in its nonrecognition of the patentability of higher life forms. However, Canada is well within its international rights to exclude the patentability of higher life forms. The World Trade Organization's Agreement on Trade-Related Aspects of Intellectual Property (TRIPs) allows the exclusion of animals and plants from patentability.[a] Not only does Canada exercise this right of exclusion, but this right is also typically embraced by developing nations, while other countries, notably the United States, may wish to limit or eliminate the exclusion.[b]

Despite the fact that Canada does not allow higher life forms to be patented, the Schmeiser decision, by a 5–4 majority, suggests that patent holders of components of higher life forms have found a way around this barrier. This decision does an apparent end run around the prohibition against patenting higher life forms by finding patent infringement in cases where a nonlicensee possesses a whole that contains a patented part. This effectively provides monopolistic protection of the whole to patent holders of the part, even though such patents are not permitted under law. The Schmeiser dissent astutely noted that "allowing gene and cell claims to extend patent protection to plants renders this provision of TRIPs meaningless. To find that possession of plants, as the embodiment of a gene or cell claim, constitutes a "use" of that claim would have the same effect as patenting the plants."[c] Aside from the Schmeiser decision, commentators have noted that the Canadian practice of issuing patents to protect the cells of plants, instead of the entire plant, has the same effect as patenting the entire plant.[d]

[a]World Trade Organization, Agreement on Trade-Related Aspects of Intellectual Property, Art. 27.3 (b).
[b]"Patenting of Higher Life Forms and Related Issues: Report to the Government of Canada Biotechnology Ministerial Coordinating Committee" June 2002, available at http://cbac-cccb.ca/epic/internet/incbac-cccb.nsf/en/ah00213e.html (accessed April 15, 2005).
[c]*Schmeiser v. Monsanto Canada* [2004] SCC 34, at para 167.
[d]Lenni Carreiro, "The Supreme Court of Canada Finds Higher Life Forms Not Patentable Subject Matter," March 19, 2003, available at www.dww.com/articles/higher_life_forms.htm (accessed April 15, 2005).

and was found on the land of farmers who did not intentionally grow it.

The *New York Times* reported that a study by the Environmental Protection Agency (EPA) found that genetically engineered creeping bentgrass could spread for miles, could pollinate test plants of the same species as far away as measured (which was 13 miles downwind), and could pollinate natural wild grass of a different species nine miles away. Previous studies indicated it could only pollinate between different varieties no more than one mile away. The Bureau of Land Management and the Forest Service opposed this product because it "ha[d] the potential to adversely impact all 175 national forests and grasslands." The Department of Agriculture had decided to complete an environmental impact statement to determine whether or not to allow the plant to be commercialized.[46] However, advocates of genetically modified agricultural plants argue that soybeans and canola do not contain the same risk, because the creeping bentgrass of the study had extraordinarily light pollen.

A large-scale study conducted in Great Britain concerning its largest crop, winter rape, indicated that wildlife suffered as a result of GM crops. The herbicide sprayed on the crops that killed the weeds resulted in one-third fewer seeds for birds and wildlife to eat than the seeds available after a conventional crop. Even when the herbicide was not sprayed again, there were still 25 percent fewer seeds for wildlife.[47]

TERMINATOR SEED TECHNOLOGY AND PATENT PROTECTION

Sterile seed technology—or "terminator seed"—self-destructs after one generation. That invention effectively would prohibit farmers from saving their seed from year to year, because the seed of the harvest would not be fertile, and it would protect the patent owners from patent infringement by protecting its patented invention and limiting the use of its invention to licensees only.

The danger of terminator seeds lay in the fact that genetically modified organisms had not been contained to only licensee farmers' lands. The GMO

Exhibit 6   **Overview of U.S. Patent Law**

The United States allows patents on higher life forms, including both plants and animals.[a] For example, a patent was granted by the U.S. Patent and Trademark Office (PTO) for the OncoMouse,[b] a genetically modified cancer-prone mouse, as early as 1988. Indeed, patents have been granted over many higher life forms.[c]

Those decisions were not made in a legal void. Since the 1980 Supreme Court decision in *Diamond v. Chakrabarty,*[d] inroads have been laid to allow the patentability of higher life forms in the United States. In that case, the subject matter was a bacteria engineered to break down crude oil components. Patent protection was allowed, after the PTO initially denied the patent because U.S. patent protection, at that time, did not extend to living things. The Patent Appeals Court reversed, and proclaimed that "the fact that microorganisms are alive is a distinction without legal significance for patent law." The Supreme Court affirmed, stating that "a live, human-made microorganism is patentable subject matter . . . [The inventor's] discovery is not nature's handiwork, but his own . . . [and] anything under the sun that is made by man" is patentable.[e]

After *Chakrabarty,* seeds were subsequently deemed patentable subject matter.[f] In 1987, the PTO announced that "non-naturally occurring, non-human, multi-cellular living organisms, including animals" were patentable subject matter.[g]

In 2001, the Supreme Court held in *J.E.M. Ag Supply v. Pioneer Hi-Bred International* that farmers could not save seed that is the subject matter of a general utility patent, including genetically modified seed. That decision effectively invalidated the protections afforded under the Plant Variety Protection Act of 1970, which allowed farmers to save the seed from sexually reproducible plants without violating the rights held by the developers of new plant varieties.[h]

U.S. courts have consistently upheld patent infringement claims against farmers who have saved GM seeds intentionally, or who unknowingly possessed GM plants on their land. However, interesting dicta in the concurring opinion in *Smithkline Beecham Corp. v. Apotex,*[i] indicates perhaps a willingness by some members of the judiciary to rethink the legal implications of wholesale patent protection for products resulting from the escape of genetically modified organisms. "[T]he implication—that the patent owner would be entitled to collect royalties from every farmer whose cornfields contained even a few patented . . . stalks . . . cannot possibly be correct."[j]

[a]"Patenting Higher Life Forms Report."

[b]Granted in 1988 to Harvard geneticist Philip Leder and Timothy Steward of the University of California, San Francisco.

[c]See e.g., *Ex Parte Allen* 2 U.S.P.Q.2d (BNA) 1425 (Bd. Pat. App. & Int. 1987), *aff'd,* 846 F.2d 77 (Fed. Cir. 1988) (oysters)

[d]*Diamond v. Chakrabarty,* 447 US 303 (1980).

[e]Ibid.

[f]*Ex parte Hibberd,* 227 U.S.P.Q. (BNA) 443 (Bd. App. & Int., 1985).

[g]L. J. Deftos, "Patenting Life: Mighty OncoMouse Squeaks About the Ethics of Biopatents," *Endocrine News* 29, no. 1 (February 2004), available at www.endo-society.org/news/endocrine_news/2004/EthicsCorner-Feb2004.cfm (accessed April 15, 2005).

[h]*J.E.M. Ag Supply v. Pioneer Hi-Bred Int'l,* 534 U.S. 124 (2001).

[i]*Smithkline Beecham Corp. v. Apotex,* 365 F.3d 1306 (Fed. Cir. 2004).

[j]Ibid.

technology had contaminated neighboring farms, and destroyed those farms' own lines of open-pollination seed with the GM gene or cell. Terminator seed technology could threaten nonlicensee seed-saving farmers' future crops by effectively sterilizing the seeds of harvests from which seeds would normally be saved.

The world had not yet embraced terminator technology, despite lobbying by large agricultural companies and trade associations. Some countries had also pressed forward with their support. For example, Canada favored terminator seed technology, but at the March 2005 United Nations Conference in Bangkok, the technology was narrowly shelved for more research.[48]

LEGAL AND ETHICAL DEFENSES TO CHARGES OF PATENT INFRINGEMENT BY FARMERS

Intellectual property rights have seemingly trumped common law property rights in the area of GM plants. The intellectual property threshold question of patent infringement had effectively foreclosed analyses under common-law property rights and tort claims. However, nonlicensee or seed-saving farmers facing patent infringement litigation could consider counterclaims and legal defenses under common law theories. For a farmer to be successful in a tort claim, he or she must show some type of physical harm. Genetic contamination of nonlicensee farmers' land could constitute trespass or negligence among other claims.

The Stray Bull Theory

Landowners had the right to claim ownership over what is found on their land. This was an ancient tradition firmly rooted and recognized at common law. What was attached to one's land could not belong to another. Historically, for example, crops, which were part of the land, could not be "lost" or "wrongfully withheld" from another because they were attached to the land. Consequently, an action to recover those goods would not stand.[49]

Commentators had argued that straying genetic material from genetically modified plants and their progeny was analogous to the progeny of a straying bull. Under settled common law, when a straying male animal wandered in another's land to breed other female animals on that land, the owner of the female owned the progeny.[50] This theory for recovery was advanced on the premises that the law of straying animals promoted neighborliness, and was stable, predictable, and grounded in common sense.[51]

Federal Court of Appeal judge W. Andrew McKay, who presided over *Monsanto v. Schmeiser,* disagreed with the stray bull analogy because "Monsanto does have ownership in its patented gene and cell and . . . has the exclusive use of its invention," apparently distinguishing the non-ownership of the product of a straying bull's libido by the bull's owner.[52] The Supreme Court of Canada simply rejected the stray bull argument without discussion, stating tersely that the issue "is not [one of] property rights, but patent protection. Ownership is no defense to a breach of the patent act."[53]

Trespass

Genetically modified agricultural product contamination was a physical entry upon land, resulting in

the use or interference with the owner's exclusive possession of the land, because patent owners were entitled to the profits derived from nonlicensee use of the patent, and when genetically modified agricultural product contamination occurred on nonlicensee land, it interfered with the owner's exclusive possession. Similarly, when a licensee terminated his agreement with the patent owner, but the patented product remained on the land, trespass had occurred because the patented product had remained after the agreed upon period had ended. In either case, the intent element could be met in the genetically modified agricultural product context if the patent owner knew that genetic contamination was likely to occur because the technology was uncontainable.

Some states had enacted statutes to protect farmers from patent owners accessing land to take samples without the farmer's knowledge and consent, which would provide additional statutory protection in the event that agents of patent owners entered land without permission.[54]

Negligence

Since genetically modified organism containment was impossible, patent owners could foresee the possibility that nonlicensee land would be contaminated with the patented product. Therefore, patent owners had a duty to protect against risk. Since nonlicensee farmers' crops were being contaminated with the patented product, this duty had been breached. The causal connection was clear, and the resulting injury could be measured in lost opportunity costs due to interference with exclusive use of land, damage or destruction of personal property, and other related injuries.

Percy Schmeiser's wife, Louise, filed a small claims complaint of negligence against Monsanto seeking $140 in damages for the cost of removing Roundup Ready Canola plants from her organic garden and a grove of trees on her property. Since the Supreme Court of Canada ruled that Monsanto owns plants that contain the patented cell and gene, and that any plant that survives Roundup spraying is a Monsanto-owned plant, then Monsanto must remove the plant. As of late 2005, Monsanto had failed to do so and the small claims court decision was still pending.[55]

Endnotes

[1]Interview with Percy Schmeiser, in Bruno, Saskatchewan, Canada, June 4, 2005.

[2]Roger Snyder, "Seed Police Sue Farmers for High Tech Piracy," January 18, 2005, available at http://printsho.station193.com/php/wordpress/archives/2005/01/18/seed-police-sue-farmers-for-high-tech-piracy (accessed September 13, 2005).

[3]Information from the U.N. World Food Programme, available at www.wfp.org (accessed June 1, 2005).

[4]Paul Elias and Anne Fitzgerald, "Monsanto Sues Farmer Customers Over Piracy Issues," *Des Moines Register,* January 30, 2005, available at www.mindfully.org/GE/2005/Monsanto-Sues-Farmers30jan05.htm.

[5]William Engdahl, "Seeds of Destruction: The Geopolitics of GM Food," *Current Concerns,* March 6, 2005, www.currentconcerns.ch/archive/2004/05/20040505.php.

[6]Martin Lee, "Food Fight—International Protests Mount Against Genetically Engineered Crops," *San Francisco Bay Guardian,* June 25, 2001, available at www.sfbg.com/reality/28.html.

[7]Elias and Fitzgerald, "Monsanto Sues Farmer."

[8]"European Union Lifts GM Food Ban," *BBC News World Edition,* May 19, 2004, available at http://news.bbc.co.uk/2/hi/europe/3727827.stm (accessed April 15, 2005).

[9]Paul Brown and David Gow, "Damning Verdict on GM Crop," *The Guardian,* March 22, 2005.

[10]Ibid.

[11]"Monsanto Chalks Up Crop of Global Biotech Victories," Associated Press, March 19, 2005, available at www.mindfully.org/GE/2005/Monsanto-Biotech-Victories19mar05.htm (accessed March 22, 2005).

[12]William Baue, "Monsanto $1.5 Million Fines for Genetic Engineering Bribe Illustrates Risks of GE Strategy," Social Funds.com, January 19, 2005, available at www.mindfully.org/GE/2005/Monsanto-$1_5M-Fines19jan2005.htm (accessed March 22, 2005).

[13]*Schmeiser v. Monsanto Canada* [2004] SCC 34, at para. 60.

[14]Ibid., at para. 17.

[15]Ibid., at para. 18.

[16]Ibid.

[17]2005 Monsanto Technology/Stewardship Agreement (limited-use license).

[18]Monsanto 2005 Technology Use Guide.

[19]Elias and Fitzgerald, "Monsanto Sues Farmer."

[20]Monsanto 2005 Technology Use Guide.

[21]Percy Schmeiser, address at the University of Texas at Austin, October 10, 2001, transcribed by Paul Goettlich, "Heartbreak in the Heartland: The True Cost of Genetically Engineered Crops," available at www.mindfully.org/GE/GE4/Heartbreak-In-The-Heartland21jul02.htm (accessed March 22, 2005).

[22]Ibid.

[23]*Schmeiser v. Monsanto Canada* [2004] SCC 34, at para 60.

[24]Schmeiser, address.

[25]*Schmeiser v. Monsanto Canada* [2004] SCC 34, at para. 60.

[26]Schmeiser, address.

[27]*Schmeiser v. Monsanto Canada* [2004] SCC 34, at para. 60.

[28]Brief for defendants at paras. 5, 9, *Schmeiser v. Monsanto Canada, Inc.* [2002] FCA 209. (Fed Court of Appeal, Court File No. T-L593-98).

[29]Ibid. at para. 10.

[30]Ibid. at para. 26.

[31]Ibid. at para. 12.

[32]Ibid. at para. 38, citing deposition of Mr. Mitchell, Monsanto's lead investigator in the Schmeiser case.

[33]Ibid at paras. 60–66.

[34]*Schmeiser v. Monsanto Canada* [2004] SCC 34, at para. 6.

[35]*Schmeiser v. Monsanto Canada* [2004] SCC 34, at para. 63.

[36]*Monsanto Canada, Inc. v. Schmeiser* [2001] FTC 256.

[37]Schmeiser, address.

[38]The Center for Food Safety, "Monsanto vs. U.S. Farmer," 2005.

[39]*Monsanto Co. V. McFarling,* 363 F.4d 1336, 1344 (Fed. Cir. 2004), *petition for cert. filed,* No. 04-31 (U.S. July 6, 2004).

[40]Ibid.

[41]David R. Moeller and Michael Sligh, "Farmers' Guide to GMOs," 2004, citing Robert Schubert, "Mississippi Farmer Gets Big Break from Appeals Court in Monsanto Biotech Seed Case," *CropChoice,* April 27, 2004, available at www.cropchoice.com/leadstry.asp?recid+2540.

[42]Center for Food Safety Report, "Monsanto vs. U.S. Farmer," p. 6.

[43]Ibid.

[44]Ibid., cited in A. V. Krebs, "Monsanto Charged with Using U.S. Patent Laws to Control Staple Crop Seeds," *Agribusiness Examiner,* January 19, 2005, available at www.mindfully.org/GE/2005/Monsanto-Patent-Control19jan05.htm.

[45]Jane Roberts, "Farmers Take on Monsanto over Seed Fines," *Knight Rider/Tribune Business News,* September 26, 2004, available at www.cropchoice.com/leadstry5eaa.html?recid+2777 (accessed April 15, 2005).

[46]Andrew Pollack, "Genes from Engineered Grass Spread for Miles, Study Finds," *New York Times,* September 21, 2004.

[47]Brown and Gow, "Damning Verdict."

[48]Stephen Leahy, "Ban Endures on Terminator Seeds," February 11, 2005, available at www.mindfully.org/GE/2005/Canada-Terminator-Seeds11feb05.htm.

[49]W. Page Keeton, *Prosser and Keeton on Torts 91,* 5th ed. (West Publishing, 1984).

[50]Drew L. Kershen, "Of Straying Crops and Patent Rights," *Washburn Law Journal 42* (2004), citing *E. G. Ark Valley Land & Cattle Co.* 130 US at 62.

[51]Ibid.

[52]Cited in Ibid.

[53]*Schmeiser v. Monsanto Canada* [2004] SCC 34, at para. 96.

[54]See e.g., S.D. Codified Laws section 38-1-45., N.D. Cent. Code section 4-24-13 (H.B. 1442), available at www.state.nd.us/lr/cencode/t04c24.pdf

[55]"Monsanto Facing Another Schmeiser Suit," Canadian Broadcasting Corporation, October 19, 2004.

ENDNOTES

Chapter 1

[1] Costas Markides, "What Is Strategy and How Do You Know If You Have One?" *Business Strategy Review* 15, no. 2 (Summer 2004), pp. 5–6.

[2] For a discussion of the different ways in which companies can position themselves in the marketplace, see Michael E. Porter, "What Is Strategy?" *Harvard Business Review* 74, no. 6 (November–December 1996), pp. 65–67.

[3] For an excellent treatment of the strategic challenges posed by high-velocity changes, see Shona L. Brown and Kathleen M. Eisenhardt, *Competing on the Edge: Strategy as Structured Chaos* (Boston: Harvard Business School Press, 1998), Chapter 1.

[4] See Henry Mintzberg and Joseph Lampel, "Reflecting on the Strategy Process, *Sloan Management Review* 40, no. 3 (Spring 1999), pp. 21–30; Henry Mintzberg and J. A. Waters, "Of Strategies, Deliberate and Emergent," *Strategic Management Journal* 6 (1985), pp. 257–72; Costas Markides, "Strategy as Balance: From 'Either-Or' to 'And,'" *Business Strategy Review* 12, no. 3 (September 2001), pp. 1–10; Henry Mintzberg, Bruce Ahlstrand, and Joseph Lampel, *Strategy Safari: A Guided Tour through the Wilds of Strategic Management* (New York: Free Press, 1998), 7; and C. K. Prahalad and Gary Hamel, "The Core Competence of the Corporation," *Harvard Business Review* 70, no. 3 (May–June 1990), pp. 79–93.

[5] Joseph L. Badaracco, "The Discipline of Building Character," *Harvard Business Review* 76, no. 2 (March–April 1998), pp. 115–24.

[6] Joan Magretta, "Why Business Models Matter," *Harvard Business Review* 80, no. 5 (May 2002), p. 87.

Chapter 2

[1] For a more in-depth discussion of the challenges of developing a well-conceived vision, as well as some good examples, see Hugh Davidson, *The Committed Enterprise: How to Make Vision and Values Work* (Oxford: Butterworth Heinemann, 2002), Chapter 2; W. Chan Kim and Renée Mauborgne, "Charting Your Company's Future," *Harvard Business Review* 80, no. 6 (June 2002), pp. 77–83; James C. Collins and Jerry I. Porras, "Building Your Company's Vision," *Harvard Business Review* 74, no. 5 (September–October 1996), pp. 65–77; James C. Collins and Jerry I. Porras, *Built to Last: Successful Habits of Visionary Companies* (New York: HarperCollins, 1994), Chapter 11; and Michel Robert, *Strategy Pure and Simple II*

(New York: McGraw-Hill, 1998), Chapters 2, 3, and 6.

[2] Davidson, *Committed Enterprise,* pp. 20, 54.

[3] Ibid., pp. 36, 54.

[4] Jeffrey K. Liker, *The Toyota Way* (New York: McGraw-Hill, 2004), and Steve Hamm, "Taking a Page from Toyota's Playbook," *BusinessWeek,* August 22/29, 2005, p. 72.

[5] As quoted in Charles H. House and Raymond L. Price, "The Return Map: Tracking Product Teams," *Harvard Business Review* 60, no. 1 (January–February 1991), p. 93.

[6] Robert S. Kaplan and David P. Norton, *The Strategy-Focused Organization* (Boston: Harvard Business School Press, 2001), p. 3.

[7] Ibid., p. 7. Also, see Kevin B. Hendricks, Larry Menor, and Christine Wiedman, "The Balanced Scorecard: To Adopt or Not to Adopt," *Ivey Business Journal* 69, no. 2 (November–December 2004), pp. 1–7; and Sandy Richardson, "The Key Elements of Balanced Scorecard Success," *Ivey Business Journal* 69, no. 2 (November–December 2004), pp. 7–9.

[8] Information posted on the Web site of the Balanced Scorecard Institute, www.balancedscorecard.org (accessed August 22, 2005).

[9] Darrell Rigby, "Management Tools Survey 2003: Usage Up as Companies Strive to Make Headway in Tough Times," *Strategy & Leadership* 31, no. 5 (May 2003), p. 6.

[10] Information posted on the Web site of Balanced Scorecard Collaborative, www.bscol.com (accessed August 22, 2005). This Web site was created by the co-creators of the balanced scorecard concept, Professors Robert S. Kaplan and David P. Norton, Harvard Business School.

[11] The concept of strategic intent is described in more detail in Gary Hamel and C. K. Prahalad, "Strategic Intent," *Harvard Business Review* 89, no. 3 (May–June 1989), pp. 63–76; this section draws on their pioneering discussion. See also Michael A. Hitt, Beverly B. Tyler, Camilla Hardee, and Daewoo Park, "Understanding Strategic Intent in the Global Marketplace," *Academy of Management Executive* 9, no. 2 (May 1995), pp. 12–19.

[12] For a fuller discussion of strategy as an entrepreneurial process, see Henry Mintzberg, Bruce Ahlstrand, and Joseph Lampel, *Strategy Safari: A Guided Tour through the Wilds of Strategic Management,* (New York: Free Press, 1998), Chapter 5. Also see Bruce Barringer and Allen C. Bluedorn, "The Relationship Between Corporate Entrepreneurship and Strategic Management," *Strategic Management*

Journal 20 (1999), pp. 421–444, and Jeffrey G. Covin and Morgan P. Miles, "Corporate Entrepreneurship and the Pursuit of Competitive Advantage," *Entrepreneurship: Theory and Practice* 23, no. 3 (Spring 1999), pp. 47–63.

[13] The strategy-making, strategy-implementing roles of middle managers are thoroughly discussed and documented in Steven W. Floyd and Bill Wooldridge, *The Strategic Middle Manager* (San Francisco: Jossey-Bass Publishers, 1996), Chapters 2 and 3.

[14] "Strategic Planning," *Business Week,* August 26, 1996, pp. 51–52.

[15] For an excellent discussion of why a strategic plan needs to be more than a list of bullet points and should in fact tell an engaging, insightful, stage-setting story that lays out the industry and competitive situation as well as the vision, objectives, and strategy, see Gordon Shaw, Robert Brown, and Philip Bromiley, "Strategic Stories: How 3M Is Rewriting Business Planning," *Harvard Business Review* 76, no. 3 (May–June 1998), pp. 41–50.

[16] For a discussion of what it takes for the corporate governance system to function properly, see David A. Nadler, "Building Better Boards," *Harvard Business Review* 82, no. 5 (May 2004), pp. 102–5; Cynthia A. Montgomery and Rhonda Kaufman, "The Board's Missing Link," *Harvard Business Review* 81, no. 3 (March 2003), pp. 86–93; and John Carver, "What Continues to Be Wrong with Corporate Governance and How to Fix It," *Ivey Business Journal* 68, no. 1 (September–October 2003), pp. 1–5. See also Gordon Donaldson, "A New Tool for Boards: The Strategic Audit," *Harvard Business Review* 73, no. 4 (July–August 1995), pp. 99–107.

Chapter 3

[1] There are a large number of studies of the size of the cost reductions associated with experience; the median cost reduction associated with a doubling of cumulative production volume is approximately 15 percent, but there is a wide variation from industry to industry. For a good discussion of the economies of experience and learning, see Pankaj Ghemawat, "Building Strategy on the Experience Curve," *Harvard Business Review* 64, no. 2 (March–April 1985), pp. 143–49.

[2] The five-forces model of competition is the creation of Professor Michael Porter of the Harvard Business School. For his original presentation of the model, see Michael E. Porter, "How Competitive Forces Shape Strategy," *Harvard Business Review* 57, no. 2

EN-1

(March–April 1979), pp. 137–45. A more thorough discussion can be found in Michael E. Porter, *Competitive Strategy: Techniques for Analyzing Industries and Competitors* (New York: Free Press, 1980), Chapter 1.

[3] Many of these indicators of whether rivalry produces intense competitive pressures are based on Porter, *Competitive Strategy,* pp. 17–21.

[4] The role of entry barriers in shaping the strength of competition in a particular market has long been a standard topic in the literature of microeconomics. For a discussion of how entry barriers affect competitive pressures associated with potential entry, see J. S. Bain, *Barriers to New Competition* (Cambridge: Harvard University Press, 1956); F. M. Scherer, *Industrial Market Structure and Economic Performance* (Chicago: Rand McNally, 1971), pp. 216–20, 226–33; and Porter, *Competitive Strategy,* pp. 7–17.

[5] Porter, "How Competitive Forces Shape Strategy," p. 140, and Porter, *Competitive Strategy,* pp. 14–15.

[6] For a good discussion of this point, see George S. Yip, "Gateways to Entry," *Harvard Business Review* 60, no. 5 (September–October 1982), pp. 85–93.

[7] Porter, "How Competitive Forces Shape Strategy," p. 142, and Porter, *Competitive Strategy,* pp. 23–24.

[8] Porter, *Competitive Strategy*, p. 10.

[9] Ibid., pp. 27–28.

[10] Ibid., pp. 24–27.

[11] For a more extended discussion of the problems with the life-cycle hypothesis, see ibid., pp. 157–62.

[12] Ibid. p. 162.

[13] Most of the candidate driving forces described here are based on the discussion in ibid., pp. 164–83.

[14] Ibid., Chapter 7.

[15] Ibid., pp. 129–30.

[16] For an excellent discussion of how to identify the factors that define strategic groups, see Mary Ellen Gordon and George R. Milne, "Selecting the Dimensions That Define Strategic Groups: A Novel Market-Driven Approach," *Journal of Managerial Issues* 11, no. 2 (Summer 1999), pp. 213–33.

[17] Porter, *Competitive Strategy,* pp. 152–54.

[18] Strategic groups act as good reference points for predicting the evolution of an industry's competitive structure. See Avi Fiegenbaum and Howard Thomas, "Strategic Groups as Reference Groups: Theory, Modeling and Empirical Examination of Industry and Competitive Strategy," *Strategic Management Journal* 16 (1995), pp. 461–76. For a study of how strategic group analysis helps identify the variables that lead to sustainable competitive advantage, see S. Ade Olusoga, Michael P. Mokwa, and Charles H. Noble,

"Strategic Groups, Mobility Barriers, and Competitive Advantage," *Journal of Business Research* 33 (1995), pp. 153–64.

[19] Porter, *Competitive Strategy,* pp. 130, 132–38, and 154–55.

[20] For a discussion of legal and ethical ways of gathering competitive intelligence on rival companies, see Larry Kahaner, *Competitive Intelligence* (New York: Simon & Schuster, 1996).

[21] Ibid., pp. 84–85.

[22] Some experts dispute the strategy-making value of key success factors. Professor Pankaj Ghemawat has claimed that the "whole idea of identifying a success factor and then chasing it seems to have something in common with the ill-considered medieval hunt for the *philosopher's stone,* a substance which would transmute everything it touched into gold." Pankaj Ghemawat, *Commitment: The Dynamic of Strategy* (New York: Free Press, 1991), p. 11.

Chapter 4

[1] Many business organizations are coming to view cutting-edge knowledge and intellectual resources of company personnel as a valuable competitive asset and have concluded that explicitly managing these assets is an essential part of their strategy. See Michael H. Zack, "Developing a Knowledge Strategy," *California Management Review* 41, no. 3 (Spring 1999), pp. 125–45, and Shaker A. Zahra, Anders P. Nielsen, and William C. Bogner, "Corporate Entrepreneurship, Knowledge, and Competence Development," *Entrepreneurship Theory and Practice,* Spring 1999, pp. 169–89.

[2] In the past decade, there's been considerable research into the role a company's resources and competitive capabilities play in crafting strategy and in determining company profitability. The findings and conclusions have coalesced into what is called the resource-based view of the firm. Among the most insightful articles are Birger Wernerfelt, "A Resource-Based View of the Firm," *Strategic Management Journal,* September–October 1984, pp. 171–80; Jay Barney, "Firm Resources and Sustained Competitive Advantage," *Journal of Management* 17, no. 1 (1991), pp. 99–120; Margaret A. Peteraf, "The Cornerstones of Competitive Advantage: A Resource-Based View," *Strategic Management Journal,* March 1993, pp. 179–91; Birger Wernerfelt, "The Resource-Based View of the Firm: Ten Years After," *Strategic Management Journal* 16 (1995), pp. 171–74; Jay Barney, "Looking Inside for Competitive Advantage," *Academy of Management Executive* 9, no. 4 (November 1995), pp. 49–61; Christopher A. Bartlett and Sumantra Ghoshal, "Building Competitive Advantage through People,"

MIT Sloan Management Review 43, no 2, (Winter 2002), pp. 34–41; and Danny Miller, Russell Eisenstat, and Nathaniel Foote, "Strategy from the Inside Out: Building Capability-Creating Organizations," *California Management Review* 44, no. 3 (Spring 2002), pp. 37–54.

[3] George Stalk Jr. and Rob Lachenauer, "Hard Ball: Five Killer Strategies for Trouncing the Competition," *Harvard Business Review* 82, no. 4 (April 2004), p. 65.

[4] For a more extensive discussion of how to identify and evaluate the competitive power of a company's capabilities, see David W. Birchall and George Tovstiga, "The Strategic Potential of a Firm's Knowledge Portfolio," *Journal of General Management* 25, no. 1 (Autumn 1999), pp. 1–16, and Nick Bontis, Nicola C. Dragonetti, Kristine Jacobsen, and Goran Roos, "The Knowledge Toolbox: A Review of the Tools Available to Measure and Manage Intangible Resources," *European Management Journal* 17, no. 4 (August 1999), pp. 391–401. Also see David Teece, "Capturing Value from Knowledge Assets: The New Economy, Markets for Know-How, and Intangible Assets," *California Management Review* 40, no. 3 (Spring 1998), pp. 55–79.

[5] See Barney, "Firm Resources," pp. 105–9, and David J. Collis and Cynthia A. Montgomery, "Competing on Resources: Strategy in the 1990s," *Harvard Business Review* 73, no. 4 (July–August 1995), pp. 120–23.

[6] Donald Sull, "Strategy as Active Waiting," *Harvard Business Review* 83, no. 9 (September 2005), p. 121–122.

[7] Ibid., p. 122.

[8] Ibid., pp. 124–26.

[9] See Jack W. Duncan, Peter Ginter, and Linda E. Swayne, "Competitive Advantage and Internal Organizational Assessment," *Academy of Management Executive* 12, no. 3 (August 1998), pp. 6–16.

[10] The value chain concept was developed and articulated by Professor Michael Porter at the Harvard Business School and is described at greater length in Michael E. Porter, *Competitive Advantage* (New York: Free Press, 1985), Chapters 2 and 3.

[11] Ibid., p. 36.

[12] Ibid., p. 34.

[13] The strategic importance of effective supply chain management is discussed in Hau L. Lee, "The Triple-A Supply Chain," *Harvard Business Review* 82, no. 10 (October 2004), pp. 102–112.

[14] M. Hegert and D. Morris, "Accounting Data for Value Chain Analysis," *Strategic Management Journal* 10 (1989), p. 180; Robin Cooper and Robert S. Kaplan, "Measure Costs Right: Make the Right Decisions," *Harvard Business Review* 66, no. 5 (September–October, 1988), pp. 96–103; and John K. Shank and Vijay

Govindarajan, *Strategic Cost Management* (New York: Free Press, 1993), especially Chapters 2–6, 10.

15 For more on how and why the clustering of suppliers and other support organizations matter to a company's costs and competitiveness, see Michael E. Porter, "Clusters and the New Economics of Competition," *Harvard Business Review* 76, no. 6 (November–December 1998), pp. 77–90.

16 For discussions of the accounting challenges in calculating the costs of value chain activities, see Shank and Govindarajan, *Strategic Cost Management,* especially Chapters 2–6, 10, and 11; Cooper and Kaplan, "Measure Costs Right"; and Joseph A. Ness and Thomas G. Cucuzza, "Tapping the Full Potential of ABC," *Harvard Business Review* 73, no. 4 (July–August 1995), pp. 130–38.

17 For more details, see Gregory H. Watson, *Strategic Benchmarking: How to Rate Your Company's Performance Against the World's Best* (New York: John Wiley, 1993); Robert C. Camp, *Benchmarking: The Search for Industry Best Practices That Lead to Superior Performance* (Milwaukee: ASQC Quality Press, 1989); Christopher E. Bogan and Michael J. English, *Benchmarking for Best Practices: Winning through Innovative Adaptation* (New York: McGraw-Hill, 1994); and Dawn Iacobucci and Christie Nordhielm, "Creative Benchmarking," *Harvard Business Review* 78 no. 6 (November–December 2000), pp. 24–25.

18 Jeremy Main, "How to Steal the Best Ideas Around," *Fortune,* October 19, 1992, pp. 102–3.

19 Shank and Govindarajan, *Strategic Cost Management,* p. 50.

20 Some of these options are discussed in more detail in Porter, *Competitive Advantage,* Chapter 3.

21 An example of how Whirlpool Corporation transformed its supply chain from a competitive liability to a competitive asset is discussed in Reuben E. Stone, "Leading a Supply Chain Turnaround," *Harvard Business Review* 82, no. 10 (October 2004), pp. 114–21.

22 James Brian Quinn, *Intelligent Enterprise* (New York: Free Press, 1993), p. 54.

23 Ibid., p. 34.

Chapter 5

1 This classification scheme is an adaptation of a narrower three-strategy classification presented in Michael E. Porter, *Competitive Strategy: Techniques for Analyzing Industries and Competitors* (New York: Free Press, 1980), Chapter 2, especially pp. 35–40 and 44–46. For a discussion of the different ways in which companies can position themselves

in the marketplace, see Michael E. Porter, "What Is Strategy?" *Harvard Business Review* 74, no. 6 (November–December 1996), pp. 65–67.

2 Porter, *Competitive Advantage,* p. 97.

3 Iowa Beef Packers' value chain revamping was first reported in ibid., p. 109. Since then the company has successfully extended its efforts to reconfigure the meat industry value chain, including an entry into the pork segment. IBP was acquired in 2001 by Tyson Foods after a heated bidding war with Smithfield Foods drove Tyson's acquisition price up to $14 billion. Tyson is now applying many of the same value chain revamping principles in chicken, beef, and pork.

4 Ibid., pp. 135–38.

5 For a more detailed discussion, see George Stalk, Philip Evans, and Lawrence E. Schulman, "Competing on Capabilities: The New Rules of Corporate Strategy," *Harvard Business Review* 70, no. 2 (March–April 1992), pp. 57–69.

6 The relevance of perceived value and signaling is discussed in more detail in Porter, *Competitive Advantage,* pp. 138–42.

7 Ibid., pp. 160–62.

8 Gary Hamal, "Strategy as Revolution," *Harvard Business Review* 74, no. 4 (July–August 1996), p. 72.

Chapter 6

1 Yves L. Doz and Gary Hamel, *Alliance Advantage: The Art of Creating Value through Partnering* (Boston: Harvard Business School Press, 1998), pp. xiii, xiv.

2 Jason Wakeam, "The Five Factors of a Strategic Alliance," *Ivey Business Journal* 68, no. 3 (May–June 2003), pp. 1–4.

3 Jeffrey H. Dyer, Prashant Kale, and Harbir Singh, "When to Ally and When to Acquire," *Harvard Business Review* 82, no. 7/8 (July–August 2004), p. 109.

4 Salvatore Parise and Lisa Sasson, "Leveraging Knowledge Management across Strategic Alliances," *Ivey Business Journal* 66, no. 4 (March–April 2002), p. 42.

5 David Ernst and James Bamford, "Your Alliances Are Too Stable," *Harvard Business Review* 83, no. 6 (June 2005), p. 133.

6 An excellent discussion of the portfolio approach to managing multiple alliances and how to restructure a faltering alliance is presented in ibid., pp. 133–41.

7 Michael E. Porter, *The Competitive Advantage of Nations* (New York: Free Press, 1990), p. 66. For a discussion of how to realize the advantages of strategic partnerships, see Nancy J. Kaplan and Jonathan Hurd, "Realizing the Promise of Partnerships," *Journal of Business Strategy* 23, no. 3 (May–June 2002), pp. 38–42; Parise and Sasson,

"Leveraging Knowledge Management," pp. 41–47; and Ernst and Bamford, "Your Alliances Are Too Stable," pp. 133–41.

8 A. Inkpen, "Learning, Knowledge Acquisition, and Strategic Alliances," *European Management Journal* 16, no. 2 (April 1998), pp. 223–29.

9 For a discussion of how to raise the chances that a strategic alliance will produce strategically important outcomes, see M. Koza and A. Lewin, "Managing Partnerships and Strategic Alliances: Raising the Odds of Success," *European Management Journal* 18, no. 2 (April 2000), pp. 146–51.

10 Doz and Hamel, *Alliance Advantage,* Chapters 4–8; Patricia Anslinger and Justin Jenk, "Creating Successful Alliances," *Journal of Business Strategy* 25, no. 2 (2004), pp. 18–23; Rosabeth Moss Kanter, "Collaborative Advantage: The Art of the Alliance," *Harvard Business Review* 72, no. 4 (July–August 1994), pp. 96–108; Joel Bleeke and David Ernst, "The Way to Win in Cross-Border Alliances," *Harvard Business Review* 69, no. 6 (November–December 1991), pp. 127–35 and Gary Hamel, Yves L. Doz, and C. K. Prahalad, "Collaborate with Your Competitors—and Win," *Harvard Business Review* 67, no. 1 (January–February 1989), pp. 133–39.

11 This same 50 percent success rate for alliances was also cited in Ernst and Bamford, "Your Alliances Are Too Stable," p. 133; both co-authors of this *HBR* article were McKinsey personnel.

12 Doz and Hamel, *Alliance Advantage,* pp. 16–18.

13 Dyer, Kale, and Singh, "When to Ally and When to Acquire," p. 109.

14 For an excellent discussion of the pros and cons of alliances versus acquisitions, see ibid., pp. 109–15.

15 For an excellent review of the strategic objectives of various types of mergers and acquisitions and the managerial challenges that different kinds of mergers and acquisitions present, see Joseph L. Bower, "Not All M&As Are Alike—and That Matters," *Harvard Business Review* 79, no. 3 (March 2001), pp. 93–101.

16 For a more expansive discussion, see Dyer, Kale, and Singh, "When to Ally and When to Acquire," pp. 109–10.

17 See Kathryn R. Harrigan, "Matching Vertical Integration Strategies to Competitive Conditions," *Strategic Management Journal* 7, no. 6 (November–December 1986), pp. 535–56; for a more extensive discussion of the advantages and disadvantages of vertical integration, see John Stuckey and David White, "When and When Not to Vertically Integrate," *Sloan Management Review* (Spring 1993), pp. 71–83.

18 The resilience of vertical integration strategies despite the disadvantages is discussed in

Thomas Osegowitsch and Anoop Madhok, "Vertical Integration Is Dead or Is It?" *Business Horizons* 46, no. 2 (March–April 2003), pp. 25–35.

[19]This point is explored in greater detail in James Brian Quinn, "Strategic Outsourcing: Leveraging Knowledge Capabilities," *Sloan Management Review* 40, no. 4 (Summer 1999), pp. 9–21.

[20]Dean Foust, "Big Brown's New Bag," *BusinessWeek,* July 19, 2004, pp. 54–55.

[21]"The Internet Age," *BusinessWeek,* October 4, 1999, p. 104.

[22]For a good discussion of the problems that can arise from outsourcing, see Jérôme Barthélemy, "The Seven Deadly Sins of Outsourcing," *Academy of Management Executive* 17, no. 2 (May 2003), pp. 87–100.

[23]For an excellent discussion of aggressive offensive strategies, see George Stalk Jr. and Rob Lachenauer, "Hardball: Five Killer Strategies for Trouncing the Competition," *Harvard Business Review* 82, no. 4 (April 2004), pp. 62–71. A discussion of offensive strategies particularly suitable for industry leaders is presented in Richard D'Aveni, "The Empire Strikes Back: Counterrevolutionary Strategies for Industry Leaders," *Harvard Business Review* 80, no. 11 (November 2002), pp. 66–74.

[24]George Stalk, "Playing Hardball: Why Strategy Still Matters," *Ivey Business Journal* 69, no. 2 (November–December 2004), pp. 1–2.

[25]Ian C. MacMillan, "How Long Can You Sustain a Competitive Advantage?" in *The Strategic Planning Management Reader,* ed. Liam Fahey (Englewood Cliffs, NJ: Prentice Hall, 1989), pp. 23–24.

[26]Ian C. MacMillan, Alexander B. van Putten, and Rita Gunther McGrath, "Global Gamesmanship," *Harvard Business Review* 81, no. 5 (May 2003), pp. 66–67; also, see Askay R. Rao, Mark E. Bergen, and Scott Davis, "How to Fight a Price War," *Harvard Business Review* 78, no. 2 (March–April, 2000), pp. 107–16.

[27]Stalk and Lachenauer, "Hardball," p. 64.

[28]Stalk, "Playing Hardball," p. 4.

[29]Stalk and Lachenauer, "Hardball," p. 67.

[30]For an interesting study of how small firms can successfully employ guerrilla-style tactics, see Ming-Jer Chen and Donald C. Hambrick, "Speed, Stealth, and Selective Attack: How Small Firms Differ from Large Firms in Competitive Behavior," *Academy of Management Journal* 38, no. 2 (April 1995), pp. 453–82. Other discussions of guerrilla offensives can be found in Ian MacMillan, "How Business Strategists Can Use Guerrilla Warfare Tactics," *Journal of Business Strategy* 1, no. 2 (Fall 1980), pp. 63–65; William E. Rothschild, "Surprise

and the Competitive Advantage," *Journal of Business Strategy* 4, no. 3 (Winter 1984), pp. 10–18; Kathryn R. Harrigan, *Strategic Flexibility* (Lexington, MA: Lexington Books, 1985), pp. 30–45; and Liam Fahey, "Guerrilla Strategy: The Hit-and-Run Attack," in *The Strategic Management Planning Reader,* ed. Liam Fahey (Englewood Cliffs, NJ: Prentice Hall, 1989), pp. 194–97.

[31]The use of preemptive strike offensives is treated comprehensively in Ian MacMillan, "Preemptive Strategies," *Journal of Business Strategy* 14, no. 2 (Fall 1983), pp. 16–26.

[32]W. Chan Kim and Renée Mauborgne, "Blue Ocean Strategy," *Harvard Business Review* 82, no. 10 (October 2004), pp. 76–84.

[33]Philip Kotler, *Marketing Management,* 5th Edition (Englewood Cliffs, N.J.: Prentice Hall, 1984), p. 400.

[34]Michael E. Porter, *Competitive Advantage* (New York: Free Press, 1985), p. 518.

[35]For an excellent discussion of how to wage offensives against strong rivals, see David B. Yoffie and Mary Kwak, "Mastering Balance: How to Meet and Beat a Stronger Opponent," *California Management Review* 44, no. 2 (Winter 2002), pp. 8–24.

[36]Stalk, "Playing Hardball," pp. 1–2.

[37]Porter, *Competitive Advantage,* pp. 489–94.

[38]Ibid., pp. 495–97. The list here is selective; Porter offers a greater number of options.

[39]For a more extensive discussion of how the Internet impacts strategy, see Michael E. Porter, "Strategy and the Internet," *Harvard Business Review* 79, no. 3 (March 2001), pp. 63–78.

[40]Porter, *Competitive Advantage,* pp. 232–33.

[41]For research evidence on the effects of pioneering versus following, see Jeffrey G. Covin, Dennis P. Slevin, and Michael B. Heeley, "Pioneers and Followers: Competitive Tactics, Environment, and Growth," *Journal of Business Venturing* 15, no. 2 (March 1999), pp. 175–210 and Christopher A. Bartlett and Sumantra Ghoshal, "Going Global: Lessons from Late-Movers," *Harvard Business Review* 78, no. 2 (March–April 2000), pp. 132–45.

[42]For a more extensive discussion of this point, see Fernando Suarez and Gianvito Lanzolla, "The Half-Truth of First-Mover Advantage," *Harvard Business Review* 83, no. 4 (April 2005), pp. 121–27.

[43]Gary Hamel, "Smart Mover, Dumb Mover," *Fortune,* September 3, 2001, p. 195.

[44]Ibid., p. 192.

[45]Costas Markides and Paul A. Geroski, "Racing to be 2nd: Conquering the Industries of the Future," *Business Strategy Review* 15, no. 4 (Winter 2004), pp. 25–31.

Chapter 7

[1]For an insightful discussion of how much significance these kinds of demographic and market differences have, see C. K. Prahalad and Kenneth Lieberthal, "The End of Corporate Imperialism," *Harvard Business Review* 76, no. 4 (July–August 1998), pp. 68–79.

[2]Joseph Caron, "The Business of Doing Business with China: An Ambassador Reflects," *Ivey Business Journal* 69, no. 5 (May–June 2005), p. 2.

[3]Extrapolated from 2002 statistics reported by the U.S. Department of Labor.

[4]Michael E. Porter, *The Competitive Advantage of Nations* (New York: Free Press, 1990), pp. 53–54.

[5]Ibid., p. 61.

[6]For more details on the merits of and opportunities for cross-border transfer of successful strategy experiments, see C. A. Bartlett and S. Ghoshal, *Managing Across Borders: The Transnational Solution,* 2nd ed. (Boston: Harvard Business School Press, 1998), pp. 79–80 and Chapter 9.

[7]H. Kurt Christensen, "Corporate Strategy: Managing a Set of Businesses," in *The Portable MBA in Strategy,* ed. Liam Fahey and Robert M. Randall (New York: Wiley, 2001), p. 42.

[8]Porter, *Competitive Advantage,* pp. 53–55.

[9]Ibid., pp. 55–58.

[10]C. K. Prahalad and Yves L. Doz, *The Multinational Mission* (New York: Free Press, 1987), p. 60.

[11]Porter, *Competitive Advantage,* p. 57.

[12]Ibid., pp. 58–60.

[13]Several other types of strategic offensives that companies have occasionally employed in select foreign market situations are discussed in Ian C. MacMillan, Alexander B. van Putten, and Rita Gunther McGrath, "Global Gamesmanship," *Harvard Business Review* 81, no. 5 (May 2003), pp. 63–68.

[14]Canadian International Trade Tribunal, findings issued June 16, 2005 and posted at www.citttcce.gc.ca (accessed September 28, 2005).

[15]George Stalk, "Playing Hardball: Why Strategy Still Matters," *Ivey Business Journal* 69, no. 2 (November–December 2004), pp. 1–2.

[16]For two especially insightful studies of company experiences with cross-border alliances, see Joel Bleeke and David Ernst, "The Way to Win in Cross-Border Alliances," *Harvard Business Review* 69, no. 6 (November–December 1991), pp. 127–35, and Gary Hamel, Yves L. Doz, and C. K. Prahalad, "Collaborate with Your Competitors—and Win," *Harvard Business Review* 67, no. 1 (January–February 1989), pp. 133–39.

[17]See Yves L. Doz and Gary Hamel, *Alliance Advantage* (Boston, MA: Harvard Business School Press, 1998), especially Chapters 2–4; Bleeke and Ernst, "The Way to Win," pp. 127–33; Hamel, Doz, and Prahalad, "Collaborate with Your Competitors," pp. 134–35; and Porter, *Competitive Advantage,* p. 66.

[18]Christensen, "Corporate Strategy," p. 43.

[19]For an excellent presentation on the pros and cons of alliances versus acquisitions, see Jeffrey H. Dyer, Prashant Kale, and Harbir Singh, "When to Ally and When to Acquire," *Harvard Business Review* 82, no. 7/8 (July–August 2004), pp. 109–15.

[20]For additional discussion of company experiences with alliances and partnerships, see Doz and Hamel, *Alliance Advantage,* Chapters 2–7, and Rosabeth Moss Kanter, "Collaborative Advantage: The Art of the Alliance," *Harvard Business Review* 72, no. 4 (July–August 1994), pp. 96–108.

[21]Details are reported in Shawn Tully, "The Alliance from Hell," *Fortune,* June 24, 1996, pp. 64–72.

[22]Jeremy Main, "Making Global Alliances Work," *Fortune,* December 19, 1990, p. 125.

[23]Prahalad and Lieberthal, "The End of Corporate Imperialism," p. 77.

[24]Ibid.

[25]This point is discussed at greater length in Prahalad and Lieberthal, "The End of Corporate Imperialism," pp. 68–79; also see David J. Arnold and John A. Quelch, "New Strategies in Emerging Markets," *Sloan Management Review* 40, no. 1 (Fall 1998), pp. 7–20. For a more extensive discussion of strategy in emerging markets, see C. K. Prahalad, *The Fortune at the Bottom of the Pyramid: Eradicating Poverty through Profits* (Upper Saddle River, NJ: Wharton, 2005), especially Chapters 1–3.

[26]Brenda Cherry, "What China Eats (and Drinks and . . .)," *Fortune,* October 4, 2004, pp. 152–53.

[27]Prahalad and Lieberthal, "The End of Corporate Imperialism," pp. 72–73.

[28]Tarun Khanna, Krishna G. Palepu, and Jayant Sinha, "Strategies That Fit Emerging Markets," *Harvard Business Review* 83 no. 6 (June 2005), p. 63.

[29]Prahalad and Lieberthal, "The End of Corporate Imperialism," p. 72.

[30]Khanna, Palepu, and Sinha, "Strategies That Fit Emerging Markets," pp. 73–74.

[31]Ibid., p. 74.

[32]Ibid., p. 76.

[33]Niroj Dawar and Tony Frost, "Competing with Giants: Survival Strategies for Local Companies in Emerging Markets," *Harvard Business Review* 77, no. 1

(January–February 1999), p. 122; see also Guitz Ger, "Localizing in the Global Village: Local Firms Competing in Global Markets," *California Management Review* 41, no. 4 (Summer 1999), pp. 64–84.

[34]Dawar and Frost, "Competing with Giants," p. 124.

[35]Ibid., p. 125.

[36]Steve Hamm, "Tech's Future," *BusinessWeek,* September 27, 2004, p. 88.

[37]Dawar and Frost, "Competing with Giants," p. 126.

[38]Hamm, "Tech's Future," p. 89.

Chapter 8

[1]Michael E. Porter, *Competitive Strategy: Techniques for Analyzing Industries and Competitors* (New York: Free Press, 1980), pp. 216–23.

[2]Phillip Kotler, *Marketing Management,* 5th ed. (Englewood Cliffs, NJ: Prentice Hall, 1984), p. 366, and Porter, *Competitive Strategy,* Chapter 10.

[3]Several of these were pinpointed and discussed in Charles W. Hofer and Dan Schendel, *Strategy Formulation: Analytical Concepts* (St. Paul, MN: West, 1978), pp. 164–65.

[4]Ibid., pp. 164–65.

[5]Porter, *Competitive Strategy,* pp. 238–40.

[6]The following discussion draws on ibid., pp. 241–46.

[7]Kathryn R. Harrigan and Michael E. Porter, "End-Game Strategies for Declining Industries," *Harvard Business Review* 61, no. 4 (July–August 1983), pp. 112–13.

[8]R. G. Hamermesh and S. B. Silk, "How to Compete in Stagnant Industries," *Harvard Business Review* 57, no. 5 (September–October 1979), p. 161, and Kathryn R. Harrigan, *Strategies for Declining Businesses* (Lexington, MA: Heath, 1980).

[9]Hamermesh and Silk, "How to Compete," p. 162; Harrigan and Porter, "End-Game Strategies," p. 118.

[10]Hamermesh and Silk, "How to Compete," p. 165.

[11]Harrigan and Porter, "End-Game Strategies," pp. 111–21; Harrigan, *Strategies for Declining Businesses;* and Phillip Kotler, "Harvesting Strategies for Weak Products," *Business Horizons* 21, no. 5 (August 1978), pp. 17–18.

[12]The strategic issues companies must address in fast-changing market environments are thoroughly explored in Gary Hamel and Liisa Välikangas, "The Quest for Resilence," *Harvard Business Review* 81, no. 9 (September 2003), pp. 52–63; Shona L. Brown and Kathleen M. Eisenhardt, *Competing on the Edge: Strategy as*

Structured Chaos (Boston: Harvard Business School Press, 1998); and Richard A. D'Aveni, *Hyper-Competition: Managing the Dynamics of Strategic Maneuvering* (New York: Free Press, 1994). See also Richard A. D'Aveni, "Coping with Hypercompetition: Utilizing the New 7S's Framework," *Academy of Management Executive* 9, no. 3 (August 1995), pp. 45–56, and Bala Chakravarthy, "A New Strategy Framework for Coping with Turbulence," *Sloan Management Review* (Winter 1997), pp. 69–82.

[13]Brown and Eisenhardt, *Competing on the Edge,* pp. 4–5.

[14]Ibid., p. 4.

[15]For deeper insight into building competitive advantage through R&D and technological innovation, see Shaker A. Zahra, Sarah Nash, and Deborah J. Bickford, "Transforming Technological Pioneering into Competitive Advantage," *Academy of Management Executive* 9, no. 1 (February 1995), pp. 32–41.

[16]Brown and Eisenhardt, *Competing on the Edge,* pp. 14–15. See also Kathleen M. Eisenhardt and Shona L. Brown, "Time Pacing: Competing in Markets That Won't Stand Still," *Harvard Business Review* 76, no. 2 (March–April 1998), pp. 59–69.

[17]The circumstances of competing in a fragmented industry are discussed at length in Porter, *Competitive Strategy,* Chapter 9; this section draws on Porter's treatment.

[18]What follows is based on the discussion in Eric D. Beinhocker, "Robust Adaptive Strategies," *Sloan Management Review* 40, no. 3 (Spring 1999), p. 101.

[19]Gary Hamel, "Bringing Silicon Valley Inside," *Harvard Business Review* 77, no. 5 (September–October 1999), p. 73.

[20]Beinhocker, "Robust Adaptive Strategies," p. 101.

[21]Kotler, *Marketing Management,* Chapter 23; Michael E. Porter, *Competitive Advantage* (New York: Free Press, 1985), Chapter 14; and Ian C. MacMillan, "Seizing Competitive Initiative," *Journal of Business Strategy* 2, no. 4 (Spring 1982), pp. 43–57. For a perspective on what industry leaders can do when confronted with revolutionary market changes, see Richard D'Aveni, "The Empire Strikes Back: Counterrevolutionary Strategies for Industry Leaders," *Harvard Business Review* 80, no. 11 (November 2002), pp. 66–74.

[22]The value of being a frequent first-mover and leading change is documented in Walter J. Ferrier, Ken G. Smith, and Curtis M. Grimm, "The Role of Competitive Action in Market Share Erosion and Industry Dethronement: A Study of Industry Leaders and Challengers," *Academy of Management Journal* 42, no. 4 (August 1999), pp. 372–88.

[23]George Stalk Jr. and Rob Lachenauer, "Five Killer Strategies for Trouncing the Competition," *Harvard Business Review* 82, no. 4 (April 2004), pp. 64–65.

[24]Ibid., pp. 67–68.

[25]For more details, see R. G. Hamermesh, M. J. Anderson, and J. E. Harris, "Strategies for Low Market Share Businesses," *Harvard Business Review* 56, no. 3 (May–June 1978), pp. 95–96.

[26]Porter, *Competitive Advantage*, p. 514.

[27]Some of these options are drawn from Kotler, *Marketing Management,* pp. 397–412; Hamermesh, Anderson, and Harris, "Strategies for Low Market Share Businesses," pp. 97–102; and Porter, *Competitive Advantage,* Chapter 15.

[28]William K. Hall, "Survival Strategies in a Hostile Environment," *Harvard Business Review* 58, no. 5 (September–October 1980), pp. 75–85. See also Frederick M. Zimmerman, *The Turnaround Experience: Real-World Lessons in Revitalizing Corporations* (New York: McGraw-Hill, 1991), and Gary J. Castrogiovanni, B. R. Baliga, and Roland E. Kidwell, "Curing Sick Businesses: Changing CEOs in Turnaround Efforts," *Academy of Management Executive* 6, no. 3 (August 1992), pp. 26–41.

[29]A study performed by Crest Advisors, a boutique investment firm and reported in Leigh Gallagher, "Avoiding the Pitfalls of Orphan Stocks," www.forbes.com, April 24, 2003.

[30]Phillip Kotler, "Harvesting Strategies for Weak Products," *Business Horizons* 21, no. 5 (August 1978), pp. 17–18.

Chapter 9

[1]For a further discussion of when diversification makes good strategic sense, see Constantinos C. Markides, "To Diversify or Not to Diversify," *Harvard Business Review* 75, no. 6 (November–December 1997), pp. 93–99.

[2]Michael E. Porter, "From Competitive Advantage to Corporate Strategy," *Harvard Business Review* 45, no. 3 (May–June 1987), pp. 46–49.

[3]Michael E. Porter, *Competitive Strategy: Techniques for Analyzing Industries and Competitors* (New York: Free Press, 1980), pp. 354–55.

[4]Ibid., pp. 344–45.

[5]Yves L. Doz and Gary Hamel, *Alliance Advantage: The Art of Creating Value through Partnering* (Boston: Harvard Business School Press, 1998), Chapters 1 and 2.

[6]Michael E. Porter, *Competitive Advantage* (New York: Free Press, 1985), pp. 318–19 and pp. 337–53, and Porter, "From Competitive Advantage," pp. 53–57. For an empirical study confirming that strategic fits are capable of enhancing performance (provided the resulting resource strengths are competitively valuable and difficult to duplicate by rivals), see Constantinos C. Markides and Peter J. Williamson, "Corporate Diversification and Organization Structure: A Resource-Based View," *Academy of Management Journal* 39, no. 2 (April 1996), pp. 340–67.

[7]For a discussion of the strategic significance of cross-business coordination of value chain activities and insight into how the process works, see Jeanne M. Liedtka, "Collaboration across Lines of Business for Competitive Advantage," *Academy of Management Executive* 10, no. 2 (May 1996), pp. 20–34.

[8]"Beyond Knowledge Management: How Companies Mobilize Experience," *Financial Times,* February 8, 1999, p. 5.

[9]For a discussion of what is involved in actually capturing strategic fit benefits, see Kathleen M. Eisenhardt and D. Charles Galunic, "Coevolving: At Last, a Way to Make Synergies Work," *Harvard Business Review* 78, no. 1 (January–February 2000), pp. 91–101. Adeptness at capturing cross-business strategic fits positively impacts performance; see Constantinos C. Markides and Peter J. Williamson, "Related Diversification, Core Competences and Corporate Performance," *Strategic Management Journal* 15 (Summer 1994), pp. 149–65.

[10]Peter Drucker, *Management: Tasks, Responsibilities, Practices* (New York: Harper & Row, 1974), pp. 692–93.

[11]While arguments that unrelated diversification are a superior way to diversify financial risk have logical appeal, there is research showing that related diversification is less risky from a financial perspective than is unrelated diversification; see Michael Lubatkin and Sayan Chatterjee, "Extending Modern Portfolio Theory into the Domain of Corporate Diversification: Does It Apply?" *Academy of Management Journal* 37, no. 1 (February 1994), pp. 109–36.

[12]For a review of the experiences of companies that have pursued unrelated diversification successfully, see Patricia L. Anslinger and Thomas E. Copeland, "Growth through Acquisitions: A Fresh Look," *Harvard Business Review* 74, no. 1 (January–February 1996), pp. 126–35.

[13]Of course, management may be willing to assume the risk that trouble will not strike before it has had time to learn the business well enough to bail it out of almost any difficulty. But there is research that shows this is very risky from a financial perspective; see, for example, Lubatkin and Chatterjee, "Extending Modern Portfolio Theory," pp. 132–33.

[14]For research evidence of the failure of broad diversification and trend of companies to focus their diversification efforts more narrowly, see Lawrence G. Franko, "The Death of Diversification? The Focusing of the World's Industrial Firms, 1980–2000," *Business Horizons* 47, no. 4 (July–August 2004), pp. 41–50.

[15]For an excellent discussion of what to look for in assessing these fits, see Andrew Campbell, Michael Gould, and Marcus Alexander, "Corporate Strategy: The Quest for Parenting Advantage," *Harvard Business Review* 73, no. 2 (March–April 1995), pp. 120–32.

[16]Ibid., p. 128.

[17]Ibid., p. 123.

[18]A good discussion of the importance of having adequate resources, and also the importance of upgrading corporate resources and capabilities, can be found in David J. Collis and Cynthia A. Montgomery, "Competing on Resources: Strategy in the 90s," *Harvard Business Review* 73, no. 4 (July–August 1995), pp. 118–28.

[19]Ibid., pp. 121–22.

[20]Drucker, *Management,* p. 709.

[21]See, for example, Constantinos C. Markides, "Diversification, Restructuring, and Economic Performance," *Strategic Management Journal* 16 (February 1995), pp. 101–18.

[22]For a discussion of why divestiture needs to be a standard part of any company's diversification strategy, see Lee Dranikoff, Tim Koller, and Antoon Schneider, "Divestiture: Strategy's Missing Link," *Harvard Business Review* 80, no. 5 (May 2002), pp. 74–83.

[23]Drucker, *Management,* p. 94.

[24]See David J. Collis and Cynthia A. Montgomery, "Creating Corporate Advantage," *Harvard Business Review* 76, no. 3 (May–June 1998), pp. 72–80.

[25]Drucker, *Management,* p. 719.

[26]Evidence that restructuring strategies tend to result in higher levels of performance is contained in Markides, "Diversification, Restructuring," pp. 101–18.

[27]Company press release, October 6, 2005.

[28]Dranikoff, Koller, and Schneider, "Divestiture," p. 76.

[29]C. K. Prahalad and Yves L. Doz, *The Multinational Mission* (New York: Free Press, 1987), p. 2.

[30]Ibid., p. 15.

[31]Ibid., pp. 62–63.

[32]For a fascinating discussion of the chess match in strategy that can unfold when two DMNC's go head-to-head in a global marketplace, see Ian C. MacMillan, Alexander B. van Putten, and Rita Gunther McGrath, "Global Gamesmanship," *Harvard Business Review* 81, no. 5 (May 2003), pp. 62–71.

Chapter 10

[1]James E. Post, Anne T. Lawrence, and James Weber, *Business and Society: Corporate Strategy, Public Policy, Ethics,* 10th ed. (Burr Ridge, IL: McGraw-Hill/Irwin, 2002), p. 103.

[2]For research on what are the universal moral values (six are identified—trustworthiness, respect, responsibility, fairness, caring, and citizenship), see Mark S. Schwartz, "Universal Moral Values for Corporate Codes of Ethics," *Journal of Business Ethics* 59, no. 1 (June 2005), pp. 27–44.

[3]See, for instance, Mark. S. Schwartz, "A Code of Ethics for Corporate Codes of Ethics," *Journal of Business Ethics* 41, nos. 1–2 (November–December 2002), pp. 27–43.

[4]For more discussion of this point, see ibid., pp. 29–30.

[5]T. L. Beauchamp and N. E. Bowie, *Ethical Theory and Business* (Upper Saddle River, NJ: Prentice Hall, 2001), p. 8.

[6]Based on information in U.S. Department of Labor, "The Department of Labor's 2002 Findings on the Worst Forms of Child Labor," www.dol.gov/ILAB/media/reports, 2003.

[7]ILO-IPEC (SIMPOC), *Every Child Counts: New Global Estimates on Child Labour,* www.ilo.org/public/english/standards/ipec/simpoc/others/globalest.pdf, April 2002. The estimate of the number of working children is based on the definition of the "economically active population," which restricts the labor force activity of children to "paid" or "unpaid" employment, military personnel, and the unemployed. The definition does not include children in informal work settings, non-economic activities, "hidden" forms of work, or work that is defined by ILO Convention 182 as the worst forms of child labor.

[8]W. M. Greenfield, "In the Name of Corporate Social Responsibility," *Business Horizons* 47, no. 1 (January–February 2004), p. 22.

[9]For a study of why such factors as low per capita income, lower disparities in income distribution, and various cultural factors are often associated with a higher incidence of bribery, see Rajib Sanyal, "Determinants of Bribery in International Business: The Cultural and Economic Factors," *Journal of Business Ethics* 59, no.1 (June 2005), pp. 139–45.

[10]For a study of bribe-paying frequency by country, see Transparency International, *2003 Global Corruption Report,* p. 267; this report can be accessed at www.globalcorruptionreport.org.

[11]Roger Chen and Chia-Pei Chen, "Chinese Professional Managers and the Issue of Ethical Behavior," *Ivey Business Journal* 69, no, 5 (May/June 2005), p.1.

[12]Thomas Donaldson and Thomas W. Dunfee, "When Ethics Travel: The Promise and Peril of Global Business Ethics," *California Management Review* 41, no. 4 (Summer 1999), p. 53.

[13]John Reed and Erik Portanger, "Bribery, Corruption Are Rampant in Eastern Europe, Survey Finds," *Wall Street Journal,* November 9, 1999, p. A21.

[14]See Transparency International, *Global Corruption Report* for 2003, 2004, and 2005; these reports can be accessed at www.globalcorruptionreport.org.

[15]For a study of "facilitating" payments to obtain a favor (such as expediting an administrative process, obtaining a permit or license, or avoiding an abuse of authority), which are sometimes condoned as unavoidable or are excused on grounds of low wages and lack of professionalism among public officials, see Antonio Argandoña, "Corruption and Companies: The Use of Facilitating Payments," *Journal of Business Ethics* 60, no. 3 (September 2005), pp. 251–64.

[16]Donaldson and Dunfee, "When Ethics Travel," p. 59.

[17]Thomas Donaldson and Thomas W. Dunfee, *Ties That Bind: A Social Contracts Approach to Business Ethics* (Boston: Harvard Business School Press, 1999), pp. 35, 83.

[18]Based on a report in M. J. Satchell, "Deadly Trade in Toxics," *U.S. News and World Report,* March 7, 1994. p. 64, cited in Donaldson and Dunfee, "When Ethics Travel," p. 46.

[19]Chen and Chen, "Chinese Professional Managers," p. 1.

[20]Two of the definitive treatments of integrated social contracts theory as applied to ethics are Thomas Donaldson and Thomas W. Dunfee, "Towards a Unified Conception of Business Ethics: Integrative Social Contracts Theory," *Academy of Management Review* 19, no. 2 (April 1994), pp. 252–84, and Donaldson and Dunfee, *Ties That Bind,* especially Chapters 3, 4, and 6. See also Andrew Spicer, Thomas W. Dunfee, and Wendy J. Bailey, "Does National Context Matter in Ethical Decision Making? An Empirical Test of Integrative Social Contracts Theory," *Academy of Management Journal* 47, no. 4 (August 2004), p. 610.

[21]P. M. Nichols, "Outlawing Transnational Bribery through the World Trade Organization," *Law and Policy in International Business* 28, no. 2 (1997), pp. 321–22.

[22]Donaldson and Dunfee, "When Ethics Travel," pp. 55–56.

[23]Archie B. Carroll, "Models of Management Morality for the New Millennium," *Business Ethics Quarterly* 11, no. 2 (April 2001), pp. 367–69.

[24]Ibid., pp. 369–70.

[25]John R. Wilke and Don Clark, "Samsung to Pay Fine for Price-Fixing," *The Wall Street Journal,* October 14, 2005, p. A3.

[26]For survey data on what managers say about why they sometimes behave unethically, see John F. Veiga, Timothy D. Golden, and Kathleen Dechant, "Why Managers Bend Company Rules," *Academy of Management Executive* 18, no. 2 (May 2004), pp. 84–89.

[27]For more details see Ronald R. Sims and Johannes Brinkmann, "Enron Ethics (Or: Culture Matters More Than Codes)," *Journal of Business Ethics* 45, no. 3 (July 2003), pp. 244–46.

[28]As reported in Gardiner Harris, "At Bristol-Myers, Ex-Executives Tell of Numbers Games," *The Wall Street Journal,* December 12, 2002, pp. A1, A13.

[29]Ibid., p. A13.

[30]Veiga, Golden, and Dechant, "Why Managers Bend the Rules," p. 36.

[31]The following account is based largely on the discussion and analysis in Sims and Brinkmann, "Enron Ethics," pp. 245–52. Perhaps the definitive book-length account of the corrupt Enron culture is Kurt Eichenwald, *Conspiracy of Fools: A True Story* (New York: Broadway Books, 2005).

[32]Chip Cummins and Almar Latour, "How Shell's Move to Revamp Culture Ended in Scandal," *The Wall Street Journal,* November 2, 2004, p. A14.

[33]Gedeon J. Rossouw and Leon J. van Vuuren, "Modes of Managing Morality: A Descriptive Model of Strategies for Managing Ethics," *Journal of Business Ethics,* 46, no. 4 (September 2003), pp. 389–400.

[34]Empirical evidence that an ethical culture approach produces better results than the compliance approach is presented in Terry Thomas, John R. Schermerhorn, and John W. Dienhart, "Strategic Leadership of Ethical Behavior," *Academy of Management Executive* 18, no. 2 (May 2004), p. 64.

[35]Anna Wilde Mathews and Barbara Martinez, "E-Mails Suggest Merck Knew Vioxx's Dangers at Early Stage," *The Wall Street Journal,* November 1, 2004, pp. A1 and A10.

[36]Archie B. Carroll, "The Four Faces of Corporate Citizenship," *Business and Society Review* 100/101 (September 1998), p. 6.

[37]Business Roundtable, "Statement on Corporate Responsibility," New York, October 1981, p. 9.

[38]Sarah Roberts, Justin Keeble, and David Brown, "The Business Case for Corporate Citizenship," a study for the World Economic Forum, www.weforum.org/corporatecitizenship, October 14, 2003, p. 3.

[39]N. Craig Smith, "Corporate Responsibility: Whether and How," *California Management Review* 45, no. 4 (Summer 2003), p. 63.

[40]Jeffrey Hollender, "What Matters Most: Corporate Values and Social Responsibility," *California Management Review* 46, no. 4 (Summer 2004), p. 112. For a study of the

corporate social responsibility reports of leading European companies, see Simon Knox, Stan Maklan, and Paul French, "Corporate Social Responsibility: Exploring Stakeholder Relationships and Program Reporting across Leading FTSE Companies," *Journal of Business Ethics* 61, no. 1 (September 2005), pp. 7–28.

[41] World Business Council for Sustainable Development, "Corporate Social Responsibility: Making Good Business Sense," www.wbscd.ch, January 2000 (accessed October 10, 2003), p. 7. For a discussion of how companies are connecting social initiatives to their core values, see David Hess, Nikolai Rogovsky, and Thomas W. Dunfee, "The Next Wave of Corporate Community Involvement: Corporate Social Initiatives," *California Management Review* 44, no. 2 (Winter 2002), pp. 110–25, and Susan Ariel Aaronson, "Corporate Responsibility in the Global Village: The British Role Model and the American Laggard," *Business and Society Review*, 108, no. 3 (September 2003), p. 323.

[42] www.chick-fil-a.com (accessed November 4, 2005).

[43] Smith, "Corporate Responsibility," p. 63. See also World Economic Forum, "Findings of a Survey on Global Corporate Leadership," www.weforum.org/corporatecitizenship, (accessed October 11, 2003).

[44] Roberts, Keeble, and Brown, "The Business Case," p. 6.

[45] Ibid., p. 3.

[46] Wallace N. Davidson, Abuzar El-Jelly, and Dan L. Worrell, "Influencing Managers to Change Unpopular Corporate Behavior through Boycotts and Divestitures: A Stock Market Test," *Business and Society*, 34, no. 2 (1995), pp. 171–196.

[47] Tom McCawley, "Racing to Improve Its Reputation: Nike Has Fought to Shed Its Image as an Exploiter of Third-World Labor, Yet It Is Still a Target of Activists," *Financial Times*, December 2000, p. 14, and Smith, "Corporate Social Responsibility," p. 61.

[48] Based on data in Amy Aronson, "Corporate Diversity, Integration, and Market Penetration," *BusinessWeek*, October 20, 2003, pp. 138 ff.

[49] Smith, "Corporate Social Responsibility," p. 62.

[50] See Social Investment Forum, *2001 Report on Socially Responsible Investing Trends in the United States* (Washington, DC: Social Investment Forum, 2001).

[51] Smith, "Corporate Social Responsibility," p. 63.

[52] See James C. Collins and Jerry I. Porras, *Built to Last: Successful Habits of Visionary Companies*, 3rd ed. (London: HarperBusiness, 2002); Roberts, Keeble, and Brown, "The Business Case," p. 4; and Smith, "Corporate Social Responsibility," p. 63.

[53] Roberts, Keeble, and Brown, "The Business Case," p. 4.

[54] Smith, "Corporate Social Responsibility," p. 65; Lee E. Preston and Douglas P. O'Bannon, "The Corporate Social-Financial Performance Relationship," *Business and Society* 36, no. 4 (December 1997), pp. 419–29; Ronald M. Roman, Sefa Hayibor, and Bradley R. Agle, "The Relationship between Social and Financial Performance: Repainting a Portrait," *Business and Society* 38, no. 1 (March 1999), pp. 109–25; and Joshua D. Margolis and James P. Walsh, *People and Profits* (Mahwah, NJ: Lawrence Erlbaum, 2001).

[55] Smith, "Corporate Social Responsibility," p. 71.

[56] Business Roundtable, "Statement on Corporate Governance," Washington, DC, September 1997, p. 3.

[57] Henry Mintzberg, Robert Simons, and Kunal Basu, "Beyond Selfishness," *MIT Sloan Management Review* 44, no. 1 (Fall 2002), p. 69.

[58] For a good discussion of the debate between maximizing shareholder value and balancing stakeholder interests, see H. Jeff Smith, "The Shareholders versus Stakeholders Debate," MIT *Sloan Management Review* 44, no. 4 (Summer 2003), pp. 85–91.

[59] Smith, "Corporate Social Responsibility," p. 70.

[60] Based on information in Edna Gundersen, "Rights Issue Rocks the Music World," *USA Today*, September 16, 2002, pp. D1, D2.

[61] This information is based on Charles Gasparino, "Salomon Probe Includes Senior Executives," *The Wall Street Journal*, September 3, 2002, p. C1; Randall Smith and Susan Pulliam, "How a Star Banker Pressed for IPOs," *The Wall Street Journal*, September 4, 2002, pp. C1, C14; Randall Smith and Susan Pulliam, "How a Technology-Banking Star Doled Out Shares of Hot IPOs," *The Wall Street Journal*, September 23; 2002, pp. A1, A10; and Randall Smith, "Goldman Sachs Faces Scrutiny for IPO-Allocation Practices," *The Wall Street Journal*, October 3, 2002, pp. A1, A6.

Chapter 11

[1] As quoted in Steven W. Floyd and Bill Wooldridge, "Managing Strategic Consensus: The Foundation of Effective Implementation," *Academy of Management Executive* 6, no. 4 (November 1992), p. 27.

[2] Jack Welch with Suzy Welch, *Winning* (New York: HarperBusiness, 2005), p. 135.

[3] For an excellent and very pragmatic discussion of this point, see Larry Bossidy and Ram Charan, *Execution: The Discipline of Getting Things Done* (New York: Crown Business, 2002), Chapter 1.

[4] For an insightful discussion of how important staffing an organization with the right people is, see Christopher A. Bartlett and Sumantra Ghoshal, "Building Competitive Advantage through People," *MIT Sloan Management Review* 43, no. 2 (Winter 2002), pp. 34–41.

[5] The importance of assembling an executive team with exceptional ability to see what needs to be done and an instinctive talent for figuring out how to get it done is discussed in Justin Menkes, "Hiring for Smarts," *Harvard Business Review* 83, no. 11 (November 2005), pp. 100–9 and Justin Menkes, *Executive Intelligence* (New York: HarperCollins, 2005), especially Chapters 1–4.

[6] Welch with Welch, *Winning*, p. 139.

[7] See Bossidy and Charan, *Execution: The Discipline of Getting Things Done*, Chapter 1.

[8] Menkes, *Executive Intelligence*, pp. 68, 76.

[9] Bossidy and Charan, *Execution*; Chapter 5.

[10] Welch with Welch, *Winning*, pp. 141–42.

[11] Menkes, *Executive Intelligence*, pp. 65–71.

[12] Jim Collins, *Good to Great* (New York: HarperBusiness, 2001), p. 44.

[13] John Byrne, "The Search for the Young and Gifted," *BusinessWeek*, October 4, 1999, p. 108.

[14] James Brian Quinn, *Intelligent Enterprise* (New York: Free Press, 1992), pp. 52–53, 55, 73–74, 76. Also see Christine Soo, Timothy Devinney, David Midgley, and Anne Deering, "Knowledge Management: Philosophy, Processes, and Pitfalls," *California Management Review* 44, no. 4 (Summer 2002), pp. 129–51, and Julian Birkinshaw, "Why Is Knowledge Management So Difficult?" *Business Strategy Review* 12, no. 1 (March 2001), pp. 11–18.

[15] Robert H. Hayes, Gary P. Pisano, and David M. Upton, *Strategic Operations: Competing through Capabilities* (New York: Free Press, 1996), pp. 503–7. Also see Jonas Ridderstråle, "Cashing in on Corporate Competencies," *Business Strategy Review* 14, no. 1 (Spring 2003), pp. 27–38, and Danny Miller, Russell Eisenstat, and Nathaniel Foote, "Strategy from the Inside Out: Building Capability-Creating Organizations," *California Management Review* 44, no. 3 (Spring 2002), pp. 37–55.

[16] Quinn, *Intelligent Enterprise*, p. 43.

[17] Quinn, *Intelligent Enterprise*, pp. 33, 89; James Brian Quinn and Frederick G. Hilmer, "Strategic Outsourcing," *Sloan Management Review* 35, no. 4 (Summer 1994), pp. 43–55; Jussi Heikkilä and Carlos Cordon, "Outsourcing: A Core or Non-Core Strategic Management Decision," *Strategic Change* 11, no. 3 (June–July 2002), pp. 183–93; and James Brian Quinn, "Strategic Outsourcing: Leveraging Knowledge Capabilities," *Sloan Management Review* 40, no. 4 (Summer 1999), pp. 9–22. A strong case for outsourcing is presented in

C. K. Prahalad, "The Art of Outsourcing," *The Wall Street Journal,* June 8, 2005, p. A13. For a discussion of why outsourcing initiatives fall short of expectations, see Jérôme Barthélemy, "The Seven Deadly Sins of Outsourcing," *Academy of Management Executive* 17, no. 2 (May 2003), pp. 87–98.

[18]Quinn, "Strategic Outsourcing," p. 17.

[19]For a more extensive discussion of the reasons for building cooperative, collaborative alliances and partnerships with other companies, see James F. Moore, *The Death of Competition* (New York: HarperBusiness, 1996), especially Chapter 3; Quinn and Hilmer, "Strategic Outsourcing"; and Quinn, "Strategic Outsourcing."

[20]Quinn, *Intelligent Enterprise,* pp. 39–40; also see Barthélemy, "The Seven Deadly Sins."

[21]The importance of matching organization design and structure to the particular needs of strategy was first brought to the forefront in a landmark study of 70 large corporations conducted by Professor Alfred Chandler of Harvard University. Chandler's research revealed that changes in an organization's strategy bring about new administrative problems that, in turn, require a new or refashioned structure for the new strategy to be successfully implemented. He found that structure tends to follow the growth strategy of the firm—but often not until inefficiency and internal operating problems provoke a structural adjustment. The experiences of these firms followed a consistent sequential pattern: new strategy creation, emergence of new administrative problems, a decline in profitability and performance, a shift to a more appropriate organizational structure, and then recovery to more profitable levels and improved strategy execution. See Alfred Chandler, *Strategy and Structure* (Cambridge, MA: MIT Press, 1962).

[22]The importance of empowering workers in executing strategy and the value of creating a great working environment are discussed in Stanley E. Fawcett, Gary K. Rhoads, and Phillip Burnah, "People as the Bridge to Competitiveness: Benchmarking the 'ABCs' of an Empowered Workforce," *Benchmarking: An International Journal* 11, no. 4 (2004), pp. 346–60.

[23]Iain Somerville and John Edward Mroz, "New Competencies for a New World," in *The Organization of the Future,* ed. Frances Hesselbein, Marshall Goldsmith, and Richard Beckard (San Francisco: Jossey-Bass, 1997), p. 70.

[24]Exercising adequate control over empowered employees is a serious issue. For example, a prominent Wall Street securities firm lost $350 million when a trader allegedly booked fictitious profits; Sears took a $60 million write-off after admitting that employees in its automobile service departments recommended unnecessary repairs to customers. Several makers of memory chips paid fines of over $500 million when over a dozen of their employees conspired to fix prices and operate a global cartel—some of the guilty employees were sentenced to jail. For a discussion of the problems and possible solutions, see Robert Simons, "Control in an Age of Empowerment," *Harvard Business Review* 73 (March–April 1995), pp. 80–88.

[25]For a discussion of the importance of cross-business coordination, see Jeanne M. Liedtka, "Collaboration across Lines of Business for Competitive Advantage," *Academy of Management Executive* 10, no. 2 (May 1996), pp. 20–34.

[26]Michael Hammer and James Champy, *Reengineering the Corporation* (New York: HarperBusiness, 1993), pp. 26–27.

[27]Ibid. Although functional organization incorporates Adam Smith's division-of-labor principle (every person/department involved has specific responsibility for performing a clearly defined task) and allows for tight management control (everyone in the process is accountable to a functional department head for efficiency and adherence to procedures), *no one oversees the whole process and its result.*

[28]Rosabeth Moss Kanter, "Collaborative Advantage: The Art of the Alliance," *Harvard Business Review* 72, no. 4 (July–August 1994), pp. 105–6.

[29]For an excellent review of ways to effectively manage the relationship between alliance partners, see Kanter, "Collaborative Advantage," pp. 96–108.

Chapter 12

[1]For a discussion of the value of benchmarking in implementing strategy, see Christopher E. Bogan and Michael J. English, *Benchmarking for Best Practices: Winning Through Innovative Adaptation* (New York: McGraw-Hill, 1994), Chapters 2 and 6; Mustafa Ungan, "Factors Affecting the Adoption of Manufacturing Best Practices," *Benchmarking: An International Journal* 11, no. 5 (2004), pp, 504–20; and Paul Hyland and Ron Beckett, "Learning to Compete: The Value of Internal Benchmarking," *Benchmarking: An International Journal* 9, no. 3 (2002), pp. 293–304; and Yoshinobu Ohinata, "Benchmarking: The Japanese Experience," *Long-Range Planning* 27, no. 4 (August 1994), pp. 48–53.

[2]Michael Hammer and James Champy, *Reengineering the Corporation* (New York: HarperBusiness, 1993), pp. 26–27.

[3]Gene Hall, Jim Rosenthal, and Judy Wade, "How to Make Reengineering Really Work," *Harvard Business Review* 71, no. 6 (November–December 1993), pp. 119–131.

[4]For more information on business process reengineering and how well it has worked in various companies, see James Brian Quinn, *Intelligent Enterprise* (New York: Free Press, 1992), p. 162; Ann Majchrzak and Qianwei Wang, "Breaking the Functional Mind-Set in Process Organizations," *Harvard Business Review* 74, no. 5 (September–October 1996), pp. 93–99; Stephen L. Walston, Lawton R. Burns, and John R. Kimberly, "Does Reengineering Really Work? An Examination of the Context and Outcomes of Hospital Reengineering Initiatives," *Health Services Research* 34, no. 6 (February 2000), pp. 1363–88; and Allessio Ascari, Melinda Rock, and Soumitra Dutta, "Reengineering and Organizational Change: Lessons from a Comparative Analysis of Company Experiences," *European Management Journal* 13, no. 1 (March 1995), pp. 1–13. For a review of why some company personnel embrace process reengineering and some don't, see Ronald J. Burke, "Process Reengineering: Who Embraces It and Why?" *TQM Magazine* 16, no. 2 (2004), pp. 114–19.

[5]For some of the seminal discussions of what TQM is and how it works written by ardent enthusiasts of the technique, see M. Walton, *The Deming Management Method* (New York: Pedigree, 1986); J. Juran, *Juran on Quality by Design* (New York: Free Press, 1992); Philip Crosby, *Quality Is Free: The Act of Making Quality Certain* (New York: McGraw-Hill, 1979); and S. George, *The Baldrige Quality System* (New York: Wiley, 1992). For a critique of TQM, see Mark J. Zbaracki, "The Rhetoric and Reality of Total Quality Management," *Administrative Science Quarterly* 43, no. 3 (September 1998), pp. 602–36.

[6]For a discussion of the shift in work environment and culture that TQM entails, see Robert T. Amsden, Thomas W. Ferratt, and Davida M. Amsden, "TQM: Core Paradigm Changes," *Business Horizons* 39, no. 6 (November–December 1996), pp. 6–14.

[7]For easy-to-understand overviews of Six Sigma, see Peter S. Pande and Larry Holpp, *What Is Six Sigma?* (New York: McGraw-Hill, 2002); Jiju Antony, "Some Pros and Cons of Six Sigma: An Academic Perspective," *TQM Magazine* 16, no. 4 (2004), pp. 303–6; Peter S. Pande, Robert P. Neuman, and Roland R. Cavanagh, *The Six Sigma Way: How GE, Motorola and Other Top Companies Are Honing Their Performance* (New York: McGraw-Hill, 2000); and Joseph Gordon and M. Joseph Gordon Jr., *Six Sigma Quality for Business and Manufacture* (New York: Elsevier, 2002). For how Six Sigma can be used in smaller companies, see Godecke Wessel and Peter Burcher, "Six Sigma for Small and Medium-sized Enterprises," *TQM Magazine* 16, no. 4 (2004), pp. 264–72.

[8]Based on information posted at www.isixsigma. com, November 4, 2002.

[9]Kennedy Smith, "Six Sigma for the Service Sector," *Quality Digest Magazine,* May 2003, posted at www.qualitydigest.com (accessed September 28, 2003).

[10]Del Jones, "Taking the Six Sigma Approach," *USA Today,* October 31, 2002, p. 5B.

[11]Pande, Neuman, and Cavanagh, *The Six Sigma Way,* pp. 5–6.

[12]Smith, "Six Sigma for the Service Sector."

[13]Jones, "Taking the Six Sigma Approach," p. 5B.

[14]Terry Nels Lee, Stanley E. Fawcett, and Jason Briscoe, "Benchmarking the Challenge to Quality Program Implementation," *Benchmarking: An International Journal* 9, no. 4 (2002), pp. 374–87.

[15]For a recent study documenting the imperatives of establishing a supportive culture, see Milan Ambroz, "Total Quality System as a Product of the Empowered Corporate Culture," *TQM Magazine,* 16, no. 2 (2004), pp. 93–104. Research confirming the factors that are important in making TQM programs successful in both Europe and the United States is presented in Nick A. Dayton, "The Demise of Total Quality Management," *TQM Magazine,* 15, no. 6 (2003), pp. 391–96.

[16]Judy D. Olian and Sara L. Rynes, "Making Total Quality Work: Aligning Organizational Processes, Performance Measures, and Stakeholders," *Human Resource Management* 30, no. 3 (Fall 1991), pp. 310–11, and Paul S. Goodman and Eric D. Darr, "Exchanging Best Practices Information through Computer-Aided Systems," *Academy of Management Executive* 10, no. 2 (May 1996), p. 7.

[17]Thomas C. Powell, "Total Quality Management as Competitive Advantage," *Strategic Management Journal* 16 (1995), pp. 15–37. See also Richard M. Hodgetts, "Quality Lessons from America's Baldrige Winners," *Business Horizons* 37, no. 4 (July–August 1994), pp. 74–79; and Richard Reed, David J. Lemak, and Joseph C. Montgomery, "Beyond Process: TQM Content and Firm Performance," *Academy of Management Review* 21, no. 1 (January 1996), pp. 173–202.

[18]Based on information at www.utc.com and www.otiselevator.com (accessed November 14, 2005).

[19]Fred Vogelstein, "Winning the Amazon Way," *Fortune,* May 26, 2003, pp. 70, 74.

[20]*BusinessWeek,* November 21, 2005, pp. 87–88.

[21]Such systems speed organizational learning by providing fast, efficient communication, creating an organizational memory for collecting and retaining best practice information, and permitting people all across the organization to exchange information and updated solutions. See Goodman and Darr, "Exchanging Best Practices Information," pp. 7–17.

[22]*BusinessWeek,* November 21, 2005, pp. 85–90.

[23]Vogelstein, "Winning the Amazon Way," p. 64.

[24]For a discussion of the need for putting appropriate boundaries on the actions of empowered employees and possible control and monitoring systems that can be used, see Robert Simons, "Control in an Age of Empowerment," *Harvard Business Review* 73 (March–April 1995), pp. 80–88.

[25]Ibid. Also see David C. Band and Gerald Scanlan, "Strategic Control through Core Competencies," *Long Range Planning* 28, no. 2 (April 1995), pp. 102–14.

[26]The importance of motivating and empowering workers so as to create a working environment that is highly conducive to good strategy execution is discussed in Stanley E. Fawcett, Gary K. Rhoads, and Phillip Burnah, "People as the Bridge to Competitiveness: Benchmarking the 'ABCs' of an Empowered Workforce," *Benchmarking: An International Journal* 11, no. 4 (2004), pp. 346–60.

[27]Jeffrey Pfeffer and John F. Veiga, "Putting People First for Organizational Success," *Academy of Management Executive* 13, no. 2 (May 1999), pp. 37–45; Linda K. Stroh and Paula M. Caliguiri, "Increasing Global Competitiveness through Effective People Management," *Journal of World Business* 33, no. 1 (Spring 1998), pp. 1–16; and articles in *Fortune* on the 100 best companies to work for (various issues).

[28]As quoted in John P. Kotter and James L. Heskett, *Corporate Culture and Performance* (New York: Free Press, 1992), p. 91.

[29]For a provocative discussion of why incentives and rewards are actually counterproductive, see Alfie Kohn, "Why Incentive Plans Cannot Work," *Harvard Business Review* 71, no. 6 (September–October 1993), pp. 54–63.

[30]See Steven Kerr, "On the Folly of Rewarding A While Hoping for B," *Academy of Management Executive* 9, no. 1 (February 1995), pp. 7–14; Steven Kerr, "Risky Business: The New Pay Game," *Fortune,* July 22, 1996, pp. 93–96; and Doran Twer, "Linking Pay to Business Objectives," *Journal of Business Strategy* 15, no. 4 (July–August 1994), pp. 15–18.

[31]Kerr, "Risky Business," p. 96.

Chapter 13

[1]Joanne Reid and Victoria Hubbell, "Creating a Performance Culture," *Ivey Business Journal* 69, no.4 (March–April 2005), p. 1.

[2]John P. Kotter and James L. Heskett, *Corporate Culture and Performance* (New York: Free Press, 1992), p. 7. See also Robert Goffee and Gareth Jones, *The Character of a Corporation* (New York: HarperCollins, 1998).

[3]Kotter and Heskett, *Corporate Culture and Performance,* pp. 7–8.

[4]Ibid., p. 5.

[5]John Alexander and Meena S. Wilson, "Leading across Cultures: Five Vital Capabilities," in *The Organization of the Future,* ed. Frances Hesselbein, Marshall Goldsmith, and Richard Beckard (San Francisco: Jossey-Bass, 1997), pp. 291–92.

[6]Terrence E. Deal and Allen A. Kennedy, *Corporate Cultures* (Reading, MA: Addison-Wesley, 1982), p. 22. See also Terrence E. Deal and Allen A. Kennedy, *The New Corporate Cultures: Revitalizing the Workplace after Downsizing, Mergers, and Reengineering* (Cambridge, MA: Perseus, 1999).

[7]Vijay Sathe, *Culture and Related Corporate Realities* (Homewood, IL: Richard D. Irwin, 1985).

[8]Kotter and Heskett, *Corporate Culture and Performance,* Chapter 6.

[9]See Kurt Eichenwald, *Conspiracy of Fools: A True Story* (New York: Broadways, 2005).

[10]Reid and Hubbell, "Creating a Performance Culture," pp. 2, 5.

[11]This section draws heavily on the discussion of Kotter and Heskett, *Corporate Culture and Performance,* Chapter 4.

[12]There's no inherent reason why new strategic initiatives should conflict with core values and business principles. While conflict is always possible, most strategy makers lean toward choosing strategic initiatives that are compatible with the company's character and culture and that don't go against ingrained values and beliefs. After all, the company's culture is usually something that strategy makers have had a hand in building and perpetuating, so they are not often anxious to undermine core values and business principles without serious soul searching and compelling business reasons.

[13]Kotter and Heskett, *Corporate Culture and Performance,* p. 52.

[14]Ibid., p. 5.

[15]Avan R. Jassawalla and Hemant C. Sashittal, "Cultures That Support Product-Innovation Processes," *Academy of Management Executive* 16, no. 3 (August 2002), pp. 42–54.

[16]Kotter and Heskett, *Corporate Culture and Performance,* pp. 15–16. Also see Jennifer A. Chatham and Sandra E. Cha, "Leading by Leveraging Culture," *California Management Review* 45, no. 4 (Summer 2003), pp. 20–34.

[17]Judy D. Olian and Sara L. Rynes, "Making Total Quality Work: Aligning Organizational Processes, Performance Measures, and Stakeholders," *Human Resource Management* 30, no. 3 (Fall 1991), p. 324.

[18]Information posted at www.dardenrestaurants. com (accessed November 25, 2005); for more specifics, see Robert C. Ford, "Darden Restaurants' CEO Joe Lee on the Importance of Core Values: Integrity and Fairness," *Academy of Management Executive* 16, no. 1 (February 2002), pp. 31–36.

[19]For several perspectives on the role and importance of core values and ethical behavior, see Joseph L. Badaracco, *Defining Moments: When Managers Must Choose between Right and Wrong* (Boston: Harvard Business School Press, 1997); Joe Badaracco and Allen P. Webb, "Business Ethics: A View from the Trenches," *California Management Review* 37, no. 2 (Winter 1995), pp. 8–28; Patrick E. Murphy, "Corporate Ethics Statements: Current Status and Future Prospects," *Journal of Business Ethics* 14 (1995), pp. 727–40; and Lynn Sharp Paine, "Managing for Organizational Integrity," *Harvard Business Review* 72, no. 2 (March–April 1994), pp. 106–17.

[20]For a study of the status of formal codes of ethics in large corporations, see Emily F. Carasco and Jang B. Singh, "The Content and Focus of the Codes of Ethics of the World's Largest Transnational Corporations," *Business and Society Review* 108, no. 1 (January 2003), pp. 71–94, and Murphy, "Corporate Ethics Statements." For a discussion of the strategic benefits of formal statements of corporate values, see John Humble, David Jackson, and Alan Thomson, "The Strategic Power of Corporate Values," *Long Range Planning* 27, no. 6 (December 1994), pp. 28–42. An excellent discussion of whether one should assume that company codes of ethics are always ethical is presented in Mark S. Schwartz, "A Code of Ethics for Corporate Codes of Ethics," *Journal of Business Ethics* 41, nos. 1–2 (November–December 2002), pp. 27–43.

[21]See Schwartz, "A Code of Ethics," p. 27.

[22]Ford, "Darden Restaurants' CEO Joe Lee."

[23]For excellent discussions of the problems and pitfalls in leading the transition to a new strategy and to fundamentally new ways of doing business, see Larry Bossidy and Ram Charan, *Confronting Reality: Doing What Matters to Get Things Right* (New York: Crown Business, 2004); Larry Bossidy and Ram Charan, *Execution: The Discipline of Getting Things Done* (New York: Crown Business, 2002), especially Chapters 3 and 5; John P. Kotter, "Leading Change: Why Transformation Efforts Fail," *Harvard Business Review* 73, no. 2 (March–April 1995), pp. 59–67; Thomas M. Hout and John C. Carter, "Getting It Done: New Roles for Senior Executives," *Harvard Business Review* 73, no. 6 (November–December 1995), pp. 133–45; and Sumantra Ghoshal and Christopher A. Bartlett, "Changing the Role of Top Management: Beyond Structure to Processes," *Harvard Business Review* 73, no. 1 (January–February 1995), pp. 86–96.

[24]For a pragmatic, cut-to-the-chase treatment of why some leaders succeed and others fail in executing strategy, especially in a period of rapid market change or organizational crisis, see Bossidy and Charan, *Confronting Reality.*

[25]Fred Vogelstein, "Winning the Amazon Way," *Fortune,* May 26, 2003, p. 64.

[26]For a more in-depth discussion of the leader's role in creating a results-oriented culture that nurtures success, see Benjamin Schneider, Sarah K. Gunnarson, and Kathryn Niles-Jolly, "Creating the Climate and Culture of Success," *Organizational Dynamics,* Summer 1994, pp. 17–29.

[27]Jeffrey Pfeffer, "Producing Sustainable Competitive Advantage through the Effective Management of People," *Academy of Management Executive* 9, no.1 (February 1995), pp. 55–69.

[28]For some cautions in implementing ethics compliance, see Robert J. Rafalko, "A

Caution about Trends in Ethics Compliance Programs," *Business and Society Review* 108, no. 1 (January 2003), pp. 115–26. A good discussion of the failures of ethics compliance programs can be found in Megan Barry, "Why Ethics and Compliance Programs Can Fail," *Journal of Business Strategy* 26, no. 6 (November–December 2002), pp. 37–40.

[29]For documentation of cross-country differences in what is considered ethical, see Robert D. Hirsch, Branko Bucar, and Sevgi Oztark, "A Cross-Cultural Comparison of Business Ethics: Cases of Russia, Slovenia, Turkey, and United States," *Cross Cultural Management* 10, no. 1 (2003), pp. 3–28, and P. Maria Joseph Christie, Ik-Whan G. Kwan, Philipp A. Stoeberl, and Raymond Baumhart, "A Cross-Cultural Comparison of Ethical Attitudes of Business Managers: India, Korea, and the United States," *Journal of Business Ethics* 46, no. 3 (September 2003), pp. 263–87.

[30]James Brian Quinn, *Strategies for Change: Logical Incrementalism* (Homewood, IL: Richard D. Irwin, 1980), pp. 20–22.

[31]Ibid., p. 146.

[32]For a good discussion of the challenges, see Daniel Goleman, "What Makes a Leader," *Harvard Business Review* 76, no. 6 (November–December 1998), pp. 92–102; Ronald A. Heifetz and Donald L. Laurie, "The Work of Leadership," *Harvard Business Review* 75, no. 1 (January–February 1997), pp. 124–34; and Charles M. Farkas and Suzy Wetlaufer, "The Ways Chief Executive Officers Lead," *Harvard Business Review* 74, no. 3 (May–June 1996), pp. 110–22. See also Michael E. Porter, Jay W. Lorsch, and Nitin Nohria, "Seven Surprises for New CEOs," *Harvard Business Review* 82, no. 10 (October 2004), pp. 62–72.

PHOTO CREDITS

INDEXES

ORGANIZATION

Note: Page numbers in *italics* indicate material in illustrations; page numbers followed by t indicate material in tables; page numbers followed by n indicate notes; page numbers preceded by C- indicate material in Cases.

NAME INDEX

Note: Page numbers in *italics* indicate material in illustrations; page numbers followed by t indicate material in tables; page numbers followed by n indicate notes; page numbers preceded by C- indicate cases; page numbers preceded by EN- indicate endnotes.